THE CAMBRIDGE URBAN HISTORY OF BRITAIN

VOLUME II

1540–1840

This second volume in *The Cambridge Urban History* offers the first wide-ranging analysis of urban growth and change during the period between the Reformation and the onset of the railway age, when Britain became the world's first modern urban nation. The contributors pay particular attention to the experiences of urban life and the changing role of different groups in urban society, and show how communities and their leaders coped with civic problems. They examine the relationship between smaller and larger towns, and assess the impact of cities on the wider society of Britain and beyond. A major innovative feature is the sustained comparative study of English, Welsh and Scottish urbanisation.

Part I examines the national and regional networks of cities and towns across the island. Part II focuses on the period 1540–1700 and looks at the urban economy, demographic and social change, the transformation of the cultural and physical landscape of towns and the role of different types of town – from a resurgent London to the smallest market centre. The third and final part investigates the urban economic and demographic take-off of the industrial age and the social, political and cultural implications for urban communities. Powerful light is shed not only on the 'new' industrial and leisure towns, but also on the many ancient cities and towns which contributed to Britain's exceptional dynamism in the early modern era.

The editor PETER CLARK is Professor of Economic and Social History at the University of Leicester. He has published extensively on urban and social history, and his study of *The English Alehouse: A Social History* (1983) was awarded the Whitfield Prize of the Royal Historical Society.

THE CAMBRIDGE URBAN HISTORY OF BRITAIN

GENERAL EDITOR

PROFESSOR PETER CLARK (*University of Leicester*)

The three volumes of *The Cambridge Urban History of Britain* represent the culmination of a tremendous upsurge of research in British urban history over the past thirty years. Mobilising the combined expertise of nearly ninety historians, archaeologists and geographers from Britain, continental Europe and North America, these volumes trace the complex and diverse evolution of British towns from the earliest Anglo-Saxon settlements to the mid-twentieth century. Taken together they form a comprehensive and uniquely authoritative account of the development of the first modern urban nation. *The Cambridge Urban History of Britain* has been developed with the active support of the Centre for Urban History at the University of Leicester.

VOLUME I 600–1540
EDITED BY D. M. PALLISER (*University of Leeds*)
ISBN 0 521 44461 6

VOLUME II 1540–1840
EDITED BY PETER CLARK (*University of Leicester*)
ISBN 0 521 43141 7

VOLUME III 1840–1950
EDITED BY MARTIN DAUNTON (*University of Cambridge*)
ISBN 0 521 41707 4

Advisory committee

THE CAMBRIDGE URBAN HISTORY OF BRITAIN

VOLUME II

1540–1840

EDITED BY

PETER CLARK

CAMBRIDGE UNIVERSITY PRESS

PUBLISHED BY THE PRESS SYNDICATE OF THE UNIVERSITY OF CAMBRIDGE
The Pitt Building, Trumpington Street, Cambridge, United Kingdom

CAMBRIDGE UNIVERSITY PRESS
The Edinburgh Building, Cambridge CB2 2RU, UK http://www.cup.cam.ac.uk
40 West 20th Street, New York, NY 10011-4211, USA http://www.cup.org
10 Stamford Road, Oakleigh, Melbourne 3166, Australia
Ruiz de Alarcón 13, 28014 Madrid, Spain

First published 2000

Printed in the United Kingdom at the University Press, Cambridge

Typeset in Bembo 10/12½   *System* QuarkXPress™ [SE]

A catalogue record for this book is available from the British Library

ISBN 0 521 43141 7 hardback

Contents

Plates

Between pages 164 and 165

Maps

Figures

Tables

Contributors

Ian A. Archer: Fellow, Tutor and University Lecturer in Modern History, Keble College, Oxford
Jonathan Barry: Senior Lecturer in History, University of Exeter
Peter Borsay: Senior Lecturer in History, University of Wales, Lampeter
Jeremy Boulton: Senior Lecturer in Social History, University of Newcastle
C. W. Chalklin: formerly Reader in History, University of Reading
Peter Clark: Professor of Economic and Social History, University of Leicester
Penelope J. Corfield: Professor of History, Royal Holloway College, London
T. M. Devine: University Research Professor in Scottish History and Director of the Research Institute of Irish and Scottish Studies, University of Aberdeen
Alan Dyer: Senior Lecturer in History, University of Wales, Bangor
Joyce Ellis: Senior Lecturer in History, University of Nottingham
Paul Glennie: Senior Lecturer in Geography, University of Bristol
P. Griffiths: Lecturer in Economic and Social History, University of Leicester
Vanessa Harding: Senior Lecturer in History, Birkbeck College, London
R. A. Houston: Professor of Early Modern History, University of St Andrews
Joanna Innes: Fellow and Tutor in Modern History, Somerville College, Oxford
Gordon Jackson: Reader in History, University of Strathclyde
Philip Jenkins: Professor of History and Religious Studies, Pennsylvania State University
J. Landers: University Lecturer in Historical Demography, All Souls College, Oxford
John Langton: Fellow and Tutor in Geography, St John's College, Oxford
Michael Lynch: Professor of Scottish History, University of Edinburgh
M. Pelling: Reader in the Social History of Medicine, Faculty of Modern History, University of Oxford
Michael Reed: Emeritus Professor of Topography, Loughborough University
Nicholas Rogers: Professor of History, York University, Toronto

David Harris Sacks: Professor of History and Humanities, Reed College, Oregon

Leonard Schwarz: Senior Lecturer in Economic History, University of Birmingham

Pamela Sharpe: Honorary Research Fellow, University of Western Australia, Perth

Paul Slack: Principal, Linacre College, Oxford

Barrie Trinder: Senior Lecturer in Industrial Archaeology, Nene University College, Northampton

R. Tyson: Senior Lecturer in Economic History, University of Aberdeen

John K. Walton: Professor of Social History, University of Central Lancashire

Ian Whyte: Professor of Historical Geography, University of Lancaster

Preface by the General Editor

British cities and towns at the end of the twentieth century are at a turning-point: their role, developed over hundreds of years, is being challenged. The redevelopment of bigger city centres in the 1960s, and of many small county and market towns during subsequent decades, has eroded much of the ancient palimpsest, the mixture of public and private buildings, high streets and back lanes, which has given them for so long a sense of place, of physical coherence and individual communal identity.[1] The decline of traditional urban industries, increasingly at the mercy of global forces, has been partially redressed by the expansion of the service sector, but the recent arrival of American-style out-of-town shopping malls has contributed to the contraction of retailing in the old central areas of towns, even affecting the business of their medieval markets, while shopping parades in the suburbs are littered with empty premises.

Just as economic activity has begun to decamp from the city, so the cultural and leisure life of town centres is being threatened by the migration of cinemas and other entertainment to the urban periphery, and the decay of municipal provision. Fundamental to the weakening position of British cities in recent times has been the erosion of municipal power and autonomy, first through the transfer of key civic functions to the state during and after the second world war and, more recently, through a brutal assault by Conservative governments of the 1980s and 1990s on the financial position of town halls and their ability to sustain their civic responsibilities. It is little wonder that, in this problematic urban world, issues of social exclusion and environmental degradation seem increasingly stark, their effects impacting on the whole of national society.

Of course, the decline of the city is not a uniquely British phenomenon. Throughout much of Western Europe there has been a loss of momentum, a

[1] Such changes have also destroyed much of the archaeological record, the buried archives of towns, so essential for understanding their early history.

decay of confidence, manifested but hardly resolved by the endless spate of European conferences, research programmes and official reports on the subject, almost an industry in itself. However, the problems and pressures seem particularly acute in Britain, raising questions about how far their current difficulties reflect longer-term structural factors related to the processes by which Britain became the first modern urban nation. Is the peripheralisation of economic and cultural activity the logical conclusion of the spatial fragmentation of British cities, including suburbanisation, which has been occurring since 1800? Why have so many of Britain's great cities fared so badly in the twentieth century? Is this related to the nature of the rapid urbanisation and industrialisation from the late eighteenth century, based on low human capital formation and cheap fuel, which made it difficult to maintain growth once other countries began to exploit cheap fuel as well?

And yet if at least some of the problems of Britain's present-day cities and towns may be rooted in the past, the historic experience of our urban communities encourages us to believe that, given greater autonomy both of leadership and funding, they can generate an effective response to many of the current challenges. As we shall see in this series, past periods of urban decline, with all their attendant social, political and other difficulties, have often been reversed or moderated by changes of economic direction by towns, whether in the late middle ages through the expansion of service trades, in the seventeenth century through the development of specialist manufacturing and leisure sectors, or in the early twentieth century through the rise of new, often consumer-oriented industries. At the present time, general images of urban decline and dereliction are countered, however selectively, by the rise of the Docklands area as the new international financial quarter of the capital, by the renewed vitality of Glasgow, Manchester and Newcastle as regional capitals, by the tourist success of towns like Bath and York marketing their civic heritage, by the social harmony and cultural vibrancy of a multi-ethnic city such as Leicester. Propelled by a strong sense of civic pride, Britain's urban system has shown, over time, a powerful capacity to create new opportunities from changing circumstances, a capacity that remains as crucial now as in the past. Certainly if many of the modern challenges to society have an urban origin then urban solutions are imperative.

Undoubtedly, Britain is an ancient urban country, remarkable for the longevity and, for much of the time, relative stability of its urban system. Though the early city barely outlasted the Romans' departure from these shores, after the seventh and eighth centuries a skeleton of urban centres developed in England, which was fully fleshed out by the start of the fourteenth century, headed by London, already a great European city, but with a corpus of established shire and market towns: the pattern established by 1300 was remarkably stable until the start of the nineteenth century. Scottish and Welsh towns were slower to become fully established and even in the early modern period new market burghs were founded in Scotland, but by the eighteenth century the island had a strong, generally affluent and increasingly integrated network of towns, which was to provide the essential springboard for the urban and industrial take-off of the nineteenth century. From the Georgian era cities and towns were centres of manufacturing and commercial expansion, public improvement and enlightenment; they were the centre stage for the enactment of a British identity. In Victoria's reign the city with its political rallies, crafts and factories, railways, gothic town halls, societies and civic amenities threatened to swallow up the country. Whether one should see the growing fascination with the countryside after 1918, that fashionable, if fanciful pursuit of Ambridge, as a new kind of anti-urbanism, or rather as the ultimate post-urban annexation of the countryside and its incorporation into the cultural hinterland of the city, remains in hot debate.[2] But the interwar period was, despite the problems of the biggest industrial cities, a time of considerable prosperity and community pride for many cities and towns up and down the country. Even in the aftermath of the second world war, many of the traditional functions and relationships of the British urban system survived – at least until the 1960s.

This is a good time for a systematic historical investigation of the rise of British cities and towns over the *longue durée*. Not just because understanding urban society is too important a task to be left to contemporary sociologists, geographers and planners, but because of the flourishing state of British urban history. Though earlier scholarly works existed, the last thirty years have seen a revolution in our understanding of the complexity of the social, political and other functions of towns in the past, of the social groups and classes that comprised the urban population, of the relationships within the urban system and between cities and the wider society, whether countryside, region or state. Initially most sonorous for the Victorian period and orchestrated by that brilliant academic conductor, H. J. (Jim) Dyos, in company with Lord Asa Briggs and Sydney Checkland, the new concert of urban historians has increasingly embraced the early modern and medieval periods, a historiographical story explained in detail in the introductions to the separate volumes. The result is that for the first time we can follow the comparative evolution of English, Scottish and Welsh towns from the seventh to the twentieth century, traversing those conventional divisions of historical labour, particularly at the close of the middle ages and the end of the eighteenth century. Mobilising the expertise of historians, geographers, archaeologists, landscape historians and others, the modern study of urban history has always sought to pursue a wide-ranging agenda, aiming, so far as possible, to comprehend communities in the round, to see the interrelation of the different parts, even if such ambitions cannot always

2 P. Mandler, 'Against "Englishness": English culture and the limits to rural nostalgia', *TRHS*, 6th series, 7 (1997), 155–75.

be fully achieved. Here urban history offers an important methodological alternative to the more fragmented study of specific urban themes, which, through micro-studies focusing on the most interesting sources and communities, runs the risk of seeing issues, social groups or particular towns in isolation, out of meaningful context. Thickets of knowledge of this type are the bane of sustained and innovative scholarly research, and have contributed much to the distancing of academic literature from the public domain. Strikingly, the last few years have seen a renewed or enhanced recognition of the overarching importance of the urban variable, both dependent and independent, in the many different areas of social, business, demographic and women's history.

In the fertile tradition of urban history, the three volumes of the *Cambridge Urban History of Britain* are the product of a collaborative project, with a good deal of friendship, fellowship, hard talking and modest drinking amongst those involved. The idea for such a series was discussed at Leicester as early as 1977, at a convivial lunch hosted by Jim Dyos, but it was not until 1990 that a proposal was made to launch the series. An advisory board was established, editors agreed, and several meetings held to plot the structure of the volumes, the contributors and the publishing arrangements. Since then regular meetings have been held for particular volumes, and the discussions have not only produced important dividends for the coherence and quality of the volumes, but have contributed to the better understanding of the British city in general. The involvement of colleagues working on Scotland has been particularly fruitful.

This series of volumes has had no earmarked funding (though funding bodies have supported research for individual chapters), and the editors and contributors are grateful to the many British and several North American universities for funding, directly and indirectly, the research, travel and other costs of contributors to the enterprise. Through its commitment to the Centre for Urban History, which has coordinated the project, the University of Leicester has been a valued benefactor, while Cambridge University Press, in the friendly guise of Richard Fisher, has been enormously helpful and supportive over the long haul of preparation and publication. The fact that the series, involving nearly ninety different contributors, has been published broadly on schedule owes a great deal to the energy, high commitment and fathomless interpersonal skills of my fellow editors, David Palliser and Martin Daunton (to whom I have been heavily indebted for wise and fortifying counsel), to the collective solidarity of the contributors, as well as to the generous support and patience of partners and families.

Thirty years ago in his introduction to *The Study of Urban History* Dyos declared that 'the field is as yet a very ragged one, and those in it are a little confused as to what they are doing'.[3] Plausibly, the volumes in the present series show that current students of urban history are less confused and somewhat

[3] H. J. Dyos, ed., *The Study of Urban History* (London, 1968), p. 46.

better dressed intellectually, having access to an extensive wardrobe of evidence, arguments and ideas, with a broad comparative and temporal design. The picture of the British town becomes ever more complex, as our greater knowledge recognises variety where once only uniformity was evident. However, we are at last nearer the point of uncovering the spectrum of historical processes, which have shaped our many cities and towns, making the urban past more intelligible and accessible, not just to academics, but to those townspeople whose identification with their own contemporary communities at the turn of the millennium is being so constantly and fiercely questioned.

Acknowledgements

In a collaborative volume of this kind the editor and individual authors wish to thank fellow contributors for their helpful comments and suggestions. The editor is particularly grateful to Peter Borsay, Penelope Corfield and Joanna Innes for their advice at critical stages in the editing of the volume, and when he took over the writing of part of Chapter 17, following the late withdrawal of a contributor. David Reeder and Richard Rodger also gave helpful advice on the Conclusion. He is also heavily indebted to Kate Crispin, James Brown and other staff and students at the Centre for Urban History, Leicester University, who have generously assisted in the myriad of tasks associated with getting this book to press.

Further thanks are due to Dr Paul Glennie and the Geography Department, Bristol University, who have taken responsibility for the preparation of most of the figures and maps in the volume. The staff of the University Library and the Central Photographic Unit, University of Leicester, have provided unfailingly helpful support on the editorial side. Linda Randall had the unenviable task of copyediting the volume for Cambridge University Press and the editor and contributors are enormously grateful to her for her meticulous care and efficiency. The index was compiled by Auriol Griffith-Jones, to whom similar thanks are due. We are indebted to the British Academy for a grant in 1996 to support a 'Population database on British towns 1550–1841' in connection with the volume.

We are indebted to the following copyright owners for giving permission for items to be reproduced here: Anhaltische Gemäldegalerie Dessau, Germany, for Plate 1; the British Library for Plates 2, 3, 4, 26; Edinburgh University Library for Plate 5; Royal Commission on Ancient and Historical Monuments, Scotland, for Plates 6, 10, 23; Guildhall Library, Corporation of London, for Plates 7, 13, 14, 16, 20, 25; Oxford City Council for Plate 8; National Monuments Record for Plates 9, 11, 21; Leicester University for Plate 12; Bristol

Museums and Art Gallery for Plate 15; Bedford Borough Council for Plate 18; The Whitworth Gallery, University of Manchester, for Plate 19; Prof. M. Reed for Plate 22; Birmingham Library Services for Plate 24; Mr Jonathan Gestetner, Marlborough Rare Books, London, for Plate 27; Bath Central Library for Plate 28; Peter Moores Foundation, London for Plate 29; Bradford Art Galleries and Museums for Plate 30; Record Office for Leicestershire, Leicester and Rutland for Plate 31. Peter Clark is very grateful to Michael Reed for his great help in selecting and editing a number of the illustrations. Thanks are also due to the following for their generous assistance: Jeremy Smith at the Guildhall Library; Mireille Galinou at the Museum of London; Dr Michels at Dessau; Miss V. Bearn at Bath; Colin Brooks of the Central Photographic Unit, and all the staff of the Special Collections Department of the University Library, Leicester University. Maps 19.2 and 19.3 are reproduced with the kind permission of Craig Spence, from Craig Spence, *London in the 1690s: A Social Atlas* (London, 2000).

Abbreviations

Add.	Additional
Ag.HEW	*The Agrarian History of England and Wales*
Annales ESC	*Annales: économies, sociétiés, civilisations*
AO	Archives Office
Arch. and NHSoc.	Archaeological and Natural History Society
BL	British Library
Bull. IHR	*Bulletin of the Institute of Historical Research* (now *Historical Research*)
C	Proceedings in the Court of Chancery, Public Record Office
CSPD	*Calendar of State Papers Domestic*
DNB	*Dictionary of National Biography*
E	Exchequer Records, Public Record Office
Ec.HR	*Economic History Review*
EHR	*English Historical Review*
GSt.	*Guildhall Studies in London History*
HJ	*Historical Journal*
HMC	*Historical Manuscripts Commission*
HR	*Historical Research*
JEcc.Hist.	*Journal of Ecclesiastical History*
JMH	*Journal of Modern History*
JUH	*Journal of Urban History*
LJ	*London Journal*
NHist.	*Northern History*
NQ	*Notes and Queries*
PP	Parliamentary Papers
P&P	*Past and Present*
PRO	Public Record Office

RCHM	Royal Commission on Historical Monuments
RO	Record Office
SHist.	*Southern History*
Soc. Hist.	*Social History*
SP	State Papers Domestic, Public Record Office
SR	*Statutes of the Realm*, ed. A. Luders *et al.*
TRHS	*Transactions of the Royal Historical Society*
UH	*Urban History*
UHY	*Urban History Yearbook* (now *Urban History*)
VCH	*Victoria County History*

· 1 ·

Introduction

PETER CLARK

WRITING HOME to the Doge and Senate, those crusty patricians ensconced in their colonnaded palace on St Mark's Square, Venetian ambassadors to the Tudor Court hymned the praises of London as one of the principal cities of Europe, but ignored or dismissed almost all the remaining English towns. Other sixteenth-century visitors from the great continental states were equally critical. Only travellers from the more remote central European countries found anything remarkable in English provincial towns. Scottish and Welsh towns barely figure in foreign reports: Edinburgh on one occasion was compared to a French country town.[1] Yet by the late eighteenth century British towns – not just London but provincial towns – were the envy of the civilised world, admired in the many travellers' accounts which rehearsed details of their affluence, manufactures, vigorous club life, bustling, friendly shops, well-lit, orderly streets, and much else.[2] Whereas at the start of our period only a minority of English people, maybe 15 per cent or so (and a much lower proportion in Scotland and Wales) resided in cities and towns, by the accession of Queen Victoria nearly half the British population was urban. Not only was there an increasingly integrated national system of towns, but British towns became notable as centres of economic and social innovation, of political discourse and cultural enlightenment, their advance having a growing impact on national society and beyond. Hitherto located on the European periphery in terms of urban development, analogous to regions like Scandinavia and central

1 *Calendar of State Papers Venetian*, 1556–7, pp. 1045 *et seq.*; *Calendar of State Papers Spanish*, 1554–8, p. 33; G. von Bülow, 'Journey through England and Scotland made by Lupold von Wedel . . .', *TRHS*, 2nd series, 9 (1895), 223–70; G. W. Groos, ed., *The Diary of Baron Waldstein* (London, 1981); M. Lynch, *Edinburgh and the Reformation* (Edinburgh, 1981), p. 2.

2 P. Kielmansegge, ed., *Diary of a Journey to England in the Years 1761–1762* (London, 1902); R. Nettel, ed., *Journeys of a German in England in 1782* (London, 1965); C. Williams, ed., *Sophie in London 1786* (London, 1933).

Europe with their low urban populations and localised towns, from the eighteenth century Britain emerged as the chief laboratory of a modernising world.

(i) THE IMPORTANCE OF TOWNS

Even in the Tudor and early Stuart era towns were hardly the marginal players in national society that foreign portraits implied. As we saw in Volume I, Britain inherited from the middle ages an established cadre of 800–900 towns.[3] London was already a major European city by the fourteenth century, but after the Reformation the island also boasted fifty or so 'great and good towns', regional centres and shire towns as well as ports, with sizeable populations, diversified economies, municipal charters and a strong sense of civic identity (see plates 1–3). The other, smaller, towns, despite their rural aspect and absence of walls (so vital for continental visions of urban identity), were much bigger and more economically advanced than villages and had an extensive role in provincial society (see plate 4). In the pre-industrial period population scale was rarely a perfect index of urban importance. Certainly, with their high mortality rates British towns contributed powerfully to population movement as tens of thousands of people a year left the hard-pressed countryside in search of work there: significantly, the story of Dick Whittington and his cat arriving and making good in London begins to circulate at the end of Queen Elizabeth's reign.[4] Urban markets and fairs were vital in the general expansion of inland trade, taking back a growing share of the commerce they had lost in the late middle ages. Towns led the way in social policy initiatives (parish rates, workhouses and settlement controls), which were often subsequently adopted by crown and parliament. Under Charles I, a core of towns served to polarise political opposition to the regime and London was the scene of an unprecedented explosion of radical activity during the 1640s, which culminated in the execution of the king. Again in the century after the Reformation, towns contributed to the growth of religious pluralism and a new print culture. London's voice was certainly strong and made itself heard in the rise of domestic and overseas commerce, national politics and the spread of social and cultural innovation, but provincial towns sang important parts in the urban chorus.[5]

Truly, however, during the 'long' eighteenth century British towns came into their own as a dynamic force on a European scale. They established new specialist industries and promoted the rise of the service sector (with shopping invented as a cultural as well as a commercial exercise). Cities and towns saw the emergence of new social groups and new social alignments. They were the forcing

[3] See D. M. Palliser, ed., *The Cambridge Urban History of Britain*, vol. I: *600–1540* (Cambridge, 2000), esp. ch. 24.

[4] C. M. Barron, 'Richard Whittington: the man behind the myth', in A. E. J. Hollaender and W. Kellaway, eds., *Studies in London History* (London, 1969), pp. 197–8.

[5] See below, Chapters 5, 7, 8, 10–11.

ground for party politics and radicalism. Accoutred with coffee-houses and taverns, societies and concerts, they shaped the distinctive character of the English and Scottish enlightenments. British cities and towns forged new patterns of leisure, time, taste and sensibility, and created new perceptions of modernity through a stress on public and private improvement, and through refashioned notions of the built environment, marked by the profusion of classical-style terraced housing and later of bourgeois suburbs.[6]

A fundamental factor in the changing image and role of British cities and towns was urbanisation, the process by which the growing proportion of population living in cities created distinct behavioural and structural changes in society. Everything in this volume demonstrates that urban growth was not a lagging indicator of British industrialisation, rather the reverse. After a century and a half of stagnation or decline in the late middle ages, the sixteenth century saw renewed urban population growth, in line with the national increase. London's advance was most spectacular, rising from about 75,000 in the 1550s to about 400,000 a century later, but many provincial towns increased their size. Limited economic expansion and other problems led to considerable social instability in the urban system before the English Civil Wars – similar to the situation in other parts of Europe.[7] However, from the late seventeenth century English towns increasingly diverged from the continental pattern in their enjoyment of sustained, real demographic growth, which served as a precondition for general economic expansion. London's momentous, apparently inexorable, rise, to nearly a million inhabitants by 1800, making it one of the greatest cities in the world, was increasingly complemented by fast-growth provincial towns; Scottish and Welsh towns followed the trend, if some way behind.[8]

Outlining the urbanisation trend is much easier than calculating precise rates of growth, an area which remains controversial. In this volume a range of estimates are provided, often reflecting different urban parameters. Thus Chapter 6 uses relatively high urban thresholds of over 5,000 to suggest that England had perhaps 5 per cent of its inhabitants living in towns by 1540, and 8 per cent in 1600. Paul Glennie and Ian Whyte (Chapter 5) take a wider definition of towns and believe that by the end of the seventeenth century the urban population of England was of the order of 30–3 per cent, with 22–5 per cent in Scotland and 13–15 per cent in Wales. In a comprehensive and radical reworking of all the available population data for towns between 1660 and 1841, John Langton (Chapter 14) argues that in the late Stuart period the English population had already achieved an urban rate of 40 per cent, with Wales at 33 per cent and Scotland at 25 per cent. By 1801 there is more agreement, aided by the census

[6] See below, Chapters 14–18.

[7] See below, Chapter 6; P. M. Hohenberg and L. H. Lees, *The Making of Urban Europe 1000–1950* (London, 1985), esp. ch. 4.

[8] E. A. Wrigley, 'Urban growth and agricultural change: England and the continent in the early modern period', in P. Borsay, ed., *The Eighteenth Century Town* (London, 1990), pp. 41–82.

evidence, and it is likely that the British population overall was 42 per cent urban, rising to 51 per cent in 1841.[9]

Calculation is difficult because, although the relative demographic order of towns is broadly agreed, estimates vary about their absolute population size (particularly of the bigger cities). As will be evident from subsequent pages, at the present time there is no consensus on this matter, and it would be premature to try and standardise our population figures. Difficulties stem both from the fragility and incompleteness of the data for the pre-census period (discussed at length below, pp. 457–62), and also from issues relating to the definition of towns. Such problems, in some ways more taxing than for many other European countries in the period, do not invalidate the urban approach, but challenge us to create sensitive, imaginative and robust methodologies in response. Certainly the usual problem of defining early towns – identifying the urban features of small places which by modern standards are hardly recognisable as towns – persists into the Tudor and Stuart period. Only the bigger centres normally combined those recognised attributes of urbanness: a substantial population density, a developed urban economy and social order, distinctive political and administrative structures, and a cultural role and influence extending beyond the immediate locality. From the eighteenth century, however, the problems are both simpler and more complex. All but the smallest towns have usually shed their bucolic image and agricultural functions, and acquired clearly urban and urbane aspects, such as shops, professional men, public improvements, new housing and sociable activities. Now problems of definition focus on recognising and identifying the frontiers of the urban community, as the traditional urban palimpsest is overlaid with new developments: the growing array of leafy suburbs for the better off; new industrial colonies on the periphery with spots of working-class housing; the emergence of the modern conurbation.[10] Already by the Restoration of Charles II the majority of London's population lived outside the civic limits and by the later Georgian era there was a penumbra of metropolitan suburban and satellite communities, many of them larger than middle-rank provincial towns, frequently with distinctive identities. At the end of our period provincial centres like Manchester, Birmingham and Glasgow were developing in a similar direction. By the early nineteenth century difficulties of definition on the ground were compounded by the growing confusion of urban administrative categories. As Britain became a modern urban nation the urban community was increasingly amorphous and elusive.[11]

However, the urban transformation of Britain in this period cannot be construed simply in terms of demographic and economic forces. Urban historians have ever to be sensitive to the importance of the political and cultural dimension. The destiny of early modern towns was shaped decisively by their relations with

[9] See below, pp. 169, 197, 462 *et seq.*

[10] See below, pp. 619–21, 644 *et seq.*, 812 *et seq.*

[11] See below, pp. 552 *et seq.*

the state. Tudor and early Stuart governments were particularly active in the urban arena, granting new charters, bolstering the power of civic oligarchies, interfering in town administration, giving corporations new official powers in regard to economic and social policy.[12] During the 1530s and 1540s one of the biggest and most successful measures of state intervention in British history, the Reformation, had a significant impact, as one sees in Chapter 8. It transformed much of the traditional fabric of the medieval town, stripped away monastic houses and fraternities, disrupted ceremonial life, depressed some urban economies and opened the door to religious and political division.[13]

A hundred years later the opposition to Charles I and the outbreak of Civil War ushered in a period of major uncertainty and instability for towns. Recent research has highlighted the demographic, economic and physical damage wrought by Civil War hostilities.[14] The long-term effects of the political and religious dissension of the English Revolution contributed to the tension and conflict in boroughs during the later Stuart period. On the other hand, after the Glorious Revolution of 1688 the state's concentration on foreign policy, war and taxation left British towns with a considerable measure of local autonomy, running their affairs in a way unknown to continental cities, where busybody central governments routinely intruded into social policy, transport, architecture, planning and intellectual life.[15] British cities assume a two-sided function in the political system of the eighteenth and early nineteenth centuries, both as the lairs of 'corrupt influence' and as arenas, theatres, where a new kind of pluralistic, participatory politics was produced. Influential in this respect was the collapse of state censorship in the 1690s, which boosted the role of towns as engines of the print revolution, with newspapers and the publishing industry wielding a powerful influence over their commercial and service development, political life, cultural image and, not least, their relations with their hinterlands and regional society.[16]

[12] See below, pp. 238 *et seq.*

[13] See below, pp. 263 *et seq.*; also R. Tittler, *The Reformation and the Towns in England* (Oxford, 1998); M. Graham, *The Uses of Reform: 'Godly Discipline' and Popular Behaviour in Scotland and Beyond, 1560–1610* (Leiden, 1996); M. Lynch, 'Preaching to the converted? Perspectives on the Scottish Reformation', in A. A. MacDonald, M. Lynch and I. B. Cowan, eds., *The Renaissance in Scotland* (Leiden, 1994), pp. 301–43.

[14] M. Stoyle, *From Deliverance to Destruction* (Exeter, 1996), esp. chs. 3–6; M. Bennett, '"My plundered towns, my houses devastation": the Civil War and North Midlands life 1642–1646', *Midland History*, 22 (1997), 35–48; I. Roy, ' England turned Germany? The aftermath of the Civil War in its European context', *TRHS*, 5th series, 28 (1978), 132–44. See also B. Coates, 'The impact of the English Civil War on the economy of London 1642–1650' (PhD thesis, University of Leicester, 1997).

[15] See below, pp. 254–62; G. S. de Krey, *A Fractured Society* (Oxford, 1985); J. Brewer, *The Sinews of Power* (London, 1988); C. Tilly and W. T. P. Blockmans, eds., *Cities and the Rise of States in Europe A.D. 1000 to 1800* (Oxford, 1994), pp. 178–80.

[16] See below, Chapters 16, 17; C. Y. Ferdinand, *Benjamin Collins and the Provincial Newspaper Trade in the Eighteenth Century* (Oxford, 1997).

Another key relationship was with rural society, and here we know more about certain aspects than others. The exchange function of towns in the agrarian economy figures prominently in this work (especially in Chapters 5 and 13), but the terms of trade between town and countryside and the patterns of urban investment and property ownership in rural hinterlands have attracted less research.[17] On the other hand, nobody can doubt the vital role of landowners in urban development in Britain, as in much of Europe. During the sixteenth century relations with local gentry ranged from the amicable to the downright acrimonious. There was a good deal of jostling over jurisdictions and privileges, and a rather condescending view of towns among the seigneurial classes. After the Restoration the upper classes' experience of great continental cities whilst on the 'Grand Tour' contributed to a landed invasion of English towns, initially London and then provincial centres.[18] Gentry and their families rented houses or lodgings in urban centres and some of them became almost residential towns in the German manner, their new fashionable areas designed (and portrayed) as extensions of landed estates. Resort towns depended heavily on landed patronage and the West End of London was developed by the aristocratic Russells and Grosvenors, among others, as a fashionable cantonment for the landed elite. Many landowners, of course, paid shorter visits to town, but the impact on the urban economy and social life of genteel demand for housing, consumer wares and leisure entertainment was profound. The retreat of the landed classes from many provincial towns, and even, to some extent, from London, after 1800 was no less decisive for their future.[19]

These major changes created both important opportunities and powerful challenges for British towns. Whether in the developed or developing worlds, urbanisation has often been associated with social disruption, social segregation and social alienation.[20] Certainly urban growth in the early modern era had negative dimensions; there were considerable costs entailed. During the sixteenth and early seventeenth centuries the failure of economic growth to keep pace

[17] For a dissection of the complexities see E. A. Wrigley, 'City and country in the past: a sharp divide or a continuum?', *HR*, 64 (1991), 107–20; for recent work on the credit links between town and hinterland see C. Muldrew, 'Rural credit, market areas and legal institutions in the countryside in England 1550–1700', in C. Brooks and M. Lobban, eds., *Communities and Courts in Britain 1150–1900* (London, 1997), pp. 155–78. [18] See below, pp. 240–1.

[19] For London see Lawrence Stone's splendid essay, 'The residential development of the West End of London in the seventeenth century', in B. C. Malament, ed., *After the Reformation* (Manchester, 1980), pp. 173–209; J. Summerson, *Georgian London* (London, 1945); for the provinces see: P. Borsay, *The English Urban Renaissance* (Oxford, 1989); L. Williams, 'Rus in urbe: greening the English town 1660–1760' (PhD thesis, University of Wales, 1998).

[20] L. Wirth, *On Cities and Social Life* (Chicago, 1964); W. A. Hance, *Population, Migration and Urbanization in Africa* (New York, 1970); T. G. McGee, *The Urbanization Process in the Third World* (London, 1971); D. J. Walmsley, *Urban Living: The Individual in the City* (London, 1988), pp. 3–7.

with demographic expansion, aggravated by the influx of poverty stricken labourers from the countryside and periodic harvest disasters and trade disruption, led to acute social problems for a number of larger and middling towns. Various studies have highlighted the tidal wave of poverty. At Warwick in the 1580s 30 per cent of the inhabitants of St Mary's parish were classed as poor; at St Martin's, Salisbury, in 1635 the comparable figure was over a third.[21] As elsewhere in Europe, numerous British towns, not least in Scotland, were affected by subsistence crises, and town elites suffered nightmarish fears over the rising tide of vagrants and the disorderly. Plague during the sixteenth century became largely an urban scourge, repeatedly decimating the poorer districts, but, despite its disappearance in the 1660s, towns remained killing fields (especially for urban infants), with mortality, if anything, higher than in the previous period.[22] Nor did urban expansion banish other problems. Trade fluctuations and changes in the urban economy – together with agricultural improvement – created cyclical crises of unemployment and large-scale poverty, while large numbers of middling traders were at risk from bankruptcy.[23]

Urbanisation caused mounting environmental problems. While rising energy use created a heat island effect in the Georgian capital, facilitating fashionable socialising even in the winter months, the pervasive metropolitan stench, fuelled by coal fires and furnaces and rotting human and animal waste (London had perhaps 100,000 horses by 1811), greeted travellers at many miles distance, while in central areas the Thames was an open sewer, fogs smothered the streets, trees withered and royal statues became so black that they were mistaken for chimney sweeps or African kings.[24] At Sheffield smoke and pollution from the iron forges

[21] P. Slack, *Poverty and Policy in Tudor and Stuart England* (London, 1988), pp. 67–85 *et passim*; A. L. Beier, 'The social problems of an Elizabethan country town: Warwick 1580–90', in P. Clark, ed., *Country Towns in Pre-Industrial England* (Leicester, 1981), p. 58; in P. Slack, 'Poverty and politics in Salisbury 1597–1666', in P. Clark and P. Slack, eds., *Crisis and Order in English Towns 1500–1700* (London, 1972), p. 176.

[22] P. Slack, *The Impact of Plague in Tudor and Stuart England* (London, 1985); J. A. I. Champion, ed., *Epidemic Disease in London* (London, 1993), pp. 1–52; E. A. Wrigley *et al.*, *English Population History from Family Reconstitution 1580–1837* (Cambridge, 1997), pp. 217–18, 272 *et seq.*; J. Landers, *Death and the Metropolis* (Cambridge, 1993), esp. chs. 4–5; but see M. J. Dobson, *Contours of Death and Disease in Early Modern England* (Cambridge, 1997), pp. 141–3.

[23] See below, Chapter 15; J. Hoppit, *Risk and Failure in English Business 1700–1800* (Cambridge, 1987), chs. 5–7.

[24] T. J. Chandler, *The Climate of London* (London, 1965), pp. 126, 147 *et seq.*; L. W. Labaree *et al.*, eds., *The Papers of Benjamin Franklin* (New Haven, 1959–93), vol. VII, p. 380; J. Evelyn, *Fumifugium: Or, The Inconvenience of the Aer and Smoake of London Dissipated* (1661; new edn, London, 1772), new preface (for the political dimension to Evelyn's original tract see M. Jenner, 'The politics of London air . . .', *HJ*, 38 (1995), 535–51); F. M. L. Thompson, 'Nineteenth-century horse sense', *Ec.HR*, 2nd series, 29 (1976), 80 (figure as proportion of national figure for non-agricultural horses); R. B. Johnson, *The Undergraduate* (London, 1928), pp. 255–6; M. W. Hamilton, 'An American knight in Britain', *New York History*, 42 (1961), 125.

wrapped the town in fumes, discolouring its buildings; in 1764 Horace Walpole baldly declared it was 'one of the foulest towns in England'. As pollution choked the lungs of townspeople, contaminated water supplies spread sickness and death among babies and children.[25]

Urban growth also posed other problems. The spatial expansion of bigger towns combined with high levels of migration and mobility created a perception of individual isolation and anomie and a more general sense of urban fragmentation: by the end of the eighteenth century observers are talking about the divisions, even the different peoples in towns. In 1797 a Londoner visiting the Borough area of south London declared 'we met and saw a variety of people who had heads on their shoulders and eyes and legs and arms, like ourselves, but in every other respect as different from the race of mortals we meet at the West End of the Town . . . as a native of Bengal from a Laplander'.[26] Newcomers (and residents as well) faced the difficulty of making their way in the city. Urban improvement and affluence removed many of the signs and symbols of traditional urban society – ancient landmarks, distinctive vernacular housing (replaced by uniform, neo-classical terraces), street signs. Distinctions of dress and life style were elided by new fashions of consumption. Inflows of gentry and professional men with their smart leisure tastes and entertainments, often aping those of London, challenged the cultural codes of many older provincial towns. Overall, towns experienced major difficulties in integrating newcomers and creating and recreating a sense of urban and communal identity.[27]

None the less, as the following chapters reveal, towns in Britain (and their inhabitants) showed a considerable resilience and capacity to cope with these pressures and problems, developing, in addition to traditional urban structures and agencies for maintaining stability, new organisations and stratagems, as urbanisation accelerated. On balance, Britain fared better in dealing with urban change than most other European countries.

In the precarious and unstable world of the sixteenth and early seventeenth centuries economic and social pressures, despite their severity, were in considerable measure contained; public order in British towns was challenged but only rarely overturned by food and apprenticeship riots; political problems, such as conflicts between the different political groups within the community, were negotiated and largely resolved. Crises were often turned to advantage. Thus the Reformation became an opportunity for a number of towns to seize command of their own governance from church control, while elsewhere town leaders

[25] R. E. Leader, *Sheffield in the Eighteenth Century* (Sheffield, 1901), p. 150; Landers, *Death and the Metropolis*, pp. 70–2.

[26] W. C. Mackenzie, ed., *The War Diary of a London Scot* (Paisley, 1916), pp. 177–8.

[27] See below, Chapters 17, 18, 20.

exploited Puritanism to attempt to consolidate their political and moral authority. During the upheavals of the Civil War there was no breakdown of the social order or of urban government; rather the dire political situation drove provincial towns to improve their political and social relations with the gentry, which facilitated the fashionable landed influx of the late seventeenth century. In the Georgian era popular action was vociferous: scores of old-style food riots were joined by recurrent political protests and agitation, by crowd attacks on the Irish, impressment and brothels, and by strike action (with nearly 150 disputes recorded in England in the last decades of the eighteenth century).[28] However, most popular action was localised and readily controlled. The exception to prove the rule were the religious-inspired Gordon riots of 1780 which led to large-scale destruction in the capital and a major reorganisation of city policing. Political radicalism in the 1790s was largely moderate and constitutional and a good deal less intimidating than the loyalist mobs which, egged on by the upper classes, threatened and sometimes attacked respectable reformers.[29]

Part of the explanation for the success of British towns in coping with the economic and other pressures of the period relates to the nature of the changes affecting them, not least industrialisation. Whereas the Industrial Revolution was conventionally identified with the introduction of new technology and the rapid spread of large-scale factory production, this industrial breakthrough generating capital concentration and class stratification, recent interpretations have suggested that most industrial advances into the early nineteenth century were small scale, incremental, technical, and workshop or domestically based, while economic expansion was seconded by the proliferation of service activities – again structured in a traditional way. It is essential, as Chapter 14 makes plain, not to downplay the dynamic importance of industrialisation in urban growth during the long eighteenth century. Rather the process should be seen as broadly manageable both in its nature and effects, at least until the turn of the century.[30]

Another key factor relates to the complex nature of the urban transformation in the pre-Victorian era. The older tripartite hierarchy of London, 'great and good towns' (the regional and county centres) and small market towns was

[28] For the situation in the 1590s see M. J. Power, 'London and the control of the "crisis" of the 1590s', *History*, 70 (1985), 371–85. P. Clark, '"The Ramoth-Gilead of the Good": urban change and political radicalism at Gloucester 1540–1640', in J. Barry, ed., *The Tudor and Stuart Town* (London, 1990), pp. 265–73; D. Underdown, *Fire from Heaven* (London, 1992); R. B. Shoemaker, *Prosecution and Punishment* (Cambridge, 1991), pp. 58, 65–6 *et passim*; N. Rogers, *Whigs and Cities* (Oxford, 1989); K. Wilson, *The Sense of the People* (Cambridge, 1995), pp. 125 *et passim*; C. R. Dobson, *Masters and Journeymen* (London, 1980), p. 22. [29] See below, Chapter 16.

[30] N. F. R. Crafts, *British Economic Growth during the Industrial Revolution* (Oxford, 1985); E. A. Wrigley, *Continuity, Chance and Change: The Character of the Industrial Revolution in England* (Cambridge, 1988).

replaced by an increasingly diffuse and polycentric system. Admittedly, London advanced exponentially: by 1840 it was the leading imperial and global metropolis and there can be no doubt that its growth had a powerful effect from the sixteenth century, promoting new markets, financial networks, the dissemination of innovation and new expectations of urban life. However, London's economic and cultural ascendancy was always sectoral, geographically incomplete, and its meteoric development should not distort our vision of the rest of the urban system.[31] After 1700 there was a growing number of new commercial and industrial cities like Birmingham, Manchester, Leeds and Glasgow, together with a tremendous upsurge of more specialist towns – resort and leisure centres, industrial towns, Atlantic ports and naval towns; almost every category with its own cluster of sub-types.[32] As a result, it is possible to conceptualise British urbanisation in the pre-Victorian era as something akin to a wave system. Major aggregate change frequently took the form of a multiplicity of small-scale alterations affecting a diversity of urban communities – alterations which rarely coincided everywhere and which by themselves could usually be absorbed at the local level. Certainly it would be blinkered to see the urban transformation of our period as an exclusively big city phenomenon. Middle-rank and market towns, small industrialising and other specialist centres all made an essential contribution to urban development into the early nineteenth century, mediating a good deal of the upheaval. There was an important political dimension to this process. The diversification of forms of urban government after the Revolution of 1688, exemplified by the rise of a bewildering array of improvement, police and other administrative agencies in both chartered and unincorporated towns, likewise served to order and contain the intense pressures of an urbanising world.[33]

At a different level, individual townspeople, groups and communities pursued their own strategies for survival and success. The challenge of urbanisation was answered on a daily basis through the personal, often grimly heroic, choices and decisions of ordinary men and women. Of exit, voice and loyalty, famously conceived by Albert Hirschmann as the standard human choices in a time of crisis, exit, in the form of migration, was the most favoured by British townspeople. In Chapter 15 we hear the story of Thomas Carter, a teenage tailor from Colchester, who travelled to London, moved around the metropolis changing masters and lodgings, when unemployed went back to his home town, and finally set up business there later in life. Men and women moved all the time,

[31] See below, Chapter 19; also M. Reed, 'London and its hinterland 1600–1800: the view from the provinces', in P. Clark and B. Lepetit, eds., *Capital Cities and their Hinterlands in Early Modern Europe* (Aldershot, 1996), pp. 57–77; P. Borsay, 'The London connection: cultural diffusion and the eighteenth century provincial town', *LJ*, 19 (1994), 27–30.

[32] See below, Chapters 20, 21, 23, 24. [33] See below, Chapters 16, 22.

forsaking oppressive masters, hoping for better conditions, leaving uncomfortable lodgings or tenements, moving away from failing trades or depressed towns: the reasons were almost infinite. Well before 1800 environmental problems in urban centres created a new type of collective movement: the genteel and then middle-class exodus to country and suburban villas.[34]

In this highly mobile urban world the family household provided one potential resource against uncertainty. Newcomers frequently lodged with kinsfolk who also helped them find work. Couples supplemented family income by sending children out to service, the woman doing laundry work or selling drink in the kitchen or backroom of the house, the husband adding another job to his occupational repertory. Family conviviality helped to consolidate kin, friend and business networks. However, as we will see in Chapter 6, the fragile nature of the urban family, its vulnerability to sickness and death, the limited scale of extended kinship links, meant that it was only a limited protection against economic disaster.[35] Neighbourhood and trades, despite being contested areas of activity, provided other defences against uncertainty. When townspeople protested over food prices, wages or other grievances, it was likely to be in gatherings with neighbours at the parish church or local alehouse or with other artisans through guild or trade meetings. Such institutions also helped in the process of urban acculturation for outsiders.[36] In spite of the constant flux of servants and other workers, in spite of the sprawling expansion of towns by 1800, the street and neighbourhood, with their matrix of public space, drinking houses, shops, lodging houses and ritual sociable activity, remained key pillars of urban loyalty and identification, indeed that function may have grown during the period. Similarly, in many larger urban communities trade guilds served as an important agency for economic and social cooperation, for integrating youngsters and the socially mobile, and for patronage and philanthropy during the Tudor and Stuart period, and, whilst guilds generally declined after 1700, occupational organisations remained a major force for cohesion and integration. Merchants, manufacturers and professional men increasingly set up their own organisations to combat excessive competition and business failure. For many artisans trade clubs became a major defence against sickness and other short-term financial problems, as well

[34] A. O. Hirschman, *Exit, Voice and Loyalty* (Cambridge, Mass., 1970); for Carter see pp. 492–3. See also generally P. Clark and D. Souden, eds., *Migration and Society in Early Modern England* (London, 1987), esp. chs. 2, 4, 7, 9–10; J. S. Taylor, *Poverty, Migration and Settlement in the Industrial Revolution* (Palo Alto, Calif., 1989); see below, pp. 491 *et seq.*, 619–20.

[35] See below, p. 223 *et seq.*; K. Westhauser, 'Friendship and family in early modern England: the sociability of Adam Eyre and Samuel Pepys', *Journal of Social History*, 27 (1994), 517–36; Y. Kawana, 'Social networks and urban space: the social organisation of a county town, Leicester c. 1550–1640' (PhD thesis, University of Leicester, 1996), ch. 3.

[36] J. Boulton, *Neighbourhood and Society* (Cambridge, 1987), chs. 8–11; P. Clark, *The English Alehouse* (London, 1983), pp. 152–3, 232–3; Clark and Souden, eds., *Migration and Society*, ch. 9.

as an important focus of male (and to lesser extent female) fellowship and solidarity.[37]

Economic organisations were only a small part of the growing army of voluntary organisations from the later seventeenth century which sought to overcome the strains of urban life. Voluntary hospitals and dispensaries relieved the sick; charitable societies like the Stranger's Friend Society and the Philanthropic Society endeavoured to relieve and control newcomers and the disorderly poor. Charity schools and the later Sunday Schools aimed to teach the young poor basic educational skills and to keep them off the streets. Prosecution societies served to reinforce the effectiveness of urban policing. Ranging from archery, bell ringing and chess clubs, to music societies and the ubiquitous masonic lodges, associations provided entertainment and relief from the increasingly relentless pressure of business life, while also offering mutual help and a mechanism for social networking and urban integration. This was a distinctly British response to the pressures of urbanisation.[38]

A number of chapters in this volume illuminate the way that changes in the urban social structure acted to stabilise urban society. In the Tudor and early Stuart period the social structure remained fragile and polarised, with a narrow elite, a cluster of middling groups and a large base of the poorer classes. By the eighteenth century the picture was much more complicated. The growth of the middling orders was striking, their modest prosperity, growing education and social networking providing a measure of social ballast, as did the emergence of a skilled artisan class. Contrariwise, there is not much evidence of general class formation before the end of the period: the rise of a distinct middle class, with interlocking political, social and cultural institutions, was at best specific to particular communities with distinctive socio-economic profiles.[39] This is hardly surprising. When one looks hard at the social structure, the differences between social groupings are often as remarkable as their shared characteristics. Take the elite, business world. Merchants, particularly great merchants, organised different social networks to manufacturers; medical men vied for social status with

[37] S. Rappaport, *Worlds within Worlds* (Cambridge, 1989), pp. 195–214; J. P. Ward, *Metropolitan Communities* (Stanford, Calif., 1997); D. Palliser, 'The trade gilds of Tudor York', in Clark and Slack, eds., *Crisis and Order*, pp. 86–112; I. J. W. Archer, *The History of the Haberdashers' Company* (Chichester, 1991); P. Clark, *British Clubs and Societies 1580–1800* (Oxford, 2000), pp. 350 *et passim*.

[38] D. T. Andrew, *Philanthropy and Police* (Princeton, N.J., 1989), pp. 49 *et passim*; T. W. Laqueur, *Religion and Respectability* (New Haven, 1976); D. Hay and F. Snyder, eds., *Policing and Prosecution in Britain 1750–1850* (Oxford, 1989), pp. 27–8, 115–207; Clark, *British Clubs and Societies*, chs. 4–6.

[39] P. Clark and P. Slack, *English Towns in Transition 1500–1700* (London, 1976), pp. 111–17; see below, Chapter 15; also P. J. Corfield, ed., *Language, History and Class* (London, 1991), chs. 2, 5; J. Barry and C. Brooks, eds., *The Middling Sort of People* (London, 1994); P. Earle, *The Making of the English Middle Class* (London, 1989). For an excellent account of the rise of the middle class in an industrialising centre see R. J. Morris, *Class, Sect and Party* (Manchester, 1990); for different social formations see A. J. Dalgleish, 'Voluntary associations and the middle class in Edinburgh 1780–1820' (PhD thesis, University of Edinburgh, 1991).

lawyers; and, within the medical profession, surgeons, physicians and apothecaries were often in bitter rivalry. Lower down the social scale, indentured apprentices in a wealthier trade had a privileged position compared to the general run of young servants. In sum, we need to be sensitive to the myriad gradations of social categories and the constant renegotiation of social relationships, both within and between social groupings. A number of groups had a crucial role in this process, as they bridged divisions within and beyond urban society. Thus lawyers frequently served as brokers between the landed classes and urban entrepreneurs, and professional men in general played a vital, intermediate role in political and cultural life, fostering (into the nineteenth century) a continued sense of urban cohesion.[40]

Life cycle and gender also help to define the nature of urban social organisation and its response to urban problems. Though young men lacked the institutional structures found in continental cities in the fifteenth and sixteenth centuries, this important urban minority crowded together at alehouses and in neighbourly games for sociable fellowship and mutual support; and from the later Stuart era their interests were catered for by a growing army of associations, which offered information, charitable aid and integrative support – as well as hard drinking, fellowship and fun. Women likewise had a vital role in the management of urbanisation. Often the majority of town inhabitants by the eighteenth century, they were active in neighbourly socialising and solidarity, they supplied crucial labour in the growth of the service and new manufacturing sectors, and they were prominent in the development of public cultural life, promoting the spread of new ideas of entertainment, sensibility and moral reform.[41]

At the communal level, towns fought hard to protect and promote their unity

[40] R. Grassby, *The Business Community of Seventeenth-Century England* (Cambridge, 1995), pp. 385–6; D. Hancock, *Citizens of the World* (Cambridge, 1995), esp. pp. 386 *et seq.*; G. Holmes, *Augustan England* (London, 1982); D. Porter and R. Porter, *Patient's Progress* (London, 1989), pp. 22, 117; but for attempts to create a wider medical community see S. Lawrence, *Charitable Knowledge* (Cambridge, 1996), pp. 250–5. I. K. Ben-Amos, *Adolescence and Youth in Early Modern England* (London, 1994), chs. 4–5; Barry and Brooks, eds., *Middling Sort*, ch. 2; P. J. Corfield, *Power and the Professions in Britain 1700–1850* (London, 1995), pp. 128, 137, 140.

[41] Clark, *English Alehouse*, pp. 127, 147–8, 224; P. Griffiths, *Youth and Authority* (Oxford, 1996); P. Griffiths, 'Masterless young people in Norwich, 1560–1645', in P. Griffiths *et al.*, eds., *The Experience of Authority in Early Modern England* (London, 1996), pp. 146–86. For women see below, esp. Chapters 6, 15, 17; see also M. Prior, ed., *Women in English Society 1500–1800* (London, 1985), chs. 2–3; and L. Charles and L. Duffin, eds., *Women and Work in Pre-Industrial England* (London, 1985), chs. 3–4; P. Earle, 'The female labour market in London in the late seventeenth and early eighteenth centuries', *Ec.HR*, 2nd series, 42 (1989), 328–46; E. C. Sanderson, *Women and Work in Eighteenth-Century Edinburgh* (London, 1996); A. Clark, *The Struggle for the Breeches* (Berkeley, Calif., 1995); L. Davidoff and C. Hall, *Family Fortunes* (London, 1987); G. J. Barker-Benfield, *The Culture of Sensibility* (Chicago, 1992). For a recent critique see A. I. J. Vickery, 'Golden age to separate spheres: a review of the categories and chronology of English women's history', *HJ*, 36 (1993), 401–12.

and identity. Confronted with a flurry of economic and social crises in the century before the Civil War corporations pioneered a range of civic measures to relieve the poor, to regulate migrants and the disorderly and to bolster the local economy.[42] Fierce competition between towns in the sixteenth and seventeenth centuries was frequently aggravated by their close proximity to one another, by the relentless growth of London and by the process of commercial integration. In response, civic elites sought to win commercial or other privileges which disadvantaged their rivals, to curry the favour of county landowners and to poach leading businessmen. The importance of great merchants or the like in the large cities – contributing to infrastructure, commercial development or charities, helping such communities to ride out the pressures of urban change – is well reported. But, if anything, wealthy figures like these had an even more decisive influence on smaller towns. Town councils spent a great deal of time keeping or courting the patronage of such worthies – rather like modern cities in hot pursuit of the new factory of a multinational company; and, if successful, this patronage could endow a small town with a measure of security against the fierce winds of external competition.[43]

Before the Civil War towns tried to exploit their relationship with the state to outflank competitors. With the diminished role of the central government after 1688, towns lobbied hard in Parliament for tariff privileges and improvement powers. However, economic expansion opened a chocolate box of other options. Increasingly competition was ameliorated by the advent of urban specialisation, as towns, first in England and later elsewhere, developed, more or less deliberately, specific leisure, transport, marketing or manufacturing functions (sometimes more than one) honed to particular sectors of demand. Specialisation in products or services underpinned much of the urban affluence of the eighteenth century, profiting small as well as large centres in much of the country.

In some places urban specialisation was the creature of heavy municipal or corporatist investment – most notably in the great ports like Liverpool and Hull (see Chapter 21). Elsewhere, there was a concerted effort to woo gentry visitors. The gentry's political interference was tolerated (preferably in return for douceurs such as a new town hall), and smart leisure amenities were installed to captivate the well-to-do. From the later Stuart period there was growing cultural one-upmanship as towns, seconded by local newspapers and magazines, sought to project new images of urbanity, improvement and modernity by demolishing town walls, promoting the building of new assembly rooms and boasting music festivals and learned societies. Travellers' reports, such as by the wonderfully acerbic John Byng, mirrored the rivalry, with sharp comparisons of the state of

[42] See below, pp. 364 *et seq*.

[43] W. T. MacCaffrey, *Exeter 1540–1640* (Cambridge, Mass., 1958), esp. chs. 4–6; D. H. Sacks, *The Widening Gate* (Berkeley, Calif., 1991), esp. chs. 1–3; e.g., P. and J. Clark, eds., *The Boston Assembly Minutes 1545–1575* (Lincolnshire Record Society, 77, 1987), pp. xiv–xv.

different towns. The Whig Sir Richard Phillips at the start of the nineteenth century actually drew up a checklist comparing (and grading) the urban attributes of nearby Derby, Nottingham and Leicester.[44]

Not that there was an uncontrolled world of urban competition. In Scotland the Convention of Royal Burghs provided a forum for concerted action up to the late seventeenth century and in England there is evidence of growing cooperation between towns. Often this was on specific issues, such as the outports' opposition to the London trading companies under James I, the opposition to itinerant traders after 1700 and the later campaigns over taxation and tariffs. But by the late eighteenth century there was more general collaboration evinced by the General Chamber of Manufacturers in the 1780s, and joint urban support for turnpike trusts and canal companies. Within regions interurban cooperation was boosted by economic specialisation and integration.[45]

As in modern-day developing countries, one can identify both integration and divergence in the British urban system. Integration is evident not only in the urbanisation process, as the upland areas of England, Scotland and parts of Wales caught up with southern England in the density and scale of their urban networks, but also in economic advances (food marketing, banking, the growth of retailing and the professions), the rise of public improvement, the cultural resurgence of towns celebrated by the circus of new style leisure activities. It was both a horizontal extension with the dispersal of new urban activities across mainland Britain, and a vertical one. By the end of the eighteenth century many minor towns in England, Scotland and Wales shared in the new developments orchestrated by the larger towns, and especially, but not exclusively, by London.[46]

Yet national integration did not choke off regional and local differentiation, indeed it may have encouraged it. As we shall see in Part I, there were marked regional differences in the distribution, size and activity of towns across the country. From the seventeenth century regional diversity seems to have been increasingly marked in terms of industrial expansion, the emergence of high growth centres and specialist urban networks. Thus one can see the stabilisation

[44] See below, Chapters 17–18, 20, 22–3; also Borsay, *English Urban Renaissance*; E. Moir, *The Discovery of Britain* (London, 1964), esp. chs. 4, 8; J. Byng, *The Torrington Diaries*, ed. C. B. Andrews (London, 1934–8); C. Grewcock, 'Social and intellectual life in Leicester, 1735–1835' (MA dissertation, University of Leicester, 1973), pp. 18–19.

[45] See below, pp. 237–8; R. Ashton, *The City and the Court 1603–1643* (Cambridge, 1979), esp. pp. 84–89 (though there was a good deal of division among the outports); *Postman*, 28 Feb.–2 March 1705/6; also *Commons Journals*, 1727–32, pp. 451–2, 459, 462; H.-C. Mui and L. H. Mui, *Shops and Shopkeeping in Eighteenth-Century England* (London, 1989), ch. 4; D. Read, *The English Provinces c. 1760–1960* (London, 1964), pp. 24–34.

[46] Cf. R. B. Potter and A. J. Salau, eds., *Cities and Development in the Third World* (London, 1990), pp. 1–6. J. A. Chartres, 'Market integration and agricultural output in seventeenth-, eighteenth- and early nineteenth-century England', *Agricultural History Review*, 43 (1995), 117–38; I. S. Black, 'Money, information and space: banking in early nineteenth-century England and Wales', *Journal of Historical Geography*, 21 (1995), 398–412.

or relative decline of the cities and towns of East Anglia and the South-West, compared to the more dynamic expansion of the urban networks of the West Midlands and parts of the North. There may also have been greater political and cultural divisions between different areas of the country. No less vital, our period saw increasingly articulated civic particularism, promoted by the print revolution, by distinctive forms of social and cultural organisation and the new waves of public and private building in towns. The British urban system of the early nineteenth century was remarkable for its pluralism and diversity.[47]

Finally, how did all these changes influence attitudes to towns? In the sixteenth and seventeenth centuries not only were outsiders, foreign visitors and gentry rather dismissive about the great majority of British towns, but, as we shall see in Part II, townspeople themselves seemed rather pessimistic, nervous about the many economic, social and other problems besetting their communities. By the eighteenth century the atmosphere was more optimistic, at least among the better off and middling classes, buoyed up by economic advances, rising living standards, urban improvement and the steady percolation through provincial society of the urban enlightenment. Social and environmental problems were never far from the surface, however, and by the start of the new century the mood had often darkened again. On the other hand, there persisted a strong belief (inherited from the Georgian period) that urban improvement could have a positive effect and that communities (finance allowing) could manage change – a perception which, combined with strenuous civic promotion (including urban historiography), was to help define the world of the Victorian city.

(ii) THE LITERATURE

Like the development of the early modern town, its study has had a checkered history. In contrast to other major European countries, and reflecting the relative backwardness of British towns, there were few town chronicles or histories before the sixteenth century: only London had any claim to a chronicling tradition. By Elizabeth's reign, however, a growing number of English provincial towns produced chronicles of varying quality and there was a small number for Scottish burghs. The first recognisable town history, John Stow's *Survey of London* appeared in 1598, followed by numerous reprints and new editions in subsequent decades; a few more town histories appeared before the Civil War, but the real expansion began in the later Stuart era, with eight published in the years 1701–20, and the number rising to over fifty in the last two decades of the eighteenth century. While early printed histories were often directed at the learned pretensions of the landed and professional classes attracted to town, by the later Georgian period one can see a greater stress on urban pride and municipal politics (marked by attacks on civic corruption) and an appeal to the growing

[47] See below, pp. 29 *et passim*.

middle-class consumer market. Such histories were hardly masterpieces of historical accuracy or literary style, but, tedious and long-winded as many of them are, they make available for the first time an assortment of economic, population, political and ecclesiastical material on urban communities.[48] The wave of town histories continued unabated through the nineteenth century. Some works, particularly for the bigger cities, were heavily concerned with the medical, sanitary and other problems – reflecting the new current of urban pessimism. Others were of the older promotional type, though containing significant evidence, culled from town archives and the recently opened Public Record Office, on the medieval and early modern town, if only to draw the contrast with Victorian modernity.[49] Towards the end of the nineteenth century interest in town records was stimulated by the Historical Manuscripts Commission (1870–) which began the task of dusting off and calendaring civic archives. A number of towns published detailed transcripts of corporation records – a practice which continued up to the second world war; and one or two civic record societies were founded. In Scotland there was a similar wave of civic record publication from the second half of the nineteenth century.[50]

None the less, before 1939 the number of serious historical studies of British towns in the early modern period could be counted on two hands. The most important included Dorothy George's magnificent *London Life in the Eighteenth Century*, F. J. Fisher's sparkling essays on economic aspects of Tudor London and W. G. Hoskins' study of industry and trade at Exeter 1688 to 1800.[51] It was Hoskins who had the most important influence after the war, reflecting the warm, enthusiastic character of his writing on all aspects of regional and local

48 R. Sweet, *The Writing of Urban Histories in Eighteenth-Century England* (Oxford, 1997); P. Clark, 'Visions of the urban community: antiquarians and the English city before 1800', in D. Fraser and A. Sutcliffe, eds., *The Pursuit of Urban History* (London, 1983), pp. 105–24; I. Archer, 'The nostalgia of John Stow', in D. L. Smith, Richard Strier and D. Bevington, eds., *The Theatrical City* (Cambridge, 1995), pp. 17–34.

49 G. Davison, 'The city as a natural system: theories of urban society in early nineteenth century Britain', in Fraser and Sutcliffe, eds., *Pursuit*, pp. 352–63; A. J. Vickery, 'Town histories and Victorian plaudits: some examples from Preston', *UHY* (1988), 58–63; e.g., J. M. Russell, *History of Maidstone* (Maidstone, 1881).

50 E.g. *HMC*, 9th Report, vol. I (Barnstaple, Canterbury, Carlisle, Ipswich, etc.); *HMC*, 11th Report, App. vol. III (Southampton and King's Lynn); *HMC*, 13th Report, App. vol. IV (Rye and Hereford); *Records of the Borough of Nottingham* (Nottingham, 1882–1956); J. P. Earwaker, ed., *The Court Leet Records of the Manor of Manchester* (Manchester, 1884–90); M. Bateson, ed., *Records of the Borough of Leicester* (London, 1899–1905); K. S. Martin, ed., *Records of Maidstone* (Maidstone, 1926); Southampton Record Society Publications (Southampton, 1905–); Bristol Record Society Publications (Bristol, 1930–); Scottish Burgh Records Society (Edinburgh, 1868–).

51 M. D. George, *London Life in the Eighteenth Century* (London, 1925; 2nd edn, London, 1965); Fisher's articles are reprinted in F. J. Fisher, *London and the English Economy 1500–1700*, ed. P. J. Corfield and N. B. Harte (London, 1990), esp. chs. 3–7; W. G. Hoskins, *Industry, Trade and People in Exeter 1688–1800* (Manchester, 1935); another pioneering study, on urban morphology, was N. G. Brett-James, *The Growth of Stuart London* (London, 1935).

history. His major investigations of Tudor Leicester and Exeter were succeeded, in the 1960s and 1970s, by the more intensive work of Alan Everitt, his colleague and successor at Leicester University, whose studies of market towns, urban inns and carriers highlighted the need to view the urban community in its regional and rural context.[52]

The period from the late 1950s also saw a wave of other scholarly work. Largely neglecting or failing to understand towns in its early (and subsequent) output, the *Victoria County History* launched a number of important volumes on Leicester, York, Warwick and Coventry. Wallace MacCaffrey drew an elegant, rounded portrait of Tudor and early Stuart Exeter, Valerie Pearl and Roger Howell published political histories of London and Newcastle during the Civil War, while Alan Rogers coordinated the first systematic investigation of a small town, that of Stamford in Lincolnshire. Of the new research, the most innovative was E. A. Wrigley's classic analysis (1967) of seventeenth- and eighteenth-century London, which examined the critical interaction between urbanisation and economic growth.[53]

By the 1970s the local history approach to the town inspired by Hoskins was being transformed by new influences – by the interests of political and economic historians, by the monumental economic and demographic studies of continental cities (notably by French scholars of the *Annales* school), by the research of social anthropologists and by the new work on modern urbanisation (in Britain strongly associated with H. J. Dyos at Leicester).[54] Whilst British studies of the early modern town remained focused on individual centres, there was growing recognition of the need for a more rigorously comparative and thematic approach. Collections of essays by Peter Clark and Paul Slack (1972) and Alan Everitt (1973) encouraged this trend, as did *Towns in Societies* (1978), edited by P. Abrams and E. A. Wrigley. Despite an effort by Abrams in his own chapter to reject the value of urban studies, mainly through the hoary ploy of exaggerating or misrepresenting the theories and ideas of writers in the field, the volume included wide-ranging and innovative pieces by Charles Phythian-Adams and

[52] W. G. Hoskins, *Provincial England* (London, 1963), esp. chs. 4, 5; W. G. Hoskins, 'The Elizabethan merchants of Exeter', in S. T. Bindoff, J. Hurstfield and C. H. Williams, eds., *Elizabethan Government and Society* (London, 1961); A. M. Everitt, 'The market town', in J. Thirsk, ed., *Ag.HEW*, vol. IV (Cambridge, 1967), pp. 467–90; A. M. Everitt, ed., *Perspectives in English Urban History* (London, 1973), pp. 91–137, 213–40; A. M. Everitt, 'Country, county and town: patterns of regional evolution in England', reprinted in Borsay, ed., *Eighteenth Century Town*, pp. 83–115.

[53] *VCH*, Leicestershire, IV (1958); *VCH*, Yorkshire, City of York (1961); *VCH*, Warwickshire, VIII (1969); MacCaffrey, *Exeter 1540–1640*; V. Pearl, *London and the Outbreak of the Puritan Revolution* (Oxford, 1961); R. Howell, *Newcastle-upon-Tyne and the Puritan Revolution* (Oxford, 1967); A. Rogers, ed., *The Making of Stamford* (Leicester, 1965); E. A. Wrigley, 'A simple model of London's importance in changing English society and economy, 1650–1750', *P&P*, 37 (1967), 44–70.

[54] For early literature surveys see H. J. Dyos, ed., *The Study of Urban History* (London, 1967), esp. pp. 1–46; P. Clark, ed., *The Early Modern Town* (London, 1976), pp. 19–28.

Martin Daunton on the early modern town.[55] The first attempt at producing a synthetic overview for students was *English Towns in Transition 1500–1700* by Clark and Slack (1976), which was followed a few years later by Penelope Corfield's pioneering volume on the *Impact of English Towns 1700–1800*. New research also came from historical geographers, such as John Patten's *English Towns 1500–1700*, based on work on East Anglian towns, and John Langton's more searching and imaginative analysis of the industrial towns of the North-West.[56] Much of the literature at this time, such as the important town studies by Alan Dyer on Tudor Worcester, Charles Phythian-Adams on Coventry, David Palliser on York and John Evans on Norwich, concentrated on the sixteenth and seventeenth centuries, and one of the central debates concerned how far English towns suffered from structural economic decline in the period before the Civil Wars – a debate which proved ultimately inconclusive because of the problematic nature of the evidence.[57]

After the 1980s the volume of publications rose sharply and here one can only sketch the main trends. Attention moved away from generalist interpretations, with all their limitations, to more specific thematic studies of urban social history, examining key groups such as widows, the poor, migrants, merchants, the professions and the middling orders.[58] The research spotlight was also turned on

[55] Clark and Slack, eds., *Crisis and Order*; Everitt, ed., *Perspectives*; P. Abrams and E. A. Wrigley, eds., *Towns in Societies* (Cambridge, 1978), chs. 1, 7, 10.

[56] Clark and Slack, *English Towns in Transition*; P. J. Corfield, *The Impact of English Towns 1700–1800* (Oxford, 1982); J. Patten, *English Towns 1500–1700* (Folkestone, 1978); J. Langton, *Geographical Change and Industrial Revolution* (Cambridge, 1979).

[57] A. Dyer, *The City of Worcester in the Sixteenth Century* (Leicester, 1973); C. Phythian-Adams, *Desolation of a City* (Cambridge, 1979); D. M. Palliser, *Tudor York* (Oxford, 1979); J. T. Evans, *Seventeenth-Century Norwich* (Oxford, 1979); for a summary of the debate see A. Dyer, *Decline and Growth in English Towns 1400–1640* (London, 1991; 2nd edn, Cambridge, 1995). Two important exceptions to this picture were Christopher Chalklin's *The Provincial Towns of Georgian England* (London, 1974) and John Money's study of eighteenth-century Birmingham, *Experience and Identity* (Manchester, 1977).

[58] Prior, ed., *Women*, chs. 2–3; V. Brodsky, 'Widows in late Elizabethan London: remarriage, economic opportunity and family orientations', in L. Bonfield, R. M. Smith and K. Wrightson, eds., *The World We Have Gained* (Oxford, 1986), pp. 122–54. On the poor see: S. McFarlane, 'Social policy and the poor in the late seventeenth century', in A. L. Beier and R. Finlay, eds., *London 1500–1700* (London, 1986), pp. 252–77; Slack, *Poverty and Policy*; T. Hitchcock, P. King and P. Sharpe, eds., *Chronicling Poverty* (London, 1997). On migrants see: M. J. Kitch, 'Capital and kingdom: migration to later Stuart London', in Beier and Finlay, eds., *London*, pp. 224–51; J. Wareing, 'Changes in the geographical distribution of the recruitment of apprentices to the London companies 1486–1750', *Journal of Historical Geography*, 6 (1980), 241–9; Clark and Souden, eds., *Migration and Society*. On magnates and merchants see: N. Rogers, 'Money, land, and lineage: the big bourgeoisie of Hanoverian London', in Borsay, ed., *Eighteenth Century Town*, ch. 9; R. Brenner, *Merchants and Revolution* (Cambridge, 1993); Sacks, *Widening Gate*. On the professions see C. W. Brooks, *Pettyfoggers and Vipers of the Commonwealth* (Cambridge, 1986), esp. ch. 3; also Porter and Porter, *Patient's Progress*; H. M. Dingwall, *Physicians, Surgeons and Apothecaries* (East Linton, 1996); and Corfield, *Power and the Professions*. On the middling orders see: Earle, *Making of the English Middle Class*; Barry and Brooks, eds., *Middling Sort*; J. Smail, *The Origins of Middle-Class Culture* (London, 1994).

different types of town. Following a surprising period of neglect, London attracted a succession of studies, some important, others more controversial. The multiplicity of small towns began to move out of the shadow, while leisure and resort towns were illuminated through works by R. S. Neale, Peter Borsay, John Walton and others.[59] On a more interdisciplinary note, landscape studies became important, building on earlier research;[60] and the Records of Early English Drama project produced an impressive series of volumes on civic pageantry, drama and ritual before the Civil War.[61]

In Scotland research has tended to lag somewhat behind the English advance. A. J. Youngson's brilliant *The Making of Classical Edinburgh*, first appeared in 1966, Michael Lynch's study of Edinburgh and the Reformation in 1981, and Nicholas Phillipson's seminal essays on the cultural life of the Augustan city from the 1970s. Early work on Glasgow was mainly interested in its commercial expansion.[62] From the 1980s, however, a growing number of more general comparative pieces by Ian Whyte, Lynch, T. Devine and others started to paint a broader picture of Scottish urban development.[63] In contrast, major Welsh studies have

59 Beier and Finlay, eds., *London*; Rappaport, *Worlds*; I. W. Archer, *The Pursuit of Stability* (Cambridge, 1991). M. Noble, 'Growth and development in a regional urban system: the country towns of eastern Yorkshire, 1700–1850', *UHY* (1987), 1–21; C. B. Phillips, 'Town and country: economic change in Kendal c. 1550–1700', in P. Clark, ed., *The Transformation of English Provincial Towns 1600–1800* (London 1984); P. Clark, ed., *Small Towns in Early Modern Europe* (Cambridge, 1995), esp. chs. 5–6. R. S. Neale, *Bath, 1680–1850* (London, 1981); Borsay, *English Urban Renaissance*; J. K. Walton, *The English Seaside Resort* (Leicester, 1983).

60 Following the earlier work of Summerson, *Georgian London*, and W. Ison's *Georgian Buildings of Bath, 1700-1830* (London, 1948; 2nd edn, 1980) and *Georgian Buildings of Bristol* (London, 1952), the recent studies include M. Girouard, *The English Town* (London, 1990); M. Beresford, *East End, West End* (Thoresby Society, 60–1, 1989); D. Cruikshank and N. Burton, *Life in the Georgian City* (London, 1990); R. Tittler, *Architecture and Power* (Oxford, 1991).

61 Particularly valuable volumes for urban historians include A. Johnston and M. Rogerson, eds., *York* (London, 1979); D. Galloway, ed., *Norwich 1540–1642* (London, 1984); A. Nelson, ed., *Cambridge* (London, 1989); A. Somerset, ed., *Shropshire* (London, 1994).

62 A. J. Youngson, *The Making of Classical Edinburgh, 1750–1840* (Edinburgh, 1966); Lynch, *Edinburgh and the Reformation*; N. Phillipson: 'Culture and society in the eighteenth century province: the case of Edinburgh and the Scottish Enlightenment', in L. Stone, ed., *The University in Society* (Princeton, N.J., 1975), vol. II, pp. 407–48; N. Phillipson, 'Towards a definition of the Scottish Enlightenment', in P. Fritz and D. Williams, eds., *City and Society in the Eighteenth Century* (Toronto, 1973), pp. 125–47; T. M. Devine, *The Tobacco Lords* (Edinburgh, 1975; repr., 1990).

63 I. D. Whyte, 'Urbanization in early modern Scotland: a preliminary analysis', *Scottish Economic and Social History*, 9 (1989), 21–35; I. D. Whyte, 'The function and social structure of Scottish burghs of barony in the seventeenth and eighteenth centuries', in A. Maczak and C. Smout, eds., *Gründung und Bedeutung kleinerer Städte im nördlichen Europa der frühen Neuzeit* (Wiesbaden, 1991), pp. 11–30; M. Lynch, ed., *The Early Modern Town in Scotland* (London, 1987); M. Lynch, 'Continuity and change in urban society, 1500–1700', in R. A. Houston and I. D. Whyte, eds., *Scottish Society 1500–1800* (Cambridge, 1989), pp. 85–117; T. M. Devine, 'The social composition of the business class in the larger Scottish towns, 1680–1740', in T. M. Devine and D. Dickson, eds., *Ireland and Scotland 1600–1850* (Edinburgh, 1983), pp. 163–73.

remained disappointingly few, with the notable exception of Harold Carter's geographical studies of the Welsh urban system, Philip Jenkins' research on urban politics, Gwyn Williams' work on the radicalism of Merthyr, and Chris Evans' study of that town's origins in the furnace of the iron industry.[64]

Recent years have seen further shifts in direction, marked by a cascade of research on the 'long eighteenth century', including studies by John Landers and Leonard Schwarz on Georgian London, Helen Dingwall on the demography of late seventeenth-century Edinburgh and Rab Houston on the social context of that city's golden era of enlightenment, Carl Estabrook on Bristol and its hinterland, Paul Gauci on Great Yarmouth, and Maxine Berg, David Hey and Theodore Koditschek on the industrial and social worlds of Birmingham, Sheffield and Bradford. Work by Paul Halliday, Nicholas Rogers and Katherine Wilson has deepened our understanding of popular politics and its crucial linkage to local urban cultures.[65] While the revival of town histories, commissioned by local authorities but written by academic authors, has generated new insights into the early modern histories of Glasgow, Nottingham, Stratford and Maidstone among others, local history groups have shone significant light on a number of smaller towns.[66] In Scotland studies of numerous burghs have been published.[67] Increasingly there is also a European perspective, encouraged by the general studies of the European city by Jan de Vries and Paul Hohenberg and Lynn Lees and the recent flowering of specialist literature on continental communities. We are starting to recognise that London's rise and impact as a capital city is best understood in comparison with Paris or Madrid, that British small

[64] H. Carter, *The Towns of Wales*, 2nd edn (Cardiff, 1966); P. Jenkins, 'Tory industrialism and town politics: Swansea in the eighteenth century', *HJ*, 28 (1985), 103–23; P. Jenkins, *The Making of a Ruling Class* (Cambridge, 1983); G. Williams, 'The Merthyr of Dic Penderyn', in G. Williams, ed., *Merthyr Politics* (Cardiff, 1966); C. Evans, *The Labyrinth of Flames* (Cardiff, 1993).

[65] Landers, *Death and the Metropolis*; L. D. Schwarz, *London in the Age of Industrialisation* (Cambridge, 1992); H. M. Dingwall, *Late Seventeenth-Century Edinburgh* (Aldershot, 1994); R. A. Houston, *Social Change in the Age of Enlightenment* (Oxford, 1994); C. Estabrook, *Urbane and Rustic England* (Manchester 1998); P. Gauci, *Politics and Society in Great Yarmouth 1660–1722* (Oxford, 1996); M. Berg, 'Commerce and creativity in eighteenth-century Birmingham', in M. Berg, ed., *Markets and Manufacture in Early Industrial Europe* (London, 1991); D. Hey, *The Fiery Blades of Hallamshire* (Leicester, 1991); T. Koditschek, *Class Formation and Urban-Industrial Society* (Cambridge, 1990). P. Halliday, *Dismembering the Body Politic* (Cambridge, 1998); Rogers, *Whigs and Cities*; Wilson, *Sense of the People*.

[66] T. M. Devine and G. Jackson, eds., *Glasgow*, vol. I: *Beginnings to 1830* (Manchester, 1995); J. V. Beckett, ed., *A Centenary History of Nottingham* (Manchester, 1997); R. Bearman, ed., *The History of an English Borough: Stratford upon Avon 1196–1996* (Stroud, 1997), chs. 6–9; P. Clark and L. Murfin, *The History of Maidstone* (Stroud, 1995), chs. 3–5; A. Henstock, ed., *A Georgian Country Town: Ashbourne 1725–1825* (Ashbourne Local History Group, 1989); J. M. Cook, ed., *Great Marlow* (Oxford, 1991); also various publications of the Faversham Society, Kent.

[67] E.g. *Historic Kirkaldy* (Edinburgh, 1995); *Historic Cumnock* (Edinburgh, 1995); *Historic Stranraer* (Edinburgh, 1995); *Historic Hamilton* (Edinburgh, 1996); *Historic Musselburgh* (Edinburgh 1996); *Historic Aberdeen* (Edinburgh 1997); *Historic Stornoway* (Edinburgh 1997); *Historic Dunblane* (Edinburgh 1998), all edited by E. P. Dennison and R. Coleman.

towns belonged to a general European phenomenon, that London's development as a city of finance learnt from the techniques and innovations of Italian and Low Countries cities, that the Enlightenment in Germany, France and Britain was energised by accelerating communication, exchange and rivalry between the greater European towns.[68]

More analytical and open-ended in approach than most continental work, British urban studies have made great strides in the last three decades. There has been an explosion of research, much of it still unpublished, on different urban groups, issues, types of town and individual communities. It is essential, however, for the overall picture not to be lost, for students of the early modern town to understand urban developments with an awareness of the wider perspective (chronological, geographic and thematic), so as to be able to relate individual studies to other work, and from that interaction to spark new insights and ideas for future research.

(iii) PLAN OF THE VOLUME

The present volume has been designed to bring together and exploit the new approaches and findings of recent and current research, in order to provide an analytical framework for the intricate investigation of the early modern town – its main structures and functions, the principal phases of development, as well as the changing relations between towns, and the interaction with the host society. The inclusion of Scotland and Wales alongside England highlights the value of a comparative dimension and the need to investigate in the pre-industrial era the origins of the increasingly integrated urban system of Victorian Britain. Our approach benefits from the way that recent research is transforming our knowledge of Scottish towns. Though Wales has been less well served in the recent literature, partly because of problems of documentation, the issues raised in this volume are designed to encourage more work on urban developments in the principality.

A comparative British approach is not without its difficulties. The institutional differences – legal, constitutional, ecclesiastical – between Scottish and English towns pose significant problems of interpretation, as does the variable chronology of urbanisation in the three countries. The shifting nature of the political relationship between England and the other mainland areas also had a major

[68] J. de Vries, *European Urbanization 1500–1800* (London, 1984); Hohenberg and Lees, *Making of Urban Europe*; also C. R. Friedrichs, *The Early Modern City 1450–1750* (London, 1995). For an exhaustive survey of the current continental literature see R. Rodger, ed., *European Urban History* (London, 1993). Clark and Lepetit, eds., *Capital Cities*; Clark, ed., *Small Towns*; H. Diederiks and D. Reeder, eds., *Cities of Finance* (Amsterdam, 1996); E. Hellmuth, ed., *The Transformation of Political Culture* (Oxford, 1990); F.-J. Ruggiu, *Les élites et les villes moyennes en France et en Angleterre (XVIIe–XVIIIe siècles)* (Paris, 1997).

effect on the urban system and complicates our understanding of it. For these reasons a number of chapters have been written jointly by English and Scottish experts.

The time span of this work is the long early modern period, stretching from the Reformation to the parliamentary and municipal reforms of the 1830s, which revamped the institutional arrangements of the old urban system. This enables a sustained analysis of the first great wave of British urbanisation and the achievements of the urban system before the main onset of the railway age. Up to now, the early decades of the nineteenth century have been treated as a transitional period and largely neglected by students of both the early modern and Victorian periods, but a major concern of this volume is to show how many of the pivotal changes of the early nineteenth century derived from developments of the previous period.

Taking the overall structure of the volume, Part I lays the foundation by surveying the broad area pattern of British towns (the distribution, local hierarchy, distinctive features and factors shaping them) with detailed sections on the English regions, Wales and Scotland. Parts II and III investigate the main thematic dimensions of urban development in our period and the experiences of different types of British town. Part II takes the period from the Reformation to the late seventeenth century and considers the changes in the urban economy and its relationship with the agrarian world, the complex demographic and social structures, the organisation of civic government, the cultural roles of towns and the built environment. Further chapters examine the different levels of the traditional urban system – London, the other major cities, the ports and the smaller market centres. In Part III the focus is on the eighteenth and early nineteenth centuries, interrogating the dynamic of urban growth and its economic impetus, and the effect on demographic and social processes, the advent of a more pluralistic political and governmental system, urban leisure and culture, and the transformation of the urban landscape. Final chapters look not only at the older types of town (London, the regional capitals, ports and smaller places), but the new specialist leisure and industrialising towns which had appeared by the end of the eighteenth century. The division of Parts II and III about 1700 is not meant to signify any watershed of the Mosaic variety. Certainly there can be no question, as noted above, that some of the most significant economic, cultural and other changes of the eighteenth century – the spread of new industries, the growth of urban sociability, for instance – can be dated back in England at least to the Restoration, or earlier. But there was an quickening pace of change after about 1700 which demands a new frame of analysis. Lastly, the collectivity of contributors to this volume took an early strategic decision not to devote separate chapters or sections to different social groups, for instance women, the young or the poor. Instead of segregating them in that way, we have sought to incorporate them into the main thoroughfare of our narrative, though recognising that this may make them less visible in the large urban throng.

The underlying object has been to present an up-to-date view of the main research literature, issues and questions in the field. Given the vitality of that research, there is, self-evidently, a range of views about a number of major issues and developments in the period, including, as already seen, urban population sizes and growth rates. During the preparation of this volume a lively debate has continued among contributors on many such points. However, there has been no editorial attempt to impose a rigid party line: rather the vision of British towns is as seen through a lattice window of different scholarly ideas, which we hope will stimulate a new generation of debate and research.

For all the size of the volume, there can be no claim to completeness. Frequently this reflects the lack of current research, some of which has already been noted. More is needed on the environmental and ecological changes in our towns, though here British scholars have been slower to develop scholarly research than their German counterparts. Work is also only just starting on the wealth of diaries, family histories and genealogical materials in order to explore the personal and other experiences of middling and lesser groups. Among many topics begging for attention are life on the street, with all its bustle, noise, sights and smells, a subject vital to the sensation of urbanness,[69] and the social and cultural patterns of elite membership and networking, which encompassed and individualised every urban community. There is more to be said too in the area of semiotics and the languages of the city (languages of urban stigma, of urban territory, of urban categorisation), as well as on visual images and the senses, perceptions of space, forms of local identity and cultural agencies. There is much still to be learnt from social anthropologists and archaeologists, while urban history has yet to engage successfully with literary scholars and musicologists – other fruitful areas for further work.[70]

This volume with all its imperfections builds on and extols the abiding strengths of British urban history. It seeks to be comparative and interdisciplinary. Its interest is not with tasting urban micro-aspects in isolation, but with the great and complex interactions of economic, social, political and cultural organisation and change, and their location in the special physical and spatial ambience of the big city or country town. Our hope is that the volume will be both a route map to past and present researches on the early modern town, and a gateway to the next generation of analysis.

[69] For a brilliant exception here see P. J. Corfield, 'Walking the city streets: the urban odyssey in eighteenth-century England', *JUH*, 16 (1989–90), 132–61.

[70] See for, instance, the UNESCO international seminar on 'Les Mots de la Ville' December 1997, coordinated by Christian Topalov, Ecole des Hautes Etudes en Sciences Sociales, Paris. For music Fiona Kisby is editing a forthcoming volume on *Music and Musicians in Urban Societies: Culture, Community and Change in Europe, 1400–1600*.

· PART I ·

Area surveys 1540–1840

Introduction

PETER CLARK

IN COMPARISON to France, the Low Countries or northern Italy, the pattern of British towns for much of the early modern period was remarkably polarised.[1] Apart from London, there were no large cities and few middle-rank centres of importance, rather a multitude of very small market centres. For England and Wales the urban hierarchy retained into the eighteenth century the thumb-print of its medieval past. London's ancient primacy as the seat of government and the country's most important port was consolidated, as the capital's population probably quadrupled in the sixteenth century (to 200,000 in 1600), and then more than quadrupled again over the next two hundred years. During the Tudor and Stuart period it was supported on the English stage by a cast of forty or so 'great and good' towns (see Chapter 11), major provincial towns but all with populations of under 10,000 in the 1520s and under about 30,000 inhabitants in 1700.[2] Of these, only Newcastle, Bristol, Exeter, Norwich and York could claim to be significant regional cities with extensive trading connections and elaborate civic privileges, and they steadily confirmed their positions as provincial capitals. Most of the rest, places like Gloucester, Leicester or Lincoln, were incorporated shire towns supported by localised trades and industries, meeting the needs of the adjoining countryside. By the Georgian period many of them were profiting from the expansion of their retailing and professional activities, sometimes complemented by specialist craft activity. These regional and county towns were surrounded by several hundred minor market centres, places with fewer than 2,000 people in the sixteenth century, quite often as low as a few hundred; their economies were heavily geared towards marketing and exchange links with the countryside, though by 1700 they had begun to acquire more specialist commercial and other functions. In Wales the vast

[1] Cf. J. de Vries, *European Urbanization 1500–1800* (London, 1984), pp. 107–20.

[2] See below, pp. 347 *et seq*.

majority of towns were in this bottom category, effectively micro-towns, and continued thus into the later Georgian period.

In sixteenth-century Scotland the traditional urban hierarchy was a miniature version of the English model. Edinburgh, with about 12,000 inhabitants in 1560, was not only the northern capital but the leading port with an important continental trade; three east coast ports (Aberdeen, Perth and Dundee) functioned as larger regional centres as well as ports; and the rest were mainly small towns, though here, unlike in England, the medieval network was considerably enlarged by the foundation of several score new baronial burghs. Urban growth was sluggish in Britain before 1700, but thereafter the pace quickened, first in England and then later in Scotland and Wales. The urban hierarchy began to fill out, with a rank size order conforming more to the picture in other urbanised regions of Europe. Provincial cities grew in size and importance. Great Atlantic ports like Liverpool and Glasgow boomed, new regional centres like Birmingham, Manchester and Leeds flourished, and there was a mounting array of specialist manufacturing, transport, leisure and naval towns.

Yet urban change was not a national process in early modern Britain, but a tessellation of local experiences. Only slowly do we see the evolution of a more integrated urban system. Orchestrating the national trend was a diversity of regional and local networks of towns, determined by geophysical factors, ancient jurisdictional arrangements, the state of agriculture, communication links and local cultural traditions (as in religious and ceremonial life). At the same time, regionalism is a fuzzy concept for Britain in this period, not least due to the long-established centralising power of the English state.[3] English regions lacked any strong political or cultural identity. There were no regional parliaments or courts (except for the Council of the North at York prior to 1640) such as one finds in France or Spain. Contemporary references to East Anglia, the Midlands or other regions were rare before the end of the eighteenth century. Even the ancient county units often provided only a problematic focus for urban networks. After 1536 the principality of Wales was annexed to the English crown but never enjoyed major regional/national institutions, and the Welsh network of towns was generally fragmented. By contrast, Scottish towns inherited from the medieval period their own institutional framework, which not only included the division between royal and baronial burghs, but the coordinating and regulating role of the Convention of Royal Burghs. Administrative and legal differences with English towns continued despite the union of crowns in 1603 and the parliamentary union of 1707. Yet within Scotland, as Chapter 4 (and later chapters) demonstrate, there were also significant regional and sub-regional variations of considerable complexity.[4]

[3] For the problems and importance of the regional perspective see P. Hudson, ed., *Regions and Industries* (Cambridge, 1989), pp. 3, 13–23, 30–3; J. Langton, 'The Industrial Revolution and the regional geography of England', *Transactions of the Institute of British Geographers*, new series, 9 (1984), 145–67; see also Langton's discussion below, pp. 462 *et seq.*

[4] See below, pp. 158 *et seq.*, 177 *et passim.*

Regions then have to be seen as fields of action, even states of mind, in early modern Britain. Many were shaped by externalities: the effect of commercial and shipping links with the continent in the case of East Anglia and the South-East; the Irish and Atlantic trades for the North and South-West. In Tudor and Stuart Wales, the small country and port towns of the central and southern shires looked for leadership to English centres like Shrewsbury and Bristol. Particularly important was the way that London's powerful economic and cultural influence extended in this period from its home territory in the South-East to penetrate (in some measure) other English regions, Wales and even Scotland.

As the following chapters illustrate, regional diversity on the ground requires sensitive interpretation: for some areas a greater recognition of institutional aspects, for others of commercial and industrial forces or of the wide variety of sub-regional networks. None the less, for all the difficulties, a regional approach remains essential, if we are to understand the complexity of British urban change in the period. As we saw in Volume I, by the close of the middle ages the English pattern already displayed significant regional variations, including the greater density of towns in the South-East and East Anglia than in the Midlands or North, the plenitude of small boroughs in the South-West, and the relatively small size of nearly all towns in the North.[5] Despite the increased integration of the British urban system during the later part of the period, one finds strong indications of greater regional differentiation, not only varying rates of urbanisation but the emergence of heavily integrated regional networks of towns in the West Midlands, central Lancashire, the West Riding, north-east and western Scotland, quite often closely associated with the advent of new regional cities.

Regional analysis also sheds light on the changing geographical balance within the urban system at this time. After the Reformation the centre of gravity was still firmly located, as during the middle ages, in the southern and eastern regions of England with their high population densities, fertile farms, river and coastal traffic, and links to the Low Countries and France. By 1840 the balance was tilting towards the uplands – the Midlands, the North, central Scotland and South Wales – as industrialisation and urbanisation in those areas predominated. But such a picture may be too linear. In the early nineteenth century, some of the towns of the South-East and East Anglia fought back, diversifying into new sectors such as military and leisure activity, or developing as transport or commuting centres: in this way they demonstrated the underlying strength and robustness of the traditional urban system.

Any regional partition of England must be essentially strategic, with a choice of scenarios available. The division between the South-East, East Anglia, the Midlands, the North, and the South-West does, however, allow us to examine

[5] D. M. Palliser, ed., *The Cambridge Urban History of Britain*, vol. I: *600–1540* (Cambridge, 2000), ch. 22.

the nature of the urban networks in different parts of the country and the forces shaping their development.[6] We can also identify the evolution of more localised networks. The studies of Scotland and Wales likewise enable both comparison with England and the English regions, and the exploration of local trends. Chapters 2 to 4 open the window on the range, depth and diversity of the British urban system, as it evolved in the three centuries after 1540. We can see the urban system at work, in harness, before we move on to study the different thematic developments and types of town in Parts II and III.

[6] The English regions in Chapter 2 have been identified as follows: *East Anglia*: Cambridgeshire, Huntingdonshire, Norfolk, Suffolk; *South-East*: Bedfordshire, Berkshire, Buckinghamshire, Essex, Hampshire, Hertfordshire, Kent, Middlesex, Oxfordshire, Surrey, Sussex; *South-West*: Cornwall, Devon, Dorset, Gloucestershire, Somerset, Wiltshire; *Midlands*: Derbyshire, Herefordshire, Leicestershire, Lincolnshire, Northamptonshire, Nottinghamshire, Rutland, Shropshire, Staffordshire, Warwickshire, Worcestershire; *North*: Cheshire, Cumberland, Durham, Lancashire, Northumberland, Westmorland, Yorkshire.

· 2(a) ·

East Anglia

PENELOPE J. CORFIELD

Regions in England have never been closely defined; and urban regions even less so. Cultural identities have been forged locally – in streets, villages, parishes, townships, counties – and also nationally or even, at times, imperially. Moreover, suspicious central governments have always refused to designate formal provincial capitals. That has been the case over many centuries. As a result, regional boundaries in England resist tidy mapping and English towns have never been constrained within distinctly designated regional networks.[1]

Yet there have also existed some broad historical affiliations that were greater than the shire counties and less than the nation. Thus were generated England's 'regions of the mind'. In concept, these were permeable and mutable, their boundaries and significance varying over time. But, by virtue of their popular origins, they had a shadowy survivability. They drew not upon formal administrative structure but upon shared geography, experience and culture. In addition, the long-term persistence of urban networks often encouraged these 'regions of the mind', since communal identities were forged when people met together – and the towns provided the classic meeting places, where residents and travellers congregated for commerce, conviviality and conversation.

(i) EAST ANGLIA AND REGIONALITY

East Anglia existed regionally in this way. Its boundaries were not rigid. It was not recognised by government as an administrative region and hence had no

[1] P. J. Corfield, 'The identity of a regional capital: Norwich since the eighteenth century', in P. Kooij and P. Pellenbarg, eds., *Regional Capitals* (Assen, Netherlands, 1994), pp. 129–31. For theoretical discussion, see R. E. Dickinson, *City and Region* (London, 1964). For full references to all literary sources cited in this chapter, please contact the author at Royal Holloway College, University of London.

official provincial capital. Its 'broad' speech was fused from a variety of dialects. Moreover, its local economy was not homogeneous. And it certainly was not cut off from the wider world. Quite the reverse. Eastern England was not remote or difficult to reach. Its inhabitants had many links – political, ecclesiastical, social, economic – outside the region. Indeed, for many centuries, traders from Lynn, Yarmouth and Ipswich played an active part in a thriving North Sea economy. But an eastern regionalism coexisted amongst these wider configurations. Norfolk and Suffolk, jutting into the North Sea, formed a compact East Anglian heartland. Meanwhile Cambridgeshire – with its secretive fenlands – and Huntingdonshire constituted an outer bulwark to the west.[2] The residents of these four counties shared a common climate and geography, shielded from the worst of the prevailing wind and rain from the south-west, but from time to time blasted by chilly east winds that sent great clouds scudding across the huge open skies of England's 'low countries'.[3]

Two examples illustrate a regional consciousness in action, as well as the haziness of the precise regional boundaries. During the winter of 1642, Norfolk, Suffolk, Cambridgeshire, Essex and Hertfordshire combined as the Eastern Association. Their well-organised troops then formed the backbone of the army that eventually defeated King Charles I. Moreover, this Association (joined in 1643 by both Huntingdonshire and Lincolnshire) was the only really effective regional group among the many that were mooted during the Civil Wars. A second instance, dating from a later period, lacks the same weightiness. Nevertheless, this example indicated a commercial willingness to invoke an eastern regional identity within England. Thus an Ipswich publisher in 1814 specified the people of Norfolk, Suffolk, Cambridgeshire, Huntingdonshire and Essex as the target audience of his short-lived literary journal *The East Anglian*.

That soubriquet was increasingly applied to the region by British antiquarians in the eighteenth and nineteenth centuries. It was an invented name for the ancient territories of the German invaders known as the East Angles, who had sailed across the North Sea to 'the smiling British shore', as hymned in a nineteenth-century 'Song of the Angles'. Needless to say, the exact boundaries of their seventh-century kingdom had long been forgotten. But the name was evocative, whilst agreeably imprecise. It suggested a dignified longevity and a freedom-loving ancestry. Moreover, the impressive ruins of the Anglo-Saxon 'royal burgh' at Bury St Edmunds also survived to testify to pre-Norman regional

2 These four counties are taken to represent East Anglia for this discussion, since Essex and Hertfordshire, the 'frontier counties', were increasingly tugged into the powerful orbit of London.

3 There were other low-lying areas – notably the Somerset Levels – but East Anglia (with the fens of south Lincolnshire) constituted much the largest area of contiguous lowland territory within England, all less than 150 metres over sea level.

glories. Interestingly, it was there that the Eastern Association held its series of key policy meetings between February 1643 and August 1648.

Bury St Edmunds did not, however, either seek or gain the title of regional capital. Nor did the Eastern Association survive beyond the Civil Wars. Nevertheless, the use of Bury as its political forum – and Cambridge as its garrison headquarters – indicated that East Anglia contained a number of significant towns that could act as rallying points.

(ii) EAST ANGLIAN TOWNS

The region was not and is not known for the absolute density of its urbanisation.[4] At the same time, however, East Anglia had a prolonged civic tradition. An interlocking mesh of pivotal towns – both large and small – had from early medieval times provided a highly distinctive feature of the local scene.[5]

An exuberant miscellany of eighteenth-century songs, poems and sayings unblushingly cheered the urban leaders. Cambridge inspired admiring respect. 'Hail, favour'd CAM! The Muses dear retreat! / Of truth and learning, awful, sacred seat!' began a woman visitor promisingly in 1756. Conversely, Ipswich was worldly. It was famed for jolly company and good cheer. 'Oh *Ipswich!* thy pleasures will ne'er be forgot, / Long as mem'ry's tablet shall last', sighed a departing guest in the 1790s. Lynn greeted guests with a peal of town music. 'No City, Dear **** [Lynn], this Borough excells / For charming sweet Sounds both of Fiddles and Bells', proclaimed a ditty in 1768. The picturesque borough of Thetford in south-west Norfolk was admired by another scribe in the 1690s: 'I congratulate thy charming site, / Fit for accommodation and delight', he enthused: 'On *Ousa's* bank's conveniently placed, / With all her troops of wanton *Naiads* graced'. Ancient Bury St Edmunds won poetic rapture too: 'Hail Bury! loveliest Spot I ever found, / To me, thou seemest like enchanted ground.' The 'water frolic' at Yarmouth in 1777 was the best entertainment 'since the days of old Noah'. Even tiny Bungay was toasted genially in the 1810s with the refrain: 'Old Bungay's a wonderful Town!'

Small surprise, therefore, that the great city of Norwich (see Plate 2) was also compared (optimistically but urbanely) to Constantinople for greenery, to a Dutch city for neatness, to ancient Athens for culture and learning, and to Jerusalem for religious potential.

Mundane realities, of course, were less romantic. Most busy townspeople had little time for such effusions. Visitors were often disappointed when urban realities failed to match the mythology. But town life meant opportunity, on

[4] 'Urbanisation' here refers to the proportion of the population living in towns rather than simply the existence of large towns.

[5] See B. Brodt, 'East Anglia', in D. M. Palliser, ed., *The Cambridge Urban History of Britain*, vol. I: *600–1540* (Cambridge, 2000), ch. 22(d).

however limited a scale. The larger centres across East Anglia played an obvious role as informal marriage marts and social meeting places, as they do today; and even small places attracted crowds for special events. One eighteenth-century Suffolk poet recorded the smiles shining 'from many a kind *Fair-going* face'. Thus there was a subdued *frisson* provided by the urban potential for social and/or sexual adventures.

Business, too, regularly attracted people to town. Trade, transport and provisioning provided staple urban employment, for men and women alike. And the market place, surrounded by inns, hostelries and eventually the urban coffee-houses, was the hub of local life. Businesses often began in informal social gatherings. Thus, just as marine insurance was launched in the 1680s from Edward Lloyd's coffee-house in London, so in the 1750s England's regulatory Jockey Club met in its own 'coffee-room' in Newmarket's High Street. Indeed, the residents of this 'metropolis of the turf' were famed equally for their hail-fellow-well-met geniality as for their keenness to place a wager.

Municipal and electoral politics also confirmed the historic importance of East Anglian towns. Nineteen places (ten of them in Suffolk) had gained the status of corporate municipalities, as shown in Map 2.1. Their constitutional diversity was considerable.[6] Most oligarchic was Castle Rising, a quondam port now a hamlet beached inland. It still appointed two aldermen, each in turn acting as mayor. More standard in its urban-constitutional format was Ipswich, with twelve portmen (two elected annually as town bailiffs) and twenty-four common councilmen. Most substantial in corporate grandeur was the City of Norwich, with its mayor, twenty-four aldermen and sixty common councillors, and with its own county jurisdiction (from 1403 onwards) over a ring of surrounding hamlets. In addition, fourteen towns were parliamentary boroughs under the unreformed constitution before 1832.[7] Here too there was a gamut: from the scandal of the fourteen voters at disappearing Dunwich to the great political importance of Norwich, with one of the largest constituencies of freemen electors anywhere in the country before 1832. All this generated business from candidates, agents, voters and lawyers.

Of course, the provision of goods and services varied from town to town. A *de facto* specialisation meant that the smallest places catered for a very localised demand, while the larger ones attracted a greater variety of custom and from

[6] The nineteen boroughs with corporate self-government pre-1835 were: *Cambridgeshire*: Cambridge, Wisbech; *Huntingdonshire*: Godmanchester, Huntingdon; *Norfolk*: Castle Rising, Lynn, Norwich, Thetford, Yarmouth; and numerously in *Suffolk*: Aldeburgh, Beccles, Bury St Edmunds, Dunwich, Eye, Ipswich, Lavenham, Orford, Southwold, Sudbury.

[7] The fourteen parliamentary boroughs before 1832 were: *Cambridgeshire*: Cambridge; *Huntingdonshire*: Huntingdon; *Norfolk*: Castle Rising, Lynn, Norwich, Thetford, Yarmouth; *Suffolk*: Aldeburgh, Bury St Edmunds, Dunwich, Eye, Ipswich, Orford, Sudbury. Most of these had returned MPs since medieval times; but Aldeburgh, Castle Rising, Eye and Sudbury were enfranchised in the later sixteenth century, and Bury St Edmunds' ancient franchise was renewed in 1608.

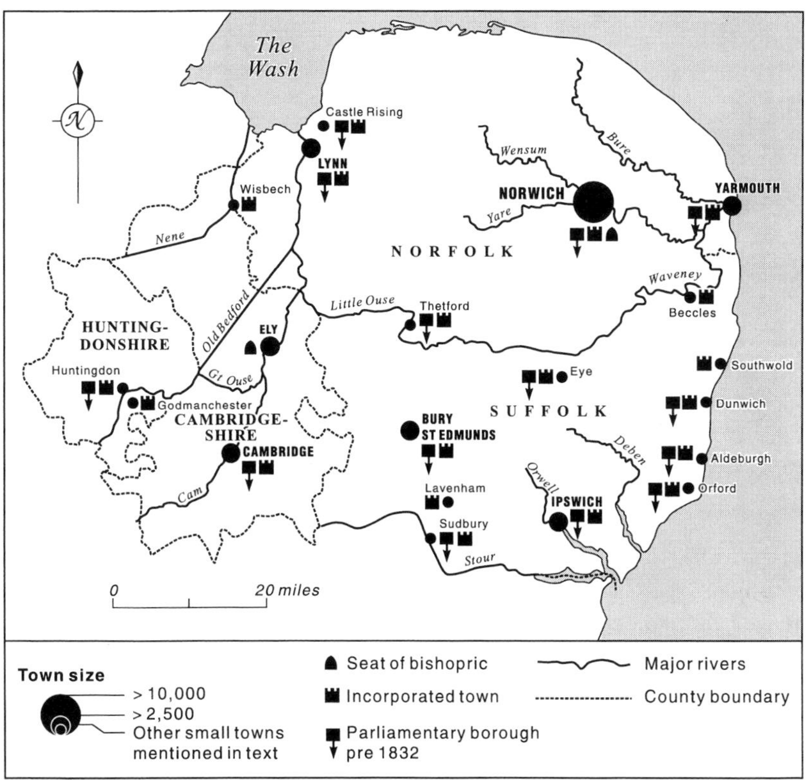

Map 2.1 Towns in East Anglia *c.* 1670

further afield. Within East Anglia, this pattern created a network of almost eighty micro-towns (as everywhere, the precise number remains uncertain, because nowhere was the small town clearly demarcated from the large village).[8] These local centres, defined by a nucleated settlement and non-agrarian employment, were scattered across the countryside. Marketing was their staple business in 1841 as in 1541. Table 2.1 tallies information about eighty-six East Anglian towns (of all sizes) in the Tudor and Stuart era. There were many very small centres, located especially in the large and historically densely settled counties of Norfolk and Suffolk. One example was Lavenham, an attractive medieval clothing town. By the seventeenth century, its industry and market had already begun to decay[9] but the borough retained the trappings of urbanism, with its own burgess corporation and an impressive guildhall (guild-built, 1529; municipalised, 1536).

[8] This imprecision allows scope for disagreement. Here a very low urban threshold has been adopted, to show the dense infrastructure of micro-towns that sustained the larger and undoubted urban centres. For definitions, see E. Jones, *Towns and Cities* (Oxford, 1966), pp. 1–12.

[9] J. Kirby, *The Suffolk Traveller: Or, A Journey through Suffolk* (Ipswich, 1735), p. 87.

Table 2.1 *Urban East Anglia in the 1670s*

	No. of towns <2,499 (with % county population)	No. of towns 2,500+ (with % county population)	All towns
Cambridgeshire	8 (12.0%)	2 (16.6%)	10 (28.6%)
Huntingdonshire	7 (21.8%)	0 (0%)	7 (21.8%)
Norfolk	32 (10.8%)	3 (14.3%)	35 (25.1%)
Suffolk	32 (17.2%)	2 (8.9%)	34 (26.1%)
Total four East Anglian counties	79 (13.9%)	7 (11.9%)	86 (25.8%)

Sources: population estimates from hearth tax data for eighty-six East Anglian towns, as identified by J. Langton (see below pp. 460 *et seq.*). County totals also estimated from hearth tax returns as Cambridgeshire: 82,100; Huntingdonshire 33,600; Norfolk 199,500; Suffolk 158,200.

Across East Anglia, the urban pattern was one of low-level pluralism, with a multitude of small towns – the Stowmarkets, East Derehams, Lintons, Kimboltons of England – punctuated by a few larger centres. By the 1670s, only seven leading towns housed more than 2,500 inhabitants. The frequency of the micro-towns, however, meant that nowhere in the region was far from a small market and/or a nucleated meeting place. In other words, East Anglia had a proto-urban heritage that countered rural isolationism. In the later seventeenth century, just over one quarter (25.8 per cent) of the region's entire population resided in towns of varying sizes: 13.9 per cent in the very small places with fewer than 2,500 inhabitants and 11.9 per cent in the centres with over 2,500.[10]

Over time, this pattern showed great durability. Within that, however, the fortunes of individual places fluctuated gently. A handful of the smallest places lost custom and returned to rural ways. For example, Yaxley in Huntingdonshire,

[10] Because of the intrinsic imprecision of information about both town and county populations, the statistics in Tables 2.1 and 2.2 indicate approximate rather than absolute orders of magnitude. For example, J. Patten, 'Population distribution in Norfolk and Suffolk during the sixteenth and seventeenth centuries', *Transactions of the Institute of British Geographers*, 65 (1975), 48–9, suggests lower county totals for both Norfolk (181,000) and Suffolk (125,000) which implies a higher percentage living in towns (27.6 per cent and 33 per cent respectively). However, John Rickman in the early nineteenth century proposed higher county totals, especially for Norfolk (229,093), which would greatly reduce its urban proportion (21.8 per cent). For the gamut of estimated county populations in the 1670s, see A. Whiteman and M. Clapinson, eds., *The Compton Census of 1676: A Critical Edition* (London, 1986), pp. cx–cxi, Table D/5.1.

Botesdale in Suffolk, and Setchey in Norfolk were medieval micro-towns that were not included even in John Adams' extensive 1690 listing of English towns. By 1750, an inn, a fine medieval church, a market square and perhaps some smart brick houses were all that marked their putative urbanity. Most notorious of the disappearing towns was Dunwich – Suffolk's medieval fishing port that gradually fell into the sea. By 1677, waves were lapping in the market-place; in 1702, the town hall was washed away; and by 1715 the gaol was under water. The coastal erosion was too systematic to be halted. 'Oh! time hath bowed that lordly City's brow / In which the mighty dwelt. Where dwell they now?', intoned a poet with gloomy relish. By the early nineteenth century, the place was esteemed as no more than 'a mean village'. Yet Dunwich retained a political role that belied its dwindling numbers, because until 1832 the vanishing Troy of East Anglia continued to send two MPs to parliament.

Most other small towns, however, continued to flourish, sometimes despite daunting setbacks. Thus serious fires at East Dereham in 1581, Bury St Edmunds in 1608, Wymondham in 1615, Southwold in 1659, Newmarket in 1682/3, and Bungay in 1688 prompted not decline but rebuilding. Earlier, in 1586, the 'statetely Towne' of Beccles had been damaged by a major conflagration, as mourned 'With sobbing sighes and tickling teares' in the contemporary *Lamentation of Beckles*. And it endured fires again in 1688 and 1699. Yet as a local nexus on the River Waveney, navigable for small craft from Yarmouth, it sustained a population of perhaps 1,700 by the 1670s. Villagers from within a ten mile radius sent announcements to be called aloud by the Beccles market crier; and shopped with Beccles tradesmen. Thus, although the redoubtable Whig traveller Celia Fiennes in 1698 feared that it was but 'a sad Jacobitish town', its inhabitants rallied to rebuild, this time in red brick.[11]

Similarly, the ravages of fire in 1689 did not halt the trading viability of Huntingdonshire's St Ives, a small inland port on the Ouse. It continued to hold its celebrated cattle and sheep markets. Moreover, the productivity of its agrarian hinterland was gradually improved by successive schemes for fen drainage. An immediate entourage of twenty-three or so villages along the Ouse valley, especially on the Huntingdonshire side of the county border, looked to the town as a local commercial centre.[12] Thus it had sufficient urban confidence to support its own paper, the *St Ives Post Boy* (founded 1718–19). And its population (multi-wived, of course, in popular rhyme)[13] grew to some 2,000 by the early 1720s.

In addition to these multitudinous small towns, there were also a significant

[11] N. Evans, 'The influence of markets', *Local Historian*, 21 (1991), 77–8; N. Evans, ed., *Beccles Rediscovered* (Beccles, 1984), pp. 38–42; and C. Morris, ed., *The Journeys of Celia Fiennes* (London, 1947), p. 145.

[12] M. Carter, 'Town or urban society? St Ives in Huntingdonshire, 1630–1740', in C. Phythian-Adams, ed., *Societies, Culture and Kinship, 1580–1850* (London 1993), pp. 77–130.

[13] Of course, the riddling ditty 'As I was going to St Ives, / I met a man with seven wives . . .' might have referred to St Ives in Cornwall, although history does not record which (if either) was intended.

few that stood out from the others. In the sixteenth and seventeenth centuries, there were seven established centres, all with over 2,500 inhabitants, that were key nodal points within the regional constellation. Some were ports: Wisbech had not yet climbed into the foothills of the urban leadership; but Ipswich[14] and Yarmouth had populations nearing 10,000 in 1700, while Lynn had over 5,000.[15] The latter two in particular were both headports for extensive inland waterways. Lynn merchants exported grain and agricultural produce from an extensive hinterland that stretched inland to six Midland counties with access to the Great and Little Ouse.[16] Meanwhile Yarmouth, with its impressively long quayside backed by its tightly packed grid of housing divided by tiny 'rows', was the centre of the herring fishery. For that, it was finely dubbed the 'Metropolis of the redde Fish' in 1599. It also transhipped bulk goods that were ferried down the sinuous Yare, Wensum, Bure and Waveney rivers in the region's distinctive flat-bottomed keels. Agreeably in tune with its nautical image, Yarmouth was thus described in 1667 as a 'place of great trade and consumption of drink'.[17]

Inland centres complemented the maritime towns. The great city of Norwich[18] attracted population by dint of its multiple roles: at once the county capital, a cathedral city for a diocese that stretched over Norfolk and Suffolk, a grand forum for agricultural exchange, a major shopping mart, a cultural meeting place, the communications headquarters for central/east Norfolk and a major textile town. Thus by 1700, its resident population of *c.* 29,000 made it the largest English provincial town.[19] Bury St Edmunds (*c.* 4,000 in the 1670s), the headquarters of west Suffolk, long remained a fashionable inland resort for the gentry of the surrounding countryside (see Plate 26); and Ely (*c.* 3,000 in the 1670s) was the seat of the compact but wealthy Ely diocese, the octagonal cathedral tower acting as a welcoming beacon to the population of the surrounding fens.

It is worth noting that these two quietly flourishing places were not county capitals. But such a role did not automatically lead to urban growth. For example,

[14] M. Reed, 'Economic structure and change in seventeenth-century Ipswich', in P. Clark, ed., *Country Towns in Pre-Industrial England* (Leicester, 1981), pp. 88–141.

[15] Lynn's population is sometimes estimated at 9,000 by the 1670s; but that would preclude any subsequent growth, since its population in 1801 was only 10,000. For data indicating a lower total of *c.* 5,000, see C. W. Chalklin, *The Provincial Towns of Georgian England* (London, 1974), p. 13 n. 26; and that is accepted in J. de Vries, *European Urbanization 1500–1800* (London, 1984), p. 270.

[16] T. S. Willan, *The English Coasting Trade, 1600–1750* (Manchester, 1938), pp. 125–35.

[17] Quoted in P. Gauci, *Politics and Society in Great Yarmouth 1660–1722* (Oxford, 1996), p. 94; and for Yarmouth society, see *ibid.*, pp. 91–9, 260–2.

[18] For its urban history, see J. F. Pound, *Tudor and Stuart Norwich* (Chichester, 1988), and J. T. Evans, *Seventeenth-Century Norwich* (Oxford, 1979). Norwich's role as a cathedral city is also highlighted in I. Atherton *et al.*, eds., *Norwich Cathedral* (London, 1996), esp. pp. 507–614.

[19] Bristol, sometimes erroneously accorded that status, had in 1700 only *c.* 20,000 inhabitants: see W. E. Minchinton, 'Bristol – Metropolis of the west in the eighteenth century', *TRHS*, 5th series, 4 (1954), 75; and P. J. Corfield, 'A provincial capital in the late seventeenth century: the case of Norwich', in P. Clark and P. Slack, eds., *Crisis and Order in English Towns 1500–1700* (London, 1972), pp. 263, 267.

Huntingdon – the quiet county town that was the birthplace of Oliver Cromwell – had in the 1670s only about 900 inhabitants. Indeed, it was mocked for its small size by the 'Saints' of St Ives in 1745, when the two towns contested informally for county leadership. The local fenlands were but thinly peopled. Huntingdon, moreover, was not a cathedral city, being under the far-flung diocesan mantle of Lincoln. Thus Huntingdonshire did not generate a capital to compare with Norwich or Ipswich. Indeed, even if the 1,240 residents (*c.* 1670) of Godmanchester, Huntingdon's twin borough immediately across the Great Ouse, were added to its total, the conurbation was still only small.

Cambridge, by contrast, became a sizeable provincial centre, with perhaps 8,000 inhabitants by the 1670s.[20] It grew, however, not as a county town but rather for its specialist educational function. The additional presence of 1,200 well-to-do university students encouraged much attendant business, licit and illicit. Hence the complaints at unauthorised plays, diversions, bear-baiting, football and fist-fights. And there was also a more decorous life of the mind. Scholars could not only visit the famous colleges but also attend the plentiful coffee-houses to admire 'the chief professors and doctors, who read the papers over a cup of coffee, and converse on all subjects', as a German traveller noted approvingly in 1710.

(iii) EAST ANGLIA AND THE WIDER WORLD

As the experience of Cambridge attested, many people came from outside the region to visit, trade, socialise, study and/or reside in East Anglian towns. Some notable religious refugees from overseas settled in Norwich. The Dutch and Walloons came in their thousands in the 1570s and 1580s; and the Huguenots in their hundreds in the 1680s. These migrants and their descendants remained for many years in contact with their homelands.[21] Others made shorter visits. For example, in 1784 the two young sons of the duc de la Rochefoucauld spent a happy year in the 'attractive little town' of Bury St Edmunds.

Moreover, with their long coastlines, the counties of Norfolk and Suffolk were readily linked into the North Sea economy. People in the ports had regular overseas contacts. 'The company you meet with here, are generally persons well informed of the world', wrote Defoe of Ipswich in 1724.[22] Yarmouth in particular was an important trading partner with Rotterdam, although Yarmouth merchants also dispatched goods to a variety of other destinations. Their overseas

[20] N. Goose, 'Household size and structure in early Stuart Cambridge', in J. Barry, ed., *The Tudor and Stuart Town* (London, 1990), p. 81.

[21] R. Esser, 'News across the Channel: contact and communication between the Dutch and Walloon refugees in Norwich and their families in Flanders, 1565–1640', *Immigrants and Minorities*, 14 (1995), 139–52.

[22] D. Defoe, *A Tour through the Whole Island of Great Britain*, ed. G. D. Cole and D. C. Browning (London, 1962), vol. 1, p. 46.

shipping in 1662 (for example) left for Ireland, the Baltic, France, Italy and the American colony of Virginia, as well as to Holland.[23] Foreign vessels also traded in the East Anglian ports. One major event in the Yarmouth calendar until the 1830s was 'Dutch Sunday', celebrated each Michaelmas, when a fleet of Dutch traders arrived to attend a popular fair on the South Downs and to join the ancient ceremony of 'wetting the nets'. That indicated the existence of cultural as well as economic links between the trim towns of Holland and those of East Anglia – just as there were many often-mentioned parallels between their economic and artistic histories.

Regular linkages also meshed the region into the wider British economy. Grain, malt, wool, textiles and agricultural products were shipped from East Anglian ports for the busy coastal trade, especially to Newcastle and to London, while coal, timber, bricks and bulk goods were brought inwards. The rivers and main roads were always busy. Cattle were brought south from Scotland to fatten on East Anglian marshlands, before being marched to metropolitan markets. Norfolk turkeys were also walked to London tables. Furthermore, before 1800 the region combined industry with agriculture. The manufacture of woollen cloths (says) continued in a cluster of south Suffolk textile towns, although the industry was declining by the later seventeenth century. In the 1720s, for example, the indefatigable traveller Daniel Defoe found Sudbury (pop. perhaps 2,000 in the 1670s) to be 'very populous and very poor'.

Textile success elsewhere, however, concealed that slow decline. A number of Suffolk men were employed in combing wool (a specialist occupation) and very many Suffolk women were engaged in spinning yarn by hand (a non-specialist but essential by-employment) for a prospering industry further north within East Anglia. The twenty-five mile region centring upon Norwich became famed from the later sixteenth century onwards for the handloom production of the light, attractive and relatively inexpensive worsted 'stuffs'.[24] Large quantities of raw materials (long-staple wool) were brought to East Anglia from northern England to be spun into fine yarn for this industry and spun yarn was also imported directly from Ireland, while the finished textiles were sold both at home and overseas. In other words, the Norwich industry depended totally upon a far-flung commercial infrastructure. Neither city nor region were isolated.

Fairs in particular provided regular venues where local and long-distance traders met together. Such events were famous at Norwich, Bury, St Ives; but, outstanding, even among such competition, was the impressive gathering at Stourbridge, held in a field outside Cambridge every September. In its heyday, from the sixteenth to the mid-eighteenth century, it was reputed one of the

23 PRO, E 190/493/5: Yarmouth Port Book, Overseas 1661/2.

24 P. Wade-Martins, ed., *An Historical Atlas of Norfolk*, 2nd edn (Norwich, 1994), p. 151, maps the weaving areas. See also Corfield, 'A provincial capital', pp. 277–87; and U. Priestley, *The Fabric of Stuffs* (Norwich, 1990), pp. 7–43.

greatest commercial fairs in Europe. Rows of wooden stalls were piled high with goods in bulk. Nearby, booths provided food, drink and entertainment for the '*Cambridge*-Youth, *London*-Traders, *Lynn*-Whores, and abundance of Ubiquitarian Strollers' who were mockingly identified there in 1700.[25] It was an 'instant city', with all its wiles and wonders. There were bawdy side-shows as well as sober transactions. No wonder that John Bunyan, from nearby Bedford, transmogrified Stourbridge in his *Pilgrim's Progress* (1678) into the temptations of 'Vanity Fair'. Or indeed that Cambridge corporation levied tolls upon these worldly transactions, which fell under its jurisdiction.

Numerous Londoners were significant among the 'prodigious' crowds of dealers from all parts of England. Yet the East Anglian traders, as later its bankers, were sufficiently well established in their own right – and sufficiently far from the City – to evade economic domination by the metropolis. London was a siphon for population and at times a rival (as Defoe worried for the shipping of Ipswich) but it was also a stimulus and a major trading partner for this accessible and productive region that tapped into the North Sea economy.

(iv) EAST ANGLIA AND REGIONAL SPECIALISATION

Profound changes then followed for East Anglia in the later eighteenth century and thereafter. The transformation was indicated, paradoxically enough, by notable continuities in the region's urban configuration. Yet apparently not to change significantly during a period of major population growth and economic innovation in itself constituted change. As Britain urbanised and industrialised, the towns of East Anglia lost their national importance. The economic powerhouse shifted from the east coast to the North-West, from the North Sea to the Atlantic. One very striking instance of that was the changing ranking of Norwich: the second city in England and Wales in 1700, its own subsequent expansion was increasingly surpassed by faster growth elsewhere. Bristol, the 'metropolis of the west' overtook it in the later 1720s/early 1730s; and others followed. As a result, Norwich was by 1851 the fourteenth largest, by 1901 the twenty-third, by 1951 the thirty-second.[26] This was the most dramatic change in terms of ranking that was experienced by any urban centre during this prolonged period of transformation.

Structural changes to the East Anglian economy underpinned this transfor-

[25] E. Ward, *A Step to the Stir-Bitch Fair* (London, 1700), p. 3. The infrastructures of town/country and town/town migration, visiting, marketing and communications of all sorts, that were necessary underpinnings of sustained urban development, deserve further study. For a pioneering contribution that paradoxically stresses the urban/rural divide, see C. B. Estabrook, *Urbane and Rustic England: Cultural Ties and Social Spheres in the Provinces, 1660–1780* (Manchester, 1998), esp. pp. 276–80.

[26] For graphic illustration of changed rankings, see B. T. Robson, *Urban Growth* (London, 1973), p. 39.

Table 2.2 *Urban East Anglia 1670s–1841*

	% Population in eighty-six towns		
	1670s	1801	1841
Cambridgeshire	28.6	32.3	36.4
Huntingdonshire	21.8	28.3	29.0
Norfolk	25.1	35.6	38.2
Suffolk	26.1	30.3	34.1
Total four East Anglian counties	25.8	32.8	35.9

Sources: for 1670s population estimates, see Table 2.1; and for 1801, 1841, see census returns as reported in PP 1852/3 LXXXV, p. cxlviii.

mation. From medieval times, the region had flourished as an area of mixed agrarian and industrial activity. That made sense for such a fertile and relatively densely populated area. From the mid-eighteenth century onwards, however, it began to focus its specialisation upon intensive agriculture.[27] That was, of course, a significant economic role, which produced considerable wealth. Hence East Anglia generated not only much-needed foodstuffs but also plentiful capital that was available for investment elsewhere in Britain. For example, the region in the early nineteenth century was a major investor in the nation's emergent railway network, most of it outside East Anglia. In particular, the array of banks and insurance companies that were established in Norwich were key institutions that orchestrated this sizeable capital outflow. Meanwhile East Anglia itself did not have major mineral reserves or easy sources of water power; and its ports had difficult harbours to negotiate. Hence it did not specialise as a location for mechanised industry – or spawn a major urban-industrial conurbation.

Nor did any new large towns emerge to upstage the existing hierarchy of towns. Its most significant new arrivals were Wisbech (8,530 in 1841), expanding as a river port on the Nene, following port improvements in 1773, and Lowestoft (4,509 in 1841), growing as a seaside resort noted for its wide sandy beaches and its 'exceedingly healthy and stimulating' sea breezes. None the less, both places were still relatively small, while Cromer, too, was tiny (1,240 in 1841). Thus East Anglia's traditional urban network broadly matched the communication and economic demands of the region. Indeed, there were no major changes within the region to the transportation network. East Anglia was not in the forefront of innovations in road, canal or, later, railway building. Certainly, that may be regarded as much as a sign of its declining economic centrality to the British economy as the root cause; yet sign it was.

Stability then remained the keynote. However, East Anglia did not experience

[27] D. C. Coleman, 'Growth and decay during the Industrial Revolution: the case of East Anglia', *Scandinavian Ec.HR*, 10 (1962), 115–27.

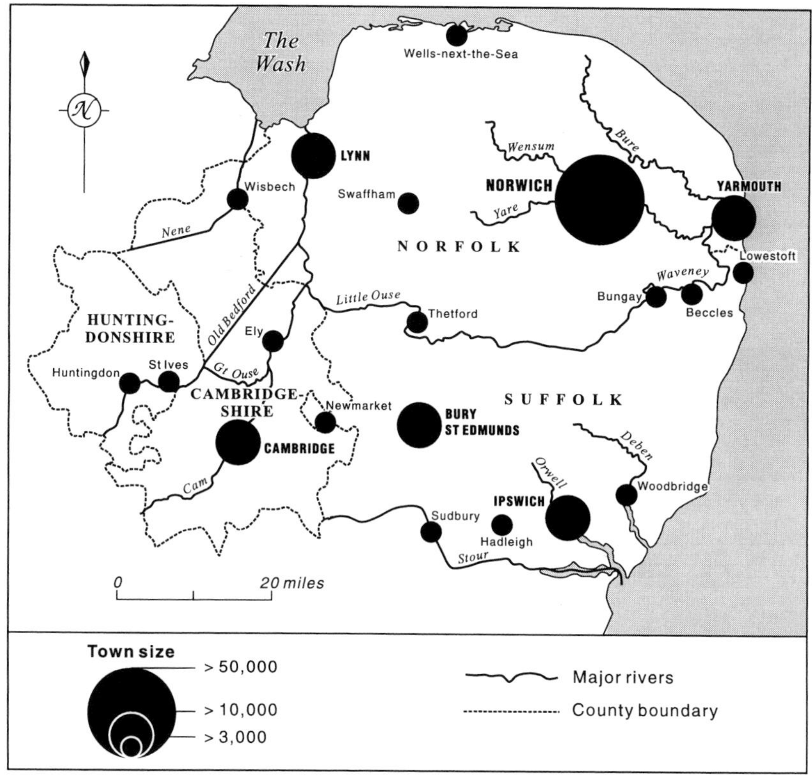

Map 2.2 Towns in East Anglia 1841

anything as dramatic as de-urbanisation. On the contrary, population growth inflated the size of most towns during the eighteenth and early nineteenth centuries. Even disappearing Dunwich, which lost population between 1670 and 1801, saw a modest recovery by 1841, as the settlement moved inland. Thus Table 2.2 shows that the East Anglian townspeople – in the eighty-six towns identified in the 1670s – had multiplied to 32.8 per cent in the relatively slow-growing regional population by 1801 and to 35.9 per cent by 1841.

Admittedly, this was not a very rapid expansion compared with that occurring in the industrialising regions of Britain. The existing towns none the less still played a traditional role as commercial centres. Map 2.2 shows the location of the twenty largest places in 1841, clustered along the main routes by river, road and sea. A commercial specialism characteristically encouraged employment in marketing, transport, services and the professions. Nor did it preclude the genesis of locally-based industries. For example, Norwich was home to a number of big brewers, making the celebrated Norwich 'Nog'. And the Quaker firm, Ransomes of Ipswich, prospered in the nineteenth century by fashioning steel agricultural implements for sale to Suffolk farmers. In other words, East

Anglia's towns retained their regional importance as local suppliers, whether through trade or the local production of specialist goods. That provided economic ballast throughout the prolonged process of national reconfiguration.

Thus it is highly misleading to state of East Anglia that 'the Industrial Revolution of the eighteenth and nineteenth centuries largely passed it by'.[28] On the contrary. All regions were deeply affected by Britain's long-term structural economic changes, however historians choose to name them. The complex process of specialisation affected all regions. Certainly, not all areas became industrial heartlands. But that was the point. Different regions concentrated upon different products, which were exchanged via an interlocking and increasingly international trading system. As East Anglia was well integrated into the national economy, it could not avoid these changes. Indeed, the region was known for its early adoption not of newly mechanised and labour-intensive industries but instead of intensive, labour-efficient farming. Those eminent Norfolk farmers, Coke of Holkham and 'Turnip' Townshend, were the East Anglian equivalents of Boulton and Watt.

To note the importance of economic factors (location, resources, communications, context) in economic matters does not imply an economic determinism over all aspects of town life. Such a view is obviously too simple. Yet economic factors are important in influencing economic outcomes. Developments outside East Anglia crucially affected those within it. Thus the earlier specialisation within the region was superseded by specialisation of the region within an emergent global economy. Indeed, the East Anglians found on a number of occasions, frustratingly, that they could not redirect their urban fortunes by policy decisions alone. Moreover, it may be noted that, across the North Sea, the Dutch towns experienced a very similar transition, as the Dutch Republic too did not industrialise despite its similar early strength in towns, trade and textiles.[29]

Continuity amidst change, however, helped most East Anglian towns to adapt. Gradual growth between 1700 and 1841 brought a degree of prosperity. Indeed, the smaller towns generally avoided the extensive grime, poverty and overcrowding of some great industrial conurbations. After all, these towns did not become magnets for long-distance migration into the region. By 1851, 84 per cent of all East Anglia's residents were locally born.[30] Moreover, the relative labour surplus and rural poverty encouraged heavy out-migration from the region to other parts of Britain (especially London) as well as overseas.[31] Thetford's Tom Paine

[28] For this verdict, see T. Williamson, *The Origins of Norfolk* (Manchester, 1993), p. 1.

[29] De Vries, *European Urbanization*, pp. 168–72, incl. Fig. 8.9 (p. 169).

[30] In 1851, the percentage of people living in the county of their birth was lower in the two smaller inland counties (Cambridgeshire 72 per cent; Huntingdonshire 70 per cent) and higher for the two larger maritime ones (Norfolk 90 per cent; Suffolk 86 per cent), averaging 84 per cent overall.

[31] A. Redford, *Labour Migration in England, 1800–50*, 3rd edn (Manchester, 1976), pp. 48–9 and Appendix Map D.

was but one illustrious son who left his native town for the wider world; and there were many others, including the textile weavers who migrated from Norwich to Yorkshire.

By thus avoiding the dangers (as well as the potentialities) of urban giantism, East Anglian towns in the eighteenth century displayed signs of modest success. Ancient Thetford, for example, attracted custom with the creation of a minor spa in the early eighteenth century. Grandees at Newmarket built lavish town residences, clustered amongst the inns and the royal palace, established by James I and retained by successive monarchs until the 1810s. Huntingdon in 1745 rebuilt its town hall in modish red-brick, with an assembly room attached (further extended in 1817). Handsome Lynn got a new freestone market cross with elaborate statuary in 1710. Emergent Wisbech, adorned with two 'impeccable' rows of Georgian town houses along The Brinks, also acquired a town hall (1801) and corn exchange (1811). Urbane Bury St Edmunds, feted in Shadwell's play *Bury-Fair* (1689) as a 'scene of Beauty, Wit and Breeding', developed its traditional old Tudor cross (1683/4) into the elegant market cross building (1774), designed by the ultra-fashionable architect Robert Adam. The 'neat elegant' market town of Swaffham, rebuilt after a fire in 1775, sponsored winter greyhound coursing from *c.* 1781. Not to be outdone by its Suffolk rivals, 'agreeable' Ipswich sponsored a new playhouse in 1736 (rebuilt 1803) and in 1751 a 'New Race Ground' with its own racing calendar. Meanwhile, Yarmouth revamped its guildhall in 1723, incorporating an assembly room; and opened a public bathhouse in 1759 for the new seaside holiday trade.

Such amenities (and there were many others) did not make fortunes for all townees. Yet the construction and reconstruction indicated a continuing urban vitality that was far removed from crisis.

Above all, East Anglia's large towns successfully weathered the shocks of change, despite periods of strain. Indeed, Table 2.3 shows that the leading towns conspicuously pulled ahead of the lesser places over time. For the ports, admittedly, there were perennial problems of harbour maintenance and river dredging. The coastline with its notoriously shifting sands made access difficult for in-shore navigation. In 1578, for example, Yarmouth had triumphantly taken possession of an offshore sandbank, only to find within four years that its new territory had disappeared. Hazards of access such as these became more problematic as the mean size of shipping increased. In 1846, to take another example, the harbour at Lynn was said to be in a 'ruinous state'. There was continued pressure for port improvements. At Ipswich, the new river commissioners (established 1805) promoted dredging schemes and later a massive wet dock was constructed (opened 1843).[32] Despite the difficulties, however, the region's export trade in grain and

[32] H. R. Palmer, *Report on the Proposed Improvements in the Port of Ipswich* (London, 1836), pp. 1–10: the wet dock protected vessels from the Orwell's tidal flow and greatly increased the draught of shipping entering the port.

Table 2.3 *Leading East Anglian towns (pop. 3,000 +) 1700–1841*

	1700	1801	1841
Cambridgeshire			
Cambridge	*c.* 10,000	10,087	24,453
Ely	*c.* 3,000	3,013	5,177
Wisbech		4,710	8,530
Huntingdonshire			
Huntingdon			3,507[a]
St Ives			3,465
Norfolk			
Lynn	*c.* 5,000	10,096	16,139
Norwich	*c.* 29,000[b]	36,238	61,846
Swaffham			3,358
Thetford			3,934
Wells-next-the-Sea			3,464
Yarmouth	*c.* 10,000	16,573	27,865
Suffolk			
Beccles			4,086
Bungay			4,109
Bury St Edmunds	*c.* 5,000	7,655	12,538
Hadleigh			3,305
Ipswich	*c.* 8,000[c]	11,277	25,384
Lowestoft			4,509
Newmarket			3,000
Sudbury		3,813	5,928
Woodbridge		3,020	4,954
Total	*c.* 70,000	106,482	229,551

[a] In 1841, the combined populations of Huntingdon and Godmanchester = 5,659.
[b] Enumerated as 28,881 in 1693.
[c] Enumerated as 7,943 in 1695.
Sources: estimated from hearth tax data and local enumerations (1700) plus census returns (1801, 1841).

other bulk goods continued. And the ports were also pleasant places that acted as local resorts. Thus, by 1841, Yarmouth had grown to 27,865; tree-girt Ipswich, with a smaller industrial hinterland but long reputed an agreeable place of sojourn, had expanded to 25,384 and was just about to launch upon its modern growth; while Lynn followed decorously enough with 16,139.

Norwich also faltered but survived. It gradually lost its staple textile industry – imperceptibly at first, as spinning was mechanised in the 1780s (putting many

Norfolk and Suffolk spinners out of work); and rapidly from the 1830s onwards, as weaving too was mechanised. It was superseded by the new cost-effective 'worstedopolis' in the form of Bradford, on the West Yorkshire coalfields.[33] In addition, Norwich's export trade faced a genuine crisis between 1793 and 1815, when its staple markets on the continent were disrupted by warfare. As a result, the city grew in numbers erratically rather than steadily. It lost population outright through emigration in the 1790s and 1800s, before recovering in the 1810s. Its attempts to mechanise textile production and to improve access to the sea with a new canal via Lowestoft (opened with much fanfare in 1833) did not succeed. The continuing importance of Norwich's role as regional commercial and professional headquarters, however, salvaged its long-term fortunes. The city also added to its portfolio a new role as a banking and insurance centre.

Functions such as these were not as labour-intensive as the earlier textile industry. But the industrious population of Norwich still continued to carry out some manufacturing (notably shoemaking from the 1840s). That meant that it retained an array of activities and ultimately shed its overdependence upon a single industry.[34] 'Fashion and its fluctuations, machinery and its progressions, iron and coal in their partial distribution, have each and all helped to lay the head of the mighty low; but there is strong vitality left within her – powerful talents and great resources', remarked a kindly chronicler of the city in 1853.[35]

And so it happened. Norwich remained the unofficial regional capital of East Anglia, as it had been since the eleventh century. Only in recent times has a serious competitor arrived,[36] in the form of modern Ipswich with its container port at Felixstowe. It means that, if regional government ever comes to East Anglia, there will now be hot debate as to which city should be the headquarters.

(v) EAST ANGLIAN URBAN IDENTITY

A strong sense of urban identity was conferred upon all these East Anglian towns by their collective history and tribulations. The continuing political and municipal role of the corporations and parliamentary boroughs also signalled the area's early and continuing importance on the national scene.

But, ultimately, urban identity depended upon much more than formal rights. East Anglia's towns drew people because there were things to do in town. They provided the ballast for the continual renewal of local life. The region housed an urban variety, both adaptable and enduring, within interlocking and overlapping

[33] See discussions in D. Gregory, *Regional Transformation and Industrial Revolution* (London, 1982), pp. 26–79, esp. pp. 48–60; and C. H. Lee, 'Regional growth and structural change in Victorian Britain', *Ec.HR*, 2nd series, 34 (1981), 438–52.

[34] C. Barringer, ed., *Norwich in the Nineteenth Century* (Norwich, 1984), pp. 119–59.

[35] S. S. Madders, *Rambles in an Old City* . . . (London, 1853), p. 163.

[36] Corfield, 'Identity of a regional capital', pp. 141, 143.

regional networks that also meshed into national and international networks. So within the region, clerical East Anglia looked to Norwich or wealthy Ely; dissenting East Anglia to Norwich or 'little Genevas' such as St Ives or Yarmouth; political East Anglia to the county and parliamentary towns, some mere pocket boroughs but others key political arenas; legal and criminal East Anglia to the assize towns, when the law courts were in session; academic East Anglia to Cambridge; commercial East Anglia to the multiple market towns and city fairs; textile East Anglia to Norwich; nautical East Anglia to the ports; 'society' East Anglia to Bury St Edmunds and the gentry resorts; holiday-making East Anglia to the seaside towns; racing East Anglia to Newmarket or to local courses as at Swaffham and Ipswich; amorous East Anglia to the fairs, resorts and 'red light' districts of Lynn or Yarmouth; theatrical East Anglia to the nineteen towns that had their own theatres by the early nineteenth century; and so on, in all multifariousness.

This was a rich heritage. Urban East Anglia could pride itself upon its persistence amidst change, change through persistence. During the many twists and turns of fortune between 1540 and 1841, the region emphatically did not deurbanise. Its towns did lose status, as Britain's economic focus shifted towards the Atlantic economy. Yet the region's urban residents continued to trade, travel and invest extensively in the wider world. Moreover, East Anglian towns in the later twentieth century may well regain some of their quondam importance, now that the economic focus is moving back towards Europe.

Tenacity over time thus created a historic identity that transcended the fluctuations of fortune. Successive generations of townees helped to nurture an enduring regional urbanity within a wider Britain. Thus East Anglia meant not only fenlands and rich pastures and great skies – but, dotted across the countryside, distinctive towns noted for their history and their adaptability.

· 2(b) ·

South-East

C. W. CHALKLIN

A mercate town [Guildford] is well frequented and full of faire inns.

(W. Camden, *Britannia*, 1607, 1977 edn, Surrey and Sussex)

[Canterbury is] a flourishing town, good trading in the Weaving of Silks . . . There is fine walks and seates [for] the Company; there is a large Market house and a town Hall over it . . . [and] the Cathedral.

(C. Morris, ed., *The Illustrated Journeys of Celia Fiennes c. 1682–1712*, 1984)

In the reign of George II, Brighton began to rise into consideration as a bathing-place . . . and it ultimately obtained the very high rank which it now enjoys as a fashionable watering-place, and its grandeur and importance, under the auspices of George IV . . . Steam vessels sail from this place to Dieppe . . . The principal branch of trade is that of the fishery.

(Lewis, *Topographical Dictionary of England*, 1840)

[Portsmouth is] a seaport, borough, market-town; [Portsea is] now the principal naval arsenal of Great Britain. (Lewis, *ibid.*)

Lewisham is a most respectable village and parish . . . inhabited by a great number of opulent merchants and tradesmen who have selected this pleasant and healthful neighbourhood as a place of retirement from business.

(Pigot and Co.'s National Commercial Directory, 1839, *Kent, Surrey and Sussex)*

THE SPECIAL features of the towns of the Home Counties and adjoining shires which these quotations illustrate were the result of several factors. Unlike much of the Midlands communications were good except in the Weald. Essex, Kent, Sussex and Hampshire had a big coastal traffic which was more sheltered than that of North-East England. Inland counties were tied by the Thames and a growing number of navigable tributaries, and the Ouse linked Bedfordshire to the Wash. Between 1790 and the 1830s several canals were added to the river network, although they were less important and necessary than in the industrial areas. Most coastal towns and villages had fishermen and many became seaside resorts from the 1740s and 1750s.

Road trade grew fast throughout the period, helped from the beginning of the eighteenth century by the plentiful spread of turnpike roads which were more numerous than in parts of East Anglia and the North. Natural resources were considerable, with much fertile soil encouraging corn, fruit and hops, and marshland, the Weald, the downland and Chilterns feeding livestock. Iron ore, chalk, copperas on the seaside, fuller's earth and timber supported manufacturing. In the earlier period people in towns and dense populations inherited from the middle ages in pastoral and woodland areas supplied its workforce.

These resources were to be found in some, though not all, of the other English regions. Two other influences were unique to south-eastern towns. London lay almost in the centre of the region, near the mouth of the Thames and as the hub of the country's road system. Its size and importance are discussed elsewhere: here we are concerned only with its relationship with the towns of the South-East. As it grew from 120,000 in 1550 to 375,000 to 1650, 650,000 in 1750 and 1,873,676 in 1841, London had many more people than all the towns of the Home Counties and adjoining areas, where the biggest towns did not exceed 5,000 in 1550 and 53,000 in 1840. Its huge wealth, and high living standards relative to England outside the South-East, based on its dominance of overseas and domestic trade, financial supremacy, its making of basic and specialised goods as the biggest English industrial area before 1800, the presence of the Court and growing administration, parliament and the law courts, numerous professional men and a wholly and partly resident or visiting peerage and gentry, influenced and shaped the South-East. Because they were nearby, the Home Counties were an excellent market for luxury goods and outlet for capital, and source of supply not only of food but also of basic craft manufactures.[1]

Again, the relative proximity of the continent affected south-eastern towns in several ways. Passenger links with it were through Dover and to a less extent Rye, and Harwich after 1700. Though the foreign trade of ports nearer London was mostly channelled through it by the eighteenth century, Dover and Southampton kept theirs. More important for some places was intermittent war with Spain, Holland or France. In the seventeenth century London needed defending against the Dutch and between 1689 and 1815 naval battles and protection of shipping against the French and Spaniards were best conducted from Channel docks and bases. Barracks and fortifications defended dockyards and Dover especially from the 1750s, and barracks were needed in southern towns in the French wars from 1793 to 1815. Because of their proximity to the Low Countries and France, Walloon refugees in the 1560s and Huguenots in the

[1] A. Dyer, *Decline and Growth in English Towns 1400–1640* (London, 1991), p. 53; A. L. Beier and R. Finlay, eds., *London 1500–1700* (London, 1986), pp. 11–12, 124–5, 127, 131, 148, 164, *et passim*.

1680s settled in Canterbury, Sandwich, Maidstone and Colchester, many with scarce skills.

(i) 1540–1650

Here urban development is discussed in three periods, 1540–1650, 1650–1750 and 1750–1840. The incomplete evidence suggests that in the South-East about 1540 there were probably at least 150 towns with between 300–50 and 5,000–6,000 inhabitants, most having under 1,000. Normally they had a market and at least half of the working people were in trades and crafts, the thirty or forty other active markets being in villages where most people were farmers and agricultural labourers.[2] Towns often had a hinterland with a radius of three to six miles, that is, easy walking distance, reflecting much arable and productive land, the proximity of London and relatively high living standards; only in the predominantly pastoral Weald where the Kentish towns of Tonbridge and Cranbrook are over twenty miles from Lewes, the nearest town to the south-west, was there an obvious gap in generally well-spread urban centres. Yet markets were more frequent in some districts than in others; the average market area in Hertfordshire was 20,000 acres, and in Hampshire and Surrey where there was extensive heath and forest more than twice this size.[3] Buyers and sellers often went to two or three markets if they were within twelve or fifteen miles. The county towns had markets and shops with customers from a bigger district.

As the living standards of the farmers increased and general population rose, country towns, including many on navigable water, prospered, particularly from the 1570s. They grew and some market villages became towns. In Buckinghamshire the population of almost all the towns fell between 1524 and 1563, probably in part because of the influenza epidemics of 1557–9; then from 1563 to 1676 it grew in all centres, though more slowly at Aylesbury and Buckingham, both without navigable rivers, than in the rest; the average was 70 per cent compared with 60 per cent for the whole county. Most towns in the South-East expanded in serving the capital's demands for food, such as High Wycombe and Maidstone, the population of the latter growing from about 1,500 in 1540 to over 3,000 by 1660. A few were hindered by physical difficulties, such as Maldon where the decay of the haven helped to keep numbers stationary. As towns expanded on balance, by 1650 there were about 170–5 towns in the

[2] In this section the South-East comprises the six Home Counties (Essex, Hertfordshire, Kent, Middlesex, Surrey and Sussex), Bedfordshire, Berkshire, Buckinghamshire, Hampshire and Oxfordshire; for populations see P. Clark and J. Hosking, *Population Estimates of English Small Towns 1550–1851: Revised Edition* (Leicester, 1993); J. Cornwall, 'English country towns in the fifteen twenties,' *Ec.HR*, 2nd series, 15 (1962), 54–69

[3] A. Everitt, 'The marketing of agricultural produce', in J. Thirsk, ed., *Ag.HEW*, vol. IV (Cambridge, 1967), pp. 473–5, 496–7.

South-East, with a minimum population between 400 and 500 and a maximum of 8,000–9,000.[4] Trade being at the heart of the economy, markets selling mainly small and perishable goods were crucial on account of the relative absence of overheads.

This was an important period in the building of town halls, usually two-storey structures with the floor level open for trade, and of market crosses. In five Home Counties (excluding Middlesex) Tittler has identified about twenty-four new town halls between 1540 and 1620, or about twenty in the years 1560–1640.[5] Shopkeepers also became more common, with retailers in all the towns and many villages of the South-East by the mid-seventeenth century. Maldon's 1,000 inhabitants between 1560 and 1640 included many bakers, butchers, brewers, inn-keepers and even several vintners among workers in food and drink, and the distributive trades were dominated by drapers, haberdashers, grocers and coal merchants. Inns lying on the main roads, especially those to and from London, were among the most important in Britain: for instance, little Dunstable on Watling Street had twelve inns in 1540. Trades were more specialised in the bigger towns, so that Canterbury had dealers in household goods such as goldsmiths, pewterers and ironmongers, and miscellaneous trades included stationers and booksellers.[6]

Much trade was in basic goods made by local master craftsmen, their apprentices and journeymen outworkers, such as shoemakers, workers in clothing, furniture makers, agricultural processors, smiths and building workers. Although these crafts were found in the country, sometimes done part-time with farmwork, they were more numerous and varied in the towns. Similarly, inhabitants of the smaller urban centres farmed land nearby, or were market gardeners, sometimes producing for sale in London by the early seventeenth century.

While most manufactures and crafts were widespread and for local use, some towns specialised in one or several goods often to sell in London. Tanning was important in centres easily supplied with oak bark and hides from cattle which supplied materials for boot and shoemaking, such as Horsham in the Sussex Weald where there were at least ten tanners at any one time in the Tudor period and about eight in the seventeenth century. Cutlery was made in Tonbridge as a by-product of the Wealden iron industry until about 1620. A character in William Bullem's *Dialogue against the Pestilence* remarks that 'I was born near unto Tonbridge, where fine knives are made.' General goods went to London from

[4] P. Clark and P. Slack, *English Towns in Transition 1500–1700* (London, 1976), pp. 24–5; M. Reed, 'Decline and recovery in a provincial urban network: Buckinghamshire towns 1350–1800', in M. Reed, ed., *English Towns in Decline 1350–1800* (Leicester, 1986); W. J. Petchey, *A Prospect of Maldon 1500–1689* (Chelmsford, 1991), pp. 13–14, 108–11.

[5] R. Tittler, *Architecture and Power* (Oxford, 1991), pp. 163–7.

[6] Petchey, *Maldon*, pp. 108–11; J. Godber, *History of Bedfordshire 1066–1888* (Bedford, 1969), p. 202; C. W. Chalklin, *Seventeenth-Century Kent* (London, 1965), pp. 258, 262.

many towns. Maldon had more brewers, glovers, shoemakers and tailors than the neighbourhood needed, and probably most of their surplus was sold in London. Its numerous butchers supplied not only local meat but also hides and tallow for leather crafts in the district and the capital. They owned or leased the great fields round the town to fatten livestock which later reached Smithfield.[7]

The effect of borough institutions and controls on urban economies needs to be considered. The South-East had more corporate towns (about sixty-seven) than most other regions. The mayor, jurats and aldermen, and councillors, normally amongst the richest men, who as elsewhere held courts, did a little administration and had intermittent relations with the central government, also tried to regulate trades and crafts through guilds. Insistence on apprenticeship, inspection of the quality of goods and restriction on trading by non-freemen probably peaked at this time. Guilds were often re-established in the sixteenth century. In Winchester, the county town of Hampshire with 3,120 people in 1604, guilds were formed anew in the later 1570s when brewers, fullers and weavers, shoemakers and cobblers, and hosiers and tailors obtained their own companies. Although regulation of crafts and trades was easier in these towns than in huge, rapidly spreading London, control was probably intermittent. In general guilds in the South-East were less developed than those in provincial towns elsewhere. Although they may have retarded local economic growth slightly, one cannot show that they had much damaging effect.[8]

In the later sixteenth century clothmaking was widespread in the South-East. Though far from exclusively urban it helped to make the towns of the region, including London, together the biggest industrial location in the country. There were various types, mostly hand crafts and labour intensive. Heavy broadcloths were made in Cranbrook, Tenterden and Tonbridge. Guildford, Godalming, Farnham, Alton and Basingstoke manufactured light, coarser textiles known sometimes as 'Hampshire kerseys', Reading, Newbury and Abingdon broadcloths and kerseys. Bays and says, the 'new draperies', were made in Canterbury and Sandwich in Kent, and in the towns of north-east Essex (Colchester, Halstead, Coggeshall, Braintree and Bocking). Clothmaking was not fully urban as most spinning and part of the weaving and finishing were done in the surrounding countryside. The clothier who put out materials to carders, woolcombers, spinners, weavers and finishers and sold the cloth in London, often for export, needed a strategic site for his workhouse and often lived in the town. In Buckinghamshire, where the domestic manufacture of lace making was

[7] Godber, *Bedfordshire*, pp. 198, 204; A. Windrum, *Horsham: An Historical Survey* (Chichester, 1975), p. 125; C. W. Chalklin, 'A Kentish Wealden parish (Tonbridge) 1550–1750', (BLitt thesis, University of Oxford, 1960), p. 66; Petchey, *Maldon*, pp. 117–24.

[8] There were fifty-two parliamentary boroughs before 1832. T. Atkinson, *Elizabethan Winchester* (London, 1963), pp. 33, 185; Chalklin, *Kent*, pp. 31, 259; Godber, *Bedfordshire*, p. 98; Clark and Slack, *English Towns in Transition*, pp. 39–40.

Table 2.4 *Tonnage of shipping of south-eastern ports in 1571–2*

London	12,265	Southampton	790	Faversham	436
Leigh	2,330	Sandwich	729	Brightlingsea	435
Rye	1,015	Maldon	599	Hythe	418
Colchester	1,005	Hastings	514	Brighthelmstone	416
Harwich	891	Dover	494		

established by 1600, 'Olney, Newport Pagnell and Stony Stratford became important centres, not only for its manufacture but also for its marketing and distribution . . . to satisfy the demands of the London market.' Clothmaking dominated work in some of these centres. N. R. Goose quotes Leland writing of Reading (about 2,500 people in 1525) that 'this town chiefly standeth by clothing.' In the sixteenth century its textile production employed 30 per cent of the males full time and mercers and drapers distributed it. About 40 per cent were in textiles between 1620 and 1659, when the population may have reached 7,000. A factor almost peculiar to South-East England, on account of its situation, was the settlement in several towns of Walloon refugees from the 1560s. They boosted the making of new draperies because of their greater skill and civic insistence that they should work on textiles in order not to compete in the basic trades and crafts. Colchester had about 200 Flemings in 1573 and 1,500 in 1622, when English were used as spinners; by then the total population may have been about 8,000. In the Dutch Bay Hall governors regulated manufacturing, and enforced the inspection and sealing of finished cloths. After 1614 broadcloth and kersey making declined in the South-East, hit by the higher wages of the region, failure to respond to changes of fashion and stoppages in continental sales.[9]

Fishing was the major employment in at least five towns, Brighton (4,000 inhabitants by 1650), Hastings (1,270 in 1603), Rye (5,000 in 1560, 2,000 in 1600), Folkestone (probably about 600 in the 1560s) and Faversham (1,300 to 1,400 in the 1560s). Herrings, mackerel and other fish were caught and sold by fishermen from the first four towns, while oysters were dredged at Faversham. In 1630 the Faversham fishermen told the privy council that with their families about 400 people were dependent on oyster-dredging. The silting of Rye harbour from the 1570s and the damage to local fishing was the main reason for

[9] Chalklin, *Kent*, pp. 117, 123–4; *VCH*, Surrey, II, pp. 342, 345; N. Goose, 'Decay and regeneration in seventeenth-century Reading: a study in a changing economy', *SHist.*, 6 (1984), 53–61; G. Martin, *The Story of Colchester* (Colchester, 1959), p. 49; C. Wilson, *England's Apprenticeship 1603–1763* (London, 1965), pp. 75–6; C. W. Chalklin, ' A seventeenth century market town: Tonbridge', *Archaeological Cantiana*, 76 (1961), 157; Reed, 'Decline and recovery'.

the sudden population decline. The Dutch were the principal market for oysters, London for herrings and mackerel, whence the catch was taken by road.[10]

As well as handling some imports and exports South-East ports had growing coastal and river commerce particularly in bulky goods such as corn, flour and malt, coal and timber. The relative volume of trade handled by the larger harbours is suggested by the total tonnage of merchant vessels belonging to them in 1571–2 as presented by Mayhew (see Table 2.4). In all these towns waterborne trade provided much work. Thus official returns (in February and October 1587) for the Kent and Sussex ports show that seamen were most numerous in Rye (285 and 325 respectively), though its trade was soon to fall dramatically; Sandwich had 106 and 102 seamen, Dover 130 and 176, and Hastings 121 and 168.

Land traffic was also important in the region. Huge numbers of livestock were driven by road, especially on account of the London market and Romney Marsh and other extensive pastures. Valuable and perishable goods went by packhorse and (increasingly) by waggon, which also carried cloth and corn when the cheaper water carriage was unavailable. Professional carriers based on market towns were rare before 1600, but were becoming common by the 1630s. Arber's *English Garner* records that 'the carriers of Buckingham do lodge at the King's Head, in the Old Change [London]; they come on Wednesdays and Thursdays.'[11]

The urban service sector acquired a growing number of professional men, boosted by improving living standards and education. By 1600 virtually all centres in the South-East had a lawyer, surgeon and schoolmaster, and perhaps a land surveyor and scrivener. The bigger towns had a growing group of professional people. Maldon had lawyers, a scrivener, surgeon and physicians in the early seventeenth century. Winchester's professional men were particularly numerous in relation to the town's size. As the location of county assizes and quarter sessions and of church courts, the administrative centre for the estates of the bishop, dean and chapter and Winchester College, the city had about thirty lawyers between 1560 and 1640; there were private as well as College schoolmasters, cathedral and parish clergy, and two or three physicians serving wealthy townsfolk and visiting gentry. A number of Puritan towns appointed preachers and lecturers from about 1570. In general because of the relative wealth of the region, and (also in the case of lawyers) the proximity of London, our towns probably had a precocious incidence of professional men, often of high standing.[12]

10 S. Farrant, *Georgian Brighton 1740–1820* (Brighton, 1980), p. 8; Chalklin, *Kent*, p. 151; G. Mayhew, *Tudor Rye* (Falmer, 1987), pp. 23, 262.

11 Mayhew, *Rye*, pp. 20, 236; D. J. Elliott, *Buckingham: The Loyal and Ancient Borough* (Chichester, 1975), p. 221.

12 A. Rosen, 'Winchester in transition, 1580–1700', in P. Clark, ed., *Country Towns in Pre-Industrial England* (Leicester, 1981), p. 152; Clark and Slack, *English Towns in Transition*, p. 72.

It is probably wrong to think of a single network of towns in the South-East. It may be suggested that these centres fell into three groups. Those within fifteen or twenty miles of the capital were essentially part of it so far as goods, trade and prices were concerned. In 1632 it was believed that the assize of bread in London should be decided by the price of wheat in the neighbouring markets of Uxbridge, Brentford, Kingston, Hampstead, Watford, St Albans, Croydon and Dartford. Part of London's food processing was done there. Business calls, consumer purchases and social visits were possible in London during a day's visit. Secondly came towns between twenty and fifty miles away such as Chelmsford, High Wycombe, Reading and Maidstone. These collected food for the capital and distributed luxury goods, groceries and coal from London. About 1600 it was still said to be fed 'principallie . . . from some fewe shires neare adioyninge'. Yet trade links also existed between towns of various sizes as farmers, traders and consumers used two or three markets, and shops in neighbouring centres. Among the third group of towns furthest from London, ties with other regions or cities were important. Sandwich and Dover, Rye in the sixteenth century and Southampton had much overseas trade. Bedford had waterborne connections with Lynn and beyond as well as by packhorse and waggon with London. The people in the smaller centres of west Berkshire had personal and trade links with Bristol.[13]

Although towns in the South-East were rather more prosperous than elsewhere urban society was still dramatically unequal in wealth. In Kent up to half of the towndwellers were on the subsistence level, living in one or two rooms with little or no heat and no artificial light and the family in a single bed. After bad harvests such as those of the 1590s there was malnutrition. As late as the 1660s half or more of the householders of inland towns in Kent, Surrey and Hampshire were too poor to pay rates. Local evidence confirms the general picture of movement between towns especially among the poorest, encouraged by economic vicissitudes and periodic epidemics which decimated urban populations. Using the Maldon view of frankpledge lists and register of freemen between 1569 and 1582 which noted all resident males over the age of twelve, Petchey showed that only 11 per cent of the population stayed there continuously over the thirteen years, and at least half were replaced. Between 1585 and 1628 only one in ten Canterbury men had been born there and not moved at all, and servants and poorer craftsmen had travelled furthest. At the same time social policy responses were often more elaborate in the South-East, encouraged by wealthy individuals and the example of London. Charitable foundations for the poor were often large: thus Archbishop Abbott's foundation at Guildford in 1619–22 has been described as a cathedral among almshouses. Long before poor

[13] F. J. Fisher, 'The development of the London food market, 1540–1640', *Ec.HR*, 1st series, 5 (1934–5), 50, 60.

rates became compulsory throughout England in 1597 towns in the South-East were making levies for the poor, as at Colchester in 1557 and Rye by 1558.[14]

On the other hand there was a relatively affluent elite of craftsmen, retailers and professional men. This is shown by the value of personal estates. In Rye between 1541 and 1603 out of 479 people for whom probate inventories were made, 79 left personal estates under £5 and 80 between £5 and £10, largely of household furnishings and tools; 106 had property between £10 and £20; and 109 between £20 and £40, mostly wealthier craftsmen and small traders. The mercantile groups (often with plate) had personal estates between £40 and £100 (81) and over £100 (24), such as John Mercer, jurat (died 1586) with £547 10s. 8d. The affluence of the higher social classes is shown in recent work on Maidstone. Between 1600 and 1640 personal assets of gentlemen averaged over £350, of shopkeepers and other distributive tradesmen about £327; while professional men (about £120) and textile manufacturers (about £99) had fewer goods, there were several wealthy brewers and papermakers. The substantial people in county towns were probably richer than those in market centres on account of more resident and visiting gentry, wholesale traders and specialised manufacturers. While further research is needed on the inventories of townspeople in other regions, Alan Dyer's work on Worcester, a West Midland county town, suggests a poorer community than Maidstone after 1600. In the 1660s and 1670s houses in Exeter and especially Leicester were smaller than those in Kent towns such as Maidstone and Rochester, confirming that at least some centres in the South-East were more prosperous than those elsewhere.[15]

(ii) 1650–1750

Of about 170 or 175 towns in the twelve counties in the 1660s and 1670s about half were still tiny, with between 450 and 1,000 people. About eighteen had over 2,000 inhabitants, fourteen at least 2,500 and five had more than 5,000 (Reading 5,000–5,500, Oxford 9,000, Colchester 8,000–9,000, Canterbury 7,431 and Deptford 6,625, both in 1676).[16] The South-East lacked regional centres of the size of the biggest in England, such as Exeter or Norwich, principally on account of the commercial dominance of London, acting as the biggest distribution

[14] Petchey, *Maldon*, pp. 37–9; P. Clark, 'The migrant in Kentish towns 1580–1640', in P. Clark and P. Slack, eds., *Crisis and Order in English Towns 1500–1700* (London, 1972), pp. 122, 129; P. Clark, *English Provincial Society from the Reformation to the Revolution: Religion, Politics and Society in Kent 1500–1640* (Hassocks, 1977), pp. 234–6; Chalklin, 'Seventeenth century market town', 160.

[15] Mayhew, *Rye*, pp. 188–9, P. Clark and L. Murfin, *The History of Maidstone* (Stroud, 1995), pp. 93–4; A. Dyer, *The City of Worcester in the Sixteenth Century* (Leicester, 1973), pp. 158–9; A. F. J. Dulley 'People and homes in the Medway towns: 1687–1783', *Archaeologica Cantiana*, 77 (1962), 171.

[16] Clark and Hosking, *Population Estimates*; Reed, 'Decline and recovery'; Goose, 'Decay and regeneration', p. 66.

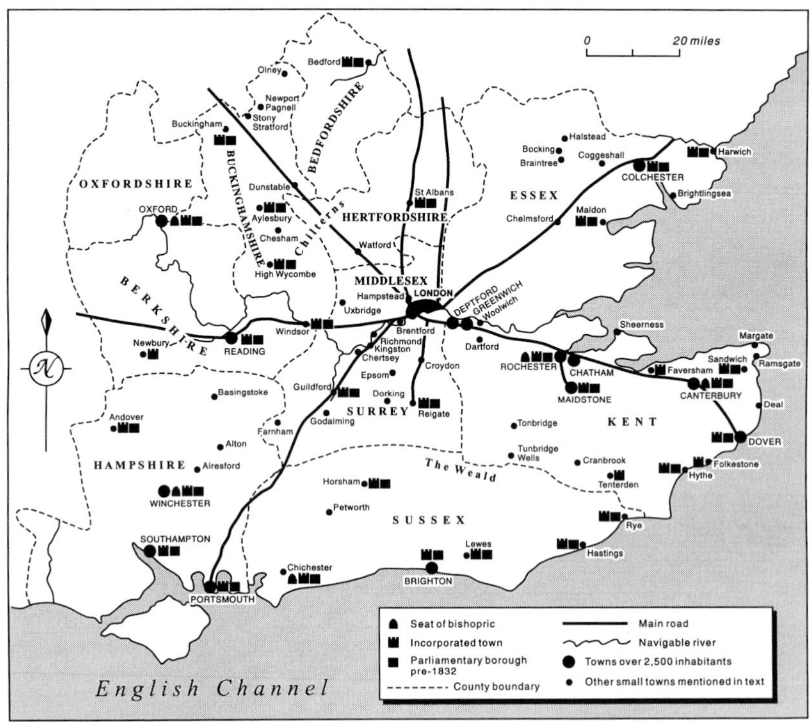

Map 2.3 Towns in the South-East *c.* 1670

centre, providing the most specialised trades such as printing, jewellery and watchmaking, and attracting many wealthy visitors who would otherwise have gone to the largest county centres. Various urban categories were present: market towns (most towns, and all with under 2,500 inhabitants), county or sub-county towns, naval dockyard towns, leisure and educational centres and London's sub-urban settlements. The last three groups are unusual in that they served the region or the whole country in a special way. While manufacturing was less important in some market and county towns, the proximity of London with its growing demand for foodstuffs was a compensation for this. A few new towns emerged or grew in this period, including Deal (because the Downs was a shipping station), Margate (dispatching corn to London by sea) and smaller Ramsgate and Sheerness (with naval docks), and two tiny spas (Tunbridge Wells and Epsom).

Market towns grew slowly as the rural population stopped expanding. Market trade was probably at its peak as several new sites were set up, including cattle markets. Markets thrived if communications were reasonable and there was no larger market nearby. In Hampshire (excluding the Isle of Wight) Dr Rosen identified twenty-one towns of which three had two weekly markets, six a major market, six a small weekly market and six markets failing or uncertainly held. Three of the small markets and all except one of the negligible markets were not on main roads. Markets were prosperous particularly if they were collecting points for sending produce to London. Thames-side ports such as Chertsey and High Wycombe sent corn, malt and flour down river; Hertfordshire towns assembled barley and malt from their own county and East Anglia. About 1720 Farnham was said to be the greatest provincial wheat market. Poultry was the speciality of Dorking, which drew supplies from as far away as Horsham.

Market trade was limited by dealing in inns and at the waterside, and shops grew fast in number and variety. In the smallest towns (such as Tonbridge with 600 people in 1664) retailers were still just general shopkeepers, named mercers or grocers. Traders of the larger market centres began to specialise, and together they sold an increasing range of goods. Buckingham (2,338 in 1676) had grocers, woollen and linen drapers, haberdashers, hatmakers, silkmen, goldsmiths and ironmongers in its Mercers' Company in 1663, adding milliners, surgeons, stationers, booksellers and hosiers in 1690. Shopkeepers were among the wealthiest working townspeople. The seventeen tradesmen in Petworth with personal estates over £500 between 1645 and 1728 included four mercers (one with the largest sum of £1,737), a haberdasher, tobacconist, draper, chandler, two butchers and an innkeeper.[17]

Crafts and manufacturing changed to some extent. Processing was ubiquitous. Malting for London was greater along the upper Thames and in Hertfordshire. In this century Reigate made oatmeal for ships' biscuits, having at one time twenty mills driven by manual or animal power. Several new industries were financed by London capital, such as gunpowder making at Faversham in the 1650s. The numerous shoemakers in some towns suggest that the region was now serving part of the capital's needs in footwear. Some crafts were linked to local raw materials. Thus Chiltern beech, ash and elm gave work to eighty-three turners, sawyers, shovelmakers, carpenters, chairmakers, spoon and trenchermakers among 705 occupied people in Chesham between 1637 and 1730. Traditional clothmaking disappeared largely in the Kentish Weald, Surrey, and Reading and Newbury. Shalloons and druggets replaced kerseys in Alton, Basingstoke and Andover. Sackcloth was made in Berkshire and blanket making became established in Witney. The new draperies prospered in Colchester and neighbouring centres. The silk industry reached a peak in Canterbury after the Restoration; in 1675 about 2,500 were said to be working in silks and worsteds. Essex and Canterbury textiles were sent to London for sale abroad, with small

[17] Rosen, 'Winchester', p. 153; P. Rogers, ed., *Daniel Defoe: A Tour through the Whole Island of Great Britain* (Exeter, 1989), pp. 54–6; Reed, 'Decline and recovery'; Elliott, *Buckingham*, p. 208; G. H. Kenyon, 'Petworth town and trades 1610–1760', Part I, *Sussex Archaeological Collections*, 96 (1958), 77, and Part II, *Sussex Archaeological Collections*, 98 (1960), 117.

quantities being sold to mercers in neighbouring towns. Faversham, Folkestone, Hastings and Hythe still concentrated on fishing, but its decay brought about the temporary decline of Brighton (with about 2,000 people in 1750). Yet another influence on towns was the fast growth of road transport in the South-East, stimulated by the early development of turnpikes around London after 1700. Organised carrier services were increasing. Services per week from London to towns and villages in the region rose from 183 in 1681 to 247 in 1738. Inns remained particularly numerous on the main roads: in Buckinghamshire one of the smaller towns, Stony Stratford on Watling Street (1,026 in 1676) had 100 beds and stabling for 127 horses in 1686, more beds than any other centre except Aylesbury (101). The number of professional people, such as attorneys, multiplied: for instance, there were eleven lawyers in Chesham between 1637 and 1730.[18]

About twelve bigger centres had commercial hinterlands with a radius of twenty or twenty-five miles, which included several lesser towns. Their markets were larger and sometimes held twice a week for different goods. Their shops had a greater variety of stock and attracted buyers from the whole district. Aylesbury was 'the principal market town in the county of Bucks'. In Hampshire traders from Alresford, Alton and Whitchurch (all with markets) brought produce to the bigger market at Winchester. Most of them were county towns which drew the leading gentry, often with their families, to assizes and quarter sessions, providing shopping and entertainment. Clusters of professional and leisured people increasingly resided there. Several had cathedrals with a chapter which increased the educated social elite. The county town of Maidstone (3,676 in 1696) was, according to Daniel Defoe, 'a town of very great business and trade, and yet full of gentry, of mirth and good company.' Spasmodic efforts were still being made by corporations and guilds to control trades and crafts, but regulations were falling into disuse. When the mayor of Reading tried to fix the assize of bread in 1723 he 'did not meet with suitable encouragement from some of my brethren' and the matter was dropped.[19] As county towns held shire and borough parliamentary elections and there were many other parliamentary boroughs, the intermittent lavish expenditure by local landowners to win support for members of parliament or electoral candidates contributed to urban economies.

The four naval dockyards (Deptford, Woolwich, Chatham and Portsmouth), to which the smaller Sheerness should now be added, and Deal grew more rapidly. Shipbuilding was an assembly industry in which the work was concen-

[18] W. Hooper, *Reigate: Its Story through the Ages*, . . . (Dorking, 1979), pp. 100–1; Reed, 'Decline and recovery'; Chalklin, *Kent*, pp. 126–8, 156; D. Gerhold, 'The growth of the London carrying trade, 1681–1838', *Ec.HR*, 2nd series, 41 (1988), 400.

[19] Rogers, ed., *Defoe*, pp. 69, 123; Rosen, 'Winchester', pp. 173–4, 177; P. J. Corfield, *The Impact of English Towns 1700–1800* (Oxford, 1982), p. 89.

trated on the spot. Naval needs in the wars led to a great influx of shipyard workers during the later seventeenth century into the Thames-side towns, and after 1700 into the Portsmouth suburb of Portsea. By 1750 the two districts had about 10,000 inhabitants, compared with 3,500 in the 1660s. Chatham had grown from under 1,000 in 1600 to over 5,000 by 1700, then it expanded more slowly. Deptford with private as well as royal dockyards grew fast in the seventeenth century. Workers in the extensive wet and dry docks, mast and ropeyards and storehouses such as shipwrights, caulkers, scavelmen, mastmakers, sailmakers, ropemakers, anchorsmiths and labourers dominated the local population. In Chatham they numbered 329 in 1664, 479 in 1688, 707 in 1712 and 1,188 in 1754. The growing wealth of London created more leisured people wanting to leave the bustle, noise and dirt of the huge congested capital for fresh air and country surroundings, sometimes for health or entertainment. Spa waters drunk for medical reasons produced two centres of a few hundred people at Tunbridge Wells and Epsom by 1700, where building and trade were partly financed by Londoners. The presence of royalty as well as pleasant views helped the growth of Greenwich, Richmond and Windsor, occupied by wealthy London people as a suburban retreat. Greenwich's population increased from about 3,000 to 5,000 in the seventeenth century, enjoying the palace and park, fine air and view above the river. Richmond benefited from the residence of the prince and princess of Wales under George I. Education helped Winchester, Eton and particularly Oxford, with over 2,000 members of the University and their servants among 9,000 inhabitants in 1667. By the early eighteenth century the navy, pleasure and teaching were making a big contribution to urbanisation in the region.[20]

(iii) 1750–1840

With resumed population increase and middle-class living standards improving further, urban growth became more rapid after 1750. Features visible in the previous century were sharpened. By 1841 there were about 180 towns with between 1,500 and 53,032 people, of which twenty-two centres had more than 10,000 and the largest was Portsmouth. The relatively high income per head in the region compared with much of the rest of England bolstered retailing, services and the professions. Yet, as elsewhere, growing population led to an increase of pauperism which was acute in such counties as Sussex and Berkshire which were mainly dependent on farming. Poverty varied in towns within twenty or thirty miles; Canterbury and Sandwich paid more poor relief per head than Maidstone in 1802–3. Yet even here in the early 1830s about 9 per cent

[20] C. W. Chalklin, *The Provincial Towns of Georgian England* (London, 1974), pp. 23–4; Chalklin, *Kent*, p. 31; Rogers, ed., *Defoe*, p. 60.

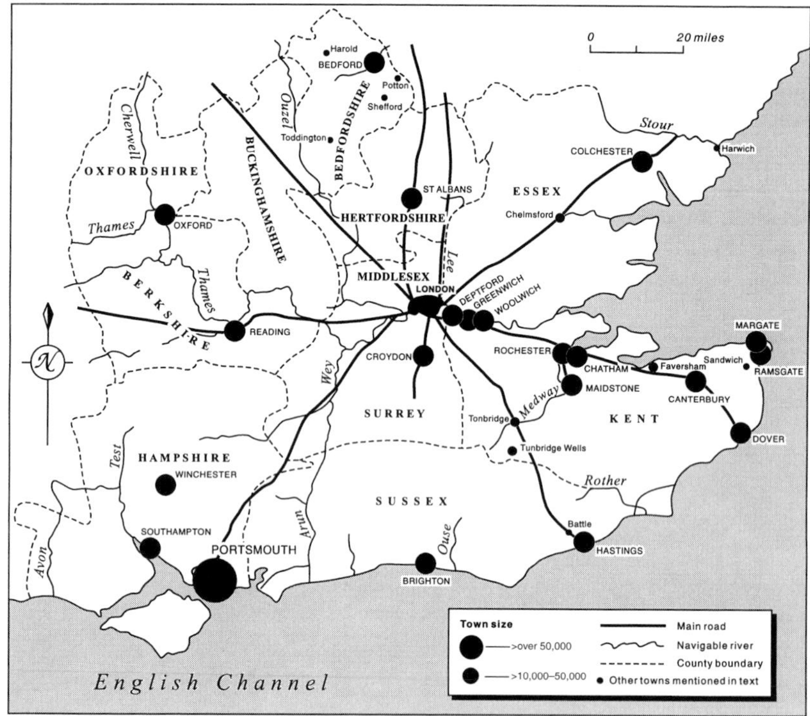

Map 2.4 Towns in the South-East 1841

were permanent paupers and 27 per cent more had temporary relief, as paupers flowed in from an impoverished countryside.[21]

Urban manufacturing such as textiles continued to decline (especially in Colchester and Canterbury). Defence and leisure were now dominating factors in the urban pattern, with both Portsmouth and Brighton the biggest provincial towns by 1821, and seaside visiting created at least three new towns. The further great economic expansion of London helped, as before, to limit the growth of the biggest county or sub-county centres such as Reading, Canterbury and Colchester. On the other hand it created satellite towns filled with wealthy retired men and women of independent means within ten or fifteen miles, and Londoners crowded the rising seaside resorts in the summer.

Turnpike roads and new waterways weakened trade in some small towns and helped the growth of larger centres. Wholesaling in shops and markets expanded and a thriving urban shopkeeping network is apparent. In the 1770s Maidstone had the best wholesale shops in Kent, supplying traders in the Weald with sugar,

[21] J. D. Marshall, *The Old Poor Law 1795–1834* (London, 1968), p. 54; Clark and Murfin, *Maidstone*, pp. 94–5.

groceries and other provisions worth £100,000 annually. Shopkeepers in the smaller towns stocked retailers in the neighbouring countryside, though the latter might also buy through riders serving London dealers. In 1791 Thomas Beeching, 'salesman, linen-draper, mercer, hosier and hatter, near Church-lane Tonbridge', advertised a rich variety of materials and clothing, 'country shops supplied, and parishes [buying for paupers] served as usual'. Some small markets became disused. While Berkshire's twelve markets all survived, in Bedfordshire eleven shrunk to nine as those at Shefford and Toddington ended, the latter's market house being pulled down in 1799; by 1819 Potton market had been declining for some years, and 'although Harold still keeps up the name of a market, it is only attended by two or three butchers, who open shambles there on Tuesdays'.[22]

Shopkeepers became ever more specialised and numerous. In Essex Chelmsford and Colchester had several booksellers before 1750 and there were insurance or estate agents in Colchester, Chelmsford and Braintree. The South-East had more shops than other parts of England. Surrey, Kent, Essex, Bedfordshire, Hertfordshire and London had twenty-nine people per shop in 1759 compared with forty-two in all England. The more prosperous markets were being reorganised with new locations and methods of sale. A covered market was opened in Oxford in 1774 with forty butchers' shops. Cattle and corn were handled wholesale on other sites. In general pitching was increasingly replaced by sample selling, making possible much larger deals. There were also more and larger inns where goods were stored and deals made.[23] With the few additions to river navigation and the relative absence of canals in the South-East, carrier services grew greatly to handle the increase of trade. In 1837 the tolls of the London road from High Wycombe were nearly ten times their value a century before, although this included private traffic. The flourishing state of transport on rivers such as the Thames, Kennet, Lea, Wey and Medway should not overshadow the less well-documented expansion of land traffic. Urban amenities promoting trade included private banks in all but the smallest towns from the later 1780s.[24] The pattern of urban manufacturing in the region continued to change. The silk industry had almost gone in Canterbury by 1800; Essex baymaking was hit by periodic depressions in the later eighteenth century as exports to southern Europe were interrupted, and, despite concentration in bigger firms the number of clothiers fell and manufacturing vanished by 1830.

22 C. W. Chalklin, 'The towns', in A. Armstrong, ed., *The Economy of Kent 1640–1914* (Woodbridge, 1995), p. 215; J. Dugdale, *The New British Traveller* (London, 1819), vol. 1, p. 10.

23 A. F. J. Brown, *Essex at Work 1700–1815* (Chelmsford, 1969), p. 67; A. Everitt, 'The English urban inn, 1560–1760', in A. Everitt, ed., *Perspectives in English Urban History* (London, 1973), p. 105; H.-C. Mui and L. H. Mui, *Shops and Shopkeeping in Eighteenth-Century England* (London, 1989), pp. 295–6.

24 L. J. Ashford, *The History of the Borough of High Wycombe from its Origins to 1880* (London, 1960), p. 206; W. Finch, *Directory of Kent* (Canterbury, 1803).

Table 2.5 *The population of leading seaside resorts in the South-East in 1801 and 1841*

	1801	1841
Brighton	7,339	46,000
Margate	4,766	11,050
Ramsgate	4,178	13,603

The cheap, skilled labour was used by Spitalfields entrepreneurs to throw and weave silk in Essex, for which steampower was harnessed from the 1820s. Naval shipbuilding and repair, particularly at Portsmouth and Chatham, grew in scale and employment. Portsmouth shipwrights and other artificers increased from 2,099 in 1759 during the Seven Years War to 3,996 at the end of the Napoleonic Wars in 1813. Population still grew later, that of Chatham rising from 10,505 in 1801 to 18,962 in 1841. Heavy fortifications at Dover and the dockyard towns and barracks created in the French wars gave a military element to many urban populations in the South-East such as those of Canterbury and Winchester. Elsewhere, many towns had substantial or small manufactures, often mainly for the London market. Faversham had large gunpowder works for the government, employing nearly 400 in the French Wars, and Battle had little works for sportsmen. Blankets were still made at Witney in the early nineteenth century, and Tunbridge Ware in Tonbridge and Tunbridge Wells.[25]

The rise of the seaside resorts was the other principal feature of urban growth in the South-East. Bathing began at Margate in the 1740s and Brighton in the 1750s. Primarily as resorts Brighton, Margate and Ramsgate were pre-eminent in 1801 and even in 1841, leading Weymouth and Scarborough outside the region, with Brighton the largest. There were at least fifteen other holiday towns in the South-East. Most grew from ports or fishing centres. The rise of Brighton was outstanding on account of the relative proximity of the capital and its fashionable demand led by the Prince Regent. Until the 1790s Margate was slightly in the lead because it began earlier and had waterborne transport on the Thames. Yet road transport was improving; in 1791 coaches took nine and in 1815 five hours to Brighton. By 1821 it had 24,429 people, the number having doubled since 1811 and more than trebled since 1801. The season lasted two or three months, especially August and September; two or three weeks stay was usual at

[25] Brown, Essex, pp. 4, 8, 22; J. Booker, *Essex and the Industrial Revolution* (Chelmsford, 1974), pp. 54–61; F. N. G. Thomas, 'Portsmouth and Gosport: a study in the historical geography of a naval port' (MSc thesis, University of London, 1961), p. 74; A. Percival, 'The Faversham gunpowder industry', *Industrial Archaeology*, 5 (1968), 15; *VCH*, Sussex, II, p. 238; J. H. Clapham, *An Economic History of Modern Britain: The Early Railway Age 1820–1850* (Cambridge, 1930), p. 47.

2–3 guineas per week per person in a lodging house. Margate had 10,000–20,000 visitors in a season by 1831 and Brighton over 4,000 in 1794 and up to 20,000 by 1840, its patrons being wealthier than at the Kentish towns. By the 1820s the steamboat carried 'artisan daytrippers on summer Sundays' numbering 30,000–300,000 to Gravesend. Sleeping in the open began here and there were over a million passengers by 1840. The London season and the inland spas provided the habit of holidays for health and diversion. While Weymouth served Bristol and Bath, and Scarborough Yorkshire, the south-eastern leisure towns were primarily for Londoners. Transport became faster, more comfortable, more reliable and even a little cheaper. Local and sometimes London capital paid for hotels, lodging houses, shops, libraries, theatres and assembly rooms. The location catered for young and old: 'visitors could bathe, walk, ride, botanize, collect shells or visit ancient monuments, or they could save up their energies for dances and card-parties'. While sea air, views and especially bathing were enjoyed best in summer, the 'beau monde' visited Brighton for a winter and spring season as well by the 1830s.[26]

Apart from the great rise of defence and leisure facilities, the expansion of London itself affected the urban network of the South-East. Towns within ten or fifteen miles became its satellites as the districts changed to market gardening (especially in Surrey and Kent), potato growing (in Essex), milling on a bigger scale, brickmaking especially in the west, cowkeeping or housing wealthy visitors, part-residents or retired people from London (notably in Kent). The growing London demand for foodstuffs increased inexorably the pressures on the economy of the more distant hinterland, making up for the decline of textiles. The area around Canterbury concentrated more on hops (which are labour intensive), north Essex became another granary for London and Reading became, above all, a collecting and processing centre of barley (malt) and wheat (flour) for the capital. On the other hand, as the national economy expanded there was some diversification away from metropolitan dominance. Although Harwich, Dover and Southampton were passenger points linking London with the continent, the last two developed more independent functions with considerable overseas as well as coastal trade, docks being built at Southampton from 1804. The Kennet and Avon and Wiltshire and Berkshire Canals, both opened in 1810, linked the towns of west Berkshire with South Wales, and the Oxford Canal in 1789 joined the Black Country with Oxford and Reading, providing an alternative source of coal. Thus new national and overseas transport connections helped to reduce the dependence of parts of the region on the capital.[27]

[26] J. K. Walton, *The English Seaside Resort* (Leicester, 1983), chs. 2, 3; J. Whyman, *Aspects of Holiday Making and Resort Development within the Isle of Thanet* (New York, 1981), *passim*; E. M. Gilbert, *Brighton Old Ocean's Bauble* (London, 1954), chs. 1–7.

[27] Brown, *Essex*, pp. 28–35, 78, 89; R. Mudie, *Hampshire: Its Past and Present Condition and Future Prospects* (Winchester, 1838), vol. I, p. 88.

The special features of the South-East created towns which were more prosperous on average than those in other regions. They were also more socially and economically varied, with the servicing of agriculture being supplemented in the sixteenth and seventeenth centuries by a range of industries and crafts, and later by the growth of leisure amenities, naval and military defence and the capital's need for suburban services including houses for rich Londoners. Again, towns differed between counties. While Bedfordshire centres, with the support of farming and servicing of hand industry, resembled those in Leicestershire, Kent was unique in the varied function of its towns. Finally, the areas round London were special in the extent of their urbanisation. In the seventeenth century a third of the population of Essex and Kent lived in towns on account of industry and the start of suburbanisation. By 1841 55 per cent of Kent's people were urban, an exceptional feature outside the industrial Midlands and North.

· 2(c) ·

South-West

JONATHAN BARRY

THE SIX counties in the South-West of England (Gloucestershire, Wiltshire, Dorset, Somerset, Devon and Cornwall) are not now associated strongly with urbanisation. Apart from Bristol and Plymouth, the region is predominantly one of small and medium-sized towns. The origins of this modern pattern, in contrast with the more heavily urbanised Midlands and (parts of) the North, lie in the period covered here. Yet it would be misleading to portray this period as one of urban decline in the South-West. Not only was there a more than threefold increase in the urban population of the region between 1660 (*c.* 225,000) and 1841 (just under 880,000), but even in 1841 the South-West, with 40 per cent of its population in towns, was as urbanised as England generally, leaving London aside (see Table 2.6).[1] If urban growth in the previous centuries was less spectacular than elsewhere, this was in part because of the strong urban infrastructure already in place, with over a quarter of the region's people living in towns by 1660, rising to almost 37 per cent by 1801. Furthermore, if the region lacked an outstanding major new town based on manufacturing and commercial success, it had many smaller ones, notably in Cornwall and in the clothing districts around Bristol, and it had the two greatest inland spas – Bath (see Plates 3 and 28) and Cheltenham, the latter the fastest growing large English town between 1801 and 1841. The leisure and tourism industry they personified was already transforming the coastal towns from Weymouth along the south Devon coast and round to Weston-super-Mare and Clevedon on the Bristol Channel. The region's towns were also deeply affected by shifts in trading patterns and, most spectacularly, by the growth of British naval power which created the port at Dock (which became Devonport) and so carried the Plymouth conurbation into second place behind Bristol in the region's urban hierarchy. The region was no less

[1] See Chapter 14 in this volume, which builds on: C. M. Law, 'The growth of urban population in England and Wales, 1801–1911', *Transactions of the Institute of British Geographers*, old series, 41 (1967), 125–43; B. T. Robson, *Urban Growth* (London, 1973).

Table 2.6 *Urbanisation in the South-West of England by county in 1660, 1801 and 1841*

County (no. of towns)	C (38)	De (63)	Do (26)	G (32)	S (42)	W (33)	B'l	All
Total pop. 1660	100.0	230.0	85.0	120.0	185.0	120.0	16.0	856.0
Total pop. 1801	188.0	343.0	115.0	195.0	270.0	185.0	58.9	1,354.9
Total pop. 1841	341.0	533.0	175.0	324.0	418.0	258.0	125.1	2,174.1
Urban pop. 1660	18.2	67.5	23.1	28.3	40.4	31.4	16.0	224.8
Urban pop. 1801	52.8	143.7	40.0	50.2	96.5	53.9	58.9	495.8
Urban pop. 1841	96.3	250.6	63.0	105.0	159.0	79.6	125.1	878.7
% urban 1660	18.2	29.4	27.2	23.6	21.8	26.1	100.0	26.3
% urban 1801	28.1	41.9	34.8	25.8	35.7	29.1	100.0	36.6
% urban 1841	28.2	47.0	36.0	32.4	38.0	30.9	100.0	40.4
Mean town 1660	478	1,089	888	883	962	950	—	956
Mean town 1801	1,388	2,317	1,538	1, 569	2,297	1,632	—	2,110
Mean town 1841	2,534	4,042	2,423	3,282	3,787	2,412	—	3,740
Median town 1660	388	620	600	650	700	600	—	600
Median town 1801	980	950	925	1,050	1,125	975	—	1,000
Median town 1841	1,465	1,510	1,500	1,375	1,738	1,500	—	1,475
Urban inc.[a] 1660–1801	190	113	73	78	139	72	268	120
Urban inc. 1801–41	83	75	58	109	65	48	113	77
Urban inc. 1660–1841	430	271	173	272	294	154	682	291
Total inc.[b] 1660–1801	88	61	35	63	46	54	268	58
Total inc. 1801–41	81	70	52	66	55	40	113	61
Total inc. 1660–1841	241	175	106	170	126	115	682	154

% of all urban[c] 1660	8.1	30.0	10.3	12.6	18.0	14.0	7.1	—
% of all urban 1801	10.6	29.0	8.0	10.1	19.5	10.9	11.9	—
% of all urban 1841	11.0	28.5	7.2	12.0	18.1	9.1	14.2	—

Notes

All figures are in thousands except those for mean and median town size.

C = Cornwall, De = Devon, Do = Dorset, G = Gloucestershire, S = Somerset, W = Wiltshire, B'l = Bristol (including parts of Somerset and Gloucestershire), All = whole region.

[a] % increase in urban population between those dates.

[b] % increase in total population between those dates.

[c] Share of urban population of the region held by that county at that date.

Sources: see text.

affected by the transformations of the nation than the Midlands and the North. Indeed, until the end of our period industrial growth based on that traditional south-western staple, the textile industry, was still capable of generating strong urban development.

In the earlier part of the period, the South-West, while containing many small towns, was also well represented at the upper end of the urban hierarchy. There is general agreement that in 1524/5 lay subsidy returns put Bristol, Salisbury and Exeter in the top five of English provincial towns (with between 5,000 and 8,000 people), though some northern cities are missing or underassessed. In all, nine towns (the others being Crediton, Plymouth and Tiverton in Devon, Bodmin in Cornwall, Taunton in Somerset and Gloucester) appear in the top fifty provincial towns. By 1600, according to Wrigley, Plymouth and Gloucester had joined Bristol, Exeter and Salisbury among the top nine towns, suggesting a peak of urban influence for the region. By 1670 or so hearth tax evidence suggests that the position of the five towns had worsened except for Bristol (still second or third in the provincial hierarchy), with Exeter, Salisbury, Plymouth and Gloucester further down the demographic rank order of the thirty or so towns with populations near or above 4,000.[2]

During the next 130 years, Bath joined Bristol, Exeter and Plymouth (including Dock) among the twenty-three English provincial towns of 15,000 or more. Bath rose to tenth town by 1801 and Plymouth to seventh, but, although Bristol replaced Norwich at the top of the hierarchy from the early eighteenth century until after 1750, and Exeter had regained fourth place by 1700, they then slipped to fourth and seventeenth places respectively in 1801. By 1841 Bristol and Plymouth had both slipped one place, but Bath and Exeter were falling behind demographically. The new star was Cheltenham, while Gloucester was also growing again after two sluggish centuries. Five other towns (Taunton, Salisbury, Frome, Truro and Bridgwater) featured in the hundred or so English towns with 10,000 or more population. While not suffering the indignity of Old Sarum, populationless and stripped in 1832 of its borough status, New Sarum (Salisbury) had suffered a decline in relative terms from fourth or fifth in the urban hierarchy to near the bottom of these hundred towns, which expresses in exaggerated form the loss of urban vitality, measured by population at least, of much of the region's older urban network.[3]

[2] A. Dyer, *Decline and Growth in English Towns 1400–1640*, 2nd edn (Cambridge, 1995), pp. 64–6; E. A. Wrigley, *People, Cities and Wealth* (Oxford, 1987), pp. 160–1; J. Patten, *English Towns 1500–1700* (Folkestone, 1978), pp. 42, 103–4, 109–13, 118–19; P. J. Corfield, 'Urban developments in England and Wales in the sixteenth and seventeenth centuries', repr. in J. Barry, ed., *The Tudor and Stuart Town* (London, 1990), pp. 35–62.

[3] Studies of the urban hierarchy in this period include: Wrigley, *People, Cities and Wealth*, pp. 160–1; P. J. Corfield, *The Impact of English Towns 1700–1800* (Oxford, 1982), pp. 12–15; C. W. Chalklin, *The Provincial Towns of Georgian England* (London, 1974), pp. 316–19; H. Carter, 'Towns and urban systems 1730–1900', in R. Dodgshon and R. Butlin, eds., *Historical Geography of England and Wales* (London, 1978), pp. 370–3.

(i) THE PATTERN OF URBANISATION

However, there is much more to a region's urban history than the fortunes of a few towns at the top, and other ways of measuring importance than population (itself a tricky thing to measure). This section explores the broader urban pattern and what, if anything, was distinctive about the towns of the South-West, both in themselves and in their relationships with their region and the wider world. This analysis will be built on the basic, if rough-hewn, building-blocks of information on population and on economic functions, especially marketing, but will also consider the political status and role of towns and their cultural identity.

Continuing with population data for the moment, we can measure the relative importance of towns of varying scale by looking at their share of the region's urban and total populations (see Table 2.7).[4] Around 1660 (the first period for which we have usable data across the region), almost 30 per cent of the urban population lived in 151 settlements (some, admittedly, of only marginal urban status at this date)[5] of less than 800 people, while almost half lived in 78 towns of between 800 and 3,199. The six towns above that size (Bristol (16,000), Exeter (11,500), Salisbury (7,000), Plymouth (5,400), Gloucester (4,750) and Tiverton (3,500)) housed only 21 per cent of the townspeople, and a mere 5.6 per cent of the estimated population of the six counties.[6] The

[4] The data used here builds on P. Clark and J. Hosking, *Population Estimates of English Small Towns 1550–1851: Revised Edition* (Leicester, 1993). In all cases except Gloucestershire, the main sources used before 1801 are the protestation returns of 1641–2, the hearth taxes of the 1660s and 1670s, the Compton census of 1676 and eighteenth-century diocesan visitation returns. Gloucestershire lacks the first of these but has an unrivalled set of ecclesiastical and antiquarian sources for population: these are summarised in A. Percival, 'Gloucestershire village populations', *Local Population Studies*, 8 (1972), 39–47 and supplement. For the problems and possibilities of the seventeenth-century material see: A. Whiteman, ed., *The Compton Census of 1676* (London, 1986); K. Schurer and T. Arkell, eds., *Surveying the People* (Oxford, 1992). For earlier efforts to establish town populations (mostly for the seventeenth century) in the region see: W. G. Hoskins, *Devon* (London, 1954), pp. 104–22; J. Whetter, *Cornwall in the Seventeenth Century* (Padstow, 1974), pp. 8–13; R. Clifton, *The Last Popular Rebellion* (London, 1984), pp. 24–33 (Somerset); D. Underdown, *Revel, Riot and Rebellion* (Oxford, 1985), pp. 293–6, and J. Bettey, *Wessex from AD 1000* (London, 1986), pp. 142–50, 189–97, 205–9, 226–35 (Dorset, Somerset and Wiltshire); Chalklin, *Provincial Towns*, p. 322 (Dorset); D. Rollison, *The Local Origins of Modern Society* (London, 1992), pp. 27–32 (Gloucestershire). The region's experience is set in national context in P. Clark, 'Small towns in England, 1550–1850', in P. Clark, ed., *Small Towns in Early Modern Europe* (Cambridge, 1995), pp. 103–8, 113–17.

[5] In 1660 11,040 people (*c.* 5 per cent of the urban total) lived in thirty-four places included here which were neither market towns at that date nor clearly already urban in character.

[6] The estimates of county population *c.* 1660 used here are based on Whiteman, *Compton Census*, adjusted by the proportion of national population, taxation and housing of each county suggested by the sources in: P. Deane and W. A. Cole, *British Economic Growth 1660–1959* (Cambridge, 1964), p. 103; J. Thirsk and J. Cooper, eds., *Seventeenth-Century Economic Documents* (Oxford, 1972), pp. 802–3; A. Browning, ed., *English Historical Documents*, vol. VIII (London, 1953), pp. 304–6, 311–12, 458–9, 513, 520–3; D. B. Horn and M. Ransome, eds., *English Historical Documents*, vol. x (London, 1957), pp. 323–4.

Table 2.7 *Population in towns of varied sizes in the South-West of England in 1660, 1801 and 1841*

	1660			1801			1841		
Town population	No.	Pop	%	No.	Pop	%	No.	Pop	%
0–199	10	1,130	0.5	5	490	0.1	2	195	0.0
200–399	50	14,315	6.4	14	4,295	0.9	6	1,875	0.2
400–799	91	49,980	22.2	71	42,105	8.5	40	26,490	3.0
800–1,599	51	52,785	23.5	70	75,780	15.3	78	88,705	10.1
1,600–3,199	27	58,475	26.0	45	98,645	19.9	49	108,060	12.3
3,200–6,399	3	13,650	6.1	23	93,890	18.9	40	173,315	19.7
6,400–12,799	2	18,500	8.2	3	23,700	4.8	13	117,255	13.3
12,800–25,599	1	16,000	7.1	1	20,500	4.1	2	28,900	3.3
25,600–51,199				2	77,500	15.6	2	73,800	8.4
51,200–102,399				1	58,850	11.9	2	135,000	15.4
102,400–204,799							1	125,100	14.2
Total	235	224,835	100.0	235	495,755	100.0	235	878,695	100.00

Sources: see text.

hundredth ranked town had 700 people and there were 63 towns with 1,000 or more population.

By 1801 the balance had shifted decidedly away from the smallest settlements.[7] Less than 10 per cent now lived in the 90 places still under 800, and only another 35 per cent in the 115 towns of 800–3,199. About a third of the rest were in the 23 towns of between 3,200 and 6,399. Bristol (58,850), Plymouth conurbation (43,500), Bath (34,000), Exeter (20,500), Salisbury (8,700), Gloucester (8,000) and Frome (7,000) together contained 13.3 per cent of the region's population (which had itself grown substantially) of whom just under half a million lived in towns. The hundredth ranking town had 1,150 inhabitants, while the top 63 towns now had populations of 2,000 or more.

Although rural population growth ensured that the proportion of the population living in towns only grew slightly between 1801 and 1841, from 36.6 per cent to 40.4 per cent, the size of towns grew dramatically. The hundredth ranked town now had 1,790 people and, neatly enough, the top 63 towns now had 3,000 or more population! A mere 3.2 per cent of townspeople now lived in the 48 towns still containing less than 800 people, and all 175 towns under 3,200 now only contained a quarter of the urban population, a smaller share than the three largest towns Bristol (125,100), Plymouth conurbation (80,000) and Bath (55,000). Together the towns over 6,400 contained about 480,000 people, approximately 22 per cent of the region's 2,174,000 souls. In all, slightly more people (878,695) lived in towns in 1841 than the entire population of the region 180 years earlier.

Unfortunately, there is a dearth of data across the region to enable one to judge the level of urbanisation either before 1660 or between that date and 1800. Where such data does exist, for Cornwall and Devon in the eighteenth century, it appears that much of the urban growth in proportion to rural population had occurred before 1750. Similarly, the major changes in the urban hierarchy seen in Cornwall had already happened by 1750.[8] If we compare the top 63 towns in 1660, 1801 and 1841, then we find 85 towns included at least once. Of these 42 remained throughout, but 20 of the 1660 towns failed to sustain their position:

[7] Information from the censuses of 1801–41 regarding parish and town populations has been modified to arrive at urban populations using evidence from other sources and from the discussions of town boundaries and populations contained in the parliamentary inquiries into parliamentary representation (especially PP 1831–2 XXVII–XLI and PP 1852 XLII) and municipal corporations (PP 1835 XXIII–XXIV). I have also benefited from a pioneering effort by Dr Tom Arkell to use census enumerators' papers to establish town boundaries for Cornwall: T. Arkell, 'Establishing population totals for small towns from the 1851 census' (unpublished paper 1992).

[8] J. Barry, 'Towns and processes of urbanization *c.* 1550–1840', in R. Kain and W. L. D. Ravenhill, eds., *Historical Atlas of South-West England* (Exeter, 1999), pp. 437–49. A similar conclusion is reached for the North-West in J. Stobart, 'An eighteenth-century revolution? Investigating urban growth in North-West England 1664–1801', *UH*, 23 (1996), 26–47.

16 had dropped out by 1801 and only 4 more by 1841. Of the 23 new towns, 20 had appeared by 1801 (three of these failed to reappear in 1841) and only three further towns appeared in 1841, all quite far down the rankings (Torquay, Westbury and St Austell, and only the first of these was growing spectacularly from nothing). The towns losing rank fastest were mostly middle-ranking inland towns from the centre of the region, such as Cullompton, Tewkesbury, Cirencester, Crediton, Sherborne and South Molton. A few ports also did relatively badly, such as Dartmouth, Lyme Regis and Minehead. The newcomers were almost all coastal and/or mining towns from Cornwall (9) and Devon (4). The port of Dock (Plymouth Devonport) should also be included here, growing from nothing in the late seventeenth century to a size that would have made it the region's third largest town in its own right in both 1801 and 1841. Only four other towns rose into the top ranks and three did so modestly (Wellington, Calne and Westbury), leaving only Stroud as an example of really major growth. Within the existing top ranks, the towns that rose furthest were Bath, Frome, Weymouth and Cheltenham. Significantly, the four towns granted parliamentary representation in 1832 were Cheltenham, Stroud (with its surrounding clothing district), Frome and Devonport (Bath and Weymouth were already represented).

(ii) AN URBAN REGION?

The towns covered here did not form an urban region in a strong sense, namely an integrated urban network whose internal linkages were central and whose fortunes were closely related. The geography of the area would make this inherently unlikely, given the predominance of water communications in establishing intra-urban links, especially in the upland parts of the region. Although road transport was always extensive – and the patterns of coach and carrier services and the inns that serviced them did much to establish small town fortunes – it was not until the arrival of the railways, creeping ever westward in 1840, that water routes lost their inland dominance.[9] The two major coastlines – of the English and Bristol Channels – each had separate trading networks, although both were also oriented towards European and, by the seventeenth century, Atlantic trade. The various river systems – Severn, Avon (Wiltshire, Bristol and Severn), Stour, Parrett, Exe, Tamar and, crucially, Thames and Kennet – linked parts of the region but also directed many of the towns towards urban and other networks outside our region – notably in those areas of Wiltshire and

[9] J. A. Chartres, 'The place of inns in the commercial life of London and western England, 1660–1760' (DPhil thesis, University of Oxford, 1973); D. Gerhold, *Road Transport before the Railways* (Cambridge, 1993); T. Barker and D. Gerhold, *The Rise and Rise of Road Transport 1700–1990* (Basingstoke, 1993). For local studies see G. Sheldon, *From Trackway to Turnpike* (Oxford, 1928), on east Devon, and N. Herbert, *Road Travel and Transport in Gloucestershire* (Gloucester, 1985).

Gloucestershire oriented towards London (see Map 2.5). Bristol and the north Devon and Somerset ports were tied into an elaborate system of exchange with Ireland, South Wales and the upper reaches of the Severn, although the goods they traded increasingly penetrated the rest of the region as improvements occurred in both water (river and canal) and road networks, which in turn boosted the growth of 'inland' towns such as Bridgwater.[10]

One way of testing the coherence of the region's urban experience is, again, to look at urban population levels. The easiest comparisons to make are betweeen the various counties, since only at this level can we make educated assumptions, before 1801 at least, about non-urban population, so as to test the varying extent of urbanisation (see Table 2.6). This is necessary, because the various counties experienced different demographic fortunes during the period. Cornwall's rural population tripled, but its share of the urban sector also grew as its urban population increased by some 430 per cent 1660–1841, compared to the regional growth of just under 300 per cent. Even so, Cornwall's starting point was so low that throughout it was the least urbanised county. In 1660 it only had 3 towns in the top 63, and although 11 of the top 63 were Cornish by 1801 and 14 by 1841, the largest town, Truro, was still only ranked tenth.[11]

Throughout the period, however, it was Devon which had the most and the largest towns, with 17 of the top 63 and the largest average size of town. Its share of the urban sector fell slightly, but it remained the most urbanised county, rising from about 30 per cent in 1660 to 41 per cent in 1801 and 47 per cent in 1841. Of course, much of Devon's urban growth was concentrated in the Plymouth conurbation which, given its location on the Tamar, should perhaps be considered as much the capital of Cornwall as of Devon. In 1630 Westcote noted of Plymouth that it was 'in every way so esteemed by Cornishmen they would claim it for their own'.[12] Its presence is certainly one reason why urban growth in Cornwall was largely concentrated in the west (Penzance, Falmouth, Truro, Penryn and so on), although the westward movement of mining and rural population was another.

10 Extensive studies of Devon's ports and maritime trade are synthesised in M. Duffy *et al.*, eds., *New Maritime History of Devon* (London, 1993–4), vols. I and II. Bristol Channel trade *c.* 1700 is reconstructed in D. P. Hussey, 'Re-investigating coastal trade: the ports of the Bristol Channel and the Severn Estuary, *c.* 1695–*c.* 1704' (DPhil thesis, University of Wolverhampton, 1995). The best guides to the trade of the English Channel ports in the seventeenth century are the many articles of W. B. Stephens, as well as papers in the series 'Exeter Papers in Economic History' and 'Exeter Maritime Studies', published by the University of Exeter. For Bridgwater see *VCH*, Somerset, VI, pp. 192–243.

11 N. Pounds, 'Population of Cornwall before the first census', in W. Minchinton, ed., *Population and Marketing: Two Studies in the History of the South West* (Exeter, 1976), pp. 11–30; D. Cullum, 'Society and economy in west Cornwall, *c.* 1588–1750' (PhD thesis, University of Exeter, 1993); P. Thomas, 'Population of Cornwall in the eighteenth century', *Journal of the Royal Institution of Cornwall*, 10(4) (1990), 416–56.

12 T. Westcote, *View of Devonshire in 1630*, ed. G. Oliver and P. Jones (Exeter, 1845), p. 382.

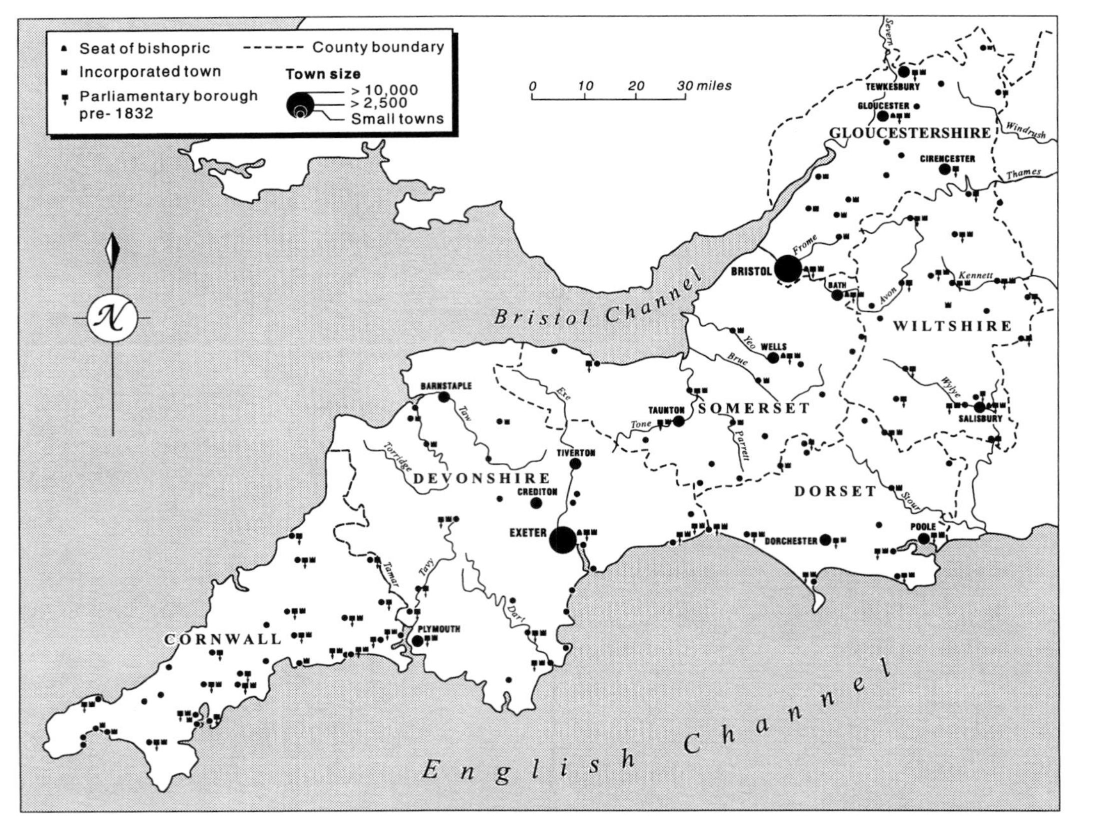

Map 2.5 Towns in the South-West *c.* 1670

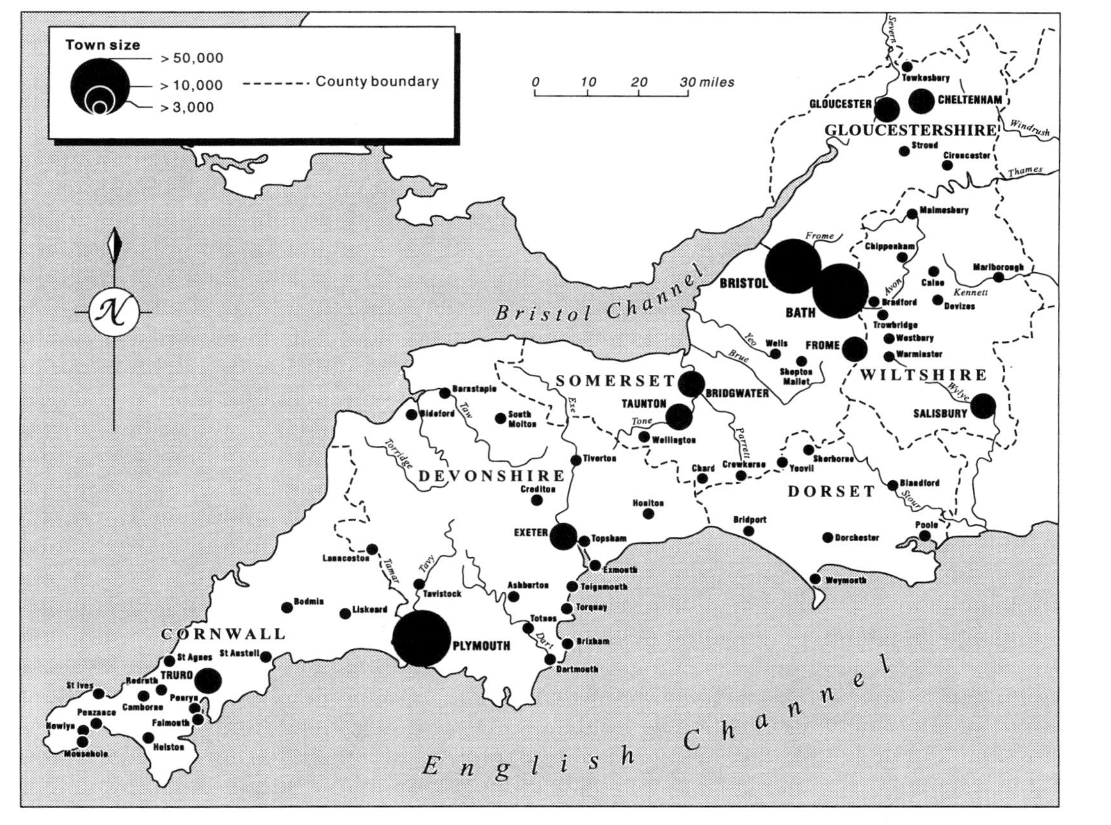

Map 2.6 Towns in the South-West 1841

At the other end of the region, we face a similar complication in considering Gloucestershire and Somerset in relation to Bristol, which straddled both counties but was legally a county in itself. In Table 2.6, we have distinguished the Bristol conurbation from both, reducing the county totals accordingly, but it could be argued that Bristol fulfilled an urban function for both counties. If Bristol's population were halved between both counties, then their urban percentage would rise, with Gloucestershire above the regional average in 1660 and 1841. Somerset would still be below average in 1660 but well above in 1801 and 1841. However, these figures are heavily distorted by the growth of Bath and Cheltenham, which greatly boosted Somerset's growth 1660–1801 and Gloucestershire's 1801–41. At all three dates Gloucestershire had only 5 towns in the top 63, but Somerset's share declined precipitately, from 17 in 1660 to 9 in 1841.

Wiltshire and Dorset saw only limited urban growth, so that their share of the urban sector fell from almost a quarter in 1660 to just over 16 per cent in 1841. To some extent this reflected the decline in their share of the region's population as a whole, but their rural populations actually grew faster than those of Devon and Somerset – in Wiltshire's case substantially before 1801 and into the early nineteenth century, before its rural and urban textile industries went into rapid decline after 1821. Wiltshire's share of the top 63 towns was unchanged at 9, but only 6 of the 10 Dorset towns reached 3,000 by 1841. To a large extent the two counties' modest showing reflected their failure to breed a large town with rapid growth of the kind which boosted the other counties. Salisbury grew very slowly and none of the clothing towns of the north-west of Wiltshire – Devizes, Trowbridge, Bradford, Chippenham and Westbury – could establish itself clearly above the others or their counterparts in adjacent parts of Somerset and Gloucestershire such as Frome, Shepton Mallet, Stroud or, indeed, Bath and Bristol, the nearest major towns. In Dorset the lack of a single major town was repeated. The county town, Dorchester, had never been a Salisbury, though like Salisbury it grew very slowly until 1801 (from 2,600 to 3,200) but more rapidly thereafter, reaching 5,750 by 1841.[13]

However, given the problematic status of Plymouth and Bristol and the major effects on county totals produced by the two national spas, Bath and Cheltenham, it is worthwhile to compare the urbanisation of the counties leaving aside these four towns, which might be regarded as standing outside the county network. If we do so, then Dorset and Wiltshire actually have a higher rate of urbanisation than any county but Devon at all three dates, with Dorset exceeding Devon in 1801. The size of the average town, without the four giants, is remarkably similar across five of the counties at all three dates, the exception being Cornwall in 1660 and 1801. As this implies, rates of urban growth apart from the four towns in the

[13] A. L. Clegg, *History of Dorchester* (n.p., 1972), and D. Underdown, *Fire from Heaven* (London, 1992) (Dorchester); *VCH*, Wiltshire, VI (Salisbury).

other five counties were broadly comparable, ranging from 154 to 176 per cent 1660–1841, whereas Cornwall's increase was 430 per cent.

(iii) TYPES OF TOWN

At a county level, therefore, we may discern a broadly similar pattern of urbanisation, save for Cornwall, but this was composed from the very varying fortunes of different towns and types of town, which need separate analysis, beginning with the town often labelled the 'metropolis of the west'. How far did Bristol play a metropolitan role?[14] Certainly it strengthened its position as the largest and richest town of the region, though this, and its claim to metropolitan status, owed at least as much to its role in southern Wales and along the Severn as to its interplay with, for example, Cornwall or Dorset (though ironically the latter was part of the diocese of Bristol from 1542 to 1836). In the first half of our period Bristol was not much larger than cities such as Exeter, Salisbury and Gloucester, or even towns such as Taunton or Tiverton. Even in 1660, Bristol's population at 16,000 was only about 7 per cent of the region's urban population and not far ahead of Exeter. Thereafter the other cities fell well behind Bristol, especially in the first half of the eighteenth century when its population doubled to approach 50,000, but there is little sign that this reflected direct competition or a growing Bristol domination of the region. The Bristol conurbation increased its share of the region's urban population to about 12 per cent in 1801 and 14 per cent in 1841, but even then it lacked 'metropolitan' dominance, being surrounded at close range by a series of substantial towns: Bath, Cheltenham, Gloucester, Frome, Trowbridge, Stroud and Bradford-upon-Avon, each with an important role both regionally and nationally independent of Bristol. Bristol's proportion of the region's population, though rising from less than 2 per cent in 1660 to 5.75 per cent in 1841, never compared with London's proportion of the national population, let alone that of its region, the South-East.

Much of the most vigorous urban growth during our period occurred in towns that not only depended little on Bristol but also, like Bristol, owed their prosperity in large measure to factors external to the region. Arguably one of the reasons for the slowing of Bristol's growth compared to that of its great rivals further north was that they forged ties with a growing industrial hinterland in a way Bristol failed to do during the high point of the West Country textile industry during the eighteenth century. Instead, it relied on colonial imported products, above all sugar, and their processing, together with new metal and other industries, only to find itself increasingly disadvantaged in these areas by the

[14] D. H. Sacks, *The Widening Gate* (Berkeley, Calif., 1991); W. E. Minchinton, 'Bristol – metropolis of the west in the eighteenth century', TRHS, 5th series, 4 (1954), 69–89; K. Morgan, *Bristol and the Atlantic Trade in the Eighteenth Century* (Cambridge, 1993); Hussey, 'Re-investigating coastal trade'.

better fuel and resource endowments of its rivals.[15] Bristol's three nearest rivals for size by 1840, Plymouth conurbation, Bath and Cheltenham, depended for their staple trade on naval or leisure requirements determined by national developments and fuelled largely by external finance. In large areas of the region urban growth and prosperity had become heavily dependent on national and international markets either in primary products – such as fish and minerals in Cornwall, for example – or in services – such as tourism in the spas and along the south coast – which required only shallow connections between growing towns and their rural and urban hinterlands.[16]

As John Langton has argued, there is no necessary contradiction between growing national and international interdependence on the one hand and the emergence of strong regional identities, based on urban centres, on the other. Indeed the two appear, in parts of the North and Midlands, to have gone hand in hand after 1700.[17] One might see the emergence of the 'West Country', as a region associated with maritime life, leisure and agriculture, as a further example of such 'regional specialisation', reflected in the changing urban hierarchy and in the changing specialisms of towns such as Exeter, Taunton and Salisbury.

Yet in this region, at least, such developments came at the expense of an older regional specialism, the cloth industry, which had not only tied many of the towns of the region together, but had also ensured a strong connection between town and countryside, given the strong rural roots of much cloth production. In the very long run the fluctuating fortunes and eventual decline of the cloth industry did more than anything else to determine the growth, or lack of it, of the majority of inland towns which sought a role greater than of market centre for a rural hinterland. Further, its decline changed the nature of urban–rural interactions, since the town often became the focus of what industrial production was left, in factories for lace, silk and other specialised textile products,[18] and became, for the countryside around, a market in which to exchange agricultural

[15] K. Morgan, 'The economic development of Bristol, 1700–1850', in M. Dresser and P. Ollerenshaw, eds., *The Making of Modern Bristol* (Bristol, 1996), pp. 48–75.

[16] For Plymouth see Duffy *et al.*, eds., *New Maritime History*. On Bath and Cheltenham see R. S. Neale, *Bath 1650–1850* (London, 1981); S. McIntyre, 'Bath: the rise of a resort town 1660–1800', in P. Clark, ed., *Country Towns in Pre-Industrial England* (Leicester, 1981), pp. 197–249; P. Hembry, *The English Spa 1560–1815* (London, 1990); G. Hart, *A History of Cheltenham*, 2nd edn (Stroud, 1990). For tourism see S. McIntyre, 'Towns as health and pleasure resorts: Bath, Scarborough and Weymouth, 1700–1815' (DPhil thesis, University of Oxford, 1973); J. Travis, *Rise of Devon's Seaside Resorts 1750–1900* (Exeter, 1993), and Chapter 23 in this volume.

[17] J. Langton, 'The Industrial Revolution and the regional geography of England', *Transactions of the Institute of British Geographers*, new series, 9 (1984), 145–67.

[18] For this pattern elsewhere see: P. Sharpe, 'De-industrialization and re-industrialization: women's employment and the changing character of Colchester', *UH*, 21 (1994), 77–96; N. Raven, 'Deindustrialisation and the urban response', in R. Weedon and A. Milne, eds., *Aspects of English Small Towns in the Eighteenth and Nineteenth Centuries* (Leicester, 1993).

produce and to buy consumer products, rather than a market from which to export the countryside's manufactured products into wider markets.

However, the region's cloth industry was never homogeneous, but rather formed a series of separate trades, each with specific urban networks and each affected very differently over time.[19] Cornwall and its towns had little or no part in the cloth industry, which may explain the small scale of its urban network in the early part of our period, by contrast with its neighbour Devon. In the sixteenth century Tiverton and Crediton (and Taunton, in the interconnected area of west Somerset) were the region's largest towns except for the county capitals. The area's cloth industry reached new heights in the late seventeenth century and Daniel Defoe in his *Tour* records his respect for the manufacturing towns of Devon and west Somerset, in sharp contrast to Cornwall's lack of cloth towns.[20] After 1700 this branch of the industry entered a protracted decline, which saw Tiverton, Crediton and Cullompton overtaken rapidly in size by other towns, including those from the rival 'West Country' cloth industry, straddling the county boundaries of north Somerset, west Wiltshire, southern Gloucestershire. Even earlier, in the seventeenth century, the towns in the south-eastern part of the region – Dorset and east Wiltshire – were losing their cloth manufactures to the same competition.

In the early eighteenth century Defoe picked out the 'West Country' region for comment, as one 'full of rivers and towns and infinitely populous, in so much, that some of the market towns are equal to cities in bigness, and superior to them in numbers of people'. He estimated that 'the country which I have now described as principally employed in, and maintained by, this prodigy of trade contains . . . 374,000 people' (a figure which he admits is 'all guesswork'). He lists twenty-eight towns (including some in north Dorset) as 'the principal clothing towns' while noting that they are 'interspersed with a great number of villages, I had almost said innumerable villages, hamlets and scattered houses in which, generally speaking, the spinning work of all this manufacture is performed by the poor people'.[21] As this remark suggests, measuring the urban population alone fails to capture the scale of this industry. By 1801 the industry was more concentrated than in Defoe's day, falling within a parallelogram from Shepton and Warminster in the south to Cirencester and Stroud in the north. Collectively the cloth towns of this region had a population (at least 47,000)

[19] P. J. Bowden, *The Wool Trade in Tudor and Stuart England* (London, 1962), pp. 45–50, 56–61; G. D. Ramsay, *The Wiltshire Woollen Industry in the Sixteenth and Seventeenth Centuries*, 2nd edn (London, 1965), pp. 2–5, 110–15; J. Youings, *Tuckers Hall, Exeter* (Exeter, 1968); W. G. Hoskins, *Industry, Trade and People in Exeter 1688–1800*, 2nd edn (Exeter, 1968); J. de L. Mann, *The Cloth Industry in the West of England from 1640 to 1880* (Oxford, 1971); K. G. Ponting, *The History of the West of England Cloth Industry* (London, 1957); K. G. Ponting, *The Woollen Industry of South-West England* (Bath, 1971); A. Randall, *Before the Luddites* (Cambridge, 1991).

[20] R. P. Chope, *Early Tours in Devon and Cornwall*, new edn (Newton Abbot, 1967), pp. 145–6, 160, 169–70.

[21] Defoe cited in Ponting, *Woollen Industry*, pp. 149–50.

approaching that of Bristol in 1801. Although in relative terms they were already falling behind the new cloth towns of the North, their absolute size was still significant. Given the growth of Bristol, Bath and Cheltenham, this area remained one of the most heavily urbanised parts of England, and thus of Europe, into the early nineteenth century.[22]

The decline of cloth manufacturing was not necessarily synonymous with the loss of urban industry. Many of the region's towns supported a range of other craft activities alongside cloth or developed a specialism to replace it.[23] Across the whole region the pastoral economy supported a variety of leather-based industries centred on towns, as well as food processing, while the grain-producing areas with good water supplies had brewing industries. As noted above, a range of other textile products – silk, lace, rope and netting, upholstery and carpeting – were developed, especially in the south-eastern parts of the region where cloth disappeared first. For example, an agricultural survey of Dorset in 1815, while noting that woollen manufacture was now 'almost confined' to Sturminster Newton (with four or five clothiers and 300 weavers) and Lyme Regis, went on to list industries such as stocking-knitting at Wareham, Corfe Castle and Wimborne, silk manufacture at Sherborne (where four silk mills employed 200 women and children) and Cerne Abbas (which also had a small dowlas factory and many shoemakers), shirt-button manufacture at Shaftesbury (employing 1,200 women and children) and Blandford, malting and brewing at Wareham and Dorchester, an iron foundry at Bridport (which still specialised successfully in rope and netting manufacture), pottery at Wareham, and so on.[24] The metal- and coal-bearing areas of the Severn estuary and Cornwall supported various forms of industrial activity, although the region lacked the spectacular growth of new industrial towns that so marked other regions after 1750. The nearest examples are Dock (whose dockyard was one of the largest industrial complexes in Europe in the early eighteenth century) and the Cornish tin, copper and china clay towns, of which St Austell and Redruth/Camborne stood out as newcomers to the urban hierarchy, although neither type fits the classic model of the 'factory town'.[25]

22 S. Jackson, 'Population change in the Somerset–Wiltshire border area, 1701–1800', *SHist.*, 7 (1985), 119–43; Rollison, *Local Origins*; A. M. Urdank, *Religion and Society in a Cotswold Vale* (Berkeley, Calif., 1990); *VCH*, Gloucestershire, XI.

23 The industries are conveniently surveyed in A. H. Shorter, W. L. D. Ravenhill and K. J. Gregory, *South-West England* (London, 1969); R. A. Buchanan and N. Cossons, *The Industrial Archaeology of the Bristol Region* (New York, 1969); F. Walker, *The Bristol Region* (London, 1972), chs. 8–10; Bettey, *Wessex*. A guide to agricultural patterns in most of the region is provided by G. V. Harrison, 'The South West', in J. Thirsk, ed., *Ag.HEW*, vol. v(1) (Cambridge, 1985), pp. 358–89.

24 W. Stevenson, *A General View of the Agriculture of the County of Dorset* (London, 1815), pp. 448–50.

25 Duffy *et al.*, eds., *New Maritime History*, I, pp. 192–208, 216–23, and II, pp. 167–9, 177–81; J. Rowe, *Cornwall in the Age of the Industrial Revolution* (Liverpool, 1953).

Another group of towns that rose into or within the urban hierarchy were fishing towns (Brixham, Mevagissey, Newlyn) and some ports emphasising the coastal trade – although other towns of this type gave up fishing and coasting in favour of a resort role. In the first half of our period a number of towns, such as Poole, Dartmouth and Falmouth on the south coast and Bideford and Barnstaple on the north, prospered on the basis of the Newfoundland trade or other colonial and Iberian trading activities, but by the mid-eighteenth century long-distance trading connections were increasingly eclipsed by coastal trading. This was true in the long run not only of middle-sized ports but also of first Exeter (as the cloth and wine trades crumbled) and then Bristol itself by the early nineteenth century.[26]

There was a complex relationship between a town's industrial or commercial function and its role as a market centre. Towns could 'export' their hinterland's specialised manufactures, for example Exeter's great serge market around 1700, or its agricultural surplus, such as the great corn markets of Warminster and Devizes. Or they might produce or 'import' the provisioning and other consumer requirements of a hinterland which was concentrating on the market production of one specialty and relying on the income to buy in other commodities, as the new market towns of Cornwall did. Attempts to enumerate and trace the fortunes of 'market towns' as if these were a single type run the risk of failing to distinguish between shifts in the overall number and distribution of market towns (fairly easy to measure) and changes in the nature of the marketing functions towns offer. This is particularly true in this period, which saw the rise of urban (and even village) retailing, not to mention itinerant peddling, and the growth of private commodity trading outside the public market system. Such changes, together with transport improvements, might render a minor market centre almost redundant, save perhaps for the butchers' and greengrocers' stalls still traditionally found in a 'market'. Contemporaries were unclear how far such places still qualified as market towns.[27]

Nevertheless, the 'market town' was the core of the urban network throughout most of our period, and significant even in 1840. Of the 235 towns in the region, only 21 never apparently had a market function at any time in the period

[26] See references cited in n. 10.

[27] A. Everitt, 'The marketing of agricultural produce', in J. Thirsk, ed., *Ag.HEW*, vol. IV (Cambridge, 1967), pp. 466–592 at 470–1 *et passim*; A. Dyer, 'Market towns of southern England 1500–1700', *SHist.*, 1 (1979), 123–34; J. Chartres, 'Marketing of agricultural produce in metropolitan western England in late seventeenth and eighteenth centuries', in M. Havinden, ed., *Husbandry and Marketing in the South West 1500–1800* (Exeter, 1973), pp. 63–74; J. Chartres, 'The marketing of agricultural produce', in J. Thirsk, ed., *Ag.HEW*, vol. V(2) (Cambridge, 1985), pp. 406–502 at 410–11 *et passim*; M. Spufford, *The Great Reclothing of Rural England* (London, 1984); H.-C. Mui and L. H. Mui, *Shops and Shopkeepers in Eighteenth-Century England* (London, 1988), pp. 38–41, 100–5, 295, 301.

1540–1840 (see Table 2.8).[28] There was a slight decline in the numbers of markets functioning, from 192 around 1673 down to 168 by 1800, but by 1840 numbers had only declined slightly further, to 161. It appears to have been the linked effects of railways and retailing in the mid-nineteenth century which led to a sharp decline thereafter. Within this figure are concealed many variations in which towns had markets. At the heart of the urban network were the 141 towns which always appear to have functioned as markets during this period, although at least 19 of them had very little but small provisioning markets left by the nineteenth century. During the period, 20 new market towns emerged, with 9 of these concentrated into the decades after 1800. During the same forty years 16 towns ceased to have markets, while 37 more had failed before 1800, making 53 in all. Moreover, larger and larger towns were apparently coping without markets. At all three dates, however, 90–2 per cent of the urban population lived in a market town and loss or absence of market status was associated with small and slow-growing towns. Of course, it does not follow that it was the marketing function which caused the population in market towns to grow faster. While some of the towns gaining markets were establishing themselves in the urban sector as marketing places, such as St Austell and Redruth in mid-seventeenth-century Cornwall, or Camborne in the same county in 1802, others required markets because they had grown, for example ports such as Falmouth (1656) or Brixham (1799) or new Devon resorts in the early nineteenth century. But for some very small towns, it was probably their marketing role which more and more distinguished them from the villages around, which might be becoming more populous. One such was Holsworthy, which was consistently the smallest market town in Devon with only 775 inhabitants in 1841.

As this last example reminds us, spatial distribution mattered: the nearest town to Holsworthy was the even smaller north Cornwall town of Stratton and the people of its hinterland had little choice but to use its marketing services. The rule of thumb, adopted by surveyors such as John Norden, that a market town was needed about every seven miles seems to have been generally accurate,[29] as there was a market town every forty-nine square miles or so in 1660, ranging from forty-two to forty-three in Gloucestershire and Cornwall to fifty-three to fifty-four in Wiltshire and Devon. By 1801 the average had increased slightly to about fifty-five, and there were almost three times as many people per market

[28] In addition to the works cited in the previous note and the primary sources they used, I have identified market towns from the following types of source: county maps; travellers' accounts and topographical writings; county histories; topographical dictionaries; trade directories; surveys of agricultural practice; secondary works such as *VCH* entries on markets. These suggest that no one source is fully reliable: the list of markets for 1792 widely cited from PP 1888 LIII is apparently full of errors and omissions. Hence my figures, especially for Devon and Cornwall, differ from those of Dyer (Chapter 13 in this volume), derived from Blome's *Britannia* of 1673.

[29] T. L. Stoate, ed., *Cornwall Manorial Rentals and Surveys* (Bristol, 1988), p. 47.

Table 2.8 *Market towns in the South-West of England c. 1600–1840*

County (no. of towns)	C (38)	De (63)	Do (26)	G (32)	S (42)	W (33)	All (235[a])
No market	2	7	3	0	3	6	21
1673 Dyer[b]	21	32	20	28	31	21	154
1673 Barry[c]	31	48	21	30	36	26	192
1800	29	41	19	25	32	21	168
1840	31	40	16	25	29	19	161
Constant full[d]	16	31	14	21	23	16	122
Constant marginal[e]	6	3	1	2	5	2	19
Constant all	22	34	15	23	28	18	141
New 1600–1800	6	2	0	2	0	1	11
New post-1800	3	4	1	0	1	0	9
New all	9	6	1	2	1	1	20
Failed pre-1800	4	11	3	7	6	6	37
Failed post-1800	1	5	4	0	4	2	16
Failed all	5	16	7	7	10	8	53
Total pre-1800	33	52	22	32	38	27	205
Total post-1800	32	45	20	25	33	21	177
Pop./mkt[f] 1660	3,226	4,792	4,078	4,000	5,139	4,615	4,792
Pop./mkt 1800	6,483	8,366	6,052	7,800	8,438	8,810	8,366
Pop./mkt 1840	11,100	13,325	10,938	12,960	14,414	13,579	13,503
Rural pop./mkt[g] 1660	2,640	3,385	2,948	3,058	4,016	3,409	3,385
Rural pop./mkt 1800	4,664	4,862	3,948	5,792	5,423	6,245	4,862
Rural pop./mkt 1840	7,894	7,060	7,000	8,760	8,930	9,390	8,046

Notes

C = Cornwall, De = Devon, Do = Dorset, G = Gloucestershire, S = Somerset, W = Wiltshire, All = whole region.

[a] Bristol is included here but not under any county.

[b] Based on Alan Dyer's chapter, see below, pp. 430–1, which uses Blome's *Britannia*.

[c] My own estimate, from a variety of sources, of markets operating in 1673.

[d] Towns constantly functioning as full market towns *c.* 1600–1840.

[e] Towns constantly referred to as market towns *c.* 1600–1840 but whose market was noted to be of marginal significance, usually towards the end of the period.

[f] Total population of that area at that date divided by number of markets then operating.

[g] Non-urban population of that area at that date divided by number of markets then operating.

Sources: see text.

town in 1841 as in 1660, while the rural population per market town had more than doubled, so non-market provision of retailing and trading activities must have been increasing very rapidly. As a few large markets, such as Taunton, grew more important, in other places occasional markets eclipsed the regular weekly market. In particular, a monthly or even less frequent market in cattle and other animals often came to represent the chief marketing role of a town, while many of the lesser centres gave up a regular market in favour of cattle or other fairs. This repeated a trend of the later medieval period when the plethora of medieval market creations was reduced to a much slimmer core, leaving many former markets with one or more fairs as signs of their former pretensions.

(iv) THE POLITICS OF URBAN STATUS

Urban regions are not purely economic in foundation or expression. If we turn to political matters, however, we find a similar pattern of diversity and decentralisation. By 1571 four towns (Bristol 1373, Gloucester 1483, Exeter 1537, Poole 1571) had 'county' status, officially placing them outside the increasingly important county structure of government: only three other southern towns shared this privilege. In Bristol's case this accurately reflected both its importance and its location on the boundaries of two counties which it could neither govern nor be governed by. Exeter, by contrast, remained the undisputed centre of Devon county government and society (and diocesan capital of Devon and Cornwall), a role which initially reflected its predominance over Plymouth as the major town and then, as Plymouth overhauled it in the late seventeenth century, increasingly became the cornerstone of its urban functions. Gloucester's autonomy was curtailed after the Restoration due to its prominence during the Civil War and its long-term economic fortunes were modest until it grew as a nineteenth-century port. Poole failed, despite early successes in the Newfoundland trade, to take off in a way that might justify its status, leaving Dorchester as county town.[30]

Bristol's county status brought it effective autonomy, which was never threatened by the surrounding gentry in the way that, for example, both Gloucester and Taunton were in the Restoration period.[31] But it did not make Bristol the political metropolis of the region. Other well-established regional (and diocesan) capitals, such as Salisbury, Exeter and Gloucester, exercised some metropol-

[30] W. T. MacCaffrey, *Exeter 1540–1640* (Cambridge, Mass., 1958); R. Newton, *Eighteenth-Century Exeter* (Exeter, 1984); R. Newton, *Victorian Exeter* (Leicester, 1968); *VCH*, Gloucestershire, IV; R. Tittler, 'The vitality of an Elizabethan port: the economy of Poole *c.* 1500–1600', *SHist.*, 7 (1985), 95–118; J. Hutchins, *The History and Antiquities of the County of Dorset*, 3rd edn, ed. W. Shipp and J. W. Hudson (Westminster, 1861–74; repr. Wakefield, 1973), vol. I, pp. 1–70.

[31] On Taunton see Clifton, *Last Popular Rebellion*; P. J. Norrey, 'Restoration regime in action', *HJ*, 32 (1988), 789–812.

itan functions in part of the region and acted as direct linkage points to the national metropolis. Partly because the region as a whole was so firmly linked into national life, there was never any attempt to set Bristol up as a regional capital for administration, as York was before 1640. Tudor concerns about unstable peripheries led only to a short-lived Council of the West based in Exeter and to the Council of the Marches (whose role in Gloucestershire was ambiguous and limited) based in Ludlow, even though Bristol was clearly the military key to the region, as seventeenth-century wars showed. The sieges of Plymouth, Exeter, Bristol and Gloucester, which helped decide the outcome of the Civil War, showed that many of the old walled towns were still substantial military assets.[32] But the growing military power of the state after 1689 was based on a scatter of ports, notably Plymouth, and directed outwards rather than towards controlling the region from the towns. Even so, after 1757, the garrisoning of the militias in substantial towns restored a military presence to inland urban life, which could have quite a social impact by the period of the Napoleonic wars, as well as bolstering the forces of law and order available to quell popular unrest during food shortages or industrial unrest.[33]

The region's government was organised not by towns but by counties and dioceses. The effect of this on urban fortunes was, by and large, further to decentralise the urban hierarchy. Three of the six counties lacked a clear county and diocesan capital. In Cornwall the old county centres of Launceston, Lostwithiel and Bodmin lost plausibility as they and their eastern inland hinterlands fell in wealth and population behind the western and coastal regions, leading eventually to Truro's emergence as the county town (unofficially at least) by the late eighteenth century. In Dorset the county town of Dorchester was surrounded by towns of similar size, while diocesan administration was delegated from Bristol to Blandford Forum. In Somerset there were two diocesan capitals – Bath and Wells – while the 'county town' of Ilchester lacked stature compared to boroughs such as Taunton and Bridgwater: eventually its puny size made it seem unsuitable even as a seat for the county gaol.[34] In these three counties the meetings of quarter sessions and assizes were rotated around the major towns in various parts of the county and no town was able to practise the 'piling of function upon function' Alan Dyer describes for the Midlands. Even in Devon,

[32] J. Youings, 'The Council of the West', *TRHS*, 5th series, 10 (1960), 41–59; P. Williams, *Council in the Marches* (Cardiff, 1958); C. Carlton, *Going to the Wars* (London, 1992), pp. 154–79; P. McGrath, *Bristol and the Civil War* (Bristol, 1981); M. Atkin and W. Laughlin, *Gloucester and the Civil War* (Stroud, 1995); M. Stoyle, *Loyalty and Locality* (Exeter, 1994); M. Stoyle, *From Deliverance to Destruction* (Exeter, 1996).

[33] M. Duffy, 'Devon and the naval strategy of the French wars 1689–1815', in Duffy *et al.*, eds., *New Maritime History*, I, pp. 182–91; J. R. Western, *The English Militia in the Eighteenth Century* (London, 1965); T. Hayter, *The Army and the Crowd in Eighteenth-Century England* (London, 1978); J. Bohstedt, *Riots and Community Politics in England and Wales 1790–1810* (Cambridge, Mass., 1983).

[34] *VCH*, Somerset, III, pp. 179–203.

Wiltshire and Gloucestershire the unquestioned county capital stood in one corner of the shire, leaving scope for other towns to emerge as predominant within their districts.

Nevertheless, if the largest urban centres were not necessarily administrative capitals, jurisdictional privileges were crucial to urban status during the early modern period, and indeed to the redefinitions of urban status under way during the 1830s as municipal and parliamentary boroughs were reshaped. Institutional complexity was a defining feature of town life. Such complexity is hard to quantify, not least because every town's institutions reflected its own individual history and needs, not a preordained national model, before 1832 at least. The most common notion is of the borough, but borough status could cover anything from full incorporation of a town council exempt from most forms of county jurisdiction, through lesser forms of legal jurisdiction, to what locals termed a 'borough' based only on old burghal tenures and customs which saw a 'borough' court or officials exercise powers that might elsewhere be held by a manorial court. The larger towns without a formal town government, such as Sherborne and Wimborne Minster in Dorset, usually found an informal substitute, namely the governors of the school and of the minster and its peculiar court respectively.[35] Many of our towns called themselves 'boroughs' in this loose sense, though only seventy-five of them ever received formal incorporation by charter or (in about nine cases) attained, by prescriptive right, a municipal status which was recognised (grudgingly) by the commissioners of the 1830s. Of the seventy-five incorporations, nine were very short-lived (mostly granted by Charles or James II and annulled in 1688) while three more lapsed, most notably that for Taunton in 1792, leaving sixty-three in 1832, though some of these were considered purely nominal by the commissioners.[36] It is somewhat arbitrary, therefore, to focus on the incorporated towns, but the autonomy and perpetuity that incorporation offered appealed strongly to urban requirements to tackle their own social problems and regulate their own economic affairs, including the provision of local legal settlement for business matters. Equally, it was their pretensions to such autonomy, especially in the smaller towns often run by ordinary tradesmen, that attracted outside criticism, whether it was from country JPs like Richard Carew in his *Survey of Cornwall* of 1603, or the visiting commissioners in 1835. Peregrine Bingham, the commissioner for Wiltshire, vented his disgust at towns such as Malmesbury, whose magistracy was 'composed chiefly of

[35] The standard study of boroughs remains S. Webb and B. Webb, *The Manor and the Borough* (London, 1908), but for the sixteenth century see the studies by R. Tittler, e.g. his *Architecture and Power* (Oxford, 1991), and for the later period D. Eastwood, *Government and Community in the English Provinces 1700–1870* (Basingstoke, 1997), pp. 57–90. I owe the examples of Sherborne and Wimborne to the research in progress of George Tatham and David Reeve respectively.

[36] M. Weinbaum, *British Borough Charters 1307–1660* (Cambridge, 1943); *HMC*, 12th Report, App. vol. VI, pp. 298–302 (charters granted 1680–8); PP 1835 XXIII–XXIV; J. Fletcher, 'Statistics of the municipal institutions of English towns', *Journal of Statistical Society*, 5 (1842), 97–167.

labourers without education and the least-instructed class of retail tradesmen', with a 'pig-keeper' as the current alderman. Their control, he claimed, 'was said to deter respectable persons from resorting to the town' and 'had a strong tendency to unsettle industrious habits and deprave the morals of the place'.[37] But many townspeople themselves became critical of existing urban government, both on grounds of efficiency and as they became enmeshed in party rivalries. Gradually municipal status became one of the problems, as well as one of the solutions, in urban life. Moreover, as Defoe pointed out, many of the growing towns lacked such institutions yet still seemed to thrive: this was true in particular of the clothing towns.[38]

However, incorporation was not merely a medieval legacy, increasingly ill-fitted to the new urban network. Almost all the incorporations were post-medieval, though often building on earlier charters. Of those still active in 1835 and not based on prescription, only four were pre-1500, twenty-five were sixteenth century and twenty seventeenth century, while Wareham was not incorporated until 1704. Many towns had several later charters: Weymouth's governing charter in 1835 was that of 1804. The largest towns in the urban hierarchy tended to be incorporated: the top eleven in 1660 and the top six in 1801, and thirty-five of the top sixty-three at each date. Generally it was the larger towns which had more extensive powers of jurisdiction: the exceptions were parliamentary boroughs in Devon and Cornwall.

About two-thirds of municipal boroughs were also parliamentary boroughs (and vice versa). In such boroughs electoral politics tended to spill over into municipal affairs (if only because the mayor or bailiff was usually the returning officer) often provoking intense faction fighting.[39] As a whole the region was well represented in both categories, with over a quarter of all incorporated towns and a third of the parliamentary boroughs. Cornwall gained notoriety, then as now, for its twenty-one small constituencies, several of which were hardly urban at all, save for their electoral status.[40] However, Wiltshire was also drastically overrepresented with sixteen boroughs, while Gloucestershire, with only three boroughs before 1832, was underrepresented even by national standards. A 1702 pamphleteer, comparing representation to county taxation, reckoned Cornwall, Wiltshire and Dorset as the third, fourth and fifth most overrepresented counties respectively.[41] When representation was altered, in 1832, the region lost more

[37] R. Carew, *Survey of Cornwall*, ed. F. E. Halliday (London, 1953), pp. 137, 157–9; PP 1835 XXIII, Appendix Part I, pp. 77–80.

[38] See his comments cited in Corfield, *Impact of English Taverns*, p. 90, and her discussion pp. 90–3.

[39] J. M. Triffitt, 'Politics and the urban community: parliamentary boroughs in the South-West of England 1710–30' (DPhil thesis, University of Oxford, 1985).

[40] For a typical critique see, 'Report of the Society of the Friends of the People on the state of parliamentary representation, 9 Feb. 1793', in A. Aspinall and E. A. Smith, eds., *English Historical Documents*, vol. XI (London, 1959), pp. 216–21.

[41] See Aspinall and Smith, eds., *English Historical Documents*, VIII, pp. 216–20, for this and earlier comments by William Petty *c.* 1685.

seats than any other, providing twenty-seven of the fifty-six seats that lost both members (including thirteen Cornish and seven Wiltshire) and thirteen of the thirty that lost one MP. Only four of the forty-two new constituencies created were in the region.[42]

Only in Cornwall and Wiltshire was the urban hierarchy mocked by the distribution of seats. The majority of boroughs had sent members to parliament before 1500 and most of these (except in Wiltshire) were large towns. Post-medieval enfranchisement was largely confined to Cornwall and Devon.[43] In 1660 the eleven largest towns were represented in parliament and in 1801 the six largest towns were represented and sixteen of the top twenty. Half of the top sixty-three towns were represented at both dates. The reforms of the 1830s, while ensuring that the top fourteen towns in 1840 all had seats, only slightly increased the share of the top sixty-three towns enfranchised. If we consider the share of the urban population living in parliamentary boroughs, this averaged 51 per cent in 1660, and the proportion actually increased by 1801 to 59.2 per cent, not far short of its post-reform level of 63.8 per cent in 1832.

Of course, living in a parliamentary borough was far from the same as having a vote. If most boroughs were in the pockets of outside patrons or had minimal electorates then there would be little chance of urban interests being represented. But the norm was not a Grampound. While a third of franchises were vested in corporations or a freeman body entirely created by such corporations, another third were based on a very wide tax or residence franchise (especially in Dorset, Somerset and Cornwall). The remaining two categories were a broad freeman electorate or a property qualification: while the latter was often open to landlord manipulation and venality, the former included some of the largest and most open of all English urban constituencies, such as Bristol, Exeter and Gloucester. The average borough had 236 electors in the early eighteenth century and 310 a century later. There were also a reasonable number of contested elections in which to exercise this right. The region's average for 1701–15 was only slightly below the national mean. The typical borough saw six or seven contests during the eighteenth century, with no great decline in numbers except in the Wiltshire seats after 1734.[44]

42 Devonport and Stroud district with two MPs each and Cheltenham and Frome with one. See J. H. Philbin, *Parliamentary Representation 1832 England and Wales* (New Haven, 1965).

43 G. Haslam, 'The duchy and parliamentary representation in Cornwall 1547–1640', *Journal of the Royal Institution of Cornwall*, 8(3) (1980), 224–42.

44 These figures are derived from: B. Willis, *Notitia Parliamentaria*, vols. I and II (London, 1716), and vol. III (London, 1750); S. T. Bindoff, ed., *House of Commons 1509–1558* (London, 1982), vol. I; P. Hasler, ed., *House of Commons 1558–1603* (London, 1981), vol. I; B. Henning, ed., *House of Commons 1660–1690* (London, 1983), vol. I; R. Sedgwick, ed., *House of Commons 1715–1754* (London, 1970), vol. I; L. Namier and J. Brooke, eds., *House of Commons 1754–1790* (London, 1964), vol. I; D. Hirst, *Representative of the People?* (Cambridge, 1975), pp. 213–26; J. Cannon, *Parliamentary Reform 1640–1832* (Cambridge, 1972), pp. 278–89; W. Speck, *Tory and Whig* (London, 1970), pp. 126–31; Philbin, *Parliamentary Representation.*

Whatever the reality, however, it was the myth of south-western decadence, given plausibility by aspects of the Cornish and Wiltshire position, that came to dominate debate by the nineteenth century. To reformers the region's boroughs came to symbolise the growing lack of connection between urban government and urban importance, as measured by population and trade or manufacturing prosperity, and this reform agenda underlay the national commissions of the 1830s whose reports have provided much of the urban data used here. They were far from neutral, reflecting a clear agenda of opposition to established urban practices and measuring towns by standards which were not necessarily shared by everyone in the 1830s, let alone in previous centuries.[45]

(v) URBAN RENAISSANCE?

In this respect the 1830s marked the culmination of a reassessment of urban identity over a century old. This reassessment was marked both by the attempt to apply a single national (indeed international) model of what a town should be, and a change in some of the key expectations of a town. Both the positive and negative dimensions of this process are particularly clear in our region. On the one hand Bath and Bristol, and later Cheltenham, epitomised the new 'urban renaissance', not only in architectural terms but also in their mixture of polite urban culture with vigorous commercial expansion. The successful cloth towns and ports shared the latter qualities, while some of the county towns and leisure resorts offered a new elegance. As Ralph Bigland noted of Cheltenham in the 1780s, its new buildings were 'so frequently and judiciously erected as to make this a very respectable specimen of a modern town and perhaps the improvement of old towns is amongst the most successful inventions of this age'.[46] On the other hand, many south-western towns appeared not to have 'improved' in either sense. Architectural symbols of this were the fire-plagued thatched towns of the region, streets without paving or lighting, or few public buildings.[47] These were often regarded as sure signs of deeper problems, such as a lack of thriving 'manufactories' or merchants and, increasingly, the statistical test of population

45 See G. Finlayson, 'The politics of municipal reform, 1835', *EHR*, 81 (1966), 673–92, and Chapter 16 below.

46 R. Bigland, *Historical, Monumental and Genealogical Collections relating to the County of Gloucester* (Bristol and Gloucester Archaeological Society Record Series, 2, 1989), vol. 1, p. 323; P. Borsay, *The English Urban Renaissance* (Oxford, 1989); M. Reed, 'The cultural role of small towns in England 1600–1800', in Clark, ed., *Small Towns*, pp. 121–47; C. Estabrook, *Urbane and Rustic England* (Manchester, 1998).

47 For changing urban topography see: M. Aston and R. Leech, *Historic Towns in Somerset* (Bristol, 1977); R. Leech, *Historic Towns in Gloucestershire* (Bristol, 1981); K. J. Penn, *Historic Towns in Dorset* (Dorchester, 1980); RCHM, *An Historical Inventory of the Historical Monuments of the County of Dorset* (London, 1952–75); *VCH*, Somerset, Gloucestershire and Wiltshire. For fire see E. L. Jones *et al.*, *A Gazetteer of English Fire Disasters 1500–1900* (Historical Geography Research Group series, 13, 1984).

size and trends. Traditional measures of urban identity such as walls, gates and crosses lost appeal, while the trappings of urban government were often now presented as symbols of old-fashioned ways, not marks of urbanity. Judged by new standards of urbanisation, much of the region's town life no longer seemed properly urban.

Doubtless, many of the criticisms and observations were correct, at one level, but there is a danger in assuming that they were universally held. By and large they are the observations of outsiders – in class or regional terms – looking in on the smaller towns, and it is hard to be sure how far the townspeople of the region (and the countryfolk coming to market) shared such views. For example, in the dispersed pastoral parts of the region where substantial villages were rare, even quite a small settlement could qualify to the locals as a town both in its marketing functions and because it stood out from the hamlets around it, while appearing insignificant to passing visitors or in the pages of a commercial or topographical directory. It may therefore be necessary to distinguish between the role of a region's towns within the national, even international, urban network, on the one hand, and the role of the towns as foci for the region's own internal networks, political, social and cultural as well as economic. In the former terms, many of the region's towns lost importance, relatively at least, but in the latter terms they surely intensified their role.

· 2(d) ·

Midlands

ALAN DYER

THE HISTORICAL Midlands is a concept which is difficult to pin down; to some extent it amounts to that area which is left when more distinctive provincial blocks are removed. For the purposes of this volume the Midlands is defined as the West Midland counties of Herefordshire and Shropshire, Worcestershire and Warwickshire, combined with the East Midland shires of Derby, Leicester and Rutland, Northampton, Nottingham and Lincoln. There do exist some natural features which help to define this region: uplands to the west and north and the Lincolnshire seacoast, but the southern border can only be defined in our period in terms of the weakening fringe of London's primary commercial region. This is shown by analysis of the bases of London-bound carriers in 1684 where there is a marked reduction at about a ninety mile radius from the capital, leaving Worcestershire, mid Warwickshire and mid Leicestershire outside, but Northamptonshire within, London's region.[1] It is no surprise to find that the major Midland towns all lie beyond this frontier.

Yet the urban networks of the Midlands do have a self-contained and consistent character which justifies thinking in these terms. While the Midland towns by their very location had vital external links, most of them looked primarily to London or to other towns within the region. And they had a great deal in common, for much of the region suffered from poor communications in the sixteenth and seventeenth centuries, and it was a truism of contemporary thought that distance from navigable water necessarily discouraged economic growth: thus in 1722 it was said of Leicestershire that 'being the most inland county in England, and consequently far from any sea or navigable rivers, you must not suppose it a county of any trade'.[2] This attitude received support from the eco-

[1] N. H., *The Compleat Tradesman* (London, 1684). A similar pattern can be seen in 1715 (J. Chartres, 'Road carrying in England in the seventeenth century: myth and reality', *Ec.HR*, 2nd series, 30 (1977), 89). [2] J. Macky, *A Journey through England* (London, 1722), vol. II, p.174.

nomic difficulties apparent over much of the Midlands in the sixteenth century. The West Midlands displayed few signs of unusual wealth in the later middle ages, but many of the wool-producing East Midland counties figure among the more prosperous parts of fourteenth-century England.

However, the subsidy of 1524/5 records a striking collapse in the Midland economy, with ten of our eleven shires in the bottom half of the ranking table; there was an inevitable deterioration in the size and importance of many of the towns involved.[3] By the later seventeenth century the hearth taxes reveal that the national position of the Midlands had been restored,[4] with six of the shires in the top half, and Warwickshire and Worcestershire among the nine most densely populated counties, indicating that the population of the Midlands had grown more strongly than that of England as a whole.[5] The first censuses of the nineteenth century confirm this recovery, with Warwickshire and Staffordshire the third and fourth most densely populated counties in England. However, some parts of the Midlands slumbered untouched by this dramatic change: western Shropshire, Herefordshire and Lincolnshire remained among the most thinly populated of the English counties. These changes in overall population levels were mirrored in the growth of Midland towns by comparison with the country as a whole: in 1650, no Midland town appears among the six centres with 10,000 or more, but by 1750, four of the nineteen towns which had attained this size lay in our region, and in 1801, eleven out of forty-five.[6] If we count only those towns with a population of 5,000 or more, then the Midlands had only about 7 per cent of the total provincial urban population in the early sixteenth century, but about 20 per cent in both the 1670s and 1801.[7]

(i) ROADS, RIVERS AND CANALS

Growth in Midland towns was closely allied to the improving communications of the turnpike roads and water routes, though we must always acknowledge that improvements in communications could follow, as well as cause, urban growth.

[3] R. S. Schofield, 'The geographical distribution of wealth in England 1334–1649', *Ec.HR*, 2nd series, 18 (1965), 483–510; A. Dyer, *Decline and Growth in English Towns 1400–1640*, 2nd edn (Cambridge, 1995), pp. 14, 33, 56–66. Rankings exclude the four most northerly English counties.

[4] A notable feature of national economic change in the period: C. Husbands, 'Regional change in a pre-industrial economy: wealth and population in England in the sixteenth and seventeenth centuries', *Journal of Historical Geography*, 13 (1987), 353–5.

[5] M. B. Rowlands, *The West Midlands from AD 1000* (London, 1987), p. 107.

[6] R. A. Dodgson and R. A. Butlin, *An Historical Geography of England and Wales*, 2nd edn (London, 1990), p. 405; H. C. Darby, ed., *A New Historical Geography of England* (London, 1973), p. 459; two extra towns have been added to cover the Potteries and the Black Country outside Dudley.

[7] National figures from E. A. Wrigley, 'Urban growth and agricultural change: England and the continent in the early modern period', in P. Borsay, ed., *The Eighteenth Century Town* (London, 1990), p. 45, with Midland figures supplied by the survey referenced at n. 15 below.

Most of the major routes between London and the northern and western provinces ran through the Midlands, creating an overland communication network of great importance, especially as the largest market for Midland products lay in London. Burton-on-Trent's largest brewery grew out of John and William Bass' carrying business, plying between Manchester and the capital.[8] When high wage costs drove industries from London, they naturally migrated along these arterial roads to the nearest point where cheap labour could be found, an origin of the Leicester hosiery manufacture and Northampton's footwear trade. However, good communications with London exposed the southern Midland towns to damaging competition from the capital when labour costs were not a crucial factor, as is illustrated by the Coventry goldsmiths, who lost what had been a domination of the Midland market to their London competitors by 1640.[9] Many smaller towns flourished on their role as staging posts along these roads, especially in the era of the stagecoach when towns such as Towcester, Daventry and Market Harborough revolved around the bustle and clamour of many scores of coaches sweeping into their inns every day; larger towns like Northampton, Stamford, Grantham or Lichfield were similarly involved.

In the sixteenth century the only major navigable rivers of the region were the Severn, which meandered from Bristol through Worcestershire and Shropshire to Shrewsbury, and the Trent which connected Nottingham to the North Sea at Hull. Neither route seems to have been vigorously exploited in the sixteenth century, but regional economies became orientated around these rivers by the later seventeenth century, stimulated by the importance of coal, by improved road links with the river ports and by the extension of navigability[10] to the Warwickshire Avon by the 1660s, the pushing of the head of the Trent navigation to Burton in 1712 (which rapidly transformed the town from poverty to industrial prosperity) and the opening up of the Derwent to Derby in 1719.[11] Important though water transport was, we should be wary of exaggerating its

[8] C. C. Owen, *'The Greatest Brewery in the World': A History of Bass, Ratcliff and Gretton* (Derbyshire Record Society, 19, 1992), pp. 1–5.

[9] A. H. Westwood, 'The development of the goldsmiths trade in the Midlands', *Transactions of the Lichfield and South Staffordshire Archaeological and Historical Society*, 5 (1963–4), 57. Elizabethan church plate shows the declining share of London makers as distance from the capital increases, with over 75 per cent London-made in Oxfordshire and Northamptonshire, 43 per cent in Leicestershire but about 25 per cent in Derbyshire and Staffordshire (S. A. Jeavons, 'Midland goldsmiths of the Elizabethan period', *Transactions of the Lichfield and South Staffordshire Archaeological and Historical Society*, 3 (1961–2), 8).

[10] Where rivers were already navigable, technical improvements could still increase the volume of traffic: the Trent was significantly improved under an act of 1772 (C. Smith, 'Image and reality: two Nottinghamshire market towns in late Georgian England', *Midland History*, 17 (1992), 63).

[11] B. Travers, 'Trading patterns in the East Midlands 1660–1800', *Midland History*, 15 (1990), 65–80; C. C. Owen, *The Development of Industry in Burton upon Trent* (Chichester, 1978). A number of minor routes were also opened, or reopened, including the Fossdyke, Welland, Witham and Nene.

significance: towns like Stratford-on-Avon or those along the Severn Valley[12] grew beyond mere market town size, but only to a limited degree, presumably because they lacked those other factors required for further development: the success of Burton-on-Trent shows how crucial were good links with nearby sources of raw materials and manufactures, and the conjunction of canal and road routes with the river.[13] Birmingham's most rapid expansion was achieved before either roads or water routes were improved very much.[14] We should see the building of the canal network as the natural extension of the improving river navigations, with the opening of the canals linking Trent, Mersey and Severn in the 1770s providing the towns of the industrial Midlands with an effective means of transporting heavy goods to and from the seaports. In conjunction with the improved turnpike roads, this creation of an interconnected water transport system allowed the Midlands to exploit its rich but untapped resources, primarily based on minerals such as coal and iron but also an abundance of cheap but willing labour. The result was an efflorescence of urban growth which transformed the medieval urban network and brought the central part of the region triumphantly emergent from the relative poverty which had hitherto accompanied its strangled development.

(ii) URBAN GROWTH

Levels of urbanisation in the Midlands were probably low in the late medieval period. By the 1670s we have the means to measure urban against total population levels in our eleven counties: the resultant mean level of urbanisation of 19.5 per cent probably compares favourably with much of lowland England.[15] Six counties show levels close to the mean, while Derby and Hereford lag behind at 12.4 and 14.5 per cent respectively, and Worcester at 26.7 per cent and Warwickshire at about 30 per cent are well ahead of it. By 1811 the general level of urbanisation had of course risen strikingly – to 42.3 per cent, and in 1841 to 46.1 per cent[16] – and the contrast between the most and least urbanised counties had increased, with Northampton and Hereford most inadequately urbanised at 20.7 per cent and 22.3 per cent (27.6 and 28.9 per cent in 1841) while the highly urbanised shires of Warwick and Stafford exceeded the 60 per cent level by 1841.

12 M. Wanklyn, 'Urban revival in early modern England: Bridgnorth and the river trade 1660–1800', *Midland History*, 18 (1993), 37–64. Unlike the Trent, the Severn could not provide ready access to the London market.

13 Owen, *Greatest Brewery*, pp. 3–17.

14 M. B. Rowlands, *Masters and Men* (Manchester, 1975), pp. 99–104.

15 Based on defining as urban in the sixteenth and seventeenth centuries all places with markets but adding some industrial settlements in 1811; urban populations based on P. Clark and J. Hosking, *Population Estimates of English Small Towns 1550–1851: Revised Edition* (Leicester, 1993), with data from standard printed sources for the major towns excluded from this study: total county populations from A. Whiteman, *The Compton Census of 1676* (London, 1986), pp. cx–cxi.

16 The 1841 percentage is probably too low, since by this date it has become difficult to distinguish between industrial towns and their satellites in the country.

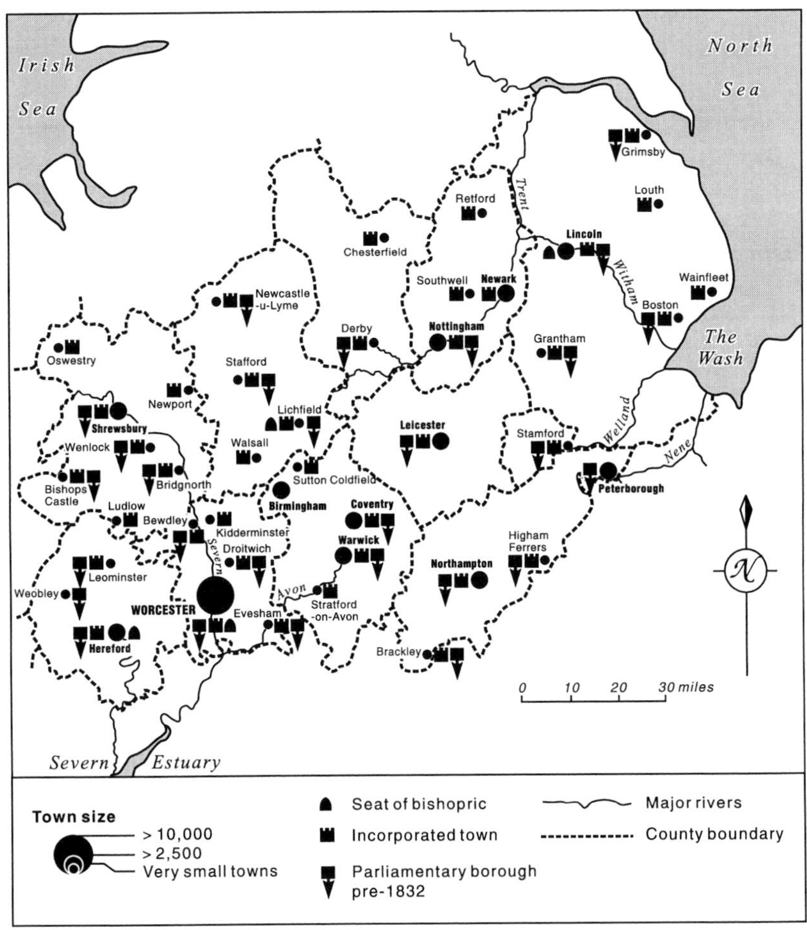

Map 2.7 Towns in the Midlands *c.* 1670

Clearly one of the effects of the economic developments of the eighteenth century had been the polarisation of the Midland urban network into areas of either dynamism or stagnation. How the situation in the 1670s compared with levels of urbanisation in the mid-sixteenth century is hard to say, since we as yet lack total population estimates for the Midland counties at the earlier date; urban populations show an increase of 55 per cent between 1563 and the 1670s which seems less than the general rural increase;[17] consequently, the level of urbanisation would have been rather below that of the 1670s. But the fact that urban populations grew faster than rural ones in the seventeenth century was not

[17] E. A. Wrigley and R. S. Schofield, *The Population History of England 1541–1871* (London, 1981), pp. 531–2, indicates an increase of over 60 per cent in a predominantly rural English sample.

necessarily positive and connected with urban economic expansion, for it was often the case that surplus people were squeezed from the land to swell the ranks of the urban poor, perhaps allowing per capita incomes in the villages to grow at the expense of those in the towns.[18] The counties of Derby and Lincoln appear to have had the thinnest urban populations and Warwick and Worcester the densest, with over double the level shown in the east. If we turn from economic growth to political development, then a picture of similar diversity presents itself.

The linked processes which involved the granting of the status of incorporation to town governments and of the right to return representatives to parliament were not particularly evident in the Midlands, unlike the South-West. Some thirty-nine towns acquired charters of incorporation and thirty-two became parliamentary boroughs, twenty before 1540 and a further twelve by 1673.[19] Their distribution varied strikingly: Leicester and Derby were the only examples of parliamentary boroughs in their counties, while Shropshire and Lincolnshire had five each; and Leicestershire, Derbyshire and Northamptonshire had only one or two incorporated towns, while Shropshire and Lincolnshire had seven and Staffordshire and Worcestershire, five. There were very few real 'rotten boroughs' in the area, though Weobley (Herefords.) and Bishops Castle (Salop.) come very close. On the whole, the larger towns of the later seventeenth century possessed the political privileges one would expect of them, since nearly all were prominent by the later middle ages; Birmingham is the conspicuous example of a large town without either incorporation or representation in parliament, and it is notable that it had acquired a good case by its general importance before the point in the seventeenth century when these rights became unobtainable; lack of a powerful local lobby which saw any advantage in them, and anxieties on the part of outside interests about the town's disorder and radicalism must account for this.[20]

Urban growth involved the development of new towns. If we define as a town everywhere with a market in 1563 and the 1670s, and add some nucleated industrial settlements to the market towns of 1811, then the total of urban places increases from 120 to 147 to 154.[21] Only Herefordshire experiences no gain or

[18] J. Goodacre, *The Transformation of a Peasant Economy* (Aldershot, 1994), pp. 58–60, 66–7, 76–7, 224.

[19] The following list (in alphabetical order of counties) covers all incorporations, with those which were also parliamentary boroughs in italic. Chesterfield, *Derby*, *Hereford*, *Leominster*, *Leicester*, *Boston*, *Lincoln*, *Grantham*, *Grimsby*, Louth, *Stamford*, Wainfleet, *Higham Ferrers*, *Northampton*, *Newark*, *Nottingham*, *Retford*, Southwell, *Shrewsbury*, *Bishops Castle*, *Bridgnorth*, *Ludlow*, Newport, Oswestry, *Wenlock*, *Lichfield*, *Newcastle-under-Lyme*, *Stafford*, *Tamworth*, Walsall, *Coventry*, Stratford-on-Avon, Sutton Coldfield, *Warwick*, *Bewdley*, *Droitwich*, *Evesham*, Kidderminster, *Worcester*. Weobley, Brackley and Peterborough returned members to parliament but were not incorporated.

[20] *VCH*, Warwickshire, VII, pp. 273–4, 327–8.

[21] There seems little point to the counting of towns between 1811 and 1840, since it becomes increasingly difficult to apply valid definitions of urban status in industrial areas. Probably the growth of new towns was roughly balanced by the dwindling number of small market towns.

loss in towns, testimony to its backward urban system. Derbyshire experienced the greatest growth, with seven towns in 1563 and seventeen by 1811; the county displays the forces which were creating new towns, for the penetration of commercial farming into the more marginal areas of Britain brought new markets to three locations in the upland north of the county in the seventeenth century. Similarly, the process of industrial expansion, which in Staffordshire and Shropshire gave rise to conglomerations of industrialised villages, in Derbyshire tended to be seated in isolated rural settlements with urbanising characteristics; by this date the absence of a market is not a crucial factor. Ilkeston and Belper look clearly urban by the early nineteenth century, but Bolsover, Dronfield and Duffield are more difficult to categorise as small towns. Other counties in a similarly marginal position also gained new market towns, with both Shropshire and Staffordshire acquiring five each.

More new towns were created by communication developments (Stourport in Worcestershire was the creation of the junction between the new canal and the River Severn) and especially by industry: the south Staffordshire iron and coal industries created several new towns, though distinguishing when they had clearly achieved an urban nucleus from the shapeless mess of industrialised countryside which characterised the Black Country is less easy to say. The north Staffordshire pottery district formed new towns which acquired clear urban status with remarkable speed, though it is again difficult to be sure whether one has a single polynuclear town or several towns in close proximity. In Shropshire the development of the coalfield in the Ironbridge area created at least two new towns and strengthened others, but definition is a problem here too.[22] While all the industrial newcomers proved to be permanent arrivals on the urban scene, a number of the new seventeenth-century markets had lost their status by the early nineteenth century. But more new markets survived than failed, for of about thirty-eight new non-industrial markets, mostly created in the seventeenth century, only about eighteen had failed by 1835, though some never achieved an unequivocal urban status. The chief new town created by none of these means was Leamington, the Midlands' only markedly successful spa:[23] in thirty years it had grown from a small village to an impressive 13,000 inhabitants in 1841, with all the trappings to be expected of a fashionable health and residential resort; the very close proximity of a traditional leisure town in Warwick must have helped the process.

The urban structure of the Midlands was influenced by the multiplication of these new centres. In 1563 only 29 per cent of the urban population was housed in the eleven big towns, modestly defined as having populations of over 2,000;

[22] B. Trinder, 'The Shropshire coalfield'.

[23] Buxton, though long recognised, and Matlock and Malvern were still very small in the early nineteenth century.

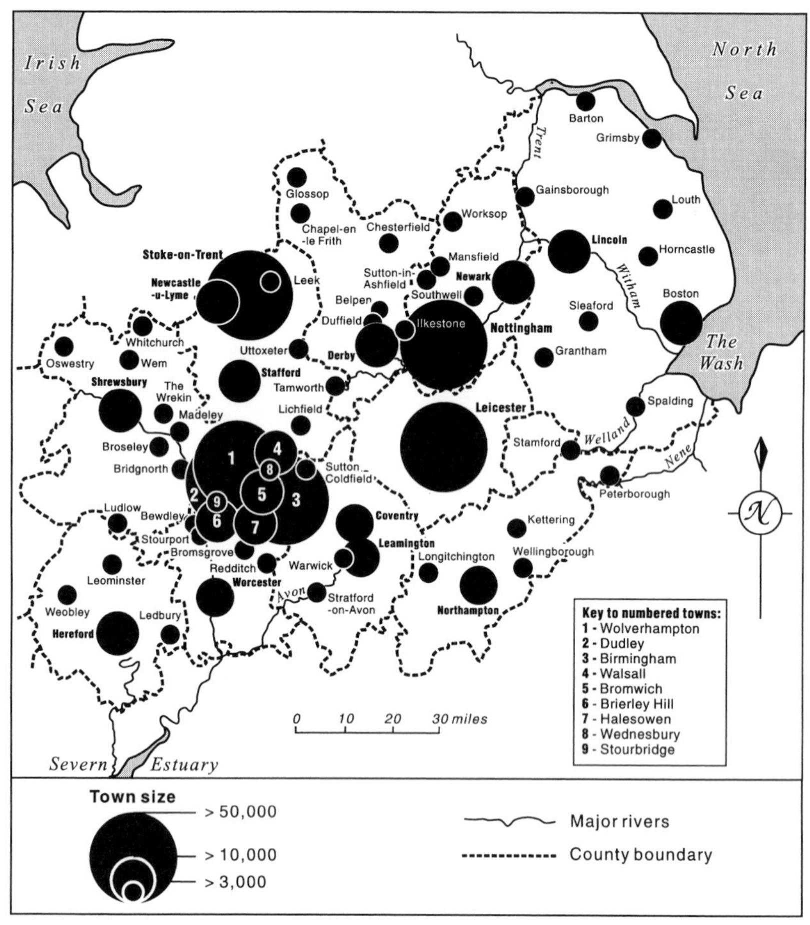

Map 2.8 Towns in the Midlands 1841

in the 1670s this remained stable with 26 per cent in nine towns of 3,500 and more;[24] the majority of the urban population before 1700 lived in large numbers of small towns. An intermediate category of middling size shows much consistency – 27 per cent in 1563, 22 per cent in the 1670s, 23 per cent in 1811 and 15 per cent in 1841.[25] This leaves us with the bulk of the urban population inhabiting genuinely small settlements before the eighteenth century – 1,000 and under in 1563, and 1,700 and less in the 1670s: here lived 44.2 per cent in 1563, 52 per cent in 1670 and even 27 per cent in 1811 and 24 per cent in 1841. The only really striking development in this structure is the emergence of exactly 50

[24] The boundaries of the categories are designed to rise in proportion to the expansion of national population over these years.

[25] This category is defined as 1,100–2,000; 1,800–3,400; 3,500–6,900 and 5,300–10,500 for these four dates.

per cent inhabiting nineteen large towns in 1811 (increasing to 61 per cent in 1841) – a doubling of the 1670s level and mostly taken from the proportion of the smallest towns. Thus for most of the period under review the urban network consists of a mass of smaller towns which are relatively similar, gathered around a limited number of relatively equally sized major towns.

(iii) COUNTY TOWNS

In the sixteenth century the most basic feature of the Midland network is the absence of a dominant provincial capital; instead, a polycentric pattern, incompletely developed, must be the concept which allows us to analyse the Midland network. The county is not an ideal framework for the analysis of urban networks, but in the Midlands it works well enough. Throughout the period we can understand the network as centred upon a series of county communities in which a major town, usually the centre of its administration, dominates the lesser towns of the shire: this pattern works well in the counties of Hereford, Shropshire, Warwick, Northampton and Leicester, joined by Nottingham in the later seventeenth century, and a little later, by Derby. This network of dominant county centres involves administrative capitals in most cases, probably because those factors which had originally made these towns the natural political centres of their shires – such as geographical location and good communications – also endowed them with a matching commercial and industrial pre-eminence. In Warwickshire, primacy was divided between the administrative and social centre in backward Warwick and its chief industrial and commercial city in Coventry, but the two were sufficiently close for us to regard the pair as together representing an eccentric binary county town.

The system is in clear existence in the mid-sixteenth century and becomes more firmly established as the centuries under review pass by. At all three points at which we have measured the population of Midland towns the average leading town absorbs about 30 per cent of the urban population of its county, which indicates the basic stability of this aspect of the urban network over time. However, two Midland counties refuse to obey these rules. Staffordshire, poor and economically marginal before the eighteenth century, contained no dominant town; its secular administration was centred in Stafford, a town which failed to establish any economic primacy,[26] while the shire's ecclesiastical and social centre lay in Lichfield, too weak to dominate yet strong enough to deny primacy to any rival town. Lincolnshire, very large, thinly populated and forced to be outward-looking by its geography, possessed no dominant shire centre either.

The emergence of these major county centres as the backbone of the Midland

[26] K. R. Adey, 'Seventeenth century Stafford: a county town in decline', *Midland History*, 2 (1974), 152–66.

urban network is an aspect worthy of elaboration.[27] The secret of their success lay in the piling of function upon function. All would have acted as suppliers of wholesale goods to their dependent market towns, though this is not easy to document: however, we have references to substantial distributive traders in the county towns with branch businesses in market towns, such as a Derby draper with a shop in Ashbourne and a Coventry ironmonger with a branch at Southam;[28] a Leicester haberdasher had branches in Lutterworth and Melton Mowbray, and an ironmonger from Leicester is recorded with subordinate businesses in Loughborough and Hinckley.[29] Up until about 1690 Nottingham supplied a site for London merchants to distribute goods through its fair, but after that date Nottingham wholesalers began to fetch goods from London themselves and to supply their region directly:[30] as Stourbridge Fair, which supplied wholesale goods to much of the Midlands, declined this process was probably replicated in other county centres. Administration was not of itself of great economic significance, but it was increasingly concentrated on the county town: in the sixteenth century we note that assizes were often shared between several towns in many of the Midland shires, but were monopolised by the county town in the seventeenth,[31] a process which led to the construction of impressive gaols and shire halls in the eighteenth century; aided by the buildings of institutions such as county infirmaries, this process made the concept of a capital town much more of a physical reality.

Such developments made these towns the natural focus for the county gentry as visitors and residents, aided by the inhospitable nature of some of the Midland countryside in winter, and around this nucleus there grew an impressive structure of social and cultural activity.[32] This can be illustrated from the history of provincial newspapers, with the major Midland county centres prominent in possessing early and long-running titles, such as the *Worcester Post-Man* (1709–) and the *Nottingham Weekly Courant* (1710–) and the others following on quite rapidly.[33] Although there are examples of small towns which could ape some of this culture sophistication, the majority of the lesser urban centres in the shires could not compete in this arena, and this elevated the county centres by providing functions which differed from their small satellites in kind as well as degree.[34]

[27] A. M. Everitt, 'Country, county and town: patterns of regional evolution in England', *TRHS,* 5th series, 29 (1979), 79–108.

[28] Lichfield Joint RO, diocesan probate records, Thomas Crychlowe 1601; Sara Bazeley 1676.

[29] *VCH,* Leicestershire, IV, pp. 81, 97.

[30] C. Deering, *Nottinghamia Vetus et Nova* (Nottingham, 1751), p. 92.

[31] J. S. Cockburn, *A History of English Assizes 1558–1714* (Cambridge, 1972), pp. 35–6.

[32] P. Borsay, *The English Urban Renaissance* (Oxford, 1989).

[33] R. M. Wiles, *Freshest Advices: Early Provincial Newspapers in England* (Columbus, Ohio, 1965).

[34] Some small towns undoubtedly performed well in this aspect (M. Reed, 'The cultural role of small towns in England 1600–1800', in P. Clark, ed., *Small Towns in Early Modern Europe* (Cambridge, 1995), pp. 121–47), but they tend to be concentrated in southern England, where road conditions and climate perhaps allowed more gentry mobility in the winter months.

The growth of large-scale industry did much to contribute to the eighteenth-century growth of these towns – textiles of one kind or another in most, whether hosiery, ribbons or lace, cotton, silk, woollen or linen; malting and brewing in Derby and Nottingham, porcelain in Derby and Worcester (see Plate 12). Often the larger towns grew at the expense of the smaller, as industry became specialised in larger units. The attraction for industry in these larger centres must lie in good contacts with distant markets, finance, labour supply and the availability of a wide range of ancillary services. Part of their industrial strength lay in providing central services for the industrialising villages and small towns in their hinterland; Nottingham and Leicester presided over the hosiery trade in their localities for instance.[35] The new turnpike roads tended to re-enforce the superior communication links of these towns – a fact especially true of the West Midlands.[36]

By the early nineteenth century the polycentric pattern can be seen perpetuated in many counties, especially in the East Midland trio of Derbyshire, Nottinghamshire and Leicestershire, all strengthened by recent industrial growth. Indeed, one of these towns might well have emerged as the dominant centre of an East Midland network spreading far beyond the confines of a single county; but each had its own peculiar strengths and was sufficiently far from its potential competitors to prevent any one of them from becoming dominant, despite the strong rivalry which developed between them.[37] The dramatic innovation in the urban network is of course the growth of industrial towns in the West Midlands. Staffordshire's lack of a central town was intensified by these developments, for the growth of the Potteries[38] in the far north and the Black Country in the extreme south provided no unifying centre. The rise of Birmingham was the single most dramatic change in the regional urban network in our period. In the 1560s it had been one of scores of middling market towns; by the 1670s it had advanced in size to equality with the six or so leading county centres and had achieved parity with them in function by the mid-eighteenth century;[39] and by 1811 its huge population of 86,000 was more than double the size of its nearest rival in Nottingham, and the 183,000 of 1841 was even further ahead.[40] When coupled with its subordinate neighbours in the Black Country, the total population of what might be almost termed a modern

[35] C. W. Chalklin, *The Provincial Towns of Georgian England* (London, 1974), pp. 40–2.

[36] E. Pawson, *Transport and Economy* (London 1977), fig. 29.

[37] J. V. Beckett, *The East Midlands from AD 1000* (London, 1988), p. 5.

[38] *VCH*, Staffordshire, VIII, pp. 80ff. The total population of the Potteries district must have been at least 25,000 by 1811, settled around several urban nuclei.

[39] It was in the seventeenth century that Birmingham's distribution system in the southern half of England and its export position were established, crucial to such a specialised manufacturing base: M. Rowlands, 'Society and industry in the West Midlands at the end of the seventeenth century,' *Midland History*, 4 (1977–8), 52–8; Rowlands, *Masters and Men*. No other Midland town had such close commercial links with other regions.

[40] E. Hopkins, *Birmingham* (London, 1989).

conurbation accounted for more than half the urban population of the whole Midland area.

Can we see in Birmingham the eventual emergence of a Midland provincial capital to replace our earlier polycentric urban structure? There may be an element of truth in this, especially in the West Midlands, but Birmingham's primacy was too narrow and too recent to subjugate its rivals.[41] In the pre-industrial period population size is probably a good indicator of the general significance of a town, but by 1800 the mere accumulation of concentrations of industrial labour is less reliable as an indicator of the existence of a wide spectrum of urban functions. Birmingham had many strengths: its location; financial and banking functions;[42] and a central position in the communication network, with a web of carrier services which was much larger than that of any other Midland town.[43] All these factors might encourage us to expect that Birmingham would be dominating the region by the late eighteenth or early nineteenth century.[44] Yet the old polycentric system had encouraged the growth of many rival centres which provided sophisticated services hallowed by centuries of usage. Worcester had most to fear from Birmingham, but the textile specialities of Coventry and the East Midland centres were quite different from the metalworking activities upon which Birmingham's rise was founded; they were also too distant. Even in the neighbouring Black Country, Wolverhampton and Stourbridge proved resistant to domination by their larger rival.[45] Although Birmingham rapidly developed a cultural and intellectual life of considerable dimensions, illustrated by the philosophers and scientists of its Lunar Society, its profusion of printers and booksellers and its musical ambitions, as well as its new public buildings (see Plate 24), the traditional Midland county towns retained – at least until the nineteenth century – the loyalty of the gentry and too lively a social and cultural life to be overshadowed by their parvenu industrial rival.

[41] J. Money, *Experience and Identity* (Manchester, 1977), pp. 1–2, 9, 24, 80–2.

[42] Rowlands, *West Midlands 1000*, pp. 216–17.

[43] *Pigot and Co.'s National Commercial Directory* (London, 1835) reveals a carrier network which extends to an approximate eighty mile radius with Bristol, Cambridge, Hull and Cheshire at its periphery, and the canal system as an unspecified adjunct: this was an unrivalled Midland distributive organisation for its date, with 1,188 departures per week to 210 specified destinations compared to 549 from Leicester and 327 from Nottingham, over smaller areas and without the same canal connections as Birmingham. See also M. J. Wise, 'Birmingham and its trade relations in the early eighteenth century', *University of Birmingham Historical Journal*, 2 (1949–50), 53–79.

[44] Birmingham was slow in forming a resident elite, and its public buildings and amenities did not catch up with its expanded size until the early decades of the nineteenth century (Hopkins, *Birmingham*, pp. 135, 141).

[45] P. Large, 'Urban growth and agriculture change in the West Midlands during the seventeenth and eighteenth centuries', in P. Clark, ed., *The Transformation of English Provincial Towns 1600–1800* (London, 1984), pp. 169–89).

(iv) MIDLAND TOWNS FROM WEST TO EAST

We may appreciate the intricacies of the character and history of the Midland urban network by surveying it in detail, beginning at the Welsh border where we are immediately faced with a distinctive sub-region within the larger one. The towns on the English side of the border lay in a commercial backwater, made clear by the striking shortage of carrier and coach services, even early in the nineteenth century, by comparison with the rest of the Midlands. Wales was poor and sparsely populated, yet the Welsh lacked towns, and were forced to cross the border to gain access to urban facilities of all sorts, so that a string of border towns from Chester in the north to Gloucester in the south prospered from these exchanges. But this prosperity could be fickle: during the disordered fifteenth century the points of exchange moved eastward to the security of the walled towns of Shrewsbury and Hereford; renewed peace in the later fifteenth century brought the border markets westward to smaller towns such as Leominster and Presteigne,[46] causing severe problems for their eastward rivals.

This damaged Shrewsbury, but its domination of its region was never challenged, and it enjoyed a quite remarkable commercial expansion in the Elizabethan period.[47] Two factors underpinned Shrewsbury's dominance: the first was its position as the effective terminus of the Severn navigation, thus allowing it to monopolise the wholesale trade of a wide area otherwise deprived of good communications. The second was its position as the marketing and finishing centre for woollen cloth woven in Wales, which gave the town an industrial function and, since the cloth was mostly exported through London, good overland links with the capital which allowed imported goods to be brought back. During the Civil War, it was the fracture of the London link, not the Bristol river connection, which deprived Shrewsbury of its imported luxuries.[48] The cloth industry was lost in the eighteenth century, but Shrewsbury's prominence as a regional, leisure and social centre amply compensated;[49] a modernised industrial renaissance between 1790 and 1820 then withered on the vine, and the town failed to make much further progress.[50] However, Shrewsbury's strength within the Shropshire urban network is an excellent example of the heyday of the county town within the Midlands. Otherwise Shropshire was, as one would expect, rather under-urbanised, and the chief interest of the

[46] W. H. Howse, *Presteigne Past and Present* (Hereford, 1945), pp. 29, 32.

[47] W. A. Champion, 'The frankpledge population of Shrewsbury 1500–1720', *Local Population Studies,* 41 (1988), 51–60; W. Champion, 'The economy of Shrewsbury, 1400–1660' (unpublished typescript, Shrewsbury Local Studies Library, 1987).

[48] H. Owen and J. D. Blakeway, *A History of Shrewsbury* (London, 1825), vol. 1, p. 437.

[49] A. McInnes, 'The emergence of a leisure town: Shrewsbury 1660–1760', *P&P*, 120 (1988), 53–87.

[50] B. Trinder, 'The textile industry in Shrewsbury in the late eighteenth century: the traditional town', in P. Clark and P. Corfield, eds., *Industry and Urbanisation in Eighteenth Century England* (Leicester, 1994), pp. 80–93.

eighteenth century is the emergence of industrial new towns in the Shropshire coalfield, looking perhaps eastwards to the Black Country rather than to the county town; as with Shrewsbury this development eventually faltered, though later on in the nineteenth century.

Hereford is an interesting parallel case to that of Shrewsbury, because Hereford declined noticeably in the sixteenth century and fails ever to achieve, in terms of size, the level of local domination reached by the other county towns. The basic fertility of the surrounding countryside, the city's eighteenth-century gloving industry, the precocious development of turnpiked roads[51] and the opening up of the Wye navigation after 1695 all seem to make little impact on Hereford's backwardness; in 1756 local roads were said to be bad despite the turnpikes,[52] so poor communications remained a crucially debilitating factor. In 1671 it was said that the only parts of England where glass windows were still unavailable to the poor were Herefordshire and Shropshire.[53] The whole area experienced eighteenth-century industrial difficulties, probably because it could not compete with more efficient towns to the east, though Hereford remained unchallenged as an administrative and shopping centre.[54] The competition of Worcester as a commercial rival and Ludlow as a gentry centre may have been relevant, but all of Herefordshire was a natural backwater and the county's towns could only echo this fact.

Worcestershire represents a classic case of a county dominated throughout our period by its county town. Worcester was the unchallenged centre of shire and church administration, the county's chief channel to the outside world by road and river and the most important industrial centre, for its cloth industry produced not only wealth and employment but, like Shrewsbury, a direct connection with the capital through cloth marketing, so that the city was the chief source of most goods and services which could not be supplied by a local market town. The decline of the cloth industry was partially compensated by the rise of gloving and the usual profitable activities of an eighteenth-century county town, not least its role as a social and cultural centre for a region extending well beyond the county boundaries. It could be termed 'the most polished city in this part of the Empire' (1814) and if 'anyone wished to see a crocodile swimming, a bear baited, a cock fighting, an exhibition of ballooning or a solar microscope', to say nothing of the Three Choirs Festival, then they came to Worcester.[55] However,

[51] Pawson, *Transport and Economy*, p. 139.

[52] *The Travels through England of Dr Richard Pococke*, ed. J. J. Cartwright (Camden Society, 2nd series, 42, 1888), p. 228.

[53] John Aubrey, quoted in C. Platt, *The Great Rebuildings of Tudor and Stuart England* (London, 1994), p. 149.

[54] J. West and M. West, *A History of Herefordshire* (London, 1985), pp. 58–62.

[55] D. Whitehead, *Urban Renewal and Suburban Growth* (Worcestershire Historical Society, Occasional Publications, 5, 1989), p. 6. The wide region dominated by the city can be illustrated from newspaper advertisements (*ibid.*) and from the work of its monumental sculptors (R. Gunnis, *Dictionary of British Sculptors 1660–1851* (London, 1982), pp. 372–3, 430–1).

the failure of the city to grow very strikingly in the eighteenth century[56] suggests that Worcester had, like Shrewsbury, reached the limit of its natural development as a county centre, especially significant in view of the rise of the industrial towns to its north.

Warwickshire was dominated commercially and industrially by Coventry until the rise of eighteenth-century Birmingham; Coventry's role as a social and cultural centre was limited by Warwick,[57] and while it might in time have absorbed some of Warwick's functions if the county town had maintained its Tudor torpidity, the stimulation administered by the fashionable rebuilding after the fire of 1694 enabled Warwick to preserve its independent role.[58] Coventry had in the fifteenth century a status which approached that of a Midland provincial capital, a distributive centre 'used then (as London is now) for the Northerne and Westerne parts'.[59] Coventry cloth was marketed in London, giving its merchants the opportunity to act as wholesalers of returning imported goods; as late as 1586 a Coventry mercer was apparently supplying mercery to shopkeepers in the smaller towns within Coventry's region, stretching as far as Worcester and into Staffordshire and Derbyshire.[60] It must have been the largest city in the region between the fourteenth and sixteenth centuries and its merchants traded through a range of provincial ports. The specialised nature of Coventry's capping and thread industries demanded an extensive distributive network (like that of Birmingham's metal trades later on), and we find a Coventry capper in 1557 leaving debts due to him from Kendal, Lancashire, Yorkshire and the East Midlands as far as Stamford.[61] The growing power of London and, above all, the industrial collapse of Coventry by the early sixteenth century undermined any pretensions that Coventry had as a Midland capital, though it remained a major urban centre throughout our period, with important textile trades. Its role as a wholesale and distributive centre was to some extent retained – Evelyn was impressed by its buildings, and especially 'the streetes full of greate Shops'[62] – due perhaps to its location just far enough away from London along a major road and as the pivot of the regional road system.[63]

In the early part of our period Staffordshire and Derbyshire lacked a dominant town. By the later seventeenth century Derby was emerging quite strikingly

[56] C. A. F. Meekings, S. Porter and I. Roy, eds., *The Hearth Collectors' Book for Worcester 1678–1680* (Worcestershire Historical Society, new series, 11, 1983), pp. 36–9.

[57] *VCH,* Warwickshire, VIII, pp. 220–5. [58] *Ibid.*, pp. 511–13.

[59] R. M. Berger, *The Most Necessary Luxuries* (Philadelphia, 1993), p. 74, quoting a Coventry corporation petition of the mid-1630s.

[60] Lichfield Joint RO, diocesan probate records, John Tailor 1586.

[61] *Ibid.*, Henry Tatenell 1557.

[62] *The Diary of John Evelyn*, ed. E. S. De Beer (Oxford, 1955), vol. III, p. 121.

[63] The road maps in Ogilby's *Britannia* of 1675 suggest that Coventry had nine routes leading from it (Worcester and Shrewsbury came second with five) and a monopoly of major routes connecting the east and the west of the region.

to fill the role of county town, after being kept back perhaps by its eccentric position towards the edge of its shire (much of the northern half of the county appears always to have looked northwards and to Chesterfield and Sheffield[64]) and perilously close to a powerfully effective rival in Nottingham.[65] Derby's rise to parity with the other county centres was a rapid one, based on the growing wealth of its locality, its nearness to the industrial wealth of the Wirksworth lead mines, its role as a social centre for the gentry and as a channel for interregional trade with the North-West; the opening of the Derwent navigation to the Trent in 1719 helped, as did industrial growth in the eighteenth century, with brewing, silk and cotton weaving, porcelain and iron manufactures.[66]

Nottingham is an interesting mirror image of Shrewsbury in the west – temporarily eclipsed in the earlier sixteenth century but recovering strongly later, always the unchallenged head of a weak county urban network at the fringe of the Midland system, and deriving a vital importance from its role as a distributive and wholesaling centre for a large area based on its function as the effective upstream terminus of a major navigable river. Up the Trent came corn, imported goods and raw materials; downstream went lead, agricultural produce and industrial goods from other parts of the Midlands, much of it bound for London. In its market place in 1641 were to be found a striking diversity of materials and goods attracting traders from neighbouring counties.[67] It was a major centre of gentry leisure and residence, despite its commercial and industrial vigour, and developed as a major textile centre specialising in stockings and lace by the eighteenth century: the large-scale employment created by these manufactures accounts for its remarkable demographic growth in the later eighteenth century. Industrial developments enhanced its relationship with the smaller towns in its hinterland, many of which (Mansfield, Castle Donington, Southwell) developed satellite branches of these textile specialities, for Nottingham was able to offer technical, financial and marketing services further to intensify its domination of its region.

Leicester appears to have been impoverished in the sixteenth century (though perhaps less than sometimes suggested), but its primacy remained unthreatened because it had no local rivals: it drew strength from its relationship with London,

64 The contacts revealed by the diary of a Chapel-en-le-Frith doctor are with Cheshire, Manchester and Sheffield: *The Diary of James Clegg of Chapel-en-le-Frith 1708–1755*, Pt 1, ed. V. S. Doe (Derbyshire Record Society, 2, 1978).

65 The Trent gave Nottingham a great advantage as a distributive centre, though one Derby ironmonger in 1610 was importing directly through Gainsborough (Lichfield Joint RO, diocesan probate records, John Burne 1610). A Derby draper's debtors reveal little business on the eastward, Nottingham side of the town but a spread to the north and south in compensation (*ibid.*, Thomas Crychlowe 1601).

66 *William Wooley's History of Derbyshire*, ed. C. Glover and P. Riden (Derbyshire Record Society 6, 1981), pp. 23–41. R. P. Sturges, 'The membership of the Derby Philosophical Society 1783–1802', *Midland History*, 4, (1977–8), 213–18.

67 'An account of Nottingham in 1641', *Thoroton Society Transactions*, 2 (1898).

far enough away to avoid competitive damage, but near enough for it to act as a collecting and distributing point for trade with the capital. It suffered from its situation in an area with poor communications – Celia Fiennes struggled from Uppingham to Leicester along 'very deep bad roads . . . being full of sloughs, clay deep way' – and this in summer.[68] It is perhaps significant that when, as late as 1770, an itinerant William Hutton had dogs set on him as an intrusive stranger,[69] the event took place in Market Bosworth, a small and out-of-the-way market town in an region with more than its fair share of such places, though many of its small towns were prospering by the eighteenth century.[70] When Evelyn rode through the Leicestershire, Rutland and Peterborough area in 1654 he found 'people living as wretchedly as in the most impoverish'd parts of France, which they much resemble being idle and sluttish'.[71] Leicester itself enjoyed the fruits of rapid expansion from the later seventeenth century on the basis of its hosiery industry, due perhaps to its relationship with London, cheap labour and the ease with which such light products could be moved along poor roads. Travellers reacted badly to its appearance – the 'old and rag[g]ed City of Leicester, large, & pleasantly seated, but despicably built' (1654)[72] – while praising Nottingham's elegance.[73] However, though it lagged behind Nottingham as a genteel centre, it did develop an impressive social and cultural life in the later eighteenth century.[74] Northampton is only marginally a Midland town, and it shares with Hereford an inability to develop beyond its role as a shopping and gentry town to become as dominant in size as the other county centres: London was too near and industrial ventures too frail until the wholesale footwear manufacture developed early in the nineteenth century.[75]

Lincolnshire was poor, thinly inhabited and an isolated backwater before the later eighteenth-century improvements in communications brought it more firmly into the Midland economy, with some impressive industrial growth in several towns. Lincoln was mainly an administrative and social centre, and although it recovered from the worst of its sixteenth-century troubles, it lacked the industrial and commercial strengths which aided the other county towns. The result was that other Lincolnshire market towns acquired an enhanced significance, Boston as a seaport and Gainsborough as a river one, these two and Grantham and Louth as major market centres.[76] *The Universal British Directory* of 1791–8 claims a surprising number of small Lincolnshire towns as centres of

[68] *The Journeys of Celia Fiennes* (London, 1983), p. 191.

[69] *The Life of William Hutton* (London, 1816), p. 45.

[70] For such a town, absorbed in its little region, see D. Fleming, 'A local market system. Melton Mowbray and the Wreake Valley 1549–1720' (PhD thesis, University of Leicester, 1980).

[71] *Diary of John Evelyn*, III, pp. 122, 135. [72] *Ibid.*, p. 122.

[73] Beckett, *East Midlands*, pp. 135ff, 223–8.

[74] P. Clark, 'Leicester society in the eighteenth century: expansion and improvement' (unpublished typescript kindly supplied by Professor Clark).

[75] R. L. Greenall, *A History of Northamptonshire* (Chichester, 1979).

[76] N. R. Wright, *Lincolnshire Towns and Industry 1700–1914* (Lincoln, 1982).

genteel social activity: Brigg, where theatre, dancing and card assemblies 'render it a scene of gaiety as well as business'; Grantham's horse racing; Louth, with concerts, assemblies and 'even masquerades' was 'one of the gayest towns in Lincolnshire', while Spalding had its famous literary society. Stamford has a peculiar interest as a town whose modest size belies a major role in the urban network, for its significance as a gentry social centre, with newspapers, inns, theatre, racecourse, assembly room and rebuilt houses allowed it to fill a conspicuous gap in the network of county towns, equidistant as it is from Lincoln, Nottingham, Leicester, Northampton and Lynn.[77]

The urban characteristics of this large and diverse area are not easy to summarise in brief. One is tempted to suggest that it reveals its Midland situation by replicating many of the features of neighbouring regions, including the early backwardness of the North and Wales and again the transforming influence of industry in the eighteenth and early nineteenth centuries in those areas. Perhaps the local networks based on dominant county centres emerge more clearly than in most other areas, and the lack of a single true provincial capital is perhaps less of a contrast with other regions than at first appears. Within the Midland regions appear most of the urban types of the inland country, whether old-established shire centre, new spa, industrial town, sleepy market or busy thoroughfare: granted the inevitable absence of seaside settlements, here is urban Britain in miniature.

[77] A. Rogers, *The Book of Stamford* (Buckingham, 1983).

· 2(e) ·

North

JOHN K. WALTON

(i) THE NATURE OF THE REGION

URBAN GROWTH in parts of northern England during the three centuries under review was spectacular even by the standards of the first industrial nation. It was spectacular in the literal sense that by the early decades of the nineteenth century not only business travellers but also tourists and social commentators were coming to marvel at the novel concentration of factories using fossil fuels in an urban setting in and around Manchester, and at the sheer scale of urban maritime and manufacturing activity in the other towns which were cohering and coalescing. The great industrial and commercial centres gathered up systems of satellite towns in their surrounding districts, conjuring up in one visiting mind the telling image of Manchester as a 'diligent spider' at the heart of its web of communications.[1] These were accelerating developments, and they reached their most dramatic, interesting and historically important phase between the late eighteenth century and the mid-nineteenth, when these new towns were at their most raw, untrammelled, dramatic, exciting and threatening: 'great human exploits'[2] which produced and distributed a cornucopia of goods under a shroud of infernal smoke and under conditions which visibly threatened life, health and social and political stability. Provincial urban developments within the North had turned it into a symbol of the future, which might or might not work in the longer term, and by the 1840s the urban concentrations of the region had become the cynosure of the informed contemporary gaze. It therefore makes sense to begin this survey with an analysis of the scale and scope of urbanisation within the region in 1840, and then to examine the roots of these unprecedented phenomena and attempt to describe and explain their development.

First of all, however, some discussion of the region itself is necessary. Putting

[1] L. Faucher, *Manchester in 1844* (London, 1969), p. 15.

[2] Disraeli's phrase about Manchester ('properly understood . . . as great a human exploit as Athens'), quoted in Gary S. Messinger, *Manchester in the Victorian Age* (Manchester, 1985), p. 93.

together the counties of Cheshire, Lancashire, Westmorland, Cumberland, Northumberland, Durham and the three Ridings of Yorkshire and presenting them collectively as 'the North', defined as the sum of nine administrative entities aggregated and divided from each other by lines on the map rather than by any deep or developed senses of shared identity, might seem somewhat arbitrary. Historians rarely use this 'North of England' as an analytical category. Helen Jewell has recently argued for the existence of a deeply rooted north of *Britain*, with a shared cultural identity going back long before the emergence of counties and indeed founded in Jurassic geology. But this pulls together the whole of North-West Britain, from Wales and Northern Ireland to the Humber, with only the development of Anglo-Saxon Northumbria preventing 'northern consciousness' (whatever that might be) from pervading the whole of this extensive area.[3] This is interesting but contentious, playing down by implication the role of industrialisation in forging northern identities; and so is Frank Musgrove's notion of the 'North' of England, defined in terms of six core counties but with borders which ebb and flow over time according to changing political circumstances. In practice, Musgrove devoted most of his attention to Yorkshire, and most writers focus on parts of the larger region, whether individual counties or composite areas which are thought to be worth analysis.[4] Within this framework assumptions about identities have varied: the 'North-West', for example, has been identified with Lancashire and Cheshire or with Lancashire and what is now Cumbria.[5] Some writers have preferred geographical units which combine parts of the North as defined here with adjoining districts which the present scheme puts elsewhere: thus Joan Thirsk combines Yorkshire and Lincolnshire as an agricultural region, though only after detaching the Pennine 'highlands of Yorkshire', while in the same volume of the *Agrarian History of England and Wales* Alan Everitt assigns Cheshire to 'western England and Wales'.[6] At the margins, at least, consensus about regional identity has been lacking.

[3] H. Jewell, *The North–South Divide: The Origins of Northern Consciousness in England* (Manchester, 1994).

[4] F. Musgrove, *The North of England* (Oxford, 1990); J. K. Walton, 'Professor Musgrove's *North of England*: a critique', *Journal of Regional and Local Studies*, 12 (2) (1992), 25–31. See also the essays in N. Kirk, ed., *Northern Identities* (Aldershot, 1999).

[5] C. B. Phillips and J. H. Smith, *Lancashire and Cheshire from AD 1540* (London, 1994); L. Castells and J. K. Walton, 'Contrasting identities: North-West England and the Basque Country, 1840–1936', in E. Royle, ed., *Issues of Regional Identity* (Manchester, 1998), pp. 44–81; J. K. Walton, 'The North-West', in F. M. L. Thompson, ed., *The Cambridge Social History of Britain 1750–1950* (Cambridge, 1990) vol. I, pp. 355–414; J. K. Walton, 'The Agricultural Revolution and the Industrial Revolution: the case of North West England, 1780–1850', in C. Bjorn, ed., *The Agricultural Revolution – Reconsidered* (Odense, 1998), pp. 65–88. Studies of *parts* of the North also include J. K. Walton, *Lancashire* (Manchester, 1987); N. McCord, *North-East England: The Region's Development, 1760–1960* (London, 1979); D. Hey, *Yorkshire from AD 1000* (London, 1986); C. M. L. Bouch and G. P. Jones, *A Short Economic and Social History of the Lake Counties* (Manchester, 1961); J. D. Marshall and J. K. Walton, *The Lake Counties from 1830 to the Mid-Twentieth Century* (Manchester, 1981); S. Marriner, *The Economic and Social History of Merseyside* (London, 1982).

[6] J. Thirsk, ed., *Ag. HEW*, vol. IV (Cambridge, 1967), pp. 28–40, 470.

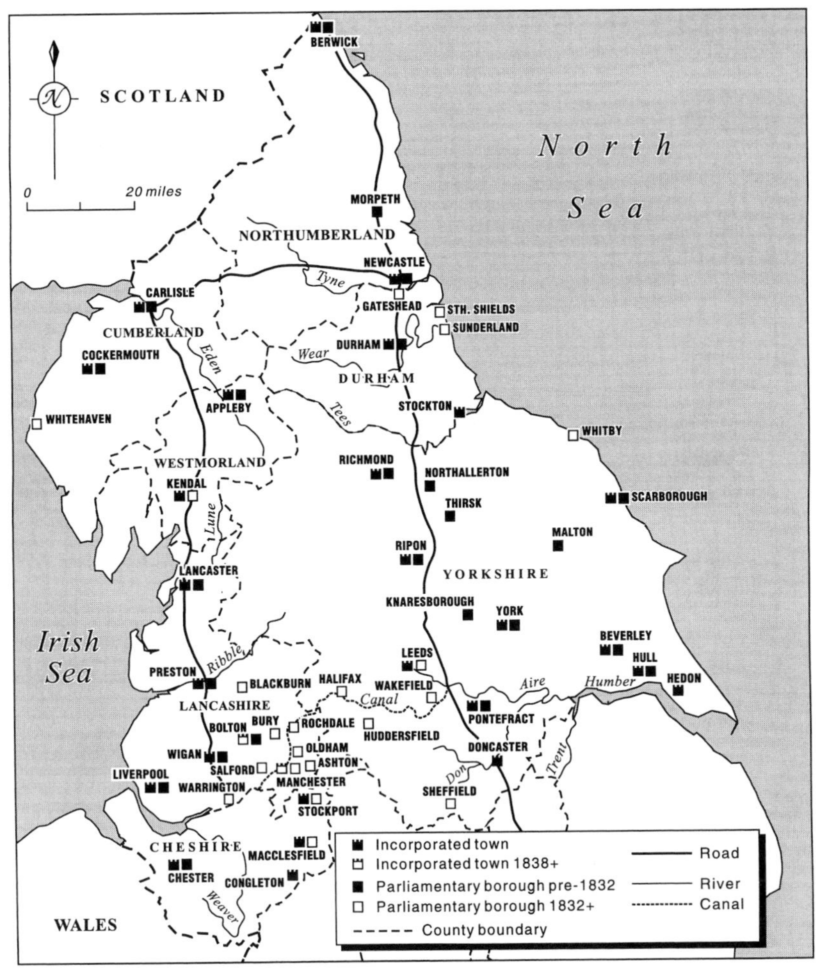

Map 2.9 Towns in the North 1540–1840

Within the North there were certainly contrasting experiences during these three centuries. The growth of international trade, and of manufacturing for diverse and distant markets, brought unprecedented and generally accelerating urban expansion to much of the region, while disrupting the rudimentary urban hierarchy which had existed in the sixteenth and seventeenth centuries. But the systems of urban interaction, competition and mutual reinforcement which mattered to people's lives operated over smaller areas within the region envisaged here. There were the ports of the west coast, which prospered (and in some cases eventually faltered) on the rise of the Irish Sea and Atlantic economies, trading and competing with each other and promoting and responding to developments in hinterlands of varying promise, from Liverpool's improvable links with developing industrial districts in Lancashire and the West Midlands (as well as North Wales) to the constraints imposed on Whitehaven's prospects by a mountainous and barren inland topography. The east coast ports looked in the opposite direction, to the North Sea and the Baltic, and to the London coal trade which fuelled the rise of Newcastle and (more single-mindedly) Sunderland. Hull's growth, like that of Liverpool, depended on navigation systems which linked it with extensive areas of the Midlands as well as (in this case) the rising textile and metalworking industries of Yorkshire.[7] Even when canals and improved stagecoach services forged stronger east/west links across the Pennines at the turn of the eighteenth and nineteenth centuries, these remained largely separate maritime systems, with centripetal consequences which pulled apart any potential regional identity.[8] A small town in the northern Pennines like Kirkby Stephen, miles from any water transport, might supply its shops from Newcastle as well as Kendal, Lancaster and Manchester in the late eighteenth century, but this could hardly form a focus for regional identity.[9] Manchester itself was acquiring metropolitan functions in the south of the region, but even at the end of the period its links to the west and north-west were much stronger than those to the east. In 1824 there were twenty-three stagecoach services between Manchester and Liverpool listed in Baines' *Directory*, but only two to Hull, although there were three competing routes by water to the east coast port by this time.[10] Leeds was the rising alternative metropolis on the Yorkshire side of the Pennines, and eleven coaches linked it with Manchester; but the extent of the Pennine divide between Lancashire and Yorkshire, cotton and wool (despite Rochdale's enduring interest in the latter) is suggested by the directory listing of Bradford stuff merchants in 1830, who were 'in fact all Leeds men, save 1 from Manchester who had a warehouse in Bradford and attended market days there'.[11] This illustrates the way in which distinctive manufacturing districts were coalescing within the border region, feeding and responding to the growth of their own urban networks and hierarchies which in turn came under the aegis of sub-regional capitals; for this was a region without a dominant city to pull it together, whether administratively, economically or culturally. This was true even at the start of the period, when York's hegemony in the mid-sixteenth century did not extend west of the Pennines. Here, moreover, the newly defined diocese of Chester was too sprawling and unwieldy for its own administrators to grasp: Bishop Chadderton in 1585, after six years in office, still did not know how far his writ was supposed

[7] Marriner, *Merseyside*; J. V. Beckett, *Coal and Tobacco* (Cambridge, 1981); G. Jackson, *Hull in the Eighteenth Century*, (Oxford, 1972).

[8] D. Aldcroft and M. J. Freeman, eds., *Transport in the Industrial Revolution* (Manchester, 1983).

[9] T. S. Willan, *An Eighteenth-Century Shopkeeper* (Manchester, 1970), p. 29.

[10] E. Baines, *History, Directory and Gazetteer of the County Palatine of Lancaster* (Liverpool, 1824–5, vol. II, pp. 397–405.

[11] R. G. Wilson, *Gentlemen Merchants* (Manchester, 1971), pp. 18–19.

to run in the north.[12] In secular matters, too, such urban economic and cultural influences as there were at this time were local and diffuse.

(ii) URBAN NETWORKS IN 1840

The history of urban networks over these three centuries is thus dominated in the North by the articulation of systems of industrial towns which, in their most impressive incarnations, had little to do with the older hierarchy of county towns and market centres, in apparent contrast with the continuing comparative vitality of the county capitals of the Midlands.[13] Most spectacular, by the time of the 1841 census whose findings will be used extensively, was the galaxy of towns, with Manchester at the hub, which had come to specialise mainly in cotton spinning, weaving and finishing. There were fifty-four such towns, with populations of more than 2,500 in 1841, in the area bounded by Preston, Todmorden, Macclesfield and Wigan within which the world's first Industrial Revolution, pulling together factories, fossil fuels and new kinds of town, was working itself out. Within this area of southern, eastern and central Lancashire, which extended into north-east Cheshire and (just) into Derbyshire, there were twenty-two centres with between 5,000 and 10,000 inhabitants in 1841; thirteen with between 10,000 and 20,000; eight with between 20,000 and 50,000; Preston, Bolton and Stockport with over 50,000; and Manchester and Salford with a combined population of 311,269, making the largest urban entity in northern England.[14] Taking a smaller area as their 'Eastern Region' of Lancashire and Cheshire the contemporary commentators Danson and Welton, using a different definition of a town (2,000 people on 180 acres), found nearly one million urban dwellers in thirty towns in 1851, 64 per cent of the total population. Half a century earlier there had been 231,000 urbanites in twenty-four towns, making just over 45 per cent of the total population.[15] Whichever detailed figures we follow, these were remarkable developments, disproportionately crammed into the post-1770 decades, which demand priority in further exploration.

The urban network of the Manchester textile region had its own sub-divisions, as cotton spinning took hold in the south (with Macclesfield specialising

[12] D. M. Palliser, *Tudor York* (Oxford, 1979), pp. 3, 7–17; D. M. Woodward, The *Trade of Elizabethan Chester* (Hull, 1970), pp. 1–4. [13] See Chapter 2(d) in this volume.

[14] These calculations, and others which follow, are based on Dr Langton's compilation of town populations for this volume. Occasional divergences will be noted: here Dukinfield's population is taken from Phillips and Smith, *Lancashire and Cheshire*, p. 136.

[15] J. T. Danson and T. A. Welton, 'On the population of Lancashire and Cheshire and its local distribution during the fifty years, 1801–51', *Transactions of the Historic Society of Lancashire and Cheshire*, 9 (1856–7), 199, 206. See also E. Butterworth, *A Statistical Sketch of the County Palatine of Lancaster* (London, 1841), pp. viii–xi, for an alternative urban classification by a contemporary.

in silk) while hand-loom weaving prevailed longer in association with a less-impressive scale of urban growth in the north and especially the north-east. Preston, Stockport, Bolton, Oldham and Blackburn stood out among the sub-centres. Preston, on the fringe of the textile belt, benefited from county administrative functions and enjoyed a wide market area for agricultural districts to the west, south-west and north, while Bolton was a particularly notable centre for industrial organisation in its own right. Subdivisions were more marked still in the West Riding of Yorkshire's woollen- and worsted-manufacturing districts, whose scale and density of interlocking urban agglomeration by 1841 was second only to the 'cotton towns'. By 1841 Leeds, with a population of 152,074, had confirmed the status to which it already aspired in the eighteenth century as 'in reality if not in name . . . the county town of the West Riding, the centre of the woollen trade and the legal and financial metropolis of the county'.[16] Bradford (see Plate 30) had become the capital of the worsted trade, pioneering new products (including, from the late 1830s, 'mixed worsteds' with a cotton warp which enhanced trade links with the cotton district), and developing a distinctive merchant community while drawing in the finishing processes. Between 1821 and 1831 it and Brighton had been Britain's fastest-growing towns, and its 1841 population of 66,715 made it the West Riding's second city, presiding over a distinctive branch of the staple trade. Below this came Halifax (27,520) and Huddersfield (25,068), each at the centre of its own sub-system of cloth production, as expressed in the origins of attenders at the cloth markets or piece halls, with Halifax specialising in lighter worsteds and Huddersfield in high-quality fancy cloths.[17] Fifth was Wakefield, whose 1841 population of 18,842 was 40 per cent the size of Oldham's, which had the equivalent rank among the Lancashire cotton towns. Here county administrative functions and the marketing of raw materials had developed while mercantile and manufacturing roles in the woollen trade had been lost to Leeds and other West Riding rivals. At the meeting-point between the textile districts to the west and a more agricultural economy to the east, Wakefield's situation was not unlike that of Preston; but the Lancashire town, developing its cotton manufacturing activities, had grown much more rapidly and was two-and-a-half times Wakefield's size.[18] Such discrepancies continued lower down the urban hierarchy: six towns in the Yorkshire textile districts had more than 10,000 inhabitants in 1841 (Pudsey joined the ranks by a whisker) as opposed to fourteen in cotton Lancashire. Twelve in all topped 5,000, compared with Lancashire's twenty-four. On the national stage,

[16] Wilson, *Gentlemen Merchants*, p. 231.

[17] T. Koditschek, *Class Formation and Urban–Industrial Society* (Cambridge, 1990), pp. 94–7; D. Gregory, *Regional Transformation and Industrial Revolution* (London, 1982), p. 118; P. Hudson, *The Genesis of Industrial Capital* (Cambridge, 1986), pp. 27–8; Hey, *Yorkshire*, pp. 245–9.

[18] W. G. Rimmer, 'The evolution of Leeds', in P. Clark, ed., *The Early Modern Town* (London, 1976), ch. 12.

developments in the West Riding clothing districts were impressive; but in this northern setting the Manchester region eclipses them.

The North's second city, Liverpool, with a population of 286,487 in 1841, had as many inhabitants as the five largest West Riding woollen towns combined; and it dominated its immediate surroundings much more than Leeds, Bradford or even Manchester. Of the cluster of mining, metalworking and salt-processing towns in its south-west Lancashire and Merseyside hinterland only Warrington, with its strategic position and diverse industries, had more than 20,000 inhabitants in 1841, when St Helens was still coalescing from a cluster of coal-mining and glassmaking colonies and hamlets to reach a five-figure total.[19] Growth on the Wirral peninsula was still very limited, and to find further clusters of thriving towns displaying rapid growth at the end of the period it is necessary to cross the region to Tyneside. Here Newcastle presided, its 70,337 denizens in 1841 making it the North's fifth most populous city, having more than doubled its population in forty years while Liverpool had increased by 248 per cent. Along the Tyne, however, there was growth at a similar rate at Tynemouth, Gateshead and South Shields, each of which had topped 20,000 by 1841; and this North Sea economy, based on a carboniferous capitalism of coal, shipping and engineering, was echoed on a smaller scale further down the coast, as Sunderland took its share of the London coal trade, Hartlepool came into the frame, pit villages began to agglomerate on an urban scale if not to acquire urban functions and identities, and Durham's growth kept pace with most of its neighbours as it added an identity as capital of a mining area to its administrative and ecclesiastical roles. Coal exports also boosted Teesside's nascent urban system, as Stockton and Darlington grew in symbiosis at almost identical rates while Middlesbrough stood at the dawning of its career as one of the most dynamic of Victorian new towns. Here, however, we are dealing with two established towns with about 10,000 people each in 1841 and a very raw newcomer which had just topped 5,000.[20] A similar kind of urban system was already well established in west Cumberland by the early nineteenth century, with the three main ports of Whitehaven, Workington and Maryport thriving on the Irish coal trade, although growth flagged in the former two places in the early nineteenth century and Whitehaven had also suffered from the decline of its transatlantic trade. The overall scale of development here was not much greater than Teesside, with less current dynamism, no dominant town like Sunderland or Newcastle and no new focus of growth like Middlesbrough.[21]

19 Marriner, *Merseyside;* T. C. Barker and J. R. Harris, *A Merseyside Town in the Industrial Revolution* (Liverpool, 1954).

20 McCord, *North-East England;* A. Briggs, *Victorian Cities* (Harmondsworth, 1968), ch. 6; M. W. Kirby, *Men of Business and Politics* (London, 1984).

21 Beckett, *Coal and Tobacco*; Bouch and Jones, *Lake Counties*; C. O'Neill, 'The contest for dominion', *NHist.*, 18 (1982), 133–52; Sylvia Collier, *Whitehaven 1660–1800* (London, 1991).

Inland, the growth of Sheffield stands out, driven first by the water-powered manufacture of cutlery and tools, then by the iron and steel industries of the Don valley. Already in 1801 it was comfortably the North's fourth city, and its population more than doubled over the next forty years: 111,091 were enumerated in 1841.[22] Rotherham, Barnsley and Doncaster might be regarded as loosely within Sheffield's orbit, but Barnsley especially had its own economic identity: it grew very rapidly as a centre of linen manufacture in the early nineteenth century, but failed to sustain this dynamism and had just over 11,000 inhabitants in 1841.[23] Doncaster looked at least as much to the agricultural east, to the river navigations which converged on the Humber, and to the Great North Road.[24] Sheffield's influence also reached southwards into Derbyshire, but without as yet stimulating significant growth in places like Dronfield or Bolsover.

Since (at least) the opening of the Don navigation in 1751, Sheffield had been closely linked with Hull, the North Sea and Baltic port which distributed imports and gathered up exports along the extensive river system which reached into the heart of emergent industrial England from the Humber. Hull was the main outlet for West Riding woollen exports and its tentacles stretched into the West Midlands, although as the Atlantic economy gained primacy and the canal network spread in the west it lost much of this trade to Liverpool. But Hull had a much longer maritime history that its upstart western rival, and in 1841 it was still the sixth city in the North, with 67,308 enumerated inhabitants. As with Liverpool, it did not stimulate much urban growth in its immediate hinterland at this stage: indeed, places like Howden, Hedon and the medieval clothworking centre of Beverley showed less urban dynamism than Liverpool's environs, boosted as the latter were by coal and salt deposits. Hull had tense relationships with river ports like Bawtry and Selby, which had passed their peak by the early nineteenth century, and with the rapidly rising new inland port of Goole.[25] But it was much more expansive than the other Yorkshire coastal towns, despite whaling at Whitby and the rise of sea-bathing at Scarborough (see Plate 29).

A further, less dynamic urban network followed a crescent around Morecambe Bay, pulled together by the hazardous oversands land transport route across the Bay and by coastal shipping. The port of Lancaster was at the core of this, although its heyday as a participant in the Atlantic economy was over by 1841, its county administrative functions were also being eroded and it was

[22] D. Hey, *The Fiery Blades of Hallamshire* (Leicester, 1991); S. Pollard, *A History of Labour in Sheffield* (Liverpool, 1959).

[23] F. Kaijage, 'Working-class radicalism in Barnsley, 1816–1820', in S. Pollard and C. Holmes, eds., *Essays in the Economic and Social Development of South Yorkshire* (Barnsley, 1976), p. 19.

[24] J. L. Baxter, 'Early Chartism and labour class struggle; South Yorkshire 1837–40', in Pollard and Holmes, eds., *South Yorkshire*, p. 151.

[25] Jackson, *Hull*, ch. 2; J. D. Porteous, *Canal Ports* (London, 1977).

looking for a new role.[26] With a population of 13,744 in 1841 it still presided over a group of small towns along the Lune valley and around the Bay, where Ulverston had its own local economic and cultural influence on a burgeoning industrial as well as agricultural region, with slate and iron coming to the fore.[27] Kendal, an important industrial town as well as a county and market centre, was an alternative node in this pattern, and its stocking-knitting industry was reaching out into the dales of Westmorland and even Yorkshire.[28] There was also a northern Cumbrian network centred on Carlisle, which developed its port facilities and a cotton industry to add to its market, garrison, ecclesiastical and administrative functions in the early nineteenth century, and more than doubled its population between 1801 and 1841. Carlisle's demand for hand-loom weavers extended beyond its own grim slums to boost urban growth on all sides, in Wigton, Longtown, Brampton and as far west as Cockermouth, which in turn also flourished modestly on cattle droving and looked westwards to the ports of west Cumberland. Carlisle also extended its influence across the Solway Firth to Dumfries and Annan. In comparative terms within the region these were modest developments, but they were far from negligible.[29]

All this urban dynamism, in its varying degrees, left York and Chester, the old pretenders to regional hegemony, on the sidelines. They did not stagnate: York, after difficult years in the sixteenth century, doubled its population to more than 28,000 between the late seventeenth century and 1841, while Chester increased more than threefold to nearly 24,000. But the impetus to growth on the grand scale was diverted elsewhere, as York lost trade to Hull and Chester to Liverpool, while the proto-industrial textile manufactures and the mineral deposits on which new industries were based lay elsewhere.[30] Nor did York or Chester become centres for constellations of subordinate towns. This failure to keep pace

[26] P. Gooderson, 'The economic and social history of Lancaster, 1780–1914' (PhD thesis, University of Lancaster, 1974); M. Elder, *The Slave Trade and the Economic Development of Eighteenth-Century Lancaster* (Halifax, 1992); S. Constantine *et al.*, *A History of Lancaster 1193–1993* (Keele, 1993), chs. 3–4.

[27] J. D. Marshall, *Furness in the Industrial Revolution* (Barrow, 1958; repr., Whitehaven, 1981); P. D. R. Borwick, 'An English provincial society: Lancashire 1770–1820' (PhD thesis, University of Lancaster, 1994), for Ulverston and district.

[28] J. D. Marshall and C. A. Dyhouse, 'Social transition in Kendal and Westmorland', *NHist.*, 12 (1976); J. D. Marshall *et al.*, 'A small town study', *UHY* (1974), 19–23.

[29] S. Towill, *Carlisle* (Chichester, 1991); J. B. Bradbury, *A History of Cockermouth* (Chichester, 1981); J. C. F. Barnes, 'Popular protest and radical politics: Carlisle 1790–1850' (PhD thesis, University of Lancaster, 1981).

[30] Palliser, *York*; Woodward, *Chester*; C. Feinstein, ed., *York 1831–1981* (York, 1981). For Chester's eighteenth-century rise as a shopping centre, see J. Stobart, 'Shopping streets as social space: leisure, consumerism and improvement in an eighteenth-century county town', *UH*, 25 (1998), 3–21, and for later developments J. Herson, 'Victorian Chester: a city of change and ambiguity', in R. Swift, ed., *Victorian Chester* (Liverpool, 1996), pp. 13–22, and C. Young and S. Allen, 'Retail patterns in nineteenth-century Chester', *Journal of Regional and Local Studies*, 16 (1996), 1–18.

with developments was not general among the older-established urban centres, however. It applied to Ripon, which was 'probably the largest town in the West Riding' in 1532 with about 2,000 inhabitants, but was to be completely eclipsed by developments elsewhere even as it grew gently through the period. Again, it lacked the new desiderata for urban dynamism.[31] But most of the towns which showed spectacular growth were already in the frame by the later seventeenth century. Of the six most populous Lancashire towns at that point, Manchester itself, Bolton and Preston featured, and the other three were Warrington, Wigan and Ashton-under-Lyne, each of which had over 20,000 inhabitants in 1841. Liverpool and Oldham were conspicuous by their absence from the upper tiers of the urban hierarchy of the later seventeenth century, however. So were Bradford and Huddersfield in the West Riding of Yorkshire, but here again Leeds, Sheffield and Halifax were already among the top five towns at this time, along with Wakefield and Doncaster. Newcastle was the North's second city in population terms in the late seventeenth century, and Hull the third, although Sunderland was nowhere. Where surrounding circumstances were propitious, then, existing urban centres were more likely to reap the benefits of economic growth in which they themselves participated, and to become the focal points of urban networks as manufacturing towns began to cluster around their older-established and more sophisticated urban functions.

There were northern urban networks, then, but to speak of an urban network covering the whole region would be to oversimplify. There is some debate as to whether northern England might be regarded as a province with a common identity, even in the negative sense of difference from the rest of England, in the sixteenth century, when York united civil and ecclesiastical governing bodies which oversaw half the kingdom.[32] However we conclude on that issue, it is clear that industrialisation brought the emergence of new kinds of economic region which specialised in production for export: the regions within the North which, or so Dr Langton has argued, crystallised with sharpening definition in the canal age.[33] Each of these regions had its own urban network and hierarchy, and developed (if it did not inherit) its own distinctive dialect and culture.[34] This sense of growing fragmentation within the region does not invalidate use of 'the North' as an heuristic device, providing an accessible level of generalised apprehension between the locality and the nation-state which helps us to understand processes of change, to make provisional comparisons and to

[31] Palliser, *York*, p. 10.

[32] *Ibid.*, pp. 6–7; B. W. Beckingsale, 'The characteristics of the Tudor North', *NHist.*, 4 (1969), 67–83.

[33] J. Langton, 'The Industrial Revolution and the regional geography of England', *Transactions of the Institute of British Geographers*, new series, 9 (1984), 145–68.

[34] J. Le Patourel, 'Is Northern History a subject?', *NHist.*, 12 (1976), 12–14.

assess interactions. Under the capacious umbrella of the 'North' of this section the emergent urban networks of the industrial age can be understood in their relationships one with another as well as in their centrifugal pulls and contrasting characteristics.[35]

(iii) NORTHERN TOWNS IN THE SIXTEENTH CENTURY

The complex urban networks of 1841 were imposed on a region where towns had been small, unsophisticated and dispersed at the beginning of the period. The market towns (most with a few hundred inhabitants) identified by Alan Everitt as operating at some point between 1500 and 1640 were particularly thin on the ground in the four northernmost counties, most obviously in the wild and vulnerable border territory of Northumberland. During this period the grid was thickening on the map where textile manufacturing was developing and its workers needed services, especially in Lancashire, where 'Several of the principal towns of modern Lancashire were emerging . . . and setting up markets of their own: Blackburn, Colne, Haslingden, Leigh, Padiham.'[36] Overall, indeed, Lancashire came to be as well endowed with market towns as Sussex, Wiltshire or Leicestershire, with a density matching the national average of seventy square miles per market town. Cheshire had a slightly lower density, and the remaining counties of the region averaged over 100 square miles per market, with half the market-goers having to travel twenty miles or more. Bleak Northumberland had 250 square miles to every market.[37]

More substantial towns were also at a premium, and their delineation is made more difficult by the shortage of plausible sources from which urban populations can be derived, especially where urban areas occupied only a small part of extensive parishes or even townships. But it is clear that only a handful of northern towns in the mid-sixteenth century had more than 2,000 inhabitants. Newcastle, the 'eye of the North', with its strategic river position, border warfare role and rising coal trade, was the North's largest town, and the third largest in England in the mid-sixteenth century, with a population in excess of 10,000; and mining, salt boiling and maritime populations on both sides of the Tyne were beginning

[35] Work on urban networks, as such, within the region has tended to concentrate on areas dominated by well-established small towns rather than the economically developing and urbanising parts of the region: R. A. Unwin, 'Tradition and transformation: market towns of the Vale of York 1660–1830', *NHist.*, 17 (1981), 72–116; J. D. Marshall, 'The rise and transformation of the Cumbrian market town, 1660–1900', *NHist.*, 19 (1983), 128–209, which contains very useful material on interactions between Cumbrian towns, including road traffic flows; M. Noble, 'Growth and development in a regional urban system: the country towns of eastern Yorkshire, 1700–1850', *UHY* (1987), 1–21. See also nn. 47 and 51, below, for work on Lancashire and Cheshire. [36] A. Everitt, in Thirsk, ed., *Ag.HEW*, IV, p. 476.

[37] *Ibid.*, pp. 485–90.

to expand around it.[38] Here was a face of the future. But York, the second urban centre in population terms, had a much broader influence through much of the region. Its economic role was in long-term decline, and in 1548 its population stood at a long-time low of about 8,000; but it concentrated institutions of regional civil and ecclesiastical government which drew litigants, supplicants and witnesses from all over the North, especially the King's Council in the Northern Parts and the archdiocese of York. Palliser sums up: 'York was, therefore, a capital to the "county community" of England's largest shire, an administrative and judicial centre for eight northern counties, and an active centre of trade and commerce in its own right.' It was the nearest approximation to a regional political capital.[39] On the relatively prosperous and accessible eastern side of the region there was nothing to challenge the dominance of York and, in its own sphere, Newcastle. The decaying cloth and minster town of Beverley, with about 5,000 inhabitants, may still have been larger than nearby Hull, while Durham housed between 3,000 and 4,000 people and nowhere else, except Ripon, approached 2,000.[40]

Towns of any size were even more sparsely distributed west of the Pennines. Chester, a parliamentary constituency and corporate borough and the most important port in the North-West, with quite extensive Irish and foreign as well as coasting trade, was the alternative metropolis here. It was a county town, and its recently acquired status as the bishopric of an extensive diocese extended its influence (at least nominally) into the northernmost parts of the region, including the northern Pennines. It had a relatively sophisticated urban structure and local government system, and its population in 1563 was probably more than 5,000. Chester had no rivals for economic, demographic or political primacy, although Nantwich, a salt-producing and transport town, may have had over 2,000 inhabitants.[41] Lancaster, the county town of the most populous north-western county, was decayed and bucolic in appearance, despite its recently recovered status as a parliamentary borough and the revival of its privileges as the assize and quarter sessions town at mid-century.[42] The problems of assessing population figures for these ill-defined urban entities are well illustrated by the case of Manchester, where confusion between the township and the (much larger) parish confounds attempts to arrive at a plausible total from the ecclesiastical return of 1563, although T. S. Willan eventually suggests 1,800 as a township population after making some heroic assumptions.[43] We have no similar estimates for other

[38] R. Howell, *Newcastle-upon-Tyne and the Puritan Revolution* (Oxford, 1967), p. 2; R. Newton, 'The decay of the borders', in C. W. Chalklin and M. A. Havinden, eds., *Rural Change and Urban Growth 1500–1800* (London, 1974), p. 9; D. Levine and K. Wrightson, *The Making of an Industrial Society: Whickham 1560–1765* (Oxford, 1991). [39] Palliser, *York*, p. 22 and ch. 1, *passim*.

[40] D. M. Woodward, *Men at Work* (Cambridge, 1995), pp. 8–9.

[41] Phillips and Smith, *Lancashire and Cheshire*, pp. 7–8, 30–2, 38–40; Woodward, *Chester*.

[42] Constantine *et al.*, *Lancaster*, pp. 54–5.

[43] T. S. Willan, *Elizabethan Manchester* (Manchester, 1980), pp. 38–9.

Lancashire towns, but none is likely to have been much larger. Further north, only Kendal in Westmorland, with its wool trade and growing administrative functions, and Carlisle in Cumberland, a county, fortress, cathedral and market town with a wide sphere of influence, seem to have had more than 2,000 inhabitants, and any notional urban network was more string and space than knots and clusters.[44] Across the region, indeed, and especially in the northern parts (where the Scottish border was still a dangerous national frontier), levels of urbanisation were very low by general English (though not Welsh or Scots) standards at this time, and despite a modestly thickening scattering of small settlements with markets and other privileges and trappings of urban local government the western half of the region was even more poorly endowed with towns than the eastern. In the whole of Cheshire in the mid-sixteenth century only Chester (which had county status), Congleton and Macclesfield sent MPs to Westminster, and some of the eleven seigneurial boroughs had scant claim to urban status. Lancashire had three incorporated boroughs (Lancaster, Preston and still-tiny Liverpool), and three additional ones with parliamentary representation, while the eight additional seigneurial boroughs again included tiny places of dubious urban status such as Hornby and Lathom.[45] This reflects the stunted political as well as economic development of an urban system at the start of the period covered here.

(iv) REFORMATION TO RESTORATION

The hearth tax records of the 1660s and 1670s offer the first general array of usable figures to provide some indication of patterns of urban growth, stagnation and change over time, and to give some purchase on an evolving urban hierarchy. What stands out is the patchy nature of what urban growth there was. Towns rarely outpaced or equalled general rates of population growth, punctuated as they were by recurrent population crises in a period of transition: Lancashire, for example, grew by 72 per cent between 1563 and 1664, Cheshire by 56 per cent, Cumberland by perhaps 46 per cent between 1563 and 1688, and Westmorland, overwhelmingly the most rural of these counties, by 9 per cent between 1563 and 1670.[46] York did grow faster than its surroundings, recovering well from early Elizabethan doldrums to increase its population by about 75 per cent, with a relatively low level of recorded poverty, while Chester also grew, but more on a par with the rest of its county.[47] The rise of Liverpool was under way, which may have held Chester back: the Merseyside port had about 1,200 inhabitants by the mid-1660s. Newcastle expanded surprisingly slowly, reaching

[44] Woodward, *Men at Work*, p. 10.

[45] Phillips and Smith, *Lancashire and Cheshire*, p. 31, table 1.5.

[46] *Ibid.*, p. 7, table 1.1, and pp. 10–12; Bouch and Jones, *Lake Counties*, p. 215.

[47] This perception of Chester's growth accepts the figure of 7,817 for its population in 1664 supplied by J. Stobart, 'An eighteenth-century revolution? Investigating urban growth in North-West England 1664–1801', *UH*, 23 (1996), 40, rather than Langton's estimate of 5,849.

perhaps 13,000 people in 1665, with some allowance for apprentices and servants. Roger Howell blames plague and emphasises poverty, pointing out that 41 per cent of the town's householders were exempt from the hearth tax and 76 per cent might reasonably be regarded as poor. These symptoms of urban crisis were certainly replicated elsewhere in the region, although in the further North-West Carlisle nearly doubled its population, while Kendal's fate is more debatable.[48]

Alongside these varying indicators of growth (though not necessarily of prosperity) in old-established towns, manufacturing and commercial centres of a newer growth like Manchester (whose population may have doubled) were making their presence felt. But some older centres were clearly in decline, and examples can be found over most of the region, from Beverley and Durham to Ripon and the old Westmorland county town of Appleby, eclipsed by Kendal. This was a difficult century across most of the North, and it is not surprising to find vicissitudes and varying fortunes among the towns of a region whose rural populations were often growing faster, fuelled by domestic manufacture and enclosure from the waste, than their urban counterparts.[49] By the mid-1660s there were still only two northern towns with populations of more than 10,000: York and Newcastle. Only three others (Chester, Kendal and Hull, which had been growing steadily) topped 5,000. Jon Stobart's detailed study finds that only 21 per cent of people living in Cheshire and Lancashire south of the Ribble in 1664 were town dwellers, on a modest definition of a town: the average size of 'urban' settlement here was 1,384, the median 883, and only five had more than 2,000 inhabitants.[50] Fifteen of Stobart's thirty towns had agriculture as their leading economic function, and ten had less than 0.5 people per acre on more than 2,000 acres of land.[51] This provides a telling perspective on levels of urbanisation in northern England more generally just after the Restoration. But impressive changes were about to get under way.

(v) THE EMERGENCE OF NEW URBAN SYSTEMS: THE 'LONG' EIGHTEENTH CENTURY

It was between the snapshot opportunities for measuring urban population which were provided by the hearth tax in the Restoration years and the census of 1801 that the urban systems of the industrial North emerged. This was an

48 Howell, *Newcastle-upon-Tyne*, pp. 6–12; J. D. Marshall, 'Kendal in the late seventeenth and eighteenth centuries', *Cumberland and Westmorland Archaeological and Antiquarian Society Transactions*, 75 (1975), 189, gives a population of 2,159 for Kendal (without Kirkland) in the census of 1695 which seems more plausible than Langton's higher figure.

49 A. B. Appleby, *Famine in Tudor and Stuart England* (Liverpool, 1978); G. H. Tupling, *The Economic and Social History of Rossendale* (Manchester, 1927); J. T. Swain, *Industry before the Industrial Revolution* (Manchester, 1986); J. K. Walton, 'Proto-industrialization and the first Industrial Revolution: the case of Lancashire', in P. Hudson, ed., *Regions and Industries* (Cambridge, 1989).

50 Stobart, 'Eighteenth-century revolution?', pp. 36–40.

51 J. Stobart, 'The urban system in the regional economy of North-West England 1700–1760' (DPhil thesis, University of Oxford, 1993), p. 227.

accelerating process, and in many places urban populations doubled over the last quarter of the eighteenth century, as we shall see; but the 'long' eighteenth century was the crucial formative and transitional period in the making of the new urban networks which had become so strongly articulated by the 1840s. The outstanding performer, admittedly, was Liverpool, which was not primarily an industrial town (although recent research has re-emphasised maritime manufactures, building and import processing),[52] and which completely overshadowed all its immediate neighbours on the coal and saltfields along the Mersey, increasing its population at least sixtyfold to rival Manchester and Salford for the title of England's second urban agglomeration, with a population (varying according to definition) of around 80,000 in 1801. In a sense, however, Liverpool played its part in all the urban networks of the western side of northern England, and beyond, from at least the middle of the eighteenth century, as the commercial heart which pumped goods, services and capital through an economic system which depended increasingly on access to materials and markets on a world stage.[53] To other north-western ports it was competitor in some ways, stimulant in others (Chester perhaps excepted). In its immediate hinterland Warrington grew more than sixfold to house more than 11,000 people, and Northwich similarly from a lower base to reach 3,600, while Prescot, the mining village which had attracted Liverpool's first turnpike road, topped 4,000 inhabitants by 1801; but Liverpool's overriding impact on urban networks was regional rather than local, diffuse rather than concentrated. Its rise completely subverted northern and national urban hierarchies, as did that of Manchester, and the two towns moved from a lowly place in the national scheme of things, to (on one reckoning) sixth and seventh place nationally in 1750, and second and third in 1801, when Leeds and newly risen Sheffield had also joined Newcastle among the ten most populous towns in England.[54]

Manchester came to preside over a distinctive urban network of its own, based on organising the production and distribution of (above all) cotton goods over an area of southern and eastern Lancashire for which it became a political and cultural as well as an economic metropolis. The twin towns of Manchester and Salford increased their combined population perhaps thirtyfold, to well over 90,000. Within what had become Manchester's sphere of influence were other towns whose populations grew more than tenfold to top 10,000 by 1801. Most impressively, Stockport became Cheshire's most populous town, eclipsing Chester itself, and combining textiles and hat manufacture with a pioneering

[52] J. Belchem, ed., *Popular Politics, Riot and Labour* (Liverpool, 1992).

[53] P. G. E. Clemens, 'The rise of Liverpool 1665–1750', *Ec. HR*, 2nd series, 29 (1976), 211–25; J. Langton, 'Liverpool and its hinterland in the late eighteenth century', in B. L. Anderson and P. J. M. Stoney, eds., *Commerce, Industry and Transport* (Liverpool, 1983). On this general theme see also J. Stobart, 'The spatial organization of a regional economy: central places in North-West England in the early eighteenth century', *Journal of Historical Geography*, 22 (1996), 147–59.

[54] E. A. Wrigley, *People, Cities and Wealth* (Oxford, 1987), pp. 160–1, table 7.1.

role in the development of urban cotton factories, especially for high-quality muslins. Oldham combined textiles and hatting with coal mining and early cotton-spinning factories, while Blackburn remained predominantly a weaving centre.[55] Significantly, Blackburn shifted its commercial allegiance from London to Manchester during the eighteenth century, reflecting a general decline in direct metropolitan influence in this part of the North; and this was followed by accelerated growth: 'It was formerly the centre of the fabrics sent to London for printing, called *Blackburn greys*, which were plains of linen warp shot with cotton. Since so much of the printing has been done near Manchester, the Blackburn manufacturers have gone more into the making of calicoes.'[56] Manchester's influence became newly important relatively late in the eighteenth century in several other Lancashire towns: indeed, Rochdale still looked to 'the Yorkshire merchants' or to its own marketing endeavours to sell its woollens in the 1790s, when Haslingden was only just emerging from Rochdale's own tutelage. Bolton was Manchester's largest satellite town in 1801, with nearly 18,000 inhabitants, and by the 1790s its trade was firmly channelled through Manchester; but in an earlier generation it had dominated its surroundings more directly, and its merchants had been instrumental in bringing the cotton industry to Bury. Preston, meanwhile, was still an agricultural produce market and centre for law courts, administration and county society until the cotton industry arrived in earnest at the end of the century.[57] It was in the last quarter of the eighteenth century that Manchester's hegemony spread and became more marked, bringing the cotton industry in its train and helping to stimulate urban growth on a novel scale and at unprecedented speed.

The population figures collected by Bishop Porteous of Chester for his visitation in 1778, coupled with a fashion for local censuses in the 1770s, enable us to chart this acceleration. Manchester itself more than trebled its population, from a base of well over 20,000; four other towns which developed or emerged in its orbit grew at a similar rate (Burnley, Chorley, Bury and Stockport); and five others more than doubled in size (Bolton, Haslingden and Blackburn, followed by Preston and Wigan on the western fringes of the textile belt).[58] These last two were old-established towns but late developers in terms of rapid population growth and the arrival of the cotton industry, and it may be relevant that they were the only old corporate boroughs (and the only parliamentary boroughs) among the dynamic towns which were coming under Manchester's stimulus. Attempts at regulating trade within and around these corporate towns were

[55] R. Lloyd-Jones and M. J. Lewis, *Manchester in the Age of the Factory* (London, 1988); R. Glen, *Urban Workers in the Early Industrial Revolution* (London, 1984); J. Foster, *Class Struggle and the Industrial Revolution* (London, 1974).

[56] J. Aikin, *A Description of the Country from Thirty to Forty Miles around Manchester* (London, 1795; repr., Newton Abbot, 1968), p. 270.

[57] *Ibid.*, pp. 248–9, 263, 267, 276–7, 279, 283–7.

[58] Stobart, 'Eighteenth-century revolution?', p. 40, table 3.

certainly made in the eighteenth century, and this may have held them back, lending some substance to the theory of a positive relationship between lack of formal urban government and ability to take up the new opportunities of the eighteenth century. Contemporaries agreed, and although some historians have been more sceptical in general terms, throughout the emergent cotton district urban government remained rudimentary at the turn of the century.[59] What is clear is the shift in the urban hierarchy of Cheshire and Lancashire south of the Ribble, as an existing tendency for the largest and fastest-growing towns to be concentrated into the eastern half of Lancashire, around Manchester, was greatly accentuated during these years.[60] It was not universal: Colne, for example, grew relatively slowly at this time, with the Craven cattle trade directing its gaze into Yorkshire, and cotton only just appearing on the scene in the 1790s.[61] But the dominant theme showed urbanisation marching in step with the rise of the cotton industry. We should also emphasise that much population growth was still spread thickly through an industrialising countryside, and that town boundaries remained difficult to delineate as small farms and hamlets proliferated on the fringes of towns and in between them.[62] But this was a crucial transitional period in the urban history of what was becoming the 'Manchester region', even though Manchester's own influence was passed on through intermediate towns, while relationships between the rural and the urban remained reciprocal and hard to disentangle.

The urban networks of the clothmaking West Riding were also taking firm shape between the Restoration and the first census; but already the Manchester region was pulling ahead, stimulated by the elasticity of demand for cotton goods and the related proximity of Liverpool and direct access to the Atlantic economy. Leeds grew fifteenfold to pass the 50,000 mark, but the dominant towns of the other cloth producing districts (Halifax for kerseys and worsteds, Huddersfield for narrow cloth and fancy woollens, Bradford for white cloth and worsteds) still hovered between 7,000 and 13,000 inhabitants, with Bradford beginning to take the lead; but none had caught up with York, and Wakefield's 10,581 inhabitants in 1801 left it still on a par with these upstart competitors to its west.[63] Subordinate settlements pulled together 2,000, 3,000 or 4,000 people, especially around Leeds itself, where Pudsey, Mirfield, Ossett, Heckmondwyke and Otley were on the cusp between large industrial villages and small straggling towns; but substantial places of the future such as Dewsbury and Batley had yet to evolve their distinctive specialisms. The urban networks of the West Riding were visibly in place by 1801, but they lacked the scale and articulation of the Lancashire

[59] P. J. Corfield, *The Impact of English Towns 1700–1800* (Oxford, 1982), pp. 91–3.

[60] Stobart, 'Eighteenth-century revolution?', pp. 40–4.

[61] Aikin, *Description*, p. 279.

[62] A. P. Wadsworth and J. de L. Mann, *The Cotton Trade and Industrial Lancashire 1600–1780* (Manchester, 1931; repr., 1965); Walton, 'Proto-industrialization'.

[63] Hudson, *Genesis*, pp. 26–8.

cotton town system. It took longer for the proto-industrial village networks, sprawling across the gritty upland countryside and linked by packhorse tracks with the cloth and piece halls of the larger towns, to cross the threshold into their own version of urbanity.[64]

Tyneside and the neighbouring coalfield had developed a more compact, highly articulated urban system, geared above all to satisfying London's hunger for coal. In contrast with Liverpool, however, Newcastle found its growth outpaced by its immediate neighbours. Its population, and that of Gateshead on the opposite bank of the Tyne, nearly trebled during the 'long' eighteenth century, reaching a combined figure of over 40,000; but North Shields grew ninefold to top 7,000 while Tynemouth and South Shields accumulated five-figure populations from tiny beginnings. The 'coaly Tyne' was losing ground to the Wear in urban growth terms: Sunderland's population multiplied twentyfold to reach 25,000 as its coal trade and shipbuilding activities grew to rival Newcastle's.[65] Further south in County Durham the county town itself rediscovered the dynamism it had lost in the post-Reformation century, and the development of mining and transport innovation allowed Stockton, Darlington, Bishop Auckland and Barnard Castle to enjoy uncannily similar growth rates as their populations trebled from small beginnings, while only Yarm stagnated as its lucrative position as the lowest crossing-point on the Tees was outflanked by Stockton's new bridge from 1771. This in turn made Stockton into a nodal point for expanding long-distance road carrier services.[66]

The leading seaports of Yorkshire also made headway as they supplied vessels to the coal trade, developed whaling and fishing industries and participated in an expansive North Sea economy which was only overshadowed by the astonishing growth of Liverpool on the opposite coast. Hull, with its improving waterway access to a developing hinterland, more than quadrupled its population to nearly 30,000, rivalling Newcastle and keeping ahead of Sunderland, while Whitby showed similar dynamism from small beginnings and Scarborough, with its fashionable spa-goers and sea-bathers, was not far behind. The latter two towns lacked improvable waterways to industrial hinterlands, however, as even Malton's comfortable but comparatively modest expansion was not echoed elsewhere; and Bridlington, Yorkshire's fourth port, seems actually to have lost population over the period, although Noble sees some evidence of growth between about 1720 and 1850. In East Yorkshire generally only four 'country towns' are said to have been 'dynamic' during this period, while five were 'expanding'; but nine were merely 'stable' and five declined for most if not

64 Gregory, *Regional Transformation*; J. Lawson, *Progress in Pudsey* (Firle, 1978), for the flavour of life in one of these industrial villages in transition.

65 T. Corfe, *History of Sunderland* (Gateshead, 1973), pp. 48–50.

66 J. W. Wardell, *A History of Yarm* (Sunderland, 1957), p. 118; D. Aldcroft and M. Freeman, eds., *Transport in the Industrial Revolution* (Manchester, 1983), pp. 90–1.

all of the period: this kind of experience was common in areas without significant industrial development but with major growth in one or two big towns.[67]

The most dramatic episode of urban expansion on the coasts of northern England, Liverpool and Tyneside apart, came on the Irish Sea in west Cumberland, where towns laid out by landowning families emerged on virgin sites, competing with each other to export coal to the hungry markets of Ireland. Whitehaven, the largest of these new towns, was also founded earliest, in the mid-seventeenth century. It had the most powerful patrons, the Lowther family, and the most diverse economy, with a long-standing interest in tobacco and other colonial goods. The Curwens' Workington and the Senhouses' Maryport were later developers – from the mid-eighteenth century, in earnest – whose promoters had slimmer purses and less political clout. But Whitehaven itself seems to have peaked in about 1785, when its population reached 16,000, and with the loss of the colonial trade it fell back to just over 10,000 in 1801. The striking aspects of growth on this coastline involved suddenness rather than scale, and the total population of the three main ports in 1801 was less than 20,000: more impressive than Teesside but far less so than Wearside or Tyneside. Difficult harbours which required disproportionate expenditure to keep up with rising optimum ship sizes, and the lack of an accessible or developing hinterland, helped to place a ceiling on growth in this remote and windswept area.[68]

West Cumberland's relative dynamism is set in perspective by the limited scale of urban growth in Carlisle's orbit (although Carlisle more than doubled its population to approach 10,000 and there was substantial percentage growth from small beginnings in the surrounding market towns) and by the similar record of the emergent Morecambe Bay urban network. Lancaster's population doubled during the eighteenth century, but it was stagnating at just short of 10,000 at the turn of the century as the colonial trade faltered and Preston took over as the county's social and (in some respects) administrative centre.[69] Kendal's growth in the eighteenth century was even more impressive, as its population more than trebled to reach 8,000 or so during the half-century after 1730. Elsewhere in this district only Ulverston showed much dynamism, albeit on a small scale, with its new ship canal at the end of the century and its social amenities for the prospering lowland yeomen and rural industries of the Furness district. There was modest urban prosperity here, perhaps, but not much growth; and some small towns in the orbit of Lancaster and Kendal actually declined during this period.

[67] Jackson, *Hull*; S. McIntyre, 'Towns as health and pleasure resorts' (DPhil thesis, University of Oxford, 1973); Noble, 'Growth and development', pp. 16–17.

[68] Beckett, *Coal and Tobacco*; Collier and Pearson, *Whitehaven*, pp. 1–4; E. Hughes, *North Country Life in the Eighteenth Century*, (Oxford, 1965) vol. II, chs. 2–4; R. Millward, 'The Cumbrian town between 1600 and 1800', in Chalklin and Havinden, eds., *Rural Change*.

[69] Constantine *et al.*, *Lancaster*, p. 126.

Patterns of this sort were widespread in the Cumbrian and Yorkshire uplands, and the epoch of market town formation seems to have ended in the late seventeenth century, in northern England as elsewhere.[70]

Away from Liverpool and the textile towns, indeed, the most spectacular urban growth in the North was in Sheffield, which increased its population more than twentyfold to reach a census figure of 45,755 in 1801. Here as in many places growth began in earnest in the early eighteenth century. The population of the central, most clearly urban, township quadrupled between 1736, when a local census was taken, and 1801. The increased population was recruited overwhelmingly from within the extensive parish and from Hallamshire (a south Yorkshire identity which had meaning for contemporaries) and north Derbyshire. Sheffield was surrounded by industrial villages, but its specialisms in cutlery and toolmaking were *sui generis* and it did not spawn an urban network as such, although Rotherham and Barnsley were growing into small towns in their own right. Significantly, the small upland centre of Penistone was able to revive its chartered market in 1699, and to sustain it thereafter, on the basis of its isolation from alternatives which included Sheffield as well as Barnsley and Huddersfield.[71]

(vi) NINETEENTH-CENTURY DEVELOPMENTS AND CONCLUDING THOUGHTS

By 1801, then, the urban networks which were apparent in the 1840s were already in being. Above all they were creations of the eighteenth century, building on very limited earlier foundations; and development accelerated sharply in the latter years of the century, as patterns formed and clarified and the larger towns grew in unprecedented ways in both scale and (usually) local and subregional influence. Existing large towns continued to set the pace between 1801 and 1841: Liverpool and Manchester each added more than 200,000 people in forty years, and Leeds 100,000. Some relatively late developers burst through to dominate their surroundings: Bradford added 43,000 to its population, Preston added nearly 40,000 and quadrupled its numbers as it embraced the cotton industry with belated enthusiasm, and the 'silk town' of Macclesfield trebled its population to over 30,000.[72] Formal local government institutions proliferated, as towns acquired improvement commissioners to deal with basic urban amenities, sometimes supplementing existing corporations; and the Municipal

[70] Marshall, 'Kendal'; Borwick, 'English provincial society'; J. Chartres, 'The market town', in J. Thirsk, ed., *Ag.HEW*, vol. v (Cambridge, 1985), pp. 409–13.

[71] Hey, *Blades*, ch. 3; D. Hey, *Packmen, Carriers and Packhorse Roads* (Leicester, 1980), pp. 164–7.

[72] Koditschek, *Class Formation*; M. Anderson, *Family Structure in Nineteenth-Century Lancashire* (Cambridge, 1971), which shows the enduring importance of short-distance migration into Preston; G. Malmgreen, *Silk Town* (Hull, 1985).

Corporations Act of 1835 precipitated incorporation in Manchester and Bolton three years later, swelling the number of chartered boroughs in the region to twenty-eight.[73] Other swollen, undergoverned industrial towns were to follow suit. Such initiatives responded in part to the sheer scale and pace of such growth, which created novel problems of housing, public health, amenity and order which were particularly arresting in Bradford and Liverpool, but became endemic everywhere. Northern industrial towns were also prominent beneficiaries of the Reform Act of 1832, as these new interests were given what turned out to be a token voice in the House of Commons. The act added twenty-three new parliamentary boroughs in the North (there had been twenty-five previously), and seven in Yorkshire (five in the West Riding textile belt). The places which orchestrated local industries also became centres for political protest, most obviously in the case of Manchester where demonstrators regularly marched in from the surrounding industrial settlements; and they were also crucibles in which a new popular culture of the printed word was forged through provincial newspapers and dialect literature.[74] The age of coal, canals and later railways, of factories and fear of disease, immorality, crime and unrest, of world markets and accentuated trade cycles, was ushered in from the turn of the eighteenth and nineteenth centuries; and a comparative study of urban networks in the North shows clearly how the strongest influence for sustained, large-scale urban growth was the cotton industry. The new century brought qualitative transformations in social relations. But they were superimposed on urban networks which had been crafted in an earlier (and resilient, and persistent) economy, founded on muscle and sinew, wind and water, workshops and small communities. The urban revolution in northern England (there certainly was one), like the Industrial Revolution with which it marched in step, had deep roots which remained enduringly influential as the pace of change quickened, towns became cities and villages became towns. The most arresting and spectacular developments were reserved for the nineteenth century, but they should not be allowed to obscure the formative significance of what had gone before.

[73] Corfield, *Impact of English Towns*, p. 152, discusses the distinctive case of Sheffield, where the town and church trusts came to provide most of the benefits of incorporation without a charter.

[74] *Manchester Region History Review*, Peterloo anniversary issue, 1989; D. Read, *Press and People 1790–1850* (London, 1961); M. Vicinus, *The Industrial Muse* (London, 1974); P. Joyce, *Visions of the People* (Cambridge, 1991).

· 3 ·

Wales

PHILIP JENKINS

THE CHAPTER examines a paradox: towns played a very significant role in Welsh social and economic life, but before about 1760, the towns that mattered most were not located on Welsh soil. This account will describe the limited importance of the specifically Welsh towns, and the strikingly small urban population of the principality. It will then discuss the networks that did exist in terms of the English regional capitals, especially Bristol, Shrewsbury and Chester; and finally, show how a distinctively Welsh urban network appeared in the south-eastern parts of the country by the end of the eighteenth century.[1]

(i) WELSH URBAN STRUCTURE 1540–1750

Welsh towns were deceptively numerous. As Matthew Griffiths remarks, 'medieval Wales had been endowed with far more boroughs and market centres than its economy could justify', the abundance reflecting the need to attract settlers, and many towns withered within a century or two of creation. Nor could they long maintain their position as islands of Norman or English influence, and Ralph A. Griffiths has shown how the later medieval boroughs became increasingly integrated into rural Welsh society. By 1540, a lengthy process of winnowing had left a small number of thriving urban centres, alongside dozens of places lacking the social or economic basis to justify their urban pretensions.

Some fifty or sixty towns in Tudor and Stuart Wales held regular markets, but we reach this figure only by including communities with 200 or 300 people. In 1756, William Owen's *Authentic Account* cited fairs at 167 centres throughout the principality, seventy of which were located in the three shires of Carmarthen,

[1] H. Carter, *The Towns of Wales*, 2nd edn (Cardiff, 1966); H. Carter, *Urban Essays: Studies in the Geography of Wales* (London, 1970); R. A. Griffiths, ed., *Boroughs of Medieval Wales* (Cardiff, 1978).

Denbigh and Caernarvon. Most of these sites were tiny and obscure, and many had only a single fair day listed each year. Using more exacting standards of definition, in Tudor Wales we find barely a dozen 'real' towns with 1,000 people or more, a small increase from the nine which met this criterion in 1400.[2]

The largest communities were Wrexham, Carmarthen, Brecon and Haverfordwest, all of which had lengthy histories and proud corporate traditions, and by 1550 probably had populations of around 2,000 each.[3] There were perhaps another eight settlements with 1,000 or more people, including Tenby, Swansea, Cardiff, Monmouth, Caernarvon, Denbigh, and probably Kidwelly and Knighton.[4] However, several of the county towns were extremely modest places, notably Flint and Cardigan.

To speak of 'urban' history in Wales before the nineteenth century is perhaps to misuse the term. Even if we include the very small towns (200 people or more), the 'urban' proportion of the population of Tudor or Stuart Wales was barely 11 per cent. The Welsh town population was little greater in the early eighteenth century than 400 years previously. Populations did grow in the seventeenth century, and quite sharply in the eighteenth, but even after decades of industrialisation, the urban portion of the landscape was less than awe-inspiring. Even by 1801, there were only twelve towns which could claim 2,000 or more inhabitants, and the largest community in Wales had around 8,000 people. By the standards of contemporary England, the only settlements in Wales which then rose above the level of 'small towns' were Swansea, Carmarthen and Merthyr Tydfil, and these only barely.

There was an ancient genre of demeaning comments about the overgrown villages that passed for towns in Wales, from Celia Fiennes' Flint ('a very ragged place') to the comparison of Dolgellau's streets with those of a grim dungeon.[5] Benjamin Heath Malkin wrote typically in 1803 that Builth 'exhibits that air of impoverished and dilapidated antiquity which so universally bespeaks the negligent and unambitious character of a thinly peopled country'. He further remarked that 'Welsh towns are universally censured by strangers for the

[2] M. Griffiths, 'Country and town', in T. Herbert and G. E. Jones, eds., *Tudor Wales* (Cardiff, 1988), p. 74; I. Soulsby, *The Towns of Wales* (Chichester, 1983).

[3] A. H. Dodd, ed., *A History of Wrexham Denbighshire* (Wrexham, 1957); G. Roberts, *Aspects of Welsh History* (Cardiff, 1969); B. G. Charles, ed., *A Calendar of the Records of the Borough of Haverfordwest* (Cardiff, 1967); W. S. K. Thomas, *Brecon c. 1093–1600: An Illustrated History* (Llandyssul, 1991); E. G. Parry, 'Brecon: occupations and society', *Brycheiniog*, 19 (1980–1).

[4] K. Kissack, *Monmouth: The Making of a County Town* (Monmouth, 1975); A. H. Dodd, *History of Caernarvonshire from the Thirteenth Century to 1900* (Caernarvon, 1968); W. Rees, *Cardiff* (Cardiff, 1969); M. I. Williams, 'Cardiff: its people and its trade', *Morgannwg*, 7 (1963). Swansea is one of the best covered of the Welsh boroughs: see for example W. S. K. Thomas, *The History of Swansea: From Rover Settlement to the Restoration* (Llandyssul, 1990); G. Williams, ed., *Swansea: An Illustrated History* (Swansea, 1990); D. T. Williams, *The Economic Development of Swansea* (Cardiff, 1940).

[5] G. H. Jenkins, *The Foundations of Modern Wales: Wales 1642–1780* (Oxford, 1987), p. 289.

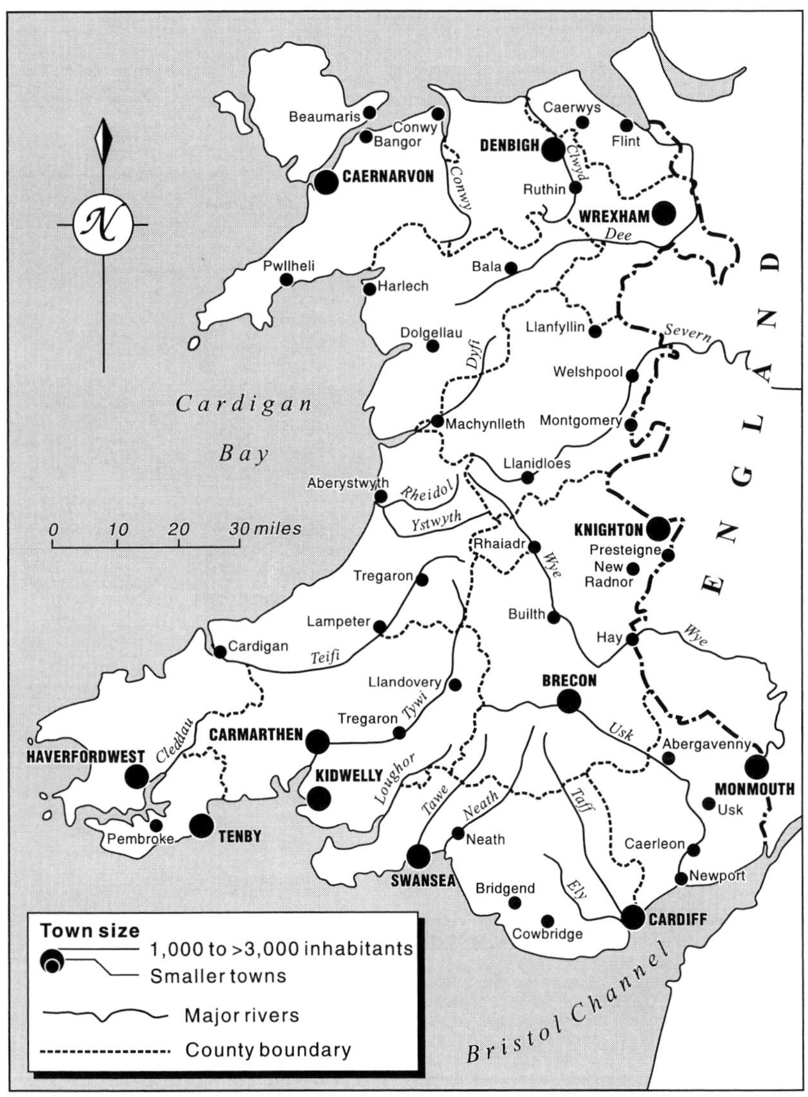

Map 3.1 Towns in Wales 1550

inelegance and inconvenience of their houses.'[6] Defoe's portrayal of Carmarthen as 'the London of Wales' (with 3,000 people) can best be described as charitable.[7] Malkin commented of the 'little London' phrase that 'In what the resemblance consists, I could not discover.'[8]

Many of the fifty or so towns were, misleadingly, 'parliamentary boroughs', in the sense that Welsh borough members after the Act of Union were elected by syndicates of the boroughs within a given county, the exact list of qualified towns varying wildly according to political fortune. This opened the way to litigation and political interference, ensuring enormous and persistent gentry interference with corporate life and borough institutions. In Restoration Monmouthshire, for example, boroughs contributing to the election of a member included Monmouth, Newport, Chepstow, Usk and Abergavenny, but in no election between 1679 and 1689 was exactly the same roster of towns involved: it might be one borough in one election year, five the next, two the following. In Montgomeryshire, participating electors originally included the burgesses of Montgomery, Welshpool, Llanidloes and Llanfyllin, until a series of partisan decisions in parliament reduced the franchise to Montgomery alone. As a result, contributory boroughs might be tiny or defunct places, like Loughor in west Glamorgan.[9] Of all the Welsh boroughs, only Haverfordwest consistently elected a member in its own right. The puny size of the towns inevitably limited their political impact.

Nor did the Welsh towns fall within a single coherent social or economic region, an inevitable consequence of the major regional distinctions within Wales. Much of the country is made up of sparsely populated mountainous areas, providing most towns with a relatively poor hinterland on which to draw. Around 1600, no town with a population of over 500 was to be found in the large empty quadrilateral bounded by Cardigan, Builth, Ruthin and Caernarvon, though a dozen or so claimed 200 or 300 residents apiece. At the same time, there were pockets of great fertility and prosperity, which in early modern times supported ports and market towns of great local significance. South Pembrokeshire was home to flourishing market towns at Haverfordwest, Pembroke and Tenby, and there were similar regions in the Vale of Tywi, the Vale of Glamorgan, in southern Monmouthshire and the eastern hundreds of Denbighshire and Montgomeryshire.

(ii) PATTERNS OF TRADE AND COMMUNICATION

The peculiar nature of the Welsh landscape put a high premium on sea communications, so that these towns were commonly linked to three English-based

[6] H. Carter, 'The growth and decline of Welsh towns', in D. Moore, ed., *Wales in the Eighteenth Century* (Swansea, 1976), pp. 48–50. [7] Jenkins, *The Foundations of Modern Wales*, pp. 116–18.

[8] Carter, 'The growth and decline of Welsh towns', 60.

[9] P. Jenkins, *A History of Modern Wales 1536–1990* (London, 1992), p. 168.

regions and metropolitan networks. Bristol and Chester were the key players in the sixteenth and seventeenth centuries, with Liverpool rising to prominence in the eighteenth. Shrewsbury played a similarly dominant role in mid-Wales. The threefold division of Wales was reinforced by the nature of the three major roads within the principality. One led from Chester to Caernarvon along the northern coast; one from Hereford to Brecon and Carmarthen, and thence to St David's; while a third was the southern coastal route, through Newport, Cardiff and Swansea, and thence to Carmarthen and points west. In addition, the towns of both the northern and southern littorals looked outside the island of Britain for commercial and social links, to the ancient sea routes of the Irish Sea. Swansea and the Pembrokeshire boroughs had historic trading links with southern Ireland, particularly to Cork, Lismore and Munster, while northern ports looked to Leinster. In the eighteenth century, Dublin became a metropolitan centre in its own right for the landed families of Anglesey and Gwynedd.[10]

Of the largest towns in the sixteenth century, the Bristol Channel trade was crucial for the survival of Cardiff, Swansea, Kidwelly, Carmarthen, Tenby and Haverfordwest. It is useful to see each of these towns not as a local capital in its own right, but as subordinate communities within the larger Bristol region. This would then place smaller settlements as Chepstow, Usk, Newport, Neath, Llanelli and Pembroke at a tertiary level.[11] These southern towns traded extensively both with each other, and with the ports on the other side of the 'Severn Sea', with centres like Minehead, Ilfracombe, Barnstaple and Bideford. The four Bristol-oriented shires of South Wales enjoyed the most vigorous commercial life in the principality, so that about 1600, these counties had half the weekly market days in the whole of Wales. In the Elizabethan period, there were over 240 Welsh fairs, almost 60 per cent of which were held in the southern coastal shires, together with Cardigan.[12] Local economic life was also based on the numerous small ports or creeks which traded with the larger coastal towns: there were a dozen such petty harbours and trading villages in Glamorgan, ten in Pembrokeshire. In the north, too, ships could be found at a dozen locations in Caernarvonshire besides Caernarvon itself.

The towns of North Wales similarly looked to Chester as their regional capital, especially the three substantial communities of Wrexham, Denbigh and Caernarvon, but also smaller centres like Conway, Bangor and Beaumaris. This orientation was reflected in social patterns, so that landed and mercantile families tended to be closely intermarried with their counterparts in Cheshire and

[10] P. Jenkins, 'South Wales and Munster in the eighteenth century', *Journal of the Cork Historical and Archaeological Society*, 34 (1979), 95–101; G. E. Mingay, ed., *Ag.HEW*, vol. VI (Cambridge, 1989).

[11] J. W. Dawson, *Commerce and Customs: A History of the Ports of Newport and Caerleon* (Newport, 1932); E. Jenkins, ed., *Neath: A Symposium* (Neath, 1974); D. R. Phillips, *History of the Vale of Neath* (Swansea, 1925); George Eaton, *A History of Neath* (Swansea, 1987); E. L. Chappell, *History of the Port of Cardiff*, 2nd edn (Cardiff, 1994).

[12] G. Williams, *Recovery, Reorientation and Reformation: Wales 1415–1642* (Oxford, 1987), pp. 55–89.

Staffordshire, with hardly any links to families in southern Wales. Meanwhile, the shires of the Welsh heartland looked to the English Midlands: to Shrewsbury, and to a lesser extent Hereford and Ludlow. Both Shrewsbury and Oswestry had a strong Welsh presence, which on market days allowed them to claim at least temporarily the position of the premier Welsh town. Under the later Stuarts, Shrewsbury was the location of the first Welsh printing press, decades before any comparable endeavour on Welsh soil.[13] Brecon was the most significant of the heartland centres, but there were also market towns of great local importance, like Machynlleth and Llanidloes, which served an enormous rural hinterland. Monmouthshire communities like Monmouth, Abergavenny and Usk looked both to Bristol and to southern border cities like Hereford and Gloucester.

Both north and south, Welsh towns dealt mainly in the agricultural products of their immediate regions, chiefly cattle and wool in the sixteenth century, but corn became a leading item of southern trade by the 1650s. Well into Victorian times, Bristol served as an endlessly hungry market for Welsh butter and cheese. The pastoral emphasis of the local hinterlands was reflected in the guild life of larger boroughs like Brecon, Carmarthen and Haverfordwest, where the main 'leather and allied' trades included glovers, tanners and saddlers. At Carmarthen about 1550, there was 'great passage of leather, tallow and hides by reason of the merchants'. In the Welsh heartland, cattle droving was the economic basis for towns like Llandovery and Builth Wells. In the mid-eighteenth century, the towns with the largest and most diverse fairs and the greatest numbers of fair days included Carmarthen, Talgarth, Trecastle and Llandovery. Lampeter, with six fair days annually, offered 'cattle, horses, pigs, sheep, pedlar's ware'; Brecon had 'leather, hops, cattle, and all sorts of commodities'.[14]

Throughout Wales, the wool trade was of great importance from the middle ages into the early nineteenth century. Though originally a southern specialty, the sixteenth century marked a decisive shift to North and mid-Wales, to Merionethshire, Montgomeryshire and parts of Denbighshire, regions dominated by the drapers of Shrewsbury. The Huguenot settlement in the 1680s further assisted the growth of industrial centres at Newtown, Llanidloes and Dolgellau.[15] This shift contributed to the prosperity of towns like Bala, the market for the Merionethshire stocking industry, and of Welshpool, which specialised in flannels. By the eighteenth century, woollen exports supported the growth of ports at Barmouth and Aberdyfi. Glanmor Williams aptly describes cloth and cattle as the 'twin pillars' of the whole rural economy, and this was equally true of the Welsh towns.[16]

[13] Jenkins, *The Foundations of Modern Wales*, pp. 215–17.

[14] Jenkins, *A History of Modern Wales*, pp. 31–4; the remark about Carmarthen is quoted in Griffiths, 'Country and town', p. 101. For fairs, see W. Owen, *An Authentic Account Published by the King's Authority of All the Fairs in England and Wales* . . . (London, 1756).

[15] J. G. Jenkins, 'The woollen industry', in Moore, ed., *Wales in the Eighteenth Century*, pp. 89–108.

[16] Williams, *Recovery, Reorientation and Reformation*, p. 83.

(iii) THE SOCIAL AND POLITICAL IMPACT OF TOWNS

There were other urban networks, involvement in which depended largely on class and social status. Prior to the Restoration, the towns relied on the patronage of local gentry as consumers of their goods, crafts and services, a connection that obviously depended on the prosperity of the local landowners. Gentry families were excellent customers in wealthy areas like the southern regions of Glamorgan, or Monmouthshire, far less so for their penurious counterparts in the western or upland shires like Cardigan or Merioneth. However, even this local custom was threatened by the tendency of wealthier landowners to satisfy their needs in London, where they usually wintered.

Though London initially drew custom away from the Welsh towns, the longer-term effects benefited them by encouraging the local imitation of London tastes and models. From the early eighteenth century, Welsh market towns were increasingly redeveloped to supply these new needs, with reproductions in miniature of the most fashionable theatres, assembly rooms, teahouses, pleasure gardens, civic buildings and race tracks.[17] These facilities were intended less for the magnates, who could indulge their metropolitan tastes at source, but for the lesser landed families and the network of stewards, lawyers, clergy and other professionals with which they overlapped so extensively. In economic life and industrial development, London acted as a metropolitan centre assisting or competing with local network capitals like Bristol or Shrewsbury. From the late seventeenth century, Bath also emerged as an extra-regional leisure centre for social elites, helping further to nationalise tastes and consumption patterns. For the landed elites of south Wales, Bath and the Bristol Hotwell served as the leisure towns which they lacked on Welsh soil, at least until the end of the eighteenth century.

Despite their small size, the towns had a major political and religious impact on the surrounding regions, as 'venues of elections, sessions, fairs, markets and other activities', and as transmission points for new ideas often stemming from a local capital like Bristol.[18] In the sixteenth century, towns like Carmarthen, Cardiff and Haverfordwest were long the only centres where Reformation sympathies made much headway, and the relative weakness of these communities explains the slow growth of Welsh Protestantism. In the Civil Wars, the parliamentarian loyalty of Pembroke, Tenby and Haverfordwest made Pembrokeshire oppose the king, with disastrous consequences for royalist war effort throughout Wales.[19] Elsewhere, nuclei of militant Puritan sentiment were found chiefly in Swansea, and in Wrexham, where dissent clearly derived from Chester. The ensuing war was a series of sieges of fortified towns, interspersed with regular scares that Welsh ports would be used for the massed landing of Irish armies.

[17] P. Jenkins, *The Making of a Ruling Class: The Glamorgan Gentry 1640–1790* (Cambridge, 1983).

[18] Williams, *Recovery, Reorientation and Reformation*, p. 395.

[19] Jenkins, *A History of Modern Wales*, pp. 124–32.

The parliamentarian capture of Bristol and Chester in 1645–6 virtually ended the royalist cause in both North and South Wales.

After the Restoration, Bristol's commercial influence in south Wales is neatly mapped by the distribution of dissenting religious groups and Quakers, and the Anglican gentry saw the greatest danger of Whiggish subversion in the southern towns: in Neath, Swansea, Pembroke and, most perilously of all, in riotous Carmarthen and Haverfordwest. The Whiggery of southern Pembrokeshire in the 1670s was explained by the 'frequent commerce' from Bristol to Milford and Haverfordwest.[20] In the eighteenth century, southern boroughs and coastal ports were the major transmission points for insurgent Wesleyan Methodism emanating from Bristol, a religious theme which appealed both to town elites and neighbouring gentry. The traditional boroughs continued to play an intermediary political role in the age of the Jacobins and even the Chartists.[21]

(iv) ECONOMIC REALIGNMENT AND URBAN CHANGE 1720–1800

Broader metropolitan regions also conditioned the emergence of newer industries which would fundamentally reshape Welsh urban structure. From the late seventeenth century, the use of coke in smelting iron placed a high premium on those areas in which coal and ore deposits were located close to easy water transport. This especially benefited the towns of western Glamorgan and eastern Carmarthenshire, in which there developed an interdependent network of coal mines, iron furnaces and non-ferrous industries, based in or near towns like Neath, Aberafan and Kidwelly. Much the most important was Swansea, which became a crucial industrial centre by the early Georgian period, and the capital of a local region in south-west Wales. Its population probably doubled in the second half of the eighteenth century. The non-ferrous industries depended on ores shipped from west Wales, where Aberystwyth now flourished, and from sources further afield in Ireland or even America.[22]

The new industrial networks derived both capital and industrial expertise from regional centres, above all Bristol in the south, and to a lesser extent Liverpool in the north.[23] This dependence also integrated Welsh towns and urban elites firmly into colonial networks. Welsh mercantile elites were involved in colonial ventures, privateering and landholding, while commercial links determined the attitudes of both gentry and merchants to imperial political issues of war and peace, commerce and slavery.

[20] T. Godwyn, *Phanatical Tenderness, or The Charity of the Nonconformists Exemplified* (London, 1684).

[21] D. J. V. Jones, *Before Rebecca* (London, 1973); D. Williams, *The Rebecca Riots* (Cardiff, 1955).

[22] Williams, ed., *Swansea*; D. T. Williams, *The Economic Development of Swansea* (Cardiff, 1940); P. Jenkins, 'Tory industrialism and town politics', *HJ*, 28 (1985), 103–23. Compare I. G. Jones, *Aberystwyth 1277–1977* (Aberystwyth, 1977).

[23] Jenkins, *A History of Modern Wales*, pp. 216–17.

By the late eighteenth century, the leading towns of Wales were still more or less those that had held this position in 1550, with Swansea, Carmarthen, Haverfordwest, Wrexham and Caernarvon all exceeding 3,500 people by 1801. However, some new centres were challenging the old. Denbigh failed to pose a serious challenge to the growth of Wrexham, Conway was finally eclipsed by Caernarvon, Brecon was giving way to Glamorgan communities like Swansea; while Beaumaris gave up the long struggle to compete both with Caernarvon, and with English ports like Liverpool. The thriving metal industries supported the rise of Aberystwyth to dominate Cardigan Bay. In Flintshire, the brass, copper and cotton enterprises of Holywell allowed it to become one of the few northern communities to compete with the industrial boom towns around Swansea Bay: its growth also proved the death-blow for nearby Caerwys.[24] In mid-Wales, Dolgellau prospered on the strength of the textile trade.

By the end of the century, the lively coastal and Irish Sea trade were sufficient to justify the creation of a number of planned towns, including Aberaeron on Cardigan Bay, and the Irish-oriented Milford Haven. The Pennant family built Port Penrhyn in order to make Bangor the crucial port for the new slate trade, which they had developed with the profits from Liverpool commerce.[25] Holyhead also boomed, briefly raising hopes in the early railway years that it might challenge Liverpool in the North Atlantic routes.[26] By 1800, a list of the dozen largest towns of Wales would omit such familiar Tudor names as Tenby, Kidwelly and Monmouth, but now included burgeoning new centres like Dolgellau, Aberystwyth, Welshpool, Holywell and the ultimate industrial upstart, Merthyr Tydfil.

The second half of the century was a time of widespread progress throughout the established towns, marked not only by improvements intended to foster economic growth, but also by a general movement towards 'civility'. In the former category, we find, for example, the extensive population growth permitted by the post-1760 enclosures at Swansea, the appearance of banking ventures in the southern towns, some new fairs and the beginnings of road improvements in the border country. In the realm of urban progress, we might point to the appearance of the Welsh printing industry at Carmarthen in the 1720s, and Cowbridge in the 1770s; the spread of cultural societies, book societies and libraries; and the creation of a well-recognised entertainment circuit travelled regularly by theatre companies and lecturers.[27] There were even some early attempts to rid the streets of the most noisome threats to public health and comfort. Cardiff, Swansea and Bridgend all tried to imitate London paving and

[24] Jenkins, *The Foundations of Modern Wales*, pp. 285–9.

[25] M. Elis-Williams, *Bangor: The Nineteenth Century Shipbuilders and Shipowners of Bangor* (Caernarvon, 1988); compare L. Lloyd, *The Port of Caernarfon 1793–1900* (Harlech, 1989).

[26] Jenkins, *A History of Modern Wales*, p. 245.

[27] C. Price, *The English Theatre in Wales* (Cardiff, 1948); Jenkins, *The Making of a Ruling Class*; D. W. Howell, *Patriarchs and Parasites* (Cardiff, 1986).

lighting in the 1760s and 1770s, and many towns acquired impressive new town halls, of which Montgomery's provides a good example. Though overwhelmed by later building elsewhere, the comfortable townscape of Georgian Wales survived until recently in the streets of Welshpool and Llanfyllin. Swansea's new metropolitan role was suggested by the appearance here of the first indigenous Welsh newspaper, the *Cambrian* (1804), followed within a decade by the first Welsh-language newspaper. The very name of the *Cambrian* suggests its aspirations to speak for the whole nation; though in 1810, this Whiggish organ was challenged by the Tory *Carmarthen Journal*.[28]

Though not an industrial town, the progress of improvement is suggested by Cowbridge, which stood in perhaps the most prosperous and gentrified landscape found in Wales, and which was long known for its grammar school and gentry social gatherings. In the 1760s and 1770s, it developed races, a book society and an assembly room, and by 1774 was praised for its 'broad and handsome' main street.[29] Monmouth similarly aspired to improve itself to attract respectable visitors from near and far. By the 1780s, every large or mid-sized town could offer at least one substantial inn as good as those of South-East England, local landmarks like the Bear at Cowbridge, the Mackworth Arms at Swansea or the Red Lion at Llandeilo. As Arthur Young remarked, good roads and inns were essential to the 'grand chain of prosperity', and the existence of this infrastructure encouraged the opening of Wales to tourism from about 1770, following the discovery of the 'picturesque'. Tourism within Britain reached a new height with the limitations on travel during the French wars after 1793. This social trend became a factor encouraging town growth, indicated by the Weymouth-inspired villas and resort facilities that made Regency Swansea 'the Brighton of Wales'.[30] Sea-bathing enjoyed a vogue at Aberystwyth and Tenby, while there was a vogue for aspiring spas like Llandrindod Wells, where an innovative hotel appeared around 1749. The presence or proximity of historical monuments and (ideally) castles was a boon for inns and shops in otherwise fading centres like Caerphilly and Kidwelly.

Masonic lodges provide a useful index of the dissemination of a town-based social and political fad, in which professional and middle-class groups participated alongside landed gentry.[31] The first Welsh lodge appeared at Carmarthen in 1726, and fourteen more followed between 1741 and 1770, all founded in either traditional or new towns, and generally meeting at one of the new inns. Most were also linked to recent economic and industrial expansion, with a defi-

[28] Jenkins, *The Making of a Ruling Class*, p. 247; R. Haslam, *The Buildings of Wales: Powys* (London, 1979); A. G. Jones, *Press, Politics and Society: A History of Journalism in Wales* (Cardiff, 1993).

[29] Jenkins, *The Making of a Ruling Class*; P. Riden, *Cowbridge Trades and Tradesmen 1660–1750* (Cardiff, 1981). [30] D. Boorman, *The Brighton of Wales* (Swansea, 1986).

[31] P. Jenkins, 'Jacobites and Freemasons in eighteenth century Wales', *Welsh History Review*, 9 (1979), 391–406.

nite concentration in the south and east. Carmarthen and Brecon each had two lodges, while other centres included Haverfordwest, Cardiff, Cowbridge, Bridgend, Swansea, Newport, Monmouth, Brecon, Dolgellau, Welshpool, Holyhead and Holywell.

(v) INDUSTRY AND URBAN GROWTH 1790–1840

These social innovations were modest when set aside the far larger developments that would transform Welsh urban structure, causing both a massive increase in the population of existing communities, and a remarkable wave of urban growth in areas that had hitherto lacked significant settlements of any size. These changes arose from factors far beyond the borders of Wales, above all the successive wars and international crises in which the British nation-state found itself engaged between 1740 and 1815. These events increased still further Welsh commitment to an imperial/colonial economic framework that depended largely on naval success, and which drew the Welsh towns into a war economy based on the production of iron, copper, tinplate, lead and brass, and the coal required to sustain these industries.

Population growth and urban development were very marked in south-east Wales between about 1780 and 1840. Initially, some established towns benefited from this growth, and by 1800 the populations of Carmarthen and Swansea both approached 6,000, a level never before reached by any urban community in Wales. By 1800, west Glamorgan was the world centre for copper smelting, and although much of the development came in neighbouring industrial villages like Landore and Llangyfelach, the town of Swansea inevitably benefited.[32] The successes of the Swansea region were symbolised by the creation of a new industrial community at Morriston, one of several innovative town-planning measures at the turn of the century. However, these western towns were being challenged and soon surpassed by the new urban centres emerging in the eastern uplands of Glamorgan and the western regions of Monmouthshire, in what had only recently been a remote pastoral hill country. Iron furnaces proliferated here from the 1760s, and by the 1820s, south-east Wales supplied about 40 per cent of British iron production.[33]

The heart of the new growth was in the four parishes of Merthyr Tydfil, Aberdare, Bedwellty and Aberystruth, where a series of unchartered settlements soon dwarfed the older corporate towns. By 1801, Merthyr Tydfil (Merthyr-

[32] Jenkins, *The Foundations of Modern Wales*, p. 293; Jenkins, *A History of Modern Wales*, pp. 211–35.

[33] Jenkins, *A History of Modern Wales*, p. 221. C. Evans, *The Labyrinth of Flames: Work and Social Conflict in Early Industrial Merthyr Tydfil* (Cardiff, 1993); Neil Evans, 'The urbanization of Welsh society', in T. Herbert and G. E. Jones, eds., *People and Protest: Wales 1815–1880* (Cardiff, 1988), pp. 7–38; Paul Jenkins, *Twenty by Fourteen: A History of the South Wales Tinplate Industry, 1700–1961* (Llandysul, 1995).

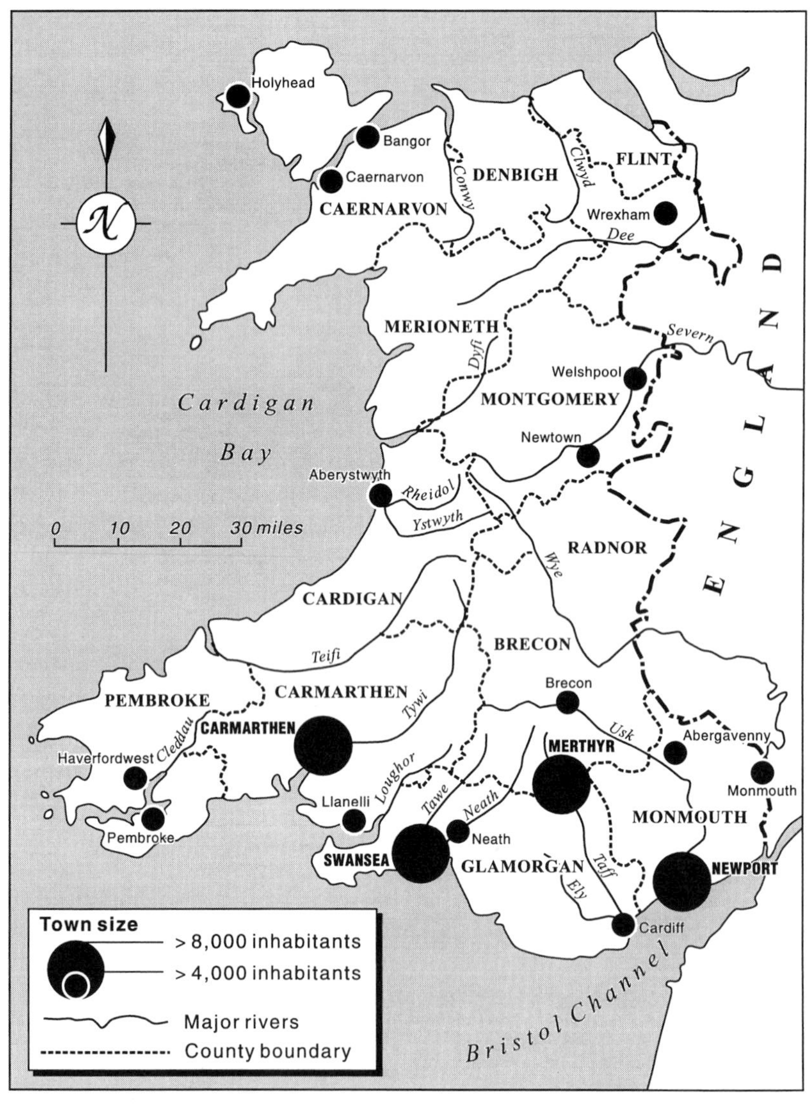

Map 3.2 Towns in Wales 1841

Dowlais) was already a real city of nearly 8,000 people, and there were 46,000 inhabitants by 1851. It was by far the largest town in Wales, and was already being regarded as a future capital. The Monmouthshire parishes of Bedwellty and Aberystruth had 1,400 people in 1801, 25,000 by 1861, while a host of middling industrial towns clustered around iron centres like Tredegar, Ebbw Vale, Beaufort, Nantyglo and Blaina. By 1840, there were probably 150,000 people directly dependent on the works at the heads of the valleys, often living in straggling and ill-defined settlements lacking much civic identity beyond that provided by the respective industrial plants. The iron they produced was chiefly shipped through Newport, which likewise expanded prodigiously, from 1,400 inhabitants in 1801 to 25,000 by 1861.

In 1840, Wales boasted six towns with 8,000 or more inhabitants: Merthyr Tydfil (43,031), Swansea (24,604), Newport (10,492), Cardiff (10,077), Carmarthen (9,526) and Caernarvon (8,001). The uplands of the south-east became the core of an industrialising region defined by the Newport–Aberdare–Abergavenny triangle, with its western extension towards Swansea Bay. This position was reinforced by new networks of roads, canals and pioneering railways. Many southern communities more than doubled their populations in the first half of the nineteenth century, so that below the triumphs of Merthyr and Swansea, there were impressive success stories, at Pontypool, Neath, Llanelli, Pontypridd, Caerphilly and so on. Much of the population growth in Glamorgan and Monmouth reflected migration from the now decaying rural counties of south-west Wales, but an Irish influx now gave the towns an unprecedented degree of religious, ethnic and linguistic diversity.

Urban expansion was reflected in national population statistics. Welsh population stood around 480,000 in 1750, and it can reliably be fixed around 587,000 in 1801. By 1851, the figure rose to 1.16 million, representing an average growth rate of almost 15 per cent for each decade in the first half of the nineteenth century, and this growth was overwhelmingly concentrated in urban industrial centres. By 1851, the increasingly urbanised shires of Glamorgan and Monmouth contained a third of the people of Wales.

Welsh urban life was revolutionised by improved communications. Wales as a distinctive linguistic community owed its existence to its very inaccessibility, and the extreme difficulty of imposing English laws or language. However, geographical obstacles also ensured that communications had to be directed outside the principality proper, either to or through one of the major English cities. This began to change from the mid-eighteenth century, with the successive construction of roads, canals and railroads, all of which opened up new industrial and commercial potential. The emerging industrialists sponsored the improvements in communications which made further development possible in these regions which had once been regarded as on or beyond the frontiers of settled life. In 1767, a leading Merthyr ironmaster sponsored the development of a new road from Cardiff to Merthyr Tydfil. In the decade after 1788, a canal building boom occurred in the powerhouse region of the south-east, roughly between Swansea, Brecon and Newport. Crucial to industrial and urban development were the Monmouthshire and Glamorganshire Canals, as well as the routes along the Swansea and Neath valleys. Between 1810 and 1820, mid-Wales and the north-east were the centres of activity, with the creation of the Brecon and Abergavenny (1811); the Montgomeryshire (1819) and the Ellesmere Canals (1819). These undertakings connected the towns of Breconshire, Monmouthshire and Montgomeryshire, and vastly benefited the local textile industry.

In mid-Wales, the development of communications was clearly undertaken within the broader economic region dependent upon Shrewsbury. From the 1750s, the first modern roads spread out from Shrewsbury to towns like Wrexham, Welshpool and Mold, and after 1815 Telford rebuilt the turnpike road from Shrewsbury to Conway, Bangor and Holyhead. Although the expansion can be seen as an attempt to improve communications with Bristol or Shrewsbury, the net effect was to improve internal links, to ensure that for the first time, it was possible to travel and trade within Wales itself. The impact of these changes on national self-consciousness would become apparent in Victorian times.

The new conditions redirected communications and marketing patterns away from the traditional coastal routes, towards the upland interior. The astonishing successes in the south-east, above all the Merthyr-Dowlais complex, utterly supplanted older communities like Brecon, Cardiff and Abergavenny, which were displaced to become staid outliers of the new industrial Wales. Also stagnating from the early nineteenth century were once dominant towns like the Pembrokeshire boroughs, and many smaller market centres like Cowbridge, Monmouth and Usk. Carmarthen reached a population of 10,000 in the 1830s, and then froze at this level for a century. In North and mid-Wales, a few older towns like Holywell accommodated themselves to the industrial age, while in 1848 the Wrexham newspaper noted that 'During the last 25 years or so, the wealth accumulated among the tradesmen, assisted by that of the neighboring gentry, has been gradually converting the town out of a decayed "genteel" one into something like an improved and improving commercial one.'[34] In the early nineteenth century, the Montgomeryshire textile industry permitted Llanidloes and Newtown to flourish. However, other traditional centres like Denbigh, Caernarvon and Dolgellau were increasingly confined to a merely local significance. As a traveller remarked typically of Brecon in 1797, 'Like most other

[34] Quoted in E. Hubbard, *The Buildings of Wales: Clwyd* (London, 1986), p. 297; compare Keith Kissack, *Victorian Monmouth* (Monmouth, 1986).

towns in Wales, this place is interesting rather for what it has been, than of account of what it now is.'[35] Throughout the country, many of the leading urban centres from Stuart times were well on the way to their twentieth century role as quaint tourist attractions.

(vi) THE NEW URBAN WORLD

The emergence of new ports and the centres in the uplands fundamentally reoriented Welsh social geography, to say nothing of the impact on culture and politics. The emergence of Swansea, Newport and Merthyr Tydfil meant that, again for the first time, the Welsh economy was effectively emancipated from the domination of the English cities. About 1790, there appeared the first Welsh urban network based on Welsh towns, and Welsh urban elites. This is suggested for example by the growth of professional communities and financial services in Welsh towns, and the heavy concentration in and around the southern industrial regions. Welsh banks began to emerge from about 1770, initially in the traditional service centres like Brecon and Cowbridge, but from the 1790s they were increasingly located in expanding towns like Merthyr Tydfil, Newport, Cardiff and Swansea. By the 1830s, there were perhaps sixteen towns in Wales with at least a core (fifteen or more individuals) active in law or medicine: ten of these centres were to be found south of Brecon, with Swansea and Carmarthen the most important. Together with the entrepreneurs and 'shopocracy' of industrial towns like Merthyr, Newport and Aberdare, these professional groups constituted the core of a new middle class, and accommodating their political demands would be a central strand of Welsh history for much of the early nineteenth century.[36]

The revolutionary changes in urban structure were accomplished so rapidly and with so little effort at planning that dire social consequences were quite inevitable. The industrial centres attracted a large labour force, but housing was provided on an utterly unsystematic basis, so the new towns were overcrowded, ill-built and lacked basic sanitary provision or decent water supplies. Merthyr by the 1830s was of special concern, wholly lacking any apparent plan or system: 'You appear entering on an extended suburb of a large town; but the town itself

[35] Carter, 'The growth and decline of Welsh towns', p. 49. W. S. K. Thomas, *Georgian and Victorian Brecon: Portrait of a Welsh County Town* (Llandysul, 1993).

[36] G. A. Williams, *The Merthyr Rising*, 2nd edn (Cardiff, 1988); Evans, *The Labyrinth of Flames*. For Cardiff as a centre of conservative and aristocratic power, see J. Davies, *Cardiff and the Marquesses of Bute* (Cardiff, 1981); H. M. Thomas, ed., *The Diaries of John Bird* (Cardiff, 1987); P. Jenkins, 'The tory tradition in eighteenth century Cardiff', *Welsh History Review*, 12 (1984), 180–96; J. Newman, S. Hughes and A. Ward, *The Buildings of Wales: Glamorgan* (London, 1995); R. Sweet, 'Stability and continuity: Swansea politics and reform 1780–1820', *Welsh History Review*, 18 (1996), 14–39.

is nowhere visible; it is without form or order . . . you can scarcely find your way along the main road, for to dignify it with the name of street is more than it merits.' It was 'a shapeless, unsightly cluster of wretched, dingy dwellings',

> having sprung up rapidly from a village to a town without any precautions being taken for the removal of the increased masses of filth necessarily produced by an increased population, not even for the escape of surface water . . . A rural spot of considerable beauty has been transformed into a crowded and filthy manufacturing town, with an amount of mortality higher than any other commercial or manufacturing town in the kingdom.[37]

Any of the growing towns could produce similar stories, as of course could some stagnant older communities like Carmarthen.

The disastrous state of urban housing and hygiene attracted acute concern during the epidemics that became commonplace in Merthyr, Cardiff and Swansea from the 1820s, and especially during the great cholera onslaught of 1849. Urban sanitary conditions naturally contributed to high death rates. The overall Welsh death rate was 20.2 per thousand in 1841, rising to 25.8 in 1849, but Merthyr and Cardiff regularly recorded rates in excess of 30 per thousand in these years. The health situation was still worse in the most notorious slums, which were usually the Irish sections: China and Tydfil's Well in Merthyr, Stanley Street and Love Lane in Cardiff, or Swansea's Greenhill. Prior to the 1830s, social and sanitary reform were inhibited by a thorough dissonance between urban needs and governmental structures. The new towns were either dominated by the stewards of aristocratic estates, as at Newport, Cardiff and Swansea, or else emerged within the ancient and quite inappropriate framework of parishes and vestries, as in the iron towns of Glamorgan and Monmouthshire. Neither arrangement was calculated to promote civic progress or development.

Urban expansion also created a political crisis for the administrative mechanisms of Church and state. By the 1830s, the most vigorously expanding Welsh towns were also the most politically radical, and the law and order situation here was at its most perilous. Merthyr Tydfil in 1831 experienced one of the most explosive urban insurrections in nineteenth-century Britain, while by end of the decade, the Chartist movement was entrenched in most of the industrial towns of the south, as well as the mid-Wales textile communities. Merthyr, Pontypool, Swansea, Newport and Carmarthen were all active centres, as were Newtown, Llanidloes and Welshpool, while in 1839 most of the new industrial towns in the southern uplands were seen as potential contributors to a general insurrection. Appropriately enough, an abortive rising in that year reached its climax in the streets of Newport, that pivotal southern centre of industry and transportation.

The geography of dissidence was generally well removed from the urban

[37] Quotations from Evans, 'The urbanization of Welsh society', pp. 21, 28; J. Gross, 'Water supply and sewerage', *Merthyr Historian*, 2 (1978), 67–78.

centres of political power and elite dominance. Both justices of the peace and Anglican clergy were found in embarrassing abundance around older and more genteel towns like Monmouth, Brecon and Cowbridge, while they were almost entirely lacking in the new industrial boom towns, which unfortunately happened to be where the bulk of Welsh people were now concentrated. The government took advantage of this displacement by situating the key military garrison for South Wales in staid and clerical Brecon, safely removed from the thriving industry of Merthyr or Pontypool, those potential hotbeds of insurrection. When riots or industrial disorders did occur, as they did with striking regularity between about 1793 and 1844, it was convenient that the ensuing trials were held and controversial sentences pronounced in the relatively safe surroundings of Cardiff, Monmouth and Brecon.[38]

By 1840, Wales had achieved something very like its modern urban structure. Still, the coming of the railways portended yet another leap in urbanisation, permitting the opening of the vast coal reserves in Aberdare and the Rhondda valley, and the creation of ports to handle them, at Cardiff and Barry. The beginning of the Welsh rail boom in 1838 thus marks an ideal transition point between the first period of rapid urban expansion, based on iron, and the second coal-fuelled era.

[38] Carter, 'The growth and decline of Welsh towns', pp. 58–9; H. Carter and S. Wheatley, *Merthyr Tydfil in 1851: A Study of the Spatial Structure of a Welsh Industrial Town* (Cardiff, 1982).

· 4 ·

Scotland

T. M. DEVINE

(i) THE SIXTEENTH-CENTURY PATTERN

IN THE early sixteenth century Scotland was undoubtedly less urbanised than England. Data on the population size of Scottish towns are very rare before the middle decades of the seventeenth century but Jan de Vries has calculated that in 1550 1.4 per cent of the Scottish population lived in towns of 10,000 inhabitants or more compared to 3.5 per cent in England and Wales.[1] Another estimate, by Ian Whyte, suggests that 2.5 per cent of Scots were dwelling in towns of over 2,000 in population in 1550 whereas in 1600 8.7 per cent of the population of England were living in towns of this size or bigger.[2] Not only was Scotland an overwhelmingly rural society in this period, more akin to countries such as Ireland and Denmark than to England or Holland, it was also one where urban development was very regionally concentrated. Whole areas, especially in the Highlands and southern Uplands, lacked any urban focus and were distant from any developed marketing centre. In the main, the Scottish towns of the sixteenth century were located in the central Lowlands, especially around the estuaries of the Forth, Tay and Clyde, along the east coast from Edinburgh to Aberdeen and in the lower Tweed valley to the south.[3] These were regions of relatively dense population and rich arable land. It is also the case that in some of these areas town development was extensive and contrasted with the national pattern of very modest urban growth. Recent demographic research on the seventeenth-century hearth taxes has shown that the five counties around the River Forth, East Lothian, Midlothian, Fife, Clackmannan and West Lothian, had by far the highest percentage of town dwellers in Scotland with a level of urbanisation which could

[1] J. de Vries, *European Urbanization, 1500–1800* (London, 1984), p. 39.

[2] I. D. Whyte, *Scotland before the Industrial Revolution* (London, 1995), pp. 174–5.

[3] M. Lynch, 'Urbanisation and urban networks in seventeenth century Scotland: some further thoughts', *Scottish Economic and Social History*, 12 (1992), 26.

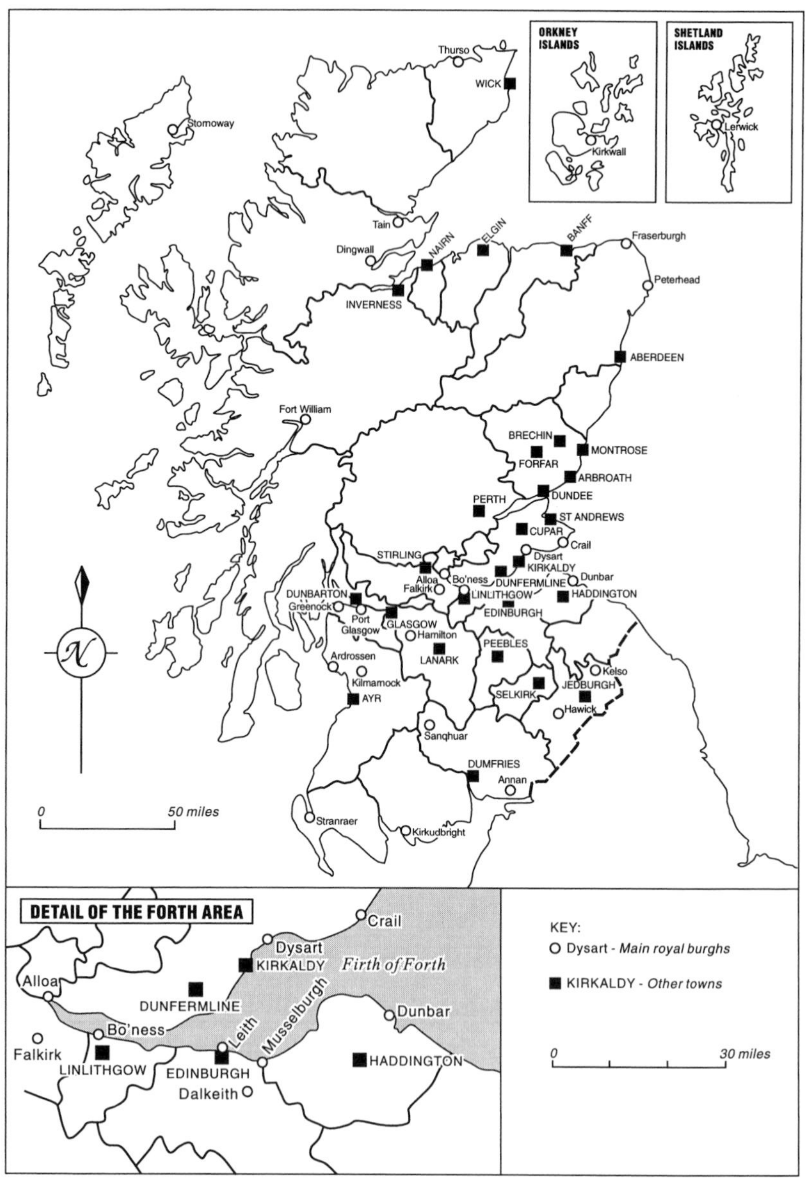

Map 4.1 Principal towns in Scotland

be compared to parts of the Netherlands.[4] It is very likely that that pattern, if not on the same scale, had already existed to some extent in earlier decades.

Scottish towns developed within a particular institutional framework. By the sixteenth century two groups of burghs had emerged: royal burghs and burghs of barony. Both existed within a system of monopolies which was very strong by the standards of the rest of Europe. Royal burghs held their charters direct from the crown, possessed a monopoly of foreign trade and also of internal commerce within a specified district which was designated as their 'liberty'. These monopolies could in theory extend for a number of miles around the burgh. Burghs of barony were authorised by the crown but created by lay and ecclesiastical landowners. They were not permitted to trade overseas but had similar legal rights over internal commerce as royal burghs. While many royal burghs were no bigger than burghs of barony, with populations numbering only hundreds, they also possessed considerable legal powers and, in addition, controlled the lucrative foreign trade. The biggest towns were usually royal burghs and they also had the right to be represented in parliament. Moreover, they possessed their own assembly, the Convention of Royal Burghs, which provided an institutional structure for the fostering of common interests and policies and, above all, for the defence of royal burgh privileges.

Yet the urban hierarchy of the sixteenth century was more complex than this simple outline suggests. First, the so-called 'four great towns of Scotland', Edinburgh, Aberdeen, Perth and Dundee, which were dominant throughout the medieval period, retained their pre-eminent position into the sixteenth century and beyond. In the 1370s they accounted for 58 per cent of the customs levied in the export trade and in 1583 together paid 54 per cent of the proportion of national taxation contributed by the burghs.[5] Secondly, Edinburgh, the capital, had a commanding position even in relation to the larger burghs. Throughout the sixteenth century its share of Scottish trade increased relentlessly, especially in the sectors of wool and leather. In 1480 Edinburgh accounted for 54 per cent of Scottish export revenues. A century later this share had risen to 75 per cent and the capital had acquired a virtual monopoly over some areas of trade.[6] Edinburgh's population (with its port of Leith) in the early seventeenth century of around 30,000 inhabitants meant that it was double the size of Aberdeen, its nearest rival in the urban hierarchy.[7]

[4] M. Flinn, ed., *Scottish Population History from the Seventeenth Century to the 1930s* (Cambridge, 1977), pp. 188–9.

[5] M. Lynch, 'Scottish towns 1500–1700', in M. Lynch, ed., *The Early Modern Town in Scotland* (London, 1987), p. 4.

[6] I. Guy, 'The Scottish export trade, 1460–1590', in T. C. Smout, ed., *Scotland and Europe, 1200–1850* (Edinburgh, 1986), pp. 62–81.

[7] R. C. Fox, 'The burghs of Scotland 1327, 1601, 1670', *Area*, 13(2) (1981), 161–7. Two recent studies of Edinburgh in the seventeenth century are H. M. Dingwall, *Late Seventeenth-Century Edinburgh* (Aldershot, 1994), and R. A. Houston, *Social Change in the Age of Enlightenment* (Oxford, 1994).

Thirdly, there were few medium-sized towns in Scotland (with between 2,500 to 5,000 inhabitants) but relatively large numbers of smaller urban centres below that level.[8] This is clearly brought out in estimates based on the burghal taxation rates of 1639. No fewer than twenty-five of the sixty towns had a population of 1,000 or less. Thirty-six had a population of 2,500 or below, while only nine, towns such as Ayr, Haddington (see Plate 4) and Stirling, had populations of between 2,500 and 5,000.[9] Towns of middling rank had been in decline throughout the medieval period and this trend continued in the sixteenth century. The long-term slump in Scottish exports together with the tightening grip of Edinburgh on key sectors of commerce put pressure on both large and medium-sized towns alike but the former were more able to diversify their economic interests than the latter.[10]

Fourthly, there was a west/east divide in the pattern of urban development. In the sixteenth century the west and south-west had only a sprinkling of small burghs. The four great towns, on the other hand, reflecting the orientation of Scottish trade to Scandinavia, the Netherlands and France, were all located on the east. Only in the seventeenth century did a western town, Glasgow, effectively challenge the historic dominance of the eastern burghs of Aberdeen, Dundee and Perth.[11]

(ii) SEVENTEENTH-CENTURY DEVELOPMENTS

It has been said that 'between the sixteenth and the late eighteenth centuries Scotland had one of the highest growth rates of urban populations in Europe'.[12] In that sense, Scotland's experience was more like England's than the pattern elsewhere in Europe, where there was more evidence either of stability or relatively sluggish urban growth. The estimated proportion of total Scottish population living in towns with over 10,000 inhabitants rose from 1.6 per cent to 5.3 per cent in 1700 and to 9.2 per cent by 1750.[13] From the early sixteenth century foreign trade experienced a pronounced recovery from the doldrums of late medieval times and such fragmentary data as are available suggest very significant increases in population for some towns in the period 1580 to 1630.[14] Edinburgh's population may have doubled between 1560 and the 1640s to

[8] I. D. Whyte, 'Urbanization in early modern Scotland: a preliminary analysis', *Scottish Economic and Social History*, 9 (1989), 21–37.

[9] Lynch, 'Urbanisation and urban networks', p. 25.

[10] M. Lynch, 'Continuity and change in urban society, 1500–1700', in R. A. Houston and I. D. Whyte, eds., *Scottish Society 1500–1800* (Cambridge, 1989), pp. 100–1.

[11] T. M. Devine and G. Jackson, eds., *Glasgow*, vol. I: *Beginnings to 1830* (Manchester, 1995), pp. 59–66; T. C. Smout, 'The development and enterprise of Glasgow, 1556–1707', *Scottish Journal of Political Economy*, 7 (1960), 194–212.

[12] Whyte, *Scotland before the Industrial Revolution*, p. 172.

[13] De Vries, *European Urbanization*, p. 39.

[14] Lynch, 'Continuity and change', p. 85.

over 30,000. Other large burghs, like Aberdeen, also experienced substantial increases.[15]

Nevertheless, the scale, duration and momentum of Scottish urban growth at this time needs to be kept in perspective. Despite town expansion most burghs were still mere villages and the vast majority of Scots remained rural dwellers. Probably as late as 1750 the ratio of country to town dwellers (assuming over 4,000 inhabitants as the base figure for a community to be regarded as a town for this purpose) was around one in eight.[16] Moreover, Scottish urban development in the seventeenth century was very complex. For one thing, several towns experienced violent short-term fluctuations in commercial activity in the early seventeenth century. Unlike the English pattern, where relative urban stability, punctuated by phases of moderate difficulty, was the norm, Scottish towns, and especially those in the middle rank, were more vulnerable to recurrent economic crisis.[17] For instance, between 1550 and 1635, Perth's taxation assessments fell seven times and rose three times.[18] In large part this reflected the economic structure of Scottish towns. Even the smallest coastal royal burghs were mainly dependent on overseas trade and were vulnerable to the fickle and volatile nature of international markets. In addition, most exports consisted of such raw materials as wool, hides, skins, salt and coal. The regular supply of these commodities was always problematic in an agricultural economy where the balance between shortage and sufficiency was easily disturbed by poor harvests and political instability.[19]

It is equally clear that the urban expansion which has been identified in the decades between the later sixteenth century and the 1630s came to an abrupt halt during the middle years of the seventeenth century. The period of the Scottish Revolution was a disastrous one for many Scottish burghs. High taxation, the quartering of troops and political crisis continued from the later 1630s until the Cromwellian Union of the 1650s. Aberdeen and Dundee suffered particularly severely. Aberdeen was sacked by the army of the marquis of Montrose in 1644 while Dundee was pillaged by the forces of General Monck after the siege of 1651.[20]

The fluctuating fortunes of individual burghs inevitably caused some changes

15 Whyte, 'Urbanization in early modern Scotland', pp. 21–37; D. Macniven, 'Merchants and traders in early seventeenth century Aberdeen', in D. Stevenson, ed., *From Lairds to Louns* (Aberdeen, 1986), pp. 58–69.

16 T. C. Smout, *A History of the Scottish People 1560–1830* (London, 1969), p. 260.

17 Lynch, 'Continuity and Change', pp. 95–6. 18 *Ibid.*

19 S. G. E. Lythe, *The Economy of Scotland in its European Setting, 1550–1625* (Edinburgh, 1960); Guy, 'Scottish export trade', pp. 62–81.

20 T. M. Devine, 'The Cromwellian Union and the Scottish burghs: the case of Aberdeen and Glasgow, 1652–60', in J. Butt and J. T. Ward, eds., *Scottish Themes* (Edinburgh, 1976), pp. 1–16; D. Stevenson, 'The burghs and the Scottish revolution', in Lynch, ed., *Early Modern Town*, pp. 167–91.

in the urban hierarchy. Until the 1640s the burghal taxation rolls reveal the continued ascendancy of the four major burghs, Edinburgh, Perth and Dundee, which had been the leading Scottish towns for over three centuries. In 1649 Glasgow displaced Perth to take fourth place and by 1670 had clearly moved ahead of both Aberdeen and Dundee. Edinburgh was still pre-eminent but Glasgow and the capital were now the dominant towns and were well ahead of the rest of the pack. In 1697 these two burghs alone were responsible for 40 per cent of burghal taxation contributions.[21]

Glasgow's performance was remarkable. There were steady signs of the growth of the commercial contacts with the Americas which were to become the main sources of the city's success in the eighteenth century. However, in this period, its development was based on more mundane domestic stimuli.[22] First, agrarian historians have shown significant increases in rural demand for consumer goods in the second half of the seventeenth century.[23] Historically, Glasgow had a much stronger manufacturing base than most Scottish burghs, particularly in textiles, and hence was well placed to exploit these new market opportunities. Second, the town's ancient trading area of Argyll and the inner Hebrides was experiencing more significant commercial development, notably with further expansion of the Highland black cattle to the markets of the south.[24] Third, and a vital influence, Ireland became a veritable pivot of Glaswegian external trade in this period. The foundation of the Ulster plantation earlier in the century and the extensive migration of many thousands of Scots from the western Lowlands, especially in the 1610s, 1620s and, above all, in the famine years of the 1690s, opened up a huge new neighbouring market for Glasgow's clothing, coal and metalwork.[25] Fourth, and finally, the overland trade to northern England gave an additional stimulus. This commerce in linen and linen yarn had gained from the pacification of the troubled border lands after the Union of the crowns. Surviving customs books of the 1620s suggest that this had become Glasgow's single most lucrative trade by that decade. Linen making steadily increased the number of textile workers in the town through the middle decades of the seventeenth century.[26]

[21] For Glasgow's rise at this time the most recent study is Devine and Jackson, eds., *Glasgow*, pp. 41–83. See also Smout, 'Development and enterprise of Glasgow', pp. 194–212.

[22] Devine and Jackson, eds., *Glasgow*, pp. 8–10, for the points discussed below.

[23] I. D. Whyte, *Agriculture and Society in Seventeenth Century Scotland* (Edinburgh, 1979), pp. 173–97; T. M. Devine, *The Transformation of Rural Scotland: Social Change and the Agrarian Economy* (Edinburgh, 1994), pp. 3–17.

[24] F. J. Shaw, *The Northern and Western Islands of Scotland: Their Economy and Society in the Seventeenth Century* (Edinburgh, 1980), pp. 115–16, 155–8.

[25] T. C. Smout, N. C. Landsman and T. M. Devine, 'Scottish emigration in the seventeenth and eighteenth centuries', in Nicholas Canny, ed., *Europeans on the Move: Studies in European Migration, 1500–1800* (Oxford, 1994), pp. 87–8; M. Perceval-Maxwell, *The Scottish Migration to Ulster in the Reign of James I* (London, 1973).

[26] Devine and Jackson, eds., *Glasgow*, pp. 47–8.

At the other end of the urban hierarchy the structures were far from static. Glasgow's rise was a story of spectacular expansion from humble beginnings and has therefore inevitably attracted the attention of scholars. But the success story in the west should not obscure the continuing power and influence of Edinburgh in the east. The capital was by far the richest town in Scotland and its relative size was not an accurate guide to its prosperity. Edinburgh paid a third of the taxation raised from the royal burghs in the later seventeenth century and as late as the 1720s, as R. A. Houston has shown, 'A third of Scotland's excise revenue came from the Edinburgh station in the 1720s – this from a city with a 4–5 per cent share of the population.'[27] As the seat of Scottish government until 1707 and the nation's legal and religious centre, the capital remained Scotland's greatest town until well into the eighteenth century (see Plates 6 and 23). Glasgow's meteoric rise could not disguise this fact.

It is also worthy of note that between 1500 and 1700 an estimated 250 new burghs of barony were founded with distinct acceleration in this trend in the last four decades of the seventeenth century.[28] Some 40 per cent of the total between 1500 and 1700 were authorised in this period.[29] In addition, between 1660 and 1707, almost 150 non-burghal markets and fairs were licensed while there was also an expansion in unlicensed market centres.[30] Inevitably many baronial burghs which were authorised were never established in reality. Others were existing trading places which were now receiving formal recognition. Yet, even when all the qualifications have been made, there was, as Ian Whyte demonstrates (see Chapter 5 below), something significant in this expansion of small-scale urbanism. It reflected primarily an increase in the internal marketing of foods and raw material and in some areas the rise of coal mining and salt burning in the decades before the Union. The Scottish economy, however tentatively, was already on the move before 1707.[31]

A basic factor in this trend was the new determination of many landowners to derive extra revenue from their estates by selling more foods and raw materials to domestic and overseas markets while also developing extractive industries on their properties. The existing rigid framework of burghal monopoly and privilege and the control of the royal burghs over foreign trade were often in direct conflict with these elite ambitions. It is not, therefore, surprising that in the later seventeenth century many of the structures of burghal privilege were effectively removed by the landlord-dominated parliament. The decisive legislation came in 1672 when the privileges of the royal burghs were significantly

27 Houston, *Social Change*, p. 3.

28 G. S. Pryde, *The Burghs of Scotland* (Glasgow, 1965).

29 *Ibid.*

30 I. D. Whyte, 'The growth of periodic market centres in Scotland 1600–1707', *Scottish Geographical Magazine*, 95 (1979), 13–26.

31 T. M. Devine, 'The Union of 1707 and Scottish development', *Scottish Economic and Social History*, 5 (1985), 23–40.

reduced. The Convention of Royal Burghs fought back and some of their monopolies were partially restored in 1690. Yet the general trend was unmistakable: the days of formal control and exclusive commercial rights were numbered. Even within the royal burghs the ancient monopolies of merchant and craft guilds were already starting to crumble before 1700, a process which intensified in the following century.[32]

(iii) URBANISATION

Despite the significant changes of the seventeenth century, Scotland remained a predominantly rural society in 1700. In a league table of European 'urbanised societies' – as ranked by the de Vries measure of the proportion of population living in towns of 10,000 or above – Scotland was estimated eleventh out of sixteen in 1600 and tenth in 1700. (Although the proportion of town dwellers in the Fife and Lothian region of the south-east, as has been indicated, was already much higher than these figures suggest.) From the later eighteenth century, however, this pattern altered drastically. By the 1760s Scotland was seventh in the league table, fourth in 1800 and second only to England and Wales in 1800. The rates of town expansion achieved between 1801 and 1831 in Scotland were the fastest of the nineteenth century, and in the same period Glasgow was growing more rapidly than any European city of its size.[33]

Despite this explosive rate of urban expansion there were considerable continuities with the older world. The four largest burghs of the seventeenth century, Edinburgh, Glasgow, Aberdeen and Dundee, were also the biggest Scottish burghs of the eighteenth century, although of course they had experienced substantial changes in size, occupational structure and economic specialisation over that period. Again, the thirteen largest Scottish towns of the early eighteenth century were the same, with only one or two exceptions, as those of 1830. The biggest urban areas, therefore, were all ancient places while the traditional county and regional capitals also continued to play a role whether as centres of administration, local government or as markets for prosperous agricultural hinterlands. But by 1830, the Scottish urban system had also developed some characteristic features typical of the new era.

First, urbanisation was mainly concentrated in the narrow belt of land in the western and eastern Lowlands. Between 1801 and 1841 never less than 83 per cent of the entire Scottish urban population (defined for this purpose as those inhabiting towns of 5,000 or more) lived in this region. Within the area there was heavy concentration in Glasgow and Edinburgh where, as early as 1800, 60

[32] T. M. Devine, 'The merchant class of the larger Scottish towns in the seventeenth and early eighteenth centuries', in G. Gordon and B. Dicks, eds., *Scottish Urban History* (Aberdeen, 1983), pp. 92–111. [33] De Vries, *European Urbanization*, pp. 39–48.

per cent of Scottish urban dwellers resided. This pattern had implications for the demographic structure of Scottish society because population concentration on such a scale could not have taken place without considerable redistribution of people over a relatively short period of time. Thus, whereas the percentage of total Scottish population in the central Lowlands rose from 37 per cent to 47 per cent of the whole between *c.* 1750 and 1821, it fell from 51 per cent to 41 per cent in northern Scotland and remained roughly static at 11 per cent in the southern region of the country over the same period. The modern population profile of Scotland was beginning to take shape.

Within the urbanising zone the fastest growth among the largest towns was in the west, with four towns in that area at least trebling in population. Paisley expanded more than six times, Greenock more than five, and Glasgow grew fourfold.[34] But the dramatic growth in this region of smaller towns and villages devoted mainly to textile production, mining and ironmaking should also be noted. In this period wide areas of the central Lowland countryside were transformed by this small-scale urbanism. The pattern in Lanarkshire was fairly typical. In the parish of Glassford population was rapidly concentrating in 'three small but thriving villages'. Clusters of industrial settlements were growing throughout the country. There were six such enclaves in the parish of Cambuslang alone. Existing small towns also expanded as weaving or mining centres. Airdrie increased its population sixfold in the second half of the eighteenth century as its textile industries enjoyed a period of remarkable prosperity.[35]

Second, there was wide diversity within the urban structure. While any attempt at neat categorisation of Scottish towns in this period is bound to be arbitrary, in very broad terms most Scottish towns after 1760 fitted into three categories: the four major cities; industrial towns; local capitals in historic sites which performed marketing and service functions for their immediate neighbourhoods.[36] In addition, there was a miscellany of other urban settlements including the fishing ports of the Fife and Moray coast, the old coal and salt burghs of the Forth estuary and the new inland spas of Bridge of Allan, Peebles and Strathpeffer. Of these groups, the industrial staple towns and some of the cities were most likely to suffer the adverse consequences of expansion which are often associated with urbanisation at this time. Such places as Paisley, Falkirk, Kilmarnock and Hawick grew swiftly, and their mainly working-class inhabitants were usually heavily concentrated in one or two industries which were

[34] Flinn, ed., *Scottish Population History*, pp. 313ff; T. M. Devine, 'Urbanisation', in T. M. Devine and R. Mitchison, eds., *People and Society in Scotland*, vol. I: *1760–1830* (Edinburgh, 1988), pp. 27–52; R. J. Morris, 'Urbanisation in Scotland', in W. H. Fraser and R. J. Morris, eds., *People and Society in Scotland*, vol. II: *1830–1914* (Edinburgh, 1990), pp. 73–102.

[35] Devine, *Transformation of Rural Scotland*, p. 152.

[36] I. H. Adams, *The Making of Urban Scotland* (London, 1978), pp. 73–104.

often geared to overseas markets and hence were vulnerable to the changes in demand for international commodities.[37]

Why Scotland should experience such a precocious rate of urban growth is a question which requires detailed consideration since its consequences for the long-run development of Scottish society were so profound. The essential foundation, though not the principal direct cause, was the revolution in agriculture which occurred in parallel with town and city expansion. Urbanisation could not have taken place without a substantial increase in food production to sustain the needs of those who did not cultivate their own food supplies. At the same time agrarian productivity had to improve in order to release a growing proportion of the population for non-agricultural tasks in towns and cities. Moreover, for much of the period of this analysis, the urban masses mainly relied on grain, milk, potatoes and meat supplied from Scottish farms. They were fed through a rise in both the production and productivity of agriculture achieved by a reorganisation in farm structure, a more effective deployment of labour and higher grain yields derived from improved fallowing of land, the sowing of root crops and the adoption of new rotation systems.[38] No authoritative measures exist of the precise rate of increase in food production but it must have been very substantial. One knowledgeable contemporary, for example, took the view that from the 1750s to the 1820s the output of corn and vegetables had doubled in Scotland while that of animal foods multiplied sixfold.[39] Grain prices rose significantly after *c.* 1780 and especially during the Napoleonic wars. Yet, though this did stimulate some social discontent in the form of meal riots, price inflation also tended to encourage innovation in better agricultural practices which in the long run continued to sustain urban expansion.[40] It was vital that this response should take place. If it had not, town growth might have been hampered by growing social unrest and diversion of too much of the society's resources to current consumption and away from investment in residential construction and the urban infrastructure.

Agrarian change was a necessary precondition for urbanisation but agricultural reform also contributed more directly to town growth at two other levels. First, the increasing orientation of agriculture towards the market further stimulated the function of urban areas as centres of exchange. There was a greater need

[37] Devine, 'Urbanisation', pp. 37–8; L. J. Saunders, *Scottish Democracy 1815–40: The Social and Intellectual Background* (Edinburgh, 1950), pp. 145–60; J. Docherty, 'Urbanisation, capital accumulation and class struggle in Scotland, 1750–1914', in G. Whittington and I. D. Whyte, eds., *A Historical Geography of Scotland* (London, 1983), pp. 244–5.

[38] The most recent study of this process is Devine, *Transformation of Rural Scotland*; see also M. Gray, 'Scottish emigration: the social impact of agrarian change in the rural lowlands, 1775–1875', *Perspectives in American History*, 8 (1973), pp. 112–44.

[39] George Robertson, *Rural Recollections* (Irvine, 1829), p. 383.

[40] C. A. Whatley, 'An uninflammable people?', in I. Donnachie and C. A. Whatley, eds., *The Manufacture of Scottish History* (Edinburgh, 1992), pp. 51–71.

than before for the commercial, legal and financial facilities which concentrated in towns. Perth, Ayr, Haddington, Dumfries, Stirling and several other towns owed much of their expansion in this period to the increasing requirements for their services from the commercialised agricultural systems of their hinterlands.[41] Regional specialisation in agrarian production also enhanced the need for growing centres of exchange. Inverness, for example, expanded on the basis of its crucial role as the sheep and wool mart of the Highlands as that area became a great specialist centre of pastoral husbandry in the first half of the nineteenth century.[42] Secondly, the prosperity of Scottish agriculture during the Napoleonic wars boosted the incomes of tenant farmers and inflated the rent rolls of many landowners. The increase in the purchasing power of these classes had major implications for urban growth because it resulted in rising demand for the products of town consumer and luxury industries, and for more and better urban services in education, in leisure and in the provision of fashionable accommodation.[43]

Yet agrarian improvement was the necessary condition for Scottish urbanisation rather than its principal determinant. Towns which acted mainly as exchange and service centres for rural hinterlands expanded only relatively modestly, at a rate which was only slightly more than the national rate of natural increase.[44] Moreover, the rise in population which occurred in all western European societies from the later eighteenth century encouraged food producers throughout the continent to increase their output to cope with enhanced demand. The nature of the Scottish Agricultural Revolution may have been distinctive but agrarian improvement was too common in Europe at this time to provide the basic explanation for Scotland's exceptional pace of urban development. It is more likely that Scottish town expansion was a direct consequence of Scotland's equally remarkable rate of general economic growth between 1760 and 1830. The Industrial Revolution before 1830 was mainly confined to mainland Britain and it is hardly a coincidence that in this same period urbanisation occurred more vigorously in England and Scotland than in any other European country. Scottish industrialisation and Scottish urban growth were both results of the same economic forces: 'Non-agrarian occupations do not absolutely demand location in an urban environment but they certainly favour it, as offering prompt access to concentrations of producers, distributors and consumers.'[45]

This process had two interlinked aspects. The first was commercial in origin. In the eighteenth century, Scotland was in a superb geographical position to take

[41] Adams, *Making of Urban Scotland*, pp. 40–73.

[42] T. M. Devine, *Clanship to Crofters' War: The Social Transformation of the Scottish Highlands* (Manchester, 1994), pp. 32–53.

[43] Saunders, *Scottish Democracy*, pp. 79–96; Devine, *Transformation of Rural Scotland*, pp. 36–59.

[44] Flinn, ed., *Scottish Population History*, p. 313.

[45] P. J. Corfield, *The Impact of English Towns 1700–1800* (Oxford, 1982), p. 94.

advantage of the changing direction of international trade towards the Atlantic world. This momentous alteration in transcontinental commerce was a highly dynamic factor in port development along the whole western coast of Europe from Cork to Cadiz. Scotland was virtually at the cross-roads of the new system and the Clyde ports grew rapidly to become the great tobacco emporia of the United Kingdom until diversifying later into the importation of sugar and cotton.[46] It was no coincidence that in the later eighteenth century four of the five fastest-growing towns in Scotland were in the Clyde basin. Commercial success was bound to foster urban expansion. The carriage and merchandising of goods in bulk were all highly labour intensive in this period and demanded large concentrations of labour. Considerable investment was also needed to build up the complex infrastructure of trade: warehouses, ports, industries, merchants' mansions, banks, exchanges, inns and coffee-houses. Greenock may be taken as the archetypal port town of the western Lowlands: it mushroomed in size from a population of 2,000 in 1700 to 17,500 in 1801 and 27,500 in 1831. By that date Greenock had become one of the six largest towns in Scotland. Irish trade, coastal commerce and continuing economic connections with Europe also stimulated port development along both the east and west coasts.[47]

But, in the long run, the expansion of manufacturing industry was even more critical for urbanisation than the stimulus derived from international and inter-regional commerce. Of the thirteen largest towns in early nineteenth-century Scotland, five at least trebled their population size between *c.* 1750 and 1821. In addition to Greenock these were Glasgow (from 31,700 to 147,000), Paisley (6,800 to 47,000), Kilmarnock (4,400 to 12,700) and Falkirk (3,900 to 11,500). Greenock apart, the inhabitants of all these towns mainly depended either directly or indirectly on manufacturing industry. It was the larger industrial towns and the constellation of smaller urban areas with which they were associated which set the pace of Scottish urbanisation. It is important to emphasise, of course, that industry did not necessarily or inevitably generate large-scale urban expansion in the short run. As late as the 1830s, for instance, around two-thirds of Scotland's hand-loom weavers of cotton, linen and woollen cloth lived in the country villages or small towns.[48] The water-powered cotton-spinning factories of the last quarter of the eighteenth century were more often to be found in rural settlements such as Catrine, New Lanark or Deanston than in the cities. Throughout most of the period under consideration both coal-mining and pig-iron manufacture were also located in small towns and country villages. The continued presence of industry in a variety of forms in the countryside helps

[46] T. M. Devine, *The Tobacco Lords* (Edinburgh, 1975; repr., 1990).

[47] Smout, *History of the Scottish People*, pp. 260–1.

[48] N. Murray, *The Scottish Handloom Weavers 1790–1850: A Social History* (Edinburgh, 1978), pp. 1–9.

to explain why a majority of the Scottish people still lived outside large urban areas by 1830.

Yet, in the long run there were obvious advantages in industrial concentration in towns. Manufacturers were able to gain from 'external economies': firms saved the costs of providing accommodation and other facilities for their workers from their own resources: they were guaranteed access to a huge pool of labour and transport costs between sources of supply, finishing trades and repair shops could be markedly reduced or virtually eliminated by the close proximity of complementary economic activities. These advantages built up a dynamic for urban expansion even before 1800. Thereafter the new technology of steam propulsion and conspicuous progress in transport developments through the construction of canals and roads steadily intensified the forces making for urban concentration. In cotton spinning, and eventually in other textile industries, steam power encouraged industrial settlements on the coalfields and removed the one major obstacle which had previously constricted the expansion of manufacturing in the larger towns. Glasgow provides the most dramatic case of the pattern of change.[49] In 1795 the city had eleven cotton-spinning complexes, but rural Renfrewshire had twelve. The fundamental need to have secure access to water power obviously diluted Glasgow's other attractions as a centre of textile industrial production. However, steam-based technology was rapidly adopted after 1800 and concentration accelerated on an enormous scale in the city and its immediate environs. By 1830 there were 192 cotton mills in Scotland employing 31,000 workers. All but seventeen were located in Renfrew and Lanark and ninety-eight were in or near Glasgow. In Paisley, or its vicinity, there was a further great network of forty factories employing almost 5,000 workers.[50] A similar process of intensifying convergence evolved over a longer time scale in the border wool towns of Hawick and Galashiels and in the linen centres of the eastern Lowlands there emerged a strong urban concentration – Dundee specialised in heavy flax and tow fabrics, Arbroath was the seat of the canvas trade, Forfar and Brechin produced heavy linens such as osnaburghs and northern Fife specialised in finer linens and bleached goods. Before 1830 textile manufacturing was the principal motor of this process of agglomeration. Up till then, for example, it was the cotton centres of Glasgow and its suburbs and Renfrewshire which grew most rapidly in the western Lowlands. Only thereafter, and especially from the 1840s, did intensive urban development spread from them to the coal and iron towns of Coatbridge, Airdrie and Wishaw in north Lanarkshire.[51] For that and the following decades the dynamic derived from the vast expansion of shipbuilding, iron and steel making and coal mining

[49] Devine and Jackson, eds., *Glasgow*, pp. 184–213. [50] *Ibid.*

[51] A. Gibb, *Glasgow: The Making of a City* (London, 1983), pp. 91–3; Adams, *Making of Urban Scotland*, pp. 90–3.

was the principal influence on the continued urban expansion of Scotland in the second half of the nineteenth century.[52]

(iv) CONCLUSION

The main theme of this chapter has been the transformation of Scottish urban life over a period of more than three centuries. In the sixteenth and seventeenth centuries Scotland was less urbanised than England and though the urban framework was far from static there was only marginal increase in the proportion of Scots living in towns and cities between the Union of crowns in 1603 and the Union of parliaments in 1707. One region, however, stood out from the rest of the country. The south-east, around Edinburgh, had levels of urbanisation on a par with the Low Countries. Edinburgh itself was by far the most important town in Scotland, dominating not only the overseas trade of the country but its civil, religious and legal administration as well.

From the later seventeenth century, but with massive acceleration from the middle decades of the eighteenth century, these traditional urban patterns were broken up. From time immemorial Scotland's most significant towns had been located along the east coast and had depended mainly on trade with Europe. The development of the Atlantic economy in the eighteenth century changed all that. The fastest-growing towns in this period were now in the western lowlands. Glasgow became the dynamic heart of a region of unprecedented urban development. Industrialisation gave further impetus to this process. But at the same time the economic revolution ensured that rapid town expansion would spread throughout the central Lowlands and not be confined solely to the west. Rural industrial villages, small textile towns and large manufacturing cities, such as Dundee in the east, all experienced major increases in population. In the century after 1750 the rate of Scottish rural–urban migration increased massively as the balance of population distribution began to swing irresistibly from county to town. By the 1850s, with England, Scotland had become one of the most urbanised societies in Europe. It was a decisive break with the patterns of the past.

[52] Morris, 'Urbanisation in Scotland', pp. 73–102.

1 London: St Paul's and the Strand: a section from the 'Copperplate Map', *c.* 1559, showing the heavy density of occupation within the city walls, but lower levels in the western suburbs.

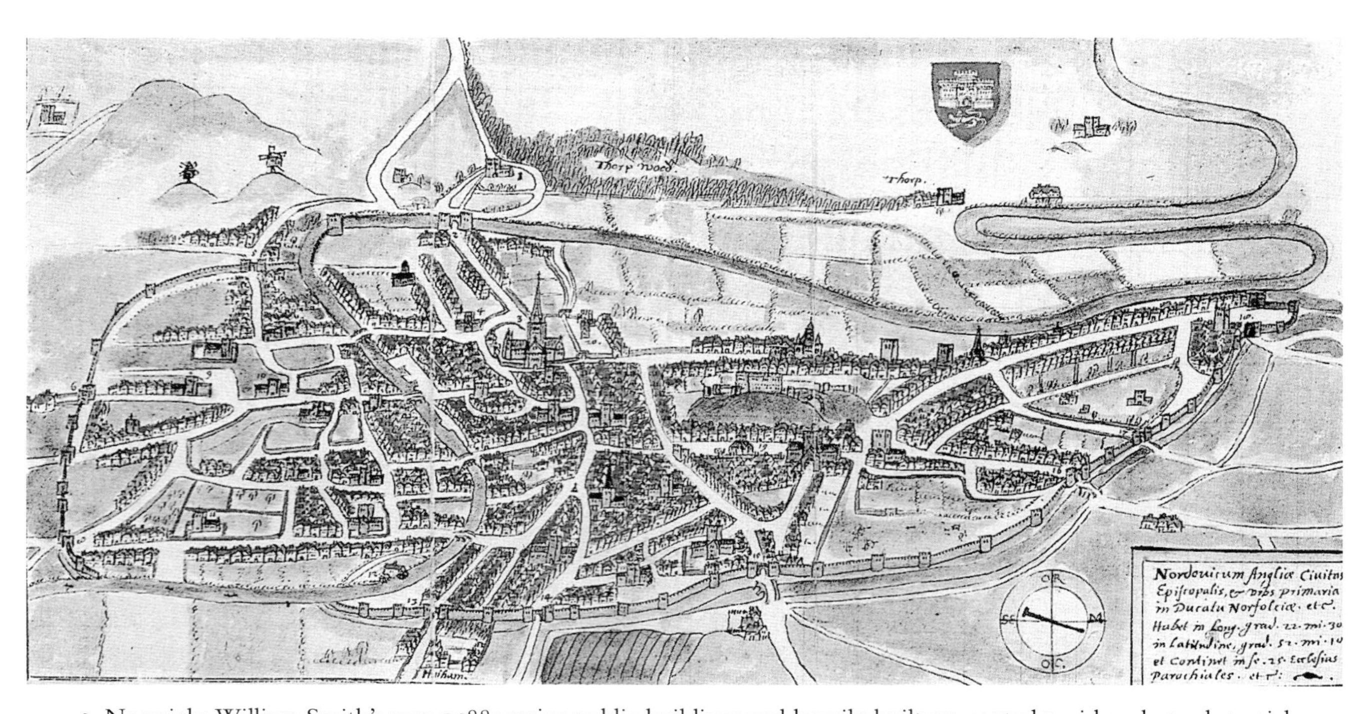

2 Norwich: William Smith's map 1588: major public buildings and heavily built-up central parishes, but substantial areas of the walled city are apparently unoccupied.

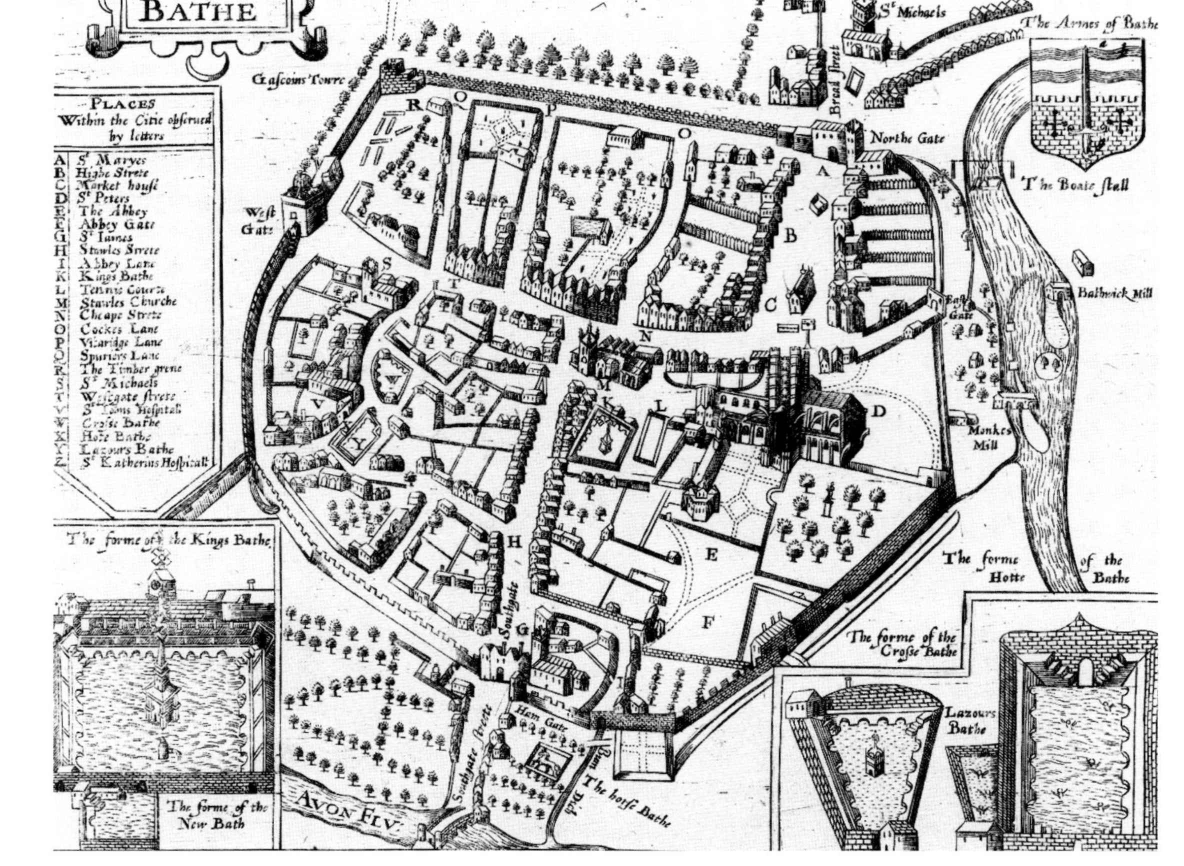

3 Bath: John Speed’s map 1611: the walled town still relatively undeveloped though the public baths are clearly established; fashionable Georgian development was to take place beyond the Northgate; compare with Plate 28.

4 Prospect of Haddington, Scotland, 1693, from Slezer's *Theatrum Scotiae*, illustrating the close relations between a smaller town and its countryside.

5 Cockenzie and Port Seton, Scotland: from John Adair's map (1688) which shows the old and new harbours at Cockenzie and the industrial complex there and at Port Seton for coal, salt and glassmaking.

6 Heriot's Hospital, Edinburgh, founded by an Edinburgh goldsmith, George Heriot; the building was begun in 1628 and completed by 1700.

7 Procession in London: the royal entry of Marie de Medici, mother of Queen Henrietta Maria, along the Strand, 1638.

8 Election in the Guildhall, Oxford, 1687, by Egbert van Heemskerk.

9 A Merchant House, Shrewsbury, built about 1575 for Robert Ireland, a wealthy wooltrader.

10 Musselburgh Tollbooth, Midlothian; this town hall was built in 1590 with additions in 1762.

11 The Banqueting House, Whitehall, London, designed by Inigo Jones and completed in 1622; the first classically inspired urban building in Britain; refaced in 1829.

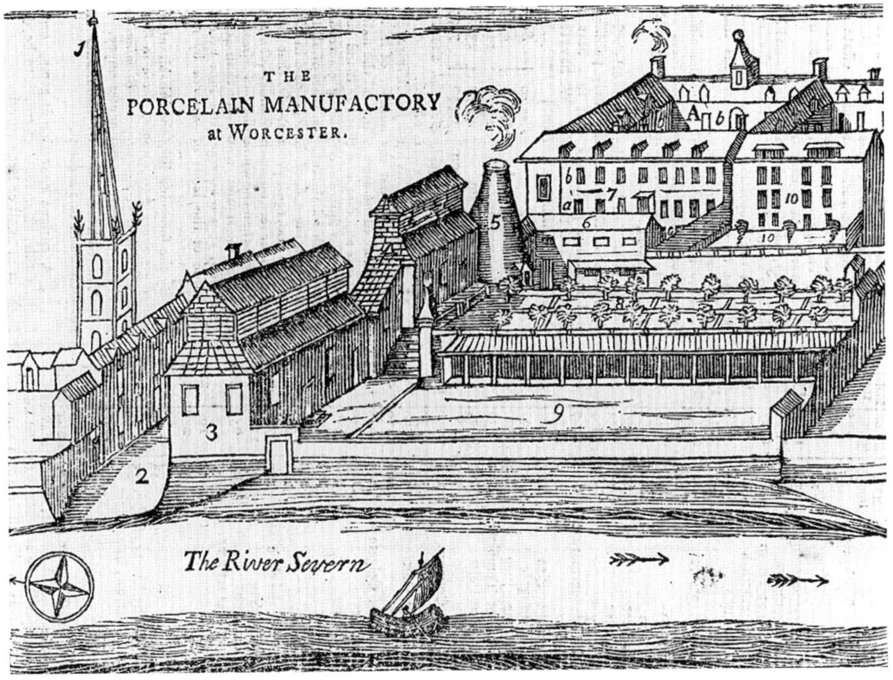

12 Porcelain factory at Worcester, depicting the different kilns (nos. 3, 5), rooms for throwing and drying (no. 7), and coalyard by the Severn; printed in the *Gentleman's Magazine* 1752.

13 London dockside *c.* 1757, with the Customs House and Tower of London: a satire on the import of luxury wares from France.

14 Billingsgate market women by Thomas Rowlandson 1810.

15 Bristol shopping arcade 1825: interior of the Upper St James St Arcade designed by James Foster.

16 Street poor in Covent Garden, London: 'Morning' from William Hogarth's 'The Four Times of the Day', first published in 1738.

17 Common Council Chamber, Guildhall, London, by A. Pugin *c.* 1809.

18 Parliamentary election at Bedford elections 1832, with its depiction of the street theatre of party politics.

19 Assembly at Bagnigge Wells, Finsbury, London, *c.* 1770, by John Sanders: a major occasion for public sociability attended by both men and women.

20 Club life: the Lumber Troop 1783: a satire on urban male sociability.

21 St George's church, Hanover Square, London; designed by John James and built between 1721 and 1724 on a West End estate being developed by the Earl of Scarborough.

22 Domestic housing, Stamford: eighteenth-century houses in the smart Barn Hill area of this small town.

23 Moray Place, New Town, Edinburgh: developed by the earl of Moray from the 1820s, with James Gillespie Graham as the principal architect.

24 Birmingham Town Hall, begun in 1832 by the town's improvement commission and designed by Hansom and Welch on the model of a Roman temple.

25 Borough High Street, Southwark, *c.* 1729: shows the interaction of commercial and convivial activity in this major market area (Borough market was closed in 1755).

26 Angel Hill, Bury St Edmunds, by John Kendall, 1774: a principal centre of fashionable sociability in East Anglia; the Angel Inn is to the right.

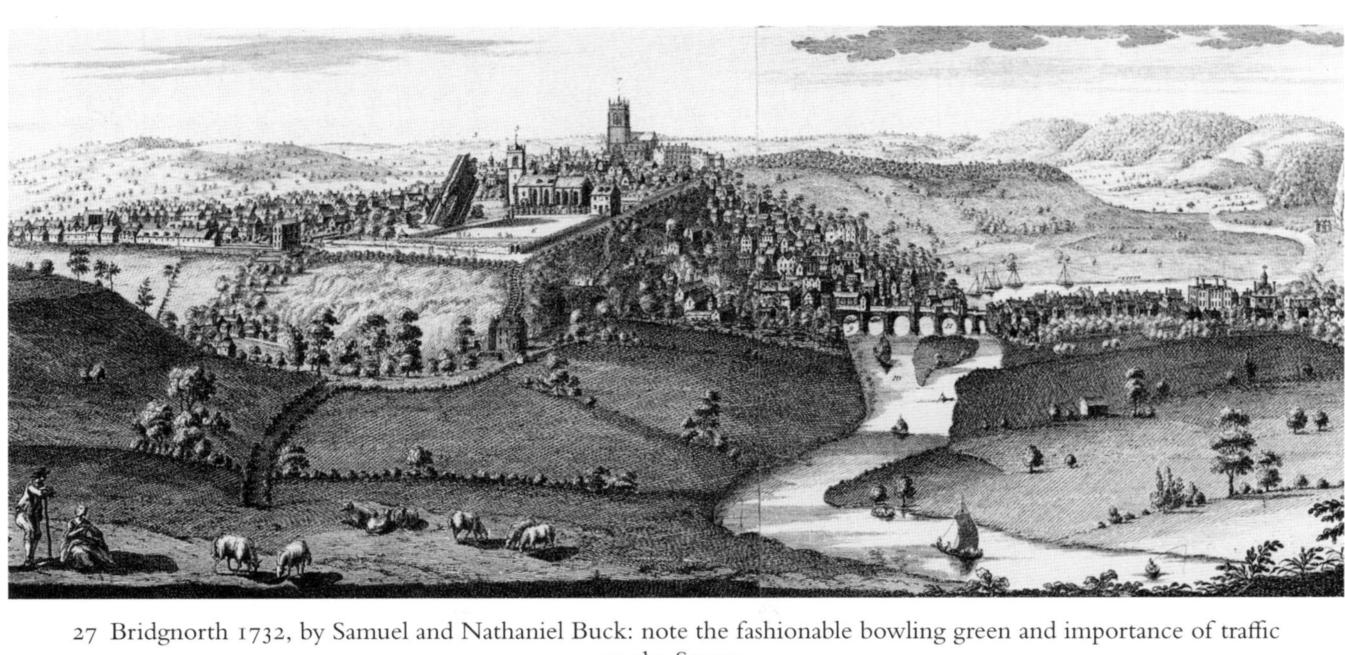

27 Bridgnorth 1732, by Samuel and Nathaniel Buck: note the fashionable bowling green and importance of traffic on the Severn.

28 A south-west prospect of Bath by T. Robins 1757: showing the town's major development as a spa complete with classical-style terraces.

29 Scarborough seaside, early nineteenth century: indicating the spa (on the left), smart houses, horse-riding socialites and the continued role of the port.

30 Early industrial Bradford: view (1825–1833) by James Wilson Anderson, with factory chimneys belching smoke.

31 Arrival of the railway into south-west Leicester *c.* 1840.

· PART II ·

Urban themes and types 1540–1700

· 5 ·

Towns in an agrarian economy 1540–1700

PAUL GLENNIE AND IAN WHYTE

'A town was never more a town than when filled with country people.'[1]

(i) INTRODUCTION

TOWNS IN early modern Britain performed many commercial, manufacturing, service, legal, political and cultural functions, and these were unevenly distributed. Even capitals as dominant as London and Edinburgh did not contain all the activities found in their respective urban systems, and different towns performed varying combinations of functions, whose fortunes shaped significant restructurings of British urban systems over this period. Urban production and trade, and their regulation, involved townspeople acting in various local, regional and national contexts. Many facets of urban life were tightly intertwined with hinterlands, and interdependences of town and country were central to many urban economic sectors. While some historiographical tension persists between work focusing on contrasting features of urban and rural life, and work focusing on urban–rural (and urban–urban) connections, the foci are substantially complementary. Contrasts grew as connectivity increased, with growing spatial divisions of labour in economic, political, social or cultural activities. This chapter considers urban life, insofar as it was distinctive, through the specialised roles connecting towns with other places. We interpret 'agrarian' broadly, since rural economies were seldom solely agricultural.

In comparative studies of European urbanisation, threshold populations of 5,000 or 10,000 have often been used, and for the demographic analysis of British towns this makes sense.[2] But from an economic perspective very many much

[1] J. Barry, 'Bourgeois collectivism? Urban association and the middling sort', in J. Barry and C. Brooks, eds., *The Middling Sort of People* (London, 1994), p. 90.

[2] For example, J. de Vries, *European Urbanization 1500–1800* (London, 1984); E. A. Wrigley, 'Urban growth and agricultural change: England and the continent in the early modern period', *Journal*

smaller places were unambiguously regarded as towns by contemporaries for whom functions, rather than population, provided 'urban' attributes. Sixteenth-century urban economic specialisations were less marked than later, but earlier commentators readily – if unsystematically – characterised towns by their specialised functions. Thus in the late sixteenth century Camden pointed to important regional corn markets (Warminster); malt entrepôts (Wallingford, Abingdon); regional trade centres and ports (Bristol, Gloucester, Norwich, Yarmouth); thoroughfare towns, especially around London (Dunstable, Royston, Ware, Uxbridge); clothing manufacture (Halifax; Newbury, Reading and Wokingham; Tenterden, Benenden and Cranbrook); centres for rural metalware industries (Birmingham, Sheffield); industrial centres (coal mining around Newcastle and Durham, alum production at Whitby); and even spas (Buxton, Matlock, Bath). Elsewhere, decay attracted his attention: towns hard-hit by declining cloth industries (Beverley, York), by the dissolution of monasteries and by rival markets.[3]

The majority of these towns contained populations of under 2,000. Most other early modern towns did. Notwithstanding their small populations, though, small towns were more than mere markets.[4] Especially in Scotland and Wales, centres of perhaps 500 people exercised several central place functions and might contain dealers, a range of artisans and various professional men.[5] Such towns formed the normal experience of urban life for many rural dwellers.

The concern of topographers like Camden with towns' economic condition, and of historians with towns as centres of information, both reflect contemporary perceptions of towns as places susceptible to instability. While the British Isles were relatively peaceful by European standards, townspeople regarded their world as one of endemic uncertainty, with households constantly threatened by disorder brought about by war, epidemics, food shortages, trade disruptions and irregular incomes. Unsurprisingly, then, urban populations maintained a practical interest in news of war, government policy and political events as prime determinants of conditions of trade and credit.

Preceding chapters have already highlighted several striking features of British urbanisation in the Tudor and Stuart period – the pre-eminence of London, the modest size of major provincial towns, the many small market towns, substan-

Footnote 2 (*cont.*)
of Interdisciplinary History, 15 (1985), 683–728; P. Bairoch, *Cities and Economic Development* (London, 1988); K. Terlouw, 'A general perspective on the regional development of Europe from 1300 to 1850', *Journal of Historical Geography*, 22 (1996), 129–46; and see below, pp. 196–8.

3 W. Camden, *Britannia* (published posthumously, London, 1607). Leland in the 1530s was less interested in urban activity than Camden or later writers such as Defoe.

4 P. J. Corfield, 'Small towns, large implications: social and cultural roles of small towns in eighteenth century England and Wales', *British Journal for Eighteenth-Century Studies*, 10 (1987), 125–38.

5 M. Lynch, 'Urbanisation and urban networks in seventeenth century Scotland: some further thoughts', *Scottish Economic and Social History*, 12 (1992), 24; T. C. Smout, *Old Aberdeen* (Aberdeen, 1983) p. 10.

tial national and regional variations in urbanisation and wide variations in the experience of individual towns. Total urban populations grew absolutely and relatively between 1540 and 1700, but growth was chronologically and geographically variable, reflecting many factors whose impacts were felt very unevenly. Using a population threshold of 5,000 and above, E. A. Wrigley estimates that 5.5 per cent of English population lived in towns in *c.* 1520 and 17 per cent in *c.* 1700, rather lower proportions than in Europe, although the gap was closing rapidly. Taking wider demographic parameters, including smaller towns, the British population appears considerably more developed. When small towns are included, the British population appears relatively urbanised: 30–3 per cent in England, 22–5 per cent in Scotland and 13–15 per cent in Wales. Much recent research has emphasised the many small towns in Britain, alongside the small number of large urban centres, and the establishment of new towns, especially in Scotland.

This chapter divides into four sections. We first discuss the changing institutional contexts that shaped the powers of towns and townspeople, and then discuss the topics of towns and agricultural change, urban industrial roles and urban service and socio-cultural industries. There were major changes in each of these three areas during the period, and in their connections with one another in shaping economic conditions in urban areas.

(ii) INSTITUTIONAL CONTEXTS

An appreciation of their diverse institutional and political contexts is essential for understanding urban economies. Several factors are involved. Some institutions were formal, such as crown regulation, the administrative duties devolved to towns or powers established by towns' chartered status. These institutions typically both resolved disputes and created various tensions between central governments and urban corporations; among towns over jurisdictions and monopolies; and between privileged elites and other townspeople. Other institutions were informal though no less influential, including the influence of local magnates, and long-run shifts in urban property ownership (not least through Henry VIII's seizure of monastic lands).

Medievalists have downgraded the importance once assigned to corporate 'borough' status.[6] Formal legal privileges played a still less important role in early modern England. Only some 20 per cent of English small towns had a borough charter, establishing self-government through an elected council, and empowering officials to administer revenues, regulate markets and so forth. However,

[6] C. Dyer, 'The hidden trade of the later middle ages: evidence from the West Midlands of England', *Journal of Historical Geography*, 18 (1992), 141–57; C. Dyer, 'How urbanised was medieval England?', in E. Thoen, ed., *Peasants and Townspeople: Studia in Honorem Adriaan Verhulst* (Ghent, 1995), pp. 169–83.

the diminishing powers of corporations and guilds often made enforcement impracticable, despite periodic attempts to enforce market monopolies, especially during grain shortages. Corporate status often did entail potential political influence, since most boroughs returned MPs. While English town MPs, unlike their Scottish equivalents, only rarely acted in concert, they contributed to a general atmosphere of urban self-interest. Unincorporated towns worked within a less formal framework of manorial and parish offices. Here, much depended on balancing the potential handicap of an anachronistic administrative system and the potential advantages of flexible and loosely regulated trading arrangements. In many cases, apparently conservative arrangements accommodated significant changes in practice, such as the numerous town officials attached to Manchester's court leet.[7] Many unincorporated towns developed rather more than manorial apparatus, including the building of town halls and market buildings.[8]

In Scotland, chartered status was much more important. By 1500, two groups of burghs had emerged: royal burghs and burghs of barony. Royal burghs held long-standing monopoly privileges, in return for taxation contributions. The merchants of royal burghs had sole rights to carry on overseas trade within large 'liberties', some covering whole sheriffdoms. Domestic trade within liberties was also notionally monopolised by royal burghs. Scottish royal burghs developed a national political lobby (before an integrated urban network) through the Convention of Royal Burghs, an assembly of representatives which apportioned burghs' taxation contributions, promoted their interests and formed a unified voice in the Scottish parliament. In practice, however, royal burghs were compelled to accommodate growing trade in numerous chartered burghs of barony. Merchants here were confined to domestic trade, and could only trade within the burgh itself, but successful baronial burghs carved out niches of considerable local significance, as economic satellites to royal burghs. Baronial burghs intruded on trade sufficiently for royal burghs to seek and obtain confirmation of royal privileges in 1633, although such protests were usually ineffectual, as at Old Aberdeen (baronial burgh) and Aberdeen (royal burgh).[9] Restrictive monopolies were increasingly attacked, and a Scottish parliamentary act of 1672 gave merchants in baronial burghs substantial access to overseas trade. Entry controls to burgesship and merchant guilds were also relaxed. By 1700 the old system of monopolies and personal restriction had been largely dismantled, narrowing institutional differences within Britain.

[7] T. S. Willan, *Elizabethan Manchester* (Manchester, 1980).

[8] Possibly building on pre-Reformation guilds and informal parish councils that had, for example, overseen the elections of churchwardens and other local officers: B. Kumin, *The Shaping of a Community: The Rise and Reformation of the English Parish c. 1400–1560* (Aldershot, 1996). For town halls, R. Tittler, *Architecture and Power* (Oxford, 1991).

[9] Lynch, 'Urbanisation and urban networks', 17; Smout, *Old Aberdeen*, pp. 38–56.

The rise of baronial burghs shifted economic power from town corporations to those rural landowners who were powerful in baronial burghs. Within the highly decentralised Scottish administrative and judicial systems, magnates offering protection to towns were in a powerful position, especially in peripheral areas remote from royal authority. Where regional landownership was fragmented, towns were less prone to magnate dominance, though even some royal burghs were subject to noble rivalries pursued through attempts to 'pack' councils.[10] Over most of Scotland, magnate dominance of urban power diminished after *c.* 1600, partly because a withdrawal of nobility left urban government to urbanites and partly because closer links were developing between burghs and central government. Royal power in the localities grew as towns were drawn into national affairs by political crises beginning with the Reformation in 1560, by increasing taxation and by initiatives encouraging a more coordinated urban voice in national politics.[11]

There was no equivalent to the Convention of Royal Burghs in England. English government was highly centralised in London, and English towns, by European standards, lacked formal political and financial powers. The provincial governing classes mainly resided either at country seats or in London, rather than in provincial towns, but they were nevertheless able to manipulate much urban parliamentary representation. Towns consequently argued and acted more individually than Scottish burghs, and lacked a distinctive national political role.[12] When large towns did exert wider influences (as in political allegiance during the English Civil War) they did not construct a specifically urban interest.

Especially before the late seventeenth century, urban food supply was far from a matter of market forces. Non-market channels of food supply were not uncommon, and food markets were regulated with regard to places and times of trading, market institutions and the personnel involved. Changing patterns of market regulation affected urban households' access to grain. The dominant 'consumer-protection' theme of anti-forestalling legislation diminished over time. This was partly due to open markets becoming less important venues for trading in grain, but also reflected a diminishing inclination to enforce it on the part of local and central authorities.

A shift away from paternalistic attitudes on part of authorities, and the breakdown of consensus on market regulation, are evident in the changing scope of the books of orders that set out magistrates' powers in periods of grain shortage

[10] Even here, there were exceptional circumstances, for example during royal minorities, when Edinburgh's capital status induced Court factions to attempt to install 'puppet' provosts: Lynch, 'Introduction', in M. Lynch, ed., *The Early Modern Town in Scotland* (London, 1987), pp. 20–5.

[11] M. Lynch, 'Continuity and change in urban society, 1500–1700', in R. A. Houston and I. D. Whyte, eds., *Scottish Society 1500–1800* (Cambridge, 1989), p. 85.

[12] D. Stevenson, 'The burghs and the Scottish Revolution', in Lynch, ed., *Early Modern Town*, pp. 167–91, at p. 168.

and high prices. These included measures for prohibiting exports, controlling prices, restricting the movement of grain and uses of grain, and regulatory powers for subsidised distribution of grain by urban or county authorities. Political debates on the framing and implementation of orders were complex, and subject to many influences.[13] Nevertheless, their changing scope and use does seem to mark an abandonment of explicit measures to protect grain supplies to urban markets. Along with restrictions on settlement, especially after the Settlement Act of 1662, these institutional changes may have substantially influenced subsistence migration patterns.

Town–country relations were also affected by the changing effects of taxation. Levels of medieval taxation in English towns relative to rural communities have been much debated.[14] Scotland as a nation was taxed much less heavily than England, and within Scotland towns were relatively lightly taxed. In the course of the sixteenth and seventeenth centuries, the total weight of taxation rose, and increasing ranges of activities were taxed in both countries. For example, Edinburgh paid more tax to the crown in the first twenty months of the reign of Charles I than it had done in the last twenty-five years of his predecessor James VI/I.[15] By the 1640s, the towns had become the most heavily taxed sector of a Scottish society that was now much more heavily taxed than hitherto.

Taxation was increasingly central to English, and then British, state finance, eclipsing revenue from crown lands and customs, largely as a means of financing wars. The introduction of indirect taxes on spending, especially the excise, exploited broader economic changes. Excise officials oversaw an increasing range of commodities and processes. Excise revenues were central to English state revenues by 1700, although they were extended to Scotland only in 1707.[16] Towns were affected both through changes in the geography of taxation and through their role as centres of fiscal administration. Disputes about apportioning taxation set urban communities against one another, and against other sectional interests within county communities. Overall, towns were contributing a greater share of British government revenue, and this reflected both their growing share of wealth, and a targeting of urban activities.[17] New taxes were

[13] J. Walter and K. Wrightson, 'Dearth and the social order in early modern England', *P&P*, 71 (1976), 22–42; A. Appleby, *Famine in Tudor and Stuart England* (London, 1978); R. B. Outhwaite, *Dearth, Public Policy and Social Disturbance in England, 1550–1800* (London, 1991), pp. 35–44.

[14] A. Dyer, *Decline and Growth in English Towns 1400–1640* (London, 1991; 2nd edn, Cambridge, 1995).

[15] Lynch, 'Continuity and change', p. 85.

[16] P. O'Brien, 'Agriculture and the home market for English industry, 1660–1820', *EHR*, 100 (1985), 773–800; J. Brewer, *The Sinews of Power: War, Money and the English State* (London, 1989).

[17] M. Braddick, *Parliamentary Taxation in Seventeenth Century England: Local Administration and Response* (Woodbridge, 1994), p. 15; A. Fletcher, *Reform in the Provinces: The Government of Stuart England* (New Haven, 1986), pp. 202–34; C. Husbands, 'Regional change in a pre-industrial economy: wealth and population in England in the sixteenth and seventeenth centuries', *Journal of Historical Geography*, 13 (1987), 345–59.

mainly administered from towns. The excise administration involved the creation of a widely distributed, almost exclusively urban, workforce. By 1700 about 1,500 excise men were employed in English provincial centres and small towns.[18]

(iii) URBANISATION AND AGRICULTURAL CHANGE

Town populations largely relied on others for crops, livestock products, fuel and other materials, but we should also recognise the significance of agricultural production *within* almost all towns. Quite apart from open ground within town boundaries, most towns possessed common grazing land, and many (including county towns and regional capitals) possessed their own fields and commons. Aberdeen ranked third among Scottish towns in 1660, but drew much of its grain from town lands, and supported several dairies. This was the townscape described by Gordon of Rothiemay in 1660: 'mony houses have ther gardings and orche-yards adjoyning. Every garding has its posterne and thes are planted with all sorts of trees . . . so that the quhole toune . . . looks as if it stood in a garding or a little wood.'[19] Most large towns had specialist dairies, and many urban households kept livestock, especially pigs and poultry. Others held land, laboured in the town's fields or took seasonal harvest work in surrounding countryside.[20] Seasonal harvest or other agricultural work was common among poorer households surviving on what P. King calls a 'jigsaw of makeshifts'.[21] In very small towns, a substantial proportion of men might work mainly in agriculture.[22]

Notwithstanding urban agricultural production, however, large quantities of food, fodder, fuel and livestock were brought into towns from beyond their immediate territories. Even quite small populations consumed the production of substantial areas of land, although these cannot be precisely reconstructed or calculated. John Chartres estimates that grain consumption in London, either as food or brewed drinks, increased from 0.5 million to 1.3 million quarters in the course of the seventeenth century.[23] Depending on crop yields and fallowing

[18] Brewer, *Sinews of Power*.

[19] Quoted by D. MacNiven, 'Merchants and traders in early seventeenth century Aberdeen' (MLitt thesis, University of St Andrews, 1977), p. 89.

[20] T. C. Smout, *A History of the Scottish People 1560–1830* (London, 1969), p. 167.

[21] P. King, 'Customary rights and women's earnings', *Ec.HR*, 2nd series, 44 (1991), 461–76.

[22] I. D. Whyte, 'The occupational structure of Scottish burghs in the late seventeenth century', in Lynch, ed., *Early Modern Town*, p. 228.

[23] J. Chartres, 'Food consumption and internal trade', in A. L. Beier and R. Finlay, eds., *London 1500–1700* (London, 1986), pp. 168–96, estimates at p. 178; food consumption, energy content and stocking density data underlying this paragraph are from D. Briggs and F. Courtney, *Agriculture and Environment: The Physical Geography of Temperate Agricultural Systems* (London, 1989); J. Tivy, *Agricultural Ecology* (London, 1990); B. M. S. Campbell, J. A. Galloway, D. Keene and M. Murphy, *A Medieval Capital and its Grain Supply: Agrarian Production and Distribution in the London Region c. 1300* (Cheltenham, 1993), pp. 31–46, 72–7; H. J. Teuteberg, *European Food History: A Research Review* (Leicester, 1992).

arrangements, this may have represented the produce of from 1,000 to over 2,500 square miles of arable land. In addition, there were the fodder requirements of the urban horse population, both working horses and those kept for riding. Metropolitan meat consumption involved scores of thousands of animals a year, in turn requiring very large areas of grazing land in districts of livestock rearing and fattening. Urban consumption of butter, cheese and eggs likewise drew on large areas of pastoral land, and heating and other uses consumed large areas of coppiced woodland, even allowing for the growing use of coal for domestic heating and various industrial purposes. Many supply areas were located at considerable distance from their markets, so the requirements of people, driven animals and draught animals on the road involved the consumption of yet further food and fodder.

Even if, for simplicity, it is assumed that urban demands for straw, leather and tallow were available as by-products from food crops and animals, and required no additional areas of supply, even towns of 1,000 people or fewer drew on output equivalent to the total production of several square miles. In practice, their supplies derived from much larger areas, since towns' immediate environs usually contained significant populations, and only a modest proportion of total output was destined for urban mouths. Areas of supply were liable to change dramatically from year to year, and to vary markedly across space, due to temporal and spatial variations in the sown area of particular crops within rotations; crop yields per sown acre; livestock grazing densities; meat and milk yields; and loads per draught animal, depending on the sizes of packs, carts and wagons.

Distant demands from large town populations were felt especially strongly along arteries of river or coastal communications. London – the extreme case – drew grain from much of England and livestock from distant parts of Britain, through an increasingly extensive network of out-markets.[24] Documentation for the provisioning of other large towns is more sketchy. Bristol drew on much of the Severn Basin, and Newcastle drew produce from many areas of eastern coastal England and Scotland that were supplied with Tyneside coal. Similarly, Edinburgh relied on chains of coastal ports around the Firth of Forth for grain and other commodities. By 1700 Edinburgh's provisioning area extended from Orkney to Berwickhire, and Glasgow imported significant quantities of grain from Ireland.[25]

If London's drawing power was writ small in the impacts of smaller centres, supplying the capital generated more distinctive effects through substantial econ-

[24] F. J. Fisher, 'The development of the London food market', *Ec.HR*, 1st series, 5 (1934), 46–64; J. A. Chartres, 'The marketing of agricultural produce', in J. Thirsk, ed., *Ag.HEW*, vol. v(2) (Cambridge, 1985), pp. 446–7; Chartres, 'Food consumption and internal trade', in Beier and Finlay, eds., *London*, pp. 168–96.

[25] E. Richards and M. Clough, *Cromartie: Highland Life 1650–1915* (Aberdeen, 1989), p. 42; L. E. Cochran, *Scottish Trade with Ireland in the Eighteenth Century* (Edinburgh, 1985), p. 100.

omies of scale, and new forms of organisation and collusion in wholesaling networks. Strongly oligopsonistic market relations concentrated power among large-scale buyers at all levels of grain trading.[26] Ultimately, London corn factors' power was exercised at the expense of arable farmers – one reason why many contemporaries perceived large towns as parasitic on the countryside.[27] The power of drovers relative to livestock farmers was, on occasion, viewed in a similar light. Drovers also made an important contribution by financial circulation by carrying money (as cash or bills of exchange) to and from urban centres.[28] Other specialised practices developed in other commodity trades, notably wool, timber and coal.

As at London's out-markets, the effective demand for food manifest in a town could greatly exceed that of the town itself. Some hinterland inhabitants, especially in rural industrial districts, also depended on town markets for food. For example, grain from East Midland counties and the East Riding was supplied to proto-industrial populations in West Riding textile districts. Market networks in the West Midlands channelled grain towards areas with various metalworking specialisms from adjoining areas of increasingly commercial arable farming.[29] Distant demand was also transmitted through towns functioning as nodes in export or interregional trade networks. Over much of eastern Britain, especially East Anglia, exports across the North Sea and English Channel consumed significant parts of regional production, especially of wheat, barley and malt. Exports in *c.* 1700 accounted for 3 to 8 per cent of English grain production, depending on domestic and international market conditions.[30] Export trade could be disproportionately important for ports that were poorly integrated into national market systems.[31]

Long-distance grain trading generally secured food supplies to large towns, sometimes at the expense of rural consumers and dwellers in out-markets. The consequences for local food supplies depended on harvest quality, the form of trading networks, regulations to restrict trading in dearths and the capacity of townspeople to pay high grain prices. The urban demographic effects of harvest

[26] Oligopsony: where small numbers of large-scale buyers exert considerable economic power over large numbers of small-scale sellers: Chartres, 'Food consumption', pp. 184–8.

[27] E. A. Wrigley, 'Parasite or stimulus? The town in a pre-industrial economy', in P. Abrams and E. A. Wrigley, eds., *Towns in Societies* (Cambridge, 1978), pp. 295–309.

[28] Chartres, 'Marketing', pp. 479–82.

[29] J. Thirsk, *English Agricultural Regions and Agrarian History* (London, 1985), pp. 17–19; P. Large, 'Urban growth and agricultural change in the West Midlands during the seventeenth and eighteenth centuries', in P. Clark, ed. *The Transformation of English Provincial Towns 1600–1800* (London, 1984), pp. 169–86; M. Rowlands, 'Continuity and change in an industrialising society: the case of the West Midlands industries', in P. Hudson, ed., *Regions and Industries* (Cambridge, 1989), p. 121.

[30] D. Ormrod, *English Grain Exports and Agrarian Capitalism, 1700–1760* (Hull, 1985), p. 70.

[31] For eastern Scotland: I. D. Whyte, *Agriculture and Society in Seventeenth Century Scotland* (Edinburgh, 1979), p. 233; Lynch, 'Continuity and change'.

failures were highly variable. In England, crises in grain supplies were not, by and large, associated with high urban mortality after the 1590s, and in some districts not even then. In parts of northern England, high mortality followed dearths of grain in 1623, but these seem not to have affected towns in particular. In general, notwithstanding the limited level of transport technology, unwieldy regulation and the large production areas needed by towns of even modest size, English urban grain supplies were robust by European standards.[32] They were certainly so by comparison with Scotland and, to some extent, Ireland. In Scotland, there were substantial improvements in urban food supply from the 1660s.[33] Nevertheless, this proved unable to prevent the famines of the later 1690s causing large-scale mortality in towns like Aberdeen which lost 20 per cent of its population (see p. 206). Whether or not the most severe impacts of food shortages were felt in towns, the most visible expressions of popular dissatisfaction were urban.[34]

Urban impacts on agriculture extended far beyond the production and movement of commodities. Changes in many aspects of agriculture were, at least in part, related to urban demand. There were many possible impacts: more specialised production; more intensive cultivation; higher land productivity; greater labour inputs; concentration of landholding and larger farm enterprises; higher rents; higher levels of investment, some of it drawing on urban capital; and the use of a diverse range of fertilisers including the use as manure of a variety of domestic and industrial refuse from towns.[35]

Increasingly specialised production occurred in the immediate vicinity of towns, especially through market gardening of fruit and vegetables, and dairying oriented to fresh milk production. More generally, if slightly further afield, urban demand for hay, wood and fresh fat livestock created commercial opportunities or institutional needs for specialised production around larger towns. Both market gardening and intensive livestock production were usually intimately connected to the by-products of urban agricultural processing industries, especially brewing and milling. Contemporaries identified many urban households as able to afford more regular meat consumption, and rising urban populations and living stan-

[32] A. Appleby, 'Grain prices and subsistence crises in England and France, 1590–1740', *Journal of Economic History*, 39 (1978), 865–87; Appleby, *Famine*; E. A. Wrigley and R. S. Schofield, *The Population History of England 1541–1871* (London, 1981), pp. 645–93.

[33] T. M. Devine, 'The merchant class of the larger Scottish towns in the seventeenth and early eighteenth centuries', in G. Gordon and B. Dicks, eds., *Scottish Urban History* (Aberdeen, 1983), p. 96.

[34] Thus most food riots reported to parliament in the 1690s occurred in towns. R. B. Outhwaite, 'Dearth and government intervention in grain markets, 1590–1700', *Ec.HR*, 2nd series, 34 (1981), 397.

[35] M. Overton, 'The determinants of crop yields in early modern England', in B. Campbell and M. Overton, eds., *Land, Labour and Livestock: Historical Studies in European Agricultural Productivity* (Manchester, 1991), pp. 284–322; M. Overton, *Agricultural Revolution in England: The Transformation of the Agrarian Economy, 1500–1850* (Cambridge, 1996).

dards often stimulated local swings from arable to livestock production, as in late seventeenth-century central Scotland, to serve Edinburgh and Glasgow.[36]

Neither large farms nor commercial orientation were novel features in *c.* 1550. Nor was the existence of considerable regional contrasts in patterns of landholding. In those areas where they have been studied in detail it is clear that urban demands for foods and investment in land by townspeople were only two factors among many in the emergence of large farm units.[37] Nevertheless, in the long run, increasing urbanisation and commercial agricultural production, especially of cereals, were broadly associated with increasing concentrations of landholding, increased average farm sizes, capitalist land tenures and agricultural wage labour. The highest degree of concentration of holdings occurred in commercially oriented arable areas, across much of southern England and the Midlands, but even here the relative scarcity of land in smaller holdings should not be exaggerated, and in some districts the bulk of holdings (although not the bulk of land) remained in small units until a very much later date.[38] In Scotland, the origins of larger, commercially oriented holdings has been less systematically examined. Multiple tenancy and smaller holdings were common in north-east Scotland and the western Lowlands, whereas large single-tenant farms, worked by hired servants, oriented to urban demand and yielding higher rents, were characteristic of the Lothians.[39] The effect on agriculture in areas with easy access to the Edinburgh market are illustrated by the Dundas estates near South Queensferry, where liming began in 1624 and an intensive farming system geared to grain production had developed by the 1630s.[40]

The precise connections between agrarian change and the penetration of urban capital are unclear for many parts of Britain. For example, what was the

[36] R. A. Dodgshon, *Land and Society in Early Scotland* (Oxford, 1981), p. 242.

[37] On the London area, M. McIntosh, *Autonomy and Community: The Royal Manor of Havering, 1200–1500* (Cambridge, 1986); M. McIntosh, *A Community Transformed: The Manor and Liberty of Havering, 1500–1620* (Cambridge, 1991); P. Glennie, 'In search of agrarian capitalism: manorial land markets and the acquisition of land in the Lea valley *c.* 1450–*c.* 1560', *Continuity and Change*, 3 (1987), 11–40. More generally, J. Yelling, 'Agriculture 1500–1730', in R. A. Dodgshon and R. Butlin, eds., *An Historical Geography of England and Wales*, 2nd edn (London, 1990), pp. 181–98; J. V. Beckett, *The Agricultural Revolution* (London, 1990), pp. 45–53; R. C. Allen, *Enclosure and the Yeoman: The Agricultural Development of the South Midlands, 1450–1850* (Oxford, 1992), pp. 78–104.

[38] R. B. Outhwaite, 'Progress and backwardness in English agriculture, 1500–1640', *Ec.HR*, 2nd series, 39 (1986), 1–18; A. Howkins, 'Peasants, servants and labourers: the marginal workforce in British agriculture, *c.* 1870–1914', *Agricultural History Review*, 42 (1994), 49–62; Overton, *Agricultural Revolution*, pp. 168–82.

[39] Dodgshon, *Land and Society*, pp. 241–55; T. Devine, *The Transformation of Rural Scotland: Social Change and the Agrarian Economy 1660–1815* (Edinburgh, 1994), pp. 2–3; I. D. Whyte, *Scotland before the Industrial Revolution* (London, 1995), p. 174.

[40] I. D. Whyte, 'Infield–outfield farming on a seventeenth-century Scottish estate', *Journal of Historical Geography*, 5 (1979), 391–402; J. Brown, 'The social, political and economic influences of the Edinburgh merchant elite 1600–38' (PhD thesis, University of Edinburgh, 1985). On transport of urban refuse as manure several miles from Edinburgh: Whyte, *Agriculture and Society*, pp. 68–70.

relative importance of motives of profit and prestige beneath the growing trend for merchants and professionals to invest in rural land, rather than exclusively in urban property, in the seventeenth century? Merchants and others may have acquired land as security for collapsed loans, in which case their holdings were an accidental result of the commercial regime rather than a coherent investment or diversification strategy.[41] Much urban capital also went into urban property ownership, of course, enlarging the rentier element within towns, and this was marked in marketing and retailing facilities themselves. At Hoddesdon, Hertfordshire, for example, as the numbers of market stalls and shops increased from twenty-eight in 1571 to thirty-five in 1585 and fifty-nine in 1639, ownership became significantly more concentrated. In 1639, just four men owned thirty-one of the shops and stalls, with the other twenty-seven owned by twenty-two men (although the average of 1.2 stalls or shops among the latter group was higher than that for the whole market sixty years earlier).[42]

Several types of evidence enable inferences about economic integration, especially in grain markets. Direct evidence for the commercial movement of goods comes from records of transport of goods, payment for goods and credit networks. Indirect evidence includes the development of areas of complementary product specialisations.[43] Such specialisms, and large-scale movements away from subsistence-oriented agricultural production, imply developed market networks for foodstuffs. Evidence for economic integration also comes from geographical analyses of price trends. At least four features in space–time patterns of prices indicate markets closely connected through the movements of goods, people and capital: first, similar short-term movements in prices in different markets, indicating the movement of goods over space in response to price differences;[44] secondly, distinctive price surfaces, with peaks 'over' large urban populations, and falling prices away from centres of demand (prices at other points represent the market centre price less transport costs, transactions costs, and marketing profits – see Map 5.1);[45] thirdly, decreased synchronicity in price fluctuations for differ-

[41] J. J. Brown, 'Merchant princes and mercantile investment in early seventeenth-century Edinburgh', in Lynch, ed., *Early Modern Town*, p. 138.

[42] J. Tregelles, *History of Hoddesdon* (Hertford, 1908), pp. 246–7; Cambridge University Library, Ee.III.6(c).

[43] J. Langton, 'The Industrial Revolution and the regional geography of England', *Transactions of the Institute of British Geographers*, new series, 9 (1984), 145–67; D. J. Gregory, 'The production of regions in England's Industrial Revolution', *Journal of Historical Geography*, 14 (1988), 50–8; A. Kussmaul, *A General View of the Rural Economy of England, 1538–1840* (Cambridge, 1990).

[44] C. Granger and C. Elliott, 'A fresh look at wheat prices and markets in the eighteenth century', *Ec.HR*, 2nd series, 20 (1967), 257–65; J. A. Chartres, 'Market integration and agricultural output in seventeenth-, eighteenth-, and early nineteenth century England', *Agricultural History Review*, 43 (1995), 117–38.

[45] N. Gras, *The Evolution of the English Corn Market* (Cambridge, Mass., 1915); J. Walter and R. Schofield, eds., *Famine, Disease and the Social Order in Early Modern Society* (Cambridge, 1989).

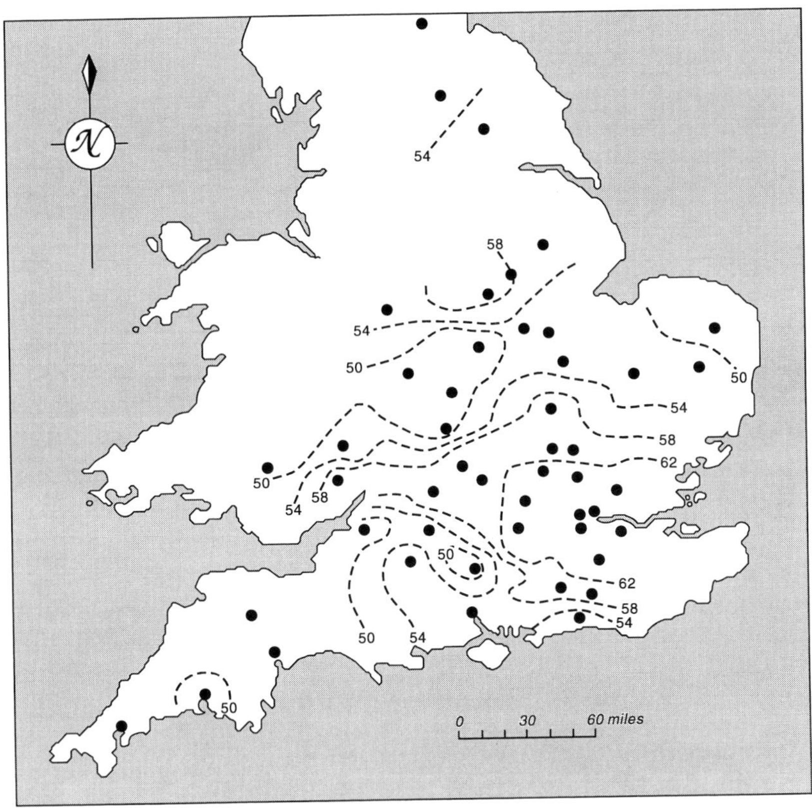

Map 5.1 Wheat prices in England and Wales December 1698 to January 1699 (shillings per quarter)

ent, but substitutable, grains;[46] finally, a decreasing amplitude of price fluctuations as they became damped by wider-scale grain movements, and prices are, in effect, averaged over wider areas. Ideally these measures would co-vary but in practice data are rarely available for all the measures to be calculated at once.

The earliest attempt to collect prices across the country was initiated in the late 1680s by John Houghton, in his commercial newspaper *Collections Relating to Husbandry and Trade*.[47] Over some fifteen years, Houghton amassed data of

[46] For example, if wheat was brought in during local shortages, in preference to substituting barley for wheat, local wheat and barley prices should fluctuate more independently than if a shortage of wheat forces higher local consumption of barley. Appleby, 'Grain prices'. Scope for such substitution varied: A. Gibson and T. C. Smout, 'Regional prices and market regions: the evolution of the early modern Scottish grain market', *Ec.HR*, 2nd series, 48 (1995), 258–82, argue that there was no real substitute for oatmeal across most of Scotland.

[47] J. E. T. Rogers, *A History of Agriculture and Prices in England* (Oxford, 1866–92), vol. IV; Chartres, 'Marketing', pp. 460–65.

varying regularity for over 100 English and Welsh grain markets, indicating that '[T]he integrated "national" market for wheat, defined as one which reacted fairly evenly to disequilibriating factors, was present in the 1690s.'[48] Nationally synchronous price fluctuations were present, but less marked, for barley. Rye prices imply several regional markets, rather than a national market. These patterns imply plausible differences in markets for different grains, and were clearly not new, but more work is needed on preceding centuries. In Scotland, too, significant changes were occurring:

> [S]ignificant developments towards the integration of local markets took place in the second half of the seventeenth century, at first as two sub-national markets, but by the end of the century as a single national one within which routine grain movements served to unite the whole of lowland Scotland into an integrated price region . . .
>
> [A] real improvement in the effectiveness of the Scottish oatmeal market occurred, . . . was clearly episodic and punctuated by periods . . . of market dislocation.[49]

Another key urban economic role within rural society lay in the provision of credit, on which many activities depended. Credit networks were dense in both town and country, involving large proportions of the population. Towns' central roles in credit networks followed from their centrality to marketing, retailing and informal trading. Various credit mechanisms facilitated both cash loans and, more importantly, complex forms of payment and consumption. Rural households received credit through urban merchants, craftsmen and shopkeepers, and farmers extended credit to urban-based dealers, drovers and processors. In late seventeenth-century Lynn, for example, the majority of households were involved in minor debt litigation, including many of the town's poor: debt litigation 'not merely penetrated deep into society but seems to have engulfed it completely'.[50]

(iv) INDUSTRIAL SPECIALISATION IN TOWNS AND THEIR HINTERLANDS

Sixteenth-century British towns contained only a limited range of industrial activity. They generally included significant numbers of craft artisans in 'basic' sectors, catering for urban and hinterland demands for food, drink, textiles, clothing, leather and everyday household items of wood and metal. Their numbers and degree of occupational specialisation varied with town size, but many urban craftsmen otherwise resembled village artisan-retailers. Such occu-

[48] Chartres, 'Marketing', p. 460. [49] Gibson and Smout, 'Regional prices', 281, 269.

[50] A. Dyer, *The City of Worcester in the Sixteenth Century* (Leicester, 1973), pp. 68–9; MacNiven, 'Merchants and traders', p. 231; C. Muldrew, 'Credit and the courts: debt litigation in a seventeenth-century urban community', *Ec.HR*, 2nd series, 46 (1993), 23–38, quote at 30.

pations were as ubiquitous a feature of towns as marketing and retailing and, although they have traditionally been accorded little importance, collectively they were a vital part of what made small towns 'urban'. Towns gradually developed more complex occupational structures, usually dominated by a broad craft base oriented to an extensive domestic market area. General trading conditions, and control over trade, were central to their industrial and commercial health.

Greater attention has been devoted to less commonplace manufacturing specialisms that gave towns distinctive characters. Relatively little production of what contemporaries referred to as 'manufactures' took place in towns, except in London and in some wool textile centres retaining their late medieval specialisms.[51] Rural textile industries thrived, however, especially in the West Country, East Anglia and the West Riding.[52] At the start of our period, many manufactured goods were imported rather than domestically produced. Many seventeenth-century commentators present a similar picture. Thus Richard Blome's *Britannia* (1673) identified a limited number of urban manufacturing specialisms, and most of these were in southern England. Gregory King's social tables, compiled in the 1690s, paint a dualistic picture of a trading-industrial metropolis and a vast agricultural hinterland. These impressions are misleading. The situation had been transformed from the decades around 1600 by several new urban manufacturing specialisms. Most produced prosaic items for regional or national markets: familiar examples include shoemaking in Northampton, saddlers' ironmongery in Walsall; buttons in Macclesfield; hosiery in Nottingham; glass in Stourbridge and Nottingham; nets in Bridport; 'carpets' (textile hangings) in Kidderminster.[53] Simultaneously, many older cloth production centres revived, sometimes by switching to lighter New Draperies. Before 1700, net imports of manufactured goods had been largely replaced by considerable manufacturing exports from England and, to a lesser extent, Scotland.

Just as urban historians have mainly been preoccupied with distinctive economic sectors rather than 'basic' activities, so they have tended to focus on men's work, and to take women's work for granted in early modern towns. In part these are connected, for many manufacturing activities were mainly male activities. A recent upsurge of work on the economic activities of women has developed earlier pioneering work.[54] The main strands of new work include the

51 On London, see also A. L. Beier, 'Engines of manufacture: the trades of London', in Beier and Finlay, eds., *London*, pp. 141–67; N. Zahedieh, 'London and the colonial consumer in the late seventeenth century', *Ec.HR*, 2nd series, 47 (1994), 239–61.

52 P. J. Bowden, *The Wool Trade in Tudor and Stuart England* (London, 1962).

53 A. M. Everitt, 'Country, county and town: patterns of regional evolution in England', *TRHS*, 5th series, 29 (1979), 79–108; J. Thirsk, *Economic Policy and Projects* (Oxford, 1978); Dyer, *Decline and Growth*, pp. 56–7; J. Houghton, *Collections relating to Husbandry and Trade* (London, 1691–1703).

54 E.g. A. Clark, *Working Life of Women in the Seventeenth Century* (London, 1919); A. Laurence, *Women in England 1500–1760: A Social History* (London, 1994) pp. 108–43.

centrality of women's work to poorer households (for whom the term 'jigsaw of makeshifts' is as useful as for their rural counterparts). In their own right, women were of greater economic importance in practice than the legal theory of the time might have suggested. They were important in relation to property, credit and the maintenance of businesses. They were directly involved in certain lines of selling and retailing, both in shops and markets. They were employed in increasing numbers, although a narrow range of roles, in certain new service sectors. To some extent these expanding opportunities, along with the increasing scale of urban domestic service by the late seventeenth century, countered a narrowing of female work in other spheres. A range of crafts and apprenticeships were less open to women than in the early sixteenth century, and many new occupations were explicitly, or implicitly but effectively, closed to women.

If expanding economies underlay urban growth, there were considerable variations in experience among towns, partly due to fierce competition among towns (especially where many towns created regional 'overcapacity' in market sites), and partly due to the streamlining of commercial networks. Increasing specialisation in particular leisure, transport, marketing or manufacturing functions offered one route out of competition among generalised trading centres, as towns catered for particular sectors of regional or national demand, rather than general local demands. Towns also capitalised on opportunities arising from transport improvements and lowered transactions costs, which created (if only temporarily) new opportunities for economic specialisation. Narrowly based urban economies, especially those most reliant on foreign trade, were clearly vulnerable to trade fluctuations, and to the growing concentration of foreign trade in the hands of London or Edinburgh merchants.[55] Urban systems also gained coherence in the distribution of specific activities. A feature of specialised trades (such as clockmaking) in the sixteenth century was their apparently random distribution among both large and small towns. Later, their distributions became more 'organised' within a more coherent urban hierarchy.

Some urban industrial specialisations grew where formerly rural industries became grafted on to towns' existing market functions. Regional proliferations of clothmaking, mining, metalworking, furniture making, leatherworking, or lacemaking were scattered across western Europe, and underlie theories of proto-industrialisation.[56] Their organisation and institutions involved varied among economic sectors and among regions, but towns commonly played several important roles. Industrial development commonly stimulated towns' ordinary market functions, in supplying of food and goods to proto-industrial

[55] Lynch, 'Urbanisation and urban networks'.

[56] S. Ogilvie and M. Cernan, eds., *European Protoindustrialization* (Cambridge, 1996); Hudson, ed., *Regions and Industries*; M. Zell, *Industry in the Countryside: Wealden Society in the Sixteenth Century* (Cambridge, 1994).

households. Within manufacturing, towns were often finishing centres taking part-finished goods from outworkers, especially where finishing processes involved specialised skills, close process control or large economies of scale, as in dyeing or tanning. Urban markets were vital for rural industries reliant on distant raw materials and distant markets. Many towns were also commercial centres, channelling local flows of wages, specifications, equipment, financial information and investment capital into and out of their hinterlands. In Scotland, the more formal control of royal burghs over their liberties sharpened the contrast between urban trading and finishing centres and rural areas of cloth production, as did the lack of Scottish urban textile production, apart from Dundee.[57]

Towards 1700, most English towns with industrial specialisms experienced considerable success, at least as measured through their increasing shares in national populations and wealth.[58] Only in the Weald have the drastic effects on towns of declining proto-industry been demonstrated: with 'great and general poverty' exacerbated by in-migration of former workers, withdrawal of clothiers and other masters, loss of specialised crafts and tradespeople, and lapsing of markets.[59]

Economic changes promoted changes in urban social structures, although in the direction of a proliferation of wealth and status positions rather than through any general processes of class formation. Perhaps unsurprisingly, given the diversity of economic experiences, urban societies were marked by a heterogeneous mix of status gradations, both occupational and personal, and relationships between and within social groupings seem to have been constantly renegotiated.

(v) TOWNS AS SOCIAL AND SERVICE CENTRES

Wide-ranging changes in urban social and cultural functions, especially after about 1660, had significant economic dimensions.[60] Towns were key social arenas for 'the middling sort', a term embracing diverse households of modest or greater prosperity, with shared commercial, recreational and administrative orientations. They both provided and consumed a range of professional and cultural services, which were most conspicuous where manufacturing growth

57 Whyte, 'Occupational structure', pp. 250–2.

58 Husbands, 'Regional change', 358–9.

59 B. Short, 'The deindustrialization process: a case study of the Weald, 1600–1850', in Hudson, ed., *Regions and Industries*, pp. 156–74, especially pp. 167–8.

60 P. Borsay, *The English Urban Renaissance* (Oxford 1989); P. Clark, *Sociability and Urbanity* (Leicester, 1988), pp. 1–22; P. Earle, *The Making of the English Middle Class* (London, 1989); J. Barry, 'Provincial town culture, 1640–1780: urbane or civic?', in J. H. Pittock and A. Wear, eds., *Interpretation and Cultural History* (London, 1991), pp. 198–234.

was limited, but manufacturing and service sectors did often expand together. New forms of consumption were seen, rightly or wrongly, by many contemporaries as distinctively urban. So was the large scale of involvement of women in services and retailing, part of the social and demographic feminisations of town life.

Several factors underlay the growth of urban service and social provision. Improved relations between towns and provincial social elites were a major factor in this 'urban renaissance'. The spending of rural and urban elites supported increased economic specialisation, retailing and new leisure and cultural activities. Patronage by rural landowners, especially by magnates, continued to be important as a focus for new activities. Urban and rural elites were increasingly interconnected by mercantile and professional investment in land, by apprenticeship of landowners' younger sons to merchants, and shared economic, cultural or administrative activity. Much county administration (sessions, musters, taxation) was decentralised to small towns, as was the growing excise system, with excisemen widely distributed through small towns from which they monitored activities within their designated rides and walks.[61] Not all administration involved elites, of course, as in the involvement of parish churchwardens in archdeaconry and episcopal visitations, and of parish constables at quarter sessions.

A social world increasingly divided (by wealth, by skills) was also characterised by 'bridging' activities, groups and places. At both high and low levels, professional and service sectors were important in mediating social relationships. Professional men of all sorts were frequently prominent urban citizens, and increasingly important to urban social cohesion. In cities as large as Edinburgh and as small as Elgin the legal profession was a considerable and wealthy presence.[62] Clergy and lawyers were key 'brokers' in social networks within and beyond towns, helping to bridge social divides between landowning and mercantile elites. Legal, educational and medical expertise was overwhelmingly urban, and spreading beyond larger towns after 1660. These sectors grew rapidly: the number of legally qualified men increased roughly tenfold between 1485 and 1640.[63] Provincial professional men frequently identified their professional skills as conferring spatial, as well as social, mobility; they identified themselves as part of a geographically widespread community of expertise, encapsulating their skills

[61] Brewer, *Sinews of Power*, pp. 101–14.

[62] Lynch, 'Urbanisation and urban networks', p. 30; H. Booton, 'Sir John Rutherford: a fifteenth century Aberdeen burgess', *Scottish Economic and Social History*, 10 (1990), 21–37; J. E. Thomas, 'Elgin notaries in burgh society and government 1540–1660', *Northern Scotland*, 13 (1993), 21–30.

[63] G. Holmes, *Augustan England* (London, 1982); C. Brooks, 'Professions, ideology and the middling sort in the late-sixteenth and early seventeenth centuries', in J. Barry and C. Brooks, eds., *The Middling Sort of People* (London, 1994), pp. 113–41; P. J. Corfield, *Power and the Professions in Eighteenth-Century England* (London, 1996).

and outlook in the many printed and manuscript compilations of draft legal agreements.[64]

Professional and commercial knowledges were not only important for urban economies, in urban cultures, and in local government. They also reshaped the ways in which elites and middling groups thought about education, intellectual skills and social status. Professional learning influenced general conceptions of the acquisition and utility of knowledge.[65] Excise and customs administration created a modest but significant addition to the professional and salaried population. Their fourteen months of full-time, mainly mathematical, training, and their incomes (£50 for ordinary officers up to over £100 for higher supervisors) made excisemen an important element among the growing urban professions. At Ipswich in 1702, for example, five excise officers and seven customs officers formed a significant group within the middling sort.[66] Their skills were a specialised form of much more widespread commercial knowledge: for example, the thirty-ninth and fortieth rules laid down for Carlisle Grammar School in 1699 stipulated that the usher assisting the schoolmaster be 'well skilled in the Art of writeing and Arithmetick, and know something of Geography, Measuring of Ground, Gaugeing, Navigation, &c'; specified that these subjects be taught every Thursday afternoon, and that the usher teach them 'at other times of vacation and as often as the parents desire', for which they are to pay him.[67] More generally, towns remained environments in which craft and trade skills were acquired. Despite uneven enforcement of regulations, apprenticeship remained a key socialising experience, especially for migrants.[68] Some towns built their economies around more specialised education: Oxford, Cambridge and Edinburgh each contained several hundred university students and staff whose economic and political power could be considerable, and there were smaller numbers in St Andrews, Aberdeen and Glasgow.

Market towns were routine meeting places for both religion and recreation, although set back by the loss of fraternities at the Reformation.[69] New religious associations of nonconformist dissent were predominantly urban. Quakers and Presbyterians were largely urban sects, but more broadly the typical territory of nonconformist meetings was the market area. Although most dissenters were country dwellers, assemblies mainly occurred in urban inns and

[64] For a manuscript example from Northampton, *c.* 1690: Northamptonshire RO, 575/40.

[65] C. Brooks, 'Apprenticeship, social mobility and the middling sort', in Barry and Brooks, eds., *Middling Sort*, pp. 52–83; Brooks, 'Professions, ideology', pp. 113–41; Barry, 'Bourgeois collectivism?'.

[66] M. Reed, 'Economic structure and change in seventeenth-century Ipswich', in P. Clark, ed., *Country Towns in Pre-industrial England* (Leicester, 1981), p. 112.

[67] Uncatalogued transcript at Cumbria RO, Carlisle, on searchroom library shelf 12.

[68] I. K. Ben-Amos, *Adolescence and Youth in Early Modern England* (London, 1994); Brooks, 'Apprenticeship'.

[69] E. Duffy, *The Stripping of the Altars* (London, 1992).

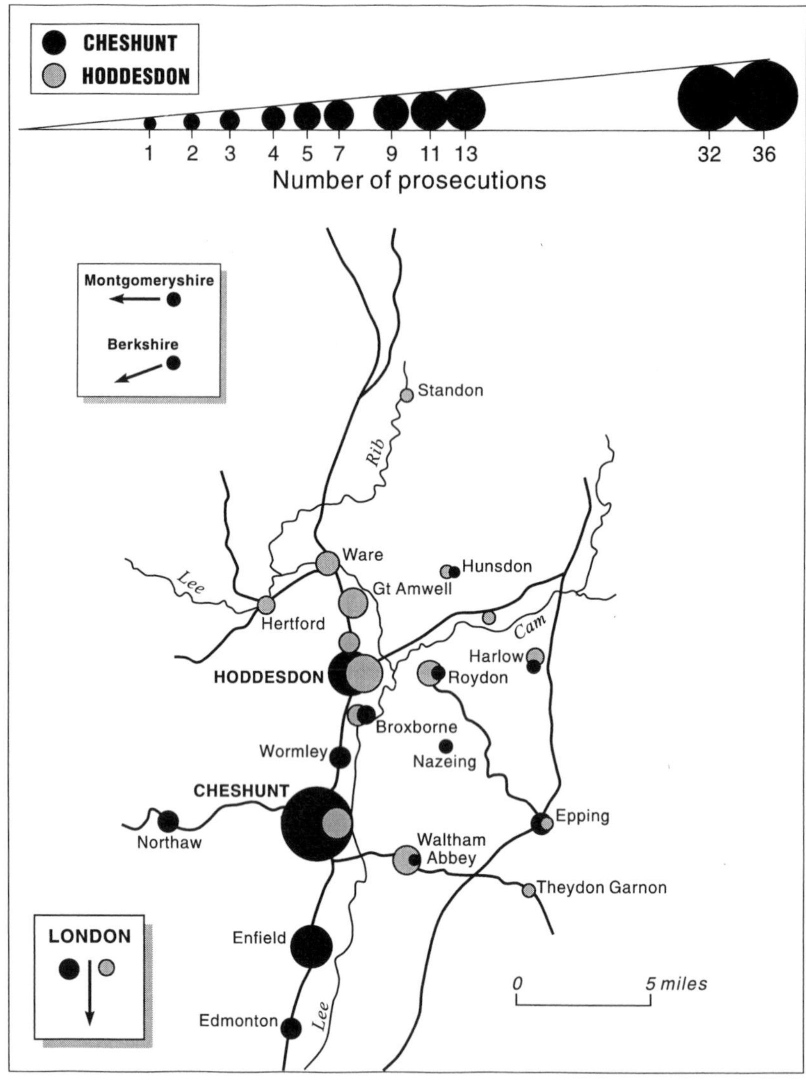

Map 5.2 Prosecuted attenders at two nonconformist meetings 1684

meeting houses (Map 5.2).[70] Numerous urban activities capitalised on urban gatherings, in growing numbers of meeting places: inns, assembly rooms, coffee-houses. Even Dorchester, 'the most Puritan place in England' in the early seventeenth century, supported two licensed coffee-houses by the

[70] M. Spufford, *The World of Rural Dissenters* (Cambridge, 1995), pp. 30, 390. Figure 5.2 maps information from Hertfordshire RO, Quarter Sessions Rolls: 1684/241–56. Rural conventicles did attract townsfolk (at Bayford outside Hertford, for example), but were smaller and usually occurred where specific local factors made an urban meeting difficult.

1670s.[71] Inns were both nodes in regional networks of information and carriage and also centres for recreation, often promoted by entrepreneurial victuallers.[72] So, increasingly, were retail shops.[73]

Urban social facilities typically displayed strong positive feedback: a range of activities encouraged visitors, and the further expansion of facilities. By 1700, major and county towns dominated many social and service facilities, but the relationship of services to town size was not straightforward. Individual towns accumulated service and social functions in an eclectic fashion (and might easily lose them subsequently). Small centres on major highways with substantial through traffic, and with active gentry, entrepreneurial or innkeeper promoters, were especially likely to possess diverse facilities.[74] That Scottish small towns lagged behind English centres in new cultural roles attracted Defoe's attention in the 1730s.[75] The failure of towns to acquire and sustain new facilities, especially inns (as distinct from mere alehouses) and shops, was one factor in the 'winnowing' of small towns.

The growing impersonality of town life as towns grew, the juxtaposition of diverse social groups and everyday conditions of social flux encouraged informal association of many kinds. Such sociability was widely seen as distinctively and ubiquitously urban.[76]

> [T]he [male] urban resident lived among a plethora of groups, formal and informal, voluntary and (in theory) compulsory that both reflected and reinforced the complexity of urban experience. The range of these associations naturally varied according to the size of the town and also over time, while opportunities for participation varied with social status, gender, wealth and pressures of work.[77]

Some voluntary association was oriented to reinforcing new civic identities, in the aftermath of religious and political disagreements during the Civil War and Restoration, acknowledging shared orientations towards security of property, personal propriety, and distancing from 'the lower sort of people'.[78] Such association provided direct economic stimulation, not just to catering and vendors of consumer goods, but to building trades through, for example, building or remodelling of town halls as architectural expressions of urban authority and identity.[79]

[71] D. Underdown, *Fire from Heaven* (London, 1992), pp. ix, 250.

[72] J. Chartres, 'Road carrying in England in the seventeenth century: myth and reality', *Ec.HR*, 2nd series, 30 (1977), 73–94; A. M. Everitt, ed., *Perspectives in English Urban History* (London, 1973), pp. 91–137.

[73] C. Shammas, *The Pre-Industrial English Consumer in England and America* (Oxford, 1990); P. Glennie and N. Thrift, 'Consumers, identities and consumption spaces in early-modern England', *Environment and Planning A*, 28 (1996), 28–45.

[74] Clark, *Sociability and Urbanity*; Barry, 'Provincial town culture', also stresses the importance of thoroughfare locations for the smallest towns.

[75] See below, p. 755.

[76] Barry, 'Bourgeois collectivism?', p. 90.

[77] Ibid., p. 84. Clark, *Sociability and Urbanity, passim*.

[78] Barry, 'Provincial town culture'; Barry, 'Bourgeois collectivism?'.

[79] Tittler, *Architecture and Power*.

This is not to propose that there was a single urban culture, or that urban cultures were coherent.[80] It is to suggest that urban mentalities possessed characteristic features, to which association and sociability were central. Much sociability bore on establishing the relations of trust central to urban economic relationships and administrative cooperation.[81] Hence the importance of education, manners, reliability and shared participation. Much late seventeenth-century association was either under the administrative control of leading citizens or only indirectly related to civic identity, but its economic effects were certainly substantial.[82]

Growing per capita consumption of commodities in Restoration England has been much investigated since the late 1980s, through analyses of consumption patterns, mainly from probate inventories, eclipsing accounts of consumer behaviour based on contemporary social commentary.[83] Numerous new goods were bought and owned by households comprising the wealthier two-thirds of English population after *c.* 1660, including new types of furniture and upholstery, new fabrics, window glass and curtains, ceramics, carpets, pictures, looking glasses, cutlery, coffee and teaware, clocks, books, globes, maps, prints, musical instruments, to name just a few. These changes were associated with changing household layouts and domestic environments.[84] Social, geographical and gender patterns in consumption have received considerable attention.[85]

Consumption changes were earliest and most rapid in towns, over and above the differences expected in virtue of urban populations' wealth and status,

[80] The extent to which 'urban cultural renaissance' was general, or particular to certain 'leisure towns', or specifically urban at all, continues to be debated: see below, Chapter 23.

[81] Brooks, 'Apprenticeship', p. 77; Barry, 'Bourgeois collectivism?', p. 101.

[82] Duffy, *Stripping of the Altars*; R. Hutton, *The Fall and Rise of Merry England* (Oxford, 1994); Barry, 'Bourgeois collectivism?', pp. 87–108.

[83] L. Weatherill, *Consumer Behaviour and Material Culture in Britain 1660–1760* (London, 1988); Earle, *Making of the English Middle Class*; Shammas, *Pre-Industrial Consumer*; building on Thirsk, *Economic Policy and Projects*; N. McKendrick, J. Brewer and J. Plumb, *The Birth of a Consumer Society: The Commercialization of Eighteenth Century England* (London, 1982). For an overview: P. Glennie, 'Consumption in historical studies', in D. Miller, ed., *Acknowledging Consumption* (London, 1995), pp. 164–203. Technical and interpretative problems in inventory analyses have been much discussed: M. Spufford, 'The limitations of the probate inventory', in J. Chartres and D. Hey, eds., *English Rural Society: Essays in Honour of Joan Thirsk* (Cambridge, 1990), pp. 139–74; J. de Vries, 'Between purchasing power and the world of goods', in J. Brewer and R. Porter, eds., *Consumption and the World of Goods* (London, 1993), pp. 85–132.

[84] R. Garrard, 'Probate inventories and the English domestic interior', *A.A.G. Bijdragen*, 23 (1980), 55–81; A. Dyer, 'Urban housing: a documentary study of four Midlands towns 1500–1700', *Post-Medieval Archaeology*, 15 (1981), 207–18; U. Priestley *et al.*, 'Rooms and room-use in Norwich housing, 1580–1730', *Post-Medieval Archaeology*, 16 (1982), 93–123; F. E. Brown, 'Continuity and change in the urban house: developments in domestic space organisation in seventeenth-century London', *Comparative Studies in Society and History*, 28 (1986), 558–90.

[85] Weatherill, *Consumer Behaviour*; Brewer and Porter, eds., *Consumption and World of Goods*; Shammas, *Pre-Industrial Consumer*; M. Spufford, *The Great Reclothing of Rural England: Petty Chapmen and their Wares in the Seventeenth Century* (Cambridge, 1984).

reflecting differential access to supply networks, and changing consumer preferences. Urban traders owned more new items than equivalently wealthy gentry; professionals were prominent consumers of positional goods; artisans out-consumed much wealthier yeomen farmers, prompting suggestions of a distinctive (and largely urban) 'consumption ethic'.[86] The profusion of new consumer goods was intimately associated with new sensibilities and social taxonomies. Consumer goods 'flagged' certain cultural discourses, and were constitutive of social structures through the accumulation and/or distinctive consumption of particular goods. A 'receptiveness to visual novelty and differentiation . . . was already present at relatively humble levels of the domestic market from the late seventeenth century' and, by the early eighteenth century, 'the forms of culture now seen as dominating town life were essentially there to be purchased by consumers'.[87]

The rapidly expanding consumption literature has inevitably focused more on some topics than others. Thus far, more work has focused on durable goods, new grocery commodities and luxuries than on housing, staple diet or clothing.[88] More work addresses patterns of possessions than their meanings. The many studies of new commodities create an impression of booming consumer markets but have not been balanced by studies of items whose use was declining.[89] There is too little work on consumption *before* the explosion of new consumer goods after the Restoration. Partly due to paucity of sources, too little work has been done on consumption among the labouring poor. Little is known about the impacts of changing work patterns on households' market involvement.[90]

Changes in society and in everyday life were making markets and shops more important as channels for access to both necessities and desirable non-essentials. The increasingly specialised production in many areas, oriented to markets, threw responsibility on to markets and retailers to supply items earlier produced locally (perhaps even domestically within the household). Many new consumer durables and semi-perishables sold mainly from retail shops. Shops were sustained by a combination of new goods (sugar, tobacco, tea, coffee) and goods formerly obtained through markets (spices, dried fruit, textiles, medicinal prep-

[86] Weatherill, *Consumer Behaviour*, pp. 78–9; see also Earle, *Making of the English Middle Class*; H. R. French, 'Chief inhabitants and their areas of influence: local ruling groups in Essex and Suffolk 1630–1720' (PhD thesis, University of Cambridge, 1993). The social depth of markets for consumer goods markets remains controversial. Thirsk, *Economic Policy and Projects*, and Spufford, *Great Reclothing*, envisage a mass market for modest consumer goods, whereas Weatherill, *Consumer Behaviour*, p. 193, argues that consumption of most new goods did not penetrate beneath 'some point between the craftsmen and the small farmers' until after 1730.

[87] J. Styles, 'Manufacture, consumption and design in the eighteenth century', in Brewer and Porter, eds., *Consumption and World of Goods*, p. 540; Barry, 'Provincial town culture', p. 208.

[88] N. Harte, 'The economics of clothing in the seventeenth century', *Textile History*, 22 (1991), 277–96.

[89] Such as painted wallcloths, wigs and some garments.

[90] De Vries, 'Purchasing power and the world of goods'.

arations) or produced at home (candles), as well as by the advantageous availability of credit.[91] The proliferation of private shops was well underway by 1660.[92] In seventeenth-century Hertfordshire, retail shop stocks and fittings were among the possessions of blacksmiths, tallow chandlers and innholders among others, while labourers, victuallers, tailors, maltsters and a blacksmith were all prosecuted for trading as grocers without due apprenticeship, showing that shops were more widespread than men specifically described as shopkeepers.[93] The spread of shops through villages and hamlets potentially weakened small towns who lost status as access points to exotic groceries and imported fabrics, but in many areas the rise of village shopkeeping came after 1700.

Townspeople's use of shops is traceable in the few surviving early shop accounts, including those of George Kelsick at Ambleside in the Lake District, comparatively remote from national concentrations of population and wealth.[94] This extensive parish contained about 2,000 people, about 550 in the town itself, and a market had been established *c.* 1650. Fifty years later, Kelsick recorded the purchases, credit and payments of more than 150 households. Around 70 lived in the town, and a bare handful lived more than three or four miles distant, or outside the parish, implying the presence of other shops in nearby centres such as Hawkshead (Map 5.3). A broad cross-section of Ambleside's population used the shop regularly: they included eight shoemakers, five stuffweavers and an array of workers in leather, wood, metal and construction (and excisemen). Only two customers were styled 'esquire', but there were six servants, and others styled 'labourer' in the parish register.[95]

(vi) CONCLUSION

Towns in early modern Britain were extraordinarily diverse, sharing only a concentration of population (albeit often modest), occupational complexity,

[91] H.-C. Mui and L. Mui, *Shops and Shopkeeping in Eighteenth Century England* (London, 1985); Shammas, *Pre-Industrial Consumer*, pp. 197–265.

[92] J. Patten, 'Urban occupations in pre-industrial England', *Transactions of the Institute of British Geographers*, new series, 2 (1977), 296–313; P. Ripley, 'Village and town: occupations and wealth in the hinterland of Gloucester, 1660–1700', *Agricultural History Review*, 32 (1984), 170–8; Large, 'Urban growth and agricultural change'; J. Pennington and J. Sleights, 'Steyning trades 1559–1787', *Sussex Archaeological Collections*, 130 (1992), 164–88; J. Stobart, 'The spatial organisation of a regional economy: central places in North-West England in the early eighteenth century', *Journal of Historical Geography*, 22 (1996), 147–59.

[93] P. Glennie, 'Shops and shopkeepers in early modern Hertfordshire' (forthcoming).

[94] Cumbria RO, Kendal, WD/TE Box 11/16. Other examples are cited by T. S. Willan, *An Eighteenth-Century Shopkeeper* (Manchester, 1970); Shammas, *Pre-industrial Consumer*, pp. 238–48. Figures for the town's population are approximate: see the different estimates of P. Clark and J. Hosking, *Population Estimates of English Small Towns 1550–1851: Revised Edition* (Leicester, 1993), and J. D. Marshall, 'The rise and transformation of the Cumbrian market town, 1660–1900', *NHist.*, 19 (1983), 162.

[95] Cumbria RO, Kendal, WPR/91/W1.

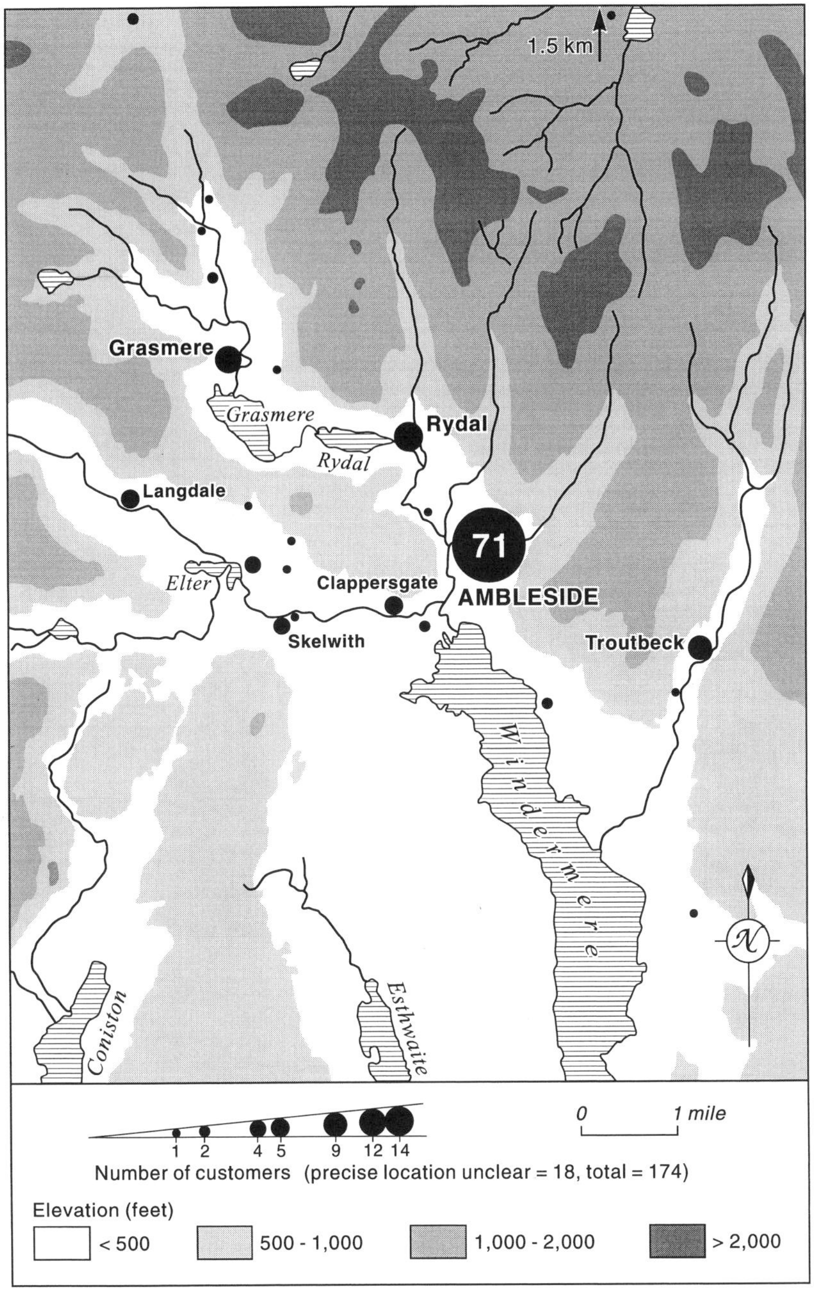

Map 5.3 Customers of an Ambleside shop *c.* 1670

marketing roles (particularly evident on weekly market days) and some degree of contemporary perception that they 'felt urban'. While everyday life in very small towns had little in common with the socio-political complexity, physical crowding, and impersonal daily life of major cities, contemporaries did not doubt that they were towns. That much urban history has been couched in terms of polarities between 'urbane' and 'rustic' life is unhelpful for the characterisation of small town economies, and can obscure how contemporaries experienced tiny centres as none the less urban, including their built landscapes.[96]

The high density of small towns in sixteenth-century England and Scotland raises the urban proportion of their populations compared with earlier estimates, and relative to parts of Europe where larger towns were more common. This is not to say that they were not lightly urbanised by European standards in 1540, but that the difference was not as great as is sometimes suggested. The scale of the contrast between the relative stability of urban hierarchies between about 1540 and about 1660, and their transformation thereafter and into the eighteenth century, remains very striking.[97] It may be, however, that urban systems changing relatively rapidly after 1660 were responding to wider economic changes that had long been underway. This appears to have been so with regard to communications, whose improvement was not so rapid as to destabilise trade networks.[98] Urban economies benefited from transport costs that were simultaneously high enough to protect and sustain large numbers of local craftsmen, yet low enough for specialised production regions to cater for distant and colonial markets. Relatively small later changes in commercial organisation, scale or strategies could precipitate substantial restructurings and 'changes of phase' into new spatial arrangements, and these could be highly disruptive for individual urban economies.

Major economic consequences flowed from the shifting cultural roles of towns, and from increasing differentiation among towns in the provision of services, commercialised leisure and civil and ecclesiastical administration. With regard to both, patterns of work and patterns of leisure distinctions between life in towns and life outside towns probably became more marked, since many new features of everyday life were mainly, or exclusively, urban. Although such distinctions later diminished, as new practices became more widespread, in 1700

[96] Small towns were more architecturally distinctive from villages in 1700 than 1540. Some public buildings and housing made greater reference to 'classical' styles, and private houses, in particular, increasingly differed in building materials and/or layout. See, for example, the comparison of Burford and neighbouring villages in D. Moriarty, *Buildings of the Cotswolds* (London, 1989).

[97] However, we acknowledge that in focusing on distinctively urban functions, there is a danger of overemphasising the more forward-looking features of those towns whose size and influence grew.

[98] It may not be coincidental that growth before 1660 was most rapid among port towns: see below, Chapter 12.

many urban–rural differences in practices and knowledges relating to work, government, literacy, consumption and timing were more pronounced than they later became.

As urban historians' attention has extended from established foci on population, trade, religion and politics to take in topics such as service industries, the professions, recreations and 'culture industries', so the typically plural character of urban economies has come into clearer, if still uneven, focus. Running through these all these areas has been an emphasis, somewhat belatedly, on women's experiences.[99] Recognition of the significance of social constructions of gender, both inside and outside households, has also proved central in sharpening and connecting debates on migration, fertility, work, household organisation and consumption patterns. To the mid-1990s, considerable spatial imbalances remain, with more work on lowland England and (since the early 1980s) central Scotland than on other parts of Britain, especially on the less well-documented economies of small towns (though see Chapters 13 and 22). Poor documentation also contributes to both thematic imbalances in work on urban economies (for example, a relative lack of work on artisan crafts, and on consumption patterns and processes at the lower end of the market), and to chronological unevenness (with much greater attention to economic change *c.* 1560–1640 and 1660–1700 than pre-1560, 1640–1660 or in the early eighteenth century). Subsequent chapters demonstrate both the achievements of urban economic historians since the 1970s, and the scope for important and interesting work over the next quarter-century.

[99] C. Hall, *White, Male and Middle Class* (London, 1992), pp. 24–7; A. J. Vickery, 'Golden age to separate spheres: a review of the categories and chronology of English women's history', *HJ*, 36 (1993), 383–414; Laurence, *Women in England*, especially pp. 108–64. It is nevertheless acknowledged that the research discussed in this chapter remains overwhelmingly preoccupied with activities in which power was largely in the hands of men.

· 6 ·

Population and disease, estrangement and belonging 1540–1700

P. GRIFFITHS, J. LANDERS, M. PELLING AND R. TYSON

WERE THE sixteenth and seventeenth centuries the first to define, for British people, 'the urban experience'? In broad terms, the answer to this would have to be in the negative, since the pattern of major towns, at least in England and Scotland, was already long-established, and the sixteenth century's increase in population can be seen as a phase of recovery as much as of expansion. On the other hand, it is in this period that London emerges as a European metropolis and as England's capital city, that urbanisation becomes linked with national identity and centralised government, and that the proportion of those resident in towns, or sharing in the experience of towns in some phase of life, begins to accelerate. In this chapter, urbanisation will first be examined in demographic terms, with reference to migration, fertility, marriage and mortality, especially in relation to subsistence and the shift from epidemic to endemic causes of death. The second section explores contemporary sensibilities and social structure as affected by changes in the pattern of disease and in the urban environment, touching on gender, work and poverty, and contemporary ideas about population, crowding and urban life. By 'environment' we mean, in particular, factors affecting townspeople's sense of the presence of others. The final section analyses the ambivalent character of two staple sources of reassurance, household and neighbourhood, which provided continuity but which can be shown to be open to challenge and renegotiation from within and without as urban pressures intensified.

(i) POPULATION

The population histories of early modern English and Scottish towns present different problems and patterns. In England, parish registers and bills of mortality

This chapter was produced collaboratively, but the sections were separately authored as follows: (i) Population, J. Landers and R. Tyson (ii) Disease, agency and the urban environment, M. Pelling (iii) Household and neighbourhood, P. Griffiths. The chapter was coordinated by M. Pelling.

permit the detailed study of urban populations which can be set alongside both those of smaller settlements elsewhere in the country, and the national-level demographic reconstruction undertaken by E. A. Wrigley and Roger Schofield. In Scotland, by contrast, demographic data are scanty before the late seventeenth century, and it is not possible either to reconstruct local experience in any detail, or to relate it to that of a well-understood national aggregate. None the less, the main lines of divergence between the two cases seem fairly clear. Both countries experienced urban growth for the first hundred years of our period, but in Scotland, unlike England, the process clearly ran out of steam around the middle of the seventeenth century, and the country remained much less urbanised than its southern – and many of its continental – neighbours. Furthermore, Scottish towns and cities seem to have displayed a more long-lasting vulnerability to mortality crises than did those in England, and to have experienced greater difficulties in recovering from them.

The question 'what is a town' is a notoriously difficult one. For practical purposes it is usually answered in terms of population size, but even on this basis there is a variety of population thresholds at which distinctively 'urban' characteristics can be recognised, depending on the observer's disciplinary, or other, interests. In some contexts these thresholds may embrace settlements comprising a few hundred inhabitants, but historical demographers have generally fixed their sights substantially higher, distinguishing, implicitly or explicitly, centres with inhabitants numbering at least in the low thousands, from the generality of smaller settlements; it is with the former that we shall be chiefly concerned. This partly reflects methodological convenience – the use of parishes as units of analysis makes it difficult to distinguish lesser towns and their inhabitants from smaller, or dispersed, settlements contained within the same parish boundaries, and aggregate population estimates for such places are very hard to come by. But there is an important theoretical issue involved as well. Recent work on historical demography has relied extensively on the concept of the 'demographic regime', conceived as an unfolding set of relationships between demographic variables, and between these and their social, economic and physical environment. There are reasons for thinking that only at this higher level do distinctively urban demographic regimes begin to crystallise as settlements become social worlds within which people live their lives, choose their marriage partners and experience characteristically elevated risks of mortality.[1]

In England urban population expanded both absolutely and proportionately throughout the period. Nationally England's population grew at an estimated annual rate of seven per thousand in the second half of the sixteenth century and five per thousand in the decades 1600–49.[2] Against this background, towns over

[1] For an extended discussion of this question, from the point of view of mortality, see J. Landers, *Death and the Metropolis* (Cambridge, 1993), ch. 1.

[2] E. A. Wrigley and R. S. Schofield, *The Population History of England 1541–1871* (London, 1981).

5,000 inhabitants probably accounted for around 5 per cent of England's population in 1540, 8 per cent in 1600 and 14 per cent by 1650 (in thousands approximately 125, 335 and 680 respectively) – corresponding to annual growth rates of roughly 1.2 and 1.0 per cent[3] – and further expansion brought the urban total to an estimated 850,000 by 1700 which, since the national population stagnated in these decades, implies a small contraction elsewhere. Lacking a tier of provincial cities above 30,000 inhabitants – or even 20,000 until well into the seventeenth century – England's urban hierarchy was overshadowed by its 'primate' metropolis.[4] London's growth from an estimated 55,000 inhabitants in 1520 to 475,000 in 1670 was proportionately double that of the provincial towns, and by the end of the century it had passed the half million mark.[5] England was also unusual in the growth of its smaller towns. Jan de Vries puts aggregate seventeenth-century English growth at a factor of 1.7 for towns in the 5,000–10,000 size range and at over 2.5 in the category 2,500–5,000, whereas elsewhere in northern Europe growth was concentrated in a small number of large centres with the lower tiers of the hierarchy apparently losing population.[6] None the less, even if the 'urban' threshold is lowered to 2,500 inhabitants, 70 per cent of English urban dwellers lived in places with over 10,000, and for most of the period four-fifths of these lived in the capital.

The data do not allow quantitative estimates of Scottish urbanisation with any confidence before the 1690s, but before 1640 growth was evidently widespread, decelerating after 1620, and going into reverse in the closing decades of the century. Taxation records for 1639 and 1691 show the towns in the 5,000–10,000 range falling from five to only two, and those numbering 2,500–5,000 increasing correspondingly from eleven to thirteen. Before then the larger Scottish towns may have performed better than their English provincial counterparts,[7]

[3] These figures are based on those presented in E. A. Wrigley, 'Urban growth and agricultural change: England and the continent in the early modern period', *Journal of Interdisciplinary History*, 15 (1985), 683–728, and are drawn from a variety of sources; see also J. de Vries, *European Urbanization 1500–1800* (London, 1984), and P. J. Corfield, 'Urban development in England and Wales in the sixteenth and seventeenth centuries', in D. C. Coleman and A. H. John, eds., *Trade, Government and Economy in Pre-Industrial England* (London, 1976), pp. 214–47.

[4] De Vries, *European Urbanization*, pp. 88–9; P. M. Hohenburg and L. H. Lees, *The Making of Urban Europe 1000–1950* (London, 1985), pp. 169–71.

[5] For recent estimates see R. A. P. Finlay and B. Shearer, 'Population growth and suburban expansion', in A. L. Beier and R. Finlay, eds., *London 1500–1700* (London, 1986), pp. 37–59; see also V. Harding, 'The population of London, 1550–1700: a review of the published evidence', *LJ*, 15 (1990), 111–12. [6] De Vries, *European Urbanization*, pp. 136–42, 255–8.

[7] For estimates of the population of Scottish towns, see M. Lynch, M. Spearman and G. Stell, eds., *The Scottish Medieval Town* (Edinburgh, 1988), p. 279; J. McGrath, 'The medieval and early modern burgh', in T. M. Devine and G. Jackson, eds., *Glasgow*, vol. I: *Beginnings to 1830* (Manchester, 1995), pp. 44–5; M. Lynch, 'Urbanisation and urban networks in seventeenth century Scotland: some further thoughts', *Scottish Economic and Social History*, 12 (1992), 24–39; H. M. Dingwall, *Late Seventeenth-Century Edinburgh* (Aldershot, 1994), pp. 3–21; M. Flinn, ed., *Scottish Population History from the Seventeenth Century to the 1930s* (Cambridge, 1977), p. 191.

but it is equally clear that levels of urbanisation in Scotland remained comparatively modest. The number of royal burghs paying taxes grew from 42 to 65 between 1550 and 1697, and 250 burghs of barony were created between 1500 and 1700, but most royal burghs numbered fewer than 1,000 inhabitants and burghs of barony fewer than 500.[8] Recent estimates put the percentage of Scots living in towns of over 2,500 inhabitants at only 9.1 in 1700, less than half that in England and one of the lowest proportions in western Europe. Whilst London had over 10 per cent of the national population, Edinburgh with Canongate had less than 3 per cent and was only one sixteenth as large, with around 35,000 inhabitants. Moreover, while Edinburgh was bigger than any English provincial town and Glasgow (with Barony parish) about the same size as Exeter with *c.* 17,000 inhabitants, there were only two Scottish centres – Dundee and Aberdeen – in the range 5,000–10,000, compared with twenty-seven in England.[9]

Urbanisation on this scale implies a substantial stream of rural–urban migration, and the English data furnish a very rough impression of its scale. Taking the figures given above for towns over 5,000 in 1540, 1600 and 1700 – with one of 678,000 for 1670 – and assuming natural decrease of five per thousand annually, we obtain annual net migration rates of 1.31, 1.65 and 2.23 per thousand of the 'rural' population. These compare with estimated growth rates for the latter of 6.05, 2.18 and −1.27 per thousand and imply that the towns 'drained off' some 40 per cent of the growth in population elsewhere for much of the seventeenth century, converting slow growth to absolute decline in its closing decades.[10] Pre-Restoration English society was permeated by geographical mobility. Church court records show some 70 to 80 per cent of deponents having moved at least once in their lives, but most such moves were over short distances. Long- and short-range forms of migration were, for the most part, distinct social and economic phenomena – generally termed 'subsistence' and 'betterment' migration. The latter, in Peter Clark's words, involved 'servants, apprentices, would-be spouses and others . . . travelling fairly limited distances, to a neighbouring town or village, usually within an area defined by a notion of a sub-regional "country"'. Thus in Norwich most apprentices came from within a radius of

[8] G. S. Pryde, *The Burghs of Scotland* (Glasgow, 1965), pp. 58–79.

[9] P. J. Corfield, *The Impact of English Towns 1700–1800* (Oxford, 1982), pp. 8–15; de Vries, *European Urbanization*, p. 39. R. E. Tyson, 'Contrasting regimes: population growth in Ireland and Scotland during the eighteenth century', in S. J. Connolly, R. A. Houston and R. J. Morris, eds., *Conflict, Identity and Economic Development* (Preston, 1995), p. 66, estimates the population of Scotland in 1691 at 1,234,575, considerably larger than de Vries' figure of 1 million for 1700. If this new estimate is correct then the percentage of Scotland's population living in towns over 10,000 is somewhat lower than that given by de Vries.

[10] The figure of five per thousand urban natural decrease may be too pessimistic, though it is probably appropriate for London at the end of the seventeenth century, but even the implausibly low figure of 0.5 per thousand yields mid-period annual migration totals of 3,000, 5,000 and 6,000, compared with 4,100, 7,200 and 9,400 on the original assumption.

eight and twenty miles of the city. London recruited apprentices from across the country; but even here, of some 1,800 immigrant apprentices and freemen whose places of origin are known for the period 1601–40, 40 per cent had travelled eighty miles or less.[11]

Subsistence migrants, by contrast, travelled longer distances, impelled by the pressures of survival and economic necessity. Of 2,651 vagrants punished under the pre-Restoration settlement laws, only a quarter had travelled twenty miles or less and a similar proportion, over a hundred miles. Individual movements might be haphazard and unprogrammed, but overall the streams of subsistence migration in England were oriented from the highland north and west to the lowland south and east, converging on London. It was, above all, towns and their environs which drew subsistence migrants – with the capital as the supreme magnet – and the experience of town life 'was decisive in the making of a vagrant . . . The further a vagabond had moved the more likely he was to have come from an urban setting.'[12]

Migration into Scottish towns was apparently similar to that in England, with the capital attracting migrants from the entire country while other towns depended largely upon their immediate hinterland. We know very little about subsistence migrants although, as in England, they were more likely to travel longer distances than apprentices and servants. The frequency of subsistence crises in Scotland, the failure of its poor law to provide relief for the able-bodied unemployed, and the lack of strictly enforced settlement laws, meant that large numbers of begging poor moved from the countryside, particularly in years of famine and particularly to Edinburgh. But most young people who came into towns were servants. The only census we have before the eighteenth century is for Old Aberdeen in 1636, where servants were 19.1 per cent of the population. Of those, 60 per cent were female but in the larger towns the ratio of females to males was much higher. In Edinburgh in 1694 there were 2.4 female servants for every male servant, in Perth 5.1 and in Aberdeen 5.5. They were more likely than apprentices to have come shorter distances, and many eventually returned home to marry.[13]

[11] P. Clark, 'Migration in England during the late seventeenth and early eighteenth centuries', in P. Clark and D. Souden, eds., *Migration and Society in Early Modern England* (London, 1987), pp. 213–52, at p. 215; J. Patten, 'Patterns of labour migration and movement of labour to three pre-industrial East Anglian towns', in Clark and Souden, eds., *Migration and Society*, pp. 77–106; J. Wareing, 'Changes in the geographical distribution of the recruitment of apprentices to the London companies 1486–1750', *Journal of Historical Geography*, 6 (1980), 241–9, table 2 p. 410.

[12] P. Slack, 'Vagrants and vagrancy in England, 1598–1664', in Clark and Souden, eds., *Migration and Society*, pp. 49–76, at p. 67.

[13] I. D. Whyte, *Scotland before the Industrial Revolution* (London, 1995), pp. 130–1; R. E. Tyson, 'Household size and structure in a Scottish burgh: Old Aberdeen', *Local Population Studies*, 40 (1988), 46–54; I. D. Whyte, 'The occupational structure of Scottish burghs in the late seventeenth century', in M. Lynch, ed., *The Early Modern Town in Scotland* (London, 1987), pp. 219–44, esp. p. 224.

International migration included refugee waves like that of the Netherlands Protestants who may have made up a third of Norwich's population in the 1570s, but this was unusual, and the proportion of overseas migrants in British towns was generally small compared with that of a continental centre such as Amsterdam, where over a third of new citizens were of foreign origin during the years 1655–9.[14] The major flow was thus outward; as many as 380,000 Britons may have crossed the Atlantic in the central decades of the seventeenth century, and in Scotland the outflow has been estimated at 85,000–115,000 in the first half of the century and 78,000–122,000 in the second – perhaps the equivalent of 40 per cent of natural increase. Many who left were soldiers, but most were civilians; as many as 50,000 (4 per cent of the population) may have left for Ireland during the harvest failures of 1695–9 alone. Such emigration in part indicates a failure of urban growth to absorb surplus rural population. The slow growth, or even decline, of many Scottish towns in the later seventeenth century also reflected economic difficulties which made them unattractive to migrants.[15]

In England net emigration combined with the effects of demographic stagnation, the growth of employment and other opportunities closer to home, and changing attitudes on the part of the elite, to effect a substantial reduction in long-range migration after the Restoration. Residential stability in the English countryside may have increased generally in these decades, but rural–urban migration was sufficient for urban growth to continue throughout the century, even if migration fields – including that of London – were contracting. At the same time, however, the composition of migration streams was evidently changing, with a growing proportion of women moving to towns and an increasing volume of upper-class 'recreational' migration.

Recent work in historical demography has underlined the importance of fertility and marriage patterns ('nuptiality') in determining long-term rates of population growth. In particular, the so-called 'low pressure' demographic regimes of western Europe were underpinned by what Malthus termed the 'preventive check' of delayed marriage and permanent celibacy – a phenomenon especially important in England – but there are unfortunately very few urban nuptiality data available from either England or Scotland. In England as a whole proportions married fell in the course of the seventeenth century, but figures for specifically urban women are unobtainable. Evidence from London suggests that 'native' women married young – in their early twenties – in contrast to the national pattern where the average age was over 25.5 years in the seventeenth century.[16]

[14] J. I. Israel, *The Dutch Republic: Its Rise, Greatness, and Fall 1477–1806* (Oxford, 1995), table 13, p. 330.

[15] T. M. Devine, 'Introduction: the paradox of Scottish emigration', in T. M. Devine, ed., *Scottish Emigration and Scottish Society* (Edinburgh, 1992), p. 4.

[16] V. B. Elliott, 'Single women in the London marriage market: age, status and mobility, 1589–1619', in R. B. Outhwaite, ed., *Marriage and Society* (London, 1981), pp. 81–100; R. Finlay, *Population*

Remarriage rates were apparently also high. In Stepney nearly half of all marriages in the early seventeenth century were found to be widow remarriages, although by 1700 the proportion had fallen to a quarter.[17] This fall may have been due in part to the effects of a declining sex ratio on opportunities for widow remarriage, but the discovery of similar trends outside London suggests that this was not the sole factor.[18]

Marital fertility was certainly no lower among urban than rural populations. English family reconstitution results generally display the so-called 'natural fertility' pattern, with childbearing continuing from marriage to the menopause without deliberate premature curtailment.[19] Overall levels were relatively low – women marrying at age twenty having on average fewer than 7.5 live births, compared to the eight to ten commonly found in studies of northern France, Flanders and southern Germany[20] – and it is likely that this reflected relatively lengthy periods of breast feeding and consequent suppression of ovulation. Marital fertility seems to have varied little in the longer term or geographically, with only a slight tendency for urban, and what Wilson terms 'urban-influenced', settlements to have higher fertility.[21] London though is an exception to this rule; here Roger Finlay found average birth intervals of under two years in two wealthy central parishes, corresponding to age-specific marital fertility levels at least 30 per cent above the natural average, and associated with the

and Metropolis (Cambridge, 1981), pp. 137–40; E. A. Wrigley and R. S. Schofield, 'English population history from family reconstitution: summary results', *Population Studies*, 37 (1983), 157–84. For a discussion of the national trends and the problems involved in estimating them see D. R. Weir, 'Rather never than late: celibacy and age at marriage in English cohort fertility, 1541–1871', *Journal of Family History*, 9 (1984), 340–54; R. S. Schofield, 'English marriage patterns revisited', *Journal of Family History*, 10 (1985), 2–20.

17 J. Boulton, 'London widowhood revisited: the decline of female remarriage in the seventeenth and early eighteenth centuries', *Continuity and Change*, 5 (1990), 323–56; V. Brodsky, 'Widows in late Elizabethan London: remarriage, economic opportunity and family orientations', in L. Bonfield, R. M. Smith and K. Wrightson, eds., *The World We Have Gained* (Oxford, 1986), pp. 122–54.

18 Evidence of sharply declining sex ratios is given by Finlay, *Population and Metropolis*, pp. 140–2, whereas L. D. Schwarz, 'London apprentices in the seventeenth century: some problems', *Local Population Studies*, 38 (1987), 18–22, argues for a smaller decline; for a critique of demographic explanations of remarriage change see B. J. Todd, 'Demographic determinism and female agency: the remarrying widow reconsidered . . . again', *Continuity and Change*, 9 (1994), 421–50. National trends are discussed in Wrigley and Schofield, *Population History*, pp. 258–9.

19 C. Wilson, 'Natural fertility in pre-industrial England, 1600–1799', *Population Studies*, 38 (1984), 225–41. Family reconstitution is a technique of demographic analysis based on the linkage of entries relating to the same family in a set of vital registers; for details see E. A. Wrigley, 'Family reconstitution', in E. A. Wrigley, ed., *An Introduction to English Historical Demography* (London, 1966), pp. 96–159.

20 Wrigley and Schofield, 'English population history from family reconstitution'; Wilson, 'Natural fertility'.

21 C. Wilson, 'The proximate determinants of marital fertility in England 1600–1799', in Bonfield, Smith and Wrightson, eds., *The World We Have Gained*, pp. 203–30.

practice of wet-nursing.[22] This seems to have been restricted to wealthy families, but elsewhere in London there is evidence that artificial feeding was practised very early in life with consequent high mortality.[23]

Births were not necessarily confined to marriage, but levels of illegitimate fertility were insufficient to offset the effects of the preventive check. A sample of 250 English parish registers analysed by Richard Adair shows births to unmarried women rising from 2.1 per cent of the total in the 1550s to between 3 and 4 per cent in the first half of the seventeenth century; this so-called 'illegitimacy ratio' then collapsed to 1.2 per cent in the 1650s and remained below 2 per cent until the last years of the century.[24] Before the Civil War, overall illegitimacy in the Highland north and west was two to three times that of the Lowlands, but this was not true of urban levels, so that towns had lower illegitimacy than the countryside in the Highlands and vice versa in the Lowlands. Adair attributes this to specifically rural cultural and economic factors promoting illegitimacy in the Highlands and leading single pregnant women to remain in the countryside, whereas their Lowland sisters were more likely to move to a town, thereby inflating urban illegitimacy ratios. In London itself illegitimacy seems to have been remarkably low, decadal averages running generally at or below six per thousand in a sample of intramural parishes. The suburban parishes had higher levels, but even here the average for the period 1571–1650 was only around 2 per cent.[25]

There are no measurements of the individual components of fertility change in Scotland before civil registration in 1855, but illegitimacy levels appear to have been considerably higher than in England. The best evidence is for Aberdeen, where 16.3 per cent of all births were illegitimate in the period 1572–91 and 14.8 per cent in the late 1650s. The departure of the Cromwellian garrison in 1659 and the rigorous punishment of offenders by both kirk session and secular

22 Finlay, *Population and Metropolis*, ch. 5; for a broader discussion of the phenomenon in the London case see G. Clark, 'A study of nurse children, 1550–1750', *Local Population Studies*, 39 (1987), 8–23.

23 J. Landers, 'Mortality levels in eighteenth century London: a family reconstitution study', in R. Porter and W. F. Bynum, eds., *Living and Dying in London, Medical History*, Supplement 11 (1991), 1–28.

24 R. Adair, *Courtship, Illegitimacy and Marriage in Early Modern England* (Manchester, 1996), pp. 48–67. Adair's is now the authoritative study of this topic and contains a full account of the substantive, interpretative and methodological problems it presents.

25 *Ibid.*, pp. 202–22. The measurement of illegitimacy in London is complicated by the appearance in the registers of the richer parishes of appreciable numbers of 'foundling' children of uncertain legitimacy. Adrian Wilson has argued forcefully that, in the eighteenth century at least, many of these were illegitimate and the conventionally defined illegitimacy ratio – which excludes such children – is thus too low (A. F. Wilson, 'Illegitimacy and its implications in mid-eighteenth century London: the evidence of the Foundling Hospital', *Continuity and Change*, 4 (1989), 103–64). Adair rejects Wilson's interpretation and assumes that most foundlings were legitimate, but the numbers of foundlings remain too small to affect the overall interpretation advanced here until close to the end of the period with which we are concerned.

justice courts reduced the level to 9.1 per cent by 1685–7, but this was still somewhat higher than that of the surrounding countryside and twice that of rural Lowland Scotland as a whole.[26]

As in England, fertility within marriage is unlikely to have changed much over time. Michael Flinn found that the mean interval between the births of the first and second child in the urban parish of Kilmarnock between 1730 and 1753 was 24.5 months, and between the second and third, 23.8,[27] which seems to have been typical of Scottish towns then and probably for earlier periods as well. As in England, urban birth intervals were affected by the incidence of wet-nursing, of which the expense – in Edinburgh 95 per cent of wet-nurses received at least twice the pay of other female servants, and 20 per cent at least five times as much – restricted it predominantly to better-off families. In Aberdeen 180 married couples pollable at 30s. (2s. 6d. sterling) or more in the 1695 poll tax register baptised forty-six infants in a twelve-month period, a ratio of one baptism to every 3.9 couples, compared with one to 7.3 among a sample of 248 couples paying less than 30s.[28] The towns, however, also had large numbers of single and widowed women so that, in the early 1690s, Aberdeen's crude birth rate of 29.2 per thousand – allowing 5 per cent for underregistration – was about the same as that of Aberdeenshire, while Edinburgh's was 30.[29]

Historical mortality studies have focused particularly on the violent short-term upswings known as 'mortality crises'. These could arise from epidemics, as well as food shortages ('subsistence crises'), or warfare whether alone or in combination, but where major towns and cities were concerned, populations were sufficiently large and dense for many immunising infections to persist in an endemic form, greatly reducing the scope for epidemic outbreaks. This was true, for instance, of smallpox, which evidently became more important as a cause of death during the seventeenth century in both England and Scotland. In London it was claiming hundreds, and sometimes thousands, of lives every year by the last quarter of the century; in smaller centres, such as the Scottish towns, the pattern was one of frequent epidemics whose impact fell particularly on young children born in the interval since the previous outbreak.[30]

In cases where immunity was lacking, however, the high densities of urban

[26] W. Kennedy, *Annals of Aberdeen* (London, 1818), vol. 1, p. 188; G. R. DesBrisay, 'Authority and discipline in Aberdeen, 1650–1700' (PhD thesis, University of St Andrews, 1989), pp. 398–400; R. Mitchison and L. Leneman, *Sexuality and Social Control: Scotland 1660–1780* (Oxford, 1989), pp. 140–4. [27] Flinn, *Scottish Population History*, pp. 276–9.

[28] Dingwall, *Late Seventeenth-Century Edinburgh*, pp. 42, 207; R. K. Marshall, 'Wet-nursing in Scotland: 1500–1800', *Review of Scottish Culture*, 1 (1984), 43–51; R. E. Tyson, 'The population of Aberdeenshire, 1695–99: a new approach', *Northern Scotland*, 6 (1985), 113–31, esp. 122.

[29] Tyson, 'The population of Aberdeenshire', p. 126; Flinn, *Scottish Population History*, p. 184 (for Edinburgh baptisms 1691–5).

[30] J. Landers, 'Mortality and metropolis: the case of London 1675–1825', *Population Studies*, 41 (1987), 59–76.

populations could lead to correspondingly severe epidemic mortality. This was the case with bubonic plague which apparently became increasingly urban-focused in the earlier part of the period, but, unlike many other urban infections, was unable to establish itself as an endemic disease on a substantial scale. Major epidemics thus reflected the introduction of new strains of plague bacillus, and urban populations failed to develop the levels of immunity associated with infections such as smallpox.[31] Hence epidemics when they occurred could display the destructiveness characteristic of outbreaks among 'virgin soil' populations. England suffered recurrent urban epidemics until the 1660s, and in London, for instance, it is estimated that between a sixth and a quarter of the population were carried off by each of the plagues of 1563, 1603, 1625 and 1665.[32]

Scotland suffered a series of outbreaks in the second half of the sixteenth century, with Edinburgh together with Leith – its satellite port and a point of entry for the disease – being most frequently affected. A severe outbreak in 1605–6 caused heavy mortality in Edinburgh, Perth, Dundee, Stirling, Ayr and Glasgow,[33] but thereafter there were only localised outbreaks of the disease before the last, and most destructive, epidemic in 1645–9. This may have been promoted by wartime troop and refugee movements and the accompanying relaxation of quarantine measures. It severely affected communities which, in aggregate, accounted for around two-thirds of burgh taxation, and claimed 20,000–30,000 lives, at least 20 per cent of the urban population.[34]

Plague mortality varied by age and sex in ways which evidently reflected specifically local factors, and no consistent pattern has yet emerged.[35] The disease was no respecter of wealth or nutritional status once individuals were infected, but there was a progressive change in the spatial, and by implication socio-economic, impact of epidemics within the larger urban centres. The London outbreak of 1563 was worst in the richer central parishes, whereas from the 1590s the poorer suburbs – where high population densities and lower standards of housing, clothing and general cleanliness combined to promote exposure to infection – suffered more.[36] The disappearance of bubonic plague may owe something to changes in these latter respects, as it may also to the cumulative effects of human agency through measures such as quarantines and *cordons sani-*

[31] P. Slack, *The Impact of Plague in Tudor and Stuart England* (London, 1985), pp. 64–9, 145–51. On the epidemiology and mode of transmission of urban plague see O. J. Benedictow, 'Morbidity in historical plague epidemics', *Population Studies*, 41 (1987), 401–32.

[32] I. Sutherland, 'When was the Great Plague? Mortality in London, 1563 to 1665', in D. V. Glass and R. Revelle, eds., *Population and Social Change* (London, 1972), pp. 287–320.

[33] J. F. D. Shrewsbury, *A History of Bubonic Plague in the British Isles* (Cambridge, 1970), pp. 188–9, 206–10, 255–63, 285–93.

[34] Flinn, *Scottish Population History*, pp. 133–49.

[35] Finlay, *Population and Metropolis*, pp. 122–3; M. F. Hollingsworth and T. H. Hollingsworth, 'Plague mortality rates by age and sex in the parish of St. Botolph without Bishopsgate, London, 1603', *Population Studies*, 25 (1971), 131–46.

[36] Slack, *Impact of Plague*, pp. 150–64.

taires. None of the wide range of explanations hitherto advanced has proved entirely convincing, however, and the phenomenon remains puzzling.[37]

The role of disease, whether epidemic or endemic, was probably very similar in England and Scotland, but this was not true of famine. In England subsistence crises brought severe mortality in the late 1550s and 1590s, and to a lesser degree in the 1620s, but thereafter things improved, and England largely escaped the mortality crises experienced elsewhere in north-western Europe following harvest failures in the 1690s.[38] Thanks to Wrigley and Schofield's reconstruction it has been possible to measure the contribution of price fluctuations to short-term movements in English mortality, and these prove to have been of secondary importance; on occasions where death rates did rise following rises in food prices, the effects were substantially offset by compensating episodes of below-average mortality in subsequent years.[39] Such analyses have, to date, been confined largely to the national level, but their conclusions are likely to hold with greater force in the case of major towns and cities which could draw raw provisions from a relatively large area.[40] Indeed, it is likely that the main effects of price fluctuations on English urban populations were felt through their role in inducing, or forcing, the migration of the indigent from the countryside to the town.[41]

Urban centres were buffered against crises, but they were not invulnerable. Where an entire regional economy collapsed in a major subsistence crisis – or military operations severed a centre from its provisioning zone – they could suffer badly, particularly since their inhabitants found it harder than country

[37] A. B. Appleby, 'The disappearance of the plague: a continuing puzzle', *Ec.HR*, 2nd series, 33 (1980), 161–73; M. W. Flinn, 'Plague in Europe and the Mediterranean countries', *Journal of European Economic History*, 8 (1979), 139–46; P. Slack, 'The disappearance of plague: an alternative view', *Ec.HR*, 2nd series, 34 (1981), 469–76; Slack, *Impact of Plague*, pp. 313–26.

[38] This account of English mortality history is based on that given in Wrigley and Schofield, *Population History*.

[39] *Ibid.*, ch. 9, 'Short-term variation: vital rates, prices and weather' (by R. D. Lee); R. S. Schofield, 'The impact of scarcity and plenty on population change in England, 1541–1871', in R. I. Rotberg and T. K. Rabb, eds., *Hunger and History* (Cambridge, 1985), pp. 67–94. In fact Lee found that, in the period 1548–1640, 22 per cent of year on year fluctuations in mortality could be statistically explained by those in wheat prices and 17 per cent could be thus explained in 1641–75. Analysis of local data, however, suggests that substantial price sensitivity was largely confined to districts in the north and west and, even there, had largely disappeared by the mid-seventeenth century (Wrigley and Schofield, *Population History*, Appendix 10).

[40] The level of agricultural productivity and distribution reached early in our period apparently extended such buffering to rural districts in central and southern England: see n. 39. In the North, by contrast, imported Baltic grain which ameliorated the famine of 1597 in Newcastle drew buyers over a radius of sixty miles despite the presence of plague in the city: A. B. Appleby, *Famine in Tudor and Stuart England* (Liverpool, 1980), p. 113.

[41] J. Landers, 'Mortality, weather and prices in London 1675–1825: a study of short-term fluctuations', *Journal of Historical Geography*, 12 (1986), 347–64; P. R. Galloway, 'Differentials in demographic responses to annual price variations in pre-revolutionary France: a comparison of rich and poor areas in Rouen, 1681–1787', *European Journal of Population*, 2 (1986), 269–305.

dwellers to fall back on famine foods or a collecting economy.[42] North of the border, towns were periodically hit by subsistence crises even if the effects were more severe in the countryside. Burial registers are lacking for the sixteenth century but prices rose even more rapidly than in England (grain prices rose sixfold and those of cattle fivefold between 1550 and 1600),[43] and famines became frequent occurrences, particularly in the 1580s and 90s. One of very few surviving burial registers reveals severe mortality in Perth in 1562–3, as witness John Knox's description of famine there in those years.[44]

The evidence for the seventeenth century is better and reveals two nationwide famines with a severe urban impact. The first, in 1623, followed disastrous harvests in 1621 and 1622. Burial registers for Dumfries, Dunfermline and Kelso all display massive increases in mortality, though many casualties were from the countryside. In Kelso burials rose from 59 in 1621 to 86 in 1622 and then to 417 in 1623, most of them in the second and third quarters of the year. There are no other burial registers for these years, but the baptismal registers for Edinburgh, Glasgow, Falkirk, Perth and Aberdeen all show substantial falls of the sort typical of subsistence crises, and the rapid urban growth that had dominated the period before 1620 came to an end.[45] Prices peaked at mid-century, and there is evidence of severe hardship in a number of towns, but none of mortality on the scale of the 1620s. Thenceforth prices fell more steeply than in England until the second great subsistence crisis, the famine of 1695–9.

This was felt across the country but was especially severe in the north-east, which probably lost 20 per cent of its population. In Aberdeen the meal market collapsed; the hinterland could not meet the town's food requirements, and it was forced back on imports as prices soared and income from overseas trade fell drastically. Burials increased by 39 per cent between 1690–4 and 1695–9, and though, as elsewhere, many casualties were beggars from the countryside seeking relief (they were so numerous in Edinburgh that the town council had to build a camp for them in Greyfriars Kirkyard), Aberdeen probably lost a fifth of its population.[46] Other Scottish towns were apparently not hit quite as badly, and in Glasgow, which could obtain food from Ireland, there was little increase in mortality.[47]

Major mortality crises, particularly plague epidemics, were impressive in their

[42] English towns and cities were spared the effect of military crises for all but a few years in the 1640s. At that time, however, centres such as York suffered severely from the combined effects of economic disruption and epidemics: C. Galley, 'A never-ending succession of epidemics? Mortality in early-modern York', *Social History of Medicine*, 7 (1994), 29–58.

[43] For urban prices see A. J. S. Gibson and T. C. Smout, *Prices, Food and Wages in Scotland 1550–1750* (Cambridge, 1995), pp. 19–68.

[44] Flinn, *Scottish Population History*, p. 109.

[45] *Ibid.*, pp. 117–26, 150–3.

[46] R. E. Tyson, 'Famine in Aberdeenshire 1695–99: anatomy of a crisis', in D. Stevenson, ed., *From Lairds to Louns* (Aberdeen, 1986), pp. 34–5. R. A. Houston, *Social Change in the Age of Enlightenment* (Oxford, 1994), p. 259.

[47] Flinn, *Scottish Population History*, pp. 183–5.

scale and destructive violence, but so were the powers of recovery displayed by many urban centres. In London, baptismal totals recovered their pre-plague levels within a few years of the major seventeenth-century plague outbreaks, and in contrast to the experience of Mediterranean Europe, the disease was unable to derail the process of urban growth.[48] In fact, the relationship between overall English mortality and the incidence and severity of crises has proved more complex than used to be thought, since the 'stabilisation' of mortality in the post-plague decades of the later seventeenth century saw an actual decline in life expectation at birth. This fell from around thirty-eight years at mid-century to below thirty-five in the 1690s, revealing the importance of so-called 'background' mortality – due to endemic diseases, or relatively small-scale epidemics – in determining overall levels. In Scotland, the defective parish registers are of little use in measuring overall mortality levels and so the relationship of these to the incidence of crises remains obscure. Crises may have played a more important role here than south of the border – certainly severe crises persisted for longer – but Aberdeen's recorded baptism surplus declined from the 1680s despite a partial stabilisation in short-term mortality.[49]

Rab Houston has measured life expectation at age thirty (e_{30}) for two groups of Scottish lawyers, advocates and writers to the signet. Both groups lived mainly in Edinburgh, and although writers to the signet came from slightly less exalted backgrounds, the life style of both was typical of Scotland's urban middle classes. For those advocates entering between 1532 and 1649, e_{30} was 25.7 years and for writers to the signet 26.9. The advocates' figure for 1650–99 rose to 27.4 years, but for writers to the signet it fell to only 23.3.[50] The differing experience of the two does not resolve the question of whether urban mortality in Scotland rose after 1650, despite the disappearance of plague, but the levels for both are low for such an elite group. For a comparable group, the Geneva ruling and upper middle classes, e_{30} was 32.7 years in 1625–84, and for London Quaker males in 1650–99 it was 28.0.[51]

The switch in interest from crises to background mortality is particularly appropriate in an urban context, for plague, however destructive its visitations, cannot explain why burial surpluses should have persisted in cities like London throughout the intervening years, whilst a recent study of York has concluded that crisis mortality in general 'is of only limited value' in explaining overall

[48] De Vries, *European Urbanization*, pp. 162–3, 207–9.

[49] Aberdeen City Archives, Kirk and Bridgework Accounts, vols. 1 and 2, Register of Baptisms, St Nicholas Parish, Aberdeen, vols. 4, 5 and 6.

[50] R. A. Houston, 'Mortality in early modern Scotland: the life expectancy of advocates', *Continuity and Change*, 7 (1992), 7–69; R. A. Houston, 'Writers to the Signet: estimates of adult mortality in Scotland from the sixteenth to the nineteenth century', *Social History of Medicine*, 8 (1995), 37–53.

[51] A. Perrenoud, 'L'inégalité sociale devant la mort à Genève au XVIIème siècle', *Population*, 30 (num. spec.), 221–43, esp. p. 236; Landers, *Death and the Metropolis*, p. 158.

levels.[52] Recent research using the method of family reconstitution has demonstrated the way in which the population size and density of larger centres allowed immunising infections such as smallpox to become endemic, so that mortality was high, particularly in childhood, but relatively stable in the short term. Adult mortality need not have been much above rural levels, as city-born adults would have acquired substantial immunity in childhood, but recent immigrants may have suffered severely.[53]

Family reconstitution is well suited to the measurement of mortality early in life – particularly of infant mortality although here the underregistration of events can create problems[54] – and urban levels prove to have been clearly above those of comparitor populations and, broadly speaking, to have worsened with settlement size. Whilst infant mortality in a set of thirteen seventeenth-century English family reconstitutions was around 165 per thousand, Finlay found rates in the range 210–70 in a sample of poorer London parishes before 1653,[55] and at the end of the century the level within the bills of mortality has been estimated at around 350 per thousand.[56] Among London Quakers the later seventeenth-century rate has been put at between 260 and 342 per thousand compared with 117 for a rural south-of-England sample,[57] whilst data from a sample of thirteen York parishes for various decades over the period yielded rates ranging from 370 to 234 with half falling between 295 and 234.

Fewer figures are available for childhood mortality, but reconstitution studies of Banbury and Gainsborough give seventeenth-century survival rates from birth to age fifteen of only 685 and 572 per thousand respectively, compared with 831 for the remote rural parish of Hartland in Devon and 708 for the thirteen-parish set.[58] Among London Quakers the proportion surviving to age ten was between 454 and 522 per thousand, as against 756 for a sample drawn from rural southern England and 625 in Bristol and Norwich.[59] In the York parish of St Martin's

[52] Galley, 'A never-ending succession', p. 30.

[53] J. Landers, 'Age patterns of mortality in London during the "long eighteenth century": a test of the "high potential" model of metropolitan mortality', *Social History of Medicine*, 3 (1990), 27–60; Landers, *Death and the Metropolis*, pp. 27–39, 89–126.

[54] E. A. Wrigley, 'Births and baptisms: the use of Anglican baptism registers as a source of information about the number of births in England before the beginning of civil registration', *Population Studies*, 31 (1977), 281–312.

[55] Finlay, *Population and Metropolis*, p. 30.

[56] Landers, *Death and the Metropolis*, p. 170.

[57] Landers, 'Age patterns'; R. T. Vann and D. Eversley, *Friends in Life and Death: The British and Irish Quakers in the Demographic Transition, 1650–1900* (Cambridge, 1992), ch. 5. The discrepancy in the London case arises from different assumptions about birth underregistration. Vann and Eversley make no corrections for this whereas Landers – whose unadjusted figures are close to those of Vann and Eversley – makes substantial corrections using assumptions which may be too pessimistic. For a further discussion see J. Landers, 'Mortality in eighteenth-century London: a note', *Continuity and Change*, 11 (1996), 303–10.

[58] Wrigley and Schofield, 'English population history from family reconstitution'.

[59] See n. 57 for sources.

Coney Street, whose infant mortality rate was close to the mean of Galley's sample, survival from birth to age ten for the period 1561–1700 was estimated at 551 per thousand.[60] The estimation of adult mortality from family reconstitution data presents major technical problems, but the available evidence suggests that urban–rural differentials were, as expected, very much narrower than was the case earlier in life. The London Quaker data indicate an e_{30} of around 28.5 years, which is very close to that of the national thirteen-parish set.[61]

The extent to which mortality in towns differed according to socio-economic status in this period is hard to assess, since such differences have to be inferred from spatial variations between parishes or similar units, and such inferences may give rise to false conclusions even where consistent spatial patterns are detected. Thus Finlay found evidence of mortality variations between parishes in seventeenth-century London, but these apparently reflected ecological factors, such as riverside location, as well as differences in aggregate wealth.[62] In the London case such differentials as existed in this period are likely to have been relatively modest compared to those which emerged in the course of the eighteenth century as growing residential segregation enabled the better-off to avoid exposure to the infectious diseases which became increasingly focused on the poorer districts.[63] Certainly, at the national level, it was only in the later eighteenth century that the social elite began to display a systematic and substantial mortality advantage over the general population.[64] Outcomes of this kind necessarily raise issues of human agency, as well as the relationship of urban dwellers to each other and to their shared environment: these will be the subject of the next two sections.

(ii) DISEASE, AGENCY, AND THE URBAN ENVIRONMENT

We are now able to summarise basic facts about baptisms, burials and (to a lesser extent) marriage with some precision, in spite of the absence of data for many individual towns. The sophistication of the methods now available should not, however, blind us either to the historical contingencies of how the data were created, or to the individual decisions and experiences which aggregates tend to

[60] Galley, 'A never-ending succession'. [61] Landers, *Death and the Metropolis*, pp. 157–9.

[62] Finlay, *Population and Metropolis*, pp. 83–110. [63] Landers, *Death and the Metropolis*, pp. 301–50.

[64] T. H. Hollingsworth, 'The demography of the British peerage', *Population Studies*, 18 (1964), supplement. For a review of long-term trends in socio-economic differentials and their possible implications see S. J. Kunitz, 'Making a long story short: a note on men's heights and mortality in England from the first through the nineteenth centuries', *Medical History*, 31 (1987), 269–80; S. J. Kunitz and S. L. Engerman, 'The ranks of death: secular trends in income and mortality', in J. Landers, ed., *Historical Epidemiology and the Health Transition*, *Health Transition Review*, Supplement to vol. 2 (1993), 29–46; R. Woods and N. Williams, 'Must the gap widen before it can be narrowed? Long-term trends in social class mortality differentials', *Continuity and Change*, 10 (1995), 105–37.

conceal. Hidden behind the figures on marriage, migration and even mortality are major questions about the balance of choice and necessity in the continued growth of towns. These questions remind us of long-established debates about the equation between towns and civilisation itself. The previous section has raised major issues about early modern towns (rates of growth, the fading of crises of subsistence, changing patterns of migration, marriage and remarriage, the 'urban penalty' of endemic as well as epidemic disease and the relationship of mortality peaks to background mortality, high mortality among infants and young children, contrasting sex ratios, increased residential segregation and growing social stratification) all of which call for explanation in terms of human agency and contemporary attitudes to urban life.

The study of British populations arguably began with the 'political arithmetic' devised by seventeenth-century Londoners. Their calculations provided a new basis for some existing impressions – notably the greater unhealthiness of towns – but contradicted other commonly held views.[65] The question of how aware people were of the demographic conditions under which they lived, and to which they inevitably contributed, is a hard one to answer for any period, but is essential to our explanations of population change. Many historical arguments tacitly presuppose that populations can assess their life chances with considerable accuracy and act accordingly, but, even if the vexed issue of 'choice' is left to one side, such decisions must always have involved a mental calculus of great complexity. Evidence bearing on this issue is extremely difficult to handle, but contemporary sources make it clear that we need to look at the felt experiences of urban dwellers – at both alienation and sources of reassurance.

In weighing up early modern responses to urbanisation and population change, we must first admit the provisional nature of many of our own estimates. Even if these prove more accurate than the perceptions of contemporaries, such perceptions would still deserve our attention, if only for considering the issues of awareness and of agency already raised. As we have seen, the period was one of major demographic change in relation to towns; for Britain, some would see it as the period in which the city (rather than 'the people') took on an identity as something beyond customary human knowledge or control.[66] 'The city is a

[65] P. Laslett, 'Natural and political observations on the population of late seventeenth-century England: reflections on the work of Gregory King and John Graunt', in K. Schurer and T. Arkell, eds., *Surveying the People* (Oxford, 1992), pp. 6–30; P. Buck, 'Seventeenth-century political arithmetic: civil strife and vital statistics', *Isis*, 68 (1977), 67–84; C. Webster, *The Great Instauration: Science, Medicine and Reform 1626–1660* (London, 1975), pp. 444–6, 454–5; L. G. Sharp, 'Sir William Petty and some aspects of seventeenth-century natural philosophy' (DPhil thesis, University of Oxford, 1977), esp. ch. 4; J. Hoppit, 'Political arithmetic in eighteenth-century England', *Ec.HR*, 2nd series, 49 (1996), 516–40. Petty was particularly influenced by his early experiences in Leiden.

[66] L. Manley, 'From matron to monster: Tudor–Stuart London and the languages of urban description', in H. Dubrow and R. Strier, eds., *The Historical Renaissance: New Essays on Tudor and Stuart Literature and Culture* (Chicago, 1988), pp. 347–74.

great wilderness', a Scottish clergyman declared towards the close of the seventeenth century, referring to London, 'few in it know the fourth part of its streets, far less can they get intelligence of the hundredth part of special affairs and remarkable passages in it.'[67] It has further been argued that this period saw the emergence of a sense of national identity based on the experience of London life shared, at the end of the sixteenth century, by an estimated one in eight English people.[68] It was also a period of violent 'mood swings' in opinion about the state of human society and its immediate future.[69] The nature of the links between demographic change and contemporary feeling about the future of human society remains problematic, but we can be certain that such links existed, and that they tended to be formed in an urban context.[70] The forms of expression which provide evidence for contemporary feeling are primarily urban – administrative records, political and religious polemic, printed literature, drama, satire, the early newspapers. To these should be added translation, since many of the impulses shaping early modern English society came from the continent. Much private correspondence also involved reporting between town and country.[71]

As we have seen, the proportion of the population living in towns was still small, and of this minority a yet smaller fraction produced the written evidence upon which we depend. There tends to be a glaring disproportion between the scale and uniformity of the effects of human behaviour influencing population structure, and the variety and particularity which can be inferred with respect to the causes of such behaviour. Yet behavioural issues are now central to the argument, which has as its polarities demographic (or economic) determinism

67 Quoted in Houston, *Social Change*, p. 148.

68 For a recent elaboration of this question which draws with varying success upon a wide range of current concepts, see L. Manley, *Literature and Culture in Early Modern London* (Cambridge, 1995). For the population estimates, see Finlay, *Population and Metropolis*, p. 9. On the concept of nationality see E. Smith, 'Sifting strangers: some aspects of the representation of the European foreigner in English drama 1580–1617' (DPhil thesis, University of Oxford, 1997).

69 J. Huizinga, *The Waning of the Middle Ages*, trans. F. Hopman (Harmondsworth, 1968); A. Heller, *Renaissance Man*, trans. R. E. Allen (London, 1978); R. Bauckham, *Tudor Apocalypse: Sixteenth-Century Apocalypticism, Millennarianism, and the English Reformation* (Oxford, 1978); K. R. Firth, *The Apocalyptic Tradition in Reformation Britain, 1530–1645* (Oxford, 1979); Webster, *Great Instauration*, ch. 1; R. Cust and A. Hughes, 'Introduction: after revisionism', in R. Cust and A. Hughes, eds., *Conflict in Early Stuart England* (Harlow, 1989), pp. 1–46. On the city as the site of ambivalence and antithesis, see G. K. Paster, *The Idea of the City in the Age of Shakespeare* (Athens, Ga., 1985).

70 For a positive view of population growth between 1540 and 1640, see D. M. Palliser, 'Tawney's century: brave new world or Malthusian trap?', *Ec.HR*, 2nd series, 35 (1982), 339–53.

71 F. J. Levy, 'How information spread among the gentry, 1550–1640', *Journal of British Studies*, 21 (1982), 11–34; R. Cust, 'News and politics in early seventeenth-century England', *P&P*, 112 (1986), 60–90; J. Raymond, 'The daily muse; or, seventeenth-century poets read the news', *The Seventeenth Century*, 10 (1995), 189–218; A. Mousley, 'Self, state, and seventeenth-century news', *The Seventeenth Century*, 6 (1991), 149–68.

on the one hand, and agency on the other. Interest has focused on patterns of marriage, because emphasis has shifted from mortality to fertility as the main source of change.[72] Both mortality and marriage patterns do, however, have a particular importance in the shifting relationship between town and country, and both can usefully be linked to the issue of mobility. Like mortality and marriage, mobility (social and geographic) can also be shown to be an issue of contemporary concern and a focus of apparently conflicting opinion. Changes in the pattern of interchange between towns, or between town and country, may come to carry a considerable part of the burden of explanation for population change.[73] As already suggested with respect to London, patterns of migration and of town visiting generally also mean that the proportion of those having some experience of urban life (positive or negative) was much greater than the estimated proportions of those resident in towns. At the same time, as other chapters will make clear, the means by which urban influences could spread were developing rapidly. We should not, however, equate more effective communication with the restoration of a sense of community.

The sources new to this period, on which modern calculations depend – parish registers, bills of mortality – require explanation in themselves. An illustration of many of these issues is provided by the bills of mortality. These originated in a personal but official certification demanded from the mayor of London by the lord chancellor confirming the safety or otherwise of the nation's capital.[74] If the city was revealed to be diseased, it was avoided. The self-interested mobility of the elite remained an issue in debates over the breakdown of social obligation, just as the spread of disease was one factor behind the fear of vagrancy. Stability was the ideal, but mobility was often the means of self-preservation sought by both rich and poor. Parish registration, on which the bills of mortality came to be based, was instituted in 1538 for England and Wales by a Tudor administration strongly influenced both by its fears of a crisis in the public health, and by the ideals and practices of the city-states of continental Europe. Parish registration was incompletely realised until the end of the sixteenth century, during another crisis period; piecemeal information emerged during the crisis of the 1550s,

[72] B. Hill, 'The marriage age of women and the demographers', *History Workshop Journal*, 28 (1989), 129–47; Todd, 'Demographic determinism and female agency'. For renewed stress on the role of mortality see P. J. P. Goldberg, *Women, Work, and Life Cycle in a Medieval Economy* (Oxford, 1992), p. 357. On the general issue of agency and fertility, see A. MacKinnon, 'Were women present at the demographic transition? Questions from a feminist historian to historical demographers', *Gender and History*, 7 (1995), 222–40.

[73] See for example M. Dobson, 'The last hiccup of the old demographic regime: population stagnation and decline in late seventeenth and early eighteenth-century south-east England', *Continuity and Change*, 4 (1989), 395–428.

[74] F. P. Wilson, *The Plague in Shakespeare's London* (Oxford, 1927), pp. 189–91, 201–2. The earliest known reference to a bill is 30 August 1519. See in general J. H. Cassedy, 'Medicine and the rise of statistics', in A. G. Debus, ed., *Medicine in Seventeenth-Century England* (Berkeley, Calif., 1974), pp. 283–312.

when a certain pleasure was taken in the fact that the 'English sweat' seemed to target the heedless and the better-off – those able to move when they needed to.[75]

Other initiatives of the Henrician period, like the London College of Physicians (1518) and the ecclesiastical system of licensing medical practitioners (1511), proved enduring but developed no effective role in national or metropolitan public health reform; the College, like physicians generally, was severely compromised by its repeated desertion of London at the first sign of a major epidemic. Another urban-based solution, the Savoy hospital, was short-lived but presaged the redevelopment of London's hospitals in mid-century.[76] The London hospitals were of course based on specific numerical estimates of the numbers of the diseased, impotent, vagrant and idle poor with which London seemed to be encumbered.[77] By the end of the sixteenth century, systems to locate and deal with the dead, the diseased and the destitute of urban parishes were in place which were to last, in one form or another, until the nineteenth century. The most neglected aspect of these systems is the underpinning provided by women, many of them poor, and, of necessity, resident.[78]

Compared with their counterparts in Europe, these systems were personal rather than institutional, fluid rather than fixed. Even in London, this kind of civic responsibility did not give itself a high profile in terms of bricks and mortar until the voluntary hospital movement of the eighteenth century, which was none the less an expression of the corporate rather than the industrial town. The voluntary hospital can be seen in part as an attempt by the 'middling sort' to distance themselves from their more intimate social obligations to dependants whom custom would earlier have made members of the household, in sickness as well as in health.[79]

The later development of the bills of mortality – which were apparently a 'purely urban manifestation' – was also dominated by the need to identify

75 Finlay, *Population and Metropolis*, p. 21; Wilson, *Plague in Shakespeare's London*, p. 191; J. A. H. Wylie and L. H. Collier, 'The English sweating sickness (*Sudor Anglicus*) – a reappraisal', *Journal of the History of Medicine*, 36 (1981), 425–45, esp. 426–7, 432.

76 C. Webster, 'Thomas Linacre and the foundation of the College of Physicians', in F. R. Maddison, M. Pelling and C. Webster, eds., *Linacre Studies: Essays on the Life and Work of Thomas Linacre c. 1460–1524* (Oxford, 1977), pp. 198–222.

77 P. Slack, 'Social policy and the constraints of government, 1547–58', in J. Loach and R. Tittler, eds., *The Mid-Tudor Polity c. 1540–1560* (London, 1980), pp. 108–14; John Howes, 'Discourse', in R. H. Tawney and E. Power, eds., *Tudor Economic Documents* (London, 1975), vol. III, pp. 418, 424–5.

78 M. Pelling, 'Healing the sick poor: social policy and disability in Norwich 1550–1640', *Medical History*, 29 (1985), 115–37, esp. 127–8; T. R. Forbes, 'The searchers', *Bulletin of the New York Academy of Medicine*, 50 (1974), 1031–8.

79 M. Pelling, 'Apprenticeship, health and social cohesion in early modern London', *History Workshop Journal*, 37 (1994), 33–56, esp. 45–6. For the locations of voluntary hospitals, see C. Webster, ed., *Caring for Health: History and Diversity*, Open University Health and Disease series (Buckingham, 1993), pp. 52–3. On plague, servants and pesthouses, see O. Grell, 'Plague in Elizabethan and Stuart London: the Dutch response', *Medical History*, 34 (1990), 424–39, esp. 426.

degrees of danger from urban disease. Other information was increasingly included, but was secondary. As with water, the rich could pay for their own supply: by the mid-seventeenth century, personal copies of weekly bills were available for a subscription of 4s. a year.[80] A network of private correspondence carried such information around the country.[81] London's example was gradually followed by other towns. By intention at least, Norwich followed suit in 1579, Lichfield in 1645–6 if not earlier, Dublin around 1658, Glasgow in 1670 and Edinburgh in 1695.[82] An attempt towards 'freedom of information' was made in the 1640s, when Henry Walker printed the bills in *Perfect Occurrences*, one of the earliest newspapers. This was consonant with proposals by Puritan reformers for making information less divisive, and for the pooling and sifting of useful knowledge, including that bearing on life and death. Their attempt at an 'information revolution' had many aspects: by this date, representatives of the 'middling sort' could assume that the urban poor had lost their instinctive knowledge of herbal lore, just as man, unlike the animals, had lost the ability to cure himself after the Fall.[83] John Graunt, 'born, and bred in the City of London' and of too low a status to qualify for the Royal Society without special consideration, was the first to analyse the bills; he criticised the trivialisation of them in the mouths of coffee-house society, and was also concerned, like Thomas Browne of England's second city, Norwich, to correct 'popular' error, claiming that men were never more wrong than about number. Both Graunt and William Petty were attempting to deal with the climate of unease following the ominous plagues and conflagrations of the first six decades of the seventeenth century – a task which arose at different times for other towns, though similar evidence might be lacking.[84]

That the city was in a sense 'natural' to man's view of himself was expressed in the revival, initiated by Thomas More, of utopian writing. This was a very

[80] Flinn, *Scottish Population History*, p. 73; *The Economic Writings of Sir William Petty*, ed. C. H. Hull (New York, 1963), vol. I, p. lxxxiii. The weekly bills were available in printed form from the 1590s: Wilson, *Plague in Shakespeare's London*, pp. 196–7.

[81] C. Webster, 'William Harvey and the crisis of medicine in Jacobean England', in J. J. Bylebyl, ed., *William Harvey and his Age* (Baltimore, 1979), pp. 1–27, esp. p. 2; J. C. Robertson, 'Reckoning with London: interpreting the *Bills of Mortality* before John Graunt', *UH*, 23(1996), 325–50.

[82] Slack, *Impact of Plague*, p. 113; D. Palliser, 'Dearth and disease in Staffordshire, 1540–1670', in C. W. Chalklin and M. A. Havinden, eds., *Rural Change and Urban Growth 1500–1800* (London, 1974), p. 60; *Economic Writings of Petty*, ed. Hull, II, p. 480; D. V. Glass, *Numbering the People* (London, 1973), ch. 1; J. K. Edwards, 'Norwich bills of mortality – 1707–1830', *Yorkshire Bulletin of Social and Economic Research*, 21 (1969), 94–113, esp. 112–13; Flinn, *Scottish Population History*, pp. 73–4.

[83] Webster, *Great Instauration*, esp. pp. 268, 262, 422, 445, 247.

[84] *Economic Writings of Petty* (includes the fifth edition of Graunt's *Natural and Political Observations*, 1676), ed. Hull, esp. I, p. xxxvi, II, pp. 333, 401; Webster, *Great Instauration*, pp. 444–6. On Graunt and his context see also P. Kreager, 'New light on Graunt', *Population Studies*, 42 (1988), 129–40.

varied genre, heavily influenced by Italian humanism, but it framed society in urban terms, gave prominence to urban problems and their control, and placed particular emphasis on health, long life and the prevention of disease. Interestingly in the present context, the representative ideal city tended to be wary of strangers, and static, even if stasis had to be achieved by barriers and enforced transfers of population. Some writers pointed to realisations of the ideal, such as Venice, Florence, Geneva, Amsterdam and San Marino: these might be 'open' cities, but they possessed successful means of self-protection.[85] There were of course a great many more pessimistic accounts of human society. In 1624, while recovering from a dangerous illness, John Donne gave classic expression to the traditional world view: 'this is nature's set of boxes: the heavens contain the earth; the earth, cities; cities, men'. He then went on to undermine it: 'And all these are concentric; the common centre to them all is decay, ruin.' Donne, who spent years in poverty outside London, exiled from company and sources of patronage, was here rendering an individualistic sense of loneliness and vulnerability.[86] Towns were valued for the sense of security they promised, through one person's observation of another; they were equally resented when such promises were not fulfilled.

One of many contemporary paradoxes was that early modern England, although predominantly rural, produced many images of itself as a crowded society. A second paradox was that with a sense of crowding came also a sense of isolation and a growing perception of urban anonymity. This was in part justified not only by the domination of London but by sharp contrasts in population density in other regions, including Scotland. During the period of demographic growth, there was concern about the erosion of social hierarchies and the abandonment of traditional obligations between the different social orders.[87] The Reformation, with its destruction of known landmarks, beautiful objects, sensuous experiences and institutions symbolic of care for the poor, could also be blamed for increasing population by overpromoting marriage and suppressing prostitution, the Popish solution cynically allowed for those too poor to marry.[88] Married priests were only one among a wide range of problems of social recognition characteristic of late Tudor and Stuart society. Playwrights and satirists, however humorously, reflected anxiety about the difficulty of recognising people

[85] See L. T. Sargent, *British and American Utopian Literature 1516–1975: An Annotated Bibliography* (Boston, 1979); M. Eliav, 'The social content of the utopias of the Renaissance, 1516–1630' (DPhil thesis, University of Oxford, 1977); J. M. Patrick, 'A history of utopianism in England in the seventeenth century' (DPhil thesis, University of Oxford, 1951). On segregation as an aspect of the definitive Renaissance city, Venice, see R. Sennett, *Flesh and Stone: The Body and the City in Western Civilization* (London, 1994), ch. 7.

[86] J. Donne, *Devotions . . . with Deaths Duell*, ed. W. H. Draper (London, n.d.), sect. x, p. 63.

[87] F. Heal, *Hospitality in Early Modern England* (Oxford, 1990), esp. ch. 8.

[88] [Francis Trigge], *An apologie or defence of our dayes* (London, 1589), pp. 27, 36.

for what they were, especially in towns. Both costume and behaviour had become deceptive; rich clothing was assumed by those with no real substance behind them, or by those out of their proper place, like apprentices, servants and citizens' wives.[89] Sumptuary legislation and an obsession with genealogy and heraldry were archaisms aimed at restoring the traditional order. Occult sciences took on a new importance as means of managing uncertainty and determining identity. Francis Bacon recommended physiognomy, especially the study of gesture, as 'a great discovery of dissimulations, and a great direction in business'.[90] The role of towns, especially that of London in the Civil War, suggested to some that growing cities were inimical to monarchy; London was thought to harbour millions rather than thousands of people.[91] At the same time, social mobility provided a sense of opportunity for many and a motive for migration to towns. 'Civility' was a common currency of behaviour which could be readily acquired.[92]

Urban anxieties focused on a number of targets: the sturdy, 'masterless' beggar, among whose cheats was the counterfeiting of disease and disability; the alehouse, where contact was promiscuous and the respectable could be tainted, physically and morally, by the lawless; the scolding woman, especially if she were 'abroad' on the streets; secrecy, rumour and the impossibility of effective surveillance in a crowded environment; and the 'pestered' suburbs where anonymity and overcrowding seemed to be greatest.[93] Although towns continued in many respects to represent (and to seek to preserve) a 'face-to-face' society, it is arguable that one response to earlier 'crowding' and mutability was a move towards greater social stratification, segregation and the growth of the 'private' household towards the end of the seventeenth century. Reassurance was also sought through comparisons with other, 'uncivil' societies, which lacked an urban structure. Although some writers idealised primitive societies, by analogy with the primitive church, nomadic peoples, like the Irish, were generally despised. In Wales, social structure was similarly 'uncivil' and towns were, as in

89 M. Pelling, 'Appearance and reality: barber-surgeons, the body and disease', in Beier and Finlay, eds., *London*, pp. 82–112.

90 F. Bacon, *The Advancement of Learning*, ed. G. W. Kitchin (London, 1965), Bk 2, IX, 2, p. 107.

91 Petty, *Treatise of Taxes and Contributions*, and Graunt, *Observations*, in *Economic Writings of Petty*, ed. Hull, I, p. 40, II, p. 383.

92 A. Bryson, 'The rhetoric of status: gesture, demeanour and the image of the gentleman in sixteenth and seventeenth-century England', in L. Gent and N. Llewellyn, eds., *Renaissance Bodies: The Human Figure in English Culture c. 1540–1660* (London, 1990), pp. 136–53.

93 See for example G. Salgado, *The Elizabethan Underworld* (London, 1977); P. Clark, *The English Alehouse* (London, 1983); A. L. Beier, *Masterless Men: The Vagrancy Problem in England 1560–1640* (London, 1987); D. Underdown, 'The taming of the scold: the enforcement of patriarchal authority in early modern England', in A. Fletcher and J. Stevenson, eds., *Order and Disorder in Early Modern England* (Cambridge, 1987), pp. 116–36. Cf. M. Ingram, '"Scolding women cucked or washed": a crisis in gender relations in early modern England?', in J. Kermode and G. Walker, eds., *Women, Crime and the Courts in Early Modern England* (London, 1994), pp. 48–80.

Ireland, dominated by the English, but the Welsh, unlike the Irish, were not seen as resisting English influence; attitudes affecting Wales in this period, as well as the thinly populated recusant northern regions, await further investigation.[94]

In spite of the major demographic changes of the period, population was fairly consistently seen as a resource, and depopulation something to be feared. This did not preclude concerns about excessive concentrations and imbalances of people, either in a given trade, in a locality, among the poor, or among 'teeming' peoples, such as the Irish. The 'political arithmetic' of William Petty and his successors was partly aimed at assuaging fears that Britain was being outdone in populousness by the French or the Dutch; particular concern was felt about the size of capitals. Graunt, also writing in the latter half of the seventeenth century, sought to explain what Gillis has called 'the celibate city'. Graunt tried to account for the comparative barrenness of urban people; to refute the belief that women outnumbered men in London by three to one; and to discredit the idea of polygamy as the solution to population decline. In the first case, he found a link between cities and the natural world in terms of reduced fertility due to promiscuity.[95] (As we have already seen, marital fertility does not seem to have been lower among urban populations.)

Like many of his numerically minded contemporaries, Graunt was effectively considering religious, political and moral questions, but to these must be added issues of gender. Concern about the sexual activity of women as well as of the poor was heightened by the threat of 'new diseases' – some of which were known to be sexually transmitted – as was women's own concern about fertility. The 'celibate' (but not necessarily chaste) life lived by many men of property in cities could simply be condemned as selfish; but the fear of being outnumbered by women reflects not only a possible feminisation of London – following a phase around the end of the sixteenth century in which the capital and larger towns such as York seem to have been unusual in having more male than female inhabitants – but also a view of the town as defined by male author-

[94] A. Laurence, 'The cradle to the grave: English observations of Irish social customs in the seventeenth century', *The Seventeenth Century*, 3 (1988), 63–84; H. C. Porter, *The Inconstant Savage: England and the North American Indian 1500–1660* (London, 1979); A. Pagden, *European Encounters with the New World* (New Haven, 1993). On the Irish see also the writings of Petty.

[95] M. Campbell, '"Of people either too few or too many": the conflict of opinion on population and its relation to emigration', in W. A. Aitken and B. D. Henning, eds., *Conflict in Stuart England* (London, 1960), pp. 169–201 (for contemporary opinion rather than estimates of emigration); Graunt, *Observations*, in *Economic Writings of Petty*, ed. Hull, II, pp. 372–8, 385–6; J. R. Gillis, *For Better, For Worse: British Marriages, 1600 to the Present* (Oxford, 1988), ch. 6. On attitudes to fertility see P. Crawford, 'Attitudes to menstruation in seventeenth-century England', *P&P*, 91(1981), 47–73; M. Fissell, 'Gender and generation: representing reproduction in early modern England', *Gender and History*, 7(1995), 433–56.

ity, as well as doubts raised by the cost to the male population of the Civil War.[96]

The 'crisis of gender' identified by some historians as developing in the first half of the seventeenth century is most convincingly demonstrated with respect to urban life, for example in terms of increased hostility to the social and economic activity of women outside the house. Women's occupational roles became more narrowly defined in the latter half of the century, as a result of which they could become more visible. Sick-nursing for example became an identifiable female occupation in towns, possibly as a result of the need to employ carers outside the household for sufferers from acute infectious diseases; while at the same time male medical practitioners disparaged female competitors and themselves intruded into midwifery.[97]

The effect of repeated outbreaks of plague in testing the social structure has been amply demonstrated.[98] Of similar significance, however, was the ominous burden of the 'new' diseases already mentioned, which seemed to signify a new (and probably gloomy) phase of human society: the sweat and other fevers, scurvy, rickets and in particular syphilis.[99] As Graunt recognised, the importance

[96] See F. Heal and C. Holmes, *The Gentry in England and Wales 1500–1700* (Basingstoke, 1994), p. 283. L. Roper, *The Holy Household: Women and Morals in Reformation Augsburg* (Oxford, 1989), is suggestive on the gendering of early modern towns. On the Civil Wars, see C. Carlton, *Going to the Wars: The Experience of the British Civil Wars, 1638–1651* (London, 1994); Webster, *Great Instauration*, esp. pp. 292, 295–300. On sex ratios and towns, see Goldberg, *Women, Work and Life Cycle*, pp. 294ff; C. Galley, 'A model of early modern urban demography', *Ec.HR*, 2nd series, 48 (1995), 448–69, esp. 457–8; Clark, 'Migration in England', and D. Souden, '"East, west – home's best"? Regional patterns in migration in early modern England', both in Clark and Souden, eds., *Migration and Society*, pp. 213–52, 292–332; and n. 18, above.

[97] See A. Clark, *Working Life of Women in the Seventeenth Century* (London, 1919; 2nd edn, 1982); M. Roberts, '"Words they are women, and deeds they are men": images of work and gender in early modern England', in L. Charles and L. Duffin, eds., *Women and Work in Pre-industrial England* (London, 1985), pp. 122–80; M. Roberts, 'Women and work in sixteenth-century English towns', in P. J. Corfield and D. Keene, eds., *Work in Towns 850–1850* (Leicester, 1990), pp. 86–102; P. Griffiths, 'Masterless young people in Norwich, 1560–1645', in P. Griffiths *et al.*, eds., *The Experience of Authority in Early Modern England* (London, 1996), pp. 146–86; M. Pelling, 'Compromised by gender: the role of the male medical practitioner in early modern England', in H. Marland and M. Pelling, eds., *The Task of Healing: Medicine, Religion and Gender in England and the Netherlands 1450–1800* (Rotterdam, 1996), pp. 101–33; M. Pelling, 'The women of the family? Speculations around early modern British physicians', *Social History of Medicine*, 8 (1995), 383–401; M. Pelling, 'Nurses and nursekeepers: problems of identification in the early modern period', in M. Pelling, *The Common Lot: Sickness, Medical Occupations, and the Urban Poor in Early Modern England* (Harlow, 1998), pp. 179–202. On midwives see H. Marland, ed., *The Art of Midwifery: Early Modern Midwives in Europe* (London, 1993).

[98] Slack, *Impact of Plague*; Grell, 'Plague in Elizabethan and Stuart London'; G. Calvi, 'A metaphor for social change: the Florentine plague of 1630', *Representations*, 13 (1986), 139–63.

[99] C. Quétel, *History of Syphilis*, trans. J. Braddock and B. Pike (Cambridge, 1990); A. Foa, 'The new and the old: the spread of syphilis (1494–1530)', in E. Muir and G. Ruggiero, eds., *Sex and Gender in Historical Perspective* (Baltimore, 1990), pp. 26–45; Pelling, 'Appearance and reality',

of these conditions can be impossible to measure quantitatively, but is shown qualitatively. Of syphilis (the pox, the great pox, morbus Gallicus) Graunt noted that while 'by the ordinary discourse of the World it seems a great part of men have, at one time or other, had some species of this Disease', the world would rarely admit that anyone had died of it.[100] It is now unfashionable among historians to regard disease as a major influence on manners and commensual behaviour; it is probable that this historiographical trend has led to a denial of the obvious, especially in the case of venereal disease.[101]

Early modern urban dwellers were not only conscious of how differently diseases affected different social groups and their interrelationships; they were also aware that social factors modified how diseases were regarded and even named or identified.[102] As plague receded and syphilis became less fulminating, smallpox and fevers became more prominent modifiers of physical life and behaviour. The importance of smallpox to changing patterns of mortality was indicated in the previous section. Although the sweating sickness can be used to highlight the intricacy of communication even between small centres in the mid-sixteenth century, it is probably smallpox, an acute fever of well-defined course and repulsive aspect which requires no vector for transmission, that best registers the extent of human interchange between early modern towns.[103] Smallpox was feared not only as a cause of death, but also because of the prejudicial effects of the visible disfigurement and disabilities suffered by many of those who recovered from it.

Practices involving social obligation which were influenced by the attempt to avoid risk include poor relief and apprenticeship. Venereal disease affected the rental sector, just as smallpox was arguably one factor in changing household structure in towns. Disease, or the fear of it, may also have contributed to the observed geographical changes in recruitment of apprentices to the larger towns. Residential patterns were also changed by the attempt to avoid urban diseases, or new 'urban penalties' such as pollution from the burning of sea coal.[104] Town dwelling among the elite was in any case always intermittent. The decamping of

pp. 95–105; L. G. Stevenson, '"New diseases" in the seventeenth century', *Bulletin for the History of Medicine*, 39 (1965), 1–21; G. Rosen, *A History of Public Health*, expanded edn (Baltimore, 1993), ch. 4. 100 Graunt, *Observations*, in *Economic Writings of Petty*, ed. Hull, II, pp. 355–6.

101 This is partly owing to the influence of Norbert Elias, especially his *The Civilizing Process*, vol. I: *The History of Manners*, trans. E. Jephcott (Oxford, 1983). One exception is Sennett, *Flesh and Stone*. 102 G. Williams, 'An Elizabethan disease', *Trivium*, 6 (1971), 43–58.

103 A. Dyer, 'The English sweating sickness of 1551: an epidemic anatomised', *Medical History*, 41 (1997), 361–83; Landers, *Death and the Metropolis*; M. Dobson, *A Chronology of Epidemic Disease and Mortality in Southeast England, 1601–1800*, Historical Geography Research Series No. 19 (Cheltenham, 1987).

104 Pelling, 'Appearance and reality', pp. 97–8; Pelling, 'Apprenticeship, health and social cohesion'; Graunt, *Observations*, in *Economic Writings of Petty*, ed. Hull, II, pp. 41–2. On air pollution and its significance, see M. Jenner, 'The politics of London air: John Evelyn's *Fumifugium* and the Restoration', *HJ*, 38 (1995), 535–51.

townspeople below the level of the nobility and gentry to property outside towns has usually been interpreted as an aspect of gentrification; the aim of restoring health, avoiding disease and ensuring the succession by improving the life chances of children has received less attention. By the middle of the seventeenth century, there is evidence of 'second homes' outside London even among the commercial classes.[105]

It is interesting, too, to reflect on new patterns of health seeking and leisure in terms not only of the 'goods' being sought, but also of what those involved were wanting to get away from. As Chapter 23 in this volume shows, many prosperous urban dwellers looked for the antithesis of what they left behind: small, relatively inaccessible places, of no great political sophistication, which, ideally at least, developed agreeable urban facilities without urban contamination, and which restored a sense of social hierarchy. Thus, diversification in the urban structure can also be seen as an effect of patterns of avoidance, which are themselves one measure of urban malaise.[106] As against this, we have to set the continuing ability of notoriously unhealthy centres to attract migrants; similarly, healthy areas could be poor. In moving to towns, early modern people often faced decisions similar to those taken by emigrants to the New World; to what extent 'choice' entered into such decisions is problematic.[107]

As already suggested, morbidity, or the incidence of sickness and disability, is far more difficult to measure than mortality, yet it is vitally linked to social conditions and social change.[108] For every premature death there was likely to be a penumbra of grief, disability and economic disadvantage. 'Political arithmetic', as well as earlier experiments in medical poor relief, included the calculation that sickness imposed a burden on the state greater than death. Moreover, as Graunt realised, the most feared diseases were not necessarily the most common causes of death; as in the present day, morbidity and mortality could be dissociated.[109]

[105] There is scattered evidence for this in records of apprenticeship disputes: London, Corporation of London Record Office, MC6. See Pelling, 'Apprenticeship, health and social cohesion'.

[106] On 'the medicine of avoidance and prevention' as it developed in the eighteenth century, see J. C. Riley, *The Eighteenth-Century Campaign to Avoid Disease* (Houndmills, Basingstoke, 1987).

[107] K. O. Kupperman, 'Fear of hot climates in the Anglo-American colonial experience', *William and Mary Quarterly*, 41 (1984), 213–40; M. Dobson, 'Contours of death: disease, mortality and the environment in early modern England', in Landers, ed., *Historical Epidemiology and the Health Transition*, pp. 77–95; Dobson, 'Mortality gradients and disease exchanges: comparisons from old England and colonial America', *Social History of Medicine*, 2 (1989), 259–97.

[108] M. Pelling, 'Illness among the poor in an early modern English town: the Norwich census of 1570', *Continuity and Change*, 3 (1988), 275ff; J. C. Riley, 'Disease without death: new sources for a history of sickness', *Journal of Interdisciplinary History*, 17 (1987), 537–63. For one attempt to build morbidity into an existing debate see Benedictow, 'Morbidity in historical plague epidemics'.

[109] Pelling, 'Healing the sick poor'; G. Rosen, 'Medical care and social policy in seventeenth-century England', *Bulletin of the New York Academy of Medicine*, 29 (1953), 420–37, esp. 430; Graunt, *Observations*, in *Economic Writings of Petty*, ed. Hull, II, pp. 349–63.

It is desirable, but very difficult, in urban history to take into account an 'index of disability', that is, the proportion of the population likely at any one time to be incapacitated by mental or physical problems.[110] Modern surveys equally find morbidity and disability hard to measure; mortality differentials according to socio-economic circumstances are undeniable, but resistant to explanation. One approach is to see survival as a balance of demands upon resources, the latter to include support from neighbours and friends.[111] This chimes with Donne's comment that 'as sickness is the greatest misery, so the greatest misery of sickness is solitude'.[112] Early modern people avoided solitude and even privacy in sickness as much as they could, and understood the paradox that to be alone and ill in a town was perhaps the worst misery of all. A currently unanswerable question is the extent to which disability was unevenly distributed between town and country as a side-effect of mobility. Disease and disability profoundly affected entry to apprenticeship or service, ability to work and chances of marriage. This was recognised at the time both in legal disputes, and by the inclusion of sickness in surveys conducted by municipal authorities, such as the censuses of the poor. Frequently, such censuses led to unanticipated results, for example the identification of large numbers of indigenous poor who were able-bodied but who could find no work.[113] What is clear is that urban dwellers, individually as well as collectively, sought forms of apprenticeship, work and even marriage for the disabled, which deflected the stigma of idleness even though at the price of downward social mobility.[114]

Urban dwellers did not react with stoicism to adverse urban conditions. The degree to which the populations of Tudor and Stuart towns were oblivious to dirt and disease has been greatly exaggerated.[115] Attempts at this period to control noxious trades or to ensure clean water have been overshadowed both by unwarrantable modern complacency and, historically, by the late seventeenth-century campaigns which were symptomatic of increased social stratification. The dark, huddled vernacular of the Tudor and early Stuart town has been imagined simply as a contrast, or at most a prelude, to the airy, spacious

110 For one comparative estimate see Pelling, 'Illness among the poor', pp. 273–90.

111 R. A. Amler and H. B. Dull, eds., *Closing the Gap: The Burden of Unnecessary Illness* (New York, 1987), pp. 125–6. For Britain see A. Bowling, *Measuring Disease: A Review of Disease-Specific Quality of Life Measurement Scales* (Buckingham, 1995).

112 Donne, *Devotions*, p. 30. On sickness and solitude see also H. Brody, *Stories of Sickness* (New Haven, 1987), pp. 99–104.

113 P. Slack, *Poverty and Policy in Tudor and Stuart England* (London, 1988), p. 27.

114 M. Pelling, 'Child health as a social value in early modern England', *Social History of Medicine*, 1 (1988), 135–64, esp. 160–1.

115 On this point see D. Palliser, 'Civic mentality and the environment in Tudor York', *NHist.*, 18 (1982), 78–115; Pelling, 'Appearance and reality', pp. 93–4; M. Pelling, 'Medicine and the environment in Shakespeare's England', in Pelling, *The Common Lot*, pp. 19–37; K. Thomas, 'Cleanliness and godliness in early modern England', in A. Fletcher and P. Roberts, eds., *Religion, Culture and Society in Early Modern Britain* (Cambridge, 1994), pp. 56–83.

policies of the Enlightenment.[116] More searching investigation may modify this long-standing perspective; recent work suggests, for example, that prescribed norms of cleanliness in London became more rigorous in the second half of the sixteenth century, and less so in the later seventeenth.[117] Similarly, urban innovations which seem later to belong to new worlds of luxury, leisure or vice, such as tobacco,[118] coffee, tea and chocolate,[119] usually owed their introduction in our period to the search for new remedies, just as the town of Bath meant health before it came to mean entertainment. Most of these anodynes and consolations gradually became as widely distributed as alcohol. Contemporaries were aware that tobacco, like alcohol, harmed as much as it healed, both directly, and indirectly as a misuse of resources; even tea and coffee could become pernicious, especially if the poor became addicted to them. Correspondingly, the increasingly respectable medical practitioners of the later seventeenth century can be seen as preceded by the less professionalised but multifarious range of town-based practitioners resorted to by all classes of early modern people in their restless search for the means to health.[120] Towns were seen ambivalently, as a source of strong remedies as well as strong diseases. The one attitude that can be ruled out is indifference. This generalisation has implications not only for the individual's view of himself or herself in the urban context, but also for the persistence of forms of interrelationship within the urban structure: family and neighbourhood.

(iii) HOUSEHOLD AND NEIGHBOURHOOD

Townspeople not only attempted to understand their changing material environments through rhetorics of inclusion and exclusion, or by plans to tackle dirt

[116] For a recent synthesis of the latter kind see Sennett, *Flesh and Stone*, part 3.

[117] M. Jenner, 'Early modern English conceptions of "cleanliness" and "dirt" as reflected in the environmental regulation of London *c.* 1530–*c.* 1700' (DPhil thesis, University of Oxford, 1991), pp. 118–19.

[118] The literature on tobacco is now considerable. See for example G. G. Stewart, 'A history of the medicinal uses of tobacco 1492–1860', *Medical History*, 11 (1967), 228–68; J. Knapp, 'Elizabethan tobacco', *Representations*, 21 (1988), 27–66; R. C. Nash, 'The English and Scottish tobacco trades in the seventeenth and eighteenth centuries: legal and illegal trade', *Ec.HR*, 2nd series, 35 (1982), 354–72; J. Goodman, *Tobacco in History: The Cultures of Dependence* (London, 1993).

[119] On different aspects of beverages, see D. Duncan, *Wholesome Advice against the Abuse of Hot Liquors* (trans. from French) (London, 1706); J. J. Keevil, 'Coffee house cures', *Journal of the History of Medicine*, 9 (1954), 191–5; P. B. Brown, *In Praise of Hot Liquors: The Study of Chocolate, Coffee and Tea-Drinking 1600–1850* (York, [1995]); C. A. Wilson, ed., *Liquid Nourishment: Potable Foods and Stimulating Drinks* (Edinburgh, 1993); P. Albrecht, 'Coffee drinking as a symbol of social change in continental Europe in the seventeenth and eighteenth centuries', *Studies in Eighteenth Century Culture*, 18 (1988), 91–103; A. L. Butler, 'Europe's Indian nectar: the trans-Atlantic cacao and chocolate trade in the seventeenth century' (MLitt thesis, University of Oxford, 1993), esp. ch. 2.

[120] M. Pelling, 'Occupational diversity: barbersurgeons and the trades of Norwich, 1550–1640', *Bulletin of the History of Medicine*, 56 (1982), 485–511, esp. 511.

and disease; they also sought reassurance in familiar places like neighbourhoods and households. It was to such communities that they turned for protection in situations where population increases were only one source of difficulty. However, the growing numbers of townspeople placed mounting pressure on the smaller structures from which towns were constructed, including the household and neighbourhood. Worse still, the leap in populations largely resulted from waves of migration, a pool of outsiders many of whom were entirely strange to the town to which they were travelling. Outsiders raised difficulties for rulers who ordered towns by tight categorisation of their people and the creation of a sense of community: a sense of belonging which partly depended on participation in stable families. As such, households and neighbourhoods were vital political as well as social and economic institutions. So, does this mean that the anonymity of urban living has been greatly exaggerated hitherto?[121] Much depends on the size of the town under review, yet in many respects families and neighbourhoods were still points in an otherwise restless environment, confirming relationships and identities, offering stability. The accuracy of this picture will be tested in the following paragraphs; its vulnerability in changing urban conditions will be emphasised, but not at the expense of its continuing significance for at least some sections of the integrated urban community.

Townspeople can be counted in households as well as in towns. Statistics of mean household size (MHS) allow us to comment on the nature of life in urban communities. Households were quite small. As in the countryside, they were usually composed of nuclear families and, sometimes, of several such families sharing a single building, though the average size of rural households (4.75 and 4.80) was slightly larger.[122] Three or four people lived in most town dwellings so far reconstructed. Towns otherwise distinguished by size or the make-up of occupational structures had roughly equivalent averages: 3.7 in Coventry, 3.8 in Southwark and Southampton and 4.1 in Cambridge.[123]

121 Arguments that urban life was characterised by anonymity have been challenged by, amongst others, K. Wrightson, *English Society, 1580–1680* (London, 1982), pp. 55–7; J. Boulton, *Neighbourhood and Society* (Cambridge, 1987); I. W. Archer, *The Pursuit of Stability* (Cambridge, 1991), p. 76; D. Garrioch, *Neighbourhood and Community in Paris, 1740–1790* (Cambridge, 1986), p. 257; and Houston, *Social Change*, pp. 147, 230.

122 Wrightson, *English Society*, p. 45; N. Goose, 'Household size and structure in early Stuart Cambridge', in J. Barry, ed., *The Tudor and Stuart Town* (London, 1990), pp. 74–120, esp. pp. 96, 114; Boulton, *Neighbourhood and Society*, pp. 122–3; P. and J. Clark, 'The social economy of the Canterbury suburbs: the evidence of the census of 1563', in A. Detsicas and N. Yates, eds., *Studies in Modern Kentish History Presented to Felix Hull and Elizabeth Melling* (Maidstone, 1983), pp. 65–86, esp. pp. 69–70; M. Pelling, 'Old age, poverty, and disability in early modern Norwich: work, remarriage, and other expedients', in M. Pelling and R. M. Smith, eds., *Life, Death, and the Elderly: Historical Perspectives* (London, 1991), pp. 74–101, esp. pp. 85–7. For rural households see P. Laslett, 'Mean household size in England since the sixteenth century', in P. Laslett, *Household and Family in Past Time* (Cambridge, 1972), pp. 125–58, and R. Wall, 'Regional and temporal variations in English household structure from 1650', in J. Hobcraft and P. Rees, eds., *Regional Aspects of British Population Growth* (London, 1979), pp. 89–113.

123 Boulton, *Neighbourhood and Society*, pp. 122–3; Goose, 'Household size'.

Flat averages, however, disguise uneven realities, and the connected factors of wealth, status, work and age were just some of the variables which caused household size to fall or rise. Houses and households were tokens of wealth, made conspicuous in the geography of urban poverty. Poverty trimmed MHS in Norwich, Warwick, Canterbury, Southwark, Salisbury and Cambridge, where the small households of the poor (in only one case above 3.3 in average size, and as low as 2.3 elsewhere) dotted suburban fringes.[124] Differences of wealth and occupation can be tracked in numbers of rooms and residents, which rise as we climb through social ranks to gentry households where it is not unusual to find ten or more residents.[125] These contrasting households are best explained by numbers of servants and apprentices, a mark of status as well as a pool of labour. Servants played a key part in occupations like Canterbury's food and drink trade, boosting household size.[126] Individual experiences were various, but they also altered over the life-course, as the birth of children or the loss of a spouse reshaped families. The impact of time was not just felt in terms of numerical age; the shifting predicaments of changing economic fortunes, plague or increased in-migration remodelled households, adding or subtracting members according to circumstance.[127]

Low household size is further attributable to the small number of co-resident kin found in many towns, including Cambridge, Worcester and Canterbury.[128] Yet the emotional and social force of kinship mattered. Kinsfolk rarely lived under the same roof, but in many well-documented episodes they are seen living nearby in the same community. The claims of kin when available were another optional resource, understood and endorsed, a fund of practical and emotional support as circumstances allowed. Moving in his large circle of kin in his tiny London parish, the deeply religious and self-questioning Nehemiah Wallington can be seen drawing up wills, striking bargains and counselling kin. In many cases kin closed ranks in the face of debt, death or other, happier, events. They might also have worked together, especially in places where sons followed fathers into the same occupation: this seems to have been more common towards the end of our period. Family ties were a source of resilience for working commu-

124 Clark and Clark, 'Social economy', pp. 69–70; Goose, 'Household size', p. 96; Boulton, *Neighbourhood and Society*, p. 124.

125 J. Langton, 'Residential patterns in pre-industrial cities: some case studies from seventeenth-century Britain', in Barry, ed., *The Tudor and Stuart Town*, pp. 166–205, esp. pp. 196–7; Goose, 'Household size', pp. 101–2, 114; Clark and Clark, 'Social economy', pp. 76–7; C. Phythian-Adams, *Desolation of a City* (Cambridge, 1979), p. 239.

126 Phythian-Adams, *Desolation of a City*, p. 241; N. Alldridge, 'House and household in Restoration Chester', *UHY* (1983), 39–52, esp. 51; Boulton, *Neighbourhood and Society*, p. 132; Clark and Clark, 'Social economy', p. 76; Goose, 'Household size', pp. 106, 114.

127 Phythian-Adams, *Desolation of a City*, pp. 238, 247–8; Goose, 'Household size', pp. 95, 118.

128 A. Dyer, *The City of Worcester in the Sixteenth Century* (Leicester, 1973), p. 179; Goose, 'Household size', p. 110; Clark and Clark, 'Social economy', pp. 73–4.

nities peripheral to civic organisations, like the bargemen along Oxford's Fisher Row, or Rye's fishermen.[129] On occasion, people helped kin to settle in a new town (residential choices were often made in this way), pooling local knowledge to find a good master, or bride or groom, though these strategies were usually only open to prosperous, propertied people.[130]

The ubiquity of the nuclear family is well established. But family or kin were just two of a set of overlapping allegiances which structured emotions and identities, just as in a political sense it was said that larger loyalties like citizenship derived from households, extrapolating in ever increasing circles. Urban dwellers had to strike a balance between several interdependent yet distinct social relationships, the sources of their affections, enmities and solidarities. The claim that 'a house is insufficient to itself without a neighbourhood' was of ancient origin.[131] Neighbourhood was arguably a more vital social commitment, emanating as it more often did from individual choice and occupation, and perpetuated by individual endeavour – an affinity to which people were not predisposed by birth or familial networks. Good neighbourhood was rarely incompatible with settled family life, but it was sometimes activated by other considerations.

One contemporary declared that London is 'a great world, there are so many little worlds in her'.[132] These little worlds, neighbourhoods and parishes, were well known to townspeople who drew mental maps of their town on these lines. They sometimes gave specific characteristics to districts felt to be filthy, shady, dangerous, prosperous or fair. Parts of the crowded parish of All Saints in Newcastle were felt to be dens of sedition. The Oxford bargemen had a deeply rooted reputation for cursing and violence. Clerkenwell and Turnmill Street ('an ill name') in and around London were centres of bawdry in popular minds.[133] In such ways, many identities existed side-by-side in the same urban space, competing for affiliations and resources, but sometimes joined by streets or overlapping jurisdictions and boundaries.

129 D. Cressy, 'Kinship and kin interaction in early modern England', *P & P*, 113 (1983), 38–69, esp. 49–50, 69; Wrightson, *English Society*, pp. 50–1; Phythian-Adams, *Desolation of a City*, pp. 149–51, 157; P. S. Seaver, *Wallington's World* (London, 1985); M. Prior, *Fisher Row* (Oxford, 1982), pp. 22, 130, 138ff; G. Mayhew, *Tudor Rye* (London, 1987).

130 P. Clark, 'Migrants in the city: the process of social adaptation in English towns 1500–1800', in Clark and Souden, eds., *Migration and Society*, pp. 266–91, esp. 271–2; Boulton, *Neighbourhood and Society*, pp. 134–6.

131 Aristotle is quoted by D. V. Kent and F. W. Kent, *Neighbours and Neighbourhood in Renaissance Florence: The District of the Red Lion in the Fifteenth Century* (New York, 1982), p. 2.

132 D. Lupton, *London and the Countrey Carbonadoed and Quartered Into Severall Characters* [1632] (Norwood, N.J., 1975), p. 1.

133 J. Ellis, 'A dynamic society: social relations in Newcastle-upon-Tyne, 1660–1760', in P. Clark, ed., *The Transformation of English Provincial Towns 1600–1800* (London, 1984), pp. 190–227, esp. pp. 208–9; Prior, *Fisher Row*, p. 170; P. Griffiths, 'The structure of prostitution in Elizabethan London', *Continuity and Change*, 8 (1993), 39–63, esp. 54; Lupton, *London and the Countrey Carbonadoed*, p. 50.

The habit of giving attributes to certain places was rooted in knowledge of social geography. Occupational clusters still persisted in some towns. They were sometimes enforced by civic and guild controls, though they were less prominent than in former centuries. Candlemakers bunched together in Edinburgh, fishmongers and vintners in Coventry, shoemakers in Reading, and clothworkers and goldsmiths in Shrewsbury. Butchers lived along Shambles in Reading, Southwark, Coventry, Norwich and Shrewsbury, though other trades were creeping in. The association of places and trades was still strong in post-Restoration London. In most towns a mixture of occupations lined streets, and trades were scattered through neighbourhoods, though few were spread evenly. In the case of noxious trades rules about residence were often imposed: the foul vapours of their trade forced leatherworkers and tanners to enclaves. Proximity to resources mattered. Watermen settled on the river's edge in Shadwell, Southwark and Oxford. Dyers also gathered close to water supplies.[134] Several tendencies emerge if we place workers in larger subcategories: retailers and food producers favoured prominent spots on high streets and busy thoroughfares; unskilled workers often packed into grubby alleys or shoddy streets.[135] In some ways more apparent than occupational clustering, however, was the social geography of wealth. Few places were untouched by social intermingling, but prosperous men of all occupations drew together in more affluent parishes ringing commercial and political town centres.

The nature of neighbourhood life depended greatly on its social composition. Sharp divisions of towns into rich and poor pockets are difficult to make and even inappropriate, but *concentrations* of wealthy people in central districts and poor in peripheral parishes have been uncovered in many places, including Newcastle, Shrewsbury, Worcester, Rye, Exeter, Cambridge, Norwich and London: a residential pattern also evident in the social topography of plague.[136]

[134] C. R. Friedrichs, *The Early Modern City 1450–1750* (London, 1995), pp. 30–1; J. M. Guilding, ed., *Reading Records: Diary of the Corporation* (London, 1892–6), vol. II, pp. 205, 321, vol. IV, p. 347; Boulton, *Neighbourhood and Society*, p. 132; Phythian-Adams, *Desolation of a City*, pp. 159–61; J. F. Pound, *Tudor and Stuart Norwich* (Chichester, 1988), pp. 53–4; J. Hindson, 'The Marriage Duty Acts and the social topography of the early modern town: Shrewsbury, 1695–8', *Local Population Studies*, 31 (1983), 21–8, esp. 25–8; M. J. Power, 'Shadwell: the development of a London suburban community in the seventeenth century', *LJ*, 4 (1978), 29–46, esp. 36; Prior, *Fisher Row*, pp. 29, 136; Houston, *Social Change*, p. 137; M. J. Power, 'The social topography of Restoration London', in Beier and Finlay, eds., *London*, pp. 199–223, esp. pp. 218–19.

[135] Boulton, *Neighbourhood and Society*, pp. 187–8; Langton, 'Residential patterns', pp. 194–5; Pelling, 'Appearance and reality', pp. 82–112, esp. pp. 84–9.

[136] P. Borsay, 'Introduction', in P. Borsay, ed., *The Eighteenth-Century Town* (London, 1990), pp. 1–38, esp. 19; Langton, 'Residential patterns', pp. 182, 200; Hindson, 'Marriage Duty Acts', 25; Mayhew, *Rye*, pp. 35–6, 141–2; Dyer, *City of Worcester*, pp. 17, 177–8; Goose, 'Household size', p. 88; Pound, *Tudor and Stuart Norwich*, p. 43; Power, 'Social topography', p. 204; Slack, *Impact of Plague*, pp. 168,133–43, 151–69. See also above, Section (i).

Yet residential social separation was rarely complete; it was a tendency. Few exclusive communities existed before 1700. Many towns could be crossed in a short time, and in such easily covered spaces social intermingling was inevitable (which could itself cause resentment). There are cases of rich and poor sharing neighbourhoods; workers are seen living in (usually) inferior streets or alleys in their employers' community, the final gasps perhaps of occupational clustering.[137] As such, it can be misleading to evaluate residence by neighbourhood, and more appropriate to reduce focus through close study of streets and alleys. The maze of alleys and courts in many towns were packed with the poor, but several alleys in London and Southwark, for example, were exclusive cloisters of rich and titled folk; the bishop of London lived in Half-Moon Court in St Botolph Aldersgate in the 1660s.[138]

Nevertheless, the early traces of residential patterns of later centuries are evident before 1700. Elegant squares appeared in some cities. Covent Garden was built in the 1630s. Other plazas and fashionable streets followed in the second half of the seventeenth century, and the first provincial squares were built in Whitehaven and Warwick towards its close. Social differentiation was expressed in spatial and architectural forms, made apparent by the drift of the better-off to suburban villages in London and elsewhere, especially after 1700 – a flight which was quickly to gather pace.[139]

In some respects these social complexities are not fully acknowledged in existing work in which they are seen as cancelled by neighbourly amity and unity. It is argued that apparent social gulfs were bridged by vertical ties, with their at times bland implications about paternalism and deference; that hands of loyalty and compassion joined across social divides; that these divisions were softened and the burdens of hard lives lightened through charity, conviviality and other neighbourly support. Yet we must note that power and control of resources were narrowly concentrated. Social pyramids were steep, and numbers of poor were rising fast in most towns at this time.

The significance of neighbourhood is clear, but we must always tease out its precise nature through study of language and context. Acts of neighbourly care are easy to find. We see neighbours swapping advice about marital choices, working, drinking and travelling together, sharing books, witnessing wills, exchanging 'cures' and information about healers, bequeathing or loaning money, and rescuing each other from fire and violence, though in the absence of banks, professional fire-fighters or police, these acts were not always motivated

137 Dyer, *City of Worcester*, pp. 177–8; Phythian-Adams, *Desolation of a City*, pp. 165–6.

138 Boulton, *Neighbourhood and Society*, pp. 175, 179–82; Power, 'Social topography', p. 209.

139 Friedrichs, *Early Modern City*, p. 30; P. Borsay, *The English Urban Renaissance* (Oxford, 1989), pp. 75, 90, 294–5; Power, 'Social topography'; M. J. Power, 'The east and west in early modern London', in E. W. Ives, R. J. Knecht and J. J. Scarisbrick, eds., *Wealth and Power in Tudor England* (London, 1978), pp. 167–85; Houston, *Social Change*, pp. 166–85, esp. p. 136.

by good will.[140] Streets were places for neighbourly commerce and conversation; alehouses were hives of such activity. These contacts, informal and instinctive, helped to impart communal feeling (so deep in places that rival communities fell to blows), which was reaffirmed by ales, feasts or parties. Such feeling was also energised by ministers and governors through perambulations, and pleas, especially in tense times like plague or dearth, that neighbourly charity be stepped up. Several historians have argued that churchgoing further encouraged fellow-feeling, though it was on occasion threatened by indifference, cultural squabbles or religious plurality.[141] Neighbourhood feelings could be as intense in towns as in villages. Nor were they usually shattered by high levels of residential mobility; many householders remained in the same house or community for a long time, providing stability, building familiarity.[142]

The neighbourhood was a physical reference point, easily imagined. But its greater felt significance was as a social description; an attribute of relations through which people were evaluated – moral or political choices, which though largely unwritten were formally expressed in cases before parish or civic institutions – and which slipped easily into conversation as neighbours swapped accusations on streets.[143] Proximity mattered because the cheek-by-jowl life of many communities gave rise to countless contacts by which neighbourly values were affirmed and on occasion contested. Above all, good neighbourhood was recognised as a set of mediations and reciprocities of a practical and emotional kind. These in turn clarified behavioural expectations, the existence of which implied a degree of self-regulation to ensure conformity and consistency.[144] The variable extent of the acceptance of this consensual code is rarely adequately discussed by historians. But it is clear that it gave at least some people a sense of amity and

[140] L. Gowing, *Domestic Dangers* (Oxford, 1996), p. 149; D. Underdown, *Fire From Heaven* (London, 1992), pp. 69–70; Guilding, ed., *Reading Records*, II, p. 262; Phythian-Adams, *Desolation of a City*, p. 166; Seaver, *Wallington's World*, p. 100; Boulton, *Neighbourhood and Society*, p. 139; M. J. Hoad, ed., *Portsmouth Record Series: Borough Sessions Papers, 1653–1688* (Chichester, 1971), pp. 59, 94–5; PRO, STAC 8, 21/7; 33/11; 62/13; 135/6; 296/9.

[141] Slack, *Impact of Plague*, pp. 40–1, 250; J. Barry, 'The parish in civic life: Bristol and its churches, 1640–1750', in S. J. Wright, ed., *Parish, Church and People: Local Studies in Lay Religion, 1350–1750* (London, 1988), pp. 152–78, esp. pp. 156, 164, 171–2; Houston, *Social Change*, pp. 154, 187.

[142] Boulton, *Neighbourhood and Society*, pp. 110, 116–17, 120–38; Finlay, *Population and Metropolis*, pp. 45–8; N. Alldridge, 'Loyalty and identity in Chester parishes, 1540–1640', in Wright, ed., *Parish, Church and People*, pp. 84–124, esp. p. 113; Gowing, *Domestic Dangers*, p. 18.

[143] R. Dennis and S. Daniels, '"Community" and the social geography of Victorian cities', *UHY* (1981), 7–23, esp. pp. 7–8; W. K. D. Davies and D. T. Herbert, *Communities Within Cities: An Urban Social Geography* (London, 1993), p. 34; Garrioch, *Neighbourhood and Community*, pp. 30–1; Wrightson, *English Society*, p. 62.

[144] Garrioch, *Neighbourhood and Community*, pp. 5, 31; Wrightson, *English Society*, pp. 51–4; D. W. Sabean, *Power in the Blood: Popular Culture and Village Discourse in Early Modern Germany* (Cambridge, 1984), p. 28.

morality powerful enough for them to issue cautions and prescriptions. The clerk of one London parish put his feelings into verse which he copied into the vestry book:

> Even as stickes may easily be broken
> So when neighbours agre not then ther is a confucion
> But a great many stickes bound in one boundell will hardly be broken
> So neighbours being ioyned in love together can never be severed.[145]

It has also been said that neighbourhoods were to some extent self-governing, formally through institutions and informally by good and bad images of neighbourly conduct circulated by gossip, itself a form of censure. Parishes and wards provided an institutional structure by which neighbourhood was cultivated and defined; a sense of belonging which though clearly coveted was also dependent on precedence, distance, officeholding and a certain amount of wealth. It was said in 1655 that the constables of Cornhill ward in London displayed 'great partiallity and indiscretion' in 'presenting yong men to be of the [wardmote] inquest who have not served as scavenger and petit jurymen . . . and ommitting other inhabitants which have byn of many yeres standing'. 'Great' discontents followed, charges were made public, a local dispute was in motion in which neighbourly feeling was deployed to canvass support and censure the upstart officers. The excluded senior residents alleged 'that union and brotherly love (among the neighbourood which is as a wall and defence to this ward) hath bin and is much ympaired and broken'. The neighbourhood could only be pieced back together again through respect to 'tyme and antiquitie', and by selecting the wardmote from those who were 'able to undergo the charge and not scandalous in their lives and conversacon'.[146] In such ways neighbourhood was defined through participation in its governing bodies, a partial sense of community, however, which planted a sense of solidarity and not a little self-esteem among those who were able to gain access to its ranks.

Another at times quite different sense of community was being constantly replenished by the stream of gossip running across all towns. News about local events or celebrities rushed around communities, probing reputations, fixing boundaries. Neighbourly opinion had moral currency both in street-talk and inside courtrooms.[147] An exemplary neighbour was one who 'carried himself to gain love and good opinion of neighbours', or who was 'well-esteemed and thought of' by 'the best and chiefest sort of inhabitants'. Such reports could make or break cases. John Freestow of Kidderminster walked free after a court was told that he 'hath ever been of honest conversation and good manners and so reputed

145 London, Guildhall Library, MS 943/1. 146 *Ibid.*, MS 4069/2, fols. 271v–2.
147 Garrioch, *Neighbourhood and Community*, pp. 33, 55; Kent and Kent, *Neighbours and Neighbourhood*, p. 53; Houston, *Social Change*, pp. 155–8.

not only amongst . . . his neighbours but also esteemed a man of good sufficiency in the country round about'.[148] There are also many cases in which neighbours intervened to settle public and domestic quarrels on the spot, or brought cases to court out of a sense of offence to neighbourly values. Neighbours also played a part in crime detection and prevention. They spotted offences through doors or windows, or gaps in walls, and tipped off officers; more controversially, neighbourhood morality was invoked to set boundaries, identify deviance and file charges.

The concerns of considerate living were expressed in neighbourly values: smell, dirt, noise, morals, crime or time. Prosecuted in this way were delinquent neighbours who kept 'bawdry' or 'ill rule', quarrelling, fighting, singing (often late at night), who let animals run free, left dunghills in streets, or quarrelled constantly, 'so that his neighbours cannot live quietly with him'.[149] These values had opposites neatly depicted in a heated row between neighbours which reached the Star Chamber. A governor of St Bartholomew's Hospital and a Star Chamber clerk were the principal participants in a long dispute about hanging clothes up to dry in an alley. The two sides swapped accusations: the governor was of 'perverse and quarrelsome disposition', lacking 'neighbourly love and friendship', 'more quarrelsome than neighbourly', despite gentle, friendly and neighbourly warning; the clerk was 'of hated and unsociable neighbourhood', and a 'contentious spirit'.[150] The street life and crowded conditions in which ties were formed were also sources of possible tension. Neighbourhoods, like households, were deeply ambivalent institutions in which order was rarely absolute or immutable.[151] People disputed common access, territory or resources, which were often ill-defined. They quarrelled about wells, yards, lights, walls, passages, gutters and washing places. Because neighbourhood was highly interdependent, it was vulnerable and sometimes fragile.[152] Yet where they were ultimately settled according to convention, disputes could clarify suitable behaviour and boost neighbourly, household or kin affiliations, even if these were only splinter groups in the community.

This last proviso is an important one, because it can be wrong to treat neighbourhoods as consensual bodies.[153] It is often unclear whether declarations of

148 PRO, STAC 8, 21/7; 11/8; J. W. Willis Bund, ed., *Worcestershire County Records: Division 1, Documents Relating to Quarter Sessions: Calendar of the Quarter Sessions Papers, Volume 1, 1591–1643* (Worcester, 1900), p. 367.

149 For example, Guilding, ed., *Reading Records*, II, pp. 394, 396, 467, III, 83, 262, 467; Willis Bund, ed., *Worcestershire County Records*, pp. 100, 450, 458; Hoad, ed., *Portsmouth Record Series*, p. 6; W. J. Hardy, ed., *Hertford County Records: Notes and Extracts From the Sessions Rolls, 1581–1850* (Hertford, 1905), vol. I, p. 89.

150 PRO, STAC 8, 93/8; 126/10.

151 For domestic disorders see P. Griffiths, *Youth and Authority* (Oxford, 1996), esp. ch. 6.

152 Archer, *Pursuit of Stability*, pp. 78–9; Gowing, *Domestic Dangers*, pp. 22, 117; Garrioch, *Neighbourhood and Community*, pp. 34, 54; Kent and Kent, *Neighbours and Neighbourhood*, p. 3; J. R. Farr, *Hands of Honor: Artisans and their World in Dijon, 1500–1650* (London, 1988), pp. 151, 164–5, 169.

153 See the discussion of 'the politics of neighbourhood' in K. Wrightson, 'The politics of the parish

neighbourhood represent a single outpouring of public opinion or the subjective or minatory commentaries of a few. Neighbourhood was significantly expressed in a partial, discriminatory vocabulary, social descriptions at once inclusive and exclusive: 'better sort' of people, 'worshipful', 'good, sufficient, and substantial' neighbours. This differentiating language was ubiquitous in government, a confirmation of the narrow compass of power in neighbourhoods where the allocation of important office followed patterns of wealth, and institutions like vestries could be characterised as much by secrecy, formality or exclusion as by popular participation, especially in larger communities in which social inequalities were more acutely felt.[154] The rhetoric of neighbourhood could therefore disguise inequalities by harmonising discordant parts in one society, an 'institutionalised unity' which several scholars treat as a real basis for communal solidarity rather than as a pretension to democracy.[155] Authority and social distance were ritually paraded and protected by elites, and made conspicuous in ceremonies, monuments, the badging of the poor, or in struggles for precedence in church seating in which elites coveted visually vital front pews.

Communities were partly defined through exclusion. Freeman status was a mark of acceptance, but outsiders often had a problematic position and they included the marginal poor, foreigners or even young people who had not yet made the transition to full adulthood. Acceptance also depended on longevity and conduct. Settled residents had a large stake in the community. Less well integrated were 'bad livers' or strangers without a past.[156] When individuals or small groups invoked neighbourhood rhetoric, it was usually to tackle practical matters like access to resources, or to obtain peace and quiet. Not all of them disagreed with the discipline which underpinned visions of the neighbourhood held by its elite. But not everybody felt the same about all issues, even when they were presented in terms of neighbourhood: women were more concerned about domestic violence; godly reformers met with resistance in places; the makeshift economy of the poor troubled elites, especially casual work and the taking-in of lodgers for small rents; and there were distinctive gendered tones to public opinion, which was itself on occasion subversive.[157]

So, neighbourhoods were riddled with judgements or different expectations.

in early modern England', in P. Griffiths, A. Fox and S. Hindle, eds., *The Experience of Authority in Early Modern England* (Basingstoke, 1996), pp. 10–46, esp. pp. 18–22.

[154] P. Griffiths, 'Secrecy and authority in late sixteenth- and seventeenth-century London', *HJ*, 40 (1997), 925–51; R. Tittler, *Architecture and Power* (Oxford, 1991), p. 128; Archer, *Pursuit of Stability*, pp. 61, 64; Alldridge, 'Loyalty and identity', p. 108.

[155] Quoting Archer, *Pursuit of Stability*, p. 59; Alldridge, 'Loyalty and identity', p. 97. See also Borsay, 'Introduction', pp. 13–17.

[156] Alldridge, 'Loyalty and identity', p. 89; Archer, *Pursuit of Stability*, p. 61; Wrightson, *English Society*, p. 57.

[157] Gowing, *Domestic Dangers*, p. 217; Underdown, *Fire from Heaven*, pp. 64, 155, and ch. 5; Garrioch, *Neighbourhood and Community*, pp. 23–6.

Above all, it is appropriate to question the levelling potential of neighbourhood in all situations. Other, larger commitments and ideologies could upset neighbourly amity. Neighbourhood was just one possible allegiance. Work or relations between rich and poor, men and women, young and old, or the godly and profane, gave rise to particular agendas and identities, which were by no means always incompatible with neighbourhood, but certainly complicated an individual's sense of self, and therefore his or her place in the community. As such, for many neighbourliness was in some respects provisional, rarely constant, something which required regular confirmation and definition.

The multiple identities of people, apparent too in administrative complexities, criss-crossing jurisdictions, and institutional identities like guild membership, affected neighbourly ties. So we must study neighbourliness as one part of the larger project of exploring social relations in motion, in terms both of the complexities of interpersonal relations and changes over time. For many urban communities were being reshaped at this time. The incremental growth of the state plainly discernible in the poor law, more vigorous manufacturing and commercial sectors, religious change, the first moves in more socially differentiated residential patterns, rising in-migration and population, the contrasting practices of stranger communities, the ever-growing number of poor: all of these and the difficulties and reconfigurations to which they gave rise presented fresh or more acute challenges, and altered the nature of perceptions. Yet, even though they were subject to change, households and neighbourhoods were valued sources of emotional and practical support before 1700 and after. For most people they were the first ports of call in a storm. Even after we disentangle the meanings of neighbourhood and community for different constituencies, solid relationships and commitments remain for many early modern people, which help us to understand how they made sense of their world and the changes they felt going on around them.

(iv) CONCLUSIONS

This chapter has outlined demographic experiences in English and Scottish towns between the sixteenth and eighteenth centuries, while emphasising the potential pitfalls in retrieving and interpreting the available data. We have also sought to describe some of the responses of townspeople and civic authorities to changes in social and physical environments, many of which were felt to be threatening and challenging. Pressures were mounting in this period: civic governors had to be (and to be seen to be) diligent, alert and even innovative in order to manage overcrowding, for example, epidemics, disease and the problems to which they gave rise. One form of response was strategies implemented by town governments, including the gathering of new forms of information, on which as historians we now depend. Another, arguably, was new forms of self-expression, protest, communication and what for later periods is called consumerism. Yet another was to turn for support and comfort to social relationships, to families, kin, friends and neighbours – relationships which at times reveal tension but which also offered reassurance.

In seeking to describe some of the essential features of social and physical environments in early modern towns, and the ways in which people attempted to come to terms with them, we have inevitably touched on matters of debate among 'optimists' and 'pessimists' about the nature of urban life at this period. One concern is with language and literary expression, and we have cautioned that rhetorics of inclusion and exclusion through which criminality or neighbourhood were defined were also freely available to be appropriated and even abused. Moreover, any form of definition of the family or the community automatically creates a category of outsiders, and can be self-regarding rather than cohesive. Contemporaries had strategies, explanations, consolations, cures and valued ties to cope with the uncertainties of daily life, but some people were excluded from these, and still others became victims (or scapegoats) in tense times like plague or harvest failure. Order was never inevitable or natural: it was always pursued through a constant process of re-evaluation and realignment by urban elites.[158] Over time, households and neighbourhoods as well as civic institutions went through this same process to meet fresh demographic and socio-economic challenges, and in so doing they too were exposed to danger and the possibility of redefinition. Neighbourly and family ties retained their force, but developments over time, including the continued growth of towns, new fears and changing residential patterns, affected both the quality and form of these social relationships.

[158] Cf. Archer, *Pursuit of Stability*.

· 7 ·

Politics and government 1540–1700

IAN A. ARCHER

(i) INTRODUCTION: A VARIETY OF URBAN POLITICAL FORMS

THE POLITICAL history of towns in early modern Europe is conventionally depicted in terms of their growing subservience to the expanding state which underpinned the consolidation of oligarchy, the displacement of merchants and craftsmen on town councils by royal officeholders and the penetration of civic government by the rural elites. It is a model which has proved influential in approaching the history of towns in the British archipelago. The later seventeenth century, in particular, is seen as a period when calculations of parliamentary electoral advantage led the crown and rural elites into massive interventions in urban affairs which curbed their autonomy. However, many of the assumptions underpinning the model have been under attack. In view of the weakness of its own resources the power of the centre could only advance by means of compromises with local groups; likewise municipal magistrates could only hope to implement their policies by involving craftsmen and tradesmen in local administration; and changes in our understanding of patronage relationships have led to the realisation that interventions by the rural elites often occurred at the instigation of townsfolk anxious to exploit the relationship with outsiders to their own ends. Civic ideals may well have retained more strength in 1700 than is often recognised, and this chapter will argue that they remained an important force in blunting the very real ideological divisions released by the Reformation and reinforced by the legacies of the conflicts of the Civil Wars and the Exclusion Crisis.[1]

Towns varied immensely both in the degree of political autonomy that they

[1] A. F. Cowan, 'Urban elites in early modern Europe: an endangered species?', *HR*, 64 (1991), 121–37; W. Reinhard, ed., *Power Elites and State Building* (Oxford, 1996), ch. 11; P. Clark and P. Slack, *English Towns in Transition 1500–1700* (London, 1976), ch. 9.

enjoyed and in the distribution of political power within them. At one end of the scale in England were the plethora of seigneurial towns, as many as two-thirds of the total in 1400. Among these towns, the level of interference by the lord and his officials and the degree of local self-government depended not only on the outcome of long-term processes of accommodation, but also on the force of individual personalities. The abbeys of Bury St Edmunds and St Albans had kept their towns in a position of almost complete subordination, and there had been repeated conflict between the abbots and the townsfolk whose religious guilds had come to act as a focus for opposition, whereas other ecclesiastical landlords like the abbots of Westminster were more indulgent, devolving many responsibilities on to the townsmen and allowing the local guild of the Assumption to become a surrogate town council. Likewise many secular lords, whose power was less consistently exercised than that of ecclesiastical landlords because of the problems of minorities, applied a light touch, sometimes confining their interference to the choice of a bailiff from candidates nominated by the tenants, and leaving the government almost entirely in the hands of the leet jury, although the lord's power over local tolls often became a flashpoint for conflict in the circumstances of increasing inland trade in the later sixteenth century.[2]

Other settlements had acquired packages of privileges from the crown giving them varying levels of self-government and jurisdictional autonomy. Key elements of borough privileges were the right to elect their own officers and the right to hold three-weekly courts for the hearing of cases concerning debts. From the fifteenth century onwards the move to formal incorporation became more common. This gave boroughs five key privileges: the rights of perpetual succession and a common seal, to sue and be sued, to hold lands and to issue by-laws. As Susan Reynolds has pointed out, many towns actually enjoyed these rights before formal incorporation granted them, 'and it was only gradually that developing legal theory made their formal expression useful'. More important were the additional grants of jurisdiction which accompanied charters of incorporation and typically gave the town a mayor and aldermen and made the mayor and some of his colleagues justices of the peace. The precise extent of jurisdiction over criminal cases varied both in scope and in the degree to which it was free from county authorities. Some civic magistrates had only a petty sessional jurisdiction, others jurisdiction over all felonies. Some sat jointly with the county justices; while the most privileged towns were constituted as counties of themselves and enjoyed a criminal jurisdiction exclusive of all interference by the county justices. Sometimes the privileges enjoyed by an urban community were exercised over a wider area than the town itself, as for

[2] M. D. Lobel, *The Borough of Bury St Edmunds* (Oxford, 1935); G. Rosser, *Medieval Westminster, 1200–1540* (Oxford, 1989), chs. 7 and 9; S. Webb and B. Webb, *The Manor and the Borough* (London, 1908).

example when a town acquired conservancy (over rivers), admiralty or market jurisdiction.[3]

Wales and Scotland show some interesting variations from the English pattern. In Wales, 70 per cent of the towns were of alien foundation, and were typically subject to the lord of the manor, the constable of whose castle exercised a formidable influence in local affairs, to the extent of often being the titular mayor. Even a closed corporation like Cardiff remained subject to the authority of the constable of the castle who was of the quorum of the bench, and chose the borough officers from a slate presented to him by the bailiffs. Welsh towns therefore found themselves particularly vulnerable to exploitation by the surrounding gentry whose feuds all too frequently were fought out in their streets.[4]

The flowering of the seigneurial town was a later phenomenon in Scotland than England and Wales, and the privileges of the royal burghs were more clearly defined because they were the subject of acts of the Scots parliament. By the end of the sixteenth century, in effect, Scottish burghs varied according to whether they held their privileges directly from the crown as tenants in chief (the royal burghs, of which there were forty-five in 1500) or whether they held from a local secular or ecclesiastical lord by royal licence (the so-called burghs of barony or regality, of which there were ninety in 1500). The key elements of royal burghal privilege were that they enjoyed a monopoly over merchandise within a given area and that they acted as the only centres of foreign trade. Dependent burghs, not all of them viable, proliferated after 1560 with 125 foundations in the following century, and no less than 110 from 1660 until the Act of Union. These were small service centres performing local marketing functions, founded often as part of an attempt by lords to establish monopolies within the areas of their influence, sometimes because it seemed the fashionable thing to do or out of rivalry with a neighbouring landowner, often tiny and distinguishable from villages only by their possession of a mercat cross. Alternatively, some new foundations were the locus for novel kinds of industrial ventures, including coal, salt, quarrying or glassmaking.[5]

A key difference between England and Scotland lay in the fact that the royal burghs developed an institution which represented their interests to the central government, the Convention of Royal Burghs. The Convention apportioned taxation among the constituent towns, developed regulations on merchandise,

3 Webb and Webb, *Manor and Borough*, I, pp. 280–9; S. Rigby, 'Urban "oligarchy" in late medieval England', in J. A. F. Thompson, ed., *Towns and Townspeople in the Fifteenth Century* (Gloucester, 1988), pp. 77–80; S. Reynolds, *An Introduction to the History of English Medieval Towns* (Oxford, 1977), pp. 113–14.

4 Webb and Webb, *Manor and Borough*, I, pp. 232–57; G. Williams, ed., *Glamorgan County History* (Cardiff, 1974), vol. IV, pp. 90, 99–100, 157–8, 160, 188–91.

5 W. M. Mackenzie, *The Scottish Burghs* (Edinburgh, 1949); G. S. Pryde, ed., *Court Book of the Burgh of Kirkintilloch, 1658–1694* (Scottish Historical Society, 3rd series, 53, 1963), pp. liv–lxxx.

negotiated trading compacts with foreign countries, acted as the conservator of the Scottish merchants' staple in the Low Countries and represented the concerns of merchants to the crown. The existence of this body reduced the interest that Scottish towns took in the business of parliament. Although by 1621 it had been established that one commissioner should be sent to parliament from each burgh with the exception of Edinburgh which sent two, these men tended to take their directions from the Convention which by 1600 was holding meetings shortly before parliaments to coordinate strategy.[6]

(ii) TOWNS AND THE STATE

In both the English and Scottish monarchies the power of the centre in the sixteenth and seventeenth centuries was strengthened. But this was not a straightforward process of centralisation because the limited resources of early modern governments meant that the consolidation of power worked through the coopting of local elites rather than their displacement. Those elites were broadened as gentry and lairds came to share power with the nobility at a local level, although the process was more muted and delayed north of the border because the monarchy was starting from a lower power base, and because in Scotland absentee monarchy after 1603 offered new opportunities for the landed classes of all sorts to exert power or influence, both over the economy and society as a whole. But the crown's ambitions in local government were extending as escalating military demands entailed the search for greater sources of revenue, and as social and economic problems became the object of more sustained attention. Moreover, confessional division and the resulting drive for uniformity in religion occasioned more frequent interventions from the centre in local affairs. Urban communities were therefore *potentially* victims of the governmental changes of the early modern period: more vulnerable to external interventions in their affairs both from local gentry and aristocratic families and from the crown. However, the developments of this period also entailed opportunities for urban communities. The attack on the power of the Church gave towns a chance to increase their own holdings of property, to curtail troublesome ecclesiastical liberties in their midst and to take over educational and charitable functions formerly exercised by the Church. Some of the interventions of the state in local affairs may have been unwelcome or even destabilising, but they more often occurred at the instigation of local groups and to serve local ends.

There is no doubt that both the Scottish and English crowns disposed of formidable powers with respect to towns. Insofar as urban privileges were derived from the crown the mere threat of their removal could induce obedience. Few

[6] T. Pagan, *The Convention of the Royal Burghs of Scotland* (Glasgow, 1926); J. Goodare, 'The estates in the Scottish parliament, 1286–1707', in C. Jones, ed., *The Scots and Parliament* (Edinburgh, 1996), pp. 11–32.

civic leaders would be prepared to stand up to a direct instruction to elect a certain man mayor or provost. The complex web of economic and social regulation in which their merchant leaders were entwined meant that the crowns could undermine local elites by the enforcement of penal legislation. Their capital cities could be cowed merely by the removal of the law courts or parliament to another location, as Mary Tudor threatened London in 1554 and James VI Edinburgh in 1596. These sanctions help explain the compliance of towns in policies (for example, those of Charles I in the 1630s) of which their ruling groups otherwise disapproved, but they were untypical of relations between crown and local community, and when they were invoked they often worked to undermine efficient local government. Henry VII's interference with the liberties of the city of London had discredited members of the ruling elite in the eyes of their subjects. In sixteenth-century Scotland it was the weaker minority regimes which engaged in the most sustained interference in local affairs, and often with unsatisfactory results.Thus Mary of Guise's regime precipitated the very conditions it sought to avert by its ham-fisted act of 1555 banning deacons of crafts, fuelling the discontents of the Perth craftsmen, while its drive for religious uniformity entailed interference in the government of Edinburgh, Perth and Jedburgh which the lords of the congregation were to denounce as arbitrary in 1560.[7]

Paradoxically, however, royal interference might work to the towns' long-term advantage. Edinburgh's magistrates found that the nobles who were imposed upon them by way of punishment for their complicity in a Presbyterian riot in 1596 acted as key conduits of influence with the king, an asset of still greater value once he had moved into his new kingdom. Advances in the power of the centre were therefore not necessarily unwelcome to civic leaders. The Tudor incorporation of Wales, for example, was a positive boon for Welsh towns, for it removed the discriminatory legislation which had prevented property holding by the native Welsh within towns, and thereby advanced the cymricisation of the towns. It also gave the towns greater leverage in London, for 'every borough being a shire town' (with the exception of Merioneth) was granted one member of parliament, in the election of which other ancient boroughs in the respective counties became involved over the course of the sixteenth century. More generally, the growing penetration of the royal courts in England, Wales and Scotland offered opportunities for townsmen to air their grievances. Although urban magistrates might groan at the number of issues removed from their ambit (often pertaining to their own conduct) and transferred to the jurisdiction of the central courts, such litigation at least had the effect of directing grievances through institutional channels

[7] I. W. Archer, *The Pursuit of Stability* (Cambridge, 1991), pp. 25–7, 32–9; M. Lynch, 'The crown and the burghs, 1500–1625', in M. Lynch, ed., *The Early Modern Town in Scotland* (London, 1987), pp. 55–65.

rather than leading to violence on the streets, and the growth of litigation ultimately served to reinforce the culture of civic order.[8]

Moreover, because the crown was the arbiter of the privileges on which urban autonomy rested, the power of the centre could also be invoked to secure benefits for towns or for groups within them. Townsfolk were sophisticated lobbyists. From 1590 the Convention of Burghs maintained an agent to represent its interests to the court and parliament, and adapted to the changed circumstances of the Union of crowns by employing one at London from 1613. In England parliament was the most important point of contact between centre and locality. Although it may have been often costly and frustrating (only 43 per cent of the seventy-four bills promoted by individual towns in the period between 1559 and 1581 were successful), the relevance of parliament should not be measured simply in terms of bills passed: it was also a matter of bills blocked, for towns played out their conflicts within the parliamentary arena. Burgesses might also use their influence to secure concessions in government legislation, like the proviso in the Chantries Act of 1547 obtained by the burgesses of Lynn and Coventry to protect the properties of trade guilds, or they might add their voices (perhaps underrepresented in the pages of the snobbish parliamentary diarists) to matters of common concern like monopolies in 1601.[9]

The importance of central institutions in the resolution of local problems has been forcefully demonstrated by Robert Tittler in his work on the response of English towns to the Reformation. Although the Reformation left former ecclesiastical boroughs vulnerable to exploitation by new gentry owners, and in other cases weakened local structures of authority by dissolving the religious guilds which had assumed important roles in the management of charitable resources, these problems could be addressed by recourse to the agencies of the Tudor state. Their acquisition of former ecclesiastical properties posed the problem of authority in an acute form. In some cases, feoffees, legal trusts created when the properties were transferred to a group of named townsmen with the power to coopt replacements, administered educational and charitable funds and assumed responsibilities in local government. Other towns, including many former ecclesiastical boroughs, sought the benefit of royal incorporation, the pace of which quickened in the mid-sixteenth century with eight between 1540 and 1547, twelve between 1547 and 1553, and twenty-four between 1553 and 1558. Other communities were able to make use of the royal courts to conduct lengthy campaigns against their gentry overlords, exploiting the weakness of individual family representatives and the vacuum of authority during minorities.[10]

Nor did the cementing of relations with the rural elites necessarily entail a

8 P. S. Edwards, 'Parliamentary representation of the Welsh boroughs in the mid-sixteenth century', *Bulletin of the Board of Celtic Studies*, 27 (1947), 425–39.

9 R. Tittler, 'Elizabethan towns and the "points of contact": parliament', *Parliamentary History*, 8 (1989), 275–88; Lynch, 'Crown and the burghs', pp. 65–6.

10 R. Tittler, *The Reformation and the Towns in England* (Oxford, 1998).

reduction in urban autonomy. It is true that sometimes relations were soured by the attentions of predatory gentlemen as at Colchester (where clashes with the Lucas family over common rights were intensified by religious antagonisms) or by conflicts over jurisdiction as at Gloucester (where the town was accused of exploiting its jurisdiction over the surrounding area to reduce the tax burden on the townsfolk). But the 'crouching observance' to the gentry so feared by the town clerk of Warwick writing in the 1640s was not necessarily typical, and towns were often able to take advantage of the factional rivaries of the local gentry. Urban patronage was used cannily. Offices like the recordership were used to secure the support of local gentlemen, while the post of high steward might be offered to an influential courtier. The practice by which members of parliament were sometimes nominated by magnates, so often dismissed as a sign of the subservience of the towns, was yet another means of securing influence at the centre as patrons reciprocated by promoting the town's concerns. Likewise the claim by an English observer of the 1580s that the Scottish burghs were 'wholly at the devotion of some nobleman or other' misconstrues what was usually a more calculating approach on the part of the townsfolk. Even the bonds of manrent into which some Scottish towns had entered did not place those centres at the mercy of their lords: a small centre like Peebles enjoyed a very profitable relationship with the Hays of Yester who were elected year after year to the position of provost, but were denied the office in perpetuity. Towns both north and south of the border benefited economically from their growing role as service centres for the rural elites, and the growing presence of professionals and gentlemen on their councils in part reflects the changing compositions of their populations.[11]

(iii) 'OLIGARCHY'

If the growing subservience of towns to the gentry and the state is one traditional conceptual framework in need of revision, so too is that other organising concept, 'the growth of oligarchy'. Although central authority was often invoked to consolidate the position of a ruling group who had appropriated the rhetoric of community, the realities of power, the fragility of urban dynasties and the constraints imposed by the adoption of that rhetoric blunted the force of oligarchy.[12]

Government became apparently more restrictive in both English and Scottish

[11] *VCH*, Essex, IX, p. 110; P. Clark, '"The Ramoth-Gilead of the Good": urban change and political radicalism at Gloucester 1540–1640', in J. Barry, ed., *The Tudor and Stuart Town* (London, 1990), pp. 262–3; A. Hughes, *Politics, Society, and Civil War in Warwickshire, 1620–1660* (Cambridge, 1987), p. 18; M. Lynch, 'Introduction: Scottish towns 1500–1700', in Lynch, ed., *Early Modern Town*, pp. 20–1; Lynch, 'Crown and the burghs', pp. 55–8, 62–5; P. Clark, 'The civic leaders of Gloucester 1580–1800', in P. Clark, ed., *The Transformation of English Provincial Towns 1600–1800* (London, 1984); H. M. Dingwall, *Late Seventeenth-Century Edinburgh* (Aldershot, 1994).

[12] S. H. Rigby and E. Ewan, 'Government, power and authority 1300–1540', in D. M. Palliser, ed., *The Cambridge Urban History of Britain*, vol. I: *600–1540* (Cambridge, 2000), ch. 13.

towns. By acts of 1469 and 1474 the Scottish parliament had reinforced the position of the mercantile ruling groups by requiring that the old council choose the new and that four members of the outgoing coucil sit on the new one. The lesser ranks might make their views felt only in the election of the provost and bailies. Although the act was only patchily observed, the trend towards exclusivity is unmistakable. The thrice annual head courts continued to meet, but their functions withered to that of rubber-stamping decisions taken in the closed councils. In the older chartered towns of England where two-tier councils often operated, power became concentrated in the hands of the upper council, and the rights of the freemen in electing councillors were curtailed. Thus mayoral elections were reorganised at Leicester and Northampton in 1489 to remove power from an assembly of burgesses and place it in the hands of a council of forty-eight nominated from above.[13]

There undoubtedly was a prejudice against the involvement of the vulgar sort. As the recorder of Nottingham put it in 1512, 'if you suffer the commons to rule and follow their appetite and desire, farewell good order'. The councillors of Dundee claimed in 1581 that theirs was a more 'civilly governed' town than Perth because of their exclusion of craftsmen, while the Convention of Royal Burghs sent packing a shoemaker delegate from Haddington. But the reasons for devising more exclusive constitutions were not always the desire for economic control and domination by an elite. It was more a question of the honour of the town being brought into disrepute by the lowly status of those elected to offices which carried judicial responsibilities and which required some financial sacrifice by those who held them. Shoemakers who served as bailiffs would hardly be able to assert themselves against the surrounding gentry, nor could their incorruptibility be guaranteed. Moreover, most civic constitutions continued to blend oligarchic and participatory elements. Even in some of the apparently closed corporations there remained some vestige of participation, as at Exeter where the freemen chose one of two nominated candidates for the mayoralty. Some of the larger corporations retained relatively open arrangements, as at Norwich where the freemen were involved in the nomination and election of all sixty common councillors, one of the two sheriffs, all twenty-four aldermen and in the nomination of two candidates for the mayoralty, or at York where the crafts continued to nominate representatives to the council until 1632. Even in London the freemen were involved in the election of common councillors and the nomination of aldermen, while the admittedly wealthier liverymen (including representatives of the city's crafts) were involved in the election of the mayor, sheriffs and MPs. In smaller boroughs many charters continued to provide for the nomination by the aldermen of two candidates for mayor from whom the freemen chose one. Likewise although the Scottish parliament exhibited a per-

[13] Mackenzie, *Scottish Burghs*, pp. 107–8, 122–8; Rigby, 'Urban "oligarchy"', pp. 77–81.

sistent hostility towards the deacons of the crafts, the latter usually succeeded in securing a voice on the councils. Thus conflicts at Perth in the 1540s and 1550s, and Edinburgh and Aberdeen in the 1580s, and Dundee and Glasgow in the 1600s led to the establishment of the right of craft representation. Most urban constitutions therefore reflected a continuing effort to find a balance between rule by the wealthy and an element of consent. Moreover, the ties enjoyed by councillors with the broader population through their roles as community brokers, extending patronage to their neighbours through ties of landlordship, credit and the sponsorship of petitions in other arenas, often made their rule more acceptable.[14]

Although certain families were usually represented by several members on town councils, urban dynasties were rare, and the accessibility of the elite to new men of talent was another way in which the concentration of authority among the wealthy may have been rendered more acceptable. This was not so much because, as William Harrison claimed, 'merchants often change estate with gentlemen', although that did occur to a limited extent, as because of a variety of economic, demographic and cultural factors, which worked to disperse urban fortunes. Because of low levels of liquidity the wealth built up by merchants was very fragile; customary practices in some towns which reserved one third of the personal estate for the widow and divided another third among the children tended to disperse mercantile fortunes. With up to one third of officeholders failing to leave male heirs, the facts of demography were also against the transmission of wealth from father to son, and mortality conditions deteriorated in the later seventeenth century. Even those children who did survive to maturity might not necessarily choose to follow their fathers' trades, seeking a career in the professions and perhaps leaving their home town for the metropolis, and those who did enter trade might not complete their apprenticeships. The inability of the elite to replenish itself from its own ranks opened up possibilities for mobility into it from other social groups. Although the newcomers tended to be recruited from the upper and middling ranks of rural society and often enjoyed a link with an existing councillor family through apprenticeship or marriage, such links were not essential to success.[15]

Moreover power was rather more dispersed in towns than the composition of their councils would suggest, as councillors were dependent on the cooperation of the middling sections of the community to implement their decisions. In

14 Rigby, 'Urban "oligarchy"', p. 177; M. Verschuur, 'Merchants and craftsmen in sixteenth-century Perth', in Lynch, ed., *Early Modern Town*, pp. 36–54; Mackenzie, *Scottish Burghs*, pp. 119–28; W. T. MacCaffrey, *Exeter 1540–1640* (Cambridge, Mass., 1958), ch. 2; J. T. Evans, *Seventeenth-Century Norwich* (Oxford, 1979); V. Pearl, *London and the Outbreak of the Puritan Revolution* (Oxford, 1961), ch. 2; D. M. Palliser, *Tudor York* (Oxford, 1979), ch. 3.

15 R. M. Berger, *The Most Necessary Luxuries* (Philadelphia, 1993), pp. 268–80; P. Gauci, *Politics and Society in Great Yarmouth 1660–1722* (Oxford, 1996), ch. 2.

England petty tradesmen and craftsmen served on juries and filled offices such as constable, collector for the poor and churchwarden on which parliament heaped ever increasing responsibilities. Likewise the ambitions of the Scottish state were reflected in the proliferation of constables who served the new commissioners of the peace; and the kirk session, three-quarters of whose members in the Edinburgh Canongate were master craftsmen in the 1630s, provided many of the opportunities for participation by the middling levels of urban society in the same way as the parish vestry did in English towns. It is true that the principle of seniority prevailed, and that wealth determined access to the more important posts in parishes and kirk sessions, but the proportion of householders holding some kind of office at any one time could be as high as 10 per cent.[16]

Likewise, craft organisations both north and south of the border provided means of representing the aspirations of the lower levels of urban society. York had over fifty different craft guilds, Chester twenty-five, Beverley seventeen, Glasgow thirteen. Guilds were usually subservient to the civic authorities: their accounts might be audited by councillors, punishments for infringements of regulations determined by the council and fines shared between it and the guild, and in Scotland their craft deacons were usually appointed by the council. But the guilds were not simple instruments of elite control. Guild ordinances with their restrictions on the numbers of apprentices protected the interests of the small producer, and sometimes members of the ruling group were among those presented for trade infractions. Even in those cases where the guild was divided between a trading and artisan group, commitment to the ideals of the collectivity could be exploited by artisans in their quest for redress of grievances.[17]

The force of oligarchy was also blunted by the civic ideology by which the rulers' position was legitimated. A variety of rituals, sermons and set-piece speeches by civic officials served to remind magistrates of their obligations to the wider community. Rituals inaugurating mayors incorporated the poor in civic processions and occasions of feasting by the rulers included token representation of the poorer sort or were accompanied by the exercise of charity. Recorders or outgoing mayors addressing mayors on the occasion of their inauguration would stress the virtues of justice and even-handedness in dealing with citizens during their year of office, while the oath made specific the mayor's duty to cherish the poor. A paternalistic language which likened the mayor's authority to that of a father over his children probably assisted in the acceptance of social inequalities, for it was in these same terms that masters might justify their rule over their households, and the commons understood that the duty of obedience implied a

[16] Archer, *Pursuit of Stability*, pp. 63–74; R. A. Houston, *Social Change in the Age of Enlightenment* (Oxford, 1994), pp. 32–5.

[17] D. M. Palliser, 'The trade guilds of Tudor York', in P. Clark and P. Slack, eds., *Crisis and Order in English Towns 1500–1700* (London, 1972), pp. 86–116; Mackenzie, *Scottish Burghs*, pp. 73–4, 117–20.

reciprocal obligation to rule in a spirit of love and charity. The duty of the elite to maintain the franchises was another element of the civic ideology which might transcend social divisions, for the freedom was not the preserve of a narrow elite, for it was often enjoyed by between 30 per cent and 40 per cent of the householders. Scottish towns lobbied through the Convention of Burghs against the creation of more 'unfrie tounis', against suburban competition and against rural industry, while their English counterparts fought vigorously against the practice of buying and selling within the town by those who did not enjoy its freedom. It needs to be emphasised, of course, that the rhetoric of civic community was a strategy of exclusion which did not necessarily incorporate all the inhabitants. To define civic identity in terms of the defence of the privileges of the freedom was to exclude the non-free and to underline the peculiar status of liberties (the precincts of cathedrals and former monastic houses, for example) in the town's midst, while those who administered charities were concerned to limit their responsibility for the relief of immigrants.[18]

Nor did magistrates always live up to their communitarian ideals, and most occasions of urban conflict have their roots in such failures. Civic leaders might use the authority of their offices to settle old scores, or they might turn a blind eye to infractions of civic regulations by their friends and fellow councillors. They might use their position to secure favourable leases for themselves or their friends and clients, or they might use their control over the assessment of taxes and local rates to punish enemies. Charges of this kind are the stuff of urban conflicts, but we should be wary of taking them at face value. Some charges have their origins in the kind of personal animosities that could be stoked up by a failure to secure a piece of civic patronage. When the charges were answered, the defences often carry conviction. Nor were the conventions of political morality clear-cut: magistrates might see a lease on favourable terms as compensation for the financial sacrifices they made in serving office, and few complained when a rough-and-ready 'moral arithmetic' was used in taxing local enclosing gentlemen over the odds. Charges of self-seeking were more likely to be directed against individuals than against the elite as a whole, and suggest that disillusionment with the principle of rule by a wealthy elite was not seriously questioned. Indeed one thread in cases of lewd words directed against town rulers was the unfitness of those of lowly fortunes to the burdens of office. More serious, however, were those instances where the corporation's handling of its property became the subject of controversy. One of the major flashpoints, for example, was the management of common lands. Town councils, increasingly strapped for cash, often came to the conclusion that these resources would better serve their interests if enclosed and leased out to realise monies which could support their

18 Gauci, *Great Yarmouth*, ch. 1; Mackenzie, *Scottish Burghs*, pp. 73–4, 145–6; Houston, *Social Change*, chs. 1, 6.

undertakings. Thus Coventry was plagued by recurrent conflict between the populace and the council over the management of the Lammas and Michaelmas lands to which townsmen looked for access after hay making and the harvest, but large sections of which the council had enclosed, while the magistrates of Cupar (Fife) were bitterly attacked for leasing the common fishing and lands to councillors. But the fact that urban identity was so frequently articulated in terms of privileges which had been enshrined in law gave a lever to those who wished to challenge the way in which the rulers exercised their power. The retaining of lawyers by trade guilds, their huge expenditures on litigation in the defence of their interests and the involvement of attorneys in challenges to corporations demonstrate that, in the words of Christopher Brooks, 'lawsuits became the medium of political disputation within towns', but insofar as disputes turned on the interpretation of the law they were thereby limited, and contained within the institutional structures of the state.[19]

Another reason for the prevalence of rule by the wealthy was the fragility of municipal finances: apart from their support for the round of municipal feasting members of the elite were expected to dig into their own pockets to provide bridging loans. At the beginning of our period English seigneurial towns with a measure of self-government seem to have enjoyed incomes of between £20 and £40 per annum, while county towns with populations of between 2,500 and 5,000 collected between £40 and £80. Although these figures rose over the period under review, income scarcely kept pace with inflation and population growth, particularly as tolls came under increasing legal challenge in the post-Restoration period. Given that there were usually substantial regular calls on revenues in the maintenance of public works, officers' expenses and fees, there was rarely a surplus for extraordinary projects such as litigation, the securing of charters from the crown or the building of a town hall or a school. As the magistrates only resorted to taxation with the greatest reluctance, they were forced to use expedients such as creations of freemen, or loans from among their own members.[20]

(iv) IDEOLOGY AND URBAN POLITICS, 1540–1650

The stability of towns depended critically on the maintenance of a degree of elite cohesion, for division within the ruling group would tend to radicalise urban opinion as factions competed for support among the lower orders. The

[19] D. M. Hirst, *The Representative of the People? Voters and Voting under the Early Stuarts* (Cambridge, 1975), pp. 51–2, 198–201, 210–12; C. W. Brooks, *Pettyfoggers and Vipers of the Commonwealth: The 'Lower Branch' of the Legal Profession in Early Modern England* (Cambridge, 1986), pp. 220–3.

[20] Tittler, *Reformation and the Towns*; E. J. Dawson, 'Finance and the unreformed boroughs: a critical appraisal of corporate finance 1660 to 1835 with special reference to the boroughs of Nottingham, York and Boston' (PhD thesis, University of Hull, 1978); cf. G. S. Pryde, ed., *Ayr Burgh Accounts 1534–1624* (Scottish Historical Society, 3rd series, 28, 1937).

most divisive forces in our period were the ideological passions unleashed by the Reformation. The Reformation was a contested phenomenon in the towns as well as in the countryside, and it had the potential to divide the ruling groups. Quite apart from the Catholic convictions of many magistrates, there was the fact that the early Protestants could all too easily be depicted as a subversive force. The early reformers brought disorder to the communities in which they operated, abusing and sometimes physically assaulting priests, desecrating cultic objects and disrupting services, while their convictions made them recalcitrant in the face of authority. There are thus signs of religious partisanship even in those communities which have been celebrated as bastions of early Reformation success. Thus in Colchester, described by the martyrologist John Foxe as 'like unto a city upon a hill', there were magistrates, like Benjamin Clere, who were prepared to collaborate with the Marian persecution; the Suffolk clothing town of Hadleigh, which had been ministered to by John Rogers, the first of the Marian martyrs, had witnessed a series of bitterly contested lawsuits between Protestants and Catholics; and in London a spirit of religious partisanship prevailed, both the reformers and their opponents being bound by ties of kinship, apprenticeship and suretyship. A similar pattern is found north of the border. Although there were striking success stories like St Andrews which seems to have achieved its Reformation overnight, the Reformation was more usually achieved only after a struggle. It is hardly surprising that Protestantism was seen as a threat to the established order in Aberdeen subject to the strongly traditionalist influence of the surrounding lairds, but more striking that the early support for the reformation in Edinburgh was confined to mercantile and legal elements, the movement acquiring a truly popular dynamic only in the 1580s under the impetus of a new generation of dynamic preachers.[21]

But by and large the tensions seem to have been contained. There were few politically or religiously motivated purges in English towns in the early years of the Reformation. In Scotland, where the Reformation was accomplished by means of an aristocratic rebellion, the Edinburgh council was purged twice in

[21] For the themes of this section, see also below pp. 268 *et seq.*; P. Collinson, *The Birthpangs of Protestant England* (London, 1988), ch. 2; M. S. Byford, 'The birth of a Protestant town: the process of the reformation in Tudor Colchester', in J. S. Craig and P. Collinson, eds., *The Reformation in English Towns* (Basingstoke, 1998); D. MacCulloch, *Suffolk under the Tudors* (Oxford, 1986), pp. 170–1; S. Brigden, *London and the Reformation* (Oxford, 1989); M. Lynch, *Edinburgh and the Reformation* (Edinburgh, 1981); J. E. A. Dawson, '"The face of ane perfyt reformed kyrk": St Andrews and the early Scottish Reformation', in J. Kirk, ed., *Renaissance and Reformation in England and Scotland* (Oxford, 1991), pp. 413–35; A. White, 'The impact of the Reformation on a burgh community: the case of Aberdeen', in Lynch, ed., *Early Modern Town*, pp. 81–101; M. Lynch, 'Preaching to the converted?: perspectives on the Scottish Reformation', in A. Macdonald *et al.*, eds., *The Renaissance in Scotland* (Leiden, 1994), pp. 301–43; M. Graham, *The Uses of Reform: 'Godly Discipline' and Popular Behaviour in Scotland and France, 1560–1610* (Leiden, 1996).

1559–60, but many Catholics found their way back over the next decade, and the purges were not usually repeated in provincial centres. Civic leaders showed themselves cautious, only offering qualified support to the lords of the congregation, and their moderation long prevailed: in the twin burghs of Aberdeen the Protestant and Catholic Churches continued to exist side by side while many Protestants remained connected to Catholics by blood or marriage ties. In most towns both in England and Scotland the councillors followed a legalistic line, cooperating with the religious policies of successive regimes because they saw obedience to duly constituted authority as an aspect of the obedience due to God. Religious differences might be sunk to further the transcendant interests of the urban community, the godly cooperating with Catholic sympathisers both on the London hospitals project in Edward VI's reign and in a scheme for the establishment of a hospital for the poor in Edinburgh in 1562. Although the Marian persecutions left a bitter legacy in many English communities, the embarrassment of collaborators who had been publicly denounced by Foxe gave them strong motives to conform, while the more recalcitrant persecutors could be eased out of office.[22]

However, there is no doubting the fact that as the Reformation progressed in the later sixteenth and early seventeenth centuries its capacity to generate internal division in urban communities became manifest. The tendency for the godly ministers, now so frequently employed by urban communities, to cast themselves in the role of Old Testament prophets denouncing the vices of magistrates could be corrosive of the traditional lines of authority. At Dundee, for example, the local minister denounced the unpopular provost, Sir James Scrymgeour, in terms which undermined the obedience due to social superiors: 'if they would choose a provost for greatness, the Devil was greatest of all'. In Scotland the alliance between the magnates and the reformed which had brought about the Reformation soon broke down as Presbyterian ministers became frustrated at the failure of the lay elites to give full backing to the cause of godly discipline. Writing of the impact of the Melvillian debates about church government in the 1580s, Lynch has detected a split in the Edinburgh kirk sessions between elders recruited from the upper ranks and deacons who came from humbler craft backgrounds, although more work is needed to determine the typicality of this phenomenon. Nor is enough known about the consequences in Scotland of the assault on the traditional festive culture which proved so divisive in England. The tensions produced by the godly programme in Elizabeth's realm have attracted more research. Their insistence on strict levels of observance, their hostility to the traditional ceremonies in the prayer book and their attack on traditional festivities and on the alehouse proved deeply divisive. These were only rarely con-

[22] Lynch, *Edinburgh and the Reformation*; White, 'Aberdeen'; Byford, 'Birth of a Protestant town'; P. Slack, 'Social policy and the constraints of government', in J. Loach and R. Tittler, eds., *The Mid-Tudor Polity, c. 1540–1560* (London, 1980), pp. 109–12.

flicts which pitted a godly elite against the poor, for the divisions generated by the godly cut vertically through society, and that is what made these conflicts so destabilising. The opponents of moral reformation included both those like Matthew Chubb and his circle at Dorchester who hankered for more easy-going patterns of sociability, and members of vested interests like the brewers and friends of the cathedral establishment who compromised the programme of godly reformation at Salisbury.[23]

One should be wary of taking the rhetoric of religious conflict at face value. The battle lines were rarely simply drawn. Rather than a Puritan group being pitted against a body of recalcitrant traditionalists, conflict was often the result of divisions within the Protestant camp. Thus although the outbreak of libelling against the elite in Colchester in the mid-1570s was a reaction to the hard-line pastoral and theological priorities of the local minister Thomas Upcher, one of his leading opponents was John Hunwick, a prominent merchant, and himself a Protestant of strong convictions, but one for whom charity demanded reconciliation. At Stratford-on-Avon the opposition to the vicar Thomas Wilson during the 1620s owed something to a drive for moral reform which was seen as serving the interests of a hypocritical elite but, because of his high conception of his clerical dignity, he also made enemies of some of those godly members of the corporation who had sponsored his appointment. Nor should we always assume that conflicts in which labels of religious abuse were used necessarily had their origins in religious disputes. The representation of the disputes at Thetford in the early 1580s as being religious in nature owes more to the fact that this chimed in with the world view of the West Suffolk justices of the peace than it does to the real issues at stake, in this case a dispute over the post of recorder and the misuse of local office.[24]

Godly Protestantism was a major factor in what one might call a process of 'popular politicisation' in towns in this period. It is sometimes alleged that the predominantly localist perspective of townsfolk gave them little interest in questions of national politics. When the populace intervened in the political process it was to protest against threats to their economic well-being, pressurising magistrates into ameliorative action in the markets in times of dearth or scapegoating alien minorities for a variety of economic ills. When towns were

[23] M. Lynch, 'From privy kirk to burgh church: an alternative view of the process of Protestantisation', in N. Macdougall, ed., *Church, Politics, and Society: Scotland, 1408–1929* (Edinburgh, 1983), pp. 85–96; Graham, *Uses of Reform*, ch. 3; Collinson, *Birthpangs of Protestant England*, pp. 56, 136–9; D. Underdown, *Fire from Heaven* (London, 1992), ch. 2; P. Slack, 'Poverty and politics in Salisbury 1597–1666', in Clark and Slack, eds., *Crisis and Order*, pp. 186–8.

[24] M. S. Byford, 'The price of Protestantism: assessing the impact of religious change in Essex: the cases of Heydon and Colchester' (DPhil thesis, University of Oxford, 1988), ch. 5; A. Hughes, 'Religion and society in Stratford-upon-Avon, 1619–1638', *Midland History*, 19 (1994), 58–84; J. S. Craig, 'The "godly" and the "froward": Protestant polemics in the town of Thetford, 1560–1590', *Norfolk Archaeology*, 41 (1990–3), 279–93.

torn by parliamentary electoral contests it was either the result of the competition of surrounding gentry or of disputes internal to the town such as the nature of the urban franchise and the performance of the elite. Such an interpretation of popular political culture within towns ignores the implications of the penetration of Protestant ideology. Some of the easy assumptions about the conflict between Puritanism and popular culture have been questioned by recent historians. Popular literary genres such as the murder pamphlets drew on world views similar to those espoused by the godly, while popular anti-Catholicism was encouraged by the development of a new Protestant ritual calendar: the celebration of Elizabeth's accession, the reigning monarch's birthday and the anniversary of the Gunpowder Plot became occasions for sermons reminding the auditory of England's miraculous deliverance from popery. Although loyal to the godly prince, their conviction that Protestants were engaged in a struggle for survival against an international popish conspiracy ensured that the godly had definite views on the policies appropriate to the godly prince. Rulers who appeared to appease Catholic powers or who tolerated Catholics at Court ran the risk of encouraging the notion of a popish plot at the centre of the kingdom. Protestantism also encouraged an active citizenship which often brought the godly into conflict with the priorities of early Stuart policies.

It was unfortunate for the Stuarts that their policies both at home and abroad seemed to call into question their commitment to the godly cause. Whereas the wars of the later 1580s and 1590s had commanded a consensus, those of the 1620s soured relations between crown and subjects. James VI and I had to be cajoled into an anti-Spanish stance on the outbreak of the Thirty Years War, while the wars fought by his son were both incompetently managed and not the kind of wars his parliaments thought they had signed up for. The inevitable consequence of parliaments' reluctance to fund the wars appropriately was a recourse to financial and military expedients like the forced loan of 1626 and the billeting of troops which undermined the confidence of subjects in the monarch's commitment to the rule of law. When these policies were combined with the drive for ceremonial uniformity and the assault on Calvinism which gathered momentum in the 1630s the notion of a conspiracy to subvert religion and the liberties of the subject achieved a horrifying plausibility. In Charles' northern kingdom a series of fiscal expedients seemed to threaten the Scottish economy, while the drive for congruity in religion between his realms entailed a still more damaging assault on the Presbyterian Church.

It is difficult to capture the blend of material and ideological reasons for the developing urban opposition to the early Stuarts. Laud's assault on predestinarian theology and his apparent sympathy for a ceremonialism which smacked of popery affronted the keenly felt religious sensibilities of many magistrates, but his curtailment of the preaching of town lecturers also threatened their drive for godly order, and the encouragement he gave to the pretensions of the clergy threatened civic jurisdiction by exacerbating quarrels between cathedral clergy and the corporations. In Scotland one can argue that it was the failure to use any of the normal channels of communication as well as the content of the prayer book itself which led to the collapse of Charles' regime. Moreover, there were undoubtedly a large number of non-religious flashpoints which contributed to a deterioration in relations between towns and the crown. Londoners, for example, were alienated by a whole series of fiscal expedients: the swingeing fine on the corporation for its failure to observe the terms of the Londonderry plantation, the activities of the commissioners for new buildings and the incorporation of the suburbs. All English urban communities shared in the increase in prerogative taxation that ship money entailed. The Scots were convinced that the Stuart policies of the 1630s were contributing to their economic weakness as the erosion of the differential tariffs between England and Scotland undermined Scottish competitiveness, and the common fishery threatened to bring the English into Scottish inshore waters. But it is also doubtful whether these economic and material issues had quite the polarising force that religion did, not least because of the way in which the rhetoric of anti-popery could incorporate all grievances since popery undermined liberties and livelihoods.[25]

Those urban communities which had been most subject to godly influence became foci for opposition to Stuart policies. The burghs were in the forefront of the opposition in the Scottish parliament of 1621 to the Five Articles of Perth which had entailed moves towards greater ceremonialism. The imposition of the prayer book was greeted with religious riots in the Scottish capital in July 1637, and although the burghs understandably awaited a lead from the nobility before revolting, they became the most committed of Charles' opponents. Of the leading burghs only St Andrews and Aberdeen failed to sign the supplication of 18 October 1637 against the prayer book, although it is noteworthy that of the smaller centres north of Montrose only Banff signed. Likewise, in England it was the godly strongholds like Banbury, Northampton, Yarmouth, Norwich, Boston and a number of the Essex clothing townships which were in the forefront of opposition to Charles I's forced loan of 1626. Differing religious affiliations may help explain the differing patterns of urban allegiance in the Civil War. David Underdown and Mark Stoyle have shown that those centres where there was the

[25] M. Stoyle, *From Deliverance to Destruction: Rebellion and Civil War in an English City* (Exeter, 1996), ch. 2; Clark, '"Ramoth-Gilead of the Good"', pp. 244–73; A. Hughes, 'Coventry and the English Revolution', in R. C. Richardson, ed., *Town and Countryside in the English Revolution* (Manchester, 1992), pp. 69–99; D. H. Sacks, 'Bristol's "wars of religion"', in *ibid.*, pp. 100–29; D. Stevenson, 'The burghs and the Scottish revolution', in Lynch, ed., *Early Modern Town*, pp. 167–91; A. I. MacInnes, *Charles I and the Making of the Covenanting Movement, 1625–1641* (Edinburgh, 1991), pp. 28–39, 102–22.

greatest popular enthusiasm for parliament were centres of godly Protestantism, whereas towns which had shown Laudian proclivities tended to produce greater popular royalism.[26]

It should be stressed that the urban populace was not monolithically godly. The king was able to attract support from centres like Stratford-on-Avon and Salisbury where the elite had been divided by religion before the Civil War. Even in London, where there was a growth of lower-class religious sectarianism in 1640–2, radicals like Praise God Barebone and Thomas Lambe had their conventicles broken up by hostile crowds. There was a surprising amount of popular resistance to the dismantling of the Laudian altar rails in 1641, and some parishes even mounted petitions in defence of episcopacy. Ruling groups were often too intimately connected with Stuart concessionary interests to give a clear lead and adherence to the cause of parliament sometimes required the application of popular pressure. At Coventry the Puritan magnate Lord Brooke and his allies on the council led by John Barker, one of the city's MPs, were able to exploit the enthusiasm of the commons for the parliamentary cause, and so compromised the corporation's quest for peace. Sometimes, as at London and Norwich where freemen sentiment was able to make its views known through elections to the common council, the so-called 'parliamentary Puritans' won decisive victories in 1641–2, and godly pressure resulted in changes in the composition of the governing body. But in other cases, as at Exeter, the adherence of the city to parliament depended on the dominance of the godly on the corporation, and their swift neutralisation of alternative power centres like the cathedral chapter, which had given a lead to the forces opposing moral reformation in the years before the war.[27]

To acknowledge the polarising force of religion within urban politics is to call into question the emphasis placed by an earlier generation of historians on the neutralism of towns and the reluctance with which they were drawn into the conflict. When groups of the commons at Bristol and Exeter attempted to prevent the entry of parliamentarian troops whom their leaders wished to admit, they were not giving vent to the expression of neutralist feeling, but were rather expressing the strength of popular royalism in opposition to the elite. In March 1643 the ruling group at Exeter actually appealed to parliament over the head of the local parliamentary commander to scotch peace negotiations which the county elites were sponsoring. Other neutralist initiatives turn out on closer inspection to be attempts by one side or the other to gain some short-term mil-

[26] J. Goodare, 'The Scottish Parliament of 1621', *HJ*, 38 (1995), 41; Stevenson, 'Burghs and the Scottish Revolution', pp. 177–9; D. Underdown, *Revel, Riot, and Rebellion: Popular Politics and Culture in England, 1603–1660* (Oxford, 1985), ch. 12; M. Stoyle, *Loyalty and Locality: Popular Allegiance in Devon during the English Civil War* (Exeter, 1994), pp. 30–110, 182–226.

[27] Hughes, 'Coventry and the English Revolution'; Pearl, *London and the Outbreak of the Puritan Revolution*, chs. 4–6; Evans, *Seventeenth-Century Norwich*, ch. 4; Stoyle, *From Deliverance to Destruction*, chs. 3–4.

itary advantage. It has been pointed out that when towns changed hands the same men tended to hold power, and from this the conclusion has been drawn that the civic rulers were time-servers, but although there were few purges of councillors in the early years of the war, opponents of the prevailing civic regime tended to withdraw from participation in government, hardly the action of men who lacked political views. More radical changes in the composition of governing bodies often followed the final parliamentary victory, but they were the end-product of long-standing rivalries within the local political establishment rather than settlements imposed by the central government on communities which had been solidly localist in sentiment.[28]

The degree to which the ruling groups were disrupted during the revolution depended on a number of factors. Those towns like Gloucester which had stood solidly for parliament were less vulnerable to purges, while those which had changed hands in the war like Hereford, Bristol and Worcester (each of which had seen two successive changes of regime) underwent more disruption. Towns like Colchester which had shown their disloyalty during the second Civil War of 1648 were more likely to secure the attentions of a hostile government, bringing a more religiously radical group to power. In Scotland religious tensions were evident in some towns by the mid-1640s; in Linlithgow, for example, the burgh church split into two separate congregations, separated by a wall built across the nave. Yet here too the key changes came in 1648–9 when the radical covenanters exploited their victory over the Engagers to remodel the burgh councils. In both kingdoms the newcomers tended to be men recruited from just outside the old ruling group, so that the revolution did not bring to power men of a markedly different stamp from those that they displaced. Changes in the structure of power were more unusual and often occurred to secure some tactical advantage for one group rather than reflecting an alternative political vision. Although the commonwealth may have supplied an opportunity for the freemen of High Wycombe and Bedford to overthrow the local oligarchies, there was no principled adherence to democratic principles by the commonwealth regime, for at Colchester the charter was remodelled in 1656 to remove direct election of aldermen by burgesses as the freemen had gradually eased out the victors of 1648. Likewise in London the commonwealth's supporters resisted pressure from the radicals for common hall to become more directly representative of the freemen rather than of the liveries of the guilds.[29]

28 R. Howell, 'Neutralism, conservatism and political alignment in the English revolution: the case of the towns, 1642–9', in J. Morrill, ed., *Reactions to the English Civil War 1642–1649* (London, 1982), pp. 67–87; Stoyle, *From Deliverance to Destruction*, pp. 66–7, 76–7, 83–4, 139–41; Hughes, 'Coventry and the English Revolution', pp. 84–6; Sacks, 'Bristol's "wars of Religion"', pp. 116–120.

29 D. Underdown, *Pride's Purge: Politics in the Puritan Revolution* (Oxford, 1971), pp. 303–6, 318–27; Stevenson, 'Burghs and the Scottish revolution', pp. 171–3.

(V) IDEOLOGY AND CIVIC POLITICS, 1650–1700

The Civil Wars had undoubtedly caused much damage to the economies of towns. They had endured often crippling sieges involving the demolition of suburbs and plundering by hostile troops; in addition to the heavy burdens of wartime taxation they had suffered free quarter; and their economies had suffered from the disruptions to internal trade and the mortality caused by the diseases troops brought in their wake. They had also been politically traumatised by withdrawals from or purges in government disrupting the workings of their administrations. But the Interregnum represented a period of stabilisation during which towns could reap many rewards. It was an opportunity to settle scores against long-standing rivals as towns asserted control over patronage to city churches, schools and hospitals, bought up crown and ecclesiastical lands and fee-farm-rents and extended their jurisdiction into the long-contested cathedral closes, or in the case of Oxford curtailed the power of the university. Towns adapted to the changed circumstances, using the leverage of their military governors with the centre to advance their causes, choosing as high stewards men closely connected with the new republican regimes and electing MPs with Oliverian connections to the Protectorate parliaments. It is less clear that the Scottish burghs were the beneficiaries of the revolution. Although they benefited from the shattering of the power of the aristocracy and the temporary abolition of heritable jurisdictions, the conditions of the forced union from 1653 gave them only limited influence at Westminster. It is true that civilian life was showing signs of a return to normalcy in the later 1650s, and that the burghs constituted a major source of support for the continuance of the union in 1659–60 against a revival of the landed interest, but the union was undoubtedly a mixed blessing because of the discriminatory English commercial policies and the unsustainably high levels of taxation.[30]

The behaviour of the towns during the Interregnum made them prime targets for Anglican and royalist reaction at the Restoration. Every corporation, declared the duke of Newcastle, was 'a petty free state against monarchy', and Clarendon referred to their 'natural malignancy'. The Corporation Act of 1662 required all municipal officeholders in England and Wales to receive the Anglican sacrament, swear an oath of non-resistance to the king and renounce the Solemn League and Covenant. The act was enforced by local commissioners recruited from the ranks of the Anglican gentry, who were empowered to

[30] I. Roy, 'The English republic, 1649–1660: the view from the town hall', in H. G. Koenigsberger and E. Muller-Luckner, eds., *Republiken und Republikanismus im Europa der Fruhen Neuzeit* (Schriften des Historischen Kollegs Kolloquien II, Munich, 1988), pp. 213–37; Underdown, *Pride's Purge*, pp. 332–5; Stevenson, 'Burghs and the Scottish revolution', pp. 172–3; F. D. Dow, *Cromwellian Scotland* (Glasgow, 1979), pp. 46–8, 105–6, 148.

displace not only those unable to meet these conditions, but also those they regarded as disaffected. The effects of the act varied according to the degree of change in the 1650s and the extent to which local communities had themselves readmitted Anglicans in the years immediately before and after the restoration. But overall about one third of the personnel of the corporations lost their places, in most cases for refusal of the declaration against the covenant rather than through the operation of the commissioners' discretionary powers. Some gentlemen seized the opportunity to extend their control over the boroughs by placing themselves on the remodelled corporations as at Ludlow and Liverpool, while in the extreme case of Taunton all the rulers were removed, the corporation dissolved and the town fell under the authority of the local gentry.[31]

However, there were tensions within the forces of reaction between those who wished to extend the central government's control over the corporations and those who sought merely to ensure that loyalists were in control. When the corporation bill empowering local commissioners to remove the disaffected was passing through parliament in 1661, amendments in the House of Lords, probably of ministerial origin, sought to give the crown the authority to remodel municipal charters, reserving to itself in the new grants the power to select recorders, town clerks and mayors from slates of the towns' nominees. That these amendments were decisively rejected in the House of Commons is an indication both of the caution of the crown's legal officers and of the strength of localist hostility to the pretensions of the central government. Thus the character of Restoration government in the towns was shaped by local circumstance which compromised the campaign against dissent. In towns like Yarmouth and Abingdon, where the dissenting interest was strongly entrenched, some of their most prominent adherents were too indispensable to have been purged in 1662, and others found their way back on to the councils in the years which followed. Apart from the practical difficulties of isolating dissenters in view of the prevalence of occasional conformity, their sheer force of numbers in many towns made persecution problematic because of the unreliability of juries, and because the crown's local managers might find their confessional instincts at odds with the parliamentary electoral considerations which made it dangerous to alienate the dissenting interest. The elimination of dissent would require large-scale external intervention which was likely to prove divisive within the urban community. Nor was the Anglican establishment a homogeneous one, many councillors and their clergy showing a sympathy towards dissent, while the declaration of indulgence of 1672 suspending the operation of the penal laws

[31] P. D. Halliday, *Dismembering the Body Politic* (Cambridge, 1998), pp. 85-105; P. J. Norrey, 'The Restoration regime in action: the relationship between central and local government in Dorset, Somerset and Wiltshire, 1660–78', *HJ*, 31 (1988), 809–12.

revealed divisions at the centre, which could only give encouragement to the dissenting interest in the provinces.[32]

The ideal of civic unity remained a powerful cohesive force capable of blunting the impact of the very real confessional tensions within Restoration towns, but the fragile coexistence of Anglicans and dissenters disintegrated with the revelations of the popish plot in 1678. The elections to the three exclusion parliaments were fiercely contested: whereas there had been thirty-two contested borough elections in 1661, there were eighty-four in March 1679, sixty-one in October 1679 and forty-five in 1681. Although the exclusion of the duke of York from the succession was by no means the only issue in these elections, and local issues often played a role, a key polarising force was the conflict of Church and dissent, which increasingly became subsumed in a party struggle of Whigs and Tories. The Whigs, while not a party of dissent, were dominated by those Anglicans who were sympathetic to the cause of dissent and who regarded popery as a threat to liberties as well as religion, while the Tories were dominated by those Anglicans who saw the threat as lying in a Presbyterian plot in a rerun of 1640–2. Feverish electoral contests nourished the process of popular politicisation and, as during the Civil War, the populace was divided. Although the Whigs were quickest to exploit the techniques of mass petitioning (the monster petition of January 1680 from London, Westminster and Southwark boasted 16,000 signatures), the Tories organised loyalist addresses from the boroughs in the wake of the dissolution of the Oxford parliament (a loyalist address from the London apprentices claimed 18,000 signatures). The ritual calendar was appropriated by both sides to drive home their own particular conspiracy theory, the Whigs utilising 5 November (the anniversary of Gunpowder treason) for pope burnings and the Tories exploiting the loyalist associations of 30 January (the regicide) and 29 May (the Restoration) for rump burnings. Rather than seeing this varied behaviour as evidence of the fickleness of the mob, historians are coming to appreciate its roots in the religiously divided society which had emerged in the mid-seventeenth century.[33]

Although the last years of Charles II's reign saw much greater intervention by central government in the affairs of towns, one should beware of exaggerating the absolutist ambitions of the crown. The crown's objective was prob-

[32] P. Seaward, *The Cavalier Parliament and the Reconstruction of the Old Regime, 1661–7* (Cambridge, 1989), pp. 151–7; Halliday, *Dismembering the Body Politic*, pp. 85–92; Gauci, *Great Yarmouth*, ch. 3; J. Barry, 'The politics of religion in Restoration Bristol', in T. Harris, P. Seaward and M. Goldie, eds., *The Politics of Religion in Restoration England* (Oxford, 1990), pp. 163–89; J. Hurwich, '"A fanatick town": the political influence of the dissenters in Coventry, 1660–1720', *Midland History*, 4 (1977), 15–47.

[33] T. Harris, *London Crowds in the Reign of Charles II* (Cambridge, 1987); M. Knights, *Politics and Opinion in Crisis, 1678–1681* (Cambridge, 1994); Barry, 'Politics of religion in Restoration Bristol', pp. 172–9.

ably to ensure that the judicial apparatus of the towns was in the hands of reliable men, although electoral considerations were present in some cases. Although the crown took the initiative in the *quo warranto* proceedings against London, where the acquittal of Shaftesbury in November 1681 had revealed its weakness, the charter policy in the provinces seems to have evolved in response to requests for intervention from local Tories. The crown initially confined its right of removal to the judicial officers, and a more aggressive policy, allowing the king to remove any future corporation member, only emerged in 1683. Lord Keeper Guildford and Secretary Jenkins who were entrusted with the details of the remodelled charters were among the more legalistically minded of the crown's ministers, and they acted sometimes to curb the excesses of their supporters in the localities. The scale of the purges was therefore often limited as it would have proved too disruptive to have removed all the leading Whigs.[34]

Whatever its intentions, the crown had undoubtedly secured a very strong position in the boroughs by 1685. This was squandered by James II, who failed to appreciate that the Anglican loyalists shared an anti-Catholic rhetoric with their opponents, however much they might differ from them over means. Confronted by the hostility of parliament to his plans to remove the disabilities under which Catholics laboured, the king decided to ditch the crown's former allies, and embarked in the early months of 1688 on the regulation of the municipal corporations in order to secure a parliamentary majority for the repeal of the penal laws and test acts. Whereas Charles II had used his powers under the new charters to remove any member very sparingly, James used it to devastating effect. Government agents reported on the complexion of town councils, *quo warranto* writs were issued, loyalist Anglicans were removed, and replaced by dissenters (usually men who had been displaced in earlier purges rather than the king's opponents of 1679–81 who had been removed in the Anglican reaction which followed). Anxieties about the king's religion were now reinforced by doubts about his commitment to the rule of law, and the policy did not succeed in building up support because of the attachment of local communities to their chartered rights. Such were the doubts about the king's intentions that even heavily purged corporations refused to vote thanks for the second declaration of indulgence. In towns like Oxford (see Plate 8) the purge of Anglican loyalists was insufficient to stop the council's unanimous opposition to a *quo warranto* in April 1688. The realisation that the king's policy had failed with the cancellation

34 Halliday, *Dismembering the Body Politic*, chs. 5–6; R. Pickavance, 'The English boroughs and the King's government: a study of the Tory reaction, 1681–1685' (DPhil thesis, University of Oxford, 1976); J. Miller, 'The crown and the borough charters in the reign of Charles II', *EHR*, 100 (1985), 53–84; C. Lee, 'Fanatic magistrates: religious and political conflict in three Kent boroughs', *HJ*, 35 (1992), 43–61.

of all the new charters in mid-October 1688 came too late to prevent William of Orange's invasion.[35]

The potential for an absolutist outcome in Restoration Scotland was rather greater. Most magnates, whatever their earlier covenanting sympathies, now supported the forces of conservatism. As the revolution in Scotland had been more radical so the reaction of the Restoration was more extreme. The Act Recissory of 1661 repealed all legislation since 1633; episcopacy was reimposed, the general assembly of the kirk outlawed and conventicles proscribed; the Act Concerning Religion placed all ecclesiastical power in the king's hands. A proclamation of 1661 instructed the burghs to keep out of office all those of 'fanatick principles and enemies to monarchicall government', and in 1663 burgh magistrates were required to sign a declaration repudiating the covenants and declaring resistance to be unlawful. Although the government toyed with a limited indulgence between 1669 and 1672, from 1674 a sustained harassment of covenanters began, entailing a much higher level of intervention by the privy council in the affairs of the burghs. Magistrates were fined for allowing conventicles and subjected to relentless pressure to take the oaths of allegiance and the declaration. From 1681 under the rule of James, duke of York, they were required by the Test Act to declare that under no circumstances was it lawful to take up arms against their ruler. Given that they were now staring a Catholic succession in the face, this was a declaration many baulked at, and several burghs (including Ayr, Cupar, Dunfermline, Irvine, Linlithgow and Queensferry) were reduced to a state of administrative paralysis as the councils refused to participate in the elections of their successors, and their officers were nominated by the privy council or its aristocratic agents. The interference of the centre reached a peak under James VII, whose pro-Catholic policies resulted in rioting in Edinburgh in 1686. The king instructed that only those burghs which had concurred with his desires in parliament should enjoy free elections; the others were required to submit names to him for approval.[36]

The Glorious Revolution did not resolve the issues which had generated the crisis of the 1680s in either Scotland or England and Wales. The crown refrained from the kind of large-scale interference in corporations which had characterised post-Restoration politics, and legislation to resolve the legal chaos of the 1680s failed in 1689–90. Whig–Tory conflicts were sustained in several towns by

[35] Halliday, *Dismembering the Body Politic*, ch. 7; Gauci, *Great Yarmouth*, pp. 166–70; P. Murrell, 'Bury St Edmunds and the campaign to pack parliament in 1687–8', *Bull. IHR*, 54 (1981), 188–206; M. Mullett, 'Conflict, politics, and elections in Lancaster, 1660–1688', *NHist.*, 19 (1983), 84–5; *VCH*, Oxfordshire, IV, pp. 124–5.

[36] P. Hume Brown and H. Paton, eds., *The Register of the Privy Council of Scotland* (3rd series, Edinburgh, 1908–33), vol. I, pp. 45–6, 296, 549, 617–18, vol. II, p. 195, vol. IV, pp. 323–6, 202, 251–2, 540–2, vol. VI, pp. 104–7, vol. VII, pp. 203–4, 220, 248–9, 249–50, 255–7, 273–4, 421, vol. VIII, pp. 264, 302–3; M. Wood and H. Armot, eds., *Extracts from the Records of the Burgh of Edinburgh 1681–1689* (Edinburgh, 1954), pp. xviii–xix.

the existence of more than one charter. At Bewdley the whigs claimed technical faults in the charter of 1685, and based their claims to office on an earlier charter of 1605, so that in Queen Anne's reign there were two competing corporations in the borough. More generally, the religious issue did not subside, because high Anglicans hoped to reverse the limited concessions made to dissenters in 1689, while the dissenters wished to remove their remaining civil disabilities. It is true that for much of William III's reign Whigs and Tories in many towns maintained an uneasy modus vivendi, the divisions between them muddied by the emergence of the court–country divisions generated by the war, but the party strife burst forth with the cry of the 'church in danger' from the mid-1690s. As the parties jockeyed for position in a series of keenly fought parliamentary contests, the integrity of the civic community was compromised by the manipulation of the freedom for party advantage, as each side manufactured freemen.[37]

The Presbyterian triumph in Scotland in 1689 led to the abolition of episcopacy, and confessional differences continued to fuel factionalism within the burghs. Although Scottish politics was dominated by the clash of rival magnate interests, these groups had a religious tinge, reflecting divisions over the status of the episcopalians and the legitimacy of the revolution, and they increasingly aligned themselves with the Whig and Tory parties in England. Thus by 1710 the councils of Haddington and Jedburgh were described as 'both somewhat Tory', while at Perth the advance of 'the Whig set' occasioned anxiety among their opponents. But the course of urban politics in Scotland in the underresearched post-revolutionary period was complicated by the economic collapse occasioned by the wars against France, which closed off traditional markets, and led to increasing tariffs in the English trade. Efforts to revitalise trade through the Company of Scotland Trading to Africa and the East Indies (which originated in efforts to buy burgh votes in parliament in 1695) ended in the fiasco of the Darien colony, which the English government had sabotaged. Rioters in Edinburgh burned the house of the unfortunate secretary of state, the earl of Seafield, but the low level of religious antagonism in the Scottish capital prevented a repeat of 1637 or 1688 in 1700. It was the failure of the Darien colony which led to the climate in which an incorporating union was conceivable. However, the union was unwelcome to urban interests.The Convention of Royal Burghs petitioned against union in 1706 by twenty-four votes to twenty with twenty-two abstentions; as parliament considered the union proposals hostile crowds filled the Edinburgh streets; and there were riots in Dumfries and Glasgow. T. C. Smout has argued there was probably a division between the interests of landowners who saw the advantages of access to English markets for the produce of their estates and urban traders and craftsmen to whom French

[37] Halliday, *Dismembering the Body Politic*, ch. 8; Gauci, *Great Yarmouth*, ch. 6.

markets would be closed after the union, or for whom English competition was threatening. Recent research has detected less clear-cut divisions between rural and urban interests. The 'Explanations' attached to some of the key economic clauses, however, reveal the different views of producers and consumers, helping to explain why the burghs were generally split on most aspects of the union debate.[38]

(vi) CONCLUSION: URBAN STABILITY

How far did the turbulence of post-Restoration politics, characterised by increased party strife and higher turnover among town magistrates, seriously undermine the stability of urban government? Politicisation extended not merely to control over civic offices and parliamentary representation, but also affected the lower tiers of government as Whigs and Tories competed for control over parish vestries and charitable institutions. Proposals for the centralisation of poor relief in corporations of the poor often originated, as at Bristol in 1696, among Whigs anxious to bypass Tory-controlled parish vestries. Even the London hospitals were not immune from the buffetings of party politics because of their extensive portfolios of property which might be used as a tool of political patronage.[39] But we should bear in mind that there were a number of forces working to blunt ideological polarisation. Although national crises like the Atterbury and Sacheverell affairs of 1701 and 1710 respectively might stoke up religious passions in the localities, confessional strife should not be seen as all-pervasive and unrelenting. In some circumstances Anglicans and nonconformists were prepared to join ranks against the common threat posed by irreligion. Towns remained profoundly concerned with their own economic well-being, and councillors of varying persuasions are found cooperating in the promotion of legislation for the benefit of their communities in parliament, or in defending incursions on urban privileges in the law courts. The advent of regular parliaments after the Glorious Revolution meant that townsmen had a greater chance of success in securing their objectives by legislative means. Paul Halliday has argued that the increasing recourse to the court of King's Bench in an intensely legalistic political culture helped to blunt the force of partisan politics, especially as its decisions often had the effect of allowing dissenters to retain

[38] D. Hayton, 'Traces of party conflict in early eighteenth-century Scottish elections', in Jones, ed., *Scots and Parliament*, pp. 74–99; T. C. Smout, 'The road to union', in G. Holmes, ed., *Britain after the Glorious Revolution 1689–1714* (Basingstoke, 1969); I. D. Whyte, *Scotland before the Industrial Revolution* (Harlow, 1995), ch. 16, C. Whatley, 'Economic causes and consequences of the Union of 1707: a survey', *Scottish Historical Review*, 68 (1989), 150–81.

[39] C. Rose, 'Politics, religion, and charity in Augustan London, *c.* 1680–*c.* 1720' (PhD thesis, University of Cambridge, 1989); J. Barry, 'The parish in civic life: Bristol and its churches 1640–1750', in S. J. Wright, ed., *Parish, Church and People: Local Studies in Lay Religion* (London, 1988), pp. 168–70.

their positions.[40] Moreover, the greater professionalisation and institutionalisation of civic administration in the later seventeenth century insulated many of the routine workings of civic government from the passions of party strife. Several towns improved the management of their finances by handing over responsibility to permanent or semi-permanent officials rather than drawing upon sometimes inexperienced citizens serving in rotation. In most urban communties the town clerk, generally recruited from among the attorneys connected with the central courts, and his assistants took on a growing number of the more mundane elements of administration.[41]

It is sometimes argued that towns were reduced to a position of subservience towards the landed elites as a result of post-Restoration political developments. It is true that there were many more gentry freemen particularly in the smaller centres and that the towns had attracted an increasing degree of political intervention by gentlemen in search of parliamentary seats in the feverish electoral environment. However, it would be misleading to present this in terms of a loss of municipal autonomy and to fail to recognise the advantages that a closer relationship with the gentry might bring. A key element in the revival of urban fortunes in the provinces was their development as leisure and service centres for the local gentry. The fact that urban elites tended to be more broadly recruited, drawing upon the growing professional element within towns, did not necessarily entail a sacrifice of mercantile or trading interests. Aristocratic patrons seeking to cultivate an urban interest could not simply coerce the townsfolk; they could only achieve their objectives by negotiation. The corporation of Yarmouth ensured that the support that they gave to their high stewards, the Paston earls of Yarmouth, was conditional upon the performance of reciprocal services for the town such as steering the bills of 1677 and 1685 for the maintenance of the haven through parliament in the face of county opposition.[42]

The impact of the interventions by the central government on Scottish burgh politics has been little studied. Doubtless charges of disloyalty to the regime often reinforced local factional rivalries as at Ayr, a leading covenanting stronghold in the later 1670s and 1680s, so that the purges did not always fulfil the objectives of the privy council. Individuals were sometimes able to exploit the favour of the Edinburgh government to consolidate their local position by holding office for long periods, bringing in their friends and kin and thereby reinforcing oligarchic trends. Thus Sir Andrew Ramsay, a client of Lauderdale and manager of the burgh representatives in parliament, aroused considerable resentment

[40] Barry, 'Parish in civic life', pp. 157–62; Gauci, *Great Yarmouth*, ch. 6; S. N. Handley, 'Local legislative initiatives for economic and social development in Lancashire, 1689–1731', *Parliamentary History*, 9 (1990), 14–37; Halliday, *Dismembering the Body Politic*, pp. 291–303.

[41] Clark, 'Civic leaders of Gloucester', pp. 327–8; Dawson, 'Finance and the unreformed borough'; Brooks, *Pettyfoggers and Vipers*, pp. 209–14.

[42] Clark, 'Civic leaders of Gloucester', pp. 323–4; Gauci, *Great Yarmouth*, pp. 78–88, 112–50, 157–65.

because of the long period for which he held office as provost of Edinburgh (1662–73). Although the burghs were more subject to resurgent aristocratic influences, like their English counterparts they retained a sense of where their economic self-interest lay. Magnates who wanted to manage a burgh had to cultivate their support. Governments which offended burgh interests, like that of Lauderdale who had supported the undermining of the trading monopolies of the royal burghs in 1672, ran the risk of running into parliamentary opposition.[43]

A major theme of this chapter has been the polarising effects of ideological division on municipal politics, but it has also sought to underline the continuing potency of a transcendant civic ideology which might unite all townsmen in defence of urban privileges and against the predatory attentions of outsiders. By the later seventeenth century those civic values were under threat not only from confessional divisions but also from economic changes. The expansion of small commodity production in the countryside undermined the position of town-based artisans; more sophisticated mechanisms of inland trade drew transactions away from the open market; economic theorists became more sceptical of the value of corporate privilege which protected urban monopolies. But it is important to realise that town magistrates did not impotently collapse before these challenges. In many cases they continued to defend the privileges of freemen in retail trade by activity against the practice of 'foreign bought and sold'; they maintained their commitment to small commodity production, placing limits on the employment of apprentices and journeymen, and the number of outlets any one individual could maintain; they spent vigorously in the defence of challenges to municipal privileges like the increasingly frequent attacks on the payment of municipal tolls. Towns north and south of the border continued to support communal projects even in the face of financial embarrassment and political conflict. If anything the ideological potency of civic 'freedom' was enhanced by the frequency of parliamentary electoral contests, in which the parties appealed to the independence of the freeman electorate. In spite of the polarising force of ideological divisions released by the Reformation, the values of the civic community remained powerful in 1700.

[43] Hume Brown and Paton, eds., *Register of the Privy Council of Scotland*, v, pp. 552–70, vii, pp. 255–7, viii, pp. 70–6, 245–70, 437–48; M. Wood, ed., *Extracts from the Records of the Burgh of Edinburgh 1665–80* (Edinburgh, 1950), pp. xvi–xviii; J. Patrick, 'The origins of the opposition to Lauderdale: the Scottish parliament of 1673, *Scottish Historical Review*, 53 (1974), 9–10, 14–17; R. M. Sunter, *Patronage and Politics in Scotland, 1707–1832* (Edinburgh, 1986), chs. 10–11.

· 8 ·

Reformation and culture 1540–1700

VANESSA HARDING

THE PERIOD 1540–1700 saw a transformation of the religious and educational institutions of English, Welsh and Scottish towns, and of the society and culture of their inhabitants. In Britain as in Europe, towns and urban society played an important part in the reformation of the Church and of its role in secular society, both in terms of institutional change and in popular and elite responses to it. Between 1540 and 1580, many of the basic institutional structures of medieval urban society were abolished or fundamentally altered. Important foci of community and civic life, such as fraternities, chantries and ceremonial, disappeared, and town populations and governments had to find a new collective spirit and new ways of organising their sociability. Many town governments came to be influenced by a Protestant or Puritan political ideology, which shaped their view of society and their response to its problems. The reformed Scottish Church achieved a very close relationship with secular urban governments, and set the agenda for action in many spheres, beyond those of religion and education. In the century and a half after the Reformation, religion continued to play an important part in the lives of townspeople in England and Wales, but the Church as a universal institution had been weakened, and the former unity of belief and observance was never recovered. Towns came to accommodate a multiplicity of beliefs and congregations. In the longer term the fragmentation of religious gatherings was paralleled by a decline in observance overall, a growing secularisation of society to which the increase in educational endowment and provision may have contributed.

(i) THE REFORMATION YEARS, 1540–1580

By 1540, the first stage of the Reformation in England and Wales – the dissolution of all monastic foundations, with the exception of some hospitals – had taken place. This had a major impact on most towns, eliminating a formerly important element in their physical, social and political environment. English medieval monasteries were by no means all based in towns, but they had had a strong influence on the development of the urban network in the middle ages, and their disappearance entailed important local changes. Ten of the twenty largest provincial English towns in 1524–5 were cathedral cities, and several of the remainder, such as Bury St Edmunds, St Albans and Reading, had been dominated by a single large monastic house. Some conventual churches became secular cathedrals or town churches, as at Bath, Bury St Edmunds, and St Albans, but many others were taken down or converted to secular use.[1] The surrender of York's monasteries must have had a 'shattering impact on the city', but in every town, the dissolution and the other institutional changes of the Reformation set a new pattern of social and political, as well as religious, relationships.[2]

The suppression in 1547 of religious guilds and fraternities and of chantry foundations marked an important change for the character and future development of urban communities. It must have been especially significant where the town's rulers had been incorporated as a guild, or where members of one or a few fraternities had dominated civic office, as at Worcester or York.[3] The attack on saints' days, images and religious processions eliminated most of the important occasions of the urban ceremonial year. Social and political life in Coventry had been structured by membership of and passage through the guilds of Corpus Christi and Holy Trinity. Several lesser craft guilds sustained the city's rich ceremonial tradition, though the city's economic difficulties had already led to an amalgamation of the two great guilds, and a reduction in observance, by the mid-1530s.[4] Corpus Christi processions and plays had served in many towns as an expression of civic unity and cohesiveness, and although there was not an immediate cessation of civic ceremony most of the urban play cycles had withered by 1580.[5] Smaller urban craft associations, mercantile guilds and livery com-

[1] S. Durston and R. M. Doran, *Princes, Pastors and People* (London, 1991) p. 167; J. J. Scarisbrick, *The Reformation and the English People* (Oxford, 1984), p. 107; C. Phythian-Adams, *Desolation of a City* (Cambridge, 1979), pp. 219, 275; J. Schofield, *The Building of London from the Conquest to the Great Fire* (London, 1984), p. 147.

[2] A. Dyer, *Decline and Growth in English Towns 1400–1640*, 2nd edn (Cambridge, 1995), pp. 64–5; D. Knowles and R. M Hadcock, *Medieval Religious Houses, England and Wales* (London, 1953), pp. 35–6; D. M. Palliser, *Tudor York* (Oxford, 1979), pp. 220–1, 235.

[3] P. Clark and P. Slack, *English Towns in Transition 1500–1700* (London, 1976), p. 129; A. Dyer, *The City of Worcester in the Sixteenth Century* (Leicester, 1973), pp. 189–90; Palliser, *Tudor York*, p. 49. Cf. Scarisbrick, *Reformation and the English People*, p. 22: 'these larger fraternities were often so dominated by the local town oligarchies that they might well be described as the local corporations at prayer – or providing for their own obsequies'.

[4] C. Phythian-Adams, 'Ceremony and the citizen', in R. Holt and G. Rosser, eds., *The Medieval Town: A Reader in English Urban History, 1200–1540* (London, 1990), pp. 238–64.

[5] Phythian-Adams, *Desolation of a City*, pp. 269–71; M. James, ' Ritual, drama, and the social body in the late medieval English town', *P&P*, 98 (1983), 3–29; P. Collinson, 'Puritanism as popular reli-

panies were also affected by the Edwardian legislation.[6] The Coventry journeymen's associations seem to have disappeared, though the more substantial mercantile crafts survived;[7] London's religious fraternities were abolished, but probably all the city's approved crafts and livery companies continued, though forfeiting the lands they had held for 'superstitious purposes', valued at some £939 per annum.[8] The guilds and companies of the larger towns still played an important role in social as well as economic organisation, contributing to stability and integration, but shorn of their religious function their character and preoccupations changed. They continued to care for members, to manage charitable bequests and to observe collective festivities, but arguably an important aspect of sociability and mutual care had been lost.

The initial processes of dissolution and suppression required the cooperation of local authorities, and several town corporations were more than compliant, though respect for the authority of national government and the principle of order may have been a strong motive. When corporations were faced with the loss of some of their own property, however, with the suppression of the guilds, or of resources they valued, such as lands, almshouses, hospitals and schools, there was a strong incentive to collective action. Many municipalities thus became direct owners and managers of lands and resources; although in general they paid heavily for this, they probably exercised fuller authority in their jurisdictions than before, no longer in competition with powerful and autonomous ecclesiastical institutions. The corporation of Coventry borrowed a large sum to buy up lands from the former Benedictine cathedral priory's large estate in and near the city, to pre-empt purchase by an outsider who would thereby have obtained a great deal of power and influence in the city.[9] The need to act quickly and collectively may also have contributed to the development of a municipal ethic translated into action in other areas of government. Some members of town elites had also profited as individuals from the dispersal of church lands, acquiring substantial urban residences and houses for rent, enhancing their local standing and control.

One effect of the Reformation felt in many towns was the closure of hospitals and schools along with the monastic houses or guilds to which they were attached. Although some of the larger hospitals were exempt from dissolution, a number of smaller hospices went in the first round of suppressions. The losses overall were considerable, but some scrupulosity on the part of commissioners, and determined efforts by urban corporations and citizens to save a valued

gious culture', in C. Durston and J. Eales, eds., *The Culture of English Puritanism, 1560–1700* (London, 1996), p. 43. [6] Scarisbrick, *Reformation and the English People*, p. 36.

[7] Phythian-Adams, *Desolation of a City*, p. 270.

[8] Scarisbrick, *Reformation and the English People*, p. 123; G. Unwin, *The Gilds and Companies of London* (London, 1908), pp. 208–14. [9] Phythian-Adams, *Desolation of a City*, p. 219.

resource, combined to prevent a complete dismemberment. At least forty-three English towns petitioned Edward VI's government for the grant or purchase of guild and chantry property. These included those asking for the free restoration of schools or almshouses (Abingdon, Chelmsford, Grantham, Guildford); those buying back properties to provide continued support for such uses, among others (Coventry, Ludlow, Wisbech); and those such as Bristol and Maidstone that bought local lands now on the market with the aim of establishing charitable foundations.[10] London made a special effort to ensure continued provision for the sick and poor, and secured the refoundation of its major hospitals and the creation of two new ones.[11] Other towns managed to save their hospitals, or to restore them after an interim; they may have been especially energetic when the hospital had been run by a civic guild. York's corporation purchased the former lands of the guild of St Christopher and St George, with which it had been closely identified, and leased those of the lesser guild of Corpus Christi, while Leicester, after nearly forty years, eventually secured property formerly belonging to town chantries, colleges and the Corpus Christi guild.[12]

Many of these developments were paralleled in Scotland, but within a different chronological and political framework. The Scottish Reformation was later than the English, and entailed more radical theological change within a short period. Although there were stirrings of reform in 1543, and evidence for some spread of Protestant teaching in the 1540s and 1550s, there was no major institutional or liturgical change until 1559–60. The political crisis of those years enabled a minority of committed reformers to frame a new ecclesiastical polity and to redefine the content and purpose of liturgy and observation in a way that had taken decades in England. Scottish townsmen and town governors played an important part in the process of religious Reformation.[13]

The Church had held an equally dominant position in Scottish urban society before the Reformation, and indeed the proportion of urban settlements primarily dependent on a religious house may have been greater. The larger towns, as in England, usually housed several convents, hospitals and friaries. There was no wholesale dissolution of monasteries in 1560: many of their resources were already substantially under the control of lay commendators, and the houses themselves were allowed to decline over a period. Their personnel were encouraged to take office in the reformed Church, but were not directly penalised for not doing so. Without support or new recruits, however, and with much of their former liturgical round proscribed, the decline in most cases was swift. In some cases a monastery church that had served the laity as well was taken over by the

[10] Scarisbrick, *Reformation and the English People*, pp. 114–15, 125–7.

[11] P. Slack, *Poverty and Policy in Tudor and Stuart England* (London, 1988), pp. 119, 69–72.

[12] Palliser, *Tudor York*, pp. 48–9, 239; Scarisbrick, *Reformation and the English People*, pp. 114–15, 131.

[13] J. Wormald, *Court, Kirk, and Community: Scotland 1470–1625* (Edinburgh, 1981), pp. 109–39.

local community, but for the most part they fell into ruin or were deliberately pulled down. The ambivalent position of the episcopate after 1560 meant that cathedral churches were also liable to decay, though that at Glasgow survived, thanks perhaps to the support of the town guilds.[14] The reforming legislation of 1560–1 abolished the mass and the observance of saints' days, and thus undermined the religious basis for many urban guilds and fraternities. Crafts like the hammermen of Edinburgh clung to the cult of saints, but they seem to have been more divided between Catholics and reformers than some of the other city guilds.[15] The hammermen of Aberdeen continued to claim rights over their altar in the town church after 1560, and more generally the craftsmen of that town resisted the loss of public and celebratory functions.[16]

Scotland was an even more emphatic example than England of a new collectivity of action to preserve resources and to establish a new ecclesiastical polity. Edinburgh's conservative council was deposed and replaced by a Protestant one in 1559, and, although there were divisions among the new men, the council played an active part in recovering resources for the reformed Church, establishing a poor hospital and supporting the town's ministers both morally and financially. Though some may have resisted reform at first, the craft guilds of Edinburgh came to play an important part in the 'trinity' of burgh government, along with council and kirk session.[17]

The extent to which the English people shared the views of prominent evangelicals and religious reformers and legislators has been one of the most disputed aspects of Reformation studies in recent years. The idea that Protestantism was the religion of the few, which they succeeded in imposing upon the many, has found wide support. In particular, it must be acknowledged that the evidence for enthusiasm for Protestant ideas and eagerness to implement liturgical and other changes may reflect only the attitudes of a small, if influential, minority within a larger community.[18] The part that town populations played in the process of reformation still lacks full documentation, though a more complex picture is emerging than the one which more or less equated urban residence with support for reformed ideas.[19]

[14] I. Cowan, *The Scottish Reformation* (London, 1982), p. 192.

[15] M. Lynch, ed., *The Early Modern Town in Scotland* (London, 1987), p. 27; M. Lynch, *Edinburgh and the Reformation* (Edinburgh, 1981), pp. 56–9.

[16] A. White, 'The impact of the Reformation on a burgh community; the case of Aberdeen', in Lynch, ed., *Early Modern Town*, pp. 89, 97–8.

[17] Lynch, *Edinburgh and the Reformation*, pp. 18, 34, 55–6.

[18] R. O'Day, *The Debate on the English Reformation* (London, 1986), pp. 102–32; C. Haigh, *English Reformations: Religion, Politics, and Society under the Tudors* (Oxford, 1993), pp. 285–95; D. M. Palliser, 'Popular reactions to the Reformation', in C. Haigh, ed., *The English Reformation Revised* (Cambridge, 1987), pp. 98–104. But cf. P. Marshall, ed., *The Impact of the English Reformation, 1500–1640* (London, 1997), p. 8.

[19] See R. Tittler, *The Reformation and the Towns in England* (Oxford, 1998).

It seems to be accepted that Protestantism was strong in London, in the urbanised South-East of England, and in many larger towns elsewhere, by the middle of the sixteenth century. Several circumstances facilitated the early success of reformed ideas among urban populations. The towns were specifically targeted by successive governments, in preaching campaigns and visitations; they probably had higher levels of general literacy than most rural communities, and certainly better access to printed and written works, both essential to the successful evangelisation of 'the religion of the book'. Some had direct contact, through their trading networks, with European centres of advanced Protestantism. Several (Sandwich, Canterbury, London, Norwich) were to have significant settlements of European religious refugees, whose congregational organisation served as a model for English reformers. While many towns had poor parishes and inadequately endowed clergy, some, especially in London, were wealthy and attracted able, educated clergy, trained at Oxford or Cambridge and in touch with developing theological and liturgical thought. By 1553 'pockets of informed Protestantism had certainly been planted in many towns', often those under the hand or eye of an active bishop or royal official.[20] London had Ridley; Bristol's clergy invited Latimer to preach in 1533; Exeter was influenced by its 'fervently Protestant' dean Simon Heynes.[21] The use of the pulpit to harangue urban populations may also have stirred up some of the more violent and disorderly aspects of the Reformation, including iconoclasm.[22]

Evidence for the spread and support for reformed ideas can be found for London, Norwich, Ipswich, Bristol and Coventry, and several smaller towns. The paradigm of commercialism and continental contact might be supported by the evidence for Protestantism in prosperous East Anglian towns, such as Colchester, Ipswich and Bury St Edmunds, which became 'organised centres of early and precocious reform' or the more rapid and widespread acceptance of reformed ideas in the port town of Hull than the small inland town of Leeds, though the latter did house a knot of Protestants.[23] Some contrast between urban and rural populations may also be drawn, for example in the South-West, where Catholic support declined more quickly in Exeter and towns like Totnes, which stood out against the (largely rural) prayer book rebels of 1549.[24]

[20] C. Cross, *Church and People, 1450–1660: The Triumph of the Laity in the English Church* (London, 1976), pp. 81–100.

[21] S. Brigden, *London and the Reformation* (Oxford, 1989), pp. 458–519; M. C. Skeeters, *Community and Clergy* (Oxford, 1993), pp. 38–46; R. Whiting, *The Blind Devotion of the People* (Cambridge, 1989), pp. 160–1.

[22] Cf. M. Aston, 'Iconoclasm: official and clandestine', in M. Aston, *Faith and Fire: Popular and Unpopular Religion, 1350–1600* (London, 1993), pp. 266–7, 276; S. Brigden, 'Youth and the English Reformation', in Marshall, ed., *The Impact of the English Reformation*, p. 71.

[23] Haigh, *English Reformations*, p. 197; P. Collinson, *The Birthpangs of Protestant England* (London, 1988), p. 38; C. Cross, 'The development of Protestantism in Leeds and Hull, 1520–1640', *NHist.*, 18 (1982), 230–8; Palliser, 'Popular reactions to the Reformation', p. 104.

[24] Whiting, *Blind Devotion*, pp. 46, 172–3.

However, evidence for Protestant beliefs or actions is usually paralleled by evidence for opposition to them, or at least for alternative views. Influential Protestants clashed with traditionalists in Bristol, Gloucester and Rye; townspeople continued to invoke the intercession of saints and prayers for the dead in their wills. The resistance of Exeter's mayor and aldermen to the prayer book rebels may have been motivated by respect for order rather than confessional enthusiasm. The Marian restoration of Catholic worship was observed as much in the towns as in the country.[25] Although there were several Protestant communities in small Yorkshire towns such as Beverley, Halifax, Rotherham and Wakefield, the North in general was slower to take on Protestant ideas and practices, and the city of York was one of the most conservative of urban centres in this respect. Priests continued to pray for the dead after the practice was declared superstitious; the city welcomed Mary's accession, and received news of Elizabeth's rather more coolly. The rulers of the city retained Catholic, or at least traditional, sympathies into the 1560s and 1570s, by which time the corporations of other leading towns were more thoroughly Protestant.[26] Nevertheless, though religious conservatives could probably be found in all urban communities, the view that the English Reformation met with quicker and fuller success in the towns seems to be justified. Over a longer period, too, the association of urban communities and governments with evangelical Protestantism and subsequently dissent becomes stronger, as those inspired by the ideology of the godly commonwealth acceded to civic power, and attempted to put their ideas into practice.

The historiography of the Reformation in Scotland has not separated urban and rural experiences to the same extent as in England, though most specific studies have been of urban communities. As with England, however, the new doctrines were better received both in the towns and in Lowland areas than in the countryside and especially the sparsely settled Highlands. Michael Lynch argues that 'the more Scotland's "urban Reformation" is studied, the more varied it has become': the influence of local lairds and active and vocal minorities within the towns helped to decide how quickly and how thoroughly the new structures were established.[27] For the burgesses of Aberdeen, the experience of the Reformation was bound up with the power struggle between burgh and local magnates, and between magnate families in the north-east; it is not clear that there was any widespread support for Protestant doctrine before an internal coup brought a 'Protestant sympathiser' to power in the burgh in 1560. The city

[25] Haigh, *English Reformations*, p. 198; Palliser, 'Popular reactions to the Reformation', pp. 103–5; Whiting, *Blind Devotion*, pp. 172–3; R. Hutton, *The Rise and Fall of Merry England* (Oxford, 1994) pp. 96–9.

[26] Palliser, 'Popular reactions to the Reformation', p. 104; Palliser, *Tudor York*, pp. 52–3, 242–4.

[27] M. Lynch, 'Preaching to the converted? Perspectives on the Scottish Reformation', in A. A. McDonald, M. Lynch and I. B. Cowan, eds., *The Renaissance in Scotland: Studies in Literature, Religion, History and Culture Offered to John Durkan* (Leiden, 1994), pp. 321–3.

continued to display a strongly Catholic character for a number of years. [28] There was some disorder and even violence during the crisis of 1559–60: the houses of friars were a particular target for 'reforming' mobs in Edinburgh, Perth, Stirling, St Andrews and Dundee. The more stable elements in urban societies, however, received the changes more cautiously.[29]

(ii) RELIGION AND URBAN SOCIETY, 1580–1700

The impact of the English and Scottish Reformations on the urban environment and the physical context of worship need not be further stressed. The effect on urban economies of the disappearance of the major religious houses, former customers for urban goods and services, centres for the redistribution of rural produce, and as attractors of religious tourism, must be set in the context of patterns of widespread and long-term economic change in the sixteenth century. The overall impact of the changes on urban corporations, however, and the status of the Church in towns after the Reformation, should be considered.

The attitudes of civic rulers played an important part in determining the character of urban religion and moral society in the later sixteenth and seventeenth centuries. Not all urban governments sought to establish a 'godly commonwealth' under their rule, but it is a widespread theme, in both contemporary and modern comment.[30] The image of the town or city as a model of human society seems to have had considerable rhetorical power. [31] The moral campaign was fought in day-to-day administration and discipline, as it was by all godly magistrates, but two areas in which civic corporations' activity was particularly noticeable were the promotion of the ministry and preaching, and the suppression of ungodly pursuits.

In the reformed Scottish Church, the creation of kirk sessions, with lay elders and deacons, who in many cases also sat on burgh councils, embodied the idea of a fully integrated religious and political society.[32] It would be wrong to take this too far, since in many burghs there may have been tension between the stricter interpreters of the new religion and its requirements and the more 'accommodating Protestant feeling' of pragmatic governors. Neither the elite nor the totality of Edinburgh government were wholly Protestant in the 1560s, but the identification was close. The deputy town clerk of Aberdeen was also bursar in civil law at King's College and a chaplain in the parish church from 1563. In a significant sense, the way in which the reformed Church evolved was

[28] White, 'Aberdeen', pp. 81–101.

[29] Cowan, *The Scottish Reformation*, p. 189; M. Lynch, 'The crown and the burghs', in Lynch, ed., *Early Modern Town*, p. 62.

[30] Cf. Clark and Slack, *English Towns in Transition*, pp. 150–1.

[31] Collinson, *Birthpangs of Protestant England*, pp. 28–32.

[32] G. Donaldson, 'Church and community', in G. Donaldson, *Scottish Church History* (Edinburgh, 1985), pp. 226–7.

conditioned by the traditions of burgh life: it owed its success to the support of burgh leaders, but it was itself shaped by the association. It took over something of the integrative function, in religion and culture, played by the medieval guild.[33] The campaign for reformation and moral and religious improvement in Scotland focused on the ministry, dependent in many cases on urban corporations for patronage and financial support. The urban endowments on which a number of chaplains and prebends had subsisted before the Reformation were assigned to support hospitals and schools, and, in the towns as in the country, parish revenues had to support old priests and new ministers.[34] The grant of former church lands and revenues to the burghs involved them intimately in the provision and payment of the ministry.[35]

Over the later sixteenth and early seventeenth centuries, the close relation of burgh council and kirk session continued, and it is impossible to think of Scottish urban society in this period without acknowledging the importance of the kirk. This close relation may have lain behind the burghs' enthusiastic support for the covenanting movement in the 1630s, responding to the threat posed to the Presbyterian polity by the religious policies of James VI/I and Charles I.[36] With episcopacy as a major issue in the Civil Wars in Scotland, and with campaigns focusing on the siege and capture of major cities, existing arrangements were liable to change, but the events may have encouraged doctrinaire Calvinistic Presbyterianism in burgh governments as it did in national political leadership. Certainly Aberdeen's council, once the Presbyterian party recovered power, continued to run the town's church before and after the Restoration, appointing and paying ministers,[37] and the final abolition of episcopacy left power in the hands of the coalition of kirk session and burgh council into the eighteenth century.

In England and Wales, a striking number of town governments saw it as their role as to establish a 'godly commonwealth', though the reasons for this were local rather than generic, and can usually be traced to the coincidence of individual enthusiasts, lay or clerical, in positions of power. Gloucester's religious and political radicalism in the Civil War, though clearly shaped by the city's social and economic problems, resulted from the dominance of municipal office by a small group of merchants and traders, sympathetic to Puritan ideas, from the 1590s; Dorchester was a relaxed and conservative small town before the

33 Lynch, *Edinburgh and the Reformation*, pp. 173, 175, 184–5, 216; White, 'Aberdeen', p. 88.
34 G. Donaldson, 'The parish clergy and the Reformation', in Donaldson, *Scottish Church History*, pp. 71–89.
35 Lynch, 'The crown and the burghs', p. 70.
36 Cf. D. Stevenson, 'The burghs and the Scottish Revolution', in Lynch, ed., *Early Modern Town*, p. 174.
37 C. R. Friedrichs, *The Early Modern City 1450–1750* (London, 1995), pp. 85–7, citing G. R. DesBrisay, 'Authority and discipline in Aberdeen, 1650–1700' (PhD thesis, University of St Andrews, 1989).

appointment of an inspiring Calvinist minister in 1605.[38] Nevertheless the structure of English urban government in the early modern period was often open to domination by self-perpetuating elites. It always relied on the willingness of the individual to shoulder office out of a sense of public obligation, and when these men were inspired also by the Puritan mission of moral reform, the opportunity and means were to hand. By the early seventeenth century, Puritan domination of urban corporations appears to have been widespread; even formerly conservative York was petitioning for extra preaching and sermons.[39]

Several urban corporations invested in purchasing the patronage of local churches, keen to take advantage of the opportunity that this offered for influencing the character of parochial worship.[40] At least sixteen town corporations had the patronage of urban livings in the seventeenth century, the mayor and aldermen of London having by then increased their four to nine or ten.[41] The significance of this depended, of course, on the outlook of the patron, but in general those who followed this course were seeking to establish a more advanced or preaching ministry. The corporation of Shrewsbury bought the advowson and impropriation of St Mary's from the crown in 1577, and hired a stipendiary curate, paying him substantially more for preaching a town lecture than for serving the cure; the rector of a Lincoln church in the seventeenth century attributed his appointment to 'the general vote of all the godly'.[42] Norwich's rulers bought up an advowson in 1630, presented a 'notorious' Puritan minister and supported his establishment of combination lectureships elsewhere in the city.[43] Bristol's rulers, however, appear to have represented a range of tastes in their appointments to the seven parishes acquired in 1627.[44]

Many municipalities also supported the establishment of lectureships. The corporation of Hull had shown their hostility to the town's conservative/Catholic incumbent by helping to ensure his deprivation at the beginning of Elizabeth's reign, and the institution of a preacher more to their taste; later

38 P. Clark, '"The Ramoth-Gilead of the Good": urban change and political radicalism at Gloucester 1540–1640', in J. Barry, ed., *The Tudor and Stuart Town* (London, 1990), pp. 244–73; D. Underdown, *Fire from Heaven* (London, 1992), pp. 7–26.

39 Cross, *Church and People*, pp. 157–8.

40 C. Hill, *Economic Problems of the Church of England* (Oxford, 1963), p. 54; Palliser, *Tudor York*, p. 229; Durston and Doran, *Princes, Pastors, and People*, p. 168; W. J. Sheils, 'Religion in provincial towns: innovation and tradition', in F. Heal and R. O'Day, eds., *Church and Society in England, Henry VIII to James I* (London, 1977), pp. 159–60.

41 Hill, *Economic Problems*, pp. 56–7, 245–74; H. G. Owen, 'The London parish clergy in the reign of Elizabeth I' (PhD thesis, University of London, 1957), pp. 238–95; D. A. Williams, 'Puritanism in city government, 1610–40', *Guildhall Miscellany*, 1(4) (1955), 3–14.

42 P. Seaver, *The Puritan Lectureships: The Politics of Religious Dissent, 1560–1662* (Stanford, Calif., 1970) p. 91; Hill, *Economic Problems*, p. 58.

43 J. F. Pound, *Tudor and Stuart Norwich* (Chichester, 1988), pp. 88–9.

44 D. H. Sacks, 'Bristol's "wars of religion"', in R. C. Richardson, ed., *Town and Countryside in the English Revolution* (Manchester, 1992), p. 114.

they instituted a lectureship as well.[45] Gloucester's Puritan magistrates invited and subsidised a Puritan preacher in 1598, and subsequently set up a twice-weekly lectureship which they similarly offered to committed Calvinists.[46] Voluntary or temporary arrangements were soon replaced by permanent endowments. Paul Seaver finds evidence for as many as seventy-four borough lectureships before 1640, of which at least fifty-two were controlled by the municipality, while Claire Cross suggests that 'almost all towns of any standing . . . had at least founded lecturing posts if they had not also set up parish lectureships'.[47]

A second aspect of the 'godly commonwealth' was the reform of public and private behaviour. This too has been the subject of some controversy: the idea that it was a specifically 'Puritan ideology' that led local elites to legislate officiously and extensively on the morality of the poorer members of their community has been questioned from several directions.[48] There is, however, adequate evidence that some urban rulers (corporations or justices, depending on local circumstances) in the later sixteenth and early seventeenth centuries saw the suppression of ungodly behaviour (drunkenness, profanity, sabbath-breaking) as an important item on their agenda.[49] Traditional activities, such as dancing, drama and popular pageantry began to decline in the face of magisterial opposition, whose hostility to ungodly pursuits was certainly enmeshed with concerns about public order. The gathering of people at plays, shows and fairs was seen as dangerous in itself, apart from the dubious nature of the activities in which they might participate.[50]

Municipal corporations thus played an important part in establishing the preaching ministry and in suppressing practices they regarded as Catholic, pagan or morally dangerous; in this, as in other matters, their aims began to conflict with those of central government in the 1620s and 1630s. The Caroline support for Arminianism ran directly counter to the views of Puritan municipalities, in England and even more markedly in Scotland, on the liturgy, the framework of worship and the proper observance of Sunday. In Worcester and Gloucester, a godly municipality clashed with a Laudian bishop and cathedral establishment;[51] in Norwich, Bishop Wren came into immediate conflict with a group of Puritan aldermen, supporters of lectures and opponents of Sunday recreations.[52] It

45 C. Cross, 'Protestantism in Leeds and Hull', *NHist.*, 18 (1982), 235.

46 Clark, '"The Ramoth-Gilead of the Good"', pp. 267–8.

47 Seaver, *Puritan Lectureships*, pp. 79–81, 90; Cross, *Church and People*, p. 157.

48 K. Wrightson and D. Levine, *Poverty and Piety in an English Village: Terling, 1525–1700* (London, 1979); M. Spufford, 'Puritanism and social control?', in A. Fletcher and J. Stevenson, eds., *Order and Disorder in Early Modern England* (Cambridge, 1985), pp. 41–57; M. Ingram, 'Reformation of manners in early modern England', in P. Griffiths, A. Fox, and S. Hindle, eds., *The Experience of Authority in Early Modern England* (London, 1996), pp. 47–88.

49 Ingram, 'Reformation of manners', p. 80.

50 Collinson, 'Puritanism as popular religious culture', p. 43.

51 Dyer, *Worcester*, pp. 233–4; Clark and Slack, *English Towns in Transition*, p. 151.

52 Pound, *Tudor and Stuart Norwich*, pp. 89–90.

would be wrong, however, to suppose that all involved in urban government were sympathetic to advanced Protestant ideas. In Norwich, Bristol and Coventry, Arminianism found some support among town councillors.[53] And by this time English 'Puritanism' had itself become more complex and divided, so that godly municipalities were beginning to be divided by faction, thus weakening their resistance to outside intervention.[54]

In the short term, the standing of the Church in England and Wales had been severely damaged by the Reformation. There can be little doubt that both the numbers and the incomes of urban clergy were seriously reduced. Many urban parishes had been abolished: York lost fifteen out of forty, Lincoln eighteen of thirty-four.[55] The dissolution of the chantries had a particularly severe impact on the towns, since chantry priests and conducts had been present in great numbers there, supplementing both liturgical performance and pastoral and educational care. Pre-Reformation London had had nearly 400 chantry priests, while rural Middlesex had only twenty or so. York had had over a hundred chantries, Bristol some forty-four; even a much smaller town like Worcester had eleven chantry priests in its ten parishes. In Exeter, where nineteen parish churches had maintained an additional mass-priest before the Reformation, few could by the reign of Elizabeth afford to support even a clerk or scholar, and most had no incumbent. Bristol's later sixteenth-century livings were poorer and less well served than before, and many could not be filled.[56]

Nor was the surviving ministry of high quality: there were simply not enough men with appropriate training and reliable views to staff the parishes of the Elizabethan Church. Urban parishes may have been in a particularly bad way, as their money incomes were undermined by inflation; the values of the Bristol livings declined markedly, and the educational attainments of their incumbents or curates appear to have done the same.[57] Reformers and counter-reformers had voiced so many criticisms of the clerical estate and of their functions, and had allowed their supporters to abuse groups and individuals, that it was difficult for the survivors to reassert their dignity and authority once the dust had settled.[58] In the Church of England, the pressing need for an educated and dedicated ministry was recognised by senior churchmen, and steps that would in time redress it were taken. By the later sixteenth century the qualifications and

[53] *Ibid.*; A. Hughes, 'Coventry and the English Revolution', in R. C. Richardson, ed., *Town and Countryside in the English Revolution* (Manchester, 1992), p. 76; D. H. Sacks, 'Bristol's "wars of religion"', p. 113. [54] *Ibid.*; Clark and Slack, *English Towns in Transition*, p. 151.

[55] Sheils, 'Religion in provincial towns', p. 160; Palliser, *Tudor York*, p. 240; M. Aston and J. Bond, *The Landscape of Towns* (Stroud, 1976), p. 110; Cross, *Church and People*, p. 92.

[56] C. J. Kitching, ed., *London and Middlesex Chantry Certificate* (London Record Society, 16, 1980), pp. xxv–xxvi; Palliser, *Tudor York*, p. 239; Dyer, *Worcester*, pp. 229–30; Whiting, *Blind Devotion*, p. 135; Skeeters, *Community and Clergy*, pp. 85, 98–104; Scarisbrick, *Reformation and the English People*, pp. 101–6. [57] Skeeters, *Community and Clergy*, pp. 93–121.

[58] Durston and Doran, *Princes, Pastors, and People*, p. 153.

quality of the parish clergy had risen again, and urban livings may have attracted a disproportionate number of this new cohort.[59]

The Scottish Church faced its own problems, in that for many years the old establishment and the new shared the revenues, and many incoming ministers had to subsist on very restricted endowments. There was also the common problem of a shortage of suitably qualified candidates for the ministry; the creation of lesser orders of the ministry was intended to supply the need for service without compromising the quality of the ministry itself. On the other hand, the Scottish Church may well have been inadequately staffed before the Reformation, and the situation was improved by the commitment of money from the Thirds of benefices to supporting reformed preachers, and by the important new role played by laymen in the community and discipline of the local church.[60]

After the upheavals of the Reformation years, no church or system of belief could command the English laity's universal support, but criticisms of the limited popular appeal of the Church established by the Elizabethan settlement underestimate the strength of conviction and attachment to it that developed over time. There may have been a reduction in churchgoing in the longer term, and in expanding cities, notably London, the provision of religious services did not meet the rising population, but there was still a high level of attendance and observance. The majority of contemporary commentators were not hostile to religion as such, only to particular kinds of churchmanship. The severest critics of the Elizabethan Church were not irreligious, but favoured further and more rigorous reform; and they found a strong following in urban congregations and corporations.

There is much evidence for the strength of belief and observance in English towns in the later sixteenth and early seventeenth centuries, and indeed of the popularity of advanced Protestant ideas, while always accepting that traditional and conservative views persisted in probably all communities. The geography of early reform was apparently repeated for acceptance of advanced Protestantism: London, the South-East and a number of provincial towns. The vestments controversy resulted in a large number of resignations or deprivations in London; the prophesyings or clerical conferences took place in Norwich, Northampton and other urban centres before they were banned in 1576.[61] Increased attention is also being paid now to the development of a popular Puritan culture in the later sixteenth and seventeenth centuries. Many traditional local and communal activities may have been suppressed or withered, but a new, secular civic culture, focused on the events of the Protestant calendar, began to establish itself, and

59 *Ibid.*, pp. 147–53.

60 G. Donaldson, *The Scottish Reformation* (Cambridge, 1960), pp. 68–72, 84–8.

61 *VCH*, London, I, pp. 309–11; Cross, *Church and People*, p. 138; Durston and Doran, *Princes, Pastors and People*, p. 149.

several aspects of advanced Protestant churchmanship, such as prayer meetings, catechising and collective fasts and sermons, can be seen as new cultural forms.[62]

One aspect of the townspeople's implementation of Protestant values may be singled out: their voluntary support for lectures and a preaching ministry. Town parishes and pulpits offered opportunities for itinerant preachers and lecturers to be heard. There were cathedral lectures in Canterbury, Carlisle, Exeter, London, Norwich, Winchester and York; whatever their tone (they were likely to be conformist, though not invariably so) they at least increased the variety and frequency of preaching which Protestants sought.[63] More directly, townsmen could buy in preachers of their choice with more advanced convictions. The 'Puritan lectureships' were largely an urban phenomenon. Several London parishes began supporting lecturers in Edward's reign, and citizens of other provincial centres were doing so in the reign of Elizabeth. Men of Coventry, where there had been some Marian persecutions, had by the summer of 1559 invited a preacher, a protégé of Bullinger, to proclaim the gospel to them, and were prepared to support him and his family 'generously'. Parish lectureships were usually the work of groups of lay persons, concerned to improve provision in their parish or neighbourhood; a similar desire prompted thirteen London parishes to buy their advowsons and appoint their own ministers.[64]

The reaction to Laudian Arminianism in the 1620s and 1630s shows how deeply internalised Calvinistic beliefs had become in England. Urban governments might be divided, but there seems to have been strong hostility among middling groups towards changes in liturgy and practice. Coventry gave Dr Prynne a hero's welcome, and Bristol's petition to the king in 1642 criticised the bishops and their activities.[65] The problem in the towns may indeed have been that religious enthusiasm, spilling out beyond the established Church, developed into advanced and separatist views in small congregations and gathered churches. London became a centre for such groups, from at least the 1560s, and Coventry was a home of Presbyterianism under Elizabeth, but the movement had limited success before the end of the century. Separatist and Anabaptist congregations were, however, established in Coventry, Lincoln, Salisbury and elsewhere, especially in East Anglia, in the early seventeenth century, perhaps borrowing ideas and inspiration from the settlements of Dutch and French refugees.[66] By 1640 a Bristol congregation had decided formally to separate from the established Church; it was followed by others in Norwich and London.[67]

[62] D. Cressy, *Bonfires and Bells: National Memory and the Protestant Calendar in Elizabethan and Stuart England* (London, 1989); Collinson, *Birthpangs of Protestant England*, pp. 94–126; Collinson, 'Puritanism as popular religious culture', pp. 46–56.

[63] Seaver, *Puritan Lectureships*, pp. 76–7.

[64] Cross, *Church and People*, pp. 133–4, 153–9.

[65] Pound, *Tudor and Stuart Norwich*, pp. 89–90; Hughes, 'Coventry', pp. 75–6; Sacks, 'Bristol's "wars of religion"', pp. 110–13.

[66] Cross, *Church and People*, pp. 138–52, 170; Durston and Doran, *Princes, Pastors and People*, p. 111.

[67] C. Cross, 'The Church in England, 1646–60', in G. E. Aylmer, ed., *The Interregnum: The Quest for Settlement, 1646–1660* (London, 1972), pp. 102, 116.

The Civil Wars offered new opportunities for reshaping religious observance and culture. The reformed Church had a firmer grip on Scottish society, and inspired strong resistance to the imposition of the English prayer book in 1637 (beginning with the demonstration in Edinburgh's town church of St Giles), and a continued commitment to extending its own polity and principles to England and Wales during the 1640s.[68] Following the adoption of the Solemn League and Covenant, bishops and religious collegiate bodies were abolished in England, and a new Directory of Public Worship replaced the prayer book. The former move obviously affected all English cathedral towns, undermining a key feature of their identity and dispersing an important group of consumers.[69] The Church in towns, as in the countryside, was purged of unacceptable doctrines and ministers. However, the attempt to impose the Presbyterian Classical system was not wholly successful, even in the capital, in the face of the diversity of religious belief and expression which had been liberated by the Civil War.[70] In several towns, like Coventry, the events of the 1640s allowed 'orthodox Puritanism' to flourish. The city became a 'second Geneva', integrating a godly magistracy and a moderate Presbyterian ministry, cooperating with respectable Independency. Though there were divisions over the details of policy, there was support for the Protector's liberal view of the Church's polity, and the extreme radical sects could gain no foothold there.[71] Independent congregations are noted in many provincial towns, though they may have been small to start with, such as the nine who founded the Canterbury congregation in 1645. Three general Baptist churches met in London in 1641, and seven London Particular Baptist churches existed in 1644.[72] In Bristol, however, the pre-war dominance of a moderate Calvinism had not prevented the establishment of separate churches, and in 1654 the city was riven by the rapid rise of the Quakers, leading to renewed political dissension. Coventry may have seen itself as a Geneva, but Nayler's 1656 entry constructed Bristol as Jerusalem.[73]

The Restoration Church of England made little attempt to accommodate the moderate Presbyterian and independent churches that had flourished within the framework of the state Church during the Interregnum. The towns in general, and their Puritan representatives in particular, were punished for their part in the Civil Wars. The legislation of the Cavalier parliament excluded nonconformists from urban government and forced congregations into hiding or out of town, and the church settlement was carried through by a reinvigorated

[68] B. Coward, *The Stuart Age*, 2nd edn (London, 1994), pp. 178–80, 213–14, 224–8.

[69] Cf. e.g. A. Rosen, 'Winchester in transition, 1580–1700', in P. Clark, ed. *Country Towns in Pre-Industrial England* (Leicester, 1981), p. 167.

[70] Cross, 'The Church in England, 1646–60', pp. 103, 107–11; Tai Liu, *Puritan London: A Study of Religion and Society in the City Parishes* (Newark, N.J., 1986), pp. 51–102.

[71] Hughes, 'Coventry', pp. 80–92.

[72] R. J. Acheson, *Radical Puritans in England, 1550–1660* (London, 1990), pp. 45–60.

[73] Sacks, 'Bristol's "wars of religion"', pp. 120–1; Acheson, *Radical Puritans*, p. 72.

episcopate.[74] The political importance of religion, and of popular religious culture, was by no means at an end, however: anti-popery was a feature of both national culture and and urban popular politics in the later seventeenth century.[75] It is clear that nonconformist congregations were submerged, not suppressed, by the Restoration. After 1689 they were free to establish churches openly, and with a further influx of Protestant religious refugees from France, London and other urban centres supported a proliferation of independent churches. Tory anxiety about the strength of nonconformity in London estimated the number of dissenters at 100,000 in the early eighteenth century; though this is clearly an exaggeration, the true number may have been over 40,000, with 74 dissenting congregations noted in the capital.[76]

(iii) EDUCATION AND LITERATE CULTURE

The higher literacy of urban populations may have contributed to their reception of reformed teachings in the early and mid-sixteenth century, and education and educational opportunity remained an important feature of British towns in the later sixteenth and seventeenth centuries. Some aspects of the production and dissemination of literate culture were necessarily urban, though the difference between metropolitan and provincial urban experience was much more marked than, for example, their experiences of Protestantism or dissent. London contained perhaps 10 per cent of England's population by the end of the seventeenth century, and a still more disproportionate amount of its wealth and literacy. If the specialisation of economic activity is to some extent a function of urban size, it is not surprising that, at least up to the end of the seventeenth century, so much educational opportunity and literate culture were concentrated in the capital.

In England, the decline of 'pious benefaction' with the Reformation, and the diversion of funds to educational and charitable uses, have been charted by W. K. Jordan, and the view of an 'educational revolution' following the Reformation examined by Lawrence Stone.[77] A number of urban schools, run by or associated with religious houses and chantry or guild foundations, fell with the dissolutions, and the elementary teaching provided by some chantry priests

[74] Hughes, 'Coventry', pp. 93–5; Cross, 'The Church in England, 1646–60', p. 120; J. Spurr, 'From Puritanism to dissent, 1660–1700', in Durston and Eales, eds., *The Culture of English Puritanism*, pp. 234–65; J. R. Jones, *Country and Court, England 1658–1714* (London, 1978), pp. 145–55.

[75] Cressy, *Bonfires and Bells*, pp. 171–89; T. Harris, *London Crowds in the Reign of Charles II* (Cambridge, 1987).

[76] M. Port, ed., *The Commissions for Building Fifty New Churches* (London Record Society, 23, 1986), p. ix.

[77] W. K. Jordan, *Philanthropy in England, 1480–1660: A Study of the Changing Pattern of English Social Aspirations* (New York, 1959); L. Stone, 'The educational revolution in England, 1560–1640', *P&P*, 28 (1964), 41–80.

must also have declined. The crown's direct provision for schools fell far short of what had been hoped or promised, and for the next generation, there may well have been a serious loss of educational opportunity. However, the value of education was widely recognised, and communities that lost schools were quick to petition for their restoration. At least twenty-six town guild or chantry schools had been re-endowed by 1553, and Mary also encouraged refoundations.[78]

It is difficult to separate out the actions of private individuals or groups, and civic initiatives, both in the Reformation period and later, but towns and townsmen continued to found and support schools and educational opportunities through the reign of Elizabeth and in the early seventeenth century. Local studies demonstrate the importance of towns as sponsors and consumers of schooling. In two archdeaconries of Stafford and Salop (Lichfield diocese), all twenty-five market towns had either a grammar or town school or some evidence of teaching; more than half the schools in Coventry archdeaconry were in market towns, and all were grammar schools. Although some schools such as Shrewsbury became famous and attracted sons of the gentry from far away, and all tended to draw on the surrounding rural population, town schools were very substantially a resource for the children of well-to-do townsmen.[79] By the later seventeenth century private charity and private enterprise schools were widely available in larger towns and in and around the metropolis. The continued growth of the capital, at the expense of the rest of the country, meant that it focused a large demand for education: in 1704 there were fifty-four charity schools there. Girls' boarding schools were perhaps particularly a feature of London and larger towns.[80]

The Scottish reformers explicitly recognised the importance of education to the creation of their new society, and called on town councils, among others, to provide for it from their own revenues or the appropriated revenues of the Church. Although local education was favoured, town schools were expected to provide a higher level of instruction, including grammar and Latin.[81] The burghs had long been providers or sponsors of education, but the new emphasis put them at the front of the Church's campaign to educate and reform Scottish society, and in the short term the provision and quality of urban schooling seems to have been much more successful than that in rural areas. There were grammar schools in many Scottish towns in the late sixteenth and seventeenth centuries, and some burgh councils played an active role in running local schools. Education was thus a key feature of Scottish urban society in the later sixteenth

[78] Scarisbrick, *Reformation and the English People*, pp. 111–19.

[79] R. O'Day, *Education and Society, 1500–1800: The Social Foundations of Education in Early Modern Britain* (London, 1982), pp. 30, 35–8.

[80] J. Sharpe, *Early Modern England: A Social History, 1550–1760* (London, 1987), pp. 273–6; O'Day, *Education and Society*, pp. 196–216.

[81] Wormald, *Court, Kirk, and Community*, pp. 181–2.

and seventeenth centuries; the Scottish universities, located in the major towns, contributed more to the character of urban culture in Scotland than did Oxford and Cambridge for England.[82]

The higher literacy of urban populations was both a cause and a consequence of the flourishing educational opportunities in towns. Literacy rates are notoriously difficult to measure, and their interpretation, for the consumption of literate culture, is contested. It seems accepted, however, that there was both a significant general increase over the sixteenth and seventeenth centuries and a noticeable bias in favour of London. Literacy among male Londoners was perhaps double that of rural males by 1640; literacy in other urban centres probably fell somewhere between the two, though there was wide regional variation.[83] The capital may also have attracted those who had already benefited from a provincial education: women who migrated to London in the later seventeenth century were more literate than those who stayed at home.[84] Rural education in Scotland was targeted for improvement by the reformers in the sixteenth century, but a rural–urban literacy differential was still noticeable in the seventeenth. In later seventeenth- and eighteenth-century Edinburgh, the urban male was more likely to be literate than the suburban, and the suburban than the rural. The evidence suggests an already high literacy rate in 1660s Edinburgh, improving quite sharply by the end of the century.[85]

In England, printing was monopolised by the London Stationers' Company, and London, as a huge concentration of population with, as noted above, higher average literacy than elsewhere, formed a ready market for their products. Higher metropolitan and urban wages must have contributed to demand.[86] Petty chapmen certainly purveyed print to the localities, but booksellers, largely urban, were a key point in the distribution network.[87] Booksellers were established in provincial towns such as Canterbury, Cambridge and Shrewsbury in the

[82] O'Day, *Education and Society*, pp. 217–37.

[83] D. Cressy, *Literacy and the Social Order: Reading and Writing in Tudor and Stuart England* (Cambridge, 1980), pp. 72, 168–71; J. Barry, 'Literacy and literature in popular culture: reading and writing in historical perspective', in T. Harris, ed., *Popular Culture in England, c. 1500–1850* (London, 1995), pp. 75–7.

[84] Sharpe, *Early Modern England*, p. 270; P. Earle, 'The female labour market in London in the late seventeenth and early eighteenth century', *Ec.HR*, 2nd series, 42 (1989), 334. Cf. R. A. Houston, 'The development of literacy in northern England, 1640–1750', *Ec.HR*, 2nd series, 35 (1982), 199–216.

[85] O'Day, *Education and Society*, p. 229; R. A. Houston, 'Literacy, education, and the culture of print in Enlightenment Edinburgh', *History*, 78 (1993), pp. 376–7. Cf. R. A. Houston, *Literacy in Early Modern Europe: Culture and Education, 1500–1800* (London, 1988).

[86] Cf. P. Burke, 'Popular culture in seventeenth-century London', *LJ*, 3 (1977), 154–7.

[87] M. Spufford, *Small Books and Pleasant Histories* (Cambridge, 1981); T. Watt, 'Piety in the pedlar's pack: continuity and change, 1578–1630', in Marshall, ed., *The Impact of the English Reformation*, pp. 308–42.

later sixteenth and early seventeenth century, though local gentry may also have made direct purchases from London and from travelling chapmen.[88] Bookselling and printselling appear among urban occupations, especially from the later seventeenth century, while bookbinders offered an additional service. By 1705 there were said to be 300 booksellers in the provinces.[89]

The potential influence of print on political and religious culture was quickly recognised, with episcopal supervision and licensing. The early output of the presses included a large number of religious works, both liturgical and didactic; though some reformers may have been wary of allowing unmediated access to religious writings, it is clear that the vernacular Bible and works such as Foxe's *Book of Martyrs* achieved wide circulation and were very instrumental in creating an informed Protestant consciousness.[90] These may have had a specific, educated audience in mind, but a significant proportion (between 30 per cent and 50 per cent) of ballads, aimed at a popular audience, registered at Stationers Hall between 1560 and 1590 were 'godly' or moralising. This must have contributed both to the dissemination of a reformed or Protestant culture and also to the spread of metropolitan influence to other towns and the countryside, though it is clear that the influence was two-way, in that London stationers responded to demand and tailored their output accordingly.[91] Seventeenth-century chapbooks included satires on rural ignorance, presumably targeted at a knowing urban audience.[92] The political turmoil of the mid-seventeenth century liberated publishing from effective censorship and saw an explosion of demand and supply. George Thomason was a London bookseller, and his collection of over 18,000 tracts published between 1640 and 1655 (and 3,000 published between 1655 and 1660) indicates both the vigour of metropolitan demand and the capacity of the industry to meet it. Pamphlet distribution was probably geographically wider, but the vast bulk of the output of the presses must have circulated in the capital. Oblique testimony to the range of printed works available to a Londoner of modest means is given by Nehemiah Wallington's notebooks, which include

[88] L. Stevenson, *Praise and Paradox: Merchants and Craftsmen in Elizabethan Popular Literature* (Cambridge, 1984), pp. 67–8. T. Watt, *Cheap Print and Popular Piety, 1550–1640* (Cambridge, 1991), pp. 315–16.

[89] See e.g. J. Pound, 'The social and trade structure of Norwich, 1525–75', in P. Clark, ed., *The Early Modern Town* (London, 1976), pp. 141, 143; D. V. Glass, 'Socio-economic status and occupations in the city of London at the end of the seventeenth century', in *ibid.*, pp. 225–6; Rosen, 'Winchester', p. 177. The figure for provincial booksellers is quoted by P. Borsay, 'The Renaissance of provincial urban culture, c. 1680–1760', in P. Borsay, ed., *The Eighteenth Century Town* (London, 1990), p. 167.

[90] Barry, 'Literacy and literature', pp. 78–9; cf. M. Ingram, 'From Reformation to toleration: popular religious cultures in England, 1540–1690', in Harris, ed., *Popular Culture in England*, p. 103.

[91] Watt, *Cheap Print and Popular Piety*, pp. 8, 39–73, 322; cf. R. Cust, 'News and politics in early seventeenth-century England', *P&P*, 112 (1986), 60–90, which also stresses the central role of London.

[92] Spufford, *Small Books and Pleasant Histories*, pp. 51–4.

many abstracts from and commentaries on printed materials which must have passed through his hands between *c.* 1620 and 1654.[93]

In the later seventeenth century towns were beginning to increase the range of consumer goods they offered to a leisured, educated class, and among these were books, prints and other printed material. Again, the capital may have offered exceptional opportunities to the book-collector. Pepys was able to collect chapbooks, prints and pamphlets in the early 1660s, though his main collecting period, when he was seeking to build up a library of 3,000 books, came later, and was not solely focused on London sources. Even a more modest collector, Daniel Thomas (d. 1704), a mercer, had 890 books and atlases, though it is unlikely that all his fellows among London's mercantile society were so well provided.[94]

The late seventeenth century also saw the growth of printed works specifically catering to urban needs and tastes: newspapers, directories and guidebooks. The earliest London directory, dating from 1677, listed the names of merchants, information rendered 'very useful and necessary' by the growth in commercial and financial business after the Restoration.[95] Edward Lloyd's coffee-house in Lombard Street was well placed to garner verbal news, but it was his weekly printed broadsheet of shipping news, first appearing in 1692, that marked it out.[96] London newspaper publishing took off after the relaxation of controls in 1695, and from the early years of the eighteenth century titles and circulation flourished. [97] In all these areas, however, late seventeenth-century growth must be seen as the precursor to much more significant development in the eighteenth century. Likewise, as provincial towns and cities began to grow more rapidly, the range of cultured and educated services they provided increased, and the pre-eminence of London in these fields began to be diluted.[98]

(iv) CHANGING SECULAR CULTURE IN EARLY MODERN URBAN SOCIETY

Between 1540 and 1700, English, Welsh and, arguably to a lesser degree, Scottish urban society became more secular, though it would be wrong to overestimate

93 G. Fortescue, *Catalogue of the Pamphlets, Books etc. Collected by George Thomason, 1640–61* (London, 1906); P. S. Seaver, *Wallington's World* (London, 1985), pp. 199–202.

94 Watt, *Cheap Print and Popular Piety*, pp. 267–8; R. Latham, *The Illustrated Pepys: Extracts from the Diary* (London, 1978), p. 11; P. Earle, *The Making of the English Middle Class* (London, 1989), pp. 295–6.

95 P. J. Corfield, ' "Giving directions to the town": the early town directories', *UHY* (1984), 24.

96 V. Harding and P. Metcalf, *Lloyd's at Home: The Background and the Buildings* (London, 1985), p. 75.

97 R. Porter, *London: A Social History* (London, 1994), p. 170.

98 This view is implicit in Borsay, 'The Renaissance of provincial urban culture', and P. Borsay, *The English Urban Renaissance* (Oxford, 1989).

the extent to which this happened.[99] Religion still played a very important part in the lives of most townspeople, but it was no longer the unifying cultural force it had been before the Reformation.[100] The traditional foci of urban association in the middle ages had been parish church, confraternity and guild. These were central elements in urban identity, whether of the individual or of the urban centre itself. Religious confraternities disappeared with the Reformation, and the meaning and importance of parish worship and guild membership changed. The following 150 years saw the emergence of new forms and occasions, shaped by their predecessors but also by the changing needs and pressures of urban life. Metropolitan society again exhibited these developments sooner and in a more marked degree than the provincial English towns and cities, while the institutionalised control that the Church had over Scottish urban society limited the scope for much change before the eighteenth century.

Although the growth of dissent is itself evidence of the continuing force of religion in the lives of townspeople, it also helped to undermine one of the traditional bases of urban religious life, the focus on the community of the parish. The comprehensive and sufficient nature of parochial worship was a central principle of the Elizabethan settlement. Both separatism and congregationalism were based on a fundamentally different organisational principle, involving self-selection and withdrawal from a wider collectivity. The principle was, obviously, divisive: its adherents rejected the idea that physical neighbours would necessarily be co-religionists, let alone co-worshippers. The system of gathered churches transcended territorial boundaries, and helped to dissolve the sense of close identification of multiple interests with the area of residence. By the end of the seventeenth century, religion had 'ceased to be something that could be taken for granted', and had become 'a matter for choice and commitment'.[101] To some extent this was paralleled within the established Church in Scotland: an important aspect of the Presbyterian polity was the fragmentation of burgh communities, many of which had been focused on a single town parish. 'Model' parishes of committed congregations were carved out of the larger whole, with the avowed aim of increasing the quality of provision but with the effect of dividing the hitherto unified religious community of the burgh.[102]

The urban parish in England and Wales gained a new role, however, with the responsibilities for poor relief which it handled from 1598 (London, and some other large towns, had instituted parish-based poor relief schemes before that date).[103] To some extent this revived the idea of the parish as a miniature commonwealth, in which the wealth of some contributed to the welfare of others, and promoted reciprocal interactions between members of the parish

[99] Cf. C. G. Brown, 'Did urbanization secularize Britain?', *UHY* (1988), 1–14, focusing on the nineteenth century. [100] Cf. Ingram, 'From Reformation to toleration', pp. 97–9.

[101] *Ibid.*, p. 99. [102] Lynch, ed., *Early Modern Town*, p. 28.

[103] Slack, *Poverty and Policy*, pp. 122–9.

community. It may also have reinforced a sense of the bounds and membership of the community, as the concepts of eligibility and entitlement were more clearly articulated. On the other hand, a situation in which relief was distributed at the discretion of a parish elite hardly promoted the real sociability of the pre-Reformation parish. The English vestry had less far-reaching authority than the Scottish kirk session, but in both cases their moral and supervisory functions may have encouraged the formation of a group consciousness. The regular and at times celebratory meetings of the body fulfilled a social, and sociable, purpose as well as a business one.[104]

Guilds, like parishes, lost an important part of their function with the Reformation and the loss of chantry endowments and commemorations. They also began to lose control of urban economic life, either through a too-rigid attitude in changing circumstances or an inability to control large flows of people and activities. In the mid-sixteenth century, the migration of young men to take up apprenticeships with the city companies was a major component of all migration to the capital; by the later seventeenth century its importance had declined markedly. Entries to the freedom were continuing to fall to the end of the seventeenth century and beyond, even as the capital continued to expand.[105] The greater guilds and companies, with less interest in the control of trade and manufacture, exercised strong social discipline over members in the sixteenth century, but also offered a focus for loyalty and sociability.[106] In the seventeenth century they built on this latter aspect of their activities, reinventing themselves as charitable and educational trusts with regular occasions for celebratory dining.[107]

Guild life could also be reinvented through the private associations, clubs and friendly societies which began to appear in provincial towns and more noticeably in London from the later seventeenth century. Jonathan Barry has recently argued for the importance of such associations among the urban middling sort in the sixteenth and seventeenth centuries, though their visibility in the historical record was limited before the spread of newspaper reporting in the eighteenth century.[108] Exactly the same problem – that informal, subscription-based

[104] Vestry and wardmote dinners were noted, and sometimes criticised: I. W. Archer, *The Pursuit of Stability* (Cambridge, 1991), pp. 73, 95; V. Pearl, 'Change and stability in seventeenth-century London', in J. Barry, ed., *The Tudor and Stuart Town* (London, 1990), p. 161.

[105] S. Rappaport, *Worlds within worlds*, pp. 76–86; M. Kitch, 'Capital and kingdom: migration to later Stuart London', in A. L. Beier and R. Finlay, eds., *London 1500–1700* (London, 1986), p. 226; J. R. Kellett, 'The breakdown of guild and corporation control over the handicraft and retail trade in London', *Ec.HR*, 2nd series, 10 (1957–8), 381–94.

[106] Rappaport, *Worlds*, pp. 215–73; Archer, *Pursuit of Stability*, pp. 100–48.

[107] Cf. W. Herbert, *The History of the Twelve Great Livery Companies of London* (London, 1834–7), *passim*.

[108] J. Barry, 'Bourgeois collectivism? Urban association and the middling sort', in J. Barry and C. Brooks, eds., *The Middling Sort of People* (London, 1994), pp. 92–3.

associations are much less well recorded than those that held property or obtained legal status, and therefore much more likely to be underestimated – occurs in the middle ages.[109] Urban life, no less challenging in the early modern period than before or later, encouraged individuals to participate in collective activity as a conscious creation of identity and continuity for themselves and their society. Barry notes many continuities, of language, form and ideology, from older civic associations. This may have been the result of conscious modelling, even appropriation, for the purposes of legitimation, but the conditions of urban life also encouraged new associations to adopt similar practices and values to the old. Public processions, calendar commemoration, collective dining were as much a feature of new charitable bodies as of civic guilds and parish fraternities. Shared values included mutual support, obedience to a collective good and sociability itself. 'Participation in established bodies like guilds, churches, or local government was not so sharply differentiated from "voluntary" participation in other associations as we might expect; both expressed involvement in civil society.'[110]

A central theme of recent writing on the Reformation and its effects is the disappearance of communal festivity and calendar celebrations.[111] Protestant reformers were responsible for a strong attack on such practices, and although they were not immediately successful in eliminating them all, it was the beginning of a long campaign of attrition, in which godly municipalities played an important part. Civic processions and celebrations with an overtly religious theme, such as the Corpus Christi processions, were lost with the Elizabethan settlement; Corpus Christi play cycles, purged of their religious content, lasted longer, but most had disappeared by the end of the century.[112] Elizabeth's government, on the whole, was not hostile to such manifestations; it was local authorities, concerned with order or imbued by Puritan views, who really determined the rate of decline. Uncertainty about what was appropriate or permissible may have helped to stifle a wide range of practices, but Puritan writers condemned dancing, Sunday sports and other activities, giving sympathetic civic officials the inspiration and justification they required. Gloucester Puritans suppressed the maypole in 1618; a few evangelical Protestants in positions of power succeeded in putting down the plays in York, Coventry and Kendal, despite popular opposition.[113]

Civic ritual did not die immediately. Godly corporations, which after all had

109 C. M. Barron, 'The parish fraternities of medieval London', in C. M. Barron and C. Harper-Bill, eds., *The Church in Pre-Reformation Society* (Woodbridge, 1985), pp. 13–37.

110 Barry, 'Bourgeois collectivism?', p. 103.

111 D. Underdown, *Revel, Riot, and Rebellion: Popular Politics and Culture in England, 1603–1660* (Oxford, 1985), pp. 68–72; Hutton, *Merry England*, p. 111.

112 Underdown, *Revel, Riot, and Rebellion*, p. 69; Hutton, *Merry England*, pp. 115–21.

113 Clark, 'The "Ramoth-Gilead of the Good"', p. 268; Hutton, *Merry England*, pp. 126–8, 137–41.

something to gain from orderly civic ritual, did not target it, but the combination of expense, and doubts about the way it might be used or interpreted, contributed to what seems like an inexorable decline. The marching watch, a procession involving the whole citizenry, was suppressed in London in 1539, ostensibly for reasons of expense and order, and had been abandoned by many other towns by 1600. York developed a Midsummer Watch, perhaps partly to compensate for the loss of other civic pageantry, but even this did not last long. The public processions (including royal entries, see Plate 7) that did survive the sixteenth century were mostly suspended during the Civil War.[114] London's Lord Mayor's Show took on some of the attributes, and indeed the pageants, of the Midsummer Watch, but it increasingly focused on the glories of the mayoralty and the company to which the new incumbent belonged; it could no longer be seen as a ritual integrating the whole civic community. The sophisticated Pepys dismissed the pageants of the 1663 Lord Mayor's Show as 'poor and absurd', even 'silly'.[115] Inauguration rituals were still a feature of many corporate towns in the later seventeenth century, in many cases with feasting, and a number of new calendar customs and anniversaries were invented and celebrated, attracting some genteel interest, but the sense that this was a crucial and defining moment of the civic year and the town's identity had faded.[116]

Traditional dramatic celebrations were succeeded by two different phenomena, the early commercial theatre and genteel entertainments and social events. The commercial theatre flourished in London from the opening of the first playhouse in 1567, with a proliferation of theatre openings on the south bank in the 1590s. Like the alehouse, the theatre was feared and condemned by godly magistrates as a source of disorder, or at least of dangerous social mixing, and specifically as a possible competitor to churchgoing.[117] Nevertheless, it was enormously popular, as the calculations of audience size suggest, until the closure of the theatres in 1642, though arguably public taste had turned away from the drama by the 1630s, either towards the private theatres and Court masques, or to ruder pleasures such as bearbaiting.[118] No provincial city had the audience to sustain the long seasons of the large open-air theatres of the metropolis, but the smaller post-Restoration playhouses appeared both in the capital and

114 Hutton, *Merry England*, pp. 121, 202.

115 M. Berlin, 'Civic ceremony in early modern London, *UHY* (1986), 15–27; S. Williams, 'The Lord Mayor's Show in Tudor and Stuart times', *Guildhall Miscellany*, 1(10) (1959), 15–16.

116 Cressy, *Bonfires and Bells*; P. Borsay, '"All the town's a stage": urban ritual and ceremony 1600–1800', in P. Clark, ed., *The Transformation of English Provincial Towns 1600–1800* (London, 1984), pp. 231–2; P. J. Corfield, 'A provincial capital in the late seventeenth century: the case of Norwich', in Clark, ed., *Early Modern Town*, p. 255.

117 R. Ashton, 'Popular entertainment and social control in later Elizabethan and early Stuart London', *LJ*, 9 (1983), 5–8.

118 *Ibid*., 6–9; A. Gurr, *Playgoing in Shakespeare's London* (Cambridge, 1987), pp. 13–44, 183–91; M. Butler, *Theatre and Crisis, 1632–42* (Cambridge, 1984).

in provincial cities, offering a different kind of dramatic experience to a more genteel audience. Norwich had a 'miniature winter season' with theatres and shows. Public concerts of classical music, including concert cycles or seasons, also found first in London, had appeared in several provincial towns by the early eighteenth century.[119] The shift from popular public spectacle to events aimed at a more restricted audience is demonstrated in Chester, where traditional plays and popular entertainments were curtailed in the sixteenth century, to be replaced by new festivities focused on the county elite such as horse racing. Peter Borsay has traced a significant growth in the number of race meetings held in the later sixteenth and early seventeenth centuries, followed by a second and more substantial boom between 1680 and 1730. [120]

If traditional urban identities were weakened as a result of religious change and the growth of dissent, and some new institutions were created to complement the social function of parish, guild and ward, urban sociability was by no means confined to organised meetings and societies, or to the elite. Inns already provided a significant venue for plays and entertainments in the sixteenth century. The number of alehouses grew markedly in the late sixteenth and early seventeenth centuries, paralleling, Peter Clark has argued, the decline of churchgoing and religious observance. Alehouses offered a locus for neighbourly *rencontre* and informal association, renewing the bonds of local community, in a way that parish celebrations and after-church meetings may have done formerly. They were in direct competition with the church for clients if they opened on Sundays, one reason for the hostility of godly magistrates.[121] While they were widely spread across the country, they clustered more densely in towns than in the countryside, and more densely still in the capital. In London they were most numerous in the suburbs, where church provision and traditional social relations were both weaker than in the centre. Westminster had 551 common alehouses in 1631; there were 228 in Southwark and Kentish Street. Of 924 licensed alehouses in the city of London in 1657, the greatest densities were in the extramural wards of Portsoken and Faringdon without. London was also well served with taverns (over 400 in 1618), again notably clustered in the inner suburbs.[122] Those areas were arguably one of the loci for significant social change and the evolution of a metropolitan (rather than a civic) culture, a process in which the alehouse could have played an important part.

Provincial alehouses provided an important point of contact between local

[119] W. van Lennep, ed., *The London Stage, 1660–1800*, Part 1: *1660–1700* (Carbondale, Ill, 1975); Borsay, *English Urban Renaissance*, pp. 117–27; Corfield, 'A provincial capital', pp. 254–5.

[120] Underdown, *Revel, Riot, and Rebellion*, p. 69; S.-B. MacLean, 'Drama and ceremony in early modern England', *UHY* (1989), 43; Borsay, *English Urban Renaissance*, pp. 180–96.

[121] P. Clark, *The English Alehouse* (London, 1983), pp. 151–60.

[122] *Ibid.*, pp. 44–53; Ashton, 'Popular entertainment', 10–11.

communities and national communications networks.[123] In town as well as country, alehouses combined something of the function of a traditional local community centre with the provision of new-style entertainments and opportunities in a relatively uncontrolled environment. They offered attractions in the form of songs and music, opportunities for sexual encounters, public shows and games, as well as drink. Football and bowling-alleys, and 'new-type indoor games', including dicing, cards, and board-games became popular. These were often seen by conservatives and religious puritans alike as dangerous pastimes, ungodly in themselves and tending to oust traditional skills and practices such as archery.[124] Taverns and alehouses also often served as meeting places for the new social gatherings noted above, such as journeymen's clubs and friendly societies, further integrating old and new social practices.[125]

(v) CONCLUSION

Religion remained an important social and cultural force in early modern towns, but its role had changed. In England and Wales, by the later seventeenth century, the Church was no longer a binding and comprehensive organisation, which all belonged to or at least respected, and through which a wide range of social and cultural experiences could be shared. Martin Ingram has argued that the effect of the sixteenth- and seventeenth-century changes, culminating in the Toleration Act of 1689, was to create 'a distinctively different context in which popular religious cultures would henceforth be shaped'.[126] This argument could be extended more widely, given the dominance of religious belief and practice in late medieval and early modern thought and culture. Nevertheless, continuities between old and new forms of association and sociability should not be underestimated. Nor should continuities between the early and the later seventeenth century, though there appears, not least in the historiography of the subject, to be something of a significant break between the Civil War and the Restoration, with an urban renaissance beginning in the 'long eighteenth century'. There are good reasons for believing in such a break, but it is worth noting that many of the records from which a changed urban sensibility can be charted in the eighteenth century are lacking for the earlier period. The religious and social world of townsmen and women was certainly transformed over the period 1540–1700, but not beyond recognition.

[123] Watt, *Cheap Print and Popular Piety*, pp. 195–6.

[124] Clark, *English Alehouse*, pp. 154–7; Ashton, 'Popular entertainment', 7.

[125] Barry, 'Bourgeois collectivism?', p. 84.

[126] Ingram, 'From Reformation to toleration', p. 123.

· 9 ·

The urban landscape 1540–1700

MICHAEL REED

(i) THE FOUNDATIONS

THE TOPOGRAPHY of British towns at the beginning of the sixteenth century was the product of the interaction between successive generations of men and women living in society, and the opportunities and constraints presented by their environment over the preceding millennium. Volume I of this work, more especially Chapters 8 and 16, gives an account of the medieval antecedents to this chapter.

Of all the features of towns inherited from the medieval centuries, the street plan, once laid down, has proved to be the most enduring, matched only by the similar longevity of the boundaries of the burgage plots which composed the spaces between the streets. The layout of both could be profoundly affected by the line of any fortifications which might be present. By the end of the medieval period well over a hundred English and Welsh towns had been fortified,[1] including Coventry, Southampton, Hereford and Newcastle-upon-Tyne, 'the strength and magnificens of the waulling of this towne', Leland thought, 'far passith al the waulles of the cities of England and of most of the townes of Europa'.[2] Numerous others, including Aylesbury, Chelmsford and Trowbridge, were not fortified, whilst in some cathedral cities the close formed a separate fortified *enceinte*, as at Salisbury.[3]

Many town walls were, by the beginning of this period, ruinous, and there was much encroaching and piecemeal destruction. A survey of Oswestry made in 1602 revealed great waste made on the castle, with stones carried away by the wagon load and whole towers taken down, with the gates of the town all very ruinous except Churchgate, where the burgesses had made their election house.[4]

1 See H. L. Turner, *Town Defences in England and Wales* (London, 1971), gazetteer, pp. 95 *et seq.*
2 L. T. Smith, ed., *The Itinerary of John Leland* (London, 1906–8; repr. 1964), vol. v, p. 60.
3 See RCHM (England), *The City of Salisbury*, vol. I (London, 1980), p. xxxv.
4 W. J. Slack, *The Lordship of Oswestry, 1393–1607* (Shrewsbury, 1951), p. 44.

Town walls were often repaired and as often damaged during the course of the Civil Wars, but it was well into the eighteenth century before they were perceived as a nuisance rather than an embellishment and their dismantling, a protracted affair, was begun, a process discussed more fully in Chapter 18 (see pp. 622–3).

The spaces between the streets were by no means entirely built up. An early seventeenth-century plan of Chester[5] shows extensive areas of gardens within the walls as well as suburbs to the north, east and across the River Dee to the south, and in this pattern of intramural gardens and open spaces and extramural suburbs Chester is by no means unique. In Exeter about a third of the walled area consisted of open spaces, and Baskerville wrote of Norwich in 1681 that the city 'is encompassed with an ancient flint wall, with towers at convenient distance for defence, and gates for entrance, and this wall is of such extent that within the compass of the city are many gardens and orchards, and enclosures, so that a man may boldly say it hath the greatest inclosures of any town in England' (see also Plate 2).[6] The fortification of Scottish towns has a different history. Only Edinburgh, Stirling and Perth had medieval stone walls. Edinburgh was established upon a superbly defensive site, the long, narrow volcanic tail that extends down from the crag upon which the castle is built. As Thomas Pennant wrote in 1769, it is 'a city that possesses a boldness and grandeur of situation beyond any that I had ever seen'.[7] Substantial stone walls had been erected by the middle years of the fifteenth century, and further walls were built between 1514 and 1560.[8] When the population of the city began to grow in the middle years of the sixteenth century, it could only be accommodated by building upwards. This physical constraint, combined with the provisions of the Scottish feu-ferm, a form of lease which disponed the property but not the superiority, leaving the feuar to pay an annual rent to the superior, in theory in perpetuity,[9] had a profound effect upon the topography of Edinburgh and in due course upon that of other Scottish towns. The superior demanded as large a feu as he could get. The feuar felt compelled to maximise his rents, something which was best done by building upwards. The result was the tenement, blocks of what were essentially flats, often seven or eight storeys high, occasionally as many as thirteen.[10] These tenements became notorious for the filth of the common stairs.

[5] G. Braun and F. Hohenberg, *Civitates Orbis Terrarum* (1572–1618; repr. with an introduction by R. A. Skelton, Cleveland, Ohio, 1966), vol. III, No.3.

[6] W. G. Hoskins, ed., *Exeter in the Seventeenth Century* (Devon and Cornwall Record Society, new series, 2, 1957), p. xii; *HMC*, Portland MSS, vol. II, p. 269.

[7] T. Pennant, *A Tour in Scotland* (Warrington, 1769; 3rd edn, 1774; repr. Perth, 1979), p. 49.

[8] I. H. Adams, *The Making of Urban Scotland* (London, 1978), pp. 37–8.

[9] See W. Ferguson, *Scotland, 1689 to the Present* (Edinburgh, 1968), p. 72.

[10] See R. Smith, 'Multi-dwelling building in Scotland, 1750–1970: a study based on housing in the Clyde valley', in A. Sutcliffe, ed., *Multi-Storey Living: The British Working Class Experience* (London, 1974), pp. 207–243; and RCHM (Scotland), *The City of Edinburgh* (Edinburgh, 1951), p. lxix.

Sir William Brereton visited the city in 1635 and found it paved with large boulder stones with water channels on both sides. The houses were very high and substantially built of stone, but the inhabitants were, he found, 'most sluttish, nastye and sloath-full people', fetching water only every other day, the houses of office being tubs which were emptied only when they were full, so that the houses, halls and kitchens 'have such a noysome tast and savour, and that so strong, as itt doth offend you, soe soone as you come within their walls'.[11]

Many Welsh towns were essentially castle towns in their origins, being primarily fortified points in a hostile countryside,[12] and this function influenced their layout. At Caernarvon, for example, the castle and town walls were planned and laid out to form a single defensive unit. There was a small market place within the walls but a larger one outside.[13] Only in the sixteenth century do the ties of Welsh towns with the surrounding countryside begin to strengthen as their functions became more truly urban and less military.

At the beginning of this period the most striking features on the skyline of any town would have been church spires and towers. All towns had at least one, and several large towns had dozens, Norwich, for example, and Lincoln and Winchester. In 1712 Gloucester was said to be 'adorned with many beautiful Towers and Spires', and the spires of Greyfriars, Trinity and St Michael's churches in Coventry gave to that town a unique and distinctive silhouette, as the prospect made by the Buck brothers in 1731 makes clear.[14] Just once Leland permits his imagination to be caught by the distant prospect of a town. 'The towne of Bewdeley', he wrote,

> is set on the syd of an hill, soe coningly that a man cannot wishe to set a towne bettar. It risethe from Severne banke by est upon the hill by west; so that a man standinge on the hill *trans pontem* by est may descrive almost every howse in the towne, and at the rysynge of the sunne from este the hole towne gliterithe, being all of new buyldinge, as it wer of gold.[15]

Ecclesiastical buildings were often the only ones in stone. Leland provides the nearest approach to a 'snapshot' view of English and Welsh towns in the 1540s. Again and again he notes that towns are 'buildid of tymbre', as at Leicester and Loughborough, Stratford-on-Avon, Oswestry and Worcester, Aylesbury and Uxbridge. Beverley was built of timber, but its gates were of brick. Wellingborough, however, was built of stone, 'as almost al the tounes be of Northamptonshire', although in Northampton itself all the old buildings were of stone and the new of timber. Doncaster was constructed of timber with slate

[11] See J. C. Hodgson, ed., *North Country Diaries, Second Series* (Surtees Society, 124, 1914), pp. 29–32.

[12] H. Carter, *The Towns of Wales*, 2nd edn (Cambridge, 1966), p. 164.

[13] H. Carter, 'Caernarvon', in M. D. Lobel, ed., *British Atlas of Historic Towns*, vol. I: *Historic Towns* (London, 1969).

[14] Sir R. Atkyns, *The Ancient and Present State of Glostershire* (London, 1712), p. 82; R. Hyde, *A Prospect of Britain* (London, 1994), plate 18.

[15] Smith, ed., *Itinerary of Leland*, II, pp. 87–8.

roofs, in spite of the presence of plenty of stone thereabouts. Sleaford was built of stone, as were most of the towns of Kesteven, whereas Wakefield was mostly of timber but with some stone.[16] In other words the limestone belt which sweeps across England from Weymouth to Whitby was already exerting its influence over the topography of the English town, something which becomes increasingly pronounced as Bath, Chipping Camden and Stamford (Plate 22) are rebuilt during the latter part of the seventeenth century and throughout the eighteenth.

The space within a town may be divided into three kinds: private, institutional and public.[17] Private space consists of those buildings and open spaces such as gardens which are privately owned or leased by individual inhabitants of a town, but there may be some ambiguity since much business and manufacture was domestic in its operation, and so parts of a private house may be open to the public at certain times during the day and many passageways and courts were shared. Institutional space is composed of that space and those buildings which are the responsibility of administrative, business and cultural organisations. It also may be used for more than one purpose. A town hall very often housed a school, and inns were frequently the settings for plays. Public space consists of the streets, lanes and open spaces within a town, including market squares and areas of public recreation such as parks and public walks. In some respects public space may also be institutional space since municipal authorities were usually responsible for the management of streets and pavements. This tripartite division of urban space is, however, nothing more than a convenient method of imposing some order upon the complexities of urban topography. The boundaries cannot always be accurately or consistently drawn, and to elaborate upon it further can serve little useful purpose.

It is probably true to say that the most rapid change of all in the topography of a town in this period comes to the physical structure of the buildings erected within the plots between the streets and to the uses to which they are put, the consequence of profound change in the ideas and ideals which underpinned these patterns of land use in the first place. The pace of change accelerates markedly during the period, with the inevitable tensions between old and new, leading to conflicts over the use of space, conflicts which could end either in violence, as with the riots over the enclosure of commons in Stair, or a lawsuit, as when John Luck, yeoman of Hastings, claimed in April of 1602 a footway through a parcel of land heretofore used in times of necessity as a churchyard to the parish church of St Clement for the burial of the dead, and now employed

[16] *Ibid.*, I, pp. 14, II, pp. 48, 3, 75, 89, 111, 113, I, pp. 47, 7, 35, 26, 42.

[17] See C. J. Bond, 'Central place and medieval new town: the origins of Thame, Oxfordshire', in T. R. Slater, ed., *The Built Form of Western Cities* (Leicester, 1990), p. 94. Henry Manship divided buildings into two kinds, 'either publick or private', and private buildings were not, he thought, 'altogether to be neglected by the magistrates': see C. J. Palmer, ed., *The History of Great Yarmouth by Henry Manship* (London, 1854), p. 62.

for garden plots.[18] The Reformation in particular precipitated very rapid change in the use of urban space, change which was by no means universally welcome. The destruction it wrought was already being lamented by the 1550s.[19]

(ii) PRIVATE SPACE

The greater part of the space within a town was given over to private use, either as housing or as gardens. Some parts were more accessible to the public than others, since the division between commercial, manufacturing and purely domestic use was often blurred. Individual house plots were often laid out when the town was first planned (see Chapter 8 of Volume I), and although there was considerable amalgamation and subdivision of these plots such change took place at a piecemeal level so that once the basic structure of the spaces between the streets was established it remained almost unchanged for centuries.

Houses in towns in the sixteenth and seventeenth centuries varied enormously in type, plan, method and materials of construction. Surveys carried out in London by Ralph Treswell between 1607 and 1612 reveal four types of post-medieval housing: one room on each floor, a type to be found both in principal streets and in courtyards, where they could be fitted into any awkward space available; houses with two rooms on each of three or more floors, with the ground floor often a shop or tavern, sometimes with a counting house or warehouse behind; houses with three to six rooms on the ground floor; and finally larger houses, often with a courtyard. The majority of London houses built before 1640 were timber framed, but there was already some use of brick.[20] Jetties went out of fashion by the end of the sixteenth century, at which time timber strap work and carved timber grotesques were at their most fashionable and most exuberant. As we shall see later in this chapter, the Great Fire swept away almost all of this vernacular extravagance.

Houses in sixteenth-century Edinburgh were rarely more than three storeys high, built either of timber or of rubble, with cellars, stables and shops on the ground floor, a hall and chamber on the first and a loft in the roof space. Some had a wooden gallery projecting at the front and the space under this might either be left open or else boarded in to form a shop or stable. During the course

[18] *The Statistical Account of Scotland* (Edinburgh, 1791–9), vol. VI, p. 113; (Manuscripts of the Corporation of Hastings): *HMC*, 13th Report, App., Part IV, p. 358; and see R. Burn, *Ecclesiastical Law* (London, 1763), vol. I, p. 247.

[19] M. Aston, 'English ruins and English history', *Journal of the Warburg and Courtauld Institutes*, 36 (1973), 231–55.

[20] See J. Schofield, ed., *The London Surveys of Ralph Treswell* (London, 1987), *passim*; and also F. E. Brown, 'Continuity and change in the urban house: developments in domestic space organisation in seventeenth-century London', *Comparative Studies in Society and History*, 28 (1986), 558–90; and A. F. Kelsall, 'The London house plan in the later seventeenth century', *Post-Medieval Archaeology*, 8 (1974), 80–91.

of the seventeenth century the wooden galleries were gradually replaced by stone structures, often carried on arcades over the street and by the middle of the century the tenement block was becoming the standard form of housing, of which Milne's Court in the Lawnmarket, an ashlar-fronted block six storeys and an attic high, is a survival. The transition to stone from wood was a protracted affair, however. As late as 1784 it was said that wooden-fronted houses were still very numerous along the Lawnmarket and the High Street.[21]

How far London and Edinburgh are typical of England and Scotland is difficult to determine. Modern attempts at the classification of sixteenth- and seventeenth-century house types can be oversubtle; fifteen have been distinguished in Stamford, for example,[22] and little attention has been paid to regional differences. Nevertheless, in spite of these problems, certain overall patterns and trends in private housing may be detected. There is a growing precision in the use of domestic space as some rooms change their functions and others become more specialised.[23] The hall gradually ceases to be the principal room in the house and by the end of the seventeenth century is often little more than an entrance room. Bed chambers cease to be miscellaneous store rooms and are essentially sleeping rooms, by the end of the period frequently known by the name of the colour in which they are furnished, whilst the parlour has lost its beds and become a family reception room.

Each house and each household is unique, and to cite but one example may give a grossly misleading impression, but it may also give at least something of the feel of what it was like to live in a town in the early seventeenth century. Henry Piper, poldavis weaver, of Ipswich, died in 1615.[24] His probate inventory reveals a personal estate of £66 9s. His house had a hall furnished with a long table, chairs and stools, a fire pan and bellows, some candle-sticks, a Bible, a musket, sword and dagger. Next to the hall was a little buttery, then a parlour, with two posted bedsteads, two cupboards, four chests, table, stools and pewterware, the room being hung with stained cloth, a cheap substitute for tapestries. There was then a little room, a buttery where the beer was kept, a brewhouse, two workshops and a yard. In the workshops were nine looms and four spinning wheels, with pieces of cloth in the course of being made, giving the impression of a working life suddenly cut short by death. In the yard was some yarn upon poles, two pigs and some poultry. There were six chambers, including one over the gatehouse, which is not otherwise mentioned, and another over the shop, which is also not mentioned. In the chamber over the parlour there was some wheat, a side saddle, a cheese rack and a pair of boots, and in the chamber over

[21] RCHM (Scotland), *The City of Edinburgh*, pp. lxvii–lxvii, No. 12, p. 73, and p. lxxi.

[22] RCHM (England), *The Town of Stamford* (London, 1977), p. 1.

[23] U. Priestley, P. J. Corfield and H. Sutermeister, 'Rooms and room use in Norwich housing, 1580–1730', *Post-Medieval Archaeology*, 16 (1982), 93–124.

[24] M. Reed, *The Ipswich Probate Inventories, 1583–1631* (Suffolk Records Society, 22, 1981), p. 82.

the shop there was some yarn, a saw, a bird cage and some rye. He also had a mare and a colt. Such was the internal structure of an early seventeenth-century house. It is not the purpose of this chapter to analyse the social structure of the household which occupied it, save to point out that in order to go to work Henry Piper had only to cross his back yard. The external structure of private property was subject to an almost continuous process of building and rebuilding during the sixteenth and seventeenth centuries, with brick or stone and tile gradually replacing timber and thatch, with the stone and bricks almost always coming from local quarries and kilns. There were sometimes particularly marked periods of rebuilding, often determined by economic prosperity, as in Totnes between about 1570 and 1640, even if W. G. Hoskins' original 'Great Rebuilding' will not now stand detailed examination.[25]

By the end of the period this rebuilding is beginning to be influenced by the reception of themes from classical architecture, bringing regularity of façade in place of the variety of the traditional vernacular building styles. This rebuilding and refacing is by no means universal, however, being very much a matter of piecemeal change. It comes in only very slowly in many towns, the first brick house in Wolverhampton, for example, dating only from 1675,[26] and much remained untouched. The lavish vernacular decoration to the Feathers Inn in Ludlow, for example, originally built as a merchant's house in 1607, still survives, and the exuberant pargetting to be seen on Sparrowe's House at Ipswich, of about 1670, is the culmination of a long regional vernacular tradition which the reception of classical themes had by no means extinguished, whilst in Totnes timber-framed construction continued until the very end of the eighteenth century.[27] Thomas Baskerville noted of York in the 1670s that in general 'the whole town is old timber buildings'.[28] Cosmo de Medici, when he visited England in 1669, found Okehampton a place of little account, with the houses built of earth and stone and thatched, whilst Basingstoke was 'wretched, both in regard to the buildings, the greater part of which are of wood, and the total absence of trade', but he would have been difficult to please, having just come from Florence.[29] Celia Fiennes visited Bury St Edmunds in 1698 and found the town had 'no good buildings'. There was, however, an apothecary's house in 'the new mode of building, 4 roomes of a floore pretty sizeable and high, well furnish'd, a drawing roome and chamber full of China and a Damaske bed embroyder'd, 2 other roomes . . . a pretty deale of plate in his wives chamber, parlours

[25] M. Laithwaite, 'Totnes houses 1500–1800', in P. Clark, ed., *The Transformation of English Provincial Towns 1600–1800* (London, 1984), esp. pp. 63–4 and 71; and see C. Platt, *The Great Rebuilding of Tudor and Stuart England* (London, 1994), esp. ch. 1.

[26] G. P. Mander, *A History of Wolverhampton*, ed. N. W. Tildesley (Wolverhampton, 1960), p. 117.

[27] See A. Clifton-Taylor, *The Pattern of English Building*, new edn (London, 1972), p. 359; and Laithwaite, 'Totnes Houses 1500–1800', p. 88.

[28] *HMC*, Portland MSS, vol. II, p. 311.

[29] L. Magalotti, ed., *Travels of Cosmo III Grand Duke of Tuscany, through England in 1669* (London, 1821), pp. 127, 139 and 157.

below and a large shop'. The rest, she found, 'are great old houses of timber and mostly in the old forme of the country which are long peaked roofes of tileing'.[30] A good example of the traditional timber-framed merchant's house can be found at Shrewsbury (see Plate 9).

The spatial distribution of houses in towns is revealed in studies of the hearth tax returns. A significant proportion of households recorded in the tax had no more than one or two hearths, perhaps indicating in many cases either small or subdivided buildings. In Ipswich in 1674, 54.3 per cent of those households which paid the tax fell into this category. A further 28.7 per cent had between three and five hearths, and only 17 per cent had six or more, of a total of 1,640 households. Further, there is a very noticeable concentration of households with a large number of hearths, suggesting bigger houses, in the two central parishes in the town. St Lawrence had only ninety-one households, but the average of hearths per household was 4.2, with 49.2 per cent with six or more. St Mary Tower, with 113 households, had an average of 3.9 hearths to each household, and 32.9 per cent had six or more. In other words, if wealth and hence social position may be equated with the number of hearths to a household, then in seventeenth-century Ipswich the well-to-do were generally to be found in large houses in the centre of the town, over and behind their shops and counting houses. The poor lived where they could, either in cottages cramped into odd scraps of land in the centre of the town or on the outskirts.[31] This social geography is repeated in every other English town, including London, and is further discussed elsewhere in this volume.

Two important social trends in private housing have their origins in the early seventeenth century and have become of considerable significance by its end. The first of these trends is the growing practice of aristocracy and country gentry alike buying houses in provincial towns, so that by the end of the seventeenth century there were few towns, especially county towns, without their quota of town houses for the rural landed classes. They came, as Cosmo de Medici noted on his visit to Exeter in 1669, 'from time to time from their country houses, which are their constant residence, to look after their affairs'.[32] Thus the earl of Bradford had built himself a town house in Shrewsbury by 1696 and the Pelham family had its town house in Lewes.

The second trend sees the expansion of suburbs. Although suburbs are a feature of many medieval towns, two important changes in their nature and structure become increasingly apparent, especially after the Restoration. Suburban devel-

[30] C. Morris, ed., *The Journeys of Celia Fiennes* (London, 1947), p. 152.

[31] See M. Reed, 'Economic structure and change in seventeenth-century Ipswich', in P. Clark, ed., *Country Towns in Pre-Industrial England* (Leicester, 1981), esp. pp. 131–3. See also J. Langton, 'Residential patterns in pre-industrial cities: some case studies from seventeenth-century Britain', *Transactions of the Institute of British Geographers*, 65 (1975), repr. in J. Barry, ed., *The Tudor and Stuart Town* (London, 1990), pp. 166–205.

[32] Magalotti, ed., *Travels of Cosmo III*, p. 129.

opment immediately outside the then built-up limits of London took the form of continuous streets, squares and terraces, and these were provided for all levels of society. One of the earliest schemes was for Covent Garden, designed by Inigo Jones for the earl of Bedford in the 1630s, with arcaded houses laid out round a square, one end of which was sealed off with a church, its roof supported on Tuscan columns. Further building took place around London, both to the east and to the west, especially in the years following the Great Fire of 1666, when 13,200 houses were destroyed. This proved to be a period of experiment in domestic planning, with many houses built of brick, no more than two or three windows wide and with only one staircase.[33] Building in the eastern suburbs was by no means intended for the well-to-do. Nicholas Barbon was putting up cheap speculative housing in Spitalfields by the 1680s. Shadwell, an almost uninhabited hamlet in Stepney in the sixteenth century, had, by 1650, 703 buildings and by 1674 a population of about 8,000, the great majority of whom made their living from the river and the sea. At the other end of the city, and of the social scale, the earl of St Albans was laying out his St James, Westminster, estate from the 1660s.[34]

However, in the scale of suburban development of this nature, further discussed in Chapter 18, London was unique. The medieval extramural suburbs lying beyond the North Gate of Bath, for example, show some modest growth by the end of the seventeenth century, but no signs of systematic planning.[35] In Glasgow Candleriggs was laid out in 1662, but was not extended into King Street until the 1720s, and no new street was laid out in Leeds between 1634 and 1767.[36] There was little extension to the built-up area of Birmingham much before 1700, the increasing population being accommodated within the old streets, many of which became very congested as a consequence, not least because the burgage plots in the town were exceptionally long. Much building took place on the 'backsides' of these plots, with access by means of narrow alleys and entries.[37] Substantial suburban growth, apart from that around London, has to wait until well into the eighteenth century.

The second aspect to this new suburban development was the building of individual country houses by wealthy merchants, usually on the outskirts of

33 A. F. Kelsall, 'The London house plan in the later seventeenth century', *Post-Medieval Archaeology*, 8 (1974), 80–91.

34 *The Survey of London*, vol. XXVII: *Spitalfields and Mile End New Town* (London, 1957), pp. 10, 29–32; M. J. Power, 'Shadwell: the development of a London suburban community in the seventeenth century', *LJ*, 4 (1978), 29–46; *Survey of London*, vol. XXIX: *St James Westminster, Part 1, South of Piccadilly* (London, 1960), pp. 2, 21 *et seq*.

35 See 'The Plan of Bath of Joseph Gillmore', in R. Peirce, *Bath Memoirs* (Bath, 1697), reproduced in M. Hamilton, *Bath Before Beau Nash* (Bath, 1978).

36 J. R. Kellett, 'Glasgow', in Lobel, ed., *Historic Towns*, I; M. W. Beresford, 'The making of a townscape: Richard Paley in the east end of Leeds, 1771–1803', in C. W. Chalklin and M. A. Havinden, eds., *Rural Change and Urban Growth, 1500–1800* (London, 1974), p. 281.

37 *VCH*, Warwickshire, VII, p. 7.

towns, sometimes in rural situations, not least to escape the increasingly congested conditions to be found in the centres of towns and the attendant threat of disease. Sometimes they settled in the vicinity of London, at Kew, for example, where what is now known as 'The Dutch House' dates from 1631.[38] Sometimes they went further afield. Great Hundridge manor, near Chesham, in Buckinghamshire, was built at the very end of the seventeenth century for a London apothecary, and Fawley manor, in the same county, was built in 1684 for William Freeman, a wealthy West Indies merchant.[39] This is a phenomenon which becomes increasingly apparent during the eighteenth century.

There was much change to the physical appearance of private housing in towns during the course of the sixteenth and seventeenth centuries, and this becomes especially marked in the years after the Restoration. Many, but by no means all, houses were at least refaced in brick and roofed with tiles. The gradual reception of the principles of classical architecture led to increasing regularity of façade. Windows became vertical rather than horizontal in their line, with wooden glazing bars and sash windows, but all of these changes took place upon an individualistic, piecemeal scale, with little sense of overall planning, save perhaps in some of the suburbs of London. Nevertheless, in spite of the new, elegant and fashionable façades, horses and pigs continued to be kept in towns, water had often to be drawn from wells, fire remained a constant threat and many townsmen still cultivated their strips in the open fields. Thomas Baskerville could call Leicester of the 1670s 'an old stinking town upon a dull river, inhabited for the most part by tradesmen'.[40]

(iii) INSTITUTIONAL SPACE

Institutional space and its buildings can take a very wide range of forms and functions, and this range becomes more varied and more complex with the passage of time. It is also a significant indicator of the ranking of a town within the urban hierarchy: the greater the number of institutions within a town the higher its rank. Such buildings may be divided into three broad categories: administrative, commercial and cultural, a word which can also be used to embrace leisure and philanthropic purposes. Administrative buildings were provided by the central government, by county justices of the peace or by municipal authorities. Commercial premises may be the responsibility of municipal authorities, whether public quays or town water mills, or of private individuals – inns and shops, for example – but these were often regulated by the town council, which licensed inns and levied tolls on those setting up stalls in market places. The largest and most numerous cultural buildings in 1540 were churches, but this

[38] J. Summerson, *Architecture in Britain, 1530–1830* (Harmondsworth, 1953), pp. 101, 158.

[39] G. Tyack, 'The Freemans of Fawley', *Records of Bucks*, 24 (1982), 130.

[40] *HMC*, Portland MSS, vol. II, p. 308.

period sees an accelerating expansion in the range of other buildings which may be subsumed under this heading, and there is again an interesting mix of municipal and private enterprise at work. Both town councils and private individuals founded schools and almshouses, public walks and bowling greens, and in the second half of the seventeenth century buildings erected by and for Protestant nonconformists make their appearance.

Both London and Edinburgh were capital cities during the sixteenth and seventeenth centuries, and Edinburgh had its status only marginally changed after the Act of Union of 1707.[41] This means that both have a range of administrative functions, and hence of building types, not to be found together in any other town within the two kingdoms. Thus both have royal palaces, the Palace of Westminster and Holyrood House, and royal palaces are to be found elsewhere within a broad radius from them: at Oatlands and Greenwich, Stirling and Linlithgow, for example. Henry VIII acquired York Place from cardinal Wolsey and this became the Palace of Whitehall. Under James I Inigo Jones was commissioned to construct there the first completely classical building in England, the Banqueting House (see Plate 11). The Palace of St James was created following the surrender of the Hospital of St James in 1531.[42] It became the centre for the royal Court only after the destruction of the Palace of Whitehall by fire in 1698. The union of the two crowns meant that the Scottish royal palaces were left unused for decades together, with serious consequences for the social and economic life of Edinburgh.

The emergence of government departments from the royal household was by no means complete at this time, giving to royal palaces an important administrative function, since government office buildings *per se* were scarcely known and certainly did not make that impact upon the urban landscape that they were to do in the nineteenth century. The Admiralty, for example, was housed within the apartments of the duke of York in the Palace of Whitehall when he became lord high admiral in 1660, and when Pepys became secretary for Admiralty affairs the clerks moved to his house in York Buildings, King Street, which became the Admiralty, and was distinguished by an anchor displayed on one of the walls. It did not move to a purpose-built office until 1695, by which time other government departments were beginning to find their own premises. The Stamp Office opened in 1684 at 7 New Square in Lincoln's Inn, just being built by Henry Serle and originally no part of the Inn. The excise office, however, established in 1643, was, even at the end of the century, still domestically based, being in the house of Sir John Frederick in Old Jewry.[43]

41 See N. Phillipson, 'Edinburgh', in *Cities and the Transmission of Cultural Values in the Late Middle Ages and Early Modern Period* (Brussels, 1996), pp. 137–49.

42 *Survey of London*, vol. XXIX: *St James Westminster, Part 1, South of Piccadilly*, p. 23.

43 R. Latham and W. Matthews, eds., *The Diary of Samuel Pepys*, vol. X (London, 1983), pp. 4 and 127.

Both capitals had buildings in which meetings of the parliaments of the two kingdoms were held. The English House of Commons met in the chapel of St Stephen, secularised in 1548, whilst the House of Lords met in a room to the south of the Painted Chamber, both being part of the ancient Palace of Westminster. The buildings for the Scottish parliament were rebuilt in Edinburgh in 1632. Both cities housed the central law courts. Kings Bench and Chancery met at one end of Westminster Hall, a medieval building with a magnificent hammer-beam roof, Common Pleas at the other. New premises for the Court of Exchequer were built, again within the Palace of Westminster, between 1569 and 1570.[44] Scotland retained its own judicial system after the Act of Union, and the supreme civil court, the Court of Session, continued to meet in Edinburgh in the Parliament House, a building provided by the city corporation.[45]

Both cities had a castle, the Tower of London and Edinburgh Castle, but whilst Edinburgh was surrounded with walls London had no further defences, it having long since expanded beyond the line of the Roman walls. The Tower of London was much more than simply a military fortress, since it housed the royal regalia, the Office of the Wardrobe, some classes of government archives and a famous menagerie, including lions and a leopard.

Outside the two capital cities many administrative functions were performed through county justices of the peace. Their power and prestige come to be expressed through their shire hall, a new building type which makes its appearance in county towns during the course of the sixteenth and seventeenth centuries. That in Cambridge was built in 1572 on the castle hill[46] and that at Derby was built in 1660. They eventually served leisure purposes as well as administrative ones in that by the end of the seventeenth century they sometimes incorporated assembly rooms. The shire hall at Carmarthen, however, had shops and shambles in its arches.[47]

Numerous towns were, by virtue of their charter of incorporation, exempt from the jurisdiction of the county justices. For these, and for many of those which were not, the symbol of their prestige and dignity was the town hall and its Scottish equivalent the tollbooth (see Plate 10).[48] The majority of towns were already provided with a town hall, however called, by the beginning of the period. Grimsby, for example, had a town hall by 1286 and it was rebuilt by 1395.[49] Various places with but the shakiest claims to urban status, such as

[44] H. M. Colvin, ed., *The History of the Kings Works*, vol. IV: *1485–1660*, Part 2 (London, 1982), pp. 291, 389, 294.

[45] J. Gifford, C. McWilliam and D. Walker, eds., *The Buildings of Scotland: Edinburgh* (Harmondsworth, 1984), pp. 118–19.

[46] *VCH*, Cambridgeshire, III, p. 118.

[47] F. Jones, 'Rent roll of Carmarthen corporation, 1678', *Carmarthenshire History*, 10 (1973), 55–63.

[48] On English town halls see R. Tittler, *Architecture and Power* (Oxford, 1991); and on Scottish tollbooths see G. Stell, 'The earliest tolbooths: a preliminary account', *Proceedings of the Society of Antiquaries of Scotland*, 111 (1981), 445–53.

[49] E. Gillett, *A History of Grimsby* (London, 1970), p. 2.

Ivinghoe, in Buckinghamshire, had one, whilst many other places which were growing rapidly at the end of the sixteenth century but still had no formal urban pretensions, places like Manchester and Birmingham, were without one. Nottingham, however, had two, one for the French borough and another for the English.[50] Many were rebuilt during the course of the sixteenth and seventeenth centuries, and this might be financed by a local landowner, by public subscription, by a legacy, from municipal funds or from a combination of these. The motives behind this rebuilding may be severely practical in that the old building had become inadequate for its purposes, but they also included a measure of civic pride and consciousness.

The traditional, vernacular town hall, often timber framed and thatched, was built with open arcading on the ground floor, offering shelter on market days, the first floor having a meeting chamber and sometimes room for the grammar school. By the end of the seventeenth century they were being rebuilt in brick and stone with the traditional design decked out in classical dress. One of the finest examples must be the town hall at Abingdon, built to designs of Christopher Kempster between 1678 and 1680. When Celia Fiennes visited Abingdon in about 1694 she found the new town hall

> the finest in England, its all of free stone and very lofty, even the Isles or Walk below is a lofty arch on severall pillars of square stone and four square pillars, over it are large Roomes with handsome Windows, above which is some Roomes with windows a little like the Theatre att Oxford, only this is a square building and that round, it makes a very fine appearance.[51]

The judicial functions of municipal authorities called for many other structures, including ducking stools, gallows, gaols, pillories and stocks. The last two are both shown in elevation on Speed's map of Bath of 1611 (see Plate 3), in the High Street, directly in front of the market house, whilst the pillory, stocks, gibbet and cucking stool at Wakefield were in 1579 ordered to be well made.[52]

Institutional space and buildings devoted to trade and commerce took a growing number of forms. Much was either provided or regulated by the municipal authority, and the larger and more sophisticated the authority the wider the range of buildings. Yet others were provided by private individuals. At Yarmouth in the sixteenth century the corporation was paying for repairs to the toll house, the crane, the market house, the pillory, the public quay and the bridge, whilst at Perth at the end of the seventeenth century four mills and a weighhouse were being maintained out of the Common Good and at Dumfries the roof and fabric of the church, a bridge of nine arches, the tollbooth, the

[50] J. Blackner, *The History of Nottingham* (Nottingham, 1815), p. 64.

[51] Morris, ed., *Celia Fiennes*, p. 39.

[52] J. W. Walker, 'The burges court, Wakefield', in *Miscellanea*, vol. II (Yorkshire Archaeological Society, Record Series, 74, 1929), p. 27.

prison, the town mills and mill dams and the school house were also being thus maintained.[53]

The trade which was the life-blood of all towns, large and small, was, by the end of the sixteenth century, being funnelled through a number of institutions. Much retail trade was still handled through weekly, sometimes daily, markets, where stallholders exhibited a very wide range of goods for sale, under the strict supervision of the town authorities. Sometimes these stalls became permanent encroachments within the market place. Sometimes the markets became specialised, so that there could be distinct parts of the streets or market places given over to poultry, meat, butter and cheese, and so on, although the medieval occupational segregation which gave rise to such street names as Milk Street, Fishmonger Row and Broiderers Lane,[54] was beginning to disintegrate at the beginning of the sixteenth century and had largely, although not entirely, disappeared by the end of the seventeenth. Wholesale trade, especially in agricultural produce such as cattle and sheep, went through fairs, bringing hundreds of visitors and thousands of animals into the streets of a town, together with the attendant problems of sanitation. Markets and fairs both required open spaces and these could occupy a significant proportion of the total surface area of a town. That at Nottingham extended over more than four acres, with full markets held on Wednesdays, Fridays and Saturdays, although some stalls were set out every day. It was said by Leland to be 'the most fairest withowt exception of al Inglande'.[55]

By the end of the sixteenth century, however, both markets and fairs were being challenged as centres of commerce and distribution by inns and by retail shops. From the fifteenth century onwards inns were often among the largest buildings in a town, coming to serve as meeting places for merchants and tradesmen, as private markets and as warehouses and storehouses. They were run by private persons but required a licence from the municipal authority. Some innkeepers became very prosperous, like Edward Marshall who became mayor of High Wycombe. He died in 1699 and his probate inventory gives full details of the rooms in his inn, with the signs by which each room was known, including the Flower de Luce, the Great Antelope and the George. There was a kitchen, a room for the ostlers, a brewhouse, a yard, granary, pantry, parlour and beer and wine cellars.[56] Inns share in that slow transformation from timber-framed vernacular styles to that more uniform, brick-built, classically inspired,

[53] P. Rutledge, ed., *Great Yarmouth Assembly Minutes, 1538–1545* (Norfolk Record Society, 39, 1970), p. 9; Sir J. D. Marwick, ed., *Register Containing the State and Condition of Every Burgh within the Kingdome of Scotland in the Year 1692* (Miscellany of the Scottish Burgh Records Society, 13, 1881), pp. 58–9 and 92. [54] Cf. *VCH*, Cambridgeshire, III, p. 89.

[55] Blackner, *Nottingham*, p. 61; Smith, *Itinerary of Leland*, I, p. 94.

[56] M. Reed, *Buckinghamshire Probate Inventories, 1661–1714* (Buckinghamshire Record Society, 24, 1988), p. 273.

style which characterises so much urban building in the late seventeenth century.

By the end of the seventeenth century there were few towns of any size which did not have a number of glass-fronted shops offering, as the probate inventories of their occupiers make abundantly clear, an astonishing range of goods drawn from all parts of the known world.[57] Even the bridge over the Tyne from Gateshead to Newcastle was lined with shops in 1647.[58] Celia Fiennes noted that the shops of Newcastle-upon-Tyne 'are good and are of distinct trades, not selling many things in one shop as is the custom in most country towns and citys'.[59]

A significant part of urban space was occupied by the buildings of institutions devoted to charitable, ecclesiastical and educational purposes, and the stock of these institutions possessed by an individual town was often added to as that movement of practical philanthropy which characterises the late sixteenth and seventeenth centuries took its course.

Hospitals began as guest houses open to all comers and were frequently to be found at town gates, at Bury St Edmunds for example. By the fifteenth century they were becoming residential, with particular concern for the elderly infirm. Most survived the Reformation and many more were founded from the middle years of the sixteenth century onwards. The Drake almshouses at Amersham, built of brick in 1657, are typical of very many similar institutions to be found in towns, great and small. They were sometimes established for members of a particular trade or occupation, like the hospital founded in Bristol in 1696 by the Merchant Venturers to care for merchant seamen. Others were established by private philanthropy, like that Drake almshouse just mentioned. It is the eighteenth century, however, before buildings are erected with the avowed purpose of providing accommodation in which sick people could be cured and then discharged.

By the early sixteenth century British towns were well endowed with churches and monastic buildings. Church building was going on right up to the Reformation, the splendid spire at Louth being built between 1501 and 1515. There is then a long gap before church building and rebuilding is taken up again, and much of what was done was to repair or restore damage inflicted in the Civil Wars. The greatest single programme of church rebuilding in the seventeenth century was that undertaken by Sir Christopher Wren in the aftermath of the Great Fire of London, culminating in his masterpiece, St Pauls, upon which he spent thirty years of his life. All of his churches are profoundly classical in their inspiration, in contrast to the Gothic of the medieval legacy, and so they and

57 See, e.g., Reed, *Probate Inventories*; J. A. Johnston, ed., *Probate Inventories of Lincoln Citizens, 1661–1714* (Lincoln Record Society, 80, 1991); and D. G. Vaisey, ed., *Probate Inventories for Lichfield and District, 1568–1680* (Staffordshire Record Society, 4th series, 5, 1969).

58 D. A. King, *Parliamentary Surveys of the Bishopric of Durham*, vol. II (Surtees Society, 185, 1972), p. 110.

59 Morris, ed., *Celia Fiennes*, p. 210.

those modelled upon his example introduce an entirely new note into urban topography in the late seventeenth century.

Scottish church building during the seventeenth century went its own way. Some buildings were rectangular in design, some were T shaped, a response to the demand for a preaching house which is peculiar to Scotland, the north aisle often having a loft with a retiring room where the laird could take his lunch between morning and afternoon services, whilst others were cruciform, such as that at Lauder, built in the form of a Greek cross to designs by Sir William Bruce in the 1670s.[60]

The Reformation wrought immense change in the topography of the early modern town. The dissolution of the monasteries meant that space hitherto ostensibly devoted to spiritual purposes had its functions quickly and permanently changed. Some monastic churches were acquired by the corporation and continued as parish churches, as at Tewkesbury, Dunstable and Romsey. At Peebles the monastery of Holy Cross was dissolved in 1560, but the church was used as the parish church until 1784,[61] and some ancient Scottish churches were divided into two or, as at Perth, into three separate churches.

Conventual buildings were sometimes converted into schools, colleges, libraries and almshouses, others became private dwellings. The Charterhouse in London was dissolved in 1537 and was granted to Sir Edward North in 1545. He turned it into a private house, added to by the duke of Norfolk in 1565–71. It was bought in 1611 by Thomas Sutton, who established a school for forty boys and an almshouse for eighty old men.[62] The public library at Ipswich was first founded under the will of Mrs Walter in 1588. In the following year William Smart gave his printed books to the town, but it was 1614 before a room in the Hospital was ordered to be fitted out with shelves. The Hospital itself, an institution for the relief of the elderly and sick and the education of poor children, was, together with the grammar school, housed in the buildings of the former Blackfriars.

Toleration of differences in Protestant religious practices came slowly to be accepted during the course of the seventeenth century, a movement culminating in the Toleration Act of 1689. The result was the building of nonconformist chapels of every denomination, at first unpretentious brick-built structures deliberately tucked away in order to avoid the attention of the authorities and of the mob. The Friends' Meeting House at Amersham, a modest building in brick, dates from 1677 and cost £26 to build.[63] That at Bridport dates from 1697 and that at Hertford from 1670. The first Jewish synagogue was opened at Bevis

[60] See G. Hay, *Architecture of Scottish Post-Reformation Churches, 1560–1843* (Oxford, 1957), *passim.*

[61] W. Chambers, ed., *Charters and Documents relating to the Burgh of Peebles* (Scottish Burgh Records Society, 10, 1872), p. lxvi.

[62] M. Seaborne, *The English School, its Architecture and Organisation, 1370–1870* (London, 1971), p. 45.

[63] RCHM (England), *An Inventory of Nonconformist Chapels in Central England* (London, 1986), p. 3.

Marks, in London, in 1700, by which time even Roman Catholics were beginning to be afforded a modicum of *de facto* toleration.

Many schools were founded during the course of the sixteenth and seventeenth centuries, often established by means of letters patent from the crown on the petition of a town corporation or of some well-meaning private person. These were grammar or free schools, usually well endowed and in any case supported by the town corporation. The reception of the New Learning led to innovations in their design and layout. One of the earliest still surviving is that at Berkhampsted, founded in 1541. The new building has a central school room with the headmaster's house at one end and the house of the usher at the other. This layout serves as the fundamental plan of schools throughout England during the course of the seventeenth century, although there is of course much individual variation upon the theme.[64] Some schools were provided with a splendid range of buildings, at Shrewsbury, for example, where a new three-storey stone-built block was added in 1627–30, complete with classical pilasters to the doorway and an inscription in Greek.[65] By 1560 most Scottish burghs had a school maintained out of the Common Good by the burgh.[66] Attendance was compulsory and private schools were not encouraged. School buildings themselves were often small, with little to mark them off from neighbouring secular buildings. The most architecturally distinguished school built in Scotland in the seventeenth century owes its existence to George Heriot, royal goldsmith, who died in 1624 leaving £23,625 sterling to found a hospital, meaning a charity school. The overall design is based upon a plan from Serlio. Work began in 1628, but it was 1659 before the first boys were admitted, and 1700 before it was finished (see Plate 6).[67] Thomas Pennant visited it in 1769, when he thought it 'a fine old building, much too magnificent for the end proposed, that of educating poor children'.[68]

The religious controversies of the Reformation prompted the founding of several new colleges in Oxford and Cambridge and of new universities in Scotland, often making use of the lands of dissolved religious communities. Trinity College, Cambridge, was established in 1546 with the avowed purpose of the extirpation of error and false teaching and the education of youth in piety and knowledge.[69] Emmanuel College, Cambridge, was founded in 1583 on the site of the Dominican friary, bought especially for the purpose.[70] In Scotland the University of Edinburgh was founded in 1583, taking over the property of the

[64] Seaborne, *The English School*, p. 16. [65] Summerson, *Architecture in Britain*, p. 183.

[66] See J. Scotland, *The History of Scottish Education* (London, 1969), vol. I, *passim*; and see D. J. Withington, ed., 'Lists of schoolmasters teaching Latin, 1690', in *Miscellany*, vol. X (Scottish History Society, 4th series, 1965).

[67] J. Clifford, C. McWilliam and D. Walker, *The Buildings of Scotland: Edinburgh* (Harmondsworth, 1984), pp. 179–81. [68] Pennant, *A Tour in Scotland*, p. 56.

[69] *VCH*, Cambridgeshire, III, pp. 456, 462. [70] *Ibid.* pp. 474, 481, 483.

church of St Mary in the Fields. The city council appointed the professors, decided the courses, awarded the degrees and paid for the erection of new buildings, including a library, and the repair of the old ones. By 1700 it had eight professors and 300 students. In Aberdeen Marischal College received its charter in 1593, so that there were two universities in the town, King's College having been founded in 1495 and built round a square with cloisters on the south side.[71] The University at Glasgow, originally established in 1451, was to all intents and purposes refounded by Andrew Melville in 1577. New buildings were begun in 1632, although it was thirty years before they were completed, and a physic garden was laid out in 1704.

(iv) PUBLIC SPACE

The streets composing public space in the early modern town were regulated by municipal authorities, which made efforts to curb encroachments, to control the use of building materials, to eradicate nuisances and to keep public buildings in repair. A number of towns obtained paving acts in an attempt to improve the condition of the streets within a town, Windsor in 1585, for example,[72] although responsibility for paving and cleansing often remained with individual property owners, their duties being enforced by the town council. The first common scavenger was appointed in Oxford in 1541, a second was appointed in 1578. In 1621 the town joined with the university to appoint one, to be paid by a levy on the colleges and a tax on houses. Inhabitants were required to sweep their refuse into heaps in front of their houses and then await the scavenger's cart, but the scheme seems to have had little long-term effect upon the cleanliness of the streets.[73] In Stirling the town council in 1529 ordered that 'middingis in the Bakraw, or on the heegait of the said burgh' should be removed within twenty-four hours or the midden was free for anyone to take away and in 1614 it was ordered that no one was to build 'furth thair biggingis nor sidwalis of thair houssis out upon the kingis hie calseyis'.[74] In Bedford regulations were made from time to time to keep the Butchers' Row clean, to scour the river bank, to keep pigs from wandering in the streets and to tile thatched houses if fire was kept in them. Statutes and ordinances made for Warrington in 1617 required pigs to be ringed, the inhabitants to keep hooks and ladders as firefighting equipment, to keep the channels and gutters clean and not to put middens in the market place.[75] Orders of this

71 Pennant, *A Tour in Scotland*, pp. 125–6. 72 *VCH*, Berkshire, III, p. 61.

73 *VCH*, Oxfordshire, IV p. 352.

74 R. Renwick, ed., *Extracts from the Records of the Royal Burgh of Stirling, 1519–1666* (Scottish Burgh Records Society, 1887), pp. 37, 135–6.

75 G. D. Gilmore, ed., *The Black Book of Bedford* (Bedfordshire Historical Record Society, 36, 1956), 37; R. Sharp France, ed., 'The statutes and ordinances of Warrington, 1617', in *A Lancashire Miscellany* (Lancashire and Cheshire Record Society, 109, 1965), p. 22.

kind were the mainstay of the business of town authorities in the sixteenth and seventeenth centuries. The frequency with which they were repeated must represent a genuine desire to keep the streets clean and free of ordure, but, in the absence of the requisite technical knowledge, they were largely to no avail. Streets throughout the period were badly paved, if paved at all, often had middens in them, were the haunt of pigs, dogs and rats, could be ankle deep in mud and filth and were cleansed only if there were a heavy downpour of rain. There were dunghills against the walls of the Sheldonian Theatre in Oxford before the end of the seventeenth century.[76] Matters were made worse by the large numbers of livestock which could pass through a town, either on their way to a fair or else to Smithfield Market in London. In 1663, 18,574 cattle paid toll in Carlisle.[77] An Exchequer suit in the time of James I reveals the trade in cattle that passed through the market at Knighton, in Radnorshire. Gruffith ap David had bought 400 oxen, 200 kine, 400 horses and 6,000 sheep, and Rees ap Meredith had bought 300 beasts, 1,000 sheep, 40 horses and 200 swine. Both were drovers and both refused to pay the market tolls in the town.[78] Conditions only really begin to improve with the appointment of improvement commissioners during the eighteenth century, and their efforts were confined to the town for which they were appointed (see below in Chapter 18).

Another major problem which affected public space was the growth of traffic of every kind. The sedan chair was introduced into England in 1581 and hackney coaches appeared in London by 1620. Vehicular traffic could on occasion be considerable and it grew rapidly in volume, more especially with the development of a countrywide network of carriers' wagons from the last years of the sixteenth century and of coaching services after the Restoration. John Evelyn, writing immediately after the Great Fire of London, advocated the replacement of carts in the city with sleds, which continued to be used in Bristol until the early nineteenth century, whilst in Yarmouth, owing to the very narrow rows, there was a special Yarmouth cart with its wheels under the seat rather than projecting on either side.[79]

The public events which would have made use of the streets of a town seem to have changed in their nature and declined in their frequency during the course of the sixteenth and early seventeenth centuries, to reappear and grow in new directions in the years after the Restoration. The medieval pageantry surrounding such feasts as that of Corpus Christi was one of the first victims of the Reformation, for example, a symptom of that long-term secularisation of the urban landscape which is becoming increasingly apparent by the end of the

76 *VCH*, Oxfordshire, IV, p. 86.

77 A. R. B. Haldane, *The Drove Roads of Scotland* (Edinburgh, 1952; repr. 1973), p. 18.

78 T. I. J. Jones, ed., *Exchequer Proceedings concerning Wales in tempore James I* (Board of Celtic Studies, History and Law Series, 15, 1955), p. 319.

79 C. J. Palmer, ed., *The History of Great Yarmouth by Henry Manship* (London, 1854), p. 274.

eighteenth century. Some ancient feasts and pageants do continue in some towns for many years, however, occasionally into the eighteenth century and beyond. An Order was made at Sussex quarter sessions at Midsummer 1645 to suppress the Yeovalls in Lewes. This seems to have been the parish feast. A sword dance was still practised at Knaresborough as late as 1775. The procession of Greenhill Bower in Lichfield on Whit Monday continues into the twentieth century[80] and bull-running through the streets of Tutbury, West Bromwich and Stamford persisted until the early decades of the nineteenth.

Other public spectacles continued, new ones make their appearance and both come to play an increasingly significant role in public civic life during the course of the seventeenth century, the processions associated with the election of the mayor, for example, and, in those towns where they were held, with the opening of the assizes, whilst attendance at quarter sessions in county towns always brought large crowds of visitors. The Lord Mayor's Procession in London began in the 1530s and became an annual event. At Gloucester the masters of the twelve companies attended the mayor upon public occasions in their gowns, something which added 'a reputation to the city'.[81] Thomas Baskerville, writing in the 1670s, noticed that the inhabitants of Newbury were a sociable people, their companies, especially the clothiers and hatters, keeping great feasts,

> they and their wives after they had heard a sermon at church were met at the Globe with the town music, who playing merrily before them, the men in their best clothes followed them, and after them the women in very good order, two and two, neatly trimmed and finely dressed all in steeple-crowned hats, which was a pleasant sight to behold.[82]

Easter, May Day, Shrove Tuesday and Midsummer's Eve continued to be celebrated by popular festivities in many individual towns,[83] whilst the polarisation of politics at the end of the seventeenth century meant that parliamentary elections became increasingly confrontational, bringing crowds of people on to the streets and hence into public space.

London, befitting its role as a capital city, had its own range of public spectacles which would draw crowds of onlookers, from public executions to processions on royal visits (see Plate 7), birthdays, marriages and coronations such as that of Edward VI recorded in a contemporary view known only from an eighteenth-century copy made by Samuel Hieronymus Grimm.[84] When the Rev.

[80] B. C. Redwood, ed., *Quarter Sessions Order Book, 1642–1649* (Sussex Record Society, 54, 1954), p. 76; E. Hargrove, *The History and Antiquities of Knaresborough* (York, 1775), p. 85; *VCH*, Staffordshire, XIV, p. 159.

[81] Sir Robert Atkyns, *The Ancient and Present State of Glostershire* (London, 1712), p. 119.

[82] *HMC*, Portland MSS, vol. II, p. 285.

[83] See P. Borsay, '"All the town's a stage": urban ritual and ceremony 1660–1800', in Clark, ed., *Transformation of English Provincial Towns*, pp. 228–58.

[84] Depicted in A. Saint and G. Darley, *The Chronicles of London* (London, 1994), pp. 60–1.

Thomas Brockbank visited London as a young man in 1695 he went to see the building work at St Paul's, 'which is now in great forwardness', Chelsea Hospital and Westminster Hall. He climbed the Monument, saw the lions, leopard and ostriches at the Tower and visited Bedlam, which he found very distressing.[85]

(v) CHANGE IN THE URBAN ENVIRONMENT

The topography of many sixteenth- and seventeenth-century towns was affected by two disruptive forces, namely war and fire. The consequent destruction must have been disastrous for those involved but the rebuilding which followed, sometimes not completed for many years, was concerned to restore within traditional structures rather than to bring about any wide-ranging replanning.

A parliamentary survey of property in the Minster Yard in Lincoln describes something of the damage caused by the sacking in 1644. No. 18 Minster Yard was not rebuilt until 1663 and No. 17 in the 1670s.[86] Lichfield cathedral and close also suffered very badly during the Civil Wars. There were three sieges, leaving the gatehouse in ruins and eight out of fourteen houses in the Close destroyed or uninhabitable. By 1660 only the chapter house and vestry of the cathedral still had any roof. Rebuilding began almost immediately after the Restoration and the cathedral was re-dedicated in 1669.[87] The siege of Colchester in 1648 left many houses destroyed. In March 1649 there were said to be at least 193 tax-paying houses still derelict. Most were fairly quickly repaired or rebuilt, but signs of the damage were still visible at the end of the century. Five churches were badly damaged and so remained for many years, the church of St Mary not being rebuilt until 1713–14.[88] The full extent of Civil War damage to English towns is only just beginning to be appreciated. It was clearly very extensive in some towns, and took decades to make good.[89]

Scottish towns had their own problems with the military. Edinburgh was almost totally destroyed by fire by an English army led by the earl of Hertford in 1544, as was Melrose, which was 'raced' in 1545, again by the earl of Hertford, whilst Jedburgh was burned in 1523 and again in 1544 and 1545. Selkirk was erected into a sheriffdom of itself in 1540 and at the same time given the right to build town walls. The town walls of Peebles were built in 1570–4 and maintained until well into the eighteenth century. A tower and about 125 yards of the wall

85 R. Trappes-Lomax, ed., *The Diary and Letter Book of the Rev. Thomas Brockbank, 1671–1709* (Chetham Society, new series, 89, 1930), pp. 85 *et seq.*

86 S. Jones, K. Major and J. Varey, eds., *The Survey of Ancient Houses in Lincoln*, vol. I (Lincoln, 1984), pp. 20, 41, 47, vol. II (Lincoln, 1987), pp. 77, 84.

87 *VCH*, Staffordshire, III, pp. 174–6.

88 *VCH*, Essex, III, pp. 105–6; P. Morant, *The History and Antiquities of the Most Ancient Town and Borough of Colchester* (London, 1748), p. 68, Book 2, p. 4.

89 For an account of Civil War damage in Exeter see M. J. Stoyle, 'Whole streets converted to ashes: property destruction in Exeter during the English Civil War', *SHist.*, 16 (1994), 67–84.

still survive.[90] The town walls of Stirling were strengthened in 1547 by using money raised from letting the Water of Forth for three years at £18 Scots a year 'upone the strengthing and bigging of the wallis of the toun, at this present peralus tyme of neid, for resisting of oure auld innimeis of Ingland'.[91] A number of Scottish towns were badly damaged during the Civil Wars (see p. 155), and it was said of Tain in 1692 that a great part of the town was ruinous by quartering of troops and of Forfar that many inhabitants had fled the town for the same reason, whilst Nairn was said to be much damaged by reason of the Highland army.[92]

The other disruptive influence affecting the fabric of sixteenth- and seventeenth-century towns was fire. Very few towns escaped one, and they could occur again and again, leading to widespread destruction. The rebuilding which followed rarely leads to any significant change in the structure of the space thus affected. Streets were sometimes widened, ancient obstructions removed, but there was no large-scale replanning.[93]

The most significant of these town fires was the Great Fire of London, which brought many important changes into the layout of houses in the City, and in due course, by example, throughout England. The fire, in September of 1666, destroyed 13,200 houses, and 87 parish churches. The Act for Rebuilding was passed in February of 1667. It laid down specifications for three sorts of houses, together with mansion houses of the greatest bigness. All rebuilding had to be done in brick and tile. Houses in by-streets and lanes were to be of two storeys, houses in streets and lanes of note were to be of three storeys, whilst houses in high and principal streets were to be of four storeys. The act also laid down details of the thickness of the walls. The houses which were built following these regulations came to serve as models throughout England. Celia Fiennes notes on a couple of occasions the presence in provincial towns of houses built in brick 'of the London mode'.[94] The actual rebuilding took place on a piecemeal basis and was undertaken by individual proprietors. Many lanes and side streets were widened and a number of the markets were moved out of the streets but only fifty-one of the eighty-seven destroyed churches were rebuilt. Queen Street was one of the very few new streets laid out, and Cornhill and Lombard Street were made into 'high streets'. Pepys found the entry into them 'mighty noble'.[95] The

[90] RCHM (Scotland), *The City of Edinburgh*, p. xlv; *ibid.*, *Roxburghshire* (Edinburgh, 1956), vol. II, p. 268 (Edinburgh, 1956), vol. I, p. 196; *ibid.*, *Selkirkshire* (Edinburgh, 1957), p. 11; *ibid.*, *Peebleshire* (Edinburgh, 1967), vol. II, pp. 277 *et seq.*

[91] R. Renwick, ed., *Extracts from the Records of the Royal Burgh of Stirling, 1519–1666* (Scottish Burgh Records Society, 1887), p. 50.

[92] Marwick, ed., *Register*, pp. 131, 136, 139.

[93] See E. L. Jones, 'The reduction of fire damage in southern England, 1650–1850', *Post-Medieval Archaeology*, 2 (1968), 140–9; M. W. Farr, ed., *The Great Fire of Warwick, 1694* (Dugdale Society, 36, 1992); and S. Porter, 'The Great Fire of Gravesend, 1727', *SHist.*, 12 (1990), 19–33.

[94] Morris, ed., *Celia Fiennes*, pp. 143, 152, 184.

[95] R. Latham and W. Matthews, eds., *The Diary of Samuel Pepys*, vol. IX (London, 1976), p. 307, and see T. F. Reddaway, *The Rebuilding of London* (London, 1940), *passim*.

London which had emerged by the end of the seventeenth century was much cleaner than the timber-framed medieval city which had been destroyed in the flames, but its sober brick façades were also much less richly varied and exuberant.

War and fire were disasters which could affect individual towns spectacularly, but not all towns were so affected, and such change as they brought was a matter of degree, not of substance. Change could also come to public space in more subtle but less dramatic ways. Urban population growth brought its own problems, and the changes this prompted become more and more apparent in the years after the Restoration as the growing numbers of gentry to be found in towns demanded improved services and facilities, of which a better water supply was one, something which a growing number of towns made some effort to provide (see Table 11.3). This entailed the laying of pipes and the building of cisterns and conduits. The water supply itself was sometimes drawn from a distance, sometimes from springs in the neighbourhood. It was often intermittent in its flow, uncertain in its quality and in any case rarely extended beyond the main streets. That provided by William Yarnold in Newcastle-upon-Tyne was available only once a week, and by 1712 there were still only 161 individual consumers, of whom 20 were in Gateshead.[96] In Leeds the water system, with a water engine to convey the river water by lead pipes to the several parts of the town, was installed in 1695 by George Sorocold, the leading water engineer of the day. He did the same for a number of other towns, including Macclesfield, Yarmouth and Portsmouth, as well as installing two separate systems in London.[97]

An improved water supply is but one facet of a growing demand for urban improvement, particularly evident in the decades after the Restoration and often leading to new forms of public space devoted to leisure and entertainment, especially for the new fashionable society now to be found in towns. This space could be either inside or outside a building. Inns, for example, like the Three Tuns, first recorded in Banbury in 1677, which had a bowling green and was used for business meetings, assemblies, balls, card parties and concerts,[98] saw the range of their functions widened and extended. Travelling companies of players put on plays in many provincial towns in England, often in the courtyards of inns, in the years up to the outbreak of the Civil War, which put an end to their activities. The earliest purpose-built theatre in England seems to be the Theatre, in

[96] R. W. Rennison, 'The supply of water to Newcastle on Tyne and Gateshead, 1680–1837', *Archaeologia Aeliana*, 5th series, 5 (1977), 179–96.

[97] R. Thoresby, *Ducatus Leodiensis* (London, 1715), p. 50; and see C. S. Davies, *A History of Macclesfield* (Manchester, 1961), pp. 79–80, 151, 156–7.

[98] *VCH*, Oxfordshire, x, p. 15. For an account of the significance of inns in the commercial life of towns see A. Everitt, 'The English urban inn, 1560–1760', in A. Everitt, ed., *Perspectives in English Urban History* (London, 1973), pp. 91–137.

Shoreditch, in London, built in 1576. The Globe, timber framed and thatched, was built in 1598 on the south bank of the Thames in Southwark. Theatres were reopened in London after the Restoration when Charles II issued letters patent for two companies to perform at what became the Theatre Royal in Drury Lane. Travelling companies of players also resumed their activities after the Restoration, but purpose-built provincial theatres were not erected until the eighteenth century, one of the earliest being in Bath in 1705.[99] The first museum in England was erected in Oxford in 1683 to house the collections given to the university by Elias Ashmole, who had in his turn acquired some of the curiosities collected by the Tradescants.[100] An entirely new building type, it is well into the eighteenth century before another appears.

Open spaces could also find their uses changed. Tennis courts are marked on Speed's plan of Bath of 1611, just to the west of the abbey (see Plate 3). Bowling greens became increasingly popular and by the end of the seventeenth century few towns were without at least one. William Schellinks, a Dutch artist, records in his diary visiting the bowling green at Guildford in 1662, next to the castle, itself in a ruinous state.[101] Thomas Baskerville records them at Bedford, in the castle ruins, at Saffron Walden, Warwick, Gloucester, in the gaol, where the townsmen come to divert themselves, and Pontefract, 'where you may have good wine'.[102] Celia Fiennes was clearly delighted with the bowling green at Newcastle-upon-Tyne, which, she wrote, was very pleasant, 'a little walke out of the town with a large gravel walke round it with two rows of trees on each side making it very shady; there is a fine entertaining house that makes up the fourth side before which is a paved walke under pyasoes (piazzas) of bricke'.[103] Many were to be found in inns, and, as the comments of Baskerville make clear, were as much centres of conviviality as of serious attention to the game of bowls.

There are also by the end of the seventeenth century a handful of examples of open spaces being deliberately dedicated to public use by being cleared, levelled and planted with trees, usually by the corporation, very occasionally by private benefactors.[104] In either case they may be seen as external manifestations of urban pride and sense of community, perhaps inspired by the laying out of Pall Mall in London in 1661.[105] At Ross on Wye John Kyrle laid out the Prospect from 1693. John Byng visited the town in 1787, 'and much admired the prospect walk (overlooking a very rich country, the bridge, castle and village of

[99] M. Hamilton, *Bath before Beau Nash* (Bath, 1978), p. 9.

[100] A. MacGregor, 'The cabinet of curiosities in seventeenth-century Britain', in O. Impey and A. MacGregor, eds., *The Origins of Museums* (Oxford, 1985), p. 152.

[101] M. Exwood and H. L. Lehmann, eds., *The Journal of William Schellinks' Travels in England, 1661–1663* (Camden Society, 5th series, 1, 1993), p. 147.

[102] *HMC*, Portland MSS, vol. II, pp. 263, 264, 290, 293, 310.

[103] Morris, ed., *Celia Fiennes*, p. 211.

[104] See P. Borsay, *The English Urban Renaissance* (Oxford, 1989), esp. Part II.

[105] *Survey of London*, vol. XXIX: *St James Westminster, Part I, South of Piccadilly*, p. 322.

Wilton, with a long sweep of the River Wye), which was planted by Mr Kyrle, the noted man of Ross . . . whose fame yet blooms'.[106] Celia Fiennes visited Shrewsbury in 1698 and noted the Abbey gardens, 'with severall fine grass walks kept exactly cut and roled for Companye to walke in; every Wednesday most of the town and Ladyes and Gentlemen walk there as in St James's Parke'.[107] This is a development which accelerates rapidly during the course of the eighteenth century (see Chapter 18).

(vi) CONCLUSION

The morphology of the early modern town experienced substantial change during this period. Of all the factors at work it is probably true to say that the Reformation had the greatest overall impact since it affected all towns to some extent, and brought widespread structural change to ancient patterns of land use. A profound shift in values leads to the destruction of many religious buildings and dramatic change in the function of others. Religious dissent eventually leads to the building of nonconformist places of worship and the need to defend the reformed faith leads to the building of new colleges and schools. Every town throughout Britain was affected in some way and its effects continued to be felt throughout the period. War and fire, although disastrous for those directly involved, were much more limited in their effects since by no means all towns were affected by them.

The reception of the principles of classical architecture, a consequence of the Renaissance, came to fruition in the years after the Restoration. New churches were built in the new style and private houses were at least refronted in it, leading to the beginning of the end for the vernacular building tradition.

The intellectual ferment which lies behind both Reformation and Renaissance leads to a demand for entirely new types of buildings, whilst the technological innovation which is associated with this ferment puts new kinds of vehicles on the streets and the voyages of discovery put a new range of merchandise on display in new shops in every town in the two kingdoms.

These changes primarily affected buildings and land use and took place within an ancient and largely unchanging structure of streets and public spaces. These were in their turn only just beginning to change in the majority of towns in the years after the Restoration, and it will be well into the eighteenth century before they are significantly affected, with change in Scottish and Welsh towns often lagging as much as a century behind that in English ones.

[106] J. Byng, *The Torrington Diaries*, ed. C. B. Andrews (London, 1934), vol. I, pp. 264–5.

[107] Morris, ed., *Celia Fiennes*, p. 227. Other walks and gardens are listed in Appendix 6 of Borsay, *English Urban Renaissance*, pp. 350–4.

· 10 ·

London 1540–1700

JEREMY BOULTON

(i) INTRODUCTION: LONDON IN EUROPEAN PERSPECTIVE

> London is the capital of England and so superior to other English towns that London is not said to be in England, but rather England to be in London, for England's most resplendent objects may be seen in and around London; so that he who sightsees London and the royal courts in its immediate vicinity may assert, without impertinence that he is properly acquainted with England.
>
> (Thomas Platter, *Travels in England in 1599*)

LONDON'S GROWTH was a phenomenon of European importance in our period. At the start, London was already a major capital city, ranking sixth in terms of size in mid-sixteenth-century Europe (see Table 10.1). It was dwarfed by the Italian city of Naples and was much smaller than either Venice (ranked second) or Paris (ranked third); and it was outnumbered by the Portuguese capital of Lisbon and London's principal trading partner, Antwerp. Within fifty years all this had changed. By 1600 London was ranked third in Europe after Naples and Paris, and its neighbour and erstwhile trading partner, Antwerp, was nowhere. Continued growth meant that London came second only to Paris by 1650 and by the end of the seventeenth century was the biggest European city containing some half a million people.

London then developed from a modest capital city, with an economy largely dependent on the export of woollen cloth, to a metropolis at the heart of the European economy. Over our period its population spilled out from the original relatively densely populated districts of the City within and without the Walls (see Plate 1) to form an urban conurbation stretching from Wapping and Poplar in the east to Westminster in the west. Its economic impact on the nation expanded from the immediately adjacent counties to the entire nation, including its overseas colonies. The task of this chapter is to provide some idea of how this extraordinary growth was accomplished and what kind of economy and society it produced.

Table 10.1 *European cities with 75,000+ inhabitants 1550–1700*

	1550	1600	1650	1700
London	75,000[a]	200,000	400,000	575,000[b]
Amsterdam	30,000	65,000	175,000	200,000
Antwerp	90,000	47,000	70,000	70,000
Brussels	40,000	50,000	69,000	80,000
Hamburg	29,000	40,000	75,000	70,000
Lyon	70,000	40,000	75,000	97,000
Marseille	30,000	40,000	66,000	75,000
Paris	130,000	220,000	430,000	510,000
Rouen	65,000	60,000	82,000	64,000
Genoa	65,000	71,000	90,000	80,000
Milan	69,000	120,000	100,000	124,000
Venice	158,000	139,000	120,000	138,000
Rome	45,000	105,000	124,000	138,000
Naples	212,000	281,000	176,000	216,000
Palermo	70,000	105,000	129,000	100,000
Madrid	30,000	49,000	130,000	110,000
Seville	65,000	90,000	60,000	96,000
Lisbon	98,000	100,000	130,000	165,000
Vienna	n/a	50,000	60,000	114,000

[a] The higher estimate presented by Harding has been adopted.
[b] This highly traditional figure has been preferred to some later estimates.
Sources: J. de Vries, *European Urbanization 1500–1800* (London, 1984), pp. 270–8; for London, V. Harding, 'The population of London, 1550–1700: a review of the published evidence', *LJ*, 15 (1990), 112; C. Spence, *London in the 1690s: A Social Atlas* (London, 1999), Table 4.1.

(ii) LONDON'S DEMOGRAPHY: LIVING AND DYING IN THE METROPOLIS

London's demography serves to introduce a number of themes of great importance to the capital's history. Its migration experience indicates the large number of links to other parts of the country possessed by its inhabitants. Experience of London life was extensive, with between one in eight and one in six of those surviving to adulthood in England living in London at some point in their lives. The demographic expansion of London underpins any informed discussion of the metropolitan economy, of its social structure and the impact that the metropolis may have had on the nation.[1]

[1] For London's demography see above, pp. 197 *et seq.*, and below, pp. 649–55. See R. Finlay, *Population and Metropolis* (Cambridge, 1981), p. 9.

A great deal of recent work has, of course, gone into estimating London's population size. Table 10.1 includes the most plausible of the current estimates of London's total population, defining 'London' as that area contained within the bills of mortality as constituted in 1636. The capital grew most quickly in the late sixteenth century, doubled in size again by the mid-seventeenth century and increased by over 40 per cent again by the end of our period. This phenomenal growth occurred at different rates in different areas of the capital. In particular it was concentrated in the western suburbs of the metropolis and was probably slowest in the built-up areas within the City walls. One recent estimate is that the population of metropolitan Westminster, Middlesex and Surrey may have increased something like eightfold between 1580 and 1695 compared to little or no overall increase within the City of London and its liberties. This suburban demographic expansion was most dramatic before the Restoration but continued at a spectacular rate in selected areas thereafter, notably in some of the parishes in the fashionable West End. By the Restoration that area of London governed directly by the lord mayor (here defined as the twenty-five wards north of the river, within and without the walls) already contained less than half of the capital's population.[2]

Migration to the capital was crucial for sustaining overall population growth. It has been calculated that later seventeenth-century London required some 8,000 migrants *net* annually to sustain the capital's rate of increase. Migrants were integral to metropolitan growth because, throughout the whole of our period, more people died in the capital than were born there. This surplus of deaths in part reflected the incidence of migration itself, many migrants contributed only to burials in the capital, dying before they could marry and have children. Such migrants, too, were peculiarly vulnerable to metropolitan diseases not encountered in their place of origin. None the less the main cause of the consistent surplus of deaths was not the vulnerability of young migrants to the capital's fearsome diseases, but the high mortality rate, notably amongst infants and young children, which exceeded the fertility of the capital's population and ensured that Londoners were not capable of reproducing themselves at any point in our period.[3]

[2] Finlay, *Population and Metropolis*, pp. 51–66; R. Finlay and B. Shearer, 'Population growth and suburban expansion', in A. L. Beier and R. Finlay, eds., *London 1500–1700* (London, 1986), pp. 37–59; V. Harding, 'The population of London, 1550–1700: a review of the published evidence', *LJ*, 15 (1990), 111–28; I. Sutherland, 'When was the Great Plague? Mortality in London, 1563 to 1665', in D. V. Glass and R. Revelle, eds., *Population and Social Change* (London, 1972), pp. 287–320; N. G. Brett-James, *The Growth of Stuart London* (London, 1935), pp. 495–515; I. W. Archer, *The Pursuit of Stability* (Cambridge, 1991), pp. 12–13; J. P. Boulton, *Neighbourhood and Society* (Cambridge, 1987), pp. 14–27.

[3] E. A. Wrigley, 'A simple model of London's importance in changing English society and economy, 1650–1750', repr. in E. A. Wrigley, *People, Cities and Wealth* (Oxford, 1987), p. 135; Finlay, *Population and Metropolis*, pp. 9, 63–9; J. Landers, *Death and the Metropolis* (Cambridge, 1993), pp. 43–9, 180–3; M. Kitch, 'Capital and kingdom: migration to later Stuart London', in Beier and

Most Londoners, then, were born outside the capital. Just 13 per cent of a sample of East Enders, 1580–1640, had been born in London, whilst a larger sample of deponents drawn from a similar period, suggested that perhaps 22 per cent were natives. In the later seventeenth century there may have been proportionally more London-born inhabitants, perhaps as many as 30 per cent.[4] Most migrants were probably in their late teens or early twenties when first coming to London. In the period before 1650 male apprentices formed a very significant proportion of newcomers but thereafter the number of male apprentices recruited by the city companies declined. The geographical origins of the migrant apprentices, as well as those of the minority who went on to become freemen, have suggested that London's migration field contracted over the seventeenth century, with increasing numbers recruited from the Home Counties and fewer from northern areas, although evidence from deposition material shows less of a contraction. Another important source of immigration was European Protestant refugees, who settled in large numbers in the 1560s and 1570s, and again in the late seventeenth century. Lastly, Londoners moved frequently within the city itself, albeit over relatively short distances, often from one street to another or even within a street or alley. It was therefore commonplace for more than half of household heads to disappear from a parish or district over a ten-year period.[5]

Until 1665 bubonic plague was responsible for a significant number of deaths in the capital. Between 6.6 per cent and 19 per cent of all those dying between 1580 and 1650 were plague victims. The disease killed most Londoners during the summer months and in particular years; in declining order of severity the most serious outbreaks were 1563, 1603, 1625 and 1665. The incidence of plague reveals much about London's topographical development. The sixteenth-century epidemics seem to have fallen as heavily in the wealthy districts of the

Footnote 3 (*cont.*)
Finlay, eds., *London*, pp. 224–51; J. Wareing, 'Changes in the geographical distribution of the recruitment of apprentices to the London companies 1486–1750', *Journal of Historical Geography*, 6 (1980), 241–9; J. Wareing, 'Migration to London and transatlantic emigration of indentured servants 1683–1775', *Journal of Historical Geography*, 7 (1981), 356–78; P. Earle, 'The female labour market in London in the late seventeenth and early eighteenth centuries', *Ec.HR*, 2nd series, 42 (1989), 333–4; D. Cressy, 'Occupations, migration and literacy in east London, 1580–1640', *Local Population Studies*, 5 (1970), 53–60.

4 Earle, 'Female labour market', 334; Cressy, 'Occupations, migration and literacy', 57.

5 V. B. Elliott, 'Single women in the London marriage market: age, status and mobility, 1598–1619', in R. B. Outhwaite, ed., *Marriage and Society* (London, 1981), p. 90; Earle, 'Female labour market', 334; Finlay, *Population and Metropolis*, pp. 45–7, 64–9; S. Rappaport, *Worlds within Worlds* (Cambridge, 1989), pp. 76–86, 295; R. D. Gwynn, 'The number of Huguenot immigrants in England in the late seventeenth century', *Journal of Historical Geography*, 9 (1983), 391–3; L. Schwarz, 'London apprentices in the seventeenth century: some problems', *Local Population Studies*, 38 (1987), 18–22; Boulton, *Neighbourhood and Society*, pp. 207–27; P. Earle, *The Making of the English Middle Class* (London, 1989), pp. 240–2.

city within the walls as in the less densely populated suburbs. Over time, however, bubonic plague became increasingly concentrated in that rapidly growing suburban area. The last case of plague was in 1679, but, none the less the overall death rate was probably higher at the end of our period than it had been 100 years earlier. In part this was because London grew large enough to act as a permanent reservoir of some killer diseases. Smallpox, in particular, appears to have become an endemic disease of childhood by the early eighteenth century. Death rates also rose because sanitation deteriorated and overcrowding became more common, particularly in those areas of the capital where susceptible migrants congregated.[6]

Continuing population expansion meant a rising demand for accommodation of all types. Another stimulus to building were the numerous fires that regularly destroyed parts of the capital's housing stock. Fires destroyed much of London Bridge in 1634, part of Wapping in 1673 and a good deal of Southwark in 1676. The danger of fire and the importance of building in brick rather than timber was recognised by a royal proclamation in 1661 but the Great Fire of London in 1666 proved the biggest stimulus to building techniques. This catastrophe destroyed the heart of the City within the walls, consuming some 13,000 houses, 44 company halls, 87 parish churches and causing destruction valued at about £10 million. Lastly, the dissolution in London saw the 'redevelopment' of the twenty-three important religious houses. They provided the five hospitals to house the sick and vagrant poor of the city and others, like the Priory of St Mary Overy, were pulled down and the land used to erect tenement dwellings. Others were converted to aristocratic mansions.[7]

London's growth meant not only the redevelopment of its existing fabric but the encroachment of new buildings into suburban fields in the west and the north-east. In the East End, too, a ribbon of buildings two miles long and half a mile wide reaching Limehouse grew up along the Thames. John Stow, writing at the end of the sixteenth century, remembered the removal of elm trees in the East End hamlet of Shadwell to make way for tenements. Such building in London occurred despite a series of royal proclamations starting in 1580, forbidding the

[6] P. Slack, *The Impact of Plague in Tudor and Stuart England* (London, 1985), pp. 114–72; Sutherland, 'When was the Great Plague?', pp. 287–320; Finlay, *Population and Metropolis*, pp. 114, 117, 155–7; T. R. Forbes, 'By what disease or casualty? The changing face of death in London', in C. Webster, ed., *Health, Medicine and Mortality in the Sixteenth Century* (London, 1979), pp. 117–39; A. Appleby, 'Nutrition and disease: the case of London', *Journal of Interdisciplinary History*, 6 (1975), 1–22; Finlay and Shearer, 'Population growth and suburban expansion', pp. 48–9; Landers, *Death and the Metropolis*, pp. 86, 139.

[7] M. J. Power, 'East London housing in the seventeenth century', in P. Clark and P. Slack, eds., *Crisis and Order in English Towns 1500–1700* (London, 1972), p. 246; K. V. Thomas, *Religion and the Decline of Magic* (Harmondsworth, 1978), p. 19; E. de Maré, *Wren's London* (London, 1975), pp. 54–5; P. S. Seaver, *Wallington's World* (London, 1985), p. 48; E. J. Davis, 'The transformation of London', in R. W. Seton-Watson, ed., *Tudor Studies Presented to Albert Frederick Pollard* (London, 1924), pp. 287–9.

erection of new housing. Development was, at first, done in a piecemeal manner, but increasing order and planning of streets began in the 1630s. When there was not enough space left, houses in London were divided and subdivided by owners and lessees. Overcrowding seems to have been a particular problem in the parts of the West End of London, the most rapidly growing area of the metropolis, where, by the middle of the seventeenth century, large numbers of houses were in multiple occupation and 'shed dwellings' were common. Much of the West End, however, was developed by perceptive aristocratic property developers like the earl of Bedford or (later) dubious property speculators like Nicholas Barebon, who were catering for the new demand for town houses from the nation's elite. Social enclaves were constructed in parts of the West End, like Lincoln's Inn Fields (1638) or the Covent Garden Piazza, one of the earliest experiments in town planning solely 'for persons of repute and quality' (1630). Observant contemporaries could appreciate at a glance the social and economic differences that were increasingly apparent in our period, such as the 'fayre' West End as opposed to the 'unsavery' East End.[8]

(iii) LONDON'S ECONOMY

An account of London's economy must begin with overseas trade.[9] The port of London, its shipping industry and ancillary trades, might have employed one quarter of the capital's population by the early eighteenth century. Many important London industries processed imported raw materials, or manufactured for export. Developments in and control of the various branches of overseas trade and commerce, moreover, determined the composition of the capital's ruling elite. Over our period London's domestic export trade consisted largely of woollen cloths. In the mid-sixteenth century this was largely undressed broadcloth or the less expensive 'kerseys', which were dyed and finished and exported

[8] V. Pearl, *London and the Outbreak of the Puritan Revolution* (Oxford, 1961), pp. 18–23; Power, 'East London housing', pp. 238–40; N. G. Brett-James, 'A speculative London builder of the seventeenth century, Dr. Nicholas Barbon', *Transactions of the London and Middlesex Archaeological Society*, new series, 6 (1933), 110–45; M. J. Power, 'The east and west in early-modern London', in E. W. Ives, R. J. Knecht and J. J. Scarisbrick, eds., *Wealth and Power in Tudor England* (London, 1978), pp. 169, 178–82.

[9] C. Clay, *Economic Expansion and Social Change: England 1500–1700* (Cambridge, 1984), vol. II, pp. 103–82; B. Dietz, ed., *The Port and Trade of Early Elizabethan London: Documents* (London Record Society, 8, 1972); B. Dietz, 'Overseas trade and metropolitan growth', in Beier and Finlay, eds., *London*, pp. 115–40; R. Davis, 'England and the Mediterranean, 1570–1670', in F. J. Fisher, ed., *Essays in the Economic and Social History of Tudor and Stuart England* (Cambridge, 1961), pp. 117–37; R. Davis, 'English foreign trade, 1660–1700', in W. E. Minchinton, ed., *The Growth of English Overseas Trade in the Seventeenth and Eighteenth Centuries* (London, 1969), pp. 257–72; R. Davis, *English Overseas Trade 1500–1700* (London, 1973); F. J. Fisher, *London and the English Economy 1500–1700*, ed. P. J. Corfield and N. B. Harte (London, 1990), pp. 81–104, 119–30; Rappaport, *Worlds*, pp. 87–122; Earle, *Making of the English Middle Class*, pp. 17–81. See also, below, pp. 390 *et seq.* and 642 *et passim*.

by the London Merchant Adventurers the short distance to the great European entrepôt of Antwerp. Statistics available for the seventeenth century indicate that the dominance of textiles in London's export trade declined particularly rapidly after 1640 but still remained by far the dominant type of commodity exported from London at the end of our period.[10]

The composition of textile exports from the capital altered dramatically from the early seventeenth century. Increasingly such exports were of the lighter and finished New Draperies, exported longer distances to the warmer countries of southern Europe and the Mediterranean. By 1640 such textiles, in terms of value, probably equalled the export trade in heavy undressed broadcloth, which latter trade had stagnated after 1615. By the end of our period the export of New Draperies exceeded the total value of 'Old Draperies'. As significant for London's economy was, however, the increase in *re-exports* in the seventeenth century. The actual value of goods re-exported from London equalled the export value of all other non-textile goods in 1640, and London merchants also profited from re-exporting goods directly between foreign ports rather than bringing them through London. By 1700 the re-export of commodities like tobacco, sugar, pepper and goods such as linens, calicoes and silks came to 38 per cent of the total value of London's exports and re-exports combined. The restructuring and growth of the capital's export trade, which led to the exploitation of longer trade routes, new overseas markets and colonisation in the New World, all had a profound impact on the metropolitan economy. New commercial organisations were set up to control branches of the new trades, more and heavier shipping was required to carry English goods, and the capital's economy benefited from the extra finishing, refining, warehousing and processing of both exported and re-exported goods. One example, however, may serve to demonstrate the beneficial effects of overseas trade expansion. Exports from London to the West Indies and North America were valued at something like £212,000 in 1686 and these were mostly manufactures. Demand for such goods stimulated the local silk industry and London's skilled artisans also made a 'large proportion' of many other manufactures, notably hats and shoes, shipped to America in the late seventeenth century.[11]

[10] J. A. Chartres, 'Trade and shipping in the port of London. Wiggins Key in the later seventeenth century', *Journal of Transport History*, 3rd series, 1(1980), 29–47; R. Davis, *The Rise of the English Shipping Industry in the Seventeenth and Eighteenth Centuries* (London, 1962), p. 390; L. D. Schwarz, *London in the Age of Industrialisation* (Cambridge, 1992), pp. 8–9; R. Brenner, *Merchants and Revolution* (Cambridge, 1993), esp. pp. 3–184; R. G. Lang, 'London's aldermen in business', *Guildhall Miscellany*, 3 (1971), 242–64; Clay, *Economic Expansion*, II, p. 144.

[11] F. J. Fisher, 'London's export trade', in Fisher, *London and the English Economy*, pp. 121–9; Clay, *Economic Expansion*, II, p. 144; Davis, 'English foreign trade, 1660–1700', pp. 270–1; N. Zahedieh, 'London and the colonial consumer in the late seventeenth century', *Ec.HR*, 2nd series, 47 (1994), 247–9, 258–9; D. Corner, 'The tyranny of fashion: the case of the felt-hatting trade in the late seventeenth and eighteenth centuries', *Textile History*, 22 (1991), 153–78.

Many London merchants earned most, if not all, of their profits from the sale of *imports*, rather than domestic exports, the overseas market for the textile element of which appears to have been finite. In particular, the period after the collapse of the Antwerp entrepôt in the 1560s saw largely import-led growth in the capital's overseas trade as London merchants sought to profit from a huge range of imported goods paid for by the sale of English cloth and the export of bullion. Figures calculated by Brian Dietz give some idea of the range of goods imported *into* London from overseas. In addition to illustrating the growing demand for luxury consumables such as wines and spices, many of the goods imported in the 1560s indicate the poverty of much native manufacturing industry then, with high values placed upon items like hats and soap and the need to import such things as pins, paper, mirrors and glass manufactures. Thereafter what statistics there are indicate the growth of the metropolitan import trade and in particular illustrate the increasing value placed upon food imports like sugar, tobacco and wines, and the development of native industries such as the silk industry, much of it located in the capital, capable of consuming raw silk valued at £344,000 by the end of the period.[12]

Although London's domination of the nation's overseas trade diminished a little towards the end of the seventeenth century (as provincial ports competed successfully in the growing trade with the colonies and proved able to build ships more cheaply) overseas trade remained of vital importance in stimulating the metropolitan economy. Some industries, such as shipbuilding or sugar refining, were stimulated directly whilst the flood of imports facilitated a process of imitation and emulation by local craftsmen, sometimes responding to policy initiatives and current mercantile theory. Foreign trade provided a significant flow of income into the metropolitan economy, with high profits available for the successful merchants. Investment in shipping and company stocks and bonds attracted perhaps one in seven of those occupying the middle station in Restoration London.[13]

Despite this emphasis on overseas trade, it is probable that domestic trade was far more important to most of those operating within London's economy. Less than half of London's Jacobean aldermen were overseas merchants and in the mid-sixteenth century foreign trade was concentrated in the hands of around 100 Merchant Adventurers. Those responsible for feeding, clothing and fuelling the city and its inhabitants, and sending London products to the provinces, greatly outnumbered those investing overseas.[14]

[12] See Rappaport, *Worlds*, pp. 88–90; Dietz, 'Overseas trade', pp. 121–7, 139 n. 35; Dietz, ed., *Port and Trade of Early Elizabethan London*, pp. 152–4; Clay, *Economic Expansion*, II, pp. 125, 158–9.

[13] Davis, *Rise of the English Shipping Industry*, pp. 33–5, 55; Dietz, 'Overseas trade', pp. 129–35; Earle, *Making of the English Middle Class*, pp. 137–47.

[14] Lang, 'London's aldermen in business', 244, 259–60; G. D. Ramsay, *The City of London in International Politics at the Accession of Elizabeth Tudor* (Manchester, 1975), p. 49.

London's domestic inward trade consisted in the growing traffic in foodstuffs needed to supply its expanding population, the burgeoning coal trade to keep that population warm and the supply of raw materials and partly finished manufactures, notably, of course, textiles, for local consumption or export. The capital's outward trade consisted of the redistribution of overseas imports by dealers and wholesale merchants, the distribution and sale of London manufactures and the transmission of provincial goods for which the port of London acted merely as a staging post. The actual volume of any branch of these trades is largely a matter of educated guesswork, but some elements in London's trade can be given a little more precision where the commodity in question was transported mainly by coastal shipping.[15]

The coastal trade of London was, as one would expect, on a considerable scale and grew enormously over the seventeenth century. There were some 352 coastwise shipments outwards from London in 1628 to about 54 different ports, but by 1683 there were 1,001 shipments to over 100 destinations. The incoming coastal trade was still more substantial. There were, for example, 4,131 shipments coastwise into London from some 68 provincial ports in 1683. The sheer number of ships, hoys and barges involved in supplying the metropolis certainly exceeded those involved in the overseas trade of the capital, although vessels plying the coasts were usually much smaller. Coal accounted for something like 40 per cent of the coastal trade shipments to London at the end of the seventeenth century, having risen from something like 200–300 shipments in the 1550s and 1560s to 2,469 in the 1690s. Otherwise feeding the capital with grain from the Home Counties was also done on a predictably large scale. Grain shipments from the ports of Kent, Essex and East Anglia in total may have exceeded the shipping devoted to coal. Otherwise the capital consumed huge quantities of butter and cheese, raw materials like the dyestuffs copperas, potash and madder, lead, iron and timber and provincial manufactures such as nails and cloth.[16]

Surviving information on London's outwards coastal trade reveals London's expected function as distributor and manufacturer, sending ranges of the manufactured goods and luxury imports to the provincial ports. Notable among

[15] J. A. Chartres, *Internal Trade in England, 1500–1700* (London, 1977); T. S. Willan, *The English Coasting Trade, 1600–1750* (Manchester, 1938); J. A. Chartres, 'The capital's provincial eyes: London's inns in the early eighteenth century', *LJ*, 3 (1977), 24–39; J. A. Chartres, 'Road carrying in England in the seventeenth century: myth and reality', *Ec.HR*, 2nd series, 30 (1977), 73–94; Chartres, 'Trade and shipping in the port of London', 29–47; J. A. Chartres, 'Food consumption and internal trade', in Beier and Finlay, eds., *London*, pp. 168–96; F. J. Fisher, 'The development of the London food market, 1540–1640', in Fisher, *London and the English Economy*, pp. 61–79; Lang, 'London's aldermen in business', *passim*.

[16] J. Hatcher, *The History of the British Coal Industry*, vol. 1: *Before 1700* (Oxford, 1993), pp. 499, 540; Willan, *Coasting trade*, pp. 203–6; Chartres, 'Trade and shipping', 39; Fisher, *London and the English Economy*, pp. 61–79; Chartres, *Internal Trade*, pp. 16–17, 29.

London-made goods sent up coastwise were ordnance, ironmongery, haberdashery, soap and hats in the early seventeenth century, whilst later on the capital also sent a great deal of paper and stationery. Most marked, however, is the distribution of imported products. Early on these were wines, groceries and oils but by 1683 this also included the product of new metropolitan refining industries such as tobacco, spirits, drugs and sometimes sugar and molasses. The coastal trade can, of course, with a few exceptions, only suggest the volume and range of products exchanged between the capital and its growing hinterland. It has been estimated recently that the coasting trade supplied just 10–14 per cent of London's needs in the early seventeenth century, and perhaps 20 per cent by 1700. Most goods were therefore transported in carts and, increasingly, wagons, or by river, and light-weight products were also distributed by pedlars and carriers.[17]

Londoners experienced significant alterations in their consumption patterns during this period. Since London represented by far the largest single concentration of people in the country, all of whom were dependent on the ability of the primary sector to feed and clothe them, it naturally represented the most important single market for food, fuel and consumer goods. Arguably, too, the capital's inhabitants possessed exceptionally high purchasing power throughout this period, so that consumption of goods and services took place on an even greater scale.[18]

Londoners made the transition from wood fuel to predominantly coal between the late sixteenth and the mid-seventeenth century. By the mid-century, therefore, if not before, air pollution from the burning of coal was an enduring feature of London's environment and trades associated with that industry were numerous and on the increase. The capital's consumption of basic foodstuffs too was naturally on a prodigious scale. In the 1690s, to cite an example, Londoners were thought to have consumed 88,400 beeves and 600,000 sheep a year. Given the capital's population increase of the period and its increasingly politically conscious inhabitants it is scarcely surprising that feeding the city was a constant preoccupation of the authorities who intervened in times of scarcity, ensuring both the stocking of granaries and the import of grain from abroad. Sixteen new suburban markets were also constructed in the seventeenth century to bring this increasing volume of produce to metropolitan consumers. Growing metropolitan demand for root crops and other vegetables also encouraged the development of capital-intensive market gardening both in and, increasingly, around the capital.[19]

[17] Willan, *Coasting Trade*, pp. 203–5; Chartres, 'Food consumption and internal trade', p. 179; D. Gerhold, 'Packhorses and wheeled vehicles in England, 1550–1800', *Journal of Transport History*, 3rd series, 14 (1993), 1–26; Chartres, 'The capital's provincial eyes', 24–39; Chartres, 'Road carrying in England', 73–94; Chartres, *Internal Trade*; T. S. Willan, *River Navigation in England, 1600–1750* (Oxford, 1936); M. Spufford, *Small Books and Pleasant Histories* (Cambridge, 1981), p. 119. [18] Chartres, 'Food consumption and internal trade', pp. 172–6.

[19] Hatcher, *History of the British Coal Industry*, I, pp. 35–40, 501–2, 534–45; W. H. Te Brake, 'Air pol-

Londoners are, of course, best known for their predilection to buy consumer durables and a range of exotic comestibles. Smoking tobacco and consuming sugar were more common in London than in the nation at large. Sugar refining, making tobacco pipes and retailing of tobacco were important and ubiquitous London industries, therefore, by the end of the seventeenth century. The late seventeenth century was a period in which ownership of books, pictures and new imported goods accelerated rapidly. Ease of supply, facilitated by the spread of shops which displayed such wares, accounted for this predilection for consumer durables.[20]

Since medieval times the aristocratic great houses sited in the capital had been foci of lavish social expenditure and display, whilst London's sixteenth-century economy also benefited from expenditure deriving from the activities of the royal Court.[21] After the Restoration disposable incomes may have increased, and an increasing tendency of provincial gentry and the aristocracy to live for part of the year in the capital redirected a substantial part of their income into the metropolitan economy. This movement of money was not simply a movement of specie. Increasingly sophisticated credit and banking arrangements, run initially by the London goldsmiths, further increased purchasing power. Moreover, the increasing prosperity and presence of professional groups boosted the capital's overall ability to consume and further encouraged the provision of manufacture and services catering for its prosperous markets.[22]

In addition to significant alterations in consumption habits, sectors of London's economy appear to have experienced some restructuring. The economy increasingly favoured large-scale heavily capitalised businesses and manufacturing concerns and there seems to have been an increase in the number

lution and fuel crises in preindustrial London, 1250–1650', *Technology and Culture*, 16 (1975), 337–59; Schwarz, *London in the Age of Industrialisation*, pp. 82–3; Earle, *Making of the English Middle Class*, p. 42; Chartres, 'Food consumption and internal trade', pp. 175, 178, 181, 183; Chartres, *Internal Trade*, p. 15; P. Clark and P. Slack, *English Towns in Transition 1500–1700* (London, 1976), p. 67; A. B. Robertson, 'The open market in the City of London in the eighteenth century', *East London Papers*, 4 (1958), 15–22; M. Thick, 'Market gardening in England and Wales', in J. Thirsk, ed., *Ag.HEW*, vol. v(2) (Cambridge, 1985), pp. 503–32.

20 C. Shammas, *The Pre-Industrial Consumer in England and America* (Oxford, 1990), pp. 78–83; Lang, 'London's aldermen in business', 258–9; Weatherill, *Consumer Behaviour*, pp. 50–1.

21 C. M. Barron, 'Centres of conspicuous consumption: the aristocratic town house in London, 1200–1550', *LJ*, 20 (1995), 1–16; J. Loach, 'The function of ceremonial in the reign of Henry VIII', *P&P*, 142 (1994), 68.

22 F. J. Fisher, 'The development of London as a centre of conspicuous consumption in the sixteenth and seventeenth centuries', in Fisher, *London and the English Economy*, pp. 105–18; Earle, *Making of the English Middle Class*, p. 18; L. Stone, 'The residential development of the West End of London in the seventeenth century', in B. C. Malament, ed., *After the Reformation* (Manchester, 1980), pp. 167–212; M. G. Davies, 'Country gentry and payments to London, 1650–1714', *Ec.HR*, 2nd series, 24 (1971), 15–36; D. Mitchell, ed., *Goldsmiths, Silversmiths and Bankers* (Stroud, 1995); Earle, *Making of the English Middle Class*, pp. 48–50; N. McKendrick, *et al.*, *The Birth of a Consumer Society* (London, 1982).

of large firms at the expense of small independent masters across a range of enterprises and in most sectors in our period. This went hand-in-hand with both a growth of economic specialisation and division of labour in the capital and also an increasing growth of specialised retailing. Given the increased cost of setting up as an independent master there was a corresponding increase in permanent journeymen, dependent workers employed by others, in many trades and crafts in seventeenth-century London.[23]

The capital possessed a relatively narrow economic base in the mid-sixteenth century, with about 40 per cent of citizens belonging to London companies involved in the manufacture, processing or distribution of cloth and clothing. Although this overstates the actual reliance on the cloth industry, there can be little doubt that there was major diversification in the next century. A 1690s poll tax assessment listed 721 different occupations just within the City of London. The silk industry alone occupied between 40,000 and 50,000 people by the early eighteenth century. The seventeenth century saw many new London industries, often highly capitalised, based on refining or finishing colonial produce, industries devoted to import substitution like glassmaking or metalworking or those catering to the new consumers of luxury commodities such as joined furniture, coaches, clocks and printed matter. The distributive trades, shopkeepers, agents, warehousemen and wholesalers also emerged as powerful players in London's economy by the end of the seventeenth century.[24]

Emphasis on manufacturing and trading should not disguise the growth of other sectors of London's economy. The number of professionals must have increased dramatically, although this is difficult to demonstrate statistically. Our period saw an immense expansion in the volume of legal business in the Westminster courts, which meant a parallel growth in the numbers of law students coming to the Inns of Court, albeit for often short periods, as well as practising barristers and attorneys. Another expanding and increasingly prestigious London profession was the medical one. Again, the expansion of government bureaucracy, notably those collecting taxes, especially after the Glorious Revolution, also benefited London's economy disproportionately.[25]

23 Corner, 'The tyranny of fashion', 153–78; M. J. Power, 'The east London working community in the seventeenth century', in P. Corfield and D. Keene, eds., *Work in Towns 850–1850* (Leicester, 1990), pp. 103–20; Earle, *Making of the English Middle Class*, pp. 26–9; A. L. Beier, 'Engine of manufacture: the trades of London', in Beier and Finlay, eds., *London*, pp. 147–8.

24 Rappaport, *Worlds*, pp. 92–4; J. Alexander, 'The economic structure of the City of London at the end of the seventeenth century', *UHY* (1989), 53; Earle, *Making of the English Middle Class*, pp. 17–34.

25 Beier, 'Engine of manufacture', p. 148; C. Brooks, '*Pettyfoggers and Vipers of the Commonwealth': The 'Lower Branch' of the Legal Profession in Early Modern England* (Cambridge, 1986), pp. 51, 112–13; W. Prest, *The Inns of Court under Elizabeth I and the Early Stuarts, 1590–1640* (London, 1972), p. 11; C. W. Brooks, ed., *The Admissions Registers of Barnard's Inn 1620–1869* (Selden Society Supplementary series, 12, 1995), p. 24; Earle, *Making of the English Middle Class*, pp. 70–2; R.

(iv) METROPOLITAN SOCIETY: SOCIAL STRUCTURE AND SOCIAL TOPOGRAPHY

London's size and administrative diversity make generalisations about its social structure particularly difficult. We have little meaningful evidence at all relating to changes in the social structure *over time*, and only partial information about the contours of metropolitan social structure in 1638 and after the Restoration. The best-documented area in our period, the City and its liberties, contained a diminishing fraction of London's population and the most rapidly expanding suburbs, in the West and East Ends, have only been studied after the Restoration. Growing poverty in the eastern suburbs in the sixteenth and seventeenth centuries might have been more than compensated for by increasing wealth in the West End. It does not always follow, too, that rapid population growth *must* mean an overall change in the social *composition* of any particular London district. Another complicating factor is that social groups might migrate *within* the metropolis, notably, of course, from the City within the Walls to the West End after the Great Fire.[26] Historians have, none the less, been quick to identify social change in London. Peter Clark and Paul Slack, for example, describe growing social and economic polarisation in early modern London while Ian Archer sees the later sixteenth century as a time when London society was 'filling out at the bottom' although Steve Rappaport presented a more optimistic view about the course of social change in the area governed by the lord mayor.[27]

The City and its liberties were probably relatively well off and experienced little dramatic social change throughout our period. The 'comfortably off' or better comprised something like half of all households in the 1690s. A similar picture was found in 1638 and the notion that those in the middle station predominated

Ashton, 'Popular entertainment and social control in later Elizabethan and early Stuart London', *LJ*, 9(1983), 3–19; J. Brewer, *The Sinews of Power: War, Money and the English State, 1688–1783* (London, 1989), pp. 65–9.

[26] See, for example, Alexander, 'Economic structure of the City of London', 47–62; J. Alexander, 'The City revealed: an analysis of the 1692 poll tax and the 1693 4s. aid in London', in T. Arkell and K. Schurer, eds., *Surveying the People: The Interpretation and Use of Document Sources for the Study of Population in the Later Seventeenth Century* (Matlock, 1992), pp. 181–200; M. J. Power, 'The social topography of Restoration London', in Beier and Finlay, eds., *London*, pp. 199–223; D. V. Glass, ed., *London Inhabitants within the Walls 1695* (London Record Society, 2, 1966), pp. ix–xlii; D. V. Glass, 'Socio-economic status and occupations in the City of London at the end of the seventeenth century', in P. Clark, ed., *The Early Modern Town* (London, 1976), pp. 216–32; C. Spence, ed., *Atlas of London in the 1690s* (forthcoming); P. E. Jones and A. V. Judges, 'London population in the late seventeenth century', *Ec.HR*, 1st series, 6 (1935), 45–63; Finlay, *Population and Metropolis*, pp. 77–81; E. Jones, 'London in the early seventeenth century: an ecological approach', *LJ*, 6 (1980), 123–33; Slack, *Impact of Plague*, pp. 170–1; R. G. Lang, ed., *Two Tudor Subsidy Assessment Rolls for the City of London: 1541 and 1582* (London Record Society, 29, 1993), pp. i–lxxvii; R. B. Shoemaker, *Prosecution and Punishment* (Cambridge, 1991), pp. 303–4.

[27] Clark and Slack, *English Towns in Transition*, pp. 64–9; Archer, *Pursuit of Stability*, p. 13; Rappaport, *Worlds*, pp. 162–73.

in this district also supports John Stow's remark in 1603 that 'they of the middle place' were most numerous. Surviving valuations of the estates of London freemen, most of whom lived in the same place, also indicate little change in the distribution of wealth. How relevant this is to the rest of the metropolis is uncertain. The City and its liberties experienced significant losses of both population and capital following the 1666 Fire. There is anecdotal information to suggest that over time the metropolitan wealth pyramid became more pointed at the very top, witness the emergence of an exceptional number of 'super-rich' merchants, government financiers and traders after 1660. Robert Shoemaker has also recently identified growing poverty as a problem in suburban Middlesex after the Restoration.[28]

What can be said more certainly about wealth in the capital was that it was distributed unequally across the metropolis. The less well off and really poor were concentrated, as one might expect, in the suburbs to the north and east, notably in Whitechapel and Shoreditch, and along riverside parishes on both banks of the Thames. Richer city parishes commonly made poor relief payments to those outside the city walls. The wealthiest inhabitants, too, lived in particular districts of the City within the Walls and in those (would-be) socially exclusive areas in the West End such as Covent Garden, St Andrew Holborn or parts of St Martin-in-the-Fields. Evidence for *growing* social polarisation within the metropolis *as a whole* over our period, then, is rather thin, although some dramatic social polarisation, with some residential segregation, occurred in parts of the suburbs outside the jurisdiction of the lord mayor.[29]

One motive for moving to London, of course, was the possibilities that the capital's economy held out for dramatic upward social mobility for the fortunate, connected, intelligent and highly skilled migrant. A notable success story would be that of Sir Thomas Cullum, draper, alderman and baronet (1587–1664). The second son of a Suffolk yeoman, he finished his apprenticeship to a London draper in 1616 with a total stock of just £292 2s. 6d. (deriving from his savings and a legacy of £200 from his father). Within four years he was worth nearly £1,000 and from that point until his death over forty years later earned between £1,000 and £4,000 per year. At his death Cullum was worth about £47,000. Cullum was, of course, highly exceptional. Many immigrants never even progressed beyond journeyman wage labour, were arrested as vagrants, died early before significant capital accumulation could be accomplished, went bankrupt

[28] Alexander, 'The City revealed', pp. 198–9; Finlay, *Population and Metropolis*, pp. 70–82; Rappaport, *Worlds*, p. 173; R. Grassby, 'The personal wealth of the business community in seventeenth-century England', *Ec.HR*, 2nd series, 23 (1970), 220–34; Shoemaker, *Prosecution and Punishment*, pp. 13–14, 289–304.

[29] Power, 'Social topography of Restoration London', p. 203; Alexander, 'The City revealed', pp. 187–96; R. W. Herlan, 'Social articulation and the configuration of parochial poverty in London on the eve of the Restoration', *GSt.*, 2(1976), 43–53; Archer, *Pursuit of Stability*, p. 151; Power, 'The east and west in early-modern London', pp. 167–85. See below, pp. 664–5.

or returned to the provinces. For those who survived the capital's high death rates, however, achievement of modest social mobility was, seemingly, a reasonable proposition at least in late sixteenth-century London. London's frenetic marriage market also proved an avenue of upward social mobility for the fortunate. In particular, many young men, like William Lilly the astrologer, made their initial (and often substantial) fortunes from marrying their masters' widows.[30]

Since social origins helped to determine one's starting point in the capital's social structure, and helped to determine the rate and direction of one's subsequent career, it is clear that the family background of the capital's immigrants did much to determine the shape of the capital's social structure. We do not actually have much information about the social origins of the majority of London's population but we know that apprentices to London companies formed a very significant part of the total migration stream and there is reasonably good evidence as to their social origins. Over time there was little change in the substantial number of mercantile tradesmen and craftsmen coming to London and the number of wage labourers who could afford to buy their sons a London apprenticeship was minimal. During the seventeenth century, however, the proportion of new Londoners claiming gentry origin increased markedly. Some 5 per cent of those becoming freemen were from gentry families in 1551–3, compared to 10 per cent in 1690. There seems to have been a marked decline, too, over the period, in apprentices with humble husbandmen as fathers. Since few of those coming to work in the City and its liberties were from the poorest social groups of early modern England, the predominance of the 'middle station' there is hardly surprising.[31]

(v) METROPOLITAN CULTURES

One well-known feature of London was the literacy of its inhabitants and the premium metropolitan society placed on possession of the ability to read and write. London apprentices were observed taking notes during sermons, placards were commonly used during street demonstrations as early as 1640 and Londoners led the way in purchasing and owning books. A veritable flood of

[30] A. Simpson, *The Wealth of the Gentry, 1540–1640* (Cambridge, 1961), pp. 115–40; Earle, *Making of the English Middle Class*,, pp. 129–30; Rappaport, *Worlds*, pp. 344, 367–76; V. Brodsky, 'Widows in late Elizabethan London: remarriage, economic opportunity and family orientations', in L. Bonfield, R. M. Smith and K. Wrightson, eds., *The World We Have Gained* (Oxford, 1986), pp. 126–7; J. Boulton, 'London widowhood revisited: the decline of remarriage in seventeenth-century London', *Continuity and Change*, 5 (1990), 323–55.

[31] For the most recent work on this, see C. Brooks, 'Apprenticeship, social mobility and the middling sort, 1550–1800', in C. Brooks and J. Barry, eds., *The Middling Sort of People: Culture, Society and Politics in England, 1550–1800* (Basingstoke, 1994), pp. 52–83; Kitch, 'Capital and kingdom', pp. 246–8.

cheap print poured from the growing number of the capital's presses from the early seventeenth century, much of it directed at Londoners and catering for a growing demand for the printed word. Regular newspapers, carrying advertising, appeared with increasing frequency after 1650. Notwithstanding this reading public, however, outside the city walls in the extramural suburbs and south of the river, illiteracy was more common.[32]

Those unable to read or write, however, could still participate in much metropolitan cultural life. Cities like London also encouraged verbal as well as printed communication. Much news and business was conducted by word of mouth, with purpose-built meeting places like the Royal Exchange (built in 1571), Gresham College (built in 1596) or less formal arenas such as Westminster Palace Hall and Yard. The new Restoration coffee-houses were also vibrant places of face-to-face contact, where gossip, news and ideas circulated freely amongst an often surprisingly mixed clientele. Both the formal and informal institutions of London life also encouraged association, feasting and communication. The guilds and companies of London increasingly over our period became social arenas, based around regular dinners, whilst the huge growth in clubs and societies, often with political leanings, catering for those in the capital's middling social groups, was a phenomenon dating mostly from the 1650s in the capital. That metropolitan social life contained a vibrant oral culture is also indicated by the fact that gossip and defamation were apparently rife in the neighbourhoods and households of London; some 200 defamation cases per year reached the London consistory courts in the early seventeenth century and equally lively gossip networks existed after the Restoration. Again, entertainment in the metropolis blended the printed with the spoken or sung word, with a host of professional actors, musicians and street traders with their distinctive cries further battering the ears of Londoners. Lastly, of course, London's 130 parish churches and venues such as St Paul's Cross were forums for a host of sermons delivered by ministers or lecturers to willing (or unwilling) hearers every week.[33]

[32] For more detail on London's literacy and cultural life, see above, pp. 280 *et seq*. J. Materne, 'Chapel members in the workplace: tension and teamwork in the printing trades in the seventeenth and eighteenth centuries', *International Review of Social History*, 39 (1994) (Supplement 2), 53–82; P. Burke, 'Popular culture in seventeenth-century London', *LJ*, 3 (1977), 143–62; T. Watt, *Cheap Print and Popular Piety, 1550–1640* (Cambridge, 1991); Spufford, *Small Books and Pleasant Histories*; R. B. Walker, 'Advertising in London newspapers, 1650–1750', *Business History*, 15 (1973), 112–30; D. Cressy, *Literacy and the Social Order: Reading and Writing in Tudor and Stuart England* (Cambridge, 1980), pp. 72–5, 135.

[33] R. C. Latham and W. Matthews, eds., *The Diary of Samuel Pepys*, vol. x (London, 1983), pp. 161–2, 357–8, 473–4; S. B. Dobranski, '"Where men of differing judgements croud": Milton and the culture of the coffee houses', *The Seventeenth Century*, 9 (1994), 35–56; B. Lillywhite, *London Coffee Houses* (London, 1963); N. E. Key, 'The political culture and political rhetoric of county feasts and feast sermons, 1654–1714', *Journal of British Studies*, 33 (1994), 223–56; D. Allen, 'Political clubs in Restoration London', *HJ*, 19 (1976), 561–80; J. Barry, 'Bourgeois collectivism?

Metropolitan culture was also a rich *visual* experience. A whole cultural world, replete with symbols and cultural references, could be found in the shop signs which hung (sometimes dangerously) in most streets and seemingly in increasing numbers in our period. A secular replacement for the religious processions and ritual of the pre-Reformation Church, was the Lord Mayor's Show which from as early as the 1530s provided a huge metropolitan civic festival, with street processions and increasingly professional and numerous pageants designed to emphasise to onlookers the power, honour and worth of the civic elite, and the importance of maintaining good order, precedence and the social hierarchy in the capital. Such processions, of course, were subject to different interpretations and were addressed specifically to the cultured and literate in the metropolitan audience; indeed, there seems good evidence to indicate that elements of the populace understood little of the messages intended, and sometimes subverted them. Such processions were, too, increasingly designed to convey political messages to onlookers, but they were paralleled and inverted by the equally large-scale and choreographed political demonstrations, particularly the pope-burning processions of the Exclusion Crisis, generated by the growth of party politics after the Restoration. Such culture, whether participatory, or passive, was not confined merely to the promulgation of civic values and particularly metropolitan cultural forms. Londoners were exposed to much royal ceremonial in their streets, whether as royal entries (see Plate 7), progresses, coronations, funerals or celebratory bonfires.[34]

It is clear that participation in much of this metropolitan cultural life was restricted by the requirements of literacy and education. Much feasting and association became increasingly imbued with consciousness of social rank and hierarchy in the later sixteenth century and the cultural life of London became culturally fragmented and elements of it socially exclusive. Arguably, too, there were increasing geographical cultural boundaries in the capital towards the end of our period, as areas with distinctive social structures and levels of literacy developed their own peculiar cultural identities. The tendency of foreign immigrants

Urban association and the middling sort', in J. Barry and C. Brooks, eds., *The Middling Sort of People* (London, 1994), pp. 84–112; P. Clark, *Sociability and Urbanity* (Leicester, 1988); L. Gowing, 'Gender and the language of insult in early modern London', *History Workshop Journal*, 35 (1993), 1–21; Earle, *Making of the English Middle Class*, pp. 225–6; S. Shesgreen, ed., *The Criers and Hawkers of London: Engravings and Drawings by Marcellus Laroon* (Aldershot, 1990); Ashton, 'Popular entertainment', 3–19; Burke, 'Popular culture in seventeenth-century London', 143–62.

[34] D. Garrioch, 'House names, shop signs and social organization in western European cities, 1500–1900', *UH*, 21 (1994), 20–48; M. Berlin, 'Civic ceremony in early modern London', *UHY* (1986), 15–27; J. Harrison, 'Lord Mayor's Day in the 1590s', *History Today*, 42 (1992) 37–43; B. Klein, '"Between the bums and the bellies of the multitude": civic pageantry and the problem of the audience in late Stuart London', *LJ*, 17 (1992), 18–26; T. Harris, *London Crowds in the Reign of Charles II* (Cambridge, 1987); T. Harris, 'The problem of "popular political culture" in seventeenth-century London', *History of European Ideas*, 10 (1989), 46–7; Loach, 'The function of ceremonial', 43–68.

to cluster in particular districts of the capital must also have reinforced this fragmentation, by creating cultural ghettos in London, especially in the 1560s and 1570s, and again in the later seventeenth century, both periods when the proportion of first-generation foreign-born immigrants were highest in the capital.[35]

The unique scale of metropolitan society was also mitigated by the fact that cities of this size tend to disaggregate into a mosaic of (sometimes overlapping) communities. Such local social systems might be produced by limited information flows about available employment or housing, by concentrations of local kin and by institutions which engendered local identity and participation. Much of the recent historiography of early modern London has stressed the importance of locality and neighbourhood sentiment in the burgeoning metropolis, all of which preserved face-to-face societies in districts of the capital. Neighbourly considerations, for example, sometimes undermined the prosecution of religious dissenters in Restoration London. Many miniature worlds comprised the social and cultural universe of the metropolis.[36]

(vi) GOVERNING LONDON: ORDER AND DISORDER IN EARLY MODERN LONDON

Historians of London have, with some differences of emphasis, remarked on the relative stability of the capital maintained in the face of the mounting pressure represented by heavy immigration and suburban growth, the mobility of much of its population and a number of short-term economic and political crises. Even the political crises of the 1640s were conducted with remarkably little bloodshed on the streets. Few London historians would now give much weight to accounts which stress social conflict, dislocation and urban anomie. How then was such 'stability' achieved?[37]

Unlike many provincial towns and cities London had no centralised governing body. Before the middle of the seventeenth century, however, the majority of Londoners lived within the jurisdiction of the lord mayor (who served annually) and the aldermen of the City of London. Their area of influence encompassed the City within and without the Walls and the so-called liberties north of the river. It did not extend to Westminster, parts of Southwark or to the northern and eastern Middlesex parishes and the Surrey parishes within the bills of mortality. This was unfortunately where the bulk of population growth took

[35] Archer, *Pursuit of Stability*, pp. 70, 93–5, 116–19; Shoemaker, *Prosecution and Punishment*, pp. 289–93.

[36] See above, pp. 225 *et seq.*, and below, pp. 654 *et seq.*; Boulton, *Neighbourhood and Society*, pp. 228–95; Harris, *London Crowds*, pp. 71–3; Gowing, 'Gender and the language of insult', 1–21.

[37] V. Pearl, 'Change and stability in seventeenth-century London', *LJ*, 5 (1979), 3–34; Rappaport, *Worlds*; Archer, *Pursuit of Stability*; F. F. Foster, *The Politics of Stability* (London, 1977); A. L. Beier, 'Social problems in Elizabethan London', *Journal of Interdisciplinary History*, 9 (1978), 203–21.

place in our period, so that the 'freedom' of the City of London with its right to trade and set up shop within the jurisdiction, was in danger, so the mayor and aldermen complained, 'to be [of] little worth' as early as 1632. The area governed by the mayor was divided into twenty-five wards each headed by an alderman, the wards being further divided into 242 separate precincts. The aldermen seem to have coordinated local government in the wards, precincts, parishes and companies. City government did allow limited democratic participation from those holding the freedom of the City. The freemen assembling in the annual wardmote meetings elected a 196–strong common council, which in turn nominated candidates from their number to the twenty-six strong court of aldermen. The court of aldermen was the true ruling body of the City: it decided which business was discussed by common council; its members served for life and chose their successors from the individuals nominated by common council. The aldermen also decided between the candidates for the mayoralty nominated by the liverymen of the City companies who met for this purpose in the 'court of common hall' or 'congregation' as it was known before 1640.[38]

The other instruments of local government within the City were the parish vestries, which appear to have been gaining power and influence at the expense of the larger and more cumbersome wards in the later sixteenth and early seventeenth centuries. Here, too, the wealthiest citizens held oligarchic control in small self-coopting groups, often running the parish via a closed 'select' vestry. Twenty-five City parishes had select vestries confirmed by the bishop of London between 1578 and 1627 alone. This trend towards oligarchy was only reversed temporarily during the commonwealth.[39]

Within the world of the City and its liberties another 'world' was represented by the one hundred or so guilds and companies which regulated the trades of their members. Only by becoming free of a London company could one qualify for the freedom of the City. Each company too was governed by an oligarchic court of assistants, who were drawn from the 'livery' of the company. Citizens who had not yet attained the livery, and many never did, were known as 'yeomanry' or perhaps 'bachelors'. The London companies performed a multitude of tasks, in addition to regulating the trades and crafts of their members, if they did that and not all did. They resolved disputes between members, provided poor relief, kept (from 1578) granaries, provided a source of troops and weapons in emergencies, and the wealthiest provided the funding and the personnel for the annual lord mayor's pageant. The twelve great companies of London had a

[38] R. Ashton, *The City and the Court, 1603–1643* (Cambridge, 1979), pp. 6–10, 164–5; a twenty-sixth, Bridge Ward Without which comprised part of Southwark was added in 1550 although its inhabitants played no other part in the City's constitution: M. Carlin, *Medieval Southwark* (London, 1996), pp. 254–5; Foster, *The Politics of Stability*, pp. 15, 28–9.

[39] Foster, *The Politics of Stability*, pp. 39–46; A. E. McCampbell, 'The London parish and the London precinct', *GSt.*, 11 (1976), 121–2.

disproportionate influence in the city government, providing nearly all its lord mayors in our period, most of the sheriffs and aldermen, and dominating common council.[40]

Recent estimates have shown that citizenship was widespread in the City and its liberties and that recruitment kept pace with population growth. For the first half of our period between two-thirds and three-quarters of all adult males were London citizens. Historians have also discovered remarkably high levels of participation in the City's local government with something like one adult male in ten participating directly in 1600: in some of the smaller (and wealthier) districts the ratio might well have been lower than one in three.[41]

However, it is worth stating again that the City and its liberties contained a shrinking percentage of the capital's population. Other parts of the metropolis continued throughout our period to be run by manorial courts and, particularly, parish vestries. Such suburban local government, moreover, proved resistant to reform. An act of 1585 provided Westminster with a government resembling London's, with twelve wards each governed by a burgess and an assistant, equivalent to the aldermen and their ward deputies in the city, but in practice local government there came to be dominated by powerful parish vestries. An initiative backed by the privy council to incorporate the suburbs came to nothing in the 1630s and plans to extend the jurisdiction of the lord mayor into such areas also proved fruitless then and again after the Restoration. Good order could often be maintained none the less. Many suburban parishes developed relatively sophisticated and well-funded bureaucracies, and some possessed some sense of institutional identity, perhaps best illustrated by the threatened dismissal of a searcher in St Martin-in-the-Fields in 1661, who had had the temerity to return a victim of starvation in the bills of mortality, thus casting 'an aspersion' on the parish, from which the ruling vestry was anxious to be 'vindicated'.[42]

An important source of that stability identified in sixteenth- and early seventeenth-century London is said to be the responsiveness and inclusiveness of its governing institutions. The chances of rising through the *cursus honorum* of the city companies were reasonably good, at least in the sixteenth century, possibly defusing the social tensions that might otherwise have arisen. Perhaps more sig-

40 The twelve companies were the Clothworkers, Grocers, Mercers, Fishmongers, Drapers, Goldsmiths, Skinners, Vintners, Ironmongers, Merchant Tailors, Haberdashers and Salters. See Foster, *The Politics of Stability*, p. 44; Rappaport, *Worlds*, pp. 162–214; McCampbell, 'The London parish', 107–24.

41 Pearl, 'Change and stability', 13,16; Rappaport, *Worlds*, pp. 49, 182.

42 W. H. Manchée, *The Westminster City Fathers (The Burgess Court of Westminster) 1585–1901* (London, 1924), pp. 1–11; J. Merritt, 'Religion, government, and society in early modern Westminster, *c.* 1525–1625' (PhD thesis, University of London, 1992), pp. 102–52; Ashton, *City and Court*, pp. 164–7; Pearl, *London and the Outbreak of the Puritan Revolution*, pp. 23–44; R. M. Wunderli, 'Evasion of the office of alderman in London, 1523–1672', *LJ*, 15 (1990), 12; Boulton, *Neighbourhood and Society*, pp. 138–45, 262–75; Westminster Archives Centre, F2003/f. 268.

nificantly the lord mayor and aldermen, and other organs of local government, were responsive to short-term crises, ensuring that the capital was well supplied with affordable corn, and appeared to have practised the rhetoric of order and social responsibility that was a commonplace not just in London but in the nation as a whole. Respect for the City's governors, therefore, was considerable. Hence, when anarchy seemed to threaten in 1641 common councilmen condemned 'such disorders & tumultuary Assemblies that bee permitted in such a Citty as this, formerly famous for the good & quiett goverment thereof' and lamented 'the great disrespect of Magistracy & Contempt of government'.[43]

Over our period, however, London's traditional government decayed. Within the City and its liberties the activities of the wardmote diminished although it retained some powers. More importantly many London companies experienced a decline in their ability to regulate trades and crafts. Decreasing numbers of city-wide searches were made and in the face of unregulated tradesmen in the suburbs many livery companies became just one other arena for merry-making. Their decline was accelerated by the increasing division of interest between controlling merchant oligarchies who ran the companies and the small handicraftsmen who made up the yeomanry. In many companies the yeomanry as a body ceased to play any part at all. The City's finances, too, were in deficit for most of the seventeenth century, with the expenses resulting from the Fire of 1666 and the Stop of the Exchequer in 1672 causing near bankruptcy in 1673. Some bodies had always had limited jurisdiction over the entire metropolis, such as the Parish Clerks' Company, but increasingly after the Restoration new bodies were given statutory rights to exercise particular powers across the whole metropolitan area.[44]

In the end one must sound a note of caution. Even before 1640 there was considerable and at times violent disorder in London, sometimes caused by the citizenry spilling outside the lord mayor's jurisdiction. London apprentices regularly attacked brothels and theatres on Shrove Tuesdays, students at the Inns of Court were notoriously riotous, foreign ambassadors faced regular xenophobic hostility and demobilised troops rioted for arrears of pay. Such disorder frequently

[43] Rappaport, *Worlds*, pp. 285–376; Archer, *Pursuit of Stability*, pp. 259–60; M. J. Power, 'London and the control of the "crisis" of the 1590s', *History*, 70 (1985), 371–85; M. Power, 'A "crisis" reconsidered: social and demographic dislocation in London in the 1590s', *LJ*, 12 (1986), 134–45; Ashton, *City and Court*, p. 214.

[44] Pearl, 'Change and stability', 26–7; W. G. Bell, 'Wardmote inquest registers of St. Dunstan's-in-the-West', *Transactions of the London and Middlesex Archaeological Society*, new series, 3 (1917), 56–70; W. F. Kahl, *The Development of the London Livery Companies* (Boston, 1960), pp. 25–7; G. Unwin, *The Gilds and Companies of London*, 4th edn (London 1963), p. 343; Ashton, *City and Court*, pp. 43–55; Wunderli, 'Evasion of the office of alderman', 3–18. For a study that claims that London guilds retained more influence and power over trades in the metropolis than is argued here, see J. P. Ward, *Metropolitan Communities: Trade Guilds, Identity, and Change in Early Modern London* (Stanford, Calif., 1997).

required the London-trained bands to suppress it, and even occasionally, as in the late sixteenth and early seventeenth centuries, the declaration of martial law in some suburban areas. After the Restoration there is some evidence that disorder on the capital's streets increased. London saw large-scale rioting against brothels involving thousands of people over a five-day period in 1668, widespread rioting occurred amongst London weavers intent on destroying engine looms in 1675, and many years saw hundreds of assaults and riots indicted at the Middlesex quarter sessions. As is well known, the 'rise of party' after the Restoration meant the rise of London crowds as a factor in national political life, with partisan mobs mounting attacks on each others' headquarters, organising huge petitioning campaigns and massing for large-scale street demonstrations.[45]

It would be unduly simplistic, then, to make a connection between the strength of the capital's government and the level of disturbance. When the ruling elites were divided ideologically, or when there was divisive political friction in the Westminster parliament, London's government proved unable to prevent large-scale disorder. Arguably, in fact, extensive participation in local government may have *facilitated* political and ideological divisions, and even sharpened the political awareness of ordinary Londoners. Sympathetic local officers made no real efforts to disperse the rioters on the streets of London in 1641 and local government posts were captured by those with religious or political agendas. The relative stability of the capital before 1640 partly reflects the ideological consensus in the city's, and indeed in the nation's, government during that period.[46]

(vii) RELIGION IN EARLY MODERN LONDON: PIETY AND PLURALISM

Turning now to a discussion of London's religion, its experience here was rich but it was also diverse. In 1540 its clergy were already the best educated in the country, its livings were the wealthiest and its laity were certainly the most literate. The landscape of the city in 1540 was dominated by the spire of St Paul's and over 130 parish churches as well as numerous chapels. Post-Reformation developments ensured that religious pluralism and a radical tradition thrived in the capital, hand-in-hand with the (probable) enduring conformity of the

45 Prest, *Inns of Court*, pp. 99–100; K. Lindley, 'Riot prevention and control in early Stuart London', *TRHS*, 5th series, 33 (1983), 109–15; Archer, *Pursuit of Stability*, pp. 1–17; T. Harris, 'The bawdy house riots of 1668', *HJ*, 29 (1986), 537–56; Harris, *London Crowds*, pp. 96–227; Shoemaker, *Prosecution and Punishment*, p. 130.

46 Lindley, 'Riot prevention and control', 123–6; D. Allen, 'The political role of the London trained bands in the Exclusion Crisis, 1678–1681', *EHR*, 87 (1972), 287–303; Pearl, *London and the Outbreak of the Puritan Revolution*, p. 233; Archer, *Pursuit of Stability*, pp. 257–8; Foster, *Politics of Stability*, pp. 155–62.

majority. The huge number of young men, living apart from their families in the capital, either as apprentices or as aspiring lawyers, made a good recruiting ground for radical religious movements both in the sixteenth and later in the seventeenth centuries. It was always relatively easy, too, to propagate radical beliefs in private houses and other meeting places in a crowded city. Religious diversity owed a great deal to the range of individuals and institutions that acted as ecclesiastical patrons to radical preachers and ministers. Each parish might appoint extra preachers, 'lecturers', to supplement the teachings of their local minister and the growth of these so-called 'puritan' lectureships was rapid. In the early 1570s just fifteen parishes are said to have had active lectureships; by the late 1580s more than three times as many did so. The development of an active preaching ministry was reinforced by the wealth of the interested laity who endowed puritan lectureships. The Inns of Court, notably Lincoln's Inn chapel, that 'focal centre of London Puritanism', also funded godly preachers. Moreover, from 1626 until their suppression by Laud in 1633, the feoffees of impropriations, funded by wealthy city puritans, bought livings all over the country, including a number in London, and inserted godly clerics to provide the correct message to their flocks. Certain parishes became identified with puritan feeling, notably St Antholin Budge Row, which had a daily lecture, and others have been suggested, although identification of such 'puritan' parishes continues to be contentious. More support for the godly could be found in City and overseas trading companies, some of whom financed their own lecturers or lent support to the puritan 'movement'. Just how strong that movement was in the capital will probably always remain debatable. But as early as the 1570s, a godly desire to reform manners is said to have motivated the governors of Bridewell in an (unsuccessful) campaign to suppress prostitution, although such action had a long history in the metropolis. Puritanism was strong in the common council in 1584 and the godly were exceptionally active in local and civic government in the late 1630s and 1640–2.[47]

Given the religious choice, radical sects and meetings flourished in the capital. Seventy-two London 'puritans' with separatist leanings were meeting at

[47] S. Brigden, *London and the Reformation* (Oxford, 1989), pp. 116, 58; Earle, *Making of the English Middle Class*, pp. 64–5; D. Keene and V. Harding, *A Survey of Documentary Sources for Property Holding in London before the Great Fire* (London Record Society, 22, 1985), pp. xv–xix; C. Kitching, ed., *London and Middlesex Chantry Certificate 1548* (London Record Society, 16, 1980); Seaver, *Wallington's World*, p. 188; Archer, *Pursuit of Stability*, pp. 46–7, 87–9, 253–4; W. K. Jordan, *The Charities of London 1480–1660* (London, 1960), pp. 284–92; Prest, *Inns of Court*, pp. 204–7, at p. 205; Pearl, *London and the Outbreak of the Puritan Revolution*, pp. 164–72, 231–6; D. A. Williams, 'London Puritanism: the parish of St Botolph without Aldgate', *Guildhall Miscellany*, 2 (1960), 24–38; J. D. Alsop, 'Revolutionary Puritanism in the parishes? The case of St Olave, Old Jewry', *LJ*, 15 (1990), 29–37; M. Ingram, 'Reformation of manners in early modern England', in P. Griffiths, A. Fox and S. Hindle, eds., *The Experience of Authority in Early Modern England* (Basingstoke, 1996), pp. 59–62.

Plumbers' Hall in 1568, and members of the Barrowist sect met frequently in London in the 1590s. Such sectarians spread their beliefs by lending books to one another, and via letters and tracts, as well as the spoken word. A better protected group were Catholics, able to hear masses in the chapels and houses of Catholic aristocrats or sympathisers, or in those of foreign ambassadors: some 500 were fined for recusancy in London between 1625 and 1629.[48]

Emphasising dissent, Puritanism and radicalism, however, probably exaggerates the capital's inhabitants' commitment to godly reform. Most were as unexceptional and conventionally pious as the Londoner admonished by his puritan neighbour for breaking the Sabbath, and sleeping during sermons and routine observance of the most basic religious exercises was probably the norm. Attachment to the Protestant sacrament of baptism was well nigh universal and the churching of mothers equally popular. Attendance at holy communion even in large suburban parishes could, on occasion, also be very high. Equally conventionally Londoners could also, particularly at times of exceptional political tension, be rabidly anti-Catholic as well as markedly xenophobic. In 1555, 500 citizens attacked some Spanish visitors on the streets of the capital and Londoners are said to have hurled mud and spat on the victims of the 'fatal vesper', when a garret where a Catholic mass was being held collapsed in 1623 at the height of the Spanish Match furore. Many London churches were also quickly purged of remaining popish images like stained glass windows in 1641 although much of this action was the work of a minority of religious zealots or was taken on parliamentary rather than on local initiative.[49]

London's religious pluralism meant that with the collapse of church discipline and the explosion of uncensored print, the 1640s saw the emergence of a multitude of religious sects in the capital, famously listed in the (highly partisan and alarmist) tract *Gangraena*. In the early 1640s, 1,000 London sectarians can be identified, and thirty-six separated congregations by 1646. Alarmed by such disorder, many London puritans (like Nehemiah Wallington, that East Cheap artisan) turned to Presbyterianism in the mid-1640s which promised, though it did not deliver, a return to religious discipline. Other Londoners preferred to subject sectarians to verbal and physical abuse. Support for the comforting ceremonies and traditional rubrics of the Anglican Church, especially its Christmas

[48] C. Burrage, *The Early English Dissenters in the Light of Recent Research (1550–1641)*, vol. II: *Illustrative Documents* (New York, 1912; repr. 1967), pp. 9–11, 27–61; Prest, *Inns of Court*, pp. 177–86; R. Lockyer, *The Early Stuarts: A Political History of England, 1603–1642* (London, 1989), p. 302.

[49] Seaver, *Wallington's World*, pp. 103, 151; Archer, *Pursuit of Stability*, pp. 88–91; Finlay, *Population and Metropolis*, pp. 22–43; Burrage, *Early English Dissenters*, II, pp. 30–1; J. P. Boulton, 'The limits of formal religion: the administration of Holy Communion in late Elizabethan and early Stuart London', *LJ*, 10 (1984), 135–54; Boulton, *Neighbourhood and Society*, pp. 279–85; Lindley, 'Riot prevention and control', 111–12, esp. n. 9; Brigden, *London and the Reformation*, p. 597; A. Walsham, '"The fatall vesper": providentialism and anti-popery in late Jacobean London', *P&P*, 144 (1994), 36–87.

holiday, however, also remained considerable. Anglicans like John Evelyn attended clandestine services in the capital and others married in secret to avoid both the new Directory of Public Worship that was intended to replace the old prayer book of 1645 and the institution of civil marriage in 1653. Such religious pluralism produced lasting religious divisions in the capital. During the 1640s and 1650s many parishioners, between 10 and 20 per cent of the total, withdrew their children from public baptism, preferring alternative services in separated congregations.[50]

Religion in London after the Restoration remained fragmented. The wills of middling Londoners, however, portray entirely conventional 'outward piety and respectability', probably characteristic of the majority Anglican faith then. Between 15 and 20 per cent of London's population belonged to some form of Protestant dissenting church after 1660, the most popular being, in descending order of popularity, Presbyterians, independent congregations, Baptists, Quakers and Fifth Monarchists. Such dissent did not always mean total separation from the local parish church. The first pew on the South Side of Allhallows Bread Street was occupied in 1701 by Sir Owen Buckingham, a notable 'Presbyterian' alderman. Bonds of neighbourliness and friendship often outweighed ideological differences in Restoration London, a toleration not, however, always extended to the capital's Catholic population. In times of political crisis latent religious tensions might still surface and spill out on to the streets, as they did during the Spanish Match, the Civil Wars and the Exclusion Crisis.[51]

(viii) POLITICS IN EARLY MODERN LONDON: LOBBYING, POPULAR PROTEST AND POLITICAL ASSOCIATION

London acted throughout our period as the political arena of seventeenth-century England. Its political life was, however, coloured by more than the location of the Court and parliament at Westminster and its huge electorate was grossly underrepresented in the House of Commons. The city always contained a disproportionate number of the political nation, and the increasing tendency

50 K. Lindley, 'London and popular freedom', in R. C. Richardson and G. M. Ridden, eds., *Freedom and the English Revolution: Essays in History and Literature* (Manchester, 1986), pp. 116–18, 127–32; M. Tolmie, *The Triumph of the Saints* (Cambridge, 1977), p. 122; Seaver, *Wallington's World*, pp. 147–50; R. Ashton, *Counter Revolution: The Second Civil War and its Origins, 1646–8* (London, 1994), pp. 133–4, 241–6, 281–94; C. Durston, *The Family in the English Revolution* (Oxford, 1989), pp. 62–86; C. Durston, 'The Puritan war on Christmas', *History Today*, 35 (1985); Finlay, *Population and Metropolis*, pp. 33–43.

51 Earle, *Making of the English Middle Class*, pp. 245, 323; Harris, *London Crowds*, pp. 66–73; J. P. Boulton, 'The Marriage Duty Act and parochial registration in London, 1695–1706', in K. Schurer and T. Arkell, eds., *Surveying the People: The Importance and Use of Document Sources for the Study of Population in the Late Seventeenth Century* (Local Population Studies Supplement, 1992), pp. 222–52; G. S. de Krey, *A Fractured Society* (Oxford, 1985), pp. 85–120.

for the gentry and aristocracy to spend time in London in the seventeenth century focused political activity still further on the capital. The increasing number of parliaments after 1640, and especially after 1688, also increased the number of (temporarily) resident MPs and was itself a significant factor in explaining the continuing growth of London in our period. The frequency with which many of those from the middling social ranks served in some sort of local government or company office, and the plurality and diversity of its governing institutions each with their own special interests and agendas, meant, moreover, that various forms of political activity took place at much more humble social levels than was normally the case in early modern England. The capital's function as a haven for political refugees, such as the future Levellers, Katherine and Samuel Chidley, who fled from Shrewsbury to London in 1629, helped to generate small networks of religious and political radicals.[52]

The opportunities for political activity were broadened, too, by the exceptional literacy of the capital's inhabitants and the range of information they encountered via the printed word, be it books, ballads or pamphlets. London, too, had been an early centre of political libels and the fashion for making either overtly political or anti-establishment comments in this way increased markedly after 1550. Libels were occasionally stuck on to the hearses that trundled the streets of London, such as the one pinned to that carrying the religious dissident Richard Rippon, a copy of which was read out publicly in Cheapside in 1592. Political comment, too, albeit only accessible to those of the requisite education and cultural background, might be encountered in the capital's private and (from 1576) public theatres or in the language, metaphors and symbols of London's civic pageantry. A particularly rich source of political allusion and metaphor were the more than 100 plays set explicitly in London, which were performed between 1580 and 1642. Political comment continued in the London theatre after the Restoration, although only two playhouses were initially licensed and they were kept under stricter state control than before 1660.[53]

52 Earle, *Making of the English Middle Class*, p. 264; Stone, 'Residential development of the West End', p. 175; A. L. Beier and R. Finlay, 'Introduction: the significance of the metropolis', in Beier and Finlay, eds., *London*, p. 12; I. Gentles, 'London Levellers in the English Revolution: the Chidleys and their circle', *JEcc.Hist.*, 29 (1978), 282–3.

53 P. Croft, 'Libels, popular literacy and public opinion in early modern England', *HR*, 68 (1995), 266–85; A. Bellany, 'A poem on the archbishop's hearse: Puritanism, libel, and sedition after the Hampton Court Conference', *Journal of British Studies*, 34 (1995), 137–64; Burrage, *The Early English Dissenters*, II, pp. 31–2; L. L. Peck, 'John Marston's *The Fawn*. Ambivalence and Jacobean courts', in D. L. Smith, R. Strier and D. Bevington, eds., *The Theatrical City* (Cambridge, 1995), pp. 134–6; A. Barton, 'London comedy and the ethos of the city', *LJ*, 4 (1978), 158–80; A. A. Bromham, 'Thomas Middleton's *The Triumphs of Truth*: city politics in 1613', *The Seventeenth Century*, 10 (1995), 1–25; P. Monod, 'Pierre's white hat: theatre, Jacobitism and popular protest in London, 1689–1760', in E. Cruickshanks, ed., *By Force or By Default? The Revolution of 1688–1689* (Edinburgh, 1989), pp. 159–89, esp. 161–7.

London's cultural function of association, moreover, facilitated all kinds of political activity. The Restoration regime frequently (and rightly) found the coffee-houses of the capital, where news was gathered and disseminated, to be politically subversive and even attempted (an abortive) total suppression of them in 1675. Some notable plotting took place over coffee in the capital, notably the Rye House Plot which implicated some twenty-five taverns and coffee-houses. Government agents kept some houses under surveillance during periods of political sensitivity and they were also used to spread false news and scare stories. Political clubs too had been known in London since at least the early seventeenth century but it was after the Restoration that the capital's burgeoning club life frequently took on a political hue, providing places of association for Whigs, Tories, Catholics and the like.[54]

The guilds and companies of London were also politically active at a number of levels. From at least the sixteenth century, London companies developed a range of lobbying tactics both at Court and in parliament, seeking to have unfavourable legislation repealed, to get their own powers to regulate trade extended and confirmed, to restrict domestic and foreign competition or to resist those courtiers who were increasingly granted powers by the crown over economic activities in which the companies had a direct interest. Divisions within companies, particularly the age-old division between capitalist employers and independent small masters, also came to have political dimensions. During the English Revolution radical political thinking, including Leveller ideas, surfaced during the constitutional conflicts that engulfed some London companies in the 1640s as the rank-and-file sought (with some temporary success) participation in their running, and to remove oligarchies who had little connection or interest in the actual trades or crafts practised by them.[55]

Perhaps the most important source of political activity, however, was the wealth of London's citizens. Loans and gifts made by Londoners, in addition to the disproportionate taxation they occasionally contributed, was an important source of funding for government. The Chamber of the City of London itself might help to support government policies, as it did in the 1580s by funding the raising of troops and money for Leicester's expedition to the Low Countries. Short-term loans from London citizens, guaranteed by the City Chamber, to James of £100,000 in 1610 and 1615 and similar sums to his son were vital to the day-to-day running of government whilst Charles II got £200,000 of the

[54] Lillywhite, *London Coffee Houses*, pp. 18, 170; Allen, 'Political clubs in Restoration London', 561–80.

[55] I. Archer, 'The London lobbies in the later sixteenth century', *HJ*, 31 (1988), 17–44; N. Carlin, 'Liberty and fraternities in the English Revolution: the politics of London artisans' protests, 1635–1659', *International Review of Social History*, 39 (1994), 223–54; Unwin, *Gilds and Companies*, pp. 339–43.

money needed to fight the Dutch from Londoners, lent against the security of the hearth tax between 1664 and 1665.[56]

Possession of the resources of London therefore was vital in the opening years of the Civil War. Since the possession of London was crucial in the struggle with Charles I, it was vital for Pym and his allies to capture the city government from the ruling aldermen who were predominantly royalist in 1641–2. This was effectively achieved via the famous 'revolution in city government' of December 1641 when elections to common council produced a politically radical majority, which proceeded to take over the London-trained bands and create a 'committee of safety' who were granted by parliament the power to choose the lord mayor. The committee installed the parliamentary radical Isaac Pennington in the place of the royalist Richard Gurney in the summer of 1642. There is some controversy over the roots of this 'revolution' in London's government, notably over a recent claim that much of the impetus came from an 'opposition' group of 'new' interloping merchants with puritan sympathies and connections engaged in overseas trades in America and the Far East and with little interest in preserving the political status quo.[57]

Generalisations about London's political allegiance, however, are difficult to make with confidence. This is partly due to the very diversity and plurality of London's institutions and the difficulty in controlling (or representing) its enormous population or the stream of ideas and news they were presented with every day. Even after the 'radical takeover' of the city in 1642 there appears to have been plenty of royalist support in London. Political opponents were always present in the capital as the range of sedition found in the capital in the 1640s testifies and the abortive 'counter-revolution' in London of 1647 demonstrates. At key political moments after 1640 the national capital was in fact paralysed by internal political divisions. Thus the desire of the ruling elite and much of the capital's population between 1646 and 1648 to espouse the Presbyterian-Scottish way foundered on the well-organised and vocal opposition led by radical sectarians and Levellers, supported by the New Model Army, which had many Londoners in its ranks and consequently much support on the streets. After the Restoration it was possible for Whigs to recruit large crowds to support the exclusion of the duke of York from the succession but equally possible for Tories to mount 'elaborate demonstrations' in support of his claim. Both parties played

[56] B. R. Masters, 'Introduction', in *Chamber Accounts of the Sixteenth Century* (London Record Society, 20, 1984), p. xxviii; Lockyer, *The Early Stuarts*, pp. 83–5; Pearl, *London and the Outbreak of the Puritan Revolution*, pp. 336–8; C. A. F. Meekings, 'The city loans on the hearth tax, 1664–1668', in A. E. J. Hollaender and W. Kellaway, eds., *Studies in London History Presented to Philip Edmund Jones* (London, 1969), pp. 335–72.

[57] Pearl, *London and the Outbreak of the Puritan Revolution*, pp. 132–59; Ashton, *City and the Court*, pp. 1–5, 201–42; Brenner, *Merchants and Revolution*, pp. 316–459; Lockyer, *Early Stuarts*, p. 10. See the review of Brenner by B. Coward, *LJ*, 20 (1995), 81–2.

on the entrenched religious differences and the enduring anti-popery of ordinary Londoners.[58]

After the Restoration the emergence of organised political parties with distinctive organisations, meeting places and leaders began to see the nation's political life increasingly reflected in London's politics. Elections to common council, the choice of aldermen and civic officers and even the governing bodies of charitable institutions and hospitals were divided and sometimes purged on party political lines. After the victory of the crown in the Exclusion Crisis, for example, the entire corporation was from October 1683 to October 1688 abolished after a successful *quo warranto* challenge and the capital was in the hands of a group of vengeful Tory royal commissioners. Whigs were forced out of the administration of the ancient London hospitals. After James II turned to the Whigs a few recalcitrant Tories were purged from London's governing institutions but after 1688 Whigs surged back into power.[59]

Notwithstanding the multiple allegiances found in its streets, the rise of the London crowd as an important and active agent in national political life began in 1640. Their precocious literacy and the multitude of opportunities for political awareness and involvement in local government meant that many ordinary Londoners attended mass street demonstrations, signed (often huge) petitions and sometimes participated in acts of political violence. The breakdown of censorship in 1640 may also have further developed Londoners' political consciousness. Between 1640 and 1650, 131 men and women below gentle rank were prosecuted for expressing political or religious opinions. After the Restoration seditious talk continued at periods of political crisis with relatively humble folk indulging in a variety of political and religious heresies and thousands (literally) signing petitions during the Exclusion Crisis.[60]

(ix) CONCLUSION: LONDON AND THE NATION: SOME INTERCONNECTIONS

There is little need here to rehearse at length the familiar economic and demographic impact that London had on the nation. It acted as a national melting pot which reduced localism and provincial insularity. Historians have long since recognised that the relationship between this giant consumer and the primary sector

[58] C. Russell, *The Causes of the English Civil War* (Oxford, 1990), p. 3; Lindley, 'London and popular freedom', pp. 132–6; I. Gentles, 'The struggle for London in the Second Civil War', *HJ*, 26 (1983), 277–305; Harris, *London Crowd*, pp. 156–88.

[59] Wunderli, 'Evasion of office', 13; C. Rose, 'Politics and the London royal hospitals, 1683–92', in L. Granshaw and R. Porter, eds., *The Hospital in History* (London, 1989), pp. 123–48.

[60] Harris, 'The problem of "popular political culture"', 43–58; Lindley, 'London and popular freedom', pp. 125, 133; Harris, *London Crowds*, *passim*; M. Knights, 'London's "monster" petition of 1680', *HJ*, 36 (1993), 39–67.

was a two-way mutually beneficial process. London's demand for fuel stimulated the coal industry of the North-East, the need to supply it with food provided an important boost to its expanding agricultural hinterland, helped develop road and river communications and boosted transport technology. All of these developments, of course, facilitated London's continued growth. Its demand for migrants acted as a brake on English demographic growth in the seventeenth century, prolonging thereby a more favourable balance between the national population and available resources.[61]

The growth of London, however, had considerable negative as well as positive feedback. Capital as well as (often expensively educated) manpower was transferred from the agricultural sector, via the purses of the gentry or via apprentice premiums to London rather than being reinvested in the agrarian economy. Much of its economic, as well as all its demographic, growth was parasitic on the rest of the country. Since the sixteenth century many ports saw their overseas trade drift inexorably towards the capital. Again, an important reason for the growth in lawsuits at Westminster before 1640 was the increasing tendency for legal disputes to be heard there rather than in local courts.[62]

Many of London's economic and social developments had their roots in its provincial hinterland. This is obviously true of the drift of the nation's gentry and aristocracy to the capital.[63] Its superior literacy, too, was produced largely by the fact that London creamed off the most literate migrants from provincial England to its own workforce. 'Possession of a skill in demand makes for ease of migration.' Reading and writing were usually taught well *before* the late teens, when most boys moved to London to begin their apprenticeships and some London companies, such as the Goldsmiths, made literacy a formal entrance requirement. London's exceptional literacy, then, was and continued to be largely a product of educational advances in the provinces. The shape and development of London's social structure as well as the ability of individuals to compete successfully in the metropolitan economy also depended both on pre-existing support networks of family and friends in the capital, but particularly on the initial size of their financial stake and the possession of skills in current demand, derived again, ultimately, from provincial origins. The growth of London was possible only by attracting an already relatively educated and skilled workforce from provincial England.[64]

Nor should it be imagined that metropolitan inhabitants were isolated from

[61] Wrigley, 'London's importance'; Chartres, 'Food and consumption', pp. 168–96; Fisher, *London and the English Economy*, pp. 61–79.

[62] A. Ruddock, 'London capitalists and the decline of Southampton in the early Tudor period', *Ec.HR*, 2nd series, 57 (1950), 137–51; Brooks, *'Pettyfoggers and Vipers'*, pp. 96–101.

[63] Fisher, *London and the English Economy*, p. 105.

[64] E. A. Wrigley, 'City and country in the past: a sharp divide or a continuum?', *HR*, 64 (1991), 118; Rappaport, *Worlds*, pp. 298–301; Cressy, *Literacy and the Social Order*, p. 154.

these provincial origins. London was a revolving door, in which not only people but also capital, information, cultural contacts, goods and services were exchanged regularly between the capital and the rest of the country. Most of London's inhabitants had been brought up in provincial England and retained tangible social and family contacts with the countryside. It was common for London kin to act as hosts for immigrant spinsters, and Samuel Pepys' diary is full of references to provincial kin seeking help, money and employment from their successful metropolitan relative. Likewise, the villagers of Myddle received news and kept in regular contact with family and friends who had moved to London. Others were trained in London but then left to exercise their talents in the provinces. An example here would be the West Country clothmaker, Benedict Webb, who, writing in the early seventeenth century recalled that he

> was brought up under my father in the trade of clothmaking until I came to sixteen years of age, and then bound apprentice in London to a linendraper and French merchant, who, after I had been with him in London some three months, sent me to Rouen where I remained certain years . . . did resolve as soon as I was quit of my service to quit London and betake myself to be a clothier again.[65]

Many apprentices coming to London left shortly afterwards and returned to provincial England, many, unlike Benedict, not even bothering to complete their apprenticeships. Ties with provincial England, over and above the frequent contacts from family of origin or via trading networks, continued even for those Londoners who chose to remain in the city. Peter Clark has described that proliferation of clubs catering for the assimilation of rural immigrants seeking out those from similar parts of the country. Many of these might have been based on earlier informal gatherings in inns and taverns associated with particular parts of the country. In the mid- to late-seventeenth century many Londoners attended county feasts, often held in the Merchant Tailors' Hall, after a sermon exhorting them to give charitable donations to the young men of their county of origin. Such sentiment was, of course, also celebrated beyond the grave. A significant proportion of London's bequeathed capital must have been returned to the provinces in the form of charitable bequests, representing a tangible return on the original capital invested in the education of a young provincial hopeful, years or more commonly decades earlier. Thus the bulk of the estate left by the wealthy London draper, John Kendrick, was squandered in an abortive attempt to revitalise the woollen industries of Reading and Newbury. Jordan noted the 'extraordinary want of parochialism' on the part of great London donors who, between 1480 and 1660, left something like one third of their total bequests outside London, and only 9 per cent of whom had been actually born in the

[65] Elliott, 'Single women', pp. 92–9; R. Houlbrooke, ed., *English Family Life 1576–1716* (Oxford, 1988), pp. 220, 231–4; Wrigley, 'City and country in the past', 119; J. Thirsk and J. P. Cooper, eds., *Seventeenth-Century Economic Documents* (Oxford, 1972), p. 206.

metropolis. Most of the growing army of attorneys lived and practised in the provinces, staying in London only during the law terms. Again, those gentry and resident nobility who crowded into London from the early seventeenth century and in greater numbers after the Restoration were rarely permanent residents. After 1660, indeed, many of the aristocracy gave up living in their great London houses in favour of more modest *pied à terres*. The 'invasion of the gentry', then, served further to blur the social and cultural differentials between the capital and the nation. If not at the beginning of our period, certainly by the end, foreign commentators might truly observe that England was in London.[66]

[66] I. K. Ben-Amos, 'Failure to become freemen: urban apprentices in early modern England', *Soc. Hist.*, 16 (1991), 155–72; Chartres, 'The capital's provincial eyes', 24–39; Key, 'County feasts and feast sermons', 223–56; C. Jackson, 'The Kendrick bequest: an experiment in municipal enterprise in the woollen industry in Reading and Newbury in the early seventeenth century', *SHist.*, 16 (1994), 44–66; Jordan, *The Charities of London*, pp. 308–18; Brooks, *'Pettyfoggers and Vipers'*, pp. 30–3, 225; F. Heal, 'The crown, the gentry and London: the enforcement of proclamation, 1596–1640', in C. Cross, D. Loades and J. J. Scarisbrick, eds., *Law and Government under the Tudors: Essays Presented to Sir Geoffrey Elton on his Retirement* (Cambridge, 1988), pp. 211–26; P. Clark, 'Migrants in the city: the process of social adaptation in English towns 1500–1800', in P. Clark and D. Souden, eds., *Migration and Society in Early Modern England* (London, 1987), pp. 281–3.

· 11 ·

Great and good towns 1540–1700

PAUL SLACK

PROVOKED BY the French charge that there was 'never a good town in England, only London', the English herald in the *Debate of the Heralds* of 1549 was moved to respond at length: 'I pray you, what is Berwick, Carlisle, Durham, York, Newcastle, Hull, Northampton, Norwich, Ipswich, Colchester, Coventry, Lichfield, Exeter, Bristol, Salisbury, Southampton, Worcester, Shrewsbury, Canterbury, Chichester?' All these, and more, 'if they were in France, should be called good towns'.[1]

The herald's list of twenty towns embraces between a third and a half of the fifty or so regional centres and major county towns of England which – with their equivalents in Scotland and Wales – are the subject of this chapter. It also contains fourteen – almost one half – of the thirty-one largest English provincial towns in the early sixteenth century, which are enumerated in Table 11.1 below. It is evident from the other six towns nominated by the herald, however, that size of population was not the only criterion for entry in his list. Lichfield, Chichester, Durham and Carlisle were there because, like others, they were cathedral cities, Hull because it was another important port, Berwick as a vital frontier citadel. Without some of these, moreover, the thinly populated North of England would scarcely have been represented at all. Status and function were as important as size in defining good towns.

The same applied to 'great towns', the other conceptual category which contemporaries applied to the upper reaches of the urban hierarchy, though in this case size came more deliberately into the frame. Thomas Wilson, describing the 'State of England' in 1601, began with the twenty-four cathedral cities, as other commentators had done. But looking then for further 'great towns', he thought there might be as many as 289 of them 'not inferior in greatness', either because

[1] R. H. Tawney and E. Power, eds., *Tudor Economic Documents* (London, 1924), vol. III, p. 7. For William Cecil's use of the term 'good towns', see PRO, SP 12/184/50.

they were walled, or because they were parliamentary boroughs, or because they were 'greater than many of the [cathedral] cities in number of people and riches'. Population and wealth might be as relevant as physical appearance and political status. Wilson was aware, however, that that involved further uncertainties at the borderline, since there were many places – he perhaps had Manchester or Halifax in mind – 'which go in the number of villages or parishes' but which had as many as 'three or four thousand communicants'.[2]

Modern historians share Wilson's difficulty, even if they avoid his hyperbole. We would probably want to leave out of account his last, unincorporated conglomerations of population, since they lacked the formal institutions, corporate articulation and civic self-consciousness which were necessary to guarantee a secure place among the good and the great. We should exclude also many of Wilson's 289 'not inferior' towns which were too small to have the regional importance which, along with civic self-consciousness, separates the great and the good from the market towns considered in the next chapter. When Gregory King counted England's 'great towns' at the end of the seventeenth century, he thought that only forty-four of them, apart from London, had 500 houses or more[3] – sufficient to bring them close to, or above, the line of 2,500 population which is taken in this volume to mark off small towns. But that still leaves us with a broad spectrum of English towns, varying greatly in size and function, though sharing other common features.

The inclusion of Welsh and Scottish towns adds further to the variety. Insofar as Wales had urban centres, it is arguable that the greatest of them lay in England, at Chester, Shrewsbury and Bristol. The Act of Union of 1536 and subsequent legislation had, however, created a number of Welsh county towns, and among them 'the four corner capitals', each with its assizes and a chancery and exchequer, 'regional capitals' as they have been termed: Carmarthen, Brecon, Caernarvon and Denbigh.[4] Of these, Caernarvon was very small, and Denbigh's growth was impeded by competition from the flourishing market of Wrexham, with which it was forced to share its assizes. But Brecon – 'a very proper walled town, well builded and well paved' – had more of the character of a regional centre, and Carmarthen certainly filled the bill: 'the fairest town in all south Wales and of most civility', where 'the King's justice is kept, by occasion whereof the gentlemen and commons of the country most resort there'. To them we might add Haverfordwest, considered 'a good town, wealthy and well governed',

[2] Thomas Wilson, 'The state of England anno dom. 1600', ed. F. J. Fisher, *Camden Miscellany*, vol. XVI (Camden Society, 3rd series, 52, 1936), pp. 11–12. Cf. William Harrison, *The Description of England*, ed. G. Edelen (Ithaca, 1968), pp. 204, 214–15, 217; and for a list of ten 'great cities' in England after London, see George Rainsford, 'Ritratto d'Ingliterra', ed. P. S. Donaldson, *Camden Miscellany*, vol. XXVII (Camden Society, 4th series, 22, 1979), p. 93.

[3] J. Thirsk and J. P. Cooper, *Seventeenth-Century Economic Documents* (Oxford, 1972), p. 791.

[4] H. Carter, *The Towns of Wales* (Cardiff, 1965), pp. 33, 35–9.

and also 'the most civil' town in South Wales (perhaps because of its large English population).[5] Brecon, Carmarthen, Wrexham and Haverfordwest may all have had populations which reached the 2,000 mark at the beginning of our period.[6]

If the union with England provided some of the institutions which gave a number of small Welsh towns civic identities like those of their larger English counterparts, the very different urban institutions of the kingdom of Scotland similarly separated off a small group of towns of distinct status. Scotland had nothing like the English administrative centre of the county town with its quarter sessions, but the royal burghs with their own Convention had a group identity in national politics never matched by English boroughs. They also had a monopoly of overseas trade and that, together with a lack of incentives for the development of craft or industrial centres, dictated the continuing predominance in size and wealth of a subset of four of them: Edinburgh, Aberdeen, Dundee and Perth. These were the 'four great towns of Scotland' which had been singled out for attention by Hansa merchants as early as the fourteenth century.[7] Edinburgh was exceptional in other ways, of course. A capital city, with its royal Court, parliament and courts of law, it sits somewhat uneasily in the company of the regional centres whose fortunes occupy the bulk of this chapter. Before 1640 it was never more than twice as big as the next largest Scottish town, and in that respect at least it was perhaps closer to the English provincial capitals like York and Norwich than to the metropolis of London. But it was an entity recognisably different in kind from Aberdeen, and it could scarcely have been further apart from even the most civil town in Wales.

Even where towns can reasonably be compared one with another – Aberdeen and Haverfordwest, say, or Bristol and Carlisle among the towns on the herald's English list – the differences between them may seem very great. To contemporaries, however, the gulf was smaller than it appears to modern eyes. Such places had in common institutions and privileges, which might be of greater or lesser elaboration, but which did not always become more elaborate with size. Haverfordwest, for example, was a county of itself, with sheriff and justices, just as Bristol was, even if the business dealt with by their common councils was vastly different in volume and quality. Most of the great and the good were physically distinguished by their walls, and their corporate consciousness was voiced in their annals and chronicles; they displayed a civic pride which made them closer to one another than any of them were to a mere market town. They formed a varied hierarchy, but it was one with some real coherence.

[5] A. H. Dodd, ed., *A History of Wrexham Denbighshire* (Wrexham, 1957), pp. 34, 36; R. R. Davies, 'Brecon', and R. A. Griffiths, 'Carmarthen', in R. A. Griffiths, ed., *Boroughs of Medieval Wales* (Cardiff, 1978), pp. 70, 155–6; Carter, *Towns of Wales*, p. 39; B. G. Charles, ed., *Calendar of the Records of the Borough of Haverfordwest 1539–1660* (Board of Celtic Studies, University of Wales, History and Law series, 24, Cardiff, 1967), p. 2. [6] See above, p. 134.

[7] M. Lynch, M. Spearman and G. Stell, eds., *The Scottish Medieval Town* (Edinburgh, 1988), p. 264.

(i) A STABLE HIERARCHY

It was also a hierarchy which enjoyed considerable stability over time. The chief towns of Wales in 1700 were still those of 1540, though Swansea had risen to join them, and they were still relatively small. There was some greater change in Scotland, particularly after 1600. By 1639, when we can first estimate the size of Scottish urban populations with any security, Glasgow had begun its phenomenal growth, thanks to new commercial opportunities which are considered elsewhere in this volume; and Perth was falling from the top rank, as the Tay silted up and it had to replace overseas trade, lost to Dundee, with overland trade in commodities such as linen. But the most radical changes occurred after 1650. Edinburgh, with a population of 40,000 or more in 1700, pulled far away from the rest (apart from Glasgow which had 18,000), and with its marked professional and service sectors it was now a city to be ranked with other European capitals. At the same time, the other large towns suffered from competition from the growth of lesser market centres, many of them newly founded. In many ways, changes which affected English towns over two centuries were telescoped in Scotland into the half-century after 1650. The overall picture of a very few major towns was, however, little distorted. In 1691 only five towns had populations over 5,000: and Aberdeen and Dundee were still there after Edinburgh and Glasgow. They were followed by Ayr, which had moved ahead of Perth and smaller regional centres like Dumfries and Inverness.[8]

Much the same pattern of change within a relatively stable overall framework can be found among the major English towns, but it was change spread over a longer period and affecting many more places. Its contours can be illustrated by comparing the largest English towns at the beginning and end of our period, using data from the subsidies of the 1520s and from taxation and other records of the 1690s. Table 11.1 shows the thirty-one largest provincial towns at each date: that is all those with populations of about 3,000 or more in 1524–5 and of 5,000 or more in 1700, a reasonable inflation of the base-line since the population of England doubled over that period.[9] No great reliance should be placed

[8] I. D. Whyte, 'Urbanization in early modern Scotland: a preliminary analysis', *Scottish Economic and Social History*, 9 (1989), 21–38; M. Lynch, 'Urbanisation and urban networks in seventeenth century Scotland: some further thoughts', *ibid.*, 12 (1992), 24–41.

[9] The sources for Table 11.1 are as follows. For 1524–5: all towns with populations over 2,750 in the tables in A. Dyer, *Decline and Growth in English Towns 1400–1640* (London, 1991), pp. 72–4, plus Beverley (see *ibid.*, p. 74n), Chester (N. Alldridge, 'The mechanics of decline: migration and economy in early modern Chester', in M. Reed, ed., *English Towns in Decline 1350–1800* (Leicester, 1986), p. 8 and n. 23), and Newcastle (C. Phythian-Adams, *Desolation of a City* (Cambridge, 1979), p. 13); and with revised totals for York and Coventry based on D. M. Palliser, *Tudor York* (Oxford, 1979), p. 112; Phythian-Adams, *Desolation of a City*, p. 197. For 1700: all towns with approximate populations of 5,000 or more listed in E. A. Wrigley, 'Urban growth and agricultural change: England and the continent in the early modern period', in R. I. Rotberg and T. K. Rabb, eds., *Population and Economy* (Cambridge, 1986), p. 126.

on the accuracy of the population totals, least of all towards the bottom of each list.[10] Neither are the cut-off points more than arbitrary. Places like Warwick, with 2,000 people at the beginning of our period, Carlisle with 1,700 and even Wells with fewer than 1,500, could certainly claim inclusion among great and good towns in 1540, not least, in the case of the two latter, because of their civic and ecclesiastical status. At the end of the period, the same might be said about Ely, Chelmsford and Sandwich, all with populations of 3,000 or so in the later seventeenth century.[11] The lists are not inclusive. But they do contain the majority of provincial towns of more than local significance, and their fortunes illustrate the history of all of them.

The most obvious feature of the Table is relative stability over time, as one might expect given the maturity of the English urban system and its already proven resilience over several centuries. Nineteen towns occur in both lists, and it is particularly notable that the top rank, as in Scotland, held their place: the regional capitals of Norwich, Bristol, Exeter and York, joined long before 1700 by Newcastle. There was even greater stability than that total of nineteen might suggest. Hereford, Reading and Northampton each had a population close to 5,000 in 1700, and were not the major casualties they might at first seem, though Hereford had fallen considerably in rank. Conversely, Nottingham, Hull and Plymouth may well have had populations around 2,000 in the 1520s;[12] and Lynn and Tiverton must have reached that figure very soon afterwards. They were scarcely fresh-faced newcomers in 1700. The seven other new arrivals in 1700 are, moreover, predictable, famous success stories to be explained, like the emergence of Glasgow, by factors considered in other chapters: Birmingham, Manchester and Leeds, the beneficiaries of new industrial development; Liverpool and Sunderland, profiting from new directions in overseas and coastal commerce; Chatham and Portsmouth, responding to the development of the navy.

The nine possible casualties by 1700 (leaving Hereford, Reading and Northampton on one side) are more interesting, because they indicate the forces which affected many other great towns. Some were victims of the changes

[10] This is especially true of the 1524–5 figures, based on lists of taxpayers and a multiplier, both of which introduce considerable uncertainties. I have therefore used only approximations drawn from Dr Dyer's calculations. The 1524–5 subsidies also exclude towns which may have had populations of between 2,500 and 3,000 such as Bath, Durham, Kendal and Rye. (I am grateful to Dr Dyer for advice on this point.)

[11] *VCH*, Warwickshire, VIII, p. 418; H. Summerson, *Medieval Carlisle* (Cumberland and Westmorland Antiquarian and Archaeological Society, extra series, 25, 1993), vol. II, p. 513; D. G. Shaw, *The Creation of a Community: The City of Wells in the Middle Ages* (Oxford, 1993), p. 47. Information on Ely, Beverley, Chelmsford and Sandwich from Dr Jack Langton.

[12] P. J. Corfield, 'Urban development in England and Wales in the sixteenth and seventeenth centuries', in D. C. Coleman and A. H. John, eds., *Trade, Government and Economy in Pre-Industrial England* (London, 1976), p. 224; C. W. Chalklin, *The Provincial Towns of Georgian England* (London, 1974), p. 18; Dyer, *Decline and Growth*, p. 74.

Table 11.1 *The largest English provincial towns 1524–5 and 1700*

1524–5		1700	
Norwich	9	Norwich	30
Bristol	*c.* 8	Bristol	21
York		Newcastle	16
Exeter	7	Exeter	14
Coventry		York	12
Newcastle	*c.* 6	Yarmouth	10
Salisbury		*Birmingham*	
Canterbury	*c.* 5	Chester	
Colchester		Colchester	
Bury St Edmunds		Ipswich	8–9
Cambridge		*Manchester*	
Chester		*Plymouth*	
Hereford		Worcester	
Lincoln	*c.* 4	Bury St Edmunds	
Oxford		Cambridge	
St Albans		Canterbury	
Shrewsbury		*Chatham*	
Winchester		Coventry	
Beverley		Gloucester	
Crediton		*Hull*	
Gloucester		*Leeds*	
Huntingdon		Leicester	
Ipswich		*Liverpool*	5–7
Leicester		*Lynn*	
Maidstone	*c.* 3	*Nottingham*	
Northampton		Oxford	
Reading		*Portsmouth*	
Rochester		Salisbury	
Southampton		Shrewsbury	
Worcester		*Sunderland*	
Yarmouth		*Tiverton*	

Approximate populations are given in thousands.
Towns in italics in 1524–5 do not appear in the 1700 list.
Towns in italics in 1700 do not appear in the 1524–5 list.
Sources: see n. 9.

which produced newcomers, as with Southampton's loss of its foreign trade, or Crediton's fall from a very recent prosperity once Devonshire kerseys gave way to serges and the town made the switch less successfully (though it started earlier) than Tiverton.[13] The long-drawn-out decline of the Old Draperies helps to explain not only the absence of Lincoln, Winchester and Beverley from the 1700 list,[14] but the steep fall in the relative position of Salisbury. But the same or similar shifts hit other towns too, without the same consequences: Chester, for example, in the case of a town's fortunes as a port, or Gloucester, in the case of its industrial base. For most of the great and good towns at the beginning of our period had more than one string to their bow, and could shift function in order to survive and often thrive. This was most obviously the case with the leaders, the provincial capitals, but it was true also of many other towns. Crediton, with nowhere else to go when its staple industry declined, is the exception which proves the rule. The largest group of apparent casualties – St Albans, Maidstone, Rochester and Huntingdon – were in fact resilient county centres, the first three of them at least flourishing again by 1700, but kept from the top rank either because they were too close to a growing metropolis or because they were in areas where there were too many competing medium-sized centres.[15] Over a period as long as a century and a half, there was bound to be some reordering of county towns, but the majority of them pulled through.

This is not to say that their task was easy, and most of them faced considerable problems in the interim. Economic change between 1540 and 1700 was nowhere smoothly linear, any more than was the demographic growth which seems to be indicated by Table 11.1. Censuses taken in Southampton show that the population had grown to 4,200 by 1596, but fallen back to 2,939 in 1696, while estimates for Lincoln suggest a fall to around 2,500 by the 1560s and then a recovery to 3,500 by 1676.[16] There were at least three outbreaks of plague between 1540 and 1700 in each of the nineteen towns which occur in both lists

[13] C. G. A. Clay, *Economic Expansion and Social Change: England 1500–1700* (Cambridge, 1984), vol. II, pp. 107–8, 111; W. G. Hoskins, *Devon* (London, 1954), p. 378; E. Kerridge, *Textile Manufactures in Early Modern England* (Manchester, 1985), pp. 25, 65, 117.

[14] It should be noted that despite relative decline, Winchester and Lincoln both had populations around the 4,000 mark in 1700, and although Beverley had a population of only 2,800 in the later seventeenth century, it was recovering as the county town for the East Riding: Corfield, 'Urban development', p. 227; Chalklin, *Provincial Towns*, p. 18 (which corrects Corfield's estimate for Lincoln); *VCH*, East Riding, VI, pp. 108, 112. On Lincoln, see also A. Whiteman, *The Compton Census of 1676* (London, 1986), p. cxix.

[15] For comparable competition between towns in the West Midlands, see A. Dyer, 'Warwickshire towns under the Tudors and Stuarts', *Warwickshire History*, 3 (1976–7), 122–35. Towns around the Medway and the Solent faced similar problems. For Maidstone, see P. Clark and L. Murfin, *The History of Maidstone* (Stroud, 1995), ch. 4.

[16] D. M. Palliser, *The Age of Elizabeth: England under the Later Tudors 1547–1603* (London, 1983), p. 204; Corfield, 'Urban development', p. 238; J. W. F. Hill, *Tudor and Stuart Lincoln* (Cambridge, 1956), p. 88; Whiteman, *Compton Census*, p. cxix.

in Table 11.1, and no fewer than nine in Norwich; and they devastated several Scottish towns in the 1640s and Haverfordwest in 1652–3.[17] Though economic recovery was generally rapid after these crises, they were a temporary brake, destroying labour resources as effectively as fires did physical plant, and undermining confidence as decisively as the floods which swept away the new jetties being built in Carlisle in 1575 and the Tay bridge at Perth in 1621.[18] Dearth, which had brought crowds of beggars and disease into rich English towns and caused heavy mortality in Haverfordwest in the 1590s, could still impose the reality of famine on Scottish towns in the 1690s, when Aberdeen lost 20 per cent of its population, Edinburgh had a refugee camp for the destitute in the new Greyfriars churchyard and the poor of Leith were 'starving and dying upon the streets'.[19] Less sporadic and more prolonged were the destructive consequences of the two major events in which great and good towns necessarily played the role of victim: the Reformation, which made the position of places such as Reading and Bury St Edmunds, once the site of rich monasteries, particularly precarious, and the Civil Wars which placed every large town under siege, either literally or metaphorically, a century later. On average, seven religious houses, hospitals and colleges were dissolved in the 1530s and 1540s in each of the nineteen 'survivor' towns of Table 11.1; and in the 1640s eleven of the nineteen found themselves besieged, in the case of Bristol on two occasions.[20]

These short- and medium-term shocks, added to the long-term economic shifts brought by industrial and commercial change, were the reality within what seems at first sight a stable urban framework. They threatened economic prosperity and social order, and tested civic capacities to respond successfully; and

[17] P. Slack, *The Impact of Plague in Tudor and Stuart England* (London, 1985), esp. pp. 61–2, supplemented by information from J. F. D. Shrewsbury, *A History of Bubonic Plague in the British Isles* (Cambridge, 1970); Whyte, 'Urbanization in early modern Scotland', 33; Charles, ed., *Haverfordwest Records*, pp. 15–16. Major fires were less common than plagues, but they affected at least eight of the nineteen 'survivor' towns of Table 11.1: E. L. Jones, S. Porter and M. Turner, *A Gazetteer of English Urban Fire Disasters 1500–1900* (Historical Geography Research Series, 13, 1984).

[18] Summerson, *Carlisle*, II, p. 548; Lynch, 'Urbanisation and urban networks', 34.

[19] Slack, *Impact of Plague*, pp. 73–5; Shrewsbury, *Bubonic Plague*, p. 251; R. E. Tyson, 'Famine in Aberdeenshire, 1695–1699: anatomy of a crisis', in D. Stevenson, ed., *From Lairds to Louns* (Aberdeen, 1986), p. 49; R. A. Houston, *Social Change in the Age of Enlightenment* (Oxford, 1994), pp. 259, 273, 286.

[20] The number of dissolutions has been calculated from information in D. Knowles and R. N. Hadcock, eds., *Medieval Religious Houses: England and Wales* (London, 1971). For a balanced account of the effects of the Civil Wars on some Scottish towns, see T. M. Devine, 'The Cromwellian union and the Scottish burghs: the case of Aberdeen and Glasgow, 1652–60', in J. Butt and J. T. Ward, eds., *Scottish Themes: Essays in Honour of Professor S. G. E. Lythe* (Edinburgh, 1976); and for the English case see I. Roy, 'England turned Germany? The aftermath of the Civil War in its European context', *TRHS*, 5th series, 28 (1978), 127–44; and R. Howell, 'Neutralism, conservatism and political alignment in the English Revolution: the case of the towns 1642–9', in J. Morrill, ed., *Reactions to the English Civil War 1642–1649* (London, 1982), pp. 67–87.

great and good towns only held their position because they had the capacity, whether by good fortune or good management, to meet the challenge.

(ii) ECONOMIC FLUCTUATIONS AND THE SOCIAL ORDER

Generalisation about the impact of economic fluctuations is made difficult by the fact that there was no single, universally applicable chronological pattern, least of all in the case of the diverse urban economies of England. With respect to the industrial function of towns, for example, the slumps in cloth exports of the 1550s and 1620s hit all of the English textile centres hard, but their longer-term effects were various. The first was fatal in Gloucester where in 1582 the capping and clothing trades were said to have been 'much decayed . . . within 20 or 30 years past'. Reading's textile industry revived after the 1550s but declined from the 1620s. That in Worcester, protected by a statute of 1534 restricting rural competition, survived both depressions and retained its dominance until 1700.[21] Worcester is the acknowledged exception to the general rule of the decline of the urban broadcloth industry, from which a few places, notably Norwich and Colchester, found an ultimate escape route in the New Draperies. But in Norwich at least that new base was only secure when domestic markets for Norwich stuffs were firmly established in the second half of the seventeenth century.[22] For most towns the prospects for the industrial sector were little more than bleak for a century after 1550, and when it came recovery was often based on diversification into new products: pins in Gloucester, boots in Northampton and stockings in Leicester, ribbon and watches in Coventry.[23]

Until that late seventeenth century revival in urban industry, the generality of established towns had to look to their other functions for economic sustenance. Marketing and distribution for a large hinterland were the most important, as regional centres profited from the expansion of inland trade in the later sixteenth century; and in this respect at least Welsh and Scottish towns benefited from the same trends as their larger English counterparts.[24] Shrewsbury's recovery from

[21] *VCH*, Gloucestershire, IV, p. 75; N. R. Goose, 'Decay and regeneration in seventeenth-century Reading: a study in a changing economy', *SHist.*, 6 (1984), 56–9; P. Hughes, 'Property and prosperity: the relationship of the buildings and fortunes of Worcester, 1500–1660', *Midland History*, 17 (1992), 45, 50.

[22] N. Goose, 'In search of the urban variable: towns and the English economy, 1500–1650', *Ec.HR*, 2nd series, 39 (1986), 176; *VCH*, Essex, IX, pp. 81–2; P. J. Corfield, 'A provincial capital in the late seventeenth century: the case of Norwich', in P. Clark and P. Slack, eds., *Crisis and Order in English Towns 1500–1700* (London, 1972), pp. 279–83. Colchester bays and says may have found their market niche earlier than the Norwich product, but they had passed their boom days by 1700.

[23] P. Ripley, 'The economy of the city of Gloucester 1660–1740', *Transactions of the Bristol and Gloucestershire Archaeological Society*, 98 (1980), 140; *VCH*, Gloucestershire, IV, pp. 107, 109; *VCH*, Warwickshire, VIII, p. 163; Dyer, 'Warwickshire towns', 123; P. Clark, ed., *Country Towns in Pre-Industrial England* (Leicester, 1981), p. 17.

the 1560s onwards was based on the exchange of goods between a pastoral west and an arable east, and on the finishing and marketing of Welsh flannel. Gloucester profited from its recognition as a port in 1580, and became a centre for the grain trade and malt making, as did Reading when it was faced with similar problems and opportunities in the later seventeenth century.[25] The importance of river traffic is evident from the difficulties of 'dry' towns like Coventry and the anxieties of those which feared they might become so, whether from the silting up of harbours and estuaries, as with Perth, or from being less advantageously situated than their rivals, as in the case of Hereford as compared with Shrewsbury.[26] Road traffic could be important, as it was for Lichfield, as a post town and coaching centre on the main route to Ireland;[27] but improvements in road transport – and, it might be added, major improvements in inland navigation – were stimulated and affordable only at the end of the seventeenth century.

The role of the larger English towns as social centres was similarly of fundamental importance to many of them from at least the 1560s, but it was a function which realised its full potential only a century later. The Palatine courts brought a host of well-to-do visitors to Chester for most of our period, and the ecclesiastical courts (and until 1640 the Council in the North) did the same for York. The grand Swan Inn showed the importance of quarter sessions for a town as small as Warwick, just as the new inns around the East gate of Leicester reflected shifts in the direction of inland transport, and the Plume of Feathers, the Vine and the Three Lions demonstrated Salisbury's role as both county centre and staging post on the road to the west.[28] But facilities for visitors, from accommodation to leisure and professional services, expanded everywhere after the Restoration, sometimes helped by special factors, like royal patronage in the case of Winchester, the settlement of political disputes with the county gentry at Gloucester, or the ambitious rebuilding at Northampton and Warwick for which fires in 1675 and 1694 provided the opportunity.[29] To describe the results as 'gentry' or 'leisure towns' runs the risk of implying too narrow a social and

[24] Cf. M. Lynch, 'Continuity and change in urban society, 1500–1700', in R. A. Houston and I. D. Whyte, eds., *Scottish Society 1500–1800* (Cambridge, 1989), p. 100.

[25] Dyer, *Decline and Growth*, p. 29; *VCH*, Gloucestershire, IV, pp. 76–8; Goose, 'Decay and regeneration', 62–3.

[26] M. Lynch, ed., *The Early Modern Town in Scotland* (London, 1987), p. 9; W. A. Champion, 'The Frankpledge population of Shrewsbury 1500–1720', *Local Population Studies*, 41 (1988), 58–9. On Hereford, see also above, pp. 105–6.

[27] *VCH*, Staffordshire, XIV, p. 16.

[28] *VCH*, Warwickshire, VIII, p. 511; *VCH*, Leicestershire, IV, pp. 154–5; RCHM (England), *The City of Salisbury*, vol. I (London, 1980), p. xlviii. See also A. M. Everitt, 'The English urban inn 1560–1760', in A. M. Everitt, ed., *Perspectives in English Urban History* (London, 1973), pp. 91–137.

[29] A. Rosen, 'Winchester in transition, 1580–1700', in Clark, ed., *Country Towns*, p. 180; *VCH*, Gloucestershire, IV, pp. 79, 101, 106–7; Ripley, 'Economy of Gloucester', 149; P. Borsay, *The English Urban Renaissance* (Oxford, 1989), pp. 18–19, 45–6.

economic foundation for what was a broadly based achievement, but it usefully points to a new and stable urban identity.[30]

The local variety implicit in these patterns of change helps to explain disagreement among historians about how far the 'urban crisis' – or more accurately urban crises – of the fifteenth and early sixteenth centuries can be said to have extended beyond 1540. There is much to be said for the view that recovery from demographic and industrial depression and from the devastation brought by the Reformation was underway from the 1570s;[31] but there remains room for doubt about the extent of that recovery before the 1630s. If inland trade was reviving in the sixteenth century on the back of agrarian prosperity, it is not self-evident that the larger towns, faced with competition from an increasing number of market centres, were quickly able to gain a major share of the profits from the new terms of trade. If urban populations were again rising, from 1560 if not earlier, it is by no means clear that all the additional hands could quickly be employed, given the problem of redeploying existing labour resources which is so eloquently reflected in the great Norwich census of the poor, taken in 1570 before the city's demographic recovery was underway.[32] It would certainly be difficult to argue that a revival of urban prosperity fed through into rising wealth *per capita* much before the second quarter of the seventeenth century.

What can be said, however, is that the larger towns had the resilience to cope, if not quickly then certainly in the medium term, with the adjustments made necessary by economic change. Something of the character of that resilience can be seen from the distribution of urban occupations, insofar as that can be reconstructed from lists of freemen and occupational designations in wills. It was one sign of the developed economies of the larger English towns, as compared with those of Scotland, for example, that substantial numbers were employed in manufacturing, commonly up to 50 per cent of the samples surveyed.[33] But it was uncommon for more than 25 per cent to be engaged in a single industry. Some of the specialised textile towns had 30 per cent or rather more of recorded occupations concentrated in the staple industry, and the fluctuating industrial fortunes of Norwich, Colchester and Reading can all be traced in the proportion falling below that threshold during depressions, in Norwich between the mid-sixteenth and mid-seventeenth centuries, in Colchester between 1540 and 1579 and in

[30] P. Clark, ed., *The Transformation of English Provincial Towns 1600–1800* (London, 1984), p. 20; A. McInnes, 'The emergence of a leisure town: Shrewsbury 1660–1760', *P&P*, 120 (1988), 53–87; P. Borsay and A. McInnes, 'Debate: the emergence of a leisure town: or an urban renaissance?', *ibid.*, 126 (1990), 189–202.

[31] For the most recent discussion, see Dyer, *Decline and Growth*, and cf. Goose, 'In search of the urban variable', 174–5.

[32] J. F. Pound, *Tudor and Stuart Norwich* (Chichester, 1988), p. 57; J. F. Pound, ed., *The Norwich Census of the Poor 1570* (Norfolk Record Society, 40, 1971).

[33] N. Goose, 'English preindustrial urban economies', in J. Barry, ed. *The Tudor and Stuart Town* (London, 1990), pp. 63–73, provides a useful survey of recent work on urban occupations.

Reading after 1630 or so. It was only in the exceptional circumstances of late Elizabethan and early Stuart Worcester, however, that the proportion employed in a single industry reached one half.[34]

In most large English towns, at least a third, and often up to one half, of employed males were in the basic trades of food and drink, clothing and building, occupations which not only catered for urban residents themselves but readily responded to demand from visitors and hence to the changing fortunes of towns as distributive and social centres. It is no accident that these were particularly prominent occupational groupings in the sixteenth century in the university towns of Oxford and Cambridge; they could expand in Elizabethan Norwich as its role as regional capital grew; and the victualling trades were particularly buoyant in later Stuart Ipswich and Shrewsbury for similar reasons.[35] It should be stressed that the sources from which such calculations are drawn usually leave out of observation sections of the population either unfree or in poverty, and hence more liable than others to be victims or beneficiaries of economic fluctuations. But there can be no doubt that these fundamental urban activities gave all the larger towns a secure base whether for retrenchment or economic growth.

Still more revealing with respect to the long-term resilience and changing fortunes of towns, however, is the number of different trades they contained. Not only does that tell us something about the functional diversity of different towns: there were as many as sixty individual trades in Elizabethan Leicester, Northampton and Nottingham, for example, and more than one hundred in Bristol, Norwich and York.[36] The fact that the number was increasing in several of our towns over the period also points to a general increase in the sophistication of urban economies, particularly after 1660. In Warwick, for example, there were twenty trades in 1604, thirty in 1661 and fifty by 1694; and Northampton had eighty-three in the later seventeenth century. Post-Restoration Winchester had its upholsterers, tobacconists, gunsmiths, booksellers, watchmakers and coachmen, and Ipswich its stationers, gardeners and periwig and fan makers, as well as those physicians and lawyers who contributed to the formation of an urban 'pseudo-gentry'.[37] For Scotland we know only the number of craft organisations, which is not the same thing as the number of crafts, for most of the period. But the fourteen guilds in sixteenth-century Edinburgh, the nine in

[34] Pound, *Tudor and Stuart Norwich*, pp. 52, 55, 59, 64; Goose, 'In search of the urban variable', 175–6; Goose, 'Decay and regeneration', 53–4, 59; Palliser, *Age of Elizabeth*, p. 245. The proportionate importance of textiles was rising again in Norwich and Colchester in the later seventeenth century, but the proportion of freemen admitted to the industry in Norwich only reached 50 per cent after 1700: *VCH*, Essex, IX, p. 77; Corfield, 'A provincial capital', pp. 275–6.

[35] Goose, 'English preindustrial urban economies', p. 65 and n. 9; Pound, *Tudor and Stuart Norwich*, pp. 55–61; M. Reed, 'Economic structure and change in seventeenth-century Ipswich', in Clark, ed., *Country Towns*, p. 102; McInnes, 'Emergence of a leisure town', 55–6.

[36] Palliser, *Age of Elizabeth*, p. 242.

[37] *VCH*, Warwickshire, VIII, p. 507; Borsay, *English Urban Renaissance*, p. 35; Rosen, 'Winchester', pp. 177–8; Reed, 'Economic structure and change', p. 130.

Dundee and Perth and seven in Aberdeen (contrasting with sixty in York) tell much the same comparative story; and Edinburgh at least had 179 notaries, thirty-three physicians and twenty-three surgeons by the 1690s.[38] At the end of the seventeenth century Edinburgh also exhibited that preponderance of females over males which is evident in the populations of some of the largest English towns, which points to the extent of domestic service and other employment opportunities for women, and which indicates a new urban prosperity.[39]

Economic change necessarily affected the social as well as the occupational and demographic structures of towns, but its differential effects are not easily reconstructed from the historical record. The snapshots provided by the English hearth taxes may throw some light upon them, albeit only in the 1660s and 1670s, at a time when adjustments to new circumstances were already underway. The source has some well-known limitations: it tells us about housing, not directly about wealth; and the figures for exemptions from the tax on the grounds of poverty are particularly fallible, given probable local variations in the criteria adopted.[40] Nevertheless, provided we deal in broad categories, it is a source too valuable to ignore. Table 11.2 gives data on the proportions of householders living in poor (one to two hearths), modest (three to five hearths) and comfortable (over five hearths) accommodation in a number of towns, as well as the proportions of the whole exempted from the tax. Comparable information about Edinburgh in 1691 has been added.[41]

[38] Lynch, Spearman and Stell, eds., *Scottish Medieval Town*, pp. 12, 261–2; Palliser, *Age of Elizabeth*, pp. 221–2; H. M. Dingwall, *Late Seventeenth-Century Edinburgh* (Aldershot, 1994), pp. 139–40, 216. For the general diversification of Scottish urban economies, see Lynch, 'Continuity and change', pp. 109–10.

[39] Dingwall, *Late Seventeenth-Century Edinburgh*, p. 28; Barry, ed., *The Tudor and Stuart Town*, p. 23; D. Souden, 'Migrants and the population structure of later seventeenth-century provincial cities and market towns', in Clark, ed., *Transformation of English Provincial Towns*, pp. 160–1.

[40] C. Husbands, 'Hearths, wealth and occupations: an exploration of the hearth tax in the later seventeenth century', in K. Schurer and T. Arkell, eds., *Surveying the People* (Local Population Studies Supplement, Oxford, 1992), pp. 65–77; T. Arkell, 'The incidence of poverty in England in the later seventeenth century', *Soc.Hist.*, 12 (1987), 23–47; N. Alldridge, 'House and household in Restoration Chester', *UHY* (1983), pp. 39–52.

[41] The sources for Table 11.2 are: Pound, *Tudor and Stuart Norwich*, p. 42 (Norwich, Bristol, York, Leicester); D. Levine and K. Wrightson, *The Making of an Industrial Society: Whickham 1560–1765* (Oxford, 1991), p. 157 (Newcastle, Chester, Coventry); W. G. Hoskins, *Industry, Trade and People in Exeter 1688–1800*, 2nd edn (Exeter, 1968), pp. 116–17; *VCH*, Essex, IX, pp. 97–8 (Colchester); Reed, 'Economic structure and change', pp. 131–3; C. A. F. Meekings, S. Porter and I. Roy, eds., 'The hearth tax collectors' book for Worcester, 1678–80', *Worcestershire Historical Society*, new series, 11 (1983), pp. 29, 39; *VCH*, Yorkshire: East Riding, I, pp. 160–1 (Hull); *VCH*, Gloucestershire, IV, p. 110, and P. Clark, '"The Ramoth-Gilead of the Good": urban change and political radicalism at Gloucester 1540–1640', in Barry, ed., *The Tudor and Stuart Town*, p. 254; A. B. Rosen, 'Economic and social aspects of the history of Winchester 1520–1670' (DPhil thesis, University of Oxford, 1975), p. 288; M. A. Faraday, ed., *Herefordshire Militia Assessments of 1663* (Camden Society, 4th series, 10, 1972), p. 21; Dingwall, *Late Seventeenth-Century Edinburgh*, p. 87. In calculating figures for Hull and Hereford, I have assumed that all the exempt were in the one to two hearth category, which may inflate the total slightly.

Table 11.2 *Housing and status from the hearth taxes: English provincial towns and Edinburgh*

Town	Percentage of households with 1-2 hearths	3-5 hearths	>5 hearths	Percent of households exempt
Norwich 1671	76	16	8	59
Bristol 1671	53	37	11	21
Newcastle 1665	76	18	6	41
Exeter 1672	70	19	11	40
York 1672	56	29	16	20
Chester 1664-5	67	22	11	40
Colchester 1674	72	21	7	53
Ipswich 1664	69	20	11	52
Ipswich 1674	54	29	17	38
Worcester 1678	70	24	7	33
Coventry 1666	68	23	8	41
Hull 1673	60	28	12	19
Gloucester 1664	54	31	15	29
Leicester 1670	70	23	7	27
Winchester 1665	59	27	14	29
Hereford 1664	73	20	7	50
Edinburgh 1691	75	20	5	—[a]

[a] No comparable data.
Sources: see n. 41.

The three-quarters of Edinburgh households in the one to two hearth category underlines the point that the hearth taxes tell us most about housing conditions, for this had for a century been one of the most densely populated cities in Europe;[42] and the dangers inherent in a snap-shot approach are nicely illustrated by the two highly contrasting sets of figures for Ipswich, perhaps explicable by an outbreak of plague which occurred between the two assessments and from which the labouring population had not fully recovered by 1674. But the extremes of the Table are nevertheless suggestive. The heavy dependence of Norwich and Colchester on the New Draperies is reflected in their exceptional proportions of exempt households, and in the high proportions in poor accommodation, despite the fact that both had, like Ipswich, recently suffered from major plague epidemics. The one to two hearth measure also highlights the importance of the rather different industrial bases of Worcester, Coventry and

[42] M. Lynch, *Edinburgh and the Reformation* (Edinburgh, 1981), pp. xiv, 14.

Leicester, of the finishing trades of Exeter and of the 'embryonic organized proletariat' created by the coal trade in Newcastle.[43] In the case of Hereford, by contrast, the comparable figure reflects, not an industrial centre, but a city of poor housing and a depressed economy, badly hit by the Civil War and with revival hampered by deficiencies in local transport.[44]

Equally interesting, however, are towns at the other extreme, with large proportions of households in the comfortable category: York, Gloucester and Winchester. These were towns now enjoying roles as social, service and marketing centres, and hence probably with social pyramids broader at the top and narrower at the bottom than those of more industrial centres, and of their less successful competitors like Hereford. In the 1520s York and Gloucester seem to have had social structures not radically different from that of Norwich, to judge by the subsidies.[45] By the 1670s they appear to have been quite distinct. The ability of some of the largest provincial towns to rest on non-industrial roles had opened up new contrasts and reflected new opportunities.

Economic change also helped to mould social and political relationships within towns. It did not disturb the universal correlation between power and wealth. The amount of wealth necessary for high office naturally varied from place to place, depending on the height of the social pyramid. In the later sixteenth century personal estates as large as £1,000 sterling were unknown among the rulers of Leicester, rare in Worcester (and in Edinburgh), perhaps average in Gloucester, very often exceeded in Exeter and Norwich.[46] But everywhere plutocracy remained the rule. What did change was the composition of the elite, as mercers and drapers rose to power in Elizabethan Oxford, for example, drapers took over (this time at the expense of mercers) in Shrewsbury at the same time, and maltsters rose to be mayors of later Stuart

[43] J. Ellis, 'A dynamic society: social relations in Newcastle-upon-Tyne, 1660–1760', in Clark, ed., *Transformation of English Provincial Towns*, p. 193. The particular industrial stimulus of coal and the labour resources needed to transport it are perhaps suggested by the very different figures for the other ports of Bristol and Hull which appear to have had proportionately much smaller labouring populations.

[44] M. D. Lobel, 'Hereford', in M. D. Lobel, ed., *British Atlas of Historic Towns*, vol. I: *Historic Towns* (London, 1969), pp. 10–11.

[45] Palliser, *Tudor York*, p. 137; Pound, *Tudor and Stuart Norwich*, p. 32; Clark, '"The Ramoth-Gilead of the Good"', p. 254. Winchester seems to have been poorer than the others in the 1520s and hence to have changed even more by the 1660s: Rosen, 'Economic and social aspects', pp. 23–4, 287.

[46] W. G. Hoskins, *Provincial England* (London, 1964), pp. 93, 111–14; A. Dyer, *The City of Worcester in the Sixteenth Century* (Leicester, 1973), pp. 224–5; M. H. B. Sanderson, 'The Edinburgh merchants in society, 1570–1603: the evidence of their testaments', in I. B. Cowan and D. Shaw, eds., *The Renaissance and Reformation in Scotland: Essays in Honour of Gordon Donaldson* (Edinburgh, 1983), p. 183; P. Clark, 'The civic leaders of Gloucester 1580–1800', in Clark, ed., *Transformation of English Provincial Towns*, pp. 318–19; W. G. Hoskins, 'The Elizabethan merchants of Exeter', in S. T. Bindoff, J. Hurstfield and C. H. Williams, eds., *Elizabethan Government and Society* (London, 1961), p. 172.

Reading.[47] The rise and fall of occupational groups prevented the formation of absolutely closed self-perpetuating urban oligarchies which might otherwise have occurred. It is possible that the same phenomenon was visible in Scotland only later, in the last decades of the seventeenth century,[48] but by then a contrary development was visible in the larger English towns. Economic equilibrium, declining immigration and close alliances between rural and urban elites, all produced a greater stability at the top. The prominent role of gentlemen of various kinds, of lawyers and even the modestly landed, in town councils[49] was accompanied by the emergence of urban trading dynasties, of what has been termed 'economic oligarchy' and hence of 'a very stable and more hereditary civic elite'.[50]

Compared with what had gone before, there was greater stability in the later seventeenth century also at the other end of the social scale, as living standards and employment opportunities began at last to improve. The many households exempted from the hearth tax were far from being in abject poverty, although in Norwich and Colchester they certainly denote populations vulnerable to crises and depressions in staple industries. In the century before 1640, however, the censuses of the poor, which were one sign of corporate consciousness of new stresses in both English and Scottish towns, produced evidence of unemployment and underemployment affecting up to a fifth of urban populations. They seemed inescapable consequences, in some places of demographic growth, in others of economic and demographic contraction; and they did much to shape the urban environment, in suburbs and alleys behind a town's grander main streets.[51]

47 *VCH*, Oxfordshire, IV, pp. 109, 137; T. C. Mendenhall, *The Shrewsbury Drapers and the Welsh Wool Trade in the XVI and XVII Centuries* (Oxford, 1953), p. 131; Goose, 'Decay and regeneration', 65.

48 T. M. Devine, 'The social composition of the business class in the larger Scottish towns 1680–1740', in T. M. Devine and D. Dickson, eds., *Ireland and Scotland 1600–1850* (Edinburgh, 1983), pp. 168–9; I. D. Whyte, 'Scottish population and social structure in the seventeenth and eighteenth centuries: new sources and perspectives', *Archives*, 20 (1993), 38. For signs of some shifts in the later sixteenth century, see Lynch in Lynch, Spearman and Stell, eds., *Scottish Medieval Town*, pp. 266–7.

49 17 per cent of Gloucester's aldermen in the last two decades of the seventeenth century were gentlemen: *VCH*, Gloucestershire, IV, p. 110. For examples of lawyers and a physician as mayors, see Rosen, 'Winchester', pp. 177–8.

50 C. Brooks, 'Apprenticeship, social mobility and the middling sort, 1550–1800', in J. Barry and C. Brooks, eds., *The Middling Sort of People* (London, 1994), pp. 71–2. Patterns of change were again rather different in the royal burghs of Scotland: cf. the 'merchant lairds' who ruled sixteenth-century Aberdeen, the importance of 'hereditary burgesses' in Edinburgh in the early seventeenth century and the proportionate decline in titled entrants to the latter's incorporations in the late seventeenth century: Lynch in Lynch, Spearman and Stell, eds., *Scottish Medieval Town*, p. 273; H. M. Dingwall, 'The importance of social factors in determining the composition of town councils: Edinburgh 1550–1650', *Scottish Historical Review*, 65 (1986), 22, 28; Houston, *Social Change*, p. 86.

51 P. Slack, *Poverty and Policy in Tudor and Stuart England* (London, 1988), pp. 73–80; Lynch in Lynch, Spearman and Stell, eds., *Scottish Medieval Town*, pp. 263, 281; see also above, pp. 216 *et passim*.

Much more important in determining the character of civic society than either the elite or the poor, however, and vital to the maintenance of social cohesion, were people in the middle of the social pyramid, the 'middling sort', the most diverse and least-studied segment of urban populations.[52] They supplied recruits to the layers of the pyramid above and below them, though social mobility upward was more limited than social mobility downward, especially in old age. Theirs was the tax base which, once it began to be properly exploited, determined the quality of public services affordable in a town, so that their greater numbers and wealth in Exeter at the end of the seventeenth century permitted pensions to the poor 50 per cent higher than were possible in Norwich.[53] As masters and employers, they conserved and transmitted skills, stocks in trade and wealth. They were vital also in maintaining the formal and informal associations which made up the warp and weft of the urban social fabric. As freemen of a town, and as overseers of the poor, wardmen and constables, they were at the base of the vertical organisation which culminated in the mayor and aldermen; as members of guilds and companies, vestries and groups of charitable trustees, they formed the horizontal networks which equally sustained senses of identity and sociability. One would give a lot to have the personal papers of just one of them, of a provincial equivalent of Nehemiah Wallington, the Puritan shopkeeper of early Stuart London.[54]

Though the historical record of it is flimsy, their crucial social position must have encouraged some self-awareness as a group. Freemen were commonly between a quarter and a half of male householders in the larger English towns, the proportion varying from town to town and within a town over time;[55] and their formal constitutional powers were equally various, extending from mere acquiescence in the choice of officers essentially made by self-perpetuating councils in Exeter and Bristol, to effective electoral influence in Norwich and Colchester.[56] In Colchester the efficacy of the freeman franchise led to recurrent disputes with the higher officeholders between the 1580s and 1620s, and in 1612 to an offer by the freemen of some restriction on the electorate which perhaps says a good deal about the self-perception of the respectable middling sort more widely. They were happy to exclude from the franchise all common bakers,

52 Barry and Brooks, eds., *Middling Sort*, is an indispensable collection of information and argument on the topic. 53 Slack, *Poverty and Policy*, p. 181.

54 P. S. Seaver, *Wallington's World* (London, 1985).

55 C. Phythian-Adams, 'The economic and social structure', in *The Fabric of the Traditional Community* (Open University, English Urban History course, Milton Keynes, 1977), p. 10; Alldridge, 'Mechanics of decline', pp. 17–18; *VCH*, Essex, IX, p. 111; Pound, *Tudor and Stuart Norwich*, p. 59. For Edinburgh, see Houston, *Social Change*, p. 32.

56 W. T. MacCaffrey, *Exeter 1540–1640* (Cambridge, Mass., 1958), pp. 29–30; D. H. Sacks, *The Widening Gate* (Berkeley, Calif., 1991), p. 163; J. T. Evans, *Seventeenth-Century Norwich* (Oxford, 1979), pp. 26–9; *VCH*, Essex, IX, p. 114. For mixed arrangements, see Palliser, *Tudor York*, pp. 67–9; R. Howell, *Newcastle-upon-Tyne and the Puritan Revolution* (Oxford, 1967), pp. 42–3.

brewers, butchers and victuallers unless ranked high on the subsidy lists, and all 'chamberers, loose journeymen, men's children not householding in their own persons, such persons as . . . have been convicted for adultery, fornication, drunkenness, theft, as common swearers, and persons receiving or asking relief of others for to relieve their poverty'.[57] Here at least is evidence of the self-consciousness of a social group, distancing itself alike from the elite and the rabble, and expecting recognition and political participation in return.

Franchise disputes like those in Colchester testify nevertheless to the pressures which were limiting some kinds of participation in the corporate life of the greater towns in the century after 1540. While the Reformation destroyed the fraternities which had embodied a wealth of voluntary and associative activity, civic magistracies backed by the crown and buttressed by a developing panoply of civic ceremony sought to control what remained. The civic response to economic and social change continued to be implemented and expressed in the middle ground of parishes, wards and craft guilds: the number of such subsidiary institutions was after all one of the main distinguishing features of these towns. But the initiative increasingly came, and was expected to come, from the top.

(iii) CIVIC RESPONSES

Even for the elite, however, corporate images and corporate ideals were indispensable in justifying and explaining action. It was legal incorporation which made these towns 'in a sort immortal', and if their magistrates enjoyed delegated authority from the crown, they must also maintain that 'fellowship' and 'brotherhood' which preserved the parallel assumption that civic affairs were governed by 'mutual consent'.[58] Patriarchal authority and the common interest were not conflicting but convergent ideals, just as they were in the little commonwealth of the family. A mayor was 'a civil husband of a civil wife', the town, according to the recorder of Lynn in 1634, and love and consent as well as deference bound them in community. Civic ordinances and by-laws were hence always two-pronged, like those in Gloucester in 1504 which were for 'the good rule and for the common wealth of this town'. The ideals were the same in the 1640s when the town clerk reminded the mayor of his duty to secure both the 'benefits of magistracy' and 'the common welfare' of the city.[59]

Civic rulers therefore had the obligation to be all-encompassing in their

[57] Essex RO, Colchester Corporation Records, Assembly Book 1600–20, ff. 109v–12. Cf. Assembly Book 1576–99, ff. 50–4.

[58] William Sheppard, *Of Corporations, Fraternities and Guilds* (London, 1659), sig. A3v, p. 4.

[59] C. Brooks, 'Professions, ideology and the middling sort in the late sixteenth and early seventeenth centuries', in Barry and Brooks, eds., *Middling Sort*, p. 129; Gloucestershire RO, GBR B2/1, ff. 19–20; J. Dorney, *Certain Speeches Made upon the Day of the Yearly Election of Officers in the City of Gloucester* (London, 1653), pp. 53, 57.

response to change, not least to that brought by the Reformation which, while removing some rival authorities, left them with new responsibilities. In England in the 1540s they were busy rescuing hospitals from the consequences of the dissolution, getting back chantry lands for grammar schools where they could, amalgamating parishes in places like York, Lincoln and Winchester where there seemed to be too many. In the 1570s and 1580s Puritan elites in many towns were seizing the opportunity to extend civic authority further, through town lecturers and new codes of discipline which built upon earlier efforts to control behaviour and popular manners.[60] In Ipswich, where old orders against excesses in apparel among 'the common and meaner sort of people' had been reissued in 1570, there seemed nothing incongruous in pursuit of moral reformation, or in civic promotion of an act of parliament in 1571 providing for assessments for paving the streets, enhancing clergy stipends and repairing chancels.[61] In Scotland the kirk resisted civic encroachment more successfully, and kirk sessions prevented burgh authorities ever having the local and social control of their English counterparts, though they might by the end of the period aspire to it: when Alexander Skene in 1685 stressed the need for 'conscientious, faithful and diligent' courts of justice, 'kept by well principled magistrates, assisted by pious, honest and zealous constables', in order to cleanse the corporate body, he was advocating what had been civic practice in England for more than a century.[62]

Among the obligations imposed by ideals of order and common weal, and underscored by the effects of the Reformation and subsequent events, regulation and relief of the poor were prominent. The earliest compulsory assessments for the poor in England, London aside, were in the leading provincial towns, in Norwich, York, Colchester, Ipswich and Cambridge before 1558. So were the first workhouses, once Bridewell had given a lead, as in Exeter in 1579.[63] Great and good towns were not only the crucibles in which the Elizabethan poor law was forged but the places which provided models of best practice in its embellishment. Here the Norwich of the 1570s took the lead, and for a century afterwards several towns sent there for masters for their workhouses, just as they looked to certain Cambridge colleges for their preachers.[64] Their magistrates were equally distinctive in the effort which they put into enforcing the new policies promulgated by the Tudor privy council for combating the crises of plague and dearth. From the 1540s onwards they were quarantining infected houses and

[60] See above, pp. 265 *et seq.*

[61] N. Bacon, *The Annalls of Ipswiche 1654*, ed. W. H. Richardson (Ipswich, 1884), p. 288; D. MacCulloch and J. Blatchly, 'Pastoral provision in the parishes of Tudor Ipswich', *Sixteenth-Century Journal*, 22 (1991), 469.

[62] G. Desbrisay, 'Menacing their persons and exacting on their purses: the Aberdeen justice court, 1657–1700', in Stevenson, ed., *From Lairds to Louns*, p. 70.

[63] Slack, *Poverty and Policy*, pp. 123, 153.

[64] *Ibid.*, pp. 149–50; Hull City RO, Bench Book 5, pp. 253–4, BRK/3/12/1; M. G. Hobson and H. E. Salter, eds., *Oxford Council Acts 1626–65* (Oxford Historical Society, 95, 1933), p. 165.

supporting their inmates, and setting up grain stocks and controlling the marketing of foodstuffs, where regional capitals like York and Exeter were particularly precocious.[65] It was not simply that these towns had the resources and manpower to invest in efforts at crisis management and close social control: they also had the ambition to show themselves as up-to-date as London in the social welfare mechanisms which demonstrated 'civility'.[66] Table 11.3, which illustrates some of the services available in several of these towns, suggests that they would all by 1600 have thought poor rates as essential as grammar schools, and the provision of work for the poor as important as some kind of civic supply of sermons.

The more narrowly economic policies pursued by municipal councils reflected the same concerns for order, welfare and reputation, and were sometimes responses to similar circumstances. Comparing two recent censuses of the poor in 1557, and concluding that poverty was increasing, councillors in Worcester discussed the causes with 'substantial clothiers': they identified deficiencies in a recent statutory prescription of minimum standards for Gloucester and Worcester cloths, which gave a competitive edge to the former, and promptly had the offending legislation amended in 1558. A century and a half later, they showed much the same awareness of the complexities of economic management when they founded a new workhouse: the relevant parliamentary bill carefully provided that cloth made in the workhouse should not be sold inside the city, in competition with private production.[67] Municipal councillors who could debate at some length the pros and cons of obtaining new fairs, as they did in Lynn in 1555, or discuss the complex problems of industrial and commercial depression, as in Hull in the 1620s, were neither blinkered economic innocents locked into outdated policies inherited from the past nor plutocrats with a single-minded eye to private profit.[68]

They were, of course, pursuing the sectional advantage of their own towns, as a multitude of examples shows, from Worcester's rivalry with Gloucester to the municipal coalitions formed in the 1690s for and against particular navigation schemes, like the alliance of Nottingham and Leicester which successfully opposed the improvement of the Derwent.[69] Civic rulers were also happiest with policies

[65] Slack, *Impact of Plague*, pp. 203–4; P. Slack, 'Dearth and social policy in early modern England', *Social History of Medicine*, 5 (1992), 4.

[66] The same points might be made about Edinburgh, though not, in the case of civic poor relief, until the seventeenth century: Dingwall, *Late Seventeenth-Century Edinbugh*, pp. 250–4; Houston, *Social Change*, pp. 246, 248–9. Cf. Lynch, *Edinburgh and the Reformation*, p. 20.

[67] Worcestershire RO, Worcester View of Frankpledge, volume 1, f. 234v; 5 & 6 Ed. VI c. 6, *SR*, vol. IV(1), 136-41; 4 & 5 Philip and Mary c. 5, *SR*, vol. IV(1), 323-6; 2 & 3 Anne, c. 8, *SR*, vol. IX, 550.

[68] King's Lynn Borough Archives, Hall Book 6, 1544–69, ff. 221, 232; Hull City RO, Bench Book 5, 1609–50, pp. 91–6.

[69] J. A. Chartres, 'The marketing of agricultural produce', in J. Thirsk, ed., *Ag.HEW*, vol. V(2) (Cambridge, 1985), p. 419.

Table 11.3 *Some urban services 1540–1700*

	Date of provision of:							
	Grammar school	Lecturer	Poor rate	First workhouse	Library	Piped water	Fire engine	Street lighting
Norwich	1547	1572	1549	1565	1608	1584, 1694	1641	1692
Bristol	bef. 1540	*c.* 1585	by 1607	1623	1613	1695	1647	1700
Exeter	1633	1600	by 1560	1579		1635, 1695	1652	1689
York	1546	1580	1550	1567		1616, 1695	1694	1687
Chester	1541	by 1603	by 1567	1576		1591, 1691		
Colchester	bef. 1540	1562	1557	1565	(1631)	1620, 1687		
Ipswich	1547	by 1568	1557	1572	by 1614	1616		
Worcester	bef. 1540	1589	?1556	?1578		1619, 1689	1641	
Coventry	1545	1561	by 1598	1571	(1601)	1629		
Gloucester	bef. 1540	1598	by 1572	1631	1658	1623, 1693	1648	
Hull	bef. 1540	1561	by 1575	1577		1613	1673	
Lynn	bef. 1540	1564	1552	1580	(by 1680)	1578		
Leicester	by 1557	1562	?1577		1633	1612	1681	
Oxford	?1576	1583	by 1579	1562		1615, 1694	1654	
Salisbury	*c.* 1559	1617	?by 1563	1564				
Reading	bef. 1540	1625	by 1607	1590		1624, 1694		
Lincoln	1568	1583	by 1592	1578	(by 1662)			
Haverfordwest	1613	by 1620	by 1581	1614				
Edinburgh	bef. 1540	1560	*c.* 1590	1619		?1674		

Notes and sources: see Appendix.

which involved tight regulation, partly in the interests of order and rule, partly in the interests of quality control, which was always assumed, rightly or wrongly, to be the cure for industrial depression. They tried to insist on apprenticeship and limit competition from 'foreign' traders, carefully vetted the ordinances of craft guilds and sometimes amalgamated them in order to achieve closer supervision. But they could also pursue contrary policies when need arose. The York corporation abolished several restrictive practices in the depth of the mid-sixteenth-century depression.[70] Many municipalities reacted to the same circumstances by seeking to introduce new trades and skills, whether New Draperies in the late sixteenth century or linen manufacture in the later seventeenth, even if that meant giving special concessions to outsiders.[71] As early as 1554 Lincoln aimed to be a 'free city', free from almost all tolls, and the scheme to make Elizabethan Ipswich another Antwerp, though equally fruitless, showed something of the same ability to consider radical solutions in the face of economic decline.[72]

Moreover, close economic control by the municipality was impossible in practice. It was often threatened by companies with the benefit of royal charters, like the Clothmakers of Ipswich or the Weavers, Tuckers and Shearmen of Exeter, pursuing separate policies which town councils had to circumvent or undermine.[73] When towns obtained new fairs, as Lichfield did in 1622, Ipswich in 1684 and Lincoln in 1695, they might be 'very beneficial . . . by the increase of . . . trade and traffic and the greater and better vent of . . . wares, commodities and cattle'.[74] But they also brought with them more 'foreign' incursions, an increase in private marketing and an opening up of the urban economy generally. Improvements in navigation often had the same consequences.[75] Despite its consistency with aspirations towards an ordered common weal, a wholly regulated economy was neither sustainable as a civic ideal nor practicable in the face of commercial realities.

The extent to which civic economic policies worked depended equally on a multitude of local circumstances. The deliberate attraction of Dutch and Walloon refugees was more successful in Norwich and Colchester than in smaller

[70] Palliser, *Age of Elizabeth*, pp. 222, 228. For a similar flexibility in corporate regulation in Scotland, see Lynch, 'Continuity and change', pp. 92–3.

[71] For seventeenth-century examples, see Reed, 'Economic structure and change', p. 125; King's Lynn Borough Archives, Hall Book 12, 1684–1731, f. 106r. The workhouse in Plymouth was intended to introduce work on hemp and flax or any other new craft to increase the trade of the borough: West Devon RO, GP/2 (1630).

[72] *HMC*, 14th Report, App. Part VIII, p. 48; Tawney and Power, eds., *Tudor Economic Documents*, III, pp. 173–99.

[73] Reed, 'Economic structure and change', p. 122; J. Youings, *Tuckers Hall Exeter* (Exeter, 1968), pp. 48, 51–3.

[74] *VCH*, Staffordshire, XIV, p. 16; Reed, 'Economic structure and change', p. 124; *HMC*, 14th Report, App. Part VIII, p. 114; H. Stocks, ed., *Records of the Borough of Leicester*, vol. IV: *1603–1688* (Cambridge, 1923), pp. 134–5.

[75] Chartres, 'Marketing', p. 420.

towns with the same ambition like Lynn, probably because of the skilled labour which already existed to be redeployed in the former.[76] In the early days the success of Norwich stuffs and Colchester bays and says may also have rested on mechanisms for quality control, pursued first by the aliens and then by their English imitators, which fitted easily with traditional policies.[77] The alternative and more common route to industrial revival, however, was unregulated growth of relatively unskilled trades, as with stockingmaking in Leicester, where the stockingmakers had to resist civic attempts to make it a freemen monopoly on the grounds that 'it is not the curious making of a few stockings, but the general making of many that is most for the public good, for that sets more people on work'.[78] In general, and especially in the seventeenth century, new kinds of demand seem to have done more for urban economies than the regulation of the supply side by means of guilds, searchers and sealers, and apprenticeship, important though these were for craft consciousness, the transmission of skills and the political ordering of established trades.

Civic authorities nevertheless had a vital role to play in maintaining the infrastructure and services necessary for any kind of economic activity. Wharves and warehouses, refuse disposal and water supply, civil courts for the resolution of disputes and some machinery for criminal policing, were all as important as welfare facilities for its smooth functioning, and more readily supplied in great and good towns than in their lesser competitors. Far from declining in significance with the advance of private marketing and unregulated activities in the seventeenth century, these basic conditions of urban life became all the more crucial if towns were to succeed in attracting customers and visitors. With respect to water supplies, for example, the public conduits carefully maintained by corporations and trusts in the 1540s[79] were being supplemented sixty years later by piped water supplies for private customers in a number of towns from Chester to Worcester; and in the 1690s private supplies were substantially improved by new engineering works sponsored by municipalities, especially those undertaken by George Sorocold in Norwich, Bristol, Nottingham, Lynn and Yarmouth.[80] Table 11.3 indicates the two distinct waves of enthusiasm for such enterprises at the beginning and end of the seventeenth century.

Other civic projects followed a similar trajectory. The new or rebuilt town

[76] Cf. Pound, *Tudor and Stuart Norwich*, p. 60; *VCH*, Essex, IX, p. 81; King's Lynn Borough Archives, Hall Book 7, 1569–91, f. 86r. In 1651 the Lynn council encouraged the immigration of Yorkshire kersey makers: Hall Book 10, 1637–58, f. 307r.

[77] *VCH*, Essex, IX, pp. 81, 94. But see Corfield, 'A provincial capital', pp. 283–4, for the Norwich industry 'shedding all internal restrictions and supervision' with expansion at the very end of the seventeenth century.

[78] Stocks, ed., *Leicester Records*, IV, pp. 563–8.

[79] E.g., *VCH*, Staffordshire, XIV, p. 15; Shrewsbury Guildhall, Assembly Book 1554–83, f. 100v.

[80] F. W. Robins, *The Story of Water Supply* (Oxford, 1946), pp. 161–5; Hughes, 'Property and prosperity', 46; F. Williamson, 'George Sorocold of Derby: a pioneer of water supply', *Journal of the Derbyshire Archaeological and Natural History Society*, 57 (1936), 43–93.

halls of the 1580s to 1620s which displayed the new authority of civic magistracy in Exeter, Gloucester, Hereford, Oxford and Salisbury, were followed by grand exchanges for the benefit of merchants in Bristol, Lynn, Liverpool, Hull and Newcastle when civic building revived in the later seventeenth century.[81] By then they were being supplemented by facilities for visitors, like the extra inns, up from fourteen to twenty-three, licensed in Gloucester in 1672, and the urban walks which had been laid out in Bristol, Exeter, Newcastle, Norwich and Shrewsbury by 1700.[82] The councillors of Winchester may have failed in their post-Restoration project to improve the Itchen navigation, but they took care to lay on entertainments for gentry visitors to the races, another facility in which provincial centres like Chester, Salisbury and York took an early lead.[83] By 1700 the provincial capitals were again setting the pace with the introduction of oil-lamps to 'enlighten' the streets, just as they had earlier been the first to set up town libraries and bring in the rudimentary but fashionable fire engines of the 1640s (see Table 11.3).

The financial resources available to municipalities to sustain these services naturally varied from one town to another, depending largely on the good fortune of property ownership and its good management. In the early seventeenth century the annual income of corporations varied from a mere £130 in Haverfordwest to £300 in Worcester, £600 in York, between £800 and £900 in Norwich and Exeter and around £1,500 in Bristol. Levies on the citizens for ordinary items of expenditure, as well as repairs to facilities such as bridges, were hence much more common in Haverfordwest, Worcester and York than in Exeter or Bristol, whose affluent council could afford to spend £120 on rebuilding a single hospital in 1627–8.[84] For all towns, however, major new undertakings incurred huge costs by comparison with regular ordinary incomes, and indicate the importance attached to them. Norwich's new waterworks of 1584 cost £700, and Exeter's refurbished guildhall of the 1590s £789, and both were overshadowed by investment in the Exeter canal, between the city and the estuary, which consumed £2,000 between 1563 and 1593 before any compensating income came in.[85]

Sudden crises added unforeseeable additional burdens if councils were to meet new obligations and expectations. In Salisbury in 1604 and Haverfordwest in

[81] R. Tittler, *Architecture and Power* (Oxford, 1991), Appendix; Borsay, *English Urban Renaissance*, p. 108 and Appendix 2; William Chambers, *Kingston upon Hull*, facsimile edition (Hull, 1985), vol. I, p. 25. [82] *VCH*, Gloucestershire, IV, p. 106; Borsay, *English Urban Renaissance*, Appendix 6.

[83] Rosen, 'Winchester', pp. 161–2, 175–6; Borsay, *English Urban Renaissance*, Appendix 7.

[84] Charles, ed., *Haverfordwest Records*, pp. 10–12; S. Bond, ed., *The Chamber Order Book of Worcester 1602–50* (Worcestershire Historical Society, new series, 8, 1974), Appendix II, and p. 38; *VCH*, York, pp. 184–5; Pound, *Tudor and Stuart Norwich*, p. 102; MacCaffrey, *Exeter*, pp. 56, 66–7; D. M. Livock, ed., *City Chamberlains' Accounts in the Sixteenth and Seventeenth Centuries* (Bristol Record Society, 24, 1966), pp. xvi, xxiv.

[85] Pound, *Tudor and Stuart Norwich*, p. 100; MacCaffrey, *Exeter*, pp. 68–9, 54.

1652 maintenance of the plague-infected and the poor cost twice the corporation's annual income, and expenditure reached £250 a week in Norwich in the epidemic of 1666.[86] In the case of social welfare, however, expenditure was met partly from charitable funds and partly from parish rates, and the growth of both made extra resources available for public purposes. In Bristol the annual amounts spent on public services are estimated to have grown from £1,154 in 1560 to £4,458 in 1630, and by the latter date nearly half of the sum was coming from parish rates and charities.[87] Bristol may have been unusually fortunate, particularly in its philanthropic endowments; Edinburgh also did well (see Plate 6). But all the larger towns were attractive to benefactors from the 1540s, when Sir Thomas White's rotating loan funds benefited a list of towns – twenty-eight in all – which is almost a complete roll-call of the great and the good;[88] and all of them may well have enjoyed unusually large incomes from rates by 1700, given their early start and the *per capita* wealth of their citizens.

Whatever the costs, and whoever paid them, however, that civility which had distinguished great and good towns in the mid-Tudor period had become by 1700 a politeness which was just as essential to the maintenance of their status in their own eyes and that of their visitors; and it had as many elements. The councillors of Norwich knew what they were doing in the 1690s and 1700s, when they promoted legislation for a new workhouse and waterworks, a court of conscience to deal with small debts and new assessments for watchmen, cleaning the streets and the provision of lights and lamps.[89] Norwich was to be 'enlightened' in part to prevent the 'lewd and disorderly' taking advantage of of dark nights; and public cleanliness was to be pursued as thoroughly as it was by the Puritan mayor of Interregnum Coventry who perambulated in order 'to observe what order the streets were in and gave special charge to remove muckhills'.[90] The years around 1700 saw the first provincial Societies for the Reformation of Manners, in towns from Bristol to Hull (as well as in Edinburgh), the first provincial charity schools, including one in Chester in 1700, and the new municipal Corporations of the Poor,

[86] P. Slack, 'Poverty and politics in Salisbury 1597–1666', in Clark and Slack, eds., *Crisis and Order*, pp. 169–70; Charles, ed., *Haverfordwest Records*, p. 17; Slack, *Impact of Plague*, p. 281.

[87] Livock, ed., *Chamberlains' Accounts*, p. xxviii. Since the revenues for public purposes accounted for centrally varied from one town to another, comparisons between towns are hazardous, and there is an urgent need for precise local studies like Dr Livock's.

[88] W. K. Jordan, *The Charities of London 1480–1660* (London, 1960), pp. 174, 370–1. Of the twenty-eight provincial towns benefiting from White's loan funds, twenty-three are on the list of the thirty-two largest towns of 1524–5 in Table 11.1: a degree of coincidence which gives some contemporary support to Table 11.1's enumeration of the great and the good. The other five were: Nottingham, Warwick, Lynn, Bath and Derby.

[89] House of Lords RO, Original Acts, 11 William III, no. 39, 12 & 13 William III, no. 16; *SR*, 10 Anne c. 15; Norfolk RO, Norwich Assembly Book 7, 1683–1714, ff. 111–14. For other new courts of conscience, see P. Langford, *Public Life and the Propertied Englishman 1689–1798* (Oxford, 1991), p. 160.

[90] L. Fox, ed., 'The diary of Robert Beake', in *Miscellany One* (Dugdale Society, 31, 1977), p. 114.

beginning in Bristol, to remove poverty as well as vice and filth from the streets.[91]

Municipal corporations were no longer trying to control all the activities of their little commonweals. Neither were they in sole command, as some Puritan magistrates had earlier striven to be, least of all of moral reform. The Reformation Societies were private associations, though they had elite membership. Charity schools were supported by voluntary organisations and private subscriptions. The Corporations of the Poor were separate from municipal corporations, although membership overlapped. But aldermen and councillors were cooperating in that provision of services which distinguished the larger towns, and which qualified them to be the centres of 'polite conversation' filled with 'people of quality' which Celia Fiennes and Defoe admired.[92]

(iv) SHIFTS OF IDENTITY

From one perspective, developments at the end of the seventeenth century might seem to have spelt the end of the regulated orderly urban common weal which great and good towns above all others represented, both as an ideal and as a necessarily flawed reality. Political intrusions since the 1640s – from sieges to the confusion caused by *quo warranto* proceedings – had done serious damage both to civic institutions and to corporate self-confidence. Social and economic change had had similar effects. Municipal corporations were threatened by other voluntary or incorporated associations. The number of apprentices was declining after probably reaching an absolute peak in the mid-seventeenth century.[93] Guilds were losing their economic rationale and becoming clubs, the elite among them for urban gentry and the 'genteel'. The freedom itself was being deprived of its old meaning as the trading monopolies of freemen disintegrated and country gentry used it as a tool for political purposes. Private marketing and private enterprises might threaten public welfare. On the one hand was the economic oligarchy, its social origins and tastes close to those of the gentry; on the other, a population of tradesmen, servants and labourers, who might have their own friendly societies[94] and other means of forging group loyalties, but who were set apart. Just as suburban growth rendered city walls redundant emblems

[91] D. W. R. Bahlman, *The Moral Revolution of 1688* (New Haven, Conn., 1957), pp. 38, 43; Houston, *Social Change*, p. 195; J. Hemingway, *History of the City of Chester* (Chester, 1831), vol. II, pp. 216–17; Slack, *Poverty and Policy*, pp. 195–200.

[92] C. Morris, ed., *The Journeys of Celia Fiennes* (London, 1947), p. 227 (Shrewsbury); D. Defoe, *A Tour Through the Whole Island of Great Britain*, ed. G. D. H. Cole and D. C. Browning (London, 1962), vol. I, p. 52 (Bury St Edmunds), vol. II, p. 143 (Nottingham).

[93] Brooks, 'Apprenticeship', pp. 62–4.

[94] Cf. P. Clark, *Sociability and Urbanity* (Leicester, 1988); J. Barry, 'Bourgeois collectivism? Urban association and the middling sort', in Barry and Brooks, eds., *Middling Sort*, pp. 84–112; and for examples of associations of labourers and servants: Ellis, 'Dynamic society', p. 211; Houston, *Social Change*, p. 89.

of old perceptions of towns as physical entities, so economic and social pluralism shattered the threads, thin as they were, of the corporate civic fabric.

Although it greatly underplays the ways in which cultural activities from town histories to civic processions could still bind rather than divide the community after 1660,[95] there is something to be said for such a view. Elements of it can be found in writing about Scottish as well as English towns, and with equal validity.[96] Yet it also contains some evident flaws. Not only does it run the risk of exaggerating the benefits that the narrowly corporate aspirations of the earlier period might have brought to the common welfare they claimed to promote. Its fundamental limitation lies in the assumption that the corporate town with its ambitious magistrates and regulatory structures of the century after 1540 was in some sense a norm, from which there had been a decline. Even if it is not an illusion, created by the bias of the historical record, and it may partly be that, it was a very temporary phenomenon. When we look back to the multi-textured civic worlds of the pre-Reformation period, when lay fraternities and the institutions of the Church played a major part in forming multiple civic identities, it is the period from 1540 to 1650 which appears exceptional. In that interval, when English and Scottish crowns were imposing new burdens on towns and insisting on control by the civic magistracy, when urban governors had to deal with problems of poverty and epidemic disease, not to mention Civil Wars, with little assistance, retrenchment was a necessity and close regulation an inevitable ambition.

In 1540 the councillors of Shrewsbury showed their hankering for the good old days when they petitioned the king for the restoration of the abbey buildings, so that the town might entertain royalty 'or any other nobility of the realm that shall resort to this town'. Their successors in 1700 must have been relieved to find themselves in charge, however nominally, of Dr McInnes' 'leisure town' with plentiful facilities for the job.[97] In making the transition, such places had not been in a permanent state of crisis. But great and good towns had had to go through a prolonged period of adjustment, involving social and cultural as well as intermittent economic impoverishment, before they could re-emerge as what might be termed polite and quality towns.

APPENDIX: SOME URBAN SERVICES

Table 11.3 is intended to be illustrative, and indicative of municipal ambitions, not to show certain achievements by a given date. The dating of grammar school foundations presents particular problems, not only in determining when

[95] Cf. J. Barry, 'Popular culture in seventeenth-century Bristol', in B. Reay, ed., *Popular Culture in Seventeenth-Century England* (London, 1985), pp. 59–90.

[96] Houston, *Social Change*, p. 11 and *passim*; Lynch, 'Continuity and change', pp. 86–9, 113–14.

[97] Shrewsbury Guildhall, Assembly Book 1532–41, f. 50v; McInnes, 'Emergence of a leisure town'.

endowments produced practical results, but in determining where there was continuity with pre-Reformation foundations and where there was not. Assessments for the poor may not always have been continuous from the given date; and workhouses were certainly discontinuous, often falling into disuse and being refounded, sometimes on different sites. In the case of the latter, the dates in Table 11.3 are simply of the first known attempt at an institution providing work for the poor (and not just for rogues, as in a house of correction). The 'lecturer' column equally embraces some variety, between the appointment of a town preacher, intended to act as godly pastor for the town, as in Colchester and Lynn, and the foundation of a set of 'guest lectures', as it were, by a succession of different clergy, as in Reading. The libraries whose dates are given in brackets were originally attached to a school or a church: they were not strictly the civic institutions of Norwich, Bristol and Leicester, although they were plainly regarded as in some sense belonging to the town. The waterworks schemes selected are those which appear to have included some provision of piped water to private consumers, and not merely to have led to public conduits, but the distinction in some cases is not entirely clear from the record.

Notwithstanding these caveats, however, it is hoped that the table shows something of the range of services which these municipalities aimed to provide. The details can be pursued in the sources listed below.

(i) *Schools*: in general, N. Orme, *English Schools in the Middle Ages* (London, 1973), pp. 293–325, and for specific towns: J. Simon, *Education and Society in Tudor England* (Cambridge, 1966), p. 227n (Norwich, Ipswich); M. C. Skeeters, *Community and Clergy* (Oxford, 1993), p. 139 (Bristol); MacCaffrey, *Exeter*, p. 123; D. M. Palliser, *The Reformation in York 1534–1553* (Borthwick Papers, 40, York, 1971), p. 17; *VCH*, Cheshire, III, p. 230 (Chester); *VCH*, Essex, IX, p. 352 (Colchester); *VCH*, Warwickshire, VIII, p. 310 (Coventry); *VCH*, Gloucestershire, IV, p. 335 (Gloucester); *VCH*, East Riding, I, p. 348 (Hull); *VCH*, Leicestershire, IV, p. 332 (Leicester); *VCH*, Oxfordshire, IV, p. 442 (Oxford); R. Benson and H. Hatcher, *Old and New Sarum or Salisbury* (London, 1843), p. 285; Hill, *Tudor and Stuart Lincoln*, p. 102; Charles, ed., *Haverfordwest Records*, p. 12; F. H. Groome, *Ordnance Gazetteer of Scotland* (Edinburgh, 1882), vol. II, p. 508.

(ii) *Lecturers*: P. Collinson, *The Elizabethan Puritan Movement* (London, 1967), p. 186; P. Collinson, *The Religion of Protestants* (Oxford, 1982), p. 141 (Norwich); Skeeters, *Community and Clergy*, pp. 145–6; MacCaffrey, *Exeter*, p. 197; *VCH*, York, p. 152; M. J. Groombridge, ed., *Calendar of Chester City Council Minutes, 1603–1642* (Lancashire and Cheshire Record Society, 106, 1956), p. xxiii; *VCH*, Essex, IX, p. 125 (Colchester); D. MacCulloch, *Suffolk and the Tudors* (Oxford, 1986), p. 198 (Ipswich); Bond, ed., *Chamber Order Book of Worcester*, p. 69; W. J.

Sheils, 'Erecting the discipline in provincial England: the order of Northampton, 1571', in J. Kirk, ed., *Humanism and Reform: Essays in Honour of J. K. Cameron* (Studies in Church History, Subsidia, 8, Oxford, 1991), p. 343 (Coventry); *VCH*, Gloucestershire, IV, p. 89 (Gloucester); C. Cross, *Urban Magistrates and Ministers: Religion in Hull and Leeds from the Reformation to the Civil War* (Borthwick Papers, 67, York, 1985), p. 14 (Hull); King's Lynn Borough Archives, Hall Book 6, f. 425r; C. Cross, *The Puritan Earl* (London, 1966), p. 132, and *VCH*, Leicestershire, IV, p. 74 (Leicester); *VCH*, Oxfordshire, IV, p. 176 (Oxford); Benson and Hatcher, *Salisbury*, p. 330; J. M. Guilding, ed., *Reading Records: Diary of the Corporation* (London, 1892–6), vol. II, p. 250; *HMC*, 14th Report, App. Part VIII, p. 68 (Lincoln); Charles, ed., *Haverfordwest Records*, p. 57; Lynch, *Edinburgh and the Reformation*, pp. 31–2.

(iii) *Poor rates*: Pound, *Tudor and Stuart Norwich*, p. 141; I. Gray and E. Ralph, eds., *Guide to the Parish Records of the City of Bristol and the County of Gloucester* (Bristol and Gloucestershire Archaeological Society, Records Section, 5, 1963), p. 1 (Bristol); MacCaffrey, *Exeter*, pp. 111–12; Slack, *Poverty and Policy*, p. 123 (York); R. H. Morris, *Chester in the Plantagenet and Tudor Reigns* (Chester, n.d.), p. 360; *VCH*, Essex, IX, p. 90 (Colchester); J. Webb, ed., *Poor Relief in Elizabethan Ipswich* (Suffolk Records Society, 9, 1966), p. 18; Dyer, *Worcester*, p. 168; Bodleian Library, MS. Top Warws.d.4, sig. 29v (Coventry); Gloucestershire RO, GBR F11/1–18 (Gloucester); Hull City RO, Bench Book 4, ff. 138v–9r; King's Lynn Borough Archives, Hall Book 6, f. 172v; Stocks, ed., *Leicester Records*, III, p. 167; *VCH*, Oxfordshire, IV, p. 343; H. J. F. Swayne, *Churchwardens' Accounts of S. Edmund and S. Thomas, Sarum* (Salisbury, 1896), p. 109; Guilding, ed., *Reading Records*, II, p. 16; Hill, *Tudor and Stuart Lincoln*, p. 89; Charles, ed., *Haverfordwest Records*, p. 190; Lynch, *Edinburgh and the Reformation*, p. 20.

(iv) *Workhouses*: Pound, *Tudor and Stuart Norwich*, p. 144; J. Latimer, *The Annals of Bristol in the Seventeenth Century* (Bristol, 1900), p. 84; Slack, *Poverty and Policy*, p. 153 (Exeter); *VCH*, York, p. 134; Morris, *Chester*, p. 364; *VCH*, Essex, IX, p. 90 (Colchester); Webb, *Poor Relief in Ipswich*, p. 16; Dyer, *Worcester*, pp. 171–2; *VCH*, Warwickshire, VIII, p. 275 (Coventry); Gloucestershire RO, Gloucester Council Minutes 1565–1632, f. 549v; Hull City RO, Bench Book 4, ff. 174v, 177; King's Lynn Borough Archives, Hall Book 7, ff. 213r, 215r; *VCH*, Oxfordshire, IV, pp. 344–5 (Oxford); *VCH*, Wiltshire, VI, p. 84 (Salisbury); Guilding, ed., *Reading Records*, I, p. 403; Hill, *Tudor and Stuart Lincoln*, p. 90; Charles, ed., *Haverfordwest Records*, p. 48; M. Lynch, ed., *The Early Modern Town in Scotland* (London, 1987), p. 26.

(v) *Libraries*: W. Hudson and J. C. Tingey, eds., *The Records of the City of Norwich*, vol. II (Norwich, 1910), p. cxlvi; Latimer, *Bristol in the Seventeenth Century*, p. 52;

VCH, Essex, IX, p. 301 (Colchester); above, p. 304 (Ipswich); *VCH*, Warwickshire, VIII, p. 220 (Coventry); *VCH*, Gloucestershire, IV, p. 100; King's Lynn Borough Archives, Hall Book 11, f. 468v; *VCH*, Leicestershire, IV, p. 365 (Leicester); *HMC*, 14th Report, App. Part VIII, p. 104, and Hill, *Tudor and Stuart Lincoln*, pp. 214–15.

(vi) *Piped water*: Hudson and Tingey, eds., *Records of Norwich*, II, pp. 392–3, and House of Lords RO, Original Acts, 11 & 12 William III, no. 39 (Norwich); Latimer, *Bristol in the Seventeenth Century*, p. 468; G. Oliver, *The History of the City of Exeter* (Exeter, 1861), p. 149; *VCH*, York, p. 460; Groombridge, ed., *Chester Council Minutes*, p. xxxvi, and Chester City RO, A/B/3, ff. 34v–5r, 38; *VCH*, Essex, IX, p. 290 (Colchester); Bacon, *Annalls of Ipswiche*, pp. 461, 472; Bond, ed., *Chamber Order Book of Worcester*, p. 44, and Worcestershire RO, Worcester Chamber Order Book 1669–1721, section B, pp. 56, 65; *VCH*, Warwickshire, VIII, p. 293 (Coventry); *VCH*, Gloucestershire, IV, p. 263 (Gloucester); *VCH*, East Riding, I, pp. 371–2 (Hull); V. Parker, *The Making of Kings Lynn* (London, 1971), pp. 133, 163; *VCH*, Leicestershire, IV, p. 164; *VCH*, Oxfordshire, IV, pp. 354–5 (Oxford); Guilding, ed., *Reading Records*, II, p. 182, and C. F. Slade, 'Reading', in Lobel, ed., *Historic Towns*, I, p. 7; Groome, *Ordnance Gazetteer of Scotland*, II, p. 525.

(vii) *Fire engines*: S. Porter, *The Great Fire of London* (Stroud, 1996), p. 23 (Norwich, Worcester); Bristol AO, Common Council Proceedings 1642–9, p. 163; G. V. Blackstone, *A History of the British Fire Service* (London, 1957), p. 28 (Exeter); *VCH*, York, p. 162; *VCH*, Gloucestershire, IV, p. 268; *VCH*, East Riding, I, p. 170 (Hull); *VCH*, Leicestershire, IV, pp. 163–4; *VCH*, Oxfordshire, IV, p. 358 (Oxford).

(viii) *Street lighting*: Borsay, *English Urban Renaissance*, p. 72, and Latimer, *Bristol in the Seventeenth Century*, pp. 491–2.

· 12 ·

Ports 1540–1700

DAVID HARRIS SACKS AND MICHAEL LYNCH

AN ISLAND nation is, commonly, a seafaring one, dependent for much of its way of life on seaborne enterprise. As Charles Lloyd put it in 1659 during the last Protectorate parliament, in which sat Scottish and Irish as well as English and Welsh members, '[w]e are islanders, and our life and soul is traffic'.[1] The existence of a seafaring nation turns in large measure on the history of its ports, great and small – their relations with the rural hinterlands which satisfy their needs for food and labour and serve as important markets for their products and services; the multi-faceted roles they play in the nation's network of urban places, the fiscal and military resources they supply to the state; and the services they provide in trade and communication with the cultures and civilisations lying over the water.

As island nations, early modern England, Wales and Scotland were simultaneously protected by the sea from potential continental enemies and points of passage. It is the tension between these two aspects of island life – the capacity of island peoples to withdraw behind the moat created by the seas surrounding them and their need to cross those same waters to find markets and supplies – that mark island nations as socially distinctive places. How their inhabitants negotiate this relationship and find a balance among its competing elements forms a defining feature of their society and culture. In early modern England, Wales and Scotland, the emphasis was increasingly on market-oriented enterprise and commercial exchange, thereby enhancing the dynamic role played by seaports.

[1] Charles Lloyd, 21 Feb. 1659, in T. Burton, *The Diary of Thomas Burton, Esq. Member in the Parliaments of Oliver and Richard Cromwell, from 1656–1659*, ed. J. T. Rutt (London, 1828), vol. III, p. 392; see also Robert Beake's very similar remark on 24 February, *ibid.*, III, p. 472. I am grateful to Steven Pincus for these references; see also S. C. A. Pincus, 'The English debate over universal monarchy', in J. Robertson, ed., *A Union for Empire: Political Thought and the British Union of 1707* (Cambridge, 1995), pp. 40–2.

Despite all that these three island nations had in common in the sixteenth and seventeenth centuries, Scotland's ports did not form a single system with those of England and Wales in the period. Wales had been incorporated under English rule in the reign of King Edward I, and formally united with England by Acts of Union in 1536 and 1543. While Wales' seafaring life was far less developed than England's, the seaports of these two nations operated in the same legal and administrative environment from the inception of the period covered in the present chapter and formed parts of a single network of waterborne trade and communication. But despite repeated efforts by the English in earlier days to enforce dominion over the Scots and the fact that from 1603 the same person was monarch in the two realms, Scotland remained an independent kingdom until 1707, with its own parliament and administration, which included an independent admiralty court, exchequer and system of customs duties. Throughout the period, except for the brief time of the Cromwellian Union, its waterborne traffic with its neighbours to the south had the same legal and administrative status as its commerce with other foreign kingdoms. Moreover, during most of the period the trade of both Scotland and England was of rather less economic significance to one another than were their independent dealings with other, foreign commercial economies, especially in the Low Countries. Indeed, Scotland's inability to share fully in the development of England's growing transatlantic and imperial enterprises and to enjoy the benefits of the thriving financial market in London was arguably a major driving force behind the desire of many Scots to seek closer ties with England.[2] Only after the achievement of this in the form of an incorporating Union in 1707 did a common history of port life emerge for the Scots and the English.

Hence, in the present chapter we shall deal first with the system of ports that had grown up in early modern England and Wales and then turn our attention to the parallel system that developed in the same period in Scotland.[3]

[2] See B. Levack, *The Formation of the British State: England, Scotland, and the Union, 1603–1707* (Oxford, 1987), pp. 138–68; T. C. Smout, *Scottish Trade on the Eve of Union, 1660–1707* (Edinburgh, 1963), pp. 239–80; T. C. Smout, 'The Anglo-Scottish Union of 1707: I. The economic background', *Ec.HR*, 2nd series, 16 (1963–4), 455–67; T. C. Smout, 'The road to Union', in G. Holmes, ed., *Britain after the Glorious Revolution* (London, 1969), pp. 176–96; C. A. Whatley, 'Economic causes and consequences of the Union of 1707: a survey', *Scottish Historical Review*, 68 (1989), 150–81; Eric Richards, 'Scotland and the uses of the Atlantic empire', in B. Bailyn and P. D. Morgan, eds., *Strangers within the Realm: Cultural Margins of the First British Empire* (Chapel Hill, N.C., 1991), pp. 67–114, esp. pp. 70–6; D. Armitage, 'The Scottish vision of empire: the intellectual origins of the Darien venture', in Robertson, ed., *Union for Empire*, pp. 97–118; M. Goldie, 'Divergence and Union: Scotland and England, 1660–1707', in B. Bradshaw and J. Morrill, eds., *The British Problem, c. 1534–1707: State Formation in the Atlantic Archipelago* (New York, 1996), pp. 220–45.

[3] In this chapter, the first section, covering England and Wales, is the work of David Harris Sacks and the second section, covering Scotland, is the work of Michael Lynch. The introductory and concluding sections represent the joint efforts of the two authors.

ENGLAND AND WALES

If the 'life and soul' of an island nation depends critically on its ports, as Charles Lloyd's 1659 parliamentary speech had implied, what was a port in the context of England and Wales? For the early modern period this simple question poses revealing complications. In early usage in English, the word 'port' – derived ultimately from Latin – referred either to an opening in a wall, a door or a passageway or to a harbour or river ford.[4] As such, the concept has always had a close connection with the idea of trade. When the term came to be applied in the middle ages to urban places it sometimes referred generically to trading towns or market centres with specific legal privileges to conduct their business, and sometimes specifically to harbour towns or river havens. Eventually, of course, the ambiguities in the term dissolved, and it became less and less common for 'port' to be employed, other than as a self-conscious archaism, to identify anything other than an urban centre with harbour facilities – a place that operated as a transit point for waterborne commerce, commonly national or international in scope. At the beginning of our period, however, both meanings and the structural interrelationships to which they referred were still in play, influencing understanding of what it meant to be an urban place and to trade.[5]

Since before the inception of power-driven forms of transportation, no urban centre of any significant size could exist very far from the sea or a navigable river, nearly all large urban centres before modern times were built along rivers or the coast. In England, we find the most important of them situated on the great tidal rivers – the Thames, Severn, Great Ouse, Trent, Humber and Yorkshire Ouse – which were navigable without obstruction from the sea and also gave good access to the hinterland through their systems of tributaries. It is 'no mere accident', as T. S. Willan has pointed out, that places such as London, Hull, Lynn, Yarmouth, Bristol and, later, Liverpool, the principal

[4] Latin dealt with the potential ambiguity between the portal and the port town by using two words derived from a single root: a feminine form, *porta*, to designate a gate or door, and a masculine form, *portus*, to refer to a haven or harbour. In the English language – where the distinction between feminine and masculine is not available – the double meaning remained in force into the early modern period and beyond; cf. *The Oxford English Dictionary*, 2nd edn, ed. J. A. Simpson and E. S. C. Weiner (Oxford, 1989), vol. XII, pp. 143–4; *Oxford Latin Dictionary*, ed. P. G. W. Glare (Oxford, 1968–80), pp. 1407, 1408–9.

[5] A similar mixture of meanings is apparent in the word 'gate'; see D. H. Sacks, *The Widening Gate* (Berkeley, Calif., 1991), pp. 11–12. In the middle ages, individuals who enjoyed specific trading rights were sometimes called 'portmen' or 'portwomen' whether or not they frequented a town possessing a harbour. In fifteenth-century Bristol, these figures were petty rural traders who enjoyed equal access with full citizens to the urban market places for purposes of retail exchange; see D. H. Sacks, *Trade, Society, and Politics in Bristol, 1500–1640* (New York, 1985), vol. I, pp. 106, vol. II, p. 793 n. 7.

'centres of collection and distribution' in the land, were simultaneously river and seaports.[6]

By the above standards, there was hardly any significant-sized urban settlement in sixteenth-century England or Wales that was not a port in a general sense – a trading centre dependent in some measure upon waterborne transportation whether by river or sea. In the South and East, from Dorset around to Norfolk, which were less well provided with navigable rivers than elsewhere, the emphasis was on the coasting trade, hauling domestic products from one location to another for redistribution by road or river to the latter's hinterland or for sale in its markets or shops. In Suffolk alone, there were thirty recognised ports, creeks and landing places, and a further thirteen in Norfolk. But this kind of trading was a significant feature of economic life in every coastal town. 'The sea', as John Patten puts it, 'was treated like a great river around the country', especially in allowing the collection and distribution of heavy goods such as coal and timber which otherwise would have been prohibitively expensive to transport. Nevertheless, not all coasting ports were seaports engaged in significant independent traffic with markets 'beyond the seas', as the saying goes.[7]

Even though many substantial inland towns depended on river traffic for their survival, only a few were also functioning seaports. For example, Gloucester, a city of around 5,000 in the seventeenth century, had separate customs records after 1575 and its own custom house after 1577, and was officially designated as an independent 'port' in 1580, but, despite the fact that it was located within one of the prime clothmaking districts in England and had a significant, if declining, role in clothmaking itself, it shipped virtually no cloth beyond the seas in the period. It was instead almost exclusively engaged in domestic trade, servicing the Severn valley and ports of the Bristol Channel. In particular it was a major grain port shipping to the entrepôt at Bristol and receiving foreign imports from there.[8]

Conversely, several large inland towns, some playing important roles in indus-

[6] T. S. Willan, *River Navigation in England, 1600–1750* (London, 1964), p. 1 and *passim*; T. S. Willan, *The English Coasting Trade, 1600–1750* (Manchester, 1938), intro., pp. ix–xiv, 189–93; T. S. Willan, *The Inland Trade: Studies in English Internal Trade in the Sixteenth and Seventeenth Centuries* (Manchester, 1976), pp. 1–49; J. Patten, *English Towns 1500–1700* (Folkestone, 1978), pp. 52, 213–16, 224–5; see also J. A. Chartres, *Internal Trade in England, 1500–1700* (London, 1977), pp. 39–46.

[7] Willan, *English Coasting Trade*, pp. 111–87; Willan, *Inland Trade*, pp. 26–41; Patten, *English Towns*, p. 224.

[8] P. Clark, '"The Ramoth-Gilead of the Good": urban change and political radicalism at Gloucester 1540–1640', in P. Clark, A. G. R. Smith and N. Tyacke, eds., *The English Commonwealth, 1547–1640* (Leicester, 1982), pp. 167–88; P. Clark, 'The civic leaders of Gloucester 1580–1800', in P. Clark, ed., *The Transformation of English Provincial Towns 1600–1800* (London, 1984), pp. 312–17; W. B. Stephens, 'The cloth exports of the provincial towns, 1600–1640', *Ec.HR*, 2nd. series, 22 (1969), 228–48, esp. App. C, 247; W. B. Stephens, 'Further observations on English cloth exports, 1600–1640, *Ec.HR*, 2nd series, 24 (1971), 253–7; J. D. Gould, 'Cloth exports, 1660–1640', *Ec.HR*, 2nd series, 24 (1971), 249–52; Chartres, *Internal Trade*, p. 17; Willan, *English Coasting Trade*, pp. 49, 69, 70, 83–4, 84n, 168–78. Gloucester used Gatcombe as its main outlet for shipping; see N. M. Herbert, 'Medieval Gloucester', *VCH*, Gloucestershire, IV, p. 43.

trial enterprise, depended mainly upon relatively nearby coastal towns for access to the sea and foreign trade. Lynn, with its command of the commerce travelling on the Great Ouse, Nene and Welland and their tributaries, served Northampton, with a population of around 3,500 in 1600, and even Leicester, with a similar population. These significant places lay more than fifty miles inland from Lynn. Even more striking is Norwich, a great regional centre in a prosperous agricultural and manufacturing district, and England's second city by population, but lacking its own custom house. As N. J. Williams points out, it was 'an important port' in the earlier middle ages, but before 1550 the River Yare became too shallow to handle sea-going vessels, and relied on Yarmouth for its access to the sea. The two towns were linked 'symbiotically' by the Yare, although carriage along it was subject to seasonal limitations in river flow and suffered after the mid-sixteenth century from a problem of silting.[9]

Similarly, York, with a population of between 8,000 in 1540 and 12,000 in 1700, another of England's largest cities, was also a major administrative and ecclesiastical centre as well as being home to its own branch of the Merchant Adventurers. In the middle ages, it had been a major foreign trading centre in its own right, concentrating mainly on the export of northern woollens manufactured near the city, but by the mid-sixteenth century it functioned only as a river port. Even though the Yorkshire Ouse was tidal and navigable up to the city, its merchants and clothiers conducted their overseas trade through Hull. In this instance, however, York retained an official connection to the customs. According to the statute of the first year of Elizabeth I's reign regulating Customs' collections, the customer at Hull was explicitly to have 'a servant or deputy continually resident at the City of York' for the purpose of registering and taxing its foreign trade, although overseas commerce represented only a small share of its overall trade in the period.[10]

For the purposes of the customs, the word 'port' had a technical or legal meaning.[11] Although the term invariably denotes a place with trading access to the sea, it too does not conform to modern usage. In the jargon of the customs,

[9] N. J. Williams, *The Maritime Trade of the East Anglian Ports, 1550–1590* (Oxford, 1988), pp. 58–9, 61–8; N. J. Williams, 'The maritime trade of the East Anglian Ports, 1550–1590' (DPhil thesis, University of Oxford, 1952), p. 63, cited in J. F. Pound, *Tudor and Stuart Norwich* (Chichester, 1988), p. 1; *ibid.*, pp. 1, 54; Patten, *English Towns*, p. 269; Willan, *Inland Trade*, pp. 20–1.

[10] 1 Eliz. I c. 11, *SR*, vol. IV(1), p. 372; Patten, *English Towns*, pp. 229–30; D. M. Palliser, *Tudor York* (Oxford, 1979), pp. 186–200, 271–4; Stephens, 'Cloth exports of the provincial towns', 232; C. W. Chalklin, *The Provincial Towns of Georgian England* (London, 1974), pp. 13–14; Willan, *Inland Trade*, p. 15.

[11] For the points in this and the next several paragraphs, see *First Report of the Royal Commission on Public Records*, vol. I, pt 2 (1912), pp. 45–7; *Descriptive List of Exchequer, Queen's Remembrancer, Port Books, Part 1: 1565–1700* (London, 1960), intro. pp. iii–ix; H. Hall, *A History of the Custom-Revenue in England: From the Earliest Times to the Year 1827* (London, 1885), vol. II, pp. 1–33; R. W. K. Hinton, ed., *The Port Books of Boston, 1601–1640* (Lincolnshire Record Society, 50, 1956), intro. pp. xiii–xvii; Stephens, 'Cloth exports of the provincial towns', pp. 228–48; Sacks, *Trade, Society and Politics in Bristol*, vol. II, pp. 737–9.

the word 'port' designated an administrative region subject to the supervision of a particular group of officials – tidewaiters and searchers, the customer and the controller. These regions were dominated by a 'headport' – normally a major trading centre such as Newcastle, Bristol, Exeter, Chester – where the custom house was located and the main officials were resident. But most had officially designated 'creeks' and 'members'. Even where the latter were not named, the territory covered by the customs officers commonly extended well beyond the jurisdictional boundaries of the port city in which they were based. The territory of the port of London, for example, extended from the mouth of the Thames to London Bridge and beyond, and included such sites as Tilbury, Gravesend, Greenwich and Southwark, even though overseas trade was limited to the north bank of the Thames from Queenhithe to Tower Wharf. Hence, each 'port' for customs purposes, with 'members' or without, in fact represented a complex of harbours, havens and inlets – some sufficiently large to stand on their own as independent marketing centres.[12]

Nevertheless, adopting the customs officials' definition of what constitutes a port avoids the difficulty of relying either on ambiguous and changing usage in the period or on the intrinsic dependence of all large urban settlements on some measure of waterborne traffic. For present purposes, therefore, a port is a seaport – an urban centre possessed of a haven or harbour, whether located on the coast or a river, whose economic activities depend in significant degree on its direct, waterborne access to the sea for overseas as well as domestic trade.

(i) SEAPORTS AND THE URBAN HIERARCHY

In his list of twenty 'good towns' recorded in 1549 by the English herald in his debate with the French, it is notable that ten are places that engaged directly in waterborne commerce beyond the seas: Berwick, Carlisle, Newcastle, Hull, Ipswich, Colchester, Exeter, Bristol, Southampton, and Chichester. The number would be eleven if we include York. Although not all these places were equally important as seaports, and a number no doubt were chosen because of the other functions they performed, or simply because of their fame, it seems clear with the inclusion of London, which the French herald from his perspective was willing to judge a *bonne ville*, that in this mock competition the honour of many of the towns had grown, directly or indirectly, from the wealth that seaborne enterprise had given them.[13] If we take population as our guide, we also

[12] For a full list of headports and their members, see Table 12.2. For the survey of London's creeks and wharfs of London, see PRO, E 159/34, rot. 222, and PRO, E 178/7075, both reprinted in *The Port and Trade of Early Elizabethan London: Documents*, ed. B. Dietz (London Record Society, 8, 1972), pp. 156–64, see also, B. Dietz, 'Introduction', in *ibid.*, pp. ix–x.

[13] *Debate of the Heralds*, 1549, in R. H. Tawney and E. Power, eds., *Tudor Economic Documents* (London, 1924), vol. III, p. 7; see also above, pp. 347 *et seq.*

find that about half of the most populous urban places in England and Wales in the sixteenth and seventeenth centuries were seaports. Their heavy presence over time in England's urban hierarchy, as delineated by Table 12.1, is itself a mark of the maritime character of English society.[14]

Table 12.1 captures the consequences for regional urban development of these long-term commercial trends. In the early sixteenth century, there were perhaps ten towns in England with populations of 5,000 or more. Of these five were seaports: London, Bristol, Exeter, Colchester and Newcastle; six if we count York. With the exception of York, all lay in the South and East, marking the persistence of England's late medieval trading patterns with its orientation towards north-western Europe, primarily between the Bay of Biscay and the Scheldt. In the later middle ages, Bristol and Exeter were especially important in the French trade, and Colchester and Newcastle in trade to the Low Countries; York, if we include it, focused on the same main continental markets as Newcastle. London was already engaged, even in those earlier days, in trade everywhere. By 1540, however, there were also signs of change, with Bristol having already emerged as a major trading centre for the Iberian peninsula and Newcastle, and York, for the Baltic. Newcastle also had already become a great supplier of coal to London via coastal routes.

By 1600, there were about twenty English towns which possessed 5,000 or more inhabitants. Of these, twelve were seaports; thirteen if we count York. Added to the list were Plymouth, Lynn, Gloucester, Chester, Hull, Yarmouth and Ipswich. The same south-east orientation is apparent. But London, Bristol, Exeter and Newcastle have all now grown; York as well. London's population was almost three times what it had been eighty years before. Newcastle had expanded twofold (mainly on the strength of the coal industry and the related carrying trade), Bristol by about 20 per cent and Exeter by a little over 10 per cent; and York too had increased by 50 per cent. Looked at another way, it would seem that urban growth in the period was being led by the port towns, and not only because London's expansion accounts for such a large share of the rise. Aside from Norwich, the largest towns in the list are seaports.

Several other features in the pattern are also noteworthy. In the North-East, Hull, with its orientation to the Baltic trade, has been added to Newcastle. Hull long had served as York's outlet to the sea, and its growth was paralleled by York's

[14] The representation of seaports at the top of England's urban hierarchy was greater than common elsewhere in Europe. Between 1500 and 1700, Paul Bairoch has observed, seaports account for only about a third of Europe's largest cities; P. Bairoch, *Cities and Economic Development from the Dawn of History to the Present* (Chicago, 1988), pp. 186–7; see also F. Braudel, *The Perspective of the World*, trans. S. Reynolds (New York, 1984), pp. 353–4; J. de Vries, *European Urbanization 1500–1800* (London 1984), pp. 141–2; P. M. Hohenberg and L. H. Lees, *The Making of Urban Europe, 1000–1950* (Cambridge, Mass., 1985), pp. 109, 111, 184, 229. For the distinction between maritime and territorial societies in political and economic geography, see E. W. Fox, *History in Geographic Perspective: The Other France* (New York, 1971).

Table 12.1 *Populations of the principal English towns and ports, c. 1520–1700*

c. 1520		*c.* 1600		*c.* 1700	
Town	Pop.[a]	Town	Pop.[a]	Town	Pop.[a]
London	55	**London**	200	**London**	575
Norwich	12	Norwich	15	Norwich	30
Bristol	10	*York*	12	**Bristol**	21
York	8	**Bristol**	12	**Newcastle**	16
Salisbury	8	**Newcastle**	10	**Exeter**	14
Exeter	8	**Exeter**	8	*York*	12
Colchester	7	**Plymouth**	8	**Yarmouth**	10
Coventry	7	Salisbury	6	Birmingham	8–9
Newcastle	5	**Lynn**	6	**Chester**	8–9
Canterbury	5	**Gloucester**	6	**Colchester**	8–9
		Chester	6	**Ipswich**	8–9
		Coventry	6	Manchester	8–9
		Hull	6	**Plymouth**	8–9
		Yarmouth	5	Worcester	8–9
		Ipswich	5	Bury St Edmunds	5–7
		Cambridge	5	Cambridge	5–7
		Worcester	5	Canterbury	5–7
		Canterbury	5	**Chatham**	5–7
		Oxford	5	Coventry	5–7
		Colchester	5	**Gloucester**	5–7
				Hull	5–7
				Lynn	5–7
				Leeds	5–7
				Leicester	5–7
				Liverpool	5–7
				Nottingham	5–7
				Oxford	5–7
				Portsmouth	5–7
				Salisbury	5–7
				Shrewsbury	5–7
				Sunderland	5–7
				Tiverton	5–7

Bold designates a recognised port. *Italics* indicates York's ambiguous status as a port.
[a] Estimate in thousands.
Sources: based on Table 7.1 in E. A. Wrigley, 'Urban growth and agricultural change: England and the continent in the early modern period', first publ. in the *Journal of Interdisciplinary History,* 15 (1985), repr. in E. A. Wrigley, *People, Cities and Wealth* (Oxford, 1987), pp. 158–9, cf. Jan de Vries, *European Urbanization 1500–1800* (London, 1984), pp. 270–1. Note that no Welsh towns had reached the level of 5,000 in population before 1700. See also Table 11.1.

own recovery as a trading centre. In the South-East there is a growing concentration in the clothing districts of East Anglia partly aimed at the markets in the Low Countries but partly also at the markets for 'New Draperies' outside those traditional centres, particularly in southern Europe and the Mediterranean. These developments, and especially the rise in importance of Yarmouth, closely parallel the growth of Norwich itself. Yarmouth also benefited from its role as a North Sea fishing centre.[15] Finally in the west, Plymouth has joined Exeter, and Gloucester and Chester have joined Bristol, also signifying a new importance in a southern and western orientation to trade, including trade between England and Ireland. Plymouth, another fishing centre, was also already playing a significant role in naval operations in this era and its economy benefited from the military activities that concentrated in it.

The picture in 1700, the end of our period, changed again. Some thirty-two towns now had 5,000 or more inhabitants. Of these sixteen were ports; seventeen if York is included. Running down the list, we can see once again that it is population growth in the ports that accounts for much of the general increase in the percentage of English population living in large towns. London had exploded by at least 300 and perhaps 400 per cent in the course of the century – although, of course, not all of this growth is attributable to the expansion of port-related activities.[16] Other port towns had also significantly grown – notably Bristol and Newcastle by about 60 per cent each. Equally of interest is the fact that ports now number four of the largest five urban places (and nine of the largest fourteen). Norwich is again the exception, but its growth of 100 per cent is matched by Yarmouth's doubling in size.

New to the list of significant-sized seaports in 1700 are Chatham, Liverpool, Portsmouth, and Sunderland. Sunderland, focused on the Baltic and on the coal trade to London, reflects the further development of the North-East region around Newcastle, which by this time had surpassed Exeter in size to become the fourth most populous city in England. Liverpool focuses attention on the North-West and its emerging role in manufacturing and in Atlantic commerce. Their advance confirms the increasing dependency of England's overseas trade in the seventeenth century on wider markets radiating in all directions away from its traditional hub in the Low Countries. The remarkable growth of the naval towns of Chatham and Portsmouth, neither of them a major overseas trading centre,[17] reveals how this expansion made it essential to professionalise naval services and

[15] Williams, *East Anglian Ports*, pp. 167–9.

[16] Finlay and Shearer give reasons to think that the population of London in 1700 has been overestimated. They argue for a figure of 490,000 instead of the more commonly given figure of 575,000. Adopting the lesser sum would not significantly affect the present argument; see R. Finlay and B. Shearer, 'Population growth and suburban expansion', in A. L. Beier and R. Finlay, eds., *London 1500–1700* (London, 1986), pp. 37–57.

[17] Chatham itself had no customs officers and while it had a significant local market and served as a centre for the regional redistribution of produce, it did very little, if any, overseas trading; see C. W. Chalklin, *Seventeenth-Century Kent* (London, 1965), pp. 31, 162–3.

subject them to bureaucratic control. In large measure, the rise of the dockyards was a sign that what Daniel Baugh has identified as Britain's 'blue water strategy' was in its nascent stage.[18]

In 1700, the orientation of the system of ports is still towards the South and East, anchored by the extraordinary commercial and financial activities concentrated at London. But there are also evident signs that the system of ports in England had ceased to be an adjunct to the urban networks of north-west Europe. The pattern had been broken after the trade depression of the 1620s, as England looked more and more beyond its traditional markets for sources of profits and increasingly became the centre of its own international and imperial trading system, focused on London. By the early seventeenth century, this great city was already on entrepôt for the tropical and subtropical products that came to it directly from India, Africa, the Mediterranean and the Atlantic. Increasingly these trades were at the heart of the era's consumer and commercial revolutions. By 1650 or so, London was no longer the satellite of the great cities of the Netherlands, but their outright competitor. The era of the Dutch Wars played out the rivalry. By 1700, England had effectively won this ongoing battle. Now London was indisputably the centre of a world-wide empire. England's system of ports reflected this new fact. London in effect had a 360 degree perspective on the world – looking to all markets and all quarters of England's commercial and imperial hegemony – while the other ports arranged around the coasts of England fell into recognisable relationships with it, servicing different regions within the kingdom and different segments of its international markets.

(ii) A SYSTEM OF SEAPORTS

Although population represents a good guide to which seaports were the most important in the English urban system during the sixteenth and seventeenth centuries, most of the largest seaports in the period grew as much from their functions as regional centres as from their role in the expansion of trade. Equally, a number of significant seaports were not great towns in terms of their popula-

[18] D. Baugh, 'British strategy during the First World War in the context of four centuries: Blue Water versus continental commitment', in D. M. Masterman, ed., *Naval History: The Sixth Symposium of the US Naval Academy* (Wilmington, Del., 1987), pp. 87–8; Daniel Baugh, 'Maritime strength and Atlantic commerce: the uses of a "grand marine empire"', in L. Stone, ed., *An Imperial State at War: Britain from 1689–1815* (New York, 1994), pp. 185–223; J. Brewer, *The Sinews of Power: War, Money and the English State, 1688–1783* (New York, 1989), pp. 59–60, 140, 168–75, 178, 199, 257 n. 94; Patten, *English Towns*, pp. 175–6; D. C. Coleman, 'Naval dockyards under the later Stuarts', *Ec.HR*, 2nd series, 6 (1953–4), 134–55; P. Clark and P. Slack, eds., *Crisis and Order in English Towns 1500–1700* (London, 1972), p. 31; Chalklin, *Kent*, pp. 3, 31–3, 105–6, and *passim*; Chatham experienced especially rapid growth in the wars of the later seventeenth century: Chalklin, *Provincial Towns*, p. 23.

tions. Along with considering the place of the ports in the urban hierarchy as a whole, therefore, we need to consider the system of seaports itself. We can capture something about the latter from the role the more important seaports played as centres for the collection of customs. At the beginning of Elizabeth's reign, the major seaports for customs purposes were designated by commission to be: Berwick, Newcastle, Hull, Boston, Lynn, Yarmouth, Ipswich, London, Sandwich and Deal, Chichester, Southampton, Poole, Exeter and Darmouth, Barnstaple, Plymouth and Fowey, Bridgwater, Bristol, Cardiff, Milford Haven, Chester and Carlisle.[19] Berwick, on the River Tweed, and Carlisle, on the River Eden, which emptied into Solway Firth, were on the list primarily because of the roles they played in relation to Scotland. Neither was a major seaport in this period by the standard of the other places on the list.[20] In addition to this group of headports, however, the customs recognised the existence of a further eighty-six lesser creeks or havens. Table 12.2 gives the breakdown by region.

The groupings of headports and members in Table 12.2 were made for the administrative convenience of the customs, rather than exclusively for their economic significance. In East Anglia and the South-East, with their numerous small and middling port towns, some lesser ports might equally well have fallen under the aegis of different headports than the ones to which they were assigned. Woodbridge, for example, would perhaps have been better placed with Ipswich than Yarmouth, with which it was officially grouped.[21] The list also does not capture all the active ports within a region; for example, it misses out such small but significant places as Cromer in Norfolk; Beccles, Orford, Lowestoft and Harwich in Suffolk; Topsham in Devon; and Haverfordwest in Wales. As regards the coasting trade in particular, the loss can give a quite false picture. Along the River Exe, for example, not only had Topsham been linked by canal with Exeter since the mid-sixteenth century, making it possible for the latter to conduct its overseas trade through the former, but tiny ports such as Starcross, Lympstone and Countess Wear also served as regular loading and unloading points; so too did small creeks like Kenton, Powderham and Cockwood. The commercial activities of places like these, insofar as they were captured at all by the customs, appear in the records for the nearest headport or

[19] 1 Eliz. I c. 11, *SR*, IV(1), 372; PRO, SP 12/38/23; *Acts of the Privy Council, 1568–1570*, pp. 278–90; *Descriptive List*, intro., pp. v–ix, 564–6. The aim was to control smuggling, see G. D. Ramsay, 'The smuggler's trade', in G. D. Ramsay, *English Overseas Trade during the Centuries of Emergence* (London, 1957), pp. 166–206; Sacks, *Trade, Society, and Politics in Bristol*, II, pp. 727–37; D. H. Sacks, 'The paradox of taxation: fiscal crises, parliament, and liberty in England, 1450–1640', in P. Hoffman and K. Norberg, eds., *Fiscal Crises, Liberty, and Representative Government, 1450–1789* (Stanford, 1994), pp. 42–5; L. L. Peck, *Court Patronage and Corruption in Early Stuart England* (London, 1990), pp. 148–9; N. Williams, *Contraband Cargoes: Seven Centuries of Smuggling* (London, 1959), pp. 1–92.

[20] Willan, *English Coasting Trade*, pp. 80n, 110–13, 187–8.

[21] *Ibid.*, p. 133; Patten, *English Towns*, pp. 234, 270; Stephens, 'Cloth exports of the provincial towns', 232.

Table 12.2 *Members and creeks of English and Welsh 'headports' 1565–1700*

NORTH-EAST

Berwick	*Newcastle*	*Hull*
none	Blyth	Bridlington
	Cullercoats	Grimsby
	Hartlepool	Scarborough
	Seaton	York
	Stockton	
	Sunderland	
	Whitby[a]	

THE WASH

Boston	*Lynn*
Fossdyke	Burnham (Norfolk)
Saltfleet	Wells-next-the-sea
Skegness	Wisbech
Spalding	
Sutton (Lincs.)	
Wanfleet	

EAST ANGLIA

Yarmouth	*Ipswich*
Aldeburgh	Colchester
Blakeney	Maldon
Dunwich	
Southwold	
Walberswick	
Woodbridge	

SOUTH-EAST

London	*Sandwich*	*Chichester*	*Southampton*
none	Deal	Arundel	Cowes
	Dover	Brighton	Portsmouth
	Faversham	Folkestone	
	Margate	Hastings	
	Milton Regis	Hythe	
	Ramsgate	Lewes	
		Littlehampton	
		Meeching (New Haven)	
		New Shoreham	
		Pevensey	
		Romney	
		Rye	
		Winchelsea	

SOUTH-WEST

Poole	*Exeter*	*Plymouth*	*Barnstaple*[b]
Lyme	Barnstaple[b]	Falmouth[c]	Bideford[b]
Weymouth	Bideford[b]	Fowey	Ilfracombe[b]

Table 12.2 (*cont.*)

SOUTH-WEST (*cont.*)				
Poole	*Exeter*	*Plymouth*	*Barnstaple*[b]	
	Dartmouth	Helford		
	Ilfracombe[b]	Helston		
		Looe		
		Mount's Bay		
		Padstow		
		Penryn		
		Penzance		
		St Ives		
		Truro		
SOUTH WALES AND THE WEST				
Milford Haven	*Cardiff*	*Bridgwater*	*Bristol*	*Gloucester*[e]
Aberdovey	Aberthaw	Minehead	Gloucester[e]	none
Aberysthwyth	Chepstow			
Cardigan	Neath			
Carmarthen	Newport			
South Burry[d]	South Burry[d]			
Tenby	Swansea			
NORTH WALES AND THE NORTH-WEST				
Chester	*Carlisle*			
Barrow Head	Whitehaven			
Beaumaris	Workington			
Caernarvon				
Conway				
Lancaster				
Liverpool				
Peel				
Poulton				
Pwllheli				

[a] For a brief period in the early seventeenth century the collector of new impositions at Bridlington, a creek of Hull, also reported collections at Whitby. But otherwise Whitby always counted as a creek of Newcastle-upon-Tyne.

[b] Until 1671, Barnstaple, Bideford and Ilfracombe were creeks of Exeter; afterwards, Barnstaple became a headport in its own right and Bideford and Ilfracombe became creeks of Barnstaple.

[c] Customs officers recorded shipments from Falmouth with those of Penryn.

[d] In Elizabeth's reign and in the earlier seventeenth century, the trading activities of South Burry were mainly recorded by the Customs officers responsible for Carmarthen, a creek of the headport of Milford Haven, but occasionally by those responsible for Swansea and Neath, creeks of the headport of Cardiff. From 1666 to 1667, however, it was regularly treated in the latter way, along with Swansea and Neath as a creek of Cardiff.

[e] Gloucester was a creek of Bristol until 1577, after which it became a headport in its own right.

Sources: based on *Descriptive List of Exchequer, Queen's Remembrancer, Port Books, Part I: 1565–1700*, comp. N. J. Williams (London, 1960); E. A. Lewis, *The Welsh Port Books 1550–1603* (London, 1927).

member.[22] Nevertheless, the list of headports and members, drawn up to facilitate the work of the customs officers in surveying trade and collecting duties, captures the main features of the regional organisation of seaborne enterprise in early modern England and Wales.

In general, the overseas trade of each of the economic regions delineated in Table 12.2 was already concentrated in the headports by the 1560s, while the creeks appear to have been primarily engaged in coastwise domestic traffic within the region and at further distances, with a growing share of it ending up in London. Although some foreign trade was regularly conducted through the more important of these lesser ports, in most regions it was light, and tended to become lighter during the seventeenth century, particularly after 1660. A year's entries normally filled at most only a folio or two of the port books issued them by the Exchequer. London, especially, overwhelmed the overseas commerce of south-eastern England, and places such as Dunwich, Aldeburgh, Orford, Woodbridge, Colchester and Maldon, once modest seaports in their own right, were its tributaries, supplying its burgeoning population with food and other supplies and offering its merchants and tradesmen access to their own marketing basins. But, to a lesser degree, a similar pattern appeared in the course of the sixteenth century around Bristol, Hull, Newcastle, Chester and other major overseas trading centres. Each region formed a 'complex' of ports on its own.[23]

In reviewing this emerging system of seaports, we need to start with London, England's premier port and by the end of our period one of the most active in the world. Continuously significant from Anglo-Saxon times, it was the kingdom's major source of sea power and state finance, and its most important trading community – an outlet for English and Welsh products in overseas trade, an entrepôt for foreign wares and a locus for shipping and shipbuilding. It long exercised a dominating influence on England's commercial and industrial economy, which intensified between 1500 and 1700, as the city grew by tenfold or more in population, gained increasing shares of the national wealth and enjoyed a greater and greater role in trade and finance in Europe and the wider Atlantic arena. At the end of the seventeenth century, about 75 per cent of England's overseas trade passed through the city, and almost half of the kingdom's merchant shipping was based there. As Eric Kerridge has emphasised, by the early sixteenth century it was becoming the nub of 'a metropolitan market

[22] Patten, *English Towns*, pp. 75, 225, 251–94; Willan, *English Coasting Trade*, pp. 99–100, 131–2, 135, 158–9; W. T. MacCaffrey, *Exeter 1540–1640*, 2nd edn (Cambridge, Mass., 1975), pp. 126–36; W. B. Stephens, 'The Exeter lighter canal, 1566–1698', *Journal of Transport History*, 3 (1957), 1–11. A similar point arises in regard to the development of the great naval dockyards at Chatham, Deptford, Woolwich and Sheerness in Kent, which grew substantially in the seventeenth century, but are also excluded from view. They appear not at all in the customs records because most of their seagoing activity did not entail the shipment of dutiable items.

[23] The term 'complex of ports' is derived from H. Chaunu and P. Chaunu, *Seville et l'Atlantique (1508–1650)* (Paris, 1959).

system'. Linking the rural hinterlands of the kingdom and its growing network of provincial ports and commercial towns with these more distant markets, its development was a cause as well as a manifestation of the emergence of an integrated national market and organised national state in England. According to Jan de Vries, by 1600 it was among the top eight cities in Europe in terms of its '"potential" for interacting with . . . people, or markets, in all other locations', particularly other urban places. By 1700, it ranked at the very top of this list and had the maximum possible 'potential' according to de Vries' scale.[24]

Although there was an intimate connection among London's functions as a national capital and major port, its extraordinary accumulation of wealth and its sustained commercial successes arose in large measure from independent geographical and economic causes – especially the advantageous access its situation on the Thames gave it looking inward to the riches of the English Midlands and outward to the wealth of the Low Countries, France and Spain and access to the Atlantic trade routes as they opened and became more important. As de Vries has pointed out, 'Atlantic ports active in inter-continental trade' like London were the 'most conspicuous' in exhibiting rapid growth in the seventeenth and early eighteenth centuries.[25] London was simultaneously a locus of political power and commercial wealth, each depending on the other.[26]

[24] E. Kerridge, *Trade and Banking in Early Modern England* (Manchester, 1988), pp. 5–6; de Vries, *European Urbanization*, pp. 155, 159. For the preceding, see D. H. Sacks, 'The metropolis and the archipelago: the growth of early modern London and Britain's "three kingdoms"', in L. C. Orlin, ed., *Material London, ca. 1600* (forthcoming). The classic statement of London's significance to English development is E. A. Wrigley, 'A simple model of London's importance in changing English society and economy, 1650–1750', *P&P*, 37 (1967), 44–70; see also F. J. Fisher, *London and the English Economy 1500–1700*, ed. P. J. Corfield and N. B. Harte (London, 1990), *passim*; P. Corfield, 'Urban development in England and Wales in the sixteenth and seventeenth centuries', in D. C. Coleman and A. H. John, eds., *Trade, Government and Economy in Pre-Industrial England* (London, 1976), pp. 214–19; A. L. Beier and Roger Finlay, 'Introduction: the significance of the metropolis', in Beier and Finlay, eds., *London*, pp. 1–33; B. Dietz, 'Overseas trade and metropolitan growth', in *ibid.*, pp. 115–40; Braudel, *Perspective of the World*, pp. 365–8; M. Reed, 'London and its hinterland 1600–1800: the view from the provinces', in P. Clark and B. Lepetit, eds., *Capital Cities and their Hinterlands in Early Modern Europe* (Aldershot, 1996), pp. 51–83. See also the discussion above, pp. 320 *et seq.*

[25] De Vries, *European Urbanization*, p. 141. 'Being the governmental centre for a large territory', de Vries concludes, 'conferred on a city' such as London 'a long-term, stable growth' that urban places, lacking this political and administrative function could not match, however large and flourishing they were; *ibid.*, p. 142. See also F. Braudel, *The Structures of Everyday Life: The Limits of the Possible*, trans. Siân Reynolds (New York, 1981), pp. 528, 547–56; Bairoch, *Cities and Economic Development*, pp. 166–7, R. Ashton, *The City and the Court, 1603–1643* (Cambridge, 1979); R. Brenner, *Merchants and Revolution* (Cambridge, 1993), pp. 3–195.

[26] London's position as both dominating national capital and primate city in England's urban network undermines the stark distinction, drawn by Charles Tilly, between strategies of coercion and strategies of capital accumulation and exchange in organising societies and states; see C. Tilly, *Coercion, Capital, and European States, AD 990–1990* (Oxford, 1990), pp. 16–20, 28–33, 45–66; see also C. Tilly, 'The geography of European statemaking and capitalism since 1500', in E. Genovese

Nevertheless, London was not alone in making commercial enterprise a critical factor in the formation of the English state and polity. The seaports in general functioned as vital go-betweens in England's developing 'dual economy'. The larger ports, in particular, absorbed a major share of the surplus production, industrial as well as agricultural, of these rural regions of England and Wales, exporting significant quantities of wool, woollens, tallow, leather and hides, as well as coal, lead and other metals which remained the mainstays of the English and Welsh export trade from the later middle ages until well into our period. The seaports functioned as vital go-betweens in the developing 'dual economy' – linking together buying and selling in regional, national and international markets with the traditional practices and customs of agrarian communities.[27]

These same major seaports, headed as always by London, also concentrated the services necessary to prepare ships for the sea – not just in assembling the skilled mariners and sailors to man the vessels but in bringing together the supplies of food, drink, cooperage, sail and gear required to keep them at sea. A ship was perhaps the most complex piece of capital equipment in use in the early modern economy; its successful operation depending not only on the mobilisation of significant investment capital but also on the effective coordination of diverse activities on shore as well as at sea. The shipping industry by its very nature drew continuously on the existing economic infrastructure of exchange in England and Wales, concentrating a large share of them in the seaports.[28]

Most obviously, however, the larger ports were the principal centres for maintaining the trades on which England's capacities to sustain its civilised way of life turned. Since Roman times, the material culture of England and Wales had relied on acquiring wares that could not be raised or manufactured in Britain:

Footnote 26 (*cont.*)

and L. Hochberg, eds., *Geographic Perspectives in History* (Oxford, 1989), pp. 158–81; C. Tilly, 'Entanglements of European cities and states', and W. P. Blockmans, 'Voracious states and obstructing cities: an aspect of state formation in preindustrial Europe', in C. Tilly and W. P. Blockmans, eds., *Cities and the Rise of States in Europe A. D. 1000 to 1800* (Oxford, 1994), pp. 1–27, 218–50.

[27] On these points, see C. G. A. Clay, *Economic Expansion and Social Change: England, 1500–1700* (Cambridge, 1984), vol. II, pp. 100–1; D. H. Sacks, 'The paradox of taxation: fiscal crises, parliament, and liberty in England, 1450–1640', in P. T. Hoffman and K. Norberg, eds., *Fiscal Crises, Liberty, and Representative Government, 1450–1789* (Stanford, Calif., 1994), pp. 27–8; see also J. Thirsk, 'Industries in the Countryside', in F. J. Fisher, ed., *Essays in the Economic and Social History of Tudor and Stuart England in Honour of R. H. Tawney* (Cambridge, 1961), pp. 70–88.

[28] The best introduction to the operations and economic significance of the early modern shipping industry remains R. Davis, *The Rise of the English Shipping Industry in the Seventeenth and Eighteenth Centuries* (London, 1962); see also G. V. Scammell, 'Shipowning in the economy and politics of early modern England', *HJ*, 15 (1972), 385–407; B. Dietz, 'The royal bounty and English shipping in the sixteenth and seventeenth centuries', *Mariner's Mirror*, 77 (1991), 5–20; D. Burwash, *English Merchant Shipping, 1460–1540* (Toronto, 1947); K. R. Andrews, 'The Elizabethan seamen', *Mariner's Mirror*, 68 (1982), 245–62; K. R. Andrews, *Ships, Money and Politics: Seafaring and Naval Enterprise in the Reign of Charles I* (Cambridge, 1991), pp. 1–61.

luxury fabrics and rare metals, salt, oils, wines, dyes, spices, drugs and subtropical foodstuffs. From the late middle ages and well into our period, this traffic depended especially on the export of woollen cloth, the largest share of which was shipped via London in an unfinished or only partly finished state to the Low Countries. Viewed from this perspective, England in the sixteenth and earlier seventeenth centuries was an economically peripheral region of north-western Europe, serving a subordinate role in a trading zone which centred on the great towns of the Netherlands. London was but 'a satellite city' subject, especially in the cloth trade, to economic rhythms in the Low Countries and north Germany. In the early sixteenth century the metropolis was Antwerp; later a similar role was played by Amsterdam.[29] Given the importance of cloth to overseas commerce as a whole, the provincial ports might themselves be viewed only as satellites of this satellite city, especially as greater and greater proportions of England's overseas trade concentrated in London.[30]

However, this conclusion is only partially correct. During our period, it speaks especially to the ports whose trade pointed in the direction of the Low Countries and the Baltic – mainly the ports, great and small, situated on the east coast of England between Berwick and Kent and Sussex. Many of them suffered declines or relative stagnation in their trading economies from the loss of the cloth trade. In a number of regions, ports that had been of considerable significance in the later middle ages dropped away in some years from the conduct of any foreign commerce at all, resulting in the customs officers returning blank port books to the Exchequer.

In the 1610s and 1620s, Whitby and Sunderland fell into this category for a few years each.[31] In the 1680s and 1690s, Hartlepool almost disappeared as an overseas trading centre; it did no foreign trade in dutiable items between

[29] G. D. Ramsay, *The City of London in International Politics at the Accession of Elizabeth Tudor* (Manchester, 1975), pp. 1–80; G. D. Ramsay, 'The Antwerp mart', in Ramsay, *English Overseas Trade*, pp. 1–33; R. Davis, 'The rise of Antwerp and its English connection, 1406–1510', in Coleman and John, eds., *Trade, Government and Economy*, pp. 2–16; B. Dietz, 'Antwerp and London: the structure and balance of trade in the 1560s', in E. W. Ives, R. J. Knecht and J. J. Scarisbrick, eds., *Wealth and Power in Tudor England: Essays Presented to S. T. Bindoff* (London, 1978), pp. 186–203; on Amsterdam's role in the world economy, see Braudel, *Perspective of the World*, pp. 175–266; see also V. Barbour, *Capitalism in Amsterdam in the Seventeenth Century* (Baltimore, 1950).

[30] F. J. Fisher, 'Commercial trends and policy in sixteenth-century England', in Fisher, *London and the English Economy*, pp. 81–103; F. J. Fisher, 'London's export trade in the early seventeenth century', in *ibid.*, pp. 119–29; L. Stone, 'State control in sixteenth-century England', *Ec.HR*, 1st series, 17 (1947), 104–8; L. Stone, 'Elizabethan overseas trade', *Ec.HR*, 2nd series, 2 (1949–50), 30–5; Stephens, 'Cloth exports of the provincial towns', pp. 228–46; J. D. Gould, 'Cloth exports, 1660–1640', *Ec.HR*, 2nd series, 24 (1971), 249–52; Stephens, 'Further observations', 253–7; R. Davis, 'English foreign trade, 1660–1700', *Ec.HR*, 2nd series, 7 (1954–5), 150–66; see also Dietz, 'Overseas trade and metropolitan growth', pp. 117–40; B. Dietz, 'England's overseas trade in the reign of James I', in A. G. R. Smith, ed., *The Reign of James VI and I* (London, 1973), pp. 106–23; Brenner, *Merchants and Revolution*, pp. 3–195.

[31] PRO, E 190/187/9; 188/6; 187/12; 189/8, 11.

Christmas 1694 and Christmas 1701.[32] These ports were losing ground in domestic as well as overseas trade to Newcastle-upon-Tyne, which grew rapidly in the period not only because of its command of coastwise shipment of coal, but also its significance in traffic with the Low Countries and the Baltic. Only at the end of the period did Sunderland itself begin to grow, mainly in consequence of being swept within the orbit of Newcastle's own impressive economic expansion.[33] A somewhat similar picture of only intermittent overseas commerce emerges for Bridlington, Grimsby and Scarborough in the earlier years of the seventeenth century, with Grimsby returning to this condition again for a few years in the later seventeenth century.[34] Here it was Hull's domination of the region's cloth trade to the Low Countries and the Baltic that made the difference. Its position at the mouth of the Humber allowed it to dominate both the coastal and overseas trade, inwards and outwards, of the West Riding of Yorkshire and the East Midlands flowing along the river systems of the Ouse, Aire, Don and Trent. The other ports in the region were becoming more and more specialised in the coastwise shipping of its agricultural products.[35]

In the region of the Wash, Boston and Lynn, the two headports, and their members together formed a tight-knit relationship among themselves dependent on the one side upon the agricultural riches of Lincolnshire, Cambridgeshire, Bedfordshire and Norfolk, and on the other upon their seaward orientation towards the Low Countries and the Baltic. In this region, overseas trade remained steady throughout the period; in no year did the customs officials in any port or member make blank returns. Both headports had long benefited from their excellent waterborne access to extensive agrarian hinterlands via intricately articulated river systems. They were able, therefore, to serve as good trans-

[32] PRO, E 190/199/ 5, 8, 11; 200/5; 204/1; 205/2, 5; 207/5, 7, 14, 16.

[33] R. Howell, *Newcastle-upon-Tyne and the Puritan Revolution* (Oxford, 1967), ch. 1, esp. pp. 20–2, 71–2, 291 n. 1, 348; R. Howell, 'Newcastle and the nation: the seventeenth-century experience', in J. Barry, ed., *The Tudor and Stuart Town* (London, 1990), pp. 274–96; J. Ellis, 'A dynamic society: social relations in Newcastle-upon-Tyne, 1660–1760', in Clark, ed., *Transformation of English Provincial Towns*, pp. 192–202.

[34] PRO, E 190/309/2, 7; 313/1, 6, 10; 315/4, 5, 11, 12; 316/2, 3; 317/12, 13, 15, 17; 319/16; 321/3; 333/2, 5; 336/1, 12; on the mixed fortunes of the economy of Grimsby, see S. H. Rigby, *Medieval Grimsby, Growth and Decline* (Hull, 1993), pp. 51–78, 113–46; E. Gillett, *A History of Grimsby* (Oxford, 1970), pp. 19–47, 98–132.

[35] E. Gillet and K. A. MacMahon, *A History of Hull* (Oxford, 1980), pp. 144–65, 180–97; R. W. Hinton, *The Eastland Trade and the Common Weal* (Cambridge, 1959), pp. 19, 21, 24, 34, 36, 52, 56, 141; H. Zins, *England and the Baltic in the Elizabethan Era*, trans. H. C. Stevens (Manchester, 1972), pp. 134–8, 174–6, 190–2; J. K. Fedorowicz, *England's Baltic Trade in the Early Seventeenth Century: A Study in Anglo-Polish Commercial Diplomacy* (Cambridge, 1980), pp. 61–2, 74, 83–7; G. Jackson, *Hull in the Eighteenth Century* (Oxford, 1972), chs. 1–4; G. Jackson, *Trade, and Shipping in Eighteenth-Century Hull* (East Yorkshire Local History Society Publications, 31, 1975); Chalklin, *Provincial Towns*, p. 13.

fer points for imported goods and for such vital items as coal from Yorkshire and Northumberland.[36]

However, in the sixteenth and seventeeth centuries overseas trade here was not extensive. Much of it had either been deflected north toward Hull or south toward Yarmouth and increasingly to London itself. Lynn, a substantial town of 4,500 inhabitants at the beginning of our period and possibly in excess of 9,000 at the end, dominated Boston, which, with a population in the range of 2,000 in the later sixteenth century, a deteriorating haven and only slow population growth, was mainly a centre for coastal traffic. Lynn did maintain a steady trade in cloth and in foreign imports such as Gascon wines. But Boston had only a tiny fleet of seagoing vessels, ranging from around eight small ships in 1565 to about double that number in the earlier seventeenth century. Although the majority of its overseas trade was in the hands of the port's own inhabitants, it is telling that its leading merchants were not invariably also its leading citizens. Equally revealing is that fact that a significant share of its overseas trade was in the hands of merchants from elsewhere, especially those of Lynn. In the latter port, despite the merchants complaining bitterly at their loss of the cloth trade to London, there continued to be a steady commerce in cloth with the Low Countries and the Baltic as well as an extensive export trade in grain, but Lynn also depended heavily on coastal trafficking. The overall picture, then, is of a region primarily devoted to exploiting the agricultural produce of the interior and serving the consumption needs of its mainly rural population, in which Lynn was effectively the leading port and Boston principally a centre for coastal trade and an entrepôt for imported items from the Low Countries and the Baltic.[37]

In East Anglia and the South-East, which abounded in lesser ports, the customs officials regularly despatched blank port books to the Exchequer. Throughout the seventeenth century, Woodbridge, Aldeburgh, Blakeney and Dunwich with its associated ports of Walberswick and Southwold, all of them creeks of the thriving port and fishing centre of Yarmouth, repeatedly had no dutiable items to report to the customs officials. The evidence from Woodbridge is especially notable. It showed remarkable weakness in overseas trade between

[36] D. M. Owen, ed. *The Making of King's Lynn: A Documentary Survey* (London, 1984), intro. pp. 41–56; V. Parker, *The Making of King's Lynn: Secular Buildings from the 11th to the 17th Century* (Chichester, 1971), pp. 11–13; Williams, *East Anglian Ports*, pp. 54–5, 97–8, 132, 138, 142, 150, 169–70, 179; P. Dover, *The Early Medieval History of Boston, AD 1086–1400* (Boston, Lincs., 1970), pp. 15–35.

[37] Willan, *English Coasting Trade*, pp. 79–80, 123–9; Hinton, *Eastland Trade*, pp. 10, 19; Zins, *England and the Baltic*, pp. 134, 136–8, 179, 180, 247, 262; Fedorowicz, *England's Baltic Trade*, p. 61; Williams, *East Anglian Ports*, pp. 97–8, 179, App. II, pp. 297–8; R. W. K. Hinton, 'Dutch entrepôt trade at Boston, Lincs, 1600–40', *Ec.HR*, 2nd series, 9 (1956–7), 467–71; Hinton, ed., *Port Books of Boston*, intro., pp. xxxiv–xlii; P. Clark and J. Clark, eds., *The Boston Assembly Minutes, 1545–1575* (Lincolnshire Record Society, 77, 1987), pp. ix–xii; Ramsay, *English Overseas Trade*, p. 9.

1595 and 1605, again in the early 1620s, early 1630s and the 1690s. But even Blakeney, which Williams identifies as 'the most flourishing creek in East Anglia', experienced intermittent difficulties with its overseas trade in the seventeenth century.[38] Maldon, creek of Ipswich, also showed periodic weakness in overseas trade, although it was not as severe as for the East Anglian ports to its north.[39] However, Colchester, which was Ipswich's other member, was quite an active port in foreign commerce, especially after 'New Draperies' began being made in the town in the later Elizabethan period.[40] Nevertheless, insofar as this region's overseas cloth trade remained in local hands, it was dominated by the merchants of Yarmouth and Ipswich.[41]

The South-East presents a somewhat more complex pattern. In the region around the ancient port of Sandwich, the creeks, especially Deal and Dover, more consistently engaged in overseas trade than was true around Yarmouth, but Milton Regis on the River Swale in Kent showed occasional weakness.[42] Around Chichester, too, there was significant overseas traffic from some of the member ports, notably Rye, one of the Cinque Ports, even though it had experienced a considerable decline in its population in the sixteenth century, as many inhabitants left, partly in consequence of the problems experienced in its haven. By the seventeenth century, however, Rye seems to have stabilised, at least as regards its overseas trading activities. Meeching (or New Haven as it came to be known) also was reasonably active. But a number of places conducted no overseas trade at all for long periods between 1565 and 1700. Chichester's haven itself was

[38] Williams, *East Anglian Ports*, p. 5. For Woodbridge: PRO, E 190/478/7, 11, 13, 20; 479/1, 8; 480/9, 15B; 481/3; 482/3, 10, 15, 17; 483/7B; 488/2, 3, 9, 11, 14, 17; 489/10, 21; 493/7; 493/7; 507/2, 10, 20; 508/11; 604/8. For Blakeney: PRO, E 190/482/18; 488/12; 489/19; 491/7; 495/4, 12; 497/10; 507/6, 16. Before England's loss of Calais, Woodbridge had served as a centre for carrying food supplies to it; this trade, an extension of Woodbridge's role as a coasting port, persisted in the subsequent period, but was especially subject to disruption in wartime; Williams, *East Anglian Ports*, pp. 112–13.

[39] PRO, E 190/594/8; 596/21; 597/6; 598/1; 600/9; 607/4, 6; see also Williams, *East Anglian Ports*, pp. 138–82.

[40] N. R. Goose, 'Tudor and Stuart Colchester: economic history', *VCH*, Essex, IX, pp. 78–87; J. Cooper, 'Port', *ibid.*, p. 238.

[41] Williams, *East Anglian Ports*, pp. 61–8, 91–2, 139, 145, 167–9, 217, 245, 246–54, 259, Table 6.3, pp. 220–1, App. II, pp. 296–7; A. Friis, *Alderman Cockayne's Project and the Cloth Trade: The Commercial Policy of England in its Main Aspects, 1603–1625* (London, 1927), pp. 21, 64–5, 115–17; M. Reed, 'Economic structure and change in seventeenth-century Ipswich', in P. Clark, ed., *Country Towns in Pre-Industrial England* (Leicester, 1981), pp. 102–6.

[42] PRO, E 190/656/18; 659/8; 663/1; 664/5; 666/4; 667/9, 12; 668/3, 15, 20. In the early Stuart period Dover's commerce benefited from the introduction of reduced customs rates to encourage trade through the port. But its strategic position on the English Channel made its overseas commerce especially vulnerable to interruption by war. It also struggled throughout the period to maintain its haven against natural forces of deterioration; see P. Clark, *English Provincial Society from the Reformation to the Revolution: Religion, Politics and Society in Kent 1500–1640* (Hassocks, 1977), pp. 50, 72, 141, 225, 303–4, 319–20, 356–7, 381; Chalklin, *Kent*, pp. 30, 168–9, 172–4, 176–8, 181–2.

unsuitable for larger ships, but its situation between the mouth of the Thames and Portsmouth gave it a trading role none the less, especially in exporting agricultural produce to the continent.[43]

The commercial successes of the nearby headports account in large measure for the history of the lesser ports in eastern England. Maldon's circumstances, for example, were significantly shaped by the fate of Ipswich. In the later sixteenth and the first half of the seventeenth century, the latter was growing rapidly not just on the basis of its long-distance trade with Greenland, France, Spain, the Low Countries, the Baltic and later with New England, but also its participation in the traffic in coal between Newcastle and London and its growing domination of the surrounding region's coastal trade in produce.[44] But these developments were compounded by the close proximity of London whose explosive expansion as an overseas trading entrepôt and as a market for agricultural produce and manufactured wares had an overwhelming influence on economic life throughout the region.[45] To return to Maldon, in 1685 it shipped almost nothing else than grain to London, and apart from some loads of coal from Newcastle and Sunderland, received in return mostly wines, grocery wares and luxury items from London.[46] In addition, in a number of places, such as Winchelsea and Dunwich, the natural deterioration of the harbour played important roles in shifting them away from their ancient overseas activities. As ports, they became increasingly incapable of reliably handling seagoing ships.[47]

It is also clear that the eastern ports, located as they were on the English Channel and North Sea, were especially vulnerable to dislocations generated by England's international wars. The worst years for international traffic all occurred in periods of intense military operations, with the sharpest declines occurring in the years between 1585 and 1604 when England was at war with Spain, in the later 1620s when it confronted both Spain and France and the 1690s when war with the French was renewed. By far, the 1690s was the worst of these periods. In Chichester's region, the headport and virtually every one of its members, save Dover and Rochester, experienced some years in this decade in which no overseas trade subject to customs duties had occurred. This was especially true for Romney, Winchelsea and Folkestone, but at the end of the period Arundel and Littlehampton, Hythe, Pevensey and even Meeching. In the last decades of the century, Romney and Winchelsea also recorded no coastal traffic

[43] *Descriptive List*, pp. 222–310; Willan, *English Coasting Trade*, pp. 146–53; Chalklin, *Kent*, pp. 172–82; A. M. Mellville, 'City of Chichester: Port', *VCH*, Sussex, III, p. 102; *Rye Shipping Records, 1566–1590*, ed. R. F. Dell (Sussex Record Society, 64, 1965–6), pp. xxxiv–xlvi and *passim*; G. Mayhew, *Tudor Rye* (Falmer, 1987), pp. 233–69; P. Clark, 'Small towns in England, 1550–1850: national and regional population trends', in P. Clark, ed., *Small Towns in Early Modern Europe* (Cambridge, 1995), pp. 97–8.

[44] Reed, 'Economic structure and change', pp. 96–7, 102–6.

[45] See text above at n. 19.

[46] PRO, E 190/613/4, 15; Willan, *English Coasting Trade*, p. 137.

[47] Patten, *English Towns*, p. 75.

in a number of years. Even Chichester itself fell into this category for several years in the 1580s and 1590s and again in the 1690s.[48] War had the capacity to create significant economic business for the new dockyard towns, as well as for larger ports capable of financing privateering activities and of supplying the military fleets with support.[49] At the same time it raised the risks of trade in the smaller ports, many of which were already struggling to maintain their positions in international trade.

However, we understand developments among the eastern ports only to a limited degree if we think primarily of losses and gains, tallying one location's growth as necessarily entailing another's decline. What we are witnessing, rather, are certain significant changes in the direction of trade in this region, especially in the growing importance of coastal traffic from the east coast ports particularly in grains and other foodstuffs. As London become the overwhelmingly dominant force in overseas traffic the remaining east coast ports more and more took on the function of collecting and redistributing points for domestic products and foreign imports. In this connection, it is notable how much of the overseas traffic, even of the more active eastern ports, represents an extension of this important coasting traffic to cross-Channel sites. The coastal trade in Northumberland and Yorkshire coal, from Hull as well as Newcastle and Sunderland, was also of major weight in these ports, not only as it was absorbed into the rapidly expanding London market but also in East Anglia and around the the south coast and even into Wales.[50]

Outside the east coast, however, the story is quite different. While London's domination of the cloth industry affected individual cloth merchants in the southern and western ports, these commercial centres had different foci for their trade. Their merchants and mariners had long looked towards France and the Iberian peninsula for their main markets; they had never depended on extensive commercial ties with the Netherlands and northern Germany, where cloth exports were essential. Declines in their cloth exports as London's share of this trade soared to 90 per cent of the English total, therefore, were not replicated in the same measure in these other aspects of their overseas activities. Such places, especially the western ports, increasingly directed their efforts towards the Mediterranean, the African coast, the offshore Atlantic islands and the shores of North America. What was important for these trades was assembling outbound cargoes sufficient to exchange for the highly valued wares – the wines, oil, dyes-

[48] *Descriptive List*, pp. 295–310.

[49] See Coleman, 'Naval dockyards under the later Stuarts', 134–55; K. R. Andrews, *Elizabethan Privateering: English Privateering during the Spanish War, 1585–1603* (Cambridge, 1964), pp. 32–3, 100–49, 222–38, App. pp. 241–64; K. R. Andrews, *Trade, Plunder, and Settlement: Maritime Enterprise and the Genesis of the British Empire, 1480–1630* (Cambridge, 1984), pp. 223–55; Davis, *Rise of the English Shipping Industry*, pp. 315–37.

[50] Willan, *English Coasting Trade*, pp. 55–69, 111–45.

tuffs and subtropical produce – they sought from continental markets. In addition, several of the western ports, headed by Bristol and Chester and including the Welsh havens, maintained a very active traffic with Ireland, shipping finished English wares and continental re-exports in return for Irish agricultural produce, raw materials and cheaper manufactured goods.[51]

This increasingly important aspect of early modern English trade is apparent as we move around the coast into the regions associated with Southampton, Poole, Exeter, Plymouth, Barnstaple, Bridgwater and Bristol. Among these places, Southampton represents an important and revealing exception to the domination of overseas trade by the headport. In the medieval period, the Hampshire port had been one of the great trading centres of England, a principal focus for Italians dealing in English wool and woollens and imported spices and wines, and for Londoners who had come there to meet them, but by 1600 it had long since been eclipsed by London's own trade, although it still maintained a respectable commerce with France and the Channel Islands. With a population of around 2,000 at the beginning of our period and 3,000 at its end, it was small for a headport, in the class of Boston rather than of Newcastle, Yarmouth, Exeter or Bristol.[52] Its principal member was the town of Portsmouth, which at the beginning of our period had experienced the same general decline in its fortunes as Southampton itself, although on a much smaller base. In 1540, its population was perhaps less than half that of Southampton, and the value of its trade only a fraction of that of the headport. But largely on the basis of its role as a naval dockyard its fortunes had changed dramatically by the end of the sixteenth century. With the labour demand and ship fitting activities generated in the yards in the later seventeenth century by the Dutch and French Wars, its population and its prosperity began a rapid expansion. In 1664 it had

[51] Sacks, *Widening Gate*, pp. 19–53, Sacks, *Trade, Society and Politics in Bristol*, I, pp. 347–54; W. B. Stephens, *Seventeenth-Century Exeter* (Exeter, 1958), pp. 3–12, 35–9, 85–166; D. M. Woodward, *The Trade of Elizabethan Chester* (Hull, 1970), pp. 5–36; D. M. Woodward, 'The overseas trade of Chester, 1600–1650', *Transactions of the Historical Society of Lancashire and Chester*, 122 (1970), 25–42; A. K. Longfield, *Anglo-Irish Trade in the Sixteenth Century* (London, 1929); L. M. Cullen, *Anglo-Irish Trade, 1660–1800* (Manchester, 1968), pp. 29–44, 75–118; R. Gillespie, *The Transformation of the Irish Economy* (Dublin, 1991); L. M. Cullen, 'Economic trends, 1660–1690', in T. W. Moody, F. X. Martin and F. J. Byrne, eds., *A New History of Ireland*, vol. III: *Early Modern Ireland* (Oxford, 1976), pp. 387–407; A. Clark, 'The Irish economy, 1600–1660', in *ibid.*, pp. 168–86.

[52] A. L. Merson, 'Southampton in the sixteenth and seventeenth centuries', in F. J. Monkhouse, ed., *A Survey of Southampton and its Region* (Southampton, 1964), pp. 218–27; A. A. Ruddock, *Italian Merchants and Shipping in Southampton, 1270–1600* (Southampton Records Series, I, 1951); A. A. Ruddock, 'London capitalists and the decline of Southampton in the early Tudor period', *Ec.HR*, 2nd series, 2 (1949–50), 137–51; C. Platt, *Medieval Southampton: The Port and Trading Community, A.D. 1000–1600* (London, 1973), pp. 152–64, 215–24, 263; Chalklin, *Provincial Towns*, p. 18; Patten, *English Towns*, pp. 174–5.

around 3,500 inhabitants, in 1676 around 4,300, and in 1700 over 5,000 and still climbing.[53]

By the mid-seventeenth century, Exeter and Bristol were well on their ways to becoming great regional entrepôts for their increasingly prosperous and populous neighbourhoods as well as outlets for the industrial wares and agricultural produce of the surrounding regions. Exeter had long had an active trade with France, especially focused on exporting the various varieties of Devonshire and West Country broadcloths. However, from the earlier seventeenth century, it became an important outlet for the region's serges, which increasingly had markets in the Iberian peninsula and later in the Netherlands as well. It also developed a growing interest in the American colonial enterprise both in the Newfoundland and New England fisheries, whose salt cod had such good markets in southern Europe, and in West Indian and American tobacco and sugar, in high demand both in England and on the continent. On this basis, Exeter was able to expand its trade in the second half of the seventeenth century, and with the benefit of the canal built in the mid-sixteenth century to link its upriver haven with seagoing facilities at Topsham, to become the leading port on the south coast both for international and coastal commerce.[54] Barnstaple, one of Exeter's members, also became significantly engaged in Atlantic commerce. It grew sufficiently in the period to become its own headport after 1671, taking Bideford and Ilfracombe with it as members. This development gave due recognition that Barnstaple's trade had approached that of Bridgwater, its near neighbour.[55]

Bristol had no involvement in the serge trade. Although it drew a portion of its cloth shipments from some of the same regional sources as Exeter, its main exports in cloth as well as shipments of lead, coal, calveskins and iron ware came more from Somerset, Gloucestershire and Wiltshire and the Severn valley. Unlike Exeter, it also had no extensive contacts in the Netherlands. Instead it flourished largely on the basis of its more intensive contacts in Spain, the Mediterranean, the Atlantic islands and later in the West Indies and the Chesapeake region in North America. Judged by the customs revenue it generated, it had ranked just below Exeter in the earlier decades of the seventeenth century, but in the 1670s and 1680s its trade was three to four times greater than the Devon port's. Simultaneously it improved its position compared to London.

53 Coleman, 'Naval dockyards under the later Stuarts', 134–55; Andrews, *Elizabethan Privateering*, pp. 32–3; Chalklin, *Provincial Towns*, p. 24; Corfield, 'Urban development', pp. 223, 228, 229; on the development of the suburb of Portsea, see C. W. Chalklin, 'The making of some new towns, *c.* 1600–1720', in C. W. Chalklin and M. A. Havinden, eds., *Rural Change and Urban Growth 1500–1800* (London, 1974), pp. 234–6.

54 Stephens, 'Exeter lighter canal', pp. 1–11; MacCaffrey, *Exeter*, pp. 126–36; Stephens, *Seventeenth-Century Exeter*, pp. 3–12, 35–9, 47–55, 103–30, 140–4, 156–65, Apps. C, J, M, pp. 168, 173, 175–7; Willan, *English Coasting Trade*, pp. 159–62.

55 Willan, *English Coasting Trade*, pp. 167–72, 174–6.

During the 1610s, its trade was valued at only about 3 to 4 per cent of the capital's; in the 1670s and 1680s it represented between 8 and 12 per cent of the value of London's commerce.[56]

The Irish trade was also important to Bristol. It was a direct outgrowth of the city's importance as a centre for the distribution of domestic and imported products in the Severn valley and West Country. Irish merchants frequented the port mainly during the time of the two annual fairs in January and July, bringing fish, agricultural products and Irish cloth and taking away a vast array of mercery, drapery and grocery wares, ironmongery and re-exported goods from the continent and later from America as well. On their return to Ireland, their customs manifests looked very similar to those exhibited in the coastal taffic leaving Bristol. Something similar may be said regarding exports to the West Indies and the Chesapeake as well, except that from the 1640s until the end of the seventeenth century the traffic normally also included significant numbers of indentured servants travelling across the Atlantic to supply the soaring labour demand of the plantations. This trade too peaked around the time of the annual fairs. On the import side, the colonial traffic was also different, since from the Chesapeake it consisted almost exclusively of tobacco shipments and from the West Indies of sugar and some dyestuffs as well as tobacco. Nevertheless, the similarities of the coastal, Irish and colonial trades tell us more than the differences. They reveal Bristol as an emporium for consumer wares – a little London in the west – as well as being a magnet for labouring men and women seeking sustenance and employment.[57]

Plymouth, too, was a booming port in the seventeenth century, its expansion conditioned by its location at the entrance to the English Channel, its fine harbour and the role it played in the fishing industry, in American colonial trade and its early importance as the most important naval port in England. In the later seventeenth century it was the kingdom's fourth-ranked port in terms of the

[56] See Sacks, *Widening Gate*, pp. 36–52; Sacks, *Trade, Society and Politics in Bristol*, I, pp. 420–8; J. Vanes, ed., *Documents Illustrating the Overseas Trade of Bristol in the Sixteenth Century* (Bristol Record Society, 31, 1979), intro., pp. 1–27 and *passim*; J. Vanes, *The Port of Bristol in the Sixteenth Century* (Bristol Historical Association, no. 39, 1977); P. McGrath, ed., *Merchants and Merchandise in Seventeenth-Century Bristol* (Bristol Record Society, 19, 1955), intro., pp. ix–xxxii and pp. 170–274, and Apps. D–K, pp. 279–95; W. B. Stephens, 'Trade trends in Bristol, 1600–1700', *Transactions of the Bristol and Gloucestershire Archaeological Society*, 93 (1974), 156–61; Stephens, *Seventeenth-Century Exeter*, pp. 8, 162 Peter Fleming, 'The emergence of modern Bristol', in M. Dresser and P. Ollerenshaw, eds., *The Making of Modern Bristol* (Tiverton, 1996), pp. 1–4. Bristol's emergence as 'the metropolis of the west', marked by W. E. Minchinton, was already a phenomenon of the seventeenth century; see W. E. Minchinton, 'Bristol – metropolis of the west in the eighteenth century', *TRHS*, 5th series, 4 (1954), 69–89.

[57] Sacks, *Widening Gate*, pp. 251–303; Sacks, *Trade, Society and Politics in Bristol*, I, pp. 347–54, 420–7; McGrath, ed., *Merchants and Merchandise*, pp. 279–94; Longfield, *Anglo-Irish Trade*, pp. 38 *et passim*, Cullen, *Anglo-Irish Trade*, pp. 29, 43, 44; Willan, *English Coasting Trade*, pp. 171–3; Minchinton, 'Bristol – metropolis of the west'.

value of its trade for customs purposes. In the period, much of its outward coasting traffic consisted of re-exports of items imported from southern Europe and America. At the end of the century, however, its role as a naval port commanded greater portions of its available labour and capital resources and took over a larger share of its economic activities and it was becoming more dependent on London, Bristol and Exeter for imports. Service in the great wars with the Dutch and the French, disruptive of trade elsewhere, became the main stimulus for its prosperity in these decades.[58]

As a headport, Plymouth also had all of the Cornish ports grouped under it. These places had some importance in the fishing industry and the coasting trade, with tin and copper forming the main items shipped in the latter, but their overseas trade was very limited even in the best years. Helston in particular experienced long periods when it did no overseas trade at all, perhaps because it lacked supplies of copper to send abroad. In consequence, the international commerce of the region in the sixteenth and seventeenth centuries was quite overwhelmed by the role played by Plymouth, even as it found itself performing a more specialised role as a naval port in the overall network of ports.[59]

Trade in the Welsh ports, operating under the aegis of Cardiff and Milford Haven in the South and Chester in the North, had a great deal in common with the pattern in Cornwall. What overseas trade there was was small, especially before 1660. A portion of it went to Ireland, leaving these ports little involved in trade with the continent or in the Atlantic. For Cardiff in the South and Conway and Caernarvon in the North, there were a number of years in which no overseas trade occurred at all.[60] Wales had no truly large urban centres in this period; even Cardiff, one of the major towns, hovered only in the range of 1,500 to 2,000 inhabitants. Welsh ports mainly engaged in coastal traffic, much of it in

[58] R. N. Worth, *History of Plymouth from the Earliest Period to the Present Time* (Plymouth, 1890), pp. 136–8, 322–31, 345–8; K. V. Burns, *Plymouth's Ships of War: A History of Naval Vessels Built in Plymouth between 1694 and 1860* (National Maritime Museum, Maritime Monographs and Reports, 4, Greenwich, 1972), pp. 3–7; Stephens, *Seventeenth-Century Exeter*, pp. 8, 39, 127, 129, 162; W. B. Stephens, 'The west-country ports and the struggle for the Newfoundland fisheries in the seventeenth century', *The Devonshire Association for the Advancement of Science, Literature and Art: Report and Transactions*, 88 (1956), 90–101; Willan, *English Coasting Trade*, pp. 162–3.

[59] A. L. Rowse, *Tudor Cornwall: Portrait of a Society* (London, 1957), pp. 54–76; Willan, *English Coasting Trade*, pp. 164–6; J. Whetter, *Cornwall in the 17th Century: An Economic History of Kernow* (Padstow, 1974), pp. 147–67; for Helston see PRO, E 190/773/34; 1026/11; 1029/11; 1031/4; 1032/3; 1035/15; 1039/11; 1044/9, 15; 1046/25, 26; 1047/5, 9, 24; 1049/20; 1050/27; 1053/11; 1055/23, 26; 1056/30 31; 1057/5, 18, 22; 1058/17; 1059/15.

[60] For Cardiff see PRO, E 190/1272/16; 1273/12; 1274/4, 6; 1275/7; 1283/2, 3, 8, 12; 1284/11, 12. For Conway see PRO, E 190/1323/11; 1327/6, 13, 17; 1328/1, 16, 18; 1331/5; 1334/4, 19, 23; 1336/7; 1337/1, 17; 1339/4; 1340/12, 22; 1344/3, 12; 1345/7, 15; 1346/4; 1348/5, 8, 13; 1349/16; 1351/11; 1353/2, 8; 1354/8; 1356/9, 12; 1358/5, 7, 14; 1359/9, 13; 1361/2, 12; 1362/6, 14. For Caernarvon see PRO, E 190/1299/3; 1324/1, 2, 15, 23; 1325/14, 16; 1328/12; 1339/3, 16; 1340/15; 1341/6, 7, 17; 1344/2, 8, 10, 11; 1350/15; 1354/2, 3, 17; 1359/21; 1360/15; 1361/20; 1362/20.

agricultural produce. Swansea, however, was already a significant coal port in the sixteenth century, and by 1700 there might have been a hundred small and middling-size sailing vessels in Swansea bay waiting to load the coal that had been mined only three miles away from the sea. Neath and Burry also participated in the same trade. The northern ports, grouped with Chester, were mainly of local importance; rarely did they ship significant cargoes much beyond Chester itself.[61]

As we shift our focus to Chester and England's north-western corner, we see further confirmation of the trends we have already observed along the southern coast in the South-West. Chester was the largest port in the region, and despite repeated difficulties with the silting of the River Dee it maintained an active international and coasting trade. In significant measure, it replicated in structure, though on a smaller scale, the picture in Bristol. In the sixteenth and early seventeenth centuries, there was a heavy emphasis on trade with France and southern Europe, concentrating on the import of wine and of subtropical produce and related specialties, to obtain which it assembled a limited range of cargoes including some varieties of northern cloths – kerseys, fustians, Manchester cottons and so on – and significant quantities of tanned calveskins shipped on licence. The Irish trade also was of importance – indeed it had greater weight for Chester than did trade with the continent. As with Bristol, there was a considerable overlap between this trade and the coasting trade. Notable in this instance are the large shipments of English and Welsh coal from the nearby region, which went in significant quantities to Ireland and to various locations along the English coast as well. However, the role of the transatlantic trades in Chester, when these become active in the later seventeenth century, was somewhat less than for Bristol, although still evident.[62]

While Chester maintained its regional leadership in foreign and domestic

[61] H. Carter, *The Towns of Wales*, 2nd edn (Cardiff, 1966), pp. 32–50; *The Welsh Port Books (1550–1603)*, ed. E. A. Lewis (Cymmrodorion Record Series, 12, 1927), pp. vii–xlvii; G. Williams, *Recovery, Reorientation and Reformation: Wales, c. 1415–1642* (Oxford, 1987), pp. 76–78, 81–3, 401–5; I. Soulsby, *The Towns of Medieval Wales: A Study of their History, Archaeology and Early Topography* (Chichester, 1983), pp. 24–8, 98, 242–7; W. Rees, *Cardiff* (Cardiff, 1969), p. 152; D. G. Walker, 'Cardiff', in R. A. Griffiths, ed., *Boroughs of Medieval Wales* (Cardiff, 1978), pp. 112–13; W. R. B. Robinson, 'Swansea', in *ibid.*, pp. 284–6; W. H. Jones, *History of Swansea and Gower* (Carmarthen, 1920); W. S. K. Thomas, 'Tudor and Jacobean Swansea, *Morgannwg*, 5 (1961), pp. 25–48; Willan, *English Coasting Trade*, pp. 176–80, 182–3.

[62] Woodward, *Trade of Elizabethan Chester*, pp. 5–72; Woodward, 'Overseas trade of Chester, 1600–1650', pp. 25–42; W. B. Stephens, 'The overseas trade of Chester in the early seventeenth century', *Transactions of the Historic Society of Lancashire and Cheshire*, 120 (1968), 23–34; T. S. Willan, 'Chester and the Navigation of the River Dee, 1600–1750', *Journal of the North Wales Architectural, Archaeological and Historic Society*, new series, 31(1) (1938), 64–7; G. M. Haynes-Thomas, 'The port of Chester', *Transactions of the Lancashire and Cheshire Antiquarian Society*, 59 (1947), 35–40; Willan, *River Navigation in England*, pp. 18, 21; Willan, *English Coasting Trade*, pp. 180–2; Longfield, *Anglo-Irish Trade*, pp. 37 *et passim*; Cullen, *Anglo-Irish Trade*, pp. 29, 32, 43.

trade, Liverpool, its principal member port, was already a commercial centre of some significance by the beginning of the seventeenth century. The good quality of its harbour on the Mersey, compared to Chester's on the Dee, made it convenient for oceangoing vessels to manoeuvre, and by the 1630s, there were some years in which wine imports into Liverpool nearly equalled those of Chester, although in both places the levels of this traffic were only modest compared to what we find in England's southern and eastern ports.[63] But it was the second half of the seventeenth century that witnessed Liverpool's rise as a major port. In part, this was the consequence of the city's ready access to the clothmaking districts of south Lancashire, whose fabrics had growing markets in Spain, France and the Mediterranean. The growth of its salt trade, made possible by the discovery in 1670 of rock salt in Cheshire near Northwich, also played a role. But the greatest contribution to its rapid expansion was made by the new colonial trades. Before the close of the seventeenth century, Liverpool was already a major sugar and tobacco trading port. Moreover, the increasing role of import trade in the region had important consequences for its coasting trade and its traffic with Ireland. It is notable, for example, that the scale of its coasting trade alone grew fivefold between the 1660s and the 1690s, with much of large outbound traffic involving the distribution of previously imported goods from abroad.[64]

The rise of Liverpool represents in miniature one of the major trends in the early modern history of England and Wales, namely their transformation into Atlantic communities. Driven by the incessant demand for imports, with their high-profit margins, the network of ports was being pulled away from its sharp focus on north-west Europe toward the Iberian peninsula, the Mediterranean and Atlantic Islands, and then North America and the West Indies. In this respect, Liverpool followed the pathbreaking of London and Bristol in the sixteenth and early seventeenth centuries.[65] Liverpool's place in the story also reveals a second side to long-term developments, since its capacity to accumulate the capital necessary to sustain its deepening involvement in Atlantic trade was due in large measure to the availability within its hinterland of the sorts of lighter-weight cloths that were in high demand in its European markets, and of rich supplies of salt as well as coal.

These same conclusions are confirmed, albeit in a somewhat less dramatic fashion before 1700, by the appearance of Whitehaven in our list of ports. It was but a tiny town in the 1670s, with around 300 inhabitants. But it enjoyed the

[63] In 1636, e.g., see PRO, E 122/198/7; Stephens, 'Overseas trade of Chester', pp. 32–3.

[64] C. N. Parkinson, *The Rise of the Port of Liverpool* (London, 1952), pp. 1–67; Ramsay, *English Overseas Trade*, pp. 152–60, 161; P. G. E. Clemens, 'The rise of Liverpool, 1665–1750', *Ec.HR*, 2nd series, 29 (1976), 211–25; F. E. Hyde, *Liverpool and the Mersey* (Newton Abbot, 1971), pp. 1–9, 25–31; Willan, *English Coasting Trade*, pp. 183–5; Cullen, *Anglo-Irish Trade*, pp. 32, 43, 44.

[65] Brenner, *Merchants and Revolution*, pp. 3–50; Sacks, *Widening Gate*, pp. 19–53.

presence of a rich coal seam and a good harbour with a westward-looking prospect. By the close of the seventeenth century, its coalpits were yielding around 20,000 tons a year, and its population grew to about 2,200 in 1693 and some 4,000 in 1713. In effect, it became an entirely new town under the entrepreneurial leadership of the Lowther family, owners of the site of Whitehaven. As with Liverpool and Chester, the chief market for its coal was in Ireland. As this trade expanded, its shipping fleet grew from a mere handful of small vessels, mainly employed in fishing, to fifty-five ships by the 1680s, a number more than adequate for large-scale trading. By the end of the century, as a result of this growth in shipping, and Sir John Lowther's enterprising spirit, Whitehaven was already a major port for the Virginia trade with ten or more tobacco-laden vessels from Virginia entering the port each year.[66]

This group of outports – the small and large – was at the leading edge of a development that was recentring the English commercial economy away from its old niche at the periphery of north-western Europe, exporting raw materials and low-priced manufactures, turning it into an Atlantic civilisation concentrated on the exchange and distribution of high-profit consumer wares. Struggling to keep themselves going against the competition of the clothtrading Merchant Adventurers based in London, they concentrated their efforts on taking profits from their import traffic, servicing the new industries that had grown up to supply the emerging consumer markets, and offering desired foreign commodities to the rich and middling buyers in their regions. In taking on these functions, they anticipated trends which took hold in London itself during Elizabeth's reign and became increasingly evident in the seventeenth century.[67]

The recentring of English and Welsh commercial activity in an Atlantic context had the effect of giving economic emphasis to new trades in London, where by the end of the seventeenth century American traffic came to dominate the scene. At the same time, it put the focus not only on groups of ports whose locations gave them ready access to the riches of southern Europe, the Mediterranean and the Atlantic, places in the south-west and west, but also on ports that were able effectively to serve the newly structured domestic market.

66 J. V. Beckett, *Coal and Tobacco* (Cambridge, 1981), pp. 7, 59, 60, 61n, 89, 102–8, 111, 112, 115, 120, 179; R. Millward, 'The Cumbrian town between 1600 and 1800', in Chalklin and Havinden, eds., *Rural Change*, pp. 216–19; Chalklin, 'Making of some new towns', pp. 231–2.

67 See G. D. Ramsay, 'The rise of the western ports', in Ramsay, *English Overseas Trade*, pp. 132–65; R. Davis, 'England and the Mediterranean, 1570–1670, in Fisher, ed., *Essays in the Economic and Social History of Tudor and Stuart England*, pp. 117–37; Brenner, *Merchants and Revolution*, pp. 3–50; Sacks, *Widening Gate*, pp. 19–53; Andrews, *Elizabethan Privateering*, pp. 159–238; see also Andrews, *Trade, Plunder, and Settlement*, pp. 1–40, 356–64; K. R. Andrews, 'The English in the Carribbean, 1560–1620', in K. R. Andrews, N. P. Canny, and P. E. H. Hair, eds., *The Westward Enterprise: English Activities in Ireland, the Atlantic, and America, 1480–1650* (Liverpool, 1978), pp. 103–23; P. McGrath, 'Bristol and America, 1480–1631', in *ibid.*, pp. 81–102.

London's massive growth alone stimulated the burgeoning trade in coal of Newcastle and Sunderland and the intensification of coasting traffic in East Anglia, Kent and Sussex. It had the effect of reducing the number of east coast ports that maintained a heavy commitment to overseas traffic, turning the remainder into effective servants of domestic trade up and down the coastline. As the boundaries of the market basins of the major ports became more clearly defined, the web of interconnections within them and between them became denser, opening room for some ports to gain more specialised roles in meeting the demand for domestic supplies.

(iii) THE SOCIAL AND POLITICAL LIFE OF THE SEAPORTS

In keeping with a Europe-wide trend, the English and Welsh seaports grew rapidly in the early modern period.[68] Seaports were able to support such increases, not only because of the diversity of their trading activities, but also because the demand for labour in the shipping industry created employment opportunities that did not exist elsewhere. This combination gave seaports a distinctive occupational structure. Just as the distribution of trades in Coventry, Worcester and Norwich demonstrated that they were textile towns, and in Northampton that it was a leather-producing one, the heavy presence in the port cities of merchants, mariners, coopers, shipwrights and related crafts marked the functions of these places as overseas trading centres.[69]

Within London's intramural parishes, perhaps 25 per cent of the population worked exclusively in overseas commerce, and perhaps another 15–20 per cent, drawn from among Londoners engaged in manufacturing and the victualling trades, also depended significantly on seaborne enterprise for their livelihoods. In the extramural parishes, the proportion of merchants was much lower, but there were large numbers of workers servicing London's shipping industry.[70] In Bristol, about half the freeman were engaged, in one way or another, in commerce or in serving the shipping industry; these same crafts also employed a very significant and growing share of all those apprenticed in the city in the

[68] Bairoch, *Cities and Economic Development*, pp. 186–7; see also Braudel, *Perspective of the World*, pp. 353–4; de Vries, *European Urbanization*, pp. 141–2; Hohenberg and Lees, *Making of Urban Europe*, pp. 109, 111, 184, 229.

[69] See Sacks, *Widening Gate*, p. 59; Sacks, *Trade, Society and Politics in Bristol*, II, p. 469; W. G. Hoskins, 'English provincial towns in the early sixteenth century', *TRHS*, 5th series, 6 (1956), 13–14; J. F. Pound, 'The social and trade structure of Norwich, 1525–1575, *P&P*, 34 (1966), 49–69; A. D. Dyer, *The City of Worcester in the Sixteenth Century* (Leicester, 1973), pp. 81–92. See also Patten, *English Towns*, pp. 146–96; L. A. Clarkson, *The Pre-Industrial Economy in England, 1500–1750* (London, 1971), pp. 80–1, 88–92.

[70] A. L. Beier, 'Engine of manufacture: the trades of London', in Beier and Finlay, eds., *London*, pp. 147–51; see also S. Rappaport, *Worlds within Worlds* (Cambridge, 1989), pp. 90–4; J. Boulton, *Neighbourhood and Society* (Cambridge, 1987), pp. 60–73, 117.

period.[71] In other seaports, the picture is comparable. In seventeenth-century Exeter, about 20 per cent of all new freemen entered in commercial occupations, and many in manufacturing trades were also engaged in supplying the needs of the export market. For example, the significant increase in the latter half of the century in the number of Exeter shoemakers becoming freemen is largely attributable to the rise in export of shoes from Exeter to the colonies. A variety of other crafts also served the needs of the port and its shipping.[72] At the end of the seventeenth century the occupational structure of Liverpool, too, demonstrated a heavy dependence on the sea; about 30 per cent of its working population were sailors.[73] A similar pattern is evident in lesser ports, places like Brighton, Hastings and New Shoreham in Sussex where marine services accounted for over half the town trades.[74]

The distribution of wealth in the major port towns also favoured entrepreneurs in overseas commerce. The picture in London of great merchant magnates with large households and vast holdings in material assets and accounts receivable is duplicated, though not on the same grand scale, in virtually all the more significant overseas trading centres, such as Newcastle, Bristol, Exeter and Chester. Since urban officeholding fell mainly into the hands of the wealthiest citizens, merchants and large-scale dealers also commonly occupied the largest share of local offices in the seaports.[75] As elsewhere in urban Britain, this arrangement helped finance local governance with the accumulated wealth of a town's most successful inhabitants, and grounded civic administration upon their business skills and experience. This nearly ubiquitous model of local government inevitably gave town governors the authority to use their office for their own benefit as well as that of their towns, in effect making them judges in their own cases, an intrinsically ambiguous moral position. The model worked well in the port towns so long as the larger body of citizens connected their own welfare with the con-

71 Sacks, *Widening Gate*, pp. 68–9; Sacks, *Trade, Society, and Politics in Bristol*, II, pp. 469–74, 477–8, 493–6, 507–8.

72 Stephens, *Seventeenth-Century Exeter*, pp. 113, 146–7, 160; see also MacCaffrey, *Exeter*, pp. 160–73.

73 A. J. Rawling, 'The rise of Liverpool and demographic change in part of south-west Lancashire, 1661–1750' (PhD thesis, University of Liverpool, 1986), p. 131.

74 Patten, *English Towns*, pp. 170–1.

75 R. Grassby, *The Business Community of Seventeenth-Century England* (Cambridge, 1995), pp. 82–107, 234–68; R. Grassby, 'The personal wealth of the business community in seventeenth-century England', *Ec.HR*, 2nd series, 23 (1970), 220–34; R. Grassby, 'English merchant capitalism in the late seventeenth century: the composition of business fortunes', *P&P*, 46 (1970), pp. 87–107; R. Grassby, 'Social mobility and business enterprise in seventeenth-century England', in D. Pennington and K. Thomas, eds., *Puritans and Revolutionaries: Essays in Seventeenth-Century History Presented to Christopher Hill* (Oxford, 1978), pp. 355–81. On the major provincial ports see Williams, *East Anglian Ports*, pp. 184–9; Howell, *Newcastle-upon-Tyne*, pp. 8–4, 350–4; Stephens, *Seventeenth-Century Exeter*, pp. 145–56; Sacks, *Widening Gate*, pp. 56–9, 149–53, 163–70, 256–7, 355–6; Sacks, *Trade, Society, and Politics in Bristol*, II, pp. 470–7, 486–96, 692–710; Woodward, *Trade of Elizabethan Chester*, pp. 106–24, 135; A. M. Johnson, 'Politics in Chester during the Civil Wars and the Interregnum, 1640–1662', in Clark and Slack, eds., *Crisis and Order*, p. 205.

tinuing prosperity of overseas trade and accepted their local leaders as just and honest men working for the general good, not just their own private gain.[76]

Nevertheless, in the seaports, especially the major ones like London, Newcastle, Bristol, Exeter or Chester, the division of labour between wholesale merchants, who bore the main risks of venturing in long-distance trade, and local shopkeepers and artisans, many of whom claimed a right to engage in such traffic when they would, sometimes created a source of rivalry in these communities, especially where the merchants formed exclusive organisations barring competition from retailers and craftsmen. London, Bristol, Chester and Exeter all experienced such episodes of disharmony and dissension in our period, particularly in regard to the import trades. Many wholesalers in luxury items, whether these came from the Low Countries, the Iberian peninsula, the Mediterranean or the Atlantic, believed they needed the protection of exclusive trading privileges to secure their credit and markets and give their trades a proper measure of predictability. In sixteenth- and early seventeenth-century London, it was the great overseas trading companies, such the Merchant Adventurers, the Levant Company and the Spanish Company, that forced the issue by imposing restrictions on the admission into their privileges of any but 'mere merchants', i.e. wholesale traders. In Bristol, Chester and Exeter, local companies of Merchant Venturers, operating under separately granted royal charters as well as local ordinances, sought equivalent protections for the same reasons. But a similar rivalry is also apparent in the coal trade from Newcastle, which operated under the aegis of the city's Company of Hostmen, formally chartered by Elizabeth in 1600 at the same time as she issued the town a new governing charter, assigning the leadership of each to the same figures.[77]

To those claiming exclusive commercial privilege, whether under royal charter or local ordinance, trade competition from fellow townsmen amounted to a form of illicit interloping; to their rivals, all citizens were judged to possess an equal freedom to trade under their town's corporate franchises, the enforcement of exclusive commercial rights amounted to a form of monopoly, depriving them of their liberties and livelihoods.[78] However, so long as large-scale

[76] On these points, see Sacks, *Widening Gate*, pp. 131–224; see also I. Archer, *The Pursuit of Stability* (Cambridge, 1991), pp. 140–8, 257–60; Rappaport, *Worlds*, pp. 23–60, 162–214, 377–87; V. Pearl, 'Change and stability in seventeenth-century London', *LJ*, 5 (1979), 3–24.

[77] See Brenner, *Merchants and Revolution*, pp. 51–389; Sacks, *Widening Gate*, pp. 59–127, 194–224; Woodward, *Trade of Elizabethan Chester*, pp. 73–105; Johnson, 'Politics in Chester', pp. 205–7; MacCaffrey, *Exeter*, pp. 124–59; W. Cotton, *An Elizabethan Guild of the City of Exeter* (Exeter, 1873); Howell, *Newcastle-upon-Tyne*, pp. 1–62, 169–217, 274–334.

[78] On the points in this and the next two paragraphs see Sacks, *Widening Gate*, pp. 251–329, 343–53; Brenner, *Merchants and Revolution*, pp. 82–195, 577–637, 709–16; see also G. S. de Krey, *A Fractured Society* (Oxford, 1985), pp. 121–76; see also D. H. Sacks, 'Parliament, liberty, and the commonweal', in J. H. Hexter, ed., *Parliament and Liberty from the Reign of Elizabeth to the English Civil War* (Stanford, 1992), pp. 93–101; D. H. Sacks, 'The countervailing of benefits: monopoly, liberty and benevolence in Elizabethan England', in D. Hoak, ed., *Tudor Political Culture* (Cambridge, 1995), pp. 272–91.

overseas trade remained focused on the continent, it was largely conducted by a limited number of merchants, since not only were continental markets narrow and highly constrained but for trade to flourish they required specialised knowledge and access to established credit networks. Under such conditions, interloping into the privileged territories of the trading companies continued to be a limited possibility.

However, in the new transatlantic trades matters were far different. The colonial economies of the Chesapeake region and the West Indies had valuable imports to offer – especially tobacco and sugar, exactly the sort of high-profit commodity that had driven the transformation of the commerce of London and the major ports towns of western England in the sixteenth and earlier seventeenth centuries. But unlike the Iberian peninsula and the Mediterranean, where long-term trading connections were an absolute prerequisite for success, in the colonies it was possible for English men and women to trade much more freely with fellow countrymen, some of whom were their own kin or former neighbours. Similarly, in those same established continental markets only a narrow selection of English products were in any demand, but the American plantations required every variety of manufactured ware as well as large supplies of labour. Any townsman or mariner with sufficient capital to send shipments of shoes, or ironware, or several indentured servants to the colonies stood able to reap rich profits in tobacco or sugar for their efforts. In these circumstances it was impossible to regulate trade through monopolistic company organisation. The number of active traders increased in port towns devoted to the colonial trades to include small-scale shopkeepers and artisans as well as rich merchants. The result was a restructuring of their local leadership away from the old company organisations in favour of traders, individually or in private firms, who were most able to use their resources to advance in this new market environment.

What was being born in these large and growing Atlantic trading ports was a complexly organised and highly integrated form of social life devoted to supplying the burgeoning demand for civilised comforts and consumption needs on both sides of the ocean through the instruments and mechanisms of market exchange. As a social form, it draws our attention to contrasting aspects of England's island way of life. In the close confines of an island, there is pressure to establish order and harmony through a system of inward regulation and control. But there is also the need to maintain links with the world beyond the coasts, not just to secure the island's forward defences, but to furnish its people with commodities they need or want but cannot themselves supply and with vent for their own produce. This market element in island life exposes its community to intrusions from without, sometimes through force of arms or foreign competition and sometimes through the corrosive influences of new products, new habits, new fashions and new ideas.

These are intrinsically difficult social functions to reconcile on whatever scale one looks: the small community, the burgeoning urban centre or the polity as a whole. Market exchange lives by what Joseph Schumpeter calls the process of 'creative destruction', regularly displacing less efficient or less profitable ways of supplying goods and services for more efficient or more profitable ones; it continuously transforms the economic environment in the process. In emphasising the measureable costs and benefits of particular choices more than their intrinsic moral virtue, it also represents a powerful challenge to the persistence of established authority and institutions, of settled social practices and traditions and of venerable and long-venerated regimes of honour and deference.[79] Nevertheless, the market place is a rule-governed arena, possessed of its own sense of morality. Those who trade in it value honesty in dealing, the keeping of promises and the productive use of skills, labour and resources.[80] Equally to the point, the market, through the mechanism of mutual exchange, also has the capacity to maintain stable social relations among large numbers of individuals and groups and to support the basic structures of society and the state.

A broadly based market society was only just coming into existence in England and Wales at the inception of our period. But in many respects, the tensions confronting the kingdom were already familiar features of life in the seaports whose very function necessarily combined an outward-facing trading life with an inward-looking civil life. Such places were testing grounds for the values, norms, habits and practices which made the emergence of modern form market society possible in the British Isles. As these port cities developed, they also provided a means to draw the component elements of the kingdom and ultimately of the entire archipelago into tighter bonds and a common, market-oriented culture. In this large-scale process, the ports became not only the principal points of contact linking the island nation to Europe and the parts beyond, but in making possible the development of an increasingly integrated and hierarchically organised urban network.

SCOTLAND

Although Scotland's population amounted to less than one tenth of that of England and Wales throughout the sixteenth and seventeenth centuries, its coastline extended to considerably more than a third of that of the British archipelago as a whole. Even more than was the case with England, ports were the hub of an economy in which the produce of rural hinterlands was variously processed, marketed and exported. Most of these ports, however, were very small, both in terms of settlement and population. It is unlikely that, before 1600, more than a handful of them – the four 'great towns' of Scotland recognised in the fourteenth

[79] J. A. Schumpeter, *Capitalism, Socialism, and Democracy* (London, 1943), pp. 81–6.

[80] For a recent discussion see Grassby, *Business Community of Seventeenth-Century England,* esp. pp. 31–9, 286–301, 388–94.

century as Edinburgh, Aberdeen, Dundee and Perth[81] – had more than 5,000 people. Most of the urban population and the vast bulk of commerce was concentrated on the 150 miles of coastline between Aberdeen and the Forth basin.

Long-established patterns of medieval trade persisted, well into the seventeenth century. There remained three main tributaries of trade: northern France, focused on Dieppe, and in the autumn with the Bordeaux wine trade; the Baltic, mostly the eastern ports such as Gdansk and Stralsund and Greifswald until new outlets for trade with Sweden developed after 1600; and the Low Countries, mostly through the small staple port of Veere on the Walcheren peninsula until new patterns of direct trading, mostly with Amsterdam and Rotterdam, emerged in the early part of the seventeenth century. The coastal trade with England began to increase in the second quarter of the seventeenth century, although it was almost all confined to the east coast and focused on the ports of Leith and Dundee. Trade with Ireland remained small scale and, apart from Dumbarton (as distinct from Glasgow), was largely confined to the coal trade out of small ports from Irvine on the Lower Clyde southwards.[82] As late as 1758, human and animal cargoes were carried across the North Channel only in small, open packet boats, plying from tiny south-west ports such as Portpatrick.[83]

(i) PORTS AND SEAPORTS

In Scotland, as in England and Wales, most of the main ports were based on tidal rivers which gave access to a large rural hinterland. Aberdeen's position, at the head of two rivers, the Dee and Don, which extended far into a very extensive and largely upland hinterland, gave it an unchallenged domination over the economy of the entire north-east; it consistently paid two-thirds of the taxation levied on the towns of the whole region. Dundee, on the north bank of the estuary of the Tay, and Perth, twenty miles upstream on its southern bank but sited at the first bridge over the river, were by far the largest urban centres in the Tay basin, controlling the regions of Angus and Perthshire and Strathmore respectively; between them, they were regularly assessed at two-thirds of the tax paid by all the towns in the Tay basin. Ayr and Glasgow, both of distinctly modest size in the sixteenth century, were the largest of a necklace of small sea and river ports based on the difficult waters of the Lower and Upper Clyde; they included

[81] M. Lynch, 'The social and economic structure of the larger towns, 1450–1600', in M. Lynch, M. Spearman and G. Stell, eds., *The Scottish Medieval Town* (Edinburgh, 1988), pp. 261–96; also *ibid.*, pp. 5–6.

[82] S. G. E. Lythe, *The Economy of Scotland in its European Setting, 1550–1625* (Edinburgh, 1960), pp. 142–86, 216–31, 232–46. For Ireland, Smout, *Scottish Trade*, pp. 178–82; L. E. Cochran, *Scottish Trade with Ireland in the Eighteenth Century* (Edinburgh, 1985); G. Jackson, 'Glasgow in transition, *c.* 1660 – *c.* 1740', in T. M. Devine and G. Jackson, eds., *Glasgow*, vol. I: *Beginnings to 1830* (Manchester, 1995), p. 77. See also *ibid.*, pp. 46–7, for Dumbarton shipping figures.

[83] J. G. Dunbar, ed., *Sir William Burrell's Northern Tour, 1758* (East Linton, 1997), p. 50.

the sea ports of Irvine and Dumbarton as well as smaller, long-established burghs such as Rutherglen, Lanark and Hamilton upstream of Glasgow.[84]

Increasingly from the fourteenth century onwards, after the loss to England of Scotland's premier port of Berwick, hub of its wool trade with the continent, the focus of both overseas and coastal trade lay in the Forth basin.[85] Edinburgh's port of Leith and the smaller ports of Bo'ness and Blackness, both used by merchants from a variety of burghs including west coast towns such as Glasgow and Ayr for eastward trade with the continent, figured so largely in the overseas trade because of their favourable site on the south side of the Forth, called by the thirteenth-century English chronicler, Matthew Paris, the 'sea of Scotland'. The waters of the Forth were tidal as far upriver as Stirling, another regional centre at the junction of an upland hinterland which, like Perth, was sited at the first point on a tidal river with either a bridge or a safe ford. On the north side of the Forth where it widened out into a large tidal basin, was a necklace of small-scale and mostly specialist ports, beginning with Culross in the west, including Inverkeithing, Burntisland, Kinghorn, Dysart, Kirkcaldy, Pittenweem and Anstruther, until the river widened out into the open North Sea near Crail and St Andrews. Ports such as these tended to specialise in specific commodities and, particularly as the sixteenth and early seventeenth centuries progressed, in coal, salt and fish. Although a few other ports, both north and south of the Forth such as Montrose and Dunbar, functioned independently in overseas trade, the activity of most east coast ports was largely confined to the coastal trade, using the main sea-based urban centres such as Leith, Dundee and Aberdeen as a funnel for both imports and exports.[86]

Much of the later medieval period and the sixteenth century saw overseas trade increasingly focused on the handful of larger ports. Leith by the last quarter of the sixteenth century had 72 per cent of the country's exports (measured by customs levied) pass through it, dominating particularly the trade in the old, established commodities of wool, fells, skins, hides and cloth. Over 54 per cent of the ships paying anchorage dues at the staple port of Veere in the 1560s came from Leith; the only serious competitors were Dundee, with 19 per cent and Aberdeen with 11 per cent respectively.[87] By the later sixteenth century even major ports such as Aberdeen were feeling the effects of the increasing strangle-

[84] For tax rolls, see the tables in M. Lynch, 'Continuity and change in urban society, 1500–1700', in R. A. Houston and I. D. Whyte, eds., *Scottish Society, 1500–1800* (Cambridge, 1989), pp. 115–17; and in Smout, *Scottish Trade*, pp. 283–4; see also P. G. B. McNeill and H. L. MacQueen, eds., *Atlas of Scottish History to 1707* (Edinburgh, 1997), pp. 309–15.

[85] McNeill and MacQueen, eds., *Atlas of Scottish History*, p. 239.

[86] For customs statistics on overseas exports to 1599, see *ibid.*, pp. 250–60; I. Guy, 'The Scottish export trade, 1460–1599', in T. C. Smout, ed., *Scotland and Europe, 1200–1850* (Edinburgh, 1986), pp. 166–74.

[87] Lynch, 'Social and economic structure of the larger towns', pp. 268–70; McNeill and MacQueen, eds., *Atlas of Scottish History*, pp. 250–5, 268; Lythe, *Economy of Scotland*, p. 244.

hold of the capital on most of the traditional areas of overseas trade; its council complained in the 1590s that many of the burgh's merchants were spending much of the year based in Leith, leaving Aberdeen a 'dry pond'. The Aberdeen shore accounts for the period 1596–1618 confirm that almost half of the shipping plying in and out of the port was coastal; by then no less than 32 per cent of Aberdeen shipping used Leith as an entrepôt.[88]

Many of the problems of seaports, however, were not man made. Most had a small draught: even Leith had only nine to ten feet at high tide and at Aberdeen the harbour mouth at low tide had a mere two feet or less, forcing larger merchant ships and men of war to anchor on the opposite bank of the river, at Torry.[89] Silting and difficulties of navigation were recurrent problems for many seaports and river ports based on tidal water. In the west, ports ranging from Dumfries and Whithorn on the Solway to Ayr and Irvine on the lower reaches of the Clyde suffered badly from silting in this period. In the east, silting had so badly hit the major burgh of Perth that its craftsmen, in their dispute with the merchant-dominated oligarchy, by the mid-sixteenth century were calling it a 'dry town far from the sea', which had lost out to its rival, Dundee, twenty miles downstream.[90] But the scouring effect of the waters of the Tay meant that Dundee, too, had severe problems with its harbour; extensive works, involving a new stone quay, sea walls and a pier were carried out in the last years of the sixteenth century under the supervision of the king's master mason, Robert Mylne.[91] Similar extensive harbour works were carried out at Montrose between 1595 and 1600, Kirkcaldy in the 1590s and at Aberdeen over the course of fifty years from 1607 onwards.[92] Yet the story with most east coast ports throughout this period, even where there had been extensive new harbour works built, is of continual and mostly ineffectual repairs stretching well into the eighteenth century, made necessary by the combination of problems of silting and the force of the North Sea storms.

88 A. White, 'Religion, politics and society in Aberdeen, 1543–1593' (PhD thesis, Edinburgh University, 1985), pp. 309, 319, 321; cited in M. Lynch, ed., *The Early Modern Town in Scotland* (London, 1987), pp. 12, 32 n. 38; J. D. Marwick, ed., *Records of the Convention of the Royal Burghs of Scotland* (Edinburgh, 1866–90), vol. 1, pp. 313–15. See L. B. Taylor, ed., *Aberdeen Shore Work Accounts* (Aberdeen, 1972); 'Ane Buik contenand in the Intress of shippis . . . at the port of Dundee, 1580–1618', in A. H. Millar, ed., *The Compt Buik of David Wedderburne, Merchant of Dundee* (Scottish History Society, 1898), pp. 193–302; the Aberdeen and Dundee lists are summarised in McNeill and MacQueen, eds., *Atlas of Scottish History*, p. 269.

89 Smout, *Scottish Trade*, p. 53; E. P. Dennison and J. Stones, *Historic Aberdeen: The Archaeological Implications of Development* (Scottish Burgh Survey, Edinburgh, 1987), p. 85.

90 Lynch, ed., *Early Modern Town*, pp. 5, 9; Smout, *Scottish Trade*, p. 53; Lynch, 'Social and economic structure of the larger towns', pp. 271–2.

91 E. P. D. Torrie, *Medieval Dundee* (Dundee, 1900), pp. 36–7.

92 G. Jackson and S. G. E. Lythe, eds., *The Port of Montrose* (Tayport, 1993), pp. 28–9; E. P. D. Torrie and R. Coleman, *Historic Kirkcaldy: The Archaeological Implications of Development* (Scottish Burgh Survey, Edinburgh, 1995), pp. 15, 55; Dennison and Stones, *Historic Aberdeen*, p. 85.

(ii) SEAPORTS, URBAN HIERARCHY AND NETWORKS

Twenty-three of the twenty-six most important towns in late sixteenth-century Scotland, as measured by their share of national taxation, were ports. Taken together, they paid over 92 per cent of all customs exports and contributed almost 90 per cent of burgh taxation.[93] No fewer than seventeen of the twenty-three were unambiguously seaports; a further six were river ports such as Perth, Stirling or Glasgow or, like Linlithgow, Haddington and Elgin, had their own ports nearby. The exceptions were all small in both size and importance – the inland market centres of Cupar, Brechin and Jedburgh. Even more than was the case with England, Scotland's was a seaborne economy. In terms of population, although that is often difficult to establish with any precision before the eighteenth century, ten of the largest dozen towns – Edinburgh, Dundee, Aberdeen, Perth, St Andrews, Dysart, Ayr, Montrose, Stirling and Dumfries – were based on the sea or tidal water; and the remaining two – Glasgow and Haddington – were river ports engaged in both coastal and overseas trade. It is no coincidence that what was by far the most heavily urbanised region of Scotland – the Forth basin – was also the hub of its seaborne economy. By the 1690s, between 39 and 55 per cent of the population of the shires or districts which fringed the Forth lived in towns.[94]

In his survey of customs and excise made in 1656, the Cromwellian official Thomas Tucker also detailed some eighty ships of above twenty-five tons burden in the whole country.[95] It is clear that the trade was routed (as was the case with England) largely through ports in the south and east, underlining the widespread persistence of the structure of medieval overseas trading patterns: Aberdeen was the only northerly port of any consequence able to take seagoing vessels of more than fifty tons; and as late as the 1690s Glasgow and Ayr were both engaged in large-scale transporting of goods thirty miles or more overland to and from the nearest available ports on the Forth.[96] Although trade increased markedly in the century after 1550, the growth of the major seaports such as Aberdeen, Dundee and Edinburgh/Leith depended (as in England) as much on their functions as

93 Table 12.3 is based on the tax roll statistics in Lynch, 'Continuity and change', pp. 96–7, 115–16; see also McNeill and MacQueen, eds., *Atlas of Scottish History*, pp. 314–15.

94 M. Lynch, 'Urbanisation and urban networks in seventeenth century Scotland: some further thoughts', *Scottish Economic and Social History*, 12 (1992), 35–7; the estimates are based on hearth tax returns.

95 Smout, *Scottish Trade*, pp. 53–4; for shipping, see Thomas Tucker, *Report by Thomas Tucker upon the Settlement of the Revenues of Excise and Customs in Scotland, 1656* (Scottish Burgh Records *Miscellany*, 1881), pp. 1–32; northern ports are mentioned at pp. 24–5. Tucker's findings are summarised in McNeill and MacQueen, eds., *Atlas of Scottish History*, p. 274, but they should be compared with *The Register of the State and Condition of Every Burgh within the Kingdom of Scotland in the Year 1692* (Scottish Burgh Records *Miscellany*, 1881), which lists 109 ships, averaging sixty-seven tons burden. See also Smout, *Scottish Trade*, pp. 53–4.

96 Smout, *Scottish Trade*, pp. 138–9, 148–9; Devine and Jackson, eds., *Glasgow*, pp. 27, 69, 71–2.

Table 12.3 *Percentages of national taxation levied on Scottish burghs 1587*

Edinburgh/Leith	28.8
Dundee	10.8
Aberdeen	9.2
Perth	6.0
St Andrews	3.5
Glasgow	3.3
Dysart	2.5
Ayr	2.2
Anstruther	2.0
Stirling	2.0
Haddington	1.9
Montrose	1.9
Dumfries	1.8
Cupar	1.6
Inverness	1.5
Brechin	1.4
Elgin	1.4
Kirkcaldy	1.3
Jedburgh	1.2
Irvine	1.2
Pittenweem	1.2
Arbroath	1.0
Crail	1.0
Kirkcudbright	1.0
Linlithgow	1.0
Wigtown	1.0

Bold indicates a seaport. *Italics* indicates a river port or burgh with its own adjacent port.

unrivalled regional centres for their hinterlands as on the rise in trade. The network of seaports reflected and exaggerated the favourable position enjoyed by a few major urban centres in the south and east.

Glasgow's rise to prominence probably needs to be fitted into the same picture rather than being explained as due to an unusual dynamic or a freer commercial atmosphere. It was the unrivalled regional centre for a vast hinterland, on both banks of the Clyde. Its transatlantic trade was distinctly modest before the union of 1707. Its occupational structure was not skewed towards commerce; it still had only about a hundred merchants engaged in foreign trade in the 1680s, not significantly more than the seventy-five Aberdeen had in the 1620s. Its new port, originally called 'Newport Glasgow', had seen building work on warehouses and quays begun in 1668 shortly after the land was purchased by the burgh, but it remained underdeveloped for some time, with its streets not yet laid out in the 1690s. Port Glasgow proved unable to dent the hold over most established sectors of overseas trade which was enjoyed by the rival Upper Clyde ports of Greenock and Dumbarton until well into the eighteenth century. Until then, Glasgow's trade still largely faced east, rather than west across the Atlantic. Although the later seventeenth century would see a substantial increase in Glasgow's trade with both the Baltic and France, importing 15 per cent of Scandinavian deals and 17 per cent of French wine, only the bulkiest items came into Glasgow's new harbour downstream at Port Glasgow, which was reportedly running at a loss in the 1690s.[97]

Despite the skewing of commercial activity towards the south and east, there was a clear recognition of both an urban communications network and a seaports network by the Convention of Royal Burghs, which represented all the royal burghs and controlled the assessment of national taxation on the urban sector of the economy; it financed the building and repair of bridges and ferries as well as harbour works. Between 1660 and 1707 alone, it funded thirty-one sets of harbour works or improvements.[98]

Although the main overseas trade routes remained the same – with the Baltic, Low Countries and France – until the third or fourth quarters of the seventeenth century, two tendencies were increasingly evident. The main east coast towns became entrepôts for both the import and export trades and many of the smaller ports increasingly specialised in one particular commodity. Anstruther, Crail and Dunbar became packing stations for herring, much of which was exported to the Baltic;[99] the Forth ports of Kirkcaldy, Dysart and Prestonpans thrived on the export of salt, mostly to the Baltic or to east coast English ports such as Hull, Ipswich and London;[100] and coal was exported direct from ports such as Culross, Burntisland, Kinghorn, Dysart and Pittenweem.[101] It was the coal and salt industries, with their respective markets heavily based in the Baltic and the Low Countries, which first prompted new developments: ports such as Culross,

[97] The view given here largely depends on the new evidence presented in Devine and Jackson, eds., *Glasgow*, see pp. 69–71, 73, 113. Cf. T. C. Smout, 'The development and enterprise of Glasgow, 1556–1707', *Scottish Journal of Political Economy*, 7 (1960), 194–212. See also S. J. Stevenson and E. P. D. Torrie, *Historic Glasgow: The Archaeological Implications of Development* (Scottish Burgh Survey, Edinburgh, 1990), pp. 237–8. For Aberdeen, see Dennison and Stones, *Historic Aberdeen*, p. 24; D. MacNiven, 'Merchants and traders in early seventeenth century Aberdeen', in D. Stevenson, ed., *From Lairds to Louns* (Aberdeen, 1986), p. 57.

[98] Lythe, *Economy of Scotland*, pp. 96–7; Smout, *Scottish Trade*, pp. 58–9.

[99] S. Mowat, *The Port of Leith* (Edinburgh, 1995), pp. 222–3.

[100] C. Whatley, *The Scottish Salt Industry, 1570–1850: An Economic and Social History* (Aberdeen, 1987), pp. 4, 33, 36, 38, 41.

[101] Lythe, *Economy of Scotland*, pp. 46–9.

which exported 89 per cent of Scottish salt in the 1590s, became the hub of miniature industrial complexes; and such was the demand for coal in the Low Countries, especially from Rotterdam, that from the 1620s onwards there were Dutch vessels queuing in the Forth to load up. By the 1680s it has been estimated that half of the ships leaving Scotland were small colliers. Such was the increasing volume of coal exports that the established infrastructure of ports, with their inadequate berthing facilities and long unloading times, proved inadequate and had to be supplemented by dedicated facilities; Methil in Fife, Port Seton in East Lothian (see Plate 5) and Saltcoats in Ayrshire, all new coal ports, had significant harbour constructions schemes begun after 1660.[102]

The extent of the coastal trade is difficult to quantify with any precision but occasional surviving lists of vessels underline how much it was preoccupied with the shipping of grain and cured herring along the east coast into Leith from small ports ranging from Thurso and Wick in the far north to Eyemouth and Dunbar in the south. A total of 155 ships carrying grain or cured herring docked in Leith in a twelve-month period in 1638–9; the fact that twenty-seven came from Montrose and a further twenty-six from Dunbar emphasises the role of these ports as both the fish and grain markets for the rich agricultural hinterlands of Angus and East Lothian. But the typical size of the coastal barks – ten of the eighteen vessels recorded in Montrose in 1692 were between ten and fifteen tons burden – together with the number of other ports given in the list of 1638–9 which shipped only a handful of cargoes – such as Tain, Findhorn or Banff – emphasises both their very modest size and the smallness of the ships involved in the coastal trade.[103]

In his survey of 1656, Tucker drew up a list of eight administrative 'precincts' on the English model, each with its headport where a collector would be based, and a survey of both ports and small creeks. Yet trade was clearly confined to the ports. The whole of the precinct based on the headport of Inverness, covering 150 miles of coastline from the River Spey to Thurso yielded only 2 per cent of customs receipts (and some 3 per cent of excise duties). Similarly, the string of tiny ports along almost 200 miles of coastline in the south-west from Ayr (the headport) on the Lower Clyde to Dumfries in the Solway Firth accounted for just over 1 per cent of customs (though over 5 per cent of excise duties). Trade in this precinct was confined to the three ports of Ayr, Kirkcudbright and Dumfries, and the numerous small creeks between these ports had only, at most, a few tiny fishing boats or small vessels involved in trade with Ireland.[104]

By contrast, the Forth basin, which had three precincts based in the headports

[102] McNeill and MacQueen, eds., *Atlas of Scottish History*, 259, 260; Lythe, *Economy of Scotland*, pp. 239–40; Smout, *Scottish Trade*, pp. 224–9.

[103] McNeill and MacQueen, eds., *Atlas of Scottish History*, p. 272; Jackson and Lythe, eds., *Port of Montrose*, pp. 98–100.

[104] Tucker, *Report*, pp. 16–32; see McNeill and MacQueen, eds., *Atlas of Scottish History*, p. 273.

of Leith, Bo'ness and Burntisland, accounted for over 71 per cent of customs dues and two-thirds of all excise duties in 1655–6. The changing nature of the Forth economy is well revealed by the individual totals for customs; Leith, which had alone paid 72 per cent of all customs in the 1590s, mostly on traditional commodities, now paid under 40 per cent as the headport of a precinct which extended from itself to the English border; but the small market town of Bo'ness, whose precinct extended from South Queensferry to Stirling on the south of the Forth and along the north bank as far as Limekilns, paid almost 25 per cent of customs, largely based on the growing importance of the chain of small salt and coal depots such as Kincardine and Culross.[105]

Tucker did not detail the revenue or excise derived from particular ports, but he did for the most part list the number of ships based in each port. Seagoing vessels ranged in size from about fifty to 250 tons. As was the case with England, each precinct had a network of ports. Within the Burntisland precinct, Kirkcaldy was fairly typical: it had twelve ships, but only three of them were larger than fifty tons and able to make crossings over to the Low Countries; the others were engaged in the coastal trade, especially in coal and salt. Pittenweem had two sizeable ships, both probably engaged in the Dutch coal trade; Anstruther, by contrast, had ten ships, all of fifty tons or less, reflecting how much the port was confined to coastal shipping. Tucker's account, however, is in places distinctly unreliable. He listed only three seagoing ships in Leith, each of 250 tons, together with 'twelve or fourteen' boats or coastal barges, which seems a small figure for a port which had over 140 skippers listed in a tax roll of 1647. A later list, drawn up for an investigation made by the Convention of Royal Burghs in 1692, seems more reliable: it listed twenty-nine vessels in Leith, totalling 1,700 tons. Of these, thirteen were seagoing ships ranging from sixty to 150 tons; the rest, ranging from fourteen to forty tons, were described as barks. By contrast, Glasgow in 1692 had twenty-three vessels, totalling 1,200 tons, although it is unclear whether most of them were based at Port Glasgow; eleven of them were of fifty tons or more.[106]

(iii) SOCIETY, INDUSTRY AND LIFE IN THE SEAPORTS

As is shown in Table 12.4, there were only a handful of ports – or indeed towns – in Scotland which had a population over 5,000, even by the end of the seventeenth century.[107] Because so many of the main ports were also regional centres,

105 McNeill and MacQueen, eds., *Atlas of Scottish History*, p. 273; Tucker, *Report*, pp. 27–9, 35–46.

106 Tucker, *Report*, pp. 17–18, 21–2; *Register*, pp. 56, 74–5; McNeill and MacQueen, eds., *Atlas of Scottish History*, p. 275.

107 This is a simplified version of a table in McNeill and MacQueen, eds., *Atlas of Scottish History*, p. 321. See Lynch, 'Urbanisation and urban networks', 24–41; and I. D. Whyte, 'Urbanisation in early modern Scotland: a preliminary analysis', *Scottish Economic and Social History*, 9 (1989), 21–27, for the basis of the calculations from hearth tax returns of 1691.

Table 12.4 *Populations of larger Scottish towns and ports 1691*

25,000	*Edinburgh*	
15,000	*Glasgow*	
10,000	**Aberdeen**	
9,000	**Dundee**	
7,000	**South Leith**	
	Canongate	
5,000	**Ayr**	
4,000	**St Andrews**	
	Inverness	
	Stirling	
	Montrose	
	Kirkcaldy	P
	Perth	
	Dumfries	
	Linlithgow	
3,000	Dalkeith	
	Dysart	P
	Hamilton	P
	Kelso	
	Bo'ness	
	Irvine	P
	Cupar	
	Brechin	P
2,000	Forfar	P
	Greenock	
	Jedburgh	
	North Leith	
	Paisley	
	Burntisland	P
	Lanark	
	Dunfermline	
	Kinghorn	P
	Crail	P
	Banff	
	Alloa	
	Arbroath	P
	Peebles	
	Selkirk	
1,000	**North Berwick**	P
	Dumbarton	
	Inverkeithing	
	Pittenweem	P

Table 12.4 (*cont.*)

	Renfrew	P
	Kinross	
	Wigtown	
	Kilrenny	P
	Hawick	
750	*Elgin*	

These estimates, based on the hearth tax of 1691, are all approximate.
P indicates where the estimate is based on the parish, landward as well as urban, and the population figure is likely to be inflated.
Bold indicates a seaport. *Italics* indicates a river port or burgh with its own adjacent port.

their occupational structure was not particularly heavily skewed either towards foreign commerce or maritime work; only about seventy-five of Aberdeen's 300 merchants in the 1620s were directly engaged in foreign trade.[108] The picture, however, would have been different in the small settlements of 1,500 or less which made up the majority of Scottish ports; here, the port would have been the main source of employment, whether in coastal trade, fishing or casual dock work. Both Inverkeithing and Pittenweem, with populations rather less than 1,000, had to provide six seamen for the Royal Navy in 1664 whereas North and South Leith, together with the adjacent port of Newhaven, which had a combined population of over 6,000, provided only twenty.[109] It is difficult to arrive at firm estimates of the number of mariners in any Scottish ports of this period. One contemporary estimate of 1643 for South Leith listed 176 skippers and seamen, which would account for between 20 and 30 per cent of adult males. The numbers in the same categories, however, are much lower in the much more complete picture available from the poll tax of 1694; here, ten skippers and twenty-two seamen are listed in South Leith and three and nineteen respectively in the smaller, fishing village of North Leith on the other bank of the river.[110] Such work, however, would have been heavily seasonal in nature: seagoing vessels engaged in foreign trade, hampered by slow turn-round times in their congested home ports and conditioned by the weather which confined voyages largely to the period between May and November, typically made a maximum of only three round voyages a year.[111]

108 MacNiven, 'Merchants and traders', p. 57.

109 Mowat, *Port of Leith*, pp. 213–14.

110 *Ibid.*, p. 179; H. M. Dingwall, *Late Seventeenth-Century Edinburgh* (Aldershot, 1994), pp. 289–93.

111 Smout, *Scottish Trade*, p. 62; Lythe, *Economy of Scotland*, pp. 133–4; T. Riis, 'Long distance trade or tramping: Scottish ships in the Baltic, sixteenth and seventeenth centuries', in T. C. Smout, ed., *Scotland and the Sea* (Edinburgh, 1992), pp. 59–75.

The only complete overall occupational profile yet made of any Scottish port is based on the 1694 poll tax of the adjacent ports of North and South Leith. The latter provided nineteen of the thirty-six coopers, twenty-nine of the 167 wrights, twenty-three of the thirty maltsters, twenty-two of the sixty smiths, forty of the 156 cordiners, and ten of the sixty brewers in Edinburgh's eleven parishes. As well as a busy port, which relied heavily on shipbuilding and parallel works such as ropemaking and sailmaking, and a large-scale warehouse, South Leith was the industrial suburb of a major metropolis, with manufacturing in areas such as soapboiling, glassmaking, brickmaking, distilling, tanning and weaving. Significantly more were employed in such manufactories than in either seafaring and directly linked maritime industry like sailmaking or in dock work; Leith formed four companies of workmen, each twelve strong, in 1695 to act as shore porters. North Leith, by contrast, although just across the narrow estuary, with eleven fishermen and twenty-two mariners out of a total of 158 adult males, was typical of other small ports, heavily oriented towards fishing and coastal trade.[112] In neither, however, was there as yet significant numbers engaged in shipbuilding. Most ships in Scottish ports had been built abroad; there would, however, have been ample regular work in ship repair and ship breaking and in some places, including North Leith, small-scale yards for the construction of modest-sized barks.[113]

The distinctly seasonal pattern of both overseas trade and the coastal trade in grain also had an effect on life in the larger ports engaged in it. Montrose, the main outport of the grain-producing area of Angus, needed large-scale storage facilities; a late seventeenth-century account describes the cluster of granaries, some three storeys in height, malt houses and kilns which had sprung up as a separate suburb threatening to 'exceed the town in greatness'.[114] In the ports, such as Montrose, Kirkcaldy, Dundee and South Leith which specialised in the import of Norwegian timber, mostly in the form of sawn deals for house building, pitch and tar, storage space must have been a serious problem and the risk of fire considerable. In Dundee, the main access to the harbour was by two lanes; even when one of them was widened in 1769 it had a breadth of a mere ten feet.[115] It was in ports such as these, where a combination of the emergence of new industries and the mushrooming of warehouse facilities made novel demands on both space and labour, that a different kind of urban society was beginning to emerge by 1700. It was, however, distinctly slow to develop outside the hothouse atmosphere of the major ports. By contrast, the other significant

112 Dingwall, *Late Seventeenth-Century Edinburgh*, pp. 143–4, 289–93. See also Mowat, *Port of Leith*, pp. 260–1. 113 Smout, *Scottish Trade*, pp. 47–8; Mowat, *Port of Leith*, pp. 154–5.

114 Jackson and Lythe, *Port of Montrose*, p. 119; A. Mitchell, ed., *Macfarlane's Geographical Collections* vol. II (Scottish History Society, 52, 1907), p. 42.

115 Mowat, *Port of Leith*, pp. 156–8; Smout, *Scottish Trade*, pp. 155–7, 241–2, 286–7; McNeill and MacQueen, eds., *Atlas of Scottish History*, p. 279; Torrie, *Medieval Dundee*, p. 41.

change of the seventeenth century lay in the emergence of small ports such as Culross, Limekilns or Methil (in Fife) or Prestonpans (in East Lothian), often financed by entrepreneurial landowners, with dedicated facilities for the coal or salt industries. Here, too, was a glimpse of the future, albeit still an uncertain one, in which there were as many failed ports as there were successful ones.

(iv) CONCLUSION: THE PORTS OF GREATER BRITAIN

By 1700 the Scottish and the English and Welsh systems of ports were on converging paths, not only as the Scots came to rely more heavily on trade with their neighbours to the south, but also as the commercial development of two kingdoms became increasingly focused on similar seaborne enterprises; as the structure of their two port networks became more alike in their organisation around regional 'headports'; and as the role of seaports in the two urban hierarchies, always large, took on increasing significance in their national economies and cultures. It is estimated that by the end of the seventeenth century perhaps half of Scottish imports went to England, although in terms of the volume of trade and its value the Baltic and the Netherlands remained more important markets to many Scottish merchants.[116] In addition, by 1700 Scotland's western ports, especially in the vicinity of Glasgow, were growing in importance, in part the consequence and in part the cause of Scotland's increasing involvement in transatlantic enterprise. Although it would be only in the eighteenth century that Glasgow itself would become fully engaged in American trade, by the end of the seventeenth century it not only was Scotland's second city in size and wealth accounting for least 20 per cent of Scottish urban taxation, but it was supporting a growing traffic in direct imports of colonial tobacco and was already supplying colonial sugar to its own refining and distilling houses. If not yet a Scottish version of Bristol, it had already laid the groundwork for the prominence in American commerce it would achieve in the ensuing period.[117]

While a variety of motives prompted the move toward the incorporating union between Scotland and England in 1707, many of them stronger than straightforward economic considerations, one of the most consistently articulated arguments on behalf of union in the seventeenth century was the desire on the part of many, especially on the Scottish side, for a commercial accord.[118] Nevertheless, it was only with the Restoration era that the matter became pressing, since the breaking of the Cromwellian Union after 1660 resulted in the

[116] Smout, *Scottish Trade*, p, 238; see also Whatley, 'Economic causes and consequences of the Union', fig. II, 172.

[117] Smout, *Scottish Trade*, pp. 144, 175–8; Smout, 'The development and enterprise of Glasgow', 194–212; T. C. Smout, 'The Glasgow merchant community in the seventeenth century', *Scottish Historical Review*, 47 (1968), 53–5, 56, 70.

[118] Smout, *Scottish Trade*, pp. 139–57.

imposition of the English Navigation Acts on the Scots and the rise of tariffs in Anglo-Scottish trade. The effects of this shift were even more pronounced after 1688. Increasing tariff and trading restrictions with England and its possessions in the 1690s had contributed to commercial difficulties. The failure of the Darien scheme had also made apparent the difficulties Scotland faced in pursuing colonial enterprises on its own.[119] In the hands of figures like William Paterson, the principal promoter of the Darien adventure, and of Daniel Defoe, acting as a political propagandist for union in England, these facts promoted not just a revival of interest in advancing some form of incorporating union for free trade between the two kingdoms, but arguments for the creation of a sovereign *imperium* between them.[120] The Treaty of Union of 1707 that resulted from these and other arguments, it has been said, 'turned Great Britain into the largest free-trade zone' in early modern Europe.[121]

Such an argument of probable cause, and of a consequent economic upturn sometime after 1707, has in recent times been confronted by new evidence of at least a partial recovery which was manifest before 1700.[122] The question remains unresolved. Yet it is clear that in the last quarter of the seventeenth century, there were already signs – resembling patterns of diversification and specialisation that had emerged in England and Wales – of a new diversity of ports in Scotland, as sectors of its long-established trade with the Baltic began to decline and its trade with France experienced repeated difficulties as a result of war. There was no direct replacement of these overseas markets for traditional commodities such as skins and hides by a substitute overseas commercial network in England. From the perspective of Scotland, what was happening was more complex, reflecting a shift in parts of the Scottish economy as a whole. This was reflected in the appearance of a significant number of small, specialised ports, often linked to a single industry, such as woollen cloth, linen, salt, coal, glass or iron. Some ports, such as Montrose, had begun to specialise in the coastal trade with England by the 1680s.[123] Grain was an increasingly prominent feature of this trade, especially out of east coast ports, such as the small north-east port of Banff.[124] Two further patterns, which were already present in Scotland in the decades before 1707, consolidated after the Union, again parallelling developments in England and Wales. Scottish trade with Ireland, much of it involving the export of coal, increased markedly.[125] The fastest growing sector, however, was transatlantic

[119] *Ibid.*, pp. 240, 244–56.

[120] Armitage, 'Scottish vision of empire', pp. 113–14; L. Dickey, 'Power, commerce, and natural law in Daniel Defoe's political writings, 1698–1707', in Robertson, ed., *Union for Empire*, pp. 75–87.

[121] Levack, *Formation of the British State*, p. 138.

[122] T. M. Devine, 'The Union of 1707 and Scottish development', *Scottish Economic and Social History*, 5 (1985), 23–40; Whatley, 'Economic causes and consequences of the Union', 150–81.

[123] Smout, *Scottish Trade*, p. 67.

[124] Dunbar, ed., *Sir William Burrell's Northern Tour*, p. 104.

[125] Devine and Jackson, eds., *Glasgow*, p. 75; Dunbar, ed., *Sir William Burrell's Northern Tour*, p. 57.

trade; by 1715 tobacco imports stood at 2 million lb per annum, a tenfold increase since the 1680s.[126]

Although no other sector came near to matching the performance of Scotland's tobacco trade in the years immediately following the Union, the picture after 1707 is nevertheless one of the increasing diversity and specialisation of Scottish, along with English and Welsh, ports, operating within the framework of a British free-trade zone which stretched, in effect, from the Elbe to the American colonies. With its birth, a new integrated system of ports and urban hierarchy became possible in the island of Great Britain, and indeed in the British Isles in general.

[126] Devine and Jackson, eds., *Glasgow*, pp. 75–6.

· 13 ·

Small market towns 1540–1700

ALAN DYER

ON MARKET days, the country came to town and the streets filled up - with buyers and sellers, cattle and sheep, cartloads of corn and bales of cloth; market places were packed with stalls, and the air was filled with the cries of frightened animals and the smell of dung. For many of the smallest market towns, this was the only day in the week when there was enough commercial bustle to make them look recognisably urban. Of course all pre-industrial towns were in some sense market towns, for all depended on public markets to supply themselves with food and raw materials, to bring in country people to deal in country products and so to patronise urban businesses, and to act as a focus for the broad spectrum of commercial and industrial activities which were the basis of the urban economy. However, for the purposes of this volume, London, larger towns, ports, leisure centres and other more specialised urban types have been assigned separate treatment, leaving this chapter to consider the life of the smaller and more nondescript inland settlements which formed the great majority of towns in this period. There were about 650 places with an operating market in England and Wales in the late sixteenth century, rising to nearly 800 a century later, and over 200 in Scotland. If we exclude perhaps ninety of this grand total because more appropriately described by some other label - provincial capital, county town, cathedral city, port - we are left with several hundred of these communities for which the term 'market town' sums up their essential character.

(i) SIZE AND DEFINITION

The upper and lower boundaries of this great class of settlement are impossible to draw with any precision. At the upper end there are larger market towns with perhaps 2,000 people in 1700, possessing a modest administrative role as the seat perhaps of one of the county quarter session meetings, or an unusual commercial

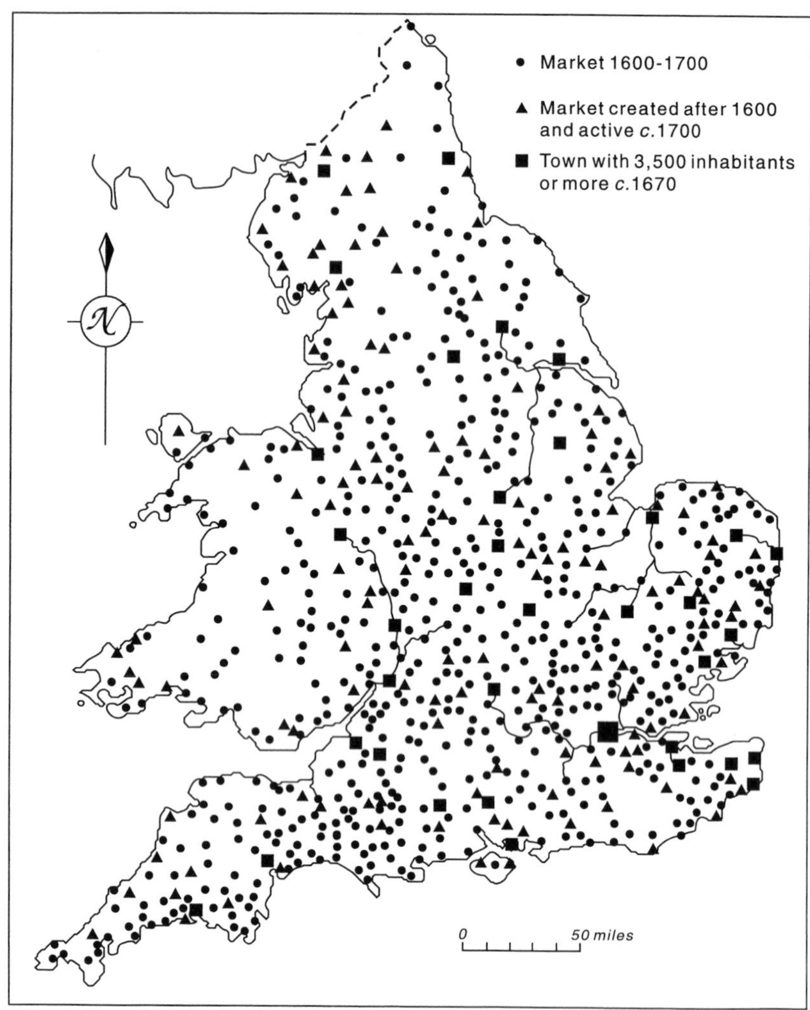

Map 13.1 Market towns of England and Wales (including large towns) 1600–1700

significance as a river port (or in Scotland a minor seaport) or major inns on an arterial road to London or Edinburgh, or an unusual concentration of industrial workers, most likely concerned with textiles. In each of these cases one should see a market town with extra functions added to it - but still a market town. Below this level are the majority of market towns, varying from thriving ones with perhaps 1,000 to 1,500 people in 1700 to those which merely serviced their immediate locality and had 800 or fewer inhabitants.

Although small by modern standards, these small towns were still considerably larger than the rural settlements which surrounded them: for instance in 1563 in the diocese of Canterbury, 171 of the 279 parishes had thirty households or less;[1] at five per household this would give us a majority of parishes (and certainly a majority of nucleated settlements) with less than 150 inhabitants. These country dwellers would find in a market town with a population of 700 a striking change of scale, and in those large parts of the country where nucleated villages were unusual and hamlets and individual farms the norm, the contrast would be all the greater. Most historians would agree that these very small markets are still to be described as *urban,* in that they were relatively large, nucleated settlements in which a majority of households supported themselves from non-agrarian activity. They also resembled larger towns in providing goods and services for the surrounding area, and possessed signs of a distinctive social structure and way of life, and possibly some administrative apparatus or cultural tradition which is distinguishable from the norm in the countryside. In Scotland it has been plausibly claimed that market centres with a population of less then 500 can often be regarded as urban, for even at this minimal size they would have contained 'a complete range of professional services, a merchant community and all the major branches of manufacturing'.[2] Indeed the majority of Scottish market centres at this date were probably even smaller than this modest figure.

The possession of a market is much the best way of distinguishing these small towns from large villages with diversified economies. For while it is very difficult to establish the sizes and occupational structures of many underdocumented settlements, published lists of market sites and crown grants of market charters do allow us to be fairly sure of the location and duration of public markets, which by definition indicate the existence of central places and in general demand a certain minimum level of commercial, craft and service activity before they can function adequately. However, there will inevitably be a proportion of the smallest settlements in which marketing was very limited and which had a considerable agrarian element in their economic structure; these might be termed more accurately 'market villages'. Two typical examples might be St David's and Newport in Pembrokeshire where in 1602 both markets were very small and held chiefly for foodstuffs on Sunday mornings, though both improved later in the century.[3] Unfortunately, it is impossible to distinguish such marginal cases from their more urbane competitors, especially as some will be in the process of further urbanisation; the best one can do is to suggest that the great majority of markets in England and Wales represented settlements which were truly, if modestly, urban, while there is a small but indefinable fringe which mixes urban and

[1] BL, Harleian MS 594, ff. 63r–84r.

[2] I. D. Whyte, 'The occupational structure of Scottish burghs in the late seventeenth century', in M. Lynch, ed., *The Early Modern Town in Scotland* (London, 1987), p. 239.

[3] H. Owen, ed., *The Description of Pembrokeshire by George Owen* (Cymmrodorion Record Series, 1, 1892), p. 141.

rural characteristics. In Scotland it was probably the case that a higher proportion of markets took place in settlements which cannot be readily accepted as 'urban' in a very meaningful sense of the word.[4]

It has been recently suggested that 'small towns' contained 54 per cent of the English urban population in 1700 but that the growth of these towns lagged behind that of the larger towns.[5] This study of small towns contains a number of larger towns which were more than mere market towns (such as cathedral cities and ports) and does not compare the performance of market towns with the countryside. By comparison we might take the Midlands [6] as a typical region: its market towns (defined by excluding the large commercial towns, administrative centres and Lincolnshire's ports) grew by 50 per cent between 1563 and the 1670s while the larger towns grew by almost exactly the same proportion. The 100 market towns of 1563 (126 in the 1670s) retained a stable 67–8 per cent of the urban population in settlements of a mean size of 863 in the sixteenth century and 1,032 a century later; these towns supplied about 13 per cent of the total population of the region in the 1670s, and possibly a little less in the sixteenth century.[7]

It is well worth pointing out that demographic growth is only one way of measuring development, and that an increasing population should not automatically be assumed to be synonymous with prosperity. Some market towns avoided the acquisition of large numbers of poor people and their demographic stability may reflect a rising per capita income and a measure of economic success. Stratford-on-Avon is a good example of this category, for its population stood at about 1,800 in both 1580 and 1730 (though it increased temporarily in the interim); yet this was a lively commercial centre for a large area with an industrial role and access to a river navigation; one can only conclude that the town controlled immigration with such care that its growing prosperity was not undermined by unnecessary demographic growth.[8] Frequently, such settlements remain unchallenged as the dominant urban centre for a specific locality over a period stretching from the twelfth century to the present day, and it seems unwise to disparage such modest but consistent success as 'urban failure' because it does not keep pace with the growth of industrialising settlements elsewhere.

[4] In 1692 it was reported that in the old-established and not particularly small burgh of Brechin, commercial activity was 'verie mean and small' and that there were only eight or ten retailers, selling mostly to their neighbours (I. D. Whyte, 'The growth of periodic market centres in Scotland 1600–1707', *Scottish Geographical Magazine*, 95 (1979), 21).

[5] P. Clark, 'Small towns in England 1550–1850: national and regional population trends', in P. Clark, ed., *Small Towns in Early Modern Europe* (Cambridge, 1995), pp. 90, 97.

[6] The region as defined in Chapter 2(d).

[7] The sources and assumptions of this survey are outlined above (Chapter 2(d)). Clearly the mere market towns kept up with their larger neighbours partly by increasing in number rather than in mean size.

[8] *VCH*, Warwickshire, III, pp. 222–5; A. Dyer, 'Crisis and resolution: government and society in Stratford, 1540–1640', in R. Bearman, ed., *The History of an English Borough* (Stroud, 1997), p. 91.

(ii) DISTRIBUTION AND NUMBERS

These hundreds of market towns were not distributed in an even, or an entirely predictable manner over the British countryside. In England and Wales an analysis of their distribution by counties in 1673 (see Table 13.1) shows that towns generally lay in market regions containing 60–100 square miles, which would suggest that they were 8–10 miles apart and that few country dwellers would have more than four or five miles to travel to a market. The medieval legal principle was that markets were entitled to a monopoly of an area 6 or 7 miles in radius, based on the assumption that peasants could be expected to spend one third of the day dealing and two-thirds travelling, and could reasonably walk twenty miles in a day.[9] This would give us a market area of 140 square miles which was in fact exceeded in our period in only five Welsh and two English counties. The more active markets would attract dealers from a wider area than this, as can be shown from the study of debt statements in probate records and other sources for towns such as Warwick,[10] but even here regular visitors uncommonly travelled more than ten or twelve miles. In Scotland, favoured Lowland areas near the eastern coast and estuaries were urbanised to an English level, but further to the north and west markets were still uncommon, and 18 per cent of the mainland still lay more than twelve miles from a market centre.[11]

We might expect that south-eastern England, economically advanced, fertile and servicing London's needs, would possess the densest network of markets, and this assumption is borne out by the example of counties such as Hertford, Bedford and Buckingham; yet the region contained shires which were far less urbanised, such as Surrey and Sussex; a complex of factors must explain this disparity, not least the proximity of London, areas of infertile down, heath or forest and the particular agrarian economy of the locality. Similarly, one can explain the paucity of market towns in the North and Wales, the regions which monopolise the bottom thirteen places in the table, in terms of economic backwardness, thin populations and large areas of upland and waste. Yet Lancashire and Cumberland, and Anglesey, Caernarvon and Pembroke in Wales, hit middling levels of urbanisation as measured in this way: here one must remember that trading in cereals gave rise to a closer pattern of market centres than did livestock dealing (since corn is heavy but animals are self-propelled) and that the constraints imposed by the topography of the Highland region will influence the number of minor urban centres to a far greater degree than in the Lowlands, where sheer distance is the crucial factor.

9 E. Lipson, *The Economic History of England* (London, 1945), vol. 1, pp. 238–9.

10 M. J. Kingman, 'Markets and marketing in Tudor Warwickshire: the evidence of John Fisher of Warwick and the crisis of 1586–87', *Warwickshire History*, 4 (1978), 16–28; A. Dyer, 'Warwickshire towns under the Tudors and Stuarts', *Warwickshire History*, 3 (1976–7), 122–35.

11 Whyte, 'Periodic market centres', 18.

Table 13.1 *Density of distribution of markets by English and Welsh counties (excluding Middlesex, and including larger towns)*

	County	Markets in 1673	Square miles per town
1	Hertford	17	37
2	Gloucester	28	45
3	Bedford	10	47
4	Buckingham	15	50
5	Dorset	20	50
6	Suffolk	29	51
7	Huntingdon	7	52
8	Somerset	31	52
9	Kent	31	53
10	Stafford	19	61
11	Warwick	16	61
12	Berkshire	12	63
13	Cornwall	21	63
14	Oxford	12	63
15	Worcester	11	64
16	Wiltshire	21	65
17	Lancashire	28	67
18	Leicester	12	69
19	Cambridge	7	70
20	Norfolk	29	71
21	Cheshire	14	73
22	Essex	21	73
23	Northampton	12	76
24	Rutland	2	76
25	Pembroke	8	77
26	Monmouth	7	78
27	Devon	32	81
28	Lincoln	31	86
29	Shropshire	15	90
30	Anglesey	3	92
31	Nottingham	9	94
32	Cumberland	16	95
33	Caernarvon	6	95
34	Hampshire	16	97
35	Sussex	15	98
36	Westmorland	8	99
37	Derby	10	101
38	Glamorgan	8	102
39	Hereford	8	105
40	Surrey	7	108

Table 13.1 (*cont.*)

	County	Markets in 1673	Square miles per town
41	Carmarthen	8	115
42	Yorkshire North	17	125
43	Durham	8	127
44	Yorkshire West	22	127
45	Flint	2	128
46	Montgomery	6	133
47	Yorkshire East	8	147
48	Denbigh	4	168
49	Cardigan	4	173
50	Brecon	4	183
51	Merioneth	3	220
52	Radnor	2	236
53	Northumberland	6	337

It is impossible to tell exactly how many market towns existed at the end of the middle ages. We know that many of the market creations of the optimistic, economically expansive period of the middle ages which ended in about 1300 led to failure, either soon after foundation or during the fourteenth and fifteenth centuries.[12] Many of these lost markets must have been chiefly engaged in small-scale dealing in food and not likely to encourage the growth of genuine urban businesses, so that we should see most of them as representing 'market villages' rather than the 'real' market towns of the kind which form the great majority of late sixteenth-century small towns. The period in which markets, whether rural or urban, were being reduced in number must have ended at some point between the mid-fifteenth century in some areas and the mid-sixteenth in others, but facts are hard to come by – the creation of new markets is usually well documented, but the slow process of attrition which leads to the extinction of failing markets, and still more the history of unofficial marketing, rarely makes an impact on the surviving record. What can be said is that by the first half of the sixteenth century it is possible to find examples of new markets being created – such as Sutton Coldfield (War.), Halstead (1562) and Waltham Abbey (1553, 1560) in Essex and Dursley (Glos.) – all of which became firmly established, but there are also a number of examples of attempted market creation which failed, such as Tollerton and Grinton in Yorkshire[13] or Princes Risborough in Buckinghamshire (1523, not recorded again until 1673) and of some established

[12] R. H. Britnell, *The Commercialisation of English Society 1000–1500* (Cambridge, 1993); C. Dyer, 'Market towns and the countryside in late medieval England', *Canadian Journal of History*, 31 (1996), 17–35.

[13] *VCH*, Yorkshire, North Riding, I, p. 238, II, p. 88.

markets mentioned by the topographer Leland in the 1530s – Whickham (Durham), Montacute (Somerset), Steeple Ashton (Wilts.), Wensley (Yorks.) which disappeared over the following decades.[14]

Probably the balance between loss and gain was about equal, and there was in any case a groundswell of change which was ever present and caused by local factors such as changes in road routes, or fires and other disasters. It seems likely that there was as yet no general demand for an expanded number of market towns, indicating that the increase in commercial farming and general agrarian prosperity, which is such a feature of the economy from the mid-sixteenth century onwards, may well have begun to enrich the existing market towns but had not yet proceeded so far as to call for the creation of new ones. But there is a significant feature in the influence of the London food market, which created commercial currents and pressures which must lie behind both the sixteenth-century elimination of uncompetitive markets in Essex and the creation of flourishing new ones, such as Hemel Hempstead (Herts.), founded in 1539 with a market place imposed on ploughed fields and rapidly prospering on the corn supply trade to the capital.[15]

During the course of the seventeenth century attempts to create market towns became more common: the process is clearly under way before the Civil Wars and during the last forty years of the century it becomes very significant (see Table 13.2). For England and Wales a highly reliable survey of 1673 allows us to measure the accumulated increase since 1588, which amounts to an extra seventy-seven markets, or a growth of 12 per cent, much of it recent, while over the next seventeen years a remarkable sixty-two new foundations had been made, so that the cumulative expansion during the course of the seventeenth century stands at about 22 per cent.[16] Some of these new foundations were inevitably speculative and competed with each other or existing centres and quickly failed. Some were wholly new and some were revived medieval foundations which had died out in the interim. Some will have succeeded without creating much more than a market village and it is clear that the expansion had come to a close by 1700 or thereabouts. But thirty years later[17] there were still 750 surviving markets, over 100 more than there had been in 1588. During the course of the eighteenth century the weakest market centres appear more clearly to be failing, yet as late as 1792 there were still 722,[18] (including some new ones in newly industrialised settlements), so that much

[14] J. Chandler, ed., *John Leland's Itinerary* (Stroud, 1993), pp. 156, 419, 502, 564.

[15] S. Yaxley, ed., *A History of Hemel Hempstead* (Hemel Hempstead, 1975), p. 42.

[16] 1588 data from William Smith, *Particular Description of England*, ed. H. B. Wheatley and L. Ashbee (London, 1878), pp. 6 *et seq.*; Wales in 1602 from Owen, ed., *The Description of Pembrokeshire*, pt i, pp. 140–1, pt iii, *passim*; and E. Pritchard, ed., *The Taylors Cussion* (London, 1906), vol. i, pp. 74–82. 1673 from R. Blome, *Britannia . . .* (London, 1673); 1690 from J. Adams, *Index Villaris* (London, 1690). [17] T. Cox, *Magna Britannia et Hibernia . . .* (London, 1720–31).

[18] PP 1888 LIII, Royal Commission on Market Rights and Tolls, First Report.

Table 13.2 *Changes in market numbers (England and Wales)*

	1588	1673	1690	1720s
South-East				
Bedford	10	10	9	10
Berkshire	12	12	12	12
Buckingham	11	14	15	15
Essex	20	21	27	28
Hertford	17	17	18	18
Kent	20	31	29	30
Middlesex	3	4	6	4
Oxford	10	12	12	15
Surrey	6	7	10	9
Total	109	128	138	141
East Anglia				
Cambridge	6	7	8	9
Huntingdon	5	7	7	6
Norfolk	30?	29	35	31
Suffolk	26	29	32	30
Total	67?	72	82	76
South				
Dorset	21	20	21	22
Hampshire	19	16	24	16
Sussex	19	15	18	16
Wiltshire	22	21	21	24
Total	81	72	84	78
South-West				
Cornwall	21	21	26	27
Devon	36	32	39	40
Somerset	31?	31	35	30
Total	88?	84	100	97
South Midlands				
Gloucester	23	28	28	26
Hereford	8	8	8	8
Northampton	10	12	13	11
Warwick	15	16	16	17
Worcester	10	11	11	11
Total	66	75	76	73
North Midlands				
Cheshire	13	14	13	12
Derby	8	10	12	9

Table 13.2 (*cont.*)

	1588	1673	1690	1720s
North Midlands (cont.)				
Leicester	10	12	11	10
Lincoln	29	31	32	25
Nottingham	8	9	9	9
Rutland	2	2	2	2
Shropshire	12	15	15	15
Staffordshire	13	19	19	18
Total	95	112	113	100
North				
Cumberland	9	16	14	14
Durham	6	8	9	9
Lancaster	16	28	30	26
Northumberland	5	6	12	11
Westmorland	4	8	8	8
Yorkshire	44?	48	50	48?
Total	84?	114	123	116?
	1602	1673	–	1720s
Wales	54	64	67?	69
	1588	1673	1690	1720s
All	644	721	783	750
Change (per cent)		+12.0	+8.6	−4.2
		1588–1690 = +21.6 per cent		

of the seventeenth-century expansion still survived and cannot be written off as a temporary phenomenon.

In Scotland there was a similar movement, in part a catching-up process in a country hitherto underurbanised: while there were over 100 new foundations between 1600 and 1660, the Restoration period saw a remarkable wave of market creation with the impressive total of 346 new burghs and market centres licensed (though not necessarily established) in the period 1660–1707.[19] Unfortunately, we can make no direct comparison with the situation in England because no contemporary Scottish source provides us with a general survey of the markets actually in operation at any one time.[20] Thus we are dependent for

[19] Whyte, 'Periodic market centres', 13–26.

[20] J. Forbes, *The Whole Yearly Faires and Weekly Mercats of this Ancient Kingdom of Scotland . . .*

Scotland on lists of grants, acknowledging that many never came into existence, or died out quite quickly, and that they were generally very small even by English standards; there were also some locations in which unlicensed and so unrecorded markets took place. But it must be true that there was a very considerable expansion in the total number of Scottish market towns in the course of the seventeenth century, and that their distribution spread from a concentration in the southern Lowlands and east coast areas further inland and into the Highlands and Islands.[21]

What lay behind this surge of market creation in later seventeenth-century Britain? The fundamental prosperity of the rural economy must lie at the base of it – a point to which we shall return below. If we see commercialised farming, with its necessary demand for access to sophisticated marketing structures, as a late medieval development in south-eastern England which slowly spread to the rest of the country, then we might expect some of the new markets to have been created in the South-East before the date of our earliest survey in 1588, and the greatest impact of the movement to be felt later, and in the more remote parts of the west and north of the Highland zone. In these regions country people were still not in the habit of visiting market towns late in the seventeenth century, for the indefatigable Celia Fiennes observed that in Derbyshire 'the common people know not above two or three mile from their home' while 'the ordinary people both in these parts of Yorkshire and in the northern parts can scarce tell you how far it is to the next place' for 'they live much at home, and scarce ever go two or ten mile from thence, especially the women'.[22] In Cumbria the factors are said to be the greater security and trade resulting from the union between England and Scotland, the rise of a yeoman class in the countryside and the importance of wool and cloth marketing.[23] This supposition is borne out by the statistics, which indicate that the greatest growth in numbers took place in Wales and the North, and in such marginal English counties as Shropshire and Staffordshire, and in these regions new markets continued to come into being in the eighteenth century too. In Scotland we can see a similar development as the market economy pushed into the more remote areas of the north and west which had never known it before.[24]

We may assume that in these regions subsistence farming was giving way to production for a local market, and then local marketing to interregional commerce. Other factors were also at work, for improved roads (and rivers) in the

(Aberdeen, 1684), appears to be the sole (inadequate) approach to such a survey; I thank Dr R. Tyson of Aberdeen University for this reference. [21] Whyte, 'Periodic market centres'.

[22] J. Hillaby, ed., *The Journeys of Celia Fiennes* (London, 1983), pp. 115, 122.

[23] R. Millward, 'The Cumbrian town between 1600 and 1800', in C. W. Chalklin and M. A. Havinden, eds., *Rural Change and Urban Growth 1500–1800* (London, 1974), pp. 206–10.

[24] R. A. Houston and I. D. Whyte, eds., *Scottish Society 1500–1800* (Cambridge, 1989), pp. 7–8; Whyte, 'Periodic market centres', 17–19.

seventeenth century accelerated these processes and encouraged more people to visit a local market and to travel further to it; but the same factor enabled the larger markets to undermine the smaller by extending their effective hinterlands. Larger markets had the great advantage of promising lower prices for purchasers and a higher likelihood of making a sale to vendors. The growth in the total quantity of marketing going on in the economy has to be set against these competitive forces in assessing the prospects of the smaller markets. The growth in disposable income during the period increased shop customers as a consumer society established itself in the seventeenth century and prosperity provided the leisure required to allow travel from home. This brought farmers' wives into town shops to buy fashionable fabrics or a clock, and tea and coffee and the china in which to sip it. While the growth in demand for marketing was spreading northward, more sophisticated marketing strategies and increased competition between markets was spreading outwards from the South-East, so that we find the market town networks of the South often losing almost as many centres as they gained, a process evident in counties such as Sussex, Surrey and Hampshire.[25] We should see this process of commercialisation as an ambiguous benefit to the smaller market towns, for it could lead to the elimination of weaker centres as well as the creation of new markets. It would seem that before about 1700 the net effect of these two opposed trends was to increase market numbers and in the eighteenth century it led to a reduction, but one should not assume from this that the market town was in some way 'in decline', for the smaller number of strengthened market towns remained for many years a major element in the urban structure of all regions.

(iii) THE ECONOMIC FUNCTIONS OF MARKET TOWNS: MARKETS AND FAIRS

An understanding of the basic economic role played by the market town in its locality is essential to an appreciation of its significance. Its existence depended on supplying country people with those goods and services which they could not find in their villages. The market allowed them to dispose of their surplus produce for cash which was then available to pay rents and taxes and make purchases. With the expansion of commercialised farming with its intrinsic specialisation, surpluses grew ever larger, creating a matching need for the importing of agricultural produce to areas of countryside which were no longer self sufficient – corn to pastoral areas and meat and cheese to cereal growing regions for instance. This principle is well illustrated in the case of Shaftesbury (Dorset) where a commentary on a map of 1615 states

[25] A. Dyer, 'Market towns in Southern England 1500–1700', *SHist.*, 1 (1979), 123–34.

> It has to the west, south-west and north-west a deep country full of pasture, yielding plenty of well-fed beeves, muttons and milch kine, and to the east, south-east and north-east is a high champion country, yielding store of corn, sheep and wool, so the town is made a great vent for the commodities on either part. It lying between them and either for the most part wanting others help, their resort thither do make a very great market on the seventh day of the week.[26]

These exchanges usually took place over a limited distance, since distinct farming regions were usually not particularly large, but in addition to these flows, market towns acted as channels for a much broader and long-distance trade between larger regions, such as the flow of corn and malt which passed from the barley-growing South and East up to the pastoral North and West. To this must be added the long-range trade created by the demand of large towns for food; Newcastle was importing Norfolk corn in exchange for coal by the later sixteenth century, and Bristol drew dairy produce from South Wales and corn from the valley of the upper Severn. This trade is generally badly documented and with only two English provincial towns having populations of more than 20,000 in 1700 the long-range effect must be limited; in Scotland, Edinburgh must have had a similar influence, judging by the highly urbanised nature of its hinterland.[27] But as some regions became industrialised they generated a demand for foodstuffs which must been larger than that of any single provincial city – Defoe was impressed by the supplies which the flourishing West Riding cloth towns drew from as far away as Cheshire and Warwickshire (cheese), Lancashire (cattle) and Lincolnshire (corn).

For most of this period it is London which represents the dominant food market and the largest and most concentrated flows of agricultural produce were heading for the capital, whether cheese from Cheshire, cereals from much of south-eastern England or cattle from Wales and the North. The involvement of the market towns lay in channelling this tide by acting as collecting (and distributive) centres. Cattle and other farm stock were often traded through fairs which might be rural in location, though the skins and leather into which they converted represented a basic urban commodity. But corn was heavy, bulky, easily spoiled and in consistent weekly demand, so that we find market towns as the funnel through which farm surpluses were supplied to the middlemen, and again possibly as points at which these bulk consignments were milled or loaded into barges. Between twenty and forty miles from London there lay a ring of market towns which acted as collecting points for London dealers – Farnham in the south, the biggest of all, might well have seen 10,000 tons of wheat in a year, and by its peak in the early eighteenth century volume could have exceeded

26 J. Hutchins, *The History and Antiquities of the County of Dorset*, 3rd edn (London, 1868), vol. III, p. 7.

27 M. Lynch, 'Urbanisation and urban networks in seventeenth century Scotland: some further thoughts', *Scottish Economic and Social History*, 12 (1992), 24–39.

1,000 tons at a single market, while at Henley-on-Thames as many as 300 cart loads (say as many tons) passed through on a good day.[28] Bedford sent corn by river to the coast for export and by wagon to Hitchin and Hertford where it was milled and sent forward to the capital.

The open market was an institution under threat in this period. Private dealing under cover of the inns which surrounded the market place was of concern to authority, which was frightened by the consequent loss of control, but the trend could be seen as strengthening the market by compensating for its greatest weakness, the British climate. But sale by sample, and dealing at the farm, were much more serious threats, and must have substantially eroded the strength of the market town by the eighteenth century. However, the marketing of livestock has remained in its traditional form into the twentieth century. The urban shop represented another sort of threat – open every weekday, displaying a wider range of goods in a more pleasing environment than the market stall and promising the evolution of shopping from a chore to a leisure pursuit. But it was not until the eighteenth century that the modern shop had developed very extensively, and then only in major towns.

The market place was not of course the sole preserve of the country visitor. Town businesses relied on it for the supply of raw materials of all sorts, for most crafts and industries of the time were based upon the processing of natural materials found in the locality. Skins and leather figure prominently here, also barley for conversion into malt; wood and sawn timber, wax and tallow, hay and coal, wool, yarn and flax, lead, iron and other metals were all required. Many traders used the market for both buying and selling, tanners buying skins and selling processed leather or weavers buying yarn and selling cloth. And of course townsmen relied on the market for the food which their concentration on trade and industry made them incapable of providing for themselves. Many townsmen did produce some food of their own, using gardens and the common fields which surrounded many market towns (and much larger ones) and urban pig keeping was very common. But town butchers and bakers relied on the market to buy in livestock and cereals, and the poor bought corn in the market too. Butcher's meat in most towns was only obtainable from the market, since the butchers had no other retail outlet than their stalls, though bakers did have shops which were open on a daily basis. Farmers' wives sold butter, cheese and poultry, often under roofed market crosses and a particular development of the seventeenth century was the growing supply of market garden produce, as vegetables such as carrots and cabbage became much more important in the urban diet; no town shopkeeper stocked these goods, except possibly the huxters, often women, about whom we know little. Many country people were also reliant on town markets

[28] J. Aubrey, *The Natural History and Antiquities of the County of Surrey* (London, 1719), p. 347; D. Defoe, *A Tour through England and Wales* (London, 1928), vol. I, p. 142; Blome, *Britannia*.

for foodstuffs, either because they were absorbed in industrial activity, as in mining or clothing districts, or because of seasonal shortages, which must explain the Devonshire yeoman William Honneywell buying cheeses and a shoulder of veal in Chudleigh market in 1602.[29]

Markets were carefully regulated by their owners, usually the town government or a landowner. Relatively few market towns had a square capable of accommodating the whole market, and so most of the main streets in the central area were taken over on market day, and a frontage on to a market space was so valuable that some of the bitterest disputes in towns at this date centred on attempts to relocate specific market areas. All but the smallest were subdivided into separate sections, often to an elaborate degree, with each commodity assigned a specific location, possibly indicated with a sign or marker, or a time sequence, indicated by a bell, as represented by Preston where the Saturday market began with linen at dawn and then moved through yarn, bread, fish, butter and cheese, with horses replacing cattle, and hides and skins giving way to barley and beans after 10 a.m.[30]

Markets required extensive administration and their own courts to deal with both commercial disputes and the many infringements of the elaborate regulations concerned with the protection of the consumer. A hierarchy of officials was appointed to operate this system, often based in upper rooms of market halls. These buildings were common in all but the smallest market places, and they represented the only conspicuous structure which expressed the civic pride of the community, and were consequently often built in a pretentious style.[31] Abingdon's arched market hall with the town hall on its first floor was judged by Celia Fiennes to be 'the finest in England, its all of free stone and very lofty', while the much older Chichester cross was 'like a Church or greate arch, its pretty large and pirramydy form with severall Carvings'.[32] Here the official weights and measures were kept, and matters which required general dissemination were publicised, whether royal proclamations or the exposure of malefactors in pillory or stocks. Markets also represented a major social occasion for the locality, in which lengthy visits to inn and alehouse were as important as the dealings in square or shop.

Fairs were held in market towns relatively infrequently – often only once or twice in the year – but were an important adjunct to the market: if the market concentrated a week's business into a few hours, the fair compressed a year's activity into several days. Here were sold commodities available so sparsely during the year that a satisfactory level of business could only be reached by this

29 'A Devonshire yeoman's diary', *The Antiquary*, 26 (1892), 254–9.

30 R. Kuerden, *Brief Description of the Borough and Town of Preston*, ed. J. Taylor (Preston, 1818).

31 R. Tittler, *Architecture and Power* (Oxford, 1991); 202 buildings in 178 towns are gazetteered, though there may have been more which are not documented.

32 Hillaby, ed., *Journeys of Fiennes*, pp. 56–7.

means – such as horses – and goods which were only available at certain times of year, such as hops and cheese. Much dealing went on at a wholesale level and involved people from a much wider area than customarily attended the market. Fairs could last for several days – the Elizabethan commercial almanacs list 304 (about a third of the total) which lasted between ten and fifteen days.[33] Most market town fairs were shorter than this. In Stuart Leicestershire, Leicester held five annual fairs, Ashby four, Hallaton and Melton Mowbray three and the other market towns one or two.[34] Fairs provided a much wider variety of goods than markets and were used by countryfolk to stock up on basics such as cloth or saltfish, and involved the suspension of the usual urban prohibition of 'foreign-bought, foreign-sold' by allowing non-townsmen to sell to each other. They were also a major social event for both town and locality, with much bigger crowds than would come in for market day,[35] bent on pleasure and meeting friends, so that nearby villages might be virtually deserted; the impact of this mass of potential customers on all town traders, but especially those dispensing hospitality, was very great.

The principal advantage to the businesses which distinguish the economies of small towns from those of their surrounding villages was the provision of customers – indeed in smaller market towns little business seems to have been done except on market day. William Stout's experience as an apprentice ironmonger in the Lancaster of the 1680s was that 'I was mostly employed in the shop in weekdays in making up goods for the market day' but 'three or four of us [were] fully employed every market day in delivering out goods'; smaller towns must have seen even less trade between markets.[36] Town traders took stalls in the market or placed one outside their shop, so that the market place was informally extended to include the principal shops of the town, which of necessity faced on to the market place and main streets leading to it. Inns and alehouses provided essential refreshment and leisure facilities to those who had travelled far, and for one day in the week even the smaller market towns functioned as true urban centres.

(iv) ECONOMIC FUNCTIONS OF MARKET TOWNS: OCCUPATIONS

The traders to be found in a typical market town can be seen as belonging to six main groups. First, the distributive traders sold goods which were imported from

33 M. T. Hodgen, 'Fairs of Elizabethan England', *Economic Geography*, 18 (1942), 389–400.

34 W. Burton, *Description of Leicestershire* (London, 1622), p. 4.

35 Leland noted that the fair at Stratford-on-Avon was 'a thing of very great concourse of people for a two or three days' (L. Toulmin Smith, ed., *The Itinerary of John Leland* (London, 1906–8; repr., 1964), vol. II, p. 27).

36 J. D. Marshall, ed., *The Autobiography of William Stout of Lancaster 1665–1752* (Manchester, 1967), pp. 79–80.

the outside world; those principally involved here are the mercer, who sold fine fabrics such as satins and velvets, the draper, who stocked the various woollen cloths and linen produced in Britain, the grocer who sold imported edible luxuries such as sugar and spices, and the haberdasher whose stock comprised a miscellany of sewing and housewives requirements, and possibly hats too. These trades were often combined, most commonly by the mercer, so that this range of goods would be available in even the smaller market town, but often in establishments which resembled a general store rather than the specialist shops which are a feature of larger towns. These trades required a good deal of capital, but produced the largest profits, so they supply a large proportion of the wealthiest traders in most towns, and are prominently represented among the ruling elite.

The second group is the artisan shopkeeper who both manufactured goods in his workshop and sold them in his shop; indeed, the two were often indistinguishable. There were always a few textile workers in most towns, weavers most commonly, and in the cloth-producing regions many towns contained large numbers of weavers and the craftsmen who finished this cloth, prominently fullers, shearmen or dyers; leather workers were everywhere, tanners and whittawers or curriers who made the material and shoemakers, saddlers, glovers, pointmakers, girdlers and the like who worked it up into finished goods; wood workers included coopers (who made the ubiquitous barrels which were in such demand for storage and transport purposes), and metalworkers such as smiths, ironmongers and pewterers. Thirdly, there were suppliers of food and drink, an essential feature of even the smallest market town; butchers, brewers and bakers comprised most of them, with the addition of a few fishmongers. Many supplied the countryside as well as the town and in some places they travelled to other towns to trade at their markets.

The fourth group provided services and included the professions such as lawyers and doctors, but also the innkeepers who were increasing in numbers and status in this period, and the tailors and barbers who were among the more numerous and poorer of these tradesmen. Alehouse keepers were very numerous, but this was usually a part-time occupation. Fifth came the building workers who often operated from the countryside and were less a feature of small towns than large ones, and the sixth group comprised the miscellaneous trades which defy classification and were again less common in smaller market towns with their less specialised trade structure, but maltmakers were widespread, especially in appropriate locations, though this was often a part-time occupation.

We can see this occupational structure in operation in Gloucestershire in 1608 where a unique muster survey lists the occupations of the adult males in the county.[37] Tradesmen are common in the countryside, especially textile workers in the clothing districts; and weavers, carpenters, smiths and a few tailors can be

[37] J. Smith, *Men and Armour for Gloucestershire in 1608* (Gloucester, 1980).

found throughout the countryside. In the larger market towns such as Cirencester and Tewkesbury (each with about 2,700 people) can be found not only the basic traders – mercers, butchers, bakers, tailors – in substantial numbers, but also a range of more specialised businesses not found in smaller towns, such as the apothecary, vintner, hatter, bookbinder and scrivener in the total of fifty-four separate occupations recorded in Cirencester, and the pewterer, cutlers, fishmonger, stationer, papermakers and saltpetreman found in Tewkesbury to a total of seventy-one[38] distinct occupations. In the smaller market towns we find a much more limited and basic range of trades: Chipping Sodbury, with few more than 500 people (and perhaps 115 households) can show eighty tradesmen in twenty-two separate occupations, including three mercers as its only distributive traders, four bakers, two butchers, twenty-four leather workers and twenty-three textile craftsmen of various kinds; modest though this occupational structure may be by comparison with the larger towns, this little town was still very urban by comparison with the villages around it in its domination by trade and craft and the variety of its occupations. Some perspective may be supplied by the village of Horton which had no market but developed one after 1660 and so could be expected to show a higher level of urban trades than the average village – yet amongst its fifty-five adult men can be found a mere ten tradesmen, of whom only the two tanners, two butchers and one tucker (fuller) could be considered as additional to the usual village occupations.

The image presented above is of a typical market town, but many of them departed from this norm by developing specialisms of various kinds. This allowed them to cater for customers living beyond their restricted market area, thus enriching and enlarging the town beyond its expected level. This phenomenon was already present by the sixteenth century, but it had developed strongly by the later seventeenth century, as revealed by the details given in Blome's *Britannia* (1673) (see pp. 748–9). The commonest specialism was the cloth industry, whether in Gloucestershire or Devon, Suffolk, Essex or the West Riding, producing textiles for other parts of Britain or for export. This was an unstable trade, liable to lose its markets in both the long and the short term, yet levels of employment and prosperity in these towns could be higher than average too. The Oxfordshire market town of Witney (population *c.* 1,200) specialised in blankets, and in the late seventeenth century had at least sixty blanket-makers with 150 looms and employment for up to 3,000 in the town and surrounding countryside.[39] Textile manufacture often involved the rapid transfer of part-finished goods between artisans – thus in Leeds the weavers sold their cloth,

[38] Shrewsbury, a major regional centre, could show only eighty-eight occupations in 1664, an indication of the relative sophistication of these larger Gloucestershire market towns: N. J. Shorthouse, 'A study in urban growth: the case of Shrewsbury 1660–1730' (MSc Econ thesis, University of Wales, 1980), pp. 20–4.

[39] R. Plot, *The Natural History of Oxfordshire* (Oxford, 1677), p. 278.

often only one piece at a time, in a cloth market which operated twice per week between 7 and 8.30 a.m. (and in virtual silence) and in Preston the yarn market operated in the evening. In both cases the timing was clearly designed to minimise any interruption to the working day.[40] Not only did the towns themselves prosper from the industrial activity, but they also acquired an enhanced role as market centres since in most clothing districts the surrounding countryside was deeply involved in the more labour-intensive aspects of the industry, such as spinning and weaving – Celia Fiennes saw in Norfolk 'lanes where you meete the ordinary people knitting 4 or 5 in a company under the hedges'.[41] This left the towns to concentrate on the more lucrative and skilled finishing, organising and marketing stages. Defoe noted that Warrington had a great linen market 'all made in the neighbourhood of the place', while Wrexham supplied similar central services to the Welsh flannel industry.[42] At the same time, the town had to supply necessities to industrialised country dwellers who had more cash but less locally produced food than was usual: in Taunton, set in the Somerset clothing district, the great Saturday market was served by the remarkable number of 140 butchers in the 1630s.[43]

Other forms of industry could be found in the metalworking districts of the West Midlands and in Sheffield: here until well on into the seventeenth century industrial production was organised around market town small-scale craftsmen, often reliant on the town market for raw materials and the sale of part-finished and completed goods, whether Walsall's metalwork for horse harness or Birmingham's and Sheffield's edge tools and knives.[44] The making of pewter was more widespread but becoming more concentrated in towns such as Wigan[45] while leather processing and manufacture was a very common specialism in the Midlands and pastoral western Britain where the supply of animal skins was abundant.[46] Large towns with industrial specialisms often were able to devote a higher proportion of their workforce to manufacture and probably few market towns could rival this degree of specialism because of their restricted access to distant markets. But activities of this kind are the principal means by which market towns grew beyond the necessary limitations of their basic function; until the eighteenth century saw the growing concentration of industrial activity in a limited number of locations, market towns could be seen as the seat of a very significant proportion of the total manufacturing activity of the country.

It would, however, be possible to exaggerate the role of industry in these small

[40] Defoe, *Tour*, II, pp. 205–6; Kuerden, *Preston*, p. 7.

[41] Hillaby, ed., *Journeys of Fiennes*, pp. 179–80.

[42] Defoe, *Tour*, II, pp. 75, 259.

[43] E. H. Bates, ed., *The Particular Description of Somerset by John Gerard, 1633* (Somerset Record Society, 15, 1900), pp. 55–6.

[44] M. B. Rowlands, *Masters and Men* (Manchester, 1975).

[45] T. C. Barker and J. Hatcher, *A History of British Pewter* (London, 1974).

[46] L. Clarkson, 'The leather crafts in Tudor and Stuart England', *Agricultural History Review*, 14 (1960), 23–49.

towns, for in many of them there was a considerable agricultural element in their economies, not only in the sense of full-time farmers based on the edges of the town, but also in part-time dabbling in farming by many tradesmen, though this seems to have dwindled as our period progressed, perhaps because it became easier to make an acceptable full-time living from regular urban occupations. Service activities were also very common, most notably the supply of refreshment and accommodation by the inns and alehouses; they were especially concentrated in the towns which lined the main roads with their ever-growing traffic, such as Daventry, 'which subsists chiefly by the great concourse of travellers on the old Watling-street Way', or Grantham, which 'lying on the great northern road is famous, as well as Stamford, for abundance of very good inns'.[47] Other small towns had developed as leisure centres, such as Westerham in Kent which was by the early eighteenth century 'full of gentry, and consequently of good company'.[48]

(v) GOVERNMENT AND ADMINISTRATION IN MARKET TOWNS

One of the distinguishing features of larger towns is their complex systems of government and administration, shown most clearly in those towns with a long history of constitutional development in the middle ages culminating in the acquisition of shire status by the sixteenth century. Market towns had much simpler governmental structures and their constitutional maturity was often not achieved before the early modern period. We may for convenience divide market town governments into two broad classes, the incorporated and the non-incorporated. Incorporated towns resembled the major cities in having acquired a series of royal charters which provided them with a measure of self-governing independence from the administration of both the crown and the shire, involving the setting up of a council of some kind with annually elected officials, a source of income and a system of courts. In the case of the unincorporated towns, the governmental apparatus was much simpler, dependence on outside powers was greater and administration was centred on an elaborated version of the manorial courts which controlled many villages. But there are a surprising number of towns which managed a hybrid status between these two systems by developing pseudo-corporations which gave a more sophisticated form of government without the formal backing of a charter of incorporation. Very little scholarly attention has been paid in recent years to these themes, so that it is not easy to develop well-founded generalisations in a field dominated by great individual variation from town to town.

Incorporated towns represented a minority of market towns, but they

[47] Defoe, *Tour*, II, pp. 86, 103. [48] *Ibid.*, I, p. 156.

included many of the more important ones. In all, some 218 grants of incorporation were made by the crown to places in England and Wales,[49] and if one excludes rotten boroughs without markets and the major towns (including major county centres, ports and cathedral cities), we are left with over 150 market towns with these relatively sophisticated forms of government. We might thus expect about a quarter of the smaller towns in an average county to have acquired a charter of incorporation, but there were substantial regional variations here: Oxfordshire with four out of eleven and Cheshire with three from fourteen were typical but some areas possessed an unusually high concentration, most notably the South-West, with Devon's twelve and Cornwall with even more; by contrast the North and some southern counties such as Bedfordshire or Cambridgeshire were markedly short of them. Chartered self-government was acquired in a similarly irregular chronological pattern, for the granting of charters owed something to the growing size and self-confidence of the more successful market towns, but much more to two processes.

The first was the consequence of the Reformation, and in particular the dissolution of the monasteries, which enabled towns which had been dominated by a great monastic house, such as Reading, Romsey and St Albans, to achieve the self-government which had been denied to them by medieval monastic power. A group of towns which was closely related were those on bishops' estates which had been similarly repressed, such as Lichfield and Banbury. The dissolution of the guilds and chantries in 1548 gravely damaged traditional small-scale governing mechanisms in many small towns, making incorporation essential to preserve existing activities; the result was a great wave of charters between 1540 and the earlier years of Elizabeth's reign which accounts for approaching half of our new town governments. The second factor was the pressure on the crown from a number of directions (most importantly local landowners) for more borough seats in the House of Commons, seats which were often given as part of incorporation charters; over 130 new seats were created during the sixteenth century alone.[50] An agreement that the size of the Commons should be fossilised led to the almost complete cessation of grants of incorporation after 1688, leaving those towns which had developed ambitions of self-government after this date to improvise or await the municipal reforms of the nineteenth century.

We may get a better idea of the nature of chartered government in a smaller town by looking at a typical example, Banbury. This major Oxfordshire market town had a population of perhaps 1,300 people in the early seventeenth century[51] and had been controlled by the bishop of Lincoln who appointed a bailiff to run the town, held courts, administered the market and owned lucrative mills and much urban property. The interests of the townsmen were probably represented

[49] M. Weinbaum, *The Incorporation of Boroughs* (Manchester, 1937), pp. 126–37.

[50] J. Loach, *Parliament under the Tudors* (Oxford, 1991), p. 35.

[51] A. Beesley, *The History of Banbury . . .* (London, 1841), p. 210.

by the Guild of St Mary, which supported an almshouse. In 1547 the bishop lost his property to the crown and the guild was dissolved, so that in 1554 the town was granted self-government through a charter of incorporation. This created a governing body consisting of an upper house of twelve aldermen and a lower one of twelve capital burgesses, all presided over by a bailiff; a civil court was created for claims under £5 in value and the new corporation took over the manorial court leet and used it to regulate minor matters.

A further charter in 1608 modified this structure by renaming the bailiff as a mayor, fusing the twelve aldermen and six of the capital burgesses into a new common council but representing the townsmen at large by a new body of thirty assistants with vague powers, though they could share in the annual election of the mayor. An expanded number of justices of the peace was created, and with them a recorder who would act as a senior legal adviser. The charter also added a wool market to the traditional markets and fairs held by the town, and forbade trade by those not formally created freemen by the council. As usual, the charter named the first members of the corporation with tenure for life and gave them the right to fill future vacancies by cooption. The activities of the government were financed by a variety of minor dues and fines, the rents from houses and land and also from the profits of the markets and fairs, which often exceeded £30 in the later sixteenth century.[52] A variety of petty officials were elected annually to carry out routine activities under the corporation's authority, including tithingmen, constables and searchers and sealers of leather; in a town of such modest size, many of the poorer but self-employed townsmen would have held minor office and a high proportion of the better-off would have joined the corporation, an assumption supported by the fact that before 1640 men were first appointed to the corporation when aged in their mid-thirties and often progressed to be mayor by their mid to late forties.[53] All of this was characteristic of the way in which larger market towns were governed.

In the majority of market towns, however, no chartered incorporation existed and government was carried on by other means. One not uncommon device was to create by unofficial means a governing body which represented the natural elite of the community. In the case of Burford, another Oxfordshire market town with a population of around 1,200 in the seventeenth century, the history of the governing body shows the way in which a town could develop its own apparatus of government without crown grants.[54] On the basis of the manorial court, guild and the trustees of charities the townsmen had created by the sixteenth century a governing body which closely resembled a legal corporation with attendant petty officials, working through the manorial court, a borough court primarily for civil cases and control of markets and fairs. Most of this structure had been

[52] J. S. W. Gibson and E. R. C. Brinkworth, *Banbury Corporation Records: Tudor and Stuart* (Banbury Historical Society, 15, 1977), pp. 45–7. [53] *Ibid.*, pp. 271 *et seq.*

[54] R. H. Gretton, *The Burford Records* (Oxford, 1920).

developed by default, and when challenged in 1620 by the first effective lord of the manor the town had recently experienced, the townsmen's pseudo-corporation collapsed; however, a representative body continued as the trustee of charitable bequests, and the town acquired its own justices of the peace in the 1650s.

There are other examples of town government by non-chartered bodies drawing their power in essence from the fact that they represented the will of the natural governing elite. Some towns claimed to be corporations by prescription, that is by long exercise of these rights, and so could hold property and behave very much as smaller chartered incorporations could. In Clitheroe the annual meeting of the court leet jury could be repeatedly adjourned so that what was in effect a town council could meet regularly during the year, manage public property, admit freemen and audit the bailiff's accounts, though the lord of the manor retained control of markets and fairs.[55] In other towns, groups of trustees bought the market rights and with them control over a vital economic institution and an income from tolls and dues, as happened in Bicester,[56] to create a pseudo-corporation.

The development of these independent and partly invisible town governments often depended on a weak lord of the manor; when an effective lord eventually appeared, he was often motivated by the wish to challenge the townsmen's growing income from market tolls, as in Farnham and Petersfield; the law courts usually found in the lord's favour, since the town had little legal documentation to support its case.[57] Towns with these pretentious but essentially manorial governments often found that their ambitions were limited by the absence of legal sanctions – Lewes regularly imposed modest general taxes on its householders (a difficult feat even for chartered towns) but found it difficult to compel defaulters to pay up.[58] Part of the power of these bodies was derived from the social prestige of their members, the urban elite, or the 'society of the wealthier and discreeter sort of the townsmen' as they were described in Lewes.[59] In many cases these governments found it possible to carry out many of the activities embraced by chartered towns – holding property and using the revenues for the supply of public amenities, regulating the use of public space, controlling poor and anti-social members of their communities and by issuing licences to trade, controlling the urban economy in a way similar to the freeman system operated in corporations. The three-weekly courts which many possessed could settle petty civil and even criminal cases,[60] but they were all limited by their

55 W. S. Weeks, 'Clitheroe in the seventeenth century', *Transactions of the Lancashire and Cheshire Antiquarian Society*, 41 (1924), 44–78. 56 *VCH*, Oxfordshire VI, p. 37.

57 *VCH*, Surrey, II, pp. 585–8; *VCH*, Hampshire, III, pp. 113–15.

58 L. F. Salzman, ed., *The Town Book of Lewes 1542–1701* (Sussex Record Society, 48, 1945–6), pp. 125–6. 59 *Ibid.*, p. 122.

60 Compare the lively activities of the Taunton borough court in the years before the town government was incorporated: R. G. H. Whitty, *The Court of Taunton in the 16th and 17th Centuries* (Taunton, 1934).

inability to use the powers of the justice of the peace, the most important agent of local government in this period, to operate courts which could deal with major commercial issues and to win independence of the shire justices. Another problem lay in the lack of that urban identity which a formal governing body would have created, so that the inhabitants of these lesser towns were forced to resort to rituals with a semblance of an official character or to social activities such as the use of assembly rooms to provide some focus for a sense of communal urban distinctiveness.

There are many other examples of towns which managed to develop a measure of sophisticated self-government without recourse to a royal charter of incorporation, but far more typical of the majority of non-chartered market town administrations were those based on manorial courts: in this respect they represented village government scaled up. A typical case is that of Henley-in-Arden (War.),[61] where under a lord of the manor the town government was headed by a high and a low bailiff, with a 'third-borough', a constable, and pairs of aletasters, chamberlains, brooklookers, leathersealers, fieldreeves and affearers. Leading officials were chosen by an annual meeting attended by former bailiffs and constables and through these offices and their membership of the jury of the biannual court leet, the leaders of this small community used their power to fine and enact bylaws to deal with the town's modest problems. Henley's court rolls are concerned with preventing the poor migrating into the town to become a burden on the rates and destroying hedges in search of fuel; pigs let loose were to be ringed and horses were not to be parked in the streets. There was a small town hall, inherited from a medieval guild, and an attempt at civic ritual when the bailiff opened the annual fair formally accompanied by his predecessors. In larger market towns which were confined to this sort of government, the enlarged burden of administration was sustained by elaborating the numbers of petty officials with specific tasks, so that in Manchester, where in 'the greatest meer village in England . . . the highest magistrate they have is a constable',[62] the court leet appointed about 120 officials by the later seventeenth century.[63] This created an urban government in which a large proportion of male householders participated, though its efficiency might be questioned. But the size and success of these towns would indicate that a sophisticated and complex system of government was not necessarily a requirement for urban growth.

In Scotland the legal basis of town government was similar, but derived from a different tradition. The royal burghs included most of the larger towns and closely resembled the incorporations of England and Wales – but there were fewer of them, with only sixty-six recorded by 1707. These burghs had a

[61] W. Cooper, *Henley-in-Arden* (Birmingham, 1946); F. C. Wellstood, *Records of the Manor of Henley in Arden, Warwickshire* (Stratford-on-Avon, 1919). [62] Defoe, *Tour*, II, p. 261.

[63] A. Redford and I. S. Russell, *The History of Local Government in Manchester* (London, 1939), vol. I, p. 73.

common organisation in the Convention of Royal Burghs which wielded considerable power, and a monopoly of sending representatives to parliament. The most striking difference from England and Wales lay in the royal burghs' monopoly of trade, foreign and domestic, within a large specified liberty around them; in 1672 they lost their control of trade in domestic products and of retailing imported goods. A fair number of these burghs could be described as market towns, though in Scotland ports combined this role more frequently than elsewhere. The other kind of Scottish burgh was the burgh of barony which enjoyed a smaller version of that monopoly of marketing in a defined area around the town which was the essential privilege enjoyed by all burghs.[64] Some 350 grants of burghs of barony were made between 1450 and 1707, with increasing frequency (and an increasing failure rate) as time went on, but about half were either never established or dwindled out of existence,[65] and perhaps only about a quarter achieved an unequivocally urban status; but this must still leave them representing the majority of Scottish market towns by the mid-seventeenth century. All burghs had courts (when granted rights of regality, with an extensive criminal jurisdiction), could elect baillies, make bylaws, set up merchant and craft guilds and administer the burgess body, and to this extent had more formal privileges than the non-incorporated English towns, especially in the sphere of economic regulation. The burghs of barony had a simpler administrative structure than the royal burghs, resembling the rural baron courts; but compared with truly rural settlements they displayed a stronger sense of community and were dominated by 'a closely-knit body of self-governing freemen'.[66] An unknown number of market towns, perhaps several score, were the result of simple grants of market charters to private owners without any other alteration to their rural administrative status.

Perhaps in conclusion we might review the state of the market town at the end of the seventeenth century. There is a good case to be made for the assertion that in England and Wales they were larger, more prosperous and making a more important contribution to the society and economy of their localities than had been the case for several centuries. Despite their limited size they could be fashionably built and make an excellent impression on the visitor – Celia Fiennes found Pontefract's houses more impressive than those she had seen in much larger York, 'the buildings so even and uniforme as well as lofty that it appears very magnificent'.[67] It is tempting to concentrate on their economic role, but small towns had a lively contribution to make to the social and cultural life of

[64] E. Torrie, 'The guild in fifteenth-century Dunfermline', in M. Lynch, M. Spearman and G. Stell, eds., *The Scottish Medieval Town* (Edinburgh, 1988), pp. 250–1.

[65] G. S. Pryde, ed., *The Court Book of the Burgh of Kirkintilloch 1658–1694* (Scottish History Society, 3rd series, 53, 1963), pp. lxxx–lxxxiii. [66] *Ibid.*, pp. lii–iii.

[67] Hillaby, ed., *Journeys of Fiennes*, p. 115.

their localities. Here happened most things which demanded the bringing together of people for specialised purposes, whether for sermons, politics, entertainment or instruction, to pay debts, make marriages or exchange news. The heyday of the small town as cultural centre lies in the eighteenth-century future, when surprisingly modest places had assembly rooms, concerts and libraries,[68] but before 1700 the church and the schoolroom, and of course the inn and the alehouse provided their distinctive services in most of them. In the seventeenth century schools for girls extended the range of educational resources found in small towns: Celia Fiennes notes the good school for girls in Leeds and in Salford 'a very fine schoole for young Gentlewomen as good as in London and musick and dancing', while her frequent references to 'very good meetings' for 'Dissenters' in many Restoration towns indicates that expansion of the role of religion in towns which followed the growth of nonconformity.[69] If the closeness of the countryside diluted their urban character, it helped them to establish a close relationship with rural folk which in larger places was replaced with some measure of distance, or even conflict.

Yet small market towns were being challenged from a number of sides. The basic institution of the market was under threat from private dealing, even if the seriousness of this development can be exaggerated. The growing concentration of industry in the major towns in time would undermine the manufacturing craft element in many small towns, though it was often possible for them to adapt their role to act as satellites to their industrial neighbours. The growth of shops in the villages undermined their monopoly of local retailing and improved road communications allowed the larger urban centres to operate more efficiently and so to eliminate smaller competing towns. But there were counter-currents in operation too – better roads brought people in to them as well as to their larger competitors and many of these damaging trends could be deflected or absorbed. The lack of entrenched vested interests – as represented in the large corporate towns – allowed the smaller towns to be more receptive to economic innovation. The mere market towns had still the prospect of a long and lively future before them.

[68] M. Reed, 'The cultural role of the small towns in England 1600–1800', in Clark, ed., *Small Towns*, pp. 121–47. [69] Hillaby, ed., *Journeys of Fiennes*, pp. 249, 252; e.g. p. 273.

· PART III ·

Urban themes and types 1700–1840

· 14 ·

Urban growth and economic change: from the late seventeenth century to 1841

JOHN LANGTON

Every schoolchild knows that an Industrial Revolution in late eighteenth-century Britain was followed by massive, rapid, urbanisation; that technological change created a world in which people interacted with nature and each other through work in new ways, and therefore lived different kinds of lives in places of a sort previously unknown; that the innovation of powered machinery sucked the British population into factory towns at hitherto remote locations. These novitiate certainties are a stark contrast to the disagreements of expert historians about the nature of economic development and urban growth, and the ways in which they were related, in Britain during the eighteenth and nineteenth centuries.

There has been vigorous argument about what, exactly, the Industrial Revolution was ever since the term was first used.[1] Recently, econometric analysis has even brought its very existence into question: whether the structure or growth trend of the British economy changed significantly before the 1840s is now hotly disputed.[2] The high rates of urbanisation standing proudly in the

[1] D. Cannadine, 'The present and the past in the English Industrial Revolution, 1880–1980', *P&P*, 103 (1984), 131–72; E. A. Wrigley, 'Introduction: what was the Industrial Revolution?', in E. A. Wrigley, *People, Cities and Wealth* (Oxford, 1987), pp. 1–17; D. C. Coleman, 'Myth, history and the Industrial Revolution', in D. C. Coleman, *Myth, History and the Industrial Revolution* (London, 1992), pp. 1–42; and P. K. O'Brien, 'Introduction: modern conceptions of the Industrial Revolution', in P. K. O'Brien and R. Quinault, eds., *The Industrial Revolution and British Society* (Cambridge, 1993), pp. 1–30.

[2] N. F. R. Crafts, *British Economic Growth during the Industrial Revolution* (Oxford, 1985); J. V. Jackson, 'Rates of industrial growth during the Industrial Revolution', *Ec.HR*, 2nd series, 45 (1992), 24–50; M. Berg and P. Hudson, 'Rehabilitating the Industrial Revolution', *ibid.*, 1–23; N. F. R. Crafts and C. K. Harley, 'Output growth and the British Industrial Revolution: a restatement of the Crafts–Harley view', *ibid.*, 703–30; and M. Berg and P. Hudson, 'Growth and change: a comment on the Crafts–Harley view of the Industrial Revoution', *Ec.HR*, 2nd series, 47 (1994), 147–9.

statistical rubble created by this demolition job[3] are not as incongruous as they might once have seemed. Complementary attacks on the idea that there was an Industrial Revolution in late eighteenth-century Britain, based on hypotheses about the processes of change rather than on trends in economic series, stress the continuing overweening significance of London through the eighteenth century,[4] and are replacing Thomas Gradgrind's Coketown with Samuel Pickwick's Eatanswill as the fictional exemplar of provincial urban life.

Rather than being a time when systems of industrial production were suddenly transformed in supply-driven economic development, the eighteenth century is now considered by some historians to have been a time of consumer revolution, when increasing commercial and landed wealth energised demand-led industrial (and other sectoral) growth. According to the most trenchant statement of this view, 'Britain was never an industrial economy, but, since the early modern period, was always essentially a commercial or commercial/financial economy with a brief interruption of factory capitalism in the first half of the nineteenth century.'[5] Other recent historians, whilst attributing more importance to industrial development, categorise the period as one of cumulating proto-industrialisation, with the accelerating growth of rural domestic handicrafts serving external markets long preceding the emergence of large-scale factory production in particular regions.[6] However different, commercial, industrial revolutionary and industrial gradualist processes need not necessarily have been mutually exclusive. One 'dual economy' model proposes the coexistence of a technologically dynamic and a laggard traditional sector.[7] Another suggests that an advanced organic economy, which might be both commercially sophisticated and technologically dynamic, but could only grow gradually within the

[3] Crafts, *British Economic Growth*, p. 67; and J. G. Williamson, *Coping with City Growth during the British Industrial Revolution* (Cambridge, 1990). It is indisputable that Britain was by far the most heavily urbanised country in the world by 1851, when over half of the population of England and Wales lived in towns, 35 per cent in the sixty-three with populations of over 20,000. R. Lawton, 'Census data for urban areas', in R. Lawton, ed., *The Census and Social Structure: An Interpretative Guide to 19th Century Censuses for England and Wales* (London, 1978), pp. 82–145, figures from p. 82.

[4] W. D. Rubinstein, *Capitalism, Culture, and Decline in Britain 1750–1990* (London, 1993), p. 158.

[5] N. McKendrick, J. Brewer and J. H. Plumb, *The Birth of a Consumer Society: The Commercialization of Eighteenth-Century England* (London, 1983); C. Shammas, *The Pre-Industrial Consumer in England and America* (Oxford, 1990); P. Langford, *A Polite and Commercial People* (Oxford, 1989); J. Brewer and R. Porter, eds., *Consumption and the World of Goods* (London, 1993); and W. D. Rubinstein, *Capitalism, Culture, and Decline in Britain 1750–1990* (London, 1993), quote from p. 24.

[6] R. Houston and K. Snell, 'Proto-industrialization? Cottage industry, social change and Industrial Revolution', *HJ*, 27 (1984), 473–92; M. Berg, *The Age of Manufactures* (Oxford, 1985); L. Clarkson, *Proto-Industrialization: The First Phase of Industrialization* (London, 1985), and S. C. Ogilvie, ed., *Proto-Industrialization in Europe*, being a special issue of *Continuity and Change*, 8 (1993).

[7] J. Mokyr, 'Has the Industrial Revolution been crowded out? Some reflections on Crafts and Williamson', *Explorations in Economic History*, 24 (1987), 293–325.

constraints imposed by diminishing returns to labour and capital in agricultural and other forms of biological production, existed alongside an energy-rich economy emerging among some proto-industrial rural crafts, from which the use of coal released those constraints.[8]

Patterns of urban growth would differ radically between such economies. A growing advanced organic economy would possess an increasingly well-articulated system of towns, with larger, better located and more specialised ones growing at the expense of others as space was more intricately organised on an increasing scale.[9] So would a proto-industrial economy, stimulating towns through which the production, capitalisation and export of regionally specific products were organised, and where rapidly increasing numbers of rural households that were progressively more dependent on industrial earnings bought what they could no longer produce for themselves.[10] A newly energy-rich economy would generate the explosive growth of different kinds of town based on the use of mineral fuel and power in the mass production of manufactures, especially at places well located on the route network which provided the cheapest means of bulk transportation, and therefore the greatest opportunities for scale economies and complementary activities.[11]

The energy-based dual economy model has much in common with ideas about the regionally constrained character of economic growth stemming from the theory of proto-industrialisation, which have recently been set against the apparent quiescence of econometrically generated eighteenth- and early nineteenth-century British national statistical series.[12] At the same time, a

[8] E. A. Wrigley, *Continuity and Change: The Character of the Industrial Revolution in Britain* (Cambridge, 1988).

[9] P. Borsay, *The English Urban Renaissance* (Oxford, 1989); H.-C. Mui and L. Mui, *Shops and Shopkeeping in Eighteenth-Century England* (London, 1989); and E. A. Wrigley, 'A simple model of London's importance in changing English society and economy, 1650–1750, *P&P*, 37 (1967), 44–70. See also J. de Vries, *European Urbanization 1500–1800* (London, 1984); and B. Lepetit, *The Pre-Industrial Urban System: France, 1740–1840* (Cambridge, 1994).

[10] F. F. Mendels, 'Proto-industrialisation: the first phase of the process of industrialisation', *Journal of Economic History*, 32 (1972), 241–61.

[11] E. A. Wrigley, 'The supply of raw materials in the Industrial Revolution', *Ec.HR*, 2nd series, 15 (1962), 1–16; R. Lachene, 'Networks and the location of economic activity', *Papers of the Regional Science Association*, 14 (1965), 183–96; F. Lukerman, 'Empirical expressions of nodality and hierarchy in a circulation manifold', *East Lakes Geographer*, 3 (1966), 17–43; D. Aldcroft and M. Freeman, eds., *Transport in the Industrial Revolution* (Manchester, 1983); P. Krugman, 'History and industry location: the case of the Manufacturing Belt', *American Economic Review*, 91 (Papers and Proceedings, May, 1991), 80–3; and P. Krugman, *Geography and Trade* (Cambridge, Mass., 1991).

[12] S. Pollard, *Peaceful Conquest: The Industrialization of Europe, 1760–1970* (Oxford, 1981); J. Langton, 'The Industrial Revolution and the regional geography of England', *Transactions of the Institute of British Geographers*, new series, 9 (1984), 145–67; P. Hudson, ed., *Regions and Industries* (Cambridge, 1989); P. Hudson, *The Industrial Revolution* (London, 1992); and S. Pollard, 'Economic development: national or regional?', *ReFRESH*, 18 (1994), 5–8.

group of iconoclastic economic theorists has been trying 'to eliminate international economics . . . and replace it with economic geography';[13] to jettison models of growth reliant on national income accounting by devising a 'new "positive feedback economics"' as 'an alternative analytical perspective . . . [to] . . . the neoclassical paradigm',[14] applicable to sub-national territorial units of analysis.[15] These new theories demonstrate that economic growth is necessarily regionally constrained, and 'path dependent' – that is, largely cumulative along lines fortuitously fixed at the outset – within regions. In any event, it might well be expected that differences between the growth rates of economic sectors dependent on organic and mineral sources of energy would have been expressed in regionally varied growth rates in eighteenth- and early nineteenth-century Britain. The use of coal for fuel and power is what constituted the energy-rich economy then, and coalfields are geographically intermittent and spatially bounded, coal was very expensive to transport relative to its intrinsic value, and the inland waterways which alone, with seaways, could carry large quantities of coal regularly, reliably and cheaply were densest on and near to coalfields.

Reliable figures of urban growth through the eighteenth and early nineteenth centuries would be of more than intrinsic interest. They would offer a convenient way of examining what happened to a national economic statistical series across a period which contained (if it occurred) the Industrial Revolution and its immediate aftermath, as well as any precursive development. Because it is in principle much easier to present data by region than according to the distinguishing criteria of the dual economy models themselves, regionally disaggregated data would provide approximate surrogates for sectoral figures and allow us to see just how far it is true that 'viewing the nation as a whole misses many of the most interesting and important parts of the story and mischaracterizes many of the ways in which the economy actually operated'.[16] What is certainly true is that 'we have run into strongly diminishing returns in analysing the same body of data over and over again',[17] and that new urban growth statistics, starting before the first national population census in 1801 and running to a terminus in the mid-nineteenth rather than the early twentieth century, are needed to do this.

[13] Krugman, *Geography and Trade*, p. 69.

[14] S. J. Liebowitz and S. E. Margolis, 'Path dependence, lock-in and history', *Journal of Law, Economics and Organisations*, 11 (1995), 205–26, quote from 205.

[15] Krugman, 'History and industry'; Krugman, *Geography and Trade*; P. A. David, 'Historical economics in the long run: some implications of path-dependence', in G. D. Snooks, ed., *Historical Explanations in Economics* (London, 1993), pp. 29–40; and P. Krugman, *Development, Geography and Economic Theory* (Cambridge, Mass., 1995).

[16] J. Hoppit, 'Counting the Industrial Revolution', *Ec.HR*, 2nd series, 43 (1990), 173–93, quote from 287.

[17] Mokyr, 'Industrial Revolution', 318.

(i) SOURCES OF DATA AND METHODS OF ESTIMATION

To calculate the extent of urban growth over a period needs a table of towns, their populations and total national populations in the terminal and intermediate years, disaggregated by region.[18] However easy in principle, each of these things is hard to do in practice.[19] The potential difficulties of regional definition were obviated by simply splitting the regions of the 'urban networks' chapters into contiguous groups of counties (as outlined on Map 14.1); but decisions about which places should be put on to a list of towns, when they should enter (or leave) it and the populations due to them are all problematical. It is impossible to decide which places were towns and exactly how big they were with any certainty. Quite different lists and population estimates could be produced, each equally plausible, by using different, equally justifiable, criteria of definition and measurement.

This is even true for Britain between 1801 and 1841, notwithstanding the existence of decennial population censuses and the amount and quality of the work done on them.[20] Because what compilers considered to be a town varied between censuses,[21] independently derived criteria must be applied to obtain comparable statistics. The most authoritative and widely used analysis is that of C. M. Law and Brian Robson, which was used as the basis of my own list of towns. It uses a minimum size of 2,500 inhabitants and threshold density and nucleation measures to define towns in the censuses between 1801 and 1911.[22] This definition was applied by Law and Robson to the administrative units of the 1911 census to produce a list of urban areas which was projected back to 1801, towns being removed when they failed to satisfy the criteria. According to this count, there were 1,129 towns in Britain in 1911, 545 of which existed in 1841.[23]

[18] I am grateful to Brian Robson, who lent me the index cards he compiled for his book *Urban Growth: An Approach* (London, 1973); Ian Whyte, who advised me on sources of Scottish data; Andrew Hann, who helped with the computation; and Peter Hayward, who drew the maps.

[19] J. de Vries, 'Problems in the measurement, description, and analysis of historical urbanization', in A. van der Woude, A. Hayami and J. de Vries, eds., *Urbanization in History: A Process of Dynamic Interaction* (Oxford, 1990), pp. 46–60.

[20] C. M. Law, 'The growth of urban population in England and Wales, 1801–1911', *Transactions of the Institute of British Geographers*, 41 (1967), 125–43; Lawton, ed., *The Census*; R. Lawton, 'Population', in J. Langton and R. J. Morris, eds., *Atlas of Industrializing Britain 1780–1914* (London, 1986), pp. 10–29; H. Carter and C. R. Lewis, *An Urban Geography of England and Wales in the Nineteenth Century* (London, 1990); and Robson, *Urban Growth*.

[21] R. Lawton, 'Census data for urban areas', in Lawton, ed., *The Census*, pp. 82–145. In the 1801 census, 136 British places were designated as towns; in that of 1831, 129; that of 1841, 969; and that of 1851, 534.

[22] Law, 'Growth of urban population', whose statistics formed the basis of the calculations of Robson, *Urban Growth*, which gives Law's list, pp. 230–40.

[23] Law's figures for England and Wales, supplemented by counts of Scottish towns with 2,500 or more inhabitants after reduction in 1841 by town parish ratios where appropriate, derived from the censuses of 1911 and 1841.

Unfortunately, this list cannot be used to measure earlier growth, and must be heavily modified to depict what happened before 1841. Many towns which had coalesced into single built-up areas governed by unitary authorities in 1911 were still separate in 1841.[24] Splitting them up, but removing places which failed on size after populations had been recalculated as described below, gives 583 towns in 1841.[25] More importantly, places with many fewer than 2,500 people might indubitably have been towns earlier.[26] The exhaustive researches of Peter Clark and Jean Hosking, who use then-current definitions of what were towns rather than arbitrary quantitive criteria (which cannot be applied before the censuses), have revealed 777 small towns in England excluding Middlesex in the 1660s and 1670s.[27] Adding large English towns,[28] and those in Middlesex,[29] Wales[30] and Scotland,[31] gives 1,005 British towns in the late seventeenth century. It seems improbable that many of them ceased to be urban over the period, and putting those which are absent from it on to the list for 1841 derived from Law's and Robson's work and my own counts for Wales and Scotland yields 1,155 towns.

These procedures for deriving a list of towns are far from satisfactory, for a number of reasons. Because there are no country-wide sources, no lists can be interpolated between those of the late seventeenth century and 1801; different kinds of criterion are used for the seventeenth and nineteenth centuries; the quantitative criteria used for the nineteenth century may well be less appropriate for the early part of the century which is the concern of this chapter than

[24] Such as the north Staffordshire and Medway towns; London's spread engulfed what had been fourteen separate towns in Surrey, Kent and Essex, and inside their bounds of 1911 Plymouth and Oldham contained settlements which were separate towns in 1841.

[25] Only Manchester/Salford and Edinburgh/Leith were retained as 'compound' towns. The definition of London in the 1851 census was used in 1841 and 1801, and in 1662 it has been defined as the area covered by the farmers of the London excise, Westminster and Southwark and its Liberties, for which figures are given in C. A. F. Meekings, *Dorset Hearth Tax Assessments 1662–1664* (Dorchester, 1951), Appendix III, pp. 107–10.

[26] P. Clark, ed., *Small Towns in Early Modern Europe* (Cambridge, 1995).

[27] P. Clark and J. Hosking, *Population Estimates of English Small Towns 1550–1851: Revised Edition* (Leicester, 1993). My total omits places on their list where the absence of population estimates in the late seventeenth century and earlier suggests that they were not even small towns by then.

[28] Meekings' *Dorset* list of the 187 'larger towns' contains fifty-five places excluded by Clark and Hosking. All are included here, as is Cranborne, Dorset, which was a borough.

[29] Brentford, Edgware, Enfield, Staines and Uxbridge, taken from J. Adams, *Index Villaris* (London, 1690).

[30] Including Monmouthshire, taken from Adams, *Index*.

[31] Including royal burghs and burghs of barony, of which reliable lists exist only from 1691. M. Lynch, 'Continuity and change in urban society, 1500–1700', in R. A. Houston and I. D. Whyte, eds., *Scottish Society 1500–1800* (Cambridge, 1989), pp. 85–117; I. D. Whyte, 'Urbanization in early modern Scotland: a preliminary analysis', *Scottish Economic and Social History*, 9 (1989), 21–37; and I. D. Whyte, 'The function and social structure of Scottish burghs of barony in the seventeenth and eighteenth centuries', in A. Maczak and C. Smout, eds., *Gründung und Bedeutung kleiner Städte im nördlichen Europa der frühen Neutzeit* (Weisbaden, 1991).

they are for the whole of it, and the Scottish, Welsh and English lists for the seventeenth century are based on amalgams of different sources, those for Scotland being forty years later than most of the others. The enumeration for each particular county can readily be challenged from more expert and thorough analysis at that scale and, therefore, so could the veracity of the whole national list.[32] Its only particular merit is that it is based on criteria which are as uniform as possible, deployed as consistently and systematically as possible, over the whole country.

Estimating the sizes of towns is even more difficult than enumerating them. This is especially so for the seventeenth century, but is also true of the nineteenth century. Law's and Robson's population statistics are for administrative areas as they existed in 1911, and for some towns they include adjacent areas into which suburbs had spread. In 1841, many urban administrative areas were much smaller, and few towns had expanded beyond the boundaries fixed after the Municipal Corporations Act of 1835.[33] On the other hand many towns, especially north of the Mersey and Trent, still sat in very extensive mainly rural parishes. Therefore, it is inevitable that the sizes of towns in the early nineteenth century are exaggerated by counting the numbers of people in administrative units projected back from 1911. Substitution of the figures given in the 1851 census for the seventy largest British towns, in constant boundaries, in 1801 and 1841[34] should

[32] It is probable that the procedures described above err on the generous side, causing the inclusion of some places without properly urban functions: six of the twenty-five Dorset towns on my list had markets which had by 1833 'fallen into disuse and are not kept, but all are equally *Towns* in the Law' (E. Boswell, *The Civil Divisions of the County of Dorset* (Dorchester, 1833), quote from p. v). Where the lower bounding line of urbanity should be drawn is an intractable problem. For Cumbria, my list of thirty-two places includes three not considered as towns by Marshall, but excludes three which he included (J. D. Marshall, 'The rise and transformation of the Cumbrian market town, 1660–1900', *NHist.*, 19 (1983), 128–209); for the Vale of York, it includes all the nineteen places considered as towns by Unwin (R. W. Unwin, 'Tradition and transition: market towns of the Vale of York 1600–1830', *NHist.*, 17 (1981), 72–116), and all but one of the twenty-five counted in east Yorkshire by Noble (M. Noble, 'Growth and development in a regional urban system: the country towns of eastern Yorkshire, 1700–1850', *UHY* (1987), 1–21); for Cheshire and south Lancashire, my list includes all the thirty towns listed by Stobart for the early eighteenth century, plus six others (J. Stobart, 'The urban system in the regional economy of North West England, 1700–1760' (DPhil thesis, University of Oxford, 1992), p. 578; and J. Stobart, 'Regional structure and the urban system: North-West England 1600–1760', *Transactions of the Historic Society of Lancashire and Cheshire*, 145 (1996), 45–73).

[33] The Report of the Municipal Boundary Commissioners in 1837 made proposals for 178 English and Welsh towns, only 54 of which were significantly enlarged. These, and similar subsequent recommendations for Scottish and other English and Welsh towns, were used in later censuses and in the back-projections to 1801 of the populations of principal towns made in the census of 1851. T.W. Freeman, 'Boroughs of the 1830s', in T.W. Freeman, *Geography and Regional Administration* (London, 1968), pp. 33–57; Lawton, ed., *The Census*; and *Census of Great Britain, 1851, Population Tables I, Numbers of Inhabitants* (London, 1852), vol. I, Report, tables XXXII and XXXIII, pp. lxviii and lxix, and appendix to the Report, table 42, p. cxxvi.

[34] *Census*, vol. I, table 42, pp. cxxvi–vii.

rectify the worst cases of such exaggeration.[35] For all other towns in large parishes for which only parish totals are given in the censuses of 1801 and/or 1841, the ratios of town to parish populations in 1841 or 1851 if possible, and if not for 1861 or 1871, were applied to earlier figures.[36] Mitchell and Deane's data were used to calculate percentages of county populations which were urban in the nineteenth century.[37]

Hearth taxes provide the best basis for English and Welsh population estimates before 1801, which is why this analysis starts in the seventeenth century, but they can only yield very speculative conjectures; they do not exist for some English counties, and are severely defective for many Welsh ones. Clark and Hosking's estimates for English small towns, which have been used here, were mainly calculated from households enumerated in hearth taxes from the 1660s and 1670s,[38] according to availability, or communicants given in the Compton census of 1676[39] for some places without tax data. These were supplemented by estimates of the sizes of other towns, as follows. Those for large English towns were based on the numbers of hearths they contained, generally in 1662.[40] Estimates for the twenty-one most important Welsh towns were derived from the number of households listed in the hearth tax of 1670.[41] The populations of fourteen English and Monmouthshire towns absent from surviving tax records were guessed from figures for nearby towns of equivalent status in the urban hierarchy; or, for Somerset, Durham and fifty small Welsh towns, they were estimated

35 For example, the 25,385 population of Wigan borough in Lancashire in 1841 was comfortably accommodated by its administrative boundaries, to which the boundary commissioners had recommended no change in 1837. However, according to Law's and Robson's method of calculation, Wigan's population was 32,344 in 1841, because it includes adjacent administrative areas which were incorporated into the borough in the twentieth century.

36 Correlation coefficients between town populations in 1801 estimated from parish totals deflated by town:parish ratios in 1851 and 1861 and the actual populations of towns given separately in the census of 1801 are above +0.90.

37 B. R. Mitchell and P. Deane, *Abstract of British Historical Statistics* (Cambridge, 1971), pp. 20–1. Populations of counties adjacent to London were modified in accordance with the spatial definition of London used here.

38 Households multiplied by 4.25, plus 35 per cent for taxes in which the exempt were unrecorded. Clark and Hosking, *Population Estimates*, pp. v–vi.

39 For fifty-six towns in the English Midlands and South; communicants multiplied by a variety of factors, as suggested by A. Whiteman and J. Clapinson, *The Compton Census of 1676: A Critical Edition* (London, 1986). Clark and Hosking, *Population Estimates*, p. vi.

40 The average ratio between Clark and Hosking's population estimates, for varying dates in the 1660s and 1670s, and hearth numbers, mainly for 1662, taken from Meekings, *Dorset*, for 123 English towns is 1.95. This was used to estimate populations from hearth numbers. Ratios for individual towns range from 0.52 to 6.1, with a majority between 1.0 and 2.5 and no pattern in the variations.

41 L. Owen, 'The population of Wales in the sixteenth and seventeenth centuries', *Transactions of the Honourable Society of Cymmrodorion* (1959), 99–113. For consistency, I used Clark and Hosking's multiplier of 4.25 on Owen's household numbers. Hearth tax records are defective for many Welsh counties, and must yield underestimates of population.

from 1801 populations.[42] Figures for the fifty-nine most significant Scottish towns are based on numbers of hearths recorded in 1691,[43] five more on poll taxes of 1694–6[44] and the remaining seventeen on burghal taxes paid in 1692.[45] Parish totals for towns in large parishes were reduced by the nineteenth-century urban:parish population ratios. Estimates of English and Welsh county populations were made from hearth totals, generally in 1662, those for Scotland from hearth totals in 1691.[46]

Because the sources of seventeenth-century urban population data are scattered in time and differ in nature, the array must contain some very large randomly variable errors.[47] All seventeenth-century Scottish figures are forty years more recent than many of those those for England and, on top of that, might be overestimated relative to them. The figures for English large towns and English and Welsh counties, based on numbers of hearths rather than households, may be a third short of truer ones,[48] which would cause urban growth

[42] For Somerset towns without records, the 1801 population multiplied by the ratio of estimated populations: 1801 populations of Dorset towns and those in Somerset with seventeenth-century records; for Durham towns, the equivalent ratio for Durham and Northumberland towns excluding Newcastle, Sunderland, Tynemouth and North Shields, and for Welsh towns, the equivalent ratio for all other Welsh towns in non-industrial areas.

[43] Given in Whyte, 'Urbanization in early modern Scotland', 24–5. Whyte's formula yields populations per hearth 73 per cent bigger than the multiplier used here on hearths in England and Wales, which might not be wholly inappropriate, given the commonness of tenemented housing in Scotland.

[44] From Whyte, 'Urbanization in early modern Scotland', 25.

[45] This assumes that the proportion of burghal tax paid by a town was equal to the proportion of the total population it contained. Tax figures from Lynch, 'Continuity and change', pp. 114–17.

[46] From Meekings, *Dorset*, and M. Flinn, ed., *Scottish Population History from the Seventeenth Century to the 1930s* (Cambridge, 1977), pp. 188–9. The multipliers used for urban hearths were also used to estimate county populations. Because larger ones might be appropriate for rural settlements, this may underestimate rural populations and overestimate the urban proportion.

[47] Different hearth taxes give widely different estimates, and hearths provide a less reliable basis than households. T. Arkell, 'Multiplying factors for estimating population totals from the hearth tax', *Local Population Studies*, 28 (1982), 51–7, and J. Patten, 'The hearth taxes 1662–1689', *Local Population Studies*, 7 (1971), 14–27. Estimates of the combined populations of twenty-two Dorset towns from household and hearth numbers in 1662 and 1674, using the same multipliers as for small English towns, vary from 9,246 (taxed households in 1662) to 18,425 (all households in 1674). The estimate from taxed hearths in 1674 is 14,592; that from taxed hearths is 156 per cent of that from taxed households in 1662 and 112 per cent in 1674. Correlation coefficients between ten pairs of estimates range from +0.84 to +0.96. Data from Meekings, *Dorset*.

[48] The total English population produced is only 62 per cent of that calculated by Wrigley and Schofield for 1662; London's is 89 per cent of Bridenbaugh's estimate for the 1640s, 66 per cent Wrigley's for 1670, and 65 per cent of Gregory King's for 1695. That for Norwich is 70 per cent of the commonest suggestion. On the other hand, my estimates for other large towns such as Exeter, Cambridge, Winchester, Lincoln, Nottingham and Northampton are larger than those given by Patten, and my total is 89 per cent of his for thirty-eight towns 1662–76. For Norfolk and Suffolk, my list contains sixty-nine towns, compared with Patten's forty-nine, and 93 per cent as many people; for the forty-seven towns in both our lists, my estimate is 83 per cent of Patten's, but well over half of the difference is due to Norwich and Lynn, where his figures are from 'doubtful' and 'partial' sources. If Dorset were typical, one cause may be the low counts of the

before 1801 to be overestimated by the same margin. The provenance of these figures gives absolutely no warrant for inferences from any but the most pronounced differences in statistics, especially those which incorporate seventeenth-century data.

(ii) THE URBAN POPULATION OF BRITAIN IN THE SEVENTEENTH CENTURY

According to the seventeenth-century estimates, well over a third of the total population already lived in towns. The impression that England (40 per cent) was more urbanised than Wales (33 per cent) or Scotland (25 per cent),[49] despite data for the last being over a quarter of a century later, is in line with received wisdom,[50] although without the Leviathan of London England's figure was only 34 per cent. Table 14.1 shows a U-shaped distribution, with an overweening metropolis and a mass of micro-towns.[51]

Even if many of the very smallest places were not really towns,[52] there were still 357 with between 500 and 2,500 people, containing 17 per cent of the total urban population. This plethora must have represented heavy commercialisation of the rural economy (in other words, the organic economy was, indeed, well advanced), and numbers of towns and sizes of regional urban populations were

Footnote 48 (cont.)
hearth tax of 1662 (although the way these were used should counteract this to some extent), and the adjustment of parish to town totals will account for some of the shortfall in my figures, though not in the cases of London and Norwich. E. A. Wrigley and R. S. Schofield, *The Population History of England 1541–1871* (London, 1981), p. 532; C. Bridenbaugh, *Vexed and Troubled Englishmen 1590–1640* (London, 1967; Oxford, 1976 edn); E. A. Wrigley, 'Urban growth and agricultural change: England and the continent in the early modern period', in E. A. Wrigley, *People, Cities and Wealth* (Oxford, 1987), pp. 160–2; P. King, *The Development of the English Economy to 1750* (London, 1971), p. 258; D. V. Glass, 'Two papers on Gregory King', in D. V. Glass and D. E. C. Eversley, eds., *Population in History: Essays in Historical Demography* (London, 1965), pp. 159–220; and J. Patten, *English Towns 1500–1700* (Folkestone, 1978), pp. 109–10 and 251.

49 The method used to estimate non-urban populations in England and Wales might well overrepresent the urban share.

50 Lynch, 'Continuity and change'; Whyte, 'Urbanization in early modern Scotland', and H. Carter, *The Towns of Wales* (Cardiff, 1965).

51 According to the Law/Robson minimum size criteria, Britain only contained seventy-eight towns, and half as many townspeople. This reinforces the emphasis placed on the significance of small towns in the pre-industrial English urban system by Clark, ed., *Small Towns*, and de Vries, *European Urbanization*. The insignificance of large towns apart from London might owe something to my estimating method and the source used, but raising the populations of towns of 2,500 or more by 25 per cent lifts the share of those with 2,500–99,999 inhabitants, excluding London, only from 29 per cent to 32 per cent of the total.

52 It is difficult to imagine that the forty inhabitants of Newtown, Isle of Wight, justified its name, and of the smallest nine of Dorset's twenty-two seventeenth-century towns, six give no topographical signs of ever having been other than the villages they now are.

Table 14.1 *Numbers and populations of British towns in different size categories in the seventeenth century*

Town size	Number of towns	Population	% of urban pop.	Cumulative %
<1,000	650	353,080	23	23
1,000–2,499	277	402,231	27	50
2,500–4,999	51	166,324	11	61
5,000–9,999	16	108,827	7	68
10,000–49,999	9	115,462	8	76
50,000–99,999	1	50,000	3	79
>100,000	1	310,941	21	100
Total	1,005	1,506,865	100	

still closely correlated with rural population densities, and therefore agricultural resources. The only regions with over 100,000 townsfolk were the Home Counties, Outer South-East, Inner South-West and East Anglia in England, and the Eastern Lowlands of Scotland, though the English East and West Midlands were not far behind. Map 14.1 shows that Lowland England and the Eastern Lowlands of Scotland, with 70 per cent of Britain's total population, had 74 per cent of its townsfolk and thirty-seven of the fifty largest towns, twenty of which were in South-East England and East Anglia alone.[53] In stark contrast, of the 250 towns in Northern England, Yorkshire less York and the East Riding, the North-West and West Midlands, only Newcastle was in the twenty biggest towns of the late seventeenth century (see Table 14.4), and only eight were in the biggest fifty and seventeen in the biggest hundred towns. Like their southern counterparts, most of them were ports, county towns and/or cathedral cities. The highest ranking of the putative industrial towns of the Highland zone were Leeds at 44th largest in Britain, then Birmingham, Macclesfield and Manchester at 56th, 79th and 82nd, respectively.

On the other hand, Map 14.1 also suggests that although some of the remotest parts of Britain had the lowest proportions of their populations living in towns – as in the Highlands and Islands of Scotland (12 per cent), Southern Scotland (12 per cent), and North (23 per cent) and South Wales (25 per cent) – other parts of upland Britain were already more heavily urbanised than the lowlands. The relatively low score of 26 per cent of the population living in towns in Inner South-East England is misleading because of the exclusion of London (it rises to well over 60 per cent if the metropolis is included), but it

53 Counting Beverley, Hull and York as lowland. The heavy Scottish representation might owe something to the later date of data for Scottish towns and overestimation of their sizes compared with large English towns.

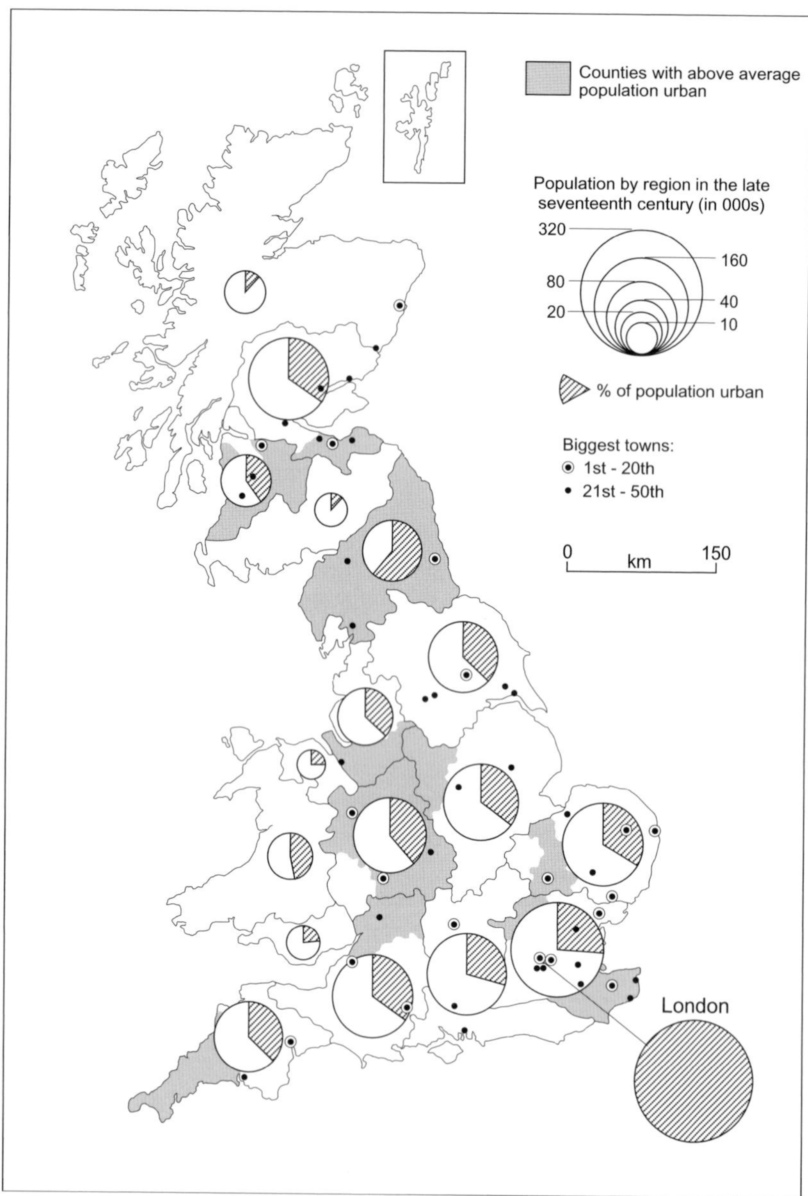

Map 14.1 Towns and urbanisation in the seventeenth century

does seem that generally the more prosperous agricultural regions, which contained most of the biggest towns, had lower proportions of their total populations living in towns than some less fertile upland regions. Thus, Outer South-East England (29 per cent) and East Anglia (33 per cent) contrasted with the South-West Peninsula (37 per cent), Rural Wales (47 per cent)[54] and Northern England (61 per cent). These statistics are consistent with London serving much of lowland England with certain urban functions, a lowland economy that was spatially integrated through the metropolis and a tier of larger urban centres below it, and more fertile soils supporting larger rural populations relatively as well as absolutely, and with urban industrial concentrations, albeit as yet on a small scale, already having developed in some resource rich upland regions.

It might, of course, be that because these rates of urbanisation incorporate unreliable estimates of both urban and total regional populations, they cannot provide a basis for any worthwhile conclusions at all. However, it is intriguing that Map 14.1 shows a preponderance of the largest towns, but relatively low rates of urbanization, in what must have been the most arable parts of the country as well as towards the extreme periphery (apart from the anomaly of Rural Wales), except where, as in the South-West peninsula and Northern England, industrial resources were already relatively heavily exploited by the late seventeenth century. Equally intriguing at the county level of spatial resolution, Lancashire and the West Riding of Yorkshire bucked the trend of upland areas having above average urban proportions of total population, which is consistent with the effects of proto-industrial development already being evident. However, it must be acknowledged that these statistics are even more prone to inaccuracy at the county than at the regional level.

(iii) URBAN GROWTH FROM THE SEVENTEENTH CENTURY TO 1841

Urban expansion can occur because pre-existing towns grow, or because new ones emerge to join them. The archetypal settlement of the conventional Industrial Revolution model of development is a new town of a novel kind, rocketing into growth where water power, ores, coal and other resources were plentiful.[55] Although the gradualist model of development has no room for such places, its consumerist version would produce resorts where resources for the

[54] Perhaps little credence can be given to this figure because of the small numbers involved and the method used to derive Welsh urban populations, although they should be relative underestimates. However, the urban percentages in rural Wales were only 18 per cent in 1801 and 23 per cent in 1841.

[55] As 'cotton mills [chose] the old abbey situations', according to J. Byng, *Rides Around Britain* (London, 1996 edn), p. 350, referring to east Lancashire in the 1790s.

Table 14.2 *The number of towns in Britain from the late seventeenth to the early twentieth century*

	Seventeenth century	1801	1841	1911
England	851	873	956	1,278
Wales	73	76	82	118
Scotland	81	87	117	145
Total	1,005	1,036	1,155	1,541

pursuit of leisure and health existed. How many new towns, of what kind, were there; how many people lived in them, and where were they?

Table 14.2 underrepresents new towns because twelve seventeenth-century towns disappeared into London by 1801, but even so, only forty-three emerged by 1801 and 119 more by 1841 (compared with 386 between 1841 and 1911).[56] Apart from seven new port and dockyard towns (with 54,930 people in total), six satellites of London (21,518), and three without particular distinguishing characteristics (9,516), the new towns that emerged before 1801 were what the advocates of an Industrial Revolution would expect. Fourteen were coalfield textiles towns (with a combined population of 43,543), seven were engaged in coal and iron production (35,000) and six in coal mining and the manufacture of pottery or glass (25,818). Three-quarters of them were in the West Midlands, the North-West and Yorkshire. This very heavy regional concentration of new industrial towns continued into the nineteenth century. Of the additional 119 new towns which emerged between 1801 and 1841, eighty-four were in those same three regions, which had now been joined by the Western Lowlands of Scotland, with twenty new towns between 1801 and 1841, compared with only three before 1801, and North Wales, with four new towns to add to its eight pre-existing ones. Only the West Midlands, the North-West and Yorkshire in England, North Wales and the Western Lowlands of Scotland contained 20 per cent or more towns in 1841 than in the seventeenth century. The biggest proportionate increase by far was in the Western Lowlands of Scotland, where 67 per cent of the towns of 1841 were new since the seventeenth century, compared with 42 per cent in the North-West, the region of greatest increase in England. As far as the appearance of new towns indicates it, an Industrial

[56] 25 per cent of the towns of 1911 emerged after 1841. This was exceeded in the English Home Counties (27 per cent), East Midlands (35 per cent), North-West (36 per cent), Yorkshire (42 per cent), North (49 per cent) and South Wales (66 per cent), but in no Scottish region. The chronology of urban orogenesis seems, therefore, to correspond to the growth trend suggested for the eighteenth- and nineteenth-century British economy by Crafts and Harley. Crafts, *British Economic Growth*; Crafts and Harley, 'Output growth'.

Revolution had occurred in three English regions by the end of the eighteenth century, then accelerated massively in those regions and spread to western Scotland and North Wales between 1801 and 1841, but did not happen in Northern England, the East Midlands, east central Scotland, or South Wales until after our period ended.[57] Nor, except in Middlesex, was the generative effect of metropolitan growth on town production in the Home Counties at all comparable with what occurred after the construction of the railway network.[58]

Of these new towns, Devonport and South Shields ranked among Britain's fifty biggest towns in 1801, but only eight had populations over 5,000 (none in Scotland). Combined, they contained 4.3 per cent of Britain's urban population. Apart from South Wales, where Merthyr Tydfil housed 25 per cent of all townsfolk, and North Wales, where Hawarden had 17.9 per cent, new towns accounted for more than 10 per cent of regional urban populations in 1801 only in the South-West peninsula (12.6 per cent, in Devonport) and the West Midlands (10.3 per cent). In North-West England, Yorkshire and the Western Lowlands of Scotland they contained 6.8 per cent, 4 per cent and 6 per cent, respectively. Of the counties, apart from Glamorgan and Flintshire (which contained Merthyr Tydfil and Hawarden), Middlesex (51 per cent) and Staffordshire (29.7 per cent) had the highest proportions of their urban populations in new towns.

By 1841 Merthyr Tydfil had joined Devonport in Britain's biggest fifty towns, and fourteen of the 162 towns that were new since the seventeenth century had over 10,000 people. Another seven urban satellites of London had emerged, and similar ones in the orbits of Manchester, Liverpool and Glasgow. The North-West, Yorkshire and the West Midlands each spawned a canal port big enough to enter the list of towns by 1841. New seaports at Middlesbrough, Birkenhead and Fleetwood, a new dockyard town at Portland, and seven coastal resorts emerged between 1801 and 1841,[59] although inland Royal Leamington Spa, also new since 1801, was much larger, with 12,838 people in 1841. But by far the biggest effluxion of new towns was again on and near coalfields, where the seventy-six predominantly mining and textiles towns that emerged between

57 This fits the late inception of rapid industrial growth in these English regions suggested in N. Evans, 'Two paths to economic development: Wales and the North-East of England', in Hudson, ed., *Regions and Industries*, pp. 201–27; and J. V. Beckett and J. E. Heath, 'When was the Industrial Revolution in the East Midlands?', *Midland History*, 14 (1989), 78–94.

58 Middlesex saw an increase from five to fourteen, but in the rest of the Home Counties more towns were swallowed by London's spread than emerged by 1841, unlike between 1841 and 1911, when fifty new towns grew beyond the (much further expanded) boundary of London. The surge of growth in the South-East from the late nineteenth century is demonstrated in C. H. Lee, *Regional Economic Growth in the United Kingdom since the 1880s* (Maidenhead, 1971).

59 Of the new coastal resorts which brook large in the list of towns in 1911, only Broadstairs, Ryde, Torquay, Abergele, Towyn, Largs and Rothesay had achieved populations of 2,500 by 1841. Like commuter towns, they were mainly a product of the railways.

1801 and 1841 housed 283,569 people. Forty-three of them were in North-West England and the West Riding of Yorkshire.

When these figures are put into the context of the national urban system as a whole, their significance is considerably dimmed. In 1841, towns which had not existed in the seventeenth century accounted for only 9.3 per cent of Britain's total urban population (about twice as many in those from before 1801 as in those of 1801–41). In some of the few regions in which they were concentrated, their significance was far greater. They contained over 12 per cent of the total urban populations of ten of the seventeen regions including, of those with half a million or more urbanites, the Western Scottish Lowlands (19.2 per cent),[60] the English West Midlands (19.1 per cent), North-West (14 per cent), Yorkshire (13.9 per cent) and Home Counties (13.3 per cent). Proportions were highest in North Wales (40.5 per cent), South Wales (37.2 per cent) and southern Scotland (23.9 per cent), but their combined urban population was only just over 200,000. Even more than in 1801, urban populations were more concentrated in new towns in particular counties. In Flintshire in 1841, 72.2 per cent of townsfolk lived in them; in Middlesex 67.4 per cent, Ayrshire 50.4 per cent, Glamorgan 49.5 per cent and Staffordshire 37.3 per cent. However, these were very exceptional pockets and generally, even in the regions where new towns were particularly numerous and eye-catching, over four-fifths of urban growth between the seventeenth century and 1841 happened in towns which had existed from the start.

The British urban population almost trebled before 1801, then more than doubled again by 1841. In 1801, 42 per cent of the population lived in towns (a 10 per cent increase from the late seventeenth century), and in 1841, 51 per cent. Table 14.3 shows marked differences from Table 14.1. The whole distribution lurched upwards. The number of towns with fewer than 2,500 people collapsed, and though their aggregate population remained about the same, their share of the urban total dwindled from one half in the seventeenth century to 25 per cent in 1801 to 9 per cent in 1841.[61] The largest towns of all grew in counterpoint. In the seventeenth century, London and Edinburgh had over 50,000 people and contained a quarter of the urban population; by 1801 there were eight towns in that size group with 34 per cent of the urban population, and by 1841 twenty-five with nearly half of the total. In the seventeenth century and 1801, only London had more than 100,000 people. By 1841 it had nearly 2 million; Manchester, Liverpool and Glasgow each had over a quarter of a million, but only another five towns had above 100,000 people (see Table 14.4). Besides the two national capitals, they were the commercial centres of the industrialising districts of North-West England, Yorkshire, the West Midlands and Western

[60] The western Lowlands of Scotland's urban population was slightly under half a million in 1841.

[61] The numbers of places with fewer than 500 people dwindled to fifty in 1801 and twenty-four in 1841, with 0.5 per cent and 0.01 per cent of the total urban population, respectively.

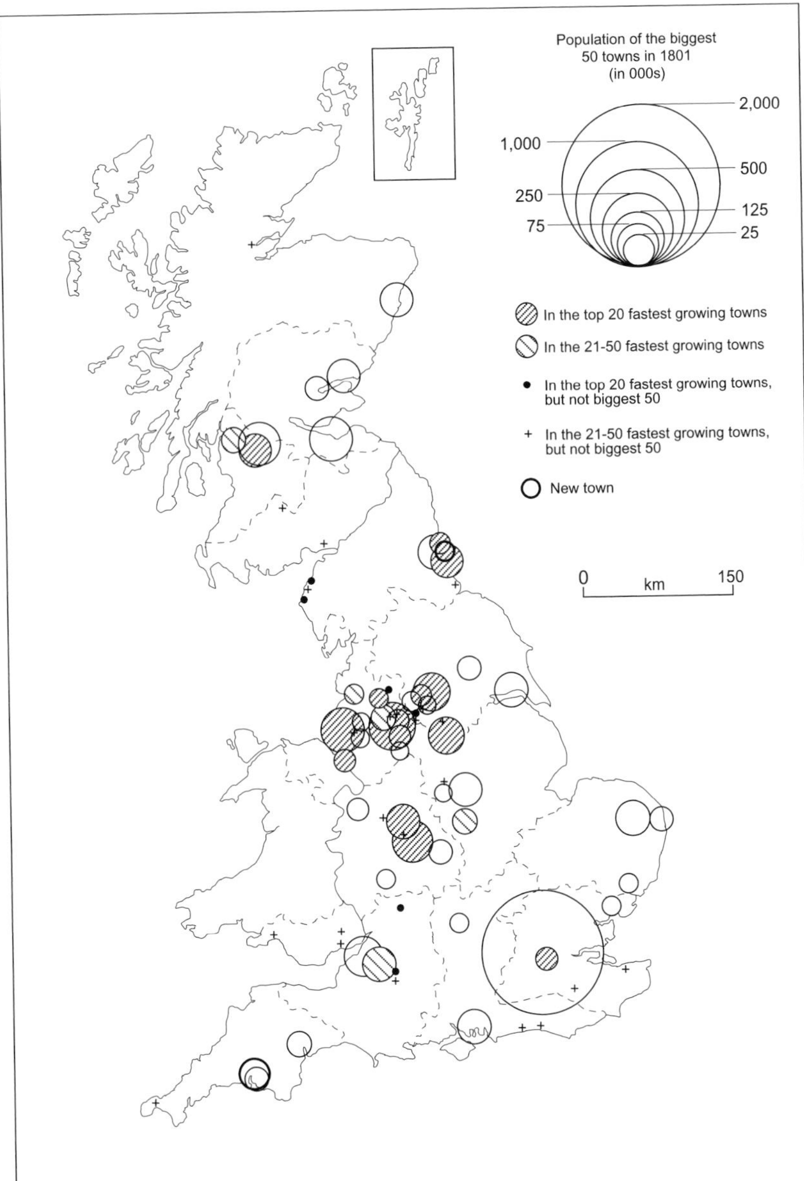

Map 14.2 The biggest fifty towns in 1801 and the fastest growing fifty towns from the seventeenth century to 1801

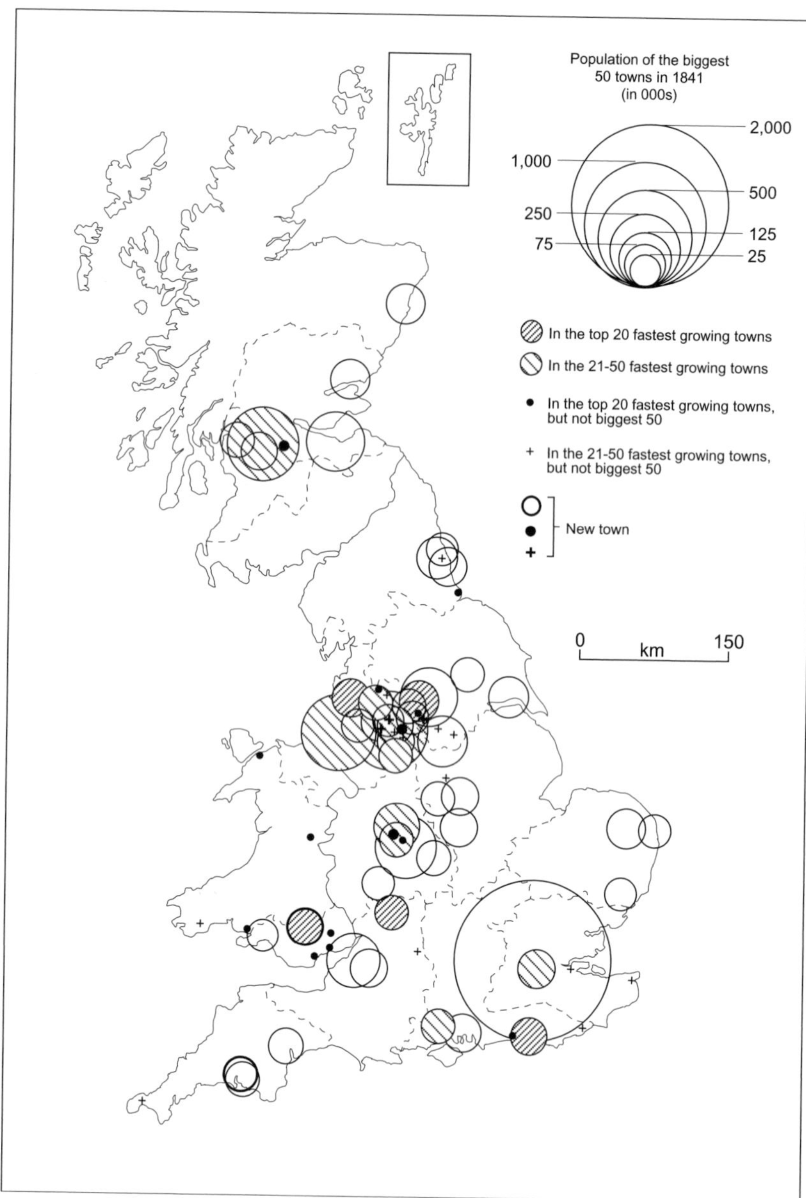

Map 14.3 The biggest fifty towns in 1841 and the fastest growing fifty towns 1801–1841

Table 14.3 *Numbers and populations of British towns in different size categories in 1801 and 1841*

Town size	1801				1841			
	Number of towns	Population	% of urban population	Cumulative %	Number of towns	Population	% of urban population	Cumulative %
< 1,000	237	158,795	4	4	113	81,028	1	1
1,000–2,499	471	751,026	17	21	374	640,650	7	8
2,500–4,999	212	722,119	16	37	392	1,351,474	14	22
5,000–9,999	58	391,035	9	46	156	1,647,843	17	39
10,000–49,999	50	880,773	20	66	95	1,285,365	14	53
50,000–99,999	7	520,618	12	78	16	956,773	10	63
> 100,000	1	958,863	22	100	9	3,542,584	37	100
Total	1,036	4,383,229	100		1,155	9,505,717	100	

Lowlands of Scotland. These towns attained strong regional predominance before the end of the eighteenth century, when it was remarked that Manchester, for example, had already 'in every respect assumed the style and manners of one of the commercial capitals of Europe',[62] then pulled away from other large towns[63] to become a distinctive tier in the national urban system and great cities of the western world.[64] The next six towns below them in size were also north-west of the Tees–Exe line, and some of the largest towns of 1801 and 1841 rose from very low seventeenth-century ranks. Table 14.4 and Maps 14.1 and 14.2 show that the British urban system beneath London was turned upside down by 1801.[65] However, Table 14.4 and Map 14.3 demonstrate that expansion in the urban system accelerated to its fastest rate only after its radically new ordinal and geographical complexions had been established.[66]

However dramatic they were, these shifts occurred within an urban hierarchy in which every set of components grew throughout the period, albeit at very different rates. The greater than tenfold increase of urban population registered in Lancashire between the seventeenth century and 1801, and thirtyfold before 1841, and the greater than tenfold increases over the whole period in Middlesex, Staffordshire, the West Riding of Yorkshire, Durham, Glamorganshire, Flintshire, Renfrewshire, Lanarkshire, Kincardineshire, Caithness-shire and Bute[67] were certainly very striking instances of growth. However, the overall annual average percentage urban population growth[68] of 1.52 per cent in England and Wales and 1.31 per cent in Scotland before 1801 was not simply due to the growth of towns in industrialising regions, but spread across the whole country. Urban population more than doubled between the seventeenth century and 1801 in most counties, even in the agricultural heartlands of England, except East Anglia. There, Norfolk had the biggest urban population increase at 94 per cent between the seventeenth century and 1801 and 215 per cent by 1841; Cambridgeshire, at 23 per cent, had the lowest before 1801, and Huntingdonshire, at 132 per cent, the lowest before 1841. Even in the most rural

[62] John Aikin (1795), quoted in M. W. Edwards, *The Growth of the British Cotton Trade, 1780–1815* (Manchester, 1967), p. 176.

[63] The cities in ranks 2–10 contained 4.38 times as many people as those in ranks 41–50 in the seventeenth century, 5.71 times as many in 1801 and 6.07 as many in 1841.

[64] R. Lawton, 'Introduction: aspects of the development and role of great cities in the western world in the nineteenth and twentieth centuries', in R. Lawton, ed., *The Rise and Fall of Great Cities* (London, 1989), pp. 1–19.

[65] The Spearman Correlation Coefficient between the population size rankings for the seventeenth century and 1801 in Table 14.4 is -0.07.

[66] The correlation coefficient for the size rankings of 1801 and 1841 is +0.90.

[67] Growth figures for the last three of these counties are very unreliable because of the small totals and insecure provenance of Scottish data for the seventeenth century.

[68] To standardise for comparison, total percentage increases in population for English and Welsh town from the seventeenth century to 1801 were divided by 130; Scottish towns to 1801 by 110; and all towns 1801–41 by 40.

Table 14.4 *Populations, ranks and growth of the largest twenty British towns in the seventeenth century, 1801 and 1841*

Town	Population			Rank on population			Average annual % growth		Rank on growth	
	Seventeenth century	1801	1841	Seventeenth century	1801	1841	Seventeenth century–1801	1801–41	Seventeenth century–1801	1801–41
London	310,941	958,863	1,948,417	1	1	1	1.41	2.58	220	205
Edinburgh	50,000	81,404	164,174	2	4	6	1.52	2.54	451	213
Glasgow	18,000	77,058	261,004	3	5	4	9.00	5.97	51	35
Norwich	14,216	36,238	61,846	4	10	16	1.97	1.77	344	378
York	14,201	16,846	28,842	5	26	40	0.61	1.78	828	375
Bristol	13,482	61,153	125,146	6	7	8	4.87	2.62	122	199
Aberdeen	12,000	26,992	63,288	7	18	15	2.85	3.36	217	118
Newcastle	11,617	33,048	70,337	8	13	11	2.97	2.82	204	169
Oxford	11,065	11,694	24,258	9	41	53	0.70	2.69	793	187
Cambridge	10,574	10,087	24,453	10	58	51	0.77	3.56	763	101
Exeter	10,307	17,412	37,231	11	23	30	1.54	2.85	446	163
Ipswich	9,774	11,277	25,384	12	45	47	0.94	3.13	681	136
Great Yarmouth	9,248	16,573	27,865	13	26	41	1.18	1.70	588	394
Dundee	8,000	27,396	64,629	14	17	14	4.72	3.40	127	112
Canterbury	7,671	9,000	15,435	15	64	80	0.60	1.79	835	372
Worcester	7,046	11,460	27,004	16	43	44	1.67	3.39	409	114
Deptford	6,919			17						
Shrewsbury	6,867	14,739	18,285	18	35	70	0.98	0.60	665	914
Salisbury	6,811	7,668	10,086	19	71	115	0.28	0.79	930	830
Colchester	6,647	11,520	17,790	20	42	74	0.99	1.36	663	525
Hull	6,600	29,580	67,308	21	15	12	5.41	3.19	103	131

Table 14.4 (*cont.*)

Town	Population			Rank on population			Average annual % growth		Rank on growth	
	Seventeenth century	1801	1841	Seventeenth century	1801	1841	Seventeenth century–1801	1801–41	Seventeenth century–1801	1801–41
Portsmouth	5,007	33,226	53,032	26	11	20	5.64	1.49	95	481
Nottingham	4,264	28,801	52,360	33	16	21	6.64	2.04	77	300
Leeds	3,501	53,162	152,074	44	8	7	24.96	4.65	11	64
Birmingham	2,745	70,670	182,922	64	6	5	38.61	3.97	5	83
Bath	2,652	33,196	53,196	71	12	19	11.21	1.51	33	466
Manchester	2,356	94,876	311,269	82	2	2	53.01	5.70	3	39
Sheffield	2,050	45,755	111,091	107	9	9	31.29	3.57	7	98
Wolverhampton	2,010	30,584	93,245	111	14	10	26.70	5.12	10	50
Paisley	1,700	25,058	48,263	149	19	27	18.26	2.32	20	253
Newington	1,406	14,847	54,606	201	33	17	22.26	6.69	16	24
Liverpool	1,210	82,295	286,487	253	3	3	138.69	6.20	1	29
Sunderland	1,147	24,998	53,335	274	20	18	26.76	2.83	9	165
Bradford	940	13,264	66,715	384	36	13	41.16	10.07	4	11

areas, therefore, urban population grew strongly. Although not in the top fifty in terms of size or growth rates, many southern towns with specialist manufacturing industries based on agricultural raw materials – such as straw (Luton and Dunstable), leather (Worcester, Woodstock and Yeovil) and hemp and flax (Bridport and Beaminster) – grew quickly in the early nineteenth century.[69] Towns nearest to London in the Home Counties grew appreciably faster than average,[70] and all leading southern towns grew in size as they declined in rank.

Of course, London itself inevitably benefited disproportionately from increased spatial integration of national economy and society, as well as from greater inputs of resources and money from, and exports of goods to, the colonies. It is true that some production for London merchants and shopkeepers moved out of the capital to other towns – such as silk to Derby and Sherborne, hosiery to Nottingham and Leicester, hatting felt to Stockport, clock and watch parts to Liverpool and Prescot, and jewellery and plated wares to Birmingham and Sheffield[71] – and that London merchants were losing control of some large colonial export trades to provincial metropolises by the end of the eighteenth century.[72] However, these losses were more than compensated by expansion in the role of London in national and imperial government, and as supplier to the whole nation of high order goods and services, which struck Defoe so strongly in the 1720s[73] and expanded prodigiously thereafter. They included ever more sophisticated home manufactures from nation-wide sources, as well as the cornucopeous 'Fruits of the Empire' which came into widespread consumption in the eighteenth century,[74] and financial and other services of increasingly varied and complex kinds.[75] The capital continued to be of a completely different order of magnitude from other British towns throughout the period: six times bigger

[69] Categorisations as in the census of 1851, which gives the populations of these and some other towns classified by dominant industry, 1801–51, in vol. I, pp. xlix–l.

[70] R. J. Morris, 'Urbanization', in Langton and Morris, eds., *Atlas*, pp. 166–7.

[71] See, for examples, W. Felkin, *History of the Machine-Wrought Hosiery and Lace Manufactures* (Nottingham, 1867), pp. 59–83; A. Sadler, *One-Hundred-and-Seventy-Five Years of the House of Christy* (London, 1948); and H. Clifford, '"The King's Arms and Feathers". A case study exploring the networks of manufacture operating in the London goldsmiths' trade in the eighteenth century', in D. Mitchell, ed., *Goldsmiths, Silversmiths and Bankers* (Stroud, 1995), pp. 84–95.

[72] Edwards, *Cotton Trade*, pp. 177–81 and 234.

[73] D. Defoe, *A Tour Thro' the Whole Island of Great Britain* (London, 1725–6). See also E. Kerridge, *Trade and Banking in Early Modern England* (Manchester, 1988).

[74] J. Walvin, *Fruits of the Empire: Exotic Produce and English Taste 1660–1800* (London, 1997).

[75] Mui and Mui, *Shops*, pp. 70–1 and pp. 262–87; Borsay, *English Urban Renaissance*, pp. 286–7; C. Y. Ferdinand, 'Selling it to the provinces: news and commerce round eighteenth-century Salisbury', in Brewer and Porter, eds., *Consumption and World of Goods*, pp. 393–411; I. S. Black, 'Geography, political economy and the circulation of finance capital in early industrial England', *Journal of Historical Geography*, 15 (1989), 366–84; I. S. Black, 'Money, information and space: banking in early nineteenth-century England and Wales', *ibid.*, 21 (1995), 398–412; and M. Buschinski and B. Polak, 'The emergence of a national capital market in England, 1710–1880', *Journal of Economic History*, 53 (1993), 1–24.

than Edinburgh (the second biggest town in the late seventeenth century), more than ten times bigger than Manchester, which was second biggest in 1801, and six times bigger in 1841 (see Table 14.4). Because of its huge size at the start of the period, the growth *rate* of London was inevitably much slower than the mercurial rise of towns which had been paltry in the seventeenth century (see Table 14.4). However, in absolute terms, metropolitan expansion was prodigious: from the seventeenth century to 1801, it took the combined population increases of the next seventeen ranking cities to equal that of London, and between 1801 and 1841 that of the next eight.

At the opposite end of the urban hierarchy, some of the the smallest towns of all seem to have dwindled away as the agrarian economy became ever more commercialised, with an increase in the working-up and longer-distance trading of agricultural surpluses and in the predilection of rural people to buy more town goods and services over longer distances.[76] It was recognised at the time that retail and wholesale dealing through open markets were becoming progressively more concentrated in the higher echelons of the urban system as they were organised over larger spatial scales:

> there were formerly, at short distance, small market towns to which, on a stated day, in every week, the corn and every product of the country was brought; and it made a little holiday; but now all these little market towns are disused, as the corn is engrossed and all other produce bought up by higglers, so these towns decay, nor are their fairs better attended, as the horse dealers go round and purchase all the nags.[77]

This must be why so many small Dorset towns had lost their markets by the early nineteenth century.[78] However, this decline of very small towns is as readily exaggerated as the commonness and significance of completely new ones. It cannot have been wholesale because, as Table 14.3 shows, most towns which left the smallest category did so as a result of growing too big to qualify for inclusion in it. These places must generally have shared in the enormous efflorescence of shops, especially those selling food and other mundane essentials, which diffused down even into small villages as the arable labour force was proletarianised, denied access to farmers' tables and increasingly deprived of rights of common, gleaning and so on, which had provided alternative sources of foodstuffs, fuel and other materials. 'The petty shop was not only a thriving institution in the eighteenth century, but also a necessary concomitant of the many changes occurring in the social and economic life of the country.'[79]

[76] For examples of this, see A. Everitt, 'The Banburys of England', *UHY* (1974), 28–38; Marshall, 'Rise and transformation'; Noble, 'Growth and development'; and C. Smith, 'Image and reality: two Nottinghamshire market towns in late Georgian England', *Midland History*, 17 (1992), 59–74.

[77] Byng, *Rides*, p. 288. [78] Boswell, *Civil Divisions*. [79] Mui and Mui, *Shops*, p. 148.

By the second half of the eighteenth century, this mass of petty shops was served by a network of specialist dealers, cascading goods from the very highest to the very lowest levels of the urban hierarchy and into the humblest homes. Low down the hierarchy, in touch with the immediate needs of rural hinterlands, even after the close of our period it was observed that 'the trade of a country market-town, especially when that market-town . . . dates from the earliest days of English history, is hereditary. It flows from the same store and to the same shop year after year, generation after generation, century after century . . . It might almost be said that whole villages go to particular shops.'[80] In larger towns, many shopkeepers were as much wholesalers as retailers, buying more than they needed from further up the hierarchy, selling on the surplus to dealers in smaller places, usually divorced from production itself. Their competitive aggression and penchants for advertising, price-cutting, disparagement of rivals and market area expansion through agencies, postal sales and free deliveries gave the larger towns of the late eighteenth century a strikingly novel aspect.[81] At the same time, more money was available in the pockets of landowners and farmers, especially in corn-growing areas, spawning specialist jewellers, booksellers, furniture makers, lawyers, medics, hairdressers and so on, who were particularly numerous in towns where potential customers were prone to congregate in large numbers from over wide areas at particular times of year.[82] They gave rise to the building of assembly rooms, race courses, theatres, reading rooms and other places of fashionable resort, as well as specialist high order craftsmen, retailers and professionals.

In this way, a distinctive hierarchical tier emerged above the smaller, more somnolent country towns, and the towns in it grew faster than their neighbours everywhere. The places which benefited disproportionately from this process – that is, the premiere venues of the 'urban renaissance' between 1660 and 1760 – were the county capitals and cathedral towns.[83] Table 14.5 shows that they did not, in fact, generally grow as fast as the average of all towns, or as London, which (*inter alia*) was the epitome of leisure towns. This is perhaps why county capitals and cathedral towns grew most slowly of all in the Home Counties, which must have felt the strongest effects of London's pulling power. At the other extreme, the county and cathedral towns of the East Midlands grew appreciably faster than the average of all towns throughout the period, which is especially intriguing because urban growth generally was relatively muted in that

80 R. Jefferies, *Hodge and his Masters* (Stroud, 1992), p. 2.

81 Mui and Mui, *Shops*, pp. 221–48.

82 For the examples of Warwick, Preston and Maidstone, see P. Borsay, 'The English urban renaissance: the development of provincial urban culture c. 1680 – c. 1760', *Soc. Hist.*, 5 (1977), 581–603; and P. Clark and L. Murfin, *The History of Maidstone* (Stroud, 1995), ch. 4.

83 A. M. Everitt, 'County, town and region: patterns of regional evolution in England', *TRHS*, 5th series, 29 (1979), 79–108, esp. 89–91; P. Borsay, 'The emergence of a leisure town or an urban renaissance?', *P&P*, 126 (1990), 189–96.

Table 14.5 *Average annual rates of growth*[a] *of fifty-five English county capitals and cathedral towns, by region*

Region	Seventeenth century–1801	1801–41	Seventeenth century–1841
London[b]	1.41	2.58	2.80
Home Counties	0.47	2.02	1.13
Outer South-East	0.73	2.89	1.88
South-West Peninsula	0.68	2.27	1.52
East Anglia	0.49	2.21	1.23
East Midlands	2.19	3.46	4.80
West Midlands	1.33	1.10	1.72
North-West	1.99	1.38	2.69
Yorkshire	0.56	1.69	1.11
North	1.07	2.59	2.27
Average (excl. London)	0.88	2.42	1.89
All English towns	1.53	2.86	3.18

[a] For method of derivation, see n. 68.

[b] These rates take account of London's expansion to include what were previously separate towns, the populations of which were included in the seventeenth-century figure from which growth rates were calculated.

region before 1841. Perhaps, uniquely in this region, early industrial and related commercial growth was as heavily focused in the biggest old towns and rural areas as proto-industrialisation theory suggests it should be, before reaching 'Industrial Revolution' proportions and spreading more widely through the urban system after 1841. In all other regions, the regional capitals which contained the leisure-based urban renaissance grew much more slowly than the average of British towns. This may have been because that stimulus was of much less relative significance than is usually supposed, or because it had largely played itself out in these venues by about the 1760s, as the market for leisure and associated activities such as the pursuit of better health and conspicuous material consumption was syphoned off over wider and wider areas by specialist resort towns.[84]

It is certainly true that the high prominence of some specialist watering places was the most obtrusive urban symptom of increasing consumerism in the British economy as a whole. Six inland spas and coastal resorts were in the fifty fastest

[84] A. McInnes, 'The emergence of a leisure town: Shrewsbury, 1660–1760', *P&P*, 120 (1988), 53–87.

growing towns of the eighteenth century (when Cheltenham ranked highest at 19th, then Tunbridge Wells at 25th), and five between 1801 and 1841 (when Cheltenham, Brighton and Worthing had the 1st, 4th and 9th highest urban growth rates). Thirty-two watering places in southern and Midland England[85] grew at an average annual rate of 1.99 per cent in the eighteenth century and 4.85 between 1801 and 1841. They were by far the fastest growing towns in the South, and Bath (12th biggest British town in 1801) was joined by Cheltenham and Brighton in the biggest fifty by the end of our period. These baubles of Jane Austen's England show, again, the high capacity for urbanisation in a technologically innovative commercial agrarian economy, swollen by imports of goods and fortunes from the colonies, with increased mobility from turnpike roads and improved means of traversing them.[86]

Maps 14.2 and 14.3 show that some of the other quickest growing towns were also scattered about the country,[87] apparently responding to a combination of the increased scale of spatial organisation in a richer, increasingly commercialised economy, and the possession of localised skills and resources. Some very rapidly growing towns existed in the eighteenth century on the Cumberland coalfield and in the Wiltshire textiles district, and in the flannel-producing area of mid-Wales between 1801 and 1841. Urban growth rates in the northern parts of Derbyshire and Nottinghamshire seem to have been in step with the those of the North-West and Yorkshire, not the rest of the East Midlands, and Northern England may have spawned few new towns before 1841, but some of its old ones grew fast. Although the cluster of high ranking towns adjacent to London in 1662 had been absorbed by it before 1801, Newington shot up from 33rd largest town in 1801 to 17th in 1841.

Thus urban growth occurred almost everywhere, in response to a variety of processes operating due to the expansion of output for sale in and the increased integration and commercialisation of an advanced organic economy. Even so, Table 14.6 shows starkly that the dynamism of the Eatanswills of Jane Austen's England was not nearly comparable with that of the Coketowns in Mrs Gaskell's stamping grounds. The effects of British consumerism on the urban system, whilst of great absolute significance, were completely overshadowed by the effects of the innovation of new technology in the mass production of manufactured goods for export markets. Even the growth rate of watering places, swollen by initially small populations, was exceeded by cotton and iron manufacturing

85 This category has only fifteen towns nationwide in the census of 1851.

86 Aldcroft and Freeman, eds., *Transport*; M. Freeman, 'Transport', in Langton and Morris, *Atlas*, pp. 80–93; E. Pawson, *Transport and Economy* (London, 1977).

87 Newtown (Isle of Wight) and Holsworthy (Devon) in the earlier, and Eccleston (Lancs.), Bolingbroke (Lincs.) and Over (Cheshire) in the later period, anomalously in the fastest growing fifty towns because of tiny initial populations, are omitted from Maps 14.2 and 14.3.

Table 14.6 *Regions with the five highest and five lowest annual average percentage urban growth*

Region	Seventeenth century–1801	1801–41
North-West	5.82	5.44
Western Scottish Lowlands	2.88	5.29
South Wales		5.11
Yorkshire	2.36	3.83
West Midlands	2.28	3.13
Northern England	2.10	
Outer South-East England		2.15
Southern Scotland		2.07
South-West Peninsula	1.08	1.98
Inner South-West England		1.92
English Home Counties	1.07	
Rural Wales	1.04	
Eastern Scottish Lowlands	0.72	
East Anglia	0.58	1.74
London[a]	1.41	2.58
London[b]	1.45	2.65
London[c]	1.05	2.65
England and Wales	1.52	
Scotland	1.31	
Britain		2.92

[a] As in boundaries of 1801 and 1841.
[b] As in boundaries of 1801 and 1841, plus satellite towns at both dates.
[c] If my figure for seventeenth-century London is underestimated by 30 per cent.

towns between 1801 and 1841, when more people were added to Manchester alone than to all the resorts.[88] Despite the initial smallness of their towns, the five coalfield industrial regions with the highest annual percentage growth rates added nearly four times as many urban people as the five regions where urban growth was slowest before 1801, and one and a half times as many between 1801 and 1841; twice as many as London (maximally defined) before and after 1801. Growth at 'commercial revolution' rates would only have added 18 per cent as

[88] Using the categorisations and populations given in the census of 1851, inland and coastal watering places had an annual average percentage increase of 4.98 between 1801 and 1841, cotton manufacturing towns 5.20, and iron manufacturing towns 5.00. *Census*, vol. I, pp. xlix–l.

many people to the five most rapidly urbanising counties before 1801, and 35 per cent 1801–41; about half as many townsfolk nationwide in both periods. London's comparatively slow expansion in the eighteenth century[89] epitomised the relatively modest performance of towns outside the 'energy rich' economies to the north.

More than that, by the early nineteenth century Britain had an increasingly dense system of waterways which spread coal thickly thoughout England.[90] The narrow regional containment of the energy-rich economy began to be broken open long before the railways. London relied on vast quantities of waterborne coal from the North-East from the sixteenth century, and the early prominence of Newcastle as the largest town of highland England in the seventeenth century was a reciprocal of that.[91] By the early nineteenth century even towns such as Bath, Leamington Spa, Oxford and Cambridge had busy coal wharves, and many other of the growing towns which were thickly spattered across southern England – such as Banbury, Basingstoke, Reading, Devizes, Trowbridge, Taunton and Wellington – had access to canal-hauled coal. Their growth, like that of many non-coalfield county towns,[92] owed a lot to the abundant availability of cheap coal by the early nineteenth century:[93] it was not simply due to the expansion of high order services in an advanced organic economy.

At the narrowly confined epicentres of these changes, where the Industrial Revolution as usually understood began earliest and cumulated fastest, the growth rates of the coalfield capitals of highland England were utterly astonishing. They were being precipitated by a Promethian economic system which was

[89] If, in fact, London initially had one third more people, the average annual percentage growth of its own and satellites' populations of 1801 put it among the five slowest growing regions. If Norwich initially had 20,000 people, its growth rate to 1801 was in the slowest growing 15 per cent of towns.

[90] G. Turnbull, 'Canals and economic growth in the Industrial Revolution', *Ec.HR*, 2nd series, 40 (1987), 537–60. Despite canals, coal prices in much of Britain were still double those on the coalfields in 1842/3. N. von Tunzelman, 'Coal and steam power', in Langton and Morris, eds., *Atlas*, p. 75; J. Langton, 'Liverpool and its hinterland in the late eighteenth century', in B. L. Anderson and P. J. M. Stoney, eds., *Commerce, Industry and Transport* (Liverpool, 1983), pp. 1–25; and A. F. Denholm, 'The impact of the canal system on three Staffordshire market towns 1760–1850', *Midland History*, 13 (1989), 59–75.

[91] Wrigley, 'London's importance'.

[92] For example, Shrewsbury, which according to McInnes changed from being a marketing and manufacturing centre to a leisure town between 1660 and 1760, saw the rapid development of large-scale factory production after being connected by canal to the east Shropshire coalfield. McInnes, 'Emergence of a leisure town'; B. Trinder, 'The textile industry in Shrewsbury in the late eighteenth century: the traditional town', in P. Clark and P. Corfield, eds., *Industry and Urbanisation in Eighteenth Century England* (Leicester, 1994), pp. 80–93.

[93] Britain had 7,200 miles of inland waterway by the mid-nineteenth century, compared with 4,170 miles in the much larger area of France. S. P. Ville, *Transport and the Development of the European Economy 1750–1918* (London, 1990), p. 31.

still unique in the world.[94] The speed with which they became world cities shows its astonishing infant potency, however spatially confined its full effects still were in 1841. If the notion of dual economy has ever been appropriate anywhere, it surely was in Britain in this period. Maps 14.4 and 14.5 show the consequences of these variations in rates of urban growth in terms of regional and county patterns. The rise of the urban West Midlands, North-West, Yorkshire and west central Scotland was spectacular. In the seventeenth century, London was 20 per cent bigger than all the towns of those regions put together; by 1841 they were 80 per cent bigger than London, whose population was exceeded by the townsfolk of Cheshire, Lancashire and the West Riding of Yorkshire alone.

Just as the growth trends for particular regions and kinds of town can only properly be appreciated when they are set in the context of all towns, so changes and geographical variations in urban populations need to be set in the context of overall demographic expansion. Changes in the proportion of the total population living in towns was neither chronologically continuous nor spatially invariant. Again, it is clear that the pattern which cumulated rapidly afterwards was already laid by 1801, except for the late surge of South Wales and, again, many intriguing embellishments existed around the most obtrusive tendencies. In 1801, the percentage of the population living in towns was higher than average in much of South-East England, Hampshire and Gloucestershire, and highest of all in parts of the central valley of Scotland (see Map 14.4). As the average rose by 1841, Hertfordshire, Kent and Hampshire slipped below it, but Warwickshire, Worcestershire, Glamorgan and Selkirkshire rose above it, and three central Lowland Scottish counties had over 70 per cent of their population in towns (see Map 14.5). During the eighteenth century the urban proportion of the population seems actually to have fallen in the South-West peninsula, Northern England, and North and Rural Wales. This tendency was characteristic of areas where mining itself, for metals and coal, was relatively important compared with manufacturing industry. In some mining counties it was pronounced, although it did not continue in any of them after 1801.[95] The urban share of the population also seems to have fallen through the eighteenth century in eleven predominantly agrarian counties,[96] perhaps because of agricultural development and the rapid swelling of crafts, shops and other services in vil-

[94] Britain produced over half of Europe's coal and pig iron, and had more than three times its spindles in the 1840s. N. J. G. Pounds, *An Historical Geography of Europe 1500–1840* (Cambridge, 1979), p. 344.

[95] In Cornwall the percentage of the population living in towns fell from 38 to 28 between the seventeenth century and 1801; Derbyshire, 40 to 26; Worcestershire, 41 to 35; Shropshire, 38 to 24; Cheshire, 39 to 35; Northumberland, 65 to 47; Cumberland, 58 to 42; Clackmananshire, 51 to 38; Fife, 26 to 23; and Ayrshire, 55 to 20.

[96] Bedfordshire, Buckinghamshire, Oxfordshire, Wiltshire, Huntingdonshire, Cambridgeshire, Rutland, Lincolnshire, Northamptonshire, Haddingtonshire and Banffshire.

lages,[97] although nowhere did this statistical trend, either, continue into the nineteenth century.

Some of this apparent relative rural growth and urban decline during demographic expansion might be due to imperfections in the seventeenth-century data. Even so, it is a salutory reminder that much early industry was rural in location. The non-urban populations of thirteen coalfield manufacturing and mining counties increased faster than the national rate of urban growth in the eighteenth century, most markedly in the West Riding of Yorkshire and Lanarkshire, where it was over three times higher. This difference continued 1801–41, although not by the same margin, in the West Riding, Lancashire and Renfrewshire. It prompts an obvious question: how far was growth in the smallest places classified as towns urban at all; was there any categorical difference between pit or factory 'villages' with 2,400 people and mining or textiles 'towns' with 2,750? Early maps and the present landscape demonstrate that the vast majority of the smaller new 'towns' of the coalfield regions were not and did not become truly urban. Nor, indeed, as their own historians have shown,[98] did many of the largest of the 'new industrial towns' by 1841, when they were still cellular straggling jumbles of pit, ironworks, potbank and factory communities, not molar entities focused on central business districts, with unitary authorities, public utilities and social institutions imposing coherence, and functional synergy had not yet created the patterned land-use zoning characteristic of towns. As Trinder argues (see below, Chapter 24), many old towns in which industry grew were hardly different, accreting 'factory colonies' on their margins which were functionally isolated from each other and from the burghal core.[99]

As we have seen, proto-industrialisation seems to have stimulated the central place activities of pre-existing larger towns, and the industrial regional metropolises quickly came to contain the full array of tertiary activities that were becoming characteristic high order towns, as well as those generated by the specialist industries of their regions: Manchester and Liverpool, for example, rivalled Chester as high order service centres by the middle of the eighteenth

97 J. M. Martin, 'Village traders and the emergence of a rural proletariat in southern Warwickshire, 1750–1851', *Agricultural History Review*, 22 (1984), 179–88; E. A. Wrigley, 'Men on the land and men in the countryside: employment in agriculture in early nineteenth-century England', in L. Bonfield, R. M. Smith and K. Wrightson, eds., *The World We Have Gained: Histories of Population and Social Structure* (Oxford, 1986), pp. 295–336; and Mui and Mui, *Shops*.

98 W. H. B. Court, *The Rise of the Midland Industries* (London, 1938); T. C. Barker and J. R. Harris, *A Merseyside Town in the Industrial Revolution* (Liverpool, 1954); L. Weatherill, *The Pottery Trade and North Staffordshire, 1660–1760* (Manchester, 1971); and C. Evans, 'Work, violence and community in early industrial Merthyr', in P. J. Corfield and D. Keene, eds., *Work in Towns 850–1850* (Leicester, 1990), pp. 121–37.

99 J. D. Marshall, 'Colonisation as a factor in the planting of towns in North-West England', in J. Dyos, ed., *The Study of Urban History* (London, 1968), pp. 215–30.

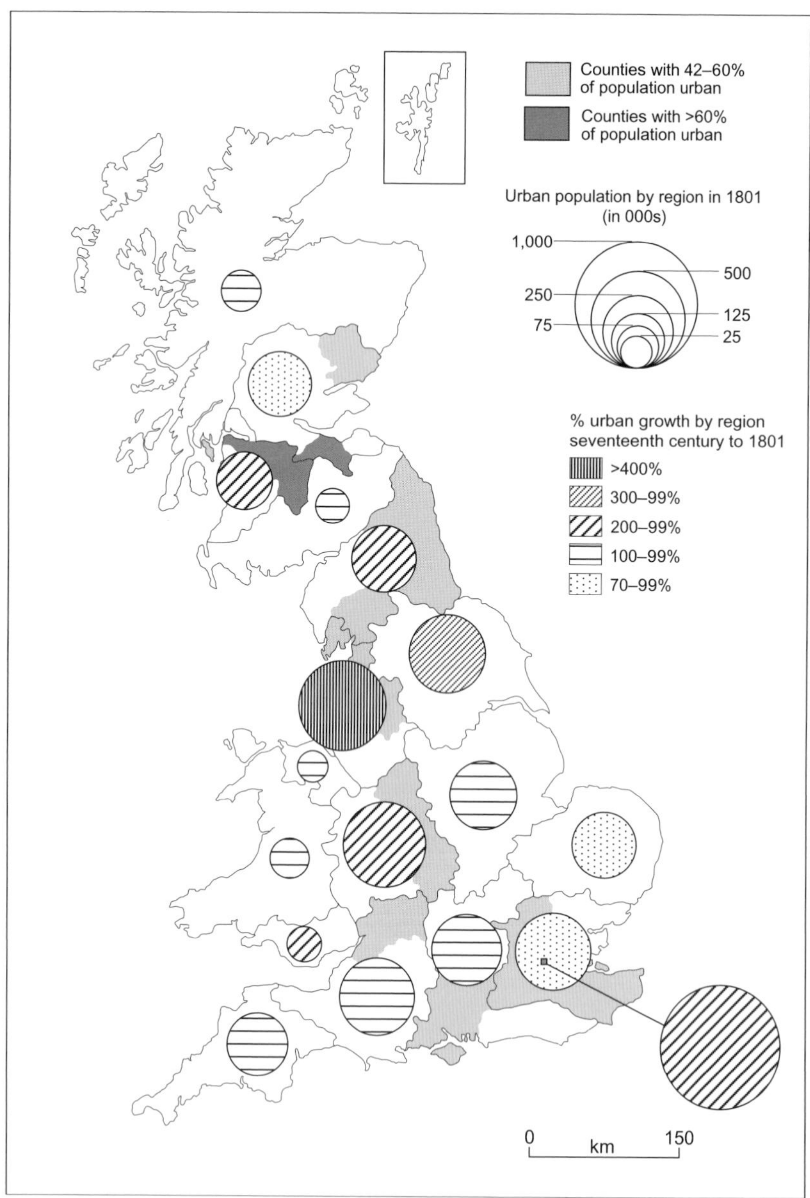

Map 14.4 Regional urban populations in 1801 and their growth from the seventeenth century to 1801, and counties with higher than average levels of urbanisation in 1801

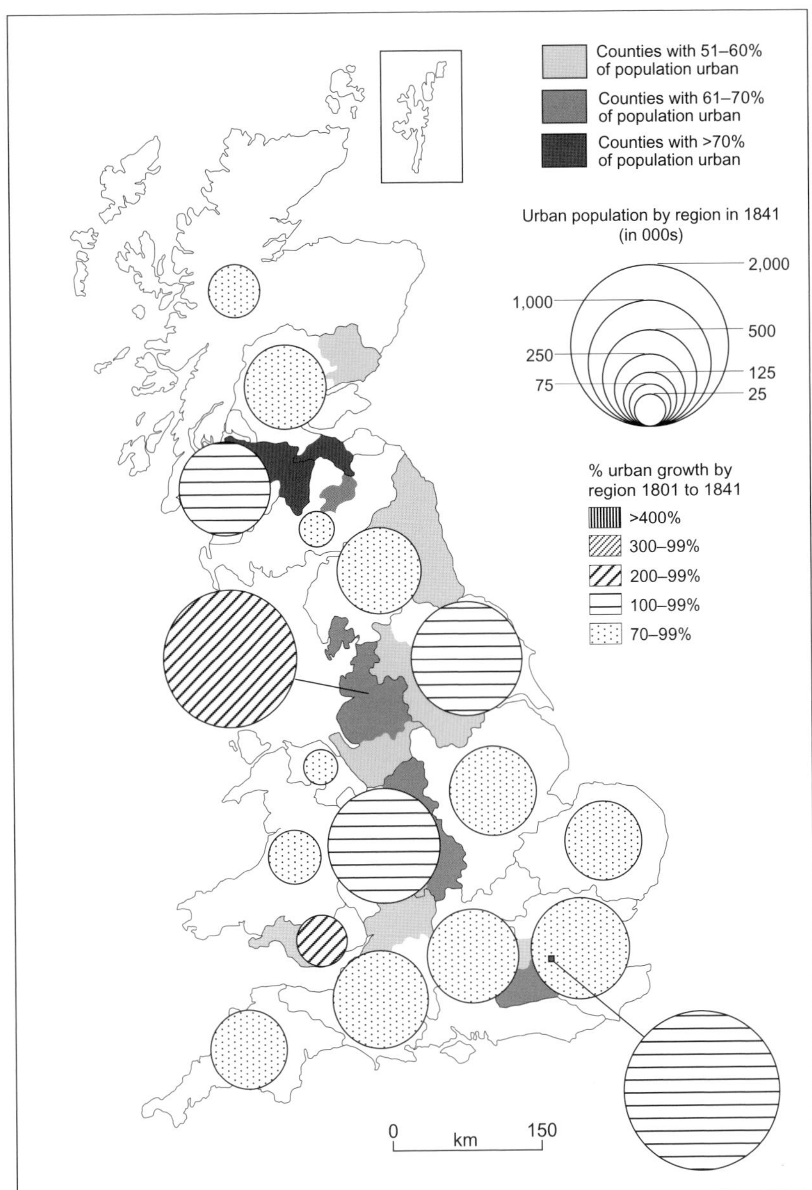

Map 14.5 Regional urban populations in 1841 and their growth 1801–1841, and counties with higher than average levels of urbanisation in 1841

century.[100] However, shops increased far less in number and variety in lesser industrial settlements than in towns of equivalent population size in agricultural areas.[101] Moreover, during our period most shops in industrialising towns seem to have emerged in back street residential areas rather than town centres.[102] Partly, this nugatory development of central retail shop facilities was because street markets and itinerant tradesmen served a much larger share of the needs of the industrial urban proletariat than of its rural agrarian counterpart.[103] Partly, it was because the larger cities of the industrial regions served smaller neighbouring towns with higher order services, in retailing and wholesaling as well as more specialised financial and mercantile activities,[104] which was perhaps because industrial regions already had well-integrated urban systems before they began their most rapid growth.[105] Whatever the exact reasons, the fastest growing industrial towns had far fewer shops per inhabitant than long-established towns in rural areas, and therefore, it may be surmised, fewer other tertiary activities, too. Not surprisingly, a completely novel economic system gave rise to settlements of an unprecedented kind: Coketown was *sui generis* in functional and topographical, even if not often so in locational, terms.

(iv) CONCLUSIONS

The inconsistencies and incomparabilities between different sources of data make it impossible to produce an accurate series of urban population totals spanning the eighteenth and early nineteenth centuries. The lack of sources between the late seventeenth century and 1801 precludes both adequate chronological depiction and any but the crudest interpretation. These are not the only reasons why urban growth and urbanisation cannot be measured and understood satisfactorily. Splitting places into urban and rural, implying that each category is uniform and remained essentially constant through history, is neat, convenient and conventional; but it is impossible to decide into which category many of the most dynamic places of this period fit.[106] This problem is particularly acute after industrialisation began to spawn settlement, but before railways, municipal, san-

[100] Stobart, 'Urban system', pp. 395–9.

[101] In *c.* 1821, there were 55 people per retail shop in York and 80 in Leicester, between 100 and 200 in Manchester, Leeds and Bolton, and 340 in Merthyr Tydfil. The ratios evened out somewhat by *c.* 1851, when they were 35, 45, 55, 70, 70 and 95, respectively. D. Alexander, *Retailing in England during the Industrial Revolution* (London, 1970), p. 93.

[102] M. T. Wild and D. Shaw, 'Locational behaviour of urban retailing during the nineteenth century: the example of Kingston upon Hull', *Transactions of the Institute of British Geographers*, 61 (1974), 101–18.

[103] Edwards, *Cotton Trade*, pp. 170–4; Mui and Mui, *Shops*, pp. 157–8.

[104] F. Collier, *The Family Economy of the Working Classes in the Cotton Industry* (Manchester, 1964).

[105] Stobart, 'Regional structure'.

[106] J. Langton and G. Hoppe, *Town and Country in the Development of Early Modern Western Europe* (Historical Geography Research Series, 11, 1983).

itary, welfare and political reforms, social movements and the full ramification of economic growth into service functions welded their fragments into unitary entities. The 'saviour city' came after 1841.[107]

However, it would be wrong to allow a nominative difficulty to distract attention from the sheer magnitude and reasonably clean coherence of the changes that occurred in the long eighteenth century. There *was* massive increase in the urban population – some of it in new towns, but most of it in pre-existing ones – and in the proportions of the total population living in towns, even if they cannot be measured accurately. The rate of urban growth was much faster everywhere after 1801, but the main features of the regional pattern of growth in the early nineteenth century were already established before it began. Most of the quickest expansion in the numbers and sizes of towns, and the fastest acceleration through the early nineteenth century, were limited to west central Scotland, Yorkshire, North-West England and the West Midlands, where rural populations also expanded prodigiously, whilst towns in most of the country (with a few very notable exceptions, which were mainly military and resort towns) grew more slowly. This is consistent both with national aggregate statistical series, which show no sharp change of trend before 1840, and with a regionally based Industrial Revolution.

Each of the four precocious regions contained cities of world-ranking status before 1841. Harbingers of similar expansion occurred elsewhere in the eighteenth and early nineteenth centuries, such as the mercurial spurt of Merthyr Tydfil into the biggest fifty British towns in a matter of decades, the uniquely rapid and sustained expansion of old regional capitals in the East Midlands and the precocity of Newcastle-upon-Tyne and the Cumberland coast in the North. However, towns in the coalfield regions of South Wales, the English East Midlands and North and east central Scotland only generally began to grow in parallel with those in the four bellwether coalfield regions during the railway era, after our period ends. And however fast and comprehensive their eventual urbanisation, only east central Scotland among them produced a regional capital of world-city status – and there were other than industrial reasons for Edinburgh's importance. In counterpoint to these regional trends in the provinces, London grew relatively slowly before 1841, but accelerated thereafter, as did towns in south-eastern England as a whole. These urban circumstances suggest that the four regions of earliest rapid economic growth contained most of the secondary and tertiary activities which spun off from their basic coal-fuelled, export-bound manufacturing industries, but that multipliers leaked out to London from the regions which launched their most rapid growth later, in a

[107] B. T. Robson, 'The saviour city: beneficial effects of urbanisation in England and Wales', in I. Douglas, R. Huggett and M. Robinson, eds., *Companion Encyclopedia of Geography: The Environment and Humankind* (London, 1996), pp. 293–309.

national space economy that was integrated by a railway network focused on the metropolis.

London's relatively slow growth rate before 1841 (although somewhat due to its very large size, and therefore simply of itself perhaps misleading) was matched over most of non-coalfield Britain, and East Anglia was perhaps archetypal of the kinds of change which characterise almost wholly organic economies. Even so, towns did grow appreciably throughout Britain, as advances in the organic economy brought greater commercialisation and increased consumption of ever higher order goods and services. At the same time wealth poured in from the colonies, and the frictional effect of overland distance on economic interaction diminished at an accelerating rate.[108] The consequent cumulating upsurge in flows of exchange and people over longer distances had the effects that would be expected in an integrated national urban system: disproportionate stimulus to the primate city and the larger provincial towns in greatest contact with it, except for those which were so near as to be in its shadow. Towns in the lowlands were not, however, simply evolving as interdependent parts of an increasingly integrated system which was changing in response to advances in organically based economy: waterway links to the North-East and along the canals which soon pushed out long spokes from their coalfield hubs stimulated a significant spatter of sporadic urban growth across lowland Britain in the early nineteenth century.

These links could not provide fuel in the cheapness and abundance possible on coalfields that had only just begun to be heavily developed, and so the scale, speed and extent of urban growth off the coalfields was modest in comparison. Although they diminished somewhat in the early nineteenth century as rapidly accelerating urban growth became more widespread, differences between the four fastest growing regions, other coalfield regions and the rest of Britain were very striking throughout the period. Even so, it is easy to push the appropriateness of dual economy models too far. However distinct in economic principle, the existence of waterway transportation meant that the advanced organic and energy-rich economies immediately became mixed and blurred on the ground. Rather than being eclipsed after the end of our period by resurgent commercial/financial economies in south-eastern England and eastern Scotland, the energy-rich manufacturing economy simply spread through the nineteenth century to activate their towns, too – at first tenuously and peripherally, but then completely after the construction of first railways, then electric power transmission lines.

Path dependence seems to have been apparent almost everywhere we look for

[108] D. Janelle, 'Central place development in a time-space framework', *Professional Geographer*, 20 (1969), 5–10; D. Janelle, 'Spatial reorganization: a model and concept', *Annals of the Association of American Geographers*, 59 (1969), 348–64; P. Forer, 'Space through time', in E. L. Cripps, ed., *Space-Time Concepts in Urban and Regional Models* (London, 1974), pp. 22–44.

it. The long gap in the eighteenth century means that the data presented here can allow only the sketchiest reconnoitre of this phenomenon. Other evidence suggests that urban growth quickened well before the last quarter of the century in North-West England, at least,[109] and it is an inevitable statistical implication of the fact that the national geography of early nineteenth-century change was already fully established by 1801. It is also clearly evident in London's continuous predominance nationally, in that of the regional capitals of the East Midlands on a smaller scale and in some remarkable geographical continuities in the regions where urban growth was most explosive. Birmingham, Manchester, Leeds and Glasgow were already the largest towns in their regions at the start of the period, even though they were insignificant nationally. Not only that: the industrial geography which underpinned their growth came into being long before growth became very rapid. Again, this was true at national, regional and local scales. Already at the start of our period, relatively rapid growth of manufacturing industry in upland Britain seems evident in relatively high rates of urbanisation; Birmingham, Manchester, Leeds and Glasgow were already performing their nineteenth-century economic functions, and glass was already being made in what was to become St Helens.[110] The processes of urban economic growth in the Industrial Revolution were as deeply rooted in time as they were narrowly spread in space. The Industrial Revolution did not come like a bolt from the blue to turn everything upside down, even in the few regions which felt its full force.

What every schoolchild knows turns out to be correct, although only up to a point. So, too, do all the other generalisations which have been proposed as alternatives, up to other points. The reason why all these ideas can be right, and therefore also wrong, is simple. Single holistic national economic and urban systems did not exist in Britain in this period, and quite different processes were operating in different places. The Industrial Revolution can disappear from national statistical series, but still be dazzlingly bright in widely scattered regional patches of massive urban growth between the seventeenth century and 1841.

[109] Economic growth in Lancashire seems to have quickened appreciably in the second quarter of the eighteenth century, and there was rapid urban growth, with the pattern of 1801 already well set before 1780. J. Langton, *Geographical Change and Industrial Revolution* (Cambridge, 1979); J. K. Walton, *Lancashire* (Manchester, 1987); and J. Stobart, 'An eighteenth-century revolution? Investigating urban growth in North-West England 1664–1801', *UH*, 23 (1996), 26–47. See also C. M. Law, 'Some notes on the urban population of England and Wales in the eighteenth century', *Local History*, 10 (1972), 13–26; and S. Jackson, 'Population change in the Somerset–Wiltshire border area 1701–1800: a regional study', *SHist.*, 7 (1985), 119–43.

[110] This is true of other geographical patterns which we might expect to have been consequences of the Industrial Revolution. J. Langton and R. J. Morris, 'Introduction', in Langton and Morris, eds., *Atlas*, pp. xii–xxx; J. Stobart, 'Geography and industrialization: the space economy of north-west England, 1701–1760', *Transactions of the Institute of British Geographers*, new series, 21 (1996), 681–96.

Despite their manifest inadequacies and the sketchiness of this interpretation of them, empirical data of urban growth between the seventeenth century and 1841 confirm utterly the unconventional theoretical truth that 'if we want to understand differences in national growth rates, a good place to start is by examining differences in regional growth'.[111]

[111] Krugman, *Geography and Trade*, p. 3.

· 15 ·

Population and society 1700–1840

PAMELA SHARPE

THIS CHAPTER aims to provide an overview of the process of demographic change in the burgeoning growth of towns and cities of the period 1700–1840.[1] The first section will consider the characteristics of migration into urban areas. English towns in this period had a preponderance of females. Why was this the case? What is the particular role of women in the process of urbanisation? The second section will examine the 'vital events' of marriage, birth and death. Notably, this time period has been dubbed 'the dark ages' of urban demography.[2] The label is justified not only because there are large gaps in our knowledge, but also as a result of the fact that this period is characterised by excess mortality associated with desperate living conditions. The chapter develops by exploring the effects of population change on the progress of urban society. How did migrants assimilate into urban life? How did urbanisation affect social structures? The 1851 census showed that by the mid-nineteenth century half of the population of England and Wales lived in towns. How did people shape the urban context?

(i) THE CHARACTERISTICS OF MIGRATION

There is no doubt that urban growth on the scale described by John Langton in the last chapter was to a large measure a result of migration. Yet there has been no detailed analysis of migration into towns and cities for this time period. The paucity of research is particularly apparent for 1750–1850, in which urbanisation

[1] For background see N. Goose, 'Urban demography in pre-industrial England: what is to be done?', *UH*, 21 (1994), 273–84; P. J. Corfield, *The Impact of English Towns 1700–1800* (Oxford, 1982). M. Flinn, ed., *Scottish Population History from the Seventeenth Century to the 1930s* (Cambridge, 1977), which, while outdated on some subjects, remains a valuable source of information for others.

[2] C. Galley, 'Urban demography 1750–1850: a glimpse into the dark ages' (unpublished paper presented at the Cambridge Group for the History of Population 6 June 1995).

and industrialisation are related processes.[3] Indeed much of the available evidence is impressionistic and based on biographical and genealogical material which is only just starting to be quantified.[4]

The 1662 Settlement Act established 'heads' of settlement, such as yearly hiring and property rental, providing all English people with a settlement parish to which they would be removed if they seemed likely to fall on the poor rates. After 1795 they were removed only if they became actually chargeable.[5] The paperwork generated by this removal process provides a valuable record of the human experience of migration. Reference will be made here to the testimonies of migrants themselves because urban dwellers often retained a poor relief settlement in the parish they had moved from, and from time to time communicated back to the parish officers there.[6] Even a brief glimpse at poor law documentation of this era reveals that for many labouring men and women the demands of sustaining their livelihood meant their lives could be very migratory.

Thomas Carter, a self-taught, bookish and rather physically frail tailor, born in Colchester, might be seen as a typical migrant. He was eighteen, single and semi-skilled when he moved to London in 1810. His knowledge of the metropolis was slight but his expectations were larger than life in terms of the cultural attractions of city life: 'I heard just enough to excite my wonder, so that for a long time I had a few extravagant notions respecting its size, wealth and curiosities.' On settling into his first lodgings in Moorfields he was struck by the awful smell of the city and commented 'I certainly did not expect to witness so great a contrast as was here presented to all that I had been accustomed to see in my native place.' He was disappointed in his aim of immediately entering intellectual society. Eventually, through a landlord, he gained access to debates at literary meetings but it was not until fifteen years after he had first arrived in London that the first master he ever had in the city elected him to become a 'poor' member of a literary society. In the meantime he had satisfied his intellectual aspirations by sampling sermons in different churches and becoming a con-

[3] On the lack of research on migration in this period see R. Lawton and R. Lee, eds., *Urban Population Development in Western Europe from the Late-Eighteenth to the Early-Twentieth Century* (Liverpool, 1989), p. 19. For a recent exception on the migration of a family see C. G. Pooley and S. D'Cruze, 'Migration and urbanization in North-West England *c.* 1760–1830', *Soc.Hist.*, 19 (1994), 339–58.

[4] J. Turnball and C. G. Pooley, 'Migration and mobility in Britain from the eighteenth to the twentieth centuries', *Local Population Studies*, 57 (1996), 50–71.

[5] For more detail see D. Marshall, *The English Poor in the Eighteenth Century: A Study in Social and Administrative History* 2nd edn (New York 1969). A good recent summary of both urban and rural poverty is M. Daunton, *Progress and Poverty: An Economic and Social History of Britain 1700–1850* (Oxford, 1995), pp. 447–76.

[6] See J. S. Taylor, 'A different kind of Speenhamland: nonresident relief in the Industrial Revolution', *Journal of British Studies*, 30 (1991), 183–208, and his *Poverty, Migration and Settlement in the Industrial Revolution* (Palo Alto, Calif., 1989). The rich collection of letters for Essex is discussed in T. Hitchcock, P. King and P. Sharpe, eds., *Chronicling Poverty* (London, 1997).

veyor of news to his fellow tailors by reading to them from an array of radical newspapers.[7]

Cities harboured ideas, but also work opportunities. Yet Carter's experience was also typical in that his work was both seasonal and casual to the greatest degree. Every day he breakfasted in the inn which held the call book of the tailor's trade and where masters would go to find workers at the appointed times of 6 a.m., 9 a.m. and 1 p.m. A shift could be as short as three hours. Out of season work was almost non-existent and Carter left for spells back in his home town. Eventually, however, in his late thirties, he left the city altogether, to set up his own tailoring business in his native town enhanced by all that his London experience had taught him. The metropolis operated, it can be said, like a vast revolving door, both attracting people and dispersing them.

The extent of migration to cities in Britain in the eighteenth and early nineteenth centuries was spectacular in comparison with the contemporary third world. The bias towards young adults as migrants was stronger than it is in developing countries today, reaching a peak in the period 1821–41.[8] Yet the degree of movement was nothing new as for English provincial towns at the beginning of the eighteenth century David Souden estimated that half to two-thirds of residents were migrants.[9] There were regional differences, migration being highest in the South of England where there were excessive supplies of rural labour. As Arthur Young famously quipped 'Young men and women in the country fix their eye on London as the last stage of their hope.'[10] Richard Lawton estimated that perhaps three-quarters of a million people out of an estimated total population increase of 1.36 million in surrounding counties in the period 1780–1830 contributed to London's growth in terms of migration.[11] Jeffrey Williamson suggests 'between 1776 and 1811 immigration accounted for a whopping 59.7 per cent of city growth in England'. For Scotland, the percentage was even higher, immigration accounting for 60.8 per cent of town growth 1801–51.[12] Whereas Scotland had been one of the least urbanised areas of Europe in the seventeenth century, it rapidly became urban in the eighteenth century and by 1850 was second only to England and Wales in terms of density of urban population.

[7] T. Carter, *Memories of a Working Man (*London, 1845) p. 35.

[8] J. G. Williamson, *Coping with City Growth during the British Industrial Revolution* (Cambridge, 1990) p. 28.

[9] D. Souden, 'Migrants and the population structure of later seventeenth-century provincial cities and market towns', in P. Clark, ed., *The Transformation of English Provincial Towns 1600–1800* (London, 1984), 133–68.

[10] A. Young, *The Farmer's Letters to the People of England*, 2nd edn (London, 1771), pp. 353–4.

[11] R. Lawton, 'Population mobility and urbanisation: nineteenth-century British experience', in Lawton and Lee, eds. *Urban Population Development*, p. 150. For a more recent estimate see Chapter 14 of this volume.

[12] Williamson, *Coping*, p. 28; T. M. Devine, 'Urbanisation', in T. M. Devine and R. Mitchison, eds., *People and Society in Scotland 1760–1830*, vol. I: *1760–1830* (Edinburgh, 1988), p. 41.

Apart from London, rapidly growing port and industrial cities attracted most migrants. Liverpool 'sucked in thousands of migrants each year' accounting for estimates of between 70 and 80 per cent of its estimated 20,000–22,000 population during the period 1790–1801.[13] Irish emigration was substantial to ports and industrial towns, with the Irish-born accounting for 4 per cent of the population of London, 8 per cent in Wigan, 12 per cent in Manchester and more than 17 per cent in Liverpool in 1841.[14] As Arthur Redford's classic study showed, many of the industrialising areas were also fed by the natural increase of their surrounding areas. He argued that early nineteenth-century migration was typically short distance, from the country to the town as a result of a complex but wave-like movement.[15] Other historians have shown that much migration was two-stage – rural people moved first to small towns, before departing for larger settlements. Such a movement might take two generations to complete.

By analysing records for indentured servants, John Wareing has shown that London's migration field was very large. Although he concurs with Souden in finding that the proportion of migrants from distant parts of England and Wales was falling by the eighteenth century, reflecting the urbanisation and hence attraction of other parts of the country, those from Scotland and Ireland grew.[16] Apprenticeship was the traditional way in which young men found a niche in city life. However, by 1700 London apprentices accounted for only 5 per cent of the population whereas in 1600 they had been 15 per cent of inhabitants.[17] A similar pattern is apparent for Scotland where the migration field of apprentices contracted during the eighteenth century.[18]

If fewer apprentices now swelled the ranks of migrants, who did so? Thomas Carter's experience shows that lack of prior indentures was no bar to finding a job in the city. Many male migrants provided the workforce for the most strenuous, menial and least remunerated jobs such as street hawking, building, portering or loading boats at the docks.[19] From John Sheppee's survey of the poor

[13] J. Langton and P. Laxton, 'Parish registers and urban structure: the example of late eighteenth-century Liverpool', *UHY* (1978), 76.

[14] R. Dennis, *English Industrial Cities of the Nineteenth Century* (Cambridge, 1984), p. 35.

[15] A. Redford, *Labour Migration in England 1800–1850* (Manchester, 1964).

[16] J. Wareing, 'Migration to London and transatlantic emigration of indentured servants 1683–1775', *Journal of Historical Geography*, 7 (1981), 356–78.

[17] R. Finlay, *Population and Metropolis* (Cambridge, 1981), pp. 66–7; I. K. Ben-Amos, *Adolescence and Youth in Early Modern England* (London, 1994) pp. 84–108 although mainly discussing the pre-1700 situation, considers the migration of young people to urban areas as apprentices. As I show below, Peter Earle and Tim Meldrum's recent work does not concur with this view. From their evidence of ecclesiastical court records the catchment area of migrants does not appear to be shrinking.

[18] A. A. Lovett, I. D. Whyte and K. A. Whyte, 'Poisson regression analysis and migration fields: the example of the apprenticeship records of Edinburgh in the seventeenth and eighteenth centuries', *Transactions of the Institute of British Geographers*, 10 (1985), 317–32.

[19] Indeed, the heavy labour of male migrants would have been vital in construction and heavy crafts. See D. M. Woodward, *Men at Work* (Cambridge, 1995), for more details.

who retained a Chelmsford settlement but were resident in London in 1823 we gain a picture of life and work for a group of ordinary migrants.[20] There was Samuel Hearsum, aged seventy-one, living in Marylebone, who sold tea by commission about London. Issac Harridge, aged sixty, resident near Elephant and Castle, received 6s. a week 'for circulating Notices of immediate Cure of a disagreeable Disorder, and of Quack Medicines' while his wife was a charwoman. William Jackson, fifty-two, of Lambeth, kept the gate at an iron foundry, his wife took in washing, but his son earned the most for the family at 10s. a week. Jackson had buried three children within the seven weeks prior to the survey but nevertheless on the strength of his son's earnings it was deemed that his assistance had to cease. David Rivenhall, forty-two, had a wife who was a fruit and vegetable stallholder in the Commercial Road; he worked as a porter and sold oysters in evening. William Scotcher, also forty-two, kept a shop, while his wife mangled. The monitoring of these individuals, some of whom were not in the best of health, reflects a process by which the economic development of large towns and cities fed off the labour of rural areas and smaller settlements, for when active workers became elderly or incapacitated they could be forced back to dependency in their settlement parishes.

Recent research on individual residential histories collected from genealogical research is beginning to suggest that the movement of family groups was perhaps more important than individual migration. A case study based on the family history of the working-class Shaws, who moved from Cumbria through north Lancashire to Preston, shows that 58.7 per cent of the moves undertaken between 1748 and 1836 were of a nuclear family group.[21] Their moves were also more complex than those described by Redford, as stages of migration did not necessarily mean moving to a larger settlement because moves to, and between, industrial villages are evident. Other married men moved alone, sending back remittances to their homes and perhaps returning to them for part of the year. This sort of migration was the inevitable outcome of the tramping system for artisans and labourers but taking up permanent residence in a city became the end result for many working men since, as poor relief documents testify countless times over, more work was available for wives and (probably even more importantly in terms of making ends meet) for children, in urban areas. Thomas Kingsbury, a Devonshire labourer from the small town of Colyton, moved to Bath in the 1790s, to join workers he already knew, with his wife and six of the children of a larger family. As he reported back 'I Can Do Beeter with my familey her Beter [*sic*] than I can Down in Devonsher.'[22]

The economic opportunities presented by urban areas for women are amply demonstrated by the evidence of migration. As one of the earliest analysts of

[20] Essex RO, D/P 94/18/42.
[21] Pooley and D'Cruze, 'Migration and urbanization'.
[22] Devon RO, 3483A/PO45.

migration to cities, A. F. Weber, put it, 'it may be confidently declared that woman is a greater migrant then man – only she travels shorter distances'.[23] Weber echoed the late nineteenth-century classic migration theorist Ernest Ravenstein, who while also finding women more migratory, suggested that women's migration field was more restricted and contracted more rapidly than men's in the eighteenth century.[24] Yet for the late eighteenth and early nineteenth centuries there was a gender bias towards females in London: 'in every decade female immigrants exceeded male immigrants' and the bias towards young people being migrants was even more pronounced for women.[25] On the face of it, the overwhelming reason for female migration to towns and cities in this period was the expanding demand from the middle class for domestic servants in a context where service was becoming increasingly feminised. Peter Earle finds that by the 1690s approximately 80 per cent of all domestic servants in London were female and even in the smart West End, where we might have expected to find more households keeping manservants, the balance was towards women.[26] However, recent revisionism by Leonard Schwarz argues that there were proportionally more female servants at the beginning of the eighteenth century than at the end.[27]

Weber recognised that the higher level of female migration to large towns, particularly older, residential towns, was not evident in heavy industrial areas which mainly provided male work.[28] Clearly, there were enormous contrasts in the labour needs of towns of different characters. Even today towns like Bath and Merthyr Tydfil seem worlds apart. Bath, in 1851, had a population of 32,517 women but only 21,737 men. Some of the women may have been genteel annuitants – the archetypal spinster aunt sojourner of the refined spa town – but the disproportion of males to females in the twenty to thirty age group, of 203 females per 100 males indicates the preponderance of female servants. In fact, a quarter of females in Bath were recorded as servants in 1851, over 14 per cent of the total population of the city.[29] Early nineteenth-century Merthyr by contrast, a sprawl of poor housing and beer shops but almost no infrastructure in the wake of the opening up of rich mineral deposits, attracted young and unattached males, particularly from the poor, agricultural areas of south-west Wales. Not surprisingly the census returns reveal a masculine sex ratio.[30]

Women migrants were also more likely to hail from large towns whence an

[23] A. F. Weber, *The Growth of Cities in the Nineteenth Century* (Ithaca, N.Y., 1899), p. 276.

[24] E. G. Ravenstein, 'The laws of migration', *Journal of the Royal Statistical Society*, 48 (1885), 167–227 and *ibid.*, 52 (1889), 214–301. [25] Williamson, *Coping*, p. 46.

[26] P. Earle, *A City Full of People* (London, 1994), pp. 39–40.

[27] L. D. Schwarz, 'English servants and their employers during the eighteenth and nineteenth centuries', *Ec.HR*, 2nd series, 52 (1999), 236–56. [28] Weber, *The Growth of Cities*.

[29] R. S. Neale, *Bath 1680–1850* (London, 1981), pp. 276–81.

[30] C. Evans, *'The Labyrinth of Flames': Work and Social Conflict in Early Industrial Merthyr Tydfil* (Cardiff, 1993), pp. 145–65.

estimated 27 per cent originated in the period 1683–1759 compared with 21 per cent of men in Wareing's sample of migrants to London.[31] More recent research goes against the grain of Ravenstein's 'laws of migration' by suggesting that a changing pattern is evident for England over time, with women moving increasing distances, and to larger cities than they had done in the earlier period, and with more movement between towns. For Scotland, I. D. Whyte and K. A. Whyte have analysed urban marriage registers which give father's residence. They find an extension of the migration field to Edinburgh as the eighteenth century advanced despite the rapid growth of other cities. In particular, they suggest a steady increase in female migrants from the Highlands, accounting for 1.2 per cent of migrants 1700–10 but 11.6 per cent 1780–99, as well as a growth of migrants from the North of England.[32] The pulling power of a centre like Edinburgh, which was significantly gentrified, is manifest. The benefits for young women were, again, cultural as well as economic. Ian Whyte shows that experience in the city spread new consumer ideas to the countryside such as the wearing of imported textiles and drinking tea.[33] This leads to speculation of how we should link women's migration experiences with marriage. How many women returned home to marry after a spell of work in the city during which they collected a dowry? This would seem to have been more common both in Scotland and on the continent than in England. London migrant women seem to have been absorbed into the city rather than returning to their native parishes. As Earle suggests, 'perhaps the melting pot melted' more effectively in London.[34]

Jan de Vries has written that 'Urban sex ratios below 100, a characteristic that continues to the present day, distinguish European urban life from that of many other world civilisations'.[35] As with the study of all migrants both 'push' and 'pull' factors can be considered. Married women who moved to towns and cities found niches in servicing and provisioning trades which proliferated with expanded consumerism. Those in the food and drink trades were often immigrants, but migrant married women also kept lodging houses, took in washing and charred.[36] Some local industries attracted a female workforce and might tip

31 Wareing, 'Migration to London'.

32 I. D. Whyte and K. A. Whyte, 'The geographical mobility of women in early modern Scotland', in L. Leneman, ed., *Perspectives on Scottish Social History* (Aberdeen, 1988), p. 87.

33 I. D. Whyte, 'Urbanization in early modern Scotland: a preliminary analysis', *Scottish Economic and Social History*, 9 (1989) 21–35.

34 Earle, *A City Full of People*, pp. 41–3.

35 J. de Vries, *European Urbanization 1500–1800* (London, 1984), p. 178.

36 Souden, 'Migrants' p. 140; W. Thwaites, 'Women in the market place: Oxfordshire *c.* 1690–1800', *Midland History*, 9 (1984), 23–42; S. J. Wright 'Sojourners and lodgers in a provincial town: the evidence from eighteenth-century Ludlow', *UHJ*, 17 (1990), 14–35. Although mainly referring to a later period there is useful material in L. Davidoff, 'The separation of home and work? Landladies and lodgers in nineteenth- and twentieth-century England', in L. Davidoff, ed., *Worlds Between* (Cambridge, 1995), pp. 151–79 and P. E. Malcolmson, *English Launderesses: A Social History 1850–1930* (Chicago, 1986).

the balance towards a female predominance even in small towns. In the time period 1650–1800, the east Devon town of Colyton, which specialised in Honiton lace making, had a population of four women to every three men.[37]

The 'push' factors include restricted work opportunities and low wages for women in the countryside and also the prospect of relief from the tedium and restriction of rural areas.[38] Some support for this is offered by Earle's suggestion that their higher literacy in ecclesiastical court records suggests that London servants were 'the cream' of provincial girls.[39] The situation was summed up by the German demographer, Johann P Süssmilch, as early as 1741: 'in the cities the proportion of females in the population is conspicuously higher than in the country, where males predominate, the causes of this are that among the rural migrants to the cities, females predominate, because they are less needed in agriculture than men, and they can easily find work as servants in the cities'.[40] Country girls were seen as stronger and healthier than girls born in cities (and not without foundation as we will see), and this also applied to servants from provincial towns. For example, William Dodd, a resident of the London West End, who was likely to have been born in Colchester, wrote to the overseers there in 1828 asking them if they would send him a country girl: 'if she conducts herself properly she might get a better place as country girls are preferable to town girls'.[41] Women's wages although lower than urban men's, graded by age, and variable due to the differing allowances given to servants, might equal those of labouring men's in the countryside. Women may have also perceived that marriage to a London man was a better economic prospect than to a country husband. For the beginning of our period, Earle found that just under 70 per cent of his sample of servants had been born outside London. Contrary to Ravenstein he found that over time they were willing to travel greater distances.[42] Tim Meldrum also finds a fall in the proportion of servants who moved to London from the South and East in the early eighteenth century, leaving a

[37] P. Sharpe, 'Literally spinsters: a new interpretation of local economy and demography in Colyton in the seventeenth and eighteenth century', *Ec.HR*, 2nd series, 44 (1991), pp. 48–9. For a more general picture see D. Souden '"East, west – home's best"? Regional patterns in migration in early modern England', in P. Clark and D. Souden, eds., *Migration and Society in Early Modern England* (London, 1987), pp. 292–332.

[38] D. Feldman, 'Migration', in M. Daunton, ed., *The Cambridge Urban History of Britain*, vol. III, *1840–1950* (Cambridge, 2000), ch. 8, makes a significant plea for further examination of the ways in which social relations affect migration.

[39] P. Earle, 'The female labour market in London in the late seventeenth and early eighteenth centuries', *Ec.HR*, 2nd series, 42 (1989), 328–53.

[40] Quoted in B. Ankarloo, 'Agriculture and women's work: directions of change in the west 1700–1900', *Journal of Family History*, 4 (1979), 115.

[41] E. Higgs, 'Domestic service and household production', in A.V. John, ed., *Unequal Opportunities: Women's Employment in England 1800–1918* (Oxford, 1986), 125–50. For the William Dodd case and this subject in general, P. Sharpe, *Adapting to Capitalism: Working Women in the English Economy 1700–1850* (London, 1996), pp. 101–29.

[42] Earle, 'Female labour market', 333.

net growth from more distant parts.[43] This must reflect a rise in service opportunities in provincial towns.

Many general servants must have obtained jobs by simply arriving in towns. Mistresses would go to coaching inns to look for appropriate maids. Others obtained positions by word of mouth or through their connections, perhaps siblings, or other relations who lived in towns. The eighteenth century also saw the development of servants' agencies, and advertisements for servants would be placed in provincial newspapers. Jonas Hanway estimated that 50,000 Londoners (both men and women) were in domestic service in 1767, in other words 7.7 per cent of the total population. Patricia Seleski estimates that there were perhaps 80,000 women in service in London by the end of the eighteenth century, although Schwarz cautions regarding the variance in the estimates made by late eighteenth-century commentators, many of whom manufactured their statistics to lace their descriptions of the abundance of luxury.[44] The 1851 census gives an almost equivalent proportion to the Hanway estimate, when 16.6 per cent of the total working population were full-time live-in servants.[45] In Scotland the poll tax records for Edinburgh and Aberdeen suggest that the four largest Scottish towns in the late seventeenth century must have employed at least 12,000 domestic servants: at a rough estimate one in ten girls in the sixteen to twenty-five age cohort in Scotland were in service. Women servants constituted 19 per cent of the pollable population in Edinburgh, 23 per cent in Aberdeen and 18 per cent in Perth.[46]

Some servants were able to save enough money in towns and cities to be apprenticed to a trade. Charlotte Blatch, a Colchester servant, had earned enough to pay a premium to learn the business of a mantua maker by 1804.[47] Work training was another reason why girls moved into towns and in branches of the consumer-orientated fashion trades such as mantua making, and millinery opportunities for girls' apprenticeship were rising over this time period.[48] These ranged from informal training, for example, a girl being put to a lacemaker in an east Devon or Bedfordshire town to learn the trade, through to formal indentures to a mistress who was a member of the company of haberdashers in London. At the lower reaches, much needlework was sweated labour and proliferated in the first half of the nineteenth century, often on a seasonal and

[43] T. Meldrum, 'Ubiquity and invisibility: domestic service in London, 1660–1750' (unpublished paper presented at Economic History Society conference, April 1993), p. 5.

[44] P. Seleski, 'Women, work and cultural change in eighteenth- and early nineteenth-century London', in T. Harris, ed., *Popular Culture in England c. 1500–1850* (London, 1995), p. 144; Schwarz, 'English servants and their employers'.

[45] Meldrum, 'Ubiquity', p. 4.

[46] Whyte, 'Urbanization in early modern Scotland' p. 33; Whyte and Whyte, 'The geographical mobility', p. 97.

[47] Sharpe, *Adapting to Capitalism*, p. 113.

[48] M. Prior, 'Women and the urban economy: Oxford 1500–1800', in M. Prior, ed., *Women in English Society 1500–1800* (London, 1985), pp. 108–9; E. C. Sanderson, *Women and Work in Eighteenth-Century Edinburgh* (London, 1996); D. Simonton, 'Apprenticeship, training and gender in eighteenth-century England', in M. Berg, ed., *Markets and Manufacture in Early Industrial Europe* (London, 1991), pp. 227–60.

casual basis and located where manufacturers were seeking to undercut traditional guild production.[49] Women also had a significant role in market trading (see Plate 14) and in managing retail outlets in towns and cities, particularly widows carrying on their former husband's businesses.[50] In Scottish cities, women's businesses appear to have been common and supported by the legal system.[51] Women were also employed in expanding professions such as teaching.[52]

The extent and characteristics of migration during British industrialisation is a gainful area for future research. However, the bias toward female migrants seems to suggest that women's labour was surplus to some areas of the capitalist farming economy. At the same time, rising demand for consumer products and services as a result of expanding wealth created a demand for women workers in urban areas. Migration was, then, perhaps as often a positive move as a result of despair. High female migration must have influenced the complexion of some towns in the early industrial period. How did the migrant experience affect demographic patterns?

(ii) URBANISATION AND THE DEMOGRAPHIC PROCESS

The background to the demographic situation in eighteenth- and early nineteenth-century urban areas is provided in Chapter 6. Chapter 14 gives details of the size and scale of the urban process. British population growth was on average 2.5 per cent per annum at the peak of the urbanisation process in the 1820s, and therefore only about half the rate of contemporary third world countries.[53] However, some cities grew at a faster rate than this and the unprecedented pace was alarming to observers at the time. Glasgow added 5,000 people to its population every year in the 1820s.[54] By the 1830s the city's rate of growth was 3.2 per cent a year. In the 1820s Manchester and Salford grew by 3.9 per cent, Bradford by 5.9 per cent and West Bromwich by 4.8 per cent. South Wales mining towns grew apace despite starting from a much smaller base. Monmouthshire's population doubled in the first decade of the nineteenth

[49] There is now an extensive literature on this for the mid- and late nineteenth century. For an earlier period see B. Lemire, 'Redressing the history of the clothing trade in England: ready-made clothing, guilds and women workers 1650–1800', *Dress*, 21 (1994), 61–74; M. Berg, 'Women's work, mechanization and the early phases of industrialization in England', in R. E. Pahl, ed., *On Work* (Oxford, 1988); S. Alexander, 'Women's work in nineteenth-century London', in J. Mitchell and A. Oakley, eds., *The Rights and Wrongs of Women* (London, 1986), pp. 59–111; P. Sharpe and S. D. Chapman, 'Women's employment and industrial organisation: commercial lace embroidery in early nineteenth-century Ireland and England', *Women's History Review*, 5 (1996), 325–50.

[50] S. D'Cruze, '"To acquaint the ladies": women traders in Colchester 1750–1800', *Local Historian*, 17 (1986), 158–62; M. R. Hunt, *The Middling Sort* (Berkeley, Calif., 1996), pp. 125–46.

[51] Sanderson, *Women and Work*.

[52] S. Skedd, 'Women teachers and the expansion of girl's schooling in England *c.* 1760–1820', in H. Barker and E. Chalus, eds., *Gender in Eighteenth-Century England* (London, 1997), pp. 101–25.

[53] Williamson, *Coping*, p. 2.

[54] Devine, 'Urbanisation', p. 49.

century, then grew by 70 per cent from 1810 to 1830. Some of the mining villages experienced tenfold population increases in this time period. Merthyr had nearly 8,000 people in 1801 but swelled by over 50 per cent in each decade to reach 27,000 in 1831, by which point it was the most densely populated community in Wales.[55]

Langton's chapter in this volume (Chapter 14), and particularly his figures, give the results of a new attempt to tabulate the size of towns and the degree of urbanisation. This suggests that 40 per cent of the population of seventeenth-century England already lived in urban areas, a position reached by the whole country by 1800. However, in concurrence with the conventional older picture the country as a whole saw the pace of urbanisation accelerate over the entire period in question. The British urban population more than doubled from 1801 to 1841. In 1801, 42 per cent of the population lived in towns (a 10 per cent increase from the late seventeenth century) while by 1841, 51 per cent were town inhabitants. By the mid-nineteenth century over 40 per cent of British people lived in cities of more than 10,000 people.[56] By contrast approximately 33 per cent of the inhabitants of the Netherlands and Scotland did so, 20 per cent of Belgians, 15 per cent of the French, 11 per cent of Germans, 10 per cent of the Irish and 6 per cent of the inhabitants of Nordic countries.[57] Scotland had the fastest rate of urban growth anywhere in Europe between 1650 and 1850.[58] The proportion of Scots living in large towns rose from an estimated 9.2 per cent to 17.2 per cent in the second half of the eighteenth century.[59] The growth of all the British cities was overshadowed by the startling growth in the size of London, by far the largest city in Europe. Taking Tony Wrigley's estimates, whereas London's population was 575,000 in 1700 by 1800 it was 900,000 (see Table 19.1 for more details). The city contained approximately 11 per cent of the country's entire population in 1750.[60] Contemporaries perceived that London's expansion was parasitic – the city was growing at the expense of other smaller settlements. Demographic historians concur in thinking that in the eighteenth century middle-rank centres lost population as migrants either moved to London or other large cities or remained in proto-industrial villages.[61]

55 G. A. Williams, *The Merthyr Rising* (London, 1978), pp. 26–7.

56 Lawton, 'Population mobility', p. 150.

57 M. Anderson, *Population Change in North-Western Europe 1750–1850* (London, 1988), p. 26.

58 R. A. Houston and C. W. J. Withers, 'Population mobility in Scotland and Europe 1600–1900: a comparative perspective', *Annales de Démographie Historique* (1990), 293.

59 R. E. Tyson, 'Contrasting regimes: population growth in Ireland and Scotland during the eighteenth century', in S. J. Connolly, R. A. Houston and R. J. Morris, eds., *Conflict, Identity and Economic Development* (Preston, 1995), p. 68.

60 E. A. Wrigley, 'A simple model of London's importance in changing English society and economy, 1650–1750', repr. in E. A. Wrigley, ed., *People, Cities and Wealth* (Oxford, 1987), p. 134.

61 R. Woods, 'What would one need to know to solve the "natural increase in early modern cities" problem?', in R. Lawton, ed., *The Rise and Fall of Modern Cities* (London, 1989), pp. 80–95. P. Clark, 'Small towns in England 1550–1800: national and regional population trends', in P. Clark, ed., *Small Towns in Early Modern Europe* (Cambridge, 1995), pp. 90–120, uses listings and aggregate

London and other cities were perceived as 'demographic sinks' until the mid-nineteenth century. They were thought to drain the countryside of people, sucking them into a sump of excess mortality and lower fertility which was associated in contemporary minds with the moral corruption of the city. It was observed that cities rarely replaced their populations by natural growth. By contrast the countryside and 'natural air' was thought to produce healthy individuals. It was the case that when life expectancy (E_0) became measurable from the 1811 census, it was less than thirty in London and all towns of 100,000 plus, whereas in rural areas it was forty-one.[62] Small wonder that London was described as 'the Great Wen' – a festering, pestilential cyst on the face of civilised life.

To go much beyond population estimates is, however, to enter a minefield where the demographic historian encounters source limitations and methodological difficulties at every turn. Most apparently, the large-scale migration to urban areas of the eighteenth century predates both national censuses and civil registration. As de Vries accurately sums up the situation: 'The demographic characteristics of urban populations in the early modern period are not well known. In fact, the impressive advances made in historical demography during the last twenty years have only made more acute our sense of ignorance about fertility, mortality and nuptiality among city dwellers.'[63] The basic evidence for historical demography before the advent of civil registration are parish registers which have been used to great effect for small towns and rural villages to elicit information on age at marriage, infant and child mortality, birth spacing and average life expectancy through the technique of family reconstitution. For large towns and cities, which contained many distinct parishes, the sheer size of the task to be undertaken in assembling the data for reconstitution is overwhelming, notwithstanding the myriad of other problems confronting the urban demographic historian. Unreliable and incomplete parish registers abound for urban areas. Nonconformist registration which may be accounted for in a small-scale study becomes a more complex obstacle in the city. All reconstitutions capture the demographic experience of settled rather than migratory individuals and the fact that migrants' baptisms and marriages are unknown is an insuperable problem in the urban context. These problems are even more serious for Wales where reconstitution is confounded by the fact that parish registers were usually

Footnote 61 (*cont.*)
population figures to suggest a more optimistic picture of how many small towns fared. Nevertheless, some towns responded to pressures more adequately than others and many towns lost out from the 1790s and in the economic difficulties of the 1820s and 1830s. For more detail see below, pp. 751 *et passim*; and E. A. Wrigley *et al.*, *English Population History from Family Reconstitution 1580–1837* (Cambridge, 1997). [62] Daunton, *Progress and Poverty*, p. 409.

[63] De Vries, *European Urbanization*, is excellent on the limitations of the sources. On Scotland's defective registration see R. A. Houston, 'The demographic regime', in Devine and Mitchison, eds., *People and Society*, pp. 10–12.

only started during the eighteenth century, patronymic naming systems were used into the nineteenth century and dissenting congregations were common.

In spite of the drawbacks, for England some partial urban reconstitutions have been carried out to great effect. For seventeenth-century populations for example, Roger Finlay has carried out a partial reconstitution of London, as has Chris Galley for York.[64] John Landers has also reconstituted sections of eighteenth-century London using the registers of Quaker meetings.[65] Omissions and overlaps mean that even basic aggregate data on the number of baptisms, marriages and burials does not exist. This leads to the greatest drawback of all – the lack of knowledge of the 'at risk' population, without which it is not possible to make estimates of either the age or sex structure of the populace.[66] A recent attempt to circumvent this problem concerns the application of a new method called Generalised Inverse Projection (GIP), which incorporates the techniques of inverse projection and back projection, but this has yet to be attempted for a British urban population.[67]

The application of this method has the potential to shed light on one of the beguiling problems of eighteenth-century demographic history. Implicit in the understanding of the continuing growth of urban areas is the possibility that mortality started to fall at some point in the late eighteenth century. But did a real fall in mortality actually take place in urban areas or was this merely an effect of the severe underregistration of parish registers? J. T. Krause, writing in the 1950s, assumed there was such an enormous omission of baptisms and burials in the post-1780 registers that a fall in death rates based on an aggregate count was unrealistic and argued that cities must have experienced a fertility rise for population growth to have been at all possible.[68] The failure of registration can be seen as a result of the inability of the established Church to keep pace with the swelling populace. For infant mortality in particular, this problem appears serious. Over the course of the eighteenth century the gap between birth and baptism widened to at least a month which means that many infants dying shortly after birth in the late eighteenth century and early nineteenth century are seen by demographers as 'missing events'. Tony Wrigley and Roger Schofield estimate that some 5 per cent of births were not registered in the mid-eighteenth century but that this figure had risen to around 20 per cent by the early nineteenth century.[69] This

64 Finlay, *Population and Metropolis*; C. Galley, 'A model of early modern urban demography', *Ec.HR*, 48, 2nd series (1995), 448–69.

65 J. Landers, *Death and the Metropolis* (Cambridge, 1993).

66 See Woods, 'What would one need to know?', p. 80, on this point.

67 M. H. D. van Leeuwen and J. E. Oeppen, 'Reconstructing the demographic regime of Amsterdam 1681–1820', *Economic and Social History of the Netherlands*, 5 (1993), 61–102.

68 J. T. Krause, 'Changes in English fertility and mortality 1781–1850' *Ec.HR*, 2nd series, 11 (1958), 52–70.

69 E. A. Wrigley and R. S. Schofield, *The Population History of England 1541–1871* (London, 1981), pp. 96–102. See also B. Midi Berry and R. S. Schofield, 'Age at baptism in pre-industrial England', *Population Studies*, 25 (1971), 453–64, for an earlier estimate.

point was considered by Bob Woods, Naomi Williams and Chris Galley when examining infant mortality in the period 1700–1840. They found that the steady fall in infant mortality rates over the period may be illusory because the parish registers became less accurate as an increasing delay between birth and baptism caused underrecording, which became evident when checked against a Quaker register.[70] A different source for evidence of mortality rates, the bills of mortality drawn up by eighteenth-century towns and recording causes of death have now also been found wanting. A comparison of the bills of mortality for Chester and Carlisle suggests that although of apparently good quality, these records have similar problems to parish registers. It is also the case that insofar as they can be used, bills of mortality have shown that levels and patterns of death in quite similar places can demonstrate markedly different mortality experiences.[71]

These shortcomings cannot be overlooked. Urban demographic historians are confounded by problems of evidence which is, to paraphrase Woods, 'at best unreliable, at worst contradictory' and yet, to be able to produce the sort of micro-community population history which is possible for villages and small towns, we need to know about the life course of individual men and women in terms of migration, marriage, reproduction and life expectancy.[72] As the concern of social history moves away from emphasis on overarching structures to concern with human agency, these problems become yet more vexing. Two further methodological points might be made. The first is that the demographic history of England, in contrast to that of Scotland, or continental Europe, has tended to place emphasis on fertility rather than mortality explanations which would now appear to have been to the detriment of urban demography. Secondly, demographic history has been largely bereft of class-specific analysis which would aid our understanding of the causes of demographic changes. While fertility and mortality have tended to be treated separately, and been given very different weightings in explanations of demographic change, the most recent views of urban growth and decline suggest that it is the interaction between migration, fertility and mortality which take us furthest in explaining population trends in the city.[73] What facts can be pieced together?

The 'urban graveyard' effect is the best-known characteristic of the demography of towns and cities. As de Vries put it, 'The implied inability of cities to

[70] R. Woods, N. Williams and C. Galley, 'Infant mortality in England 1550–1950: problems in the identification of long-term trends and geographical and social variations', in C. Corsini and P. P. Viazzo, eds., *The Decline of Infant Mortality in Europe 1800–1950: Four National Case Studies* (Florence, 1993).

[71] W. A. Armstrong, 'The trend of mortality in Carlisle between the 1780s and 1840s: a demographic contribution to the standard of living debate', *Ec.HR*, 2nd series, 34 (1981), 94–114; C. Galley, N. Williams and R. Woods, 'Detection without correction: problems in assessing the quality of English ecclesiastical and civil registration', *Annales de Démographique Historique* (1995), 161–83.

[72] Woods, 'What would one need to know?', p. 84.

[73] Galley, 'A model of early modern urban demography'.

sustain themselves by natural generation constitutes what is easily the single most widely noted demographic feature of early modern cities.' The urban graveyard constitutes 'the venerable orthodoxy of urban natural decrease'.[74] This echoes the view of contemporaries. As Malthus saw it, cities were killers, snuffing out life at the source:

> There certainly seems to be something in great towns, and even in moderate towns, peculiarly unfavourable to the very early stages of life: and the part of the community on which the mortality principally falls, seems to indicate that it arises more from the closeness and foulness of the air, which may be supposed to be unfavourable to the tender lungs of children, and the greater the superior degree of luxury and debauchery usually and justly attributed to towns.[75]

Allen Sharlin produced a speculative rebuttal of the 'urban graveyard thesis' for early modern cities. He suggested that high death rates only applied to migrants; natives would have experienced natural increase and therefore the population would not have declined except for immigration. He sought to distinguish between temporary and permanent residents. The temporary migrants, such as artisan journeymen and servants, were prevented from marrying prior to the nineteenth century due to restrictive practices in their employments or households, or simply due to the sexual imbalances in urban areas.[76] This view has been controversial.[77] De Vries argued that city life was more open than Sharlin portrayed and that migrants did marry natives. Not only would this result from the unbalanced sex ratio because native women would need to take partners who were migrant men but a migrant man seeking urban citizenship and a job would do well to marry a native woman. But both Sharlin and his critics seem to be floundering with a paucity of evidence. Distinguishing between the settled and permanent residents of cities is difficult given the available records. Generalising about the limitations on young people's lives needs more qualification. Indeed, whereas we now know a good deal about youth, service and apprenticeship, as well as the social history of marriage in the sixteenth and seventeenth centuries, for the eighteenth century – the transitional era of early industrial Britain – a great deal less research has been carried out.[78] It may be

74 De Vries, *European Urbanization*, esp. pp. 178–80.

75 T. R. Malthus, *An Essay on the Principle of Population* (London, published 1803, printed 1973), quoted p. 242 in Woods, 'What would one need to know?', p. 80.

76 A. Sharlin, 'Natural decrease in early modern cities: a reconsideration', *P&P*, 79 (1978), 126–38. K. A. Lynch, 'The European marriage pattern in the cities: variations on a theme by Hajnal', *Journal of Family History*, 16 (1991), 79–96, supports the view that only a limited number of economic niches were available in early modern urban society.

77 R. Finlay, 'Natural decrease in early modern cities' *P&P*, 92 (1981), 169–74, and rejoinder by A. Sharlin in same volume, 175–80. De Vries, *European Urbanization*, pp. 185–92.

78 For the early modern period, P. Griffiths, *Youth and Authority* (Oxford, 1996); Ben-Amos, *Adolescence and Youth*; J. Lane, *Apprenticeship in England, 1600–1914* (London, 1996). However, see J. Gillis, *For Better, for Worse: British Marriages 1600 to the Present* (Oxford, 1985), on urban marriage.

that migrants were both more thrifty and determined to establish themselves in urban areas before marriage, whereas in rural areas, certainly by the second half of the century, the decline of live-in service along with expanding poor relief encouraged early marriage. Given these caveats, however, recent research confirms some of the broad tenets of Sharlin's argument.

Landers' detailed investigation of London's demography shows that the city experienced particularly high mortality in the period 1700–75. Mortality was highest for migrants, bearing out Sharlin's case. Smallpox 'constituted a particular threat to the lives of migrants many of whom seemed to have lacked immunity to the disease'.[79] His reconstitution of Quaker records showed that a quarter to a third of all smallpox casualties were aged fifteen to thirty and almost all had recently migrated to London. However, fertility was also high. The Quakers' birth rate was 20 per cent or more higher than in other English reconstitutions and dropping in the late eighteenth century. It is not clear whether this was due to lower marital fertility or nuptiality but birth intervals appeared to be shortened by the first quarter of the eighteenth century, perhaps because wealthier people were less keen to breastfeed.[80] Sarah Hanmer, a young West Country woman newly married into the gentry in 1717, explained to her apparently incredulous aunt in Dorset that during their sojourn in London for the season, for her baby son Walden 'i am not a Nurse my self but have a wett nurse in the house, one of this town'.[81]

The latest intervention in the Sharlin debate is by Galley who has developed a model to explain urban demography.[82] Galley shows that variations in the proportion of women who married are indeed important. Declining nuptiality and fertility in late seventeenth-century York was associated with the increased proportion of female migrants. He suggests that both mortality and fertility interacted with each other and with the economy so that in the case of London a higher than normal proportion of the population would have to marry and procreate for natural increase to occur. However, other evidence has shown that immigrants who married each other did so at late ages and that bachelors, spinsters and the widowed predominated in urban areas.[83] The fact that marriage seems to have taken place at later ages or not at all in urban areas presents some problems for the predominant neo-Malthusian demographic explanations which suggest that availability of resources determined marriage age and chances.[84]

[79] Landers, *Death and the Metropolis*, p. 160. [80] *Ibid.*, pp. 190–4.

[81] Pinney papers, Bristol University Library Special Collections, letter from Sarah Hanmer 10 May 1718.

[82] Galley, 'A model of early modern urban demography'. It is instructive to compare Galley's results with P. J. P. Goldberg, *Women, Work and Life Cycle in a Medieval Economy* (Oxford, 1992).

[83] De Vries, *European Urbanization*, p. 190, finds that immigrants marrying each other do have late marriage ages. See also Weber, *The Growth of Cities in the Nineteenth Century*, p. 3, on marriage chances.

[84] This central issue is explored in the special issue of *Journal of Family History*, 16 (1991).

Work opportunities and access to earnings would then seem to have a more complex relationship with nuptiality than has hitherto been ascribed by Wrigley and Schofield's model.[85] Celibacy does not seem to have been confined to the elite; it was not only the practice of professionals and those waiting to inherit land, but had much wider social applicability as a feature of town life.[86]

Illegitimacy used to be thought high in urban areas, in line with the peak in national illegitimacy ratios in the early decades of the nineteenth century.[87] As Nicholas Rogers put it for eighteenth-century London, 'Rich and poor lived cheek by jowl in this luxury-driven economy which was persistently fuelled by new recruits from the countryside. It was the type of milieu in which illicit sexual activity was likely very high and in which illegitimacy was a perpetual hazard.'[88] Anomie in urban areas, the presence of foundling hospitals and high levels of cohabitation have all been seen to contribute to illegitimate births.[89] Sexual behaviour in London has been seen to be courtship-led whereas it was marriage-led in the countryside.[90] However, recent research by Richard Adair finds both illegitimacy and bridal pregnancy levels to be low in urban areas before 1750.[91] The early-nineteenth century high also seems to be a mainly rural phenomenon. To a large degree, then, the evidence is for a celibate culture in towns and cities in which customary norms were not carried over from the countryside.

However, recent results of reconstitutions, which provide information on the demography of towns such as Banbury and Gainsborough, have refined our knowledge of fertility in urban areas. First, there was a rise in marital fertility over the course of the 'long' eighteenth century. The reconstitutions show a particularly striking rise in the fecundity of older women (aged thirty-five and over), contributing to an increase in marital fertility of some 8 per cent between the late seventeenth and the early nineteenth centuries. Not only did birth intervals become shorter, but combined with a fall in average age of female marriage by two years over the course of the eighteenth century (in both rural and urban areas), and an overall rise in the proportion of illegitimate birth from 1.5 to 6 per

85 Wrigley and Schofield, *Population History*.

86 Sharpe, 'Literally spinsters', 46–65. Based on evidence from the Netherlands, van der Woude argues that 'urban disamenities' had not disappeared when the population started to show natural increase, so that in an earlier period there was unrealised potential for excess fertility. A. M. van der Woude, 'Population developments in the northern Netherlands (1500–1800) and the validity of the urban graveyard effect', *Annales de Démographie Historique* (1982), 55–75.

87 P. Laslett, K. Oosterveen and R. M. Smith, eds., *Bastardy and its Comparative History* (London, 1980), pp. 26–7.

88 N. Rogers, 'Carnal knowledge: illegitimacy in eighteenth-century Westminster', *Journal of Social History*, 23 (1989), p. 357.

89 Gillis, *For Better, for Worse*, pp. 181–2.

90 A. Wilson, 'Illegitimacy and its implications in mid-eighteenth-century London: the evidence of the Foundling Hospital', *Continuity and Change*, 4 (1989), 103–64.

91 R. Adair, *Courtship, Illegitimacy and Marriage in Early Modern England* (Manchester, 1996), pp. 188–223.

cent, the results from the Cambridge Group suggest an overall rise in gross reproduction rate (GRR) of more than 40 per cent.[92]

Turning to death rates, the patterns that emerge are perhaps clearer but explanations remain speculative and the full picture is beguilingly complex. Thomas McKeown propounded the thesis that until well into the late nineteenth century doctors could do little to reduce mortality, especially that derived from airborne disease. He argued that there was no understanding of infection before 1850. He thought hospitals spread disease and smallpox prevention was ineffective and may have actually spread disease as isolation was not rigorously applied. However, Peter Razzell has strongly argued for the effectiveness of inoculation which was in widespread use from the 1740s. He suggested in 1965 that smallpox made such a large contribution to eighteenth-century death rates that its control could provide a wholesale explanation for natural increase from the late eighteenth century.[93] More recent research has also modified McKeown's view, revising the role of health care and suggesting that there was an increased awareness of cleanliness, particularly the use of soap and cheap, washable, cotton clothing.[94]

McKeown argued that nutritional standards were important for disease resistance and, indeed, they certainly affect susceptibility to measles, tuberculosis and cholera. However, correlating the incidence of disease with high prices has not been decisive when tested across Europe. The late eighteenth century, in fact, shows declining responsiveness of mortality to price changes and life expectancy does not appear to correspond with rising average real wages. Massimo Livi-Bacci concludes that great epidemic cycles across Europe have been independent of the state of nutrition of populations.[95] Landers also found no clear correlation between real wages and mortality for eighteenth-century London although the incidence of smallpox and the ever-present 'fevers' do concur with high food prices, as in the very cold winter of 1740–1.[96]

P. R. Galloway has found a correlation between deaths from epidemic diseases such as smallpox, typhus and 'fevers' in London at times of high grain prices during the period 1670–1830, although through more complex mechanisms than simply the price of provisions.[97] Poor harvests led to rural migration to the city which would mean increased chances of contracting an infectious disease.

[92] Wrigley *et al.*, *English Population History*, pp. 383–93.

[93] T. McKeown, *The Modern Rise of Population* (London, 1976); P. E. Razzell, 'Population change in eighteenth-century England: a reappraisal', *Ec.HR*, 2nd series, 18 (1965), 312–32.

[94] Contemporaries such as Francis Place commented on the increased use of washable cotton for clothing. See also S. Cherry, 'The hospitals and population growth: the voluntary general hospitals, mortality and local populations in the eighteenth and nineteenth centuries', *Population Studies*, 34 (1980), 59–75 and 251–65. J. C. Riley, *The Eighteenth Century Campaign to Avoid Disease* (London, 1987).

[95] M. Livi-Bacci, *Population and Nutrition* (Cambridge, 1991).

[96] Landers, *Death and the Metropolis*, pp. 278–9. However, L. D. Schwarz, *London in the Age of Industrialisation* (Cambridge, 1992), p. 146, finds a less clear-cut picture. See also below, pp. 649 *et seq.*

[97] P. R. Galloway, 'Annual variations in deaths by age, deaths by cause, prices and weather in London 1670 to 1830', *Population Studies*, 39 (1985), 487–505.

However, it is his research on disease in urban France which provides some much needed class differentiation. He showed that the elite's increased access to food supply meant they had no extra protection from infection. During food shortages infectious diseases spread to all classes in densely populated Rouen. He suggested that domestic servants stood at the nexus between rich and poor. They gave food to migrant relatives who came into town in bad harvests and thus spread disease from the poor to the better-off. A similar set of circumstances may have operated in early eighteenth-century London.[98]

As cities became more segregated along class lines however, such disease environments became more confined. Thus Landers finds emerging geographical differences in London's mortality over the course of the eighteenth century. Disease was increasingly being conducted along 'pathways' due to social segregation, differences in the provision of housing, water and sanitation. The areas lacking infrastructure were, not surprisingly, those in which migrants lived. There is evidence that London was becoming cleaner from the mid-eighteenth century. Roads were paved and provided with gutters, scavenging and cleansing were carried out and manure was carted out of the city to sell.[99] But such improvements were least likely to apply in areas where migrants settled. R. A. Houston also finds an improved life expectancy for the Scottish urban elite over the course of the 'long' eighteenth century by analysing records of advocates and writers to the signet. Despite the fact that their work meant they would have been exposed to infection from all classes, distancing in terms of residence may have been operative.[100]

This points to the importance of what economic historians have termed 'urban disamenities' and the need to associate mortality with economic and social conditions. While Wrigley and Schofield have stressed the lack of correlation between death rates and real wages both Mary Dobson and John Landers argue that disease and mortality are closely tied to prevailing environmental conditions, and draw on evidence of regional variations in demographic patterns.[101] The long-running 'standard of living debate' for the Industrial Revolution period suffers from befuddled attempts to compare dissimilar and incomplete

98 P. R. Galloway, 'Differentials in demographic responses to annual price variations in pre-revolutionary France', *European Journal of Population*, 2 (1986), 269–305.

99 Landers, *Death and the Metropolis*; Schwarz, *London in the Age of Industrialisation*, pp. 151–2, 234–6, and see Schwarz's chapter in this volume.

100 R. A. Houston, 'Mortality in early modern Scotland: the life expectancy of advocates', *Continuity and Change*, 7 (1992), 47–69; R. A. Houston, 'Writers to the signet: estimates of adult mortality in Scotland from the sixteenth to the nineteenth century', *Social History of Medicine*, 8 (1995), 37–53.

101 J. Landers and A. Mouzas, 'Burial seasonality and causes of death in London 1670–1819', *Population Studies*, 42 (1988), 77–9, suggest that the early eighteenth century saw a rise in typhus mortality due to deteriorating economic and social conditions. On the link between environment and mortality more generally see M. J. Dobson, *Contours of Death and Disease in Early Modern England* (Cambridge, 1996).

types of evidence and to construct a national picture from a myriad of regional differences.[102] From the 1960s to the 1980s historians could be broadly divided into 'quantitative' (broadly, 'optimistic') and 'qualitative' (generally 'pessimistic'). Quantitative historians' efforts centred on the attempt to construct a realistic real wage index. Peter Lindert and Jeffrey Williamson's index suggested that industrialisation brought impressive gains of up to 140 per cent to all workers, but particularly argued that the lower middle class had prospered.[103] The qualitative debate, drawing on the writings of foregoing socialist historians such as Toynbee, the Webbs and the Hammonds, and expressed in the trenchant arguments of E. P. Thompson and Eric Hobsbawm, centred on the dehumanisation of the industrialisation process.[104] These writers stressed the desperate work and housing conditions and lack of infrastructure in industrial areas. They emphasised the loss of freedom and skills of the proletarianised worker, especially the former skilled artisans such as hand-loom weavers whose livelihood could be undercut by their own children being sent to harsh labour in factories and mills, thus supposedly hastening the disintegration of the family unit. Above all, the 'pessimists' described the breakdown of the traditional paternalist system of work and wages, of prices and retail. An implicitly just system of local moral economy was now replaced by the harsh and unremitting logic of *laissez-faire*. Even if evidence could be found for rising real wages, the optimists had taken insufficient account of chronic unemployment and underemployment.

In many ways the argument echoed the views of contemporaries who had debated the 'Condition of England' question. There is now little debate about the late eighteenth century, which prior to the inflation of the French wars saw relatively low food prices. The main arena of contest is the period 1820–40 which apparently saw the greatest gain in real wages but also the direst consequences of 'urban disamenities'. Illnesses derived from contaminated food and water remained at a high level until the late nineteenth century, indeed dysentery and typhus may have increased due to deteriorating economic and social conditions. More recently, attempts have been made to forward the debate using new types of evidence. Roderick Floud, Kenneth Wachter and Annabel Gregory's work on the average heights of conscripts suggests significant improvements in nutrition and that height inequalities within the working class narrowed in the late eighteenth and early nineteenth centuries; however, from the second quarter of the nineteenth century, average heights declined, corresponding with higher national mortality in Wrigley and Schofield's results.[105]

[102] A good recent summary is Daunton, *Progress and Poverty*, pp. 420–46.

[103] P. H. Lindert and J. G. Williamson, 'English workers' living standards during the Industrial Revolution: a new look', *Ec.HR*, 2nd series, 36 (1983), 1–25.

[104] E. P. Thompson, *The Making of the English Working Class* (London, 1963); E. J. Hobsbawm, *Labouring Men* (London, 1964), pp. 64–125.

[105] R. Floud, K. Wachter and A. Gregory, *Height, Health and History* (Cambridge, 1990). For a summary see R. Floud, 'Standards of living and industrialisation', *ReFRESH*, 16 (1988), 1–4.

Between the 1820s and 1850s the gains in real wages seem to have been offset by the effects of urbanisation, diet and possibly work intensity. Exposure to work accidents and occupational diseases may have also increased.[106] Recent research has concentrated on the effect of industrialisation on women. Stephen Nicholas and Deborah Oxley have used records of heights of convict women for the period 1795–1820 to compare the well being of women relative to men in Irish and English rural and urban areas. They conclude that the burden of the industrialising process fell on women as English women show declining heights in comparison with Irish women.[107] Sara Horrell and Jane Humphries' large-scale project on family budgets also indicates falling female living standards due to declining female wage rates and increasing unemployment.[108]

The evidence on the slowness of government intervention amid appalling urban sanitary conditions is well known and contained in the first parliamentary reports to appear when metropolitan filth became a national issue.[109] The impact of urbanisation was even more severe in Scotland in the second quarter of the nineteenth century because it was so rapid. Whereas the population of Glasgow had been 77,385 in 1801 by the 1841 census it stood at a massive 274,533. Migrants moved in from the poorest regions of the British Isles – Ireland and the south-west Highlands. Notorious slums such as Gorbals developed, as former villages were overrun. Attempts to provide poor relief, sanitation or any civic amenities were overtaken, leading to a sharp rise in death rates in the early nineteenth century. No other Scottish city had a comparable level of mortality, with a death rate of 31.5 in 1841. In the 1837 typhus epidemic Glasgow was thought to have the highest recorded number of fever deaths in Britain. The population expansion ran alongside economic growth but the local economy was dominated by a textile industry heavily dependent on unstable overseas markets. In the long run urban growth simply outran economic possibilities with huge unemployment bringing the collapse of wages in the 1815–30 period.[110]

When cholera arrived in the new industrial town of Sunderland from Asia in 1831, it ravaged places like the poor districts of Glasgow, as it was transmitted by

[106] C. G. Spence, 'Dangerous work: occupational mortality in late seventeenth-century London' (unpublished paper presented at the Social History Conference, Glasgow, January 1996), has assembled casualty information from bills of mortality.

[107] S. Nicholas and D. Oxley, 'The living standards of women during the Industrial Revolution, 1795–1820', *Ec.HR*, 46 (1993), 723–49.

[108] S. Horrell and J. Humphries, 'Women's labour force participation and the transition to the male-breadwinner family, 1790–1865', *Ec.HR*, 48 (1995), 89–117.

[109] A. S. Wohl, *Endangered Lives: Public Health in Victorian Britain* (Cambridge, Mass., 1983); M. W. Flinn, ed., *The Sanitary Condition of the Labouring Population of Great Britain*, by Edwin Chadwick, 1842 (Edinburgh, 1965); PP 1844 XVII and 1845 XVIII, First and Second Reports on the State of Large Towns and Populous Districts.

[110] Explored further in T. M. Devine and G. Jackson, eds., *Glasgow*, vol. I: *Beginnings to 1830* (Manchester, 1995), p. 404, who find that no Scottish town had comparably high mortality rates. The comparative crude death rate in 1841 for Aberdeen was 16.0, Dundee 22.1, and Edinburgh 25.4.

drinking water contaminated by sewage. It spread rapidly through the country in 1832 affecting 431 English towns and villages, afflicting 82,528 people and leading to 31,376 deaths due to ineptitude, slowness or panic in dealing with the disease.[111] In the long run the shock effects convinced the authorities to act. Local boards of health were created, and specific acts were passed for cities to cleanse themselves but none of these measures were effective in anything other than a very localised way during the time period considered here. Indeed, cities remained reservoirs of lethal infections beyond 1840.

The most significant barometer of the economic and social condition of a society is the infant mortality rate (IMR). This was recognised by contemporary commentators as the quotation from Malthus indicated. Demographic historians have recently argued that its importance as a critical variable in population change has been overlooked in favour of marriage and fertility.[112] Since infant deaths accounted for up to 50 per cent of all deaths in urban areas in the eighteenth century, the importance of the IMR in an assessment of the 'urban graveyard' is obvious. Due to the problems discussed above regarding the growing gap between birth and baptism in the course of the eighteenth century the sources are particularly problematic. Landers found that infant mortality accounted for some 330 per 1,000 live births in London in the early eighteenth century with the number dropping towards the end of the century.[113] Infant and child mortality were exceptionally high (twice the level of other English reconstitutions and for 1725–50 two times higher than in the London of 1840) due mainly to gastric disease and smallpox.

The difference between urban and rural areas elsewhere in the country is apparent from family reconstitutions. In the first half of the eighteenth century child mortality in Gainsborough, Lincolnshire, was 272 per 1,000, whereas in Hartland, a rural parish in Devon, it was three times lower at 85 per 1,000 in 1700–49. Recent research by Paul Huck for nine industrialising parishes in the early nineteenth-century North and West Midlands has found a substantial and sustained increase in infant mortality except in the smallest parishes. Thus when infant mortality fell in London it was rising in other areas which lacked social

[111] J. Walvin, *English Urban Life 1776–1851* (London, 1984), pp. 27–8.

[112] Galley, Williams and Woods, 'Detection without correction'. While maternal mortality made only a very small contribution to overall death rates, it is worth noting that maternal mortality rates were consistently higher in London than in other areas but they were dropping everywhere in the course of the 'long' eighteenth century. See R. S. Schofield, 'Did mothers really die? Three centuries of maternal mortality in "the world we have lost"', in L. Bonfield, R. Smith and K. Wrightson, eds., *The World we Have Gained* (Oxford, 1986), pp. 231–60; I. Loudon, *Death in Childbirth: An International Study of Maternal Care and Maternal Mortality 1800–1950* (Oxford, 1992).

[113] Landers, *Death and the Metropolis*, p. 170. See also J. Landers, 'Age patterns of mortality in London during the "long eighteenth century": a test of the "high potential" model of metropolitan mortality', *Social History of Medicine*, 3 (1990), 27–60.

and economic infrastructures and where population density was high.[114] The close association between mortality and economic and social conditions is shown by Glasgow where childhood deaths from smallpox declined in the 1790s–1810s but increased again in the 1830s and 1840s.[115]

However, for urban areas in the country as a whole the picture is one of relative improvement for survival chances of infants under the age of two over the period 1700–1840.[116] For Scotland, R. A. Houston found that child mortality, which accounted for from a fifth to a quarter of all live births in the mid-eighteenth century, had dropped to an eighth a century later.[117] Nevertheless, the urban/rural differential was still much higher in 1841 than it was to be in 1901. Huck's study of the seasonality of infant mortality finds a change from a winter to a summer peak over the course of the nineteenth century and he attributes this to reduced breast feeding which confers some immunity from disease to babies, possibly due to malnutrition making mothers unable to breast feed.[118]

As Woods suggests, a fall in infant and child mortality, an increase in nuptiality and a newly balanced sex ratio among the young with some economic encouragement to marry would have been sufficient 'to take Georgian London from natural decline to Victorian growth'.[119] Such an overview, set in a different time frame, might similarly apply to urban areas outside of London.

(iii) MAKING SOCIETY

How did migrants adapt and did their presence shape the circumstances of urban life? What were the effects of the demographic situation on urban society? As we have seen, most migrants were poor, and many, like Thomas Carter, or the thousands of nameless domestic servants alighting at coaching inns, arrived alone. Death rates were high, marriages were late, fertility may have been low overall, and infant and child mortality were high. Even if these circumstances eased over time and were both relative and localised, the general conditions stand

114 P. Huck, 'Infant mortality in nine industrial parishes in northern England, 1813–1836', *Population Studies*, 48 (1994), 513–26; P. Huck, 'Infant mortality and living standards of English workers during the Industrial Revolution', *Journal of Economic History*, 55 (1995), 528–50.

115 Anderson, *Population Change*, p. 58.

116 P. Laxton and N. Williams, 'Urbanization and infant mortality in England: a long term perspective and review', in M. C. Nelson and J. Rogers, eds., *Urbanisation and the Epidemiologic Transition* (Uppsala, 1989), pp. 109–31.

117 Houston, 'The demographic regime', p. 14.

118 P. Huck 'Shifts in the seasonality of infant deaths in nine English towns during the nineteenth century: a case for reduced breast feeding?', *Explorations in Economic History*, 34 (1997), 368–86. V. Fildes, *Breasts, Bottles and Babies: A History of Infant Feeding* (Edinburgh, 1986), pp. 398–400, finds that it became fashionable for middle-class women to feed their own babies from the mid-eighteenth century. The situation is less clear for poor women and probably varied depending on female work opportunities.

119 Woods, 'What would one need to know?'.

for the whole period 1700 to 1840. As a result, many people were single, or at least lived in small family units or in other people's households. However, this is not to say that migrants remained solitary. Research has shown that urban dwellers were not necessarily isolated or disorientated but could draw on a variety of informal social networks.[120] Whereas the history of the family has stressed the self-sufficiency of the nuclear unit, in the long run urban historians may challenge this by drawing attention to the mutuality of households in urban areas. Sociologists traditionally made distinctions between *Gemeinschaft* and *Gesellschaft*, charting a change from a small, intimate, immobile world to a large-scale, impersonal, individualistic one. Aside from the implicit Whig standpoint, and oversimplicity, this view overlooks both the 'urban village' context of life in developing cities as well as the multiplicity of both horizontal and vertical links which individuals needed to live by.

On arrival in an urban area most migrants who could do so went to kin or 'friends' unless they had already arranged a live-in job with an employer. Michael Anderson found lodgers present in 23 per cent of Preston households in his sample from the 1851 census. Of these, 48 per cent were unmarried. At least half of all Preston couples lived with kin or in lodgings for the first few years after marriage.[121] He argued that kin were an essential source of functional assistance for migrants in finding jobs and becoming established in other ways. When David Spearman from Braintree tried to get a job as a manservant in London in 1834 he first stayed with his brother and his young family who lived in Bishopsgate-without parish. Finding a suitable post took longer than he had anticipated. His knowledge as a footman was not sufficient for sophisticated London and he was forced to set lower sights on being a groom.[122] Even distant relatives, and family acquaintances or god-parents, could be helpful in the city. Contacts were established with people from the same town or general area of the country. Using kin as servants was likely to have been also common, particularly in gentrified and residential towns.[123]

Some of the poor who wrote to parish overseers for financial support mention lack of kin or contacts as the greatest of their difficulties. This situation may have been even more straitening for women than for men due to their low earnings and greater difficulty in ensuring social credibility. Sarah Withnell, a silk weaver who moved from Colchester to Spitalfields in 1815 asked the overseers to consider her situation 'A wider [widow] with 2 children in a strange Place, it was a grate favour for anyone to give me credate [credit].' She had moved to join her

[120] C. Lis and H. Soly, 'Neighbourhood social change in western European cities: sixteenth to nineteenth centuries', *International Review of Social History*, 38 (1993), 11.

[121] M. Anderson, *Family Structure in Nineteenth-Century Lancashire* (Cambridge, 1971), pp. 46, 53.

[122] Essex RO, D/P 264/18/24.

[123] D. Cooper and M. Donald, 'Households and "hidden" kin in early-nineteenth-century England: four case studies in suburban Exeter, 1821–1861', *Continuity and Change*, 10 (1995), 257–78.

aunt but nevertheless her greatest concern, in order to find work and become financially secure, was to get known and established. Elizabeth Ann Manning, a widow living in London but originally from Rochford, in the late 1820s complained that she needed help from her home parish because she had not got 'any Friends to do the lest trifle for me'.[124] A study of industrialisation and emigration into the port of Antwerp in this period stresses the importance of proletarian networks which offered mutuality by caring for the sick, taking in children and other acts of reciprocal assistance. Catherina Lis' analysis of migrants to Antwerp in 1817 found that only 20.4 per cent had relatives or friends to go to on arrival.[125] She points out that those who did not have strong contacts in the city prior to their move or who did not marry (and then preferably to a native) had great difficulty in integrating in the sense that they were far more likely to have to draw on public relief than those with connections. Thomas Carter seems to have led a fairly solitary life in terms of social pursuits but he fostered people he knew. These were the contacts who found him work, an abode and encouraged his literary leanings.

Catherina Lis and Hugo Soly argue that 'Lodging was not only financially profitable for both parties, it also formed the basis of reciprocal relations.'[126] Being a sojourner was a normal feature of even small town life and some of it recreational rather than work related. Sue Wright found that in the Shropshire town of Ludlow roughly one in seven households contained inmates.[127] They comprised a tenth to a twelfth of the total adult population of the town and were most likely to be female and single as the eighteenth century advanced. Some of the sojourners were glovers but others were wealthy temporary residents as Ludlow became a social centre. In larger settlements, Peter Clark finds lodging houses, some catering for regions and some specific to certain occupations such as sailors, 'Men (and sometimes their wives) were supplied not only with beds, but victuals and clothes – usually on credit.'[128] Irish lodging house keepers in the East End of London met boats arriving from Irish ports to look for potential inmates among the immigrants.[129] Lodging houses were important institutions in the life of the itinerant lower orders, sometimes retaining their character over successive generations of different owners. One lodging house in Shrewsbury in 1861 housed two pedlars, a hawker, a Welsh tailor, a drover from Somerset, an Irish army pensioner, two carpet weavers, a plate engraver and Asam Ali, a Mecca-born tract distributor with his wife who was born in Cork.[130]

[124] Sharpe, *Adapting to Capitalism*, pp. 42–3, 147.

[125] C. Lis, *Social Change and the Labouring Poor* (New Haven, Conn., 1986), p. 150–60.

[126] Lis and Soly, 'Neighbourhood social change', p. 12.

[127] Wright, 'Sojourners and lodgers'.

[128] P. Clark, 'Migrants in the city: the process of social adaptation in English towns 1500–1800', in Clark and Souden, eds., *Migration and Society*, p. 284.

[129] L. H. Lees, *Exiles of Erin* (Manchester, 1979), p. 86, for a slightly later period and as noted by Mayhew.

[130] B. Trinder, *History of Shropshire* (Chichester, 1984), p. 99.

Eighteenth-century Jewish travelling pedlars gravitated towards certain lodging houses in which the landlord kept a cupboard with utensils for the preparation of kosher food.[131]

Support for migrants was available on a number of fronts: from trade clubs, unions and benefit societies. It is possible to go as far as to suggest that friendly societies could make a crucial difference in terms of whether a migrant who fell ill or into difficulties had to return home or not. As a man who had obviously regularly been sending back remittances for his children wrote home to Colchester from Whitechapel:

> I am very sorry to inform you that it is not in my power to send any money to support my four Children on Account of my Affliction. I have been afflicted for these 18 or 20 Days and what I should have done in my affliction had it not been for the support of my Brother Journeymen God knows what wou'd have become of me.[132]

Martin Gorsky's recent research on friendly societies shows that they played a vital role for migrants in asserting their claim to membership of the local community and providing a breadwinner with health insurance. He finds that membership density was highest in urban areas, and those expanding due to migration, and suggests that in leaving the poor prospects of the country migrants relinquished customary, familial and parochial support structures. 'The friendly society therefore operated as "fictive kin", meeting the needs which arose through the provision of social networks, conviviality and personal and financial support at times of life crisis.'[133] Some friendly and benefit societies also operated specifically for women.

Other migrants gained informal support from their employers or neighbours. In 1824 Widow Marsh's poverty led to the householders of one neighbourhood in Shoreditch, for whom she took in washing, to petition the overseers of her home parish of Chelmsford to give her support during the cold winter months when there was less work to do. The charity and beneficence of masters and mistresses to employees in small but probably significant ways, now invisible to the historical record, should not be ignored. The extent of support for Widow Marsh also defines for us the size of the 'urban village': here a street and an alley.[134] People's awareness of their neighbourhood constituted not more than a small area, perhaps a street with alleys and courts, akin to the size of the country village. When people moved to a new habitation, their mobility was within a limited area, which suggests that a sense of neighbourhood was important to

[131] B. Williams, *The Making of the Manchester Jewry* (Manchester, 1976), p. 2.

[132] Essex RO, D/P 203/13/4A 10/7/1816.

[133] M. Gorsky, 'The growth and distribution of friendly societies in the early nineteenth century', *Ec.HR*, 2nd series, 51 (1998), 501–2, 507. This point is also made by Clark, 'Migrants in the city', p. 282.

[134] Essex RO, D/P 94/18/42 11/10/1824.

them. This formed the boundaries of a community of which the limits of normal behaviour were bounded by gossip. The community established people's personal credit and claims to honour, usually defined in terms of male honesty in trade and female sexual propriety in a society where public slander and defamation with the term 'whore' and its various permutations was still current.[135] Privacy was in short supply and in the openness of the street everyone's actions were on public display. Sometimes the street was also still an occupational area as in clothmaking areas of towns, or docklands. In a purely practical sense the arena of poor people's operation was also limited to that where they had sufficient standing for credit, for borrowing money and, perhaps, where they regularly pawned goods. Begging also had a specific spatial dimension (see Plate 16).

The greatest importance of locality to the English poor, however, prior to 1834 may have been their attempt to gain a settlement for poor relief and this would have been conferred on many servants by being in service for a year in a certain parish. While the individuals mentioned in this chapter were writing back to their parishes because they were in receipt of non-resident poor relief, many of them also sought a settlement in their new parish and make this explicit.[136] Poor relief in city parishes has not been extensively researched for this period but many pauper letters contain the perception that provision by London parishes was better than by country parishes.[137] Indeed, some London parishes were perceived as being particularly generous in terms of support. As Daniel Rust wrote to his wife in Chelmsford workhouse from London in 1825, 'the Pore men tell me this is a Verry good Parrish and that they Pay thare Pore men with famely 3 shillings per Day and if i should be so Luckey I will try to settle my selfe thare'.[138] London parishes were understandably more in tune with the high cost of living in the city and seasonal shifts in employment. William Mathewman wrote back to Colchester from City Road, London in 1831: 'I Wish that i Do not belong to you for it Wode been Better for Me if To belong To London then to the Country for if i belonge he [here] i should [have] had Relief all the Winter for that i Wish i Deed belonge To them.'[139] By contrast, the parish-based Scottish poor relief did not prove equal to the strain of

135 A. Clark, 'Whores and gossips: sexual reputation in London 1770–1825', in A. Angerman *et al.*, *Current Issues in Women's History* (London, 1989), pp. 231–48; L. Gowing, *Domestic Dangers* (Oxford, 1996). On plebeian culture in cities more generally see A. Clark, *The Struggle for the Breeches* (Berkeley, Calif., 1995).

136 Taylor, 'A different kind of Speenhamland'; Taylor, *Poverty, Migration and Settlement.*

137 However, see the essays in L. Davison, T. Hitchcock, T. Keirn and R. B. Shoemaker, eds., *Stilling the Grumbling Hive: The Response to Social and Economic Problems in England 1689–1750* (Stroud, 1992); M. E. Fissell, *Patients, Power and the Poor in Eighteenth-Century Bristol* (Cambridge, 1991).

138 Sharpe, *Adapting to Capitalism*, p. 116. Williamson, *Coping*, pp. 188–90, finds city rents for the working class were 2.5 times higher than those in rural England. For England as a whole the cost of living for unskilled workers was 12.3 per cent lower in rural areas.

139 Essex RO, D/P 245/18/6 28/2/1831.

population growth in the 1820s and 1830s and provision was complicated by dissenting religion. Many fell through the net of support in cities with the collapse of what had been a face-to-face system. Others were excluded because denying relief was seen as having more social and moral benefit than providing help.[140]

How did migrants develop a sense of belonging? Some must have done so through churches or chapels. Methodists formed societies around themselves by building chapels in mining and other new industrial areas. Quakers carried tickets or testimonials to serve as an introduction to a new meeting. For many migrants churches would have served as their point of entry to a new milieu. Another focus might have been places where migrants went for refreshments such as local cook-shops or drinking houses. Inns and alehouses were the arrival locations for most immigrants. In many occupations they were the rendezvous for workers who wanted to find employment and they housed the 'box' of the friendly society. Furthermore, as migrant letters show, they were the places where many migrants received their mail and messages. The public house would be the hub of a neighbourhood and a place of conviviality and contacts. In cities they often had regional connections. Regional identities seem to have been cohesive rather than divisive. Migrants from certain areas of the country would settle in the same neighbourhoods. Those from Essex favoured either Spitalfields or the Elephant and Castle. Links with others who also lived in the city might be forged by trips home for annual events such as the harvest, or the town fair. Thus working people who moved to cities located themselves within a variety of overlapping communities, only one of which was their work.

David Garrioch has said of neighbourhood formation in eighteenth-century Paris: 'In a sense immigrants had no past'.[141] Cities certainly offered opportunities for people to reinvent their lives if they wanted to, yet the need for support meant that for many retaining and strengthening links with home was a defensive mechanism.[142] This is most apparent for groups like the Scots, Welsh and Irish in English cities. Several Welsh societies existed in eighteenth-century London.[143] The migration of Irish to London increased in the 1820s and 1830s. By 1841 between 75,000 and 80,000 Irish were settled there. Most lived in Irish enclaves such as the Rookery near Seven Dials. Seven Dials was 'a shopping emporium for the poor . . . residents could buy food, drink and clothes without leaving working-class territory'.[144] Irish pubs are not just a contemporary fashion but existed as early as the 1800s and functioned as information centres for newly

[140] R. Mitchison, 'The Poor Law', in Devine and Mitchison, eds., *People and Society*, pp. 262–319. Devine and Jackson, eds., *Glasgow*, p. 413, found formal provision for the poor declining based on the actual amounts of money expended in the early nineteenth century.

[141] D. Garrioch, *Neighbourhood and Community in Paris, 1740–1790* (Cambridge, 1986), p. 227.

[142] See, for example, P. Sharpe, 'Bigamy among the labouring poor in Essex 1754–1857', *Local Historian*, 24 (1994), 139–44. Much bigamy was associated with military mobility.

[143] E. Jones, 'The Welsh in London in the seventeenth and eighteenth centuries', *Welsh History Review*, 10 (1981), 461–79.

[144] Lees, *Exiles of Erin*, pp. 46, 85.

arrived migrants. Some provided a deeper and richer cultural experience. In the 1830s, John Savage's pub in St Pancras, London, was a centre for Irish singing and radical politics. At the end of each evening's session Savage would denounce the English Establishment. He later formed the Great Radical Association and eventually became a Chartist. As Lynn Lees has argued, the 'urban village' was in fact 'more a cultural than a physical community'. The social world of the London Irish 'consisted of a multitude of Irish networks that criss-crossed the working-class territory they inhabited'.[145]

Some other immigrant groups to eighteenth- and nineteenth-century Britain formed their own communities and were slow to assimilate. The kernel of the Jewish community in mid-eighteenth-century Manchester was the development of a Synagogue Alley in an area where Jewish hawkers of small luxury goods were accustomed to congregate, and later set up small shops. The permanent settlement consolidated in the aftermath of the 1793 Aliens Act after which Jews had to produce licences to be able to trade. By the end of the French wars there were an estimated 10,000 Jews in the provinces and some 15,000 in London. Although the immigration of substantial Jewish merchants only took place in the 1830s, not all of the eighteenth-century Jewish pedlars remained poor. In the 1790s Samuel Solomon's miracle 'cure' the 'Balm of Gilead' sold so well in England and America that he was soon able to build a substantial mansion just outside of Liverpool.[146]

Huguenots, almost all of whom arrived from France in 1685–6, formed an obvious separate community in early eighteenth-century England, dominating certain residential areas of Norwich, Canterbury and Spitalfields. The largest congregation, at Threadneedle Street in the City, had 7,000 members. Huguenots formed their own friendly societies, many based around regional affiliations retained from the continent. These societies met for meals and sermons but also the mutual relief of the poor and sick and for burial, in a parallel organisation to parish poor relief.[147] Huguenot communities, active in the production of intricate craft articles such as fine Spitalfields silks, glass and metalwork, also formed around workplaces. By the early nineteenth century, however, the dwindling congregations and decline in number of weavers registered with the London Weaver's Company showed that the Huguenots had assimilated rather than retained their separate identity. To an extent this was part and parcel of social acceptance; as Natalie Rothstein describes them, the Huguenots were 'an intensely orthodox community, intelligent, skilled and enlightened within limits, but on the whole, generally anxious to be accepted as "gentlemen"'.[148]

145 *Ibid.*, p. 87. 146 Williams, *Making of the Manchester Jewry*, pp. 3–16.

147 R. D. Gwynn, *Huguenot Heritage: The History and Contribution of Huguenots in Britain* (London, 1985), pp. 165–71.

148 N. Rothstein, 'Huguenots in the English silk industry in the eighteenth century', in I. Scouloudi, ed., *Huguenots in Britain and their French Background 1550–1800* (London, 1987), pp. 125–40.

The other readily identifiable group of migrants in eighteenth-century England were the blacks, almost all of whom were colonial slaves, brought by their planter masters to be household servants. Contemporaries estimated that there were some 30,000 black slaves in eighteenth-century England but judging by the size of the servant population as a whole, about half this figure seems more realistic. Certainly not as despised as the Irish, in most cases Pompey (as the black page was stereotypically named) lived and died in service but this was not always the case. Soubise, a slave boy brought to England under aristocratic patronage from St Kitts, became a noted equestrian. He then denied his slave background and claimed descent from African nobility. His later career was as a beloved riding and fencing master at Eton. Henry Mayhew's *Morning Chronicle* surveys of the early 1850s noted blacks in a variety of menial jobs. He interviewed a crippled black street-sweeper and sometime beggar from Jamaica who had previously served in the navy and merchant marine but after injury forced the amputation of both of his legs he settled in London. He married an English woman (also of black descent) from Leeds and commented to Mayhew on his drinking and cursing Irish neighbours who derided him with 'Cripple', 'Uncle Tom' or 'Nigger'. In the early nineteenth century William Cobbett objected to the number of 'debased foreigners' particularly '*Jews, Negroes* and *Mullattoes*' but perhaps because of the servile status of most eighteenth-century blacks, the crowd's xenophobic chant of 'No Popes, no Jews, no Wooden shoes' appears to have ignored them.[149]

(iv) DIVIDING SOCIETY

If migrants developed a sense of belonging by various means, if they in different ways assimilated to an urban way of life as towns and cities sprawled and solidified, to what extent was an urban identity also a class identity? The demographic experience shows that social division brought epidemic diseases which almost exclusively affected poor areas of towns and cities. When and how did ordinary people become aware of social inequality? Historians suggest that class consciousness in England is a development of the time period 1700–1850, and perhaps more specifically of the period 1780–1830. It can be suggested that in most areas of the country until the late eighteenth century, people felt less identification with their social peers than they did with those above and below them in the social hierarchy. In other words, given a patronage and dependency-based culture, people envisioned social relationships in a vertical rather than a horizontal way. Only perhaps in relatively isolated cases, such as the independent Derbyshire lead miners or the cosmopolitan sailor

[149] D. A. Lorimer, *Colour, Class and the Victorians: English Attitudes to the Negro in the Mid-Nineteenth Century* (Leicester, 1978), pp. 25–42.

population, might something approximating to class consciousness be evident in early modern society. For the lower orders, it was the status and favour of an individual's master or patron which was crucial to the progress of an individual. Historically legitimated hierarchical and occupational distinctions between trades were maintained because most workplaces were small units of production and workers had little opportunity or desire to form horizontal attachments.

We can, then, argue that the process of urbanisation was crucial for the development of class consciousness for both the working class and the middle class. Eighteenth-century historians have noted the emergence of a language of class which started to supplant that of ranks, orders and degrees.[150] As Penelope Corfield notes, the use of the word 'class' implied a dynamic; it had the potential for change and social mutability rather than the continuance of a fixed social hierarchy. The term 'middle class' appears in English writings in 1812. 'Working classes' appears in the radical free-thinker Robert Owen's writing from 1813.[151] From around 1820 contemporary writings describe the complexion of urban areas in terms of their social structure.[152] By the 1830s and 1840s people thought in terms of three classes and their writings and demagogy recognised that conflict developed from a clash of interests resulting from the distribution of wealth and power.[153]

E. P. Thompson's vastly influential writings on eighteenth-century society see working-class consciousness as developing from 'an identity of interests'. In a much-quoted passage: 'In the years between 1780 and 1832 most English working people came to feel an identity of interest as between themselves, and against their rulers and employers . . . the working-class presence was, in 1832, the most significant factor in British political life.' Thompson's avowed project was to rescue the poor stockinger, the overlooked shoemaker and their forgotten cousins, 'from the enormous condescension of posterity'.[154] Most historians would now see the claim about the influence of the working class by 1832 as overrated. This is partly because a turn in the historiography means that research has moved from trying to understand the rise of the working class (almost the sole concern of social historians in the 1960s and 1970s), to attempting to comprehend the solidification of the middle class, whereas Thompson saw the eighteenth century in terms of a polarisation between patricians and plebeians thus

150 P. J. Corfield, 'Class by name and number in eighteenth-century Britain, *History*, 72 (1987), 38–61; D. Wahrman, *Imagining the Middle Class* (Cambridge, 1995); J. Seed, 'From "middling sort" to middle class in late eighteenth-century and early nineteenth-century England', in M. L. Bush, ed., *Social Orders and Social Classes Since 1500* (Harlow, 1992), pp. 114–35.

151 R. Owen, *A New View of Society* (London, 1813).

152 R. J. Morris, 'Introduction: class, power and social structure', in R. J. Morris, ed., *Class, Power and Social Structure in British Nineteenth-Century Towns* (Leicester, 1986), p. 4.

153 R. J. Morris, *Class and Class Consciousness in the Industrial Revolution 1780–1850* (London, 1979), p. 9.

154 Thompson, *The Making of the English Working Class*, pp. 12–13.

attributing no agency to the middling orders. Nevertheless, the search for an 'identity of interests' is a useful way to approach an understanding of class consciousness for both the working class and the middle class.

In Thompson's vision, the background to the development of working-class consciousness lay first with late eighteenth-century patriotic mobs, the 'Church and King' riots of the early 1790s, then with French revolutionary agitation. Plebeians appropriated the long-heralded trope of the 'freeborn Englishman'. The nucleus of radicalism, the first true working man's organisation, was the London Corresponding Society, established in 1792, led by a radical shoemaker and migrant Scot, Thomas Hardy. Tailors, shoemakers and other handicraft workers reduced to casualised work met together, absorbed and argued through radical ideas, while waiting for jobs at houses of call (like the ones Thomas Carter frequented in the 1810s). They discussed books such as Tom Paine's *Rights of Man*, a bestseller variously reprinted from 1790 to 1792. Paine advocated democracy and deism. He was avowedly anti-aristocracy and anti-tax. Although Thompson was dismissive of the role of Methodism, and historians have debated whether or not dissenting religion served to fire or quell revolutionary spirit, there can be no doubt that it provided a counterweight to the established Church and that it gave workers practice in reading and organising committees. Springing up in sprawling mining areas, near far-flung quarries and in the midst of industrial squalor, the more 'primitive' branches of Methodism certainly held the seeds, if not the fruits, of urban radical identity.

In the Thompsonite interpretation, class consciousness was also forced by the Combination Acts of 1799/1800 which outlawed large meetings. Incipient unions were driven underground where they merged with insurrectionary activists such as machine-breakers. Although the late 1810s activities of the East Midland machine-breakers led by the mythical Ned Ludd may be interpreted as the desperate actions of men faced with declining income and trade reorganisation, for Thompson and his followers, their actions were part of a greater plan – nascent class warfare. Perhaps inhabiting the misty interstices between myth and reality, organisations like the Black Lamp in the Pennines held mass meetings with secret arming and drilling. But the failed 'Pentrich rebellion' of 1817 was no fiction. Around 300 industrial workers, without any middle-class support, marched on Nottingham with the eventual aim of storming London. In the hungry years following the wars, they were quashed by the authorities – a measure of the perception that the workers were dangerous. More decisive, was the savage suppression of the reform meeting held at Peterloo fields in Manchester in 1819. Eleven people were killed and hundreds injured out of the peaceful crowd who had gathered to hear Henry Hunt advocate universal suffrage. The subsequent outrage galvanized the development of a distinct working-class radicalism which opposed both the values of the elite and the middle class. Later, links and shared sentiments developed between Chartists,

Owenite socialists, factory reformers and anti-poor law agitators, in and around the betrayals of the 1832 Reform Act and the New Poor Law of 1834. More broadly, the background to the agitation, and the reaction to it, was the end of the paternalism–deference relationship – as the nineteenth-century historian Thomas Carlyle called it 'the abdication on the part of the Governors' – occurring at the same time as workers were propelled forcibly into the throes of a boom/slump economy.

Thompson's argument is potent, but has not been without critics.[155] Of most relevance for the urban context, John Foster analysed the development of working-class consciousness in the three industrial towns of Oldham, Northampton and South Shields in the early nineteenth century.[156] Foster found working-class consciousness to be a development of the 1830s and 1840s rather than earlier, and argued that workers were first politicised by industrial problems and later went on to develop revolutionary ideas. In a rather overlooked 'five part model', Ron Neale differentiated types of working-class consciousness, finding 'proletarian' consciousness in urban and factory areas, 'deferential' consciousness applying to women and agricultural labourers and 'privatized' consciousness espoused by skilled artisans and small shopkeepers who believed in self-interest and self-help. More recently, a study which largely concentrates on artisans in London and Glasgow has attempted to inject some much-needed gender analysis into the Thompsonite picture. Anna Clark probes the gender conflicts inherent within the rhetoric of plebian urban culture and argues that sexual crisis pervaded working-class urban communities in the early nineteenth century and imbrued the shape of working-class formation.[157] Studies of different immigrant groups in early nineteenth-century society, particularly of Irish workers, and the lack of homogeneity of occupational experience, further serve to splinter and render romantic a view of the identical interests of workers. Yet while there may have been competing aims and outlooks of working men and women, horizontal alliances may have been forged in reaction to the imposition of middle-class values and needs.

Historians tend to place the development of the middle class in parallel to the emergence of the working class. If we are to analyse this in terms of an 'identity of interests', the formation of the middle class was largely an urban phenomenon but with its roots in the countryside.[158] The catalyst was rising wealth and expectations from the late seventeenth-century 'financial revolution'. Indeed,

155 H. J. Perkin, *The Origins of Modern English Society 1780–1880* (London, 1969), for a different model. C. Calhoun, *The Question of Class Struggle: Social Foundations of Popular Radicalism during the Industrial Revolution* (Oxford, 1981).

156 J. Foster, *Class Struggle and the Industrial Revolution* (London, 1974).

157 Clark, *The Struggle for the Breeches.*

158 It remains to be seen whether this is a result of the fact that historians have ignored the rural middle class.

early modern historians argue for the existence of a substantial middling sort before that.[159] Over time, however, the size of this middle group was growing. For the early eighteenth century John Brewer suggests that one in seven people were of 'middling order' status. By the early nineteenth century perhaps one in four or one in five of the population could be described as 'middle class'.[160] This growth arose from several interrelated circumstances. First, from the late seventeenth century there was an upwardly mobile group of merchants and financiers. Often with agrarian origins, they developed trade but sought to invest again in land. Secondly, there was a proliferation of the professions, most of which were urban based. Thirdly, the many international wars led to the growth of army and public administration posts. The concomitant rise in wealth stimulated the production of consumer products, providing new niches for master craftsmen producing luxury goods and increased manufacture of standardised consumer items. Growing affluence meant people pursued luxury, refinement and all the trappings of genteel status. This is visibly encapsulated for posterity in the Regency housing of Edinburgh's New Town or the Clifton area of Bristol. Education and culture placed a new stress on politeness and other defined codes of conduct. This, in itself, created the demand for more occupations, whether for teachers of reading and writing or dancing masters.[161] As T. C. Smout viewed it for Scotland, a dizzy sense of opportunity pervaded towns from around 1760. Farmers and landowners prospered. Merchants enjoyed the profits of the opening of new trades to North America, Russia, the West Indies, Europe, India and China. There were entirely new business opportunities as bankers and manufacturers. The upturn in trade brought fresh sources of patronage, for example, for excise officers. As a result there were more lawyers, doctors, ministers and booksellers. Clockmakers were even mentioned in rural areas in the *Statistical Account* of the 1790s but had been an unusual occupation a century earlier. Smout remarked: 'It is difficult to think of any middle-class calling that was not expanding in numbers and affluence in the half century after 1760.'[162] In the early nineteenth century professions proliferated further due to specialisation. Whereas the eighteenth-century attorney was something of a jack of all legal trades, by the nineteenth century solicitors, surveyors, estate agents, auctioneers and stockbrokers pursued separate businesses.

A stimulus to the growth of the middle class has been seen as the openness of the elite. Harold Perkin claimed England had 'an open aristocracy based on

[159] Hunt, *The Middling Sort*; J. Smail, *The Origins of Middle-Class Culture* (Ithaca, N.Y., 1994); J. Barry and C. Brooks, eds., *The Middling Sort of People* (London, 1994). See also the review article by J. Barry, 'The making of the middle class?', *P&P*, 145 (1994), 194–208.

[160] J. Brewer, 'Commercialization and politics', in N. McKendrick, J. Brewer and J. H. Plumb, eds., *The Birth of a Consumer Society: The Commercialization of Eighteenth-Century England* (London, 1982), p. 24. Hunt, *The Middling Sort*, p. 17, provides a recent estimate.

[161] P. Langford, *A Polite and Commercial People* (Oxford, 1989).

[162] T. C. Smout, *A History of the Scottish People 1560–1830* (London, 1969), p. 340.

property and patronage' to an extent unique in Europe.[163] Foreigners commented on the openness of the landed elite to new wealth and the lack of legal barriers to middle-class advancement. This view has not gone unchallenged. It may be that openness only went as far as the level of gentry.[164] Judging by later evidence, Bill Rubinstein, who used nineteenth-century probate records and income tax documents, suggested that it was lawyers and other professionals who were upwardly mobile, rather than businessmen.[165] Rogers' study of aldermanic records describes the development of a purely urban-based 'big bourgeoisie' in London. These successive generations of extremely wealthy bankers and merchants did not invest in land except for buying country seats at convenient proximity to the City.[166] In some senses, of course, it is difficult to separate the rural and the urban middling sort. Many landowners of necessity spent much time in towns, and flocked to London and pleasure resorts for the season. It was common for eighteenth-century men and women to spend large periods of their lives living in lodgings and making use of clubs.[167] As a result, they enhanced and assimilated the urban identity without permanently residing there. As communications improved, this admixture of rural and urban experiences increased. Bath had 12,000 visitors a year in 1749 but 40,000 in 1800 and was said to be fit to be the capital of a small kingdom.[168] Both of Jane Austen's novels published in 1818, *Persuasion* and *Northanger Abbey*, give us a good flavour of the fleeting atmosphere of this leisure town in the 1810s.

Rubinstein's data also show the greater wealth of the metropolitan and commercial middle class compared with the northern industrialists. As a result he identified two distinct middle classes with different forms of property, ideology, status priorities and relationships with the elite.[169] But it is probably still possible to attribute some core social values to the middle class. They espoused sobriety, hard work, order, respect for property and authority, respectability, honesty and self-interest, and were antithetical to some aspects of elite society such as idleness and excess. Common aspirations and values do not make a class, however, especially when upward mobility and a capitalistic ethos clearly imply competition. How do common values actually form an 'identity of interests', and how

163 Perkin, *The Origins of Modern English Society*.

164 J. Cannon, *Aristocratic Century: The Peerage in Eighteenth-Century England* (Cambridge, 1984); L. and J. C. F. Stone, *An Open Elite? England 1540–1880* (Oxford, 1984).

165 W. D. Rubinstein, 'The Victorian middle classes: wealth, occupation and geography', *Ec.HR*, 2nd series, 30 (1977), 602–23.

166 N. Rogers, 'Money, land and lineage: the big bourgeoisie of Hanoverian London', *Soc. Hist.*, 4 (1979), 437–54, but see also the reply by D. T. Andrew, 'The aldermen and the big bourgeoisie of London reconsidered', *Soc. Hist.*, 6 (1981), 356–64, and the rejoinder by Rogers in the same volume. H. Horwitz, '"The mess of the middle class" revisited: the case of the "big bourgeoisie" of Augustan London', *Continuity and Change*, 2 (1987), 263–96, suggests that only the very richest of the middling orders could aspire to landed status.

167 See below, pp. 587–9. 168 Neale, *Bath*, pp. 46–7.

169 Rubinstein, 'The Victorian middle classes'.

does that coalesce into class consciousness? In what ways did the power of association operate for the middle class?

As R. J. Morris has written, 'The assumption that class experience is dominated by, and can be best elucidated by political experience, is a powerful one in British culture.'[170] Middle-class political action was a recognisable nineteenth-century phenomenon. Power was not only dissipated and localised in the eighteenth century, it was also almost universally male. The only major political organisation to include women before the nineteenth century was the anti-slavery movement.[171] The local context of power in terms of the magistracy, the vestry and other trappings of local authority explain why the urban setting is so vital to understanding the development of the middle class. In a pioneer article, Asa Briggs suggested that middle-class consciousness formed around specific early nineteenth-century political issues such as opinion making during the French wars, parliamentary reform agitation in the early 1830s especially in Manchester, Leeds and Birmingham, the campaign for the repeal of the Corn Laws up to 1846 and also Chartism.[172]

More recent interpretations, while accepting the importance of these historical moments, ascribe a greater role to culture. Historians such as Harold Perkin see religious belief as crucial to the development of class consciousness – 'the midwife of class'.[173] The equivalent of Methodism's influence for the working class is the emphasis given to the evangelical revival from about 1780, for the emergence of middle-class identity. Obviously, however, this was not a unified movement. There were, for example, clear divisions and even antagonisms between Baptists, Congregationalists and Independents. Morris suggests that a secular public sphere overcame these divides, particularly through the development of voluntary societies after 1780. He stressed their role in the development of health care by subscribing to hospitals and dispensaries; in promoting public order; in science and culture by setting up libraries or chambers of commerce. He argues: 'Only the voluntary society as a social form, allowed that variety of patterns of association, participation and action, which was so essential if a fractured and divided socio-economic group was to act as a class.'[174] For example, the Leeds Philosophical and Literary Society can be seen as central to the creation of an elite-led middle-class culture in that city.

Embellishing this view, Davidoff and Hall argue that it is necessary to see the language and formation of the middle class as gendered.[175] Their analysis stresses

170 Morris, 'Class, power and social structure', p. 8.

171 C. Midgley, *Women Against Slavery: The British Campaigns 1780–1870* (London, 1992).

172 A. Briggs, 'Middle-class consciousness in English politics, 1780–1846', *P&P*, 9 (1956), 65–74.

173 Perkin, *The Origins of Modern English Society*.

174 R. J. Morris, 'Voluntary societies and British urban elites 1780–1850', in *HJ*, 26 (1983), 95–118, and R. J. Morris, *Class, Sect and Party* (Manchester, 1990), pp. 161–203, quote on p. 167.

175 L. Davidoff and C. Hall, *Family Fortunes* (London, 1987).

the growing centrality of separate spheres, suggesting that public and private were constructed as part of middle-class culture and identity. The palpable evidence of this was that home and work became physically separated in the development of residential suburbs like Edgbaston in Birmingham. Business was increasingly seen as the male sphere and took place away from the home. In the private sphere the family was central to a sense of 'middle classness' and was shaped by the prescriptive literature of the evangelical revival. Influential writers, such as the conservative Hannah More, advocated the ideal domestic life and the subordinate role of women. Domesticity is evidenced by the declining involvement of women in family businesses and because it became a mark of gentility for women to stay at home. Whether or not all this amounts to a convincing explanation for the development of urban class identity during the time period 1780–1830 has been questioned.[176]

Nevertheless, it is clear that the experience of urban living cannot but have promoted a novel sense of societal awareness. Urbanisation brought migration, greater demographic uncertainty and probably attendant disparate class experiences of fertility and mortality. Life in urban areas was qualitatively different in 1840 from 1700. Both a consideration of neighbourhood and of class formation reminds us that towns and cities were not only disease-ridden, unhealthy mires but also dynamic centres in which people forged viable and vital lives for themselves.

(v) CONCLUSION

Britain was even more urbanised than has previously been thought, and the period 1700–1840 was crucial in terms of the movement of people from rural areas, and from other parts of the world, to form and develop heterogeneous urban societies. This chapter has described the effects of this population change on the nature of urban society. By the late nineteenth century, the life experience of the majority of British people took place within the context of a town or city. This chapter has also suggested that in terms of our knowledge of the demography of urbanisation, much remains to be researched. In fact, we know far more about rural demography than urban population processes. We know even less about the interjacency and interconnections between rural and urban areas. More research is needed on migration in the eighteenth and early nineteenth centuries, especially on the role of women. Demographic historians are hampered by evidence deficiencies but further investigation of towns will undoubtedly be undertaken as increasingly sophisticated demographic methods

[176] Hunt, *The Middling Sort*, casts some doubt on the timing. A. J. Vickery, 'Golden age to separate spheres: a review of the categories and chronology of English women's history', *HJ*, 36 (1993), 383–414, also questions any assumption of a sudden change and argues that the supposed 'middle-class' values were also espoused by the gentry.

are developed. In particular, patterns of marriage and fertility for the period from 1800 through to 1870 must be examined as well as the apparent class differences in demographic experience. Towns offered people new experiences and fresh exposures. As William Cowper put it, in the middle of our time period, 'God made the country and man made the town.'[177] The intermingling of increasing numbers of people created dangerous disease environments but the fusion of ideas and the fomentation of new possibilities.

[177] William Cowper, 'The sofa', *The Task* (London, 1785), p. 749.

· 16 ·

Politics and government 1700–1840

JOANNA INNES AND NICHOLAS ROGERS

IN THE 1830s, critics of the 'borough system' – of a parliament heavily weighted towards the representation of small boroughs – and of 'unreformed' municipal government portrayed British urban governmental institutions as hidebound, as having failed to adapt to changing times. It is true that, from 1700 to the 1830s, there was little change in the formal institutions either of parliamentary representation or of borough government. Scottish burghs gained representation in the Westminster parliament after the Union of 1707 (and Irish boroughs after the Union of 1800). From the 1770s, would-be parliamentary reformers succeeded in getting the constituency boundaries of three notoriously corrupt parliamentary boroughs redrawn, and one such borough disfranchised. But more radical changes – the disfranchisement of dozens of smaller boroughs, and enfranchisement of large unrepresented towns – had to await the Reform Act of 1832. Similarly, very few new corporate charters were issued after 1700 (though in Scotland, a scattering of burghs of barony were created). Even passage of the 1835 English and Welsh Municipal Corporations Act did not radically change the picture here: among the major unincorporated towns, only Manchester and Birmingham sought incorporation in the remainder of that decade.

By contrast, this was of course an era of striking social, economic and cultural change. National population tripled; the urban share of population grew and there were changes in the urban hierarchy as various industrial and other economically specialised kinds of town rose towards the top of the pile. Towns became the sites of more or less vigorous associational life (now formally tolerated dissenting congregations being among the earlier manifestations of voluntarism). The rise of the newspaper press both reflected and reinforced local

Though this piece is the joint work of the two authors, Nicholas Rogers is primarily responsible for sections (vii) and (ix), and Joanna Innes for the remainder. Joanna Innes would like to express especial thanks to Roey Sweet for her generous readiness with information and comments.

interest in supra-local issues. The entrenchment of parliament in a central place within the machinery of government was associated with the rise of 'party' conflict, vigorously waged in numerous parliamentary boroughs. In the later decades of the period parliament became a key arena for the working out of 'reform' projects: though a key target for reform itself, it was also the favoured instrument for effecting reform.

It falls to this chapter to explore this apparent disjuncture – between the institutional and the social and cultural – and the ways in which it was perceived and dealt with by contemporaries. Clearly, by the 1830s at least, contemporaries did perceive there to be a problem: the reform acts of that decade represented an attempt to put things right. Yet exploring the disjuncture must also involve complicating our understanding of it. It is possible to portray the era down to 1830 as an era of institutional stasis – but only by a certain wilful selectiveness (something to which reformers were not averse). *Some* institutions remained, at least formally, unchanging. But people often found new ways of operating within them, they also developed alternative institutions.

There were reasons for preferring accommodating, eclectic, piecemeal strategies. Seventeenth-century experience had made many wary of ambitious, centrally directed reconstructive projects. Intervention might also be feared inasmuch as it might lead to the redistribution of power between political factions or social classes. Even many of those who would have liked *more* institutional change sometimes thought it could, and might best be, brought about gradually, with careful attention to the spirit of inherited institutions.

The Whig reforms of the 1830s did not go far enough to meet radical demands. Though they were more dramatic than many had expected, the changes they wrought were none the less carefully judged. Sweeping enough to allay some discontents, and to allow government to present itself as inaugurating a bold new era, they yet fell far short of completely rationalising complex, unevenly developed, inherited institutional structures, and they held fast to the notion – a reformist notion in its origins, though increasingly one challenged by the populist left – that the distribution of power in society should mirror the distribution of property.

(i) FORMS OF TOWN GOVERNANCE

In 1730 there were said to be some 750 market towns in England and Wales. Dr Langton's somewhat more broadly conceived, partly size-based definition of a town produces higher totals: over 900 towns in England and Wales in the late seventeenth century, a further eighty-odd in Scotland, rising to a joint total of 1,163 by 1841. In England and Wales, only a minority of towns were incorporated. In 1835, Municipal Corporations Commissioners identified a mere 246 corporations: between a third and a quarter of all towns. The remainder were at most seigneurial boroughs – often relying on a locally improvised mix of institutions to order their affairs.[1]

In Scotland, the burgh status of most urban settlements of any size was more clearly established. The great majority of Langton's 'towns' figured among the sixty-six royal burghs. Most of the remainder were 'burghs of barony', as were many smaller settlements. (There were more than 300 burghs of barony by 1700, a total expanded by further foundations especially in the earliest and latest decades of our period.)[2] Scottish Municipal Corporation Commissioners, reporting in 1836, recommended that even quite small settlements be endowed with something of the apparatus of town government (by then understood to mean elective government): as they saw it, all settlements with populations of over 1,500 should elect their own councils. (The absence in Scotland of anything entirely comparable to the English parochial system provides an important part of the context for this recommendation).[3]

The standard form of the corporation had of course been set long before, and changed little before 1835.[4] Corporations (see Plate 17) characteristically comprised a governing elite – a mayor or other chief magistrate and one or more councils – and perhaps, though not invariably, a larger or smaller body of freemen (in this period, usually a shrinking minority of adult male residents).[5]

1 For numbers of towns, see Chapter 14 in this volume. For the reports of the Royal Commission on Municipal Corporations in England and Wales, PP 1835 XXIII–XXVI, XL, 1837 XXXV, 1837–8 XXXV.

2 A convenient list in I. H. Adams, *The Making of Urban Scotland* (London, 1978), pp. 278–82, draws on G. H. Pryde, *The Burghs of Scotland* (Oxford, 1965). See also Pryde, 'The Scottish burgh of barony in decline, 1707–1908', *Proceedings of the Royal Philosophical Society of Glasgow*, 73 (1949), 43–64.

3 PP 1836 XXIII, Report of the Royal Commissioners on Municipal Corporations in Scotland, pp. 97–8. For the Scottish parish, A. Whetstone, *Scottish County Government in the Eighteenth and Nineteenth Centuries* (Edinburgh, 1981), pp. 33–6, 85–6; R. Mitchison, 'The making of the old Scottish poor law', *P&P*, 113 (1974), 63ff; R. Mitchison and L. Leneman, *Sexuality and Social Control: Scotland 1660–1780* (Oxford, 1989), ch. 1.

4 For elaboration of the following paragraphs, see PP 1835 XXIII–XXVI, XL, 1836 XXIII, 1837 XXXV, 1837–8 XXXV. Data contained in the reports were further analysed in J. Fletcher, 'Statistics of the municipal institutions of the English towns', *Journal of the Statistical Society of London*, 5 (1842), 97–169. S. Webb and B. Webb, *The Manor and the Borough* (London, 1908), draws heavily on the report, but also on many urban archives (their ch. 5 is devoted to Wales, but they do not include Scotland). H. Dickinson, *The Politics of the People in Eighteenth-Century Britain* (London, 1995), ch. 3, unusually extends to Scotland. There exists no survey of Scottish burgh government in this period, but for a local study see I. Maver, 'The guardianship of the community; civic authority prior to 1833', in T. M. Devine and G. Jackson, eds., *Glasgow*, vol. I: *Beginnings to 1830* (Manchester, 1995). Printed corporation records of this period include *Records of the Borough of Leicester*, vols. V–VII, ed., G. A. Chinnery (Leicester, 1965–74); *Oxford Council Acts* (Oxford, 1933–62); *Records of the Borough of Northampton* (London, 1898); *Records of the Borough of Nottingham* (Nottingham, 1882–1952); and *A Selection from the Southampton Corporation Journals*, ed. A. T. Patterson (Southampton, 1965).

5 Leeds provides an example of a town without freemen – though some attempt to institute them was made in the late seventeenth century (Webb and Webb, *Manor and Borough*, II, p. 417). For freemen as a proportion of urban populations in 1835, PP 1835 XXIII, pp. 32–4, 92–3.

Corporations commonly (though not invariably) owned property and drew revenue from that, also from market tolls and other dues. Often, they were responsible for administering charitable revenues, and in this way might have a stake in hospitals, almshouses or schools, or, in the case of certain Scottish towns, universities. They might also control clerical livings.

One or more corporate officers was usually *ex officio* a justice of the peace. Over a quarter of English and Welsh boroughs had rights of exclusive jurisdiction in criminal cases: county magistrates had little or no authority within their bounds. Many corporations maintained civil courts. There would be a town gaol, perhaps also a bridewell. Watching, street cleaning and lighting arrangements were often governed by municipal by-laws.

Corporate bodies engaged in a variety of ways with urban economic life. Freemen (if there were such) might enjoy monopoly or privileged trading rights. Guilds might regulate aspects of the production or trading process. Market trading was always regulated to some extent. In return for the various dues they collected, corporations were expected to maintain key components of the economic infrastructure, such as market and port facilities. They were expected to defend corporate rights and privileges, and the town's interest generally, against assault or challenge, and to make representations to central bodies as the need arose.

Where corporate institutions did not exist, some of these functions might be performed by manorial institutions: indeed, the corporation, seigneurial borough and manor stood in a continuum, rather than being distinct species.[6] A manorial bailiff or constable might, for example, discharge functions performed by the mayor elsewhere; a court leet might serve as an administrative body. In unincorporated Manchester, notoriously, the court leet long remained a key institution of urban government (demonstrating its capacity for adaptation when it began charging ill-kept factories as nuisances).[7] In some places, townsmen had taken over manorial privileges before 1700; elsewhere, lords of the manor remained potentially or actually a force to be reckoned with. The Moseley family of Manchester did not sell out until 1846, following the incorporation of the town.[8]

Where neither corporate nor manorial institutions were available, or where such institutions did not suffice, there were alternatives. Four forms of alternative governmental resource deserve notice.

First, the county magistracy. From the later middle ages, and especially from the sixteenth century, statutes had endowed justices of the peace with many powers analogous to those exercised by corporate officers – indeed, since senior corporate officers were usually JPs *ex officio*, these statutes helped to define the

[6] Webb and Webb, *Manor and Borough*, I, ch. 3; M. B. Rowlands, 'Government and governors in four manorial boroughs in the West Midlands', *Journal of Regional and Local History*, 13 (1993), 1–19.

[7] F. Vigier, *Change and Apathy: Liverpool and Manchester during the Industrial Revolution* (Cambridge, Mass., 1970), pp. 128–9.

[8] *Ibid*., pp. 96, 99, 113, 125.

nature of authority in corporate towns. Justices sitting singly or with others in petty or quarter sessions had a wide range of legal and administrative powers. They could judge criminal cases and petty delinquencies; in Scotland, from the 1790s, they could hear small debt claims. They had responsibilities for the upkeep of prisons, bridges and highways; they licensed alehouses, could adjudicate employment disputes; enforce marketing regulations and set certain wage rates and prices.[9]

A county magistrate or magistrates prepared to exercise these powers in an unincorporated urban area might *de facto* provide much in the way of town government. Manchester and Salford benefited in just this way from the attentions of successive justices of the peace for the Salford division of the county of Lancashire. A much smaller town – suburban Hackney – similarly benefited from the attentions of the local justices who staffed Hackney petty sessions.[10]

The burdens on such 'urban' magistrates might be very heavy – meaning that it was by no means always easy to find suitable people to serve. The stipendiary magistracy was pioneered in urban Middlesex, by an act of 1792, to solve just that problem. In 1830, the same solution was adopted to meet the needs of the booming industrial settlement of Merthyr Tydfil.[11]

In England and Wales (much less so in Scotland), the parish also provided an important urban governmental resource. Sixteenth-century English statutes had made parishes key units in the administration of poor relief and highway maintenance; constables, orginally manorial officials, sometimes also came to be regarded as parish officers. Even the smallest parishes commonly ran budgets of tens, if not hundreds, of pounds by 1700. By the early nineteenth century, the budgets of urban parishes might equal or exceed those of corporations.[12]

From the beginning of our period, some parishes were governed by long-standing, self-electing 'select vestries'; elsewhere, vestries were open meetings of ratepayers. As such, they might be disorderly and contentious gatherings. In Whitechapel in the 1730s, vestry meetings were open to some 1,300 ratepayers; a local gentleman attested that he had 'heard such Cursing and Swearing and Noise, at the choosing of Parish Officers, and making the Rates, that the

[9] S. Webb and B. Webb, *The Parish and the County* (London, 1906), pp. 387–479. See also *Manor and Borough*, index under 'Justices, County'. For the powers of JPs in Scotland, Whetstone, *Scottish County Government*, ch. 2.

[10] For one of the most active Manchester magistrates, see T. Percival, *Biographical Memoirs of the Late Thomas Butterworth Bayley* (Manchester, 1802); for Hackney, R. Paley, ed., *Justicing in Eighteenth-Century Hackney* (London, 1991).

[11] Webb and Webb, *Parish and County*, pp. 572–80. For the establishment of a stipendiary magistrate in Manchester, see PP 1828 VI, p. 492. The Merthyr Act was 10 Geo IV c. xcv. G. A. Williams, *The Merthyr Rising* (London, 1978), pp. 21–2, 34, 50, 88–9, sets it in context.

[12] Webb and Webb, *Parish and County*, pp. 9–276, remains the most comprehensive account. For parish budgets, see the data gathered by various parliamentary inquiries into the poor laws, e.g. *Reports of Committees of the House of Commons* (London, 1803), vol. IX; PP 1803–4 XIII.

Churchwardens have been obliged to adjourn the vestry.'[13] Through the institution of the vestry, the parish defined a local political community. In 1835, the English and Welsh Municipal Corporations Act built on notions of political personhood developed in this context by designating the parochial ratepayer the municipal elector (in Scotland, where the kirk sessions had a somewhat different character, and where parish rates were not standard, the municipal franchise was instead based on the parliamentary, £10 householder franchise).[14]

The issues aired at parish level were various. Some parish functions invited deliberation, if not contention, notably the levying and distribution of poor rates. In the 1820s, provoked by the levying of rates for new churches under the 1818 Church Building Act, dissenters began to challenge the levying of church rates on non-Anglicans. Parish meetings also provided a convenient forum in which issues not formally assigned to the parish could be addressed. In the expanding metropolitan fringe, the parish was often the administrative unit chosen when local legislation was sought, in relation not only to poor relief, but also to lighting, watching and general 'improvement'. From the later eighteenth century, parish meetings were often coopted to make representations relating to national or local political issues. Thus, in London in the late 1790s, parish meetings protested against proposed new national 'Assessed Taxes'; in Manchester, critics of the performance of the street commissioners made the vestry their forum, where they expounded a radical view of both local and national affairs.[15]

Sturges Bourne acts of 1818 and 1819, drafted against this background of burgeoning 'parish democracy', attempted to strengthen the hands of richer ratepayers, by providing that their votes should carry more weight in the decision as to whether or not to establish a 'select vestry'; conversely, the Whig Hobhouse's act of 1831 provided that select vestries might be dissolved by simple majority vote. The principle of one-ratepayer-one-vote triumphed in the 1835 municipal franchise; by contrast, the 1834 New Poor Law, which transferred most relief decision-making functions from parishes to elected boards of guardians, provided for a weighted franchise on the Sturges Bourne model.[16]

A third, at least quasi-governmental, resource for urban areas was the volun-

[13] *Journals of the House of Commons*, vol. XXII, pp. 270–1.

[14] 5&6 Wm IV c. 76, cl. 9, 29; 3&4 Wm IV c. 46, cl. 9. B. Keith-Lucas, *The English Local Government Franchise* (Oxford, 1952), chs. 1–2, cover parishes and reformed municipal corporations respectively. For Scottish parish government, see n. 3 above.

[15] Webb and Webb, *Parish and County*, pp. 91–103; D. Fraser, *Urban Politics in Victorian England* (Leicester, 1976), ch. 2. J. Parry, *The Rise and Fall of Liberal Government in Victorian Britain* (New Haven, 1993), pp. 59–60, for the origins of conflict over church rates. D. Wahrman, *Imagining the Middle Class* (Cambridge, 1995), p. 114.

[16] 58 Geo III c. 69; 59 Geo III c. 12; 59 Geo III c. 85; 1&2 Wm IV c. 60; B. Keith-Lucas, *The Unreformed Local Government System* (London, 1980), pp. 23–36; J. Prest, *Liberty and Locality: Parliament, Permissive Legislation and Ratepayers' Democracies in the Nineteenth Century* (Oxford, 1990), pp. 9–11.

tary society, that fecund new social form, and its fiscal counterpart, the 'subscription'. Voluntary societies could operate in contexts where neither charter nor statute provided a basis for official action. Their limitation was, of course, that their promoters could not compel compliance.[17]

Voluntary societies and subscriptions flourished in a wide variety of fields. In the field of law enforcement, for example: in the form of 'societies for the reformation of manners', and 'societies for the prosecution of felons'. Crises of dearth or unemployment were often addressed in towns by special subscriptions; Strangers' Friend societies dealt especially with those who fell outside the parish relief system; in the early nineteenth century, visiting societies began to attend charity recipients in their homes. Evangelicals were especially fertile in founding societies for the relief and improvement of the poorer classes – perhaps carrying them into small towns where they had not previously existed – but they built upon older traditions. Voluntary societies also had a long history in the field of education, while hospitals were often substantially dependent on subscriptions.[18]

Interesting syntheses were sometimes developed between the continuing reality of aristocratic power and the new bourgeois voluntarist mode. Cardiff, in the early nineteenth century a booming industrial port, illustrates this. The marquis of Bute, lord lieutenant of the county, occasional inhabitant of the castle, dominant landowner in the town and key promoter of its industrial development, also assiduously contributed to local societies. Thus, in 1840 he subscribed to Cardiff's Infirmary, Reading Room, Dorcas Society, Sympathetic Society, Auxiliary Bible Society, Visiting Society and Literary and Scientific Society, as well as to other good causes in the county, Swansea and Bristol.[19]

In some towns, improvements in lighting and watching arrangements were funded, at least in the first instance, by voluntary subscription. But the need to

[17] See below, pp. 586–9, 611–12. In addition to works on particular forms of association listed in the following note, J. Cookson, *The British Armed Nation 1793–1815* (Oxford, 1997), esp. pp. 237–45, interestingly discusses the functions and significance of military 'volunteering' in an urban context.

[18] For the reformation of manners, R. B. Shoemaker, 'Reforming the city: the reformation of manners campaign in London 1690–1738', in L. Davison *et al.*, eds., *Stilling the Grumbling Hive* (Stroud, 1992), pp. 99–120; J. Innes, 'Politics and morals: the reformation of manners movement in later eighteenth-century England', in E. Hellmuth, ed., *The Transformation of Political Culture* (Oxford, 1990), pp. 57–118. For other associative ventures, essays by P. King and D. Philips in D. Hay and F. Snyder, eds., *Policing and Prosecution in Britain 1750–1850* (Oxford, 1989), pp. 113–207; M. G. Jones, *The Charity School Movement* (London, 1964); T. Laqueur, *Religion and Respectability: Sunday Schools and Working Class Culture 1780–1850* (New Haven, 1976); J. Woodward, *To Do the Sick No Harm: A Study of the British Voluntary Hospital System to 1875* (London, 1974); F. K. Brown, *Fathers of the Victorians* (Cambridge, 1961), ch. 9. Local studies of the diffusion of charitable voluntarism in the provinces include G. B. Hindle, *Provision for the Relief of the Poor in Manchester 1754–1826* (Manchester, 1975), chs. 6–8; T. Koditschek, *Class Formation in Urban-Industrial Society* (Cambridge, 1990), ch. 11; and R. J. Morris, *Class, Sect and Party: The Making of the British Middle Class* (Manchester, 1990), chs. 7–12.

[19] J. Davies, *Cardiff and the Marquesses of Bute* (Cardiff, 1981), p. 92.

ensure that the costs of the more costly public services were spread across the ranks of those able to contribute often prompted a bid for parliamentary sanction. Such acts constituted the fourth 'alternative resource'. Acts of parliament endowing corporations with powers to provide public services beyond those sanctioned by their charters issued from as early as the fourteenth century. After 1688, annual, prolonged, sessions of parliament increased opportunities to seek such authorisation.[20]

Prominent among urban local acts of the 1690s were acts establishing corporations of the poor, with jurisdiction over several parishes. These acts were significant, among other things, for establishing special-purpose statutory authorities. Statutory commissioners came to be charged with managing many different local services: small debt courts, turnpike trusts, river improvements and canals, street lighting, watching and other improvements, harbours and docks. The opportunity to establish a new body was, of course, attractive when none had jurisdiction over the whole area affected. Furthermore, when acts gave power to raise rates, the chance to have the relevant authority elected by and accountable to ratepayers, or open to any propertied resident, was probably often necessary to mobilise the broad base of propertied support for which parliament looked.

Figure 16.1 charts the chronological and geographical spread of one of the most common kinds of urban act, the 'improvement act' (included in the graph are all acts providing for the paving, lighting, watching and other 'improvement' of towns). It reveals that numbers of such acts took off from the mid-eighteenth century (earlier acts on the graph were mainly specialised watching acts). London originally dominated, but the provinces and Scotland subsequently made a stronger showing. In all there were some 600 new improvement acts over the period, of which 150 plus applied to the metropolis, 400 to provincial England, some fifteen to Wales and fifty to Scotland. Most major towns were affected by such legislation: of the forty-odd English towns with populations over 11,000 in 1831, only four were not subject to improvement acts.[21]

[20] See J. Innes, 'The local acts of a national parliament: parliament's role in sanctioning local action in eighteenth-century Britain', in D. Dean and C. Jones, eds., *Parliament and Locality 1660–1939* (Edinburgh, 1998), pp. 23–47, for references to the wider literature.

[21] Leicester, Nottingham, Wenlock and Wigan. Welsh towns served ranged from Cardiff and Swansea to Aberystwyth (pop. 1841: 4,956); Scottish towns, from Edinburgh and Glasgow to Banff (pop. 1841: 3,202). The Scottish figures used here represent a minimum in that they exclude acts described only as imposing local duties on beer, some of which in fact served to finance improvements (for further discussion of Scottish legislative patterns see Innes, 'Local acts'.) In my calculations, 'new' acts means acts other than those specifically described as continuing, amending or repealing earlier acts. A total for the number of towns affected would be lower, which probably accounts for the Webbs' rather smaller totals: by their account, some 100 improvement commissions were created to serve the metropolitan area before 1835, 200 to serve the rest of England (*Statutory Authorities for Special Purposes* (London, 1922), pp. 242–3). I am grateful to Ben Collins for his assistance in compiling the data on which the graph is based.

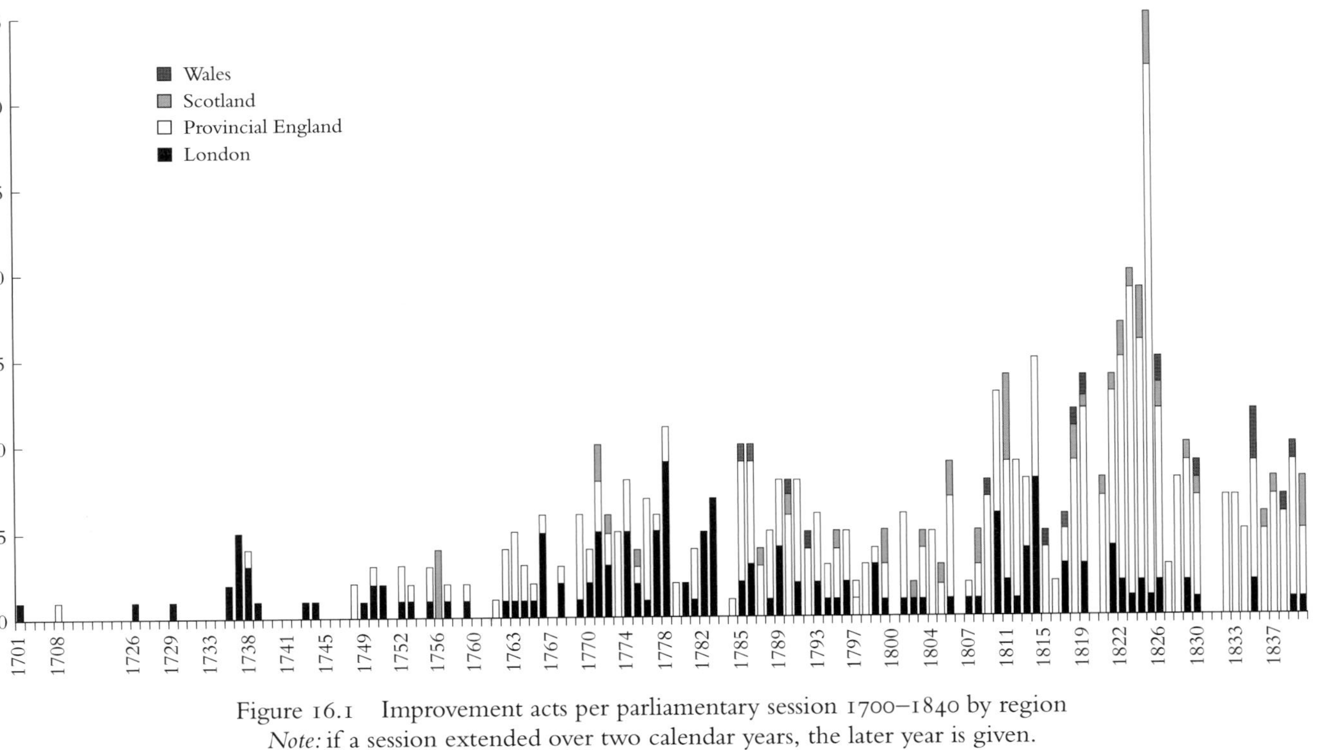

Figure 16.1 Improvement acts per parliamentary session 1700–1840 by region
Note: if a session extended over two calendar years, the later year is given.

From the 1830s, a series of general acts, some permissive, some compulsory, drew upon what was by then a formidable body of local experience in an attempt to generalise best practice. The English Lighting and Watching Acts of 1830/33 were the first such; the Scottish Burgh Police Act of 1833 the second. (Reflecting a national difference already noted, the first gave power to parishes, the second to burghs.) Subsequently, the English New Poor Law of 1834 compelled the grouping of parishes in larger administrative units, while the County Courts Act of 1846 created a national network of small debt courts.[22]

Passage of these acts ended some forms of application, for small debt courts and corporations of the poor (though existing poor authorities could continue to operate if they wished, and numerous towns in practice gained partial exemption from the operation of the New Poor Law in this way). Improvement acts, by contrast, continued until a much later date.[23] Like the Municipal Corporations Act itself, most of the general acts enshrined the principles of elective authority, and vested electoral power in the hands of property owners large and small (in England and Wales, ratepayers) – following the model popularised by almost a century and a half of local legislation.

(ii) TOWN GOVERNMENT: SOCIAL COMPOSITION

Contemporaries often suggested – and historians have largely agreed – that the early modern period saw a trend towards the concentration of corporate power in the hands of a relatively narrow elite of townsmen.[24] In the eighteenth century, as in previous centuries, little men sometimes opposed the domination of the great. Thus, in London, the pre-eminence at the highest levels of the corporation of financiers and overseas merchants, and in Newcastle, the similar pre-eminence of coal-shipping 'hostmen' generated antagonisms which from time to time fuelled conflict.[25]

[22] Prest, *Liberty and Locality*, p. 8; F. Driver, *Power and Pauperism: The Workhouse System 1834–84* (Cambridge, 1993), ch. 3; H. Arthurs, *'Without the Law': Administrative Justice and Legal Pluralism in Nineteenth-Century England* (Toronto, 1985), pp. 38–49.

[23] Driver, *Power and Pauperism*, pp. 42–7; Prest, *Liberty and Locality*; Webb and Webb, *Statutory Authorities*, p. 347 and n.

[24] Thus PP 1835 XXIII, pp. 19–20. See above, pp. 241 *et seq.*, and see also the discussion in P. Gauci, *Politics and Society in Great Yarmouth 1660–1722* (Oxford, 1996), esp. chs. 1–2. Other local studies include P. Styles, *The Corporation of Warwick 1660–1835* (Oxford, 1938); R. G. Wilson, *Gentlemen Merchants* (Manchester, 1971), esp. chs. 2, 8; and P. Clark, 'The civic leaders of Gloucestershire 1580–1800', in P. Clark, ed., *The Transformation of English Provincial Towns 1600-1800* (London, 1984), esp. pp. 327–36. Insight into the life of members of the corporate elite is provided by the *Georgian Tiverton Political Memoranda of Beavis Wood 1768–98*, ed. J. Bourne (Devon and Cornwall Record Society, new series, 29, 1986); *The Oakes Diaries: Business, Politics and the Family in Bury St Edmunds 1778–1827* ed. J. Fiske (Suffolk Records Society, 32–3, 1990–1) – or, at a more formal level, *A Journal of the Shrievalty of Richard Hoare esq 1740–1* (Bath, 1815).

[25] N. Rogers, *Whigs and Cities* (Oxford, 1989), esp. chs. 1–4 on London, and see also ch. 8 on Bristol. For Newcastle, K. Wilson, *The Sense of the People* (Cambridge, 1995), pp. 288–303 and 315–75. For Glasgow, Maver, 'The guardianship of the community', pp. 256–8.

Equally problematic, however, could be the *failure* of corporate power structures to mirror other structures of power and status. Corporate officers sometimes included certain local gentry, but were commonly largely drawn from the local trading community. Gentry and 'pseudo-gentry', occasionally or permanently resident in towns, might regard such urban dignitaries as vulgar and self-important, mistrust their management of corporate funds or question their priorities.[26]

A rather more common focus for discontent was the concentration of power in the hands of a group whose political or religious views did not represent those of the whole community. The fact that many corporate bodies were self-electing facilitated such divergences. Some corporations were notoriously Whig or dissenting strongholds (thus early eighteenth-century Coventry, or Nottingham) some notoriously Tory or Anglican strongholds (thus early nineteenth-century Leeds).[27] In fact, not even self-electing bodies were necessarily all of one mind. Coopted members furthermore sometimes voiced views other than those expected. Still, at no time was it easy for those outside 'closed' bodies to affect their stance.[28]

These various oligarchic tendencies were in practice often offset in one or more ways. First, although the commanding heights of the corporation were usually dominated by some form of elite, other offices might be held by lesser men, and corporate structures might ramify downwards into urban neighbourhoods (in the form, for example, of 'ward-mote inquests'), in this way offering status or power to small shopkeepers, craftsmen and the like.[29] Secondly, as we have noted, corporations usually coexisted with – and in some towns were wholly replaced by – other structures of governance. These other structures were sometimes more easily penetrable. Paul Langford has noted, for example, that the obligation to take Anglican communion, which still formally attached to corporate offices, was almost never attached to office on statutory commissions. Even though they sometimes came to be monopolised by alternative cliques, at least the existence of such other bodies helped to create a more pluralistic urban scene.[30]

Finally, of course, any account of a system of government which focuses only on its personnel tells only a part of the story. Two equally narrow elites might

26 P. Langford, *Public Life and the Propertied Englishman 1689–1798* (Oxford, 1991), pp. 220–2, and for tensions in Southampton, A. T. Patterson, *A History of Southampton 1700–1914*, vol. I: *An Oligarchy in Decline 1700–1835* (Southampton, 1966), pp. 44–8, 75–7.

27 PP 1835 XXIII, pp. 94–5, for modes of election. For general discussion, see J. Bradley, *Religion, Revolution and English Radicalism: Non-Conformity in Eighteenth-Century Politics and Society* (Cambridge, 1990), pp. 69–80.

28 G. Bush, *Bristol and its Municipal Government 1820–51* (Bristol Record Society, 29, 1976), pp. 25–6, 34–7.

29 J. M. Triffitt, 'Town politics and the urban community: parliamentary boroughs in the South-West of England 1710–30' (DPhil thesis, University of Oxford, 1986), ch. 4, develops the theme.

30 Langford, *Public Life*, pp. 76, 128–30; Koditschek, *Class Formation*, pp. 157–60; Morris, *Class, Sect and Party*, pp. 123–4.

operate, in one case with a narrow, in one case with a broad, view of a town's interests. There were, in fact, good, self-interested reasons why commercial elites should at least intermittently have judged it proper to attend to the views of local gentry, whose patronage and custom they desired, to the concerns of inhabitants of their rural hinterlands, who helped to sustain urban markets, and to the circumstances of the local working class, who might turn threatening if conditions of work or the cost of living changed for the worse.[31]

When they did not satisfy expectations, governing groups might face more or less vigorous or hostile representations, be criticised in print, or at public meetings. In that context, their restricted social base might be one of the charges brought against them – but this did not usually constitute the whole burden of a complaint.

(iii) THE PRACTICE OF TOWN GOVERNMENT: IMPROVEMENT

The theme of improvement – broadly interpreted – provides one basis for structuring an account of changing practice in urban government. Tracing the course of 'improvement' entails noting first the appearance then the diffusion of those devices and expedients which most commended themselves to town dwellers.

Expedients for improving urban life were often pioneered in the largest towns. If not, their adoption by a major city, especially by some part of the metropolis, might yet play a vital part in their diffusion. Paul Slack, in Chapter 11, describes some of the improvements pioneered in major cities at the end of the seventeenth century: improvements in lighting technology, for example, pioneered in London, and quickly imitated in the greatest provincial cities of the day, Bristol and Norwich. London in a sense pioneered the corporation of the poor, having established one in 1649 – but it was Bristol's revival of the notion in 1696 that spurred a wave of, mostly West Country and East Anglian, provincial foundations. The first of the new-style voluntary hospitals was a metropolitan foundation: the Westminster Infirmary. According to the Webbs, it was Liverpool – whose rapid growth had by mid-century carried it into the ranks of the major cities – whose 1748 improvement act inaugurated the mid-century take-off in such legislation.[32]

[31] Though generally critical of the introversion and secrecy of corporations (thus *Manor and Borough*, II, pp. 729–35), the Webbs praised some for public spiritedness (thus, II, p. 485). The general tone of subsequent historiography has been critical, but see Gauci, *Great Yarmouth*, chs. 1–2, for an argument about the need for oligarchies to justify themselves, worked through with particular reference to Yarmouth, and also Clark, 'Civic leaders', p. 337; R. Sweet, 'Stability and continuity: Swansea politics and reform 1780–1820', *Welsh History Review*, 18 (1996), 30; and R. A. Houston, *Social Change in the Age of Enlightenment* (Oxford, 1994), pp. 343ff. For sensitivity to others' concerns, nn. 44 and 56, below.

[32] P. Slack, *Poverty and Policy in Tudor and Stuart England* (London, 1988), pp. 195–200; Woodward, *To Do the Sick No Harm*, pp. 11–12; Webb and Webb, *Statutory Authorities*, p. 242.

Some projects pursued in the largest towns were not well suited for adoption by their smaller counterparts. Hospitals, for example, were generally conceived on a scale and entailed an expense that only the largest towns could bear. Innovations pioneered in smaller towns, and suited to their needs, had, in that regard, a better chance of securing wide adoption – if means could be found to draw them to wider public notice. The chronology and geography of workhouse diffusion is suggestive in this respect. Corporations of the poor, characteristically associated with ambitious workhouse-building projects, were established mainly in larger towns in the 1690s and early eighteenth century; by 1715, interest in their establishment seemed to be spent. What gave the workhouse movement a new lease of life in the 1720s was the propagandistic efforts of the Society for Promoting Christian Knowledge (SPCK) – whose publicity material focused especially on (supposedly) successful experiments carried out in such smaller towns as Bedford, Cirencester and Maidstone. Hundreds, indeed thousands, of workhouses were established in the next two decades: by the late 1730s there can have been few market towns without a workhouse.[33]

It is clear that Scottish towns were on the circuit through which ideas for improvement circulated, though it is hard to think of an eighteenth-century improvement pioneered in a Scottish town.[34] In the second half of the century, none the less, Scotland was clearly gaining a reputation as the home of a literate, independent, law-abiding populace (thus, it was noted that there were fewer prisoners in Scottish than in English prisons.) In the early nineteenth century, schemes of improvement traceable to Scottish influence often seem to have been those linked with these associations. Thomas Chalmers, a Glasgow minister, published several books about problems associated with provision for the poor in large towns in the 1810s and 1820s. The example of Glasgow's practice, as publicised by him, seems to have helped to inspire a wave of foundations of 'visiting societies' in London and other English towns in the 1820s. The first British temperance society was established in Glasgow in the 1820s; the scheme was carried thence to Bradford by a Scottish-born manufacturer.[35]

Schemes for improvement quite frequently generated controversy. Characteristically, however, the notion that a proposal embodied an improvement was not itself attacked. Controversy focused rather on the ways in which implementation might affect various interests. Challenges might be brought in the name of ratepayers' interests, it being argued that they would have to bear the cost, without commensurate benefit. Alternatively, they might be mounted

[33] *An Account of Several Workhouses* (London, 1725); T. Hitchcock, 'Paupers and preachers: the SPCK and the parochial workhouse movement', in Davison *et al.*, eds., *Stilling the Grumbling Hive*, pp. 145–66.

[34] The first voluntary hospital founded outside London was in Edinburgh: Woodward, *To Do the Sick No Harm*, pp. 15–16, 147–8.

[35] S. Brown, *Thomas Chalmers and the Godly Commonwealth* (Oxford, 1982), esp. pp. 93–149; H. Rack, 'Domestic visitation: a chapter in early nineteenth-century evangelism', *JEcc.Hist.*, 24 (1973), 357–76; B. Harrison, *Drink and the Victorians* (London, 1971), pp. 103ff.

in the name of established authorities – a corporation, or a lord of the manor – who thought they stood to lose either power or income. There was, therefore, a 'politics of improvement' – yet at the same time, the term essentially connoted an evolving consensus about best practice.[36]

Contemporary accounts of towns often celebrated their improvement in terms that verged on bland triumphalism. To avoid that fault, we should stress not only the occasionally controversial character of 'improvement' but also its limitations in practice.

First, we might note that many improvement schemes disproportionately benefited wealthier inhabitants. Beautification projects commonly targeted town centres, main thoroughfares and elite residential districts, not the alleyways and courts where the poor were more likely to live, or the poorer districts. Old watch and new police forces likewise did not always patrol back alleys (though they might harass their residents for 'misconduct' if they treated thoroughfares as recreational space).[37]

A list of improvements too easily suggests cumulative progress. Yet not all acts were implemented. Moreover, enthusiasm for playing a part in new ventures might quickly wane. In the 1770s, an MP commenting sceptically on a proposal for a poor relief incorporation remarked that he well remembered local gentlemen eagerly taking part when such a body was launched in his own Westminster parish in the 1750s – however, later, their zeal had waned.[38] Improvers sometimes had to run to keep pace with urban change. Proliferating metropolitan relief acts testify not so much to the progress of improvement as to the continuing expansion of the built-up area; statutory authorities accreted in ever-expanding layers around the metropolitan core.[39]

The sheer intractability of some of the problems innovators engaged with also needs stressing. Poverty and crime were both such. The era was fertile with new expedients for relieving want and promoting independence, and combating crime both at the root and in its most flagrant manifestations – but, in the last analysis, what repeated surges of innovation bear witness to is the intractability of the task.[40]

Contemporary assessments of the achievements and prospects of urban government seem to have shifted in the course of the period from predomi-

[36] For a local study of such politics, see Sweet, 'Stability and continuity'. Fraser, *Urban Politics*, ch. 4, for the final decades of our period.

[37] Vigier, *Change and Apathy*, pp. 137–42, for inequities in provision in Manchester; R. Paley, '"An imperfect, inadequate and wretched system": policing the metropolis before Peel', *Criminal Justice History*, 10 (1989), 95–130.

[38] *Parliamentary History*, ed. W. Cobbett (London, 1806–20), vol. XVIII, pp. 427–31.

[39] Webb and Webb, *Statutory Authorities*, pp. 276–97; L. Clarke, *Building Capitalism: Historical Change and the Labour Process in the Production of the Built Environment* (London, 1992), pp. 144–8.

[40] For this pattern, see esp. J. Beattie, *Crime and the Courts in England 1660–1800* (Oxford, 1986), esp. chs. 9–10.

nantly optimistic, in the eighteenth century, to increasingly tinged with pessimism, in the early nineteenth. While local histories and guidebooks remained predominantly upbeat in tone, an incipient fashion for social inquiry encouraged the production of other, less optimistic forms of survey. Doctors produced some of these: the growth of interest in medical statistics encouraged some doctors to survey their home towns from the 1770s. Those charitably inclined people, or their agents, who undertook the work of charitable visiting, a practice gaining in favour from the later eighteenth century, had their own grim tales to tell.[41]

The growth of steam-powered factory production in industrial towns did perhaps produce a real deterioration in living conditions; certainly as such towns grew once-pleasant districts deteriorated into slums. At the same time, what were to some extent traditional concerns – about the idleness, fecklessness and ignorance of the poor – were recast within a new discourse about the evils of 'large towns' and of 'industrial society': a presentation that encouraged pessimism, inasmuch as it suggested that these evils were the dark side of progress. The cholera epidemic of 1832 helped to catalyse some of these anxieties. When MP Robert Slaney moved in 1840 for the establishment of a House of Commons select committee to consider conditions in 'large towns', he helped to set in motion a process that would lead to a reconsideration and extension of the powers and responsibilities of urban authorities.[42]

(iv) THE PRACTICE OF URBAN GOVERNMENT: URBAN ECONOMIES AND THEIR REGULATION

Accounts of town governments' engagement with urban economic life, and of municipal finance, cannot be organised wholly around the theme of improvement – though certainly that has a place. Many town governments did exert themselves to improve towns' economic infrastructure. Whole classes of local legislation were devoted to the improvement of roads and rivers, the building of canals, the improvement of harbours and port facilities and the construction of docks. Corporations were among the sponsors of these – though petitions

[41] R. Sweet, *The Writing of Urban Histories in Eighteenth-Century England* (Oxford, 1997), esp. ch. 3; D. V. Glass, *Numbering the People: The Eighteenth-Century Population Controversy and the Development of Vital Statistics in Britain* (Farnborough, 1972), esp. p. 67; J. M. Eyler, *Victorian Social Medicine: The Ideas and Methods of William Farr* (Baltimore, 1979); D. M. Lewis, *Lighten their Darkness: The Evangelical Mission to the Working Class: London 1828–60* (New York, 1986), esp. chs. 6–7.

[42] For cholera, R. J. Morris, *Cholera 1832* (London, 1976). Most modern work on urban mortality has concentrated on the period after 1840, when data improve. However, Simon Szreter's work in progress aims to extend our knowledge backwards: see S. Szreter and G. Mooney, 'Urbanization mortality and the standard of living debate: new estimates of the expectation of life at birth in nineteenth-century British cities', *Ec.HR*, 2nd series, 51 (1998), 84–110. For Slaney: P. Richards, 'R. A. Slaney, the industrial town, and early Victorian social policy', *Soc. Hist.*, 4 (1979), 85–101.

favouring them were also presented by groups of local inhabitants, and individuals supplied most of the investment funds.[43]

Striving to make towns attractive to genteel visitors – one object of improvement – represented, among other things, an economic strategy. This was the spirit in which the corporation of York encouraged the establishment of a theatre, in 1733, and sponsored the local races. In the early nineteenth century, in the same spirit, the corporation of Boston financed an assembly room.[44]

Some corporations owned substantial swathes of urban property, and had by virtue of this power to influence the economic development of towns. In Bath, the corporation contributed little to the development of the town in the early eighteenth century, constrained by its own small income and by uncertainty as to whether the spa's booming popularity would last, but, assisted by a rising rental, pitched in more vigorously in the second half of the century. In Hull, the corporation not only vetted plans for all new building on its own extensive properties, but also insisted, successfully, that *all* new building needed the approval of the mayor. In Scottish royal burghs, officers called deans of guilds often enjoyed certain powers to regulate urban building.[45]

Control over sometimes very extensive open fields and common lands on the edge of towns presented special problems and opportunities. In Newcastle in the 1770s, freemen successfully brought suit against the corporation to prevent the leasing of the town moor; in Nottingham, the common lands which encircled the town were opened up for development only after parliamentary and municipal reform had diminished the influence of the freemen. In Bath, by contrast, freemen accustomed to profit from a share of the proceeds of the commons estate complained in the 1780s that the corporation was not doing enough to develop its potential.[46]

One function town governments had long been expected to perform was to

43 No study on transport improvements that I have seen pays sustained attention to the role of corporations (with the exception of J. R. Kellett, *The Impact of the Railways on Victorian Cities* (London, 1969) – who, however, includes among his sample several towns not incorporated before the 1830s). However, it seems that corporations were quite prominent in petitioning for legislation, less so among investors – not surprisingly, considering the financial constraints they commonly operated under. For the effect of these constraints on their response to problems discussed in the previous section, J. G. Williamson, *Coping with City Growth during the British Industrial Revolution* (Cambridge, 1990), chs. 9–10.

44 P. Borsay, *The English Urban Renaissance* (Oxford, 1989), pp. 218–9; E. J. Dawson, 'Finance and the unreformed boroughs: a critical appraisal of corporate finance 1660 to 1835 with special reference to the boroughs of Nottingham, York and Boston' (PhD thesis, University of Hull, 1978), p. 536.

45 S. McIntyre, 'Bath: the rise of a resort town', in P. Clark, ed., *Country Towns in Pre-Industrial England* (Leicester, 1981), pp. 197–249; G. Jackson, *Hull in the Eighteenth Century* (Oxford, 1972), p. 310; PP 1836 XXIII, p. 56.

46 T. Knox, 'Popular politics and provincial radicalism: Newcastle-upon-Tyne, 1769–85', *Albion*, 11 (1979), 224–41; Wilson, *Sense of the People*, pp. 343–6; M. Thomis, *Politics and Society in Nottingham 1785–1835* (Oxford, 1969), pp. 122ff; R. A. Church, *Social and Economic Change in a Midland Town: Victorian Nottingham 1815–1900* (London, 1966), pp. 162–70, 183–4; McIntyre, 'Bath', p. 236.

lobby to defend and promote towns' economic interests when national economic and fiscal policies were being formed. Sometimes undertaken by corporate bodies, such efforts were also made by particular guilds or trading companies, and by less formal groupings of merchants, traders and inhabitants.[47]

Scottish burghs had their own special forum in which to canvass their concerns: the Convention of Royal Burghs. Its existence had once offset such disadvantages as Scottish burghs suffered from operating in a unicameral legislature. After the Union, it had a role within the British polity as a promoter of distinctively Scottish interests, lobbying successfully, for example, for the use of Scottish tax revenues to promote the linen and fishing industries. But the Convention did not keep pace with changing times. Its membership was static, and heavily weighted towards the once more commercially active east coast; it was not well equipped to deal with shift towards the Atlantic coast, or with other changes in the urban hierarchy. Furthermore, as a lobbying body it was relatively unwieldy.[48]

From the 1770s, economic interests in some English and Scottish towns established alternative fora for themelves in the form of 'chambers of commerce'. Most early foundations did not stay the course – sometimes rent apart, as Manchester's was in 1801, by conflicts between competing interests *within* the town. But Edinburgh and Glasgow chambers of commerce have had a continuous existence from the 1780s, and elsewhere, such chambers were refounded in the early nineteenth century: at least sixteen were in existence by 1840.[49]

Traditionally, town governments had not merely striven to promote towns' economic interests, but also, in various ways, to regulate local economic activity. In the course of this period their activities in this sphere declined, in part eroding autonomously, in part being undercut by parliamentary action.

'Regulation' was bound up with systems of privilege and exclusion, which operated both at the national and at the local level. In England, until 1689, many branches of foreign trade were at least formally the monopoly of London-based trading companies. Agitation from provincial ports helped to secure abolition of most such monopolies before 1700, though the East India Company monopoly survived as a bone of contention, coming under vigorous provincial attack in the 1730s, and again in 1813, when the 'free traders' finally triumphed.[50] In Scotland,

47 J. Brewer, *The Sinews of Power: War, Money and the English State 1688–1783* (London, 1989), ch. 8.

48 T. Pagan, *The Convention of the Royal Burghs of Scotland* (Glasgow, 1926). See also *Extracts from the Records of the Convention of the Royal Burghs of Scotland* (1677–1759; Edinburgh, 1880–1915).

49 V. E. Dietz, 'Before the age of capital: manufacturing interests and the British state, 1780–1800' (PhD thesis, Princeton University, 1991), now forthcoming as a book; R. Lloyd Jones and M. J. Lewis, *Manchester and the Age of the Factory* (London, 1988), p. 64 and n. 4; L. Brown, *The Board of Trade and the Free Trade Movement in England 1830–42* (Oxford, 1958), p. 182.

50 C. G. A. Clay, *Economic Expansion and Social Change: England 1500–1700* (Cambridge, 1984), vol. II, pp. 191–202; R. Grassby, *The Business Community of Seventeenth-Century England* (Cambridge, 1995), pp. 60–1; L. Sutherland, *The East India Company in Eighteenth-Century Politics* (Oxford, 1952); pp. 27–30; P. Marshall, *Problems of Empire: Britain and India 1757–1813* (London, 1968), pp. 78–101.

royal burghs had traditionally claimed a monopoly on all foreign trade, other than in basic foodstuffs and certain other raw materials. However, from the late seventeenth century, trying to make a virtue out of their difficulties in enforcing this, they offered to tolerate other burghs' trade in return for a contribution to the share of the land tax they traditionally bore.[51]

At town level, systems of exclusion and privilege were most commonly found in corporate boroughs – although they were not unique to them: in unincorporated Sheffield, the Cutlers' Company strove to reserve to its members the right to engage in the town's primary manufacture.[52] In their most extreme form, restrictive regulations might allow only freemen to maintain shops or workshops, while outsiders trading in the market might be subjected to special dues. Freemen themselves might also be subject to restrictive regulations: their work might be subject to inspection, and there might be limits as to the numbers of apprentices they might take on. These systems were by no means defunct. Indeed, the late seventeenth and early eighteenth centuries saw the foundation or refoundation (after Civil War disruptions) of large numbers of guilds, and prosecutions of non-freemen for trading were brought intermittently down to 1835.[53]

Ultimately, however – as at the national level – the tendency was for these systems to lose their force; for authorities to compromise, in an attempt to come to terms with a changing situation, and for parliament to pronounce in favour of the freeing of trade. Local studies suggest that guild membership declined, first in larger towns and richer trades, later in smaller towns and poorer trades. In parliamentary boroughs with freeman franchises, admissions to freedom often came to cluster in election years – suggesting that their main attraction was the conferral of the right to vote. In London at mid-century, and in some other towns, licensing systems were developed, giving non-freemen the right to trade on payment of certain fees. Time after time, in place after place, trade after trade, masters responded to the growth both of demand and of competition by taking on more apprentices. The Sheffield Cutlers' Company enacted a common sequence of responses in the early eighteenth century when it first tried to enforce restrictive rules, then opted instead for a policy of encouraging expansion.[54]

51 Pagan, *Convention of Royal Burghs*, pp. 138–50.

52 D. Hey, *The Fiery Blades of Hallamshire* (Leicester, 1991), pp. 56, 140–3.

53 M. Walker, 'The extent of guild control in England c1660–1820: a study based on a sample of provincial towns and London companies' (PhD thesis, University of Cambridge, 1986), esp. ch. 4; C. Brooks, 'Apprenticeship, social mobility and the midding sort', in J. Barry and C. Brooks, eds., *The Middling Sort of People* (London, 1994), p. 65.

54 In addition to the works listed in the preceding note, J. R. Kellett, 'The breakdown of gild and corporation control over the handicraft and retail trade in London', *Ec.HR*, 2nd series, 10 (1957–8), 381–94. Hey, *Blades*, pp. 140–3, and Gauci, *Great Yarmouth*, pp. 40–8 and Appendix 3. For Edinburgh, Houston, *Social Change*, pp. 346–71.

The forces driving these developments were undoubtedly complex. Both masters' and workers' immediate interest (in maximising profit, getting a job or being able to practise a trade) might conflict with their medium-term interest (in limiting competition, and maintaining conditions of work) which in turn might conflict with their longer-term interest (in maintaining competitiveness within national and international markets).

The Municipal Corporations Act of 1835 removed a central plank of the old regulatory order when it prohibited the exclusion of the unfree from trading rights. The more limited Scottish Burgh Reform Act of 1833 had not included a similar provision, but Scottish Municipal Corporations Commissioners, appointed subsequently, recommended its adoption. They noted that their inquiries had not revealed much popular sentiment in favour of trading privilege 'except among the incorporations in Glasgow' – where it perhaps reflected less traditionalism *per se* than the strength of artisan radicalism, striving to devise systems for the protection of working men's rights out of the debris of the past.[55]

Although certain forms of economic restriction and regulation were especially associated with corporate bodies, others, though perhaps exercised by corporate bodies, were also very widely exercised by other authorities: manorial bodies or magistrates. In practice, these powers seem to have been unevenly employed, some of them chiefly coming into their own in times of crisis.[56]

From the later eighteenth century, under the sway of free-trade ideology, parliament began to deplete this arsenal. The repeal of laws against forestalling and engrossing in 1772, and of the apprenticeship clause of the Statute of Artificers, in 1813–14, were both significant moments. The assize of bread was abolished for London in 1822, for the country as a whole in 1836, though it had already fallen into disuse by that time. The fixing of wage rates was a declining practice from the early eighteenth century. Parliament usually resisted agitation by workers to give it new force. Even restraints on the sale of beer were abolished in 1830.[57]

55 5&6 Wm IV c. 76 cl. 14; PP 1836 XXIII, pp. 77–89.

56 For the regulation of food marketing, especially in times of dearth, see now A. Randall and A. Charlesworth eds., *Markets, Market Culture and Popular Protest in Eighteenth-Century Britain and Ireland* (Liverpool, 1996), esp. chs. 2, 5–7. For the use of regulative powers in responding to other kinds of urban disorder, J. H. Clapham, 'The Spitalfields Acts, 1773–1824', *Economic Journal*, 26 (1916), 459–71; J. Rule, *The Experience of Labour in Eighteenth-Century Industry* (London, 1981), p. 154.

57 E. P. Thompson, 'The moral economy of the English crowd in the eighteenth century', originally in *P&P*, 50 (1971), now repr. in E. P. Thompson, *Customs in Common* (Harmondsworth, 1993), ch. 4, with his thoughts on the extensive discussion provoked in ch. 5; T. K. Derry, 'The repeal of the apprenticeship clauses of the Statute of Artificers', *Ec.HR*, 1st series, 3 (1931–2), 67–87; C. Petersen, *Bread and the British Economy, c. 1770–1870* (Aldershot, 1995), ch. 4; R. K. Kelsall, 'Wage regulation under the Statute of Artificers', in W. E. Minchinton, ed., *Wage Regulation in Pre-Industrial England* (Newton Abbot, 1972), pp. 190–5; and see also Rule, *Experience of Labour*, chs. 4, 6; P. Clark, *The English Alehouse* (London, 1983), ch. 14.

Such changes were not always to urban authorities' taste. They had to bear the brunt of disturbances in times of dearth or labour conflict; at such times, the opportunity to intervene between seller and buyer, employer and worker, might represent a vital resource. Some furthermore regarded protecting the interests of the urban populace as a worthwhile task in its own right, an element of their own *raison d'être*. In the 1780s, the corporation of London clashed with dominant parliamentary opinion when it sought new powers to regulate meat marketing. In the early nineteenth century, Lanarkshire magistrates tried to help agitating Glasgow weavers obtain better wages. The agitation for free trade in beer was also opposed by local magistrates, who saw their ability to maintain orderly communities threatened.[58]

In fact, though the trend was for parliament to cut regulatory powers back, the purge was not total. Magistrates retained responsibility for securing the use of proper weights and measures. They retained and extended powers they had been developing to license and regulate urban transport services: powers over porters, chairmen and hackney coachmen were extended from the 1830s to new-fangled omnibus services. Even the tradition of passing laws for the protection of workers acquired new form in the factory acts, which in their early form gave new powers of inspection to local magistrates.[59]

(V) THE PRACTICE OF URBAN GOVERNMENT: MUNICIPAL FINANCE

Town government finances were intimately bound up with the various forms of their engagement in local economies.[60]

Many corporations' largest source of income was rental income from property – though some of the newer foundations (such as the cloth towns of Leeds and Tiverton, both incorporated in the early seventeenth century) had little or no property. Another important income source was dues and tolls, levied for the use of harbour facilities, on river traffic, or on those bringing goods to market. A third source was 'fines', leviable on a wide variety of grounds: for the renewal of leases; on wealthy inhabitants refusing to serve corporate office (who might be targeted

58 *Parliamentary Register*, ed., J. Debrett, vol. XXII (London, 1787), pp. 366–70; C. A. Whatley, 'Labour in the industrialising city, *c*. 1660–1830', in Devine and Jackson, eds., *Glasgow*, p. 376; Clark, *English Alehouse*, p. 335.

59 J. Hoppit, 'Reforming Britain's weights and measures 1660–1824', *EHR*, 108 (1993), 82–104. Transport regulation powers were bestowed by local act. London for example got an act providing for omnibus licensing and regulation 1838: T. C. Barker and M. Robbins, *A History of London Transport* (London, 1963), vol. I, pp. 14, 33–5. B. L. Hutchins and A. Harrison, *A History of Factory Legislation* (London, 1911), pp. 16–18, 32, 35–40.

60 Dawson, 'Finance and the unreformed borough', offers the fullest treatment of this topic. Local studies include R. Newton, *Eighteenth-Century Exeter* (Exeter, 1984), ch. 6, pp. 116–17, 149ff; McIntyre, 'Bath', esp. p. 226; and Bush, *Bristol*, ch. 4.

for that very purpose); for admission to the freedom; or by way of penalty for an offence judged in a local court. Many corporate bodies administered charitable trusts, which sometimes found their way into corporate coffers; at the very least, corporations might draw upon them to cushion themselves in difficult times.

The sums arising from these various sources were not usually very great. At the beginning of our period, fair-sized towns, such as Hull, York, Nottingham and Bath, reckoned their income only in hundreds of pounds a year – even by the early nineteenth century, only in thousands. In 1835, among English towns, only London, Liverpool and Newcastle had annual incomes exceeding £20,000. The historical contingencies of corporate property ownership meant that there was no consistent relationship between a town's size and its income. Newcastle, thus, had an income several times that of Norwich – though it surpassed it in size only at the end of the eighteenth century.[61]

Though corporate income usually increased markedly, with demographic and economic upturn, in the later eighteenth century, expenditure increased still faster. Many corporations borrowed, often by the sale of bonds or annuities, chiefly to raise money for urban improvements. Debt servicing became a major item of expenditure in its own right.

Some corporations had anciently imposed rates on inhabitants. Those dozen or so towns which were counties in their own right could impose rates 'in the nature of a county rate' for purposes specified by statute: chiefly prison building, the removal of vagrants and upkeep of certain bridges. In 1740, a tidying-up statute clarified the right of all towns not subject to the jurisdiction of county justices to raise such rates.[62] In practice, however, neither ancient nor general statutory powers were much employed: in part, it seems, because they did not provide a sufficiently secure legal basis for the range of things urban communities wanted to do, in part because corporations specifically were not always trusted to use public monies wisely. Local legislation provided a way through these problems, either by securely establishing corporations' powers to rate, or by arming new, more broadly based, bodies with rating powers.[63]

Unincorporated towns sometimes benefited from the expenditure of county rate income by county justices. In some such places, trustees held property in trust for the benefit of the town. Manorial bodies collecting market tolls might have money to spare for market improvements. And of course, when such towns obtained local acts, they often gained the power to rate themselves.[64]

61 PP 1835 XXIII, p. 97. M. Girouard, *The English Town* (London, 1990), pp. 28–9; Dawson, 'Finance and the unreformed borough', p. 62 (cf. population figures pp. 33–5).

62 12 Geo II c. 29; 13 Geo II c. 18 s. 7.

63 Langford, *Public Life*, pp. 222–4; Innes, 'Local acts'.

64 For Salford house of correction, built by Manchester magistrates to serve Manchester and Salford, M. de Lacy, *Prison Reform in Lancashire 1700–1850* (Manchester, 1986), pp. 25, 74, 76–7, 80, 173–7. For the Sheffield Town Trust, Hey, *Blades*, pp. 202–6. Of course, such bodies also existed in incorporated towns: thus Morris, *Class, Sect and Party*, pp. 169–70.

Finally, any (but especially small) parliamentary boroughs might benefit from the munificence of a current or would-be political patron, either in the form of cash gifts, for example to pay off corporate debts, or in the form of expenditure on public works.[65]

Property-owning corporations usually laid out much of their income on expenses associated with the ownership of property: maintenance and development; also quit rents, and property taxes. Salaries were commonly paid to corporate officers – though some were remunerated by being given the right to collect some form of town revenue, and keep the proceeds. Corporations often contributed to the cost of public services: building and maintaining prisons, contributing to hospitals and schools and towards the expenses of improvement commissions.

A portion of corporate expenditure was commonly devoted to legal services – routinely, for purposes associated with property ownership, less routinely, but not uncommonly, for the defence of corporate rights, especially those associated with the collection of dues and tolls, and the requirement that traders and craftsmen should be freemen of the town. In the later eighteenth and early nineteenth centuries, these rights were more frequently challenged (an aspect of the growth of a specifically urban form of radicalism, further discussed below.) Corporations then had to calculate whether the value of the income arising from those rights, and such other more nebulous value as they might attach to them, sufficiently justified the expense and trouble associated with defending them. Growing expenditure on litigation suggests that they did fight hard to defend at least some of their claims, but over time, more and more were abandoned or some compromise negotiated.

All these purposes, together with debt servicing, characteristically consumed the bulk of corporate income. What remained was usually directed towards the corporation itself, narrowly conceived: being spent on entertainments, or amenities for corporate officers, such as mayoral mansion houses, or plush new town halls. Elizabeth Dawson has shown that in the genteel town of York, which received many royal and other important visitors, in the mid-eighteenth century, entertainment (exceptionally) accounted for as much as 40 per cent of corporate expenditure. At the same time, she argues of the several towns she has studied that rising entertainment costs in the late eighteenth and early nineteenth centuries reflected the growth of corporate business: the cost, for example, of supplying wine to those attending increasing numbers of meetings. She also shows that, in her towns, such items represented a declining *proportion* of rising total expenditure. None the less, the fact that noticeable fractions of corporate expenditure were devoted to such purposes needs to be borne in mind if the resentment corporations often incurred is to be understood.[66]

[65] PP 1835 XXIII, p. 31. Girouard, *English Town*, p. 27; M. Humphreys, *Crisis of Community: Montgomeryshire 1680–1815* (Cardiff, 1996), p. 27.

[66] Dawson, 'Finance and the unreformed borough', pp. 611–61.

It can be argued that corporations, by such means, added colour to town life: supplied pomp and circumstance which could provide a focus for local identity. Certainly the installation of a new mayor, for example, could serve as a form of local festival. Yet not all inhabitants derived vicarious enjoyment from the spectacle of corporate dignitaries living it up. In the 1730s, for example, a dissatisfied group in Warwick brought suit against the corporation for having used revenues which should (they claimed) have been devoted to charity to rebuild their 'court house', to serve for their feasting and card playing. Chancery found in favour of the complainants, and the building was sequestered.[67]

Post Municipal Reform Act corporations, which not only inherited corporate property, but also a clear right to rate, characteristically had much higher incomes than had 'unreformed' corporations. An element of puritanical disdain for the ways of their less well-endowed predecessors is none the less suggested in the radical cuts in entertainment budgets they sometimes effected, and the high priority they gave to paying off corporate debts.[68]

(vi) CENTRAL-LOCAL RELATIONS

Systematic oversight of urban government was not a feature of any part of our period. The flurry of *quo warranto* writs and reissuing of charters under Charles II and James II gave central interference a bad name. Ministers remained keenly interested in seeing that town governments were in the hands of 'reliable' people – especially in parliamentary boroughs. But it was not always in their power to achieve that, and the means they used were commonly indirect: a matter of influence rather than direct intervention.

It has not often been noted that *quo warranto* informations continued to issue in substantial numbers throughout the eighteenth and early nineteenth centuries, to serve political ends. Local malcontents struggling for advantage would identify technical violations of charters, and bring suit against the corporation accordingly. The fact that both friends and opponents of government used these tactics suggests an expectation, apparently not wholly misplaced, that the post-Revolutionary judiciary would deal with such cases on their technical merits.[69]

National leaders were certainly not above manipulating local conflicts, however – and were probably suspected to be orchestrating such challenges, or their resolution, even more often than they were. Walpole especially attracted

[67] For urban ceremonial: P. Borsay, '"All the town's a stage": urban ritual and ceremony 1660–1800', in Clark, ed., *Transformation of English Provincial Towns*; Sweet, *Writing of Urban Histories*, pp. 261–4. Girouard, *English Town*, p. 30.

[68] Bush, *Bristol*, p. 186.

[69] Though see now P. Halliday, 'Partisan conflict and the law in the English borough corporations 1660–1727' (PhD thesis, University of Chicago, 1993), and P. Halliday, *Dismembering the Body Politic* (Cambridge, 1998). Lord Mansfield's efforts to systematise the law in this as in many other areas won praise even from the oppositionally inclined: thus J. W. Willcock, *The Law of Municipal Corporations* (London, 1827), p. iii, and H. A. Merewether and A. J. Stephens, *The History of Boroughs and Municipal Corporations of the United Kingdom* (London, 1835), vol. III, p. 2162.

such suspicions. During his ascendancy, constitutional disputes in London and Norwich were resolved by act of parliament (the effect, in each case, being to strengthen oligarchical elements within corporations.) Many other corporation cases were brought to the Court of King's Bench. Walpole's supposed role in corporation disputes was cited to the secret committee set up after his fall, and a bill 'for further quieting corporations' was brought in, but defeated in the Lords.[70]

Suspensions of charters as a result of legal conflicts sometimes provided the background to the issuing of a new charter. In other cases, corporations sought new charters in order to restructure themselves in some way: Tewkesbury's new charter of 1798, for example, extended the jurisdiction of borough magistrates over the larger parish. However, relatively few charters were issued for any reason. A survey compiled by Whig lawyers Merewether and Stephens in 1835 mentions only thirty-two town charters issued between 1700 and 1835; according to them, numbers had not been so low since the reign of King John. Only one town concerned – Wareham (1703) – appears not previously to have possessed a royal charter, and even that had long functioned as a borough.[71]

Towns figured within national administrative systems of this period in a variety of ways. Sometimes boroughs – or selected boroughs – figured alongside counties as units within a larger administrative scheme. Commissioners of the land tax, for example (an important tax at the beginning of the eighteenth century, though one being phased out at its end), were appointed (by statute) both for counties and for certain boroughs. The same was true of the militia (though in both cases, the vast majority of towns were subsumed into the county system).[72]

Towns as places often provided bases for the administration of larger districts. County administration was traditionally town based, insofar as it had a physical location.[73] The customs system was based in a series of port towns. New administrative matrices, developed in the later seventeenth and early eighteenth centuries, followed the same pattern: thus, postmasters were town based, and excise

[70] I. Doolittle, 'Government interference in City politics in the early eighteenth century: the work of two agents', *LJ*, 8 (1982), 171–6; Rogers, *Whigs and Cities*, pp. 35ff, 320ff; P. Yorke, *The Life of Lord Chancellor Hardwicke* (Cambridge, 1913), vol. I, p. 291, vol. II, p. 541.

[71] T. W. Freeman, *Geography and Regional Administration in England and Wales 1830–1968* (London, 1968), p. 53; Merewether and Stephens, *History of Boroughs*, III, pp. 1844, 1949, 2003, 2037, 2160, 2197.

[72] Annual land tax acts listed the areas for which commissioners served. The first income tax used existing land tax jurisdictions (see 39–40 Geo III c. 49; 43 Geo III c. 162); Western, *The English Militia in the Eighteenth Century* (London, 1965), pp. 21, 131, 135, 196–7, 217–18, 277–85. For attitudes in Scottish burghs when extension of the militia to Scotland was under consideration: J. Robertson, *The Scottish Enlightenment and the Militia Issue* (Edinburgh, 1985), pp. 98, 108, 111, 114, 131, 138, 150.

[73] Girouard, *English Town*, ch. 3, for physical manifestations of this.

districts, town centred. The New Poor Law of 1834 provided machinery for the definition of a new set of town-centred districts.[74]

Though cities and boroughs in general were not as such structured into most centralised administrative networks, there were many *ad hoc* exchanges between urban authorities and central government – usually with the secretary of state or home secretary, though economic issues might entail exchanges with the Treasury or Board of Trade. Urban authorities could request – though they did not always obtain – military assistance in dealing with rioters. Central government sometimes came down heavily on corporations or corporate officers who failed to keep order, suggesting the importance attached to this function. Under Walpole, Glasgow and Edinburgh were heavily fined for their failure to contain the Malt Tax Riots and the Porteus Riots respectively. From the 1790s – troubled as that decade was by dearth-related labour and political unrest, and by fears of revolution – contacts between urban authorities and the (newly specialised) 'home secretary' probably increased in frequency.[75]

Many forms of interchange between towns and central government focused on parliament, rather than on departments. Borough MPs were not the only channels for this business. County members recognised a responsibility for doing business on behalf of boroughs not otherwise represented. MPs also showed special alertness to the interests of places where they owned property, or had other connections. Town governing bodies, or townsmen, might also approach parliament directly, by way of petition.[76]

Scottish parliamentary burghs had given a very mixed reception to the Union proposals of the early eighteenth century: probably in part because they feared for the survival of the kirk under new arrangements; in part because, whereas some merchants anticipated that the Union would open up new fields for their endeavours, others feared that they might lose from English competition in both export and import trades. Perhaps also they thought a Westminster-based parliament would be less sensitive to their interests thereafter.[77] In fact, though Scottish issues did not loom large on the British parliamentary agenda, Scottish interests, as represented by their governing classes, were attended to – in return

[74] E. Hoon, *The Organisation of the English Customs System 1696–1786* (repr., Newton Abbot, 1968), pp. 167–8; K. Ellis, *The Post Office in the Eighteenth Century* (London, 1958), pp. 6, 32; Brewer, *Sinews of Power*, p. 102; Driver, *Power and Pauperism*, pp. 38–40. Freeman, *Geography*, ch. 2, notes municipal boundary commissioners striving to distinguish urban and rural districts, at much the same time that Poor Law Commissioners were striving to unite them.

[75] T. Hayton, *The Army and Crowd in Mid-Georgian England* (London, 1978), provides the only systematic study of a form of central-local interaction.

[76] P. Langford, 'Property and "virtual representation" in eighteenth-century England', *HJ*, 31 (1988), 83–115. For petitions see e.g. S. Handley, 'Local legislative initiatives for economic and social development in Lancashire 1689–1731', *Parliamentary History*, 9 (1990), 14–37.

[77] T. C. Smout, 'The road to Union', in G. S. Holmes, ed., *Britain after the Glorious Revolution* (London, 1969), pp. 186–9; R. Mitchison, *Lordship to Patronage: Scotland 1603–1745* (London, 1983), pp. 129–32.

for overwhelmingly pro-government votes. By the end of our period, the unholy compact between Scottish corporate elites and the ministry was a source of grievance. Political considerations helped to deafen parliament to Scottish pleas for reforms in the internal government of burghs, pressed intermittently from the 1780s to the 1830s.[78]

After fighting the courts in the 1704 'case of the Aylesbury men', the Commons obtained recognition for their claim to be the sole body competent to determine such electoral disputes – and by this means became the arbiter of contested borough franchises. Parliamentary determinations in the early eighteenth century often had the effect of narrowing, sometimes of broadening, these. Until 1770, committees dealing with disputed elections were open, and might be swayed by party feeling. Thereafter, members were chosen by lot, and a more judicial form of proceeding attempted. These later hearings resulted in a number of acts effecting more drastic remodellings.[79]

After the conclusion of the Napoleonic wars, in 1815, the *quality* of relations between central bodies and the localities changed, as government and parliament became more intrusive and interventionist. These changes in part reflected a broader process of cultural change, which affected the localities as much as the centre – supplying central bodies with the local sympathisers they needed to pursue new policies. Thus, central bodies' growing hunger for information reflected a larger growth of interest in empirical social and economic inquiry, manifest in, for example, the formation of local statistical societies from the 1830s.[80] The reformist spirit which powered many central interventions also had many exponents within towns.

The early nineteenth century saw a revival in the use of royal commissions as instruments of government. Commissions on education and charities conducted detailed inquiries in towns. The 1830s brought the royal commission on the poor laws (with their 'Town queries'), and English and Scottish Municipal Corporations Commissions.[81] The Poor Law Commissioners, as permanently constituted by the New Poor Law of 1834, were empowered to send directive

[78] For Scottish voting patterns D. Szechi, 'John Bull's other kingdoms: Scotland', in C. Jones, ed., *Britain in the First Age of Party* (London, 1987), pp. 253–5; J. Brooke, *The House of Commons 1754–1790: Introductory Survey* (Oxford, 1968), pp. 251–7. For reform, see below n. 123.

[79] J. Cannon, *Parliamentary Reform 1640–1832* (Cambridge, 1973), pp. 33–4; P. Lawson, 'Grenville's Election Act 1770', *Bull. IHR*, 153 (1980), 218–28. The proposal to transfer the representation of corrupt boroughs to unrepresented towns was actively debated in parliament from 1818, when the case of Grampound was first considered.

[80] D. Eastwood, '"Amplifying the province of the legislature": the flow of information and the English state in the early nineteenth century', *HR*, 62 (1989), 276–94; M. J. Cullen, *The Statistical Movement in Early Victorian Britain* (New York, 1975).

[81] R. Tompson, *The Charity Commission in the Age of Reform* (London, 1979), pp. 207–9, explores the confusion arising from the overlapping of charity and municipal corporation inquiries. For 1830s commission reports: PP 1834 XXXV–VI, Report of the Royal Commission on the Poor Laws; PP 1835 XXIII–XXVI, XL; PP 1836 XXIII; PP 1837 XXXV; PP 1837–8 XXXV.

circulars not only to boards of guardians of new urban poor law unions, but also to the governing bodies of those older statutory incorporations which survived.[82] The 1830s also saw the institution of the first central inspectorate of an urban governmental function, by the Prison Act of 1835.[83]

The municipal reform acts of the 1830s focused primarily on the abolition of problematic features of older arrangements, and only secondarily on the creation of an effective urban infrastructure. Though Brougham in 1833 announced, on behalf of the government, a plan to introduce a bill establishing reformed institutions in all 'large towns', in fact, the English and Welsh Municipal Corporations Act applied only to the larger corporate boroughs; unincorporated towns had to apply individually for incorporation if they wished to be governed by its provisions. While Manchester and Birmingham did quickly apply, other urban giants of recent growth were slower to come forward. Many smaller English urban districts long continued to rely on parish-linked governmental forms.[84]

In truth, policy makers at the centre were far from having resolved problems of agency. The next half-century was to see much experimentation and eclecticism, as attempts were made to find acceptable ways of organising the work of governing different sizes and kinds of urban community.

(vii) UNREFORMED POLITICS: PARLIAMENTARY AND NATIONAL POLITICS

In the early 1780s, the Society for Constitutional Information began to collect information about patterns of influence in parliamentary boroughs: identifying the nobility and gentry with substantial property in or near boroughs who were able to influence boroughs' choice of members. In the 1790s, Thomas Oldfield, a member of the Society, published a substantial treatise on the subject, which was revised and reissued in the early nineteenth century.[85] In the mid-twentieth century, this approach found a latter-day echo in the work of Lewis Namier, a fascinated student of eighteenth-century English political culture, who explored

[82] *Official Circulars of Public Documents and Information, Directed by the Poor Law Commissioners to be Printed, Chiefly for the Use of Boards of Guardians and their Officers* (London, 1840–51; repr. New York, 1970).

[83] S. McConville, *A History of English Prison Administration*, vol. I: *1750–1877* (London, 1981), pp. 170–6.

[84] *Hansard*, vol. XX, cols. 821ff. D. Fraser, *Power and Authority in the Victorian City* (Oxford, 1979), p. 150, lists the towns incorporated in the two decades following the act: Devonport, Birmingham, Manchester and Bolton in the 1830s; ten more in the 1840s, all from the industrial North or South-West. For the persistence of other approaches to local self-government, Prest, *Liberty and Locality*.

[85] For Oldfield and his work, E. C. Black, *The Association: British Extraparliamentary Political Organisation 1769–1793* (Cambridge, Mass., 1963), pp. 283–8.

with loving care the ways in which a more or less cohesive English ruling class, dominated by nobility and gentry, though also comprising other elements, had managed to sustain itself within the setting of a formally elective political system. Through his influence, the tradition lives on in the pages of the reference works produced by the History of Parliament Trust.[86]

There is much to be said for an account of borough politics especially which emphasises the role of 'influence'. Most of the seats in the House of Commons were borough seats (432 to the counties' 122),[87] and many of these were responsive to influence. Ministries commonly relied heavily on the votes of borough MPs for the support that sustained them in power (a fact recognised, if exaggerated, by reformers when they dubbed the pre-Reform political system 'the borough system'). Government influenced few boroughs directly – indeed, even the boroughs termed Treasury and Admiralty boroughs sometimes proved to have fallen under the personal influence of those supposedly managing them for government. But many of those who did have weight in boroughs lent support to the ministry of the day through some mixture of inclination and calculation.[88]

The immediate exerters of 'influence' were by and large the nobility and gentry. Landownership in the borough often provided a context for their efforts. They sometimes held local manorial rights. Law or practice in certain Welsh corporations gave local landed families extraordinary powers vis-à-vis corporations: the Beauforts were thus placed in Swansea, the Butes in Cardiff.[89] A long-standing relationship with a corporation might be acknowledged by appointment to such (often largely or wholly honorific) positions as lord high steward or recorder. Some seats were open to monied carpetbaggers, especially those where willingness to dispense huge sums at elections was the key to influence: Colchester, Hereford and Canterbury, for example, all had reputations as places where 'money will do a great deal'.[90]

Though boroughs had to be nurtured, and this consumed time and money, there were many men of substantial property eager to have this power. Influence is suggested to have increased in the three decades before the Reform Act, to

86 L. B. Namier, especially his *The Structure of Politics at the Accession of George III* (London, 1929); R. Sedgwick, *History of Parliament: The House of Commons 1714–54* (London, 1970); J. Brooke and L. B. Namier, *History of Parliament: The House of Commons 1754–90* (London, 1964); and R. G. Thorne, *History of Parliament: The House of Commons 1790–1820* (London, 1986).

87 In addition, Oxford and Cambridge Universities returned two members each.

88 See thus the breakdown of voting on 'Dunning's motion' 1780: Brooke, *House of Commons*, pp. 298–9. For government boroughs, *ibid.*, pp. 78–81; Thorne, *History of Parliament 1790–1820*, I, pp. 57–8.

89 Brooke, *House of Commons*, pp. 67–78. For Swansea, Sweet, 'Stability and continuity', p. 16; for Cardiff, Davies, *Cardiff*.

90 PP 1835 XXIII, p. 23; Sedgwick, *History of Parliament 1715–54*, I, pp. 241, 258, 266. J. J. Sack, 'The House of Lords and parliamentary patronage in Great Britain 1802–1832', *HJ*, 23 (1980), 913–37.

the point where some 75 per cent of all borough seats were vulnerable to some kind of magnate influence, 40 to 45 per cent to nomination, that is, it was said that they would return one or more MPs as directed.[91]

Not uncommonly, there was more than one such source of influence in a borough, and this could give rise to rivalry, and sometimes to electoral contest.[92] But this was by no means the only difficulty encountered by would-be borough patrons. Borough electors were far from being entirely plastic in their patrons' hands. On the contrary, they realised and vigorously exploited the fact that their position gave them power.

There were a variety of kinds of borough franchise, the most common being those in which votes were vested in freemen (resident and non-resident). Freemen boroughs in turn divided into those with large and those with small numbers of freemen (the latter of course being more susceptible to influence – or, conversely, better placed to demand a return for their support). Second most common were boroughs where voting rights were concentrated in the hands of the corporate or senior corporate body (mayor and aldermen); all Scottish burghs were of this type (most Scottish, and some Welsh boroughs were, moreover, grouped for electoral purposes, the final choice of a representative being vested in a small group of delegates). Burgage franchises, which attached votes to property, were often associated with very small electorates; freeholder, scot-and-lot and householder franchises, with large poor electorates, sometimes eager to trade votes for money.[93]

Though all forms of borough constituency could prove hard to manage, the nature of the challenge posed varied from place to place. Corporate bodies often expected exchanges of hospitality; subsidies for corporate expenses, and attention to local interests in parliament – indeed, at least some of these were expected from MPs in most borough constituencies. 'You must be forthcoming on every occasion not only of distress, but of fancy, to subscribe too largely to roads, as well as every other project that may be started by the idlest of the people', wrote Lord Shelburne of his experiences at Calne and Chipping Wycombe; 'add to this, livings, favours of all sorts from Government . . . and a never ceasing management of men and things.'[94] Members of larger electorates often expected treating, and sometimes direct payment. Some 10 per cent – 20 out of 203 – of English boroughs have been characterised as venal, and the proportion of venal

[91] See *English Historical Documents 1783–1832*, ed. A. Aspinall and E. A. Smith (London, 1959), no. 168, pp. 224–6; and F. O'Gorman, *Voters, Patrons and Parties* (Oxford, 1989), p. 21n.

[92] O'Gorman, *Voters, Patrons and Parties*, pp. 113–14; R. M. Sunter, *Patronage and Politics in Scotland, 1707–1832* (Edinburgh, 1986), ch. 10.

[93] The various volumes of the various sections of the *History of Parliament* all provide analyses of borough franchises. O'Gorman, *Voters, Patrons and Parties*, pp. 28–58, classifies boroughs not on the basis of their formal electoral arrangements, but rather according to the ways in which their elections were (or were not) controlled.

[94] Cited by Brooke, *House of Commons*, p. 69.

Scottish burghs was even higher.[95] The constant across all these cases was that loyalty was contingent. Contests indeed might be relished, as tending to increase the value of a vote.

If some borough electors looked for material rewards, there were others who cast their votes on the basis of their views, looking for candidates who shared and would represent them. Attitudes to religious dissent might be crucial. Sometimes more crucial were attitudes to the concentration of power. 'Independents', resenting the power of a local corporation, might be attracted by the rhetoric of candidates who assumed an anti-court stance. Finally, voters might be influenced by their ideas about particular issues or policies, and the stance candidates took on these. So, Burke alienated the electors of Bristol by his stances on the treatment of debtors, removal of restrictions on Irish trade and toleration for Catholics.[96]

Urban voters were not found only in parliamentary boroughs. If town dwellers met the county voting qualification (in England and Wales, possession of a forty shilling freehold, which might be an urban freehold) they might vote in the appropriate county; others qualified as non-resident freemen of parliamentary boroughs. So, the 'unrepresented' town of Birmingham helped to influence election results in Warwickshire and surrounding counties, in Lichfield, Newcastle-under-Lyme and Bridgnorth.[97]

Table 16.1 provides what might appear to be an index of declining urban political activity. As it reveals, fewer English boroughs went to the polls as time progressed, under a third after 1768. A similar trend is visible among those counties where the urban freeholder vote was substantial; that is, higher than 25 per cent of the total in 1831. Although the electoral participation of these counties was more impressive than that of the counties as a whole, there was a significant decline in the number of seats contested after 1715, a decline only partially arrested after 1802. Welsh constituencies were less vigorously contested than English ones before 1715 – but here too later eighteenth-century decline was evident. The exception was the Scottish burghs, where the number of contested elections increased in the early nineteenth century.

Yet also significant was the high number of large towns and cities that persistently went to the polls. Participation in large freeman or inhabitant boroughs of 1,000 or more voters actually increased over time, with over half contested on a regular basis. Because these 70,000 or so voters comprised the bulk of the borough electorate, the paradox was that while fewer boroughs were contested after 1722, still the majority of urban voters actively participated in the electoral process. Indeed, taking the intermediate boroughs into account, as many as

[95] *Ibid.*, p. 63. [96] For the role of opinion, O'Gorman, *Voters, Patrons and Parties*, ch. 5.

[97] Cannon, *Parliamentary Reform*, pp. 248–9; J. Money, *Experience and Identity* (Manchester, 1977), pp. 159–60.

Table 16.1 *Contested general elections in boroughs and counties 1701–1831*

	1701–15	1722–68	1768–1802	1806–31
No. of elections n =	7	7	7	8
	%	%	%	%
English boroughs (203)	40.9	34.8	32.3	32.8
Large boroughs (28)	53.6	56.6	59.7	59.4
English counties (40)	45.7	20.7	16.4	23.1
'Urban' counties (10)	60.0	25.7	21.4	30.0
Welsh boroughs (12)	13.1	28.6	10.7	18.8
Scottish burghs (15)	n/a	27.6	26.7	38.3
Welsh counties (12)	17.9	29.8	15.5	7.3
Scottish counties (30)	n/a	26.7	23.3	22.5

Scottish figures in the final column relate to the four general elections 1806–18 only. *Sources:* calculated from J. Cannon, *Parliamentary Reform 1640–1832* (Cambridge, 1973), appendix 3. For the top ten 'urban counties', see appendix 5. For Wales and Scotland, *History of Parliament* (see n. 86); W. A. Speck, *Tory and Whig: The Struggle in the Constituencies 1701–15* (London, 1970), appendix; F. O'Gorman, *Voters, Patrons and Parties* (Oxford, 1989), table 3.1.

66 per cent of the English borough electorate regularly went to the polls, excepting only the mid-eighteenth-century decades.[98]

Local studies suggest high levels of political engagement and consciousness in the larger boroughs. Voter turnout was high, usually over 70 per cent, and arguably increasing with time.[99] Voters displayed a high degree of party loyalty, with relatively few 'splitting' their two votes in deference to local patrons.[100]

Voting patterns in the borough sector generally both shaped and reflected changes in the nation's political culture. At the opening of the eighteenth century, towns sent large numbers of both Whig and Tory members to parliament – and the shifting outcomes of borough elections helped to determine the balance of power in the Commons. Scottish burgh MPs, appearing after the Union, rapidly became supporters of government. In the era of 'Whig

[98] See J. A. Phillips, 'The structure of electoral politics in unreformed England', *Journal of British Studies*, 19 (1979), 94.

[99] O'Gorman, *Voters, Patrons and Parties*, p. 184; see also J. A. Phillips, *The Great Reform Bill in the Boroughs* (Oxford, 1992), p. 32, and G. Holmes, *The Electorate and the National Will in the First Age of Party* (Lancaster, 1976), pp. 22–3.

[100] O'Gorman, *Voters, Patrons and Parties*, pp. 372–3; Rogers, *Whigs and Cities*, pp. 228–9, 268.

oligarchy', boroughs in general tended towards support for Whig ministries – though with important exceptions: large open boroughs increasingly supported 'country' opponents of Walpole, and, when the prince of Wales and earl of Islay turned against Walpole, their ability to influence Cornish and Scottish urban votes helped to bring about his fall.[101]

From 1784, boroughs followed a shift in electoral opinion nationwide in swinging behind Pitt (dissenting support for Pitt may, however, have been more of a factor in boroughs than elsewhere). Boroughs' tendency thereafter to support Pitt and successor ministries led to their being labelled 'Tory' by some new-style reformist Whigs and radicals. The Whigs' further lost support in closed boroughs during the French Revolutionary and Napoleonic wars. The rise of borough 'Toryism' was not simply a matter of consistent support for government attracting different labels at different times. The late eighteenth and early nineteenth centuries saw long-entrenched Whig cliques losing control over some corporations: for example, those of Bristol and Coventry.[102]

A series of indicators can be used to argue that, in the decade 1820–30, the borough system was not subjected to exceptional strain. Neither numbers of contests nor of petitions complaining about the conduct of such contests ran at an especially high level. None the less, from the late 1820s especially, increasingly highly charged political debate made certain features of the borough system highly visible. The Catholic emancipation crisis revealed that borough patrons could not control their own MPs' votes on highly contentious matters. Some borough electorates grew markedly; boroughs in general were said to be growing more expensive to contest. Ferocious local struggles led to complaints being made to parliament and courts about the methods used by those desperate to maintain political control. By 1830, even erstwhile defenders of the borough system were beginning to wonder if 'reform' might not offer the only route to civil peace.[103]

Political ideas were not monopolised by electors. The growth of the newspaper press and of political pamphleteering helped to make information about public affairs, and samples of political argument, more widely available. The politically concerned sometimes assembled in local political clubs (vestries sometimes served as rallying points for the 'Church' party). Consciousness of national events was both reflected and encouraged by the staging of local

[101] W. A. Speck, *Tory and Whig: The Struggle in the Constituencies 1701–15* (London, 1970), pp. 76–8 and appendix C; Rogers, *Whigs and Cities*, p. 232. For Scottish MPs, see above n. 78.

[102] J. Parry, 'Constituencies, elections and MPs 1790–1820', *Parliamentary History*, 7 (1988), 154–8. In the absence of a *History of Parliament* volume extending beyond 1820, subsequent developments are less clear. For Bristol and Coventry: Bush, *Bristol*, pp. 25–6, 34; Brooke and Namier, *History of Parliament 1754–90*, eds., I, pp. 400–2, and Thorne, *History of Parliament 1790–1820*, II, pp. 401–2.

[103] Cannon, *Parliamentary Reform*, pp. 197–9; M. Brock, *The Great Reform Act* (London, 1973), pp. 89–102.

celebrations and demonstrations to mark national events. Petitioning to express a point of view on a national issue was another form of political activity open to the unenfranchised.[104]

'Influence' never insulated towns from broader forces on the national scene. In the highly charged partisan atmosphere of the early eighteenth century, when the issue of a disputed succession haunted national politics, local celebrations of national festivals were often confrontational, with Whig and Tory mobs rampaging through the streets, traversing each other's territory, singing or whistling seditious or provocative tunes and burning their opponents' symbols or leaders in effigy. From 1710 until 1722 virtually every town of significance in England experienced some serious disorder on a public anniversary. This calendar of seditious revelry continued in the Tory heartlands of Lancashire and the West Midlands until mid-century, declining only as Jacobitism lost its pungency as an idiom of sedition and defiance.[105] Contentious gatherings associated with festivals and other events – including elections themselves – remained a critical component of urban political culture until well into the nineteenth century. Armed with only rudimentary policing capacities, magistrates frequently gave crowds a wide berth, tolerating raucous behaviour and insult.

A glance at the pattern of local activity prompted by the trial of Admiral Keppel in 1779 suggests something of the scope and character of popular urban political culture.[106] The court martial of this opposition Whig admiral for an inconclusive battle against the French off Ushant became something of a *cause célèbre*, especially because Keppel was brought to trial by a political foe and subordinate officers with the complicity of the Admiralty Board. The trial attracted enormous media attention, and when Keppel was acquitted, over 150 'demonstrations of joy' were reported in the London and provincial press, even reaching Ramsey on the Isle of Man. Of the 150 places specifically listed in the newspapers, forty-nine were significant towns, including some such as Birmingham, Manchester and Leeds not formally represented in parliament. A further seventy-five were small towns of under 5,000 inhabitants, including a few such as Banbury, where a thousand or so celebrants defied their patron (in this case the prime minister, Lord North) by championing the opposition admiral. In fact, of the fifty-nine boroughs that commemorated Keppel's acquittal, no less

104 Relevant studies include Speck, *Tory and Whig*; G. S. Holmes, *The Trial of Dr Sacheverell* (London, 1973); Rogers, *Whigs and Cities*; Wilson, *Sense of the People*; A. Goodwin, *The Friends of Liberty: The English Democratic Movement in the Age of the French Revolution* (London, 1979); J. E. Cookson, *The Friends of Peace: Anti-War Liberalism in England 1793–1875* (Cambridge, 1982); I. Prothero, *Artisans and Politics in Early Nineteenth-Century London* (Folkestone, 1979).

105 See N. Rogers, 'Riot and popular Jacobitism in early Hanoverian England', in E. Cruickshanks, ed., *Ideology and Conspiracy: Aspects of Jacobitism 1689–1759* (Edinburgh, 1982), pp. 70–88; and P. Monod, *Jacobitism and the English People 1688–1788* (Cambridge, 1989), chs. 6–8.

106 For a fuller account N. Rogers, *Crowds, Culture and Politics in Georgian Britain* (Oxford, 1998), ch. 4.

than twenty-five (42 per cent) had returned a full slate of ministerial candidates in the general election five years before.

The larger freeman and inhabitant boroughs were the pacemakers of this increasingly vibrant urban political culture. Of the 111 English provincial newspapers published in 1745, sixty-two (56 per cent) emanated from these largest constituencies.[107] Outside the metropolis, large provincial towns with freeman electorates were also the first to develop provincial clubs and societies. Thus in Norwich, the Loyal Society of Worsted Weavers, the dominant craft of the electorate, organised journeymen voters for city elections. In Bristol, the Steadfast Society and the Union Club performed similar functions, coordinating parish electoral societies into rival party machines.[108]

In the decades following the Hanoverian succession, when the reigning Whigs under Sir Robert Walpole attempted to muzzle urban electorates, the big cities emerged as their most outspoken critics, with large freeman boroughs (along with some of the English counties) dominating the agitation against Walpole, instructing their MPs to oppose the Excise Bill and the Spanish Convention of 1739, and demanding his dismissal in 1742. The same places were active in demanding an inquiry into the fall of Minorca in 1756. Sympathisers hailed them as representing 'the sense of the people' in an increasingly sclerotic electoral system.

This trend continued into the second half of the eighteenth century, as Table 16.2 shows. It charts the participation of larger urban constituencies in some of the major political agitations of the period. The City of London predictably led the list, addressing the crown or petitioning parliament on ten of the eleven occasions listed.

What the Table does not disclose is the sheer numbers of people involved. In the petitioning movements of 1769, 1775 and again in 1784, over 50,000 signatures were successfully solicited, a number equivalent to about 18 per cent of the total electorate or 3 per cent of all adult males.[109] The petitions certainly drew on a majority of voters in many constituencies in 1769 and 1775, and at times ran deeper. The combined total of addressers and petitioners for Poole in 1775 was double that of the electorate. Moreover, in that year, as the Table hints, petitions drew on the unrepresented towns for the first time; in this instance upon the residents of Leeds, Halifax and Bolton, who together mustered over 5,000 signatories.[110]

The precedent set in 1775 quickly became part of the new repertoire of polit-

[107] Calculated from R. M. Wiles, *Freshest Advices* (Columbus, Ohio, 1965), appendix B.

[108] Rogers, *Whigs and Cities*, pp. 277–8, 292–9; Wilson, *Sense of the People*, pp. 61n, 64.

[109] G. Rudé, *Wilkes and Liberty* (Oxford, 1962), pp. 105, 211; J. Bradley, *Popular Politics and the American Revolution in England* (Macon, Ga., 1986), pp. 3–4; J. Cannon, *The Fox–North Coalition: Crisis of the Constitution 1782–4* (Cambridge, 1969), p. 188n; O'Gorman, *Voters, Patrons and Parties*, p. 179.

[110] Bradley, *Popular Politics*, p. 67.

ical mobilisation. In 1784 the addresses to the crown thanking the monarch for dismissing the Fox–North coalition drew from a wide circle. This pattern became more marked in the campaigns to abolish the slave trade, which drew increasingly upon unincorporated bodies, and upon the unrepresented towns of the North, with as many as 10,000 signatories hailing from Manchester in 1788. By 1792 the abolitionists had also succeeded in mobilising many trades and friendly societies in Scotland.[111]

Perhaps the most dramatic mobilisation of the late eighteenth century was the campaign against Tom Paine's *Rights of Man* in 1792–3. In the wake of a call by John Reeves to defend the existing constitution against popular radicalism and republicanism, over 1,000 and perhaps as many as 1,500 societies agreed to associate.[112] Just how many people were involved in this movement is impossible to say, but it is very clear that it involved many middling property holders as well as some of humbler rank, either clients of the powerful or members of local friendly societies who were alarmed by Paine's brand of distributive radicalism. Few towns or county hundreds were without their loyalist association, and while a few loyalist associations were demonstrably reformist,[113] the vast majority were King and Country to the core, aggressively appropriating public space and often intimidating radicals from openly canvassing for an expansive male citizenship, a new spirit of internationalism and structural political change. It was not until the very end of the Napoleonic wars, in fact, that radicals gained the initiative, and the popular radical movement embarked on a 'mass platform' for democratic reform.

After 1815, the number of contentious gatherings grew exponentially, but the repertoire of collective action shifted increasingly away from the crowd interventions of the past towards public meetings, parades, petitions and more orderly forms of demonstration.[114] In the Queen Caroline agitation of 1820–1, there were plenty of examples of crowd exuberance, including effigy burnings of the principal Italian witnesses against the queen and the forced illumination of windows on the abandonment of the Bill of Pains and Penalties. But it was the orderly processions of the London and Lancashire trades and the countless

[111] Cannon, *Fox–North Coalition*, pp. 185–8; S. Drescher, *Capitalism and Antislavery* (Oxford, 1986), ch. 4.

[112] Reeves claimed that he had fostered 2,000 societies, but most historians believe this an exaggeration. For differing accounts of the loyalist movement, E. C. Black, *The Association: British Extraparliamentary Political Organization 1769–93* (Cambridge, Mass., 1963), ch. 7; H. T. Dickinson, 'Popular conservatism and militant loyalism 1789–1815', in H. T. Dickinson, ed., *Britain and the French Revolution* (London, 1988), pp. 103–25; D. Eastwood, 'Patriotism and the British state in the 1790s', in M. Philp, ed., *The French Revolution and British Popular Politics* (Cambridge, 1991), pp. 146–68; M. Philp, 'Vulgar conservatism 1792–3', *EHR*, 110 (1995), 42–69, and most recently Cookson, *The British Armed Nation*, esp. ch. 8.

[113] See A. Mitchell, 'The Association Movement of 1792–3', *HJ*, 4 (1961), 56–77; and D. E. Ginter, 'The Loyalist Association Movement of 1792–3 and British public opinion', *HJ*, 9 (1966), 179–90.

[114] C. Tilly, *Popular Contention in Great Britain 1758–1834* (Cambridge, Mass., 1995).

Table 16.2 *Extra-parliamentary agitations 1769–95*

	No. of electors	1	2	3	4	5	6	7	8	9	10	11
Bristol	5,000	x	x	x	x	x		x	x		v	
Colchester	1,500			x	x			x		x	v	v
Coventry	1,500	x	x	x	x			x		x	p	
Exeter	1,500	x			x			x	x	x		
Gloucester	2,000				x	x	x			x		
Hull	1,200				x			x				p
Liverpool	2,000	x	x		x			x			pv	p
Leicester	2,500		x		x			x		x	v	p
London	7,000	x	x	x	x	x	x	x	x		v	p
Newcastle	2,500	x		x	x	x		x	x	x	v	p
Norwich	3,000		x					x	x	x	v	p
Nottingham	2,000			x	x	x			x	x	v	p
Southampton	500			x	x			x	x		v	p
Southwark	2,000	x		x	x		x	x		x	pv	pv
Westminster	12,000	x				x	x	x			v	
Worcester	2,000	x		x	x			x	x	x		
Yarmouth	800		x	x	x		x	x		x		
York	2,500				x	x	x	x	x	x	pv	p
Birmingham								x	x	x	p	p
Halifax				x	x			x		x	v	
Leeds				x	x				x	x		
Manchester									x	x	p	p

1 = Petitions protesting Wilkes' expulsion as Middlesex MP 1769.
2 = Addresses supporting Wilkes' expulsion.
3 = Petitions requesting conciliation with America 1775.
4 = Addresses supporting government's coercive policy 1775.
5 = Petitions for economical reform 1780.
6 = Petitions for parliamentary reform 1783.
7 = Addresses commending king for dismissing the Fox–North coalition 1783.
8 = Petitions against the slave trade 1788.
9 = Petitions for the abolition of the slave trade 1792.
10 = Petitions for and against the Gagging Acts 1795 (p = pro; v = against).
11 = Petitions for and against peace 1794/5 (p = pro; v = against).

Sources: (1) G. Rudé, *Wilkes and Liberty* (Oxford, 1962), pp. 113, 211; (2–4) J. Bradley, *Popular Politics and the American Revolution in England* (Macon, Ga., 1986), *passim*; (5) *Parliamentary History*, ed. W. Cobbett (London, 1806–20), vol. xx, pp. 1370–2; (6) *Journals of the House of Commons*, vol. xxxix (1782–4), pp. 41ff; (7) *London Gazette*, Jan.–May 1784; (8) *Journals of the House of Commons*, vol. xliii (1787–8), pp. 159ff; (9) *Journals of the House of Commons*, vol. xlvii (1792), pp. 127ff, vol. xlviii (1792–3), p. 610; (10) *Journals of the House of Commons*, vol. l (1795), pp. 93ff; (11) *Journals of the House of Commons*, vol. l (1795), pp. 74ff.

deputations to the queen that caught the public eye.[115] Among the many addresses that the queen received were twenty-five from women, signed by well over 70,000 supporters. These addresses hailed not only from the established radical centres of London, Bristol, Leicester, Newcastle and Nottingham, but from seven unenfranchised towns in Yorkshire and Lancashire, including Halifax, Leeds, Sheffield and Manchester. They exemplified the changing sociological and geographical dimensions of urban politics in the age of reform.

(viii) UNREFORMED POLITICS: THE POLITICS OF THE URBAN SCENE

National and municipal political life interacted in complex ways.[116] In most corporate towns – including Bristol, Liverpool, Coventry, Leeds and Exeter – corporations were 'close': self-electing. In such towns, municipal political life was chiefly a matter of conflicting opinions being vented – sometimes very energetically vented. Elsewhere – London, Newcastle, Norwich, Maidstone – there were contested local elections. Some corporate officials or councillors were elected, directly or indirectly, by freemen. Elections to statutory commissions and posts in voluntary bodies were also sometimes contentious, and sometimes took on party political colouring.[117] Institutionalised contests for power of this kind could help to nurture and sustain the political convictions and loyalties that shaped townsmen's conduct in the national arena. But they were not a precondition for national political consciousness. Local contests furthermore often revolved around issues unconnected or only obliquely connected with national issues.

Religious attitudes provide an outstanding example of a set of ideas which might, in the right circumstances, shape both national and local allegiances. Sometimes, national and local allegiances shaped each other, as it were, at one remove. Those who opposed a corporation might oppose the national political grouping the corporation supported; conversely, those out of sympathy with a corporation's stance in national politics might be moved to challenge its management of local affairs. The interplay of local and national politics might produce odd conjunctions. In the late 1760s, many dissident, 'independent' groups in corporate towns were pitted against corporations supportive of the ministry: their rhetoric of rights and liberty neatly corresponded with the rhetoric of anti-ministerial, Wilkite agitators on the national scene. But in Coventry,

115 N. Rogers, 'Royal soap? Class and gender in the Queen Caroline affair', *Left History*, 11 (1994), 5–26.

116 Dickinson, *Politics of the People*, pp. 106–23, provides a helpful overview; see also J. A. Phillips, *Electoral Behavior in Unreformed England 1761–1802* (Princeton, N. J., 1982).

117 Webb and Webb, *Manor and Borough*, II, ch. 9, is devoted to 'Municipal democracies'. They list some nineteen boroughs which might be considered such, and examine five in some detail (Berwick, Ipswich, Morpeth, Norwich and London). Langford, *Public Life*, pp. 129–31. No study comparable to Fraser's *Urban Politics* exists for the eighteenth century.

where the highly politically manipulative corporation was a stronghold of dissenting Whiggery, slogans of right and liberty were deployed by 'Tory', pro-ministerial freemen.[118]

Constitutional conflicts, focusing on the nature and limits of corporations, or of select bodies within them, were a common feature of urban life in this period (though not one which historians have very fully explored).[119] These conflicts had an intellectual dimension. In the late seventeenth century, the historical evolution of burgesses' rights had been the subject of both popular and scholarly debate. One view of the matter was that towns had initially been controlled by adult male inhabitants – but that over time a more restricted group of burgesses had come to be distinguished within these. An alternative view had it that charters had never empowered more than a select group; there was no basis for quasi-democratic claims of right not grounded in strict charter terms.[120]

The outstanding scholarly studies of the late seventeenth and early eighteenth centuries took a Tory view: thus Robert Brady's 1690 *Treatise of Boroughs* and Thomas Madox's 1726 *Firma Burgi*.[121] But these studies by no means put paid to local debate about the rights and wrongs, and whys and wherefores, of borough constitutions. A kind of democratic antiquarianism became the hallmark of a certain sort of urban radicalism. The Municipal Corporations Commissioners were well aware of this politico-historical debate. They commented cautiously, 'As far as we can judge, neither the opinion of those who treat every extension of authority, beyond the select body, as a popular usurpation, nor of those who view every municipal corporation as formed out of a symmetrical and uniform organisation of the people, can be supported.' (Though rejecting an ultra-radical line, they did endorse the view that the trend had been increasingly to concentrate power.)[122]

Though we know all too little about these constitutional conflicts, and about

[118] Money, *Experience and Identity*, pp. 266ff.

[119] Halliday, *Dismembering the Body Politic*, has now carried the story up to 1720s, but not beyond. There is relevant material scattered throughout Webb and Webb, *Manor and Borough*, and see esp. II, pp. 699–705; also Sweet, *Writing of Urban Histories*, esp. ch. 5; Dawson, 'Finance and the unreformed borough', ch. 6. Relevant local studies include H. Cam, '*Quo Warranto* proceedings in Cambridge 1780–90', *Cambridge Historical Journal*, 8 (1946), 145–65; J. Phillips, 'From municipal matters to parliamentary principles: eighteenth-century borough politics in Maidstone', *Journal of British Studies*, 27 (1988), 327–51, esp. 334–6; P. Cadogan, *Early Radical Newcastle* (Durham, 1975); and G. E. Welch, 'Municipal reform in Plymouth', *Transactions of the Devonshire Association*, 96 (1964), 318–38. A helpful guide to the law, including a historical sketch of its development, is Willcock, *Law of Municipal Corporations*. J. Barry, 'I significati della libertà: la libertà urbana nell'inghilterra del xvii e xviii secolo', *Quaderni Storici*, 89 (1995), 487–513; and R. Sweet, in 'Freemen and independence in English borough politics *c.* 1770–1830', in *P&P*, 161 (1998), 84–115, explore the practical and imaginative context for these conflicts.

[120] J. G. A. Pocock, *Virtue, Commerce and History* (Cambridge, 1985), pp. 260ff.

[121] Brady and Madox, though not their views on boroughs in particular, are discussed by D. Douglas, *English Scholars 1660–1730* (London, 1939).

[122] PP 1835 XXIII, p. 16.

the ways in which they related to broader trends and controversies, it is clear that they were not confined to any part of the period. None the less, such printed material as survives, and such research as has been done, suggests an intensification of criticism from the later eighteenth century.

In Scotland, there are indications that a burgh reform movement was taking shape from as early as the 1770s. By the late 1780s, that cause was being pressed on parliament.[123] No such coherent movement ever took shape in England, but by the 1820s at the latest people critical of the rights and powers that corporations claimed were exchanging ideas and information, and trying to coordinate their campaigns, at least within regions. Thus, during that decade, towns throughout Lincolnshire and elsewhere on the English east coast were agitating and litigating against corporate tolls and duties; Cambridge agitators in the same cause sent Lincolnshire colleagues a copy of their newsletter for information.[124]

Common claims advanced by critics of corporations were, first, that select bodies within corporations (such as mayor, aldermen, common councilmen) had usurped powers properly vested in freemen at large, including powers to elect both to parliament and to local office, and decision-making powers. Second, that corporations were failing properly to manage corporate property, notably by keeping their accounts secret and not submitting them to proper audit. Third, that the revenues they mismanaged were in any case improperly or at the very least ill-advisedly derived, arising, as a large part of them often did, from the imposition of tolls and duties that injuriously restrained trade. Critics of corporations often rehearsed such arguments in the courts, to underpin *quo warranto* contests, or applications for *mandamuses*. Sometimes they succeeded in extorting concessions from reluctant corporate elites; sometimes the courts delivered victory into their hands. The corporation of Plymouth was largely democratised, and the conduct of its business rationalised, as the result of a series of freemen's campaigns and lawsuits between the 1770s and the 1830s. (The Municipal Corporations Commissioners judged it in many ways a model corporation.)[125]

These constitutional disputes nurtured a form of corporate reformism which associated hope for the future with a revival of what was seen as the democratic

123 Cannon, *Parliamentary Reform*, pp. 112–14; Pagan, *Convention of Royal Burghs*, pp. 95–105. No extended study of the Scottish burgh reform movement exists, though see for its early years R. C. Primrose, 'The Scottish burgh reform movement, 1783–1793', *Aberdeen University Review*, 37 (1957–8), 27–41, and, with an emphasis on Glasgow, Maver, 'The guardianship of the community', pp. 260ff. H. Home, Lord Kames, *Sketches in the History of Man* (Dublin, 1774), vol. IV, pp. 289–94, gives some early thoughts on this theme. Many other relevant documents are listed in C. Gross, *A Bibliography of British Municipal History* (Leicester, 1966), pp. 127, 136–40.

124 Dawson, 'Finance and the unreformed borough', p. 396.

125 Increasing corporate indebtedness, noted in the discussion of finance above, of course provided a part of the context for concern. For the content of criticisms, see works listed in n. 119 above. For Plymouth see Welch, 'Municipal reform'.

potential of traditional institutions. The radical restructuring undertaken by the Whigs in the 1830s left proponents of this alternative approach abandoned, their carefully honed analyses suddenly of little more than antiquarian interest.[126]

Constitutional and legal arguments appropriate to corporate towns overlapped with and shaded into more generally conceived or pragmatic arguments also deployed by critics of urban elites elsewhere. Select vestries and self-electing or merely unpopular statutory commissions were attacked as 'aristocratic'. The claims of lords of manors were denounced as 'feudal'. All sorts of bodies were criticised for want of economy in their financial management; alternatively, criticism might be targeted on abuses in corporation courts, or on oppressive proceedings in statutory courts of requests.[127]

(ix) PARLIAMENTARY REFORM

Some of the larger English boroughs began demanding parliamentary reform from the third decade of the eighteenth century. As soon as it became clear that 'influence' could seriously compromise the preference of most electors – as was manifest from the 1734 general election, when the unpopularity of Walpole's Excise Bill brought little perceptible change in the composition of the Commons – then parliamentary reform of some kind became part of the political agenda in the most open and independent boroughs.

Interest in a 'Country' programme of reform revived in the final years of the American war, when a wide range of propertied opinion became disillusioned with the government's intransigent and increasingly unsuccessful policy of coercion. But parliamentary reform proposals evoked disagreement and scepticism outside parliament, and this was echoed and intensified within. Even Pitt's modest reform proposal of 1785, which strove to redistribute the seats of thirty-six rotten boroughs to London and the counties, with subsequent further redistribution of seats in favour of other towns, failed in the Commons by 248 votes to 174.[128]

Parliamentary reform made little headway in mainstream political circles during the French Revolutionary wars (though a Scottish parliamentary reform

[126] Thus corporation law experts Willcock (of the *Law of Municipal Corporations*) and Merewether and Stephens (of the *History of the Boroughs*). Willcock in fact states (pp. 512–14) that his preference would be for an annulling of all charters, reincorporation of the kingdom in extensive districts and the recognition of all non-paupers as freemen. But he says that he does not expect this to happen.

[127] See D. Gadian, 'Class formation and class action in north-west industrial towns, 1830–50', p. 54, and J. Seed, 'Theologies of power: Unitarianism and the social relations of religious discourse, 1800–50', p. 143, both in R. J. Morris, ed., *Class, Power and Social Structure in British Nineteenth-Century Towns* (Leicester, 1986). For diverse grievances, Bush, *Bristol*, pp. 55–8; Newton, *Eighteenth-Century Exeter*, pp. 82, 86, 101–2, 127–8, 135–6, 150; Patterson, *History of Southampton*, I, pp. 71–89, 119–24, 162–3.

[128] Cannon, *Parliamentary Reform*, pp. 92–3.

movement did join forces with the English one at this time). The cause was too closely identified with Jacobinism or Foxite whimsy to gain much support from MPs, despite growing distaste for wartime taxation and state patronage. Yet grass-roots support for parliamentary reform grew markedly, especially in the years of post-war distress. The 1817 parliamentary session saw more than 700 petitions from over 350 towns, including petitions from Scotland (although not from Wales) and from major unrepresented towns of the Midlands and North. Indeed, the nucleus of this petitioning activity lay in areas that a few years earlier had been notable for their Luddism and insurrectionary temper. The post-1815 reform campaigns were altogether more extensive and democratic than their predecessors. This expansion of support brought on fears of renewed popular insurgency, especially after the trauma of Catholic emancipation in 1828.[129]

The Reform agitation of 1830–2 brought extra-parliamentary politics to fever pitch (see Plate 18), although the existence of 120 political unions across the country – from manufacturing cities such as Manchester, Leeds and Glasgow to ports, to mining towns such as Merthyr Tydfil, to weaving villages in the West Country – may in fact have helped to contain a very volatile situation.[130] The elections of 1830–1 suggested that almost all the more open boroughs supported some version of reform; there was also strong support in the counties.[131] Opposition from the less open boroughs in this context merely underlined their unrepresentative character, and further incensed reformers. Though Tories were shocked by the number of borough disfranchisements the Whigs proposed, their scheme fell far short of radical aspirations. Yet most radical leaders (Henry Hunt excepted) recommended that their followers support the Whig Reform Bill, in the hope that it would be productive of further change. This proved illusory, as the subsequent history of Chartism was to show.[132]

The Reform Bills of 1832 largely achieved the government's intention of consolidating a pluralistic propertied order. They broadened the base of propertied power without markedly weakening landlord influence in the counties, and replaced the old, variegated urban electorate with a uniform £10 householder franchise (although resident 'ancient right' voters were allowed to retain their franchise for their lifetime).[133] In England, dozens of the smallest boroughs were

129 *Ibid.*, pp. 171–2.

130 N. LoPatin, 'Political unions and the Great Reform Act', *Parliamentary History*, 10 (1991), 105–23, and references there.

131 Brock, *Great Reform Act*, pp. 196–7; Cannon, *Parliamentary Reform*, pp. 197–9, 220–1. John A. Phillips, *The Great Reform Bill in the Boroughs: English Electoral Behaviour 1818–41* (Oxford, 1992), pp. 297–8, notes that in the 1831 election, with only one exception, the Tories lost all boroughs with over 600 voters.

132 For a rich account of reform politics in London and its links with other popular movements, see Prothero, *Artisans and Politics*, ch. 14.

133 Sons of freemen might indeed inherit the vote. The English and Welsh reform act was 2 Wm IV c. 45; the Scottish act, 2&3 Wm IV c. 65.

disfranchised, and large unrepresented towns given the vote (elsewhere in Britain, such changes were less dramatic). However, in general only towns with populations over 10,000 were enfranchised, and only those with populations under 2,000 were disfranchised – so that there remained many 'unrepresented' towns larger than the old 'represented' ones, and the smaller boroughs remained highly vulnerable to influence. Though many closed constituencies *were* opened up (in Scotland, the vote passed out of the hands of corporations for the first time), the enfranchisement clauses did not significantly alter the socio-economic composition or distribution of the vote in the more open constituencies – save by disfranchising future generations of working-class voters in former potwalloper and inhabitant boroughs. In England as a whole, the percentage of adult males eligible to vote did not rise beyond levels reached in the late seventeenth century in the era of triennial elections.[134]

Reform and the registration of votes may have strengthened and in some cases generated partisanship, but in terms of overall urban electoral practice, urban political practice was marked as much by continuity as by change.[135] Post-reform elections had more polling booths, but the old arts of wooing and cajoling electors continued, and significant influence could still be brought to bear on those in dependent situations. Among the more independent voters, religious affiliation remained an important determinant of electoral behaviour, more important than the class identities that could be found in the wider political sphere. Inhabitants of the largest towns gained electoral strength as a result of the Reform Bill. Yet against this, it is worth remembering that the status of the large towns as the political pulse of the nation was already firmly established.

(x) MUNICIPAL REFORM

Both the Scottish Burgh Reform Act of 1833 and the English and Welsh Municipal Corporations Act of 1835 followed on the heels of parliamentary

[134] Borough representation pre- and post-reform was as follows:

	Pre-reform		Post-reform	
England	202 boroughs return	403 MPs	168 boroughs return	324 MPs
Wales	12 borough constituencies return	12 MPs	13 borough constituencies return	13 MPs
Scotland	15 burgh constituencies return	15 MPs	21 burgh constituencies return	23 MPs
Totals:	229 borough constituencies return	430 MPs	222 borough constituencies return	360 MPs

Note: English pre-reform totals allow for the disfranchisement of Grampound. Some Welsh and most Scottish contituencies comprised groupings of boroughs. There were of course from 1801 also Irish members in the Commons.

The figures make it plain that borough seats lost were almost all lost in England, whereas new urban seats were more widely spread.

[135] For two recent, and contrasting, assessments of the impact of the 1832 act upon urban politics, see Phillips, *Great Reform Bill*; and J. Vernon, *Politics and the People* (Cambridge, 1993).

reform, and in a sense represented a codicil to it.[136] The unhitching of borough franchises from corporate structures deprived corporations of an important part of their *raison d'être*. The Whigs furthermore did not wish to see so many 'Tory' bodies left entrenched in power. The establishment of elective town councils can be seen as part of a larger project: the creation of political and governmental structures which would allow emergent liberalism to flourish.

Municipal reform was imposed from above, by parliament. But government and parliament were also subject to pressure from below. Some large towns – Bristol, Liverpool – were considering remodelling urban constitutions by local act; they desisted only when it became plain that the government had plans for more comprehensive reform. When Brougham in 1833 proposed to bring in a bill to establish elective councils in all 'large towns' (a proposal not followed through in that form) he was apparently trying to pre-empt a private member's proposal to the same effect.[137]

Scottish burgh reform, as implemented in 1833, had two components. One act focused on the establishment of elective muncipal governments; the other was a permissive act, adoptable by any burgh with more than 3,000 inhabitants, providing a simple framework for the management of lighting, watching, cleansing, supplying with water and general 'improvement'. English and Welsh Municipal Corporations Commissioners, appointed in the same year, and Scottish Commissioners appointed three years later, by contrast worked to a more complex agenda, adumbrated in a long tradition of criticism of corporate bodies.

In the spirit of that tradition, the English and Welsh Municipal Reform Act of 1835 concentrated more on the supersession of problematic structures and cutting back of powers than on the creation of new capacities. The act, which applied only to 178 larger corporations, established elected town councils, and indirectly elected mayors and aldermen. Its ratepayer franchise was so hedged around with qualifications that it proved in practice narrower than the parliamentary franchise.[138] The new bodies were not immediately endowed with any substantial powers. Indeed – reflecting the importance traditionally attached to the preservation of order in towns – the only specific function positively conferred on new town governments was that of maintaining a watch force; they were also empowered to extend lighting to unlit parts of boroughs.

At least as notable was what the act took away. It took judicial powers away from mayors and aldermen; they retained only the right to nominate magistrates,

[136] 3&4 Wm IV c. 46; 5&6 Wm IV c. 76. G. B. A. M. Finlayson, 'The politics of municipal reform, 1835', *EHR*, 81 (1966), 673–92, summarises the conclusions of his Oxford 1959 BLitt thesis. Little appears to have been written about the impact of the Reform Act on the political life of Scottish burghs.

[137] Bush, *Bristol*, p. 60; Vigier, *Change and Apathy*, p. 177; Webb and Webb, *Manor and Borough*, II, p. 710n.

[138] Keith-Lucas, *Local Government Franchise*, pp. 55–8.

power to appoint passing to the lord chancellor. Borough courts also lost the power to try capital cases, and towns lost admiralty jurisdiction. Trusteeship over charitable funds was henceforth to be exercised by distinct bodies. Rights of presentation to livings were to be sold, under the guidance of the Ecclesiastical Commissioners. All kinds of exclusive or privileged trading right associated with admission to the freedom were abolished. No payments were to be made but on the order of town councils, and auditing procedures were prescribed. Any surplus of funds was to be applied to the 'improvement' of the town; any deficiency might be supplied by rate. (Since it was not envisaged that such rates would necessarily be collected, the ratepayer franchise was defined with reference to the parochial poor rate, not the borough rate).[139]

In the short term, the Municipal Corporations Act did fulfil its promoters' political objectives. In many boroughs, some members of old corporations were re-elected – but overall, the first municipal elections under the new regime produced significant gains for Whigs and reformers. As at the parliamentary level, however, the restructuring of the political system was within a few years to prove simply to have recast the framework within which political struggles were fought out. Whigs and liberals would find their position eroded on the right by Tory revival, on the left by Chartism.[140]

APPENDIX

The totals of towns follow lists compiled by John Langton (see Chapter 14), which give numbers of towns appearing in late seventeenth-century lists, and all those with populations of 2,500+ in 1801 or 1841. The Midlands, North and Scotland stand out for the numbers of settlements of 2,500+ by 1801 and/or 1841 not appearing as 'towns' in late seventeenth-century listings.

Corporations and boroughs are distinguished into 'Major corporations', those judged significant enough to be brought within the terms of the 1835 Municipal Corporations Act, and others. In most regions, more corporations were brought within the terms of the act than not, but in Wales the reverse was true, emphasising the tiny size of most Welsh corporate towns. The Scottish chart shows not 'major' and 'minor' corporations but royal burghs and burghs of barony: it is clear that more Scottish towns had royal burgh status than English towns corporate status; burghs of barony included many tiny settlements.

[139] Studies of the impact of municipal reform on urban administration include E. P. Hennock, *Fit and Proper Persons* (London, 1973); Fraser, *Power and Authority*; Fraser, *Urban Politics*, esp. ch. 6; and D. Fraser, ed., *Municipal Reform and the Industrial City* (Leicester, 1982). See also Bush, *Bristol*. Less has been written about Scotland, but see K. Carson and H. Idzikowska, 'The social production of Scottish policing, 1795–1900', in Hay and Snyder, eds., *Policing and Prosecution*, pp. 283–8, and for Glasgow, Maver, 'The guardianship of the community', pp. 267–70.

[140] For the political impact of municipal reform, see Phillips, *Reform in the Boroughs*, p. 228, and the works listed above. Few studies have set Chartism in municipal political context, but see P. Searby, 'Chartists and freemen in Coventry 1838–60', *Soc. Hist.*, 6 (1977), 761–84.

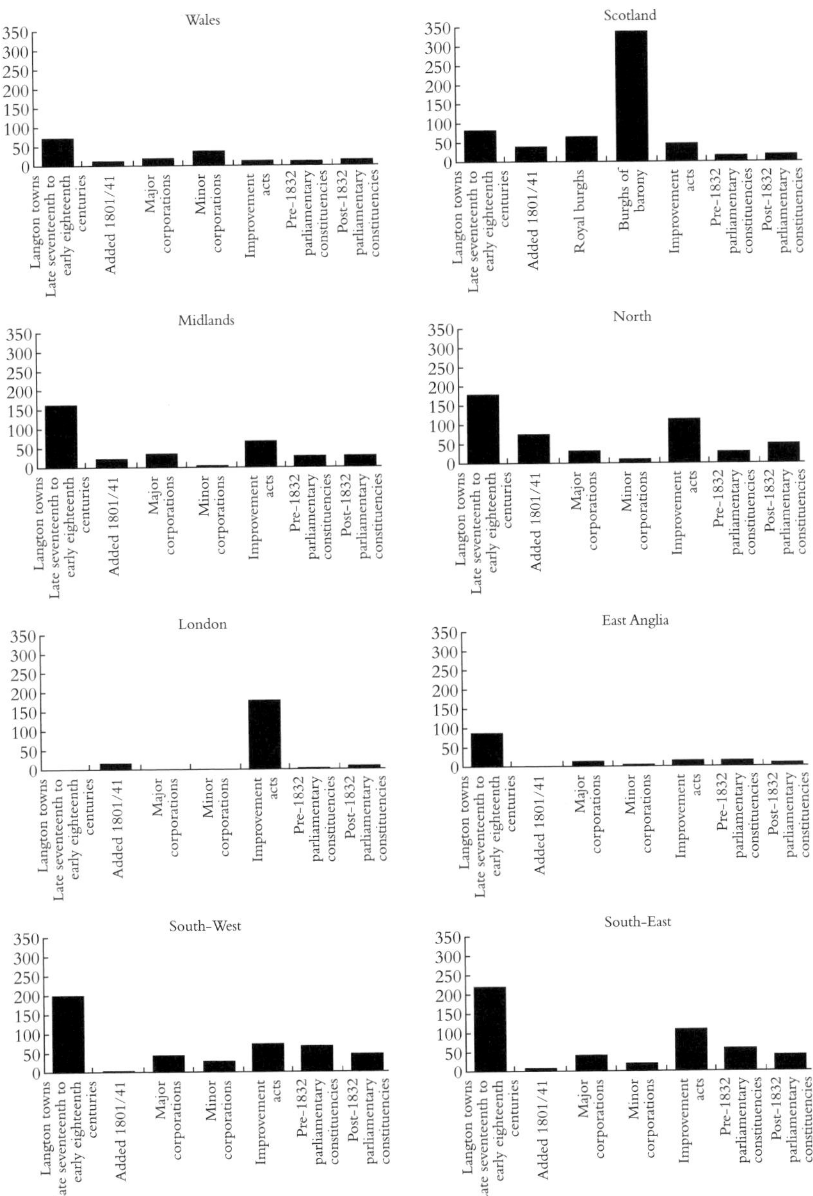

Figure 16.2 Urban communities, corporate forms, improvement acts and parliamentary representation by region

Total (i.e. urban+rural) populations of these regions, following Deane and Cole's estimates for English regions, in 00,000s

	1701	As % total	1831	As % total
Scotland	2[a]	3	3	2
Wales	4	8	9	6
North	11	17	38	25
Midlands	11	17	25	16
East Anglia	5	8	9	6
London	6	9	14	9
South-East	15	23	37	24
South-West	11	17	20	13

Notes:
[a] Estimates vary between 1 and 2.
Regions:
Wales: incl. Monmouthshire
North: Cheshire, Cumberland, Durham, Lancashire, Northumberland, Westmorland, Yorkshire
Midlands: Derbyshire, Herefordshire, Leicestershire, Lincolnshire, Northamptonshire, Nottinghamshire, Rutland, Shropshire, Staffordshire, Warwickshire, Worcestershire
East Anglia: Cambridge, Huntingdonshire, Norfolk, Suffolk
South-East: Bedfordshire, Berkshire, Buckinghamshire, Essex, Hampshire, Hertfordshire, Kent, Oxford, Surrey, Sussex
South-West: Cornwall, Devon, Dorset, Gloucestershire, Somerset, Wiltshire

Improvement acts here as in the chapter means all new acts (i.e. excluding those described as continuing, amending or repealing previous acts); the totals are not totals of towns to which acts applied: many towns obtained more than one such act. East Anglia and Wales both appear to have been relatively poorly endowed with improvement acts; the North by contrast was well endowed (the meaning of these patterns could only be determined by a more refined investigation into the distribution of acts across towns of different sizes).

Changes in numbers of *parliamentary constituencies* show the geographically diverse effects of parliamentary reform, which reduced the number of borough constituencies in the South-East and West, and East Anglia, and increased their number in the Midlands, North and Scotland – and marginally in Wales.

· 17 ·

Culture and leisure 1700–1840

PETER CLARK AND R. A. HOUSTON

This iron age departed, we behold,
An age of pleasure, luxury, and gold;
No more exist those opposites to Life,
A social husband, and domestic wife . . .
Triumphal entries and their dull parades,
Are chang'd for Op'ras, Balls and Masquerades;
No longer Sunday's dull employment cloys,
For Church we substitute politer joys . . .

THUS IN mildly satirical vein a poetaster of the 1770s described the smart new cultural world of Georgian Britain.[1] The sense of cultural transformation, of the new sociable importance of women, of new entertainments, of the secularisation of social life, is striking, acute – and exaggerated. As we shall see in this chapter, such changes do figure prominently in the dynamic, and increasingly pluralistic, cultural landscape of British cities during the Georgian era, but they were only part of the painting.

In contrast to the earlier period, there can be little question that cities and towns after 1700 became vital centres for cultural mixing and dissemination, affecting not only the elite classes but a good part of national society as well. The leading cities, particularly London and Edinburgh, became cultural bazaars, increasingly cosmopolitan, importing and translating cultural ideas, goods and practices from continental Europe and beyond. Urban communities became exposition centres, exhibiting the fashionable models of cultural activity, whether performances of Handel's oratorios, meetings of a newly established

Peter Clark was primarily concerned with south of the border and Rab Houston north of it; but we have sought to make the analysis as united as possible. Peter Clark wishes to thank Anne Borsay for suggestions about reading and John Walsh for his invaluable counsel on the final section.

[1] *Epistle To Mrs. M*ll*r* . . . (Bath, 1776), p. 6. For the Batheaston poetry circle see J. Brewer, *The Pleasures of the Imagination* (London, 1997), pp. 601–4.

learned society or the latest taste in furnishings, dress or speech. Yet British cities in the Georgian era were more than sites or stages for cultural exchange: they were also seedbeds of innovation. They generated new forms of leisure entertainment, including more gender-defined activities, new perceptions of time and space and, later on, new concerns about social and moral behaviour.

If there was a secularisation of religion during the eighteenth century, there was also an urbanisation of culture. In Britain new Enlightenment ideas and activities were largely an urban phenomenon, rather than one patronised by the state or the nobility as we find in other European countries.[2] Cultural change and innovation in this country were closely associated with economic and other developments in towns: the influx of the landed class and other migrants (notably women), improved living standards, the growth of new social groups, the expansion of the commercial entertainment and information industries, urban improvement and, also, the accumulating social problems of urban growth. Cultural changes both mirrored and were a response to the new currents and pressures generated by urbanisation.

At the same time, one must see cultural change – the replacement of an 'iron age' with an 'age of pleasure' – in perspective. The new entertainments, operas, balls and masquerades, did not sweep away all the more traditional activities, such as rituals and games linked to the home, neighbourhood and drinking houses. Nor were all the new developments limited to the golden world of the metropolitan elite: indeed what is striking about the eighteenth century is how quickly and widely new practices were disseminated among the middling and artisan classes and across the urban system. At the same time, local cultural autonomy remained important and in the early nineteenth century it is arguable that religion reasserted its central and powerful role in urban society. In Scotland it may never have lost it.

This chapter takes a broad definition of culture to include shared attitudes, meanings and values in urban society. The analysis is necessarily selective. It looks, first, at the new cultural developments of the eighteenth century, including new entertainments and attitudes towards time and space; secondly, it examines the causes of change and then considers traditional counter-currents; the last section sketches the role of the urban Church and its contribution to the resurgence of cultural high seriousness by 1840.

(i) CULTURAL INNOVATION

Though as we saw in Chapter 8 a number of new cultural entertainments, in music, sport and learning, gained an important footing in English towns after the Restoration, some even appearing before the Civil War, there can be little

[2] For the European picture cf. R. Porter and M. Teich, eds., *The Enlightenment in National Context* (Cambridge, 1981).

question that it was in the century following the Glorious Revolution that they flourished in abundance. In London during the 1760s the duchess of Newcastle described a cascade of entertainments, among them four opera houses, two sets of strolling players, four pleasure gardens, seven major assemblies, three fashionable lecture series, over seventy exhibitions, menageries and learned societies, besides '20 inferior assemblies, 100 lectures on anatomy, law, astronomy etc etc; debating clubs including the Robin Hood, concerts, billiard tables and cockpits'. A few years later Lady Mary Holland wrote from the capital 'what a rage there is for amusement [here] . . . masquerades, balls, and assemblies without end'.[3] By the close of the century London newspapers published social calendars, 'arrangements in high life', which often listed half a dozen fashionable events each evening. If the metropolis was the Vatican of pleasure in all its new forms, provincial towns partook of a growing share. In 1731 a visitor to Cambridge noted one evening going 'to coffee-house, chapel, supper, music club', while during the Bury St Edmunds fair 'all the neighbouring nobility and gentry come there every afternoon where they divert themselves in raffling, and [then] . . . go to the comedy . . . and afterwards . . . to the assemblies'. Of Salisbury under George III, it was said 'every amusement, though inferior [in] degree to London, may be found'. By this time Gloucester boasted county cockfights and horse races, plays at the two city theatres, card assemblies, concerts by the music society, promenades on the cathedral green (entertained by a military band), scientific lectures, masonic lodges, florist feasts and the triennial gatherings of the Three Choirs Festival.[4] The rising spa towns were also significant centres of new-style sociability, albeit limited in most cases by the shortness of the season. Smaller English towns had a more modest array of activities (as did Scottish equivalents like Moffat), but Louth in Lincolnshire could claim not only 'frequent assemblies and concerts but even masquerades'. Provincial standards were not always high: socialising at Hereford, according to Mrs Delany, was distinguished by 'dirty beaux, awkward belles, bad dancing and worse fiddles'.[5]

The pace of change varied between different parts of Britain. There was a scattering of assemblies, balls and hunt clubs in the towns of North Wales by the 1770s and some of the more important Welsh centres like Carmarthen, Cowbridge and Wrexham enjoyed a range of entertainments. But the pattern

[3] See above, pp. 286–8. For the standard account see P. Borsay, *The English Urban Renaissance* (Oxford, 1989). J. Greig, ed., *The Diaries of a Duchess* (London, 1926), pp. 206–7; Kansas University Library, Special Collections, MS 203A (4).

[4] E.g., *The Star*, 21 Mar. 1791; *Morning Chronicle*, 2 May 1791. R. Parkinson, ed., *The Private Journal and Literary Remains of John Byrom*, vol. II (2) (Chetham Society, 1st series, 34, 1855), p. 431; J. Macky, *A Journey through England* (London, 1724), vol. I, p. 6; *St James Chronicle*, 26–8 Jan. 1769; *Gloucester Journal*, 18 Mar. 1760, 25 Oct. 1762, 2 Jan. 1764, 20 Oct. 1766, 3 Apr. 1769, 10 June 1771 *et passim*.

[5] See below, p. 786 *et seq.*; *A Short Tour in the Midland Counties of England . . . 1772 . . .* (London, 1775), pp. 23–4; Lady Llanover, *The Autobiography and Correspondence of Mary Granville, Mrs Delany: First Series* (London, 1861), vol. I, p. 572; R. Morris and F. Morris, *Scottish Healing Wells* (Sandy, 1982).

was less pronounced than in England and new developments tended to occur a couple of decades behind, reflecting the lagging nature of Welsh urbanisation. Thus at Swansea the 'age of improvement' – of the local press, assemblies and other leisure facilities – had to wait until the late 1780s. In Scotland Edinburgh was becoming a major centre for new-style sociability under George II and by the 1770s Edward Topham could declare: 'we have an elegant playhouse and tolerable performers; assemblies, concerts, public gardens and walks, card parties, and a hundred other diversions'. Elsewhere, advances occurred later, reflecting not only the slower rate of economic and urban growth but also the initial opposition of the kirk. However a middle-rank town like Kelso had its gentleman's club, library and assemblies by mid-century.[6]

The efflorescence of new forms of cultural and leisure activity after the Glorious Revolution undoubtedly owed a good deal to the expanding role of drinking houses – already one of the pillars of public sociability in the preceding era. The number of premises probably continued to increase into the early eighteenth century, though at a declining rate. More significant, however, premises became larger, more lavish and commercial, acquiring specialist facilities including club rooms and assembly rooms, while their landlords became energetic social and cultural entrepreneurs, financing, organising, hosting and marketing many of the new entertainments. The old trinity of inns, taverns and alehouses was joined by new kinds of premises – elite and lower-class coffee-houses, gin-shops and later gin-palaces. From the later seventeenth century inns developed as the prime venue for many of the new entertainments already mentioned: balls, assemblies, plays, lectures, exhibitions, scientific experiments, sports, concerts, society meetings, along with a great variety show of equestrian feats, displays of birds, wild animals and human freaks, and acts by magicians, mountebanks and jugglers. Smaller in scale taverns and alehouses (increasingly referred to as public houses) went down a similar route. Commercial concerts were staged for the first time in Europe at John Bannister's London alehouse in the 1670s, while it was at the Goose and Gridiron, another London public house, that the first national masonic grand lodge was established in 1717, launching one of the most successful associational movements in the western world.[7]

6 *Adams Weekly Courant*, 31 Jan., 7 Nov., 14 Nov. 1775, 5 Jan. 1779 *et passim*; see above, pp. 134 *et seq.*; R. Sweet, 'Stability and continuity: Swansea politics and reform 1780–1820', *Welsh History Review*, 18 (1996), 18–19; Edward Topham, *Letters from Edinburgh Written in the Years 1774 and 1775* (London, 1776), p. 90; J. B. Paul, ed., *Diary of George Ridpath* (Scottish History Society, 3rd series, 2, 1922), pp. 4, 66, 71, 115, 162.

7 P. Clark, *The English Alehouse* (London, 1983), pp. 51–3, ch. 9; A. Everitt, The English urban inn 1560–1760', in A. M. Everitt, ed., *Perspectives in English Urban History* (London, 1973), pp. 100–20; J. A. Chartres, 'The capital's provincial eyes: London's inns in the early eighteenth century', *LJ*, 3 (1977), 24–39; J. Harley, *Music in Purcell's London* (London, 1968), pp. 137, 141; A. S. Frere, ed., *Grand Lodge 1717–1967* (Oxford, 1967), pp. 48–51.

Coffee-houses also played a significant part in promoting the new activities. By 1700 there may have been 2,000 in London, supplemented by small clusters, some of them converted taverns, in the provinces. They were closely associated with new-style sociability. In 1737 we hear 'there's scarce an alley in city and suburbs but has a coffee-house in it which may be called the school of public spirit'. Most provided daily and weekly newspapers, others had their own library. After the Glorious Revolution they hosted a growing variety of clubs and societies. Thus the Spalding Gentleman's Society, a learned society with its own museum, originated under Queen Anne in a circle of local worthies reading the *Tatler* and *Spectator* magazines at the town's coffee-house. Though their number and significance in elite social life generally declined in the second half of the eighteenth century, towns like Leicester, Nottingham and Derby gained a new breed of coffee-house with newsrooms attached, attracting mainly shopkeepers and small manufacturers. After 1800 popular coffee-houses also filtered north of the border, furnishing basic social facilities (including a newspaper) for artisans and the semi-skilled. Other new drinking premises had a lesser role in the growth of new leisure and cultural activities. The gin-shops which mushroomed in the early Georgian capital, and subsequently elsewhere, tended to be rudimentary, illicit premises, providing a focus for old-style drinking.[8]

While the more respectable drinking houses played an active part in promoting the development of new-style entertainments, by the second quarter of the eighteenth century many of the principal activities, such as music-making, assemblies, the theatre, sporting events and clubs and societies, had gained their own organisational momentum. In a number of areas this process was hastened by the advent of specialist bodies and promoters to run them and specialist buildings and dedicated premises to house them. Michael Reed highlights in Chapter 18 the upsurge of smart assembly rooms, theatres, race-grounds (with grandstands) and concert rooms not just in London but in towns across the kingdom.[9]

In the case of music, the commercial concerts under Charles II introduced a slow crescendo of activity. Towards the end of the seventeenth century fashionable concerts on St Cecilia's day were organised in the capital by a society of gentlemen and inspired lesser events at Oxford, Winchester, Salisbury and elsewhere. Semi-operas appeared which soon gave way to Italian operas and these in turn were eclipsed by Handel's oratorios, which increasingly dominated the London and provincial music scene. From the 1720s there was a major series

[8] A. Ellis, *The Penny Universities* (London, 1956), pp. xiv, chs. 6–8 *et passim*; see also B. Lillywhite, *London Coffee Houses* (London, 1963); *Daily Gazetteer*, 4 July 1737; W. Moore, *The Gentlemen's Society at Spalding* (London, 1851), pp. 5–6; Clark, *English Alehouse*, p. 14; R.A. Houston, *Social Change in the Age of Enlightenment* (Oxford, 1994), pp. 222–7; R. A. Houston, 'Fraud in the Scottish linen industry: Edinburgh's charity workhouse, 1745–58', *Archives*, 21 (1994), 43–5; P. Clark, 'The "mother gin" controversy in early eighteenth-century England', *TRHS*, 5th series, 38 (1988), 63–71. [9] See below, pp. 629 *et seq*.

of subscription concerts at Hickford's Room in London, together with others given by the Academy of Vocal Music (after 1731 the Academy of Ancient Music), the Swan tavern society and the Castle tavern society. Accompaniment was provided by a multitude of benefit and individual concerts, and grand annual occasions arranged by philanthropic bodies such as the Sons of the Clergy.[10]

Organised music making spread quickly outside the capital, and was established at Bristol, Gloucester, Norwich, Oxford, Salisbury, Wells, Worcester and Edinburgh by the 1720s. At mid-century at least twenty English provincial towns supported public concert series. In East Anglia concerts are found not only in the larger centres but in the small market towns. Edinburgh's St Cecilia's Hall was the mid-Georgian city's premier concert venue, and there were strong links with the emerging musical scene at Aberdeen.[11] Provincial towns also saw the arrival of music festivals, lasting two or more days. Earlier ones such as the Three Choirs Festival at Gloucester, Hereford and Worcester followed metropolitan models, but by George III's reign provincial towns were vying with one another to organise successful meetings, often focused on secular charities such as local infirmaries and involving performances of Handel's oratorios complete with expensive London soloists. 'There is now hardly any town of the least note in this country, we hear in 1787, which is not distinguished by its music meetings.' That year Birmingham's festival made nearly £2,000 profit, compared to £1,000 at Liverpool and £200 at Coventry.[12]

By the later eighteenth century music festivals were only part of a rich musical programme. Principal events in London during the 1789–90 season included Italian and English operas (twice weekly and nightly), two series of modern concerts, three series of ancient music (twenty-four concerts in all), two oratorio series, concerts by at least five music societies, twenty-six benefit concerts and multifarious private, Court and church performances. Rivalry between ancient music, notably Handel and the Italians (patronised by the king), and the new modern repertoire (supported by the middle classes), was balanced by a medley of singing societies, some like the Catch Club with elite members, others attracting the middling and lower orders. Concert promoters like Bach and Abel and

[10] W. H. Husk, *An Account of the Musical Celebrations on St Cecilia's Day* (London, 1857); S. McVeigh, *Concert Life in London from Mozart to Haydn* (Cambridge, 1993), pp. 3–4; see also W. Weber, *The Rise of Musical Classics in Eighteenth-Century England* (Oxford, 1992), pp. 29 *et seq.*; W. F. Gray, 'The musical society of Edinburgh and St Cecilia's Hall', *Book of the Old Edinburgh Club*, 19 (1933), 189–246; D. Johnson, *Music and Society in Lowland Scotland in the Eighteenth Century* (London, 1972).

[11] Borsay, *English Urban Renaissance*, pp. 122–3, 332–5; Norfolk and Norwich RO, MSS 427, 434–5, 443; Johnson, *Music*.

[12] B. W. Pritchard, 'The music festival and the choral society in England in the eighteenth and nineteenth centuries: a social history' (PhD thesis, University of Birmingham, 1968); *Farley's Bristol Journal*, 29 Sept. 1787; Brewer, *Pleasures of the Imagination*, ch. 14.

later Salomon were increasingly influential, as metropolitan music making became big business.[13]

William Gardiner's *Music and Friends*, first published in the 1830s, reveals the extraordinary wealth of provincial music making in the later eighteenth century. As well as music festivals and commercial concerts, bigger towns often now had several music societies (with their own collections of instruments and scores). There were also informal music clubs, singing clubs (like the Bristol and Canterbury catch clubs), and a growing number of choral societies in northern towns.[14]

The end of the eighteenth century marked something of a watershed. The Napoleonic wars led to a decline of concerts in London and music festivals in provincial towns. Singing clubs with their bawdy songs were affected by the new-found respectability and religiosity of public sociability. Ancient music was steadily eclipsed by the new classical repertoire, which gained powerful momentum after the establishment in London of the Philharmonic Society in 1813. Patronage by the wealthy middle classes led to a sharp increase of orchestral and chamber music concerts in the capital from the 1820s. In provincial towns music making remained largely semi-amateur, though Paganini's concert tour of Britain in the 1830s took in not only London, Edinburgh Glasgow, Leeds and Sheffield, but Perth, Cheltenham, Chester, York, Yarmouth and Southampton. Mechanics institutes sponsored concerts, while choral societies, often as in the past linked to nonconformist churches, became leading centres of urban musical life: the Sacred Harmonic Society was formed in London in 1832, and the Huddersfield Choral Society four years later.[15]

The success of urban music making in the eighteenth century derived in part at least from the fact that it involved the participation of both sexes. Music was seen as 'peculiarly a female accomplishment. It brings into view the finest feelings of a woman's mind and imparts a grace to society.' Women took part as performers, sang in choral societies, attended concerts in considerable numbers: only the salacious singing clubs were largely out of bounds. In the early

13 McVeigh, *Concert Life*, pp. 5, 53–7, 73 *et seq.*; Weber, *Musical Classics*, pp. 194–5, ch.8.

14 W. Gardiner, *Music and Friends* (London, 1838–53), vol. I, pp. 14, 66–7, 286, vol. II, pp. 512–13, vol. III, pp. 32, 52; S. Sadie, 'Concert life in eighteenth century England', *Proceedings of the Royal Musical Association (1958–9)* (1959), 18–28; see also R. P. Sturges, 'Harmony and good company: the emergence of musical performance in eighteenth-century Derby', *Music Review*, 39 (1978), 178–91; J. G. Hooper, 'A survey of music in Bristol with special reference to the eighteenth century' (MA thesis, University of Bristol, 1963), pp. 201–5; Pritchard, 'Music festival', pp. 119–46.

15 T. B. Milligan, *The Concerto and London's Musical Culture in the Late Eighteenth Century* (Ann Arbor, Mich., 1983), p. 18; Hooper, 'Music in Bristol', pp. 205–6; H. Raynor, *Music and Society since 1815* (London, 1976), pp. 58–9, 93–6, 101, 107–8; W. Weber, *Music and the Middle-Class* (London, 1975), pp. 7, 25, 95, 103 *et seq.*

nineteenth century the spread of domestic music making – aided by the invention of the pianoforte – further enhanced the role of women. But women were equally prominent in many other new forms of urban cultural activity in the Georgian period, not least assemblies, masquerades and the theatre.[16]

Assemblies were being held in London (see Plate 19) and many bigger towns by the early years of the eighteenth century, and most small towns hosted them by George III's reign. The essence was social meeting and display, along with dances and music, normally interleaved with cards; it was a place to meet marriage partners and afterwards to show off the wedding finery. Attendance became a social imperative. Writing from near Maidstone in 1747, Fanny Burney confessed 'this is assembly night and I shall have all my Kentish friends upon my back for not going' there. In contrast to the mainly public assemblies, increasingly regulated by rules, drums and routs were usually more private and informal affairs, noisy and crowded; as Elizabeth Carter conjugated, 'a drum, a rout, a racket, a hurricane, an uproar'. As with assemblies, however, women were often prominent (in London they were often organised by women). Masquerades enabled the greatest extent of gender mixing: 'women changed into men and men into women', as the *Guardian* noted, and women attended unescorted. Such events challenged established norms in further ways, not least by permitting a confusion of the upper and middle classes. In spite of official criticism of masquerades, strong demand and commercial promotion kept them in vogue up to the 1790s. Then economic recession and the new stress on moral reform brought their demise, together with the routs and drums.[17]

The theatre was another of the prime entertainments of Georgian towns. In early eighteenth-century London the most popular venues were the Lincoln's Inn Fields theatre and the Theatre Royal in Drury Lane, and from the 1730s the new Covent Garden theatre became fashionable. Despite legislation in 1737 to regulate and censor the stage, productions were increasingly elaborate, performers like David Garrick and Kitty Clive turned into stars and profits were high.

[16] Gardiner, *Friends*, III, pp. 284 303; Weber, *Music and the Middle-Class*, p. 55; BL, Add. MS 27,951, f. 62–v; T. Castle, *Masquerade and Civilization* (London, 1986), pp. 28, 32–4; R. A. Houston, 'Women in the economy and society of Scotland 1500–1800', in R. A. Houston and I. D. Whyte, eds., *Scottish Society 1500–1800* (Cambridge, 1989), pp. 118–47; Brewer, *Pleasures of the Imagination*, p. 76 *et seq*.; P. A. G. Monro, ed., 'The professor's daughter. An essay on female conduct by Alexander Monro (primus)', *Proceedings of the Royal College of Physicians of Edinburgh*, 26 (1996), Supplement 2.

[17] A. Dain, 'Assemblies and polite leisure in East Anglia 1715–1825', *Suffolk Review*, new series, 28 (1997), 1–22; Borsay, *English Urban Renaissance*, pp. 150–62, 336–49; *Selections from the Family Papers Preserved at Caldwell*, vol. I (Glasow, 1854), p. 267; M. Reed, 'The cultural role of English small towns in England 1600–1800', in P. Clark, ed., *Small Towns in Early Modern Europe* (Cambridge, 1995), pp. 136–7; C. Aspinall-Oglander, *Admiral's Wife . . . from 1719 to 1761* (London, 1940), p. 60; C. Aspinall-Oglander, *Admiral's Widow* (London, 1942), p. 16; Castle, *Masquerade*, pp. 5, 28, 71 *et passim*.

A flexible tariff of seat prices enabled a broad range of the upper and middling classes to attend, with women prominent: a significant part of the entertainment involved the interaction of personalities and social groups in the auditorium. Large-scale theatre rebuilding at Covent Garden and Drury Lane in the 1780s and 1790s, seating audiences of over 3,000, opened the door to the lower orders, who crowded the pit and galleries.[18]

In the provinces metropolitan travelling companies and itinerant players were increasingly replaced by local town companies: York, Norwich and Bristol had them by the 1720s, and Birmingham, Plymouth and Salisbury by George III's reign. Early productions smacked of vaudeville, as at Exeter where audiences watched 'some diverting play . . . with antics, sarabands and masquerades', as well as moving tableaux. But in the later period theatres became larger, equipped with extended stages and better lighting, while productions became ever more lavish. During the early nineteenth century, however, the growing size of playhouses in London and the provinces, together with greater artisanal attendance, led to an exodus of the wealthier classes (also influenced by the religious awakening).[19]

Unlike provincial music and the theatre, the fine arts remained largely metropolitan focused; in John Sell Cotman's words, 'London with all its fog and smoke is the only air for an artist to breathe in.' At the start of the period the Society of the Virtuosi of St Luke provided a rendezvous for portrait painters, carvers, sculptors, engravers and so on and led to the establishment of the Academy of Painting in 1711, as a training school for artists. In following decades, fashionable London societies like the Roman Club (1723), the Society of Dilettanti (1732?) and the Egyptian Society (1742) cultivated lay interest in the Mediterranean civilisations. In addition, a dense network of informal clubs gathered together artists and patrons on a more equal footing, de-emphasising old-style, seigneurial patronage relationships in favour of more commercial arrangements. The importance of the consumer was increasingly recognised in other ways too. In 1760 the first public exhibition of works of art was held in the capital organised by a society of artists. Two years later the Free Society of Artists was established, which held extensive exhibitions, while another group was chartered in 1765 as the Incorporated Society of Artists; dissension within this led to the creation of the Royal Academy in 1768. Basking in the king's favour the Academy organised exhibitions, a training school and an institutional

18 G. Rudé, *Hanoverian London 1714–1808* (London, 1971), pp. 65–7; A. Nicoll, *A History of English Drama 1660–1900*, vol. III (Cambridge, 1927), ch. 1; M. R. Booth *et al.*, *The Revels History of Drama in English*, vol. VI (London, 1975), pp. 29 *et seq.*, 96–133; M. Baer, *Theatre and Disorder in Late Georgian London* (Oxford, 1992), pp. 20–2.

19 Borsay, *English Urban Renaissance*, pp. 118–22; *Brice's Weekly Journal*, 11 Feb. 1725/6; Baer, *Theatre and Disorder*, pp. 48–52.

focus for British artists. If the Academy's impact was generally conservative, the metropolitan art scene became heavily commercialised through the development of an industry marked by stiff competition, the division of labour and standardised production and prices. Independent professional artists emerged working for a middle-class market. Most painters made only modest profits themselves, but there was an expanding urban market for works of art, encouraged by the rise of dealers and auctions, the growth of foreign imports, public exhibitions and the lucrative promotional work of print manufacturers, who produced thousands of copies of famous works. Outside London only Norwich, with its Society of Artists (1803) and painters like Crome and Cotman, formed a significant school of English artists, though Bath attracted large numbers of visiting artists (and clients) and after 1800 there was some minor activity at Liverpool, Birmingham and elsewhere. North of the border, Edinburgh had its own school during the eighteenth century and among successful artists we find Allan Ramsay, Henry Raeburn and David Wilkie.[20]

On top of these indoor entertainments, there was a growing volume of new-style activity outside including pleasure gardens, promenades and sports. Small pleasure or tea gardens (some with springs) developed in and around the capital during the later Stuart era, usually associated with taverns, and these continued through the eighteenth century. Samuel Curwen lauded the gardens at the Shepherd and Shepherdess at Islington, where the company played bowls, listened to an organ and had a peerless pool for swimming. But in the 1730s and 1740s the two gardens at Spring Gardens (later Vauxhall) and Ranelagh (at Chelsea) were remodelled on a grand scale, and attracted up to 10,000 visitors on some occasions. These places combined the fashionable interest in gardening and botany with music, assemblies, the fine arts, plays and promenades. Visiting Vauxhall in the early 1760s the German Count Kielmansegge admired its large orchestra and organ, its statues by Roubillac, the ballroom, many avenues of fine trees and the garden brilliantly lit at night by 1,500 lamps. Though the prime concern was to attract the smart classes, the commercial nature of the operation

[20] T. Fawcett, *The Rise of English Provincial Art* (Oxford, 1974), p. 209; W. T. Whitley, *Artists and their Friends in England 1700–1799* (London, 1928), vol. 1, pp. 7–14, 74–7, 157–9; L. Lippincott, *Selling Art in Georgian London* (London, 1983), pp. 16–45; I. Pears, *The Discovery of Painting: The Growth of Interest in the Arts in England 1680–1768* (New Haven, 1988), pp. 49, 53, 63, 127; J. Barrell, ed., *Painting and the Politics of Culture* (Oxford, 1992), pp. 23, 93–5; S. C. Hutchinson, *The History of the Royal Academy 1768–1968* (London, 1968), chs. 2–8; L. Lippincott, 'Expanding on portraiture: the market, the public, and the hierarchy of genres in eighteenth-century Britain', in A. Bermingham and J. Brewer, eds., *The Consumption of Culture 1600–1800* (London, 1995), pp. 75–86; N. L. Goldberg, *John Crome the Elder* (Oxford, 1978), vol. 1, ch. 6; S. L. Sloman, 'Artists' picture rooms in eighteenth-Century Bath', *Bath History*, 6 (1996), 132–54; Fawcett, *Rise of English Provincial Art*; T. C. Smout, *A History of the Scottish People 1560–1830* (London, 1969), pp. 455–6.

meant that it was difficult to exclude those from middling and lesser backgrounds. For the French traveller Pierre Jean Grosley the pleasures of Vauxhall united both sexes and 'all ranks and conditions'.[21]

Numerous provincial towns opened similar, if smaller, premises, usually linked to drinking houses. At Canterbury in 1752 Vauxhall garden was 'already extremely beautiful . . . because of the elegant improvements made in its walks and plantations'; Leicester's gardens had a large assembly room in 1774, a new bowling green by 1779, and later a pleasure boat and billiard room. The smart set of Edinburgh flocked to the Shore at Leith (the city's port) to watch horse-racing and archery contests in the early and mid-eighteenth century or to eat curds and whey at the farms between Edinburgh and Leith where the New Town began to be built from the 1760s. However, by the 1790s pleasure gardens in both London and provincial centres felt the cold wind of cultural change, as economic uncertainty and religious criticism compounded the pressures of suburban and industrial development, and many closed down at this time.[22]

A key attraction of the pleasure garden was the tree-lined walks and from Charles II's reign public promenades were highly fashionable. In London Pall Mall and the royal parks were the favourite resort, whilst provincial towns corporations began to lay out formal walks by 1700, often with views of a river or the local countryside; in cathedral towns the close was often appropriated. For the Edinburgh elite, according to one observer, structured promenading was part of the ritual of social meeting and fashionable behaviour, it being 'customary for them to drive in their carriages to the sands at Leith and Musselburgh, and parade back and forwards, after the manner of Scarborough'. By the late eighteenth century, as shopping developed into a fashionable leisure pursuit, London (and provincial towns) began to create distinct shopping streets, such as Oxford Street, which became fashionable promenades (with window shopping at night). The problem, as with other entertainments, was that walks and promenades attracted not just the fashionable classes but lesser folk. Towns tried to regulate such public places, but there was also increasing temporal segregation, the upper classes parading when the lower orders were at work. Another alternative for the better-off was to go promenading on the river. Mixed parties, clubs, guilds, and concert subscribers hired boats and, often escorted by a band, voyaged to a select place outside town where they could feast, booze, dance and frolic undisturbed. Even

[21] W. Wroth, *The London Pleasure Gardens of the Eighteenth Century* (London, 1896); A. Oliver, ed., *The Journal of Samuel Curwen, Loyalist* (Cambridge, Mass., 1972), vol. 1, p. 50; T. J. Edelstein, *Vauxhall Gardens* (New Haven, Conn., 1983), pp. 11–32; F. Kielmansegge, *Diary of a Journey to England in the Years 1761–1762* (London, 1902), pp. 167–8; P. J. Grosley, *A Tour to London* (Dublin, 1772), vol. 1, p. 170.

[22] *The Kentish Post*, 18 July 1752; C. Grewcock, 'Social and intellectual life in Leicester 1763–1835' (MA thesis, University of Leicester, 1973), p. 23; Topham, *Letters*, pp. 38, 51, 84, 256; Wroth, *London Pleasure Gardens*, pp. 217–18, 276, 314 *et seq.*

here, however, social emulation was unavoidable. By the 1780s Bristol apprentices were 'going down the river on parties of pleasure on the Sabbath day', a practice also enthusiastically pursued by young Londoners with their cutter clubs.[23]

The decades from the late seventeenth century saw the emergence of a wide range of urban or urbanised sports, often run on a semi-commercial basis, with rules, governing bodies and a growing spectator presence. Though drinking houses kept their own bowling alleys, after the Restoration many towns acquired fashionable bowling greens, often decked out with rails and other fancy facilities. At early Georgian Ashby, which had a good green, 'the neighbourly noblemen and gentlemen resort thither to dine together and bowl in the season'; later on many greens were organised by clubs. Other ball games became urbanised more slowly. A country game in the South-East, cricket won national attention through various well-publicised matches played in the metropolitan area in the 1730s. Clubs began to be formed in the capital and, *pace* the prestige of the rural Hambledon club in Hampshire, metropolitan teams came to dominate the sport, drawing up rules. Cricket never caught on in Scotland, but golf was increasingly organised as a respectable sport: Edinburgh had two societies by the 1740s with others following at St Andrews, Bruntsfield and Musselburgh; after 1766 London Scots were also playing the game at Blackheath. Curling followed a similar pattern of consolidation, though this retained strong rural roots.[24]

Whether as participants or spectators, townspeople could choose by the 1780s from an ever-growing range of sports, including archery (highly fashionable), riding, skating, sailing, trap-ball, running, boxing, fencing, rowing, ballooning and numerous animal sports. Cockfighting, frequently linked to inns, the gentry, county rivalry and heavy gambling, and staged in many large and small towns in the early eighteenth century, was in decline in England by 1800, although it enjoyed a late boom in Scotland. By contrast fox hunting came in from the rural cold and was often run on a subscription or society basis, accompanied by a good deal of conviviality in country towns. Angling too became more urban, with London tradesmen setting out early in the morning for the rivers and ponds of Shepperton, Carshalton and other 'places of diversion'. Fishing tackle,

23 Rudé, *Hanoverian London*, pp. 72–3; Borsay, *English Urban Renaissance*, pp. 162–72; *Gloucester Journal*, 10 June 1775; Topham, *Letters*, p. 94. Leith was Edinburgh's port, then a separate town to the north of the city proper. *St James Chronicle*, 26–9 June 1790; *Farley's Bristol Journal*, 17 Oct. 1789; M. D. George, *London Life in the Eighteenth Century* (London, 1925), p. 272.

24 Macky, *Journey*, II, p. 170; J. Arlott, ed., *From Hambledon to Lords* (London, 1948); P. Clark, *British Clubs and Societies 1580–1800* (Oxford, 2000), p. 81; G. Cousins, *Golf in Britain* (London, 1975), chs. 1–3; I. T. Henderson and D. I. Stirk, *Royal Blackheath* (London, 1981), pp. 7–35; D. B. Smith, *Curling: An Illustrated History* (Edinburgh, 1981); C. E. S. Chambers, 'Early golf at Bruntsfield and Leith', *Book of the Old Edinburgh Club*, 18 (1932), 1–10.

along with shooting goods and children's toys, could be bought at Thomas Henderson's shop at the Cross Well in Edinburgh in 1759.[25]

Undoubtedly, the most successful of all urban sports in this period was horse racing, boosted by improvements in native bloodstock and a growing equine obsession among the gentry. Before legislation in 1740 England had over 130 race courses with more than 400 prizes, though the numbers were subsequently reduced, confining them to towns. In Scotland town races generally flourished later: thus the now famous Ayr and Musselburgh races were established in the late eighteenth century. Corporations offered prizes for races, fanning the flames of heavy gambling; but the smart classes were also attracted by other entertainments staged in town at race time. Once again there was the difficulty of controlling social access, as races drew in large crowds of less respectable spectators. At Newmarket it was said a country grazier could bet 'with the same freedom as the greatest lord of them, for here is no ceremony'. The 1740 act and the establishment of the Jockey Club about 1750 led to some moves towards greater regulation, but the most effective response was the building of grandstands for the better-off, which not only enabled social segregation but, combined with other entertainments on offer, attracted a growing female presence at race meetings (unlike for most other sports). Not everyone had fun: after a visit to Tetbury races the duchess of Beaufort observed that attendance obliged 'a considerable share of patience and good humour, to hold out through the venison dinner, the broiling tedious races, and the stewing, stifling balls . . . smiling and smirking through the day'.[26]

By George III's reign many of these new-style urban activities were run on an associational basis, but this was only the tip of the iceberg. During the eighteenth century in the region of 12,000 clubs and societies were established in English towns, with another 3,000 in Scottish towns and up to 750 or so in Welsh towns; the numbers continued to multiply in the next century. No less striking was the kaleidoscope of different types – well over a hundred in the period. As well as those already mentioned, the litany included alumni associations, book, benefit and bell-ringing societies, debating and gambling clubs, florist feasts, literary societies, a profusion of masonic and pseudo masonic societies (like the Khabainites, Gormogons, Free Sawyers and Noble Order of Bucks), medical societies, neighbourhood clubs, philanthropic, political, professional and prosecution societies,

[25] Borsay, *English Urban Renaissance*, pp. 176–80; R. Carr, *English Fox Hunting* (London, 1976), pp. 45–60; [T. Legg], *Low-Life: Or One Half of the World Knows Not How the Other Half Live* (London, 1752), p. 39; *Edinburgh Chronicle*, 12–14 Apr. 1759; W. F. Gray, 'An eighteenth-century riding school', *Book of the Old Edinburgh Club*, 20 (1935), 111–60.

[26] P. Borsay, 'Town and turf: the development of racing in England *c.* 1680–1760', in *Life in the Georgian Town* (London, 1986), pp. 53–9; Topham, *Letters*, pp. 38, 51, 84, 256; Macky, *Journey*, I, p. 135; Aspinall-Oglander, *Admiral's Widow*, p. 35.

regional and ethnic societies, scientific and learned associations and a legion of drinking, dining and social clubs, such as the Sols, Mahometans, Fandangoes, Sampsons, Kiddies, Judges, Fumblers, Sons of Momus, Knights of the Moon and Lumber Troop (see Plate 20).[27]

Predictably London was home to the greatest collection of voluntary societies. One writer declared that 'all the little clubs and societies that are dispersed throughout this great metropolis were' impossible to count; another claimed that the capital was 'one great complexion of societies'. It is likely that there were over 3,000 societies established in London by 1800, comprised of nearly 100 different types. But growing numbers were found at most levels of the urban system. Bristol probably had between 200 and 300 clubs and societies in the eighteenth century, and over twenty different types; at Norwich the total may have exceeded 300 with twenty to thirty types. Middle-rank centres had a lower incidence: for instance, at the county town of Maidstone in Kent the total was nearer forty clubs and societies. Outside England Edinburgh supported the heaviest concentration of associations in the eighteenth century, with over 200 societies and about forty different types; but by 1800 Glasgow was catching up fast. Regional centres like Aberdeen and Perth also boasted growing clusters of associations.[28]

At the time of the Glorious Revolution clubs and societies recruited primarily from the upper classes in towns – incoming landowners, professional men, some merchants and prosperous traders. In the following decades support widened to include the middling and artisan ranks, and this representation became increasingly pronounced by 1800 – evinced by the large numbers of mutual aid societies as well as leisure clubs for skilled workers. Urban associations generally admitted members from certain broad social categories, with smaller numbers coming from wider social bands: in eighteenth-century England there was little exclusively class-based recruitment. Scottish clubs may have been more socially divided. Edinburgh groups like Alan Ramsay's Easy Club (1712–15) and the Rankenian Club (1716–74) met to cultivate conversation, friendship, taste, politeness and improvement. Some urban bodies were controlled by landowners or lawyers, others by merchants (Glasgow's Hodge Podge) and manufacturers. Edinburgh's masonic lodges were dominated by masters who used their meetings as an extension of their power over apprentices and journeymen, for whom separate lodges existed from the early eighteenth century. Lodges like this were probably no more egalitarian than the society which spawned them.[29]

27 Clark, *British Clubs and Societies*, chs. 3–4; *Ars Quatuor Coronatorum*, 4 (1891), 94.

28 *Fog's Weekly Journal*, 2 May 1730; Clark, *British Clubs and Societies*, pp. 131 *et seq*.

29 Clark, *British Clubs and Societies*, ch. 6; P. H. J. H. Gosden, *The Friendly Societies in England 1815–1875* (Manchester, 1961), pp. 2–6; N. Phillipson, 'The Scottish Enlightenment', in Porter and Teich, eds., *The Enlightenment*, p. 27. Houston, *Social Change*, pp. 217–18.

In contrast to most other new kinds of public sociability in the Hanoverian period, clubs and societies were largely masculine organisations: only towards the end of the period do women start to encroach on this largely male-defined space. Male predominance probably owed a good deal to the origin of many such bodies in drinking houses, from which women were conventionally excluded except on special occasions. Certainly for most of the period up to 1800 a vital part of the sociable vocabulary of associations was alcohol rich refreshment. As the *Spectator* famously observed, 'our modern celebrated clubs are founded upon eating and drinking, which are points wherein most men agree'. But by mid-century many associations showed a growing commitment to improvement, whether scientific, medical, agricultural or cultural. In England the London Society of Arts (1754) was the most fashionable and prominent of a series of metropolitan and provincial societies concerned with promoting innovation. In Scotland Edinburgh had a series of bodies like the Honourable Society of Improvers and the Select Society (with its offshoot the Edinburgh Society for Encouraging Arts, Sciences, Manufactures, and Agriculture in Scotland), which were dedicated to trying to catch up with England in economic and cultural terms, in order to assert a new sense of national identity. From the 1780s these society concerns with improvement were increasingly complemented, as we shall see, by new emphases on social and moral discipline and religious reform, and, for the lower classes, by a greater distinction between work and leisure.[30]

(ii) ATTITUDES TO TIME AND SPACE

New-style sociability in towns along with the changing tempo of economic activity and the changing nature of social relationships had important implications for attitudes towards time and space. In bigger towns there was a growing consciousness of time – visitors spoke of the hurry and bustle of passers-by, of the punctuality of Londoners. Consciousness was facilitated by the increased use of chronometers: in the 1730s well over a third of the better-off inhabitants of Bristol had a clock, and a quarter watches; for those without, many public buildings by the 1770s had clocks with dials. As well as the growing consciousness of time, there was greater definition of the periods of the day, and changes in traditional prandial arrangements in urban society, at least for the better-off. Basic here was the shift of dinner time from about 1 p.m. or 2 p.m. in 1700 (noon

30 D. F. Bond, ed., *The Spectator*, vol. I (Oxford, 1965), p. 42; D. Hudson and K. W. Luckhurst, *The Royal Society of Arts 1754–1954* (London, 1954), pp. 4–18; D. G. C. Allan and J. L. Abbott, eds., *The Virtuoso Tribe of Arts and Sciences* (London, 1992); S. Wilmot, *'The Business of Improvement': Agriculture and Scientific Culture in Britain c.1700–c.1870* (Historical Geography Research Series, 24, 1990); D. D. McElroy, *Scotland's Age of Improvement* (Pullman, Washington State, 1969); T. C. Smout, 'Problems of nationalism, identity, and improvement in later eighteenth-century Scotland', in T. M. Devine, ed., *Improvement and Enlightenment* (Edinburgh 1989), pp. 18–19.

earlier) to 5 p.m. or 6 p.m. in the later Georgian era. In its place arrived breakfast and luncheon (a light meal), freeing the afternoon for greater business or sociable activity, including tea parties and visiting for women, sports for men. In turn a late dinner allowed the rest of the evening to be devoted to leisure activity, such as visits to inns and coffee-houses, clubs, assemblies and concerts. Fashionable assemblies and balls in London increasingly started about 9 p.m. or 10 p.m., with supper after midnight, followed by renewed dancing, cards and heavy drinking till dawn. 'Scarce a lady of quality in Great Britain, one magazine claimed, ever saw the sun rise.' Metropolitan socialising, aided by new urban improvements like public lighting, increasingly involved the colonisation of night.[31] Late-night socialising was probably less pronounced in provincial towns – 'night-walker' remained a pejorative term in Scottish towns – but generally there was a marked contrast to the countryside, where sociable events were less time specific and more extended through the day. Marriages became more evenly distributed between months in the growing towns of the later eighteenth and early nineteenth centuries, replacing the highly seasonal patterns of the rural world. In towns new-style socialising increasingly articulated the changing seasonal rhythms of urban life; the upper classes concentrated their activity into the late winter and spring, whereas the middling and lesser orders retained a greater loyalty to traditional ritual times such as Easter and Whitsun.[32]

New sensibilities to time also influenced urban perceptions of the past, at least among the better-off classes. From the end of the seventeenth century the old town chronicles, often in manuscript, with their shallow notions of antiquity, often no more than a litany of mayors and events, gave way in many places to largely printed urban histories, which attempted coherent, if often mythic, accounts of urban origins and growth, and related this story to current economic and cultural improvements. If the early Georgian histories, such as Charles Deering's *Nottinghamia Vetus et Nova* (1751), were quite elaborate and expensive, written for the genteel classes, by the start of the nineteenth century, a mount-

[31] R. B. Johnson, ed., *Bluestocking Letters* (London, 1926), p. 70; W. A. L. Bettany, ed., *Diaries of William Johnston Temple 1780–1796* (Oxford, 1929), p. 9; J. Taylor, *A Journey to Edenborough in Scotland*, ed. W. Cowan (Edinburgh, 1903), p. 50; P. J. Corfield, 'Walking the city streets: the urban odyssey in eighteenth-century England', *JUH*, 16 (1989–90), 143–4; Grosley, *Tour*, I, p. 115; J. Barry, 'The cultural life of Bristol 1640–1775' (DPhil thesis, University of Oxford, 1985), pp. 133–4; A. Palmer, *Movable Feasts* (London, 1952), pp. 8–17; A. Chalmers, ed., *The British Essayists* (London, 1808), vol. v, pp. 246–7; also T. Burke, *English Night-Life* (London, 1943), pp. 23–70.

[32] Houston, *Social Change*, pp. 225; R. A. Houston, 'The demographic regime', in T. M. Devine and R. Mitchison, eds., *People and Society in Scotland*, vol. I: *1760–1830* (Edinburgh, 1988), pp. 1–18; R. A. Houston, *The Population History of Britain and Ireland, 1550–1750* (Cambridge, 1995), p. 21; R. A. Houston and M. P. C. van der Heijden, 'Hands across the water: the making and breaking of marriage between Dutch and Scots in the mid-eighteenth century', *Law and History Review*, 15 (1997), 215–42; M. Harrison, 'The ordering of the urban environment: time, work and the occurrence of crowds, 1790–1835', *P&P*, 110 (1986), 134–68.

ing number of histories, often in a cheaper, simpler format were aimed at the middle classes, emphasising, in many cases, civic growth and success, and, in others, the need for urban reform: here a growing sense of the past was being used to shape the present, and to create a new sense of urban identity. In the case of Edinburgh William Maitland's 1753 chronicle of the city was followed in 1776 (and later editions) by Hugo Arnot's *History*, both presenting overviews of its history, archaeology, topography, folk and literary traditions. Kincaid (1787), Stark (1806) and Stevenson (1839) catered to the growing demand for celebratory, antiquarian volumes for middle-class readers, often borrowing shamelessly from the earlier publications.[33]

The growth of new-style sociability was also associated with the creation of new forms of urban space. We have already noted the evolution of more clearly accented gender and class space in towns, but no less significant was the emergence of a new kind of social space, an area of social interaction distinct from both private family life and old-style institutional or public space identified with state, civic or institutional bodies. In the semi-commercialised world of public drinking premises, coffee-houses, libraries, concerts, assemblies, clubs and societies and shops, the better-off classes in town could meet, hear news and engage in social and political discourse: as David Hume observed, 'being every day more accustomed to the free discussion of public affairs', men will be improved in their judgement of them. Social space, so important for the growth of cultural pluralism in towns, was given growing physical meaning by civic improvement, remodelling the centres of towns, pulling down the old gates and walls, removing markets and fairs, and opening up urban society to the wider world.[34]

In sum, British towns during the eighteenth century, for long on the outer district line of European cultural development, moved now to the metropolitan axis of the Enlightenment, receiving more or less quickly the latest continental fashions and ideas in music, architecture, art, historiography, literature, scientific ideas, dress and the like. The biggest centres were the most dynamic. Clearly for

[33] P. Clark, 'Visions of the urban community: antiquarians and the English city before 1800', in D. Fraser and A. Sutcliffe, eds., *The Pursuit of Urban History* (London, 1983), pp. 114–24; R. Sweet, *The Writing of Urban Histories in Eighteenth-Century England* (Oxford, 1997); H. Arnot, *History of Edinburgh* (Edinburgh, 1816); A. Kincaid, *The History of Edinburgh* (Edinburgh, 1787); J. Stark, *Picture of Edinburgh Containing a History and Description of the City* (Edinburgh, 1806); R. Stevenson, *Annals of Edinburgh and Leith . . . AD 320 – AD 1839* (Edinburgh, 1839).

[34] J. Stobart, 'Shopping streets as social space: leisure, consumerism, and improvement in an eighteenth-century county town', *UH*, 25 (1998), 3–21; D. Castiglione, 'Opinion's metamorphosis: Hume and the perception of public authority', in D. Castiglione and L. Sharpe, eds., *Shifting the Boundaries: Transformation of the Languages of Public and Private in the Eighteenth Century* (Exeter, 1995), p. 168; T. A. Markus, ed., *Order in Space and Society* (Edinburgh, 1982); T. A. Markus *et al.*, 'The shape of the city in space and stone', in T. M. Devine and G. Jackson, eds., *Glasgow*, vol. I: *Beginnings to 1830* (Manchester, 1995), pp. 106–38; A. J. Youngson, *The Making of Classical Edinburgh 1750–1840* (Edinburgh, 1966).

much of the eighteenth century London and Edinburgh were the leading spring boards for cultural and intellectual innovation, but by the close of the century the new generation of regional, commercial and industrial cities like Newcastle, Glasgow, Birmingham, Manchester and Leeds were developing their own cultural initiatives. Yet new cultural ideas and entertainments were increasingly adopted across the urban system, including county towns and smaller market centres.[35] The momentum for change was clearly impressive, not least to the many overseas visitors who flocked to London and the other major cities of late Georgian Britain.

(iii) THE REASON WHY

What were the forces shaping these new dynamic and pluralistic developments in British towns? In contrast to the situation in England before the Civil War or in many continental countries during the eighteenth century, the state had a limited role in reshaping the cultural image of British towns after 1700. Apart from sporadic legislation (the Theatre Act in 1737, the Racing Act in 1740), occasional subventions (as to the Royal Society), displays of royal patronage (the founding of the Royal Academy, the staging of the Handel festivals at Westminster Abbey in the 1780s) or the granting of charters (to a limited number of cultural bodies), government intervention was minimal. No attempt was made to use cultural agencies to promote centralisation, as happened in France: the British Museum owed little to state support. Official interference in the functioning of societies was generally short-lived. Most state regulation, as over theatres in 1737, was at the behest of private interest groups.[36]

The genteel influx into towns from the late seventeenth century had a more crucial effect on the cultural life of towns. The several thousand major landowners in early Georgian London generated a great volume of demand for urban cultural services, while even at a shire town like Northampton we hear that 'within and about it live many gentry who are the support of the town'. In Scotland the largest concentration of landowners was at Edinburgh, but smaller numbers appeared at Aberdeen, Perth and Dumfries. There were likewise small clusters in the bigger Welsh towns. Not all came for an extended stay; in smaller places they might stop for just a few days or come in as day trippers. As well as having deep pockets, visiting landowners had time on their hands and felt like fish out of water, away from their county networks, surrounded by a sea of strange faces. 'They don't know what to do, and they are anxious to get acquain-

[35] See below, pp. 690–7, 763 *et seq*.

[36] Cf. J. Queniart, *Culture et Societé Urbaines dans la France de l'Ouest au XVIIIe Siècle* (Paris, 1978); R. van Dülmen, *The Society of the Enlightenment* (Cambridge, 1992); P. Langford, *A Polite and Commercial People* (Oxford, 1989), pp. 319–20; Clark, *British Clubs and Societies*, pp. 97–8, 175–6; J. Loftis, *The Politics of Drama in Augustan England* (Oxford, 1963), pp. 128–53.

tances', the actor Thomas Sheridan remarked.[37] One remedy was through participation in many of the fashionable social and cultural activities in town.

Of course, the rural elite and their wives were not the only newcomers to Georgian towns. Communities were crowded with strangers, often young people, looking for a pathway into urban society. For many, a number of the traditional mechanisms for social integration, such as guilds and apprenticeship and living-in service, were in decline in England by the early and mid-eighteenth century – somewhat later in Scotland. Drinking houses in all their different types remained an important first port of call for outsiders, but the new forms of sociability also afforded opportunities for social networking. At York, the 'assemblies are great helps to strangers . . . to become acquainted with all the good company male or female'. Edinburgh's social assemblies, held from the 1720s, had as one of their functions, mixing residents and newcomers, 'to afford some ladies an opportunity to alter the station that they had been long faithfully continued in [maidenhood], and to set off others as they should prove ripe for the market'. Clubs and societies were particularly helpful. For Oliver Goldsmith 'a countryman who comes to live in London finds nothing more difficult' than to make friends and contacts, and may try to overcome this by being 'enrolled in societies, lodges, convocations and meetings'. The Manchester physician and advocate of shorthand, John Byrom, used a series of associations – the Royal Society, the Deists Club, clubs at the Anchor and Baptist, at Chancery Lane, a shorthand club, masonic lodges and others – as a way of consolidating his own position in London society. Societies frequently had special procedures for welcoming visitors to their gatherings. If associations of this type catered primarily for men, many other types of sociable entertainment offered similar opportunities for better-off women to establish contacts and enjoy themselves. On a visit to London in 1748 Ireland Greene, the young daughter of a Liverpool lawyer, went out to eight plays, three oratorios, two concerts, one burlesque, three routs, two ridottos, four dinners and twenty-one teas, as well as going to Ranelagh and Vauxhall nine times: all in a matter of ten weeks.[38]

Not all newcomers were easily assimilated, nor did all want to join a uniform

[37] M. R. Wenger, ed., *The English Travels of Sir John Percival and William Byrd II: The Percival Diary of 1701* (Columbia, Miss., 1989), pp. 161–2; Houston, *Social Change*; R. A. Houston, 'Writers to the signet: estimates of adult mortality in Scotland from the sixteenth to the nineteenth century', *Social History of Medicine*, 8 (1995), 37–53; see above, p. 142; F. A. Pottle, ed., *Boswell's London Journal 1762–1763* (London, 1950), p. 93.

[38] P. Clark, 'Migrants in the city: the process of social adaptation in English towns 1500–1800', in P. Clark and D. Souden, eds., *Migration and Society in Early Modern England* (London, 1987), pp. 269–86; J. H. Jamieson, 'Social assemblies of the eighteenth century', *Book of the Old Edinburgh Club*, 19 (1933), 31–91, quotation at 41; O. Goldsmith, *Essays, 1765* (Menston, 1970), pp. 21–2; R. Parkinson, ed., *Private Journal of John Byrom*, vol. 1 (1) (Chetham Society, 1st series, 32, 1854); also vol. 1(2); Clark, *British Clubs and Societies*, pp. 209 *et seq.*; R. Stewart-Brown, *Isaac Greene, a Lancashire Lawyer with the Diary of Ireland Greene* (Liverpool, 1921), pp. 33–46.

urban culture. In Scotland trade with Europe and the wider world, exchanges with Dutch universities and prolonged stays by French prisoners during the Revolutionary and Napoleonic wars created a cosmopolitan feel to Edinburgh and Glasgow. Cultural diversity was enhanced by significant concentrations of Gaelic speakers (including monoglots), as a result of heavy migration from the Highlands to Lowland industrial cities in the late eighteenth and early nineteenth centuries. Nine major Scottish towns had Gaelic chapels by 1800, forming foci of separate identity as, for example, the Welsh day school in Liverpool did from 1804. Gaelic school societies existed in Glasgow, Edinburgh and Inverness by 1818 – with auxiliary societies in other towns. Immigration also contributed to the new religious pluralism in cities like Dundee and Glasgow: there were almost no Catholics recorded in Glasgow in 1791 but 13 per cent of the population followed this faith by 1831, mostly Irish incomers. Where sufficiently numerous, the Irish and, to a markedly lesser extent, the Welsh and Scots, were residentially, socially and culturally segregated in mid-nineteenth-century cities.[39]

New-style public sociability not only helped in the integration of certain types of outsiders into urban society, it also provided a response to the growing social uncertainty and confusion within towns. Economic growth created a profusion of new occupations. The emergence of secondary professions such as accountants, bankers, architects and dentists was particularly noticeable, but so was the expansion of retailing and manufacturing trades. William Creech used the number of perfumers as an index of civilisation in *fin de siècle* Edinburgh. Rising social mobility, compounded by high levels of physical mobility, caused mounting concern about social recognition and identity. Status terms like gentleman and esquire became debased and even dress and speech, blurred by rising affluence, consumption and education, no longer provided an accurate indicator to social standing. One of the attractions of the new forms of sociable activity was that they sought to provide a controlled arena for social contact among the respectable classes. The problem, already noted, was that too often commercial considerations and pressures of demand meant that such events failed to ensure social selectivity. Assemblies, routs, pleasure gardens, promenades and bowling greens were frequently invaded by social parvenus. Clubs and societies with their rafts of regulations over admission and behaviour had more success at controlled social mixing, fashionable societies, for instance, bringing together different groups of the urban elite. Thus the London Virtuosi of St Luke not only embraced artists but merchants, gentlemen, bankers and surgeons. In the same way middle-rank societies brought together masters, shopkeepers and lesser professions. As well as facilitating social recognition and advancement, societies frequently had a prudential function, members rallying around to help brethren

[39] Houston, 'Demographic regime'; C. W. J. Withers, 'Kirk, club and culture change: Gaelic chapels, Highland societies and the urban Gaelic subculture in eighteenth century Scotland', *Soc.Hist.*, 10 (1985), 172–92; T. M. Devine, 'Urbanisation', in Devine and Mitchison, eds., *People and Society in Scotland*, p. 49.

when they experienced personal adversity, just as assemblies could double as a means of raising funds for poor relief or other good causes.[40]

Lubricating the ascent of new-style sociability was rising affluence among the better-off and artisanal classes, since entertainments of this sort, though competitive, were not cheap. Up to the 1780s at least ticket prices meant that theatres were largely the preserve of the upper and middling classes. The engraver George Vertue complained that belonging to clubs meant 'continual expense'. For an artisan membership of a single club might cost a twentieth of his weekly wage. Yet income-led demand was only part of the story. No less crucial were commercial developments, including the growth of the leisure and entertainment industries. By the eighteenth century the earlier promotional work of innkeepers and other victuallers was increasingly complemented by that of commercial entrepreneurs. Concert impresarios on the London scene had as their provincial counterparts local worthies, organists and musicians promoting music festivals and concert series, dancing masters organising assemblies, booksellers running circulation libraries and book clubs, professional men initiating all kinds of associations, and printers and publishers marketing a host of sociable activities. The proliferation of dancing academies was remarked upon from Inverness to Dumfries in the mid- and late eighteenth century.[41] Sociability and profit were never far apart.

In addition to the role of printers, newspapers and magazines were powerful dynamos in the dissemination of new cultural ideas and practices. The end of censorship in 1695 released a tidal surge of newsprint: in the mid-1730s London had three daily and four evening papers and within forty years the number had risen to four daily and eight to nine evening papers; by the 1780s around fifty provincial newspapers had been founded in England. Newspapers proliferated in Scotland too, integrating the nation by disseminating information about British urban life and values to a geographically diverse audience of both urban and rural dwellers. By 1840 almost every Lowland town of any size had a printer and bookseller, while some had newspapers of their own.[42]

Numbers of titles and editions multiplied even faster in the early nineteenth

40 P. J. Corfield, 'Class by name and number in eighteenth-century Britain', *History*, 72 (1987), 38–46; Langford, *Polite and Commercial People*, pp. 66–7; B. M. Benedict, '"Service to the public": William Creech and sentiment for sale', in J. Dwyer and R. B. Sher, eds., *Sociability and Society in Eighteenth-Century Scotland* (Edinburgh, 1993), pp. 119–46; BL, Add. MS 39,167, ff. 75–6; Clark, *British Clubs and Socieites*, ch. 6.

41 Rudé, *Hanoverian London*, pp. 65–6; *Vertue Note Books*, vol. III (Walpole Society, 22, 1934), p. 120; Clark, *British Clubs and Societies*, pp. 221–2; McVeigh, *Concert Life*, ch. 10; C. T. Probyn, *The Sociable Humanist* (Oxford, 1991), ch. 7; J. Barry, 'Cultural patronage and the Anglican crisis', in J. Walsh *et al.*, eds., *The Church of England c. 1689–c. 1833* (Cambridge, 1993), pp. 196–7; P. J. Corfield, *Power and the Professions in Britain 1700–1850* (London, 1995), pp. 180–1, 232–3 *et passim*.

42 M. Harris and A. Lee, eds., *The Press in English Society from the Seventeenth to Nineteenth Centuries* (London, 1986), pp. 48, 81; J. P. S. Ferguson, *Directory of Scottish Newspapers* (Edinburgh, 1984); A. Murdoch and R. B. Sher, 'Literary and learned culture', in Devine and Mitchison, eds., *People and Society*, p. 136.

century. The impact of the press was increasingly extensive. Subscription numbers by 1800 were often over 2,000 per paper, and given that public houses, coffee-houses and the like kept copies and ordinary townspeople sometimes clubbed together to buy a paper, the total readership was probably several times greater. Distribution likewise advanced – the *York Chronicle* in 1775 went to eighty-five places, while its Shrewsbury counterpart reached over thirty, its network embracing a large area from the West Midlands into North Wales. From George II's reign metropolitan papers and increasingly their provincial cousins carried massed columns of notices and advertisements on social events of all types. Papers supplied the marketing life-blood of urban sociability, just as advertising of this kind helped boost the image and profits of the press (the advertising income of London dailies rose fivefold from 1770 to 1820). No two papers were alike, their coverage depending on the printer's interests and the prospective readership. Thus the York papers in the late eighteenth century carried three times more notices of sports, music, plays and clubs than those at Leeds, which catered more for business. Metropolitan magazines like the *Spectator*, *Tatler* and later *Gentleman's Magazine* were also important conduits of news and attitudes about public socialising and by the later eighteenth century a bevy of specialist and regional publications modulated social news for particular audiences. Between 1739 and 1817 the monthly *Scots Magazine* contained news, literature and social material. The *Edinburgh Review*, refounded in 1802, marked the decline of cultural dependency and the establishment of a new climate of confidence and achievement. It created a national intellectual consciousness for Scotland and new recreational fashions. Overall the press was crucial in reshaping the general image of Georgian towns as centres of urbanity and sociability, as well as highlighting the distinctive cultural identity of individual towns.[43]

The growth of the press was only part of the print revolution in British towns, encouraged by the end of censorship, rising consumer demand and technical innovation. Sales of printed works rose tenfold between 1700 and 1800 with a not dissimilar increase over the next forty years. Though London remained the headquarters of the printing industry significant publishing centres emerged at Bristol, Oxford and Edinburgh. With 6,033 titles, Edinburgh came second out of forty-one British towns (printing more than fifty items) during the eighteenth century. A long way behind London, which produced 97,360 titles or 84 per cent of the total in these forty-one towns, Edinburgh still produced more than three times as many items as its nearest rival, Oxford, and more than four times as many as the fourth placed Glasgow; Aberdeen came twenty-first equal with

[43] R. M. Wiles, 'The relish for reading in provincial England two centuries ago', in P. J. Korshin, ed., *The Widening Circle: Essays on the Circulation of Literature in Eighteenth-Century Europe* (Philadelphia, 1976), pp. 88–90, 97; J. F. Looney, 'Cultural life in the provinces: Leeds and York, 1720–1820', in A. L. Beier *et al.*, eds., *The First Modern Society* (Cambridge, 1989), pp. 483–510; also C. Y. Ferdinand, *Benjamin Collins and the Provincial Newspaper Trade in the Eighteenth Century* (Oxford, 1997); Murdoch and Sher, 'Literary and learned culture', pp. 130–7.

Carmarthen (135 items). The rate of growth of imprints between 1700 and 1779 was fastest at Newcastle and Bristol (exceeded among imperial cities only by Philadelphia) followed by Glasgow with a fivefold rise and Aberdeen next in the ranking.[44]

Along with this print revolution, leading to a sharp fall in the price of books, there took place a major expansion on the retailing side. Booksellers appeared in considerable numbers in provincial towns: Newcastle for instance had ten to fifteen firms in the years 1736–71, and thirty-eight in 1787; Bristol had forty-two six years later, but a typical figure for the general run of middle-rank towns was around five; bigger market towns usually had one or two. Booksellers expanded their business through heavy advertising and catalogues, and by running circulating libraries and promoting book clubs and library societies. By 1821 there may have been nearly 900 book clubs and societies in England, many disposing of their stock on a regular basis or operating for short periods, others like those at Bristol, Bradford, Worcester and Liverpool with extensive collections (the Liverpool Library had a collection of over 8,000 volumes, plus a newsroom and coffee-room). A French visitor, colonel de la Rochette, spotted more than fifteen libraries in Edinburgh in the 1760s and there were significant numbers of commercial subscription and public libraries in Scottish towns by 1800.[45]

Book readership and ownership extended down the social scale. 'The book collection and language knowledge of English artisans', was recognised by Sophie von la Roche in the 1780s. A key factor was improved educational standards in towns, which was due only in part to institutional schooling. Town grammar schools, as in the past, had highly erratic careers, dependent on the success or otherwise of their masters. More important probably in many towns was the increased number of charity schools – including those promoted by the SPCK (SSPCK north of the border). It is likely too that there were many private schools and academies for the children of the respectable classes, while evening classes sprang up for artisans. At Bristol there may have been 100 or more teachers in the city by the 1770s.[46] Adam Ferguson opined of Edinburgh in 1759 that 'the wit and ingenuity of this place is still in a flourishing way, and with a few corrections . . . is probably the best place for education in the island'. Scottish

44 C. J. Mitchell, 'Provincial printing in eighteenth-century Britain', *Publishing History*, 21 (1987), 20–1.

45 J. Feather, *The Provincial Book Trade in Eighteenth-Century England* (Cambridge, 1985), pp. 29–30, 41–2; P. Kaufman, *Libraries and their Users* (London, 1969), pp. 36–64, 188–208; J. E. Vaughan, 'The Liverpool Library: another chapter', *Library History*, 5 (1979–81), 61; National Library of Scotland, MS 3803, f. 55v.

46 C. Williams, ed., *Sophie in London, 1786* (London, 1933), p. 176; R. A. Houston, *Literacy in Early Modern Europe* (London, 1989), pp. 10–75; R. A. Houston, *Scottish Literacy and the Scottish Identity* (Cambridge, 1985), pp. 74–9; J. Mason, 'Scottish charity schools in the eighteenth century', *Scottish Historical Review*, 33 (1954), 1–13; M. G. Jones, *The Charity School Movement* (London, 1964), pp. 23–7, 56–61, 69–72 *et passim*; Barry, 'Cultural life of Bristol', p. 30.

girls requiring extensive formal education were sent to Edinburgh's 'finishing schools', the capital's dominance being recognised in advertisements for provincial ladies' academies of the 1760s and later which offered instruction 'as complete as at Edinburgh'. In Scottish towns private and charity schools increasingly supplemented the numerous but small parish schools, accounting for two-thirds of all pupils in day schools by 1818. By then education seems to have been accessible to the lower orders in the large cities of the central Lowlands, which had the highest proportion of children at school.[47]

Basic literacy (measured by the ability to sign one's name on a document) was nearly universal for the urban elites as early as 1700 and for the middling ranks by *c.* 1750. By then over 70 per cent of Bristol bridegrooms and 92 per cent of their counterparts in central London could sign their names. However, women and the labouring sort experienced only slow change: signing ability among lower-class women in Edinburgh was in the range 5–15 per cent at the start of George III's reign. From the 1780s there are signs of stagnation and even regression as rapid urbanisation affected towns like Halifax, Ashton-under-Lyne, Dundee, Paisley and even Edinburgh. Their social superiors, by contrast, were qualified by a more varied and prolonged education to partake of an extensive and widening range of newspapers, periodicals, novels and histories.[48]

No less important than the provision of schooling was the growth of demand and of self-education, as ambitious young people from the middling and artisan classes pored over teach-yourself manuals, either individually or more commonly in clubs and societies dedicated to improvement: hence the growth of various middle- and lower-class mathematical societies. Desire for self-improvement and social acceptability extended to many areas of cultural life. English – as opposed to vernacular Scots – had become established as 'the medium of a polite, urbane Scottish culture in the universities and cities' by the mid-eighteenth century. Catering for the inhabitants' desire to appear less provincial, the Irishman Richard Brinsley Sheridan gave a well-attended series of lectures in 1761 on the 'correct pronunciation and elegant reading' of English, said to be 'indispensable acquirements for people of fashion' in non-metropolitan society.[49]

[47] Quoted in R. B. Sher, *Church and University in the Scottish Enlightenment* (Edinburgh, 1985), p. 108; C. Beveridge, 'Childhood and society in eighteenth-century Scotland', in J. Dwyer *et al.*, eds., *New Perspectives on the Politics and Culture of Early Modern Scotland* (Edinburgh, 1982), p. 280; D. J. Withrington, 'Schooling, literacy and society', in Devine and Mitchison, eds., *People and Society*, pp. 177–9.

[48] Barry, 'Cultural life of Bristol', p. 39; Houston, *Literacy in Early Modern Europe*, p. 140; R. A. Houston, 'Literacy, education and the culture of print in Enlightenment Edinburgh', *History*, 78 (1993), 373–92.

[49] Murdoch and Sher, 'Literary and learned culture', p. 129; Smout, *History of the Scottish People*, p. 269. M. E. Ingram, *A Jacobite Stronghold of the Church* (Edinburgh, 1907), p. 71. The use of English – as opposed to vernacular Scots or even Gaelic – was a mark of membership of polite society among intellectual and social elites by the mid-eighteenth century.

In Scotland urban education, society and culture were much more heavily influenced by the universities than south of the border. There were five institutions in four towns – Aberdeen (two), Edinburgh, Glasgow and St Andrews. Edinburgh grew most rapidly from *c.* 1,000 in 1700 to 4,400 in 1800. In comparison, Oxford and Cambridge had a lower total number of students, a lower participation rate per head of population, a more restricted (elite) social range, and less intellectually dynamic subjects and teaching. The Scottish Enlightenment was firmly located within the universities, with academics taking a prominent role among the urban literati; and certain fields like medicine were dominated by Scottish institutions, which produced nine out of ten British doctors academically trained in the eighteenth century.[50]

Educational improvement not only contributed to mounting public interest in a wide range of learned, scientific and sociable activities in town, as well as increasing economic skills: it undoubtedly stimulated political awareness, serving to underpin the progressively animated and sophisticated political and party discourse in many British towns towards the end of the eighteenth century, a trend exemplified by the spread of political and debating societies. Yet it is evident that many of the new kinds of sociable activity which surfaced during the period were perceived not as mechanisms for political mobilisation but as refuges from the rough and tumble of party and religious dispute. 'The Royal Society is of all parties, Benjamin Franklin declared, but party is entirely out of the question in all our proceedings.'[51] New-style public sociability flourished in Georgian towns because it interfaced in so many respects with the major economic, social and political changes affecting urban society.

(iv) COUNTER-CURRENTS

None the less, for all their impressive success the new cultural activities did not monopolise the social and cultural stage in British towns. Many traditional entertainments survived, indeed attracted extensive support, while even some new-fashioned activities betrayed important older features. Equally significant, there were major local variations in the reception of public sociability.

At the communal level the eighteenth century saw the resurgence of older-style ceremony and ritual, encouraged by the apparently more relaxed attitude of the authorities towards public order. In spite of the decay of the English town

50 Houston, *Literacy in Early Modern Europe*, pp. 76–90; L. Rosner, *Medical Education in the Age of Improvement* (Edinburgh, 1991), pp. 2, 12, 24, 86–91, 102; R. L. Emerson, *Professors, Patronage and Politics* (Aberdeen, 1992); N. Phillipson, 'Culture and society in the eighteenth century province: the case of Edinburgh and the Scottish Enlightenment', in L. Stone, ed., *The University in Society*, vol. II (Princeton, N.J., 1975), pp. 407–48; N. Phillipson, 'The Scottish Enlightenment', pp. 19–40.

51 V. W. Crane, 'The club of honest Whigs: friends of science and liberty', *William and Mary Quarterly*, 3rd series, 23 (1966), 211.

guilds there were numerous trade processions. At Norwich in 1750 the anniversary of St Blaze saw 'the grandest procession of the journeymen woolcombers of this city' headed by the bishop 'in his episcopal robes in an open chaise, drawn by four light grey horses, a book in one hand and a wool comb in the other'. Twenty years later the Bury St Edmunds shoemakers 'made a grand procession on horseback from the south gate through all the principal streets with trumpets in front and the rest of the band joined with drums, fifes etc.'. Bradford's feast of St Blaze was still being celebrated in the 1810s with thousands attending and the mills standing idle. A major occasion for junketing in Scottish towns was the election by the trade incorporations (guilds) of their deacons (leader and representative) every autumn, an important social and political event in a country which had less than 3,000 parliamentary voters. Corporation ceremonies, particularly mayor making, were also lavish events; at Leicester heavy refreshment at the mayor's feast meant 'cheerfulness and joy sit pleasantly on every countenance, the great and the small happily forget distinction', until the inevitable drunken unpleasantness ended proceedings. For all their commercial decline, fairs (and to a lesser extent markets) remained occasions for popular socialising and entertainment, as did parish wakes. Music and dancing were supplemented by wrestling or boxing, bowling, cockfights, stalls and theatrical shows.[52]

Public ceremonies in the Georgian era were frequently associated with events in the political calendar. From the Restoration, the king's birthday was a major public festivity in the urban ritual year: a form of orchestrated festivity involving bonfires, bells, flags, noise and protracted drinking. These patriotic celebrations became an important focus of British identity from *c.* 1780 as Scots and English alike came to idealise George III. Scottish towns were less well endowed with certain other types of public spectacle. At four to five a year the rate of executions per head in late eighteenth- and early nineteenth-century Scotland was roughly a third that of England where sixty to seventy a year were hanged.[53]

At the neighbourhood and domestic level, workshops celebrated the completion of apprenticeships and other events with feasts and street processions, while householders organised convivial welcomes and foys (or farewells) for new arrivals and those departing. Family rites of passage attracted large neighbourly gatherings. Marriage celebrations often lasted several days, with fiddlers and dancing, and funerals were major public occasions, despite the advent of commercial

[52] *Norwich Mercury*, 20–8 Jan. 1749/50; Kansas University Library, Sp.Collections, MS B 39 (unfol.); W. B. Crump, ed., *The Leeds Woollen Industry, 1780–1820* (Thoresby Society, 32, 1929), pp. 113–14; J. Throsby, *The History and Antiquities of the Ancient Town of Leicester* (Leicester, 1791), p. 375; for the survival of civic junketing well into the nineteenth century see D. Cannadine, 'Civic ritual and the Colchester oyster feast', *P&P*, 94 (1982), 109–22. R. Malcolmson, *Popular Recreations in English Society 1700–1850* (Cambridge, 1973), pp. 17–24.

[53] C. A. Whatley, 'Royal day, people's day: the monarch's birthday in Scotland, c.1660–1860', in N. MacDougall and R. Mason, eds., *People and Power in Scotland* (Edinburgh, 1993), pp. 170–88; V. Gatrell, *The Hanging Tree* (Oxford, 1994), p. 8.

undertaking: in Georgian Manchester, for instance, John Clayton complained how weddings and funerals drew great crowds of spectators into the streets gazing at the events. Clubs and societies escorted deceased brethren with pomp and ceremony to the grave. A good deal of urban socialising still focused around traditional times of the year, as at Easter when 'the middle and lower ranks . . . will spend the week with buxom joy'. On May day popular celebrations persisted in Georgian London. The sexual licence which ushered in the day was still being condemned by magistrates in the 1780s, though the rustic festivity of milkmaids dancing through the streets with their garlands and pails was increasingly eclipsed by a parade of blackened chimney sweeps, personifying an increasingly polluted urban world. In the case of the holiday of St Monday, the focus of a great deal of artisanal leisure activity into the nineteenth century, the custom seems to have been confirmed, even perhaps invented during the early eighteenth century as work pressure accelerated in the rest of the week.[54] Popular rituals were rarely long-standing but constantly invented and reinvented.

Drink was the nectar of traditional fellowship and leisure. Alcohol sluiced down throats at labour initiations and rites such as banging out, footings and maiden garnish. Drinking matches were common and binges remained as important for industrial workers as they did for village labourers. Publicans sponsored many popular games and entertainments, including skittles, quoits, dancing, football matches and other sports. Gaming and gambling pervaded popular leisure activities – not just the ubiquitous card games, but the profusion of foot races and other feats. There was an under-current of cruelty not only in bullbaiting, cockfights and other animal sports but in crowds assailing competitors in matches and races. Popular singing was another vital aspect of traditional entertainment which continued until the end of the century. As well as the bawdy singing prevalent at public houses, streets resounded to women singing crude songs for money, matching the words with obscene gestures. The success of patriotic songs in the 1790s was twofold, encouraging nationalist sentiment and steadily drowning out the chorus of dirty ditties.[55]

Whilst the new urban environment and all its economic and political pressures influenced traditional social events, the process was by no means one way. Many of the new-style entertainments and cultural activities of the eighteenth

[54] J. Clayton, *Friendly Advice to the Poor* (Manchester, 1755), p. 13; *Morning Chronicle*, 25 Apr. 1791; Marylebone District Library (Archives), Vestry Minutes 1782–6, p. 453; C. Phythian-Adams, 'Milk and soot: the changing vocabulary of a popular ritual in Stuart and Hanoverian London', in Fraser and Sutcliffe, eds., *Pursuit*, pp. 83–104; D. A. Reid, 'The decline of Saint Monday 1766–1876', *P&P*, 71 (1976), 77–84.

[55] J. Rule, *The Experience of Labour in Eighteenth-Century Industry* (London, 1981), pp. 198–9; C. Aspin, *Lancashire: The First Industrial Society* (Preston, 1969), pp. 37, 102; Clark, *English Alehouse*, pp. 297–8, 317–18; Malcolmson, *Popular Recreations*, pp. 43–9; cruelty to animals as a precursor to, and integral with, that to humans was satirised in Hogarth's 'Four stages of cruelty'. BL, Add. MS 27,825, ff. 144, 147v, 154, 157.

century incorporated more traditional elements, indeed this was one of their attractions for participants. We have already noted how heavy drinking, associated with traditional conviviality and victualling houses, was a vital feature of clubs and societies, but it also pervaded race meetings, balls and assemblies, pleasure gardens and the theatre, frequently provoking brawls and disorder. In the same way, huge bets were staked on cricket matches or horse races, and endemic wagering occurred in clubs and societies of all sorts. The *Edinburgh Advertiser* and other newspapers regularly carried advertisements for lotteries in Britain and Ireland during the late eighteenth and early nineteenth centuries. Also loud among smart society entertainments (at least until the 1790s) were traditional songs, while irrationality retained a strong appeal, presiding over many arcane and bizarre rituals at fashionable learned bodies as well as at masonic, pseudo-masonic and drinking societies.[56]

Opposition to the new cultural innovations may have come from particular social groups. According to Jonathan Barry, the middling ranks may have sought to hang on to older practices as a way of maintaining or consolidating their own collective identity. Thus at Bristol and some other towns older-style town annals continued to circulate in manuscript among such groups, in contrast to the printed town histories favoured by the better-off. But it is difficult to generalise about middling groups and their preferences. Many shopkeepers, masters and artisans joined the new religious societies at the end of the seventeenth century and a generation or so later flocked to the growing numbers of masonic lodges and benefit clubs. Frequently many of the so-called elite entertainments of the Georgian era opened the door (through commercial pressures and force of demand) to a wider range of social groups, both as spectators and participants.[57]

Cultural differentiation was probably stronger at the local community level. The vital point is not that certain urban social groups maintained older practices, but that some towns did. Or, even more important, that some urban communities adopted new cultural forms, whereas others failed to, or did so much later. We have already noted that although the metropolis was a powerful engine of cultural exchange, particularly in the early eighteenth century, different centres of cultural innovation emerged during the period, in the old regional capitals

[56] *Edinburgh Advertiser*, 27 Sept. 1782; Borsay, *English Urban Renaissance*, pp. 190–1, 249, 302; D. Stevenson, *The First Freemasons* (Aberdeen, 1988); e.g. L. Cust, *History of the Society of Dilettanti* (London, 1914), pp. 25, 29; W. H. Rylands, 'A forgotten rival of masonry: the noble order of Bucks', *Ars Quatuor Coronatorum*, 3 (1890), 140–63; L. C. Jones, *The Clubs of the Georgian Rakes* (New York, 1942). R. L. Emerson, 'Science and the origins and concerns of the Scottish Enlightenment', *History of Science*, 26 (1988), 333–66; R. L. Emerson, 'Sir Robert Sibbald, Kt, the Royal Society of Scotland and the origins of the Scottish Enlightenment', *Annals of Science*, 45 (1988), 31–72.

[57] J. Barry, 'Provincial town culture, 1640–1780: urbane or civic?' in J. H. Pittock and A. Wear, eds., *Interpretation and Cultural History* (London, 1991), pp. 209–16; Freemasons Hall, London, Registers of Grand Lodge; Bodleian Library, Rawlinson MS D 1312.

and the major industrialising centres. At the same time, there were areas where certain types of cultural activity seem much less important than elsewhere. Freemasonry for instance appears more vigorous during the eighteenth century in the towns of the South-West and the North, but less favoured in the urban centres of the Home Counties or Midlands.[58]

Regional variations may be important in urban cultural development at this time, echoing growing economic and demographic differentiation on a regional basis. More crucial probably was the role and response of local communities to cultural changes, a response shaped by their economy, social and occupational structure, external connections and the strength of older cultural institutions, such as the Church and dissenting congregations. What one can recognise is a kind of negotiation between the new cultural activities (propelled often by metropolitan example and commercial pressures) and local urban communities, as the latter sought to use and adapt them to their own needs, not least to assert their own attractiveness and identity in a competitive urban system. In Scotland Edinburgh's powerful landed and professional presence parented a fine array of fashionable social and associational activities. Glasgow with its merchants and crowds of migrants from the Highlands and Isles developed its own portfolio of bodies, including many philanthropic organisations and distinctive regional societies. At the market town level too there were variations in the level of associational activity between different towns, dependent in part on the size of their respectable clienteles.[59] When we know more about the precise geography of other forms of public sociability, we may be able to identify similar strong divergences between communities. But overall we should be concerned less with finding cultural innovations than not discovering them – and asking why.

Recent work has also suggested that there was greater resistance to cultural and social change in the countryside as well. Certainly there was no inevitable invasion by a town of its hinterland, at least during the early eighteenth century. Admittedly, landowners, increasingly addicted to coach-borne travel to town, to comfortable neat town houses, and the new urbane symbolism of visiting, became intolerant of the slowness, isolation and discomfort of rural life, bereft of new-style entertainments. As Boswell put it, his ultimate rural nightmare was to be stranded all winter in 'an old house in the north of Scotland and being burdened with tedium and gnawed with fretfulness'. But for many middling and lesser folk it was not until nearer 1800 that towns began to extend their cultural influence into the villages, with modest men like Peter Pownall, a Cheshire farmer, going to plays, sporting events and clubs in their local towns. Paradoxically, it was at this time that the urbanised elite began to rediscover a fashionable interest in 'country' styles – in archery contests, crenellated houses,

58 Cf. J. Lane, *Masonic Records 1717–1894* (London, 1895).

59 R. B. Sher, 'Commerce, religion and the Enlightenment in eighteenth-century Glasgow', in Devine and Jackson, eds., *Glasgow*, pp. 312–59.

druids' feasts, seascapes and poetic village scenes, even the first suburban villas with their gardens. Criticism of the world of the big cities – for their anonymity, their social disintegration – had recurred earlier, but now it had an increasing intellectual and cultural justification, linked to the newly discovered cult of nature. British anti-urbanism was already on the horizon, underlining the fact that the triumph of the urban renaissance was never more than partial.[60]

(v) RELIGION AND MORAL AND CULTURAL REFORM

Accepting the importance of cultural pluralism and commercialisation during the eighteenth century, one cannot forget that religion remained a powerful force in the lives of many townspeople, and that its influence was growing again before the end of the century. The Anglican Church continued to be a central pillar of communal, parish and domestic life in many towns: through its control over the rites of passage, its association with the provision of welfare and education and its identification with public institutions. Fashionable ministers and churches attracted large congregations, but most urban parishes organised more regular services than their rural counterparts, their ministers normally recruited from the urban better-off. After a century of neglect following the Reformation there came a wave of church building and refurbishment. London led the way, its construction boom triggered by the Great Fire of 1666 and by Tory legislation in 1711 for 'fifty new churches' in the metropolitan area (see Plate 21). At the same time, other expanding centres benefited: thus Liverpool raised three new churches between 1700 and 1763. The refurbishment of church interiors included the building of galleries, the decoration of the altar and chancel and the purchase of brass chandeliers, silver plate, sculpture and works of art. In many places the church aligned itself with the new cultural developments in town, conscious of the need to keep secular leisure activities at bay. Parishes established their own libraries, church organists sponsored concerts, music festivals were staged in town churches and many public events including society anniversaries involved sermons at the town church. Highly fashionable, many churches had societies of bell-ringers engaged in competitive change-ringing against teams from other towns.[61]

[60] C. Estabrook, *Urbane and Rustic England: Cultural Ties and Social Spheres in the Provinces 1660–1780* (Manchester, 1998), esp. ch. 9; C. Ryskamp and F. A. Pottle, eds., *Boswell: The Ominous Years* (London, 1963), p. 54; H. Coutie, ed., *The Diary of Peter Pownall: A Bramhall Farmer 1765–1858* (Congleton, 1989). S. Pigott, *Ruins in a Landscape* (Edinburgh, 1976), chs. 6–8; also H. Trevor-Roper, *The Romantic Movement and the Study of History* (London, 1969); C. Campbell, *The Romantic Ethic and the Spirit of Modern Consumerism* (Oxford, 1987); A. J. Weitzman 'Eighteenth-century London: urban paradise or fallen city?' *Journal of the History of Ideas*, 36 (1975), 469–80.

[61] W. M. Jacob, *Lay People and Religion in the Early Eighteenth Century* (Cambridge, 1996), pp. 52, 62, 202, 208–17; Walsh *et al.*, eds., *Church of England,* pp. 11, 89, 198, 203; J. Summerson, *Georgian London* (London, 1945), ch. 6. E. Morris, *History and Art of Change-Ringing* (London, 1931), pp. 216, 239, 251–2.

In England the Glorious Revolution and the Toleration Act inaugurated a new era of social recognition for dissenting congregations and in the wake of buoyant commercial and middling incomes nonconformist groups became important groups in the urban community, not just in London. Dissenting ministers like Phillip Doddridge of Northampton were influential figures in provincial society. Dissenting chapels became larger and more elegant, their public visibility fronting a dense network of charitable and social meetings.[62]

In Scottish towns the kirk remained an equally powerful cultural and political institution controlling many aspects of poor relief and parish schooling. Scotland's established Church remained Presbyterian after the Union of 1707, but within a decade the kirk's monopoly of religion in Scotland had been removed and toleration assured. As the eighteenth century wore on, the English fashion for 'lukewarm' religion was adopted among the upper ranks of society and among intellectuals. Presbyterian theology, church discipline and social attitudes were gradually weakened. By the mid-eighteenth century the Church had two wings, 'moderate' and 'evangelical', the former linked to the political establishment, the latter more radical. At the same time, the established Church in Scotland came to accept and even promote Enlightenment ideas. There was vitality within the cultural forms surrounding ecclesiastical observances, including a revival in church music from the 1750s. 'Evangelical Protestants, far from dismissing ritual, displayed a wide range of performative expression and a notable confidence in rituals to symbolise, and even to make manifest, the divine.' In the 1770s, churches were heavily attended, the Sabbath was well observed, and there was said to be none of 'the excess of idleness and riot' which characterised London Sundays.[63]

The continuing vitality of religion in urban cultural life was manifested by the widespread support for the moral reform movement before and after 1700. Fears about moral and social decline in London were exploited by the bishops and committed laity to galvanise Protestant support in urban society and to launch a prosecution campaign against the marginal classes, including drunkards and prostitutes. Moral reform societies multiplied, first in the capital (twenty or so by 1701), and then in a great swathe of provincial towns. Edinburgh already had a prominent society for the reformation of manners after 1690; and others sprang up. Complementing such bodies, there was an upsurge of religious societies (for young men), clerical societies and charity schools. The SPCK established in London in 1699 promoted urban schools, libraries and religious societies both in the metropolis and beyond. Whilst Anglicans made much of the initial running in the reform movement, the dissenters sought to join the crusade,

62 G. S. de Krey, *A Fractured Society* (Oxford, 1985), esp. ch. 4; G. Rupp, *Religion in England 1688–1791* (Oxford, 1986), ch. 11.

63 L. E. Schmidt, *Holy Fairs: Scottish Communions and American Revivals in the Early Modern Period* (Princeton, N.J., 1989), p. 216; Topham, *Letters*, pp. 190–1, 237.

though the revival of Tory Anglicanism during the last years of Anne's reign led to renewed division in Protestant ranks.[64]

Under George I the religious reform movement lost momentum in English towns, in part due to internal problems but also because of wider religious trends. Under the benign effect of toleration and affluence, the urban dissenting churches seem to have become more complacent, inward-looking and fissiparous, beset by growing division among the Presbyterians in particular. During the 1730s dissenting ministers bemoaned the decay of the dissenting interest. And without the competition from dissent Anglican churches may have stagnated. Even if there was no absolute decline in religious activity, the extraordinary vitality and variety of new-style cultural entertainments left church attendance one piece in the progressively complex mosaic of public socialising. Already from the 1730s evangelicals and early Methodists were starting to take over somnolent religious societies of differing complexions, though the religious revival movement did not take off before the last decades of the century. In Scottish towns the evangelicals, also known as the 'Popular Party', formed breakaway churches in the mid- and late eighteenth century which had religious and social similarities with contemporary evangelicalism and Methodism in England (though Methodism itself attracted only a few thousand Scottish adherents before 1830). Evangelical revival meetings in the proto-industrial towns of the west-central Lowlands during the 1740s (Cambuslang is the most famous) marked a resurgence of enthusiasm. Evangelicalism and moderatism were 'tendencies' rather than separate churches, though the Secession Church arose from a dispute over a burgess oath to exclude Catholics from public office imposed on Glasgow, Edinburgh and Perth 1745–7. But the real growth of religious pluralism in towns only came with the religious revival movement.[65]

The religious awakening of the late Georgian period was never exclusively an urban phenomenon, but it had a powerful urban edge and occurred on numerous fronts: hence the growth of new churches, the resurgence of older dissenting congregations, the advance of evangelical Anglicanism, the explosion of church-centred religious, philanthropic and educational societies and the

[64] G. V. Portus, *Caritas Anglicana* (London, 1912), pp. 28–106, 146–53; also A. G. Craig, 'The movement for reformation of manners 1688–1715' (PhD thesis, University of Edinburgh University, 1980); R. B. Shoemaker, 'Reforming the city: the reformation of manners campaign in London 1690–1738', in L. Davison *et al.*, eds., *Stilling the Grumbling Hive* (Stroud, 1992), pp. 99–115; T. C. Curtis and W. A. Speck, 'The societies for the reformation of manners: a case study in the theory and practice of moral reform', *Literature and History*, 3 (1976), 45–64. Houston, *Social Change*, pp. 188–9

[65] Walsh *et al.*, eds., *Church of England*, p. 57; Jacob, *Lay People*, pp. 91–2; D. Hempton, 'Religion in British society 1740–1790', in J. Black, ed., *British Politics and Society from Walpole to Pitt 1742–1789* (Basingstoke, 1990), pp. 214 *et seq.*; C. G. Brown, *The Social History of Religion in Scotland Since 1730* (London, 1987), pp. 27–8, 35–6; A. J. Hayes, *Edinburgh Methodism, 1761–1975* (Edinburgh, 1976); C. G. Brown, *Religion and Society in Scotland Since 1707* (Edinburgh, 1997); N. C. Landsman, 'Presbyterians and provincial society: the evangelical enlightenment in the west of Scotland', in Dwyer and Sher, eds., *Sociability and Society*, pp. 194–209.

growing impact of religious and moral reform ideas on the cultural activities and social behaviour of townspeople. The revival was generated in part by national concerns: a sense of failure and divine retribution after the debacle of the American war, and the need by the 1790s for the nation to gird itself in religious armour against the menace of French revolutionary atheism. Such concerns were heightened by a sense of general religious, moral and social collapse in towns as a result of accelerating urbanisation. High levels of migration from the countryside, the growing influx of Irish, increased economic polarisation, together with the quickening pace of spatial transformation and segregation, as the respectable classes decamped to villas and later suburbs, caused many respectable people to see popular urban society drifting out of control, contaminated by irreligion: in 1815 Richard Yates proclaimed that the great urban areas were becoming 'a mine of heathenism'.[66]

The orthodox urban Church (despite local successes in expanding parochial provision to meet demographic demand) was seen as ineffectual in stemming this tide. These concerns were not limited to London and the biggest cities; many county towns at the end of the century faced similar difficulties, if in less massive form: thus the Sunday School movement at Gloucester in the early 1780s began as a response to the sight of multitudes of young people in the poor suburbs who 'spend their time in noise and riot and playing at chuck, and cursing and swearing'. But it is important not to see the urban revival entirely from an upper-class perspective. Rapid urban change with its high levels of mobility, particularly among women, and the need for newcomers to find a foothold in the community, the development of new towns and other semi-urban industrial settlements without established institutions, the shock of the new as many country people flooded into rapidly expanding communities where their position was frequently challenged by economic vicissitude, created strong demands among many lower-class people for new forms of social and cultural organisation; new bodies through which they might obtain social recognition, mutual aid, help when migrating, spiritual and emotional comfort in times of distress and panic (for instance, during the cholera outbreak of 1832) and also opportunities for self-improvement. It is important to emphasise that at least some of the new and traditional forms of social and cultural organisation, including drinking houses and clubs, continued to answer those needs as well. However, there can be no question that the religious revival movement provided a wide-ranging response to the pressures of later eighteenth- and early nineteenth-century urbanisation.[67]

The growth of congregations is striking. Among the older churches, the

[66] D. W. Bebbington, *Evangelicalism in Modern Britain* (London, 1989), ch. 2; H. McLeod, *Religion and the Working Class in Nineteenth-Century Britain* (London, 1984), pp. 20–1; E. R. Norman, *Church and Society in England 1770–1970* (Oxford, 1976), pp. 16–25; Walsh *et al.*, eds., *Church of England*, pp. 18–19.

[67] For local successes: M. Smith, *Religion in Industrial Society* (Oxford 1994), pp. 34–5. T. Laqueur, *Religion and Respectability* (London, 1976), p. 23; McLeod, *Religion*, pp. 23–5.

number of Congregationalists and Particular Baptists, the large majority living in towns, rose about eight times between 1750 and the 1830s; the Methodists increased their support tenfold in the years 1781–1836. Aided by their greater institutional flexibility dissenting churches rapidly increased their places of worship: in the West Riding, for instance, licences for temporary places of worship increased from 73 in the 1780s to 401 in the 1790s. In Scotland the Secession Church grew strongly in towns after 1780, though suffering further splits in its ranks. Congregationalist and Baptist congregations were the most popular offshoots of Presbyterianism in the big centres. Helped by their own Sunday Schools from the 1780s, the evangelicals attracted a strong following in the industrial and fishing towns; the evangelical sects were united in 1820 as the United Secession Church. By the 1830s less than half the churchgoing population of Edinburgh and Glasgow attended worship in the established Church. In the same way a major growth of dissenting congregations occurred in the new industrialising settlements of South Wales, notably after 1800.[68]

Slower to respond, despite the impact of evangelical enthusiasm in England, the Anglicans were increasing their attendance by the end of the period. After 1809 the government provided financial help for poor livings and in 1818 the Church Building Society was established, followed by state funding for new churches: up to 1830, 134 new churches had been built, with 50 more under construction, the vast majority in urban parishes. Nor was growth confined to the Protestant churches: the Catholics recorded a threefold increase in Manchester, Liverpool, Preston and Wigan during the last decades of the eighteenth century.[69]

The churches sought to reassert their central position in urban social and cultural life not only through expanding church attendance but by recovering their powerful position in education. Following local initiatives at Gloucester and elsewhere, the Sunday School Society was formed in 1785, and by 1840 at least 17,000 schools had been established, a high proportion in towns and more than half nonconformist. Though such schools provided some elementary teaching, the main upper- and middle-class stress was on religious and moral instruction, drawing poor children and their families away from disorder and irreligion. Not that they were simply agencies of social control. Some local schools in the early nineteenth century were taken over by artisans and other lower-class people anxious to furnish educational opportunities for their children. An English importation, Sunday Schools were never as significant in Scotland as they were

[68] A. D. Gilbert, *Religion and Society in Industrial England* (London, 1976), ch. 2; McLeod, *Religion*, p. 21; Brown, *Social History of Religion*, pp. 35–6; C. G. Brown, 'Protest in the pews. Interpreting Presbyterianism and society in fracture during the Scottish economic revolution', in T. M. Devine, ed., *Conflict and Stability in Scottish Society, 1700–1850* (Edinburgh, 1990), pp. 83–105; E. T. Davies, *A New History of Wales: Religion and Society in the Nineteenth Century* (Llandybie, 1981), ch. 2.

[69] Norman, *Church and Society*, pp. 53–5; Hempton, 'Religion in British society', p. 218.

south of the border. They tended to have a sectarian as well as an educational function. Indeed, during the period of the French wars they were actively suppressed because of their identification with religious dissent and political radicalism.[70]

The churches also took an active role in the promotion of charity schools. In addition to earlier foundations, the end of the century saw an upsurge of schools established by local congregations. Anglican schools were brought under the coordinating umbrella of the National Society in 1811, and by 1824 the society supervised and supported 3,000 schools, many in manufacturing towns. The dissenters responded to the challenge with the British and Foreign School Society in 1814 which had a similar role. In 1833 government funding for schools was allocated to the two societies which gave them powerful leverage over public education until the last years of the nineteenth century.[71]

Religious influence was also manifest in the scores of new philanthropic and similar organisations established in London and other centres from the 1780s. At Glasgow in 1815 there was over a score of such bodies including the Society for the Deaf and the Dumb, the Magdalene Asylum, Female Society, Benevolent Society for Clothing the Poor, Old Man's Friend Society, Aged Women Society, Glasgow Dispensary, Sick and Destitute Strangers Society, and Humane Society. By 1800 all the main denominations had their own missionary societies, mostly based in London, though with auxiliary branches in provincial towns, and these were as important for mobilising congregational support in Britain as in promoting Christianity among the heathen. In the 1780s there was a resurgence of the moral reform movement through the establishment in London of the Proclamation Society and after 1802 the Society for the Suppression of Vice with its various local committees. In a concerted way, churches around the start of the nineteenth century exploited the new structures of voluntary societies to extend their outreach in urban communities. During the 1830s and after some evangelicals questioned this reliance on organisational action, and called for greater recognition of the role of the supernatural, but in general voluntarism remained a vital component of the churches' response to urbanisation throughout the Victorian era.[72]

What was the impact of the renewed concern for moral reform on urban

70 Laqueur, *Religion and Respectability*, p. 44, ch. 7; for criticism of Laqueur's view, cf. M. Dick, 'The myth of the working-class Sunday School', *History of Education*, 9 (1980), 29–31. Houston, *Scottish Literacy*, pp. 224–5; Withrington, 'Schooling, literacy and society', pp. 157–8.

71 Norman, *Church and Society*, pp. 55–61, 113.

72 J. Cleland, *Annals of Glasgow* (Glasgow, 1816), vol. I, pp. 271–3; N. Goodall, *The 'Fundamental Principle' of the London Missionary Society* (London, 1945); J. Innes, 'Politics and morals: the reformation of manners movement in later eighteenth-century England', in E. Hellmuth, ed., *The Transformation of Political Culture* (Oxford, 1990), pp. 59–118; M. J. D. Roberts, 'The Society for the Suppression of Vice and its early critics, 1802–1812', *HJ*, 26 (1983), 159–76; Bebbington, *Evangelicalism*, p. 76.

cultural life? Public drinking and other traditional aspects and institutions of sociability came under attack. From the 1780s zealous magistrates increasingly regulated public drinking houses, restricting opening hours and reducing the number of licensed premises in town. Sunday observance legislation in 1780, succeeded by a series of early nineteenth-century measures, challenged one of the key days for artisanal celebration, while the traditional festivities of St Monday started to come under pressure. A Manchester newspaper in 1834 condemned the campaign 'to debar the poor from all kinds of amusement, their ancient wakes are suppressed, their walks are shut up, their commons enclosed, and their pastimes discouraged'. Instead the churches sought to set up their counter-attractions, among them tea parties, school anniversaries, excursions and concerts.[73]

The actual effect of these restrictive measures on the cultural world of the lower orders was at best partial. In towns with more traditional economies St Monday retained its significance as a popular festive day into the late nineteenth century. Many customary activities including wakes persisted in and around industrialising towns, often encouraged by the drink trade. Licensed publicans, backed by wholesale brewers through the tied house system, designed purpose-built premises with glass windows, and advertised and sponsored a variety of commercial entertainments such as organs, bands, dancing, musical clocks and displays of butterflies and stuffed birds. Tighter licensing controls in the late Georgian period also led to a surfeit of illicit beer and gin-shops, which provided a focus for drunkenness among the poor. 'In many [Liverpool] streets every third house [about 1814] is a public-house', the landlords often having 'but a few shillings to do the business'; in addition there is 'the great number of liquor vaults'. The problems of regulating this squalid subterranean drinking world contributed to the ending of many licensing controls in 1830. For the upper and middling orders the religious influence was more powerful and immediate, signalled by a growing reaction away from heavy drinking, lubricious songs and the like in public, though many traditional pursuits probably continued *sotto voce* in private social clubs.[74] In the late 1820s the temperance movement was established, although its impact was delayed until the 1850s. Likewise certain traditional animal sports, including cockfighting and bullbaiting, came under attack – a process accelerated by the establishment in London of the Royal Society for the Prevention of Cruelty to Animals during the 1820s[75]

[73] Clark, *English Alehouse*, pp. 55–9, 254–60; Reid, 'Decline of Saint Monday', pp. 83 *et seq.*; H. Cunningham, *Leisure in the Industrial Revolution* (London, 1980), pp. 25, 44, 85 *et seq.*; *Manchester Guardian*, 3 May 1834.

[74] D. A. Reid, 'Weddings, weekdays, work and leisure in urban England 1791–1911', *P&P*, 153 (1996), 135–63; University College, London, Archives Dept, Chadwick MS 12; also Clark, *English Alehouse*, pp. 273–8; Liverpool City RO, Holt Papers (942 HOL 5), p. 9.

[75] B. Harrison, *Drink and the Victorians* (London, 1971), chs. 4–5; K. Thomas, *Man and the Natural World: Changing Attitudes in England 1500–1800* (London, 1983), pp. 159–60.

The moral reform movement also put growing pressure on the more frivolous of the new social entertainments of the eighteenth century. Masquerades and routs largely disappeared from the 1790s; assemblies went into a genteel decline; pleasure gardens faded. As noted earlier, the theatre lost much of its upper-class support in the early nineteenth century. Religious pressures were compounded by the economic recession after the end of the French wars and the steady retreat of the landed classes from provincial towns.[76]

The religious awakening had mixed results. While it consolidated church attendance and family religious practices among the respectable classes, it failed to do much to halt the spread of irreligion and apathy among the urban lower classes. Though there was a proliferation of church building and new congregations, religious division and fragmentation became widespread in urban society as almost every denominational group, with cash to spare, set up their own, often short-lived church. Yet there can be little doubt that the advent of many interconnected religious, missionary, charitable and other organisations created powerful forms of cultural networking in towns, helping to define the social and cultural identities of individual urban communities in the early nineteenth century.[77]

The new religious seriousness had a ripple effect on many wider aspects of urban cultural life. Among the better-off classes it gave added impetus to the domestication of certain types of cultural activity such as music making. In the public domain societies, both old and new, became a major feature of the cultural life not just of the big centres as before 1800, but of smaller towns as well. The famous and fashionable Walter Scott could brag in 1829, 'what a tail of the alphabet I should draw after me were I to sign with the indications of the different societies I belong to, beginning with the president of the Royal Society of Edinburgh and ended with Umpire of the Six foot high Club'; and indeed he subscribed to over a score of learned, scientific, artistic, sporting, social, political and other societies in London, Edinburgh and Glasgow. But even minor lawyers and shopkeepers in market towns had their membership of philanthropic, learned, political and other bodies. There was a continuing growth of older voluntary organisations – music and flower societies, political and sporting clubs, professional organisations and masonic lodges (500 in England and Wales by 1830). Friendly societies, mainly for the artisanal classes in towns, multiplied, though after the 1830s local clubs gave way to those affiliated to national orders like the Oddfellows and Foresters, the initial impetus for these coming from Lancashire and Yorkshire. Distinctive of the new cultural mood, however, was the proliferation of scientific and learned societies together with

[76] Castle, *Masquerade*, pp. 332–5.

[77] B. Harrison and B. Trinder, *Drink and Sobriety in an Early Victorian Country Town* (London, 1969), esp. pp. 36–40; R. J. Morris, 'Clubs, societies and associations', in F. M. L. Thompson, ed., *The Cambridge Social History of Britain 1750–1950* (Cambridge, 1990), vol. III, pp. 406–14.

mechanics institutes in the early nineteenth century; these fused older themes of public improvement and the new predeliction for morality, politeness and respectability. Literary and philosophical societies and similar bodies which had begun in various provincial centres in the late eighteenth century spread to most larger English towns (and some Scottish ones). As well as organising lecture courses on literature, science, economics, travel and archaeology, the societies established laboratories, museums and libraries. In 1831 the British Association for the Advancement of Science was established to foster and coordinate activity on a national scale, often exploiting urban rivalries.[78] Mechanics institutes were initially envisaged as more popular versions of the provincial learned societies, appealing to the lower orders. In 1823 the Glasgow Mechanics Institute was established, offering courses in natural philosophy, chemistry, mathematics and mechanics with a library and museum, and the model was soon copied in London and elsewhere: by 1826 over 100 were operating with a good number in Scotland and Wales as well as in England; by 1841 the number had reached over 300. In some instances they were the result of middle-class initiative, in others pressure came from workers. In general they failed to attract ordinary working men but the institutes, usually in their own premises, furnished educational and cultural opportunities for artisans and the lower middling orders in towns. In addition to courses and small libraries, some promoted interest in the history of art and architecture as well as music.[79] This new respectable improving world was a far cry from the traditional popular leisure activities of the lower orders still largely associated with public drinking houses.

(vi) CONCLUSION

By the end of our period, a national urban culture had emerged affecting much of Britain. The urban renaissance of the eighteenth century, initially at least London-inspired, had infiltrated many English provincial towns to a greater or lesser extent. But its impact elsewhere in Britain was tardier and less complete. The revolution in material culture came late to Scotland and even prosperous merchants and professionals in the early eighteenth century had fewer fashionable and decorative items than would have been found among comparable social groups in English provincial towns. New-style cultural and leisure activities made a major impact on Edinburgh, but diffused much more slowly to the

[78] W. E. K. Anderson, ed., *The Journal of Sir Walter Scott* (Oxford, 1972), pp. 528–9; Clark, *British Clubs and Societies*, pp. 472 *et seq*. Gosden, *Friendly Societies*, ch. 2; T. Kelly, *A History of Adult Education in Great Britain* (Liverpool, 1992), pp. 107–9; E. Kitson-Clark, *The History of One Hundred Years of Life of the Leeds Philosophical and Literary Society* (Leeds, 1924), pp. 26–7; O. J. R. Howarth, *The British Association for the Advancement of Science: A Retrospect 1831–1931* (London, 1931).

[79] Sher, 'Commerce, religion and the Enlightenment'; Kelly, *Adult Education*, ch. 8.

regional centres and smaller towns in Scotland. The Scottish Enlightenment largely focused in Edinburgh – what Smollett's Humphrey Clinker called 'a hotbed of genius' – developed its own particular character, shaped by nationalistic, political, cultural and religious tensions, and nurtured by a sense of collective identity among thinkers. Conversely, new cultural activities in Welsh towns were not only slow to develop but thinly spread. By the early nineteenth century all that had changed: the bourgeoisie of Edinburgh and Glasgow had become as evidently affluent as their fellows in Bristol or Liverpool, and the respectable classes of Scottish and Welsh towns shared many of the same cultural interests – in missionary, philanthropic and educational work, science and music, associational activity, religious revivalism and moral reform – as their English cousins. For a good part of the eighteenth century there had been some resistance to change from more traditional urban groups but this was increasingly eroded. Changing patterns of work had implications for cultural forms as one can see in Scotland. 'By 1830 . . . the idea of regular, supervised work had been accepted, albeit reluctantly, by many labouring Scots.' The division between work, leisure and commitments outside the workplace became more distinct as work became constant rather than intermittent. Large groupings of a particular occupation, such as the thousands of Glasgow weavers in the 1790s and 1800s, coupled with changing social and political attitudes allowed the development of workers' associations with specific cultural patterns. There were similar developments elsewhere in Britain helping to restructure the cultural life of better-off workers. Only the lowest urban classes, increasingly seen as marginal or dangerous, were left out of the picture.[80]

And yet if there was growing cultural homogeneity, this was counter-balanced by greater pluralism and particularism. In the earlier period the local response to cultural change was often defensive: by the early nineteenth century there was a stronger sense of accepting and adapting cultural innovations to project a new cultural identity, keeping a city or town ahead in the urban steeple chase with other provincial centres. It was partly about economics. From the late Georgian period county and spa towns were acutely aware of the commercial benefits of leisure and other cultural activities, and the danger of business going elsewhere. But increasingly a strong cultural identity – with museums, libraries, art galleries, learned societies and the like – was seen as consecrating the success of rising provincial towns, even new industrial towns.[81] This distinctive kind of urban culture – at once national and autonomous – was to dominate the world of the Victorian city.

[80] Quoted in Sher, *Church and University*, p. 155; D. Daiches, 'The Scottish Enlightenment', in D. Daiches *et al.*, eds., *A Hotbed of Genius: The Scottish Enlightenment, 1730–1790* (Edinburgh, 1986), pp. 1–42; C. A. Whatley, 'The experience of work', in Devine and Mitchison, eds., *People and Society in Scotland*, pp. 240–6. W. H. Fraser, 'Patterns of protest', in *ibid.*, pp. 268–91.

[81] E.g. G. Firth, *Bradford and the Industrial Revolution* (Halifax, 1990), pp. 207–16.

· 18 ·

The transformation of urban space 1700–1840

MICHAEL REED

(i) INTRODUCTION

THE FABRIC of the urban environment experienced accelerating change during the course of the eighteenth century, and the pace of change in some towns, although by no means all, underwent a dramatic gearshift from the 1780s onwards. These changes were driven by rapid population growth and migration, and by technological innovation, leading to the mechanisation of transport and of many manufacturing processes. Central government and municipal authorities contributed very little to this metamorphosis, unlike the experience of many European cities. The traditional pattern of urban social geography, in which the well-to-do lived in the centres of towns and the poor in the suburbs, was shattered in many towns in the late eighteenth and early nineteenth centuries and replaced by suburban residential segregation based upon socio-economic status and the separation of home and work, in its turn dependent upon ease of transport. Everywhere it is a subtle, complex process of transformation. In some towns, such as Glasgow, it takes place within a generation. In other towns, unaffected by the first stages of industrialisation, it was the end of the nineteenth century before these processes had fully worked themselves out.

Much of this growth and change had to be accommodated within ancient boundaries and administrative structures, creating problems of health, sanitation and housing upon an unprecedented scale. These problems were widely recognised by the 1830s, but it is the 1840s before central government begins to take the first tentative steps towards putting things right.

The distinctions between private, institutional and public space made in Chapter 9 continue to be useful, but the pace of change brings increasing fluidity into the use of urban space, particularly with the emergence, as suggested in Chapter 17, of what may be called a semi-commercialised social space, so that it becomes ever more difficult to draw clear-cut boundaries between them.

(ii) PRIVATE SPACE

The provision of private houses, whether in the old centres of towns or in new suburbs, was influenced by a number of general factors in addition to those specific to any one town. First of all, the building industry itself was organised upon a very small scale, with individual craftsmen working together on perhaps no more than three or four houses at a time, bartering their individual skills, so that very little actual money changed hands.[1] Only in the first decades of the nineteenth century do large-scale contractors appear, at first in London, with Thomas Cubitt by far and away the most successful.[2] The industry itself was profoundly affected by long-term economic trends, with increasingly obvious periods of boom and bust. Thus it would seem that the years 1715–30 were years of expansion, followed by a slow-down in the following decade. There was a renewal of building activity from the 1750s, but a return to almost slump conditions after 1793 and the outbreak of war with France.[3] Secondly, by the end of the seventeenth century the basic themes of classical architecture were well known and understood, and their use by provincial builders grew rapidly during the course of the eighteenth century in response to the pressures of fashion (see Plate 22). By the last years of the century new themes are beginning to appear, some of them oriental in origin. There is a revival of interest in both Gothic and Greek architecture, widespread use of stucco and the emergence of the semi-detached house, all making for rapid and far-reaching change in the physical appearance of towns. There was also a long-term trend towards submerging the façades of individual houses within one overall grand design. This is noticeable in Bath, for example, and in the development of Edinburgh's New Town (see Plate 23). It is reinforced by the use of brick, tile and stone, the two processes combining to introduce a measure of external uniformity into streets in place of the variety of the vernacular tradition.[4] Thirdly, fire continued to present a very real risk and on occasion it devastated the centres of old towns, but the long, slow replacement of timber and thatch by brick and tile seems to have prompted an equally long and slow decline in the numbers of town fires. The opportunities for replanning which fire created were never seized upon on a large

[1] See D. Cruikshank and P. Wyld, *London: The Art of Georgian Building* (London, 1975); J. Summerson, *Georgian London* (London, 1945, and later editions); and C. W. Chalklin, *The Provincial Towns of Georgian England* (London, 1974).

[2] See H. Hobhouse, *Thomas Cubitt, Master Builder* (London, 1971), *passim*.

[3] Cruikshank and Wyld, *London*, pp. 1–2.

[4] The earliest known semi-detached houses in series are the three pairs of brick houses in the Grove, Highgate, of 1688: see J. Summerson, 'The beginnings of an early Victorian suburb', *London Topographical Record*, 27 (1995), 3. W. Ison, *The Georgian Buildings of Bath, 1700–1830* (Bath, 1948; 2nd edn, 1980); A. J. Youngson, *The Making of Classical Edinburgh* (Edinburgh, 1966); E. L. Jones, 'The reduction of fire damage in southern England, 1650–1850', *Post-Medieval Archaeology*, 2 (1968), 140–9.

scale. Some obstructions were removed, streets were occasionally widened and straightened, but nothing more.

The open spaces which were so characteristic of the centres of seventeenth-century towns were gradually built over to provide accommodation, often of the poorest kind. Stables, workshops and outhouses were converted into dwellings, and larger houses were subdivided to accommodate several families. This growing overcrowding in inner areas led to a movement into more salubrious suburbs by those who could afford it. The houses thus built were used entirely for residential purposes, a break from the traditional practice of living over the shop still to be found in the centres of towns. A garden was increasingly sought after, summerhouses and greenhouses became *de rigueur*, and a five bay front to the house became almost a standard requisite.[5]

London in particular was almost encircled by the beginning of the eighteenth century with pleasant villages much frequented by retired or semi-retired city merchants, a phenomenon noted again and again by Daniel Defoe. In the villages of Stratford, Walthamstow, Woodford, Wansted and West Ham, for example, he says over a thousand new houses have been erected since the Glorious Revolution, and 'this increase is, generally speaking, of handsom large houses . . . being chiefly for the habitations of the richest citizens', and it was said of Carshalton in 1770 that there were many fine houses of citizens of London, 'some of which are built with such grandeur and expence that they might be rather taken for the seats of the nobility, than the country house of citizens and merchants'.[6] At the same time, from 1689 onwards, parliament met every year, so that the London winter season developed, and wealthy gentlemen from all over the country bought houses in the rapidly growing fashionable districts of the West End of London in order to spend four or five months of each year savouring the delights of the capital. The processes are immensely complex and vary over space and time. As new suburbs emerge, older ones sometimes descend the social scale. Covent Garden went downhill from the end of the seventeenth century, particularly after the establishment of the market in 1670, and Soho Square, one of its fashionable successors, went the same way at the end of the eighteenth century.[7]

The interiors of houses, the most private of private spaces, underwent important changes during the course of the eighteenth century. The hall ceases to be an all-purpose room and becomes only an entrance room. By the early eighteenth century it is usual to find a parlour on the ground floor, but not entered

[5] J. T. Smith, *English Houses: The Hertfordshire Evidence, 1200–1800* (London, 1992), pp. 162–6.

[6] D. Defoe, *A Tour through England and Wales*, ed. G. D. H. Cole (1724; repr. London, 1948), vol. I, p. 6; H. Chamberlain, *A New and Compleat History and Survey of the Cities of London and Westminster* (London, 1770), pp. 636–7.

[7] *Survey of London*, vol. XXXVI: *Parish of St Paul Covent Garden* (London, 1970), pp. 82 *et seq.*; *Survey of London*, vol. XXXIII: *St Anne Soho* (London, 1966), pp. 42 *et seq.*

directly from the street. Separate dining and withdrawing rooms appear, often on the first floor. Dinner as a meal was eaten later and later in the day and developed its own rituals. Men and women dined together, but the ladies then withdrew to the drawing room to prepare tea and coffee, leaving the gentlemen in the dining room to their port. As one French visitor remarked, 'Then the pleasure: there is not an Englishman who does not feel contented at that moment.'[8] Later, sometimes very much later, the men would rejoin the ladies in the drawing room. An even more exclusively male domain, the smoking room, appears early in the nineteenth century. Bed chambers become increasingly private and are often provided with closets. The kitchen is to be found in the basement, and servants' quarters are either there or else in the garrets. The larger the house the more extensive the stabling required, and the back lanes and side streets of the Grosvenor and Belgravia estates become a warren of stables, hay lofts and coach houses.

The external appearance of Scottish towns of the eighteenth century was quite unlike that of English towns. When Thomas Pennant visited Dunbar in 1769 he noted that the houses were built of stone, 'as is the case with most of the towns of Scotland', and he described Glasgow at the same date as 'the best built of any modern second-rate city I ever saw, the houses of stone, and in a good taste . . . many of the houses in the principal street are built over piazzas'.[9] Rebuilding in Scottish towns often lagged as much as a century behind that in English towns, and it is the last years of the eighteenth century before it takes place upon any scale. The contributors to *The Statistical Account of Scotland* in the 1790s note again and again how handsome new houses are rising every year; as at Crieff, where the new houses were almost universally of two storeys, with blue slate roofs; at Kinross, where between sixty and seventy houses had been added within the last thirty years; at Lanark, where roofs of turf and straw had been replaced with slate; at Thurso, where above twenty had been built within the last five years, 'some of them rather in a style of elegance for a country town'; and at Dumfries, where there were new houses of brick and red freestone.[10]

Houses of the middle ranks in society in Scottish cities, especially in Edinburgh, were usually composed of three or four rooms and a kitchen, normally to be found on one level in a tenement block. There is greater precision and uniformity in room names from the mid-eighteenth century. In the early eighteenth century the bed was the most valuable item of domestic furniture. By the end of the century it was the dining table and from the 1820s it was the piano, the outward manifestations of social transformation.[11]

[8] N. Scarfe, ed., *A Frenchman's Year in Suffolk* (Suffolk Records Society, 30, 1988), p. 23.

[9] T. Pennant, *A Tour in Scotland* (Warrington, 1769; repr. Perth, 1979), pp. 44, 230.

[10] *The Statistical Account of Scotland* (Edinburgh, 1791–9), vol. IX, p. 590, vol. VI, p. 165, vol. XV, p. 29, vol. XX, p. 493, vol. V, p. 123.

[11] See S. Nenadic, 'Middle rank consumers and domestic culture in Edinburgh and Glasgow, 1720–1840' *P&P*, 145 (1994), 122–56.

The results of these changes as far as English houses are concerned may be illustrated by advertisements from *The Times.* On Tuesday 2 January 1798 a genteel brick newly erected sashed messuage in the centre of Bedford was advertised. It had four parlours, a well-fitted kitchen, a good cellar, brewhouse and washhouse, ten bed chambers with closets, a laundry room, a stable with six stalls, a coach house, a pleasant garden with a new-built greenhouse, a kitchen garden and yard. A commodious pew in St Paul's Church gallery went with it. The division between home and work was by no means complete, however. *The Times* of Thursday 4 January 1798 carries an advertisement for a suite of elegant and commodious shops with modern sashed fronts at 149, Cheapside, a house with eight bed chambers with dressing rooms and closets, a handsome drawing room and dining parlour, and a distinct family entrance.

The building of new suburbs accelerates rapidly during the course of the century. The history of the Grosvenor Estate in London illustrates many of the problems and consequences of this movement.[12] It took two private acts of parliament of 1711 and 1726 to authorise the development of the estate. The landlord, Sir Richard Grosvenor, built the sewers at his own expense, although in due course he recovered this money, and he provided loans on mortgage to individual builders. The main lines of the estate were laid out on a lavish scale. Grosvenor Square itself covered eight acres, and the main east to west streets, Grosvenor and Brook Streets, were each sixty feet wide. Much of the actual building was carried out on a system of barter and many individual craftsmen were involved. The whole scheme took over fifty years to complete, with a long slack period in the 1740s and 1750s. The principal streets of the estate became increasingly fashionable but never socially exclusive. A survey of the inhabitants carried out in 1789–90 reveals thirty-one titled householders out of forty-seven in Grosvenor Square itself, but of the total number of inhabitants on the estate nearly 60 per cent were engaged in trade, following 120 different occupations, from muffin makers to herald painters, with a house of ill-fame in Norfolk, now Dunraven, Street, and seventy-five public houses.

Each suburban estate development is of course unique, but in almost every town across Britain, from Edinburgh and Glasgow to Bristol and Birmingham, many of the main themes of the development of the Grosvenor Estate repeat themselves. A private act of parliament was usually necessary to enable the leases to be granted. Much of the actual building was carried out on a small scale and took many years to complete, with the ability and indeed the willingness of the ground landlord to impose regular frontages growing only very slowly during the course of the century, and although many landlords hoped for social exclusiveness for their new estates it was almost impossible to secure or to maintain. Belgravia, almost from the first, was, and remained, socially very exclusive,

[12] See *Survey of London*, vol. XXXIX: *Grosvenor Estate in Mayfair, Part 1, General History* (London, 1977).

although for years it must have resembled a builder's yard, whereas Bloomsbury lost its social cachet from the 1820s onwards. Other estates, such as Somers Town, had no pretensions to gentility, and yet others quickly deteriorated, in Glasgow, for example, where Gorbals, a separate parish and barony to the south of the Clyde, was extensively feued out in the late eighteenth century. The Laurie brothers planned a middle-class suburb. Carlton Place was laid out in 1802, just as William Dixon, who owned an ironworks immediately to the south, built a wagon way across undeveloped land to a coaling quay on the Clyde. As a consequence Laurieston rapidly declined into some of the worst slums to be found anywhere in Britain.[13]

A new and distinctive kind of suburb begins to appear in the early nineteenth century, especially after 1815 and particularly around London. It is characterised by rows of detached and semi-detached houses built in an astonishing variety of styles, set wherever possible in gardens marked off by gates, fences and hedges from the neighbours. Privacy was all-important. The division of home from work now becomes complete, made easier by the introduction of the horse-drawn omnibus in 1829 linking the new suburbs in Paddington with the City. One consequence was the growing isolation of middle-class married women from their husband's working life.[14]

Housing for the 'industrious classes' was built to provide cheap, basic accommodation within walking distance of the place of employment. Population growth, often caused by immigration, combined with the increasing mechanisation of manufacturing processes, conspired to produce in some towns insanitary, ill-lit accommodation which came very slowly to be recognised as a national disgrace. In Nottingham by 1815 a distinctive working-class house type had already emerged. It was brick-built, with a cellar, a room to dwell in, a chamber and a work room over together with a cock-loft, in other words a four-room four-storey house.[15] Many were built back-to-back and drainage was almost non-existent. By 1812 there were already more than 300 courts in the town and the slums of Nottingham became notorious in the following decades. Such conditions were repeated, with local variations, wherever rapid industrial-

[13] See A. Gomme and D. Walker, *The Architecture of Glasgow* (London, 1968); R. Smith, 'Multi-dwelling building in Scotland, 1750–1970: a study based on housing in the Clyde valley', in A. Sutcliffe, ed., *Multi-Storey Living* (London, 1974), pp. 207–43; J. R. Kellet, 'Property speculation and the building of Glasgow, 1783–1830', *Scottish Journal of Political Economy*, 8 (1961), 211–32.

[14] See D. J. Olsen, *The Growth of Victorian London* (London, 1976), esp. p. 187 *et seq*., F. M. L. Thompson, 'The rise of suburbia', in R. J. Morris and R. Rodger, eds., *The Victorian City* (London, 1993), p. 149 *et seq*.; L. Davidoff and C. Hall, *Family Fortunes* (London, 1987), esp. ch. 8.

[15] S. D. Chapman, 'Working-class housing in Nottingham in the Industrial Revolution', *Thoroton Society*, 67 (1963), 67–92; S. D. Chapman, 'Working-class housing in Nottingham during the Industrial Revolution', in S. D. Chapman, ed., *The History of Working-Class Housing* (Newton Abbot, 1971), pp. 133–63; J. Blackner, *The History of Nottingham* (London, 1815), p. 66.

isation was taking place. Industrial housing is further discussed in Chapter 24. Industrialisation did bring some benefits, however. At Forfar, where the manufacture of osnaburghs had been introduced in about 1745 and since had grown considerably, thatched roofs were now, that is in 1792, scarcely to be seen. Instead new two-storey four-room houses were making their appearance, with garrets and accommodation for a loom. The prosperity that the new manufacture brought to the town meant that 'tea kettles, hand bellows and watches were now the necessary furniture of the poorest houses'.[16]

(iii) INSTITUTIONAL SPACE

Institutional space may still be divided into three kinds, but growth in the role of government, mounting technological innovation and cultural diversification led to dramatic change across all three, not least because the traditional urban hierarchy is turned upside down and the rapidly growing new industrial and commercial centres, particularly Liverpool, Glasgow, Manchester and Birmingham, develop their own patterns of institutional space, very quickly becoming important centres of business and cultural activities in their own right.

London and Edinburgh, as capital cities, performed a wider range of functions than any other places in Britain. London remained the principal residence of the monarch, and hence the main seat of government. The old Palace of Whitehall was all but destroyed by fire in 1698 and so the eighteenth-century monarchs made the Palace of St James their principal London residence until in 1762 George I bought Buckingham House as a residence for Queen Charlotte. It remained the Queen's House until 1820. In 1821, George IV, dissatisfied with the recently finished Carlton House, decided to pull it down, redevelop the site and move to Buckingham House. He employed John Nash to prepare new designs, which developed into a full-scale transformation into Buckingham Palace.[17]

By this time, however, the royal palaces had become purely residential. There was a slow but accelerating expansion of central government during the course of the eighteenth century and this led eventually to the erection of purpose-built government offices.[18] The site of the old Palace of Whitehall was progressively built over with them, beginning with the Admiralty in 1723–6, and the Treasury in 1733–6. One of the most splendid of government buildings followed upon the demolition of the sixteenth-century Somerset House. Rebuilding began in 1776 under the direction of Sir William Chambers, the surveyor-general, to

[16] *Statistical Account of Scotland*, VI, p. 516.

[17] Hobhouse, *Thomas Cubitt*, pp. 373–5, 394–5, and see also M. H. Port, 'Buckingham House' and 'Buckingham Palace', in H. M. Colvin, ed., *The History of the King's Works*, vol. VI: *1782–1851* (London, 1973), pp. 261–2 and 263–92.

[18] See M. H. Port, *Imperial London: Civil Government Building in London 1850–1915* (London, 1995).

house, *inter alia*, the Navy Office, the Duchy of Cornwall Office, the Exchequer Office, the Privy Seal Office, the Audit Office and the Stamp Office, as well as the Royal Society, the Royal Academy and the Society of Antiquaries. The Navy Office included some official residences, but in this it was unusual.[19] The journey to work became a normal experience of life for the great majority of those employed there.

In Edinburgh the Palace of Holyrood remained throughout the eighteenth century a block of exclusive flats for noblemen who had obtained grants of lodging there, the duke of Hamilton, for example, as hereditary keeper of the palace and the duke of Argyll as hereditary keeper of the household.[20] The palace came to life again only in 1822, with the visit of George IV to Scotland. The Act of Union of 1707 deprived Edinburgh not only of a resident monarch but also of its parliament. The parliament of Great Britain met in the ancient Palace of Westminster. This was almost totally destroyed by fire in 1832, to be replaced in due course by the new Victorian Gothic Houses of Parliament. Considerable rebuilding of the Scottish Parliament House in Edinburgh took place early in the nineteenth century when a new Exchequer Court, Signet Library, Advocates' Library and further accommodation for the Lords Ordinary and the Court of Session was built. Robert Adam provided some designs, but the work was actually carried out by Robert Reid.[21] It would be long before the English law courts were housed in such dignified surroundings.

Central government kept up naval dockyards at Woolwich, Chatham, Portsmouth and Plymouth, whilst the first purpose-built barracks erected anywhere in Britain were built at Berwick-upon-Tweed in 1719.[22] The maintenance of the fortifications of towns was the responsibility of the town authorities. Town walls and gates, once the pride of the corporation, were gradually recognised as impediments to the easy flow of trade and were demolished in the cause of urban improvement. At Perth it was reported in 1796 that the town had formerly been surrounded with high walls and towers but that the town had been for many years laid quite open, the last of the large towers, the Spey Tower, having been taken down some thirty years ago.[23] It took a private act of parliament, passed in 1807, to demolish the town walls of Carlisle, then ruinous and very inconvenient.[24] By the eighteenth century the North Gate at Oxford was a vaulted tunnel some seventy feet long, with a prison above it. It

[19] N. Pevsner, revised by B. Cherry, *The Buildings of England: London*, vol. I: *The Cities of London and Westminster* (Harmondsworth, 1985), pp. 332–5; see also J. M. Crook, 'Somerset House', in Colvin, ed., *The King's Works*, v, pp. 480–4.

[20] J. Gifford, C. McWilliam and D. Walker, eds., *The Buildings of Scotland: Edinburgh* (Harmondsworth, 1984), pp. 128–9.

[21] *Ibid.*, pp. 118–25.

[22] H. Tomlinson, 'The Ordnance Office and the king's ports, 1660–1714', *Architectural History*, 16 (1973), 5–25. N. Pevsner, *The Buildings of England: Northumberland* (Harmondsworth, 1957), p. 90.

[23] *Statistical Account of Scotland*, XVIII, p. 529.

[24] D. R. Perriam, 'The demolition of Carlisle city walls', *Transactions of the Cumberland and Westmorland Antiquarian and Archaeological Society*, new series, 76 (1976), 184–98.

was demolished in 1771 by the paving commissioners. When John Byng visited the town in 1781 he thought that 'the old gateways to the town, which added dignity to the entrance, and bespoke it to have been a place of arms, and antiquity, might have been preserv'd'.[25] At Chester, however, as Thomas Pennant noted in 1769, 'the walls of the city . . . are kept in excellent order, being the principal walk of the inhabitants: the views from the several parts are very fine'.[26]

Customs houses were to be found in both coastal and inland ports. The Custom House in London has its own complex history. It was destroyed in the Great Fire and then rebuilt to designs by Sir Christopher Wren. This was burned down again in 1718, rebuilt, destroyed once more by fire in 1814 and again rebuilt.[27] In provincial port towns the stock of customs houses was added to, rebuilt and extended, with the result that the physical presence of central government was similarly extended. The Old Customs House at Gloucester and that at Peterborough were both built in about 1700. That at Lancaster was described by an enthusiastic Thomas Pennant in 1769 as 'a small but most elegant building, with a portico supported by four ionic pillars, on a beautiful plain pediment . . . a work that does much credit to Mr Gillow, the architect, an inhabitant of this town'.[28]

The administration of justice at a local level was carried on in shire and county halls built and maintained by the county justices in county towns. They were used for meetings of county quarter sessions and of the assizes, and often also contained ball rooms and assembly rooms. The Shire Hall at Hertford was built in 1768–9 to classical designs by John Adam, since, like all public buildings of the eighteenth century, from the new buildings for the Royal Mint erected on Tower Hill from 1807 to the new Guildhall built in Queenborough in 1793, shire halls shared in the prevailing fashion for classical architecture.

The range of public buildings was much extended during the course of the eighteenth and early nineteenth centuries. In York, for example, the 1720s and 1730s see the building of the Mansion House, the Judges' Lodgings and the Assembly Rooms. In the 1770s the Women's Prison, Assize Court and County Lunatic Asylum were built.[29] Institutions providing for the mentally ill were for centuries almost non-existent. Bethlehem Hospital, for the care of the insane, was founded just outside Bishopsgate in 1247, but it was unique. A handful of county asylums were built in the late eighteenth century, but it was the Lunacy Act of 1808 which precipitated the building of asylums in county towns throughout the country. Institutional space was becoming both more extensive and more varied.

Within towns themselves the symbol of the authority of the corporation

[25] *VCH*, Oxfordshire, IV, pp. 302–3; C. B. Andrews, ed., *The Torrington Diaries* (London, 1934), vol. I, p. 5. [26] Pennant, *A Tour in Scotland*, p. 2.

[27] T. H. Shepherd and J. Elmes, *Metropolitan Improvements* (London, 1827–31; repr. New York, 1968), pp. 132–3. [28] Pennant, *A Tour in Scotland*, p. 261.

[29] See K. Downes, *The Georgian Cities of Britain* (Oxford, 1979), p. 9; *VCH*, City of York, p. 535.

continued to be the town hall (see Plate 24). These were built and rebuilt during the course of the eighteenth century. Primarily erected to provide a meeting room for the town council, they could serve a number of other functions – to house the town records and treasure, as a court room and gaol, as a school, market house, theatre and assembly room. By the end of the seventeenth century they were being built according to the rules of classical architecture. By the first years of the nineteenth they share in that dissolution of accepted standards and practice which is characteristic of architecture generally at the time, and by 1840 they could be built in a wide variety or medley of styles, and occasionally in none.

In the tollbooth, the Scottish equivalent, the principal rooms were often on the first floor, which was reached by an external stair (see Plate 10). There was also usually a clock tower, and internally the ceilings were sometimes painted.[30] In Stirling the Town House was rebuilt in 1703–5 to designs by Sir William Bruce, to provide one of the earliest Scottish town houses to be treated in the classical style, although it retained the traditional steeple. The functions of a tollbooth were summarised in 1798 in the account of that at Banff, where the foundations of a new Town House were laid 'last season'. It was to house the sheriff court and the county record office as well as a council room, the town clerk's office, two houses of correction and two civil prisons.[31]

Some corporations took an active part in building and development within their town, almost always with an eye to improvements in trade. Others played little part at all and such amelioration of the urban environment as took place was almost entirely the work of groups of private citizens, usually with powers conferred by a private act of parliament. Liverpool corporation promoted turnpike trusts in order to improve access to coal mines, and obtained the act of parliament for the building of the Sankey Brook canal, with the same objective. At Bristol, however, the corporation dithered for fifty years over plans to improve the port, which was rapidly becoming choked with shipping. Successive plans were shelved, and it was 1803 before a private act of parliament was finally obtained for a New Cut and floating harbour. In Hull an act of parliament was obtained in 1774 for the building of a new dock. It was to be run by a private company, but the corporation took ten shares each of £500. Two further docks were built and together these had a profound influence upon the subsequent layout of Hull, since they formed an arc joining the Humber and the Hull rivers, encircling the old heart of the town.[32]

30 G. Stell, 'The earliest tolbooths, a preliminary account', *Proceedings of the Society of Antiquaries of Scotland*, 111 (1981), 445–53. 31 *Statistical Account of Scotland*, XX, pp. 366–7.

32 F. A. Bailey, 'The minutes of the trustees of the turnpike roads from Liverpool to Prescott, St Helens, Warrington and Ashton in Makerfield, 1726–1789, Part 1, 1726–1753', *Transactions of the Historical Society of Lancashire and Cheshire*, 88 (1936), 159 *et seq.*; A. F. Williams, 'Bristol port plans and improvement schemes of the eighteenth century', *Transactions of the Bristol and Gloucestershire Archaeological Society*, 81 (1962), 138–88; *VCH*, Yorkshire: East Riding, I, pp. 186 *et seq.*

Some corporations paved their streets and made half-hearted attempts to suppress nuisances, but resources were limited and effective technical knowledge almost non-existent. It was improvement commissioners, sometimes called Police Commissioners, appointed under private acts of parliament for individual towns, who really brought about improvements in paving, lighting, cleansing and policing the streets of their own towns. Indeed, in some towns, the improvement commissioners formed the only effective local authority, in Manchester, for example, where they cleansed and paved the streets, numbered the houses, made some attempt to regulate water supplies and in 1817 built a gas works.

There were eventually about 400 improvement acts for provincial towns in England, and a further 150 for London.[33] A number of Scottish towns also obtained them, Aberdeen, for example, in 1795.[34] Such improvement acts present an almost endless diversity of constitution, powers, membership and effectiveness. In addition to paving, lighting and cleansing the streets, the commissioners could regulate hackney coaches and sedan chairs, name streets and number houses, build sewers, market houses and slaughterhouses and maintain fire engines, but their efforts depended very much upon the enthusiasm of individual commissioners and in any case their attention was often confined only to the main streets of their town. Nevertheless, slowly and with much hesitation, conditions in some towns began to improve.

Until the invention of the Newcomen steam engine the only sources of mechanical power were wind and water mills. Few sixteenth- and seventeenth-century towns were without at least one of both kinds. By the early eighteenth century water power in particular was being applied to a wide range of industrial processes. The stream which flowed through Halifax was said to power eleven corn mills, eight fulling mills, two mills for the grinding of wood for dyers, one for making paper used by clothworkers, a shear-grinder's forge and one for frizing cloth.[35] Water mills evolved into factories as the number of people working in them increased and as the machinery became more complex. Their location was determined by the presence of a suitable stream to provide the motive power, so that the earliest factories were by no means always to be found in towns. One of the first urban factories must have been Thomas Cotchett's silk-throwing mill at Derby, built in about 1704 on the banks of the River Derwent. John Byng visited the Derby silk mills in 1789, writing 'the silk mills quite bewildered me; such rattlings and twistings! Such heat, and stinks! that I was glad to get out: we shou'd be full as happy, if silk worms had never been.'[36]

Only when the steam engine was adapted to provide rotary motion could it be used in textile factories, which of necessity had to be as close as possible to adequate supplies of coal (see Plate 30). The result was the growth of new towns

[33] See above, p. 536. [34] *Statistical Account of Scotland*, XIX, p. 168.

[35] J. Watson, *The History and Antiquities of the Parish of Halifax* (London, 1775), p. 68.

[36] Andrews, ed., *The Torrington Diaries*, II, p. 62.

at a pace which contemporaries found breath-taking. Thus, when John Byng visited Stockport in 1790 he wrote,

> astonishing is the increase of buildings about this town, and they go on most rapidly; (Stockport contain'd about 10 years since, about 700 houses, now they exceed 2,000, which are insufficient to hold the inhabitants) . . . Where the old castle stood, are cotton works built in a castellated stile, with battlements, etc., looking like one of the grandest prisons in the world. All the houses of this town were formerly built of oaken timber; this, now, in general, has given way to brick.[37]

By the 1840s churches were no longer the most prominent buildings in such towns as Manchester and Leeds, Oldham and Coventry, Bradford and Paisley. Their traditional dominance of the skyline had been displaced by the factory chimney. The Scottish linen industry made its own unique contribution to the urban environment. Linen requires to be bleached and bleach fields were laid out either by the manufacturers or by the municipal authorities. There was, for example, one at Banff, another at Thurso and at Perth there were four public bleach fields.[38]

But the factory was by no means the only new building type produced by technological innovation. William Murdock, employed in the Soho works of Messrs Boulton and Watt, had succeeded in lighting the foundry there by gas in 1803. The use of gas to light the streets of towns spread very quickly. The Gas Light and Coke Company was laying gas mains in Pall Mall for house lighting in 1814.[39] By 1830 only a handful of towns with more than 10,000 inhabitants did not have at least their main streets lit by gas, replacing with dramatic effect the lamps using train oil which had been used from the first years of the eighteenth century.[40] When the paving commissioners of High Wycombe eventually provided a gas lamp in 1832 it was, a contemporary wrote, 'a revelation . . . the light rendered by this lamp has rendered nearly useless those which are close to it'.[41] The accompanying gas holders and street lamps are entirely new building forms and lamp lighter a new occupation.[42]

The act of parliament authorising the construction of the Sankey Brook canal was passed in 1755 and the canal itself was open by November of 1757. Wharves, warehouses and locks appeared as the canal system evolved, together with some

[37] *Ibid.*, p. 179. [38] *Statistical Account of Scotland*, XX, pp. 356 and 516, XVIII, p. 516.

[39] *The Survey of London*, vol. XXIX: *St James Westminster, Part 1, South of Piccaddilly* (London, 1960), pp. 352–3.

[40] See E. L. Jones and M. E. Falkus, 'Urban improvement and the English economy in the seventeenth and eighteenth centuries', in P. Borsay, ed., *The Eighteenth Century Town* (London, 1990), pp. 133–4.

[41] Quoted in L. J. Ashford, *The History of the Borough of High Wycombe from its Origins to 1880* (London, 1960), p. 274.

[42] M. E. Falkus, 'The British gas industry before 1850', *Ec.HR*, 2nd series, 20 (1967), 494–508.

astonishing feats of civil engineering, the Barton aqueduct, for example. The first passenger railway in the world was opened on 15 September 1830 for traffic between Liverpool and Manchester, creating another entirely new building form. Railway stations were built at both ends of the line, and that in Manchester still survives. By 1852 the only major towns in England without a railway station were Hereford, Yeovil and Weymouth. Both canal and railway companies created their own towns, complete with houses, churches, schools and gas works, as at Runcorn, Grangemouth and Goole for example, and at Crewe and Wolverton.[43]

If the coming of the factory meant a sharp discontinuity in the traditional patterns of life in some towns during the last decades of the eighteenth century, many other trades and professions continued to be domestically based. Specialised business and commercial buildings make their appearance only very slowly. Designs for merchants' houses made in 1724 have, in one example, a central vestibule, with a compter immediately to the left and a private parlour behind it, and on the right a withdrawing room and a parlour behind that.[44]

The Bank of England opened for business on 27 July 1694 in rented premises in Mercer's Hall, Cheapside, with a staff of seventeen clerks and two gatekeepers. In 1724 it bought an estate in Threadneedle Street, including the house of Sir John Houblon, its first governor, and in January 1732 it decided to build new offices on its Threadneedle property. The new premises, probably the first purpose-built bank in the world, opened for business on 5 June 1734.[45] Further additions were made which, it was said in 1770, when finished will make it 'in all probability . . . the most magnificent building of a public nature in the whole universe'.[46] In contrast, James Oakes, a successful businessman of Bury St Edmunds, engaged John Soane to add two new wings to his substantial five-bay house in Guildhall Street in Bury St Edmunds. The northern wing was built to serve as a banking office, with a dining room over in which to entertain customers on market days. The rest of the house remained his private residence.[47]

Purpose-built commercial premises were still something of a rarity, even in 1840. The first office building in London designed as such seems to be the County Fire Office, completed in 1819.[48] The creation of the central business district, composed of non-residential shops and offices, had scarcely begun in

43 D. Semple, 'The growth of Grangemouth', *Scottish Geographical Magazine*, 74 (1958), 78–85; D. K. Drummond, *Crewe: Railway Town, Company and People, 1840–1914* (Aldershot, 1995).

44 K. Downes, 'The King's Weston book of drawings', *Architectural History*, 10 (1967), 9–88, esp. figs. 76 and 80. The doll's house made for Petronella Oortman in about 1695 and now in the Rijksmuseum in Amsterdam has a similar arrangement.

45 R. Roberts and D. Kynaston, eds., *The Bank of England* (Oxford, 1995), pp. 225–7; also N. Pevsner, *A History of Building Types* (London, 1976), p. 201.

46 Chamberlain, *A New and Compleat History*, p. 473.

47 J. Fiske, ed., *The Oakes Diaries*, vol. 1 (Suffolk Records Society, 32, 1990), pp. 71–2.

48 Pevsner, *A History of Building Types*, p. 213.

1840, even in London, where the City had 128,000 inhabitants in 1801, and 123,000 in 1841, but only 112,000 by 1861. The City was still a place in which to live as well as to work.

Markets and fairs have been significant users of urban space for centuries, combining business and pleasure (see Plate 25), but even these ancient institutions did not escape change. They continued to be held in many towns throughout the eighteenth and nineteenth centuries, but the commercial importance of some fairs declined considerably during the century as they became 'toy' or 'pleasure' fairs. Many markets continued, but they were increasingly concerned with basic foodstuffs and other commodities at the lower end of domestic demand, whilst retail shops came to monopolise the more expensive and luxury end. A leap forward in market hall design came in 1827, with the erection of Covent Garden Market to designs by Charles Fowler. He made effective use of iron in its construction and it set the pattern for many new market halls of the nineteenth century, in Birmingham, for example, where Charles Edge designed a building with two main entrances flanked by enormous Doric columns.[49]

Shopping arcades and department stores make their appearance at the beginning of the nineteenth century. The Burlington Arcade was built between 1815 and 1819, and James Foster built two arcades in Bristol, leading from St James Barton to Broadmead, in 1825 (see Plate 15). Charles Fortnum opened his shop in Piccadilly in about 1770. Dickens and Jones was founded in 1803, Swan and Edgar in 1812, Kendal Milne in Manchester in 1831 and Marshall and Snelgrove in 1837.[50]

Inns continue to be important throughout this period. Well before the end of the seventeenth century many of the inns of London were developing regional connections. Thus inns in Aldersgate Street became markets for meal from Bedfordshire and Hertfordshire and the Bell in Friday Street was the terminus for carriers from Gloucestershire.[51] Daniel Defoe, when he visited Northampton in the 1720s, found the George, a great inn at the corner of the High Street, 'more like a palace than an inn'. The town was, he thought, the centre of all the horse markets and horse fairs in England, a trade which could only have added to the prosperity of the inn. He thought both Grantham and Stamford were famous for their abundance of very good inns, 'a great advantage to the place'.[52] In the last decades of the eighteenth century some of the better inns were being transformed into hotels.[53] William Hutton, writing in 1781, notes the erection in 1772 at the head of Temple Row, in Birmingham, of a new building called Hotel.[54]

[49] *VCH*, Warwickshire, VII, p. 43.

[50] D. J. Olsen, *The Growth of Victorian London* (London, 1976), p. 122.

[51] J. A. Chartres, 'The capital's provincial eyes: London's inns in the early eighteenth century', *LJ*, 3 (1977), 24–39.

[52] Defoe, *A Tour through England and Wales*, II, pp. 86 and 103.

[53] P. Clark, *The English Alehouse* (London, 1983), p. 10.

[54] W. Hutton, *A History of Birmingham to the End of the Year 1780* (Birmingham, 1781), p. 131.

Claridge's and Brown's hotels, both in London, date from the early nineteenth century, and the first railway hotel, the Midland, was opened in Derby in 1840, by which time alehouses, hitherto ordinary dwelling houses, were being replaced by purpose-built public houses and these became increasingly extravagant in their design and appearance, with gas lamps, clocks, large glass windows and polished brass fittings.[55]

The rapid growth in coaching, more especially from the 1780s, brought more and more people on to the roads, whether for business or for pleasure, since tourism also expands dramatically in the second half of the eighteenth century. In many respects this is the golden age of the stage-coach and hence of the coaching inn, whether in town or country. It collapses dramatically with the coming of the railway in the 1830s and 1840s. John Byng was an incurable traveller during the 1780s and 1790s, and he made acid comments on the inns in which he stayed. 'Most inns, now,' he wrote in 1790, 'are kept by, and for a change of post horses, as fine gentlemen never step out of their chaises in the longest journies; and others travell in the mail, or post coaches: so that the tourist who wants only a supper, and a bed, is consider'd as a troublesome unprofitable intruder'.[56]

The cultural functions of towns became increasingly diversified during the course of the eighteenth century, and this is reflected in an equally wide range of building types, themselves a function of the place of the individual town in the urban hierarchy. So diversified is the cultural life of towns by the 1840s that it is impossible to give a satisfactory account of every facet, but some generalisations are possible.

First of all the new provincial centres, towns such as Manchester, Liverpool and Birmingham, develop their own distinctive cultural life, taking pride in being independent of London. Thus the Liverpool Royal Institution was founded in 1814 with a grant of £1,000 from the corporation, its founding collections being those amassed by William Roscoe, the failed Liverpool banker whose *Life* of Lorenzo de Medici achieved a European reputation.[57] Secondly, even the smallest of provincial towns had some informal group or club with ostensibly 'cultural' pretensions, although in practice they were often more convivial than anything else. Forfar, for example, was said in 1793 to be a place of resort for the enjoyment of society in clubs and assemblies.[58] Finally, 'popular' as opposed to 'polite' culture, insofar as this is a valid or sustainable distinction, continued to flourish and often came to have its own distinctive building forms. The grandstand at the Knavesmore race course at York was built in 1754 and that at Doncaster in 1776. Thomas Lord established a private cricket ground in Dorset Square, London, and the Marylebone Cricket Club, founded in 1787, made its headquarters there. He moved to the present site of Lord's Cricket Ground in

[55] Clark, *English Alehouse*, pp. 273–7. [56] Andrews, ed., *The Torrington Diaries*, III, p. 314.

[57] E. Morris, 'The formation of the Gallery of Art in the Liverpool Royal Institution, 1816–1819', *Transactions of the Historic Society of Lancashire and Cheshire*, 142 (1993), 87–98.

[58] *Statistical Account of Scotland*, VI, p. 522.

1813, taking with him his precious turf. The cock-pit in Edinburgh was said in 1790 to be much frequented.[59]

Clubs and societies of every kind proliferate in towns from the end of the seventeenth century (see Plate 20). A French visitor wrote:

> Clubs are established in England in every province of the realm, in every town and every country district . . . Those in the capital are nothing more than associations for debauchery and expense, etc. . . . Clubs of a more useful kind, and which are more widespread, . . . are associations of people who are experts and amateurs in the same art or useful science.[60]

Initially they almost always met in inns or taverns or in private houses. By the end of the eighteenth century purpose-built premises begin to make their appearance, in London and Edinburgh at first. White's, in London, dates from 1787, Boodle's from 1775 and Brooks's from 1778. The Athenaeum was founded in 1824 and its splendid building dates from 1828, whilst the New Club at Edinburgh was built in 1834, and the masonic hall in Bath, designed by Wilkins in Greek revival style, dates from 1817.[61]

In the early nineteenth century many other towns, large and small, acquired similar buildings and these in turn became more and more specialised as cultural entertainments themselves became more diverse. The Bridport Literary and Scientific Institute was built in 1834, the Liverpool Lyceum club dates from 1800–2 and the Camborne Literary Institute was built in 1829. One of the most elegant concert rooms of the eighteenth century, St Cecilia's Hall, was built in 1761–3 in the Cowgate, Edinburgh, for the Musical Society of Edinburgh.

The number of provincial theatres grows rapidly during the course of the eighteenth century. The town hall in Sheffield was let to players in 1727. A playhouse was built in the yard of the Angel inn in 1730 and a theatre and assembly rooms were built by subscription in 1762.[62] The history of the provincial theatre is thus neatly encapsulated. It was rebuilt in 1773, and when John Byng visited it in 1789 he found it 'a neat, well-built theatre, and they say it will hold, at the advanced prices of next week, £100, for then Mrs Siddons will act here'. On the other hand, when he visited the theatre in Buxton he found it 'a mean, dirty boarded, thatched house; and can hold but few people'.[63] There was no theatre in Hastings in 1824 'to prevent the demoralisation of the lower classes', but there was a small one about a mile and a half from the town and one in the town was planned.[64] At Dumfries a theatre was said to be in the course of construction in 1793, whilst the town was already accommodated with 'an elegant suit of assembly rooms'.[65]

[59] *Ibid.*, p. 615. [60] Scarfe, ed., *A Frenchman's Year*, pp. 188–9.

[61] Ison, *Georgian Buildings of Bath*, p. 44.

[62] F. T. Wood, 'Sheffield theatres in the eighteenth century', *Transactions of the Hunter Archaeological Society*, 6 (1946), 98–116. [63] Andrews, ed., *The Torrington Diaries*, II, pp. 25, 134, 188.

[64] W. G. Moss, *The History and Antiquities of the Town and Port of Hastings* (London, 1824), p. 156.

[65] *Statistical Account of Scotland*, V, p. 124.

Assembly rooms became an essential focus for the social life of very many towns during the course of the eighteenth century (see Plate 19). All large towns and very many small ones came to have them, and they continued to be built until almost the end of the nineteenth century, those at Tamworth dating from 1889. Their functions are admirably described in the account of the assemblies at Nottingham given by Charles Deering in 1751. There were, he wrote, two monthly assemblies for the genteel part of the town for both sexes, where the younger divert themselves with dancing, whilst the senior or graver part enjoy themselves over a game of quadrille or whist. One of these places was in Low Pavement, built purposely, a handsome, lofty and spacious room, with a gallery for the music at the upper end. The room was sixty-seven feet long by twenty-one wide, with two withdrawing rooms and a place where a person attends who sells all kinds of refreshments. There was also a tradesmen's assembly room at Thurland Hall in Gridlesmith Gate.[66] Thus are the social distinctions nicely preserved.

The most splendid assembly rooms erected anywhere in Britain must surely be those at York, designed by the earl of Burlington and built between 1730 and 1735. Francis Drake published a view, plan and elevation of the Aedes Concentus Eboracensis in his *Eboracum* in 1736. However, when John Byng went to see them in 1792 he thought Lord Burlington 'surely the most tasteless Vitruvius, and has left the saddest Egyptian Halls, and woeful walls to record his invention!'.[67]

The first museum to be built in Britain was the Ashmolean, built in Oxford between 1678 and 1683. The library of books and manuscripts collected by Sir Robert Cotton before his death in 1631 was described in an act of parliament of 1700 as 'the best of its kind now extant'. A disastrous fire in 1731 was eventually followed by an act of parliament of 1753 to found the British Museum, where the Cotton library could be housed. A lottery raised £10,000 to buy the manuscripts collected by the earl of Oxford and a further sum was raised to buy Montagu House, in Bloomsbury, as a home for the museum.[68] The magnificent Ionic colonnade which now adorns the façade to Great Russell Street was designed by Sir Robert Smirke in 1823 but it was not finished until 1847. Other museums followed only very slowly. The Yorkshire Museum opened in 1830,[69] Saffron Walden Museum in 1834 and Scarborough Museum was built 1828–9.

Art galleries are even later in making their appearance. The National Gallery in London was begun only in 1832 to house the collection of paintings formed by John Angerstein, a wealthy Lloyds underwriter, after his death in 1823.[70] The

66 G. C. Deering, *Nottinghamia Vetus et Nova* (Nottingham, 1751), p. 75.

67 Andrews, ed., *The Torrington Diaries*, III, p. 36.

68 See J. M. Crook, 'The British Museum', in Colvin, ed., *The King's Works*, V, pp. 403–20.

69 RCHM (England), *York*, vol. V: *Historic Buildings of the Central Area* (London, 1981), p. 166.

70 M. H. Port, 'The National Gallery', in Colvin, ed., *The King's Works*, V, pp. 461–70.

government paid £57,000 for his collection and it was opened to the public in what had been his private house, 100, Pall Mall. It was at first proposed that the National Gallery, as this collection was now called, should be housed in the new buildings of the British Museum then being erected to take the library of George III, but it was eventually decided that a site to the north of Charing Cross, then being developed as Trafalgar Square, should be used for an entirely new building.[71] This was finally completed, to rather weak neo-classical designs by William Wilkins, and opened in 1838. The National Gallery in Edinburgh was not begun until 1848.

Museums and art galleries in other towns and cities in Britain were very slow to appear. Lord Fitzwilliam made his bequest to the University of Cambridge in 1815, but it was 1848 before temporary buildings were provided. Sir Peter Bourgeois bequeathed his collection to Dulwich College in 1810 and a gallery was opened in 1817. The Liverpool Royal Institution was founded in 1814 and thirty-seven paintings, almost all from the collections of William Roscoe, were put on exhibition in 1819.

At the same time traditional centres of cultural life continued to have a major impact upon the urban landscape. Church building and rebuilding was more common throughout Britain in the eighteenth century than is generally thought, but the fabric of many existing churches was sometimes neglected.[72] The building of new churches (see Plate 21) failed to keep up with patterns of population growth and movement. New parishes were formed to take some account of this and some parishes were amalgamated, but such action was often too little and too late. By the last years of the eighteenth century it was clear that the Church of England was in crisis. There were not enough seats in church for the population of such towns as Manchester and Oldham, Wolverhampton and Bolton. In 1818 the New Churches Act was passed, allocating £1,000,000 for the building of new churches. By 1834, 134 new ones had been erected,[73] often in a sad, rather spindly, imitation Gothic style, but in spite of every endeavour building simply could not keep up with population trends.

The passage of the Toleration Act in 1689 saw the proliferation of nonconformist sects and the building of meeting houses and chapels to accommodate them. The sects themselves were often riven by internal dissent, and splinter groups formed and reformed, so that the denomination of any one chapel could change with sometimes bewildering rapidity. The fragmentation to which Christianity had been brought by the end of the eighteenth century may be illustrated by the example of Aberdeen, in 1797 a city of 16,000 inhabitants. It had

[71] F. Owen, 'Sir George Beaumont and the National Gallery', in *'Noble and Patriotic': The Beaumont Gift, 1828* (London, 1988), pp. 7 *et seq*.

[72] Norwich Cathedral was in a deplorable state by mid-eighteenth century. See I. Atherton, *et al.*, *Norwich Cathedral* (London, 1996), p. 598.

[73] E. R. Norman, *Church and Society in England, 1770–1970* (Oxford, 1976), pp. 53–4.

two parish churches and five chapels of ease, three English and two Scottish Episcopalian churches, one chapel for Burghers, one for Anti-Burghers, one Relief, one Roman Catholic, one Methodist, one for Bereans, one for Independents and one for Quakers.[74]

Toleration *de jure* was not extended to Roman Catholics until 1829, although a Relief Act of 1791 permitted worship in registered places. The result was that until the very end of the eighteenth century Roman Catholic churches and chapels were often to be found in private houses and even when purpose-built ones were erected they were at first deliberately kept inconspicuous.

Almshouses continued to be built throughout the eighteenth and well into the nineteenth centuries. A new development from this traditional method of providing for the elderly infirm makes its appearance in the eighteenth century. The first voluntary hospital devoted exclusively to the care of the sick was opened in 1720. This, the Westminster Infirmary, was quickly followed in London with Guy's Hospital (1726), St George's (1733), the London Hospital (1740) and the Middlesex Hospital (1745). The first one opened outside London was the Edinburgh Hospital for the Sick Poor, opened in 1729. Provincial infirmaries then follow, with Winchester in 1736 and Bristol in 1737, so that by the end of the eighteenth century twenty-eight infirmaries had been opened in provincial towns.[75] They were often financed by public subscription, like the General Hospital at Hereford, started in this way by Dr Thomas Talbot in 1783. The Infirmary in Hull was opened in 1782 in a house in George Street. It moved two years later to new buildings, a brick-built block fifteen bays wide and three storeys high, a building which took thirty years to complete.[76] An infirmary was founded in Aberdeen in 1739 and a dispensary was established in 1781. The infirmary in Dumfries was established in 1777, and that in Glasgow was said in 1793 to be just begun.[77]

Institutional space was transformed between 1700 and 1840. Entirely new kinds of buildings make their appearance, from gas works to railway stations, from asylums to theatres, with the result that the proportion of urban space given over to institutional use shows a significant increase during the period.

(iv) PUBLIC SPACE

Public space, composed of the streets and squares of a town, was managed, more or less, by municipal corporations, although there is an increasingly significant contribution from private landlords and statutory authorities. Municipal

[74] *Statistical Account of Scotland*, XIX, p. 185.

[75] See J. Lane, 'Worcester Infirmary in the eighteenth century', *Worcestershire Historical Society*, Occasional Publications, 6 (Worcester, 1992), p. 1; and G. B. Risse, *Hospital Life in Enlightenment Scotland* (Cambridge, 1986), pp. 19–20.

[76] *VCH*, Yorkshire: East Riding, I, p. 383.

[77] *Statistical Account of Scotland*, XIX, pp. 188, 193, V, pp. 127, 524.

authorities in England, with only a few exceptions, took a very narrow view of their responsibilities, normally confining themselves either to providing certain basic facilities, such as a market, or else to checking nuisances. In many towns in Scotland, however, the dean of guild came to exercise a wide control over 'neighbourhood', so that by 1698 Edinburgh, for example, had a coherent body of building regulations aimed primarily at preventing fire. By 1715 the city had a special committee on public works. Of the sixty-six royal burghs in Scotland forty-one eventually came to have a dean of guild and their practices owed much to the example of Edinburgh. By the early decades of the nineteenth century, however, their powers were declining, so that by 1868 only twelve were still in operation.[78]

Streets themselves were paved, particularly the main ones in a town, sometimes by householders fronting the street under threat of fine by the town council, sometimes by the council itself employing paviours and charging the cost to householders. Neither method was at all satisfactory, and so the management of this public space was increasingly transferred to improvement commissioners, whose powers and effectiveness have already been discussed. They could have considerable influence over the public space of the towns for which they were acting. It was the commissioners appointed under the 1791 Paving Act for Chichester, for example, who moved the gutters from the middle to the sides of the streets in that town, and those for Southampton, working under the Paving Act passed in 1770, who had street names painted on boards and houses numbered.[79]

New street forms make their appearance in the eighteenth century. The crescent and the circle, even if not the actual invention of John Wood senior, were first used on any scale in the new suburbs which he laid out to the north of the medieval city of Bath, but, although they were much admired, they were also a long time building, so that their full impact could not be appreciated much before the 1760s, and their influence upon town planning elsewhere in Britain was slow to take effect. Wood began the King's Circus in 1754, the year of his death, and his son began the Royal Crescent, the most splendid building in Bath, in 1767.[80] The Crescent in Buxton was built to designs by John Carr between 1779 and 1781. Atholl Place was laid out as a crescent in Perth at the very end of the eighteenth century. The Royal Circle in Edinburgh was built between 1820 and 1823 and Lewes Crescent, Kemp Town, Brighton, was planned in about 1825.

The movement, already discernible at the end of the seventeenth century and discussed in Chapter 9, to improve appearances and amenities in towns gathers

[78] R. G. Rodger, 'The evolution of Scottish town planning', in G. Gordon and B. Dicks, eds., *Scottish Urban History* (Aberdeen, 1983), pp. 71–91.

[79] A. Temple Patterson, *A History of Southampton, 1700–1914*, vol. I: *An Oligarchy in Decline, 1700–1835* (Southampton, 1966), p. 49.

[80] See Ison, *Georgian Buildings of Bath*, pp. 32–4.

momentum during the course of the eighteenth century, impelled either by purely practical reasons, better paved streets were good for business, or else by conscious civic pride, itself sometimes driven by personal rivalries. The duke of Rutland remodelled much of Bakewell from about 1800, replacing timber-framed buildings with stone ones and laying out gardens in an attempt to emulate the improvements being made by the duke of Devonshire in Buxton.[81] The *Proposals* of 1752, which led eventually to the building of Edinburgh New Town, were largely the work of George Drummond, lord provost of the city on at least five occasions. They contrasted the 'neatness and accommodation' of the private houses in London, 'the beauty and conveniency of its numerous streets and squares . . . its large parks and extensive walks' with the 'steepness, narrowness and dirtiness of the lanes' of Edinburgh, 'the height of the buildings, leading to a great want of free air, light, cleanliness, and every other comfortable accommodation' and the 'great deficiency of public buildings'. The final accomplishment of the scheme owed a great deal to Drummond's determination and commitment to improving the appearance of the city.[82]

Other improvements were less ambitious. The New Walk in Lichfield on the south side of the Minster Pool was laid out in 1772.[83] At Stirling a noble walk along the summit of the rock, at the very foot of the south wall, from one end of the town to the other, shaded from the sun by a thicket of fine thriving trees, was said, in 1793, to have been lately finished at considerable expense.[84] It was written of Perth in 1769 that it 'is large and in general well-built: two of the streets are remarkably fine: in some of the lesser are yet a few wooden houses in the old style; but as they decay, the magistrates prohibit the rebuilding them in the old way'.[85] The corporation of Doncaster was described in 1750 as being very rich.

> They have laid out lately £1,000 on a mansion house only for publick dinners and assemblies, besides offices and other convenient rooms; there is one which is sixty foot long and thirty wide and high. There are three windows like those of the banqueting house, with galleries to each, which rests on the rustick story below, at the angles and between the windows are couples of Corinthian pillars, which support a pediment of the wideth of the building.[86]

The range and architectural pretensions of public buildings are clearly accelerating rapidly by the last half of the eighteenth century.

There were even some tentative beginnings towards street embellishment. The monument commemorating the Great Fire was erected in London between

81 J. T. Leach, 'Buxton and the Cavendish families', *Derbyshire Archaeological Journal*, 108 (1988), 54–65.

82 Youngson, *Making of Classical Edinburgh*, *passim*, esp. pp. 16–17.

83 *VCH*, Staffordshire, XIV, p. 163.

84 *Statistical Account of Scotland*, VIII, p. 275.

85 Pennant, *A Tour of Scotland*, p. 75.

86 J. J. Cartwright, ed., *The Travels Through England of Dr Richard Pococke*, vol. I (Camden Society, new series, 42, 1888), p. 183.

1671 and 1677 to designs by Sir Christopher Wren. In Bristol a statue of Neptune was erected in about 1723 in the middle of Temple Street at the conduit head where water from a spring at Totterdown came into the city. The inhabitants of Lewes decided in 1786 to build a new tower to house the town clock, with another tower for the bell on the spot where the old clock house formerly stood.[87] Lord Weston commissioned an equestrian statue of Charles I from the French sculptor Henri Le Sueur in 1633. It escaped being melted down during the Commonwealth years and was eventually erected upon a stone pedestal at Charing Cross in 1667.[88] There was an equestrian figure of Charles II near the site of the present Mansion House, in London. An equestrian statue of William III by Peter Scheemakers was erected in the market place in Hull by public subscription in 1735.[89] There is another in Bristol by Rysbrack, finished in the same year, and Defoe noted of Lynn that 'there is, in the market-place of this town, a very fine statue of King William on horse-back, erected at the charge of the town'.[90] This movement reaches a splendid climax in Edinburgh. The David Hume monument, to designs by Robert Adam, was built in the Old Calton Burying Ground in 1777. Calton Hill became the setting for a group of public buildings which, when taken together, are without equal for their monumentality. The Nelson Monument was completed in 1807, to be followed by the Playfair Monument of 1825–6, the Dugald Stewart Monument of 1831 and, finally, the National Monument, an attempt to build the Parthenon in the Athens of the North, but left unfinished in 1829.

More practical, less pretentious, improvements were sometimes more difficult to carry through. In the growing industrial towns access to open space was becoming almost impossible by the end of the eighteenth century, just as an awareness of its benefits was beginning slowly to emerge. It was pointed out in 1833 that the rapid growth in population of many towns had led to a great increase in the value of property and a consequent neglect in the provision of public walks and open spaces 'fitted to afford means of exercise or amusement to the middle or humbler classes'.[91] There were no public walks in Birmingham, Bristol, Hull, Bradford, Blackburn, Bolton, Bury or Sheffield. Solutions to the problem came only very slowly. Joseph Strutt paid for the laying out of the Arboretum at Derby in 1840 and the first park to be laid out at public expense was designed by Sir Joseph Paxton for Birkenhead in 1843.

The main streets in many, but by no means all, towns were often paved and lit with gas by 1840, the crescent and circus had become the small change of every jobbing builder, and some open spaces had been laid out, although they were still missing from towns where they were most needed. Nevertheless, many

87 V. Smith, ed., *The Town Book of Lewes, 1702–1837* (Sussex Record Society, 69, 1972–3), pp. 73, 88.

88 M. Whinney, *Sculpture in Britain, 1530 to 1830* (Harmondsworth, 1964), pp. 36 and 243 n. 11.

89 *VCH*, Yorkshire: East Riding, I, p. 408.

90 Defoe, *A Tour through England and Wales*, I, p. 74.

91 PP 1833 XV, Report of the Select Committee on Public Walks.

side streets were still noisome, irregular and dangerous, and responsibility for the maintenance of public space remained divided and uncertain until long after 1840.

(v) THE USES OF PUBLIC SPACE

Towns, however, are not islands unto themselves. They are linked together by a communications system and the parts of a town are integrated by the use of the public spaces as thoroughfares. Through traffic was often considerable, and grew very rapidly during the course of the period. Markets and fairs could bring crowds of people into towns. The cloth market at Leeds was described in 1715 as the 'Life not of the Town alone, but those parts of England'. It was held twice a week in the street in Briggate. It was then cleared and other 'professions' were allowed in, country line drapers, shoemakers, hardwaremen and the sellers of wood vessels, wicker baskets, wanded chairs, flakes and fruit of all sorts, together with milk cows and fish.[92] The market place in Nottingham was said in 1815 to be the finest in England. There were folds for sheep and pigs, farmers selling corn by sample, stalls for fruit, butter, baskets, chairs and coopers' wares, fish and earthenware, with which it was always well supplied, together with town and country butchers. The cattle market had only recently been removed, and the poultry market was held in Poultry.[93] In all of this Nottingham was by no means unusual. Dr Pococke visited Exeter in 1750 and noted the long High Street, running from east to west. 'It is surprising', he wrote', 'to see how the great street is filled on a market day with people, and great plenty of all sorts of provisions.'[94]

The noise, confusion and mounds of ordure created by markets in general and cattle markets in particular meant that many were moved out into semi-suburban sites during the course of the early years of the nineteenth century. The markets in Birmingham were one of the chief concerns of the improvement commissioners from the moment their empowering act was passed in 1769. The cattle market was moved out to Dale End. The general market was moved from the High Street to the Bull Ring in 1806. In 1817 the Smithfield market was opened on the site of the moat of the old manor house, and a new market hall was opened in 1835.[95] Through traffic and the influx of visitors going to the market or fair, or to quarter sessions in county towns, or, more frequently, to the shops, the theatres and the other amenities which towns had to offer, combined with the activities which constituted the everyday lives of the inhabitants themselves to produce the confusion, congestion and noise for which the larger towns in Britain were notorious. As John Byng wrote when he visited Derby in 1789, every house in the town was adorned with 'oaken boughs in honor of the old

[92] R. Thoresby, *Ducatus Leodiensis* (London, 1715), p. 14.

[93] Blackner, *History of Nottingham*, p. 63.

[94] Cartwright, ed., *Travels of Dr Pococke*, I, p. 99.

[95] *VCH*, Warwickshire, VII, p. 251.

29th of May; and the boys preparing and begging for their bonfires. The Derby militia are assembled here; and disturbing (as at Northampton) the sick, and quiet, by their uproar.'[96] More basic pleasures could also bring the crowds on to the streets. In 1763 there were said to be no more than five or six brothels in Edinburgh, but by 1783 the number had increased twentyfold, 'and every quarter of the city and suburbs was infested with multitudes of females abandoned to vice'.[97]

In London much of the intercourse between individuals and families was conducted on foot. Walking the streets and parks in search of friends and with friends in order to take the air was a very common practice.[98] The streets themselves, in spite of the efforts of improvement commissioners, were often dirty, ill-paved and poorly lit, even in the most fashionable quarters, but this did not prevent much coming and going, on foot as well as in carriages of every kind, and late into the night. Events in the Court Calendar, such as a royal birthday, brought large crowds on to the streets, as could public executions and cultural events such as theatre performances. Further examples are given in Chapter 19. Some events were very popular, the Handel festivals in Westminster Abbey, for example, were attended by a thousand musicians as well as the audiences. As Boswell wrote, 'the immense crowd and hurry and bustle of business and diversion, the great number of public places of entertainment, the noble churches and the superb buildings of different kinds, agitate, amuse and elevate the mind'.[99] The same could be said of Edinburgh,

> a crowded metropolis, which, with its noise and clamour, its sounds of trade, of revelry and of licence, its variety of lights, and the eternally changing bustle of its hundred groups, offers, by night especially, a spectacle which, though composed of the most vulgar materials when they are separately considered, has, when they are combined, a striking and powerful effect on the imagination.[100]

The extent to which this activity was to be found in other towns would depend upon the range of amenities on offer, and this range was considerably extended in individual towns during the course of the eighteenth century. London was by no means the only place to have pleasure gardens. Vauxhall Gardens, described so brilliantly in Chapter VI of *Vanity Fair*, was imitated, more or less, in other major cities, including Bath, Liverpool, Newcastle, Birmingham and Norwich, where the New Spring Gardens were laid out in 1739. They were bought in 1776 by James Bunn. He arranged flower shows, exhibitions of paintings, concerts, at which J. C. Bach, Haydn and Stamitz performed, and balloon

96 Andrews, ed., *The Torrington Diaries*, II, p. 163.

97 *Statistical Account of Scotland*, VI, p. 613.

98 For a detailed analysis of urban street life in the eighteenth century see P. J. Corfield, 'Walking the city streets: the urban odyssey in eighteenth-century England', *JUH*, 16 (1989–90), 132–74.

99 F. A. Pottle, ed., *Boswell's London Journal, 1762–1763* (London, 1950), pp. 68–9.

100 Sir Walter Scott, *Guy Mannering* (Edinburgh, 1815), ch. 36.

flights, including a manned one in 1785.[101] In Dorchester the walks laid out along the line of the town walls became a popular resort for the townspeople. Similarly, at Colchester, when St Mary's church, destroyed during the siege, was finally rebuilt in 1713–14, handsome gravel walks were laid out, at a cost of £65 17s. 4d., and planted with lime trees 'which being kept cut are very shady and pleasant in the summer: and they being the best walks about the whole Town, are much resorted to by people of the best fashion'. Such people, especially if they were visitors, demanded an ever-increasing range of amenities. Among leisure towns Bath had the largest array (see Plate 28), but Margate by 1790 had a newly erected assembly rooms, a theatre and a new library. In none of this was it unusual, but seaside towns needed their own new building types. The first bathing machine was erected at Lowestoft in 1768, from a model procured in Margate. The chain pier at Brighton was built in 1823 and a new pier at Margate in 1815.[102]

By 1840 the noise and confusion had been compounded by the traffic created by the new railway stations, the introduction of the horse-drawn omnibus, and the tidal waves of people arriving for work, whether at the factory gate, the shop or the office, and leaving when their working day was over.

(vi) CHANGE IN THE URBAN ENVIRONMENT

The three centuries covered in this Chapter and in Chapter 9 brought profound and complex change into the topography of towns the length and breadth of Britain. By 1840 the main streets of most towns, the principal component of public space, were adequately paved and drained. Gas lighting was to be found, certainly in main streets, and kerb stones were almost everywhere used to mark off pedestrian areas from vehicular traffic. Streets themselves now bore sign boards with their names and houses were numbered, the use of pictorial signs having long been discontinued except for inns, some of which still bear their eighteenth-century wrought iron sign boards, as at the Cock inn, in Stony Stratford. Responsibility for the upkeep of public space still remained uncertain and fragmented, however.

Private space was undergoing profound and complex social change by 1840. In larger towns the central business district was just beginning to take shape, as people moved out of the centres of towns into the newly developing suburbs,

101 T. Fawcett, 'The Norwich pleasure gardens', *Norfolk Archaeology*, 35 (1973), 382–99.

102 P. Morant, *The History and Antiquities of the Most Ancient Town and Borough of Colchester* (London, 1748), Book 2, p. 4; *Hall's New Margate and Ramsgate Guide* (1790), p. 9; J. Whyman, 'A Hanoverian watering-place: Margate before the railway', in A. M. Everitt, ed., *Perspectives in English Urban History* (London, 1973), pp. 138–60; E. Gillingwater, *An Historical Account of the Ancient Town of Lowestoft* (London, 1790), p. 51; E. W. Gilbert, *Brighton: Old Ocean's Bauble* (London, 1954), p. 124.

leaving the centres of towns to shops and offices. At the same time industrialisation meant that much manufacture which had traditionally been performed in workshops attached to private dwellings was starting to move into factories, with the result that employees now had to travel to work. The separation of home and work was by no means complete in 1840, however, although the occupational segregation which was so marked a feature of medieval towns had long broken down, to be replaced by new patterns of residential and economic segregation. Much rebuilding had taken place in the centres of many, although by no means all, towns by 1840, prompted by fire, by the replacement of thatch and straw by brick and tile and by modernisation at the increasingly imperious dictates of fashion or the needs of commerce. The centres of those towns unaffected by the first stages of industrialisation, places such as York, Shrewsbury and Ludlow, still retained many timber-framed buildings. Successive waves of rebuilding in towns such as Sheffield and Manchester have removed all but a handful of such buildings, and those that survive, like Staple Inn in High Holborn, are heavily restored and rather disconsolate survivors from a lost world. To compare the rather monotonous regularity of the façades to Gower Street in London, for example, with the variety of the fronts to the Market Place in Buckingham serves only to reinforce the point.

In many respects institutional space has suffered the most profound change. It is often only a street name which recalls the presence of a medieval ecclesiastical community, Greyfriars Lane in Leicester, for example, and by 1840 factory chimneys were higher and more numerous than church spires. The multiplication of the functions of central and local government added many new types of buildings, from shire halls to county lunatic asylums. New departures in cultural and intellectual interests have added yet further types of buildings, including museums and theatres. Technological innovation had, by 1840, brought in entirely new methods of transport with the building of the railways and at least the main streets of towns were safer places at night after the introduction of gas lighting. Nevertheless, walking remained the most usual method of getting about in towns, and horses were even more numerous in 1840 than they were in 1540.

All of this change, however, took place within ancient frameworks. Old streets may have been better paved in 1840 than they were in 1540, but they still followed the same route. There had been comparatively little realignment of streets in the centres of towns, even after the most devastating fire, so that the medieval street plan can still be recognised behind the most modern façades. When towns began to expand beyond their medieval limits their new streets were aligned according to ancient property boundaries. Pre-industrial field boundaries lie behind the nineteenth-century streets and courts of Leeds, for example. Municipal corporations were not reformed until 1835 and their ancient boundaries were not redrawn until 1837. The new wine of nineteenth-century urban expansion was poured into some very old bottles.

· 19 ·

London 1700–1840

LEONARD SCHWARZ

(i) LONDON: PORTENT OF THE FUTURE

IN 1737 Samuel Johnson, having failed to make a very successful living hitherto, made his way to London, at the age of twenty-eight, and wrote a gloomy prognostication of his chances of survival:

> For who would leave, unbribed, Hibernia's land,
> Or change the rocks of Scotland for the Strand?
> There none are swept by sudden fate away,
> But all whom hunger spares, with age decay:
> Here malice, rapine, accident, conspire,
> And now a rabble rages, now a fire;
> Their ambush here relentless ruffians lay,
> And here the fell attorney prowls for prey;
> Here falling houses thunder on your head,
> And here a female atheist talks you dead.[1]

Johnson had not yet visited Scotland, or he might have revised his views on the comparative safety of life in the Highlands. It was in London that he found the company that he most longed to frequent and in London that he made his career. He did not leave London often and it was in London that he died forty-seven years after his arrival, having made his famous remark that a man who was tired of London was tired of life, as there was in London all that life could afford. Most of the poem had in fact little to do with London, although it was quite correct in pointing out that the capital had its highwaymen and that the older houses

I would like to thank Pat Garside, David Green, Nigel Wood and the seminar on Metropolitan History at the Institute of Historical Research for their comments on earlier drafts of this article. The literature on London is vast: the indispensable guide is H. Creaton, *Bibliography of Printed Works on London History to 1939* (London, 1994). There is a short guide to the literature of the last thirty years in L. Schwarz, 'London, 1700–1850', *LJ*, 20 (1995), 46–55.

[1] *London* (London, 1738), lines 9–18.

occasionally fell into the street. Johnson used London to typify decadence. This was, from one point of view, part of an anti-urban tradition that long predated Johnson and long outlived him. Cities were easy to denounce. They were the dwelling places of the economically rational man, applauded by Mandeville and denounced ineffectually by clergymen of all persuasions as well as, on this occasion, by Johnson:

> By numbers here from shame or censure free,
> All crimes are safe but hated poverty . . .
> Couldst thou resign the park and play content,
> For the fair banks of Severn or of Trent;
> There might'st thou find some elegant retreat,
> Some hireling senator's deserted seat;
> And stretch thy prospects o'er the smiling land,
> For less than rent the dungeons of the Strand.[2]

However, to Johnson's more educated contemporaries the significance of his poem was the announcement at the beginning that it was 'in imitation of Juvenal's third satire'. They would not have failed to draw the parallels with Rome, to have noticed the combination of irony, distaste and admiration with which Johnson described England's capital, sentiments that they were likely to have shared. The English Rome – the English Babylon to many – was the shock city of the eighteenth century. During the first half of the nineteenth century it retained its capacity to shock and attract but had to share the accolade with Manchester and the Coketowns of the North.[3] As Jeremy Boulton has shown (see above, Chapter 10), during the course of the seventeenth century London expanded to be the largest city in Europe, even exceeding Paris by 1700. Only one country, wrote L.-S. Mercier, the great eighteenth-century celebrant and describer of Paris, has stood out against France: 'London, neighbour and rival, must inevitably be considered when talking of Paris' and accordingly visited London in 1781 to make notes for a book that he never published.[4] And although London was England's only 'world city' it was indeed international in its orientation. Only Amsterdam could rival it in this respect and Amsterdam was far smaller. Imperial capital, one of the great nodal points of the global economy,

[2] *Ibid.*, lines 158–9, 210–15.

[3] For an example of a celebration of this, see Pierce Egan's best-selling *Life in London; or The Day and Night Scenes of Jerry Hawthorn Esq and his Friend Corinthian Tom, in their Rambles and Sprees through the Metropolis* (better known as Tom and Jerry) appearing in 1820 and preceding Dickens; Marilyn Butler, 'Hidden metropolis: London in sentimental and romantic writing', in C. Fox, ed., *London – World City, 1800–1840* (New Haven, Conn., 1992), p. 189. Obvious allusions were made in Blake's *Jerusalem* and Byron's *Sardanapalus* (*ibid.*, pp. 195–8). For shock cities: A. Briggs, *Victorian Cities* (Harmondsworth, 1968), p. 96.

[4] L.-S. Mercier, *Parallèle de Paris et de Londres*, ed. C. Bruneteau and B. Cottret (Paris, 1982), p. 53; L.-S. Mercier, *Tableau de Paris*, vol. XI (Paris, 1788), p. 371: 'Londres, voisine et rivale, devient inévitablement le pendant du Tableau que j'ai tracé'.

London lay at the confluence of national and international trade, largest of the European entrepôts, markets and manufacturing towns, the prime European contender for the term 'Megalopolis'.[5] The docks built at the end of the eighteenth century had warehouses over half a mile in length. Its food supply came from far beyond its base in the South-East of England; its demands for fuel led to a large import of coal, almost certainly far larger, than the total imports of any other European country; it attracted large numbers of Huguenots from France in 1685, it had a large black community by the 1760s and many other national communities were to be found.[6] London was a source of denunciation and pride, often combined.

As befits shock cities, it was also a fearful warning of the future, a potentially dangerous cauldron. It had a great deal more policing than historians used to believe but there were regular riots. The worst fears appeared to be justified by the Gordon riots in 1780 when the rioting lasted for a week, the rioters destroyed Newgate Gaol and the Fleet, attacked the Bank of England, reputedly did ten times as much damage as in Paris throughout the French Revolution,[7] with order finally restored by the army firing down the streets and killing at least 290 people. There are no figures for those wounded. It was a death toll that well exceeded the early casualties of the French Revolution and was twenty-six times that of Peterloo. Only in London did lord chief justices have their houses sacked. It did indeed appear to be a portent of the future.[8] That it should have been sparked off by a protest against a mild alleviation of the penalties on Roman Catholics was a further insult to the Enlightenment. At the same time, only in London was city growth so well managed as it was in parts of Westminster, with its paving and lighting acts. That only the wealthy parts of Westminster gave themselves good pavements and gas lighting would not have surprised any eighteenth-century observer; what was surprising was that the acts were successful and furthermore were so in a part of the town that had a population of 70,000 in 1700 and 150,000 in 1801, in itself larger than any other city in Britain and apart from London the thirteenth largest urban conglomeration in Europe at the time.

5 T. C. Barker, 'London: a unique megalopolis', in T. C. Barker and A. Sutcliffe, eds., *Megalopolis* (London, 1993), pp. 43–60.

6 P. Earle, *The Making of the English Middle Class* (London, 1989), p. 39; P. Earle, *A City Full of People* (London, 1994), pp. 47–9; G. Rudé, *Hanoverian London 1714–1808* (London, 1971), pp. 7–8. F. Shyllon, *Black People in Britain 1555–1833* (Oxford, 1977), pp. 101–2, considers the figure of 20,000 that was commonly quoted during the 1760s as too high and suggests a figure of 10,000 for the whole of Britain to be a plausible maximum. See also P. Linebaugh, *The London Hanged* (London, 1991), pp. 348–56.

7 R. Porter, *English Society in the Eighteenth Century* (Harmondsworth, 1982), p. 116, for the estimate of £100,000.

8 E. P. Thompson, 'Eighteenth-century English society: class struggle without class?', *Soc. Hist.*, 3 (1978), 133–56; E. P. Thompson, 'Patrician society, plebeian culture', *Journal of Social History*, 7 (1974), 382–405.

London came to be more methodically policed and considerably less riotous. Nothing like the Gordon riots ever came again. Fear that they might do so remained. 'What can be stable with these enormous towns?' lamented Lord Liverpool when showing a foreign visitor the view from the roof of Downing Street in 1819. 'One serious insurrection in London and all is lost.'[9] Echoes of the past returned spasmodically – with the Queen Caroline riots of 1819–20, the Reform Act of 1832, the Chartists in 1848 and the Hyde Park demonstrations of 1866. Perhaps the inhabitants had become more peaceful; considering the capital's high crime rate it is more plausible to suggest that alternative ways of making a point had come into existence. Nevertheless, a century after the Gordon riots, when 'Bloody Sunday' referred to a handful of injuries and no deaths at all (around the extremely well-paved streets of Westminster) something had indeed changed.

(ii) LONDON: THE ELUSIVE TOWN

As is the case now, what individuals meant when they spoke of 'London' varied enormously.[10] 'London' had long been the built-up core of a diffuse region of satellite towns and villages; increasingly during the eighteenth century, and overwhelmingly during the nineteenth century the ever-expanding core took on the characteristics of an urban region in itself. This core – never contained within city walls, so nobody could be sure where it ended – contained only about 2 per cent of the population of England and Wales at the start of the sixteenth century but had grown to between 10 and 11 per cent by the end of the seventeenth century, remaining around that level until 1801, growing steadily after 1811, to reach 14 per cent in 1851. The process slowed down thereafter, but still attained 16 per cent in 1901. By European standards this was a degree of national dominance achieved only by Amsterdam in its Golden Age. The populations of Edinburgh and Glasgow combined managed by 1801 to form a similar proportion of Scotland's population. In 1700 London's built-up area was essentially confined to some five miles along the north bank of the Thames, a century later it was twice as large. But as a legal entity London did not exist until the creation of the London County Council in 1888 – which itself had dubious and rapidly outdated boundaries. Before then, the census makers of the nineteenth century were forced to refer to various entities – the City of London, Westminster, the various and increasing numbers of parishes. At the start of the eighteenth

[9] The various forms of improvement are discussed by Joanna Innes and Nicholas Rogers in Chapter 16 of this volume. European urban figures from B. R. Mitchell, *European Historical Statistics 1750–1975*, 2nd edn (London, 1981), pp. 86–8. For Lord Liverpool's alarm see E. Halévy, *A History of the English People in the Nineteenth Century*, vol. II: *The Liberal Awakening* (London, 1961), p. 103.

[10] K. Young and P. L. Garside, *Metropolitan London: Politics and Urban Change 1837–1981* (London, 1982), pp. 14–22, P. L. Garside, 'London and the Home Counties', in F. M. L. Thompson, ed., *The Cambridge Social History of Britain 1750–1950* (Cambridge, 1990), vol. I, p. 471.

century, contemporaries implicitly agreed that one of the unique characteristics of London that distinguished it from any other town in Britain was that it was impossible to know all of it, or to agree what it was. Pope, in common with other Augustan writers, described parts of the town in loving detail, and expected his readers to know quite a lot about them. Aristocrats – to whom 'the Town' meant Westminster – were presumed to know that Grub Street was in Cripplegate Ward near Smithfield and Bedlam, that the walks of Moorfields were a haunt of prostitutes, with the walk dividing upper and lower Moorfields traditionally allocated to homosexuals.[11] But they were not expected to be acquainted with the topography of the East End. London merchants had a different geography: that of the City and the East End. To sailors London meant the riverside, to silkweavers Spitalfields, to drovers Smithfield. Then as now, London appeared to the visitor as a patchwork of local areas. 'When I consider this great city in its several quarters and divisions, I look upon it as an aggregate of various nations distinguished from each other by their respective customs, manners and interests' wrote Addison in *The Spectator*, in 1712.[12] The town had, complained Swift in 1736, 'grown to such an enormous size, that above half a day must be spent in the streets going from one place to another.'[13] 'When one goes into Rotherhithe or Wapping, which places are inhabited chiefly by sailors', wrote Sir John Fielding in a 1776 guide to the town, 'but that somewhat of the same language is spoken, a man would be apt to suspect himself in another country. Their manner of living, speaking, acting, dressing, and behaving are so very peculiar to themselves'.[14] Boswell was recommended by Johnson to visit Wapping, but he did not do so until thirty years after his first visit to London. South London remained difficult to reach: until Westminster Bridge was completed in 1750 there was only one bridge across the Thames.[15]

The core was diffuse, the region even more diffuse. That eighteenth-century urbanisation affected the greater metropolitan region as much as it affected the metropolis is made clear by the statistics of the employers of manservants in 1780. Since liveried manservants cost more to employ than women servants, were taxed and did not do much that women servants could not do (except possibly display themselves on the front of coaches), they tended to be employed principally for the status that they gave their employer. As will be shown later, very many were employed in London. What is interesting is how many employers of manservants lived in the environs of London: 196 in Croydon, 66 in Clapham, 66 in

[11] P. Rogers, *Hacks and Dunces: Pope, Swift and Grub Street*, 2nd edn (London, 1980), pp. 37, 47. See also p. 74: readers of the *Dunciad* were assumed to have some knowledge of Rosemary Lane in the East, St Giles Cripplegate, Fleet and Farringdon, St Giles-in-the-Fields and Covent Garden in the West. [12] *Spectator*, no. 403 (12 June 1712).

[13] Quoted in Rogers, *Hacks and Dunces*, p. 4.

[14] J. Fielding, *A Description of the Cities of London and Westminster* (London, 1776), p. xiii.

[15] Westminster Bridge was completed in 1750, Blackfriars in 1769. London Bridge was widened 1758–62.

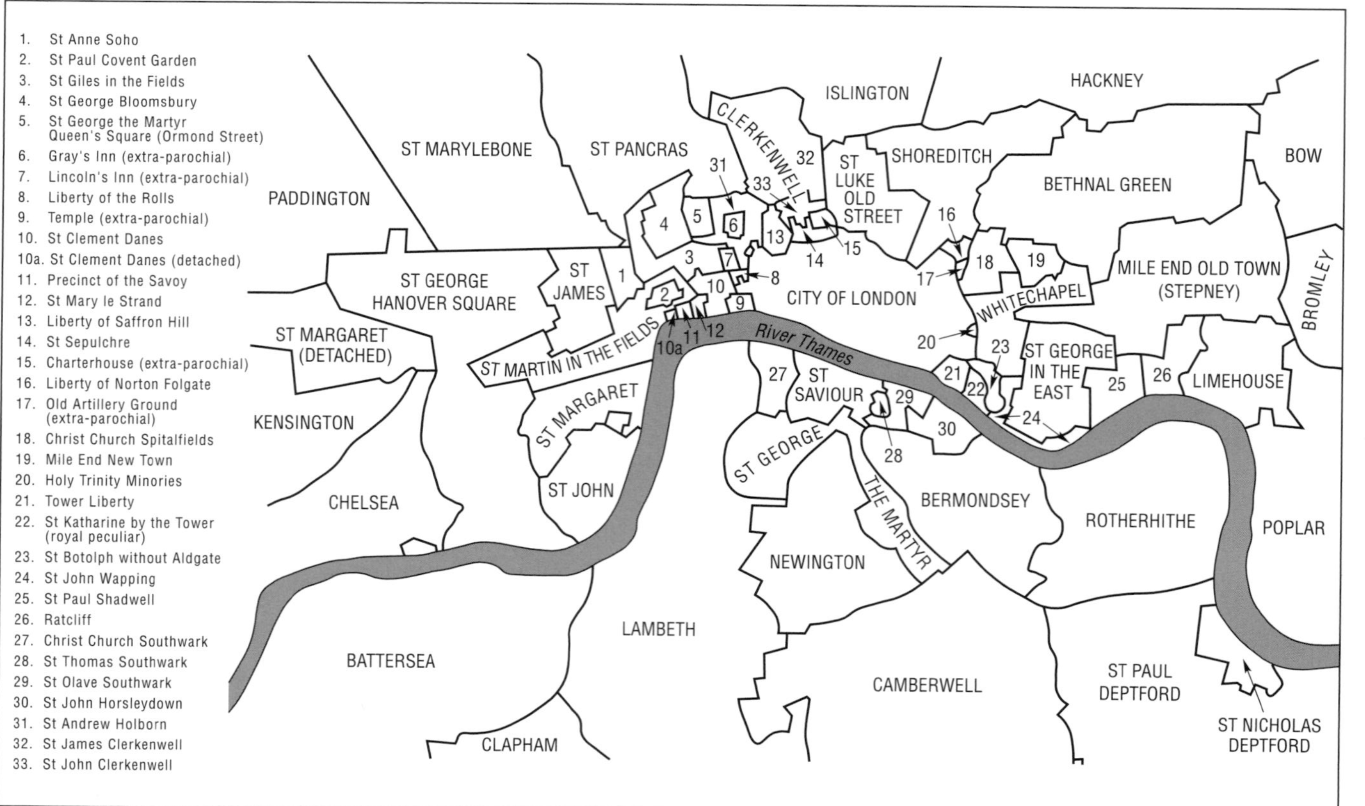

Map 19.1 Metropolitan parishes outside the City of London 1763

Hampstead, 56 in Kensington, 58 in Leyton, 49 in Tottenham. This was not a new phenomenon[16] and should be compared with provincial county towns such as Worcester with 66 employers of manservants, Shrewsbury with 72 or Lancaster with 39. Overall, 'rural' Middlesex and Surrey had far more 'towns' with large numbers of manservants than any other county in England. During the earlier seventeenth century urban centres within a twenty mile radius of London 'were essentially part of it so far as goods, trade and prices were concerned'.[17]

Transport improvements accelerated suburbanisation and led to the rise of suburbs that dwarfed most English or European cities. St Pancras with 166,596 inhabitants in 1851 and St Marylebone with slightly fewer were each larger than Bristol or Bradford and if counted separately would have been the eighth and ninth largest cities in Britain and the twenty-fourth largest in Europe, larger than Hamburg, Munich or St Petersburg, approaching Rome's 175,000 while in France surpassed only by Paris, Lyons and Marseilles;[18] of the sixteen English urban places in 1851 that contained a population of at least 100,000 seven were located in London.[19] It is open to doubt whether London's influence on southern England was ever greater than during the later seventeenth century, but transport improvements subsequently made this influence felt more immediately while the growth of a wealthy service sector during the eighteenth century made more obvious the influence of the Great Wen against which Cobbett fulminated so ineffectually.

London can therefore be seen as a built-up area, itself a kaleidoscope of neighbourhoods, set amidst a large and amorphous urban region. Nevertheless, at least six of the capital's major attributes remained unchanged throughout this period. As the chapters on both late medieval and sixteenth and seventeenth-century London have shown, many of these characteristics were not new and as Boulton has shown great care needs to be taken when asserting that they were specific to London and were the product of a certain 'metropolitan culture'.[20]

The first characteristic of London, that it was by far the largest town in Britain, had for long been beyond dispute. Secondly, it was the prime cultural centre of the country. As far as High Culture was concerned almost all the major departures in art and music commenced there, with only eighteenth-century Edinburgh beginning to rival London, and then only in part. Despite this, it is remarkably difficult to point to specific cultural creations of the largest grouping of bourgeoisie in the world. The national culture – at whatever level it is defined – was sufficiently integrated for the search for a 'London taste' to be very elusive. This is a large problem which has not been systematically studied and

[16] D. M. Palliser, ed., *The Cambridge Urban History of Britain*, vol. I: *600–1540* (Cambridge, 2000), ch. 9.

[17] See above, p. 56. [18] Mitchell, *European Historical Statistics*, pp. 86–8

[19] D. R. Green, *From Artisans to Paupers: Economic Change and Poverty in London, 1790–1870* (Aldershot, 1995), p. 3. [20] See above, pp. 344–6.

cannot be studied here.[21] However, taking a wider definition of culture, many new national practices, such as coffee and tea drinking, first became widespread in the capital. London was of course the centre of fashion, from silks to porcelain. Thirdly, London's financial role, already very important with the financial revolution of the 1690s, continued to expand. The South Sea Bubble was not allowed to prevent this. Institutions central to the working of the City such as the East India Company, the Sun Fire Office (1708), the Exchange Assurance Company (1720) and Lloyds continued to grow. Amsterdam was soon outranked.[22] This was a departure of immense national and international importance, but its direct impact on London, in terms of employment and geography, was limited. It was not until the second half of the nineteenth century that the City came to attain the characteristics of a central business district, although there was a continuous but gradual exodus of inhabitants which by the 1840s finally undermined its residential function.[23] As late as 1780 the City still had 1,209 employers of manservants. This was fewer than the 1,939 of Westminster, but as a proportion of its population nevertheless double that employers of manservants formed of the population of Surrey, Berkshire and Essex, treble that of Suffolk or Hampshire and six times that of Devon. Much less limited was the fourth factor which will, for convenience, be referred to as the Court, the annual attendance of the aristocracy and gentry in the capital for a few months during each year. This generated an immense seasonal demand and employment, being central to occupations as varied as coachmaking, a large part of scientific instrument making (in which London was a major international centre), much of London's large silkweaving manufacture, the legal professions or the theatre. Fifthly, with a very large effect on employment, is the fact that London was by far the largest port in Britain, comparable only with a small handful of major European ports, such as Amsterdam, Naples and Hamburg. During this period, London's predominance within England's overseas trade declined somewhat, from three-quarters of the total in 1699–1701 to 63 per cent in 1790, but it remained overwhelming. The oft-quoted estimate that a quarter of eighteenth-century's London population may have depended on the Port 'directly or indirectly' is no more than an unprovable estimate. There is no evidence on direct employment: in 1801 the riverside parishes east of the City and Southwark had

21 See, for example, A. Wilton, 'Painting in London in the early nineteenth century', in Fox, ed., *London – World City*, pp. 167–86, which endeavours to limit itself to London but could nevertheless serve as a good introduction to the history of English (if not British) painting during this period.

22 P. J. Cain and A. G. Hopkins, *British Imperialism: Innovation and Expansion 1688–1914* (London, 1993), pp. 60–3.

23 Green, *From Artisans to Paupers*, p. 187; D. Kynaston, *The City of London*, vol. 1: *A World of its Own* (London, 1994), p. 59: 'In 1823 the great majority of those [City merchants] whose surnames began with "A" lived either in the City, or, more commonly, pretty nearby in such places as Islington, Vauxhall, Walworth and Kentish Town.'

a total population of only a tenth of the metropolis,[24] while the definition of indirect employment is infinitely variable. But the numbers were certainly large. Inseparable from the capital's role as port and Court, London was also the largest manufacturing town in the western hemisphere.

The combination of these six factors led naturally to the seventh, that long before the eighteenth century London had been the indisputable centre of national wealth and the hub of the professions. The largest concentration of aristocracy, the wealthiest bankers and merchants, the wealthiest capitalists and the largest concentration of taxpayers were all to be found there. At least a quarter of the nation's attorneys and solicitors lived in London in 1729 and a third in 1800; a third of the nation's doctors in 1783.[25] During the 1690s the proportion of servants (both male and female) in the capital's population was two or three times as high as it was in quite prosperous provincial cities such as Norwich, Bristol or Gloucester; in 1780 London and Middlesex, with about a tenth of the nation's population, had 28 per cent of England and Wales' manservants; in 1851, with 13 per cent of the nation's labour force, the region had 21 per cent of its manservants, in 1812 it was responsible for nearly 40 per cent of the total raised by direct taxation in England and Wales.[26]

Space forbids discussing each of these factors in detail. Those not so discussed below must be borne in mind.

(iii) POPULATION AND MIGRATION

Until the nineteenth-century census the statistics of London's total population are inexact. In particular the range of error for the mid-eighteenth century is wide, as Table 19.1 shows. As regards the growth of the population, our knowledge is also imprecise, but certain broad conclusions stand out. London grew not by its own powers of growth – until the last quarter of the eighteenth century deaths outnumbered births – but by drawing on a large share of the national population growth. As Jeremy Boulton has shown in Chapter 10 of this volume, seventeenth-century London was an unhealthy town, with a crude death rate (CDR) during non-plague years in the region of forty per thousand. Infant and

[24] R. Davis, *The Rise of the English Shipping Industry in the Seventeenth and Eighteenth Centuries* (London, 1962), p. 390; L. D. Schwarz, *London in the Age of Industrialisation* (Cambridge, 1992), p. 9.

[25] Schwarz, *London in the Age of Industrialisation*, p. 27; P. J. Corfield, *Power and the Professions in Britain 1700–1850* (London, 1995), p. 217 for doctors in 1783 and attorneys in 1780.

[26] Schwarz, *London in the Age of Industrialisation*, p. 18; W. D. Rubinstein, 'The Victorian middle classes: wealth, occupation and geography', *Ec.HR*, 2nd series, 30 (1977), 602–23; A. D. M. Phillips and J. R. Walton, 'The distribution of personal wealth in English towns in the mid-nineteenth century', *Transactions of the Institute of British Geographers*, 2nd series, 64 (1975), 35–48; L. D. Schwarz and L. J. Jones, 'Wealth, occupations and insurance in the late eighteenth century: the policy registers of the Sun Fire Office', *Ec.HR*, 2nd series, 36 (1983), 365–73.

Table 19.1 *Estimated figures for London's population 1700–1851*

1700	575,000
1750	600,000–675,000
1801	900,000
1811	1,050,000
1821	1,247,000
1831	1,595,000
1841	1,948,000
1851	2,362,000

Sources: V. Harding, 'The population of London, 1550–1700: a review of the published evidence', *LJ*, 15 (1990), 111–28; L. D. Schwarz, *London in the Age of Industrialisation* (Cambridge, 1992), pp. 125–8. 'London' can be taken as approximating to the continually built-up area of the time.

child mortality was particularly high. The balance of evidence suggests that non-plague mortality rates rose during the second half of the seventeenth century, and were even higher during the first half of the eighteenth century.[27] From the mid-eighteenth century, there was a tendency for the CDR to fall and by the 1780s London had begun to move into surplus. Table 19.2 provides some very approximate indications of the process. With demographic calculations of this nature the margins of error are very large and no single decade should be regarded as accurate (especially the period 1800–10), but the trends are unmistakable. Starting in the 1770s there was a complete change in the relationship between London and its hinterland and this is one of the few factors that indisputably made London during the second half of this period different from what it had been previously. Traditionally, large cities were demographic parasites.[28] There were three reasons why their death rate was so high. In the first instance, the sanitation was rudimentary, barely existing in some parts. Secondly, they had many very poor people, living in bad housing conditions. But this alone does not explain why large cities had higher death rates than smaller but equally poor and unhygienic cities. What was decisive was the factor of size. London was the national reservoir of infections. Parasites need hosts, and the larger the town the greater the number of potential hosts. Tuberculosis, which thrives in damp and dark conditions and remains infectious for a long time was not a specifically urban disease in the manner of measles, which struck briefly and became endemic in London when the town's population passed three-quarters of a million.[29] Smallpox was highly prevalent, not inoculated against widely until

[27] See above, pp. 203, 207–9, 318–19. [28] See above, ch. 6.

[29] Schwarz, *London in the Age of Industrialisation*, pp. 142–3.

Table 19.2 *Crude vital rates in London 1730–1830*

	Pop. estimate	CBR per 1,000	CDR per 1,000	Surplus/deficit, p.a. Per 1,000	N. per decade
1730s	675,000	43.1	48.6	−5.5	−37,000
1740s	675,000	34.4	46.0	−11.6	−78,000
1750s	675,000	40.5	44.8	−4.3	−29,000
1760s	740,000	36.5	42.2	−5.7	−42,000
1770s	811,000	40.2	42.1	−1.9	−15,000
1780s	890,000	37.4	36.0	1.4	12,000.
1790s	975,000	37.4	34.6	2.8	27,000
1800s	1,162,000	33.1	33.2	−0.1	-1,000
1810s	1,434,000	34.0	28.9	5.1	73,000
1820s	1,595,000	32.2	26.7	5.5	88,000

Sources: the CBR and CDR estimates are derived from J. Landers, *Death and the Metropolis* (Cambridge, 1993), p. 175. The population sizes are derived from the traditional estimate of 675,000 for 1750, the census data (with the midpoint between the two census years taken) and the assumption of a constant growth rate between 1750 and 1801. The figures of surplus/deficit per decade have been rounded to the nearest thousand. It must be stressed again that this exercise is only intended to be indicative of trends and should not be quoted as precise data.

comparatively late into the eighteenth century and it was virtually impossible to grow up in eighteenth-century London without being exposed to it. To reach adulthood in London one needed a large supply of antibodies, far more than in the rest of England. Out of every thousand children born to London Quakers between 1650 and 1699, 478 failed to survive until their tenth birthday; during the first half of the eighteenth century the figure was as high as 582, and during the next half-century it fell to an average of 490.[30] However, once one had reached this age, one had a rather good chance of surviving. This could not be said for rural immigrants, for whom immigration to London was a measured risk. Johnson was not wrong to be gloomy about his chances of survival.

Maintaining a balance between demographic growth, food supply and a

[30] Death rates per thousand of population, from birth to age nine, from sample of English parishes (outside London) and London Quakers (J. Landers, *Death and the Metropolis* (Cambridge, 1993), p. 136):

	English parishes	London Quakers
1650–99	284	478
1700–49	310	582
1750–99	277	490

wealthy hinterland might therefore be precarious. A prosperous hinterland communicated more with its town, which in turn meant increased exposure to urban infections. The death rate in many parts of South-East England increased during the late seventeenth and early eighteenth centuries, as communication with London became more intense. This in turn reduced the population surplus that was able to migrate to the capital. With net urban immigration decreasing, and urban demand in its turn failing to increase, the danger was a cycle of depressed demand, late marriage and low population growth in the hinterland.[31] That this danger was not hypothetical is shown during the second third of the eighteenth century. This was a period of relative stagnation – certainly of very slow growth – in the capital's economy and population. A vicious circle was at work – the death rate was higher during the first half of the eighteenth century than it had been during the non-plague years of the second half of the seventeenth century. At the same time, there are signs that the catchment area of immigrants to London narrowed and certainly within a general context of slow population growth London required an inordinate share of the national growth of population – during the second half of the seventeenth century at least twice the national increase and between two-fifths and two-thirds during the next half-century (depending on our estimates of the capital's population in 1750). There is disagreement over whether the slow population growth caused the slow economic growth or vice versa;[32] the more significant point is that the two interacted in a manner which makes the influence of one upon the other difficult to disentangle, and which was typical of the urban system before the nineteenth century. What is clear is that, contrary to the views of some eighteenth-century moralists and earlier twentieth-century historians, the taste for gin drinking that was accused of sweeping over London during the earlier eighteenth century was not only limited but had little effect upon mortality.[33]

By the 1760s the process began to change, and the change seems to have been inexorable. The capital's economy boomed, the population increased more rapidly than during the previous century and the crude death rate fell. The combination was historically new. The crude death rate continued to fall until it reached the national average level of twenty-three per thousand in the 1840s. By the last quarter of the eighteenth century births roughly balanced deaths, and by

[31] M. J. Dobson, 'The last hiccup of the old demographic regime: population stagnation and decline in late seventeenth-and early eighteenth-century South-East England', *Continuity and Change*, 4 (1989), 395–428.

[32] Landers, *Death and the Metropolis*, pp. 83–6; Schwarz, *London in the Age of Industrialisation*, pp. 80–4.

[33] M. D. George, *London Life in the Eighteenth Century*, 2nd edn (London, 1965), pp. 41–55, is the classic text. Gin is noticeable by being entirely absent from the index of the authoritative account of English population history: E. A. Wrigley and R. S. Schofield, *The Population History of England 1541–1871* (London, 1981). For the final demolition, which suggests that gin drinking was not even very widespread, see P. Clark, 'The "mother gin" controversy in early eighteenth-century England', *TRHS*, 5th series, 38 (1988), 63–84.

the nineteenth century there was a surplus. This cannot be attributed to improved living standards or better nutrition. The highest death rate was experienced amongst infants and children under the age of two – not a section of the population famed for its gin-drinking habits – where the CDR fell to a third of its eighteenth-century level. For those aged under ten the fall was two-thirds.[34] Between 1730–9 and 1838–44 deaths from consumption, smallpox, fever and typhus fell from nearly 17.8 to 6.9 per thousand.[35] If these diseases had been at their seventeenth-century levels in 1841, then an additional 20,000 Londoners, or 1 per cent of the population would have died during that year. If infant and child mortality had been at its eighteenth-century peak then another 30,000 would have died and in order to maintain growth the drain on the population of southern England would have become correspondingly greater.

London overcame the demographic challenge and continued to grow. The combination of large-scale immigration, high death rate and, for most of the time, rapid economic growth produced a situation that appeared paradoxical at first: the combination of rapid turnover of population with identifiable neighbourhoods. Again, this was not new. Estimates should be treated with reserve, but Boulton has estimated that during the course of the seventeenth century the proportion of London-born inhabitants may have risen from 22 to 30 per cent of its inhabitants. Landers has estimated that between 1735 and 1765 'native' Londoners aged ten to nineteen formed a little under 60 per cent of this age group living in London. For those aged twenty-to twenty-nine, the comparable figure was around 80 per cent.[36] In the 1851 census 84 per cent of those under the age of twenty about whom information was supplied had been born in London, but only 46 per cent of those above that age. Immigration was therefore at a very high level. During the period 1670–99 it is possible to suggest an annual net immigration total of 6,800 for a town with a total population of 575,000.[37] These figures are liable to be misleading, because they ignore emigration. As other chapters in this volume, particularly that of Pamela Sharpe, have shown, towns were 'revolving doors'.[38] Considering the period 1650–1750 Wrigley has suggested that while one tenth of the population of England and Wales was living in London at any one time, one sixth may have spent some part of his or her life there. From the experience of nineteenth-century American or German towns, this may well be a conservative estimate. Furthermore, it was unusual for those who remained in London to stay for very long in any single

[34] Schwarz, *London in the Age of Industrialisation*, p. 134. The CDR of 51.8 for 1730–9, originally based on J. Landers and A. Mouzas, 'Burial seasonality and causes of death in London 1670–1819', *Population Studies*, 42 (1988), has been brought down to 48 in the light of Landers' subsequent figures: (*Death and the Metropolis*, p. 175) and the figures have been adjusted accordingly.

[35] Schwarz, *London in the Age of Industrialisation*, p. 135, adjusted as explained above.

[36] See above, p. 318. Landers, *Death and the Metropolis*, pp. 180–3.

[37] J. Landers, private communication. This figure is not very different from Wrigley's estimate of 6,000 p.a. [38] See above, pp. 492 *et seq*.

residence, or even single parish. Mobility was rendered easy by the near universality of rent rather than house purchase among most of London's population, but this degree of mobility had been common during the seventeenth and eighteenth centuries, and London was by no means exceptional. That a street should 'lose' 80 per cent of its surnames in the course of a decade was common.[39]

Nevertheless, contemporaries were firmly of the view that London was a patchwork of neighbourhoods, each with its own distinct character. The 'seeming paradox' between London's 'extreme disorderliness' and 'essential orderliness' was commented on long ago by Dorothy George and the paradox has remained at the heart of studies of the metropolis ever since.[40] No interpretation of London that does not deal with this problem can hope to grasp the essential nature of the town. Neighbourhoods were in permanent flux and yet were remarkably stable. The high turnover within neighbourhoods was moderated by three factors. In the first place, the poor moved more than the rich. Secondly, most people only moved a few streets at a time. Francis Place, a successful, well-informed tailor who rose from the ranks to be an employer, knew his London better than most and changed his address eight times between 1791 and 1833, yet never lived more than a kilometre from St Clement Danes' church. He shared this pattern of circular migration with about half the paupers who applied for poor relief to the parish of St Giles between 1832 and 1862.[41] Thirdly, new immigrants to London did not target the town indiscriminately. They aimed to find communities of their 'countrymen', whether from Kent or from Ireland.[42] Unlike the more established inhabitants, they might subsequently move considerable distances within London, but their choice of location was informed.

An important corrective to the older views of the impersonality of large towns is that the larger a town, the more it is capable of supporting a substructure of local cultures. London was a prime example of this. London had always supported a wider range of ethnic communities than any other British town; it also supported the congregation of immigrants from other parts of the country. The 1851 census shows this process clearly. Two-fifths of those born in Kent lived south of the Thames, one-eighth of them in Greenwich. Two-thirds of those from Surrey lived south of the Thames. Once they had settled, they might move a great deal, but many of them were selective in their movement. New and

39 P. Laslett, *The World We Have Lost – Further Explored* (London, 1983), pp. 75–7.

40 George, *London Life*, pp. 9–10.

41 Green, *From Artisans to Paupers*, pp. 93–4. See also 'An investigation into the state of the poorer classes in St. George's-in-the-East', *Statistical Society of London*, 11 (1848), 193–249.

42 L. H. Lees, *Exiles of Erin* (Manchester, 1979), pp. 55–87; J. O'Neill, 'Fifty years' experience of an Irish shoemaker in London', *Saint Crispin*, 1–2 (1869–70). On arrival in London he was promptly directed to the Irish part of town, and when there was passed on to those from his own county and eventually his own village, who promptly found a job for him. Earle, *A City Full of People*, pp. 38–54.

rapidly growing areas were themselves selective: Kensington in 1851 attracted migrants from Essex, Hampshire, Berkshire, Somerset and Gloucestershire at twice the rate of Marylebone, and there is no reason to believe that such selectivity had not been the case earlier.

(iv) THE ELUSIVE METROPOLITAN CULTURE

A stress on neighbourhoods may also provide part of the answer to the elusive question of a 'metropolitan culture'. On a superficial view, London culture polarises into a 'high' culture dominated by the aristocracy, and a mix of bourgeois and plebeian traditions, usually restricted to particular trades or localities. For almost all this period, 'high' culture was dominated not by the bourgeoisie but by the aristocracy who, gathered in the capital for a few months each year, clearly considered themselves the capital's trend setters. This, in turn, casts some doubt on the thesis of the consumer revolution, at least as far as it relates to the consumption of high culture. Within the narrowly defined field of 'high culture' the London bourgeoisie was on the whole happy to follow rather than lead. Architects appealed mainly to the aristocracy, as did painters. Musicians were subsidised by them and the best musicians strove hard to obtain aristocratic patronage. During the 'season', a ticket to the best music societies needed aristocratic patrons: during the early 1760s Mrs Cornelys, the chief procuress of the best orchestral players in London, distributed her season tickets among suitable aristocratic ladies who could pass them on according to their judgement.[43] On his first arrival in London careful attempts were made to shelter Haydn from the bourgeoisie.[44] The great musical festivals – the coronations of course, but also the great Handel commemoration of 1784 – were dominated and often managed by the aristocracy.[45] The pattern of art was similar: it was exhibited in London because that was where the wealthy patrons were, but there was nothing particularly metropolitan about the patrons' tastes. Until the nineteenth century few provincial towns had more than the odd resident artist and provincial art societies suffered from persistent problems.[46] There was more 'high' culture than anywhere else, and the great national festivals and artistic events almost invariably took place in the capital. When the eighteenth-century musical equivalent of the Great Exhibition came to be presented – the great Handel

43 S. McVeigh, *Concert Life in London from Mozart to Haydn* (Cambridge, 1993), pp. 14–15.

44 *Ibid.*, p. 12.

45 *Ibid.*, pp. 182–202. The problem with this analysis is that of the definition of the aristocracy, which, after all, was not a caste. Rogers and Andrew have debated the extent to which the City's aldermen linked themselves to the aristocracy and the extent to which intermarriage took place: N. Rogers, 'Money, land and lineage: the big bourgeoisie of Hanoverian London', *Soc. Hist.*, 4 (1979), pp. 437–54; D. T. Andrew, 'The aldermen and the big bourgeoisie of London reconsidered', *Soc. Hist.*, 6 (1981), 359–64.

46 T. Fawcett, *The Rise of English Provincial Art* (Oxford, 1974), pp. 1, 12–14, 204–14.

Commemoration of 1784 – it was naturally presented in London, at Westminster Abbey and the Pantheon. Only London could be guaranteed to have 500 high-class vocal and instrumental performers, and an audience to match.[47] It was so successful that it was repeated during 1785–7 and 1790–1.[48] The first museum in the country was the Ashmolean,[49] but the significant public and permanent art galleries were in London, the most important being that opened by Hogarth in 1735, followed by the exhibition in the Foundling Hospital and eventually the Royal Academy in 1768.[50] The Industrial Revolution came, and most of it took place far from London, but it was almost inevitable that the Great Exhibition to commemorate it would be held in London. The one notable exception, the Great Shakespeare Jubilee of 1769 was held in Stratford but needed London talent for its organisation. It was masterminded and overseen by Garrick, with specially commissioned music by Thomas Arne, backdrops by Joshua Reynolds, a new ode by Garrick and Boswell as the press officer.[51]

However, excessive concentration on the aristocracy is misleading. A monolithic approach to the British aristocracy is dangerous; furthermore there was in London a market for the consumption of culture reaching far beyond the aristocracy. As far as music and the theatre were concerned, this market does not seem to have had its own distinct tastes in any formal sense, nor to have set itself apart from the rest of the country, and much of what it did like had been handed down by the aristocracy, but it was large. Only in London were concerts common events. The public rehearsal of Handel's *Music for the Royal Fireworks* had an audience of over 12,000 and a three-hour jam of carriages.[52] From the 1760s until a sudden righteous, counter-revolutionary collapse in concert-going during the 1790s London's concert life 'flourished . . . as never before, and no European capital (not even Paris) could rival the scale and variety of entertainments on offer'.[53] Concerts flourished again after the war, with London's concert promoters increasing the sale of their product faster than Lancashire cotton lords: it has been calculated that there was a threefold increase in the number of London concerts between the mid-1820s and the mid-1840s.[54] During the eighteenth century at any rate the aristocracy foreclosed on the top performers

[47] C. Burney, *An Account of the Musical Performances in Westminster Abbey* (London, 1785).

[48] W. Weber, *The Rise of Musical Classics in Eighteenth-Century England* (Oxford, 1992), pp. 223–42.

[49] See above, p. 631.

[50] D. Mannings, 'The visual arts', in B. Ford, ed., *The Cambridge Guide to the Arts in Britain*, vol. v (Cambridge, 1991), p. 108.

[51] P. Rogers, 'Literature', in Ford, ed., *The Cambridge Guide*, v, p. 195.

[52] N. Anderson, 'Music', in Ford, ed., *The Cambridge Guide*, v, pp. 275–303.

[53] McVeigh, *Concert Life*, p. 53; Weber, *The Rise of Musical Classics*, p. 146: 'Nowhere else in the Western world did public concerts develop on the scale they did in London' (referring to the second half of the eighteenth century).

[54] C. Ehrlich, *The Music Profession in Britain since the Eighteenth Century* (Oxford, 1985), p. 59; W. Weber, *Music and the Middle Class* (London, 1975), pp. 159–60 tables 1 and 4.

and compounded exclusivity by exorbitant prices for subscription series. But lesser performers, less competent instrumentalists and popular pieces could always be heard at the pleasure gardens. Ranelagh charged 2s. 6d. (12.5p), Vauxhall – representing 'a quintessentially eighteenth-century form of refined but not precious amusement' – was putting on concerts from the mid-1730s and charging 1s. 0d. (5p), raised to 2s. 0d. (10p) in 1792.[55] This was less than a day's wage for an artisan, who would, of course, need to dress in a manner above his station.[56] Below Vauxhall and Ranelagh were many cheaper pleasure gardens, such as the Pantheon in Spa Fields frequented chiefly by 'journeymen tailors, hairdressers, milliners and servant maids', the New Wells in Clerkenwell where the purchase of a pint of wine served as an admission ticket, Marylebone Gardens frequented by Macheath, and a host of other venues, often short-lived, often combining the functions of public house and music hall, putting on dramatic shows, pageants, plays, music and circus performances in a manner supposed by some only to have become widespread during the later nineteenth century.[57]

That there was a specific 'metropolitan taste' is debatable: from the point of view of theatrical and musical entrepreneurs the important characteristic of London was that it was large and potentially profitable to exploit, that audiences could be obtained, but that their tastes were to a very large extent dependent upon what their betters thought. Seventeenth-century London merchants had not copied their Dutch counterparts and developed their own symbolic domestic architecture, nor did their patronage bring about a creative explosion; this remained the case in the eighteenth century, but did not prevent them from desiring a wide range of consumer durables.[58] The Spitalfields silk industry had long known this, and made a point of closely observing the first balls of the season. There were truly popular ores to be mined – probably not specifically metropolitan, but more present in the metropolis because of its larger size. Taking a wider definition of culture, it is difficult to show London's 'demonstration' effect, although such an effect is highly probable. The most important cultural departures did not necessarily begin in London, but it was in London that they reached their apogee. Newspapers are an obvious example, attaining their mass market in London and spreading out from there. This was the typical pattern, also repeated with pleasure gardens which reached their apogee in London, and with coffee-houses which as with museums did not begin in London but in Oxford in 1652 but spread rapidly through London from the 1660s. In the mid-1730s London had nearly nine-tenths of the nation's dealers

55 McVeigh, *Concert Life*, pp. 39–44.

56 E. D. Mackerness, *A Social History of English Music* (London, 1964), pp. 100, 103–6.

57 W. Wroth, *The London Pleasure Gardens of the Eighteenth Century* (London, 1896), pp. 25, 33, 94 and *passim*.

58 R. Grassby, *The Business Community of Seventeenth-Century England* (Cambridge, 1995), pp. 359–60.

in tea and coffee.[59] By the 1690s if not earlier there were specialist coffee-houses, such as Lloyds for shipping, Garraway's, closely allied to the Royal Exchange, or John's in Cornhill which in the heady days of the South Sea Bubble was the address for a subscription of £2 million 'for erecting salt-pans in Holy Island'.[60] Writers, poets, stockbrokers, merchants congregated in their own coffee-houses to an extent to which smaller towns obviously could not aspire; by the earlier nineteenth century the coffee-houses had become clubs from which women and undesirable men could be barred.[61]

For those more secure members of the bourgeoisie, whose numbers increased during this period, London probably led the way with a new form of upper-middle-class, essentially female-led housekeeping which seems to have begun in London around the 1660s, becoming a cumulative process from about the 1680s with inventories showing increasing amounts of china, comfortable chairs and better-furnished bedrooms – London builders, cheesemongers, soapmakers did not waste their money on bedrooms, but 'most merchants, mercers and drapers made very sure that they would not be found dead in a bedroom worth less than £15' and usually a great deal more.[62] There is some debate concerning the extent to which London took the lead in this process, as well as the extent to which women willingly adopted these roles. But even a reasonably well-off married woman could only have a place in the home if there were a wide range of services on which she could draw, from servants to cook-houses, bakers, brewers, tailors and laundresses. By the end of the seventeenth century London had become a fast food city. To a great extent this was a result of London's greater purchasing power rather than of any specifically metropolitan taste, but the demonstration effect of this purchasing power should not be underestimated.[63]

At the same time, as Margaret Hunt has demonstrated, the presence of large numbers of bourgeoisie, many of them posed precariously between security and ruin, made London a forcing ground for a more diffuse set of values where the insecurity of life fostered a stress on moral seriousness and kinship reliance as well as on a serious religion. So of course London had most of the nation's playhouses, prostitutes, obscene publications and all the temptations designed to lead astray the sons of struggling entrepreneurs, including a fairly visible homosexual

[59] L. Weatherill, *Consumer Behaviour and Material Culture in Britain 1660–1760* (London, 1988), p. 62.

[60] B. Lillywhite, *London Coffee Houses* (London, 1963), pp. 17, 20, 216–24, 295–6, 330–5.

[61] For an example see A. Wedgwood, 'The Athenaeum', in B. Ford, ed., *The Cambridge Guide to the Arts in Britain*, vol. VI (Cambridge, 1990), pp. 255–61. For the seventeenth century see above, pp. 330, 341.

[62] Earle, *Making of the English Middle Class*, pp. 290–6, 165–6.

[63] Earle, *A City Full of People*, pp. 106–13. C. Shammas, *The Pre-Industrial Consumer in England and America* (Oxford, 1990), pp. 86–92, believes that the spread of these items was a function of income, not of geography, and Earle's data are confined to London. Examining this in detail would require a much more detailed chronology than is currently available. Shammas' data derive from east London and south Worcestershire during the 1660s and the 1720s, and if London was a powerful centre for imitation, the process would have spread to Worcestershire by the 1720s.

culture. Unsurprisingly, the fathers reacted. During the earlier eighteenth century London boasted its societies for the reform of manners; in the mid-century it was host to a remarkable outpouring of nationalistic, mercantile benevolence designed to restore the population to a useful existence – whether by saving new-born infants, foundlings or prostitutes, or by sweeping London street children into the navy. Later in the century this developed into the evangelical revival. It all highlighted irreconcilable contradictions between notions of female domesticity and female spheres of activity.[64]

(v) FINANCE, POLITICS AND ADMINISTRATION

London's politics and administration have been much studied. The subject can be approached at various levels. As already pointed out, this large inchoate sprawling urban region lacked any unified administration until the formation of the London County Council in 1888. The City governed itself, of course, but the City formed a steadily declining part of the whole. Westminster obtained its own paving and lighting acts and other parts of the town followed. Outside the City the usual unit of government was the parish, and some parishes rivalled large provincial cities. These continually spawned their own administrative bodies. The Public Health Act of 1848 did not provide a great deal of rationalisation and in 1855 *The Times* could comment that London's local administration was carried on by 300 different bodies deriving their powers from about 250 local acts of parliament.[65]

Before the advent of the Metropolitan Police in 1829 the City and parishes controlled their own police, and the lack of coordination was of course anathema to the government, which sought a degree of coordination with the Middlesex Justices Act of 1792 which appointed a number of stipendiary magistrates for the entire built-up area.[66] The Metropolitan Police force was the final product of a long history of parallel policing, where carefully chosen magistrates worked in cooperation with the government to watch the pulse of London and report directly to the secretary of state. Henry Fielding in the 1750s had been a celebrated but isolated example, Patrick Colquhoun during the 1790s was as celebrated but less isolated.[67] All of these carefully omitted the City from their official jurisdiction. The forces that they controlled were few in number: Henry Fielding had only a dozen 'thief-takers' at Bow Street, while in 1828 the

64 M. R. Hunt, *The Middling Sort* (Berkeley, Calif., 1996), pp. 101–24, 136–7; D. T. Andrew, *Philanthropy and Police* (Princeton, N.J., 1989), pp. 44–73, 98–134, 163–96.

65 Quoted in Young and Garside, *Metropolitan London*, p. 21. See also F. H. W. Sheppard, *Local Government in St. Marylebone 1688–1835: A Study of the Vestry and the Turnpike Trusts* (London, 1958), for a rare description of how an individual parish sought to achieve coordination.

66 L. Radzinowicz, *A History of English Criminal Law and its Administration from 1750* (London, 1956), vol. III, pp. 123–37. 67 *Ibid.*, pp. 31–62, 211–46.

government paid for 427 constables. The parishes employed far greater numbers. The Metropolitan Police itself in 1833 had only 3,389 men. In the last resort, their significance was less an impact on crime than the capacity to forestall large-scale disorder, and their direct and immediate connection to the government and from there, if necessary, to the army.[68] However, at the same time there was a much larger magistracy that dealt with routine matters, and it may well have been easier and cheaper to obtain justice in London than elsewhere – the courts were near, and met more frequently than was usually the case elsewhere; the absence of other gentry increased the role of magistrates as intermediaries and conciliators as well as prosecutors. By contemporary English standards London was rather well policed.[69]

Political movements, petitions, protests also had their parallel side. On the one hand, there were the uncoordinated parishes and the bodies within them, not to mention the wards within the City. On the other hand, there were continual efforts to create movements across the entire town. The City had a long tradition of corporate solidarity (see Plate 17). It was divided into 26 wards and 242 precincts; some 12,000 to 15,000 resident freemen ratepayers elected the 236 members of the common council each year and the poorer ratepayers could still elect ward and precinct officers.[70] This helped to create a 'City opinion', and the more important the City within the metropolis, the easier it was for it to give shape to London's political stance. As London expanded and the City itself was inexorably 'improved' to the detriment of its popular character, its role declined. It never came anywhere near regaining the role it had in the 1640s, but the Wilkite agitation of the 1760s showed that the City's capacity to be at the epicentre of national radical agitation remained. Other centres, particularly Westminster, were always important, its elections attracting considerable Court intervention.[71]

Historians have tended to approach London politics as the politics of radicalism. The City was sufficiently free of government influence to be able to express its radicalism if it so wished. Westminster in the mid-eighteenth century was

[68] A great deal of literature on this: for an accessible introduction see F. H. W. Sheppard, *London, 1808–1870* (London, 1971), pp. 30–40. For an example of the London magistracy in action with the army see John Stevenson, 'The Queen Caroline Affair' in J. Stevenson, ed., *London in the Age of Reform* (Oxford, 1977), pp. 117–48 at pp. 136–9.

[69] R. B. Shoemaker, *Prosecution and Punishment* (Cambridge, 1991), pp. 9–10. R. Paley, ed., *Justice in Eighteenth-Century Hackney: The Justicing Notebook of Henry Norris and the Hackney Petty Sessions Book* (London Record Society, 1991), for an example of one such magistrate.

[70] Rudé, *Hanoverian London*, pp. 118–27; S. Webb and B. Webb, *The Manor and the Borough* (London 1908), pp. 569–692 at p. 579. Estimate of 10,000–12,000 ratepaying households in 1689, *ibid.*, p. 580 (estimate of 12,000 liverymen, 40,000 freemen in 1832, *ibid.*, p. 584: 12,000–15,000 freemen who lived within the City boundaries).

[71] N. Rogers, *Whigs and Cities* (Oxford, 1989), pp. 168–96; N. Rogers, 'Aristocratic clientage, trade and independency: popular politics in pre-radical Westminster', *P&P*, 61 (1973), 70–106.

much less able to do so,[72] but gradually developed this capacity. There were always parallel streams in London radicalism, both geographically and socially. During the eighteenth century there had been a tendency towards cooperation but the French Revolution brought the cooperation to breaking point, with the artisan-led London Corresponding Society's enthusiastic espousal of Thomas Paine. From then, cooperation, while not infrequent, changed its character. From 1807 a revived and electorally successful Westminster radicalism flanked but was no longer led by a revived streak of opposition from the City. The Queen Caroline affair provided a brief moment of unity but by then London had become too large and the City no longer able to provide the focus for organised oppositional movements to the government. The same lack of focus was apparent in 1832 and thereafter radical politics, taking their new shape of National Union, Owenism and Chartism, lacked the institutional focus available to the earlier radicals.[73] The publicity that had been achieved during the eighteenth century by petitions now had other means of propagation. Nineteenth-century political movements took place *within* London, but they were not generated outwards from London as had been the case with many of the major eighteenth-century agitations.[74]

However, this is only a part of the story. Politically the centrality of the City may have declined; financially it continued to grow. Its financial aristocracy had an important role within the City but was a crucial part of the settlement that evolved during the years after 1688 and financed the national debt, the wars, overseas trade and overseas expansion. Its members often combined their role as financiers with that of merchants; the wealthiest of them, whose wealth rivalled the wealthiest aristocracy and who mixed socially with the latter, were often members of parliament, and by the later nineteenth century had merged with them almost to the point of invisibility. The extent to which they did so during the eighteenth century has been much debated by historians; there is no doubt that they were close.[75]

(vi) SOCIAL STRUCTURE AND SOCIAL GEOGRAPHY

Details about the social structure of the capital's population are not easily attainable. The nineteenth-century census data is more suitable for analysing occupations than incomes. However, an analysis of the tax data of 1798 provides a

72 Rogers, *Whigs and Cities*, p. 193; 'When we consider the armoury of interest at the Court's disposal [during the 1740s] it is surprising that their opponents made any showing at all.'

73 Much has been written on this: see J. Stevenson, *London in the Age of Reform* (Oxford, 1977); Sheppard, *London, 1808–1870*, pp. 297–344; D. Goodway, *London Chartism, 1838–1848* (Cambridge, 1982); I. Prothero, *Artisans and Politics in Early Nineteenth-Century London* (Folkestone, 1979).

74 See above, pp. 562–5, for the expansion of the geographical basis of popular mobilisation after about 1770.

75 Cain and Hopkins, *British Imperialism*, pp. 60–3, 66–7.

reasonable starting point, which subsequent research is unlikely to change to any very considerable extent, either for the preceding century or for the subsequent half-century. It must be stressed that this data covers the entire metropolis, a wider area than the City and its Liberties that Boulton has drawn from in a preceding chapter.[76] In 1798 the upper income group – aristocracy, wealthier gentry and wealthier merchants with average incomes of over £200 – formed not more than 3 per cent of the capital's population. Of more note, numerically, were the 'middling classes' with incomes of about £80 upwards who formed between a fifth and a sixth of the population. Their upper echelons consisted of fairly well-defined groups, most of them in the service sector, who would have fitted comfortably into the highest income group, but these were the peaks of the visible part of the iceberg. Many of them were in the professions; it is probable that the professions expanded most rapidly between about 1680 and 1730, thereafter probably doing no more than maintain their share of the capital's population.[77] Below the prestigious and expensive doctors, lawyers and a few writers, musicians, sculptors and painters was a pyramid of insecure hangers-on, only a few of whom could ever hope to attain even a moderate degree of financial security, and mostly invisible to subsequent historians.[78] Government employees were not very different. Shopkeepers ranged from those keeping prestigious establishments in the West End, with capital not much less than wealthy merchants, to humble chandlers' shops by the riverside. 'Dealers' ranged from those few City merchants who achieved the traditional legendary wealth to struggling poulterers and fishmongers. Manufacturers were, of course, present, although they tended to be less wealthy than the other groups.[79]

The remaining working-class population of London formed about three-quarters of the total population. They were, of course, a very disparate group, but the most important distinction was between artisans, lesser shopkeepers (sometimes artisans themselves) and others. Artisans were – by working-class standards – reasonably well paid, and expected to be paid sufficiently regularly to belong to friendly societies, which required weekly subscriptions in order to pay out benefits. Friendly society members formed a large group of the population: if (and it is an unresolved question) they were overwhelmingly comprised of those employed rather than of small capitalists and shopkeepers, they would have comprised a third of the adult male population, or some 40 per cent of the working population and have outnumbered the middle classes. It would, however, be a mistake to believe that artisans were usually self-employed. Data on the number of shops in London during the 1790s suggests that, with the

[76] See above, pp. 327–8. [77] Schwarz, *London in the Age of Industrialisation*, p. 28; Corfield, *Power and the Professions*, pp. 28–34. [78] Corfield, *Power and the Professions*, pp. 176–7, 184–6, 230–1.
[79] Schwarz, *London in the Age of Industrialisation*, pp. 57–73; Earle, *Making of the English Middle Class*; Earle, *A City Full of People*; G. Holmes, *Augustan England* (London, 1982); Corfield, *Power and the Professions*.

exception of the building trades, self-employed artisans formed no more than 3 to 4 per cent of the male population, or 5 to 6 per cent of the working population.

Aggregate figures are of limited use. London had its geography – the West End and City had always contained large numbers of rich people, while most of the built-up part of the East End contained few of them. This geography took time to make itself clear and as late as the second half of the eighteenth century the area north of the crowded strip along the Thames was relatively rural with quite large numbers of wealthy residences. Nevertheless in 1798 there was no extensive region of London, and hardly a parish, where the working population did not form a majority of the population. This was not unusual in large European cities: it was the case in Dublin at the same time; it would be the case in Paris during the 1840s. Residential segregation was confined to comparatively small areas. Transport was too expensive and the demand for labour-intensive services too great to permit the wealthy to dominate areas larger than a few squares or streets. Between the 1690s and the 1840s, as the capital's perimeter widened, its social geography showed two consistent and related characteristics. The first, a very slow process, was a gradually increasing concentration of wealth in the west and centre and the transformation of the City into a central business district. The second was the persistence of large pockets of poverty in the midst of areas of affluence.

Maps 19.2 and 19.3, showing the poor and wealthy areas of London during the 1690s, demonstrate the first of these processes. During the 1690s the poorest areas arched around the central districts of the city from Wapping and Whitechapel in the east to Saffron Hill in the west. In addition, much – but certainly not all – of the Tower Division in the east was poor.[80] The rich areas were in four groups: a part of the City Within, from St Dunstan in the west to Covent Garden, north of Charing Cross, and the region south of Piccadilly. By the 1840s, the situation was not so different, except that the West End had raised itself more. 'In the 1840s the main distinction in terms of poverty was between a belt of impoverished inner districts surrounding the City and those wealthier areas further out'.[81]

As long-standing as this process of differentiation was its opposite: the persistence of the poor in wealthy areas. The rich made life more difficult for the poor by building larger houses and by a tendency to drive wide roads through the middle of insalubrious slums. It was called 'improvement'. Within the City of London, improvement predated the Great Fire, but the brick houses built in the aftermath of the Great Fire accelerated it markedly. Improvement then slowed down, with relatively little taking place during the first half of the eighteenth

[80] I would like to thank Mr Derek Morris for showing me his work on Mile End Old Town (quite a wealthy area) between 1740 and 1790. [81] Green, *From Artisans to Paupers*, p. 196 and ch. 7.

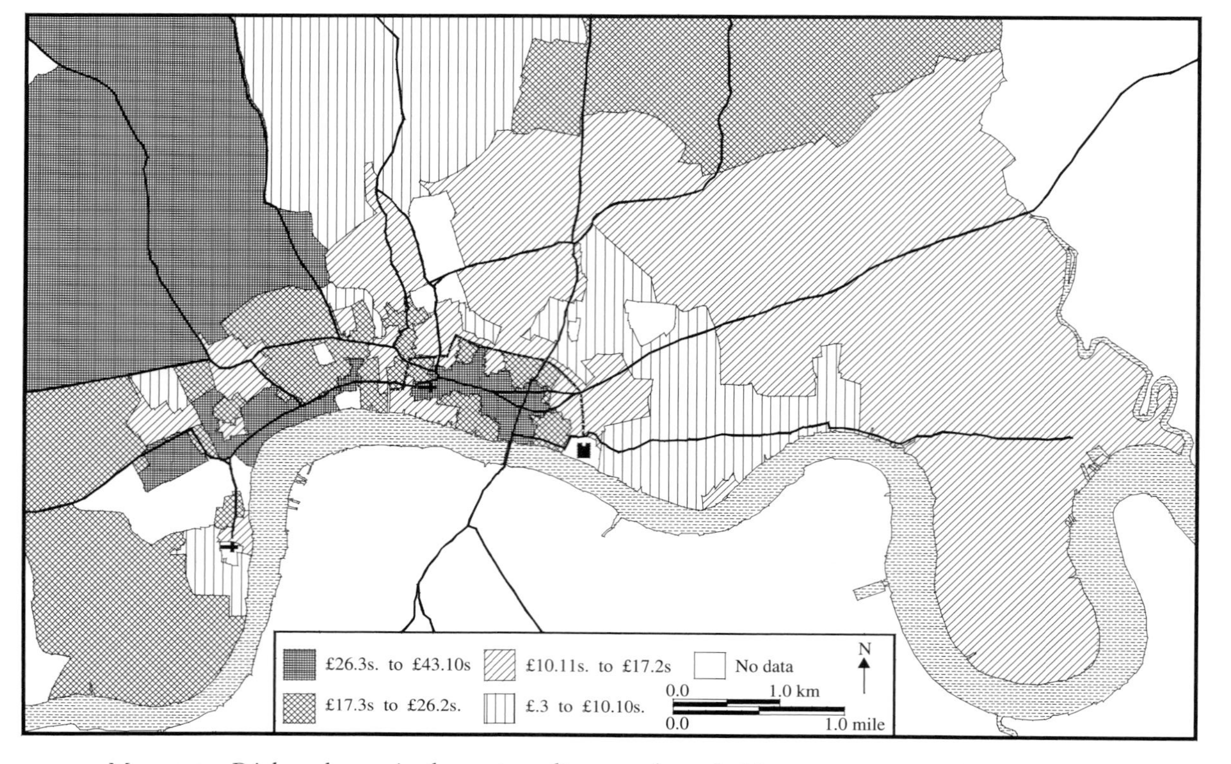

Map 19.2 Rich and poor in the metropolis: mean household rent per annum 1693–1694

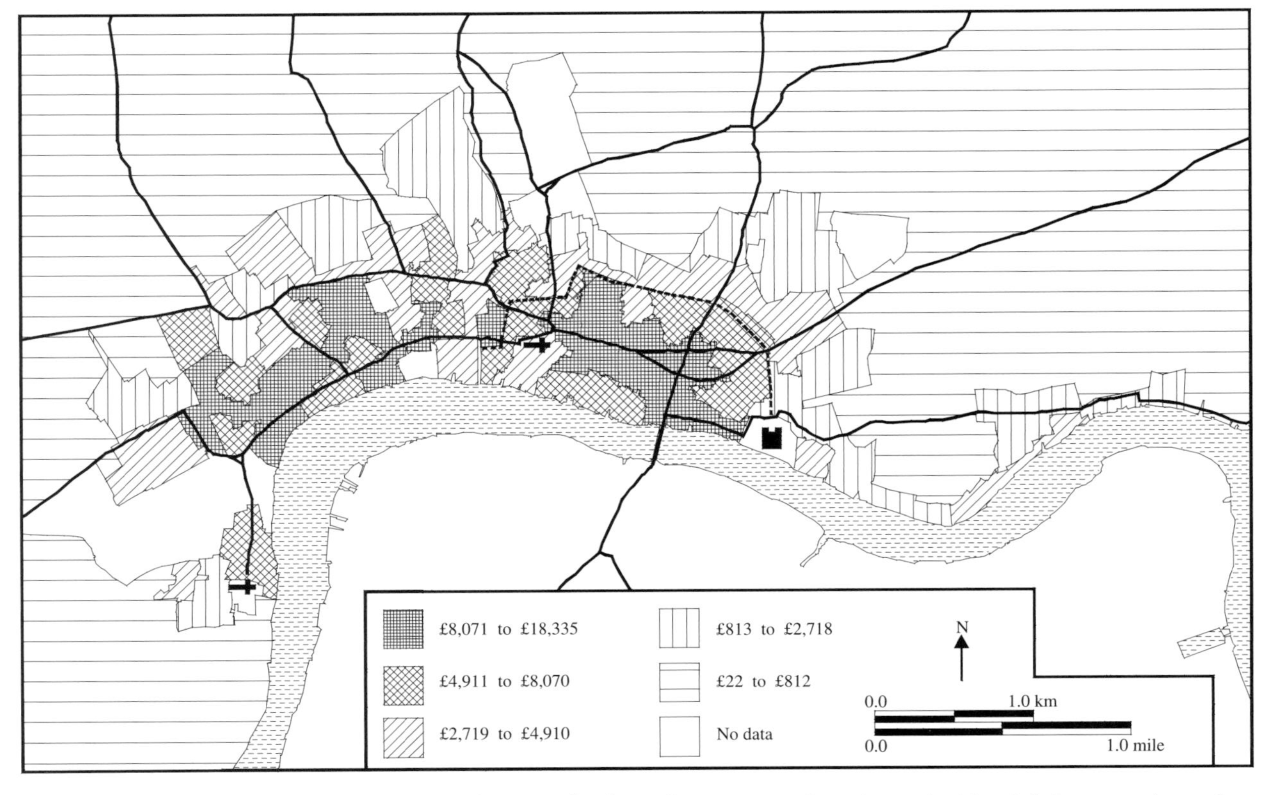

Map 19.3 Rich and poor in the metropolis: capital value of property and stock per (residential) hectare 1693–1694

century, more thereafter. The West End improved itself in a serious manner under the Regency, while subsequent railway building and systematic Victorian urban road cutting accelerated the process. However, the poor remained, because the wealthy needed and attracted them. In the West End (and to a large extent in the City) there was a demand for two different types of labour. The first was that of the well-paid artisan, almost invariably male, producing luxury goods, working and living locally. As the nineteenth century progressed, he was less and less likely to live in the City. He might well have a shop, perhaps managed by his wife. The second type of labour force was at the other end of the spectrum, a largely casual labour force of servants, prostitutes, criminals, porters, market-traders, fetchers of wood and drawers of water, a labour force that was to a large extent female (see Plate 14). 'Immediately behind some of the best constructed houses in the fashionable districts of London are some of the worst dwellings, into which the working classes are crowded', remarked Chadwick in 1842.[82] One reason why this was so was reported in 1786:

> By enquiry an honest charwoman, to support the place of a woman-servant, may be procured for 1s. a day. If such are hired to wash, their wages are larger: 1s. 6d. [7.5p] with tea and a dram twice a day, and strong beer and supper; but for this they slave hard, will begin to work at 2 in the morning, and continue it till 9 of the next evening.[83]

The local poor (see Plate 16) increased in numbers during the eighteenth century as the wealth of the City and the West End increased. The building of Regent Street forced them into the Strand and Westminster, and subsequent improvements and railway building localised them even more into ever tighter and more crowded slums, with rents higher and overcrowding greater than in the East End.[84]

The two largest foci of employment, the port (see Plate 13) and the Court, influenced immensely both the geography of manufacturing and the nature of employment itself within London, with the division between rich and poor, male and female, adults and children. The nature of the labour attracted to the West End has just been described. The port was very different. The age of sail, seasonality and labour-intensive methods of loading and unloading ships produced a casual, often underemployed labour force of riverside workers, mostly male, and prostitutes, mostly female. The wives of the former needed employment and during the nineteenth century they increasingly found it in what would be called the 'sweated trades' – tailoring and shoemaking – with long hours and very low pay, often conducted from home. It was a form of urban proto-industry that historians have commonly described for eighteenth-century

[82] *Report on the Sanitary Condition of the Labouring Population of Great Britain* (E. Chadwick), PP 1842 XXVI (repr. Edinburgh, 1965), p. 232. [83] G. Kearsley, *Table of Trades* (London, 1786), p. 97.

[84] Green, *From Artisans to Paupers*, pp. 183.

rural manufacture. Those who employed them sought to live north of the slums, as long as there remained rural parts of Hackney and Stepney.

The geography just described was a function of the port and the Court. London displayed another parallel geography, that of manufacturing. As pointed out earlier, London was the largest manufacturing centre in the western hemisphere. It was well integrated with the port and the Court but, unlike these, it had the potential to provide more regular employment. 'Regular' meant that it was available for several months, maybe most of the year. It did not preclude seasonal unemployment. Hobsbawm has divided the London labour market of the later nineteenth century into three geographical regions. South London had a substantial degree of heavy industry and relatively little connection with the rest of London. Westminster had many skilled artisans. North and east London contained large masses of unskilled labour.[85] This was the case long before the later nineteenth century and was a reflection of the nature of manufacturing in the capital. The peak of London's manufacturing prominence was during the later seventeenth and earlier eighteenth centuries, when the capital dominated a wide range of industries. From London's point of view the Industrial Revolution can be defined as a process of provincial economic development to which London adjusted. It did so by developing its strengths – its skilled labour and its proximity to the finished market. The obverse of these strengths was that labour was expensive and rents were high, so the natural response was to develop workshop manufacture, with high quality labour being carried out in highly specialised small workshops in specialised regions of the capital. Spitalfields produced – or finished – silks, Long Acre coaches, Clerkenwell watches. Division of labour was by workshop, and the production line ran through the street. In that respect London was similar to Birmingham, but on a much larger scale.[86] As provincial England industrialised, there was a continuous tendency for the London trades to move towards the finished end of the production process, downstream and up-market. This had not been a new process during the seventeenth century when silkweaving replaced fustian; it continued during the eighteenth century when trades such as framework weaving and silk ribbon weaving left London while broad silk weaving, for the luxury end of the market, grew. During the eighteenth century the process of adaptation tended on the whole to be fairly successful; during the nineteenth century it became more stressful. Silkweaving, having gone as far up-market as possible, was in crisis when the prohibition of

85 E. J. Hobsbawm, 'The nineteenth-century London labour market', in E. J. Hobsbawm, *Worlds of Labour* (London, 1984).

86 M. Berg, *The Age of Manufactures* (Oxford, 1985), pp. 75, 274; M. Berg, *The Age of Manufactures*, 2nd edn (London, 1994), pp. 72–5. This is not to ignore the large-scale engineering works, tanning, hat making, brewing or shipbuilding works in London. Most of them, with the exception of shipbuilding, were south of the Thames, where the land was cheaper and the capital's labour market different (Schwarz, *London in the Age of Industrialisation*, p. 32).

imported French silks was lifted in 1826. Watchmaking, similarly, could not maintain its position. Other industries, such as shipbuilding, which typically boasted that it made the best ships in the country, thrived for longer, but never recovered from the depression of 1866.[87]

(vii) LIVING STANDARDS AND TRADE DILUTION

Some trades neither declined nor went up-market. They grew, but they adapted their labour force, often painfully. In the process, the tension between formal and informal structures of employment increased. Until the end of the Napoleonic wars, the analysis of wage rates and living standards in London is reasonably straightforward.[88] Wage rates rose until the mid-eighteenth century, and then tended to fall gradually until the 1790s, when they fell quite sharply, to rise somewhat thereafter and considerably between 1815 and 1825, when prices fell and wages did not. The eighteenth-century fall was moderated by increased employment and much influenced by cyclical effects. The latter were caused to some extent by an incipient trade cycle and to a greater extent by wars which usually produced slumps on their outbreak, then a labour shortage following mobilisation, with a glut of labour and a crime wave when the wars ended. Warfare was endemic up to 1714 and from 1739 to 1815, and so was this pattern. Industrialisation produced a longer-term change, but only during the nineteenth century. As with contemporary de-industrialising Britain, averages are meaningless by the second quarter of the nineteenth century.[89] The gap between formal and informal structures, between contemporary myth and reality grew to the point where it cannot be ignored. The myth assigned only a small, supportive role to women and children. It pretended that a town with 30 per cent or more of the population aged between ten and thirty and usually unmarried[90] would be practising sexual continence, that – at least during the eighteenth century – apprentices would remain under the watchful eyes of their employers, law-abiding and sexually continent. The myth became considerably more stretched during the nineteenth century when low-paid female domestic work in London expanded simultaneously with the strengthening of the 'male breadwinner wage' amongst artisans, and not accidentally. The expectation that women should not contribute to the family income grew from the 1820s, in large part

[87] G. Stedman Jones, *Outcast London* (Oxford, 1971), pp. 152–5; S. Pollard, 'The decline of shipbuilding on the Thames', *Ec.HR*, 2nd series, 3 (1950–1), 72–89; G. Crossick, *An Artisan Elite in Victorian Society: Kentish London, 1840–80* (London, 1978); Prothero, *Artisans and Politics*, pp. 24–5, 46–50, 305–6; Green, *From Artisans to Paupers*, pp. 156–76.

[88] L. D. Schwarz, 'The standard of living in the long run', *Ec.HR*, 2nd series, 38 (1985), 24–41.

[89] That is why it is possible for historians considering identical evidence to disagree whether the changes in London during this period were great or not: Green, *From Artisans to Paupers*, pp. 156–76; Schwarz, *London in the Age of Industrialisation*, pp. 38–40, 179–207.

[90] Landers, *Death and the Metropolis*, p. 180.

as a defence against female 'sweated' labour, although it remained exceedingly difficult even for artisans to realise in practice and met with considerable difficulty when expectations came up against the reality of women who were neither servants nor married.[91]

The capital's concentration on the finished, up-market sector led to a large number of relatively small trades with high proportions of skilled artisans, overwhelmingly male, the envy of their peers across the nation. On their own, these trades could never have employed all those requiring work, but beneath them there was a wide range of male-dominated and tolerably paid trades such as tailoring or shoemaking many of whose practitioners were not particularly skilled, but who had acquired sufficient skills to erect flimsy barricades against the flood of workers that continually threatened to engulf them. This flood consisted of women, children and males formally unskilled but willing and able to learn fairly rudimentary skills at short notice. The feminisation of those parts of the trade that had hitherto been predominantly male was a result of provincial industrialisation, but it was not a response to new machinery. London trades never competed directly with the provinces, an effort that with London's more expensive rents and labour would have been doomed from the start. By specialising in the finishing process, London benefited from the cheaper materials that industrialisation provided. In its turn, this created an opportunity to manufacture cheaper clothes, and therefore made it worth while for employers to employ cheaper labour, a process that took place on a large scale during the second quarter of the nineteenth century, a period of relatively slow growth in the capital's economy. The result was an enormous rise in female employment in these trades, a fall in the wage rates of those hitherto slightly protected, a fall quite possibly stabilised by more constant (if appallingly paid) female employment. The same process was taking place in many other towns of continental Europe, as well as in New York.[92]

The trades that were diluted tended to have certain facets in common. They were trades where the 'male breadwinner wage' that the men claimed so loudly was being undermined had always been rather uncertain. They were trades which supplied the basic demands of the domestic population, trades with a large market, trades with some scope for de-skilling through division of labour rather than machinery, most of which tended to see the growth of large-scale capitalist control over distribution.[93] These would include tailors, shoemakers, furniture makers. The Industrial Revolution produced an increase in the number of

[91] A. Clark, *The Struggle for the Breeches: Gender and the Making of the British Working Class* (Berkeley, Calif., 1995), pp. 198–203, 220–32; P. Seleski, 'The women of the laboring poor: love, work and poverty in London, 1750–1820' (PhD thesis, University of Stanford, 1989), p. 302.

[92] For references, see Schwarz, *London in the Age of Industrialisation*, p. 159.

[93] J. Breuilly, 'Artisan economy, artisan politics, artisan ideology', in C. Emsley and J. Walvin, eds., *Artisans, Peasants and Proletarians* (London, 1985), pp. 199–201.

hand-loom weavers, but it also produced a very large, and longer lasting, increase in the number of tailors, many of them female. A different, although not altogether dissimilar, process was taking place within the building trades.[94]

In the last resort, London's growth was a function of national growth. Of course, London was too dominant an economic centre for it not to affect national growth, but during the age of the Industrial Revolution its dominance was gradually declining. From the vantage point of London, the Industrial Revolution can be seen as a process of provincial industrial growth, to which London responded by increased specialisation, first by moving downstream in the production process towards finished, labour-intensive goods, and, secondly, by moving up-market. Some trades left London entirely but as late as 1851 London maintained its role as the largest manufacturing town in Europe, where the number of men and women involved in manufacturing was almost equal to the entire population of Liverpool, the second largest city in Britain at the time, and greater than the population of Manchester or Glasgow. However, as a third of the employed population of the capital this was a lower proportion of the labour force than was the case in many other towns. Services, in the broadly defined sense of the port and the Court, had always dictated the principal contours of manufacturing in London, provided the greatest wealth and demand and ultimately dominated the geography of the capital. Finance eventually added itself to these.

Whether the town was 'improved' in the way that nineteenth-century commentators continually asserted is another matter. As London expanded, the ever-increasing number of coal fires made the London smog an ever-more celebrated feature of life in the capital.[95] Wordsworth, who in 1802 had stood on Westminster Bridge and declared that earth had not anything to show more fair rarely visited the capital thereafter, and never wrote in praise of it again.[96] Staying away from Westminster Bridge was in fact increasingly advisable as more and more of the town's sewers were connected to each other and in turn directed into the Thames, a process that reached its nadir with the Great Stink of 1858. Meanwhile, despite the self-serving congratulations of the urban improvers, slums remained, although less obtrusively than previously. The one incontestable improvement, the fall in the death rate, was not obviously due to better sanitation, better building practices or improved living standards, at least not during the second half of the eighteenth century, although it may have been thereafter. However 'moral' improvements – for Victorian observers the prerequisite for all other improvements – were clearer. That the London poor behaved themselves in a more orderly manner appears difficult to contest. Whether by choice

[94] L. Clarke, *Building Capitalism: Historical Change and the Labour Process in the Production of the Built Environment* (London, 1992), pp. 61–84.

[95] For one interpretation of the effects of urban improvement, see Schwarz, *London in the Age of Industrialisation*, pp. 234–7.

[96] Sheppard, *London, 1808–1870*, p. xv.

or otherwise, they rioted less, foreigners found them less insulting, while artisans sought to separate themselves ever more clearly from the disreputable poor below them. This was, of course, a national phenomenon, that was by no means confined to London. They continued the long process of becoming more literate, educating their children a little better than they themselves had been educated, washed themselves more, took advantage of cheap cotton clothing, perhaps drank a little less and upheld the ideal of the male breadwinner wage and the paterfamilias, many with no realistic chances of stemming the tide of female labour, others with much more success, while the ever-growing world city took advantage of the Industrial Revolution and the Empire to become the service centre of the world.

· 20 ·

Regional and county centres 1700–1840

JOYCE ELLIS

It is now widely recognised that towns played a central role in the development of a new, more modern British economy and society in the years between 1700 and 1840. However, it is often assumed that the expansive element in urban society, the new social attitudes and cultural values that were helping to change patterns of consumer demand, to mobilise capital resources and to generate novel industrial processes and products, were confined to the great metropolis of London and the specialist ports, resorts and industrial towns whose growth attracted so much attention from contemporary observers. Nevertheless, it would be a mistake to ignore the role played in this process by the established regional centres and historic county towns, many of which retained their importance well into the late eighteenth and early nineteenth centuries. Their experiences during this period of substantial and sometimes dramatic change in the urban system encompass every possible permutation from explosive population growth to sullen stagnation and raise pertinent questions about the very nature of 'success' in the context of urban development. Rather than being passive spectators of a drama taking place elsewhere, regional and county centres were fully involved in the action.

(i) STATUS, FUNCTIONS AND PATTERNS OF DEVELOPMENT

A substantial number of the 'Great and Good towns' of early modern England fell into the category of county centres, towns whose social and economic influence over a broad hinterland beyond their immediate market area was recognised by their contemporary classification as 'the capital of all the county' or simply 'county town'.[1] In practice these centres varied widely in size and significance.

[1] D. Defoe, *A Tour through the Whole Island of Great Britain*, ed. G. D. H. Cole and D. C. Browning (London, 1962), vol. II, p. 162; D. Defoe, *The Complete English Tradesman*, 2nd edn (London, 1727), p. 80. For 'Great and Good' towns, see above, pp. 347 *et seq.*

There was a world of difference between substantial provincial towns such as Ipswich or Worcester, with around 8,000 inhabitants in the early eighteenth century, which were able to exert a major impact over their localities, and equally historic but much less successful towns such as Buckingham and Dorchester, with barely 2,000 inhabitants, which struggled to compete with their local rivals.[2] It should also be noted that the terms 'county' or 'shire-town' can in themselves be misleading, since county centres rarely occupied the geographical centre of their 'official' administrative area. In many cases the counties concerned simply covered too large or too disparate an area to manage with one single centre: thus Kent was served by Maidstone, 'the Shire Town for all publick business', as well as by the ecclesiastical centre of Canterbury, Derbyshire by Chesterfield as well as by its formal county town of Derby, and Yorkshire by Beverley, Wakefield and Doncaster as well as by York itself. In some cases the effective hinterlands of these subsidiary centres even crossed county boundaries: Lichfield, for instance, drew in both trade and visitors from Derbyshire and Warwickshire as well as Staffordshire, while Carlisle's 'neighbourhood' took in a substantial tract of territory on both sides of the border with Scotland.[3] But despite these anomalies and reservations, it is undeniable that county centres derived both their status and their livelihood from the support of a particular county or a substantial portion of it. It was the influence of both their administrative and social roles within the county and their position as the natural focus of their economic hinterland that shaped their distinctive economy and society.[4]

Above them in the urban hierarchy stood a handful of regional capitals, 'universal towns' which dominated the county centres within their extensive hinterlands and earned their special status because of the enormous range and depth of their influence. At the opening of the eighteenth century there were probably about eight major provincial towns which fell into this category, including Norwich, the second city in the kingdom, Bristol and Newcastle-upon-Tyne, the two largest ports outside London, and the smaller centres of Exeter, York, Chester and Shrewsbury.[5] Each of these cities lay at the heart of a complex web of social and economic relationships, held together by well-developed systems of communication. All were significant cultural and social centres, providing an

[2] Defoe, *Tour*, I, pp. 45, 210, II, pp. 43–6; M. Reed, 'Decline and recovery in a provincial urban network: Buckinghamshire towns 1350–1800', in M. Reed, ed., *English Towns in Decline 1350–1800* (Leicester, 1986), pp. 25–6, appendix 2.

[3] R. Hyde, ed., *A Prospect of Britain* (London, 1994), plate 46; Defoe, *Tour*, II, p. 80; *VCH*, Staffordshire, XIV, pp. 21–4; J. Money, *Experience and Identity* (Manchester, 1977), p. 82; W. Hutchinson, *History of the County of Cumberland and Some Places Adjacent* (Carlisle, 1794), vol. II, pp. 660–1.

[4] A. M. Everitt, 'Country, county and town: patterns of regional evolution in England', in P. Borsay, ed., *The Eighteenth Century Town* (London, 1990), pp. 83–115; C. W. Chalklin, *The Provincial Towns of Georgian England* (London, 1974), pp. 8–11; E. A. Wrigley, 'City and country in the past: a sharp divide or a continuum?', *HR*, 64 (1991), 107–20.

[5] P. Borsay, *The English Urban Renaissance* (Oxford, 1989), pp. 8–10; Chalklin, *Provincial Towns*, pp. 9, 13–19.

ever-increasing range of leisure facilities and personal services to visitors as well as to the wealthy residents of their extensive 'neighbourhoods'.[6] All were major centres of wholesale and retail trade, drawing in supplies and dispatching goods along the interlocking networks of road and waterborne carriage that served these provincial entrepôts. All, except York and Chester, were closely associated with local industrial developments: many were not only centres of broad-based manufacturing activity in their own right but also acted as the main focal points of wider industrial regions, supplying capital, credit, raw materials and commercial expertise to manufacturers throughout their hinterlands. Thus Bristol, the 'metropolis of the west', was not only a magnet for much of the social and economic activity of the five largely rural counties of the West Country but also exercised a powerful attraction over a wider area that included the West Midlands and much of South Wales.[7] Newcastle-upon-Tyne, the only major urban centre between York and Edinburgh, functioned in a similar manner as 'the great Emporium of all the Northern Parts of England, and of a good share of Scotland', channelling both agricultural produce and manufactured goods to the industrial workforce of the north-eastern coalfield while reaping the benefits of the port's buoyant coastal and export trade.[8] The impact of Norwich and Exeter was in some respects more localised but they still exercised a powerful influence on East Anglia and the south-western counties: it has indeed been argued that Norwich's influence on its relatively compact industrial region was stronger than that of Bristol over its more extensive commercial hinterland.[9] Despite its relative eclipse in the mid-seventeenth century, York retained its regional influence as an administrative and social centre, while the smaller cities of Chester and Shrewsbury, with populations of around 7,000, drew much of their prosperity from servicing the 'urban desert' of Wales.[10] Shrewsbury dominated a huge

[6] Everitt, 'Country, county and town', pp. 94–6; J. Stobart, 'Regional structure and the urban system: North-West England 1700–1760', *Transactions of the Historic Society of Lancashire and Cheshire*, 145 (1996), 45–73; G. A. Cranfield, *The Development of the Provincial Newspaper 1700–1760* (London, 1962). See also above, pp. 579 *et passim* and below, 690 *et seq*.

[7] Defoe, *Tour*, I, pp. 36–7; W. E. Minchinton, 'Bristol – metropolis of the west in the eighteenth century', in P. Clark, ed., *The Early Modern Town* (London, 1976), pp. 297–313; K. Morgan, 'The economic development of Bristol, 1700–1850', in M. Dresser and Ollerenshaw, eds., *The Making of Modern Bristol* (Bristol, 1996), pp. 63–4.

[8] T. Cox, *Magna Britannia et Hibernia,Antiqua et Nova* (London, 1720–31), vol. III, p. 608; H. Bourne, *The History of Newcastle on Tyne: Or, the Ancient and Present State of that Town* (Newcastle, 1736), pp. 54, 158; J. Ellis, 'A dynamic society: social relations in Newcastle-upon-Tyne, 1660–1760', in P. Clark, ed., *The Transformation of English Provincial Towns 1600–1800* (London, 1984), pp. 190–227.

[9] P. J. Corfield, 'A provincial capital in the late seventeenth century: the case of Norwich', in P. Clark and P. Slack, eds., *Crisis and Order in English Towns 1500–1700* (London, 1972), pp. 263– 319; W. G. Hoskins, *Industry, Trade and People in Exeter 1688–1800*, 2nd edn (Exeter, 1968); R. Newton, *Eighteenth-Century Exeter* (Exeter, 1984), especially pp. 18–25.

[10] J. Hutchinson and D. M. Palliser, *York* (Edinburgh, 1980), pp. 55–74; N. Alldridge, 'The mechanics of decline: migration and economy in early modern Chester', in Reed, ed., *English Towns*, pp. 2–5; S. I. Mitchell, 'The development of urban retailing 1700–1815', in Clark, ed., *Transformation of English Provincial Towns*, pp. 260–2.

hinterland stretching right through central Wales to the west coast: Defoe reported that although 'they all speak English in the town . . . on a market-day you would think you were in Wales'.[11]

As this indicates, in the early years of the eighteenth century the influence of Bristol, Shrewsbury and Chester was so pervasive that Wales lacked any comparable regional centres of its own, while the Welsh border counties were inclined to look to Gloucester, Hereford and Worcester rather than to their own administrative capitals to fulfil most of the functions normally supplied by a county centre.[12] Indeed, given its many acres of barren, mountainous countryside, it is not surprising that only four or five of the twenty or so Welsh towns which hosted regular meetings of the assizes could be regarded as county towns by the standards of contemporary England. The largest urban populations were probably those of Carmarthen, Brecon, Wrexham and Haverfordwest, each with no more than 3,000 inhabitants: English travellers commented with some surprise that the latter, 'a large, populous and Trading town', was 'a better town than we expected to find, in this remote Angle of Britain'.[13] Scotland too was a predominantly rural society and thus relatively poorly endowed with regional and county centres as the eighteenth century opened. Moreover, although existing regional centres such as Aberdeen and Dundee retained a significant influence over their localities, it appears that Glasgow and Edinburgh were the only Scottish cities which were actually expanding in the early years of the century.[14]

Glasgow's steady rise up the urban hierarchy in the century before 1700 had rested primarily on its role as the only major regional centre of the west coast. Although the opening up of new transatlantic trade routes had increased the volume and value of the cargoes handled by its merchants, overseas trade was not the main source of its economic and demographic success in this period. On the contrary, its expanding influence over the other towns of the western Lowlands was based on its well-established role as the market place of the region as well as on the broad manufacturing base which made it the natural finishing centre for local industry. The spectacular expansion of the tobacco trade in the early eighteenth century undoubtedly boosted the overall importance of overseas trade to

[11] Defoe, *Tour*, II, pp. 75–7; Hyde, ed., *Prospect of Britain*, plate 73; A. McInnes, 'The emergence of a leisure town: Shrewsbury 1660–1760', *P&P*, 120 (1988), 53–87.

[12] P. Jenkins, *The Making of a Ruling Class: The Glamorgan Gentry 1640–1790* (Cambridge, 1983), pp. 244–6. See also above, pp. 136–8.

[13] Hyde, ed., *Prospect of Britain*, plate 30; Defoe, *Tour*, II, p. 57; H. Carter, *The Towns of Wales* (Cardiff, 1965), pp. 33–50; E. G. Parry, 'Brecon: occupations and society, 1500–1800', *Brycheiniog*, 19 (1980–1), 60–7; A. H. Dodd, ed., *A History of Wrexham Denbighshire* (Wrexham, 1957). See also above, p. 134.

[14] M. Lynch, 'Continuity and change in urban society, 1500–1700', in R. A. Houston and I. D. Whyte, eds., *Scottish Society 1500–1800* (Cambridge, 1989), pp. 104–5; M. Lynch, 'Urbanisation and urban networks in seventeenth century Scotland: some further thoughts', *Scottish Economic and Social History*, 12 (1992), 24–41. See also above, pp. 155 *et seq*.

its economy: colonial merchants invested heavily in shipping and new port facilities, while industrial production in the city itself as well as in its thriving hinterland expanded to meet the voracious colonial demand for manufactured goods.[15] Although its character was still that of a regional centre serving a mainly rural hinterland rather than that of a world-class entrepôt, by the middle of the century Glasgow was unmistakably 'a city of business', uncompromising in presenting to visitors 'the face of trade'. As yet, however, trade had promoted rather than detracted from its role as a social centre. Its flourishing economy sustained many of the trappings of fashionable civility as well as a wide range of professional and personal services: in 1764 an English tourist described it as 'one of the pleasantest and most elegant cities, and much superior to old Edinburgh'.[16]

However, Glasgow's rapid expansion should not obscure the fact that Edinburgh remained 'the metropolis of this ancient kingdom' long after the Act of Union in 1707 had removed the Scottish parliament to Westminster. The fact that Scotland's legal, financial, educational and ecclesiastical systems retained their independence meant that Edinburgh continued to exercise considerable control over 'North British' affairs and made the city a magnet for salaried professionals. In social and cultural terms, too, Edinburgh functioned as a regional centre whose region embraced virtually the whole of Scotland. Students trained in the capital carried its influence far beyond its immediate hinterland, while its buoyant consumer industries and service sector catered for 'all our nobility who cannot afford to live in London' as well as for its resident population of wealthy merchants and professionals. Meanwhile it continued to benefit from its traditional role as the major commercial and manufacturing centre of the fertile Lothians, exchanging agricultural goods for the products of its strong industrial base and conducting an extensive coastal and overseas trade through its satellite port of Leith. Thus despite its relatively modest size – in 1700 its 50,000 inhabitants made up only 5 per cent of Scotland's population – it was easily the richest town in the country and was far more prosperous than its relative size would suggest: even in 1750 it was still the second largest conurbation in Britain.[17]

As the Georgian age unfolded, however, the rapid growth of Glasgow and the other towns of the central Lowlands, fuelled by commercial and industrial development, threatened Edinburgh not only with relative economic eclipse but also with the loss of its previously unquestioned status as Scotland's principal

[15] Lynch, 'Continuity and change', pp. 105–7; G. Jackson, 'Glasgow in transition, *c.* 1660–*c.* 1740', in T. M. Devine and G. Jackson, eds., *Glasgow*, vol. I: *Beginnings to 1830* (Manchester, 1995), pp. 63–105.

[16] Defoe, *Tour*, II, pp. 335–7; Nottingham RO, anonymous diary, M 380, f. 49; T. M. Devine, 'The golden age of tobacco', in Devine and Jackson, eds., *Glasgow*, p. 139; T. M. Devine, *The Tobacco Lords* (Edinburgh, 1975).

[17] Lynch, 'Continuity and change', pp. 109–13; H. M. Dingwall, *Late Seventeenth-Century Edinburgh* (Aldershot, 1994), pp. 9–11, 20–1; R. A. Houston, *Social Change in the Age of Enlightenment* (Oxford, 1994), pp. 1–4 (quotation, p. 4).

city.[18] Nor was Edinburgh alone in feeling the chill wind of competition. Although the urban system as a whole exhibited considerable continuity in the century and a half after 1700, there were also significant changes in the rankings of individual towns, changes which gathered pace in the later eighteenth century and which undermined the relative prosperity of many other established county and regional centres. As the long-sustained rise in real incomes, which had underpinned widespread urban growth in the later seventeenth and early eighteenth centuries, died away, many historic county towns and regional centres found that their rate of population growth began to fall well below the national average. Although very few actually declined in size, their share of Britain's total population began to fall markedly so that they experienced the sort of relative 'failure' which had already afflicted York in the mid-seventeenth century. By the time of the 1801 census Edinburgh, Glasgow, Bristol, Newcastle-upon-Tyne and Norwich were the only traditional regional centres which remained among the country's fifteen largest towns and in the case of Norwich the census revealed that its population was actually lower than it had been twenty-five years earlier (see Table 20.1).[19] It is hardly surprising, therefore, that many provincial cities which had, as E. A. Wrigley puts it, 'for many centuries . . . exchanged places in the premier urban league', greeted the results of the census with dismay and disbelief. The response in Newcastle-upon-Tyne, for instance, was 'universal surprise' and its outraged citizens virtually demanded a recount: since the town had in their eyes 'not only maintained its rank, but even risen in the scale of national importance', the figure of 33,038 which resulted from the official enumeration was simply unacceptable.[20]

Explanations of the relative eclipse of so many traditional county and regional centres in the century after 1750 have to take into account a variety of factors. Many contemporary writers argued that it was precisely the historic character of these towns and the entrenched privileges of their leading citizens that had weakened their ability to adapt to change: it became axiomatic that 'Charters and Corporations are of eminent Prejudice to a Town, as they exclude Strangers, stop the Growth of Trade, and . . . prevent Ingenuity and Improvements.'

[18] R. A. Houston, 'The demographic regime', and T. M. Devine, 'Urbanisation' both in T. M. Devine and R. Mitchinson, eds., *People and Society in Scotland*, vol. I: *1760–1830* (Edinburgh, 1988), pp. 9–26 and 27–52.

[19] See Table 20.1. Urban population estimates for 1700 are taken from Chalklin, *Provincial Towns*, pp. 1–25; E. A. Wrigley, 'Urban growth and agricultural change: England and the continent in the early modern period', in Borsay, ed., *Eighteenth Century Town*, pp. 42–3, and sources cited there. Other figures supplied by J. Langton.

[20] Wrigley, 'Urban growth and agricultural change', pp. 42–3, 47–50; J. Brand, *The History and Antiquities of the Town and County of Newcastle upon Tyne* (London, 1789), vol. I, p. 19n; E. Mackenzie, *A Descriptive and Historical Account of the Town and County of Newcastle, including Gateshead* (Newcastle, 1827), p. 197. As Mackenzie's title indicated, local perceptions of Newcastle's size and status would have included the 8,597 inhabitants of Gateshead on the south bank of the Tyne, raising the *de facto* total to 41,645 as reflected in Table 20.1.

Table 20.1 *The largest provincial towns c. 1700–1841*

1700		1801		1841	
Edinburgh	50,000	*Manchester*	95,000	Manchester	311,000
Norwich	30,000	*Liverpool*	82,000	Liverpool	286,000
Bristol	21,000	*Edinburgh*	81,000	Glasgow	261,000
Glasgow	18,000	*Glasgow*	77,000	Birmingham	183,000
Newcastle[a]		*Birmingham*	71,000	Edinburgh	164,000
Exeter	14,000	*Bristol*	61,000	Leeds	152,000
Aberdeen	13,000	*Leeds*	53,000	Bristol	125,000
York	12,000	Sheffield	46,000	*Sheffield*	111,000
Yarmouth	10,000	*Newcastle*	42,000	*Wolverhampton*	93,000
Colchester	9,000	*Plymouth*[b]	40,000	Newcastle	90,000
Plymouth[b]		*Norwich*	36,000	Plymouth	70,000
Worcester		Bath	33,000	Hull	67,000
Birmingham	8,000	*Portsmouth*		*Bradford*	
Dundee		Wolverhampton	31,000	Dundee	65,000
Ipswich		*Hull*	30,000	Aberdeen	63,000
Manchester		*Nottingham*	29,000	Norwich	62,000
Portsmouth		*Dundee*	27,000	Sunderland	53,000
Chester	7,000	*Aberdeen*		*Bath*	
Coventry		Paisley	25,000	Portsmouth	
Lynn		*Sunderland*		Nottingham	52,000
Leeds		Tynemouth	20,000	*Bolton*	51,000
Shrewsbury		Bolton	18,000	*Preston*	
Bury St Edmunds	6,000	*Exeter*	17,000	Leicester	
Cambridge		Greenock		*Stockport*	50,000
Canterbury		*Leicester*		*Brighton*	49,000
Hull		York		*Paisley*	48,000
Leicester		Yarmouth		*Oldham*	
Liverpool		Coventry	16,000	*Merthyr Tydfil*	43,000
Nottingham		Perth		*Blackburn*	37,000
Oxford		Chester	15,000	Exeter	
Salisbury		Oldham		*Greenock*	36,000
Sunderland		Shrewsbury		*Derby*	33,000
		Stockport		*Macclesfield*	
				Tynemouth	

Notes

Approximate populations are given in thousands.

Towns in italics in 1700 do not appear in the 1841 list.

Towns in italics in 1801 appear in all three lists.

Towns in italics in 1841 do not appear in the 1700 list.

[a] Figures for Newcastle-upon-Tyne include Gateshead.

[b] Figures for Plymouth include Devonport.

However, this apparently unambiguous connection between incorporation and stagnation, whereby all towns subject to 'Corporation-Tyranny' were inevitably doomed to remain 'mean, poor, and ill-inhabited', was not in fact as simple as it appeared. Although many unincorporated towns did indeed 'flourish in People, Riches and Trade', Manchester and Birmingham being the examples most often cited in this context, it was much less easy to explain why the corporate status of Liverpool and Leeds had not hindered their almost equally rapid growth over the same period.[21] Modern versions of this argument tend therefore to focus not on the mere fact of corporate government but on the alleged complacency and business conservatism that could develop among the leading citizens of long-established towns that were accustomed to virtually unchallenged domination of their hinterlands. Thus Bristol's relative demographic and economic 'decline' has been attributed to the fact that its merchants were 'to a degree unable and to a degree unwilling' to invest in local enterprise and infrastructure while Newcastle's backwardness in improving its river navigation and port facilities has similarly been blamed on the complacent short-sightedness of its entrenched oligarchy.[22]

However, it has to be accepted that many of the problems faced by long-established urban communities in the later years of the eighteenth century were not susceptible to easy solutions and that even the most astute, energetic civic leadership could struggle in vain to adapt to changing circumstances. In the case of many county centres their main problem was, somewhat ironically, closely linked with their relative buoyancy in the earlier part of the period. The gradual provision of better transport and communications had initially given these larger settlements an advantage over smaller towns within their spheres of influence by making them more accessible to a wider circle of potential visitors. As capital expenditure on better bridges and investment in the spread of turnpikes after the 1690s raised the often appalling standards of overland transport and opened up new routes between inland towns, trade was diverted to larger towns which could offer travellers, prosperous farmers and wealthy consumers comfortable inns, permanent shops selling a wider variety of goods and regular visits from substantial London-based salesmen. Few market towns in Essex, for example, could compete with Chelmsford, which had a population of fewer than 2,800 inhabitants in 1775, but which could boast over forty shops, including bookshops and coffee-houses, and no fewer than forty-eight inns, many of them

[21] T. Short, *New Observations on City, Town and County Bills of Mortality* (London, 1750), p. 79; Defoe, *Tour*, II, p. 37; W. Richards, *The History of Lynn* (London, 1812), pp. 783, 972. The arguments on both sides are summarised in P. J. Corfield, *The Impact of English Towns 1700–1800* (Oxford, 1982), pp. 90–3.

[22] Morgan, 'Economic development', pp. 48–75; B. W. E. Alford, 'The economic development of Bristol in the nineteenth century: an enigma', in P. McGrath and J. Cannon, eds., *Essays in Bristol and Gloucestershire History* (Bristol, 1976), pp. 252–83 (quotation, p. 263); J. M. Ellis, 'The taming of the river dragon: Newcastle-upon-Tyne in the eighteenth century' (typescript, 1996).

having their own market room.[23] As long-distance travel increased, many county centres along the improved road network also developed a lucrative coaching trade: Georgian Lichfield, for instance, prospered as a post town and coaching centre on the main route from London to Ireland. In the case of several other county towns, notably Lincoln and Reading, these beneficial effects were reinforced by the impact of river navigations and canal networks on their waterborne trade. Improved communications and the willingness of increasing numbers of people to travel further from home in search of better facilities also had an effect in Wales and in Scotland, where historic centres such as Perth and Inverness enjoyed modest expansion.[24]

As the pace and scale of improvement increased, however, many of these towns began to suffer themselves from increasing competition as the roads, rivers and canals opened up the countryside and hastened existing trends towards concentrating trade in bigger, well-positioned and increasingly specialised towns. Whereas previously only the great provincial cities had been able to boast of a direct connection with London, by the 1780s every region in England, and some in Wales and Scotland, had a turnpike network of its own, part of a larger national system. Contemporaries were bemused not merely by the comparative ease and speed of travel but also by the readiness of the population to take advantage of their new opportunities. 'Who would have believed, thirty years ago', inquired one character in a novel published in 1779, 'that a young man would come thirty miles in a carriage to dinner, and perhaps return at night?' Moralists and conservatives may have deplored the fact that the population was 'All running to and fro, like mad dogs' but they could do little to prevent the consequences.[25] Faster transport systems and changing patterns of regional growth and development could leave previously prosperous county centres isolated in economic backwaters or drained of their vitality by better-placed rivals.[26] What made matters worse for many struggling county towns, and even for some of the smaller regional centres, was that the process of relative decline could all too easily become self-reinforcing as well-travelled visitors developed increasingly high expectations. One visitor to Exeter in 1760 disputed its reputation as 'the

[23] E. Pawson, *Transport and Economy* (London, 1977), pp. 323–9; A. F. J. Brown, *Essex at Work 1700–1815* (Chelmsford, 1969), pp. 63, 116–77. Note that by 1800 the number of inns in Chelmsford had fallen to thirty-one.

[24] Borsay, *English Urban Renaissance*, pp. 25–6; *VCH*, Staffordshire, XIV, pp. 24–5, 45–6; Hutchinson, *History of Cumberland*, p. 662; Chalklin, *Provincial Towns*, pp. 30–2; J. W. F. Hill, *Georgian Lincoln* (Cambridge, 1966), pp. 122–35; Carter, *Towns of Wales*, p. 56; Parry, 'Brecon', 62–3; Devine, 'Urbanisation', pp. 32–3.

[25] P. Langford, *A Polite and Commercial People* (Oxford, 1989), pp. 397–405 (quotation, p. 404); J. Byng, *The Torrington Diaries* ed. C. B. Andrews (London, 1934–8), vol. IV, p. 1.

[26] W. T. Jackman, *The Development of Transportation in Modern England*, 2nd edn (London, 1962), p. 275; Pawson, *Transport and Economy*, pp. 277–9, 324–6; Hill, *Georgian Lincoln*, pp. 122–36; Langford, *Polite and Commercial People*, p. 419.

"London of the West"' on the grounds that 'it principally consists of one very long street, tolerably broad but not very straight, the houses every one of which are shops of a most ancient model; indeed we saw not any that can be call'd good in this grand city'. Thirty years later she was equally disappointed by Canterbury, which she described as 'a melancholy, dirty town', with 'hardly any smart shops, whereas now in most country towns there are many capital ones'.[27] As shops spread out into these smaller towns and even into the villages, the number and especially the quality of a town's shopping facilities could indeed be used as a basic measure of its prosperity and relative status. Thus Chester retained its competitive edge over neighbouring Stockport and Macclesfield, despite their rapid population growth, because it succeeded in raising the quality of its shopping facilities to meet this sort of discriminating demand, concentrating on the luxury end of the market.[28]

Despite this relative and localised success, however, there can be little doubt that Chester, like many similar towns throughout Britain, was eclipsed by the rise of new regional centres. Many of these so-called 'new' towns were in fact old-established urban communities which had already begun to experience rapid population growth in the later seventeenth century as their buoyant economies attracted large numbers of migrants. As the eighteenth century progressed, ports such as Liverpool, Glasgow and Greenock undoubtedly profited from the increasing wealth of the Atlantic trade, but on the whole the key factors at work in the changing patterns of urban development were the rapid growth of industrial production and the shift of industry towards the major coalfields. All the fastest growing regional centres of the early nineteenth century, including the leading ports, depended to a large extent either directly or indirectly on manufacturing industry.[29] The 1820s and 1830s in particular saw a sharp readjustment in the traditional parameters of economic activity as steam-based technology encouraged industrial production to concentrate in urban or suburban locations. Although smaller centres such as Shrewsbury attempted to take advantage of the new conditions by establishing power-driven factories, they rarely enjoyed long-term success. In contrast, by 1839, 92 of Scotland's 192 cotton mills were located

[27] P. L. Powys, *Passages from the Diaries of Mrs Philip Lybbe Powys*, ed. E. J. Climenson (London, 1899), pp. 66–7, 307. For the 'de-urbanisation' of shopping in the later eighteenth century with the spread of petty shops into smaller urban and village centres, see H.-C. Mui and L. H. Mui, *Shops and Shopkeeping in Eighteenth-Century England* (London, 1989).

[28] S. I. Mitchell, 'Retailing in eighteenth- and early nineteenth-century Chester', *Transactions of the Historic Society of Lancashire and Cheshire*, 130 (1981), 37–60; J. Stobart, 'Shopping streets as social space: leisure, consumerism and improvement in an eighteenth-century county town; *UH*, 25 (1998), 302–23.

[29] Corfield, *Impact of English Towns*, pp. 15–16; H. Carter and C. R. Lewis, *An Urban Geography of England and Wales in the Nineteenth Century* (London, 1990), pp. 53–66; Devine, 'Urbanisation', pp. 33–6. For population figures, see Table 20.1.

in or near Glasgow and the 1830s also saw considerable local investment in the coal, iron, chemical and engineering industries, investments which were to prove crucial once cotton production faltered in the later 1840s.[30] In northern England too the growth of the textile industry fed directly into the expansion of the local textile towns and promoted the rise of Manchester, Liverpool and Leeds as major regional centres. Just as in the case of Glasgow, their economies benefited from a continued process of industrial diversification while continued investment in transport improvements and in professional and commercial services integrated their fast developing hinterlands ever more closely into their spheres of influence.[31]

The speed and scale of these urban transformations excited in contemporary observers a mixture of exhilaration and alarm. Just as early modern London had been condemned as a parasite, devouring the nation's wealth and luring migrants to an early grave, so Manchester in the 1820s and 1830s was portrayed as a smoky, ravening monster, 'a diligent spider . . . placed in the centre of the web', a vortex which sucked in and consumed the 'art, science, industry, activity and wealth' generated by its productive hinterland.[32] What these critics overlooked, however, was the vital role which Manchester, Glasgow and the other great cities of industrial Britain played in stimulating and sustaining this productive activity. As they grew in size and significance, they inevitably assumed many of the economic and social functions that had been primarily associated with more traditional regional centres. It seems clear, for instance, that the emerging industrial and commercial cities played an equal, if not greater, part in diffusing the new scientific, technical and financial ideas throughout their localities and even in setting new educational, cultural and intellectual standards.[33]

It would be a mistake, however, to assume that all regional centres developed

[30] R. H. Campbell, 'The making of the industrial city', in Devine and Jackson, eds., *Glasgow*, pp. 184–213; A. Slaven, *The Development of the West of Scotland 1750–1960* (London, 1975), pp. 10–16; J. Docherty, 'Urbanisation, capital accumulation and class struggle in Scotland 1750–1914', in G. Whittington and I. D. Whyte, eds., *A Historical Geography of Scotland* (London, 1983), pp. 251–3.

[31] Chalklin, *Provincial Towns*, pp. 32–40; G. S. Messinger, *Manchester in the Victorian Age: The Half-Known City* (Manchester, 1985); J. Langton, 'Liverpool and its hinterland in the late eighteenth century', in B. L. Anderson and P. J. M. Stoney, eds., *Commerce, Industry and Transport* (Liverpool, 1983), pp. 1–25; R. G. Wilson, *Gentlemen Merchants* (Manchester, 1971).

[32] J. Butterworth, *A Complete History of the Cotton Trade* (London, 1823), p. 26; L. Faucher, *Manchester in 1844; its Present Condition and Future Prospects*, repr. (London, 1969), p. 15; Messinger, *Manchester*, pp. 5–16; V. Pons, 'Contemporary interpretations of Manchester in the 1830s and 1840s', in J. D. Wirth and R. L. Jones, eds., *Manchester and Sao Paulo: Problems of Rapid Urban Growth* (Stanford, Calif., 1978), pp. 51–76.

[33] See for example T. Fawcett, 'Self-improvement societies: the early "Lit. and Phils."', in *Life in the Georgian Town* (London, 1986), pp. 15–25; I. Inkster and J. Morrell, eds., *Metropolis and Province: Science in British Culture 1780–1850* (London, 1983); R. H. Kargon, *Science in Victorian Manchester: Enterprise and Expertise* (Manchester, 1977).

along exactly the same lines or that their influence over their ever-widening hinterlands was indistinguishable from that of their historic predecessors: the resort town of Bath, for example, was unique in that its distinctive 'Province of Pleasure' extended throughout the kingdom.[34] Some regions, the West Midlands, for example, developed an extremely complex urban network in which the influence of Birmingham, which was by far the largest and most dynamic urban community throughout this period, was exercised in a climate of creative tension with that of the older county centres of Coventry, Warwick and Lichfield and of the rising industrial town of Wolverhampton. Meanwhile, in the North-East the old pattern of regional linkages based on the almost unchallenged hegemony of Newcastle-upon-Tyne was gradually undermined by the development of new riverside conurbations, creating what has been termed 'an urban doughnut' coupling together the economies of the Tyne and the Wear.[35] By 1840 a new urban world had evolved, one in which the traditional county boundaries and structures had very little influence and in which successful cities reformulated their local spheres of influence on the basis of shared economic interests. As a result it could be argued that the early stages of the Industrial Revolution did not merely exchange new regional centres for old: the great provincial cities of the early nineteenth century were in many ways more diversified as well as much, much larger than their counterparts in 1700.[36]

(ii) OCCUPATIONAL STRUCTURE AND SOCIAL CHARACTER

One of the distinguishing characteristics of traditional county and regional centres in this period was the fact that their wide range of administrative, social and commercial functions tended to produce a correspondingly wide and increasingly varied occupational structure (see Table 20.2). County towns were by definition local administrative centres and, since many were also cathedral cities, their administrative functions were enhanced by their role as diocesan centres. As the legal capital of Scotland, Edinburgh was notoriously full of lawyers and it is equally unsurprising that a visitor to Canterbury in 1739 found it to be full of 'Deans, Prebends, Minor Canons, . . . and the Church militant upon earth'. Indeed, the rich legacy of small urban parishes in many of the historic regional and county centres, combined with their substantial populations, meant that even towns without a cathedral were well supplied with clergymen

[34] Corfield, *Impact of English Towns*, p. 125; Jenkins, *Making of a Ruling Class*, pp. 245–6; see also below, pp. 777 *et passim*.

[35] M. J. Wise, 'Birmingham and its trade relations in the early eighteenth century', *University of Birmingham Historical Journal*, 2 (1949–50), 53–79; Money, *Experience and Identity*; G. Burke, *Towns in the Making* (London, 1971), pp. 132–5; Ellis, 'Taming of the river dragon', pp. 15–24.

[36] Carter and Lewis, *Urban Geography*, 42–66; D. Gregory, *Regional Transformation and Industrial Revolution* (London, 1982); J. Langton, 'The production of regions in England's Industrial Revolution: a response', *Journal of Historical Geography*, 14 (1988), 170–3.

Table 20.2 *Trades and professions in regional centres*

Edinburgh 1774		Birmingham 1777		Manchester 1772		Newcastle 1778	
217	Merchants	248	Innkeepers	140	Innkeepers	175	Innkeepers
188	Advocates	129	Buttonmakers	75	Fustian manufacturers	55	Butchers
171	Writers	99	Shoemakers	58	Warehousemen	50	Tailors
169	Grocers	77	Merchants	49	Check manufacturers	36	Grocers/tea sellers
141	Clerks to HM Signet	74	Tailors	46	Hucksters	35	Peruke makers
110	Vintners	64	Bakers	44	Smallware manufacturers	32	Attorneys at law
94	Lords/advocates clerks	56	Toymakers	27	Shoemakers	32	Cabinet makers
86	Baxters	52	Platers	26	Barbers	31	Shoemakers
80	Shipmasters	49	Butchers	25	Tailors	27	Schoolmasters
79	Shoemakers	48	Carpenters	24	Clergy	22	Linen drapers
64	Wrights	46	Barbers	24	Grocers	21	Cheesemongers
61	Brewers	46	Brassfounders	23	Carpenters/joiners	21	Flour shops
56	Schoolmasters	39	Bucklemasters	23	Hatters	20	Coal fitters
52	Tailors	39	Shopkeepers	21	Lawyers	18	Flax dressers
46	Barbers	36	Gunmakers	17	Yarn manufacturers	18	Gardeners
45	Milliners	35	Jewellers	15	Butchers	18	Woollen drapers
45	Smiths	26	Maltsters	15	Linen drapers	17	Pilots
45	Stablers	24	Drapers	14	Corn factors	16	Bakers
39	Physicians	23	Gardeners	14	Fustian dyers	16	Coopers
35	Clergy	21	Ironmongers	13	Fustian callenders	16	Hatters
33	Surgeons	21	Plumbers/glaziers	13	Toy/hardware shops	15	Hackney horsekeepers
30	Bankers			12	Bakers	15	Whitesmiths
24	Painters			11	Cabinet makers	15	Surgeons
21	Booksellers			11	Gardeners	13	Clergymen
21	Goldsmiths/jewellers					13	Hardwaremen

Sources: Williamson's Directory of Edinburgh (1774); A. Pearson and J. Rollason, *Birmingham Directory* (1777); *Manchester Directory* (1772); *Whitehead's Newcastle Directory for 1778*. On the use of commercial directories, see P. J. Corfield and S. Kelly, 'Giving directions to the town: the early town directories', *UHY* (1984), 22–35; E. P. Duggan, 'Industrialization and the development of urban business communities', *Local Historian*, 11 (1975), 457–65.

serving both the established and the nonconformist churches.[37] Although Nottingham in the early eighteenth century had a relatively small professional sector, most of Britain's county and regional centres benefited from a significant concentration of financial, medical, educational and cultural expertise. The influx of wealthy visitors and residents attracted by the annual round of meetings to transact the legal and political business of the county, as well as by the social life that accompanied these occasions, sustained a thriving trade in professional and personal services, and was one of the main reasons why rival centres competed for the privilege of holding the assizes.[38]

The local gentry also played a part in promoting the commercial and dealing sectors of the urban economy in these 'places of great resort'. According to Defoe, the economy of Bury St Edmunds depended chiefly on 'the gentry who live there, or near to it, and who cannot fail to cause trade enough by the expense of their families and equipages' (see Plate 26) and these wealthy consumers undoubtedly encouraged the increasing diversity and specialisation of retail outlets in county and regional centres throughout Britain. Comfortable inns, rebuilt or refaced in the latest architectural styles, colonised the main routes into the town centres, shops lined their major streets and infiltrated the yards and alleyways behind them, while regular wholesale and retail markets catering for their immediate hinterlands as well as their own resident populations spilled into the roadways and obstructed the traffic. In some cases their markets had national as well as regional significance and their merchants and dealers flourished accordingly. Moreover, as the period progressed their principal shopkeepers began to compete with London wholesale dealers to service petty shops in smaller towns and villages within their regional spheres of influence, enhancing the role traditionally played by regional and county centres as inland entrepôts.[39]

Although merchants, traders and shopkeepers thus formed significant occupational groupings, they were in most cases outweighed by the large numbers employed in all significant urban centres in the industrial crafts. In an occupa-

[37] See Table 20.2; Dingwall, *Late Seventeenth-Century Edinburgh*, pp. 217–22; J. Gilhooley, *A Directory of Edinburgh in 1752* (Edinburgh, 1984), pp. 100–1; E. Montagu, *Elizabeth Montagu: Her Correspondence 1720–61*, ed. E. J. Climenson (London, 1906), vol. 1, p. 35; J. Barry, 'The parish in civic life', in S. J. Wright, ed., *Parish, Church and People* (London, 1988), pp. 152–70; but see Corfield, 'A provincial capital', p. 257.

[38] G. C. Deering, *Nottinghamia Vetus et Nova* (Nottingham, 1751), pp. 94–5, 101; G. Holmes, *Augustan England* (London, 1982); Borsay, *English Urban Renaissance*, pp. 205–7; P. Clark, 'Introduction', in *Transformation of English Provincial Towns*, pp. 27–9; Corfield, 'A provincial capital', pp. 256–7; J. Aikin, *A Description of the Country from Thirty to Forty Miles Around Manchester* (London, 1795), pp. 284–5.

[39] Defoe, *Tour*, I, p. 52; Borsay, *English Urban Renaissance*, pp. 208–11; D. Collins, 'Primitive or not? Fixed-shop retailing before the Industrial Revolution', *Journal of Regional and Local Studies*, 13 (1993), 23–38; N. Cox, 'The distribution of retailing tradesmen in north Shropshire 1660–1750', *Journal of Regional and Local Studies*, 13 (1993), 2–22; Mui and Mui, *Shops and Shopkeeping*, pp. 70–1.

tional study of Bristol in the 1770s, for example, artisans made up 48.4 per cent of the population under consideration. It is generally accepted that this 'kaleidoscopic' sector of the urban economy continued to expand and to diversify well into the nineteenth century as buoyant consumer demand encouraged the spread of new, specialised trades alongside the traditional staples: butchers, bakers and candlestick makers now flourished alongside watchmakers, jewellers, cabinetmakers and milliners.[40] However, it would be a mistake to argue from the sheer variety of occupations to be found in many well-established towns that their economies were incapable of specialisation. On the contrary, the fastest growing regional and county centres of this period were successful precisely because they were closely associated with a specialist function or trade. Many had profited from the late-seventeenth-century revival of urban industry to develop specialised industrial sectors which were important sources of employment among labouring men, women and children, groups notoriously underrepresented in occupational breakdowns based on freemen's rolls, parish registers and other contemporary sources. Norwich, Colchester and Exeter were textile-producing towns as well as marketing centres for cloth produced in their regions; Nottingham and Leicester specialised in hosiery; Derby in silk weaving and brewing.[41] Several of the great regional centres were among the country's major ports, with large numbers of their inhabitants employed in shipping and related trades.[42] A few could even be classed as specialist leisure towns where the energies of a significant section of the population were directed towards the lucrative task of catering for the increasingly sophisticated consumer economy.[43] Indeed, regional and county centres were doubly fortunate in that the breadth of their economies allowed them to change direction and harness new sources of growth when long-standing specialisms began to lose momentum. Thus in

[40] E. Baigent, 'Economy and society in eighteenth-century English towns: Bristol in the 1770s', in D. D. Denecke and G. Shaw, eds., *Urban Historical Geography* (London, 1988), p. 116; Dingwall, *Late Seventeenth-Century Edinburgh*, pp. 127–70; Everitt, 'Country, county and town', pp. 104–11.

[41] J. M. Ellis, 'Consumption and wealth', in L. K. J. Glassey, ed., *The Reigns of Charles II and James VII and II* (London, 1997), pp. 191–210; Hyde, ed., *Prospect of Britain*, plates, 17, 20, 24, 50, 52; Deering, *Nottinghamia*, pp. 94, 100–1; E. Hopkins, 'The trading and service sectors of the Birmingham economy 1750–1800', *Business History*, 28 (1986), 76–97. N. Goose, 'English pre-industrial urban economies', *UHY* (1982), 24–30, is also concerned to stress the importance of industrial specialisation.

[42] D. Defoe, *A Plan of the English Commerce* (London, 1728), p. 85; Baigent, 'Economy and society', pp. 115–16; Ellis, 'Dynamic society', pp. 194–5; P. Langton and P. Laxton, 'Parish registers and urban structure: the example of late eighteenth-century Liverpool', *UHY* (1978), 77–82; but see Corfield, *Impact of English Towns*, p. 45.

[43] Defoe, *Tour*, II, pp. 75, 230, 234; McInnes, 'Emergence of a leisure town', 55–87. The extent to which such developments were the product of a general 'urban renaissance' rather than concentrated in specialist leisure towns is debatable: see P. Borsay, 'The English urban renaissance: the development of provincial urban culture c1680–c1760', in Borsay, ed., *Eighteenth-Century Town*, pp. 159–87; P. Borsay and A. McInnes, 'Debate: the emergence of a leisure town or an urban renaissance', *P&P*, 126 (1990), 189–202.

the course of the eighteenth century the port city of Chester and the manufacturing town of Colchester both survived temporary economic difficulties by developing into 'gentry' towns, capitalising on the attractiveness of their new-found tranquillity to wealthy residents, while in the later years of the period Preston moved in the opposite direction, developing into a busy, 'industrious' textile town.[44]

As these examples indicate, the new urban world was dynamic rather than stable and this dynamism was reflected in the larger towns' demographic performance in the years between 1700 and 1840. Despite the fact that the evidence available to those few demographers who have attempted to work on the population history of regional and county centres is both limited and in many respects far from conclusive, it is possible to discern significant variations over time in their experience and relative success.[45] Chester, for instance, compared very favourably with its faster growing neighbours in the North-West in the later eighteenth century in terms of its relatively low mortality rates, prompting contemporaries to praise its 'proportional healthiness'. On the other hand, Chester's birth rates were equally sluggish, indicating perhaps that its increasingly specialised role as a shopping and residential centre acted to curb fertility through restricting the employment and marriage prospects of its poorer inhabitants. In Liverpool, on the other hand, high burial rates as the result of worsening environmental conditions and the spread of disease were countered by high and sustained baptismal rates as industrial and commercial growth encouraged earlier marriage among young adult workers, 'among whom the greatest principles of increase and decrease are to be looked for'.[46] It was possible, therefore, for towns with high mortality rates to achieve a surplus of births and thus make a positive contribution to their overall rate of population growth: despite the massive challenge posed by the well-known 'urban graveyard' effect, some natural increase was certainly possible. However, in analysing the complex interaction between

[44] Aikin, *Description*, pp. 283, 286, 388–92; R. Craig, 'Shipping and shipbuilding in the port of Chester in the eighteenth and early nineteenth centuries', *Transactions of the Historic Society of Lancashire and Cheshire*, 116 (1964), 39–68; A. F. J. Brown, 'Colchester in the eighteenth century', in L. M. Munby, ed., *East Anglian Studies* (London, 1968), pp. 146–73; P. Sharpe, 'De-industrialization and re-industrialization: women's employment and the changing character of Colchester 1700–1850', *UH*, 21 (1994), 77–83; Newton, *Eighteenth-Century Exeter*, pp. 65–84, 140–1; A. J. Vickery, 'Town histories and Victorian plaudits: some examples from Preston', *UHY* (1988), 58–64; J. V. Beckett, 'An industrial town in the making 1750–1830', in J. V. Beckett, ed., *A Centenary History of Nottingham* (Manchester, 1997), pp. 189–219.

[45] J. Landers, *Death and the Metropolis* (Cambridge, 1993), pp. 162–95; R. Woods, 'What would one need to know to solve the "natural increase in early modern cities" problem?', in R. Lawton, ed., *The Rise and Fall of Modern Cities* (London, 1989), pp. 80–95.

[46] J. Haygarth, 'Observations on the population and diseases of Chester, in the year 1774', *Philosophical Transactions of the Royal Society*, 68 (1778), 311–14; Aikin, *Description*, pp. 343, 592; Langton and Laxton, 'Parish registers', 75–82; I. C. Taylor, 'The court and cellar dwelling: the eighteenth-century origins of the Liverpool slum', *Transactions of the Historic Society of Lancashire and Cheshire*, 122 (1970), 67–72.

fertility and mortality in regional and country centres, as in all other towns and cities of the period, it is impossible to ignore the impact of migration. Only migration could have initiated and maintained the level of population growth experienced by the faster growing centres in the eighteenth and early nineteenth centuries in the face of what Pamela Sharpe has termed 'the massive penalty of urban living'. Even in Nottingham, where natural increase made a significant contribution to growth from the mid-1740s, migration was responsible for nearly 60 per cent of the rise in population between 1780 and 1801 as the local framework-knitting industry expanded and turned the previous trickle of just under 200 in-migrants a year into a flood.[47] In Birmingham, too, 'numbers of people crouded upon each other, as into a Paradise', drawn by the irresistible lure of employment opportunities in a vibrant urban economy despite the evident dangers that were inseparable from living and working in such an environment.[48]

Although many of these migrants came from the town's immediate hinterland and therefore would not have looked or sounded particularly alien to their new surroundings, they nevertheless contributed to the obvious mobility and fluidity of urban populations as they moved both between town and country and between transitory lodgings and employments within particular urban neighbourhoods.[49] Their presence within the community, together with the underlying dynamism of the regional and county centres as a whole, was reflected in the diversity and accessibility of urban society. The regional and county centres were relatively open and heterogeneous communities, understandably so since their prosperity depended on their ability to attract both business and custom from a wide catchment area. Their residents could not afford to display the 'small-town mentality' which greeted a German visitor to Burton-on-Trent in 1782, 'where all the people were standing at their doors on both sides, and I had to run the gauntlet of their curious gaze and hear behind me the sound of their hissing'.[50]

[47] See above, pp. 502 *et seq.*; J. D. Chambers, 'Population change in a provincial town: Nottingham 1700–1800', in L. S. Pressnell, ed., *Studies in the Industrial Revolution* (London, 1960), pp. 110–24; A. Henstock, S. Dunster and S. Wallwork, 'Decline and regeneration: society and economic life', in Beckett, ed., *Centenary History*, pp. 132–6, 191–2.

[48] W. Hutton, *A History of Birmingham to the End of the Year 1780*, 2nd edn (Birmingham, 1783), pp. 41, 8*; R. A. Pelham, 'The immigrant population of Birmingham 1686–1726', *Transactions of the Birmingham Archaeological Society*, 61 (1940), 45–80; A. Parton, 'Poor-law settlement certificates and migration to and from Birmingham 1726–57', *Local Population Studies*, 38 (1987), 23–9.

[49] Dingwall, *Late Seventeenth-Century Edinburgh*, p. 54. See also J. R. H. Holman, 'Apprenticeship as a factor in migration: Bristol 1675–1726', *Transactions of the Bristol and Gloucestershire Archaeological Society*, 97 (1979), 85–92; E. L. Buckatzch, 'Places of origin of a group of immigrants into Sheffield 1624–1799', in Clark, ed., *Early Modern Town*, pp. 292–6; C. G. Pooley and S. D'Cruze, 'Migration and urbanization in North-West England circa 1760–1830', *Soc. Hist.*, 19 (1994), 339–58.

[50] R. Nettel, ed., *Journeys of a German in England in 1782* (London, 1965), p. 149; W. Hutton, *The Life of William Hutton*, 2nd edn (London, 1817), p. 115; P. J. Corfield, 'Small towns, large implications: the social and cultural roles of small towns in eighteenth-century England and Wales', *British Journal for Eighteenth-Century Studies*, 10 (1987), 128–9.

Their social pluralism was also reflected in a commercialised, flexible social system, one in which occupational mobility could raise a successful tradesman from humble beginnings as an apprentice to affluent retirement as one of the leisured elite. Yet this relative flexibility was not carried so far as to undermine the fundamental stability of their societies, a stability which contemporaries found reassuring. Despite the swelling numbers of migrants within their populations, most regional and county centres had a substantial core of comparatively stable business and professional families whose activities were central to their social and political life as well as to the smooth functioning of their economies.[51] Population listings also reveal that most of their inhabitants lived in stable family groupings, forming a network of fairly small households based on the nuclear family which lived so close to one another in the densely packed streets of these historic towns that privacy and daylight were both rare luxuries. Tolerance and adaptability were essential in this sort of busy, crowded urban environment.[52]

(iii) SOCIAL LIFE AND CULTURE

The vitality and diversity of urban society in the century after the Restoration made even the smallest towns centres of sociability whose attractions were felt throughout their local spheres of influence. The larger county and regional centres drew in hundreds of people on a regular basis not simply to transact business but to meet friends and exchange gossip in the many inns, taverns and coffee-houses that lined the main streets and clustered round the market place. The fairs, festivals, celebrations and commemorations that punctuated the urban year could bring thousands into the town to enjoy the sights and sounds of the 'big city': colourful processions, public entertainments and the unaccustomed excitement of being part of a crowd.[53] What really distinguished regional and county centres from smaller towns in this respect, however, was the annual influx of the landed elite of their hinterland to attend short but glittering social 'seasons' that were timed to coincide with the arrival of the assize judges on their summer

[51] See for example Dingwall, *Late Seventeenth-Century Edinburgh*, pp. 196–291; S. D'Cruze, 'The middling sort in eighteenth-century Colchester: independence, social relations and the community broker', in J. Barry and C. Brooks, eds., *The Middling Sort of People* (London, 1994), pp. 184–7. The composition of the urban social elite is discussed below, p. 691.

[52] Corfield, *Impact of English Towns*, pp. 126–9; Houston, *Social Change*, pp. 162–3; R. Houston, 'Fire and filth: Edinburgh's environment 1660–1760', *Book of the Old Edinburgh Club*, new series, 3 (1994), 33–4; Hutton, *History*, p. 53; L. Weatherill, *Consumer Behaviour and Material Culture in Britain 1660–1760* (London, 1988), p. 83.

[53] Defoe, *Tour*, I, p. 45; *The Leicester and Nottingham Journal*, 26 Sept. 1761; P. J. Corfield, 'Walking the city streets: the urban odyssey in eighteenth-century England', *JUH*, 16 (1989–90), 158; M. Harrison, 'The ordering of the urban environment: time, work and the occurrence of crowds 1790–1835', *P&P*, 113 (1986), 134–68; but see P. Borsay, '"All the town's a stage": urban ritual and ceremony 1660–1800', in Clark, ed., *Transformation of English Provincial Towns*, pp. 228–58, which suggests that public ceremonies and outdoor festivities tended to decline in this period.

circuit or with a traditional local event such as St Dennis' Fair in Colchester. Some local residents may have been ambiguous in their attitudes to race or fair week, resenting the annual gentry invasion of their home towns or simply reacting against the inevitable disruption of their normal lives, but in general they seem to have basked in the reflected glory of the 'numerous and numerous Company, . . . some of the first Quality and Fashion, who by the Elegancy of their Dress display'd the most brilliant Appearance'.[54]

Each town thus lay at the centre of a circle of gentry sociability, a local 'neighbourhood' whose size and character varied considerably according to the number and quality of the families who maintained country houses in the vicinity. Contemporaries regarded the 'neighbourhood' of Newcastle-upon-Tyne, for example, as exceptionally large and hospitable, while the respectable society of Canterbury surprised visitors used to the ways of more fashionable towns by going home to bed before ten o'clock at night.[55] However, these substantial landowning families shared the social leadership of county and regional centres with a specifically urban elite made up not only of minor gentry, retired professionals and tradesmen, delicately referred to as 'other persons disengaged from business', but also the upper ranks of the active trading and professional communities. The number of so-called 'town gentry' living in most county centres may have been fairly small, representing no more than 4 per cent of the population even in the smarter county towns. In the larger regional centres, however, there tended to be a much higher concentration of high status occupations, as many as 14 per cent of those recorded in a major port such as Bristol, occupations which brought with them considerable social prestige as well as great personal wealth. In Edinburgh it was lawyers and advocates who commanded the most respect; in Glasgow it was the 'Tobacco Lords' who had made fortunes in the Virginia trade; in Newcastle-upon-Tyne it was the 'Lords of Coal', whose vulgarity both amused and horrified fashionable visitors from London.[56] In these powerful regional centres, however, it is evident that there was no clear-cut distinction between a landed and a commercial elite, between 'true' and 'pseudo-gentry'. They had often been educated at the same local grammar schools, they attended the same churches and assemblies, they belonged to the same book clubs and antiquarian societies as well as to the same drinking and gaming clubs,

54 *Cresswell and Burbage's Nottingham Journal*, 7 Aug. 1779; Brown, 'Colchester', p. 167; Montagu, *Correspondence*, II, pp. 205, 207; Powys, *Diaries*, pp. 315–18; J. Oakes, *The Oakes Diaries: Business, Politics and the Family in Bury St Edmunds 1778–1827*, ed. J. Fiske (Suffolk Records Society, 32, 1990), vol. I, pp. 193–4.

55 Montagu, *Correspondence*, II, p. 137; Powys, *Diaries*, p. 315; Hill, *Georgian Lincoln*, pp. 5–14.

56 Aikin, *Description*, p. 388; Everitt, 'Country, county and town', p. 101; Baigent, 'Economy and society', pp. 115–17; S. Nenadic, 'The rise of the urban middle class', in Devine and Mitchison, eds., *People and Society in Scotland*, pp. 111–14; Devine, *Tobacco Lords*, pp. 3–33; Montagu, *Correspondence*, II, p. 137; M. Elwin, ed., *The Noels and the Milbankes: Their Letters for Twenty-Five Years 1767–92* (London, 1967), pp. 107–8.

they employed the same architects and painters, they visited the same resorts, they sent their daughters to the same genteel boarding schools and their sons on the Grand Tour. They also shared the same interest in the economic fortunes of their local metropolis: in Bristol, for example, 'Even the very clergy talk of nothing but trade and how to turn the penny', while a visitor to Newcastle in 1758 noted that 'Every gentleman in the county, from the least to the greatest, is as solicitous in the pursuit of gain as a tradesman.'[57]

It could be equally difficult to differentiate between the lower reaches of 'polite' society and the most prosperous of their neighbours in middle-rank occupations, the solid but not necessarily prosperous tradesmen who formed the backbone of the urban economy: indeed Peter Borsay has described the attempt as 'a labour of Sisyphus'.[58] It has been suggested that the employment of one or more male servants could be used as a significant indicator of genteel status within this broad band. However, this argument has been undermined by a close examination of the taxation returns of 1780, which demonstrate conclusively that in the urban context manservants were an expensive luxury confined to a very small, mostly aristocratic elite, whereas female servants could be found throughout the whole broad category of the 'middling sort'. The largest concentrations of manservants outside London and Bath were indeed to be found in the major regional centres, as might be expected, but the numbers involved were relatively low. On the other hand the ratio of female servants to families can undoubtedly provide valuable evidence of the extent and character of the middle class in different types of urban settlement. In Scotland, for example, listings dating from 1792 demonstrate that the social structures of Edinburgh and the county town of Dumfries, with servant ratios of one in eight and one in ten families, were appreciably different from those of Glasgow and the regional centre of Aberdeen, with ratios of one in fourteen and one in fifteen. It is evident, therefore, that although the middle class was growing in significance as well as in numbers in every county and regional centre in this period, its growth was heavily influenced by the character of the local economy.[59]

[57] Cox, *Magna Britannia*, IV, pp. 744–5; Montagu, *Correspondence*, II, p. 149. This issue is discussed at length in P. J. Corfield, 'The rivals: landed and other gentlemen', in N. B. Harte and R. Quinault, eds., *Land and Society in Britain 1700–1914* (Manchester, 1996), pp. 8–12; see also Borsay, *English Urban Renaissance*, pp. 225–32; Wilson, *Gentlemen Merchants*, pp. 220–37; Oakes, *Diaries*, I, pp. 194–200; Nenadic, 'Rise of the urban middle class', pp. 119–20.

[58] Borsay, *English Urban Renaissance*, p. 307. The nature of this broad middle band of urban society is examined by several of the contributors to Barry and Brooks, eds., *Middling Sort*: see D'Cruze, 'Middling sort', pp. 181–207; also Baigent, 'Economy and society', pp. 116–17; S. Nenadic, 'The middle ranks and modernization', in Devine and Jackson, eds., *Glasgow*, pp. 278–85.

[59] J. Chartres, 'English landed society and the servants tax of 1777', in Harte and Quinault, eds., *Land and Society*, pp. 34–56; Dingwall, *Late Seventeenth-Century Edinburgh*, pp. 44–9, 118–20; E. Hopkins, *Birmingham* (London, 1989), p. 92; P. Earle, *The Making of the English Middle Class* (London, 1989), p. 218; Nenadic, 'Rise of the urban middle class', p. 112. Domestic service outside London in this period is still woefully under-researched.

The prevalence of domestic service in middle-class urban society meant that servants played an important role as intermediaries between the more prosperous sections of that society and the more precarious world of the struggling artisans, petty dealers and wage labourers. Again, there seems to have been an appreciable difference between regional centres with an industrial or commercial specialism, where up to 65 per cent of the population could be classified as actually or potentially living in poverty, and those with a larger leisured or professional class, towns where contemporaries identified a 'much less proportion of the lowest class of the poor'.[60] In the larger, more expansive towns it is clear that the poor were becoming marginalised by the rise of the middling sort since they had neither the leisure nor the purchasing power to share in the cultural or material benefits of the 'urban renaissance'.[61] There are also clear signs that by the 1770s social polarisation was beginning to be reflected in a more polarised urban landscape as the gentry, wealthy merchants and professionals moved out of congested city centres to newly built fashionable housing developments on the edge of the built-up area. Despite such well-known examples as the building of the New Town in Edinburgh (see Plate 23), it would be a mistake to exaggerate the speed of this process: in many county and regional centres the pre-industrial pattern of socially mixed neighbourhoods radiating out from a wealthy central district to poorer suburbs survived late into the eighteenth or even the early nineteenth century. It would also be a mistake to be unduly sentimental about the extent of social mixing within the pre-industrial pattern since there is unmistakable evidence of sharp segregation at street level, in some cases between different floors of the same building, reflecting the extent of social divisions and disunities even within traditional, relatively stable urban communities.[62]

Women featured disproportionately in the ranks of the urban poor and therefore suffered more than their fair share of distress and discrimination in both county towns and regional centres throughout the period. It may therefore seem paradoxical that these were precisely the towns where the female population was

[60] Aikin, *Description*, pp. 389, 392; Hutton, *History*, p. 70; Baigent, 'Economy and society', p. 117; Corfield, 'A provincial capital', pp. 235–6; Ellis, 'Dynamic society', pp. 197–8; T. M. Devine, 'The urban crisis', in Devine and Jackson, eds., *Glasgow*, pp. 411–2.

[61] Borsay, *English Urban Renaissance*, esp. pp. 284–307; Houston, *Social Change*, esp. pp. 214–33; D. Levine, 'Consumer goods and capitalist modernization', *Journal of Interdisciplinary History*, 22 (1991), 67–77.

[62] I. H. Adams, *The Making of Urban Scotland* (London, 1978), pp. 73–86; Houston, *Social Change*, pp. 8, 132–46; Ellis, 'Dynamic society', pp. 198–9; Langton and Laxton, 'Parish registers', 80–2; Beckett, 'Industrial town', pp. 204–6; Nenadic, 'Middle ranks', pp. 285–6; E. Baigent, 'Assessed taxes as sources for the study of urban wealth: Bristol in the later eighteenth century', *UHY* (1988), 40–5; Baigent, 'Economy and society', pp. 118–21. D. Cannadine, 'Residential differentiation in nineteenth-century towns', in J. H. Johnson and C. G. Pooley, eds., *The Structure of Nineteenth-Century Cities* (London, 1982), pp. 238, 245, argues that Victorian towns were also more socially mixed than either contemporaries or most historians have assumed.

expanding most rapidly as a result of in-migration from smaller rural settlements, producing what one demographer has called 'a remarkable predominance of women' in contrast with the more balanced or emphatically male-dominated populations of smaller country towns and villages. By the 1690s the sex ratio (the number of males per 100 females) in larger towns had already fallen to an average of 83.4 and indeed in Bristol the ratio was as low as 80.2. This female bias in urban populations continued unabated well into the next century: indeed, the 1801 census revealed that the largest provincial towns all housed a majority of women.[63] Poorer women were attracted into the towns primarily because they offered a wider range of economic opportunities than were available in an increasingly inhospitable countryside. Although they were thought to have a special gift for retailing, they could be found working in every sector of the urban economy: their activities were by no means confined to occupations that could be regarded as extensions of traditional domestic tasks. Indeed, it would be possible to identify significant numbers of women successfully running their own businesses in every regional and county centre in Britain in this period.[64] However, women were subject to so many restrictions in their choice of employment that it is unsurprising that they remained most often in the low status trades or in the domestic sector and that they invariably outnumbered men among those applying for poor relief. Their role in society was emphatically subordinate to that of even the humblest townsmen, a hierarchy of worth symbolised by the celebrations organised in Bury St Edmunds in June 1814 to enable the poor of the town to celebrate the great victory of Waterloo: sixty deserving men sat down to a public dinner in the market place while the town's poor women were restricted to taking tea and snuff in the afternoon and running races for tea kettles.[65] Most middle-class women in county and regional centres seem to have spent the major part of their time either working in their own households or, in their rare hours of leisure, in the company of other women. Even women from the upper ranks of urban society were segregated in a way which

[63] D. Souden, 'Migrants and the population structure of later seventeenth-century provincial cities and market towns', in Clark, ed., *Transformation of English Provincial Towns*, pp. 133–68; I. D. and K. A. Whyte, 'The geographical mobility of women in early modern Scotland', in L. Leneman, ed., *Perspectives in Scottish Social History* (Aberdeen, 1988), p. 97; Dingwall, *Late Seventeenth-Century Edinburgh*, pp. 92, 561.

[64] Little work has been done on urban women outside the capital cities of London and Edinburgh: see B. Hill, *Women, Work and Sexual Politics in Eighteenth-Century England* (London, 1989); P. Earle, *A City Full of People* (London, 1994), pp. 107–55; S. Seleski, 'The women of the labouring poor: love, work and poverty in London 1750–1820' (PhD thesis, University of Stanford, 1989); E. S. Sanderson, *Women and Work in Eighteenth-Century Edinburgh* (London, 1996); Dingwall, *Late Seventeenth-Century Edinburgh*, pp. 201–8, 210; S. D'Cruze, '"To acquaint the ladies": women traders in Colchester 1750–1800', *Local Historian*, 17 (1986), 158–62; Sharpe, 'De-industrialization', 73–83.

[65] Oakes, *Diaries*, I, p. 186; J. Walvin, *English Urban Life 1776–1851* (London, 1984), pp. 52–4; Baigent, 'Economy and society', pp. 116–18; Sanderson, *Women and Work*, pp. 136–67, 169.

surprised many foreign visitors. They were completely excluded from many public and private male functions, particularly clubs (see Plate 20), and it was noticeable that they were often left to their own devices even at ostensibly 'mixed' events such as assemblies while their menfolk, 'these lords of creation', retired to the card room or hogged the conversation in the middle of the floor.[66]

However, contemporaries were in no doubt that women from the upper ranks of society enjoyed considerably more freedom of action in the town than in the countryside. Towns offered such women a variety of respectable occupations, amusements and companions, all of which they could enjoy in a degree of physical comfort. Young single women and widows were particularly prone to boredom in the countryside and had a greater incentive to settle permanently in town but even married women felt the need of regular visits 'to brush off the Rust a little'. As a result, many of the 'urban gentry' of this period were in fact widowed or spinster gentle*women*: both Preston and the New Town at Edinburgh were notoriously full of 'old maids' whose families either could not or would not afford a dowry sufficient to secure a husband of suitable rank but who could find a comfortable niche in urban society. The greater concentrations of both people and wealth found even in provincial centres meant that women could socialise on a much wider scale without sacrificing their status and respectability by mingling with those too far beneath them. The relatively compact built-up area of most towns was also an advantage, putting this wider circle of acceptable acquaintances within easy reach, especially as improvements in the urban environment, including better pavements and more efficient street lighting, and in public transport, such as sedan chairs and hackney carriages, meant that women were much more mobile in the town than in the country. Women were sometimes allowed to take a leading role in organising social events: the assembly at Derby, for instance, was administered by a succession of lady patronesses, each of whom kept the accounts and was expected to turn over a surplus to her successor.[67] They could even wield considerable influence over the intricate workings of national and local politics, areas from which they were publicly excluded. 'Husbanding' an electoral interest, for instance, was a continuous political process which demanded the deployment of a wide range of tactics

[66] Weatherill, *Consumer Behaviour*, p. 164; B. Hill, ed., *Eighteenth-Century Women: An Anthology* (London, 1984); A. Parreaux, *Daily Life in England in the Reign of George III* (London, 1969), p. 121; Oakes, *Diaries*, I, pp. 184–5; Elwin, ed., *Noels*, p. 108; Powys, *Diaries*, p. 75; J. Coke, *Letters from Lady Jane Coke to her Friend Mrs Eyre at Derby 1747–58*, ed. A. Rathbone (London, 1899), p. 10.

[67] J. M. Ellis, '"On the town": women in Augustan England 1688–1820', *History Today*, 45 (1995), 20–6; W. Goldsmith, *She Stoops to Conquer* (London, 1773), act I, scene I; R. A. Houston, 'Women in Scottish society 1500–1800', in Houston and Whyte, eds., *Scottish Society*, p. 131; R. Pococke, *The Travels through England*, ed. J. J. Cartwright (Camden Society, 2nd series, 42, 1888), p. 12; M. Girouard, *The English Town* (London, 1990), pp. 112–14; Corfield, 'Walking', 133–4; Houston, *Social Change*, p. 133; Rathbone, ed., *Letters*, p. 8.

including judicious use of the candidates' wives, whose behaviour was recognised as having an appreciable impact on their political standing. Aristocratic ladies found themselves 'obliged to be the *Pink of Courtesy* to all the Aldermen & their Wives to the Hundredth Cousin', afraid to alienate the touchy sensibilities of the urban elite by appearing too proud and haughty or, worse still, refusing to appear at all. The women who were missing from the grand processions to welcome visiting dignitaries or celebrate great public events, processions which are sometimes described as 'a perfect mirror of county society', had a role to play behind the scenes which raised them above the level of passive spectators.[68]

Such processions symbolising the close links between city and country took place within a ceremonial context that punctuated the entire year with highly orchestrated public events in which urban rather than county society took a leading role. On such occasions the highly visible presence of the civic leadership in all its glory served to emphasise a civic consciousness that defined and asserted the special nature of towns in general but which was particularly strong in traditional corporate towns. Even the newer, unincorporated regional centres demonstrated a growing self-confidence and pride in their achievements, a self-confidence exemplified by William Hutton's dogmatic assertion that 'when the word Birmingham occurs, a superb picture instantly expands in the mind, which is best explained by the other words grand, populous, extensive, active, commercial and humane'. There was an almost tangible local pride which found vivid expression not just in public buildings and ceremonials, or in the printed town histories, maps and views which became available in ever cheaper editions as the period progressed, but also in popular ballads and keen local rivalries.[69]

As this indicates, it was not only the upper reaches of urban society which identified civility and urbanity with cooperative endeavour. The clubs and voluntary societies that were formed in increasing numbers by affluent citizens in the later years of the period to promote medical and educational charities, to encourage intellectual, scientific or agricultural improvement, or simply to enjoy an agreeable hobby in congenial company had their counterparts among the

[68] Elwin, ed., *Noels*, p. 216; Montagu, *Correspondence*, II, p. 207; Borsay, 'Urban ritual', pp. 230–3. D'Cruze emphasises that male participation in civic government and politics often depended on the willingness of wives and daughters to cover for their absence from the family business: 'Middling sort', pp. 196, 207.

[69] Hutton, *History*, p. 23; J. Barry, 'Bristol pride: civic identity in Bristol *c.* 1640–1775', in Dresser and Ollerenshaw, eds., *Modern Bristol*, pp. 25–47; Ellis, 'Dynamic society', pp. 200–2; Money, *Experience and Identity*, pp. 24–50; Nottingham RO, anonymous diary, M 380, ff. 110–12; P. Clark, 'Visions of the urban community: antiquarians and the English city before 1800', in D. Fraser and A. Sutcliffe, eds., *The Pursuit of Urban History* (London, 1983), pp. 105–24; R. Hyde, *Gilded Scenes and Shining Prospects: Panoramic Views of British Towns 1575–1900* (New Haven, Conn., 1985), pp. 61–131; Corfield, *Impact of English Towns*, p. 188.

lower ranks of artisans and tradesmen.[70] Naturally every urban ceremony was organised on the basis of strict rules of hierarchy and precedence: corporations and guilds, clubs and societies, all marched and prayed, feasted and drank in an order that embodied the traditional values of community life. Seniority, status and seemly public behaviour were the guiding principles of their organisation, principles which in the early years of the period still commanded the support of the wider urban community. Despite frequent, sometimes acrimonious, disputes over precedence and despite the almost total exclusion of women and wage labourers from their formal structures, for much of the eighteenth century local institutions attracted the active participation of the whole broad category of the 'middling sort'.[71] It was recognised that these institutions played a vital role in providing the infrastructure and services that underpinned urban society. Thus civic support of the poor in regional and county centres provided a necessary safety net, accepted by wealthier citizens as 'a means of [their] long prosperity and preservation against all the attempts of [their] enemies', since it helped to underpin social stability. And if that stability was threatened by popular protests sparked off by high prices or low wages, the civic authorities were expected to act as peace-makers as well as peace-keepers, invoking a tradition of negotiated settlements 'upon Terms' which tended to produce an equally structured and orderly response from the crowd.[72]

(iv) THE PARTING OF THE WAYS?

However, there are clear signs that this civic ideal was coming under pressure in the later eighteenth and early nineteenth centuries, that the consciousness of the urban elite was becoming more and more distinct from that of poorer towns-men and women. One such sign was the increasing unpopularity of urban cor-porations as their composition became more socially exclusive and as a more

[70] J. Barry, 'Bourgeois collectivism? Urban association and the middling sort', in Barry and Brooks, eds., *Middling Sort* pp. 84–112; P. Clark, *Sociability and Urbanity* (Leicester, 1988); Borsay, *English Urban Renaissance*, pp. 135–7; Houston, *Social Change*, pp. 216–18; Langford, *Polite and Commercial People*, pp. 99–100; Anon., *Four Topographical Letters Written in July 1755* (Newcastle, 1757), pp. 63–4; Hutton, *History*, pp. 15– 25; Money, *Experience and Identity*, pp. 98–120.

[71] *The Leicester and Nottingham Journal*, 26 Sept. 1761; Borsay, 'Urban ritual', pp. 228–43; Houston, *Social Change*, pp. 48–54; D'Cruze, 'Middling sort', pp. 181–207; Ellis, 'Dynamic society', pp. 201–2; J. Black, 'Eighteenth-century political history: the local dimension', *Local Historian*, 23 (1993), 103–10.

[72] Houston, *Social Change*, pp. 318–19; I. Maver, 'The guardianship of the community: civic author-ity prior to 1833', in Devine and Jackson, eds., *Glasgow*, pp. 239–77; M. Harrison, *Crowds and History: Mass Phenomena in English Towns 1790–1835* (Cambridge, 1988); L. H. Lees, 'The study of social conflict in English industrial towns', *UHY* (1980), 34–43; J. M. Ellis, 'Urban conflict and popular violence: the Guildhall riots of 1740 in Newcastle-upon-Tyne', *International Review of Social History*, 25 (1980), 332–49; Ellis, 'Dynamic society', pp. 215–17.

hawkish attitude towards the poor spread among heavily burdened ratepayers. By the 1830s the political structure of most regional and county centres had come to reflect the new horizontal, class-based social divisions that had been visible in the major regional centres since the 1770s, a process which helped to undermine their long-established role as 'places of resort' for genteel society.[73] As the years passed, contemporaries reported a worrying decline in the number and quality of the company attending both the winter assemblies and the main summer or autumn occasions. Given the increasing ease of travel and their own rising wealth, many county families were no longer prepared to settle for a 'little London' in the winter when they could now visit the original, while the superior attractions of Bath in the winter months and of the new seaside resorts in the summer were also slowly but inexorably eroding the appeal of the county towns as centres of fashionable leisure. Even in the 1770s many race week balls were described as no more than tolerable in comparison with the 'brilliant' gatherings of the past and by the 1820s at the latest their glory was no more than a memory: the leading gentry families were taking their custom elsewhere.[74]

At the same time, the increasing scale and pace of economic development in many of the larger regional and county centres was eroding their traditional appeal as places of genteel residence for the wealthy and leisured sections of eighteenth-century society. It had long been a commonplace that 'Towns of a considerable Business and a flourishing Trade, seldom give Gentlemen great Encouragement to be fond of settling in them': indeed, the noise, dirt and congestion that were inseparable from industrial and commercial activity were so distasteful that some of the wealthier residents of Colchester in the early years of the period were said to have welcomed the decline of its once-flourishing cloth industry.[75] On the other hand, towns which lost their staple means of employment and were unable to replace it ran the risk of falling into a downward spiral of poverty and neglect, becoming literally as well as figuratively 'decayed'. Genteel society appreciated the aesthetic and historical value of Roman antiquities and ancient churches but it also expected 'spacious, dry and airy streets', smart housing and modern amenities. Historic cities such as York and Canterbury which had not kept pace with these changing standards were there-

[73] S. Poole, 'To be a Bristolian: civic identity and the social order 1750–1850', in Dresser and Ollerenshaw, eds., *Modern Bristol*, pp. 76–95; Baigent, 'Economy and society', pp. 122–3; Harrison, *Crowds and History*, pp. 196–201, 260–7; Money, *Experience and Identity*, pp. 246–74; Houston, *Social Change*, pp. 332–78; R. Newton, 'The membership of the chamber of Exeter 1688–1835', *Devon and Cornwall NQ*, 108 (1976), 282–6, 333–6.

[74] Powys, *Diaries*, pp. 134, 234; Borsay, *English Urban Renaissance*, pp. 188–93; Everitt, 'Country, county and town', p. 100; Newton, *Eighteenth-Century Exeter*, pp. 140–1. See below, pp. 777 *et seq*.

[75] Deering, *Nottinghamia*, p. 6; Hutton, *History*, p. 26; J. Macky, *A Journey through England* (London, 1714), vol. II, p. 221; T. Marcy, 'Eighteenth-century views of Bristol and Bristolians', in P. McGrath, ed., *Bristol in the Eighteenth Century* (Newton Abbot, 1972), pp. 11–40; Brown, 'Colchester', pp. 155–6.

fore almost universally condemned as 'indifferent' or even downright 'ugly'.[76] However, towns which had a well-established reputation as attractive residential centres tended to maintain that reputation well into the later eighteenth and early nineteenth centuries despite dramatic changes in the local economy. One formerly desirable residence in the 'garden city' of Nottingham, for instance, was still described in the 1820s as 'an enchanting country seat in the heart of the town' although it was now hemmed in by a miscellaneous collection of workshops, warehouses and framework-knitters' cottages, not to mention a Wesleyan chapel whose windows had to be partly boarded up to preserve some measure of privacy for the remarkably resilient householder. Rapid population growth combined with speculative building within the congested city centre to produce an urban environment that in the following decade became notorious for its 'unparalleled overcrowding and squalor'.[77]

In the case of towns like Nottingham, whose character had been transformed within a generation by intensive economic development, the social threat posed by newly rich but irredeemably vulgar industrialists seems to have been just as influential as the deteriorating urban environment in prompting a flight to the country. One well-born resident of Preston is recorded as leaving the town 'in a towering passion' within a few hours of discovering that the fishmonger had sold his finest turbot to a wealthy cotton spinner. 'This was too much for [his] sense of dignity.'[78] This sudden fracture of 'Proud Preston's' ruling class seems to indicate that the earlier reconciliation between the rural and urban elites, between polite and civic culture, so persuasively described by Peter Borsay, could not survive the demographic and economic stresses which accumulated in nearly every regional and county centre in the decades after 1770.[79] The apparent harmony which reigned in so many of these towns during the 'urban renaissance' of the later seventeenth and early eighteenth centuries had depended on the urban elite's willingness to offer due deference to their social superiors and to observe the many subtle distinctions of rank and status which pervaded every aspect of social intercourse. It had also depended on the eagerness of the 'Trading

[76] L. Simond, *An American in Regency England: The Journal of a Tour*, ed. C. Hibbert (London, 1968), pp. 61, 108; Powys, *Diaries*, pp. 16–17, 307; Aikin, *Description*, pp. 386–8; G. Poulson, *Beverlac; or the Antiquities and History of the Town of Beverley* (London, 1829), p. 26.

[77] A Henstock, 'County house, high pavement; a Georgian and Regency town house', *Thoroton Society*, 78 (1974), 54–67; Chambers, 'Population change', p. 99; Beckett, 'Industrial town', pp. 189–208.

[78] R. Edgcumbe, ed., *The Diary of Frances, Lady Shelley 1787–1817* (London, 1912), vol. I, p. 3; Aikin, *Description*, pp. 286–7; Vickery, 'Town histories', 58–9.

[79] The classic exposition of this case is Borsay, *English Urban Renaissance*. See also G. S. Holmes, 'The achievement of stability', in J. Cannon, ed., *The Whig Ascendancy* (London, 1981), pp. 1–23; P. Borsay, 'Culture, status and the English urban landscape', *History*, 67 (1982), 2–12. An extended critique of this approach is offered by J. Barry, 'Provincial town culture, 1640–1780: urbane or civic?', in A. Wear and J. Pittock Weston, eds., *New Directions in Cultural History* (London, 1990), pp. 198–234.

parts of the Town' to join with the 'principal Gentlemen' in excluding most of their fellow citizens from their definition of what constituted 'proper company', an enterprise that appeared increasingly futile in an urban setting as the commercialisation of leisure continued to lower the price of fashionable culture.[80]

The tensions revealed by these attempts at social differentiation should not, however, distract attention from the profound political, religious and cultural conflicts that split the urban elite into rival and often bitterly hostile factions. The legacy of the divisions that had crystallised during the Civil Wars meant that regional and county centres became potential arenas for ideological warfare as much as for social display: indeed in York in the 1720s these two birds were killed with one stone since there were rival Tory and Whig assemblies held on different days.[81] The use of cultural events to promote political causes was part of a wider phenomenon which made it very difficult to promote any form of non-partisan activity since every initiative was inevitably associated with one or other of the town's competing 'interests'. Charitable subscriptions and improvement societies, for example, were rarely simple expressions of generosity or public spirit: instead they became platforms for the assertion of divisions within the elite, divisions that were often fostered by the competitive nature of society in the most dynamic regional centres. The merchants of Bristol, for instance, were notorious for their 'sharp and hard dealings', while John Wesley identified internal recriminations as the 'the sin which, of all others, most easily besets the people of Newcastle'. Such was the intensity of the conflict that contemporaries feared its public expression could undermine the very basis of social relations by bringing the elite into disrepute and encouraging the lower orders to enter the political arena.[82]

These fears became much more acute in the second half of the period as renewed conflicts between Whig and Tory were exacerbated by new political and religious issues arising from the growing social divisions between rich and poor. Rapid population growth among the poor at a time, when the wealth and well-being of the upper and middle orders of society seemed to be increasing at

[80] Oakes, *Diaries*, II, 8 May 1802; Nenadic, 'Rise of the urban middle class', p. 120; J. Brewer, *The Pleasures of the Imagination* (London, 1997), pp. 547–9. Brewer, *ibid.*, pp. 507–12, argues that urban businessmen were increasingly concerned to redefine 'gentility' in such a way as to elevate wisdom and experience at the expense of rank and 'mere fortune' (p. 511).

[81] Girouard, *English Town*, pp. 133–4; Macky, *Journey*, II, p. 211: though it should be noted that the two York assemblies merged in 1732 with the opening of new rooms. Borsay, *English Urban Renaissance*, pp. 279–80, stresses the tendency for town culture to develop 'an apolitical, even anti-political complexion'.

[82] J. Black, 'The press and the politics of culture in Bristol 1660–1775', in J. Black and J. Gregory, eds., *Culture, Politics and Society in Britain 1660–1800* (Manchester, 1991), pp. 49–81; S. Nenadic, 'Middle ranks', pp. 292–301; M. Gorsky, 'The pattern of philanthropy: endowed charity in nineteenth-century Bristol' (typescript, 1991), p. 6; D'Cruze, 'Middling sort', pp. 199–206; Ellis, 'Dynamic society', pp. 202–5, 214–15; S. Curwen, *The Journal of Samuel Curwen, Loyalist*, ed. A. Oliver (Cambridge, Mass., 1972), pp. 399–400.

an unprecedented rate, polarised attitudes in the county and regional centres just as it did in the industrialising towns. On the one hand, some contemporaries denounced the growing inequalities that had sharply demarcated the 'smart' areas of town from the narrower, dirtier and disease-ridden alleyways where the common people were herded together in increasing numbers. Critics of early nineteenth-century Manchester, for instance, condemned its 'unnatural' society, 'associated but not united, contiguous but not connected'. With inverted pride they asserted that 'there is no town in the world where the distance between rich and poor is so great, or the barrier between them so difficult to be crossed': 'in one portion, there is space, fresh air, and provision for health; and in the other, everything which poisons and abridges existence'.[83]

On the other hand, the sheer concentration of urban problems in the poorer districts of the old town centres was beginning to erode the relative tolerance that had characterised urban society in the early eighteenth century and to sever the traditional connection between paternalism and deference. The swelling numbers of the poor now seemed to threaten the very existence of urbane society, overwhelming the resources of local councils and improvement commissions.[84] They were at best expensive and at worst positively dangerous, each one a potential criminal prone to fraud and violent disorder. In Glasgow, for instance, public fears were exacerbated by hysterical images of Irish immigrants, 'these modern Huns', burrowing into the heart of the ancient city and 'nightly issue[ing] to disseminate disease and to pour upon the town every species of abomination and crime'.[85] They also encouraged a tendency to blame the 'ignorance and moral errors' of the poor for their all-too-apparent misery: hence the increasing popularity among the elite of measures that were designed both to reduce the cost of relief and to draw a clear distinction between the 'deserving', deferential poor and those who were stigmatised as marginal and 'undeserving'. Even in Bury St Edmunds, an apparently stable and genteel county centre, these anxieties prompted heated arguments about whether it was advisable to badge those receiving parish relief or establish a night watch to prevent disorder in its rural hinterland from spilling over into the town itself.[86]

83 R. Parkinson, *The Present Condition of the Labouring Poor in Manchester* (London, 1841), pp. 11–12; Faucher, *Manchester in 1844*, pp. 69–70; R. Dennis, *English Industrial Cities of the Nineteenth Century* (Cambridge, 1984), pp. 48–92; I. Taylor, 'The court and cellar dwelling: the eighteenth-century origins of the Liverpool slum', *Transactions of the Historic Society of Lancashire and Cheshire*, 122 (1970), 67–90; Devine, 'Urban crisis', pp. 402–6; A. K. Chalmers, *The Health of Glasgow 1818–1925: An Outline* (Glasgow, 1930), pp. 2–26; M. Beresford, *East End, West End* (Thoresby Society, 60–1, 1989). 84 See above, Chapter 16.

85 Quoted in Devine, 'Urban crisis', p. 406; J. Pagan, ed., *Glasgow, Past and Present* (Glasgow, 1884), p. 32; J. G. Robb, 'Suburb and slum in the Gorbals: social and residential change 1800–1900', in G. Gordon and B. Dicks, eds., *Scottish Urban History* (Aberdeen, 1983), pp. 135–44.

86 J. Kay, *The Moral and Physical Condition of the Working Classes Employed in the Cotton Manufactures in Manchester* (London, 1832), pp. 5–6; Pons, 'Contemporary interpretations', pp. 51– 76; Houston, *Social Change*, pp. 234–89; Oakes, *Diaries*, II, 4 Nov. 1800, 26 Jan. 1809, 6 May 1816.

Disorder in itself was nothing new: the streets and market places of county and regional centres had for centuries been the natural venue for a wide variety of riots, protests and demonstrations. However, in the past popular protests had tended to express the grievances of a broad spectrum of local society. In the more abrasive, more polarised society which was developing in the later eighteenth century, crowds came more and more to represent narrower sectional interests, while the urban elite proved increasingly unlikely to sanction any form of protest in which 'the mob' played such an active role. Even public participation in traditional urban rituals was gradually abandoned as the perceived threat to good order and social discipline posed by the lower orders increased. The changing social climate was clearly demonstrated on Coronation Day in 1821, when the elaborate processions and expensive festivities organised by city authorities throughout the land were greeted with a sullen hostility that occasionally boiled over into boisterous, subversive dissent.[87] A rumbling threat of violence menaced the urban elite in the great regional centres in the 1820s and 1830s: the 'apocalypse' of the Reform riots in Bristol and Nottingham was recalled by a speaker to a vast Chartist rally on Newcastle Town Moor in 1838 when he urged the crowd of more than 40,000 people to arm themselves and burn the city to the ground should the authorities attempt to implement the New Poor Law. The growing assertiveness of the urban population in many regional and county centres should perhaps be counted alongside growing environmental degradation as contributing to their declining appeal as places of genteel residence: living in a city constructed 'upon the infinite abysses' of violence and fear appeared increasingly undesirable.[88]

(v) CONCLUSION

These dramatic changes in the character of many of Britain's historic cities, together with the equally dramatic rise of the commercial and industrial towns of the North and West, raised the question of whether it was still possible for a city to be perceived as both 'great' and 'good'. Public perceptions of what constituted a city as opposed to a town had indeed been changing throughout the

[87] Houston, *Social Change*, pp. 290–331; G. A. Tressider, 'Coronation day celebrations in English towns c. 1685–1821: elite hegemony and local relations on a ceremonial occasion', *British Journal for Eighteenth-Century Studies*, 15 (1992), 1–16; C. A. Whatley, 'Royal day, people's day: the monarch's birthday in Scotland c1660–1860', in R. Mason and N. MacDougall, eds., *People and Power in Scotland: Essays in Honour of T. C. Smout* (Edinburgh, 1992), pp. 170–88; R. D. Parker, 'The changing character of Preston Guild Merchant 1762–1868', *NHist.*, 20 (1984), 108–26.

[88] Poole, 'Civic identity', pp. 290–331; R. Challinor, *A Radical Lawyer in Victorian England: W. Roberts and the Struggle for Workers' Rights* (London, 1990), p. 198; C. A. Whatley, 'Labour in the industrializing city c1660–1830', in Devine and Jackson, eds., *Glasgow*, pp. 360–410; S. J. Davies, 'Classes and police in Manchester 1829–80', in A. J. Kidd and K. W. Roberts, eds., *City, Class and Culture* (Manchester, 1985), pp. 30–1; T. Carlyle (1843), quoted in Messinger, *Manchester*, p. 90.

period. Even in the 1720s Defoe had been distinctly uneasy about the convention that accorded a higher status to minor cathedral cities, yet denied it to a substantial regional centre such as Shrewsbury which in his view was 'equal to many good cities in England, and superior to some'.[89] As the pace of urbanisation increased, numbers came increasingly to dictate status and the great cities of Liverpool, Glasgow, Manchester and Birmingham (see Plate 24) developed a robust sense of pride in their achievements and confidence in their own distinctive urban identities. And yet in each case this pride and self-confidence had to battle against the widespread public perception that economic and demographic growth were inseparable from dirt, squalor, disorder and disease: whereas in the eighteenth century docks and factories had attracted the admiration of well-born tourists, by the 1840s horrified travellers tended to avert their gaze. Given that few of the older centres of the South and East had experienced a similar transformation, the urban world appeared to have split decisively between the places where money was made and the few remaining centres of elegance and refinement, between Milton and Barchester.[90]

It would in some ways be a mistake to exaggerate the novelty of this division between 'neat and elegant' county towns like Canterbury and Chester, on the one hand, and the grimy urban environment of Birmingham, Manchester or Glasgow, on the other. Edinburgh's Old Town, for instance, had an unenviable reputation in the early eighteenth century as one of the 'Nastiest Citys in the World', whose residents had to contend with offensive smells, excrement piled 'like mountains' in the streets, and bug-infested lodgings. Bristol too had been renowned for its dirt and disorder long before the rise of Liverpool, while the impression made by Newcastle-upon-Tyne, that 'nasty, sooty, smoky chaos of a town', on eighteenth-century visitors ranged from 'exceeding unpleasant' to 'horrible'.[91] What was new in the early nineteenth century, however, was the gap that had opened up between the biggest regional centres and the traditional county towns. Whereas in 1700 Salisbury with a population of around 6,000 had been regarded as a 'large and pleasant city' only five times smaller than Norwich and eight times smaller than Edinburgh, in 1841 it was more than thirty times

[89] Defoe, *Tour*, II, p. 76; Corfield, *Impact of English Towns*, pp. 4–5.

[90] Anon., *Four Topographical Letters*, pp. 62–3; Byng, *Torrington Diaries*, I, pp. 48–9; Nettel, ed., *Journeys*, p. 146; W. MacRitchie, *Diary of a Tour through Great Britain in 1795* (Edinburgh, 1897), pp. 42–5; Vickery, 'Town histories', 59. Note, however, that Byng had already stigmatised Manchester as 'a dog hole' in 1792: J. Byng, *Byng's Tours: The Journals of the Hon. John Byng*, ed. D. Souden (London, 1991), p. 183.

[91] J. Taylor, *A Journey to Edenborough in Scotland* (Edinburgh, 1903), pp. 130–4; Houston, 'Fire and filth', 25–30; C. Anstey, *The New Bath Guide* (London, 1776), letter VII; Marcy, 'Bristol', pp. 20–3; Defoe, *Tour*, II, p. 252; Montagu, *Correspondence*, II, p. 138; Elwin, ed., *Noels*, pp. 116, 145; MacRitchie, *Diary*, pp. 137–8. Anti-urban rhetoric had, however, been largely focused on London: see R. Williams, *The City and the Country* (London, 1973); W. A. Speck, *Society and Literature in England 1700–60* (London, 1983), pp. 116–38; K. Thomas, *Man and the Natural World: Changing Attitudes in England 1500–1800* (London, 1984), pp. 243–54.

smaller than Manchester, 'a little old city, very ugly, and of which there is nothing to say'.[92] As their patterns of development diverged, so contemporary opinion began to polarise and the status, indeed the whole moral standing, of the great cities became a matter of dispute.[93] On the one hand, the inhabitants of Sheffield, Wolverhampton and the other 'industrious' towns and cities of Victorian Britain could bask in the virtues of their 'improved and improving' communities, leaving their less fortunate neighbours to dwindle into obscurity. From this perspective, at least, the period as a whole could be regarded without any hint of apology as one of progress. On the other hand, the challenges of urban life in Victorian Britain made 'success' a problematic concept: notions of progress and improvement were difficult to reconcile with the terrors of cholera and revolution that stalked the slums of the inner city. 'We are,' concluded one resident of Manchester, 'as it were, a *debris* which the whirlpool of human affairs has deposited here in one of its eddies': by 1840 the 'Augean pandemonium' of wealth and commercial hegemony achieved only at the price of dirt, disease and overwhelming misery had to a large extent undermined public confidence in the future of the great regional centres.[94]

[92] Defoe, *Tour*, I, pp. 188–92; Simond, *Regency England*, p. 61. For population figures, see Table 20.2.

[93] It should be noted that traditional religious and political rivalries were often transposed into this new discourse: thus Anglicans linked the perceived evils of urban society with the rise of irreligion, while dissenters were notably more optimistic. See above, pp. 565 *et seq*.

[94] Vickery, 'Town histories', 58–64; Parkinson, *Present Condition*, p. 11; Chalmers, *Health of Glasgow*, p. 5; A. Briggs, *Victorian Cities* (Harmondsworth, 1968), p. 134.

· 21 ·

Ports 1700–1840

GORDON JACKSON

(i) THE DIVERSITY OF PORTS

PORTS WERE among the most dynamic towns during the commercial and Industrial Revolutions in Britain. They were also exceedingly diverse. By definition they were all boroughs or burghs with members of parliament, and councils controlling their domestic affairs. They enjoyed monopoly rights over foreign and most coastal trade. An English law of 1558 restricted trade to specified places and designated Legal Quays within them where all customable goods *must* be handled.[1] There were approximately seventy-two English ports from 1696, when the customs service was reformed.[2] In Scotland only designated royal and certain baronial burghs could trade overseas, and these were organised in thirteen precincts before the Union and approximately thirty ports thereafter.[3] Although ports were separate entities, to some extent they competed with each other as part of the general or regional transportation system, but they shared characteristics that can be dealt with across the spectrum of places and activities.

By definition ports grew round a waterfront, preferably the mouth of a river linking them to a hinterland, or, less successfully, a stretch of seashore enclosed by a pier or piers and dependent on land carriage.[4] Almost universally throughout northern Europe this waterfront was lined originally with private warehouses backing on to merchants' houses facing the main street, maximising

I am grateful to the Economic and Social Research Council for supporting the Scottish part of the work on which this essay is based.

[1] R. Jarvis, 'The appointment of ports', *Ec.HR*, 2nd series, 11 (1959), 460–3.

[2] E. E. Hoon, *The Organization of the English Customs System, 1696–1786* (New York, 1938), pp. 168–9, quotes official lists of fifty-one in 1696 and seventy-two in 1786, but the first omitted Welsh ports. The few ports added between these dates were unimportant.

[3] For Scotland, see T. C. Smout, *Scottish Trade on the Eve of the Union, 1660–1707* (Edinburgh, 1963), ch. 2 and appendix 1.

[4] For a more sophisticated analysis of early ports, see above, pp. 380 *et seq*.

ground area while minimising expensive water frontage. There was usually a secondary centre round a market serving the local distribution network. In the eighteenth century the ground plan was elaborated in busy ports, with further streets for warehouses. However, the high cost of cartage and government failure to extend Legal Quays encouraged concentration round the waterside, raising land values and confirming the economic domination of those who owned it, with unfortunate effects for later developments. Burgage plots were intensively built over and domestic housing was gradually driven from the centre as ports reorganised urban space for the sake of essential infrastructure.

Ports can be categorised in various ways, most obviously by volume of trade and tonnage of shipping owned, though type of trade was also significant, whether coal, cotton or eastern spice. The largest were general trade ports seriously engaged in foreign and coastal trade, or coal exporters; places of bustle and wealth. The rest engaged in varying amounts of coastal traffic, with restricted foreign interests; and the smallest had few coasters and no foreign trade. Many had port-related industries distinguishing them from inland towns, though a few developed industries usually found inland. Their merchants enjoyed protection of various sorts; they sold knowledge rather than goods; they had easy access to capital and credit. By any standards their leaders were rich indeed. Serious ports were also unique among towns in the compulsion to maintain or develop social overhead capital.

In effect, the incremental trade of the commercial and Industrial Revolutions went mostly through existing ports with distinct comparative advantages, their performance determined by changes in their hinterlands and in the direction and composition of trade.[5] The rising ports were chiefly in the 'North' of England and central Scotland, corresponding to the industrialisation of the interior, while few of the 70 per cent of English ports lying south of the Severn–Wash line had dynamic hinterlands. Change and decay were inherent in the system. England's early European trade went through East Anglia and the South-East, whose poor harbours and hinterland were discounted by shorter voyages. Things changed as the economy moved northwards. The Cinque Ports, long on splendour, short on trade, were thoroughly distressed and now served local market functions, except for Dover, whose passenger and packet traffic made it one of the largest ports by tonnage, though not by volume of goods.

By contrast, the rising ports built on their geographical advantages.[6] They occupied the prime positions on the principal estuaries. The importance of roads for development has been emphasised recently, and certainly ports of all description had their tentacles of inland routes that stretched many miles. Poor roads

[5] The detailed trade of all ports was recorded by HM Customs until *c.* 1783 in England and 1829 in Scotland, so we know more about the core activity of ports than of other sorts of town.

[6] The standard work on port sites is J. Bird, *Major Seaports of the United Kingdom* (London, 1963), ch. 1.

thwarted long-distance carriage of heavy, bulky or cheap goods, holding back the development of Whitehaven's transatlantic exports vis-à-vis Glasgow's around 1750.[7] Glasgow city council invested in bridges and improvements to the roads to England and the east coast, and Dundee, by 1834, had 130 carriers maintaining links with at least fifty towns and villages. All port *Directories* show the same thing. Nevertheless, waterways and short coal railways stimulated manufacturing and mining regions with growing populations and were the main volume arteries. Superior water connections gave major ports their head start and sustained them until the railways confirmed their position.[8] Major ports also enjoyed – and were able to extend – good harbours in which they catered for substantial and growing contacts with foreign countries and balanced this with the largest share of the country's coastal traffic. Within those harbours they owned substantial fleets.

Finally, most ports, certainly the serious ones, had complex business and social structures. In theory the whole coastline fell within the precinct of some port, and goods could be moved between shore and ship in the presence of a customs 'riding officer'. Such activity was, however, rare. Trade, shipping, business, credit and vital information flows tended to concentrate in ports with proven success. A pretty village at the seaside, with a pier, quay or beach, was no more a serious port than a rural mill was a cotton town!

Among the busy ports London was pre-eminent.[9] Its huge market and manufacturing sector supported a well-developed coastal distribution and collection function. It had the East India monopoly, and was strong in the transatlantic trades; Glasgow's exports stood little chance in the 1670s in New England and Jamaica when the London ships came in.[10] Much regional specialisation was directed to serving London's large population. Indeed, the magnetism of its market, the expertise of its merchants, the availability of capital and the ease with which ships could be found for any destination blighted the foreign trade of ancient ports from the Humber to the Exe, Daniel Defoe noting especially Ipswich, Dartmouth, Weymouth and Southampton 'swallowed up' by London.[11] However, despite Defoe's pessimism, Southampton survived and was growing fast. Exeter, an important regional centre, was near enough to the Western Approaches to nourish transatlantic trade, and well connected for shipping cloth to southern Europe and importing wine. However, it chiefly shipped agricultural products

[7] J. V. Beckett, *Coal and Tobacco* (Cambridge, 1981), ch. 6.

[8] T. H. Barker and D. Gerhold, *The Rise and Rise of Road Transport* (Cambridge, 1993), pp. 8–30; T. S. Willan, *Early History of the Don Navigation* (Manchester, 1965), pp. 1–40; T. S. Willan, *River Navigation in England, 1600–1750* (Oxford, 1936), p. 1.

[9] For the early history and comparative size of the major ports and their markets, above, pp. 380 *et seq.*, 411 *et seq.*

[10] G. Jackson, 'Glasgow in transition', in T. M. Devine and G. Jackson, eds., *Glasgow*, vol. 1: *Beginnings to 1830* (Manchester, 1995), p. 72.

[11] D. Defoe, *A Tour through England and Wales* (London, 1928), vol. 1, p. 43.

along the south coast and, since it still cost more to ship from the Exe to Bristol than to London in the 1830s, its main long-distance venture was the transhipment of North-East coal for smaller southern ports.[12]

While London dominated the South-East, and had clear advantages in breaking bulk from the Indies or Mediterranean, there was a line beyond which other ports asserted a measure of independence and operated their own long-distance and regional distribution trades. Such places were already by 1700 the 'major' ports, interspersed with the smaller places that were linked to them, that would soon carry most of the outports' foreign trade. There were fewer than a dozen of them, their growth and relative standing apparent in Table 21.1.

Bristol on the Severn was the commercial capital of the South-West, unique, according to Defoe, in its 'more entire independency [*sic*] upon London'.[13] To North American fish and oil had been added investment in West Indian sugar, and a deep involvement in the slave trade, an exercise in enterprise and initiative beyond the scope of the old Merchant Venturers.[14] A wide-ranging hinterland of major and minor rivers covered Gloucestershire, Warwickshire, Worcestershire, Hereford and Monmouth, much of this reached by barge from the great transhipment port of Gloucester. It held good markets and was a storehouse of cloth, wool, grain, cider and cheese, while the rising industries of Shropshire were the earnest of industrial intent. Bristol was undoubtedly the second port by trade value and wealth in the early decades of the eighteenth century, but the South-West's initiatives did not lead the Industrial Revolution for long and its relative position declined during the second half of the century. The ending of the slave trade in 1807 was a serious blow, both directly to slave shippers, and indirectly through its negative effects on West Indian sugar producers.

Liverpool was the leading long-term beneficiary of the rise in transatlantic trade. Its hinterland in Lancashire and Cheshire, improved considerably from the 1720s by turnpikes to St Helen's, Warrington and Northwich, and most notably by the St Helens and Bridgewater Canals, held salt and coal; a range of industries answered settlers' demands; and it also pursued the slave trade.[15] Better still, in the long run, was the importation of American cotton and exportation of cottons for settlers and slaves. Moreover, while Bristol dithered, Liverpool built docks and became a cheaper port to use, the product of superior enterprise and more sensible initiatives, or simply a more expansive hinterland. Without doubt the cotton industry offered a huge symbiotic stimulus, but it is important to emphasise the complexity of trade serving all aspects of a rapidly growing industrial region's needs for housing, factories, mines, foodstuffs and luxuries, all of which paid their percentage to 'Liverpool gentlemen', to the chagrin of

[12] E. A. G. Clark, *The Ports of the Exe Estuary, 1660–1860* (Exeter, 1960), p. 93.

[13] Defoe, *Tour*, I, p. 36.

[14] D. H. Sacks, *The Widening Gate* (Berkeley, Calif., 1991), pp. 262–7.

[15] S. Marriner, *The Economic and Social Development of Merseyside* (Liverpool, 1982), pp. 15–16; F. E. Hyde, *Liverpool and the Mersey* (Newton Abbot, 1971), chs. 2–3.

Table 21.1 *Tonnage of shipping entering and clearing the major ports in foreign trade, sample years 1716–1772 and 1790–1841 (nearest 000 tons)*

	Inwards						Outwards					
	1716	1730	1751	1772	1791	1841	1716	1730	1751	1772	1791	1841
Bristol	24	29	30	39	79	75	24	25	27	36	71	70
Hull	11	12	24	44	115	342	9	8	16	18	53	256
Liverpool	17	18	32	77	268	995	19	19	34	93	275	1,029
London	—	—	174	247	547	1,316	—	—	174	247	397	1,064
Newcastle	8	14	22	22	35	299	40	46	58	74	100	594
Whitehaven	10	15	11	33	40	23	32	45	113	193	212	28

These figures are based on owners' and customs' estimates. Those for 1716–72 and 1791–1841 are not strictly comparable, but changes in order of magnitude are borne out by the growth in the number of ships and volume of goods. London figures are not available for 1716–30.

Sources: 1716–72, BL, Add. MS 11256; 1791, PRO, Customs 17/13; 1841, PP 1842 (259) XXXIX, p. 626.

'Manchester men'. Such ironic descriptions reflect a distaste for the middleman, but also the wealth of the mercantile class. Nothing escaped its ledgers.

However, for sheer dash and daring those who gained fastest – but not most – from the American miracle were the upstarts of Glasgow. They were in the 'English' colonies from the 1660s, with agents in Whitehaven, Liverpool, Bristol and London. The Union of 1707 encouraged a drive to capture the tobacco trade through credits to Virginia and contract sales to Europe. By 1740 the city dominated the trade, and its industrial structure was responding swiftly to American demand.[16] Linen production was overtaken by a massive cotton industry, by machinery, metal goods, chemicals and coal. Glasgow was the only major port that became a major industrial city – a sort of Liverpool and Manchester combined (and early nineteenth-century people spoke in these terms).

European trade was a natural corollary to colonial trade. In the 1740s and 1790s two-thirds of Glasgow vessels traded with Europe (including Ireland, source of food and consumer of coal),[17] and both Whitehaven and Liverpool had extensive European interests. But the eastern ports predominated here. Aberdeen, with a regional network offering agricultural and fishery products and linen, and taking wood and flax, was nevertheless by English standards a small port. Nor did Dundee rise to prominence until the end of the eighteenth century, and then largely on the strength of its own industrial growth, involving heavy imports of flax and hemp for linen, sacking and 'slave cloth' shipped to the colonies.[18] In fact, for most of our period the only serious general ports on the Scottish east coast were Bo'ness, an eastern gateway for Glasgow with a greater tonnage inwards than English second-rank ports, and Leith, the port of Edinburgh.

Leith had in a minor way the advantages of London. The capital, though lacking a parliament, hosted the aristocracy of land and law. A great place for the wine and grocery trades, and of course for the wood trade, it also had an interest in things such as printed books and type, carriages, mirrors and whalebone, reflecting both literary enlightenment and good living. It linked central Scotland to the culture and manufactures of Europe, while its coastal network stretched southwards to the border, and northwards to Wick. In the early nineteenth century it also handled considerable trade on behalf of Glasgow merchants who since the 1770s had easier transport through the Forth and Clyde ship canal.

16 Jackson, 'Glasgow in transition', T. M. Devine, 'The golden age of tobacco', and R. H. Campbell, 'The making of the industrial city', in Devine and Jackson, eds., *Glasgow*, *passim*.

17 Jackson, 'Glasgow in transition', p. 75, and Jackson, 'New horizons in trade', in Devine and Jackson, eds., *Glasgow*, p. 217.

18 For Dundee, see G. Jackson, *The Trade and Shipping of Dundee, 1780–1850* (Dundee, 1991), *passim*. Jute, for which Dundee is famous, was not imported directly until the 1860s, though it was imported coastwise from Liverpool and London from the 1830s.

Leaving aside, for the moment, the Tyne, Wear and Tees, the only major eastern outport was Hull, least of the great English ports with London, Liverpool and Bristol far ahead in exports, though its import tonnage passed Bristol's in the third quarter of the century, when it was growing fast as supplier, *par excellence*, of European materials – malleable iron, wood, vegetable fibres, alkali, dyestuffs, oils and other things. Its position was based firmly on superior inland transport connections, with early improvements to the Don, to Sheffield; the Aire and Calder, to Wakefield, Leeds and Halifax; and the Trent, to Gainsborough (a great transhipment centre), Stockwith (for the Chesterfield–Stockwith canal), Nottingham and Burton, and, by canal extension, to Derbyshire (Arkwright built his mills with timber from Hull), Leicestershire and the Potteries.[19] No other port enjoyed so wide an effective hinterland before the trunk canals linked Liverpool, Hull, Bristol and London in the early nineteenth century.

After 1750 an increasing amount of activity involved minerals, chiefly coal. First Sunderland and then Newcastle rose to prominence through shipping it to Europe, and including coastal trade were the busiest ports in Britain. They were dirty, coal-dusty places, made worse by their prodigal use of coal for domestic hearths and manufacturing salt, glass and bottles. Coal ports were also attractive to landowning speculators. On the west coast Whitehaven, developed by the Lowthers, shipped coal to the colonies and Ireland in return for tobacco and foodstuffs, without ever becoming a general port or even a large town; by the end of the century the marquis of Bute was developing Cardiff. In 1791 the leading coal ports[20] accounted for 32 per cent of tonnage leaving Britain, compared with 52 per cent from the major general commercial ports.[21] Such places grew rich on their agency and shipment skills, attracting a large workforce and a good number of forceful entrepreneurs, not least in the integrated profession of shipowning. But it should be noted that some major commercial ports also developed coal exports: one of Liverpool's comparative advantages was Lancashire coal, and Lanarkshire coal was the bulkiest commodity shipped from Glasgow by the 1840s.[22] Hull's trade was comparatively small until the late nineteenth century precisely because its hinterland was such that it neither imported nor exported coal.

The large coal ports remained dominant but, since coal, copper, slate or china clay did not require sophisticated mercantile facilities, mine owners often preferred the shortest route to a suitable shipment place which might be little more than a pier and a drop. The Scottish coalfields relied on many small ports. The

[19] Hull's hinterland is discussed in detail in G. Jackson, *Hull in the Eighteenth Century* (Oxford, 1972), ch. 2.

[20] Newcastle, Stockton, Sunderland, Swansea and Whitehaven; Alloa, Ayr, Irvine and Kirkcaldy.

[21] Bristol, Hull, Liverpool and London; Glasgow and Leith.

[22] G. Jackson and C. W. Munn, 'Trade, commerce and finance', in W. H. Fraser and I. Maver, eds., *Glasgow*, vol. II: *1830–1912* (Manchester, 1996), pp. 62–3.

Ayrshire field shipped through the Lower Clyde 'ports' of Ayr, Irvine, Saltcoats, Troon and Ardrossan, chiefly to Ireland, though Ayr in particular used its larger vessels in transatlantic trade and sailed out of Glasgow in the tobacco trade.[23] Clackmannan and Fife coal went through – among others – Alloa, Airth, Pittenweem, Methil, Leven, Dysart and Kirkcaldy, of which only the first and last were legal ports.[24] Some Northumberland and Durham collieries favoured Blyth, Cullercoats and Seaton, and the first steam railway was, of course, built to take Darlington coal to the new 'Port Darlington' on the Tees, a set of coal drops that never made the grade and were replaced eventually by Middlesbrough. Cumberland coal-owners created Harrington, Maryport and Workington in rivalry to Whitehaven. In Cornwall, where inland communications were so difficult, owners of resources usually created private 'ports' consisting of simple stone piers, with the occasional spectacular cove port: Hayle, for example, built for copper in the 1780s and dwelling in the 'gloom of its poisonous atmosphere'; and Charlestown with its all-pervading china 'clay' in the 1790s.[25] Charlestown in Scotland shipped only lime; Easdale shipped only slates. These smaller mineral 'ports' were rarely wealthy towns on that account; and some were scarcely villages.

Beneath the great commercial ports and the busier coal shippers there was a wide range of places. First, were those such as Bideford, Boston, Grimsby, Harwich, Maldon, Padstow, Dumfries and Inverness, with minimal or no foreign trade in our period, whatever their past might have been.[26] As towns they varied, depending on their catchment areas. Grimsby Haven was reopened *c.* 1800 by Lincolnshire landowners and the county was criss-crossed by turnpikes carrying agricultural produce there and to Boston, the second largest town and principal port in Lincolnshire during our period. But, as happened elsewhere, the roads also went to the Trent and Barton-on-Humber, which siphoned off trade to Hull, and though Boston was one of the larger coastal ports only two or three foreign shipments a year left its silted haven, and its main import was occasional cargoes of wood.[27]

Secondly, there were those with larger amounts of foreign trade, again chiefly wood imports offered by Norwegian ships passing down the coast. In 1791 there were thirty-one places, such as Aldeburgh, Blakeney, Deal, Gweek, Lyme, Woodbridge, Sandwich, Dunbar, Fort William and Wigtown, that received less

[23] E. J. Graham, *The Shipping Trade of Ayrshire, 1689–1791* (Ayr, 1991), *passim*.

[24] B. F. Duckham, *A History of the Scottish Coal Industry*, vol. I: *1700–1815* (Newton Abbot, 1970), pp. 222–34; B. Lenman, *From Esk to Tweed: Harbours, Ships and Men of the East Coast of Scotland* (Edinburgh, 1975), pp. 30–9.

[25] R. Ayton, *A Voyage round Great Britain* (London, 1814), vol. I, p. 15; G. Jackson, *The History and Archaeology of Ports* (Tadworth, 1983), pp. 36–8.

[26] For the early history of the minor ports and creeks see above, pp. 387 *et seq.*, 411 *et seq.* They are listed, with comparative tonnages for 1791 and 1841, in G. Jackson, 'The ports', in M. Freeman and D. H. Aldcroft, eds, *Transport in Victorian Britain* (Manchester, 1988), pp. 246–9.

[27] N. R. Wright, *Lincolnshire Towns and Industry, 1700–1914* (Lincoln, 1982), pp. 20–1.

than 1,000 tons of shipping per annum – perhaps ten handy-sized European traders (equivalent to five West Indiamen or three whalers) and do not show the characteristics associated with thriving ports, though they reflected their maritime core. Thirdly, there were more impressive places such as Berwick, Chester, Lancaster, Lynn, Poole, Rochester, Whitby and Yarmouth, Aberdeen, Ayr and Dundee, which enjoyed a wider internal and international connection which imported wood, flax and hemp, and Irish foodstuffs where appropriate, and exported agricultural products, fish and sometime manufactures. They might also be engaged occasionally in more exciting ventures to America or the Mediterranean. Kirkcudbright, for instance, supported its agricultural hinterland and experimented internationally by capitalising on the connections, in Liverpool and abroad, of members of its leading shipping company.[28] Many ports had small ventures which for them were exciting and big. Not least were occasional forays into whaling, a sea-based industry which did not require a hinterland because the products could be sent coastwise. Grimsby, hardly a town, let alone a port, had two whalers for a time around 1800; Montrose made a great thing of whaling for a quarter of a century.[29]

In most – perhaps all – ports coastal trade exceeded foreign, and coal was its dominant feature, accounting for some 40 per cent of all tonnage clearing coastwise *c.* 1780–1830.[30] Though London was by far the principal market, ports without 'local' supplies imported it for their own or inland use, even if it meant beaching the collier and lumping its cargo over cobbles, dunes and fields. 'The quay', it was said of Portreath (the Cornish mineral port), 'is thronged with men and mules, in a state of equal and incessant action, clearing the [Welsh] colliers.'[31] Most small ports maintained facilities for its sake, but their coal 'merchants' were hardly great men.

For the most active middling ports, especially those in East Anglia and the south, regional specialisation meant foodstuffs. Lynn and Yarmouth were both busy exporting to London grain brought by their own navigable rivers, and Yarmouth also supplied herring.[32] Hull's navigations produced an apparently endless supply of grain, dairy produce and, after mid-century, potatoes, but from being the chief exporter of grain in 1781–6 Hull became the second largest

[28] C. Hill, 'Kirkcudbright Shipping Company, 1811–1817', *International Journal of Maritime History*, 9 (1997), 69–91. I am grateful to Mrs Hill for allowing me to use her work.

[29] For small-port whaling, see, for example, R. C. Michie, 'North-east Scotland and the northern whale fishing, 1752–1893', *Northern Scotland*, 3 (1977–8), 61–85; W. R. H. Duncan, 'Aberdeen and the early development of the whaling industry, 1750–1800', *Northern Scotland*, 3 (1977–8), 47–59; G. Jackson, 'The battle with the Arctic; Montrose whaling, 1785–1839', in G. Jackson and S. G. E. Lythe, eds., *The Port of Montrose* (Tayport, 1993), pp. 200–24; C. Dixon, 'Exeter Whale Fishing Company, 1754–1787', *Mariner's Mirror*. 62 (1976), 225–31; and A. G. E. Jones, 'The whaling trade of Ipswich, 1786–1793', *Mariner's Mirror*, 40 (1954), 197–203.

[30] J. Armstrong and P. S. Bagwell, 'Coastal shipping', in D. Aldcroft and M. Freeman, eds., *Transport in the Industrial Revolution* (Manchester, 1983), pp. 152–5.

[31] Ayton, *Voyage*, I, p. 18.

[32] Armstrong and Bagwell, 'Coastal shipping', pp. 156–9.

importer in 1819–27.[33] Stockton sent Yorkshire butter. Dundee, drawing on the fertile Carse of Gowrie, provided a similar service for Leith, but also sent potatoes, beef and salmon on the coastal liner smacks to London by the 1830s.[34] Montrose, also from *c.* 1760, sent grain, lobster and salmon by fast smacks to London and the northern industrial markets.[35] For most ports the coastal trade also brought necessities and luxuries from the major ports.

A number of ports cannot be categorised easily by size because they performed different functions from those outlined above. Packet ports such as Dartmouth, Falmouth and Port Patrick handled postal and passenger traffic to Ireland and the Channel Islands, but while they had facilities associated with the packet boats and some measure of private freight traffic, their chief purpose was rapid transit involving a low ratio of vessels owned to vessels active, and little in the way of warehousing and other port infrastructure.[36] However, for a time Port Patrick (the Irish link) had the largest tonnage of traffic in Scotland sheltering in its minute harbour, and Dover, most important of all, had a very substantial rapid transit business supporting a large shipping sector, though again it was a pier port without significant warehousing. It follows that the size and wealth of such places was not proportional to the tonnage of their traffic.

Harbours of refuge were also unusual ports. Since long stretches of the east and south coasts were dangerous in storms and lacked good harbours, acts of parliament imposed coal duties to allow Bridlington (1697), Whitby (1701) and Scarborough (1732) to improve their harbours for sheltering colliers. More impressively, a huge harbour at Ramsgate, costing the state almost £2 million, sheltered around 13,000 vessels per annum between 1820 and 1850, chiefly London traders waiting in the Downs to enter the Thames.[37] Some East Anglian estuaries were also used for laying up colliers; at Ipswich, Defoe recorded, 'they lie as safe as in a wet dock'.[38] Of course harbours of refuge also engaged to some extent in ship repair, victualling, coastal trade and fishing. The Yorkshire ports, in particular, owned and overwintered portions of the collier fleet, and had more of the 'port' about them with large numbers of shipbuilders, shipowners, seamen and their families.

(ii) THE DEVELOPMENT OF PORT FACILITIES

Port communities grew by balancing their inland and overseas connections, developing shipping technology and deployment, and investing their capital or

[33] Jackson, *Hull*, pp. 82–9 and appendices 13–16; Armstrong and Bagwell, 'Coastal shipping', pp. 156–8. [34] Jackson, *Dundee*, ch. 4 and appendices 4.1–4.2.

[35] D. G. Adams, 'Trade in the eighteenth and nineteenth centuries', in Jackson and Lythe, eds., *Port of Montrose*, pp. 133–6.

[36] See, for instance, P. S. Bagwell, 'The Post Office steam packets, 1821–36, and the development of shipping on the Irish Sea', *Maritime History*, 1 (1971), 4–28.

[37] Jackson, *Ports*, pp. 39–42. [38] Defoe, *Tour*, 1, p. 41.

organising their credit to best advantage. However, more and larger vessels soon created bottlenecks in havens originally chosen for their safety, not their size. Greenville Collins condemned most of the southern harbours: 'I might have said more of these Bar-harbours, but I leave it to Coasters, and do not recommend it to strangers, they being harbours of little trade or resort.'[39] Some were lost beyond recall; even the best fell short of new demands. The period 1695–1725 witnessed the first attempts by many ports (the corporations of which owned and were responsible for port facilities) to organise large, expensive engineering works often requiring local taxation and agreement within the elite amounting to community responsibility for local transport 'policy'.[40] In large ports the problem was initially the seasonal laying-up of ships. London, despite an excellent river and extensive quays (see Plate 13), was hit first and the Bedford estate built the Howland Great Wet Dock, *c.* 1700, for empty ships, away from the legal quay by the Tower of London.[41] Encouraged by this initiative, Exeter, Bristol, Chester, Grimsby, Colchester and Yarmouth worked on their havens, but apart from Exeter they largely wasted their time and money; several grand schemes on the south coast (some by private landowners) were never successfully completed. At Portreath 'the entrance to the harbour is singularly frightful, and has an air of preposterousness and grotesque inexpediency about it, very striking to those who have always considered a harbour as obviously presenting a place of safety and security for ships'.[42] A more important category of work improved the coal harbours of the English and Scottish coal ports and the supporting collier ports.

By comparison with some of the smaller places mentioned above, merchants with determination and money moved mountains of mud and changed the physical nature of the larger ports. The most successful was Liverpool, whose tiny harbour failed to answer demand. 'Here', wrote Defoe, 'was no mole or haven to bring in their ships and lay them up . . . for the winter; nor any key for the delivering their goods, as at Bristol, Bideford, Newcastle, Hull and other sea ports.'[43] Making use of London expertise, Thomas Steers converted the 'pool' into the first commercial dock in Britain, opened in 1715, and another five were built between 1753 and 1796. By the 1820s, when Liverpool was contemplating a massive dock-building programme, Glasgow was aggrieved that its rival's superior facilities offered comparative advantages in American trade.[44]

Other major ports experienced severe congestion from the mid-eighteenth

[39] G. Collins, *Great Britain's Coasting Pilot* (London, 1753 edn), p. 1.

[40] D. Swann, 'The pace and progress of port investment in England 1660–1830', *Yorkshire Bulletin of Economic and Social Research*, 12 (1960), 32–6.

[41] Howland dock sheltered the South Sea Company's whaling fleet, 1725–33, hence its later name of Greenland Dock; G. Jackson, *The British Whaling Trade* (London, 1978), pp. 45–7.

[42] Ayton, *Voyage*, I, p. 18; Jackson, *Ports*, pp. 33–4.

[43] Defoe, *Tour*, II, p. 258; Jackson, *Ports*, pp. 46–8.

[44] Report of the lord provost to HM government on state of trade and employment, 16 Feb. 1823, printed in J. Cleland, *Statistical Tables Relative to the City of Glasgow* (Glasgow, 1823), p. 55.

century. The first, Hull, might serve as a cautionary tale of the hazards involved. Proposals to supplement the inadequate haven with a laying-up dock were opposed by the Exchequer, which demanded a commercial dock with a Legal Quay.[45] Since a commercial dock would be more expensive the government offered a subsidy and all the land on which the first three docks were subsequently built. The elite promptly formed a joint stock company with monopoly rights to all dues and no obligations to build further docks. Moreover, the 'north walls' site was reached via a crowded haven and right-angle turn, and wags reckoned it took longer than the trip from St Petersburg (a common assertion in ports more concerned with price than topography). So blatant was the greed that no other major port got itself into such a mess.

Learning from Liverpool and Hull, other growing ports relieved their overcrowding with varying success. Bristol, where the size of the harbour was less problematic than remaining afloat, impounded the quay area to make a seventy-acre 'Floating Harbour' *c.* 1803, though the port dues required to finance it were twice those of London and Liverpool, and six times those of neighbouring Gloucester, competing for traffic on the Severn.[46] In Scotland docks were built in Greenock at the turn of the century to cater for the larger transatlantic vessels; Dundee built one for the linen trade; and Edinburgh spent so much on two in Leith that its bankruptcy was accelerated, and the state was forced to subsidise them.[47]

When London needed docks, again around 1800, there was no corporation capable of initiating activity because the port had long outgrown the ancient 'City', the maritime interest had lost its homogeneity and the huge capital costs were entangled in arguments over who should benefit from, and pay for, docks. *Ad hoc* private enterprise (following Hull) achieved a great deal in a short time, but, though initially effective, it was in the long run less systematic and cohesive than subsequent port building on the continent, where major ports were owned by their cities and generally subsidised by the state. The West India interest acted first, building an exclusive dock with fortress walls and vast secure warehouses to control pilfering from sugar cargoes, paid for by monopoly dues on West Indiamen. North American and European interests followed with London dock for tobacco, wine and brandy; the East India Company built a dock for its own goods; and the northern European raw material traders followed with the Baltic, Commercial and East Country Dock Companies.[48] These docks were monumental structures for their age, and functioned well for almost half a century before slipping out of date. Ironically, the last of the 'old' docks, St Katharine's, was opened in 1828 as a *competitive* warehouse dock with almost no quay space

[45] All space for trade, apart from a few public staiths, was privately owned. Jackson, *Hull*, pp. 243–58.

[46] Jackson, *Ports*, pp. 52–4. [47] Lenman, *From Esk to Tweed*, pp. 63–72.

[48] These amalgamated as the Surrey Commercial Dock Co. in 1864. A useful modern account is J. Pudney, *London's Docks* (London, 1975), chs. 3–8.

and inadequate access when steam ships and trains were already running, and one of its least desirable consequences was that it nudged the capital's dock system towards bankruptcy. St Katharine's Dock marked the virtual end of the first phase of harbour and dock building in Britain. By then London alone had spent over £7 million on docks, and altogether some 400 acres of dock space had been provided in England.[49]

Although most ports were in ancient locations offering various comparative advantages, advancing pier and lock engineering enabled new facilities to be constructed for mineral traffic or (as disgruntled merchants mistakenly hoped) to offer rival facilities undercutting established ports. The former commonly thrived; the latter did not. Grimsby, built to secure political advantages for competing landowners, is the best example of a failed speculation. Grimsby Haven Company built a large dock for which John Rennie constructed what was probably the first sea lock 'floated' on bottomless mud. But Grimsby's ambition exceeded its trade, and though some merchants came from Hull, they did not stay. The problem was that there was no decent inland transport from Grimsby. By 1825 the enterprise was dead.[50]

Clearly a port could only attract another's trade with comparative advantages outweighing existing facilities, connections, expertise and loyalty of shipowners. Since they must have at least equal access to inland transport, those most successful were built where a canal met an estuary.[51] The Aire and Calder Canal Company, for instance, built Goole as a transhipment port, opened in 1828 and almost immediately a threat to Hull's coastal trade and for a time to that part of its foreign trade involving west Yorkshire.[52] In a variant of this theme, the Gloucester and Berkeley Canal Company revitalised the river port of Gloucester by cutting a ship canal to the lower reaches of the Severn, a far more rewarding venture than Norwich and Lowestoft Navigation Company's new creation at Lowestoft, which went bankrupt in 1835 and was only rescued by railway development.[53] Other canal towns developed, most notably Runcorn where the Bridgewater canal met the Mersey (though it remained part of the port of Liverpool).[54] At the other end of the scale both Lancaster and Carlisle – though the chief distribution centres for Cumbria – failed to make much out of over-optimistic canal ports.[55] The breakthrough in the creation of 'new' general ports

[49] Swann, 'Pace and Progress', 38.

[50] See G. Jackson, *Grimsby and the Haven Company, 1796–1846* (Grimsby, 1971), *passim*; G. Jackson, 'The Claytons of Grimsby: local trade and politics in the eighteenth and early nineteenth centuries', *Lincolnshire History and Archaeology*, 9 (1974), 43–51.

[51] Jackson, *Ports*, pp. 62–4; J. D. Porteous, *Canal Ports* (London, 1977), *passim*.

[52] B. F. Duckham, *The Yorkshire Ouse: The History of a Navigation* (Newton Abbot, 1967), chs. 5, 7.

[53] W. J. Wren, *The Ports of the Eastern Counties* (Lavenham, 1976), *passim*.

[54] H. F. Starkey, *Schooner Port: Two Centuries of Upper Mersey Sail* (Ormskirk, 1983), chs. 2–3.

[55] Jackson, *Ports*, pp. 87–8; J. D. Marshall, 'The rise and transformation of the Cumbrian market town, 1660–1900', *NHist.*, 19 (1983), 144–53.

came with the railways, and even then it was easier to make a mineral than a commercial port, as West Hartlepool's struggles show.

Steamers affected ports long before the railways. Starting on the Clyde in 1812, they soon dominated estuaries and by 1830 brought their time-tabled liner operation to the cream of the coastal routes. Although expensive to build and run, their rapid turn-around and passage times enabled trade to grow faster than shipping. Three entered Glasgow's steamship harbour every half-hour in the 1830s, and passenger boats turned round in an hour and cargo boats in a day. Lines down to Liverpool and Bristol added a new dimension to the integration of foreign trade, and the same thing was true on the east coast, where the Aberdeen and London, the Dundee, Perth and London, the Dundee and Hull, the Leith and London and several Hull shipping companies beat a regular passage with magnificent liners for which the Thames had only three suitable steamship wharves as late as 1830. By the 1840s steamers were in the western European trades and were beginning to cross the Atlantic.[56]

The impact of all this on ports was electrifying. The leading ports were transformed. They were also 'industrialised', as was their workforce. Shipowners objected to delay, while investment costs also rose because lines required reserve vessels. The clutter in ports – especially sailing coasters – became intolerable. Steam owners in Aberdeen *opposed* a dock in the 1830s because of time wasted passing the lock and awaiting tides, while in Hull, Liverpool and London steamers were soon too big to enter docks. Once they carried substantial cargoes their owners clamoured for access. Dedicated steamship facilities followed Clarence Dock in Liverpool (1830), as all major and some medium ports invested to keep abreast of the times. Railways, on the other hand, were to a large extent financed in the hinterland.

The costs of transport were rising in terms of local investment in docks and shipping during the Napoleonic wars, and this helped to change the economic and social structure of ports during the period. At the highest level the shipowner began to displace the merchant. A small coaster might be had for £50, and vessels owned by 'mariners' were not unknown.[57] While sailing coasters (except liners and superior colliers) remained small, foreign-going vessels grew rapidly at the end of the century. A large ship was 300 tons in 1780, only East Indiamen approaching 1,000. The opening of the Canadian Maritime Provinces by British wood merchants and shipbuilders during the Napoleonic war raised large vessels over 1,000 tons, and by 1830 they were over 3,000. With increases in both size and numbers, the ownership of capital began to move from merchants to specialist shipowners, and shipbrokers and agents emerged to provide the necessary information structure. The colliers already had a tradition of own-

[56] For a brief modern discussion of the relationship between coastal steam and foreign-going steam, see G. Jackson, 'The shipping industry', in Freeman and Aldcroft, eds., *Transport in Victorian Britain*, pp. 262–8. [57] Jackson, *Dundee*, pp. 58–62.

Table 21.2 *Number and tonnage of vessels registered at major shipowning ports 1791 and 1841*

	1791		1841	
	No.	Tons	No.	Tons
Bristol	301	43,469	197	43,117
Dartmouth	298	17,055	164	24,171
Exeter	152	13,288	131	15,637
Hull	443	54,677	323	67,795
Liverpool	528	83,696	1,097	307,852
Lynn	150	17,350	129	17,156
Newcastle	534	115,426	1,143	259,571
Poole	223	20,834	81	12,155
Scarborough	179	25,629	157	31,010
Sunderland	338	55,939	803	174,252
Whitby	250	49,327	291	47,837
Whitehaven	461	54,585	341	55,501
London	1,842	378,514	2,405	598,554
Aberdeen	184	13,467	377	54,457
Alloa	99	3,855	127	18,797
Dundee	116	8,509	347	52,482
'Glasgow'[a]	455	45,724	946	195,974
Leith	177	18,349	256	26,149

[a] Glasgow includes Greenock and Port Glasgow.
Source: 1791, PRO, Customs 17/13; 1841, PP 1842 (409), XXXIX, p. 633.

ership in ports with almost no trade: Scarborough and Whitby, for instance, had comparatively huge fleets (see Table 21.2), and the best-known sailing-collier owners – Henley and Company – also ventured their vessels abroad as opportunity arose.[58] Whalers, the most expensive vessels after East Indiamen, were also vessels outside general trading which had specialist owners. In particular the timber/shipbuilding firms were beginning to retain and operate more of their own large vessels. Kidstones and Pollok & Gilmour crop up with monotonous regularity in the Clyde shipping registers; Thomas Wilson, a Hull iron merchant, took his first steps to being one of Britain's largest shipowners in 1837.[59] New opportunities in shipping attracted men to the expanding ports: Swires,

[58] S. P. Ville, *English Shipowning during the Industrial Revolution: Michael Henley & Sons, London Shipowners, 1770–1830* (Manchester, 1987), pp. 52–62.

[59] J. Rankine, *A History of our Firm, being Some Account of the Firm of Pollok, Gilmour & Co., and its Offshoots and Connections, 1804–1920* (privately printed, 1921), *passim*; Hull Shipping Registers and Wilson papers, Hull University Archives, *passim*.

Brocklebanks, Holts and others to Liverpool; Samuel Cunard from shipbroking in Halifax, Nova Scotia, to Glasgow and Liverpool.[60] The identification of specialist shipowners increased substantially with steamers because of the need to assemble larger funds: steam lines were big business demanding modern business organisation.[61] Shipowners who were no longer principally merchants gained in influence in larger ports and specialist shipowning centres, and they tended to lead in port improvements.

(iii) PORT-BASED INDUSTRIES

Merchants and shipowners were at the heart of a port's business, but their interests ranged wider, instigating port-related industries and sustaining the shipbuilding sector. Shipbuilding was almost universal, though yards were often only a shelving beach and highly 'mobile', while their products were more often boats than ships. For many ports ship repairing was more valuable than building. Coasters were the staple output of the larger builders, who could not compete with ocean-going vessels from America before the Revolution and Canada after it. British oak was more or less finished by 1750, and all masts and spars were imported, usually from Riga, which encouraged a concentration of building along the east coast, especially around the coal ports (with Sunderland leading by 1800).[62] Building was also traditionally strong on the Thames, where Wells' Brunswick Dock was famous for fitting out and sheltering the East India fleet. It was not until the early nineteenth century that steam power drew shipbuilding to industrialising ports where engine building was initially more important than shipbuilding.[63] Glasgow was from the start a leading steamship builder, with the brilliant, innovative Napiers, but London was not far behind. The ancillary sailcloth manufacture also emerged in several ports towards the end of the century, and native roperies replaced Russian cordage around mid-century; two – Hall's Barton Ropery (Hull) and Gourock Rope Works (Greenock) – reached world class.

A more specialised branch of shipbuilding and repairing occurred in the royal dockyards at Chatham, founded in 1550 and reflecting Tudor interest in maritime adventures (it was there that Francis Drake grew up), and later at

[60] Hyde, *Liverpool and the Mersey*, pp. 46–7; P. L. Cottrell, 'The steamship on the Mersey, 1815–80: investment and ownership', in P. L. Cottrell and D. H. Aldcroft, eds., *Shipping, Trade and Commerce* (Leicester, 1981), pp. 144–9.

[61] See, for instance, G. Jackson, 'Operational problems of the transfer to steam: Dundee, Perth & London Shipping Company, 1820–45', in T. C. Smout, ed., *Scotland and the Sea* (Edinburgh, 1992), pp. 154–81.

[62] S. P. Ville, 'Rise to pre-eminence: the development and growth of the Sunderland shipbuilding industry, 1800–50', *International Journal of Maritime History*, 1 (1989), 65–86.

[63] S. R. Palmer, 'Shipbuilding in Southeast England, 1800–1913', *Research in Maritime History*, 4 (1993), 45–74.

Portsmouth and Plymouth. They grew in importance from the Dutch wars, thriving on naval conflicts and imperial ventures, and though they played little direct part in *general* trade or economic development, heavy government expenditure encouraged very large populations and brought considerable local and regional importance, not least in terms of male employment. Their peculiar consumption, rather than normal trading patterns, is revealed in huge foreign and coastwise importation of 'naval stores' compared with their minimal export trade; their product, of course, was the royal navy. It is a pity, perhaps, that naval work was so narrowly confined, thus denying to other places the experience of building and servicing large vessels, but in practice good private builders in the outports did get a share of naval building in wartime.[64]

Needless to say, the emphasis on construction rather than deployment of ships gave the dockyard towns a somewhat different atmosphere and social structure from commercial ports. Though many crafts contributed to naval shipbuilding, the whole productive effort was more concentrated towards one end than was the case in any other sort of industrial town before the specialised cotton towns of the late eighteenth century or, more closely, the metal shipbuilding centres of the mid-nineteenth. The labour was also 'industrialised' and disciplined, and since sailors were only drafted into the navy during wartime there was no proportionally large band of them within dockyard populations. The mutinies at Spithead (Portsmouth) and the Nore (Chatham) imply that the less sailors fraternised with landsmen – or each other – the better, for they might prefer the freer world of trade.

In the period from 1700 to 1840 most medium to large ports probably devoted less effort to shipbuilding than to processing imports. Sugar, from the start, was boiled up in the ports, which also made candles, tanned hides and ground snuff; add in spirits, tobacco, porter, blubber-boiling and bone-crushing (French, it was said, from the road to Moscow) and ports were places of wondrous smells! Imports of unsawn 'timber' from *c.* 1750 depended on saw mills and vast seasoning yards in ports, and continental oil seeds encouraged the seed-crushers, expanding into paint and putty long before Hull became the centre of the British paint industry after 1815.[65] Ports dealing in china clay, such as Hull, Liverpool and Glasgow, opened their own potteries, and Newcastle became a centre for the production of glass bottles. Indeed, Glasgow and Newcastle both excelled in the handling of heat, which stood them in good stead when they turned to engine and iron ship construction, but most ports had foundries for the metalwork of ships, docks, cranes and quays.

[64] For one example, see Jackson, *Hull*, pp. 179–81.

[65] Detailed examinations of port-based industries are in Jackson, *Hull*, ch. 8; Jackson, 'Glasgow in transition'; Campbell, 'The making of the industrial city; C. A. Whatley, 'From handcraft to factory: the growth and development of industry in Montrose, *c.* 1707–1837', in Jackson and Lythe, eds., *Port of Montrose*, pp. 256–76.

Foundries also made 'whaling irons' for companies of merchants and speculators responding to bounties and shortages during war in America (the 'normal' source). Between 1749 and 1762 some sixteen ports[66] equipped whalers, before peace ruined profit. Revived interest after 1783 took in others, though their involvement was brief as whaling gravitated to the consuming ports, London, Hull and Liverpool. By 1815 only Hull, London, Whitby and Scottish ports (including Peterhead and Montrose) were serious contenders, and in the 1830s only Hull, Newcastle and the Scottish ports remained. London, however, also had the Southern Whale Fishery established there by American loyalists in the 1780s, but this also declined rapidly after the Napoleonic war. William Wilberforce was probably right in describing whaling as 'rather . . . a species of gambling than any sort of regular trade'.[67] Nevertheless, it was, briefly, a valuable trade, with great investment, endeavour and bravery of owners and crews, and emotional involvement of local people. Few vessels were so fêted; few caused such heart-ache and grief.

Compared with whaling, fishing was widespread and cheap. There were no fishing ports in the modern sense before the railways eased inland distribution, but many ports, piers and coves from Wick to St Ives supported inshore boats for local consumption or – as at Brixham and Dover – for London. In Scotland, which specialised in curing herring for the European market, fishing was subsidised after the 1745 rebellion to employ and feed crofters. On a larger scale, Aberdeen and Montrose caught lobsters and salmon for Leith and London; the Clyde ports sent fish down the west coast. Herring also fed ports in the north; Glasgow's industrial success was attributed to cheap living off herring and oats.[68] And, then as now, visitors to the seaside could gorge themselves on fish just landed at Anstruther, Scarborough or Lyme.

Fishing places were not therefore noticeably big, and few reached the status of towns on that alone. Indeed, the fishers, with their womenfolk, followed the herring round the northern and southern coasts, with great gatherings in Wick and Yarmouth, and then went home. More significantly, the over-fishing of the southern coast for London's sake brought semi-permanent migrations of line-fishing families to exploit the North Sea, from Brixham to Lowestoft, Cromer and Scarborough, for example. They still served London, with its taste for cod and sole, but when fast routes to the new industrial towns were developed they congregated at the road or railheads and fishing towns were born, or fishing suburbs sprang up, most of all in Aberdeen, Hull and Grimsby. For a short time

[66] Glasgow, Campbeltown, Whitehaven, Liverpool, Bristol and Exeter, Aberdeen, Dundee, Kirkaldy, Bo'ness, Leith, Dunbar, Newcastle, Whitby, Hull and London – by far the leader; Jackson, *British Whaling Trade*, chs. 3, 4.

[67] Hansard, *Parliamentary History*, vol. XXV, col. 1379, 12 Apr. 1786.

[68] J. Gibson, *The History of Glasgow from the Earliest Accounts to the Present Time* (Glasgow, 1777), pp. 5–6, 112; M. Gray, *The Fishing Industries of Scotland, 1790–1914* (Oxford, 1978), *passim*.

this smack-based 'rural' peasant enterprise operated out of sophisticated modern urban centres, before it, too, became industrialised.

(iv) THE PORT ELITE: A COSMOPOLITAN SOCIETY

Port towns in many regards were special. The more active ones had corporations enjoying considerable wealth drawn from port dues, and their councils exercised strong control over urban structure (much of which they owned) because the safety of goods and ships demanded it. Fire engines and water supplies, for instance, came early to ports and a general political awareness was vital. Harbour works required acts of parliament to authorise capital formation, compulsory purchase and dues; trade and shipping were deeply affected by diplomatic bargains and acts of navigation; in matters such as slavery and American independence moral enthusiasm was tempered by economic necessity; seamen were regularly press-ganged. Understandably, ports took their parliamentary representation seriously and 'organised' elections to suit their perceived economic needs. Merchants went into parliament; William Wilberforce from Hull, Kirkman Finlay from Glasgow and Robert Gladstone from Liverpool were giants of their age, though only one of them – Robert Smith of Wilberforce and Smiths – became an English peer while still in trade. Behind and supporting the corporations were the other elements of port life: ancient guilds and merchants societies, Trinity Houses and late eighteenth-century chambers of commerce which pronounced on everything, but chiefly the West Indies, the East Indian monopoly, and free trade. Many of these organisations also engaged in 'good works'.

The society these people headed was complex. From major ports the 'county set' were kept at bay, though minor ones might be their fiefdom. Leading merchants were gentlemen, mixing with landed gentry in business, pleasure and marriage. 'West India Princes', 'East India Nabobs', 'Tobacco Lords', and 'Baltic Barons' did not, like the industrialist hero of *North and South,* need to learn gentility from broken-down southern clergymen; nor, at the lower end of the scale, did the Tennysons of Grimsby and Hull, whose best-known son 'Saw the heavens filled with commerce, argosies of magic sails, Pilots of the purple twilight, dropping down with costly bales.'[69] Costly bales produced a standard of living that many envied: 'with the splendour of the best gentlemen, . . . with the luxury and expence of a Count of the Empire', as Defoe put it.[70] Exeter in decline and Liverpool in growth both shared a 'county-town' life style at the top, with crumbs from the great men's table to keep the rest happy, though Exeter, like Whitehaven, sang the gentry's song in its 'Georgian High Noon'.[71]

Merchants traded in information, and that was gained by connections and

[69] Lord Tennyson, 'Locksley Hall'.

[70] D. Defoe, *A Plan of the English Commerce* (London, 1730), p. 100.

[71] R. Newton, *Eighteenth-Century Exeter* (Exeter, 1984), ch. 5.

passed through generations like the family silver, from the seventeenth century to the nineteenth. Successful merchants married well, but also intermarried, at home and abroad, to extend their networks, discount their bills and open their banks. In the early eighteenth century they were university-educated in England, Scotland, Holland or Germany, and their apprenticeship was often abroad. Many were nonconformists inspired by the international brotherhood of dissenting Protestantism centred on Holland, the source also of commercial and industrial expertise which they brought into Britain. Some of them came from abroad to an increasingly cosmopolitan society. Religious refugees in the early eighteenth century – French Huguenots and southern Jews – offered commercial, language or industrial skills; empire loyalists from America, in the 1780s, established Southern Whaling and became important London shipowners; Scandinavians and Germans began replacing British factors abroad with their own agencies in Britain around 1800. Greek exiles commenced their notable contribution to British maritime affairs, especially in London and Liverpool, around 1810.[72] Moreover, ports were gateways for ideas as well as goods and people. Early on it might be those of Boerhaave of Leiden. Later on they read Adam Smith, or debated with him if they lived in the hothouse of the Glasgow or Edinburgh 'Enlightenment'.[73] The trade in tin plate was not the only one in which exportation replaced importation around 1750.

As trade makers, mercantile youths and wayward uncles were sent off to explore the production and market potential of the Baltic. Around 1700 Adam Montgomery in Stockholm worked up Baltic trade for his family in Glasgow, Whitehaven and London (his father was an MP); the Narva banking house of Thorley and Ouchterloney sprang from a Hull-Montrose partnership, a useful reminder that 'minor' ports could still maintain respectable niche operations;[74] London men were everywhere. In a different way – because the labour had also to be supplied – British merchants explored America. Kirkman Finlay, one of the greatest merchant-manufacturers of the Industrial Revolution, was described in 1833 as 'General merchant in . . . London, also in the city of Glasgow' and until lately in Liverpool, and also in Charlestown, New York and New Orleans.[75] One cannot emphasise sufficiently the extent to which ports were not at the end of the line but in the middle of a network. No port was an island; the largest served foreign economies as well as their own.

By 1800 the grand merchants were withdrawing their presence if not their funds from ports, not least because of pressure on land for harbours and warehouses. Terraces of fine Georgian houses and classical tenements had risen on

[72] G. Harlaftis, *A History of Greek-Owned Shipping* (London, 1996), pp. 39–40.

[73] R. Sher, 'Commerce, religion and the Enlightenment in 18th century Glasgow', in Devine and Jackson, eds., *Glasgow*, pp. 312–59.

[74] Jackson, *Hull*, p. 124; and Jackson and Lythe, eds., *Port of Montrose*, p. 141.

[75] PP 1833 VI, Select Committee on Manufactures, Commerce and Shipping, p. 618.

the edge of port districts (Gladstone, in Liverpool, lived only ten minutes walk from the docks), and even minor ports had their dash of splendour as their wealthy built their modern houses, in Lynn, Boston or Poole. Few lived over the counting house by 1800, and though merchants and shipowners boasted of rigorous apprenticeship, their clerks were doing the routine work, and sometimes more. More seriously, the work of export merchants was increasingly done by shipping agents, and their role in shipping was also declining. The richer sort retired finally to country estates purchased over generations as safe backing for credit-worthiness. All the great – and many lesser – ports were ringed by Georgian mansions, in Scotland by pseudo-baronial castles. It follows that merchants withdrew gradually from direct political activity, not always without local battles with craftsmen and shopkeepers, until municipal reform in the 1830s changed the nature of city government. Whether it improved the government of ports is a matter for debate, but it was inevitable as many ports, and principally London, saw a rapid increase in their non-port activities and populations.

Not everyone was rich – or poor. Sea captains might be numbered among a growing middle class in all ports, especially after steam raised their wages (and engineers were paid nearly as much). The middling sort of people grew in number, designing ships, teaching languages and navigation, interpreting law, refining sugar; all of them, hopefully, upwardly mobile. They, too, were engaged in the business of cultural diffusion, importing dock and nautical engineering, industrial techniques and medicine from France and Holland in the early eighteenth century and exporting steam technology to Europe in general in the early nineteenth. But in truth, while port populations were growing the benefits were spread unevenly. Port communities as a whole were becoming *relatively* less wealthy after 1800, as merchants' profits were replaced by agents' commissions and fees. Although the new shipowners soon rivalled merchants in wealth, the trend was towards larger amounts of capital and influence in fewer hands, especially in costly steam lines. These changes were most obvious perhaps in Goole, built in the 1820s with no merchants or shipowners to grace the working-class terraces in what was promised to be 'the handsomest town in the North of England'.[76]

(v) SEAMEN AND DOCKERS

As trade increased, the number of sailors and dockers necessarily rose, and both were increasingly 'industrialised' in the early nineteenth century. But the experience of labour varied. Larger ports were all bustle, constantly seeking labour, with overlapping trades levelling out the worst of seasonal fluctuations. Coal ports, with mechanical loading machinery, made more efficient use of labour

[76] J. D. Porteous, *The Company Town of Goole: An Essay in Urban Genesis* (Hull, 1969), pp. 32–5.

than London, where coal was unloaded by hand or small crane. Coastal ports dealt with small vessels easily handled – often by the crew or customers – and foreign traders were insufficient to justify permanent labour. The Thames wharfingers employed their own lumpers, but the confusion of 'aquatic labourers', as Patrick Colquhoun called them, enabled 'depraved characters [to] prowl the wharfs, quays and warehouses', asking for work but looking for plunder, which he thought was as much as a million pounds a year.[77] In effect, semi-permanent, organised labour – whose 'liberal wages arising from labour' would put an end to 'profligacy and idleness' – came with the huge enclosed warehouse-docks in London, requiring a military-style discipline to organise complex day labour reaching a thousand at peak season and encourage it with a mixture of rewards and punishments.[78]

Port labour outside London was very little noticed before the steam age, but the problems of sailors were obvious. Small coasters might still be family-run, and even men in the larger colliers spent time ashore. Both foreign-going and coastal liner men were regularly on shore, their seagoing lives structured in company systems. But men in long-haul trades were seasonal strangers in their own land as shipowners moved in the 1770s and 1780s towards maximum deployment of vessels, and some men, like the owners, maximised their income by switching vessels and rarely visiting their 'home' port. In fact most men left the physically demanding and socially intrusive foreign trade before middle age, moving to the coastal trade with its opportunities to live more regularly at home; others manned the quays, or opened dock gates. However, port life was certainly distinct with men frequently away, and women as effective heads of household were probably more common than in other towns, their tight-knit communities and kinship groups bonding in mutual comfort. Mortality, accidents, men caught in Baltic or Arctic ice, all upset family incomes, while sailors' superannuation schemes – most ports had them – were not always adequate. Places such as Bristol, Hull and Glasgow had their own poor laws, with hospitals and workhouses providing a cushion against seasonal depression.[79] Wars and depressions brought many dependants on to the poor law, and corporations in ports, which knew all about cyclical inactivity and men at sea, were often generous in their provisions, as were the public in ports hit by maritime disasters. Let it be noted, however, that the worst disasters for port people – except for the privateering thugs and the slaving men – were the insecurity of life, limb and labour in the constant warfare of the long eighteenth century, including the monstrously

[77] P. Colquhoun, *A Treatise on the Police of the Metropolis* (London 1796), pp. 58–63.

[78] A. R. Henderson and S. R. Palmer, 'The early nineteenth century port of London: management and labour in three dock companies, 1800–1825', in S. P. Ville and D. M. Williams, eds., *Management, Finance and Industrial Relations in Maritime Industries* (Research in Maritime History, 6, 1994), pp. 31–50.

[79] S. Webb and B. Webb, *English Local Government* (London, 1922), vol. IV, pp. 110 *et seq.*; Jackson, *Hull*, pp. 320–6.

unfair operations of the press gang, which took thousands of sailors in wartime, to the degradation of their families. Compared with this, the industrialisation of port labour was probably a blessed relief.[80] The impact of war-induced poverty is evident in Hull, where poor rates rose dramatically from £2,080 in 1785 to £8,320 in 1798, and one can understand rioters in ports disrupting food shipments at the turn of the century and the growing reluctance of councils to involve themselves in poor relief.[81]

There are no adequate statistics for seamen before 1772, and from 1788 official sources give either seamen required – theoretically – to man all registered vessels, or all seamen active in a year, including repeated voyages. However, we may presume that by the 1770s some 50,000 men were engaged in English sea service, and about a tenth of these were fishermen. Another 9,000–10,000 served in Scottish vessels, of whom a quarter were fishermen.[82] By the 1790s the registered fleet required approximately 100,000 in Britain, and 140,000 by the end of the Napoleonic war, though war demands reduced the number active. In 1808, for instance, only 90,000 Britons sailed abroad, compared with 16,000 foreigners. Distribution of seamen was always lumpy. A third of English seamen worked from London, a third of Scottish ones from Port Glasgow/Greenock. In terms of local impact, in the mid-1780s, London had 14,000 in foreign trade, Liverpool had 6,600, Bristol 3,600 and Hull 1,300, and the leading coal ports – Whitehaven, Newcastle and Sunderland – had between them around 4,500. Most ports had far more men in coastal than foreign trade, and some with insignificant trade of any sort still had many ships and mariners – Poole and Scarborough, for instance – who were more likely than most to be away from home for long periods. Other towns, such as the new foundations at Grimsby and Goole had few seamen because they had few of their own ships, another factor depressing aggregate port income.

Quite apart from this movement of vessels, it should not be assumed that all men sailing from a port lived there. Sailors were highly mobile and, throughout our period, small maritime communities, especially fishing villages, sent their surplus men to the nearest busy port, though not necessarily permanently. Aberdeen and Montrose attracted men from neighbouring fishing villages; Dundee Greenlandmen came from rural Fife; the Tyne and Tees drew colliers' crews from Whitby and Scarborough; Hull mariners owned strips in the common fields of Lincolnshire; East Anglians moved around their ports; Welshmen went to Liverpool, and so on. Some switched happily between fishing and coasting. Others were attracted from the hinterland by more money or adventure in the long-haul trades and tended to be more permanent.

However, while merchants and bankers were welcomed to a cosmopolitan

80 The urban comment in Gaskell's *Mary Barton* is well known, but not the port-specific comment in *Sylvia's Lovers* (1863), exploring seamen's experiences and press gang influence *c.* 1800.

81 Jackson, *Hull*, appendix 36; G. Bush, *Bristol and its Municipal Government, 1820–51* (Bristol Record Society, 29, 1976), pp. 10–11.

82 PRO, Customs 17/1, 17/8, 17/27.

mercantile elite, Britain differed from most of Europe in excluding third-party ships and restricting the inflow of foreign sailors, normally forbidden or restricted to a quarter or fifth of a British crew. Even Shetlanders were excluded in peacetime. Nor were British shipowners inclined to use slave labour (illegal in England, 1772, and Scotland, 1778), and colonial and Indian subjects made no substantial 'ethnic' contribution to labour in our period. One might expect this protection to raise seamen's wages, but in fact there was a European-wide norm during peacetime – around £1 a month, all found – from which there was little local deviation, though the nature of shipping was such that British sailors were able to strike, when need arose, to keep wages up; they did it in the coal trade when winter stocks were building, and very effectively in early nineteenth-century coasters when timetabled operations began. The lower status of the 'stoker' came after our period with the increase in steam power, as did 'colonial' workers after the manning restrictions were finally abandoned in 1853; 47,000 British seamen petitioned against the change.[83]

Of course, in wartime more European and American sailors arrived in foreign ships, rowdy in legend, haunting the quays in a half-dark world of booze and brothels. There were 21,000 of them entering British ports by 1795, an increase matching the fall in British ships and men.[84] The situation was aggravated in the major ports by the rapid rise in long-haul exotic voyages for which all sort and conditions of men were signed up, some highly competent and some less so. The latter were not usually local men, but drifters or discharged men, stranded between voyages, falling into the system known as crimping where, in a babel of foreign tongues, lodging house keepers supplied skippers with men in their power, ensnared by young girls, financial advances and drink. The worst-off were probably Lascars (and some Chinese) replacing pressed-men on East India ships, around 200 in London in 1803 and six times as many by 1813.[85] Ill-paid, ill-fed, sickly and cold, they eked out a meagre existence – and died in large numbers – in a company barracks in Shoreditch, from which they went begging and frequently sold their – or the East India Company's – bedding and clothes.[86] Even the hard men of the sea could be careless of their own interests amid slop-shops, victuallers and ships chandlers in London, Liverpool or the largest coal ports, though local men in smaller ports, exhibiting their status symbol souvenirs to their peer network, escaped to some extent the system and the worst of its abuses.[87]

[83] S. R. Palmer, *Politics, Shipping and the Repeal of the Navigation Laws* (Manchester, 1990), p. 176. Lascars were specifically legislated against, though some ended up destitute in British ports because by a curious provision they could not be discharged in Britain or employed on outward voyages. *Ibid.*, p. 50.

[84] PRO, Customs 17/17, Preface.

[85] N. Myers, 'The black poor of London: initiatives of eastern seamen in the eighteenth and nineteenth centuries', in D. Frost, ed., *Ethnic Labour and British Imperial Trade: A History of Ethnic Seafarers in the UK* (London, 1995), pp. 10–11.

[86] *Ibid.*, pp. 13–16. Their conditions improved after 1813.

[87] See the interesting comparative discussion in W. Rudolph, *Harbor and Town: A Maritime Cultural History* (Altenburg, 1980), ch. 2, 'Sailortown'.

By the 1760s a growing urban sophistication and social morality often saw sailors as brutes, distinguishing the 'town', where the decent folks lived, from the 'sailortown', where the depraved lived badly. 'The trade and inhabitants, and consequently the houses, are increasing swiftly,' John Wesley wrote of the very plebeian Greenock, Glasgow's sailortown, in 1772, 'and so is cursing, swearing, drunkenness, Sabbath-breaking, and all manner of wickedness.'[88] From the 'hoary women' of Glasgow in the 1690s to the 'fallen women' of Hull in the 1810s, and 'Maggie May' in 1830s Liverpool, the hearts of ports were deemed immoral. Perhaps ports were different, needing the goad of the Bethel flag. With transient men and hungry women, crowded lodgings and insecurity and the brutality learned in ill-managed vessels, ports drew the same anguished fire as the theatre – 'especially hurtful to a trading city',[89] and in neither case was it fully deserved. Nevertheless the seamen's societies and Bethel associations springing up in ports spread accusations of degradation which are widely believed. Fortunately, seamen were sometimes human: 'I was a god-dam fool in the port of Liverpool.'[90] There were also those, like the Rev. Thomas Dikes of Hull, who thought the dregs were not to blame: 'Suppose that, instead of being brought up in a decent and virtuous neighbourhood, you had lived from your infancy in those lanes of moral turpitude, from which are emitted fumes of pollution that might almost corrupt an angel of light – can you say what, under these circumstances, you might have been?'[91]

Hull was small enough for a smart congregation to know that those in the lanes of moral turpitude were, inevitably, poor. However organised, 'aquatic labour' was irregular. Even larger ports, with some capacity for balancing demands, had seasonal fluctuations resulting from ripening sugar, migrating whales or freezing seas. But since the busiest ports catered for maximum demand, overmanning and underemployment was endemic.

Irregularity of work and income lay at the heart of poverty among lumpers who did not enjoy the same institutional relief as sailors and turned more often to the poor law. There was also insidious competition for work, in Mayhew's (*c.* 1850) words, among 'decayed and bankrupt master-butchers, master-bakers, publicans, grocers, old soldiers, old sailors, Polish refugees, broken-down gentlemen, discharged lawyers' clerks, suspended government clerks, almsmen, pensioners, servants, thieves – indeed, everyone who wants a loaf, and is willing to work for it'.[92] He forgot the Irish, but brought them in – with the cheap Jew's

88 *The Journal of John Wesley* (London, 1906), vol. III, p. 467.

89 John Wesley, referring to Bristol, quoted in T. B. Shepherd, *Methodism and the Literature of the Eighteenth Century* (London, 1947), p. 191. The first Glasgow theatre was burned down by 'the mob', blamed variously on George Whitefield's preaching and on mercantile hard work leaving no time for the evening theatre; Devine and Jackson, *Glasgow*, p. 318; Shepherd, *Methodism*, pp. 194–6.

90 'Maggie May', 1838 version, S. Hugill, *Songs of the Sea* (Maidenhead, 1977), pp. 68–9.

91 J. King, *Memoir of Rev. Thomas Dykes* [*sic*] (London, 1849), pp. 451–2.

92 P. Quennell, ed., *Mayhew's London* (London, 1969), pp. 565–6, 572–7.

shops and costermongers' carts, the ragged, unwashed, shoeless children and tarts asleep on doorsteps – in approaching a stable-looking lodging house 'usually frequented by the casual labourers'. There he found a smoke-bound kitchen full of men (with matted hair 'like flocks of wool', greasy, black and shiny clothes and evidence of famine) dozing, toasting herrings and drying out cigar-ends from the gutters. But the eighty-four bunks – at twopence a night – generally held around sixty, and only ten or fifteen of these were actually labourers! The well-known squalor round London's docks was partly the accumulated squalor of a great city, and smaller ports had less of it, depending on the size and mix of trades involved.

(vi) CONCLUSION

While the smaller, older ports are renowned for their mediaeval guildhalls and Georgian mansions, those catering for industrialisation were full of people and short of space. They were commonly, like Liverpool, half circles fronting the water; Hull (contained by the Rivers Humber and Hull) was a quarter circle. Bristol was more or less a complete circle. As in the case of London, the water at the heart of ports was often a divisive intrusion into street plans and a block to easy development. The waterside was occupied by trade, and docks or harbours were built out into the water or into the land, either way confirming the central core for trade and shipping. Warehouses and industries hovered near to the water, interspersed by poor housing. Fortress docks of the London sort were 'ports within ports' which effectively cut off the population from the waterfront, while even open docks kept people at arms length. When the time came for extension, ports became elongated, with miles of quays, a degree of specialisation of function which complicated employment patterns, and dockers' housing either crowded behind the warehouses or at some distance from their work. In smaller ports these things were less of a problem, and certainly this was the case in the mineral ports where loading devices and wagonways reduced the number of men required to handle ships of a given size. Transport was, nevertheless, a problem in many ports, and none more so that London, where the fortress docks were not easily entered or left.

By the end of our period the leading ports – London, Bristol, Liverpool, Glasgow, Leith and Hull, together with the leading coal ports – had taken on the air of industrialised nastiness in the popular imagination, not least because of the later writings of Mayhew and Dickens. But ports were, after all, economic entities vital for the industrialisation process, and in this regard were no different from the industrial towns. Their business was making money. Nevertheless, the *general* unattractiveness of ports in the eighteenth and early nineteenth centuries should not be exaggerated. Most big ports were reasonably well governed. They tried to shift the dirt and grime associated with towns in general, though they ran out of funds in the general crisis of towns in the years after 1815. (Cholera, an *imported* disease, is a comparative red-herring: one would expect ports to suffer badly from it!) They had at least one advantage in that, with the exception of London, their people were never very far from fresh sea air, sometimes too much of it; even in London Wordsworth could still observe 'the beauty of the morning'.[93] The unindustrialised ports were already 'resorts'; Yorkshire gentry drank the water at Scarborough (see Plate 29), while south-coast creeks played host to half-pay naval families visited by Jane Austen's heroines; and if Dickens described homes in upturned boats, his own house at Broadstairs looked down on a warren of 'picturesque' lanes that most small ports still have because they were not cleared away by progress. The pier at Margate was as much for pleasure as business when the steamer 'trips' began, and 'doon the watter' from Glasgow became the rage. Sandwich, Blakeney, Rye and Aldeburgh have the ghostly air of forgotten ports; but that is what they are and have been for a very long time, supplementing their income by their alternative trade in fish and recreation.[94] The variety of experiences in ports was, therefore, immense, and it is as well to remember that ports as they developed in Britain could be either pretty or prosperous, but rarely both.

[93] 'Earth has not anything to show more fair', 1802.

[94] An evocative survey is G. G. Carter, *Forgotten Ports of England* (London, 1951), full of 'crooked old roofs', 'gaily painted small cottages' and 'infinite space' (p. 44).

· 22 ·

Small towns 1700–1840

PETER CLARK

BRITAIN'S MYRIAD of small towns remained at the heart of economic and social life into the early Victorian era, bridging the urban and rural worlds. Diaries like that of the Sussex shopkeeper Thomas Turner of East Hoathly reveal an almost constant interaction between villagers and small towns. Turner records how he went to the nearby town of Lewes to buy cottons and cheese, to attend property sales, pay debts, get a doctor, scotch rumours about the disharmony between him and his wife, to participate in church events, to 'see the finest horse-race that ever I see run' and as often as not to get drunk and come rolling home.[1] While the traditional open market, the nucleus of most small towns since their inception, was often in decline after 1700, these communities consolidated their position in Georgian provincial society, growing in population and prosperity, as they acquired retail shops and specialist crafts, as

This chapter draws on material and data-sets collected as part of the project on Small Towns in England 1600–1850, at the Centre for Urban History, Leicester University; this was funded by the Economic and Social Research Council 1985–93. It also uses data-sets on urban functionality and nineteenth-century British populations assembled for a project on European Urbanisation (EUROCIT) funded by the European Union (1993–6) through the Human Capital and Mobility programme. Further grants for research have come from the Nuffield Foundation, and the Leicester–Loughborough universities joint research fund. I am grateful to these funding bodies and also to the large number of persons, research and computing staff, students, volunteers and others involved in the Small Towns project over the last decade or more, in particular R. Weedon, K. Gaskin, A. Wilson, E. Sullivan, A. Milne, A. Young and M. O'Loughlin. I am further indebted to I. Buckley, D. Powell, V. Martins, P. Barnes, P. Forton, A. Mason, D. Williams and N. Gohel for their assistance in the preparation of this chapter. David Souden kindly gave advice on the demographic sections, and Robert Anthony and Roger Bellingham supplied information on specific points. I am very grateful to Penny Lane for helping with a major technical problem at a critical juncture.

[1] D. Vaisey, ed., *The Diary of Thomas Turner 1754–65* (Oxford, 1984), pp. 1, 13, 15, 19, 28, 52, 160, 300–1 *et passim*. For a detailed study of the interaction of small towns and rural hinterlands see M. Carter, 'Town or urban society? St Ives in Huntingdonshire, 1630–1740', in C. Phythian-Adams, ed., *Societies, Culture and Kinship, 1580–1850* (London, 1993), pp. 77–100.

well as new leisure activities. The transformation did not occur overnight. In the 1720s the antiquarian and polymath William Stukeley, fresh from London, was dismayed at the small town of Stamford in Lincolnshire, where there was 'not one person . . . that had any taste or love of learning'; but within a few years things began to improve, as music making and club life blossomed, and he concluded eventually that this 'is true life, not the stink and noise and nonsense of London' . By the 1760s Fanny Burney could talk of the 'perpetual round of constrained civilities . . . unavoidable in a country town'.[2] Cleaner and less sleepy than the countryside, less frenetic and open than the bigger cities, ornamenting their landscape with a modest array of classical-style public buildings and fashionable housing, creating new administrative structures, small towns began to acquire a more distinctively urban and urbane identity, while at the same time becoming more closely integrated into regional and national networks of towns.

Not that there was a single type of small town. Differences in their origins, size and functions were compounded by variations between England, Scotland and Wales. In fact, the period witnessed growing regional diversity and the appearance of a minority of high growth towns. During the early nineteenth century the image of small town prosperity was increasingly fractured in other ways, affected by tough competition between towns and the problems of minor centres, with those in the agrarian counties sometimes reduced to village status. None the less, in many ways the long eighteenth century was a golden age for most of Britain's small urban communities.

Towns having less than about 2,500 or so inhabitants towards the end of the seventeenth century were widely regarded by contemporaries as belonging to a separate category of community, functioning usually as small local or market towns, below the level of more significant shire and regional centres.[3] Small towns comprised the great majority, about nine in ten, of urban centres in early Georgian Britain, and, after prolonged neglect by historians, new research is starting to expose the main lines of their development. As in much else, England was in the van, witnessing widespread urban growth from the later Stuart period, the ranks of medieval towns being joined by a contingent of new communities. In Scotland the great wave of baronial burghs created during the sixteenth and seventeenth centuries was largely over and many of the planned landowner set-

[2] W. C. Lukis, ed., *The Family Memoirs of the Rev. William Stukeley, M.D.*, vol. I (Surtees Society, 73, 1880), pp. 109, 379, 385, vol. II (Surtees Society, 76, 1883), p. 292; L. E. Troide, ed., *The Early Journals and Letters of Fanny Burney*, vol. I (Oxford, 1988), pp. 83–4

[3] P. Clark, 'Small towns in England 1550–1850: national and regional population trends', in P. Clark, ed., *Small Towns in Early Modern Europe* (Cambridge, 1995), pp. 91–2; for a list of English small towns (excluding Middlesex) see P. Clark and J. Hosking, *Population Estimates of English Small Towns 1550–1851: Revised Edition* (Leicester, 1993).

tlements of the eighteenth century failed to become towns, but by the 1790s there was substantial expansion among established small towns, as Scottish urbanisation quickly caught up with that of England.[4] Though almost wholly a country of small towns in the earlier period, Wales saw the least dynamic change, but by the start of the nineteenth century industrial towns were starting to emerge, particularly in the south. In the words of Robin Ddu Eryri who visited the burgeoning textile centre of Newtown in 1833:

> Thy flannel goes as quick as one can tell . . .
> To every part of Britain and its known world,
> The gas light bright, thy new built houses high
> Thy factory lofts seem smiling on the sky . . .[5]

A number of small towns soared in size during this period. Most were long-established market centres like Sheffield, Bradford (see Plate 30), Wolverhampton and Paisley, their rise fuelled by industrialisation; others were ports such as Liverpool, Greenock and Cardiff, or burgeoning leisure centres, for example Brighton. Rather fewer were *ab initio* industrialising towns such as Stoke, Burslem or St Helens, which like urban comets passed rapidly through the small town phase before rushing over the horizon as large fully fledged towns of the nineteenth century. The story of these major specialist towns is discussed elsewhere in this volume. Here the focus is on the great mass of small towns which until the early Victorian era remained relatively small (under about 5,000 inhabitants in 1811).[6] We need to investigate: the changing pattern of small centres on the ground, in the different parts of the country; demographic trends, as indicated by parish register evidence; economic performance; social and cultural developments; and the administrative and political dimensions of small town evolution.

(i) PATTERNS ON THE GROUND

At the start of the period there were probably about 730 English small towns with less than about 2,500 inhabitants; in Wales the number was just over 50 with only perhaps Monmouth and Wrexham above the threshold. In Scotland

[4] Clark, 'Small towns in England', pp. 94–102; I. D. Whyte, 'The function and social structure of Scottish burghs of barony in the seventeenth and eighteenth centuries', in A. Maczak and C. Smout, eds., *Gründung und Bedeutung kleinerer Städte im nördlichen Europa der frühen Neuzeit* (Wiesbaden, 1991), pp. 14–25; also D. G. Lockhart, 'The construction and planning of new urban settlements in Scotland in the eighteenth century', in *ibid.*, pp. 31–66; see also above, pp. 159 *et seq.*

[5] See above, pp. 140 *et seq.*; quotation in L. Williams, 'A case study of Newtown Montgomeryshire', *Montgomeryshire Collections*, 64 (1975), 57.

[6] See above, pp. 465 *et seq.*, 708 *et seq.*, and below, pp. 788 *et seq.*, 807 *et seq.* 1811 population threshold increased from the seventeenth-century level to take into account national population growth.

approximately 150–60 towns can be classed in this way.[7] A standard threshold may, of course, distort the picture because of the lower population levels outside England, but reducing the ceiling to about 1,500 inhabitants does not radically change the picture: Wales on this basis had 46 small towns and Scotland about 145. Adopting the standard parameter, about 12 per cent of the English population lived in towns of this size; in Scotland and Wales the figures were probably of the order of 5–7 and 12 per cent respectively. Generally, the high level of British small towns was similar to the pattern evident in the more peripheral regions of northern and central Europe (Scandinavia, Poland and Hungary) during the early modern period.[8]

From the later Stuart period English towns were toured by a procession of inquisitive visitors, armed with a set of questions about the local economy, urban facilities and the like. Their reports indicate that they recognised a broad spectrum of small towns, if not a hierarchy. One of the most comprehensive surveys of English small towns was by Richard Blome in his *Britannia* (1673) who counted 94 'mean' or lesser market towns and 142 'flourishing' centres. These distinctions were no figment of the imagination. Correlating Blome's list with population estimates for this time derived from the hearth tax we find that the mean market towns had an average of about 560 inhabitants compared to 1,030 for those Blome praised as flourishing.[9] Other evidence confirms the existence of a rank order of English small towns. At its head were larger, usually early established, centres, a number of them boroughs, benefiting from good communications and a variety of functions, sometimes overlapping with lesser county towns; here one thinks of Chichester, Stamford, Lichfield, Huntingdon and Chelmsford. Then came a run of middling market towns, such as the principal unincorporated market towns of Leicestershire (Melton Mowbray, Hinckley, Loughborough, Lutterworth, Market Harborough and Ashby de la Zouch), which had a complex of trades and crafts and substantial local hinterlands. Finally, there appeared a crowd of minor centres, some micro-towns, having fewer than 800 inhabitants at the end of the seventeenth century, places where

[7] Clark and Hosking, *Population Estimates*; figures adjusted to include about eight small towns in Middlesex (this figure is subject to a significant margin of error, because of the rapid pace of urban growth in the metropolitan area). For the somewhat different figures calculated by Dr Langton see above, pp. 466 *et seq*. For Wales see L. Owen, 'The population of Wales in the sixteenth and seventeenth centuries', *Transactions of the Honourable Society of Cymmrodorion* (1959), 107–13; also H. Carter, *The Towns of Wales*, 2nd edn (Cardiff, 1966), p. 35. Scottish figures calculated from Whyte, 'Function and social structure', pp. 25–7.

[8] Clark, ed., *Small Towns*, chs. 2–4; also Maczak and Smout, eds., *Gründung und Bedeutung kleinerer Städte*, pp. 103–69, 193–233.

[9] Cf. M. R. Wenger, ed., *The English Travels of Sir John Percival and William Byrd II* (Columbia, Miss., 1989), pp. 22 *et seq.*; R. Blome, *Britannia; Or, a Geographical Description of the Kingdoms of England, Scotland, and Ireland* (London, 1673). Hearth tax estimates from Clark and Hosking, *Population Estimates*.

rural aspects persisted, despite the general growth of small town urbanity during the eighteenth century. Thus when John Yeoman, a Somerset man, turned up in the little town of Berkhampsted in Hertfordshire during the 1770s, he found that 'the people are so countrified as in any town is I know. They will stare at you as if they had never seen no one before.'[10]

Outside England, similar broad distinctions are evident among small towns, though with a greater stress on minor centres. In Scotland during the 1690s a number of lesser county centres and ports – royal burghs like Elgin, Cupar and Irvine – had populations of 1,000 or more. But there were large numbers of tiny places, including recently created burghs of barony, with 800 to 500 inhabitants, or less. Thus the Perth area had numerous small towns, which (apart from the diocesan centres of Dunkeld and Dunblane) supported no more than 500 or so people.[11] In Wales several county towns could boast a modest degree of prosperity and importance: Denbigh was said in the 1720s to be 'fair and populous', having an active market and fairs, while Monmouth and its 2,500 inhabitants was 'very considerable and populous'; the port of Haverfordwest, distinguished by its corporation, good trade, convenient harbour, markets and free school, was another sizeable centre. However, the great majority of basic market towns in Wales had below 1,000 inhabitants in the early eighteenth century, a reflection of low population densities and the sluggish, underdeveloped nature of the economy.[12]

Already visible from the middle ages in the overall distribution of small towns, regional variations can now be seen in their rank order. For England, Blome's 'flourishing' market towns were predominantly in southern parts of the country; well over half of those listed in East Anglia came into that category. In Yorkshire, by contrast, only a quarter of those noted by Blome were described as 'flourishing', and the incidence was not much higher in other northern districts. Moreover, it was in these regions that Blome's 'mean' towns were pervasive,

10 P. Clark, 'Changes in the pattern of English small towns in the early modern period', in Maczak and Smout, eds., *Gründung und Bedeutung kleinerer Städte*, pp. 72–9; H. Gräf, 'Leicestershire small towns and pre-industrial urbanisation', *Transactions of the Leicestershire Archaeological and Historical Society*, 68 (1994), 98–120; M. Yearsley, ed., *The Diary of the Visits of John Yeoman to London* (London, 1934), p. 38.

11 I. D. Whyte, 'Urbanization in early modern Scotland: a preliminary analysis', *Scottish Economic and Social History*, 9 (1989), 24–5, 30–1; M. Lynch, 'Urbanisation and urban networks in seventeenth century Scotland: some further thoughts', *Scottish Economic and Social History*, 12 (1992), 35.

12 E. Bowen, *Britannia Depicta or Ogilby Improved (1720)*, new edn (Newcastle, 1970), pp. 38, 57, 204; M. S. Archer, *The Welsh Post Towns before 1840* (Chichester, 1970), pp. 48, 54, 84 *et passim*; W. T. R. Pryce, 'Parish registers and visitation returns as primary sources for the population', *Transactions of the Honourable Society of Cymmrodorion* (1971), 275; W. T. R. Pryce and J. A. Edwards, 'The social structure of the embryonic town in rural Wales: Llanfair Caereinion in the mid-nineteenth century', *Montgomeryshire Collections*, 67 (1979), 46–50.

Table 22.1 *Population distribution of English small towns c. 1670 (percentages)*

Region	0–900	901–1,800	1,801–2,750	*n*
East Anglia	58.0	37.7	4.3	69
Midlands				
East	54.2	34.7	11.1	72
West	56.1	40.9	3.0	66
North				
northern	63.4	33.3	3.3	30
North-West	69.4	20.4	10.2	49
Yorkshire	64.6	29.2	6.2	65
South-East	64.4	29.9	5.7	177
South-West	76.9	18.8	4.3	117
Mean	64.3	29.8	5.9	645

Figures exclude Middlesex towns.

against much lower proportions in the South (21 per cent in East Anglia, 18 per cent in the South-West). In the same manner, we find differences in the size distribution of small towns, particularly high numbers of lesser centres being located in north-western shires and the South-West, and more middle size towns in East Anglia and the West Midlands (see Table 22.1). For Scotland, likewise, recent work has pointed to the developed networks of small towns in the central and eastern regions by the late seventeenth century, with the Fife region, for instance, having more than a third of its population living in towns – a high density 'hinged on the chain of small ports from Anstruther to St Andrews'. The size and importance of small towns in the west and south-west of Scotland was considerably less.[13]

During our period small town hierarchies and regional patterns were transformed by general urbanisation, economic and transport changes and the volatility of smaller communities. Under the pressure of competition from larger centres (including larger small towns) a sizeable contingent of minor places failed to preserve their urban status. In England by the close of our period somewhat over 100 towns appear to have de-urbanised, of which the highest proportion was concentrated in East Anglia, and only a handful in the West Midlands. Minor towns which failed included Methwold, reduced by 1830 to being 'a large village'; Mendlesham, 'formerly a market town . . . the inhabitants are mostly

[13] Lynch, 'Urbanisation and urban networks', 35–7.

employed in agriculture'; and Ludgershall, once a market town of some note but now 'a mere village'. In Scotland various lesser burghs of barony suffered problems of viability in the eighteenth century, as did minor towns in mid- and North Wales.[14]

Only a modest number of new towns emerged in Britain in our period. England's new small towns probably totalled no more than a few dozen, among them an assortment of industrial towns like Burslem, transportation centres such as Stourport and Wolverton, dockyard towns (for instance, Sheerness) and a coterie of leisure towns like Tunbridge Wells, Buxton, Leamington and Harrogate.[15] In Scotland only a few planted settlements of the eighteenth century grew into small towns, and most expansion took place in established centres, though after 1800 one sees the spread of industrialising and urbanising villages in the western Lowlands.[16] Awakening economically towards the end of the eighteenth century, Wales generated several new industrialising and mining towns, particularly in the south-eastern shires of Glamorgan and Monmouth (Merthyr, Pontypool); also new ports such as Milford, and resorts like Llandrindod and Aberystwyth.[17]

In broad terms, the demographic increase for English small towns during the eighteenth century was close to the national urban trend. Scotland's small towns suffered setbacks during the early Georgian era, and their subsequent growth, though accelerating, lagged behind that of the biggest centres; in Wales the evidence is too incomplete to tell. What is evident is that across Britain regional differentiation was gaining momentum, having a transforming effect on the urban system as a whole, not least on the army of small towns. Thus, the demographic expansion of Yorkshire's small towns was probably twice that found in East Anglia; small town networks in the Midlands and the North likewise achieved buoyant growth rates compared to the more sluggish South-West and South-East.[18] In the case of Scotland's small towns the regional balance increasingly focused on western central Lowlands around Glasgow, though the north and east and Lothian–Fife regions continued to do relatively well. In Wales the small towns of the south-east forged ahead.[19]

[14] Clark, 'Changes in the pattern', p. 69; *Pigot and Co's National Commercial Directory* (London, 1830), pp. 589, 775, 803; Whyte, 'Function and social structure', pp. 18 *et seq.*; G. S. Pryde, ed., *The Court Book of the Burgh of Kirkintilloch 1658–1694* (Scottish History Society, 3rd series, 53, 1963), p. lxxxiii; S. Lewis, *A Topographical Dictionary of Wales* (London, 1834), not paginated but see under Aberavon, Aberconway, Aber-Fraw, Estyn, Lampeter *et passim*.

[15] Clark, 'Changes in the pattern', p. 70; P. J. Corfield, *The Impact of English Towns 1700–1800* (Oxford, 1982), pp. 15 *et passim*.

[16] Lockhart, 'Construction and planning', pp. 31–65.

[17] H. Carter, 'Urban and industrial settlement in the modern period, 1750–1914', in D. H. Owen, ed., *Settlement and Society in Wales* (Cardiff, 1989), pp. 270, 278; *Aris' Birmingham Gazette*, 13 July 1767.

[18] Clark, 'Small towns in England', pp. 99, 108–12.

[19] *Ibid.*, p 99; see above, pp. 143 *et seq.* and 158 *et seq.*

Table 22.2 *Population distribution of English small towns c. 1811 (percentages)*

Region	0–1,650	1,651–3,300	3,301–5,000	5,001 +	*n*
East Anglia	54.4	38.0	6.3	1.3	79
Midlands					
East	39.1	32.2	11.5	17.2	87
West	21.4	30.0	20.0	28.6	70
North					
northern	26.9	19.2	19.2	34.7	52
North-West	0.0	20.4	12.2	67.4	49
Yorkshire	16.4	28.4	16.4	38.8	67
South-East	33.0	40.0	17.0	10.0	200
South-West	39.9	39.4	12.2	8.5	188
Mean	32.6	34.3	14.3	18.8	792

Turning to the early nineteenth century, regional changes are highlighted by the distribution of small towns in 1811 (taking places with under about 5,000 inhabitants). For England as a whole (see Table 22.2), about a third of our late seventeenth-century sample of towns still had less than 1,650 inhabitants; somewhat over one in ten had between 3,300 to 5,000; while nearly one in five had leapt the 5,000 barrier. However, when we look at the regional areas, we find that by 1811 the North-West had no towns in the smallest category and over two-thirds of its small centres now exceeded 5,000 people. Similarly in Yorkshire, the northern shires and West Midlands, about a half or more of the earlier small towns were in the top categories. This is in sharp contrast to East Anglia, where the majority of small towns in 1811 were at the bottom of the range, a situation echoed in the South-West and South-East.

Over the next forty years the onward rush of urbanisation was accompanied by a growing divergence between big cities and small towns, as growth rates for the former ran at twice those of lesser places. Even so, by 1851 a third of our small towns had forged above the 5,000 threshold, leaving less than one in five in the demographic basement of under 1,650 inhabitants (see Table 22.3). Regional differentiation was ever more pronounced, with Yorkshire and the West Midlands the most expansive areas in terms of demographic increase. In these and other industrial districts the urban system was now overshadowed by large towns, whilst in East Anglia well over a third of the small towns languished in the lowest categories, a pattern more or less repeated in the eastern Midlands and the South-West. The South-East was exceptional in experiencing a sharp reduction in minor centres, due in considerable measure to metropolitan suburbanisation and government military investment, which spawned a string of

Table 22.3 *Population distribution of English small towns c. 1851 (percentages)*

Region	0–1,650	1,651–3,300	3,301–5,000	5,001 +	*n*
East Anglia	38.0	31.6	20.3	10.1	79
Midlands					
East	24.1	25.3	16.1	34.5	87
West	7.0	28.2	22.5	42.3	71
North					
northern	18.9	16.9	5.7	58.5	53
North-West	0.0	11.5	13.5	75.0	52
Yorkshire	12.7	14.3	23.8	49.2	63
South-East	14.0	33.5	22.5	30.0	200
South-West	26.8	33.3	20.8	19.1	183
Mean	18.8	27.9	19.7	33.6	788

satellite towns around the capital, including Brentford, Greenwich and Woolwich.[20]

The Scottish picture increasingly converged with that for England, as the proportion of very small centres diminished and a sizeable number of older small towns vaulted the 5,000 level (see Table 22.4). Pivoting on Glasgow the central and western regions clearly had the most dynamic development, which was powered by a strong cluster of bigger centres. The Lothian and Fife region had more minor towns, but the most traditional areas were the border counties, where there was an overwhelming number of medium size small towns and few larger ones. After 1811 the shift towards larger towns in the west and central area of Scotland accelerated: by 1851 only about one in seven of the earlier set of small towns were in the bottom two bands, as against over a half with more than 5,000 inhabitants (see Table 22.5). Elsewhere the advance was more laggardly.[21]

By the start of the nineteenth century Wales had experienced only limited change. No more than three of its old small towns exceeded 5,000 in 1811 and these were in the north (Holywell, Mold, Wrexham); there was a lumpy distribution of other places with nearly half minor centres. However, this pattern masked the first emergence of new towns in the south, though most of these (except for Merthyr) were fairly small. At the end of our period the Welsh urban system was more flourishing and on the move; one in three of the older small

[20] Clark, 'Small towns in England', pp. 99, 113–18; see above, p. 65.

[21] Tables 22.4–5: towns based primarily on Whyte's list of eighteenth-century centres in 'Function and social structure', pp. 26–30. The censuses for 1811 and 1851 have been used, taking parish figures because of the difficulty of identifying the urban component. Individual figures may be exaggerated but the regional comparisons are instructive.

Table 22.4 *Population distribution of Scottish small towns c. 1811 (percentages)*

Region	0–1,650	1,651–3,300	3,301–5,000	5,000+	*n*
Borders	31.6	52.6	15.8	0.0	38
Central and west	8.8	44.1	20.6	26.5	34
Lothian and Fife	20.0	55.0	22.5	2.5	40
North-east	29.6	40.7	22.2	7.5	27
Highlands and Islands	15.4	61.5	15.4	7.7	13
Mean	21.7	50.0	19.7	8.6	152

Table 22.5 *Population distribution of Scottish small towns c. 1851 (percentages)*

Region	0–1,650	1,651–3,300	3,301–5,000	5,000+	*n*
Borders	13.2	50.0	18.4	18.4	38
Central and west	0.0	14.7	32.4	52.9	34
Lothian and Fife	12.5	45.0	17.5	25.0	40
North-east	18.6	29.6	25.9	25.9	27
Highlands and Islands	0.0	46.2	30.8	23.0	13
Mean	9.9	36.8	23.7	29.6	152

towns had risen above 5,000 inhabitants (Cardiff soaring to over 18,000), just as the proportion of minor centres had fallen to one fifth, though the plight of market towns in the poorer, rural areas remained unresolved.[22]

By the Victorian era the position of British small towns, particularly the lesser ones, was coming under pressure, and considerable numbers were experiencing retardation or even eclipse. This was notable in the more agrarian regions. None the less, for much of the preceding century or more many small towns across Britain benefited from sustained demographic and economic growth and a greater sense of urban identity. We must now try to understand the nature of these changes.

(ii) THE DEMOGRAPHIC MECHANISMS

What were the demographic mechanisms of eighteenth-century expansion and what do they tell us about the process of urban change in our small communities? How far were Georgian small towns, like their predecessors, generating growth through their own natural surpluses and to what extent were they becoming dependent, like bigger cities, on net immigration from the country-

[22] Carter, *Towns of Wales*, pp. 50–75.

side? Here our evidence is confined to England where parish register aggregations provide the best illumination. Analysis of this kind is fraught with difficulty in the case of small towns. As well as the inevitable problem of the underregistration of events, there are questions concerning the parochial unit of analysis (quite often more extensive than the urban centre), and the scale of nonconformist absenteeism (though detailed work on this would suggest that it was less of a problem than has sometimes been thought, or at least that it was not just an urban problem).[23] From a sample of parish registers[24] chosen to provide a reasonable cross-section of small towns across the English regions (excluding the North and North-West – because of the great size of many parishes there), we find that overall the baptismal and burial rates were not so very different from the national trend outlined by E. A. Wrigley and Roger Schofield. From the later seventeenth century into the early years of the next the indices broadly converged: small towns enjoyed very small surpluses (see Figure 22.1); this compares to the substantial ones before the Civil War. At the start of the eighteenth century any significant urban growth was fuelled by immigration. From the

[23] M. K. Noble, 'Growth and development of country towns: the case of eastern Yorkshire c.1700–1850' (PhD thesis, University of Hull, 1982), p. 356; M. Ryan and G. Mackay, 'Non-conformity in Loughborough – a demographic study' (unpublished paper, Centre for Urban History, University of Leicester, 1994).

[24] The sample is based on parish register aggregations for ninety-seven small towns, comprising those collected by the Small Towns project team and others collected by the Cambridge Group for the Study of Population and Social Structure and generously made available to the project (I am indebted to Sir Tony Wrigley and Roger Schofield for their help). Towns were selected to give the sample a good representation of the population distribution of small towns in each region. Only aggregations with data covering a major part of the period were analysed here; additional aggregations for the North-West and North were excluded because of the extensive non-urban areas in the parishes. New aggregative data were checked according to Cambridge Group procedures and defective registrations identified and corrected using revised but compatible versions (designed by Ms J. Harding) of the Cambridge Group computer programmes (see E. A. Wrigley and R. S. Schofield, *The Population History of England 1541–1871* (Cambridge, 1989), pp. 694–707). National trends in Figures 22.1–4 have been calculated from *ibid.*, pp. 496–502. The following towns were included in the sample by region: East Anglia – Attleborough, Eye, Framlingham, Hadleigh, Lavenham, Linton, Mendlesham, Mildenhall, North Walsham, Saxmundham, Swaffham, Woodbridge; West Midlands – Alcester, Bromyard, Broseley, Eccleshall, Ledbury, Ludlow, Penkridge, Solihull, Stone; East Midlands – Castle Donington, Dronfield, East Retford, Gainsborough, Great Grimsby, Hinckley, Loughborough, Lutterworth, Market Bosworth, Matlock, Melton Mowbray, Oakham, Southwell, Tuxford, Waltham on the Wolds, Worksop; South-West – Bridgwater, Bruton, Camborne, Colyton, Crewkerne, Fairford, Hartland, Minchinhampton, Modbury, North Petherton, Truro, Winchcombe; Yorkshire – Bridlington, Doncaster St George, Great Driffield, Hedon, Howden, Otley, Patrington, Skipton, Thirsk, Yarm; South-East – Ampthill, Ashford, Aylesbury, Bampton, Banbury, Bedford, Chipping Norton, Berkhampsted, Cranbrook, East Grinstead, East Ilsley, Eltham, Farringdon, Fordingbridge, Goudhurst, Gravesend, Haslemere, Hemel Hempstead, Hitchin, Hythe, Lenham, Maldon, Odiham, Princes Risborough, Potton, Reigate, Ringwood, Romford, Romsey, St Albans (Abbey), Sevenoaks, Sittingbourne, Tenterden, Thaxted, Tonbridge, Watford, Westerham, Woburn.

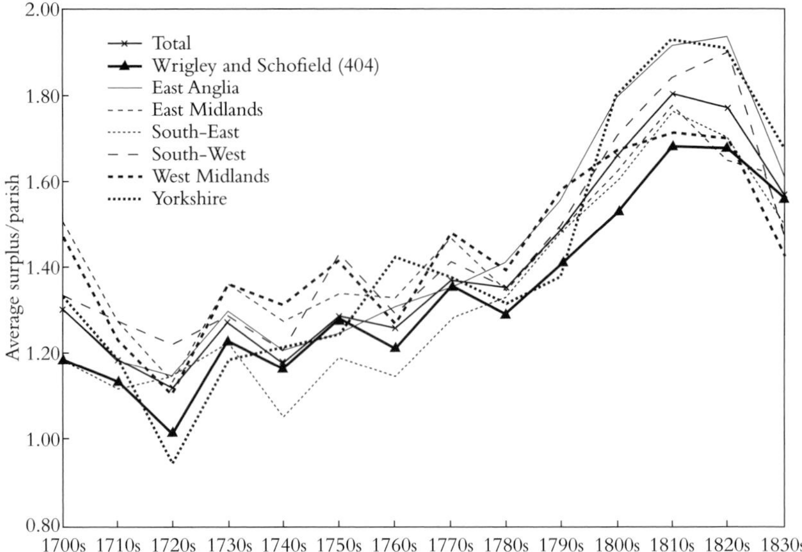

Figure 22.1 English small towns: demographic surpluses: ten year averages by region (excluding North and North-West) 1700–1837

second quarter, however, the demographic surpluses begin to mount; a substantial expansion occurred in the last third of the century.[25]

Such aggregate trends hide significant variations, however. Focusing on the relationship of baptisms to burials, we discover that unlike the period before the Civil War, when there seems to have been a wide degree of regional oscillation, the long eighteenth century saw a more consistent pattern for all regions, with the fairly modest surpluses of the earlier decades giving way to the marked upturn of the last years of the century. On the other hand, the South-East records low surpluses, as does Yorkshire in the earlier period, though in the second half of the century, as industrial take-off occurs, it leads the picture. The industrialising West Midlands enjoy significant surpluses, in common with the less dynamic South-West and East Anglia.

Yet urban surpluses are the confection of two unstable elements. Examining baptismal and burial rates for the period after 1700 separately (see Figures 22.2–3) one finds that East Anglia was not doing well on the baptismal front, its sluggish advances until the close of the period a reflection, perhaps, of declining industrial activity and so reduced employment and marriage opportunities for young people. But in the demographic swings and roundabouts this was compensated

[25] Wrigley and Schofield, *English Population History*, especially ch. 7.

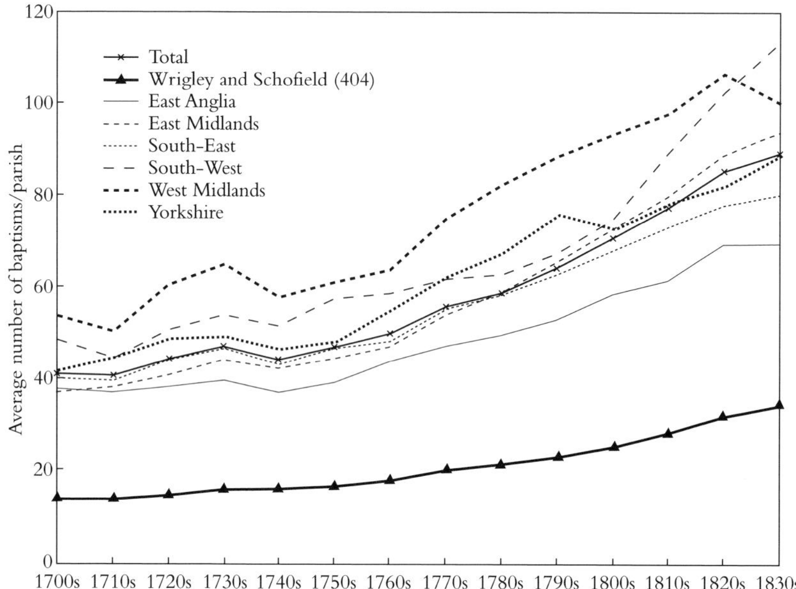

Figure 22.2 English small towns: baptisms: ten year averages by region (excluding North and North-West) 1700–1837

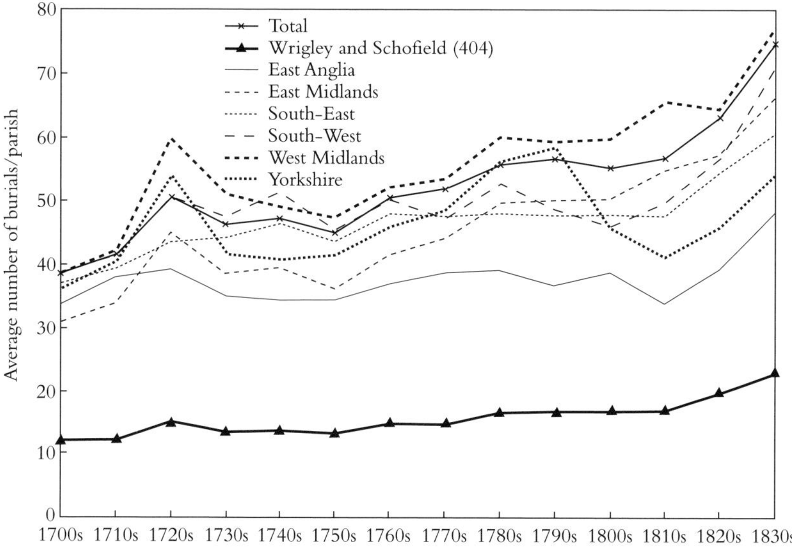

Figure 22.3 English small towns: burials: ten year averages by region (excluding North and North-West) 1700–1837

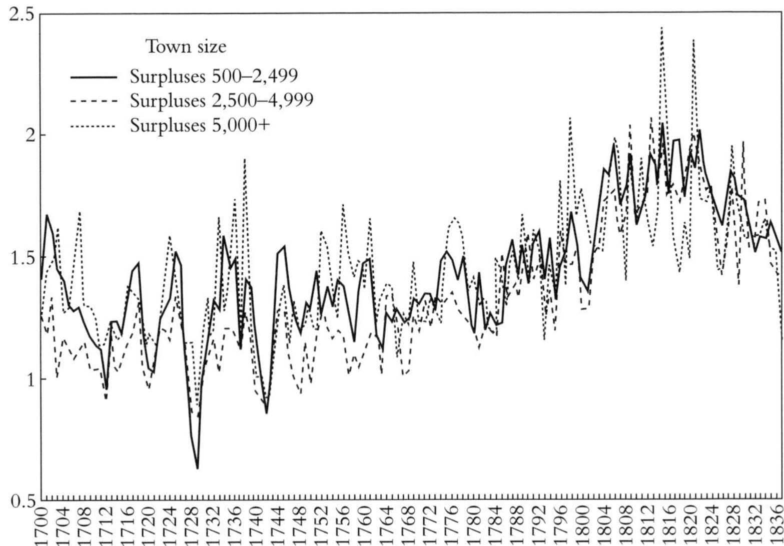

Figure 22.4 English small towns: surpluses: ten year averages by population band 1700–1837

for by relatively static burial rates, as improved agricultural ouput led to falling grain prices, and, more important, commercial contact with higher mortality areas, particularly the metropolis, may have stagnated.[26] West Midland centres enjoyed high and sustained baptismal rates, as industrial growth in the region not only encouraged earlier marriage but also attracted young adults to town (usually from the locality);[27] but this was at the price of relatively high though lagging burial rates, linked probably to environmental factors and the vulnerability of outsiders to sickness. The small towns of the South-East were towards the bottom of the league for baptismal growth, arguably because of the heavy demand for young adult migrants from the capital; given higher burial rates, influenced no doubt by metropolitan mortality, this caused a serious squeeze on natural growth.[28]

Correlating demographic trends with the ranking of small towns, one finds at

[26] D. T. Jenkins and K. G. Ponting, *British Wool Textile Industry 1770–1914* (London, 1982), p. 4 *et passim*; P. Sharpe, 'De-industrialization and re-industrialization: women's employment and the changing character of Colchester 1700–1850', *UH*, 21 (1994), 77–83.

[27] For migration in the West Midlands: J. M. Martin, 'The rich, the poor, the migrant in eighteenth century Stratford-on-Avon', *Local Population Studies*, 20 (1978), 43–7; also R. A. Pelham, 'The immigrant population of Birmingham 1686–1726', *Transactions of the Birmingham Archaeological Society*, 61(1937), 45–80.

[28] M. Dobson, 'Population 1640–1831', in A. Armstrong, ed., *The Economy of Kent 1640–1914* (Woodbridge, 1995), pp. 9–12, 23 *et seq.*; J. Landers, *Death and the Metropolis* (Cambridge, 1993), pp. 89, 107–9.

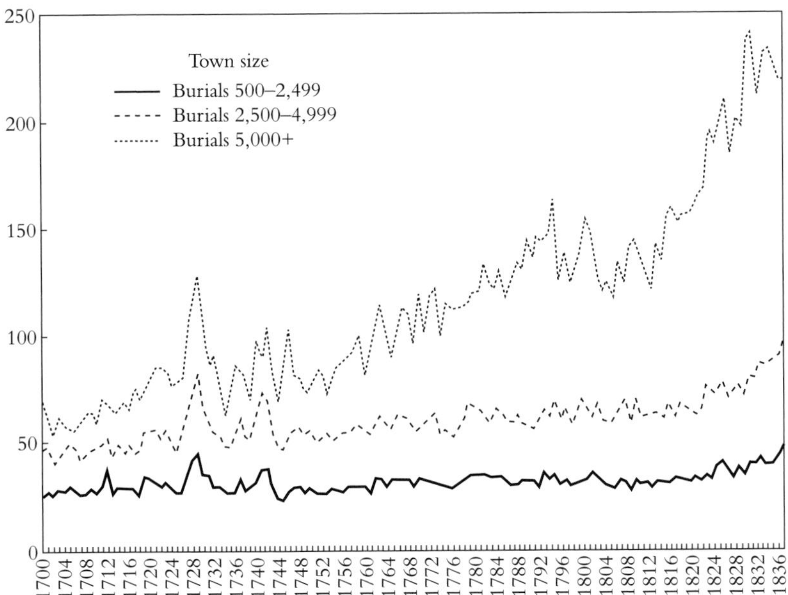

Figure 22.5 English small towns: burials: ten year averages by population band 1700–1837

first sight a considerable measure of convergence, with similar levels of surplus among the big, medium and lesser centres from the later seventeenth century until 1800 or so, when the bigger centres experienced a relative downturn (see Figure 22.4). However, disaggregating the indices and focusing on burials (see Figure 22.5), it is evident that the most dynamic small towns had rising burial rates from the 1770s, with a modest pause at the close of the century before another sharp rise subsequently, probably due to deteriorating housing and other environmental factors. Medium size and lesser towns had flatter burial trends.

The problem with this kind of analysis is that one knows relatively little in this period about that other crucial variable, migration flows. Church court data for the early part of the century suggest that English small towns experienced substantial mobility, though with more localised movement than for bigger towns.[29] For the later decades the most extensive evidence comes from lower class movers under the settlement acts and those getting married; and here again the predominance of localised movement is striking even for more dynamic centres. Information on the volume of movement is sparse, although David's Souden's

[29] P. Clark, 'Migration in England during the late seventeenth and early eighteenth centuries', *P&P*, 83 (1979), 75; D. Souden, ' Migrants and the population structure of later seventeenth-century provincial cities and market towns', in P. Clark, ed., *The Transformation of English Provincial Towns 1600–1800* (London, 1984), p. 146.

analysis of movers and stayers from parish register reconstitutions is instructive. In the West Midlands the small towns of Alcester and Banbury apparently experienced reduced mobility in the late seventeenth century, but substantially rising levels during the eighteenth centuries, in line with population increase and economic expansion. In less dynamic Lincolnshire Gainsborough's flow of incomers appears to have been more stable through the eighteenth century. Stagnant towns seem to have suffered growing out-migration. As in the case of bigger towns, migration may well be the basic key to understanding population change in small towns for most of this period.

All this is rather abstract, the outcome of a multitude of personal or family decisions (about mobility, marriage, the conception of children) and demographic incidents like outbreaks of smallpox or an inrush of rural migrants, which even on a small scale may well have had a more disruptive effect on the more fragile demographic (and social world) of a market town than larger-scale events in a big city.[30] The evidence for the demographic mechanics of small town growth is also far from conclusive, limited as it is at present to England. In broad brush terms, the trends in vital events appear broadly in line with the national picture. But when the evidence is disaggregated a number of regional and hierarchical variations emerge, which supports the argument for increasing regional differentiation in small town networks. At the same time, there is much here which calls for further research and analysis, particularly close-textured study at the local level.

(iii) ECONOMIC TRENDS

Small town growth in Georgian Britain was determined in large part by those national processes of industrial and commercial expansion discussed elsewhere in this volume, but the economic life of such communities was also affected by specific developments, with significant variations between regions and levels of town. Already in the seventeenth century, when public markets remained central to their economies, visitors to small towns reported on their growing economic specialities. Nearly a third of the English small towns surveyed by Richard Blome in the 1670s were described as multi-functional, in other words having more than a market role (see Table 22.6).[31] About one in ten of those listed had a recognised manufacturing specialism, whilst service activities also started to prolife-

[30] C. C. Pond, 'Internal population migration and mobility in eastern England in the eighteenth century century' (PhD thesis, University of Cambridge, 1980); A. Constant, 'The geographical background of inter-village population movements in Northamptonshire and Huntingdonshire 1754–1943', *Geography*, 33 (1948), 81, 83; D. Souden, 'Pre-industrial English local migration fields' (PhD thesis, University of Cambridge, 1981), pp. 194–6, 214–15; see also Gräf, 'Leicestershire small towns', 108. For the pattern in declining Yorkshire towns see Noble, 'Growth and development of country towns', p. 433. For a discussion of the personal experience of demographic incidents see above, pp. 495 *et seq.*

[31] Blome, *Britannia*.

Table 22.6 *Multi-functional specialisms in English small towns c. 1673*

Region		*n*		%
East Anglia		14		57.1
Midlands				
East		26		23.1
West		19		31.6
North				
northern		13		30.8
North-West		13		23.1
Yorkshire		20		15.0
South-East		56		42.8
South-West		17		35.3
	Total	178	Mean	32.4

rate: about a quarter boasted schools, inns, spas and similar functions (or a combination of them). In general, Blome's figures may understate the scale of specialisation (we know, for instance, that numerous markets at this time were trading in specific commodities, such as corn and cattle), but the evidence from *Britannia* is important because of its illumination of regional trends. Most notable is the high incidence of specialisms in East Anglia, with over half of the small towns surveyed having one or more; there were also above average levels in the South-East, and South-West. In comparison, the small towns of the Midlands and North of England had below average rates of specialisation – as low as 15.0 per cent in Yorkshire.

Unfortunately, evidence for Wales is much less detailed, limited to twenty-four small towns, mostly larger settlements. According to Blome, about half of these were multi-functional centres, but only five had specialist mining or manufacturing activities; a similar number were ports, and others had legal or other service functions. No comparable information is available for Scotland for the same period.[32]

During the eighteenth century economic specialisation provided the momentum for accelerating urbanisation, as new activities spread across the country, transforming the regional landscape. England clearly led the way. Manufacturing specialities, already evident by the late seventeenth century, surged ahead among small towns in the rising industrial areas of the West Midlands and the North. Metalworking was widespread in north Worcestershire and west Warwickshire; in north Staffordshire Newcastle became the nexus of a set of specialist ceramic centres at Burslem, Hanley and elsewhere; while ribbon making and other

[32] *Ibid.* Blome lists Scottish towns with only limited detail.

textile trades figure in the small towns of the Coventry area.[33] In the North-West urbanisation quickened, creating fast-growth textile, later cotton, towns in eastern Lancashire (such as Burnley and Blackburn), and a cluster of mineral towns in the south-west of the county such as St Helens, Prescot and Warrington, which was described by one visitor as 'another of the great manufacturing towns', its glass and copper houses seconded by a sailcloth industry.[34] Frequently, the higher priced output of larger cities was complemented by the cheaper, lower quality production of the small towns in the area. These places often served as conduits of capital and materials to the domestic industry of the countryside. On the other hand, in the West Riding rural industry seems to have enjoyed a more symbiotic relationship with local towns, some industrialising townships acquiring sub-urban functions.[35]

Especially notable, during the eighteenth century manufacturing specialisms were not confined to the heartland of industrialising regions. They also developed on their periphery: for instance, the growth of textiles in the West Riding was paralleled in some of the small towns of the North Riding. New industries also blossomed on their own in small places away from the industrial mainstream. Thus Tewkesbury from the Stuart period had a prosperous hosiery industry and Witney in western Oxfordshire its blanket trade.[36] At Banbury the old shoemaking industry gave way to the manufacture of plush, whilst at Kettering (Northants.) there developed a flourishing worsted industry employing up to 1,000 framework-knitters – perhaps half the population.[37] The growth of the royal navy and state funding led to the development in Kent and Essex of several small dockyard towns at Harwich, Sheerness and Strood, in the slipstream of the

[33] M. B. Rowlands, *Masters and Men* (Manchester, 1975); P. J. Bemrose, 'Newcastle under Lyne. Its contribution to the growth of the North Staffordshire pottery industry 1650–1800' (MA thesis, University of Keele, 1972); also J. Ward, *The Borough of Stoke-upon-Trent* (London, 1843); J. Prest, *The Industrial Revolution in Coventry* (Oxford, 1960), pp. 44–5.

[34] J. Stobart, 'An eighteenth-century revolution? Investigating urban growth in North-West England 1664–1801', *UH*, 23 (1996), 35–47; J. Langton, *Geographical Change and Industrial Revolution* (Cambridge, 1979); T. Maurice, *Memoirs of the Author of Indian Antiquities* (London, 1819–22), part II, pp. 80–1.

[35] J. Nichols, *The History and Antiquities of Hinckley* (London, 1782), p. 28; P. Hudson and S. King, 'Rural industrialising townships and urban links in eighteenth century Yorkshire', in P. Clark and P. Corfield, eds., *Industry and Urbanisation in Eighteenth Century England* (Leicester, 1994), pp. 41–63.

[36] J. McDonnell, ed., *A History of Helmsley, Rievaulx and District* (York, 1963), pp. 172–3; N. Raven, 'De-industrialisation and the urban response: the small towns of the North Riding of Yorkshire c.1790–1850', in R. Weedon and A. Milne, eds., *Aspects of English Small Towns in the Eighteenth and Nineteenth Centuries* (Leicester, 1993), pp. 50 *et seq.*; T. Rath, 'The Tewkesbury hosiery industry', *Textile History*, 7 (1976), 140–8; A. Plummer, *The Witney Blanket Industry* (London, 1934), ch. 1.

[37] *VCH*, Oxfordshire, x, p. 64; A. Randall, *The Kettering Worsted Industry of the Eighteenth Century* (reprinted from *Northamptonshire Past and Present*, 4 (1972)), pp. 3, 15.

great shipyard centres at Chatham, Deptford and Woolwich.[38] Also in the metropolitan area, food processing towns boomed, among them Abingdon and Henley, key suppliers of the metropolitan market: Henley's inhabitants, it was said, 'are generally bargemen and by carrying away much corn and good store of wood . . . in their barges to London do enrich the neighbourhood'. Buckinghamshire's small towns like High Wycombe made niche products including furniture for smart London consumers.[39]

Towards the end of the eighteenth century older specialisms (particularly textile trades) came under mounting attack in southern and eastern England from more mechanised production in the North. The decline of textiles in East Anglia's small towns is well documented, their industrial problems exacerbated by the growing profitability of agriculture. Yet decline was not always inevitable. In north Essex a number of small communities, deprived of their clothing trades, moved into silk weaving when that industry abandoned the capital because of high costs.[40] In Bedfordshire the exodus of industry from London led to the growth or consolidation of small town specialities, such as hat making at Luton and Dunstable.[41]

Even when industrial crafts failed to prosper there were other avenues for specialisation. Service towns, already significant by the time of Blome, continued to multiply in number and importance during the Georgian era catering for the enlarged urban and rural elites. Some of the larger small towns became fully fashionable social towns, and offered a range of facilities for the county well-to-do: new brick-built houses, local newspapers, piped water, town walks, race courses and stands, assembly rooms, bowling greens, a cluster of retail shops – as well as social entertainments. Beverley, Lichfield, Warwick, Ludlow and Stukeley's Stamford all came to thrive as Georgian gentry towns.[42] At Ludlow in the 1760s

[38] C. W. Chalklin, 'The towns', in Armstrong, ed., *Economy of Kent*, pp. 209–10, 213, 222; T. M. Harris, 'Government and urban development in Kent: the case of the royal naval dockyard town of Sheerness', *Archaeologia Cantiana*, 101 (1984), 245–76; L. T. Weaver, *The Harwich Story* (Dovercourt, 1975), chs. 6, 12, 16.

[39] J. Townsend, *A History of Abingdon* (London, 1910), p. 156; J. Brome, *Travels over England, Scotland and Wales* (London, 1707), pp. 99–100; M. Reed, 'Decline and recovery in a provincial urban network: Buckinghamshire towns 1350–1800', in M. Reed, ed., *English Towns in Decline 1350–1800* (Leicester, 1986).

[40] N. Evans, *The East Anglian Linen Industry* (Aldershot, 1985), chs. 5–6; N. Raven 'City and countryside: London and the market town economies of southern England' (paper at the Economic History Conference, Nottingham University, 1994).

[41] J. G. Dony, *A History of the Straw Hat Industry* (Luton, 1942), chs. 2–3; L. Schwarz, 'The de-industrialisation of eighteenth-century London' (unpublished paper at ESRC colloquium on Industry and Urbanisation in the Eighteenth Century, University College, London, 1993).

[42] Cf. M. Reed, 'The cultural role of small towns in England 1600–1800', in Clark, ed., *Small Towns*, ch. 6; *VCH*, County of York, East Riding, VI, pp. 112–18, 131–2; *VCH*, Staffordshire, XIV, pp. 21–4; *VCH*, Warwickshire, VIII, pp. 507–8, 511–13; A. Rogers, ed., *The Making of Stamford* (Leicester, 1965), pp. 61, 72–3, 83 *et seq.*

gentlemen and professions comprised nearly 10 per cent of householders, and the dependent food and drink traders another 14 per cent. Thirty years later Beverley was 'chiefly supported by the genteel private families that reside there in continuance'.[43]

Gentry towns of this kind sometimes tried to add a spa or mineral spring to their fashionable bow, but most spa and later seaside towns were specialist centres, either new towns like Epsom, Buxton, Harrogate, Tunbridge Wells and Margate, or towns drawn from the bottom ranks of the small town hierarchy – thus Cheltenham, Matlock and Lyme Regis. Some of the early centres were close to the metropolis, but later ones were scattered across the regions, in response to rising provincial prosperity, improved communications and that fashionable yearning for the picturesque uplands. With their limited social facilities and often poor communications such places could only attract gentle visitors for a few weeks in the summer months.[44] Winter at Brighton was said to be 'very disagreeable' in the later eighteenth century as sociable activity and the population melted away. Unlike many of the fast growth industrialising towns, most small leisure towns stayed select and small until the impact of steamships and railways in the second quarter of the nineteenth century.[45]

A few of the seaside resorts were also ports but in general small ports prospered in their own right during the long eighteenth century. If, like Bideford, they were pushed out of overseas trade by larger competititors, they found plenty of business in the booming coastal commerce. Maldon shipped agricultural produce for the London market and supplied imports to central Essex, while Boston served as the leading entrepôt for coastal trade in Lincolnshire.[46]

The growing volume of inland trade and transport improvements led to the increased transport role of small towns. Northallerton in the North Riding was described by Roger Gale about 1740 as 'no corporation, neither is there any particular manufacture carried on here; [but] it is a great thorough-fare to the north, with good inns'. On the Gloucestershire border, Lechlade prospered after the upper reaches of the Thames were cleared for traffic, Bridgnorth did well from

43 I owe this information from the Ludlow Easter Books to the kindness of Dr Sue Wright. K. A. MacMahon, ed., *Beverley Corporation Minute Books (1707–1835)* (Yorkshire Archaeological Society, Record Series, 122, 1958), p. xxi.

44 For more see below, pp. 776 *et seq.*; also J. K. Walton, *The English Seaside Resort* (Leicester, 1983), chs. 2–3.

45 W. C. Ford, 'Diary of William Greene, 1778', *Massachusetts Historical Society Proceedings*, 54 (1920–1), 86; J. Whyman, 'A Hanoverian watering place: Margate before the railway', in A. M. Everitt, ed., *Perspectives in English Urban History* (London, 1973), pp. 138–60; P. E. Jones, 'Bathing facilities in Bangor, 1800 to the present day', *Caernarvonshire Historical Society Transactions*, 36 (1975), 124 *et seq.*

46 E. Starr, 'Bideford: a directory survey of occupations 1793–1850' (Certificate dissertation, Centre for Urban History, University of Leicester, 1991); J. R. Smith, 'The borough of Maldon 1688–1768' (MPhil thesis, University of Leicester, 1981), pp. 32–7.

Severn river trade and service activity (see Plate 27), while the *Yorkshire Memorandum Book* in the 1780s drew attention to small towns like Keighley, Yarm, Snaith, Skipton and Selby, which had benefited from river navigation.[47] Selby and Pocklington not only gained from river improvement but from canals, like the Leeds and Liverpool, and a series of turnpikes. In both places townspeople seem to have taken the initiative in some of the schemes, compared to the more passive attitude at Market Weighton, which did less well.[48] Similarly, Loughborough gained and maintained a commercial head-start on other Leicestershire towns after 1777 because of its canal link to the Trent navigation system (and other canal links later); its role as a major distribution centre in the shire yielded substantial dividends for the town's industry. On the other hand, there were relatively few specialist transport centres before 1800 – only a few canal towns like Stourport, Ellesmere and Runcorn (with Goole in the 1820s).[49] At the end of our period these began to be overshadowed by the advent of railway towns such as Wolverton in Buckinghamshire and Swindon, a declining market town transformed after 1840 into the booming locomotive workshop of the Great Western Railway.[50]

As well as the advance of specialist service towns of different kinds, the service sector of small town economies continued to thrive. Even towns which did not become fully fledged gentry centres could often claim a programme of cultural and social activities to attract in local gentry (and their families) for the day: thus the Lancashire landowner Nicholas Blundell's diary is full of references to short visits to neighbouring Ormskirk for the bowling green, club meetings, and more informal, boozy socialising at the inns and fairs. Boosted also by the expansion of inland trade and road traffic, inns increased in number, size and importance; for instance, at places like Kingston, Chelmsford, Stamford, Grantham and Sittingbourne.[51] Many places had small, but powerful, clusters of attorneys who sometimes dominated the governing body; schoolteachers were also increasingly

[47] W. C. Lukis, ed., *The Family Memoirs of the Rev. William Stukeley, M.D.*, vol. III (Surtees Society, 80, 1887), pp. 338–9; A. Williams, *Lechlade* (Cirencester, 1888), p. 9; *The Yorkshire Memorandum Book* (York, 1782), pp. 15, 21, 22, 24.

[48] I am indebted for these data to my student Mr Roger Bellingham.

[49] J. Griffiths, 'A study of the economic development of three Leicestershire small towns – Loughborough, Lutterworth and Melton Mowbray' (Certificate dissertation, Centre for Urban History, University of Leicester, 1994), pp. 11–12, 20–1; C. Hadfield, *The Canals of the East Midlands* (Newton Abbot, 1970), pp. 36–9, 82–4; J. D. Porteous, *Canal Ports* (London, 1977), pp. 50–2.

[50] M. Reed, *The Buckinghamshire Landscape* (London, 1979), pp. 232, 238–9; L. V. Grinsell *et al.*, *Studies in the History of Swindon* (Swindon, 1950), pp. 94–104.

[51] J. J. Bagley, ed., *The Great Diurnal of Nicholas Blundell*, vol. I (Record Society of Lancashire and Cheshire, 110, 1968), pp. 58, 110, 175, 179, 184, 196 *et passim*; J. Whitter, 'A survey of the economic and administrative life of Kingston-upon-Thames' (MSc (econ.) thesis, London School of Economics, 1932–3), p. 235; M. R. Innes, 'Chelmsford: the evolution of a county town' (MA thesis, University of London, 1951), pp. 363–4; A. M. Everitt, 'The English urban inn 1560–1760', in Everitt, ed., *Perspectives*, pp. 95–7.

ubiquitous. Other professional men, such as physicians and booksellers, tended to be located mainly in the larger centres. From Wells Claver Morris gave medical advice to virtually all the landed families within a thirty mile radius. In Norfolk booksellers were located on a more or less regular basis in nine of the county's thirty or so small towns – mostly in bigger fashionable places such as Thetford and East Dereham.[52] Other kinds of retail shops appear in virtually all towns, creating a class of modestly affluent shopkeepers like Abraham Dent of Kirkby Stephen, whose family grocery and mercery business was combined with the wine trade, hosiery manufacture and dealing in bills. This growth of the retail sector was partially offset by the decline of traditional fairs and open markets; perhaps forty to fifty small centres lost them entirely between the 1690s and 1790s, especially in the South-West and East Anglia. And while these traditional urban institutions decayed, there came a parallel penetration of general stores into much of the countryside, producing further competition for small towns.[53] But in other directions the special status of small towns was confirmed and consolidated towards the end of our period through an accession of administrative activities. In Leicestershire, for instance, Lutterworth became the venue for local petty sessions and the county court, and also acquired parish and union workhouses, a post office and, later on, the district police station.[54]

North of the border the later seventeenth century and early decades of the eighteenth may have been a time of difficulty for many small towns. Various topographical reports, including Daniel Defoe's *Account and Description* in the 1730s, present a generally gloomy picture, except for a circle of small centres in the Glasgow and Stirling area and patchy specialisation in the east coast shires, where small towns supplied linen, fish, salt and foodstuffs for the Edinburgh market. Elsewhere, the story is often one of communities depending on general markets and fairs, and of old staple industries in decay (often due to competition from England); small towns in the borders experienced serious setbacks.[55] A more

[52] K. R. Adey, 'Aspects of the history of the town of Stafford 1590–1710' (MA thesis, University of Keele, 1971), pp. 60, 65, 67; E. Hobhouse, ed., *The Diary of a West Country Physician AD 1684–1726* (London, 1934), p. 27; T. Fawcett, 'Eighteenth-century Norfolk booksellers: a survey and register', *Transactions of the Cambridge Bibliographical Society*, 6 (1972–6), 1–18.

[53] I. Mitchell, 'The development of urban retailing 1700–1815', in Clark, ed., *Transformation of English Provincial Towns*, ch. 8; C. Shammas, *The Pre-Industrial Consumer in England and America* (Oxford, 1990), ch. 8; T. S. Willan, *An Eighteenth-Century Shopkeeper* (Manchester, 1970); A. Dyer, 'The market towns of southern England 1500–1700', *SHist.*, 1 (1979), 129; J. A. Chartres, 'The marketing of agriculture produce', in J. Thirsk, ed., *Ag.HEW*, vol. v(2) (Cambridge, 1985), pp. 409–12.

[54] J. McCormack, 'Lutterworth: a comparative study of economic and social structure in Leicestershire' (Certificate dissertation, Centre for Urban History, University of Leicester, 1992), p. 2.

[55] D. Defoe, *A Tour through the Whole Island of Great Britain*, ed. G. D. H. Cole and D. C. Browning (London, 1962), vol. II, pp. 291, 324–6, 328–9, 360, 377. Various descriptions of towns in the 1720s are printed in A. Mitchell, ed., *Geographical Collections relating to Scotland* (Scottish History Society, 1st series, 51–2, 1906–7); there are only a few references to industrial specialisms.

buoyant scene is described by the first *Statistical Account* in the 1790s. The growth of economic specialisation was particularly impressive in the Lowlands, in the central and western areas around Glasgow. Small towns, including Galston, Renfrew, Lanark, Lochwinnoch, Hamilton, East Kilbride, Strathaven and Rutherglen, developed as major centres of assorted branches of the textile industry, manufacturing stockings, cottons, linen, muslin and carpets. Glasgow merchants provided the capital for local developments and marketed the output. Other specialist industries also proliferated in the area, among them glass making at Dumbarton and Clackmannan, and coal mining at Saltcoats. Industrial specialisms evolved in other regions too, although in a less integrated way. Lothian and Fife saw weaving at Leslie, sugar making at Burntisland, coal mining at Bathgate, textiles and mining at Dysart and linen at Dunfermline, Kirkcaldy and Coupar Angus. The linen industry benefited from heavy investment by the government Board of Trustees for Fisheries and Manufactures. Among the small towns of the north-east production developed at Arbroath, while Huntley had its yarn and cotton traders. In the Highlands and Islands Rothesay on Bute employed many young and old people in spinning, one cotton mill having 300 workers.[56]

Not all Scottish centres acquired industrial specialisms. Various small towns like Culross and Crail lost their traditional crafts. Problems such as this were particularly common in the border counties: Sanquhar had a declining stocking industry; Coldstream was destitute of manufactures; and Coldingham suffered out-migration for similar reasons. Other centres expanded their traditional port role, like Dunbar and Jedburgh engaged in the export and coastal trades. Yet others, especially in the north, developed more commercial fisheries, with Cullen exporting fish as far as London, and Nairn selling salmon to Aberdeen for export. Trade was also boosted by waves of road construction. Nearer the major cities a number of small towns built up specialist provisioning markets; Falkirk became a great cattle market and Dalkeith a large grain centre supplying Glasgow and Paisley.[57] In the 1730s Defoe had remarked upon the general absence of social activities, but by the turn of the century a sizeable service sector can be identified in many towns, incorporating inns, professional men and the like. However, fewer Scottish small towns became social centres, at least before 1800. Stranraer had a cluster of resident gentry in the 1790s; Forfar was 'a place for resort for freeholders for the enjoyment of society in clubs and assemblies'; but other traditional centres were content to fall back on their old administrative and

[56] J. Sinclair, ed., *The Statistical Account of Scotland* (Edinburgh, 1791–9). For the rise of the linen industry at Kirkcaldy: E. P. Dennison and R. Coleman, eds., *Historic Kirkcaldy* (Edinburgh, 1995), pp. 18–19. C. McWilliam, *Scottish Townscape* (London, 1975), p. 67. For an account of the growth of the linen and other manufactures: D. Turnock, *The Historical Geography of Scotland since 1707* (Cambridge, 1982), pp. 52–61.

[57] Sinclair, ed., *Statistical Account*; G. R. Curtis, 'Roads and bridges in the Scottish Highlands . . . 1725–1925', *Proceedings of the Society of Antiquaries of Scotland*, 110 (1978–80), 476 *et seq.*

educational functions (St Andrews as a university town, Kirkcudbright as a legal and customs town). Only one or two places, such as Portpatrick and Moffat, started to develop as spas. Outside the Glasgow region, many minor burghs of barony failed to specialise.[58]

In Wales urban specialisation was even more regionally specific, mainly concentrated in the southern shires. In North Wales sociable activities surfaced at places like Holywell, Conway, Ruthin, Denbigh and Beaumaris, but Wrexham alone seems to have become a lively social centre, building on its long-established commercial and craft importance in the area. Only after about 1800 does Bangor grow up as a seaside town. In middle Wales most small towns remained sleepy, looking, as ever, to the towns of the English border counties for commercial and cultural services; local crafts, as at Brecon, were in decline.[59] This is in sharp contrast to south-east Wales, which saw a mounting number of small towns prosper through industrial, commercial and service expansion – boosted by the spread of canals. The rapid growth of the ironworks around Merthyr Tydfil from the 1760s is well known: by 1801 the community had over 7,000 inhabitants though its urban functions were slow to develop. Newport imported and exported iron; Neath became an important mining and coal export town; Cardiff followed suit.[60] Inland places like Cowbridge and Monmouth won fashionable acclaim as social centres. Mrs Boscawen on a visit in 1770 to the latter lauded the 'public breakfasts of 400, races, public dinners, balls at the townhall; in short *divertimenti sans fin et sans cesse*'; though other English visitors by 1800 were more critical.[61] Broadly speaking, the burgeoning small towns of South Wales appeared closer to the urban network of the English South-West than to the rest of Wales.

In such ways and at differing speeds British small towns were caught up in the general process of urban transformation in the Georgian period. Yet they also continued to experience special problems and challenges, not least the powerful competition from other towns, both large and small. Minor towns which had

[58] Defoe, *Tour*, II, p. 324; E. P. Dennison and R. Coleman, eds., *Historic Dunblane* (Edinburgh, 1997), p. 43; E. P. Dennison and R. Coleman, eds., *Historic Stranraer* (Edinburgh, 1995), pp. 20–1.

[59] *Adams' Weekly Courant* [Chester], 31 Jan., 7 Nov., 14 Nov. 1775, 5 Jan., 23 Feb. 1779 *et passim*; Pryce and Edwards, 'Social structure of the embryonic town', 49–50, 55–6; W. Minchinton, 'The place of Brecknock in the industrialisation of South Wales', *Brycheiniog*, 7 (1961), 3–4.

[60] M. Atkinson and C. Baber, *The Growth and Decline of the South Wales Iron Industry 1760–1880* (Cardiff, 1987), esp. pp. 2–11; M. I. Williams, 'Observations on the population changes in Glamorgan, 1800–1900', *Glamorgan Historian*, 1 (1963), 109–10, 112–13; D. M. Rees, The industrialisation of Glamorgan, *ibid.*, 17–24. For the growth of textiles at Newtown see Williams, 'A case study of Newtown', 63 *et seq*.

[61] P. Jenkins, *The Making of a Ruling Class* (Cambridge, 1983), pp. 247–8, 267–8; J. Byng, *The Torrington Diaries*, ed. C. B. Andrews (London, 1970), vol. I, pp. 20–2; C. Aspinall-Oglander, *Admiral's Widow* (London, 1942), p. 29. T. Lewis, ed., *Extracts of the Journals and Correspondence of Miss Berry* (London, 1865), vol. II, pp. 96–8.

failed to consolidate their position through specialist activity were particularly vulnerable. In Yorkshire the little town of Howden was eclipsed by Selby and the new canal port of Goole. In the near hinterland of Leicester the minor market centres of Hallaton and Billesdon disappeared in the face of the rising commercial success of the county town.[62] Chester's developing role as a shopping town may have blighted lesser market towns in the western part of Cheshire. Wetherby was overshadowed by the larger towns of the Vale of York, while Grimsby was affected not just by fierce competition from Hull, but by the decay of its haven, becoming 'a little poor town not a quarter so great as heretofore'.[63] That other natural disaster, fire, could also have a major effect on small towns, though the spread of insurance, fire acts and building regulations helped most communities to combat and overcome the problem; indeed the classical rebuilding of Warwick and Blandford after serious fires contributed to their rise as fashionable gentry towns.[64]

Relations with the countryside remained much more critical for small towns than their larger counterparts. While the proportion of the small town's inhabitants engaged in agricultural occupations steadily diminished, the rural hinterland still played a key role in its development. We have already noted how small towns regularly had intimate links with domestic industries in the countryside. At Hinckley in Leicestershire the 1,000 stocking frames in the town were complemented by another 200 in the adjoining villages, many of them owned by Hinckley masters. Around the end of the eighteenth century, as rural crafts came under pressure from more mechanised production and agricultural specialisation, such trades frequently migrated into local small towns; in north Buckinghamshire and south Northamptonshire, for instance, lace making became concentrated in towns like Olney, which retains remnants of the workshops in its back streets.[65]

Again, country landowners wielded a powerful economic influence in small towns. At Neath in Glamorgan Sir Henry Mackworth took over the borough's lands and mineral rights and was instrumental in turning coal production into a major export business. In Yorkshire local gentry were involved in transport improvements affecting small towns, investing heavily in canal schemes, which boosted interregional trade. In Scotland landowners were no less powerful. At Inverary the dukes of Argyll effectively reconstructed the town, and established new linen, woollen and carpet industries; at Cumnock the earls of Dumfries tried to develop mines and ceramics; at Hamilton the noble family sought to

62 Noble, 'Growth and development of country towns', p. 407; Gräf, 'Leicestershire small towns', 106

63 Mitchell, 'The development of urban retailing', pp. 261–2; R. Unwin, *Wetherby* (Leeds,1987), p. 80; C. Jackson, ed., *The Diary of Abraham de la Pryme* (Surtees Society, 54, 1869), pp. 153–5.

64 P. Borsay, *The English Urban Renaissance* (Oxford, 1989), p. 46.

65 Gräf, 'Leicestershire small towns', 102, 103; Reed, 'Decline and recovery'.

transform both the economy and the townscape.[66] Elsewhere, landowners planted new planned settlements some of which turned into small towns. In addition to new manufactures and commercial developments, landowners actively promoted other specialisms. At Buxton the duke of Devonshire, who owned the spa's wells, planned the building of the Crescent, crowned by its splendid assembly room. In Dorset Swanage was designed as a seaside town by William Morton Pitt.[67] As already noted, the patronage of local gentry, quite often spending several weeks a year in the bigger places, or riding in for the day for shopping and leisure activities, helped sustain the service sector in many market centres.

By the end of the eighteenth century, however, this continued dependence, greater or lesser, on the countryside was proving problematic for many smaller towns. Rising agricultural productivity, the decay of rural crafts and the growth of village populations caused mounting rural poverty, the stagnation of local demand and an influx of country poor into town. Meantime, landowners began to spend less time there, preferring the attractions of their newly improved country houses or, with better communications, visits to larger and more fashionable cities, increasingly (after the Napoleonic wars) abroad.[68]

None the less, at the start of the nineteenth century the prosperity and success of British small towns was striking, certainly compared to their counterparts in many other parts of Europe. A detailed analysis of the town descriptions in the *Universal British Directory* for the 1790s[69] shows the growth of multi-functional activities, with service, manufacturing and port activities complementing marketing or distribution roles (see Table 22.7). Just over half of the English small towns listed (325) had a spread of functions, a substantial increase on the later seventeenth century. The proportion was highest – over two-thirds – in the West Midlands and the North-West. The East Midlands by contrast had less than a quarter in this category, the rest of its small towns being single function centres (predominantly markets). However, the picture was complex. The old specialist regions identified by Blome – East Anglia, the South-East and South-West – all retained quite high levels of multi-functionality. On the other hand, industrialisation (and de-industrialisation) was starting to have an impact. In East Anglia

66 D. T. Williams, 'The port books of Swansea and Neath 1709–19', *Archaeologia Cambrensis*, 95 (1940), 197 *et seq.*; Noble, 'Growth and development of country towns', pp. 271–5; I. G. Lindsay and M. Cosh, *Inverary and the Dukes of Argyll* (Edinburgh, 1973), p. 145 *et passim*; E. P. Dennison and R. Coleman, eds., *Historic Cumnock* (Edinburgh, 1995), pp. 18–19; E. P. Dennison and R. Coleman, eds., *Historic Hamilton* (Edinburgh, 1996), pp. 25 *et seq.*

67 I. E. Burton, 'The Buxton Crescent', *Derbyshire Miscellany*, 7 (1974–6), 238–43; Clark, 'Changes in the pattern', p. 77.

68 J. D. Marshall and C. A. Dyhouse, 'Social transition in Kendal and Westmorland', *NHist.*, 12 (1976), 131.

69 *Universal British Directory* (London, 1790–8). For the various problems of this directory see C. W. Chilton, '"The Universal British Directory" – a warning', *Local Historian*, 15 (1982), 144–6.

Table 22.7 *Primary functions of English small towns in the 1790s*

Region	*n*	Single function %	Multi-functional: primary function Market %	Port %	Service %	Industrial %
East Anglia	25	52.0	50.0	25.0	16.7	8.3
Midlands						
East	36	77.8	75.0	0.0	0.0	25.0
West	32	28.1	73.9	0.0	0.0	26.1
North						
northern	29	72.4	50.0	37.5	0.0	12.5
North-West	29	31.0	15.0	0.0	15.0	70.0
Yorkshire	30	76.7	50.0	12.5	0.0	37.5
South-East	76	44.8	59.5	16.7	2.3	21.5
South-West	68	20.6	37.0	29.6	3.8	29.6

three-quarters of the small towns (both single and multiple function) were identified as primarily market towns with a number of the others ports; only one or two were described as principally industrial centres. At the other end of the spectrum, in the North-West, over three-quarters of the total (single and multi-function centres) were categorised as primarily industrial towns, and only about one in eight as market towns. Even in the industrialising regions, however, the picture was sometimes blurred. In the West Midlands the proportion of industrial centres was not much higher than for the South-West despite the latter's slowly declining textile industries. The South-East maintained a broad mix of marketing, port, service and manufacturing centres.

It is possible that our evidence for the 1790s may be somewhat out of date: the *Universal British Directory* tended to rely on cannibalising earlier directories. The sample is also incomplete, excluding in particular those very new growth centres evolving at the end of the eighteenth century, especially in the West Midlands. Yet at face value the data suggest the complicated, partial nature of economic change at this time. Regional differentiation was probably accelerating, but the general prosperity of Georgian small towns ensured some continuing degree of cohesion in the urban system until the start of the nineteenth century.

During the following decades even those small town industries which had flourished through the previous century were coming under pressure. This was particularly a problem outside the main industrialising regions. Thus Tewkesbury's hosiery trade decayed, stranded technically by its distance from the main manufacturing centres in the Midlands. Even in the industrialising regions minor towns that failed to move towards mechanised production risked being side-lined from expansion. Poulton le Fylde in Lancashire stagnated from the 1820s, while Atherston suffered from the concentration of the ribbon-making and hatting industries at Nuneaton and Coventry.[70] Small towns on the periphery of industrial districts were particularly vulnerable. In the North and East Ridings, for instance, several small towns, active in the textile industry up to the 1820s and 1830s, subsequently went into decline. Regional concentration was taking place. Even towns which managed to attract new industries to replace old ones, like the north Essex towns, experienced a high turnover of businesses and the limited durability of firms.[71]

Small town economies suffered not only fierce industrial competition but other difficulties. In the 1820s and 1830s problems in the financial sector affected numerous country banks whose main offices or branch offices were located in the bigger small towns. The accelerating pace of transport change also took its toll. Already before the railways, improvements in coaching curtailed the number of intermediate stops required and this had adverse consequences for a number of small towns. But the advent of the railways, spreading across the country from the 1830s, was much more serious. The earliest and most important waves of railway construction were highly selective, marked by a strong regional bias. In East Anglia nearly half of all the small towns had failed to acquire a railway connection by the 1840s, with the figure as high as two-thirds in Norfolk. In the West Midlands, by contrast, less than a third of small towns were omitted (the highest level in outlying Shropshire). The Home Counties came out even better; only 31.4 per cent of small towns were not linked in this way. Networking here was boosted by the frenetic activity of the metropolitan railway companies and strong demand from prospective commuters. In Surrey only 6.0 per cent of all small towns were without a station, though the proportion was higher in the outer areas of the region.[72] Railways both responded to regional and local economic trends and exaggerated them. Even well-established small towns had their marginality finalised by the absence of a railway link. Thus Atherston's defeat in its struggle against nearby Nuneaton was underlined by the latter's railway connection to London.[73]

Such changes are in some measure documented by trade directory descrip-

[70] Rath, 'Tewkesbury hosiery industry', 149–51; D. Foster, 'Poulton- le-Fylde: a nineteenth-century market town', *Transactions of the Historic Society of Lancashire and Cheshire*, 127 (1977), 92–4; W. McGarvey, 'The demographic and occupational structure of small towns in Nottinghamshire and Warwickshire, 1801–50' (Certificate dissertation, Centre for Urban History, University of Leicester, 1992), pp. 2–3, 12–13.

[71] Raven, 'De-industrialisation and the urban response', pp. 50–67; Raven, 'City and countryside'.

[72] Williams, 'A case study of Newtown', 64. Calculations on railway coverage from *The Parliamentary Gazetteer of England and Wales* (London, 1844).

[73] McCormack, 'Lutterworth', p. 20; McGarvey, 'Demographic and occupational structure', pp. 2–3; also Noble, 'Growth and development of country towns', pp. 241–2.

Table 22.8 *Primary functions of English small towns c. 1850*

Region	*n*	Single function %	Multi-functional: primary function Market %	Port %	Service %	Industrial %
East Anglia	30	10.0	76.8	10.0	6.6	6.6
Midlands						
East	49	40.8	91.8	2.0	6.2	0.0
West	32	9.4	75.0	0.0	0.0	25.0
North						
northern	15	53.3	20.0	26.7	0.0	53.3
North-West	41	17.0	9.8	4.9	4.9	80.4
Yorkshire	24	25.0	4.1	0.0	8.4	87.5
South-East	123	24.4	62.6	12.2	8.9	16.3
South-West	72	18.1	84.7	9.7	2.8	2.8

tions for towns about 1850, just after the end of our period (see Table 22.8).[74] Comparing the leading functions or activities of well over 300 small towns, we see a rising proportion of marketing centres in the less dynamic regions: over three-quarters in East Anglia, higher still in the East Midlands. Most striking was the collapse of the textile industry in the South-West, where four-fifths of all our towns were now designated as primarily market centres – roughly twice the level of the 1790s. Predictably, in the North, North-West and Yorkshire (West Riding) high proportions were listed as principally manufacturing and mining towns. Once again the West Midlands is a puzzle, given its apparently low proportion of manufacturing centres, and more work needs to be done to try and explain it.

On top of these regional divisions, what is also noticeable is the continuing advance of multi-functional activity among our English small towns: there was a steady decline of towns described as single activity centres – down to a quarter of the sample, from a third in the 1790s. In part this may an artefact of better directory coverage, but it also probably mirrors the reality on the ground. When small towns prospered as manufacturing centres they extended their range of support sectors, not least services. Paradoxically, when they declined industrially, they sought to compensate by developing alternative areas such as services.

This may help to explain the preliminary evidence from a large-scale investigation of small town occupations for East Anglia and the West Midlands in the 1830s (see Table 22.9). Occupational data are notoriously difficult to handle,

[74] Based on town description data collected from nineteen trade directories for England covering the years 1844–58 including national, regional and county directories.

Table 22.9 *Occupations in small towns in East Anglia and the West Midlands c. 1830*

Occupational group	East Anglia (%)	West Midlands (%)
Agriculture, etc.	1.6	0.8
Fishing	0.0	0.0
Mining	0.6	0.4
Building	7.3	6.5
Manufacturing	34.8	34.3
Transport	1.4	1.1
Dealing	28.3	33.6
Industrial service	3.1	2.5
Labour	0.0	0.0
Professional and public service	13.4	11.9
Service	0.8	1.1
Independent	6.6	2.7
Dependent	0.0	0.0
Unspecified	2.1	5.1
n	10,035	8,830

while to compound the diffficulties our source, trade directories, provide only a partial, uneven picture of the urban economy, though the data may have a greater degree of internal consistency and reliability than has sometimes been thought. Here occupational data have been used to show the range of economic activities in small towns not the scale: in other words it is horizontal information not vertical. Data have been categorised into classes according to an edited version of the Booth–Armstrong occupational schema. What one finds is a considerable, perhaps surprising, degree of convergence in the overall structure of small town economies in both the dynamic West Midlands and more sluggish East Anglia. Manufacturing occupations in the two regions were broadly comparable, with dealing slightly greater in the West Midlands, confirming the suggestion of complementary sectoral developments. The professional and public service sectors were likewise on a similar level. On the margins one can see a higher level of agricultural and independent (rentier) occupations in East Anglia, but such differences were limited.[75]

More work needs to be done on other regions and different levels of small

[75] Occupational data derived from Pigot and Slater directories for Cambridgeshire and Huntingdonshire; Pigot directories for Norfolk and Suffolk (all 1830) (East Anglia); Pigot directories for Shopshire, Staffordshire, Warwickshire, Worcestershire (1835) (West Midlands). For the original Booth–Armstrong schema see W. A. Armstrong, 'The uses of information about occupation', in E. A. Wrigley, ed., *Nineteenth-Century Society* (Cambridge, 1972), pp. 191–310.

town. Moreover, aggregate data of this sort are unable to unravel the great occupational diversity of individual places, understating the changes occurring within particular sectors of the local economy. In towns affected by declining staple trades there was often a desperate search for new industries, quite often those geared to the agrarian economy. A number of small towns in eastern England attempted to establish agricultural machinery trades, though only the bigger centres were successful. Other country towns saw the growth of wholesale brewing, taking over the domestic and public house trade. By the 1840s consumers across southern England were buying beer from wholesale brewers based in larger and small towns, men who frequently controlled chains of tied houses in the local hinterland.[76] In the East Midlands a number of places, such as Melton Mowbray, acquired the trappings of specialist hunting towns. Elsewhere, towns increasingly relied on more traditional industries, tailoring, shoemaking and so on, which catered for local demand, probably taking away business from the village artisans of the area. Overall, our evidence underlines the relatively sophisticated nature of the small town economy by the start of Victoria's reign; in the middling and larger places at least, retailing and professional trades provided fairly solid pillars of the urban economy, thereby helping to safeguard its stability, even if industrial specialisms started to decline.[77]

In conclusion, the long eighteenth century saw sustained expansion for many English small towns, as they enlarged their economic role to embrace manufacturing, commercial and service functions and specialisms. A growing measure of regional differentiation is evident, confirming the demographic trends observed earlier. Small town networks in the industrialising Midlands, Yorkshire, the North and North West were particularly dynamic and increasingly integrated, as were those in western central Scotland around Glasgow and in south-west Wales. At the same time, a growing rump of minor towns, particularly in the more agrarian regions, failed to retain their earlier specialisms and often experienced decay in the Victorian period.

(iv) URBAN SOCIETY AND CULTURE

The urban identity of Hanoverian small towns was shaped not merely by their expansive economies, but by their enhanced social and cultural significance, in considerable part defined by their provision of fashionable leisure activities and entertainments for the wealthier classes. By George III's reign numerous English market towns were kitted out with a range of social activities – plays, assemblies, musical activities, clubs and societies. As in bigger towns, assemblies became *de*

[76] P. Matthias, *The Brewing Industry in England* (Cambridge, 1959), pp. 128–9 *et passim*.

[77] Gräf, 'Leicestershire small towns', 103. See also the important discussion here in S. Royle, 'The development of small towns in Britain *c.* 1851–1951', in M. Daunton, ed., *The Cambridge Urban History of Britain*, vol. III: *1840–1950* (Cambridge, 2000), ch. 9.

rigeur, attended especially by gentlewomen desperate, like Jane Austen's Bennet girls, to escape the monotony, gloom and dirt of the countryside. East Anglia had a sequence of subscription assemblies and concerts, together with music society meetings, held in about ten of the principal small towns.[78] In the East Midlands Spalding, Stamford, Peterborough, Boston and other market towns could all muster learned and antiquarian societies of different kinds, whilst the market towns of Northamptonshire and Oxfordshire saw a flowering of horticultural feasts and singing competitions.[79] During the late eighteenth century at least sixty book clubs and literary societies gathered in small towns across the country, with a clustering in the Midlands. In 1781 over fifty English small towns had race meetings, often, like those at Ludlow, important social occasions.[80]

In Wales social activities were on a more modest scale, though we find dancing assemblies, hunts, prosecution societies, meetings of Druids and social clubs in the small market centres of North Wales. Tory and Jacobite clubs were prominent at Wrexham and in several small towns of the south-west – these subsequently dressed up as masonic lodges.[81] In Scotland likewise there was a strong presence of masonic lodges in small towns by 1800, together with political and benefit societies, sports clubs and other bodies. About a hundred small towns had agricultural clubs and societies between the 1740s and 1830s, frequently established by local grandees.[82]

Metropolitan models were patently influential in the flourishing of new-style social and cultural activities in provincial towns, but the pattern on the ground was far from uniform and mirrored local preferences and pressures, as we have already noted. Detailed evidence for this is provided by a map of modern and ancient masonic lodges in smaller English towns about 1800 (see Map 22.1). This indicates a strong bias towards expansive Lancashire and the West Riding, with moderate numbers in the West Midlands, the South-West, and the area close to London. The declining small towns of East Anglia are noticeable for their absence.[83]

[78] Norfolk and Norwich RO, Mann Collection, MSS 427, 442–3, 448.

[79] J. Nichols, *Literary Anecdotes of the Eighteenth Century* (London, 1812), vol. VI, pp. 2–5; Lukis, *Stukeley Memoirs*, I, p. 93 *et passim*; Northampton Central Library, Northamptonshire Collection, Cuttings 591 (*Northampton Mercury*); *Jackson's Oxford Journal*, 24 Aug. 1754 *et passim*; 22 May 1782, 17 June 1783 *et passim*.

[80] P. Kaufman, *Libraries and their Users* (London, 1969), pp. 39–43; J. Weatherby, *Racing Calendar* (London, 1781), p. 31.

[81] *Adams Weekly Courant*, 31 Jan., 7 and 14 Nov., 5 Dec. 1775; P. Jenkins, 'Jacobites and freemasons in eighteenth century Wales', *Welsh History Review*, 9 (1978–9), 393–9.

[82] G. S. Draffen, *Scottish Masonic Records 1736–1950* (Edinburgh, 1950); I. MacDougall, *A Catalogue of Some Labour Records in Scotland* (Edinburgh, 1978); D. B. Smith, *An Illustrated History of Curling* (Edinburgh, 1981), ch. 3; R. C. Boud, 'Scottish agricultural improvement societies 1723–1835', *Review of Scottish Culture*, 1 (1984), esp. 76–7.

[83] Map based on *The Free-Masons Calendar* (London, 1800) [Moderns], and *The Constitution of Free-Masonry or Ahiman Rezon* (London, 1807) [Ancients]. For more on the spread of the masonic order see P. Clark, *British Clubs and Societies 1580–1800* (Oxford, 2000), ch. 9.

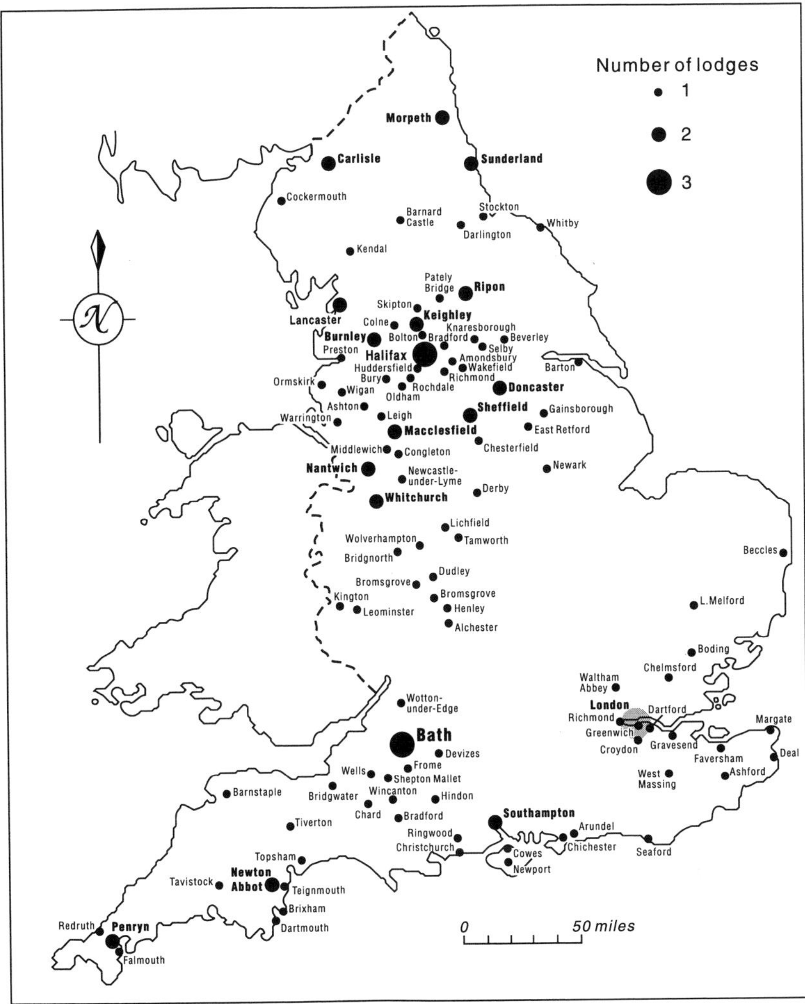

Map 22.1 Distribution of freemason lodges in smaller English towns *c.* 1800

By the early years of the nineteenth century the bigger small towns had often constructed a calendar of social events. As well as its lucrative inauguration as a tourist town (after the Shakespeare jubilee of the 1760s), Stratford-on-Avon could take pride in its card and dancing assemblies, an annual dinner for the king's birthday, dispensary ball, plays, hunt ball, and meetings of the local SPCK, prosecution society, Warwickshire and Stratford hunts, the Stratford Medical Book Society, a Church Missionary Society and masonic lodges. Though gentry patronage may have been declining in some places after 1800, the proliferation of church and church-related organisations, schools and voluntary associations helped consolidate the social function of the larger market towns. Early

Victorian Banbury was awash with sectarian congregations appealing to the town bourgeoisie as well as respectable folk from the countryside.[84] Minor small towns frequently had to make do with sporadic balls and the like, though there was a growth of race meetings in some of these places in the early nineteenth century.

At the local level, the small size of urban elites served as a constraint on the development of new-style activities. In minor towns sociable activity might depend on one enlightened individual like the jovial, generous lawyer Edward Hasted, who lived near Dartford and instituted a monthly concert there, while his wife organised a weekly public breakfast for the ladies on market days.[85] As well as the small size of the clientele, there was often the problem of adequate accommodation. In many lesser places, inns, sometimes with special assembly rooms, remained the main venue for social entertainments. In the bigger towns, however, the Georgian era saw other premises appearing, including classical style town halls (in boroughs) as well a number of assembly rooms, market houses, theatres, new parish churches and dissenting chapels. Investment in the urban infrastructure might be considerable. In the West Riding, Knaresborough, Pontefract and Ripon – all with under 5,000 inhabitants in 1811 – expended between £10,000 and £27,000 on public buildings during the period 1700–1840, including a substantial amount on churches. Admittedly, these figures look less impressive when set beside the £355,000 spent by Leeds and £280,000 by Sheffield over the same period. In Wales after 1800 large nonconformist chapels became temples of the new-found urbanity in small towns.[86]

The public image of small towns was boosted by a wave of parliamentary improvement acts passed for English communities in the last part of the eighteenth century: seventy-one were enacted for small towns between 1751 and 1800 (excluding those for harbour improvement). Urban improvement also occurred in Welsh market towns and Scottish small burghs. At Stranraer, for example, the town council was active in widening the main street, building a new school house and rebuilding the church. A number of small towns also gained Palladian-style town halls. An English visitor to Ayr in 1800 praised it as 'a pretty lively smart town' with 'new and modern edifices'.[87] Across Britain new

[84] J. Thomas, 'The pursuit of leisure: a study of cultural activities in Warwickshire small towns' (Certificate dissertation, Centre for Urban History, University of Leicester, 1993), pp. 23–4; Noble, 'Growth and development of country towns', p. 305 *et seq.*; B. Trinder, *Victorian Banbury* (Chichester, 1982), ch. 4.

[85] Nichols, *Literary Anecdotes*, p. 137; A. Everitt, 'Kentish family portrait: an aspect of the rise of the pseudo-gentry', in C. W. Chalklin and M. A. Havinden, eds., *Rural Change and Urban Growth 1500–1800* (London, 1974), p. 180.

[86] K. Grady, *The Georgian Public Buildings of Leeds and the West Riding* (Thoresby Society, 62, 1989), p. 40; Carter, 'Urban and industrial settlement', pp. 286–7.

[87] Figures for improvement acts taken from *Statutes at Large*. Dennison and Coleman, eds., *Historic Stranraer*, pp. 19–20; F. Wood and K. Wood, *A Lancashire Gentleman: The Letters and Journals of Richard Hodgkinson 1763–1847* (Stroud, 1992), p. 141.

public buildings were joined by improved private housing. Though there was little of the large-scale construction of the bigger cities, individual houses and small terraces of new classical-style housing appeared in the main streets of numerous small towns, usually in brick. Where money was less abundant, older vernacular structures were smartened up by the cosmetic addition of fashionable frontages. While the formal style was borrowed from the metropolis, builders often deployed local building materials and architectural customs, thereby articulating and preserving the physical personality of the small town (see plate 22). In Scotland new-fashioned merchant houses and civic buildings combined neo-classicism with traditional Scottish features, such as 'Dutch' gables.[88]

Urban identity was increasingly celebrated in other ways – in prints and paintings and town histories (at least for the bigger centres). Here paintings and engravings were distinctive for their concern with the traditional urban setting. Instead of the artist concentrating on the built-up area as with larger towns, we see the small town encircled, embraced by the fields and neighbouring farms, reminding the viewer of the essential link with the countryside. In other works the town was simply the backcloth for leisure activities. Antiquarian histories which appeared for most larger towns in the eighteenth century were also published for a small number of market towns. Once again these tended to include discussion of neighbouring rural parishes and local landowners, who also figured in the lists of subscribers.[89] Generally, national metropolitan values were renegotiated at the small town level, not only to assert its identification with the urban world but its long-standing and close relationship with rural society.

The smart social and cultural world which developed in small towns in the long eighteenth century was often shallow and precarious, dependent on small elites; most vigorous in the larger improved towns and in the more prosperous regions, weakest in minor towns; often with strong local and traditional features. Social life in country towns might be both restrained and petty, where, in Fanny Burney's words, 'all the conversation is scandal, all the attention, dress, and almost all the heart, folly, envy and censoriousness'. There was less opportunity for the more open socialising and mixing and reforming of social ranks found in big cities.[90] The smallest centres may well have had lower levels of social mobility than bigger places, due to less migration and fewer economic opportunities. The development of anything approaching a middle class was probably limited

[88] Reed, 'Cultural role', pp. 131–3; M. Laithwaite, 'Totnes houses 1500–1800', in Clark, ed., *Transformation of English Provincial Towns*, pp. 87 *et seq*.; McWilliam, *Scottish Landscape*, pp. 70–4.

[89] V. Martin, 'Cultural life of Suffolk small towns 1700–1850' (unpublished paper, Centre for Urban History, Leicester University, 1996), pp. 12–13. E.g. F. Peck, *Academia tertia Anglicana or the Antiquarian Annals of Stanford* (London, 1727); M. Dunsford, *Historical Memoirs of the Town and Parish of Tiverton* (Exeter, 1790); R. Pocock, *The History of the Incorporated Town and Parishes of Gravesend and Milton* (Gravesend, 1797); *The Ludlow Guide* (Ludlow, 1797); T. Hinderwell, *The History and Antiquities of Scarborough*, 2nd edn (York, 1811).

[90] Troide, ed., *Early Journals of Fanny Burney*, II, p. 14.

to some of the bigger manufacturing centres. Traditional social relationships were underpinned by the survival of old topographical arrangements right into the nineteenth century. As in the past, the houses of wealthier inhabitants clustered in the main streets near the centre of town; poorer folk lived in back alleys and courts, and on the outskirts. Suburban villas are only starting to make an impression even in the bigger small towns by the time of the Great Reform Act.

The relative fragility of the social order was emphasised by the growing influx of poorer people from the countryside at the end of the century. This was particular serious in the increasingly agrarian regions of southern England. Frederick Eden in the 1790s remarked on the great number of unemployed crowding into Winslow in Buckinghamshire due to the enclosure of the local common fields and reduced demand for labour. In Dorset the rapid rise of the poor rate at Blandford was blamed on the high price of provisions, the low level of wages and the consolidation of small farms, driving people into the town. Indigence was particularly acute in lesser towns where resources for relief were most limited. At Hungerford in Berkshire close to half the parish of 2,000 souls (the town in 1811 numbered less than 1,000) were on the bread line and up to 20 per cent received relief. Some small towns established unions with neighbouring parishes but these were increasingly overwhelmed by the destitute. Regional trends are evident. In East Anglian market towns poverty levels rose sharply through the later eighteenth century, but relief expenditure in 1803–4 (per 100 population) was only half that of the West Midlands, where the problems were mainly cyclical and where growing employment relieved structural poverty.[91]

Social and cultural developments tended to enhance the urban image and identity of small towns, drawing them into the urban system. Indicative of this increasingly interconnected urban world, John Osbourne, a prosperous clothier at Wotton under Edge in the Stroud valley was able by the 1760s to attend plays and scientific lectures in his own small town, as well as supporting the grammar school, but he also went off to Gloucester to the Three Choirs music meeting, and to social events at Cirencester, Bristol and Bath.[92] Yet viewed at the local level, the mix and variety of cultural activities in small towns undoubtedly helped to articulate regional and local differences, as well as to energise the continuing relationship with the countryside. In the long term, such developments tended to polarise the position of larger and lesser small towns. For minor places, the exiguous size of their local elite, the sporadic character of sociable events, the absence of public buildings or improvements and the inrush of rural poor were further factors in their eventual eclipse as urban centres.

[91] F. M. Eden, *The State of the Poor*, ed. A. G. L. Rogers (London, 1928), pp. 142–3, 177; D. S. Stafford, 'A Gilbert Act parish: the relief and treatment of the poor . . . of Hungerford, Berkshire 1783–1834' (MPhil thesis, University of Reading, 1983), pp. 60–1; PP 1803–4 XIII, Abstract of the Answers and Returns . . . relative to the Expense and Maintenance of the Poor in England.

[92] Gloucestershire RO, D2930/1.

(v) POLITICS AND GOVERNMENT

At the start of the eighteenth century there remained major institutional distinctions among small towns. In England and Wales the main difference (discussed in Chapter 13) was between the minority with borough charters (135 in England), which often enjoyed parliamentary representation as well, and the several hundred others whose privileges were largely confined to market rights and manorial liberties. In Scotland a much higher proportion of small towns had burghal charters but here the contrast was between royal burghs and burghs of barony. During the eighteenth century the importance of some of these institutional differences diminished. From the 1670s royal burghs in Scotland generally lost their official monopoly on overseas trade. In England the growth of new quasi-administrative bodies affected both corporate and unchartered towns. On the other hand, the political importance of the parliamentary boroughs probably increased before the 1832 Reform Act, as landowners and party activists jostled and lobbied to win elections.[93]

As in the bigger cities, municipal activity seems to have diminished in chartered small towns, affected by the growth of civic oligarchy, party factionalism and recurrent charges of corruption and abuse. In many places magistrates abandoned earlier strategies for dealing with social problems and by mid-century had largely ceased to intervene directly in the urban economy. At Tewkesbury the infrequent meeting of the council in the 1710s 'has very much lessened the power, authority and interest of this corporation'. At Rye in Sussex most civic activity, from the leasing of town lands to the celebration of mayoral elections, took place away from the town hall at the Reindeer Inn, and municipal government at Tiverton likewise gave way to club rule. The process of municipal decline was accelerated in some places by opposing factions setting up rival corporations, which could trigger the suspension of the charter.[94]

In general, however, municipal decline did not lead to the decay of urban government. Rather there was a decentralisation of policy making with a mixture of old and new bodies taking over the reins of administration. Social problems, particularly poverty, were dealt with by parish vestries and towards the end of the century by workhouse boards with their salaried officials. General meetings or associations of better-off townsmen took over various administrative functions. The town of Lewes was said to be 'governed by gentlemen' who

[93] See above, pp. 444 *et seq.*, *Statutes of the United Kingdom (1832)*, (London, 1832), pp. 725 *et seq.*; W. M. Mackenzie, *The Scottish Burghs* (Edinburgh, 1949), pp. 145 *et seq.*; J. A. Phillips, *The Great Reform Bill in the Boroughs* (Oxford, 1992), especially ch. 5.

[94] F. Redmond, 'The borough of Tewkesbury 1575–1714' (MA thesis, University of Birmingham, 1950), p. 10; G. S. Bagley, *Some Inns and Alehouses of Rye* (Rye, 1958), p. 4; J. Bourne, ed., *Georgian Tiverton* (Devon and Cornwall Record Society, new series, 29, 1986), p. xxiii; S. McIntyre, 'The Scarborough corporation quarrel, 1736–1760', *NHist.*, 14 (1978), 208.

promoted its growth as a gentry centre. At Bedford leading inhabitants and gentry banded together to finance a new town organ, the focus of urbane musical life. Prosecution societies proliferated in many small towns (often with support from the adjoining countryside) to support joint action against felons.[95] Towards the end of the century there was a steady increase of charitable societies to look after the poor and needy. Transport improvements including turnpikes, river navigation and canal construction were promoted by private trusts and companies. Other forms of civic improvement, including public hygiene, police, street widening and lighting, were increasingly promoted by new statutory improvement commissions, whose membership was often recruited from a wider urban group than the old corporations. Acts were passed for over fifty small boroughs in the second half of the eighteenth century. In Scotland where there were fewer improvement acts, clubs and societies sought to direct and invigorate municipal action. Thus Stirling's Port Club, which met every Saturday, urged the council to improve the town, making proposals for the introduction of new manufactures, the deepening of the river and the enclosure of the town lands.[96]

Just as the boroughs devolved much urban policy making on to these new often voluntary bodies, so in the unincorporated small towns parish vestries, committees of leading inhabitants, private individuals, voluntary associations and improvement commissions took an active role, and generated a coherent response to urban expansion. At Ashford in Kent a committee of principal townsmen managed much of the town's business, supervising the workhouse, taking a hand in setting up a new market, and paving the streets. Improvement legislation for unchartered towns came later than for boroughs, but in the 1780s and 1790s acts were passed for a couple of dozen towns, mostly in southern England.[97]

In such ways the larger unincorporated market towns became engaged in the general process of urban administrative restructuring and expansion in the eighteenth century. Only the lesser market centres were left behind, dependent on their manorial courts and parish bodies. Where small towns, chartered or otherwise, were different governmentally from their bigger brethren was in the extent of outside interference – by landowners and county justices. Scottish

[95] Stafford, 'Hungerford', pp. 51 *et seq.*, 130 *et seq.*; J. Macky, *A Journey through England* (London, 1724), vol. 1, pp. 100–1; Bedford Town Hall, Town Minute Book 1688–1718, ff. 116v, 129v–30; P. J. R. King, 'Prosecution societies and their impact in eighteenth-century Essex', in D. Hay and F. Snyder, eds., *Policing and Prosecution in Britain 1750–1850* (Oxford, 1989), pp. 171–207.

[96] Clark, *British Clubs and Societies*, pp. 105–9; E. Pawson, *Transport and Economy* (London, 1977), esp. ch. 7; see also generally, E. L. Jones and M. E. Falkus, 'Urban improvement and the English economy in the seventeenth and eighteenth centuries', in P. Borsay, ed., *The Eighteenth Century Town* (London, 1990), pp. 128–55; *Statutes at Large*; National Library of Scotland, Edinburgh, Manuscripts Dept., Misc. Accession 7862.

[97] Eden, *State of the Poor*, pp. 207–8; *Statutes at Large*.

landowners were not only busy in urban improvement, but took a hand in town appointments. In Wales even the relatively important town of Wrexham experienced repeated interference by the county justices at the start of the period.[98]

Landed involvement in small towns was particularly important where parliamentary seats were at stake. Though the frenzy of party rivalry and electioneering under William and Anne may have abated somewhat after the Septennial Act of 1716, the later decades of the century saw a renewed spate of contests in small boroughs, as in bigger towns. Political involvement by the gentry was hardly new, but was encouraged by greater landed residence and socialising in towns. Given the rising cost of electoral campaigns, there can be no doubt that small boroughs were major beneficiaries. At election times freemen were showered with largesse including heavy feasting and drinking, the profits from which irrigated the whole local economy. At Newcastle-under-Lyme in 1790 large crowds of freemen and their families took up residence for the week in local pubs where they regaled themselves at the candidates' expense. There were also longer-term dividends. At Brackley the earl of Bridgewater secured the town's seats in the early eighteenth century at the price of a 'very neat townhall'. At Banbury the dominant North family rebuilt the town's almshouse in 1711 and endowed the Blue Coat school.[99] For many small boroughs allegations about their electoral corruption and abuse was a price worth paying if the outcome was a modest dowry of new-style public buildings, which helped to confirm the community's distinctive urban identity.

By the start of the nineteenth century urban government in small towns had become more organised and effective, led by professional officials. None the less, one finds mounting protests about civic and electoral abuse, fanned in many instances by party conflict and to a lesser extent by political radicalism. The Great Reform Act had only a limited effect on electoral abuse, which persisted into the late nineteenth century, but it did entail the complete disenfranchisement of fifty-six small boroughs and the partial loss of seats by another thirty. Most of those towns deprived were located in the South-West and South-East. It is arguable that the disappearance of parliamentary seats contributed to the general decline of landed interest and activity in small towns and so to their worsening economic problems in southern England. The Municipal Corporations Act in 1835 led to fewer changes. Though the preceding commission report had excoriated the corruption and malpractices of many small boroughs, the Act struck only at the worst abuses. It paved the way for the formal chartering of the great

[98] Dennison and Coleman, eds., *Historic Hamilton*, p. 28; D. G. Evans, 'The market towns of Denbighshire' (MA thesis, University of Wales, 1978), p. 80.

[99] Phillips, *Great Reform Bill*; Staffordshire RO, D593/S/1610/8; W. A. Speck, 'Brackley: a study in the growth of oligarchy', *Midland History*, 3 (1975–6), 31–8; *VCH*, Oxfordshire, x, p. 90; also M. E. Clayton, 'Ye subtlety of electioneering: election practices in Haslemere 1715–80', *SHist.*, 17 (1995), 54–5.

unincorporated towns but it did not disturb the charters of existing small boroughs, apart from removing sessional jurisdiction from about fifty centres, many located in southern England.[100]

In many small towns, both chartered and unincorporated, voluntary bodies and non-civic organisations continued to maintain a powerful position in town government into Victoria's reign, but, with declining landed and professional interest, they came to be dominated by conservative bourgeois groups with a narrower, reactive interest in urban improvement. Small town government showed itself ineffectual against mounting social and environmental problems. After the end of the period there was an increasing gap in terms of the quality of urban government between Britain's many small towns and their larger urban counterparts. This was especially true in the agrarian regions and among the middling and lesser small towns.[101]

(vi) CONCLUSION

Any discussion of Britain's multitude of small towns in this period must be superficial and selective. As we have seen, there is a kaleidoscope of regional, hierarchic and local experiences which have only been touched on here, though a number of themes are further explored elsewhere in this volume. Some tentative conclusions can be suggested, however. In the first place, many small towns, particularly in England, but also to a considerable, if later, extent in Scotland and Wales, became integrated into the urban system during the long eighteenth century, incorporated into more clearly defined regional networks of towns. In England at least they appear to have enjoyed marked growth during the eighteenth century, with higher rates of urbanisation than almost anywhere else in western Europe. It seems that they acquired more urban demographic characteristics such as enhanced levels of mortality. Their economies became increasingly complex through the development of service and retailing functions, as well as manufacturing specialisms. Their social and cultural image, at least until the start of the nineteenth century, acquired a more visibly urbane character, displaying a redesigned townscape and an efflorescence of smart entertainments. For most of the rural elite the local market town – not London or Bath – was the regular and most accessible gateway to fashionable social life in Georgian England. Lastly, there was a broadening of administrative organisation and enhanced political visibility for many parliamentary boroughs.

Yet these general trends were qualified by growing regional differences: in England between the industrialising Midlands, Yorkshire and Lancashire and the

[100] *Statutes of the United Kingdom (1832)*, pp. 725–48; *Statutes of the United Kingdom (1835)* (London, 1835), pp. 389–463.

[101] R. M. Gutchen, 'The government and misgovernment of Hitchin', *Hertfordshire Past and Present*, 15 (1975–6), 32–65.

southern and eastern areas; in Scotland between the Strathclyde area and the border counties; in Wales between the southern valleys and the rest. The picture was also varied by the more limited ability of minor towns to share in the mainstream of urbanisation, as they suffered a decline of industrial specialisms particularly in the agrarian regions.

During the early decades of the nineteenth century these variations undoubtedly became more visible and pressing. In the agrarian districts the problems of agriculture and the collapse of traditional crafts left many small towns, particularly lesser ones, scrabbling for business. The situation was compounded by the decline of elite patronage and the problem of rural poverty cascading into these communities. Here that umbilical connection with the countryside proved less of a safeguard than a liability. The spread of the railways often tended to accentuate problems, though bigger small towns may have stabilised their fortunes by acquiring new administrative agencies. Small towns in industrialising regions undoubtedly did better, but they suffered from a contraction of the core area of activity, and minor towns were vulnerable to economic consolidation. Politically and socially, small towns, increasingly deserted by the 1830s by the landed and wealthier professional classes, came under the ascendancy of a petty bourgeoisie sharing limited ambitions and horizons. With the decayed elegance of their classical façades and modest legacy of Georgian public buildings, many of the old market towns, particularly in southern England, North and mid-Wales and parts of Scotland, stagnated and slumbered, not to be awakened until after the first world war with the spread of new industries and new services, a petrol-driven transport revolution, and middle-class tourism.

· 23 ·

Health and leisure resorts 1700–1840

PETER BORSAY

LONG BEFORE the orthodox onset of the Industrial Revolution, and well before Europe was facing a similar shake up, the traditional urban order in Britain was experiencing the forces of change that were to reshape its character.[1] An important feature of the transformation underway was the emergence of the so-called 'new towns', and among these one of the most novel and distinctive categories was watering-places – inland and coastal resorts devoted to the provision of health and leisure.[2] This chapter will examine the evolution of the resort from about 1700 until the arrival of the railways, an event whose influence can be exaggerated but which none the less represented a watershed.[3] Four sets of issues will be explored. First, the chronology and pattern of development. Second, the broad factors responsible for this. Third, the urban status of watering-places, their relationship to other towns providing similar services, and their typology. Fourth, the particular economic, social, political and cultural characteristics of resorts. Because of their newness and distinctive profile, spa and seaside centres provide a litmus test of the urban transformation unfolding in the long eighteenth century. Though apparently very different from the classic 'new

I am grateful for comments from Anne Borsay, and from those who heard earlier versions of this chapter, delivered as a paper to meetings at the University of Wales conference centre Gregynog, and at the University of East Anglia.

1 P. J. Corfield, *The Impact of English Towns 1700–1800* (Oxford, 1982), esp. pp. 1–16; J. de Vries, *European Urbanization 1500–1800* (London, 1984), pp. 255–65; E. A. Wrigley, 'Urban growth and agricultural change: England and the continent in the early modern period', *Journal of Interdisciplinary History*, 15 (1985), 705–12. For an overview of the development of resorts see J. K. Walton, 'Le cittá di villeggiatura in Inghilterra e Galles, dal tardo seicento agli anni settanta di questo secolo', *Storia Urbana*, 67–8 (1994), 177–207.

2 P. Clark and P. Slack, *English Towns in Transition 1500–1700* (London, 1976), pp. 33–45; Corfield, *Impact of English Towns*, pp. 51–65.

3 J. K. Walton, 'Railways and resort development in North West England, 1830–1914', in E. M. Sigsworth, ed., *Ports and Resorts in the Regions*, Papers submitted to the Conference of Regional History Tutors (Hull, 1980), pp. 120–37.

towns' of the Industrial Revolution, they were to form a vital element in the urban network which emerged.

(i) CHRONOLOGY AND PATTERN OF DEVELOPMENT

In Britain the earliest commercial development of spas as a health cure for the social elite dates from the late Tudor and early Stuart era. This parallels the beginnings of a period of discovery and rediscovery of springs in France, though in Italy there seems to have been a network of widely used watering-places since at least the later medieval period, whose clientele included the aristocracy. In the case of Britain, Phyllis Hembry has located the foundation of sixteen spas in the late sixteenth and early seventeenth centuries, and there are clear signs of exploitation of the springs at Buxton, Harrogate, Tunbridge Wells and most notably Bath (see Plate 3), which saw substantial investment in the health and visitor facilities.[4] This important formative phase in the rise of the watering-place was curtailed by the disruptive impact of the Civil Wars;[5] but as stability returned the trend set in motion before the conflict led in the post-Restoration era to a multiplication of new 'discoveries'. Hembry identifies thirty-nine spa foundations in the years 1660 to 1699, and thirty-four between 1700 and 1749; and Thomas Short's *History of Mineral Waters* manages to include 131 'spaws' in the first volume of 1734 and a further ninety-four in the second volume of 1740.[6] Many of Short's roll-call could not be remotely classified as resorts, but they do represent a pool of potential recruits, from which a select band were to rise to prominence – and, significantly, did so by offering recreation as well as recuperation. This was a mixture the French springs largely eschewed, though Spa (Belgium) did represent a fashionable continental competitor. In Britain the leading centres were located predominantly in southern England. They included Epsom, in its heyday 1690–1710 and the chief among the cluster of spas on the periphery of London; Tunbridge Wells, the most dynamic of the watering-places at the turn of the century; Scarborough, which became widely fashionable from the 1720s;

4 P. Hembry, *The English Spa 1560–1815* (London, 1990), pp. 4–52, 355–60; R. Palmer, ' "In this our lightye and learned tyme": Italian baths in the era of the Renaissance', and L. W. B. Brockliss, 'The development of the spa in seventeenth-century France', both in R. Porter, ed., *The Medical History of Waters and Spas* (London, 1990), pp. 14–22, 23–47; L. W. B. Brockliss, 'Taking the waters in early modern France: some thoughts on a commercial racket', *Bulletin of the Society for the Social History of Medicine*, 40 (1987), 74–6; R. G. Heape, *Buxton under the Dukes of Devonshire* (London, 1948), p. 23; *Historic Buxton and its Spa Era* (Buxton, 1971), pp. 1–4; B. Jennings, ed., *A History of Harrogate and Knaresborough* (Huddersfield, 1970), pp. 219–21; T. B. Burr, *The History of Tunbridge Wells* (London, 1766), pp. 30–3; A. Savidge, *Royal Tunbridge Wells* (Tunbridge Wells, 1975), pp. 25–31; J. Wood, *A Description of Bath* (repr. Bath, 1969), pp. 200–16; P. R. James, *The Baths of Bath in the Sixteenth and Early Seventeenth Centuries* (Bristol, 1938).

5 Hembry, *English Spa*, pp. 58–65; Burr, *Tunbridge Wells*, pp. 37–8.

6 Hembry, *English Spa*, pp. 355–60; R. Lennard, 'The watering-places', in R. Lennard, ed., *Englishmen at Rest and Play: Some Phases of English Leisure 1558–1714* (Oxford, 1931), p. 36.

and Bath (see Plates 28 and 29). The last of these entered a new phase of investment in visitor facilities from about 1700, and from the mid-1720s began the remarkable extramural building programme of high class residential blocks that was to guarantee its status as the premier Georgian inland resort.[7]

As a network of spas took shape in the early eighteenth century, so the first tantalising signs of a new type of watering-place emerged. Practical evidence of elite sea-bathing can be found from about 1720. By the 1730s Brighton, Margate and Scarborough (which combined the roles of spa and seaside resort), and by the 1740s Weymouth, all show indications of accommodating the new fashion.[8] It was these four fishing towns and ports which were to develop in the second half of the eighteenth century into the earliest substantial seaside resorts.[9] From the end of the century they were joined by a proliferating body of sea-bathing centres, and by 1851 John Walton is able to identify a corpus of seventy-one coastal resorts.[10] This was an area of urban development in which Britain led the way; it appears that serious investment in continental sea-bathing resorts only began to occur (first in Germany) from the 1790s.[11]

By far the most important concentration of seaside watering-places, before the coming of the railways, was in the London zone of influence, particularly Sussex and Kent. Brighton was the dominant centre, from the 1780s breaking out beyond the confines of the old town and spawning large-scale suburban

[7] Brockliss, 'Spa in seventeenth-century France', 36–8; J. Black, *The British and the Grand Tour* (Beckenham, 1985), pp. 125–8; Hembry, *English Spa*, pp. 66–122, 159–73; F. L. Clark, 'The history of Epsom spa', *Surrey Archaeological Collections*, 57 (1960), 1–41; Burr, *Tunbridge Wells*; Savidge, *Tunbridge Wells*, pp. 33–69; C. W. Chalklin, *Seventeenth Century Kent* (Rochester, 1978), pp. 156–8; C. W. Chalklin, 'The making of some new towns, *c.* 1600–1720', in C. W. Chalklin and M. A. Havinden, eds., *Rural Change and Urban Growth 1500–1800* (London, 1974), pp. 233–4, 243–6; A. Rowntree, ed., *The History of Scarborough* (London, 1931), pp. 247–62; S. McIntyre, 'Towns as health and pleasure resorts; Bath, Scarborough, and Weymouth 1700–1815' (DPhil thesis, University of Oxford, 1973); S. McIntyre, 'Bath: the rise of a resort town, 1660–1800', in P. Clark, ed., *Country Towns in Pre-Industrial England* (Leicester, 1981), pp. 198–249; R. S. Neale, *Bath 1680–1850* (London, 1981), pp. 1–225; T. Fawcett and S. Bird, *Bath: History and Guide* (Stroud, 1994), pp. 44–57; G. Davis and P. Bonsall, *Bath: A New History* (Keele, 1996), pp. 28–62.

[8] J. A. R. Pimlott, *The Englishman's Holiday: A Social History* (Hassocks, 1976), pp. 51–2; J. K. Walton, *The English Seaside Resort* (Leicester, 1983), pp. 10–12; S. Farrant, *Georgian Brighton 1740–1820* (Brighton, 1980), pp. 4–5; J. Whyman, 'A Hanoverian watering-place: Margate before the railway', in A. M. Everitt, ed., *Perspectives in English Urban History* (London, 1973), p. 139; *A Journey from London to Scarborough* (London, 1734), p. 36; McIntyre, 'Towns as health and pleasure resorts', pp. 192–4, 302; *The Great Diurnall of Nicholas Blundell*, ed. J. J. Bagley (Record Society of Lancashire and Cheshire, 114, 1972), pp. 52, 81.

[9] E. W. Gilbert, *Brighton: Old Ocean's Bauble* (London, 1954), pp. 56–110; Farrant, *Georgian Brighton*, pp. 13–25; Whyman, 'Hanoverian watering-place', pp. 138–60; McIntyre, 'Towns as health and pleasure resorts'; Rowntree, ed., *Scarborough*, pp. 247–72; J. Hutchins, *The History and Antiquities of the County of Dorset* (repr., East Ardsley, 1973), vol. II, pp. 467–71.

[10] Walton, *Seaside Resort*, p. 53.

[11] A. Corbin, *The Lure of the Sea*, trans. J. Phelps (Cambridge, 1994), pp. 250–81; Pimlott, *Englishman's Holiday*, pp. 197–200.

development. Its population rose from about 2,000 in 1750, to 7,000 by 1801, 24,000 by 1821 and 47,000 by 1841. Elsewhere in Sussex, Hastings and Worthing also rose to the status of important resorts.[12] By 1851 almost 30 per cent of Kent's urban population resided in its nine leading coastal resorts, of which the most significant concentration was on the Isle of Thanet – including Ramsgate (15,000 people in 1851), Margate (10,000), and Broadstairs (3,000).[13] Further centres – such as Southsea, Southampton, Weymouth and Lyme Regis[14] – were strung out along the south coast, but the second major concentration of early coastal resorts was in the South-West. Despite signs of growth from the mid-eighteenth century, it was between 1789 and 1815 that 'tourism rocketed' in south Devon; thereafter development slowed in the south, with the exception of Torquay (the largest resort in Devon by 1841, with a population of 6,000), while northern resorts experienced their first major phase of expansion between 1816 and 1843.[15] A further, as yet limited, pocket of development was also emerging on the coast of Lancashire. Both Southport and Blackpool were attracting well-off sea-bathers before the turn of the century, but it was from about the 1820s that these resorts began to take off. The number of visitors to Blackpool at the height of the season tripled from around 1,000 in 1830 to 3,000 in 1840, while the population of North Meols (the township which included Southport) expanded from 2,763 in 1821 to 7,774 forty years later.[16] By the 1830s and 1840s resort growth in many areas of the country was slackening off, in some cases sharply. It may be that the seaside 'industry' had reached a plateau in demand, and was experiencing a bottleneck in supply, which the arrival of the railways was partly to relieve.[17]

[12] Farrant, *Georgian Brighton*, esp. p. 14; B. R. Mitchell and P. Deane, *Abstract of British Historical Statistics* (Cambridge, 1962), p. 24; S. Farrant, 'Sussex by the sea: the development of seaside resorts 1730–1900', in Sigsworth, ed., *Ports and Resorts*, pp. 168–75.

[13] J. Whyman, ed., *Kentish Sources*, vol. VIII: *The Early Kentish Seaside (1736–1840)* (Gloucester, 1985), pp. 1–31; R. Craig and J. Whyman, 'Kent and the sea', in A. Armstrong, ed., *The Economy of Kent 1640–1914* (Woodbridge, 1995), pp. 196–204.

[14] R. C. Riley, *The Growth of Southsea as a Naval Satellite and Victorian Resort* (Portsmouth Papers, 16, 1972), pp. 4–6; E. M. Sandell, 'Georgian Southampton: a watering-place and spa', in J. B. Morgan and P. Peberdy, eds., *Collected Essays on Southampton* (Southampton, 1958), pp. 79–87; J. Fowles, *A Short History of Lyme Regis* (Wimborne, 1991), pp. 28–33.

[15] J. F. Travis, *The Rise of the Devon Seaside Resorts 1750–1900* (Exeter, 1993), pp. 7–93; P. Russell, *A History of Torquay and the Famous Anchorage of Torbay* (Torquay, 1960); G. Holmes, *Sidmouth: A History* (Sidmouth, 1987), pp. 46–71; B. May, 'The rise of Ilfracombe as a seaside resort in the nineteenth and early twentieth centuries', in H. E. S. Fisher, ed., *West Country Maritime and Social History: Some Essays* (Exeter, 1980), pp. 137–45; J. Travis, *An Illustrated History of Lynton and Lynmouth 1770–1914* (Derby, 1995).

[16] F. A. Bailey, *A History of Southport* (Southport, 1955), esp. p. 59; J. Porter, *History of the Fylde of Lancashire* (repr., East Ardsley, 1968), pp. 316–36; W. I. Curnow, 'The growth of Blackpool as a health and holiday resort', in A. Grime, ed., *A Scientific Survey of Blackpool and District* (London, 1936), pp. 76–8; J. K. Walton, *The Blackpool Landlady: A Social History* (Manchester, 1978), pp. 13–16.

[17] Pimlott, *Englishman's Holiday*, p. 74; Gilbert, *Brighton*, pp. 109–10; Walton, *Seaside Resort*, pp. 58–9.

In the second half of the eighteenth century many of the older spas, located in the South-East of England, stagnated. Tunbridge Wells displayed few signs of significant growth and as a watering-place Epsom had long been a fading force, increasingly dependent on its role as a residential and racing centre.[18] Competition from the rising coastal resorts of the region was probably taking its toll. However, this was hardly the case for Britain as a whole, where a new wave of spa creation and expansion – situated this time in the West, the Midlands and the North – was underway in the later eighteenth and early nineteenth centuries; Phyllis Hembry traces thirty-nine new foundations to the years 1750–99, and eighteen to the period 1800–15.[19] Bath continued to build on its early pre-eminence, growing from a town of between 6,000 and 8,000 people in 1750, to a major city of 33,000 by the close of the century – about the tenth largest city in England and Wales.[20] Prominent among the 'new' generation of inland resorts were Buxton, Matlock, Harrogate, Malvern, Cheltenham and Leamington. The last two were the most dynamic, Cheltenham forging ahead from the start of the century (mushrooming from 3,000 inhabitants in 1801 to 20,000 by 1826, and 36,000 by 1841), Leamington expanding rapidly from the 1820s (leaping from a population of only 543 in 1811 to 12,600 by 1841).[21] However, the picture was by no means one of unalloyed success. 'Irreversible decline' set in at Bristol Hotwells from the 1790s, Buxton's boom was over by the early nineteenth century, as on a grander scale was that at Bath, while by the 1830s there were clear signs that the meteoric rise of both Cheltenham and Leamington was faltering.[22]

Resorts came to the Celtic periphery of Britain later and on an altogether smaller scale. In Scotland the Firth of Forth – under the influence of Edinburgh – was an early focus of development. Portobello was the most rapidly evolving of the east coast resorts, its population growing from 1,912 in 1821 to 2,781 a decade later. Aberdour also displayed signs of the impact of the tourist industry

[18] Hembry, *English Spa*, pp. 231–42; Savidge, *Tunbridge Wells*, pp. 51, 71, 97; D. Hunn, *Epsom Racecourse: Its Story and its People* (London, 1973), pp. 27–48.

[19] Hembry, *English Spa*, pp. 111–301, 355–60.

[20] McIntyre, 'Bath', p. 214.

[21] Hembry, *English Spa*, pp. 216–30, 245–69, 284–301; P. Hembry, *British Spas from 1815 to the Present: A Social History*, ed. and completed by L. W. Cowie and E. E. Cowie (London, 1997), pp. 8–53, 115–45; *Historic Buxton*, pp. 6–9; Heape, *Buxton*, pp. 19–64; Jennings, *Harrogate and Knaresborough*, pp. 219–38, 286–303; B. S. Smith, *A History of Malvern*, 2nd edn (Stroud, 1978), pp. 171–94; G. Hart, *A History of Cheltenham* (Leicester, 1965), pp. 124–210, 224; R. Chaplin, 'The rise of Royal Leamington Spa', *Warwickshire History*, 2(2) (1972–3), 13–29; E. G. Baxter, 'The social life of visitors to Leamington Spa in the first half of the nineteenth century; Part I', *Warwickshire History*, 3(1) (1975), 15–37, and 'Part II', *Warwickshire History*, 3(2) (1975–6), 46–70.

[22] Hembry, *British Spas*, pp. 30, 46–7, 54–70, 115–21, 123–4; B. Little, 'The Gloucestershire spas: an eighteenth-century parallel', in P. McGrath and J. Cannon, eds., *Essays in Bristol and Gloucestershire History* (Bristol and Gloucestershire Archaeological Society, 1976), pp. 179–80; Hembry, *English Spa*, pp. 227, 270–83; Heape, *Buxton*, p. 33; Fawcett and Bird, *Bath*, pp. 77–81; A. Barbeau, *Life and Letters at Bath in the Eighteenth Century* (London, 1904), pp. 298–309; D. J. Jeremy, 'The social decline of Bath', *History Today*, 17 (1967), 242–9; Hart, *Cheltenham*, pp. 184–5, 209; Baxter, 'Visitors to Leamington Spa . . . Part I', 34–7.

in the early nineteenth century, though this provided no obvious boost to its tiny population, 840 in 1790, 903 in 1841.[23] Scotland also had its spas. In the eighteenth century these included Moffat (discovered in the previous century) and Strathpeffer. Moffat appears to have been well patronised, and in 1825 it embarked upon a programme of expansion in response to the project to launch Bridge of Allan as a health resort. By the 1840s the latter had a daily routine and structured season, catering to different clienteles at different times of the year.[24] In Wales taking the waters at Llandrindod and Builth dates back at least to the eighteenth century, and both by the 1830s were established but still small spas – a treatise was published on the Llandrindod waters as early as 1756, and a guide to the spa in 1825.[25] More significant as resorts were Swansea, Aberystwyth and Tenby, whose rise as watering-places dates from the 1780s and 1790s, and which by the early nineteenth century were offering a credible range of fashionable facilities – though by the 1830s and 1840s Swansea's role as a polite resort was being undermined by commercial and industrial expansion.[26]

(ii) THE FACTORS BEHIND RESORT DEVELOPMENT

What were the broad forces responsible for the rise of resorts, and the pattern of development which emerged? To answer these questions historians generally refer, implicitly or explicitly, to an explanatory model based on the interaction between demand and supply, though with varying degrees of emphasis on the two factors. A trip to spa or seaside, and a proper engagement in their commercialised health and leisure routines, was an inherently costly business. In these circumstances the sustained growth in demand for watering-places can only be explained in terms of an increasingly wealthy or numerous aristocracy, gentry

23 A. J. Durie, 'The development of the Scottish coastal resorts in the central Lowlands, *c.* 1770–1880: from Gulf Stream to golf stream', *Local Historian*, 24(4) (1994), 206–9; E. Simpson, 'Aberdour: the evolution of a seaside resort', in G. Cruickshank, ed., *A Sense of Place* (Edinburgh, 1988), pp. 177–80. I am grateful to Alastair Durie for his help on the subject of Scottish resorts.

24 A. J. Durie, '"The queen of Scottish spas": the nineteenth century development of Bridge of Allan as a health resort' (typescript), pp. 1–5; Hembry, *British Spas*, pp. 207–15.

25 C. Price, 'A Welsh spaw', *Welsh Review*, 5(1) (1946), 42–4; *Leigh's Guide to Wales and Monmouthshire* (London, 1831), pp. 79, 185–6; J. B. Sinclair and R. W. D. Fenn, *Llanfair Ym Muallt: Builth Wells* (Stroud, 1993), pp. 9–11; G. H. Jenkins, *The Foundations of Modern Wales 1642–1780* (Oxford, 1993), p. 288; Hembry, *British Spas*, pp. 215–22.

26 D. Boorman, *The Brighton of Wales* (Swansea, 1986); P. Stead, 'The entertainment of the people', in G. Williams, ed., *Swansea: An Illustrated History* (Swansea, 1990), pp. 246–51; W. J. Lewis, 'Some aspects of the history of Aberystwyth: II, "The Brighton of Wales"', *Ceredigion*, 4(1) (1960), 19–35; W. J. Lewis, *Born on a Perilous Rock: Aberystwyth Past and Present*, 3rd edn (Aberystwyth, 1980), pp. 194–9; R. C. B. Oliver, 'Holidays at Aberystwyth: 1798–1823', *Ceredigion*, 10(3) (1986), 269–86; *The Tenby Guide*, 2nd edn (Swansea, 1810); *An Account of Tenby*, 2nd edn (London, 1820); M. A. Bourne, *Guide to Tenby and its Neighbourhood* (London, [1843]); W. Harrison, 'Some aspects of Tenby's history', *Pembrokeshire Historian*, 2 (1966), 54–74; J. Tipton, *Fair and Fashionable Tenby: Two Hundred Years as a Seaside Resort* (Tenby, 1987), pp. 5–16.

and 'middling sort'. It was the last of these groups, particularly the swelling ranks of the *haute bourgeoisie* (the professions, merchants, manufacturers, prosperous farmers, etc.), who provided the most dynamic ingredient in demand, though lower-middle-class elements also stimulated the growth of a 'popular' resort like Margate. At this stage working-class incomes were not a major force in resort development, and – outside the day excursion – they only became so from about the 1870s.[27] The expansion in the quantity of demand, and its widening social distribution, was a major factor in the emergence of the seaside resort. Opening up the coast enlarged, almost infinitely, the stock of watering-places available, permitting the resort system to absorb not only a greater volume of clientele, but also to respond to the market's increasingly diverse requirements for status, health and culture. The second wave of spa creations in the later eighteenth and early nineteenth centuries, located especially in the Midlands and the North, can also be seen as a response to the expansion in demand generated by regional economic growth during the early Industrial Revolution. War with France between 1793 and 1815, though initially a destabilising force – it contributed to the building crash in Bath in the 1790s – created, with the effective closure of the continent, an artificial boom in domestic demand, which provided a temporary springboard for the development of spas like Cheltenham and Leamington, and for launching the tourist industry in Devon.[28]

A critical influence in determining the demand for and geographical pattern of watering-places was urbanisation. Expanding towns and cities represented a concentrated market of resort consumers in search of an environment and life style – free from pollution, and devoted exclusively to health and leisure – which was the antithesis of their own. The influence of London – during the eighteenth century doubling in size from half a million to one million people and accommodating one in ten of the population of England and Wales – was huge, skewing the early network of resorts heavily towards the South-East. In 1724 Defoe commented on Epsom, ''tis very frequent for the trading part of the company to place their families here, and take their horses every morning to London', and in 1810 it was reported of Margate, 'this place is crowded with company, and indeed it may be considered as London in miniature, being in many circumstances an epitome of that vast metropolis'.[29] But it was not just London which exerted this type of impact. In Scotland the proximity of Edinburgh and Glasgow was critical in the early growth of watering-places like

[27] Walton, *Seaside Resort*, pp. 5–44; Whyman, 'Hanoverian watering-place', pp. 155–60.

[28] Hembry, *English Spa*, pp. 240, 243–4, 255, 285–301, 310–11; Fawcett and Bird, *Bath*, p. 69; Travis, *Devon Seaside Resorts*, pp. 26–7.

[29] Corfield, *Impact of English Towns*, pp. 8–9; D. Defoe, *A Tour through the Whole Island of Great Britain*, ed. G. D. H. Cole and D. C. Browning (London, 1962), vol. 1, p. 161; the *Morning Chronicle*, quoted in Whyman, 'Hanoverian watering-place', p. 143; Walton, *Seaside Resort*, pp. 12–14, 48–9.

Bridge of Allan, Portobello and Aberdour.[30] Resorts in the South-West of England, together with Swansea, owed much to visitors from Exeter, Tiverton, Bristol and Bath.[31] The rapidly expanding towns of the North were the driving force behind the rise of the Lancashire resorts. In 1841 Granville commented, 'As the Manchester people have their favourite sea-bathing at SOUTHPORT, so have those of Preston at BLACKPOOL'; during the season 'one may see the walls of that smoky city [Manchester] placarded with "Cheap travelling to Southport" – "Only five hours to Southport" – "Excursion to Southport;" and vociferations from a hundred throats to the same effect, are to be heard from the top of every species of vehicle in the principal streets'.[32]

On the supply side of the equation historians have traditionally placed considerable emphasis on accessibility and communications. Thus the Kent seaside towns flourished because of their excellent low-cost water links, first by sail then (after 1815) by steamboat, with London.[33] Bath profited from its proximity to Bristol and the West Country clothing industry, whose presence encouraged the early turnpiking of the roads to London. But the spa also enhanced its own position by acting with foresight to improve the poor thoroughfares in its immediate vicinity, through the navigation of the Avon to Bristol from 1727, and by pioneering – under the auspices of Ralph Allen – developments in the postal service.[34] At a general level, the arrival of the steam packet foreshadowed the impact of the railways, providing an important boost to the growth of many resorts.[35] On the other hand, poor communications and a slowness in adopting road improvements have been claimed to have restricted the early development of Cheltenham and the coastal resorts of the South-West, and within Devon to have been a factor in the differential evolution of the tourist industry in the south

[30] Durie, 'Bridge of Allan', p. 4; Durie, 'Scottish coastal resorts', 206–10; Simpson, 'Aberdour', p. 178.

[31] Travis, *Devon Seaside Resorts*, p. 11; J. Travis, 'Lynton in the nineteenth century: an isolated and exclusive resort', in Sigsworth, ed., *Ports and Resorts*, p. 155; Boorman, *Brighton of Wales*, p. 3.

[32] A. B. Granville, *The Spas of England and Principal Sea-Bathing Places*, vol. I: *The North* (London, 1841; repr., Bath, 1971), pp. 346–7; Bailey, *Southport*, pp. 59–73; J. Walvin, *Beside the Seaside: A Social History of the Popular Seaside Holiday* (London, 1978), pp. 29–30; Walton, *Blackpool Landlady*, pp. 14–15.

[33] J. Whyman, 'Water communications and their effect on the growth and character of Margate, circa 1750 to circa 1840', in Sigsworth, ed., *Ports and Resorts*, pp. 138–51; J. Whyman, 'Water communications to Margate and Gravesend as coastal resorts before 1840', *SHist.*, 3 (1981), 111–38; Whyman, *Kentish Seaside*, pp. 19–28.

[34] McIntyre, 'Bath', pp. 200, 208–11; B. J. Buchanan, 'The Great Bath Road', *Bath History*, 4 (1992), 71–94; B. Boyce, *The Benevolent Man: A Life of Ralph Allen of Bath* (Cambridge, Mass., 1967), pp. 10–55.

[35] Travis, 'Lynton in the nineteenth century', pp. 154–5; D. Neave, 'Transport and the early development of East Riding resorts', in Sigsworth, ed., *Ports and Resorts*, p. 107; R. W. Ambler, 'Cleethorpes: the development of an east coast resort', in Sigsworth, ed., *Ports and Resorts*, pp. 180–1; May, 'Rise of Ilfracombe', p. 140; Simpson, 'Aberdour', p. 178; Durie, 'Scottish coastal resorts', 209; Durie, 'Bridge of Allan', p. 2.

and north.[36] However, in explaining the pattern of resort growth we should avoid placing too much emphasis on ease of access and facility of communications. Southend was about half the distance of Margate to London, and by water that represented much the calmer portion of the journey along the Thames Estuary; yet, despite showing signs of development as a bathing place from the 1760s, it was still in the 1840s only a small resort.[37] It also, at this stage, retained its fashionable image, and it could be contended that the success of exclusive resorts, such as those in North Devon and Wales, depended upon their *inaccessibility*. The sheer difficulty and cost of a journey to Lynton, Tenby and Aberystwyth filtered out 'popular' elements and secured the high social tone of these places.[38]

The pattern and pace of development among watering-places depended not only upon their ease (or otherwise) of access, but also upon how they catered and competed for the patronage of the visitor population. It appears that resorts originated in places whose economies were particularly open to change, and that they developed a culture especially conducive to entrepreneurial activity. These issues will be explored later in this chapter. What is clear is that competition was a key factor in determining the way the resort system evolved. Spas and sea-bathing centres were part of a fiercely contested market for urban health and leisure services, which was regularly reinvigorated by new entrants. This encouraged innovation and investment in facilities, a sensitivity to pricing and a need to shape as well as respond to demand. It also led resorts to play an increasingly differentiated role. Early rivalry between Bath, Epsom and Tunbridge Wells may have led the Somerset spa to adopt a spring and autumn season, leaving the summer open to its competitors.[39] In staking a claim for the special qualities of Tenby, Mary Bourne in 1843 advanced an early version of niche-marketing:

> it cannot . . . boast the soft verdure and garden-like fertility of the Isle of Wight, the wooded luxuriance of the shores of Devon, the real magnificence of Brighton, or the advantages which their vicinity to the metropolis affords to watering-places on the southern and eastern coasts of England; but to none of these does it yield the palm of distinction to which its own unrivalled attractions entitle it . . . its smooth, firm and extensive sands – its healthful situation – the peculiar transparency of its ocean waters – its pure invigorating breezes.[40]

Competition existed not only between but also within resorts. Spas might be split into rival settlements, such as Great Malvern and Malvern Wells, the old and new towns at Leamington, Lower and Higher Harrogate, and

[36] Hart, *Cheltenham*, pp. 146, 232; Travis, *Devon Seaside Resorts*, pp. 11–14, 23–4.

[37] W. Pollitt, 'Southend: 1760–1860', *Transactions of the Southend-on-Sea Antiquarian and Historical Society*, 3(4) (1939), 212–49.

[38] Travis, 'Lynton in the nineteenth century', pp. 156, 159–64; Travis, *Lynton and Lynmouth*, pp. 23–36; *Tenby Guide* (1810), pp. 18–19; Lewis, 'Aspects of the history of Aberystwyth', 29–31.

[39] Hembry, *English Spa*, p. 92.

[40] Bourne, *Guide to Tenby*, pp. 1–2.

Southborough, Rusthall, Mount Ephraim and Mount Sion in seventeenth-century Tunbridge Wells.[41] Cheltenham had five different wells operating in the 1830s;[42] and Bath, Tunbridge Wells, Leamington and Cheltenham all had more than one set of assembly rooms vying for custom.[43]

Competition stimulated the provision of facilities; it encouraged both proliferation and rationalisation, uniformity and diversity; and as a force it was continuously reshaping the network of watering-places. Yet, countervailing this, and itself a factor in moulding the resort system, was the influence of mutuality. Within towns there had to be a degree of cooperation between entrepreneurs to facilitate an adequate provision of public facilities and services, and to ensure that suppliers did not cut each other's throat. It is significant that in Bath an agreement was arrived at to use the rival sets of rooms for balls on different days of the week.[44] The relationship between towns could also be of a non-competitive, supportive nature. Malvern benefited from the expansion of Cheltenham in the early nineteenth century, acting as an overflow for it.[45] Small watering-places might profit from the proximity of larger ones. In 1805 it was said that 'Filey is resorted to in the summer season by numerous parties from Scarborough and Bridlington', while in Sussex South Lancing and Heene were able to piggyback on the development of Worthing, and Rottingdean on that of Brighton.[46] The resorts of Kent, as well as competing with each other, also constituted two mutually supportive systems – Folkestone, Sandgate and Hythe on the one hand, and the Thanet bathing towns on the other – able to share visitors and facilities because of their contiguous location.[47] Through the mechanism of seasonal timing, neighbouring resorts could develop a relationship which complemented and strengthened rather than contradicted and weakened each other. Bristol Hotwells was a summer spa, Bath a spring, autumn and (increasingly) winter one, and at the end of the season visitors and tradesmen moved from one to the other. Torquay's success was built on its role as a winter watering-place, while Paignton – its satellite – developed as a summer bathing place.[48] It could be argued that whereas mutuality encouraged clustering in the resort network, competition enhanced the tendency towards dispersal.

41 Smith, *Malvern*, pp. 171–94; Baxter, 'Visitors to Leamington Spa . . . Part I', 32, and 'Part II', 47, 55; Jennings, *Harrogate and Knaresborough*, p. 228; Burr, *Tunbridge Wells*, pp. 38–9, 44–6.

42 S. Blake, *Pittville 1824–1860* (Cheltenham, 1988), p. 5.

43 Wood, *Description of Bath*, pp. 319–20; J. Savage, *The New Bath Guide* (Bath, 1809), pp. 19–25; Savidge, *Tunbridge Wells*, pp. 64–5; Baxter, 'Visitors to Leamington Spa . . . Part I', 32; Hart, *Cheltenham*, pp. 134–5.

44 Wood, *Description of Bath*, p. 411; C. Pope, *The New Bath Guide* (Bath, [1762]), pp. 28–9; R. Cruttwell, *The New Bath Guide* (Bath, 1784), pp. 22–3.

45 Smith, *Malvern*, p. 174.

46 Quoted in Neave, 'East Riding resorts', p. 104; Farrant, 'Sussex by the sea', p. 171.

47 Whyman, *Kentish Seaside*, pp. 17–19.

48 Little, 'Gloucestershire spas', p. 175; B. Little, *The City and County of Bristol: A Study in Atlantic Civilisation* (London, 1954), pp. 231–2; Travis, *Devon Seaside Resorts*, p. 70.

(iii) URBAN STATUS, RELATIONSHIP AND TYPOLOGY

The chronology and pattern of resort development, and the broad forces behind this, have been briefly surveyed. But to what extent were the entities being created actually *urban*? How did they compare and relate to other towns in the business of providing high status commercialised health and leisure? And what was the nature of that principal distinction in resort typology, between inland and coastal watering-place?

By orthodox defining characteristics[49] – such as size, political structure and appearance – a high proportion (perhaps the majority) of Georgian resorts would find it difficult to pass muster as a town. Many were only small, indeed tiny, settlements. John Walton's list of seventy-one seaside resorts in 1851 contains only nine with a population of over 10,000 (two of these were 'considerably inflated by non-resort elements' in their make up), and over half had under 3,000 inhabitants. In 1841 only three of the principal resorts in Devon possessed a population of over 4,000, and none exceeded 6,000.[50] All this was after a century or so of growth among coastal watering-places. Of the 173 spas Phyllis Hembry catalogues as founded between 1558 and 1815, a great many were located in villages and hamlets that could never have contained more than a handful of inhabitants.[51] Even spas of some significance were often only small. Buxton, after its late eighteenth-century burst of growth, still only contained 760 people in 1801, and scarcely much more than 1,000 in 1861; Great Malvern, a spa which had been commercially developed from the mid-eighteenth century, had under 1,000 inhabitants in 1801, a figure which only just passed the 2,000 mark in 1831, despite considerable investment in the 1820s.[52] Many resorts possessed no more than village political institutions, and contemporary observers frequently seemed ambivalent as to the urban character of such places. In 1749 Elizabeth Montagu could write of Tunbridge Wells: 'the houses are scattered irregularly . . . [it] looks, from the window I now sit by, a little like the village you see from our terrace at Sandleford'. Seventeen years later Thomas Burr confirmed this impression, when he described the Kent spa as a 'populous and a flourishing village'; but then in the same work he depicted it as having 'the appearance of a town in the midst of woods', and declared that the four settlements of Mount Ephraim, Mount Pleasant, Mount Sion and the Wells, 'all united together, form a considerable town'.[53] A writer in the *St James' Chronicle* of 1790 maintained that 'every watering place is a kind of urbs in rure', which though it attested to the urban character of spas, also emphasised their rural context.[54] One commen-

[49] Clark and Slack, *English Towns in Transition*, pp. 2–7; Corfield, *Impact of English Towns*, pp. 4–6.

[50] Walton, *Seaside Resort*, p. 53; Travis, *Devon Seaside Resorts*, pp. 68, 85.

[51] Hembry, *English Spa*, pp. 355–60.

[52] *Ibid.*, pp. 216–27, 250–4; Heape, *Buxton*, esp. p. 47; Smith, *Malvern*, especially p. 188.

[53] Montagu quoted in Savidge, *Tunbridge Wells*, p. 63; Burr, *Tunbridge Wells*, pp. 98–9, 103, 273.

tator in 1723 called Margate 'a small fishing town', another in 1763 'only a large village'.[55] In 1841 Granville adjudged that,

> While Cheltenham and Leamington have converted themselves, in the course of a few years, from mere villages that they were, into smart and pert towns, Harrogate has remained a village still. It has been brushed up a little to be sure, and extended somewhat . . . ; but so wildly and irregularly . . . that pretension to any thing above a village it has none.[56]

Given such evidence it may seem doubtful whether resorts as a body of settlements should be included in a history of urban Britain, at least before 1840. Yet we should be wary about excluding them. Population figures can be misleading, and can omit the influx of visitors who swelled the size of a watering-place during the season. Many (but not, of course, all) resorts were proto-towns, and though during the early stages of growth they remained village-like in size and political structure, they already displayed urban characteristics and contained the seeds of urbanism within them. Indeed, some tendency towards becoming a town was probably essential for long-term survival and success. A small and isolated spa like Astrop in Northamptonshire, which between the late seventeenth century and about 1800 seems to have maintained a credible social season, ultimately suffered from its failure to develop an infrastructure of urban services, and today virtually all trace of it has vanished.[57] However, in the ultimate analysis the argument for treating resorts as urban, even if they were very small, is that their social life and culture was that of a town and not a village. The presence of facilities like a pump room, assembly room, fine walks, library, theatre, luxury shops, lodging houses and inns; of the sophisticated social routine that tied these together; and of a high status, leisured visitor population – all these features pointed to a town in spirit, if not in hard demographic fact. It was probably this which a poet of 1693 had in mind when he wrote of Tunbridge Wells (which in the early eighteenth century possessed only about 150 houses):

> The pretty Walk, the Crowd, the splendid Street,
> Of Shops above the Market Folks that meet,
> The frequent People, Gentry mix'd with Clown,
> Makes up a something, something like a Town.[58]

The rise of the resort was not an isolated phenomenon. It was part of a much broader tendency, distinguishable from at least the late Stuart period, for towns

[54] *St James' Chronicle*, 28–31 Aug. 1790. I am indebted to Peter Clark for this reference.

[55] Whyman, 'Hanoverian watering-place', p. 144.

[56] Granville, *Spas of England*, p. 38.

[57] C. Tongue, 'Thomas Thornton at Astrop Spa', *Northamptonshire Past and Present*, 4 (1970–1), 281–5; Hembry, *English Spa*, pp. 70–1; N. Pevsner, *The Buildings of England: Northamptonshire*, 2nd edn, revised B. Cherry (Harmondsworth, 1973), p. 96.

[58] *Metellus, His Dialogues*, quoted in Savidge, *Tunbridge Wells*, p. 41; Chalklin, 'Some new towns', p. 234.

to cater to the needs of the social elite for leisure and luxury.[59] It was a trend which affected many of the larger centres in the urban system, most noticeably London, the provincial capitals and the county towns. A number of the last of these established their own small spas – such was the case at Canterbury, Durham and Northampton[60] – and acquired recreational facilities, like assembly rooms and theatres, to be found in watering-places. But county towns and resorts were different types of settlements. The former usually enjoyed a broad range of economic functions, including commerce and manufacture, displayed strong traditions of civic government and culture, built its elite recreational life around the winter season and drew patrons with strong regional ties; the latter's economy was based far more exclusively on health and leisure, it usually had a less sophisticated political system, it was influenced to a much greater extent by the seasonal cycle (which was normally orientated around the summer), and enjoyed a more cosmopolitan clientage.[61] Because the two types of centre were distinctive, operating to different seasonal cycles, it is unlikely that they damaged each other through competition – at least until the early nineteenth century, when some resorts began to make inroads into the markets for winter holidays and permanent residence.

Within the category of resorts the most obvious distinction which began to appear from the mid-eighteenth century was that between inland and coastal watering-places. How far contemporaries perceived the two types of settlements as different, particularly early on, is a debatable point. Both provided water-based therapies, and many seaside resorts – such as Brighton, Scarborough, Swansea, Tenby (at nearby Gumfreston) and Aberystwyth – developed their own springs to supplement sea water treatment. Brighton, as well as a chalybeate spring, which was commercially exploited from the 1750s, also possessed from 1825 the German Spa, where artificial mineral waters were manufactured and dispensed.[62] The similarities between the two types of watering-place were reinforced by the way, well into the nineteenth century, coastal resorts aped the facilities, daily routine and architecture of their inland counterparts, particularly deploying Bath as model.[63]

59 P. Borsay, *The English Urban Renaissance* (Oxford, 1989).

60 C. Morris, ed., *The Journeys of Celia Fiennes* (London, 1947), pp. 125, 216; *VCH*, Northamptonshire, III, p. 23.

61 For a discussion of these issues, though from different perspectives, see A. McInnes, 'The emergence of a leisure town: Shrewsbury 1660–1760', *P&P*, 120 (1988), 53–87; P. Borsay and A. McInnes, 'Debate: the emergence of a leisure town: or an urban renaissance?', *P&P*, 126 (1990), 189–202.

62 Gilbert, *Brighton*, pp. 60–1, 73–5; J. D. Parry, *An Historical and Descriptive Account of the Coast of Sussex* (Brighton and London, 1833; repr., London, 1970), pp. 135–6; Rowntree, ed., *Scarborough*, pp. 247–72; Sandell, 'Georgian Southampton', p. 80; Boorman, *Brighton of Wales*, p. 17; *Account of Tenby* (1820), pp. 120–4; Lewis, 'Aspects of the history of Aberystwyth', 23–4; see also Neave, 'East Riding resorts', pp. 105–6.

63 Walton, *Seaside Resort*, pp. 156–7; Travis, *Devon Seaside Resorts*, pp. 18, 38–41; Pimlott, *Englishman's Holiday*, p. 59; Corbin, *Lure of the Sea*, pp. 254–7; Neave, 'East Riding resorts', pp. 101–2.

However, there were important differences which encouraged the growing popularity of coastal centres.[64] On the practical front the seaside often had the advantage of easy access by water. The cost of a visit was probably less than that to a spa; the season was shorter and therefore the length of stay less, and the compulsory round of subscriptions, a heavy burden at an established centre like Bath, would not be so onerous at a coastal resort still developing its facilities. Whereas personal behaviour and social routine at the traditional spa became highly structured, the seaside offered a more informal ambience. The very character of the beach and sea, their wide expanses resistant to formal landscaping in the manner of a garden or walk, encouraged a more relaxed approach to holidaying. For a visitor market wearying of the formulaic nature of spa culture, or at least desiring a change of tempo, this may well have proved very attractive. One authoress in 1845 described the somewhat anarchic scene on the 'sands' at Margate, which appeared 'one indiscriminate moving mass of cabs, cars, carts and carriages; horses, ponies, dogs, donkies, and boys; men, women, children, and nurses; and, the least and the biggest – babies and bathing machines'.[65] Young children, a well nigh invisible group in accounts of Georgian spas, would have found the seaside far more accommodating, and the rise of the coastal resort may reflect a new emphasis on childhood and the middle-class family holiday.[66] Finally, in assessing the appeal of the coast we should not underestimate the simple factor of the sea itself, which was beginning to occupy a quite new prominence in the cultural construction of health and leisure.[67] All this said, it must be remembered that spas continued to flourish in the late Georgian period, so that inland and coastal watering-places should be seen as much complementing as competing with each other.

(iv) ECONOMIC, SOCIAL, POLITICAL AND CULTURAL CHARACTERISTICS OF RESORTS

What sorts of urban organisms were resorts? What were their central characteristics? These are the questions which will be addressed in the final section of this chapter, exploring the particular economic, social, political and cultural features displayed by watering-places.

Many seaside resorts developed in settlements facing economic difficulties, primarily through a decline in their trading activities and fishing industry. Brighton, for example, had flourished between the late sixteenth and mid-seventeenth centuries through fishing and to a lesser extent cargo carrying, so that its population at least trebled and it became (with 4,000 inhabitants) the largest

[64] Walton, *Seaside Resort*, pp. 16–18, 217–18; Pimlott, *Englishman's Holiday*, pp. 55–6; Farrant, *Georgian Brighton*, pp. 3–4.

[65] Mrs Stone, *Chronicles of Fashion* (1845), in Whyman, *Kentish Seaside*, p. 197.

[66] J. H. Plumb, 'The new world of children in eighteenth-century England', *P&P*, 67 (1975), 64–95.

[67] Corbin, *Lure of the Sea*.

town in Sussex. Yet between 1650 and 1750 a withdrawal from North Sea fishing, prompted in part by the erosion of the town's foreshore, led to long-term decline and a halving of its population.[68] Tenby had been facing economic problems since Elizabethan times, was already in a physically ruinous condition by the late seventeenth century, and in 1813 was described as 'a poor neglected fishing town' until 'rescued by its attractions for sea-bathing'.[69] By the late eighteenth century the west Fife village of Aberdour seems to have been stagnating, and during the early decades of the next century its native industries (especially weaving) continued to decline.[70] In 1806 Edmund Bartell observed that Cromer, then just emerging as a genteel resort, 'must formerly have been a place of much more consequence than it is at present', and that 'The mercantile trade here is small; the want of a convenient harbour, where ships might ride in safety, will ever be an obstacle.'[71] Such problems provided a powerful stimulus for depressed settlements to embrace enthusiastically the new opportunities offered by tourism. It is less easy to find evidence of spa development being encouraged by decline, though the depression in Bath's textile industry in the late sixteenth and early seventeenth centuries may have accelerated the city's rise as a watering-place.[72] In the long run, of course, the resort function could itself be undermined by new opportunities for commercial and industrial expansion, as the cases of Southampton and Swansea were to demonstrate.[73]

Resort economies were naturally geared towards the tertiary sector; they were service towns *par excellence*. The effect of this is illustrated by the case of Brighton, where 'Between 1750 and 1780 the town's employment structure was profoundly altered by the transition from seafaring town to seaside resort.' Jobs in the maritime trades declined in significance whereas those directed towards the needs of fashionable visitors and residents expanded. Services (excluding accommodation) accounted for over 40 per cent of the entries in the town's late Georgian directories, representing by far the largest sector in Brighton's economy.[74] The most direct impact on resort employment was in the leisure and

[68] S. Farrant and J. H. Farrant, 'Brighton, 1580–1820: from Tudor town to Regency resort', *Sussex Archaeological Collections*, 118 (1980), 331–41; Farrant, *Georgian Brighton*, pp. 6–13.

[69] C. Norris, *Etchings of Tenby* (London, 1812), p. ii; *Account of Tenby* (1820), pp. 21–30, 34, 125–30; T. Rees, *The Beauties of England and Wales . . . South Wales . . . Volume XVIII* (London, 1815), p. 767; Harrison, 'Tenby's history', 54–7; B. Howells, *Pembrokeshire County History*, vol. III: *Early Modern Pembrokeshire, 1536–1815* (Haverfordwest, 1987), pp. 293–4, 328.

[70] Simpson, 'Aberdour', p. 177.

[71] E. Bartell, *Cromer, Considered as a Watering Place, with Observations on the Picturesque Scenery in the Neighbourhood*, 2nd edn (London, 1806), pp. 3, 21. For other cases of economic decline prior to resort development see Walton, *Seaside Resort*, p. 49; Travis, *Devon Seaside Resorts*, p. 17; Travis, 'Lynton in the nineteenth century', pp. 153–4; Travis, *Lynton and Lynmouth*, pp. 8–13; Whyman, 'Hanoverian watering-place', p. 144; Sandell, 'Georgian Southampton', p. 79; May, 'Rise of Ilfracombe', pp. 138–40; Holmes, *Sidmouth*, p. 44.

[72] McIntyre, 'Bath', p. 201.

[73] Sandell, 'Georgian Southampton', p. 87; Boorman, *Brighton of Wales*, pp. 94–5.

[74] Farrant, *Georgian Brighton*, pp. 43–8.

health fields (musicians, bathing attendants, etc.), but numerically far more important was the plethora of jobs generated indirectly by the presence of the wealthy *beau monde.* Retailing assumed a central position. There were busy food markets purveying high quality produce. Specialist luxury shops (such as booksellers, jewellers, souvenir sellers, milliners and confectioners) were a marked feature, often clustered together in a prestigious retailing zone – the Pantiles in Tunbridge Wells, Orange Grove and later (as the focus of the city shifted northwards) Milsom Street in Bath, Castle Street and the eastern end of North Street in late eighteenth-century Brighton.[75] The provision of accommodation was another important source of employment. Between 1773 and 1800 the number of lodging and boarding house keepers listed in the Bath guides rose from 263 to 430, and to their ranks must be added the large volume of servants hired for use in these establishments.[76] The visitors had high mobility needs – for their bodies, goods and correspondence – and this created many jobs in the areas of intra- and extramural transport and communications. By 1799, for example, Bath supported some 340 registered chairmen, who constituted a distinctive, and occasionally militant, occupational group. [77] The leading resorts were also home to a concentration of educational services, including not only a multiplicity of private schools – by 1851 Brighton had 189 such establishments catering for over 4,000 children – but also specialist instructors in fashionable accomplishments. The 1812 *Improved Bath Guide* listed fifteen teachers of art and drawing, seven of languages, thirteen of dancing and thirty-seven 'professors of music, teachers of the harp, piano-forte, flute, &c. and music-sellers'.[78] In highlighting the importance of the tertiary economy to resorts it would be a mistake to ignore the impact of other sectors, and the variation in occupational structure between different watering-places. In many small spas and seaside resorts it is probable that agriculture and fishing remained major areas of activity. Several sizeable coastal towns, such as Yarmouth and Lowestoft in East Anglia, managed to combine the role of successful resort, port and fishing centre.[79] Industry, of one type or another, was almost inevitably an aspect of a flourishing resort. Rapid physical expansion boosted the building industry, and the presence of well-heeled con-

[75] Morris, ed., *Celia Fiennes*, pp. 133–4; Burr, *Tunbridge Wells*, pp. 100–2, 107–8: T. Fawcett and M. Inskipp, 'The making of Orange Grove', *Bath History*, 5 (1994), 24–50; P. Egan, *Walks through Bath* (Bath, 1819), pp. 68–9, 140; T. Fawcett, 'Eighteenth-century shops and the luxury trade', *Bath History*, 3 (1990), 49–75; Farrant, *Georgian Brighton*, p. 47. [76] McIntyre, 'Bath', p. 218.

[77] *Ibid.*, p. 220; T. Fawcett, 'Chair transport in Bath: the sedan era', *Bath History*, 2 (1988), 113–38.

[78] Gilbert, *Brighton*, p. 197; *The Improved Bath Guide* (Bath, [1812]), pp. 129–30; *Letters from Bath 1766–1767 by the Rev. John Penrose*, ed. B. Mitchell and H. Penrose (Gloucester, 1983), pp. 144, 146, 167, 171–2; T. Fawcett, 'Dance and teachers of dance in eighteenth-century Bath', *Bath History*, 2 (1988), 27–48; T. Fawcett, *Voices of Eighteenth-Century Bath: An Anthology* (Bath, 1995), pp. 121–30.

[79] J. H. Druery, *History and Topography of Great Yarmouth* (London, 1826); C. Lewis, *Great Yarmouth: History, Herrings and Holidays* (North Walsham, 1988), pp. 15–24, 29–30; P. Clements, *Lowestoft: 200 Years a Seaside Resort* (Lowestoft, 1994), pp. 5–7.

sumers stimulated the clothing trades and craft manufacture. Moreover, a health and leisure function by no means precluded a town capitalising on trends in the broader national economy. Fom the late eighteenth century Bath experienced a process of what R. S. Neale has dubbed 'incipient industrialization', one feature of which was a thriving engineering industry.[80]

Because of their newness and potential for growth, resorts were particularly conducive to entrepreneurial activity. Aristocratic and gentry landowners were frequently involved in promotion and exploitation; for example, the fifth duke of Devonshire at Buxton, Lord Courtenay at Teignmouth, Sir William Johnstone Pulteney in Bath, Sir Robert Abercrombie at Bridge of Allan and Thomas Read Kemp in Brighton.[81] The opportunity to maximise the returns on property holdings provided the obvious stimulus in these cases. For another major group of promoters, medical men, it was the occasion to exploit their professional skills and expand their practices that encouraged them to become heavily committed to advancing and publicising watering-places; Dr Russell in Brighton, Dr Jephson in Leamington or the apothecary John Livingston at Epsom are examples.[82] Hoteliers and innkeepers were also an important element in stimulating resort development.[83] A range of other well-off middling men – such as merchants, solicitors and bankers – searching for an outlet for their surplus capital might be involved in promoting a resort, or an extension to one. The successful Cirencester attorney, Joseph Pitt, directed his wealth not only towards banking, politics and becoming a country gentleman; he also made heavy purchases of property in Cheltenham, promoting from the 1820s the development of Pittville, a new spa and superior residential district on the edge of the town. Pitt may have initiated and overseen the project, but much of the capital for building was drawn from professional people and leisured society, and the responsibility for construction was carried by a host of individuals (especially those in the building industry and the professions) who erected a few properties each for speculative gain.[84]

The scale of the Pittville scheme was exceptional (though not unique) among resort development in the Georgian period; what was typical was the widespread

[80] McIntyre, 'Bath', pp. 215–16; Neale, *Bath*, pp. 268–74; Davis and Bonsall, *Bath*, pp. 87–99.

[81] Hembry, *English Spa*, pp. 218–27, 166–75, 361–4; Heape, *Buxton*, pp. 19–41; Travis, *Devon Seaside Resorts*, p. 38; Neale, *Bath*, pp. 226–42; *Beyond Mr Pulteney's Bridge* (Bath, 1987); Durie, 'Bridge of Allan', p. 4; Gilbert, *Brighton*, pp. 98–9; A. Dale, *The History and Architecture of Brighton* (Brighton, 1950), pp. 68–9.

[82] Hembry, *English Spa*, pp. 106–7, 251; Hembry, *British Spas*, pp. 12–13; Gilbert, *Brighton*, pp. 56–62; Baxter, 'Visitors to Leamington Spa . . . Part I', 19–20; Clark, 'Epsom spa', 1–41.

[83] Hembry, *English Spa*, pp. 202–30; Jennings, *Harrogate and Knaresborough*, pp. 290–6; Smith, *Malvern*, pp. 178–9; Farrant, *Georgian Brighton*, p. 26.

[84] Blake, *Pittville*; R. K. Howes, 'Joseph Pitt and Pittville', *Gloucestershire Historical Studies*, 6 (1974–5), 58–60; R. K. Howes, 'Joseph Pitt, landowner', *Gloucestershire Historical Studies*, 7 (1976), 20–4; R. K. Howes, 'The rise and fall of Joseph Pitt', *Gloucestershire Historical Studies*, 8 (1977), 62–72.

involvement of the middling orders as developers, investors and speculators.[85] Some capital and expertise came from London, and resorts in the South-East were particularly subject to this influence; Tunbridge Wells from the late seventeenth century, and Brighton from the 1780s, benefited from metropolitan investment.[86] But most finance was probably generated locally, and – in terms of the relationship between county town and watering-place – it is significant that capital for the early development of Brighton came from Lewes and for Leamington from Warwick.[87] Examples of civic promotion of facilities, something frequently found in county towns,[88] are less easy to find, but this may simply be a reflection of the undeveloped character of corporate government in resorts, and a lack of public monies. Bath corporation's response to the growth of the town as a spa was relatively sluggish, only releasing its extensive property holdings for building from the mid-eighteenth century. However, private enterprise in the city did not need a helping hand; moreover, later in the eighteenth century as their income began to grow substantially, the city fathers did spend heavily on civic improvement.[89] Swansea was one town where the corporation displayed an impressive level of commitment to the development of the resort, investing in bathing facilities, walks, horse and boat racing and taking over the financing of the assembly rooms (opened in 1822) when a scheme to raise private capital failed.[90]

Often located in settlements which were relatively undeveloped, or which were suffering economic decline, watering-places encouraged change and innovation, particularly in the fields of services and property development. They also tended to attract those with surplus capital and who were willing to take a risk, from theatre managers to bankers, since the scope for investment, and the *potential* returns, were high. All this ensured that resorts nurtured an economy, and an economic culture, that was opportunistic and entrepreneurial.

Watering-places were also characterised by a special sort of social environment, the product of the pursuit of sociability on the one hand, and social difference or status on the other. Georgian resorts can be likened to exclusive holiday camps, or as Pimlott describes them 'a cruising liner or a winter-sports hotel', in which there are intense pressures to behave in a corporate fashion.[91] This was reflected in the notion of the 'company', which was intended to be the principal unit of social interaction, and to whose norms and practices the visitors were expected to demonstrate loyalty. In the language of the anthropologist Victor

[85] C. W. Chalklin, *The Provincial Towns of Georgian England* (London, 1974), esp. pp. 74–80; Neale, *Bath*, pp. 151–69; Farrant, *Georgian Brighton*, pp. 27–43; Walton, *Seaside Resort*, pp. 110–15.

[86] Chalklin, 'Some new towns', pp. 248–9; Hembry, *English Spa*, pp. 80–3; Savidge, *Tunbridge Wells*, pp. 108–15; Farrant, *Georgian Brighton*, p. 27.

[87] Farrant, 'Sussex by the sea', p. 169; Hembry, *English Spa*, pp. 295–6.

[88] Borsay, *English Urban Renaissance*, pp. 218–19.

[89] McIntyre, 'Bath', pp. 222–37.

[90] Boorman, *Brighton of Wales*, pp. 14–16, 41–53, 67–81.

[91] Pimlott, *Englishman's Holiday*, pp. 40–3.

Turner, the holiday might be seen as a 'liminal' phase in the year, in which fashionable society was thrown together to reinforce the ties of 'communitas'.[92] Such a bonding experience played an important role in integrating new recruits into the social elite and in mitigating the severe religious and political divisions evident in the ruling order since the mid-seventeenth century. A wide variety of mechanisms were deployed to weld together the company. A form of domestic architecture was adopted – in the classical terrace, square and crescent – which subsumed individual dwellings into a larger residential unit; a daily routine was constructed, in many spas of a rigorously formal character, designed to ensure that everyone was doing the same thing in the same place at the same time; in several resorts a master of ceremonies emerged (the most famous being Richard Nash at Bath and Tunbridge Wells) whose responsibility it was to promote order, sociability and conformity within the company; there arose a method of payment (the subscription system) for the use of the recreational facilities which pressurised and committed the visitors to participate in the resort's social life; and these facilities – such as walks, theatres, concerts and assemblies – were of a character which maximised the opportunities and obligations to engage in social intercourse.[93] In some resorts, particularly the spas of the Midlands and North, responsibility for integrating the company rested with lodging houses, inns and hotels, which were the real focal points of social life rather than public facilities. Samuel Essington's hotel in early nineteenth-century Malvern operated a series of rules, one of which required 'the company to assemble and dine together, at the public table, in the great room, at three o'clock each day; – the first bell to be rung at half-past two, and the dinner bell at three o'clock. – No lodger to dine privately in the house, unless sickness render it necessary.'[94]

The ideal of the unified 'company' would always be a difficult one to sustain, given the inherent competitiveness of Georgian society. At times, such as at Bath in the late 1760s or Cheltenham in the early 1780s, the visitors split into two separate factions.[95] In the long term, however, a more serious threat to the corporate principle was posed by the rise of private clubs and parties, something detectable in Bath from the late eighteenth century, the resorts of South Devon from about the 1820s, and Cheltenham and Leamington in the 1830s and 1840s.[96] The trend towards privatisation was a reaction to the growing social

92 V. Turner, *The Ritual Process: Structure and Anti-Structure* (Chicago, 1969), ch. 3.

93 Borsay, *English Urban Renaissance*, pp. 219–20, 267–83.

94 Smith, *Malvern*, p. 180; Hembry, *English Spa*, p. 202; Borsay, *English Urban Renaissance*, p. 274; Heape, *Buxton*, p. 27.

95 *The Bath Contest* (Bath, 1769); *The Conciliade; Being a Supplement to the Bath Contest* (Bath, 1769); Hart, *Cheltenham*, p. 131.

96 Suffolk RO, E2/25/3, Lady M. Cullum to E. Hanson, 13 Jan. 1789; Barbeau, *Bath*, pp. 298–300; R. Mainwaring, *The Annals of Bath, from the Year 1800 to the Passing of the New Municipal Act* (Bath, 1838), p. 67; Travis, *Devon Seaside Resorts*, pp. 72–3; Hart, *Cheltenham*, p. 205; Baxter, 'Visitors to Leamington Spa . . . Part I', 36–7.

heterogeneity of the clientele attracted to resorts – a result, in particular, of the accelerating flow of middle-class visitors – and the consequent need to create ghettoes of exclusivity. This reminds us that watering-places were not only places for social mixing, but also for the expression of status and class. There were long traditions of popular sea-bathing and usage of springs,[97] but the sustained trip to spa or seaside during the Georgian period was very largely an upper- and middle-class activity, and part of their strategy to acquire social prestige.

Resorts varied considerably in their social tone, and therefore in the degree of kudos they provided for their patrons. In 1724 Daniel Defoe described how in the vicinity of London, 'as the nobility and gentry go to Tunbridge, the merchants and rich citizens to Epsome; so the common people go chiefly to Dullwich and Stretham'.[98] In the early nineteenth century there was a considerable difference between aristocratic Brighton and middle-class Margate, the latter's image lowered by the easy and cheap access to it by boat from London.[99] The proliferation of small coastal resorts from the late eighteenth century reflects the urge, particularly with the continent closed during the war, of the aristocracy, gentry, and *haute bourgeoisie* to explore further and further afield in Britain to escape the swelling ranks of the middle-class holidaymakers. Tiny pockets of exclusivity were created, especially in the relatively remote and inaccessible South-West and Wales, at resorts such as Lynton, Tenby and Aberystwyth.[100]

Since status was one of the commodities dealt in by watering-places, then establishing social tone was of paramount importance. Royal patronage was the ultimate mark of distinction, and several resorts – such as Bath, Brighton, Weymouth, Cheltenham and Leamington – received a major (perhaps critical) boost from this quarter. Leamington obtained the ultimate accolade when in 1838 it was permitted by Queen Victoria to append the 'Royal' prefix to its name.[101] The publishing of visitor lists in the local newspaper was another means

[97] Porter, *Fylde of Lancashire*, p. 319; Lewis, 'Aspects of the history of Aberystwyth', 23; Walton, *Seaside Resort*, pp. 9–11; Walvin, *Beside the Seaside*, pp. 23–4, 31; K. Thomas, *Religion and the Decline of Magic* (Harmondsworth, 1973), pp. 54–5; J. and C. Bord, *Sacred Waters: Holy Wells and Water Lore in Britain and Ireland* (London, 1986); Jennings, *Harrogate and Knaresborough*, pp. 221–3, 297. [98] Defoe, *Tour*, I, p. 157.

[99] Whyman, 'Water communications and their effect on the growth and character of Margate', pp. 141–2; Whyman, 'Hanoverian watering-place', pp. 155–9.

[100] Travis, 'Lynton in the nineteenth century', pp. 155–6; *Tenby Guide* (1810), pp. 25–8; Rees, *Beauties of England and Wales*, p. 765; Tipton, *Fair and Fashionable Tenby*, p. 11; Lewis, 'Aspects of the history of Aberystwyth', 31; Lewis, *Born on a Perilous Rock*, p. 196; Oliver, 'Holidays at Aberystwyth', 269–86.

[101] Wood, *Description of Bath*, pp. 85, 204, 206–7, 216–17, 221, 259–61, 324, 333, 342–3, 347–8; P. Egan, *Walks through Bath* (Bath, 1819), pp. 64–5; Mainwaring, *Annals of Bath*, pp. 17, 138, 183–90; Gilbert, *Brighton*, pp. 16, 88–91, 105–6, 125–6; Hutchins, *Dorset*, I, pp. 469–71; McIntyre, 'Towns as health and pleasure resorts', p. 308; Hart, *Cheltenham*, pp. 138–43, 161, 188; Little, 'Gloucestershire spas', pp. 190–8; Baxter, 'Visitors to Leamington Spa . . . Part I', 15, 'Part II', 51–2; Chaplin, 'Royal Leamington Spa', 28; and also Pimlott, *Englishman's Holiday*, pp. 60–1; J.

by which a watering-place could proclaim the social caste of its clientele. Within resorts a whole series of mechanisms existed for asserting and securing exclusivity. Different seasons could be demarcated for the different classes. The charitable hospital opened in 1826 at Harrogate to offer water treatment for the poor was closed annually between early July and early September, so that its patients' presence would not – it was alleged – offend the sensibilities of the wealthy summer visitors. In 1841 it was said of Brighton that 'the summer months are abandoned to the trading population of London, the early autumn is surrendered to the lawyers; and when November summons them to Westminster, the *beau monde* commence their migration . . . secure from any participation of the pleasure with a plebeian multitude'.[102] Access to polite recreations would be restricted by the heavy formal costs of subscription and (even heavier) informal expenses of dressing for the occasion. More overt barriers also existed to the use of fashionable facilities like clubs,[103] walks,[104] and assemblies. The 'trading part of the inhabitants of Bath, however respectable', were excluded from the balls in the Upper Rooms, and the 1826 rules for the High Street assembly rooms in Cheltenham declared 'that no clerk, hired or otherwise, in this town or neighbourhood; no person concerned in retail trade; no theatrical or other performers . . . be admitted'.[105] The creation of select residential blocks and estates – such as the crescents and squares in Bath, Pittville in Cheltenham, Kemp Town and Brunswick Town in Brighton and Calverley Park in Tunbridge Wells – provided further opportunities both to protect and assert status.[106]

One of the most striking characteristics of resorts was the female profile of their population. At Tunbridge Wells in 1831 for every 100 males there were 122 females, at Tenby in 1811, 148, and Bath in 1801, 159.[107] The key factor responsible for this was undoubtedly the dominance of the service sector, with its high demand for female labour, especially as domestic servants. But the presence of large numbers of affluent women visitors and residents also made an important contribution. Of the visitors of independent means listed in the 1841 census for

Barrett, 'Spas and seaside resorts, 1660–1780', in *The Rise of the New Urban Society* (Open University, Milton Keynes, 1977), p. 50; Burr, *Tunbridge Wells*, pp. 62–4; Sandell, 'Georgian Southampton', pp. 79, 82; Riley, *The Growth of Southsea*, p. 5.

102 Jennings, *Harrogate and Knaresborough*, p. 298; *New Monthly Magazine*, 61 (1841), quoted in Gilbert, *Brighton*, p. 109; Corbin, *Lure of the Sea*, pp. 277–8; Baxter, 'Visitors to Leamington Spa . . . Part I', 19.

103 J. Savage, Meyler and Son, *The Original Bath Guide* ([Bath], 1811), pp. 114–15; *Improved Bath Guide* (1812), pp. 102–3; Baxter, 'Visitors to Leamington Spa . . . Part I', 58.

104 Rowntree, ed., *Scarborough*, p. 274; Boorman, *Brighton of Wales*, pp. 69–70.

105 Savage, Meyler and Son, *Original Bath Guide* (1811), p. 107; Hart, *Cheltenham*, p. 191.

106 Barrett, 'Spas and seaside resorts', pp. 55–7; Blake, *Pittville*, p. 24; Dale, *History and Architecture of Brighton*, pp. 67–76; Savidge, *Tunbridge Wells*, pp. 108–15.

107 Savidge, *Tunbridge Wells*, p. 116; Rees, *Beauties of England and Wales*, p. 765; McIntyre, 'Bath', p. 214; and also Neale, *Bath*, pp. 275–81; Davis and Bonsall, *Bath*, p. 69; Walton, *Seaside Resort*, pp. 98–101.

Margate, 63 per cent were women.[108] It is possible that this created and reflected a social system in watering-places which for well-off women was more than usually geared to their needs and aspirations, allowing them *comparatively* more autonomy in fields such as human relationships, marriage brokering, charitable work, gambling and leisure in general. It is probably for this reason that women of independent means, such as wealthy spinsters and widows, were so attracted to resorts. Such a system did not, of course, undermine the fundamentally gendered character of social behaviour. There were, for example, growing pressures to introduce and enforce separate bathing regimes for the sexes, and Alain Corbin has argued that submersion in the sea was designed and represented to be wholly different activities for women and men; for the former, passive, submissive and voluptuous, for the latter active, independent and explorative – in other words, a parallel of what was taken to be the 'nature' of sexual relations in general.[109]

Focusing on the life style of the wealthy visitors and residents should not conceal the fact that though resorts undoubtedly had a marked concentration of the social elite compared to the national population (in some cases two to three times as high a proportion),[110] by far the majority of the inhabitants were working people. In nineteenth-century Bath, for example, about three-quarters of the townspeople enumerated in the censuses were working class.[111] Catering to the needs of the affluent was a labour-intensive business, spawning myriads of support workers; of the 5,620 persons returning an occupation in the census for Leamington in 1841, no less than 2,442 (or 43 per cent) were domestic servants.[112] The larger resorts proved highly attractive to poor migrants, and by the later Georgian period could harbour slum districts – such as Kent's Court in Brighton, or Holloway, Avon Street and the Dolemeads in Bath – which contrasted sharply with the elegant terraces and crescents of the fashionable quarters.[113] A significant contributory factor to poverty, given the nature of resort economies, was seasonal unemployment, which must have exerted a persistent downward pressure on the living standards of working people.[114]

Vagrancy, pauperism and environmental deterioration all posed 'problems' which needed effective local government to tackle. Yet though a few watering-places – such as Bath, Scarborough, Southampton, Weymouth, Yarmouth and

108 Whyman, 'Hanoverian watering-place', p. 158.

109 Corbin, *Lure of the Sea*, pp. 73–7; Pimlott, *Englishman's Holiday*, p. 58; Neave, 'East Riding resorts', p. 102; Boorman, *Brighton of Wales*, p. 19; May, 'Rise of Ilfracombe', p. 144; Bailey, *Southport*, pp. 57–8, 71–2, 83; Porter, *Fylde of Lancashire*, p. 322.

110 Walton, *Seaside Resort*, pp. 77–8.

111 Davis and Bonsall, *Bath*, pp. 87–8.

112 T. H. Lloyd, 'Chartism in Warwick and Leamington', *Warwickshire History*, 4(1) (1978), 1.

113 Hart, *Cheltenham*, pp. 195–6; Neale, *Bath*, pp. 71–7, 271–5, 286–92; G. Davis, 'Beyond the Georgian facade: the Avon street district of Bath', in M. Gaskell, ed., *Slums* (Leicester, 1989), pp. 144–85; Mainwaring, *Annals of Bath*, pp. 228–9, 249–51, 444; Gilbert, *Brighton*, p. 101; Farrant, *Georgian Brighton*, p. 28.

114 Farrant, *Georgian Brighton*, p. 47; Neale, *Bath*, pp. 77, 336.

Swansea – possessed corporations, the vast majority depended during the early years of their expansion upon what were essentially village structures of government; court leet, vestry and local magistrates. Incorporation had to wait at Brighton until 1854 and Cheltenham until 1876. One way of strengthening the local administrative system was to establish an improvement commission (responsible for specific problems like paving and lighting), but this device – adopted in English provincial towns on a significant scale from the 1750s – came relatively slowly to resorts; Bath acquired a commission in 1766, Brighton 1773, Cheltenham 1786, Swansea 1809, Ilfracombe 1827 (not strictly a town commission), Torquay, Aberystwyth and Tunbridge Wells 1835, Harrogate 1841 and Southport 1846.[115] Brighton enhanced the powers and status of the commissioners with further legislation in 1810 and 1825, and the construction of a town hall in 1830, and from about 1812 petty sessions were meeting in the resort. Outside the formal institutions of local administration other quasi-governmental organs might be introduced where there was enough demand and support. Voluntary organisations were frequently formed, concentrating upon charitable activities or law and order; from about 1792 Bath had a Society of Guardians which was established to cover subscribers' expenses in 'advertising, apprehending, and prosecuting offenders', and in 1816 an Association for Prosecuting Felons was set up in Tunbridge Wells.[116] At the latter town the supervision and maintenance of the Walks (together with the running of the charity school) was in the hands of the trustees of the Chapel of King Charles the Martyr, a body which raised revenue by collections on the Walks and charity sermons.[117]

John Walton has argued that 'Until the 1830s and 1840s, at best, local government at the seaside remained patchy in organization and limited in scope', and his verdict might, with a few exceptions, stand for watering-places as a whole.[118] To some extent, this simply reflected the 'newness', small size and 'village' origins of many of the settlements involved. But it may also be a result of the inherently entrepreneurial character of resorts, whose evolution was a consequence of private rather than public initiative. Local government was constructed on the hoof, reacting to rather than leading development. Too much bureaucratic control might cramp the forces of free enterprise. For example, during the early eighteenth century the corporation at Bath attempted on occasions to inhibit the development of fashionable facilities and housing outside the

115 E. L. Jones and M. E. Falkus, 'Urban improvement and the English economy in the seventeenth and eighteenth centuries', in P. Borsay, ed., *The Eighteenth Century Town* (London, 1990), pp. 137–45; McIntyre, 'Bath', p. 241; Farrant, *Georgian Brighton*, pp. 48–53; Dale, *History and Architecture of Brighton*, pp. 59–65; Hart, *Cheltenham*, p. 136; Boorman, *Brighton of Wales*, pp. 9–10; May, 'Rise of Ilfracombe', p. 145; Russell, *Torquay*, p. 82; Lewis, *Born on a Perilous Rock*, p. 20; Savidge, *Tunbridge Wells*, p. 122; Jennings, *Harrogate and Knaresborough*, p. 295; Bailey, *Southport*, pp. 123–4.

116 Cruttwell, *New Bath Guide* (1800), pp. 46–7; Savidge, *Tunbridge Wells*, p. 121.

117 Savidge, *Tunbridge Wells*, pp. 49, 96–7; Hembry, *English Spa*, p. 234.

118 Walton, *Seaside Resort*, p. 132.

old town because of the perceived threat to their economic interests and power.[119] Some major entrepreneurs sought to restrict the development of local government to protect their business and political autonomy. In the 1830s Joseph Pitt successfully overcame in parliament the attempt of the Cheltenham paving commissioners to extend their powers to Pittville, and in Tunbridge Wells John Ward – who was busy developing his Calverley estate – initially resisted the introduction of an improvement commission, only acquiescing when the bill was redrafted along lines more favourable to him.[120] Georgian resorts, therefore, tended to resemble a sort of enterprise zone; a characteristic which, though it may have encouraged rapid market-orientated development, inhibited the evolution of urban government and, consequently, of civic consciousness.

Resorts, as much as industrial towns, were in the business of manufacturing and delivering products; in this instance the objects for sale were of a fundamentally cultural character, health and leisure. Though there is some tendency now to underplay the therapeutic role of watering-places, and to see this as a cover for the really important business of pleasure seeking, the provision of health was a vitally important function of resorts. Georgian society was as obsessed about its physical and mental well-being as we are today, and for those feeling unwell a visit to spa or seaside, if they could afford it, represented a major opportunity to obtain relief; contemporary collections of correspondence from a spa like Bath leave us in little doubt about this.[121] However, fashions in treatment did shift substantially during the period, emphasising their cultural character. Bathing at the spas, popular under the Elizabethans and early Stuarts, increasingly gave way – particularly after the Restoration – to drinking. At the same time cold bathing continued to have its advocates and facilitators; commercially run cold bath houses were built at Bath in about 1704 (with a plunge-bath installed in 1707) and Tunbridge Wells in 1708.[122] This paved the way for the great change in perception that came to identify the sea and seaside not as an object of danger but as something medicinally beneficial.[123] Drinking the waters (including, initially, sea water) continued to be practised, while by the early nineteenth century coastal resorts were becoming as much valued for the invigorating quality of their air as of their waters.[124] The health appeal of resorts rested on their capacity to combine traditional magico-religious elements of therapy with new empirical 'scientific' ones (published analyses of the contents of waters

[119] Bath City RO, Council Minutes, 7 May 1711; Wood, *Description of Bath*, pp. 225, 247–8, 379–80; McIntyre, 'Bath', pp. 223, 225.

[120] Blake, *Pittville*, p. 43; Howes, 'Joseph Pitt and Pittville', 59–60; Savidge, *Tunbridge Wells*, p. 122.

[121] See, for example, *Letters from Bath 1766–1767 by the Rev. John Penrose*, ed. Mitchell and Penrose.

[122] Wood, *Description of Bath*, pp. 268–9; W. Ison, *The Georgian Buildings of Bath*, 2nd edn (Bath, 1980), pp. 102–3; Burr, *Tunbridge Wells*, pp. 59–60.

[123] Corbin, *Lure of the Sea*, pp. 1–18, 57–96; Gilbert, *Brighton*, pp. 13–14, 56–75; Pimlott, *Englishman's Holiday*, pp. 49–54.

[124] Gilbert, *Brighton*, pp. 76–86; Travis, *Devon Seaside Resorts*, p. 28.

abounded);[125] on the sheer availability of the cure, particularly when sea-bathing was 'discovered', and the relative freedom of control this gave patients over handling their personal health;[126] and on the potential of watering-places to provide an escape from, or an antidote to, the deteriorating environment to be found in late Georgian cities. On the last point one magazine writer suggested in 1803 that 'if any one seeks . . . a retreat from the dust, bustle and bad air of the capital, to an air freshened amidst the heats of summer by breezes from the sea, I can venture to recommend the town of Cromer'.[127]

The distinction between health and leisure as practised at resorts was a thin, and probably in visitors' minds unreal, one. Drinking and bathing could be both therapeutic and pleasurable activities, while the sociable and elevating character of polite pastimes would be seen as mentally invigorating. What was on offer was a total regime geared at the individual's well-being as a whole. As with health, the recreational element in this package was a dynamic one. Peter Burke has argued that the early modern period witnessed the 'invention of leisure',[128] and the emergence of the resort can be seen as the culmination of this formative process. During the Georgian era watering-places, whether inland or coastal, offered a highly standardised package of entertainment services, whose contents had been pioneered at the early spas; assemblies, plays, concerts, libraries, racing, gaming, card playing, luxury shops and a town guide. Even small resorts possessed most of these basic facilities. In the early nineteenth century Tenby supported assembly and card rooms, a theatre, a circulating-library, regularly maintained walks, horse races, several specialist retailers and a printed guide; Lyme Regis possessed a public promenade (in addition to the famous Cobb), three 'well-conducted boarding-schools', assembly and card rooms, two circulating-libraries and a guide; and Aberystwyth had assembly and card rooms, a theatre, a circulating-library, walks, races and a guide.[129] The shift to the coast to some extent modified and extended the prescribed parcel of spa facilities; most notably with the development of the bathing-machine, the evolution of the pier into a place of recreation as well as commerce – an admission charge was imposed in 1812 for those using the pier at Margate, and in 1823 the chain pier at

125 See the essays by Coley and Hamlin in Porter, *Medical History of Waters and Spas*, pp. 56–81; T. Fawcett, 'Selling the Bath waters: medical propaganda at an eighteenth-century spa', *Somerset Archaeology and Natural History*, 134 (1990), 193–206.

126 R. and D. Porter, *In Sickness and in Health: The British Experience 1650–1850* (London, 1988), p. 197.

127 *The Monthly Register and the Encyclopaedic Magazine*, quoted in A. C. Savin, *Cromer . . . A Modern History* (Holt, 1950), pp. 25–6.

128 P. Burke, 'The invention of leisure in early modern Europe', *P&P*, 146 (1995), 136–50.

129 *Tenby Guide* (1810), pp. 16, 18, 25–8; Bourne, *Guide to Tenby* (1843), pp. 21, 26–7; Lewis, 'Aspects of the history of Aberystwyth', 22–9; *Picture of Lyme Regis and Environs* (Lyme Regis, 1817), pp. 9–10, 12–13; Fowles, *Lyme Regis*, pp. 28–33; Oliver, 'Holidays at Aberystwyth', 269–86.

Brighton was opened, with its extensive pleasure facilities[130] – and the growth in boat racing, pleasure boating, and excursions into the surrounding area. However, until at least the 1840s the seaside watering-place was still modelled largely in the image of its inland precursor.[131]

One pastime catered to in all resorts was the consumption of 'nature'. From early on watering-places had been constructed and projected to reflect the ideal of *rus in urbe*. Spas in close vicinity to the metropolis, such as Epsom and Tunbridge Wells, were particularly prone to this treatment, clearly intended to satisfy Londoners' appetite for the pastoral myth.[132] But an established and more distant town like Bath was also deeply affected by the rural idyll, from the 1760s witnessing the erection of a rash of elevated crescents and terraces which enjoyed spectacular views of the surrounding countryside, and which seemed to draw the rural world into the urban. This reflected the whole trend, originating in the early modern period, towards the discovery, exploration and celebration of the natural world.[133] It was a process which caught the imagination of polite society in Georgian Britain, and one which resorts were well equipped to cater for, offering the geologist, naturalist and aesthete exceptional opportunities to indulge their pleasures. Bristol Hotwells, the spas of Derbyshire and the coastal resorts of Devon and Wales, with their 'wild' indigenous landscapes, possessed a rich array of resources with which to feed the picturesque and romantic sensibilities of their patrons.[134] One aspect of the 'discovery' of nature was, as Alain Corbin has argued, a fundamental change in attitudes towards the sea, no longer perceived as a location of horror and danger to be shunned, but as a place of pilgrimage, pleasure and wonder.[135] The sea became for tourists a huge psychic resource, capable of stimulating in visitors – often, one suspects, desensitised by the routine of their work or the boredom of their life style – a cocktail of emotions. As Mary Bourne wrote of Tenby in 1843:

> Whether beheld in the tranquillity of a calm summer-day . . . with the crystal expanse extending in dreamy beauty to the far horizon . . . whether seen under the animating influence of fresh sea breezes, curling the bright glancing waves and cresting them with foam . . . or when the angry tempest howls through the darkened sky, when the waves, lashed into fury by the force of the fitful winds, hurl

[130] Pimlott, *Englishman's Holiday*, pp. 131–2; Parry, *Coast of Sussex*, pp. 137–9; Gilbert, *Brighton*, pp. 124–30.

[131] Walton, *Seaside Resort*, pp. 9, 156–63; Travis, *Devon Seaside Resorts*, pp. 18–21, 72–5.

[132] Defoe, *Tour*, I, pp. 159–62; Burr, *Tunbridge Wells*, esp. pp. 102–3, 111.

[133] K. Thomas, *Man and the Natural World: Changing Attitudes in England 1500–1800* (Harmondsworth, 1984).

[134] Little, 'Gloucestershire spas', pp. 176–8; *HMC*, Verulam MSS, pp. 232–3; I. Ousby, *The Englishman's England: Taste, Travel and the Rise of Tourism* (Cambridge, 1990), pp. 131–7; Travis, *Devon Seaside Resorts*, pp. 46, 51–2, 56; Travis, 'Lynton in the nineteeth century', pp. 152–3; Travis, *Lynton and Lynmouth*, pp. 14–22; May, 'Rise of Ilfracombe', p. 139.

[135] Corbin, *Lure of the Sea*, *passim*.

> their loud surges on the craggy rocks, and fling their glistening spray over the surrounding hills . . . the effect has ever an interest and novelty that cannot weary or cease to charm.

Edmund Bartell, in his early nineteenth-century guide to Cromer, confirmed that 'the sea furnishes an almost never-ending source of amusement'. He also alludes to the sea (and resorts) as places of pilgrimage, capable of inducing in observers a visionary-religious experience:

> towards the close of a fine summer's evening, when the sun declining in full splendour tints the whole scene with a golden glow, the sea-shore becomes an object truly sublime. The noble expanse of blue waters on the one hand; . . . contrasted on the other by the rugged surfaces of the impending cliffs; the stillness of the scene, interrupted only by the gentle murmurs of the waves falling at your feet . . . What can give a more adequate idea of the Divine Creator than such a scene?[136]

Bourne's and Bartell's accounts should remind us not only of the cultural experiences to be found at resorts, but also how these experiences were made. Watering-place culture was a manufactured phenomenon. There was nothing inherently stimulating about the sea; for centuries, it appears, people had blithely ignored its aesthetic (and therapeutic) virtues. What was essential was that writers and painters created representations that could structure the visitors' perceptions of what they were to see and feel. In this context, one of the resorts' greatest assets was their capacity to generate and attract positive images of themselves. An avalanche of quasi-scientific treatises were produced which invested the waters and environment of their favoured settlements with medicinal virtues.[137] Such publications purported simply to be describing intrinsic qualities, but in effect they were creating these in the minds of the readers. Resorts were a favourite subject for topographical artists, making images which visitors could draw upon to help them visualise the landscape.[138] In this respect it is significant that Bartell in his Cromer guide observes that 'to the artist . . . the sea . . . is a constant moving picture', and specifically discusses the painting of marine views; that the artist Charles Norris chose to settle permanently in Tenby (of the town and neighbourhood of which he produced some 300 drawings) in 1805, just as it was developing as a resort; and that the London print seller John Wallis dispatched his son to the small but select resort of Sidmouth in about 1800 to establish a sea-front business trading in topographical

[136] Bourne, *Guide to Tenby* (1843), p. 5; Bartell, *Cromer*, pp. 25–7; see also *Account of Tenby* (1820), pp. 68–9; *The Cambrian Tourist*, 5th edn (London, 1825), p. 97; Pimlott, *Englishman's Holiday*, pp. 106–9; Bailey, *Southport*, p. 65.

[137] Hembry, *English Spa*, pp. 160, 167–9; Barrett, 'Spas and seaside resorts', pp. 44–5; Porter, *Medical History of Waters and Spas*, pp. 56–81; Fawcett, 'Selling the Bath waters', pp. 193–206.

[138] P. Howard, *Landscapes: The Artists' Vision* (London and New York, 1991), pp. 33–7, 71–2, 74–5; J. Lees-Milne and D. Ford, *Images of Bath* (Richmond-upon-Thames, 1982).

material.[139] Perhaps the watering-place's most powerful image-making machine was the printed guide, a *sine non qua* for a resort of any pretensions, which provided visitors with the sort of mental map that permitted them to plot the physical and psychological layout of their new surroundings.[140] But not all representations of resorts were of a positive nature; imagery could be a contested area, a tool in the struggle for power and status that lurked behind the apparently serene façade of watering-place life.[141]

Resorts, in several respects, exemplified the urban transformation Britain experienced between the late seventeenth and early nineteenth centuries. Many were new admissions to the ranks of towns, and therefore contributed to a creative phase in the British urban system unparalleled since the twelfth and thirteenth centuries. A number experienced dynamic growth, and two – Bath and Brighton – became major towns (with around 50,000 people each in 1841). However, Georgian watering-places were most typical not in that they grew to be large cities – ports and industrial centres far outpaced them in this respect – but rather in that they represented the vitality of many small towns, which it is now being realized was as much a feature of the long eighteenth century as the success of the big manufacturing centres.[142] The rise of resorts also reflected the trend towards specialisation of economic function.[143] A common economic rationale, allied to the recent acquisition of urban credentials, invested watering-places with shared and distinctive characteristics; an entrepreneurial service-based economy, a social regime balanced between meeting the needs of sociability and status, relatively undeveloped forms of local government and civic consciousness and a visitor culture based on the provision of health and leisure. A network of resorts emerged, characterised by specific geographical clusterings, and shaped by the countervailing forces of competition and mutuality. But this network, though distinctive, was also part of the wider urban system. Despite often being small, resorts were qualitatively towns. Their growth was being driven by the same underlying socio-economic forces, such as the expansion of

139 Bartell, *Cromer*, pp. 27–31; Norris, *Etchings of Tenby*; A. L. Leach, *Charles Norris 1779–1858* (Tenby, 1949), esp. pp. 13, 31; J. Tipton, *Charles Norris 1779–1858 and his Legacy to Tenby* (Tenby, 1997); Holmes, *Sidmouth*, pp. 50–1.

140 J. Vaughan, *The English Guide Book c.1780–1870: An Illustrated History* (Newton Abbot, 1974), especially pp. 15–26, 76–7, 104–5, 108–9, 126–9; R. J. Goulden, *Kent Town Guides 1763–1900* (London, 1995).

141 P. Borsay, 'Image and counter-image in Georgian Bath', *British Journal for Eighteenth-Century Studies*, 17(2) (1994), 165–79.

142 See the essays by P. Clark and M. Reed in P. Clark, ed., *Small Towns in Early Modern Europe* (Cambridge, 1995), pp. 90–147; P. J. Corfield, 'Small towns, large implications: social and cultural roles of small towns in eighteenth-century England and Wales', *British Journal for Eighteenth-Century Studies*, 10(2) (1987), 125–38; Borsay, *Eighteenth Century Town*, pp. 5–6.

143 Corfield, *Impact of English Towns*, p. 16.

the middling orders, which affected towns as a whole. Moreover, their development was often connected umbilically with urbanisation elsewhere in the system, through a supplier-receiver relationship based upon flows of people and capital. The rise of Tunbridge Wells and Brighton, for example, was tightly linked to London's expansion, the emergence of Southport and Blackpool to the dynamic textile towns of the North. Resorts were part of an increasingly sophisticated urban system whose members fulfilled different but complementary roles.

· 24 ·

Industrialising towns 1700–1840

BARRIE TRINDER

INDUSTRIAL TOWNS in the early nineteenth century were seen as sources of social and economic problems. 'Degeneracy', wrote Richard Ayton in Swansea in 1813, 'results from the increase of manufactories, and the consequent attraction of a larger population to one point'.[1] The expansion of manufactures was perceived during the debate on the 'Condition of England' question in the early 1840s to be responsible for many social ills, some of which were urban. The town of the mid-nineteenth century has come to be represented by a series of pessimistic images, like the view of the cotton mills alongside the Rochdale Canal at Ancoats, Manchester, published by George Pyne in 1829,[2] and by several much-quoted descriptions: Engels and de Tocqueville on Little Ireland in Manchester, or Reach on the east end of Leeds.[3] Peter Gaskell summarised a popular perception when he observed that 'the universal application of steam-power . . . separates families; and . . . lessens the demand for human strength, reducing man to a mere watcher or feeder of his mighty assistant'.[4]

Contemporaries were nevertheless aware that the development of manufactures was not synonymous with urban growth, that the factory system needed to be understood in rural as well as in urban contexts, at Egerton and Styal as well as in Manchester and Leeds. None of the industries which most conspicuously expanded in the century before 1840 – coal mining, textiles, the mining and processing of non-ferrous metals, ironmaking, hardware, glassmaking, ceramics – was essentially urban. Towns were significant in these industries, but

[1] R. Ayton, *A Voyage Round Great Britain Undertaken in the Summer of 1813* (London, 1814), p. 70.

[2] F. Klingender, *Art and the Industrial Revolution* (London, 1972), p. 180.

[3] F. Engels, *The Condition of the Working Class in England*, ed. W. O. Henderson and W. H. Chaloner (Oxford, 1958), pp. 71–4; A. de Tocqueville, *Journeys to England and Ireland*, ed. J. P. Mayer (London, 1958), pp. 105–8; P. E. Razell and R. W. Wainwright, eds., *The Victorian Working Class: Selections from Letters to the Morning Chronicle* (London, 1973), pp. 213–15.

[4] P. Gaskell, *Artisans and Machinery* (London, 1968), p. 7.

they encompassed much activity outside urban limits. A French visitor to Derbyshire commented in 1785 that the English 'turn out a great quantity of manufactured goods which they sell in competition with the other nations, and which makes a living for everyone in the countryside as well as in the towns'.[5]

It is traditional to envisage a taxonomy of towns in the early nineteenth century, in which 'old' towns, particularly regional capitals like York, Exeter and Norwich, are regarded as being undeveloped in terms of industry, while 'new' towns, like those involved with cotton in Lancashire or woollens in Yorkshire, had prospered through the rise of manufactures. This is too simplistic a division. There were many contrasts between large industrial settlements, even those involved in the same industries. Wolverhampton, an ancient town which had prospered through iron manufactures, had a medieval church, elegant eighteenth-century mansions and a network of carriers' carts linking it with the nearby countryside, and was very different from Merthyr, an accumulation of settlements around a concentration of blast furnaces in what had previously been sparsely populated uplands. Some of the fastest growing towns of the period, like Brighton, owned little to manufacturing industry. Urbanisation and industrialisation were distinct but connected processes, and their interconnections are characterised by paradox.

Manufacturing for the population of a hinterland is a basic urban function. Even in the smallest eighteenth-century settlements with claims to urban status there were concentrations of shoemakers, tailors and bakers. In all but the smallest towns there were cabinet makers and blacksmiths together with a few doctors or lawyers. With the exception of the goods sold by mercers, fabrics, hosiery, paper goods, dry groceries and chemicals, the drugs retailed by apothecaries and the hardware stocked by ironmongers, most of what was consumed in 1700 was produced locally, and was still produced locally in 1840. Traders in London and in such large provincial cities as Norwich and Bristol supplied wider markets – the Shropshire ironmaster Abraham Darby III, for example, purchased a red leather hat box and some patent chocolate from merchants in Bristol in 1776, and hats, shoes and stockings from retailers in London in 1785.[6] There were some specialised products, like mail coaches or tortoiseshell, for which London was a monopoly supplier. Manufacturers of consumer goods in most towns did not send them beyond the limits of the local carriers' cart network.

It is precisely this sector of the economy that appears to have experienced no kind of revolution in the period up to 1840; to quote Professor Crafts, 'much of British "industry" in the first half of the nineteenth century was traditional and small-scale, and catered to local domestic markets. This sector, responsible for

[5] N. Scarfe, ed., *Innocent Espionage: The La Rochefoucauld Brothers' Tour of England in 1785* (Woodbridge, 1995), p. 51.

[6] Shropshire Records and Research (formerly Shropshire RO), 1987/19/20, Cash Books of Abraham Darby III, 1770–80, f. 25, 1784–9, f. 15.

perhaps 60 per cent of industrial employment, experienced low levels of labour productivity and slow productivity growth – it is possible that there was virtually no advance during 1780–1860.'[7]

Some trades, like malting, corn milling and tanning, omnipresent in market towns, had always required large, specialist buildings. A source of water power for grinding grain was essential in a medieval town. Most town mills were used for grinding grain, but during the eighteenth century urban water power was increasingly put to other uses. There were fulling mills in most towns in regions which produced woollen cloth, while water in Birmingham and Sheffield was extensively used to work iron. The application of water power reflected changing economic circumstances. At the town mills in Birmingham Charles and Sampson Lloyd added the slitting of iron to the grinding of grain in 1728–9. At Mansfield the town corn mill was converted to spin cotton in 1795. The mill on the island below the ancient bridge at Burton-on-Trent was used for fulling cloth in the early eighteenth century. It was converted to hammer and plate iron in 1719–21, and in 1814 was adapted to work a cotton mill for Sir Robert Peel.[8] Town mills lost some of their significance with the development of the steam engine, but most remained important sources of power in 1840.

Most of the materials from which towns were constructed were still in 1840 obtained near the places where they were used. Maps provide abundant evidence of the brickfields on the urban fringes of London, one of which was memorably described by John Hollingshead in 1861,[9] but more than a century earlier Gonzalez remarked, 'It is amazing to see in the neighbouring fields the . . . bricks and tiles which are daily making for the supply of new buildings.'[10] London was so large that bricks made on the spot were supplemented by supplies shipped from the Medway.[11] The edges of the built-up areas of most growing towns were marked by brickyards, or in towns like Bradford, where stone was abundant but clay was lacking, by quarries. Lord Torrington in 1790 noted the presence of brick kilns as evidence for the growth of Macclesfield.[12]

Daniel Defoe commented in 1728 on a particular class of manufacturing town, which lacked both resident gentry and formal institutions of government, quoting as examples Manchester, Warrington, Macclesfield, Halifax, Leeds,

7 N. F. R. Crafts, 'British industrialisation in an international context', *Journal of Interdisciplinary History*, 19 (1989), 425.

8 H. Lloyd, *The Quaker Lloyds in the Industrial Revolution* (London, 1975) p. 205; M. Palmer and P. Neaverson, *Industrial Landscapes of the East Midlands* (Chichester, 1992), p. 109; C. C. Owen, *The Development of Industry in Burton upon Trent* (Chichester, 1978), p. 108.

9 J. Hollingshead, *Ragged London in 1861* (London, 1986), pp. 78–82.

10 M. Gonzales, 'The tour of Don Manoel Gonzales of Lisbon' (1730), in J. Pinkerton, ed., *A General Collection of the Best and Most Interesting Voyages and Travels in All Parts of the World* (London, 1908), vol. II, p. 19.

11 J. M. Preston, *Industrial Medway: An Historical Survey* (Rochester, 1977), pp. 91–8.

12 J. Byng, *The Torrington Diaries*, ed. C. B. Andrews (London, 1934–8), vol. II, pp. 171–2.

Wakefield, Sheffield, Birmingham, Frome, Taunton and Tiverton, which he regarded as 'Full of wealth and full of people, occasioned by the mere strength of trade and growth of the manufactures established in them.'[13] Eighteenth-century writers often categorised towns with phrases like 'great deal of company', 'thoroughfare' or 'of great trade'. In this context the use of the word 'manufacture' in the early eighteenth century can be seen to indicate the production of goods for markets beyond the town's normal hinterland. Every town made malt and produced shoes for local consumption, but to regard malt in Devizes or Reading, or shoes in Northampton and ceramics in Worcester (see Plate 12), as 'manufactures' indicated that they were being supplied to wider markets, in each case to London. Conversely, a town which had 'no manufacture considerable enough to merit mention', which was Pennant's description of Shrewsbury in 1773, may be assumed to have produced nothing of note which was sold beyond its immediate vicinity.[14] While Defoe's classification provides an insight into the way in which industry was perceived in the early eighteenth century, too credulous an acceptance of his list would obscure the importance of manufactures in larger towns which had other functions, in Bristol, Norwich, Exeter, Newcastle and above all London.

(i) TEXTILE TOWNS

Many of the principal English towns in the eighteenth century, whatever their other functions, were centres of textile manufacture. Common characteristics were shared by most towns active in textiles in the eighteenth century. They were collection and distribution points for manufacturing enterprises which were domestically based and extended through surrounding regions. Defoe observed that weavers in Norwich were supplied with yarn from all the country round. The homes of entrepreneurs and later their warehouses were the hubs around which the trade revolved.[15] The four-storey 'factory' in Devizes built by John Anstie in 1785 appears to have been designed for this kind of function, with a counting house, storage lofts and workshops which lacked any source of power.[16] In cities which prospered most from the new fabrics of the eighteenth century and early nineteenth century, Manchester from cottons, Bradford from worsteds (see Plate 30), Nottingham from machine-made lace, warehouses continued to be the focus of the textile trades long after domestic manufactures ceased, and they often accommodated finishing processes. In 1815 there were

[13] Quoted in P. J. Corfield, *The Impact of English Towns 1700–1800* (Oxford, 1982), p. 23.

[14] T. Pennant, *Tours in Wales 1778–1810* (London, 1883), vol. III, p. 224.

[15] D. Defoe, *A Tour through England and Wales* (London, 1959), vol. I, pp. 62–3.

[16] M. Stratton and B. Trinder, *Longs Buildings, Devizes, Wiltshire: An Evaluation* (Telford, 1992), *passim*; L. Haycock, *John Anstie of Devises 1743–1830: An Eighteenth Century Wiltshire Clothier* (Stroud, 1991), pp. 33, 79–81.

some 1,450 warehouse establishments in Manchester, 57 of them in Cannon Street.[17] James in 1857 considered that one reason for the prosperity of Bradford from the mid-1820s was the colony of foreign merchants, and the merchants' and manufacturers' warehouses which served them.[18]

The marketing of cloth was an urban activity in the eighteenth century, and specialist buildings to accommodate buyers and sellers were constructed as the scale of textile manufactures increased. The Kirkgate Cloth Hall in Leeds was built in 1711, to be followed in 1756 by a White Cloth Hall in Meadow Lane, a Mixed Cloth Hall on the edge of the city in 1758, and a new White Cloth Hall in Call Lane in 1775. The Piece Hall in Halifax was completed in 1779, and there were halls in Huddersfield by 1766 and Bradford by 1773.[19] In Shrewsbury until the mid-1790s the Drapers' Company bought Welsh cloth every Thursday in the square around the Elizabethan market hall to which they processed when the market ended. As Welsh weavers turned to make flannel, commercial activity in the region migrated to market halls opened at Welshpool in 1797, Newtown in 1832 and Llanidloes in 1836.[20] In Chester a linen hall was built in 1778 by linen merchants importing fabrics from Ireland.[21]

Much cloth woven in the countryside in the homes of hand-loom weavers was finished in towns in the eighteenth century. In towns which specialised in woollen cloth water-power resources were used to power fulling mills. In Exeter a system of leats extended from the Head Weir on the River Exe to the Custom House some 400m. downstream, and powered several fulling mills. Shaw noted in 1789 that 'the suburbs consisting of dye houses and drying frames, spread in crowds upon the banks of the river,' and Tozer's map of Exeter of 1793 confirms that extensive areas of the riverside meadows and the Bull Mead were covered in tenter frames.[22] In the course of the eighteenth century urban water power was applied to other stages of the manufacture of textiles. In Derby the silk-throwing mill, constructed by Thomas Lombe in 1721, stood adjacent to the city's ancient corn mill. By the 1780s a water-powered cotton mill was operating alongside it.[23] William Green's map of Manchester of 1787–94 shows water-powered mills along the Medlock and the Irk, one of which in Walkers Croft

[17] R. Lloyd-Jones and M. J. Lewis, 'The economic structure of Cottonopolis in 1815', *Textile History*, 17 (1986); R. Lloyd-Jones and M. J. Lewis, *Manchester and the Age of the Factory: The Business Structure of Cottonopolis in the Industrial Revolution* (London, 1988), pp. 44–130.

[18] J. James, *A History of the Worsted Manufacture in England* (London, 1968), pp. 289–91.

[19] M. Beresford, *East End, West End* (Thoresby Society, 60–1, 1989), p. 102; B. Trinder, *The Making of the Industrial Landscape* (London, 1982), p. 68.

[20] A. H. Dodd, *The Industrial Revolution in North Wales*, 3rd edn (Cardiff, 1971), pp. 231, 241.

[21] P. Broster, *The Chester Guide* (Chester, 1782), p. 25.

[22] S. Shaw, 'A tour to the West of England in 1788' (1789), in Pinkerton, *General Collection*, II, p. 262.

[23] A. Calladine, 'Lombe's mill: an exercise in reconstruction', *Industrial Archaeology Review*, 16 (1993), 82–99; Scarfe, ed., *Innocent Espionage*, pp. 38–45.

off Long Millgate was clearly a former fulling mill. Along the Irwell as well as the Irk and the Medlock were numerous dyehouses, drawing process water from the river. Many meadows were covered with frames for drying cloth. There was a dense concentration of such frames east of Ardwick Bridge on the Medlock. Water power was used to power cotton mills in other Lancashire towns like Bury, Accrington, Darwen, Middleton and Bolton and was responsible for the rapid growth of Stockport in the late eighteenth century. In West Yorkshire water power formed the basis of woollen manufacture in the small towns along the Calder, like Hebden Bridge, Sowerby Bridge and Brighouse, as well as in Leeds where most of the best sites were occupied by fulling mills, and the tributary streams were lined with dyehouses from which arose the noxious vapours described in 1757 by the poet John Dyer as the 'incence of thanksgiving'.[24]

The cotton sector of the textile industry set the pattern for urban manufacturing. The first building in which Richard Arkwright's innovations in spinning technology were applied was a horse-powered mill in Nottingham, which commenced operation in 1769. It was the prototype for numerous small-scale horse- and human-powered 'mills' which worked in towns in the following decades, small, unheroic buildings, of which scarcely any purpose-built examples survive. Arkwright's first water-powered cotton mill of 1771 was erected at Cromford in Derbyshire, an isolated site, and many of the 200 or so Arkwright-style mills constructed by 1787 were in similar rural settings, where the machines could be operated by water power and workers were free from the temptations of urban society.[25] The number of urban water-power sites adequate for the operation of large-scale manufacturing operations was limited, for no town in Britain possessed the luxuriant water-power resources of Lucerne, Trollhättan or Lowell, Massachusetts. Steam power made possible the proliferation of mechanised textile production in towns. The first large purpose-built cotton-spinning factory in Manchester appears to have been Shudehill Mill, a five-storey structure built by partners of Richard Arkwright about 1782, which used a steam engine to recirculate the water which powered its waterwheel. The development of the rotative engine made possible the direct application of steam power to the working of textile machines. The first use of rotative power in a cotton mill appears to have been in a rural setting at Papplewick, Nottinghamshire, in 1786, but soon afterwards steam-powered mills began to proliferate in Manchester, Preston, Stockport and elsewhere, many of them situated alongside canals which provided water for boilers as well as enabling the convenient delivery of coal. Williams has demonstrated that while some were designed to accommodate particular groups of machines, others simply provided room and power which

[24] Beresford, *East End, West End*, p. 103.

[25] S. D. Chapman, 'The Arkwright mills – Colquhoun's census of 1788 and archaeological evidence', *Industrial Archaeology Review*, 6 (1981–2), 5–27.

entrepreneurs could utilise to their own requirements.[26] The mills along Union Street in Ancoats, which included the eight-storey structure built by A. and G. Murray in 1798, were perceived to typify the industry, but closely mixed with the terraced houses of Manchester and Salford were many small cotton mills, as well as other textile establishments of modest size, fustian cutting shops, spindle manufactories, dyehouses, sizing works and printworks.[27]

The steam engine accelerated the growth of mechanised textile manufactures in other regions. The first Boulton and Watt rotative engine to power a Yorkshire textile mill was installed in 1792. By 1800 over eighty steam engines were employed in the manufacture of wool textiles, and by 1840 steam was the dominant source of power in West Yorkshire mills. It made possible the growth of manufacturing in Bradford, whose population rose from 13,000 in 1801 to 104,000 in 1841. The historian of the worsted trade acknowledged in 1857 that 'Bradford is particularly indebted to the steam engine for the colossal greatness to which it has in such a short time reached compared with its obscure position only fifty years ago.'[28] The extent to which steam liberated entrepreneurs from the constraints of water power is shown by the growth of John Marshall's flax mills in Leeds, which opened in 1791 with a small steam engine recirculating the water which powered the mill machinery. By 1821 there were six steam engines in the complex providing a total of 234 hp.[29] In Macclesfield three water-powered silk-throwing mills were operating before 1780. Construction of mills accelerated in the following decades, and over forty mills for the manufacture of silk and cotton were built in the town in the first quarter of the nineteenth century. Some were steam powered, but many were small and powered by horse gins. A local historian writing in 1866 considered that 'within the living memory of a large proportion of the inhabitants now living . . . the machinery of our silk mills was turned by means of a horse gate'.[30] Some of the first flax mills in Dundee, constructed in the 1790s, were steam operated but others were worked by blind men turning cranks. The industry grew hesitantly until the late 1820s but fourteen new mills were erected between 1822 and 1834, three of them iron framed, and all steam powered.[31]

Some textile manufactures took place in workshops intermediate in size between loomshops within dwellings and powered factories. In Leicester by the 1840s many knitting frames were located in small shops adjoining dwelling

[26] M. Williams, *Cotton Mills in Greater Manchester* (Preston, 1992), p. 53.

[27] Richard Thornton, *Plan of Manchester and Salford, 1831* (repr., Swinton, 1982); Ordnance Survey large-scale plans, *Manchester Victoria 1849, Salford Adelphi 1848* (repr., Newcastle, 1987–91).

[28] James, *Worsted Manufacture,* p. 350.

[29] C. Giles and Ian Goodall, *Yorkshire Textile Mills: The Buildings of the Yorkshire Textile Industry 1770–1930* (London, 1992), pp. 135–6.

[30] A. Calladine and J. Fricker, *East Cheshire Textile Mills* (London, 1993), pp. 36, 56–7, 65–9.

[31] M. Watson, *Jute and Flax Mills in Dundee* (Tayport, 1990), pp. 12–13, 123–4.

houses.[32] In the West Riding groups of cottages with top-floor loom shops clustered round many spinning mills, both urban and rural.[33] In Kidderminster several workshops have been identified which, when operating in the 1830s, could have accommodated between four and six carpet looms. Similar premises were to be found in early nineteenth-century Dundee.[34] Most fustian cutting in Manchester and much dressing of lace in Nottingham took places in 'low-roofed garrets in back alleys'.[35] Peter Gaskell observed in 1836 that 'The universal application of steam-power as an agent for producing motion in machinery, has closely assimilated the condition of all branches of manufacturing industry, both in their moral and physical relations. In all, it destroys domestic labour.'[36]

His view of the significance of steam power in textile towns was valid, if unremarkable for its time. His opinion of its effects on domestic labour might have seemed self-evident in the 1830s but would have been unsustainable forty years earlier. The construction of steam-powered spinning mills stimulated in some towns the growth of colonies of houses designed for hand-loom weaving. In Lancashire houses with ground floor and cellar loomshops were built in great numbers. Cottages incorporating loomshops were to be found in at least a third of the streets of Blackburn in the early nineteenth century. In Wigan there were 520 houses with cellar loomshops in 1849, which would have comprised about 15 per cent of the town's housing stock in the 1820s.[37] The cotton industry began to grow in Preston after the construction of the 'Yellow Factory' by John and Samuel Horrocks in 1791, which was followed by other steam-powered spinning mills, and by the construction of well over 1,000 houses with cellar loomshops, most of them concentrated around the Horrocks works in the south-east of the town, and in the north-west, near the canal. Almost all were built before 1825, the majority in streets laid out before 1809.[38] Dwellings of this type have disappeared from the principal Lancashire towns, but many survive in smaller settlements, like Horwich, or Top o'the Lane at Brindle, which provide evidence of different house types, and of the propensity to build colonies.

Contemporaries acknowledged the existence of colonies linked to particular entrepreneurs. A colony off the Oldham Road in Manchester in the early 1830s consisted of 145 cottages, and was said to have capacity for over 600 hand-looms. Some urban colonies were the property of cotton masters – one manufacturer

[32] PP 1863 XVIII, First Report from the Commissioners on the Employment of Children and Young Persons, p. 291. [33] Giles and Goodall, *Yorkshire Textile Mills*, pp. 19–20.

[34] Watson, *Dundee*, p. 88.

[35] PP 1863 XVIII, First Report from the Commissioners on the Employment of Children and Young Persons, pp. 160–2, 183. [36] Gaskell, *Artisans and Machinery*, p. 7.

[37] J. G. Timmins, *The Last Shift: The Decline of Handloom Weaving in Nineteenth Century Lancashire* (Manchester, 1993), pp. 60–5.

[38] N. Morgan, *Vanished Dwellings: Early Industrial Housing in a Lancashire Cotton Town* (Preston, 1990), pp. 7, 40–7.

in Blackburn, for example, owned eighty-four houses with cellar loomshops in the early 1840s – but some were owned by others, even though they were identified with particular factories.[39]

Similar colonies existed in other textile districts. A Barnsley linen manufacturer between 1801 and 1806 constructed sixteen cottages with looms fixed in vaulted cellars.[40] Cottages with cellar loomshops for linen weavers were built in Newark in the early nineteenth century by Scales & Co.[41] In Macclesfield the construction of steam- and horse-powered cotton-spinning and silk-throwing mills between 1800 and 1825 was accompanied by the building of about 600 terraced houses with garrets for weaving, most of them three-storey structures in brick, with the top floors approached by ladders and lit by broad, small-paned windows. Some were owned by the town's principal entrepreneurs.[42] Many of the fabrics woven from the linen yarns produced at Dundee's steam-powered spinning mills in the 1830s were made in weavers' homes.[43] Hundreds of two-storey dwellings designed specifically for weaving were built in Bethnal Green and other parts of east London in the first two decades of the nineteenth century.[44] There were distinct colonies of houses with topshops for ribbon weaving in Coventry, as well as isolated colonies in the city's suburban fringes built in the early nineteenth century which were later engulfed by the conurbation.[45] Around Nottingham were many colonies of dwellings 'built expressly to contain machines in their upper storeys'.[46]

Textile colonies were a positive factor in urban growth between 1780 and 1820. They were not just isolated developments that were later overtaken by suburban sprawl. As John Marshall acknowledged in 1966, the evidence for deducing that a particular collection of dwellings was a colony, with links of whatever kind to a particular entrepreneur, is unlikely ever to be conclusive.[47] There could be conflict between an entrepreneur's wish to recruit young people to operate a new factory and his longer term ambition to establish a self-sustaining, disciplined colony. The language used by nineteenth-century social critics suggests

[39] Timmins, *Last Shift*, pp. 60–5; P. Joyce, *Work, Society and Politics: The Culture of the Factory in Later Victorian England* (Brighton, 1980), p. 121.

[40] Giles and Goodall, *Yorkshire Textile Mills*, p. 19; PP 1840 XXIII, Hand Loom Weavers, p. 483.

[41] PP 1840 XXIII, Hand Loom Weavers, p. 350.

[42] Calladine and Fricker, *East Cheshire Textile Mills*, pp. 54–5.

[43] Watson, *Dundee*, p. 88.

[44] PP 1840 XXIII, Hand Loom Weavers, p. 239.

[45] D. Hardill, 'The survival of Coventry and north Warwickshire's silk ribbon weaving archaeology' (unpublished dissertation, Ironbridge Institute, 1991), pp. 24, 25, 38; PP 1840 XXIV, Hand Loom Weaving, pp. 3–332.

[46] PP 1861 XXII, The Expediency of Subjecting Lace Manufacture to the Regulation of the Factory Acts, p. 77.

[47] J. D. Marshall, 'Colonisation as a factor in the planting of towns in North-West England', in H. J. Dyos, ed., *The Study of Urban History* (London, 1968), pp. 215–230; Joyce, *Work, Society and Politics*, pp. 134 *et seq*.

that the colony was regarded as an ideal. Robert Owen's apologias for New Lanark can be read, not just as eloquent statements of socialist principles, but also as an account of his success in establishing a colony.[48] Andrew Ure commented in 1835 that 'the pure unmixed effect of factory labour is best and most easily found in the country, where it affords regular employment over the years to the same families'. He upheld the example of the Strutts' colony on the edge of Belper, which he regarded as a manufacturing village which 'had for half a century furnished steady employment and comfortable subsistence to a population of many thousands'.[49] Peter Gaskell similarly commended rural manufacturing communities like Quarry Bank which he described as 'one great family, bound together by common ties and dependent on one common master', regretting that the ties between employer and employee were less strong in towns, but implying that the colony was an urban as well as a rural ideal, even if imperfectly realised.[50]

Franklin Mendels ascribed a specific role to urban textile centres in the classic model of proto-industrialisation. Towns provided facilities for marketing and finishing fabrics, and were the source of the capital which financed putting-out systems.[51] Contemporary writers acknowledged that towns were essential to the overall process of textile manufacture in the eighteenth century. Gonzales in 1730 observed that 'Lancashire abounds with many good trading towns, especially in the fustian, linen check and narrow both linen and woollen wares',[52] and nine of Defoe's manufacturing towns of the 1720s were concerned with textiles.

As textile production was mechanised, traditional water-power sites in towns were adapted to power manufacturing processes, silk throwing in Derby and Congleton in the first half of the eighteenth century, cotton-spinning and later flax, woollen and worsted spinning in many towns from the 1770s. Nevertheless, most mechanised as well as most hand-operated preparation, spinning and weaving took place in rural areas until the 1790s when steam power made possible the concentration in towns of factories, around which clustered purpose-built colonies for domestic workers. By 1840 few textile processes remained unmechanised, but residual hand working proved persistent.

The prosperity of urban textiles in the mid-nineteenth century depended on relationships with surrounding rural areas. Manchester was famously the city of

[48] R. Owen, *A Statement Regarding the New Lanark Establishment* (Glasgow, 1973); *A New View of Society* (London, 1972), pp. 93–129.

[49] A. Ure, *The Philosophy of Manufactures,* 3rd edn (London, 1861), pp. 342–3.

[50] Gaskell, *Artisans and Machinery*, pp. 89–91.

[51] F. F. Mendels, 'Proto-industrialization: the first phase of the industrialization process', *Journal of Economic History*, 32 (1972); L. A. Clarkson, *Proto-Industrialization: The First Phase of Industrialization?* (London, 1985), pp. 25–6, 53–4; M. Berg, *The Age of Manufactures*, 2nd edn (London, 1994), pp. 66–70.

[52] Gonzales, *Tour*, p. 19.

100 mills and market for the products of another 2,000.[53] Leeds, Glasgow, Bradford, Nottingham, Leicester, Dundee, Aberdeen and Coventry performed similar functions within their regions. Even smaller towns within Lancashire and Yorkshire had close relationships with mills and domestic workers in their surrounding regions. The fortunes of the flax industry in Shrewsbury show how essential it was for a textile town to have roots within its region. Mechanised flax spinning was transplanted to Shrewsbury from Leeds in the 1790s, and three steam-powered mills were built to accommodate it. For a decade flax spinning expanded, but it had no foundations in the surrounding countryside, there were no buyers for one of the mills when its owners died, and in the 1830s the industry shrank to a single concern, whose activities as an offshoot of a Leeds company gradually contracted in the following decades.[54] While most textile towns added manufacturing to their other functions between 1780 and 1820, they remained centres of regional networks. The growth of the textile industry was to some extent organic, the long-term prosperity of large concerns being dependent upon the vitality of a range of smaller firms located throughout a region. There were similarly complex relationships between the large and the small towns in the principal textile regions. Places like Bury, Morley and Hyde were more than mere agglomerations of factories, even if their commercial activities were on a much smaller scale than those of Manchester, Leeds or Bradford. Samuel Bamford memorably described his regular childhood journeys around 1800 from the family home at Middleton to the warehouse of Samuel and James Broadbent in Cannon Street, Manchester, bearing with his uncle wallets filled with woven handkerchiefs, lunching in a deferential relationship to the Broadbents' putter-out, and returning in the convivial company of other weavers.[55] Such a journey epitomised the connections between textile towns and their hinterlands, relationships established long before Bamford's birth, which continued into the twentieth century.

(ii) COALFIELD TOWNS

Coal mining is the least urban of industries but towns in the eighteenth century and early nineteenth century served distinctive roles in the coal trade. It is possible to recognise distinctive features in towns located on or in the vicinity of coalfields, some of which, like Manchester or Leeds, also fulfilled roles in other industries.

The most straightforward function of a such towns was the transfer of coal between modes of transport. Whitehaven, laid out on a grid pattern by Sir John

[53] Williams, *Cotton Mills in Greater Manchester*, p. 18.

[54] B. Trinder, 'The textile industry in Shrewsbury in the late eighteenth century: the traditional town', in P. Clark and P. Corfield, eds., *Industry and Urbanisation in Eighteenth Century England* (Leicester, 1994), pp. 80–90; B. Trinder, *The Industrial Archaeology of Shropshire* (Chichester, 1996), pp. 140–9.

[55] S. Bamford, *Early Days* (London, 1967), pp. 36–7.

Lowther from the 1660s, had a population of over 2,000 by 1690, 6,000 in 1730 and about 9,000 in 1770. Pococke described it in 1750 as 'a very thriving town in the coal trade to Ireland'. Eighteenth-century growth at nearby Maryport and Workington similarly followed formal plans.[56] Goole, built by the Aire and Calder Navigation Company from the early 1820s, and the first stages of the development of Middlesbrough in the 1820s and 1830s were also laid out on grid plans and had similar patterns of rapid initial growth.[57] Newport (Monmouthshire) grew from a modest parish of 750 inhabitants in 1791 to a port with more than 10,000 inhabitants in 1841, and nearly twice as many in 1851. The Monmouthshire Canal, which opened in 1796, brought to the coast the produce of an expanding coal-mining and iron-producing region. Cargoes were transferred to seagoing vessels at riverside wharves until 1842 when the Old Town Dock, authorised by an act of parliament of 1835, came into operation.[58] Cardiff, Neath and Swansea likewise developed by trading coal delivered by canal.

Newcastle-upon-Tyne and Sunderland similarly prospered through the export of coal, the population of the former growing from 33,000 in 1801 to 70,000 in 1841, and of the latter from 24,000 to 43,000, but both developed coal-using industries. Until towards the end of the eighteenth century much of the coal trade of Sunderland had consisted in the loading of seagoing ships from keels, the small boats which brought down coal from the upper reaches of the River Wear. The construction on the south bank of the river between 1815 and 1822 of the Lambton Drops and the Hetton Staiths, and the railways which served them, and the staiths serving Wearmouth Colliery on the north bank in the 1830s, brought the handling of coal to the town itself. Lime burning, glassmaking, shipbuilding, rope making and pottery manufacture were flourishing along the banks of the river by the 1840s.[59] A similar proliferation of manufactures extended along the banks of the Tyne above and below Newcastle.

Other coalfield towns gained much of their sustenance from using in their own manufactures coal and semi-finished products made with coal in their hinterlands. The opening of the Birmingham Canal in 1768 was greeted with optimistic ballads, and the principal coal wharf was subsequently fronted by a monumental archway. The perceived effects of the canal were noted in 1791 by Arthur Young, who observed that Birmingham could be regarded as 'the first

[56] R. Pococke, *Travels through England of the Revd. Dr. Richard Pococke*, ed. J. J. Cartwright (London, 1988–9), vol. I, p. 16; C. Bell and R. Bell, *City Fathers* (Harmondsworth, 1972), pp. 150–4; S. Collier, *Whitehaven 1660–1800* (London, 1991).

[57] Bell, *City Fathers*, pp. 168–71, 176–93; A. Briggs, *Victorian Cities* (Harmondsworth, 1968), pp. 241–76.

[58] C. Hadfield, *The Canals of South Wales and the Border* (Cardiff, 1960), pp. 127, 147.

[59] T. Robson, *Plan of the Borough, Docks and Port of Sunderland* (Sunderland, 1844).

manufacturing town in the world', and by W. Blakey who considered that 'Birmingham may be looked upon to be the greatest magazine of hardware on earth, so much has fuel given life to numbers of Manufactories, while many die upon the Continent for lack of firing.'[60] Sheffield similarly prospered from the manufacture of hardware in the city itself, and in its region, and as the 'capital' of the coal-mining region of Hallamshire.

Some towns benefited from the construction, usually in the third quarter of the eighteenth century, of a short canal or railway which delivered abundant supplies of coal. The Sankey Brook Navigation and the Leeds and Liverpool Canal did this for Liverpool in 1757 and 1774, the Bridgewater Canal for Manchester in 1760, the Birmingham Canal Navigation for Birmingham in 1768. A French observer noted in 1785 that 'there is a canal that brings cheap coal to Coventry'.[61] Sheffield was served from 1774 by a railway from the duke of Norfolk's colliery at Arbourthorne, and from 1819 by the Sheffield Canal, and Leeds by the Middleton Railway, which guaranteed in 1758 to deliver 23,000 tons of coal per year.[62] Nottingham benefited from the Erewash Canal, opened in 1779, and the Nottingham Canal completed in 1802, as well as from improvements to the Trent Navigation.[63]

It is difficult to define the smaller towns in the principal coalfields. A series of lengthy terraces constructed around a large, recently constructed colliery in south Lancashire, south Durham, the East Midlands or Yorkshire, and populated by young and fertile couples, could soon attain a population in excess of a thousand, equivalent to that of many places in rural counties which were unquestionably regarded as towns. Such settlements rarely contained more communal facilities than a few shops and one or two places of worship, and on qualitative evidence it is difficult to regard them as towns. The larger coalfields gradually developed urban forms and institutions. Visitors to the North Staffordshire Potteries in the 1840s, where it was estimated that the population had grown from 4,000 to over 70,000 in a hundred years, were unimpressed with the region's urban virtues. Some potbanks had formal façades to the street, which hid untidy ranges of workshops and kilns, perpetually subject to alteration, and they were surrounded by waste tips and the irregularly constructed houses of the working poor. By 1840 the first traces of the urban foundations of the Six Towns had been established, although none had then gained borough status. A town hall was erected on the site of the maypole in Burslem in 1760, an example copied

[60] Trinder, *Industrial Landscape*, p. 56; A. Young, *Tours in England and Wales* (London, 1932), pp. 253–61; W. Blakey, *Observations on the Progress of the Iron and Steel Trade in Great Britain* (London, 1791), p. 74. [61] Scarfe, ed., *Innocent Espionage*, p. 118.

[62] M. Walton, *Sheffield: Its Story and Its Achievements* (Sheffield, 1948), pp. 113–14, 151; Beresford, *East End, West End*, p. 100.

[63] R. A. Church, *Social and Economic Change in a Midlands Town* (London, 1966), pp. 5–6.

in all six of the towns by 1831, when the market hall was built in Fenton. In Tunstall the erection of a market hall in 1816 provided the opportunity for its trustees to insist on uniform patterns of building in the streets which surrounded the market square. In Hanley and Shelton some landowners of modest means had laid out grids of streets where houses were built on ordered plots in contrast to the squatter-like dwellings which were the norm for the region.[64]

In south Lancashire the settlements surrounding the Ravenhead works of the British Cast Plate Glass Co. and the copper smelters of the Parys Mountain Co. were only beginning to show signs of urban order in 1840. Tontine Street, the first planned thoroughfare in the area, was laid out about 1797, and a terminating building society provided a vehicle for investment and a means of developing ordered housing between 1824 and 1843. It was not until 1833 that a market square was created, on the side of which a town hall 'in the modern Italian style with a Corinthian portico' was constructed in 1838, which subsequently formed a focus for social, cultural and civic activities. Only with the establishment of an improvement commission in 1845 did St Helens gain a form of government appropriate to urban status.[65]

Towns which lacked sources of cheap energy were perceived to be disadvantaged. Whatley found the dearness of fuel put forward as a reason for the constraint of growth in Northampton in 1750, and in the 1820s the high price of coal in York, between 5s. and 6s. a ton dearer than in Leeds, was blamed for the apparent lack of manufactures in the city.[66] The significance of cheap fuel is best illustrated by the example of Liverpool, which from the 1770s flourished as a manufacturing city, exploiting the benefits of coal delivered by the Sankey Brook Navigation and the Leeds and Liverpool Canal. Coal-using industries included salt manufacture, sugar refining, glassmaking, iron founding, pottery manufacture, copper smelting, cotton spinning, tobacco curing and sulphuric acid manufacture. During the 1790s the advantages of cheap fuel were lost as coal exports from the Mersey rose and the consumption of coal near to the points of production increased. From 1792 the price of canal-borne coal moved upwards, the scale of manufacturing in Liverpool diminished and the city became an entrepôt, dependent on overseas trade and on inland manufactures.[67]

[64] J. G. Kohl, *Ireland, Scotland and England* (London, 1844), p. 21; D. Baker, *Potworks: The Industrial Architecture of the Staffordshire Potteries* (London, 1991), pp. 60–70; D. M. Smith, 'Industrial architecture in the Potteries', *North Staffordshire Journal of Field Studies*, 5 (1965), 81–94; C. Hawkes-Smith, 'The Potteries landscape 1500–1820 AD', *Staffordshire Archaeological Studies,* new series, 5 (1987), 94–124.

[65] T. C. Barker and J. R. Harris, *A Merseyside Town in the Industrial Revolution* (Liverpool, 1954), pp. 290–304.

[66] S. Whatley, *England's Gazetteer* (London, 1751), *sub* 'Northampton'; A. Armstrong, *Stability and Change in an English County Town* (Cambridge, 1974), p. 23.

[67] J. Langton, 'Liverpool and its hinterland in the late eighteenth century', in B. L. Anderson and P. J. M. Stoney, eds., *Commerce, Industry and Transport* (Liverpool, 1983), pp. 1–25.

(iii) METALWORKING TOWNS

The centres of hardware production in Britain, the Black Country and Hallamshire, already commanded overseas markets in 1700. The latter was centred on Sheffield, the seat of the Company of Cutlers established in 1624, the source of capital, and the point of contact with London. Birmingham fulfilled similar functions in the West Midlands. Both cities consisted predominantly of small manufacturing units. Several mid-nineteenth-century commentators compared Birmingham with Manchester and concluded that it was a city of small workshops. J. G. Kohl found it to have a central business district of less than half a square mile, surrounded by a suburban sprawl in which there were few buildings larger than dissenting chapels.[68] In gunmaking and jewellery the workshops of interdependent craftsmen were clustered along particular streets. Water power was utilised in Birmingham, but it was essential in the development of Sheffield, where by 1770 over 100 waterwheels were operating within the parish, grinding cutlery and edge tools. A steam engine was first employed for grinding in 1786, and by 1850 over 100 engines were working in the city, but steam power did not cause dramatic change in the form of urban industry.[69] Most enterprises in Sheffield in 1840 were on a small scale. The first cutlery factory, the Sheaf Works, was opened in 1823 and there were no more than six establishments with more than 100 workers by the middle of the century. Many Sheffield manufactures were produced by complex outworking systems, in some cases involving craftsmen in the outer townships of the parish. The making of steel, whether by the cementation or the crucible process, was a small-scale operation, often undertaken by the cutlers who used it.[70]

Birmingham shared some functions with other Black Country towns. Wolverhampton in 1840 was a hardware manufacturing town of some 93,000 people, most of whom worked in small workshops, but its prosperity, the subject of much comment from visitors, derived from its role as an entrepôt for the nailmakers and locksmiths of the Black Country. R. H. Horne estimated in 1842 that there were six warehouses in the town with a value above £20,000, some of them worth more than £60,000.[71] The nature of the products traded dictated the use of warehouses, but transactions took place at inns rather than at an exchange.[72] The smaller Black Country towns of Dudley, Stourbridge and

[68] Kohl, *Ireland, Scotland and England*, p. 8.

[69] D. Hey, *The Fiery Blades of Hallamshire: Sheffield and its Neighbourhood 1660–1740* (Leicester, 1991), p. 179; S. Pollard, *A History of Labour in Sheffield* (Liverpool, 1959), pp. 50–4; D. W. Crossley, *Water-Power in Sheffield* (Sheffield, 1989).

[70] M. Berg, 'Technological change in Birmingham and Sheffield in the eighteenth century', in Clark and Corfield, eds., *Industry and Urbanisation*, pp. 20–32.

[71] PP 1842, Mining Districts, p. 367; L. Faucher, *Etudes sur l'Angleterre* (Paris, 1845), vol. II, pp. 167–75.

[72] M. B. Rowlands, *Masters and Men* (Manchester, 1975), p. 114.

Walsall had performed similar commercial roles in the eighteenth century. The expansion of hardware manufacturing capacity and the growth of blast furnace and forge complexes in the region from the 1770s owed nothing to urban order, but more to the stimulus of enclosure and the construction of a canal network. The urban centres performed essential functions in the developing exploitation of the iron and coal resources of the Black Country, but the energy which created that development was exercised in the collieries, blast furnaces, forges and workshops which sprawled untidily across the region from Cradley Heath to Walsall.

Some metalworking regions failed to develop urban centres or did so only slowly. The Coalbrookdale coalfield in Shropshire, where the Iron Bridge was constructed in 1777–81, was one of the most celebrated manufacturing regions in late eighteenth-century Britain, with extensive ironworks and potteries and innovative glass and chemical manufactories, yet it developed no significant urban centre – its shops, elites and seats of government were dispersed.[73] Similarly, the settlements which grew up around the blast furnace complexes of South Wales had acquired few urban characteristics by 1840. Even Merthyr, which in the 1840s claimed to be the largest iron-smelting settlement in the world, was scarcely a town. It had one shop in 1822 for every 400 of its inhabitants, compared with a ratio of 1:70 at York. Patterns of housing were dispersed, following patterns set by pre-existing fields and property boundaries rather than those of order and convenience.[74]

Cornish tin was authenticated and traded at the duchy's stannary towns, but tin sustained only parts of the economies of such places as Penzance, Truro and Bodmin. In the principal concentration of tin and copper mines in Cornwall, around Redruth and Camborne, the tradition that mining families built their own houses ensured that the region by 1840 had few urban features.[75] As for lead, Wirksworth in Derbyshire seat of the barmoot court was regarded as important in the early eighteenth century trade,[76] and Nenthead in County Durham, built by the London Quaker Lead Company in the eighteenth century, has a minimum of urban characteristics, but the mining and smelting of lead were essentially activities of the remote uplands. The lead mines of Shropshire, Somerset, mid-Wales and north Yorkshire had few influences on towns beyond providing cargoes to be handled at river and sea ports like Shrewsbury and

[73] B. Trinder, ' The Shropshire coalfield', in Clark and Corfield, eds., *Industry and Urbanisation*, pp. 33–9.

[74] C. Evans, 'Merthyr Tydfil in the eighteenth century: urban by default?', in Clark and Corfield, eds., *Industry and Urbanisation*, pp. 11–19; C. Evans, *'The Labyrinth of Flames': Work and Social Conflict in Early Industrial Merthyr Tydfil* (Cardiff, 1993), pp. 145–77; B. Thomas, 'Merthyr Tydfil and early ironworks in South Wales', in J. S. Garner, ed., *The Company Town: Architecture and Society in the Early Industrial Age* (Oxford, 1992), pp. 17–42; H. Carter and S. Wheatley, *Merthyr Tydfil in 1851: A Study of the Spatial Structure of a Welsh Industrial Town* (Cardiff, 1982).

[75] J. A. K. Hamilton, *The Cornish Miner* (Newton Abbot, 1972) p. 252.

[76] Defoe, *Tour*, II, p. 159.

Aberystwyth. The processing of lead was more commonly an urban occupation. The manufacture of piping, shot, sheet lead for roofs and of white and red lead for paints was carried on by 1840 in Newcastle, Chester, Hull, Derby, Shrewsbury, Newcastle and above all in London. Panoramic views of the capital of the 1840s and 1850s show the dominance of the shot towers of the riverside lead works between Hungerford Bridge and Lambeth.[77]

The smelting of copper from Cornwall and Parys Mountain was the principal stimulus to the growth of Swansea in the eighteenth century. The landscape of the lower Swansea Valley became possibly the most polluted in Britain, while the 'dirty town of Neath', as Skrine described it in 1798, was similarly shrouded in toxic fumes from smelters. Neither town was wholly reliant on copper for its growth. Both can be regarded as primarily coal ports, which prospered on the trade brought by canals in the late 1790s. At Neath by 1800 there were blast furnaces, foundries, a lead smelter and a sulphuric acid works. Swansea in 1813 seemed to one visitor to be a handsome watering place, with lodging houses, hotels and circulating libraries, as well as manufactories of pottery, soap and sailcloth.[78] Stephen Hughes has shown that entrepreneurs involved in copper smelting in Swansea established colony-style settlements in the style of the hand-loom weaving colonies of urban Lancashire.[79]

On a smaller scale, copper smelting was responsible for the growth of the Cornish port of Hayle, the point of dispatch for ores bound for Swansea or Merseyside, and the place of arrival of Welsh coal for firing Cornish steam engines. The advantages of manufacturing at the port stimulated the growth in the early nineteenth century of two substantial engineering works, Harvey and Co. and the Copperhouse Foundry, which supplied world markets with large steam engines and pumps.[80] By contrast, Cornwall's other celebrated heavy engineering works, the Perran Foundry, was located in a wholly rural setting.

In North-West England in the second half of the eighteenth century copper smelting with silk manufacture stimulated the growth of Macclesfield, and was one of the many coal-using industries of Warrington. An urban setting was not a prerequisite for smelting copper, however, and the principal works in the region from 1779 flourished at Ravenhead, St Helens, in a context which remained non-urban for some decades, and the secondary processes of working

[77] M. Stratton and B. Trinder, *Industrial Monuments in England: The Lead Industry* (Telford, 1989), pp. 8–9; D. J. Rowe, *Lead Manufacturing in Great Britain: A History* (Beckenham, 1983).

[78] H. Skrine, *Two Successive Tours through the Whole of Wales with Several of the English Counties* (London, 1798), in Pinkerton, *General Collection*, II, p. 593; C. Hadfield, *The Canals of South Wales and the Border* (Cardiff, 1960), pp. 45–75; R. Ayton, *A Voyage round Great Britain Undertaken in the Summer of 1813* (London, 1813), p. 69.

[79] S. Hughes, *Copperopolis* (forthcoming), Royal Commission on the Ancient and Historical Monuments of Wales, Aberystwyth.

[80] PP 1843 XIV Children's Employment Commission, Second Report, Part II, pp. 757/S1–10.

copper were carried on at such remote locations as Oakamoor, Havannah, Alton and the Greenfield Valley.[81]

Bristol was a centre of brass production by the early eighteenth century, but few of the works were located near the centre of the city, and the industry is best regarded as a regional activity, utilising the coal of the Bristol coalfield, the water power of the River Avon and the commercial expertise of the city.[82] During the early nineteenth century stamping and casting became the principal means of working brass, and the manufacturing side of the trade came to be concentrated in Birmingham. Some of the larger factories had formal street frontages, similar to those of north Staffordshire potbanks, with yards and workshops extending to canalside wharves. The factory of R. W. Winfield and Sons on the corner of Cambridge Street and Easy Row was established in 1820. By 1860 it extended over more than two acres, and employed 1,000 men, and set the pattern for other substantial works.[83]

(iv) TRANSPORT TOWNS

Of all the 'industries' which flourished in Britain in the eighteenth century and early nineteenth century the influence of transport was perhaps the most profound. 'Thoroughfare' towns like Stone or Towcester gained their livings from road transport, but most large towns were centres of coach and wagon networks. The nature of thoroughfare is perhaps best captured by John Drinkwater's description of his ancestors' work at the Mitre in Oxford.[84] J. D. Porteous has shown that a specific kind of canal town grew up at the points where narrow canals met existing broad waterways, at first gaining a living from the transhipment of coal and other commodities, but later developing manufactures. He demonstrated the similarities between Runcorn, Ellesmere Port, Goole and Stourport. Oxford had the same characteristics, but also had other urban functions, while Shardlow, in a similar location, failed to develop as a town.[85] Railways by 1840 had long been influencing the growth of towns, but they had yet to create substantial new settlements.

Seaports are considered in Chapter 21. By 1840 there had developed a range of characteristic port industries, sugar refining, tobacco processing, oil seed crushing, the processing of whale and fish oils, as well as shipbuilding and the range of service trades connected with the fitting and provisioning of oceango-

[81] M. Stratton and B. Trinder, *Industrial Monuments in England: The Copper, Brass and Tin Industries* (Telford, 1989), pp. 6–7.

[82] J. Day, *Bristol Brass: A History of the Industry* (Newton Abbot, 1973).

[83] Stratton and Trinder, *Copper, Brass and Tin*, pp. 26–8.

[84] J. Drinkwater, *Inheritance: Being the First Book of an Autobiography* (London, 1931), pp. 99–116.

[85] J. D. Porteous, *Canal Ports* (London, 1977), pp. 38–53; M. Prior, *Fisher Row* (Oxford, 1982), pp. 180–253.

ing vessels.[86] The ports which most significantly influenced the general development of manufactures were the naval dockyards. The shipbuilding and repairing facilities at Devonport, Portsmouth, Chatham and Woolwich were more extensive than any in the private sector, while the victualling yards at Plymouth, Gosport and Deptford had breweries which ranked amongst all but the largest in the country, and biscuit bakeries and abattoirs on a scale unknown in other contexts.[87]

(v) THE PROLIFERATION OF MANUFACTURES

'Industry' in 1840 may be characterised by images of Manchester and Birmingham, but it can be argued that the changes which were beginning in most towns at that time had economic and social consequences which were as significant as the growth of the centres of textile-manufacturing and coal-mining regions. Many towns were beginning to manufacture products for distant markets which were not directly related to the resources of their hinterlands.

Even in the eighteenth century some towns were supplying the traditional products of craftsmen to national markets. In 1751 Whatley noted that shoes from Northampton were sent in great numbers beyond the seas.[88] Manufacturers of the humblest products could develop businesses of significant size. Pins from Warrington were distributed nationally. William Harrison of Wolverhampton, a bend cooper who died in 1712, had warehouses at Dudley, Stourbridge, Walsall and Wolverhampton, where he kept huge stocks of pails, sieves, strainers and dishes.[89] Some confectionery products were widely distributed. The Gloucester port books show a steady and considerable downstream trade in gingerbread in the early eighteenth century.[90] Malt loaves were traded from Dartford.[91] Banbury Cakes were dispatched in willow twig baskets 'by coach, chaise, waggon, cart horse and foot into all parts of this kingdom', as well as to Australia, the United States and the East Indies.[92]

The pattern of change in such manufactures is illustrated by the manufacture of biscuits in Reading. Joseph Huntley, whose son in 1841 formed a partnership with George Palmer, established a biscuit bakery in 1822. From an early date he marketed his products in tinplate boxes, made by his younger son's company, and used machinery for mixing dough, made by William Exall, a local iron founder, who had commenced his business by making agricultural machines. Huntley

[86] G. Jackson, *Hull in the Eighteenth Century* (Oxford, 1972).

[87] J. G. Coad, *The Royal Dockyards 1690–1850* (Aldershot, 1989).

[88] Whatley, *England's Gazetteer*, *sub* 'Northampton'.

[89] Lichfield Joint RO, MY 171 2HRRW. I am grateful to Mrs Nancy Cox of the University of Wolverhampton for this reference.

[90] University of Wolverhampton, History Department, Gloucester Port Books Data Base.

[91] Information from Mr C. W. Chalklin. [92] B. Trinder, *Victorian Banbury* (Chichester, 1982), p. 32.

used the canal system to distribute his biscuits nationally, and his successors utilised the Great Western Railway, not just for distribution but for marketing, drawing the attention of travellers on the line from Paddington to their factory, and providing small complimentary packets of biscuits for those travelling first class.[93] At least one other substantial biscuit manufactory was subsequently established in Reading. By 1900 there were manufacturers of consumer goods whose businesses had developed from traditional urban trades in many towns. There were few in 1840 but the beginnings of a widespread and varied pattern of urban manufactures were widely evident.

Some brewers had succeeded by 1840 in establishing for themselves national markets. The London breweries were already some of the largest manufacturing enterprises in England by the early eighteenth century. By 1829 four breweries in the capital produced more than 150,000 barrels of beer per annum, and another four made more than 70,000 barrels.[94] The predominance of Edinburgh in Scottish beer production was even more marked – the city's beer production was five times that of Glasgow in the 1830s, and the proportion increased further in the second half of the nineteenth century. By 1840 about thirty provincial brewers were producing more than 20,000 barrels of beer per annum, which may be taken as a benchmark for a concern which was of more than local significance. Most had grown by acquiring tied public houses and seeking distant markets.[95]

It was acknowledged in the 1680s that Derby ales were consumed beyond the limits of the town, and in the early eighteenth century they were being carried in barges on the lower Severn. One consignment of forty hogsheads passed downstream through Gloucester, probably from Bewdley, on 26 April 1719. Whatley noted in 1751 that Derby 'makes malt and brews ale, of both of which great quantities are sent to London'.[96] Brewing on a significant scale in Burton-on-Trent appears to have begun in the first decade of the eighteenth century when several of the town's inns gained a reputation for the quality of their beer. From about 1740 entrepreneurs from Derby began to invest in the town, and by 1780 there were thirteen breweries in Burton, although none produced more than 2,000 barrels a year. Perhaps 40 per cent of the town's total output of about 20,000 barrels was exported, much of it to the Baltic, where it formed part of a pattern of trade which also involved the import of iron, flax and timber. Brewing in Burton declined following the collapse of the Baltic trade in 1807, but revived

[93] D. Phillips, *The Story of Reading* (Newbury, 1980), *passim*; T. A. B. Corley, *Quaker Enterprise in Biscuits: Huntley & Palmer of Reading 1822–1972* (London, 1972), pp. 21, 78.

[94] P. Mathias, *The Brewing Industry in England 1700–1830* (Cambridge, 1959).

[95] T. R. Gourvish and R. G. Wilson, *The British Brewing Industry 1830–1980* (Cambridge, 1994), pp. 111–13.

[96] University of Wolverhampton, History Department, Gloucester Port Books Data Base, 1259/02/09/16; Whatley, *England's Gazetteer*, *sub* 'Derby'.

after Samuel Allsopp's production in 1822 of a pale ale which could be exported to India. By the 1830s seven or eight breweries in Burton were producing in total about 50,000 barrels of beer per annum.[97] Alloa came to have a similar position in the Scottish brewing industry, its breweries producing about 80,000 barrels per annum in the 1840s. Other significant English breweries included Steward and Patterson of Norwich, a city in which the proportion of beer brewed by common brewers rather than publicans was exceptionally high; Lacon of Yarmouth, which prospered by dispatching its ale to London; Simonds at Reading and Breakspear at Henley.[98] The brewery in Banbury established by the canal engineer James Barnes already had twenty-three tied houses in 1814, when the concern was valued at £37,061. By 1840 Barnes' successors were sending beer to Birmingham, the Black Country and London, as well as exporting casked ale to India via Liverpool.[99] Brewing was the first of the characteristic market town manufactures in which entrepreneurs prospered by creating significant distant markets.

Mechanical engineering, the manufacture of machines, also became a characteristic urban activity. During the first half of the nineteenth century engineering techniques spread from the coalfields and the largest cities to almost every town of consequence in the country. Most large machines manufactured in the eighteenth century were assemblages of parts made by blacksmiths, iron founders, carpenters and workers in non-ferrous metals, put together by millwrights, often, as in the case of a steam engine or a corn mill, forming an integral part of a building. Most eighteenth-century foundries, like Pippingford in Sussex which produced munitions, or Coalbrookdale in Shropshire which made steam engine cylinders, were appendages to blast furnace complexes, and the relatively small number of foundries in large cities chiefly produced architectural and household castings.[100] Arthur Young noted in 1777 that the foundry in Waterford made 'pots, kettles weights and all common utensils'.[101] The development during the 1790s of the cupola furnace, in which scrap or pig iron could readily be melted, made it easier to establish foundries in areas distant from blast furnaces.

From the mid-1790s engineering concerns with foundries producing castings, smiths' shops making forgings, and woodworking shops were assembling complete machines. The best known was the Soho Foundry of Boulton and Watt in Smethwick, which began production in 1796. The previous year the Leeds engineer Matthew Murray, with partners, set up the Round Foundry, which took

97 Owen, *Burton upon Trent*, pp. 31–73; Gourvish and Wilson, *British Brewing Industry*, pp. 89–93.

98 Gourvish and Wilson, *British Brewing Industry*, pp. 105, 113–14.

99 Trinder, *Victorian Banbury*, p. 35.

100 M. Stratton and B. Trinder, *Industrial England* (London, 1996), pp. 74–89.

101 A. Young, *A Tour in Ireland Made in the Years 1776, 1777, 1778 and Brought Down to the End of 1779* (London, 1780), pp. 332–3.

its name from its circular assembly shop. Aikin in 1795 noted the existence of six foundries in Manchester, mostly drawing their pig iron from Shropshire. He regarded their principal products as stoves and grates,[102] but the foundries of Brodie, McNiven and Ormrod and of Joshua Wrigley were by that time producing steam engines, and engineering works proliferated in the city in the first decade of the nineteenth century. The principal nursery of British engineering talent was the London workshop of Henry Maudslay, in Oxford Street between 1798 and 1810, and subsequently at Lambeth, where early products included the machines for making wooden pulley blocks in Portsmouth Dockyard, designed by Sir Marc Brunel.[103]

Engineering also flourished in smaller towns. In the mid-1790s William Hazledine established a foundry in Shrewsbury, where the beams and columns of the town's Ditherington flax mill, the first iron-framed building, were cast in 1796–7, and numerous parts for large bridges in subsequent years, while his brother John set up a works alongside the Severn at Bridgnorth, where within a few years products included steam engines and other machines designed by Richard Trevithick, some of which were exported to Latin America.[104] By 1840 foundries flourished in most market towns. Coastal shipping and inland navigation created national markets for the foundryman's raw materials, pig iron and coke. In 1849 a founder at Plymouth was using Scottish iron or Welsh iron from Clydach. A foundry in Hornchurch mixed scrap with pig iron from the Old Park Co. in Shropshire. A Brighton founder used mostly Shropshire iron but sometimes mixed it with Scottish pig. The St Peter's foundry in Ipswich used iron from Blaenavon, Derbyshire and Tyneside. Founders from Huntingdonshire and Northampton commended the qualities of coke from Elsecar near Sheffield, while a Southampton foundry preferred Durham coke.[105] Machine tools were available from manufacturers in London and Manchester, while a mobile population of pattern makers, moulders and fitters from traditional ironworking regions took their skills to towns of modest size. They were the 'skilful and scientific men' of the kind the Hereford Iron and Brass Foundry boasted that it employed to make stoves, grates, iron chests and millwrights' castings on the occasion of its first anniversary in 1836.[106] The Great Exhibition of 1851 displayed the growth of engineering in British towns during the previous half-century. The catalogues list many machines made in towns of modest size, like the steam engine displayed by William Crosskill of Beverley, the cheese press

[102] J. Aikin, *A Description of the Country from Thirty to Forty miles around Manchester* (London, 1795), pp. 177–78.

[103] J. A. Cantrell, *James Nasmyth and the Bridgewater Foundry: A Study of Entrepreneurship in the Early Engineering Industry* (Manchester, 1984), pp. 4–7.

[104] Trinder, *Industrial Archaeology of Shropshire*, pp. 39–76.

[105] PP, 1849, Report of the Commissioners Appointed to Enquire into the Application of iron to Railway Structures, Appendix, pp. 426–32.

[106] *Hereford Journal*, 17 Feb. 1836.

made by W. and J. Rodenhurst of Market Drayton, and the chaff machine produced by Joseph Grant of Stamford.[107]

Engineering works emerged from traditional urban trades. Some were developed by ironmongers, some by millwrights and some by blacksmiths. Most manufactured agricultural machines, many made steam engines, and by 1840 some were assembling locomotives. Many made machines for local manufacturers, for textile mills in Lancashire, biscuit makers in Reading or bobbin makers in the Lake District. Some supplied national or international markets, whether from large cities like Manchester, where Edward Cowper pioneered the manufacture of powered printing machines, from spas like Bath where Stothert and Pitt made cranes, or Leamington, where Sidney Flavel manufactured the 'Leamington kitcheners', sold by ironmongers throughout Britain, or from small towns like Leiston, where Richard Garrett made traction engines. Engineering was the most wholly urban of the manufactures which grew during the century before 1840.

(vi) CONCLUSIONS

The pattern of urban industrial growth in Britain before 1840 was untidy. It was most dramatic in those towns which were seen at that time as centres of concern, in Birmingham, Leeds, Liverpool, Sheffield and above all Manchester. Such cities were the centres of substantial regions for whose products they served as commercial centres. Within these regions were hierarchies of other towns, which served the commercial needs of the industries which had most significantly expanded in the past century, textiles, coal and metalworking. These were all places 'full of wealth and full of people, occasioned by the mere strength of trade and growth of the manufactures established in them', to use Defoe's expression of more than a century earlier. By 1840 most towns were beginning to produce goods for sale beyond the town's immediate hinterland. York might seem an archetypal example of those cities 'full of quietness and interest', where it was claimed in 1827, 'We have no manufactures, we have no complicated machinery in operation.' Nevertheless, the city found employment in 1841 for 54 in glassmaking, 118 in linen manufacture and 107 in producing combs.[108] While it remained true that few towns other than those producing textiles or those drawing energy from nearby coalfields gained the greater part of their livings from manufactures, many were beginning to develop new forms of manufacture which were not directly dependent on local resources.

Those which did shared a range of common characteristics. All had benefited from turnpike roads, and by 1840 had some means of water transport. Many had

[107] *Great Exhibition of the Works of Industry of All Nations, 1851, Official Descriptive and Illustrated Catalogue* (London, 1851), *passim.*

[108] Armstrong, *Stability and Change*, pp. 16–19.

short distance transport links which provided cheap coal. Many had utilised water power, at least as a nucleus of manufacturing. Many made use of process water from rivers. Most had developed financial and commercial services, one or two banks and a newspaper in smaller towns; ranges of banks, exchanges, wholesale markets, insurance companies and several newspapers in the largest cities. Many new urban cultural institutions, mechanics' institutes, literary and philosophical societies, temperance societies and organisations providing concerts developed in the decades before 1840, and were credited with stimulating urban economic growth. In some cities large-scale manufacturing enterprises had transformed the social and economic roles of women and children.

Those towns which had prospered in the decades before 1840 from their involvement with textiles or coal-based and metal-using industries lay within regions which sustained and stimulated their growth. A rigid separation of urban and rural was not necessarily observed by town dwellers of the 1840s, many of whom cultivated allotment-style gardens on town edges, and returned to native villages to help with the harvest or to participate in wakes. Socially and economically the region rather than the town was more the home of particular industries.

Many towns without guilds or ancient trading companies developed large-scale manufactures but it seems unlikely that such institutions seriously impeded potential growth elsewhere. The preferences of landowners might shape towns – as the Calthorpe estate did in Birmingham – but it may be doubted whether the growth of manufactures in any town was wholly impeded by such forces. Unenclosed fields around Coventry, Nottingham, Leicester and Cambridge affected the patterns of growth of those towns, but economic dynamism found ways rounds the obstacles which they posed. Parts of several towns were developed through deliberate planning processes. In Sheffield, in Ashton-under-Lyne, in Manchester and in Birmingham streets were laid out in grids, creating plots which could be used for industrial premises or for housing, but towns could equally grow one field at a time at the edges of built-up areas, or in patches along radial roads.

A supply of amenable labour might be a factor in persuading an entrepreneur to invest in a particular town, as it was for Sir Robert Peel at Tamworth in the 1790s, or for John Heathcoat at Tiverton after 1816.[109] Alternatively, urban manufactures could be seen as a means of providing occupations for the poor. Defoe commended manufactures in Salisbury 'which employ the poor of the great part of the country round' while Bray in 1777 commented that the great silk mill in Derby employed 200, 'to the great relief and comfort of the poor'.[110]

[109] Young, *Tours*, p. 273; W. Felkins, *A History of the Machine-Wrought Hosiery and Lace Manufactures* (Nottingham, 1867), pp. 180–270.

[110] Defoe, *Tour*, I, pp. 188–92; W. Bray, *A Tour through Some of the Midland Counties into Derbyshire and Yorkshire* (London, 1777), pp. 226–7.

Entrepreneurs doubtless pondered questions about location. A rural site offered the prospect of creating a contented colony of workers, but at the cost of investment in housing and social facilities, and the possible loss of contact with fellow manufacturers, customers and suppliers. In a town with surplus labour, like Shrewsbury or Tamworth, housing could probably be supplied by market forces, but if it lay outside an acknowledged manufacturing region, a new enterprise could wither through isolation. In a large town workers would be prone to temptation, although they might be controlled through the informal mechanisms of a colony. For entrepreneurs themselves a town offered the stimulus of intellectual contacts, which might compensate for labour difficulties and pollution. Alfred Marshall viewed a town as a place where 'Good work is rightly appreciated, inventions and improvements in machinery, in processes and the general organisation of a business have their merits promptly discussed; if one man starts a new idea it is taken up by others and combined with suggestions of their own, and thus it becomes a source of further new ideas.'[111]

This was not purely an intellectual phenomenon. Manufactures prospered most where there was variety, where growth stimulated the establishment of new activities supplying or being supplied by those already established. Engineering works, timber yards and corn mills were to be found in most substantial industrial towns, regardless of their specialisms. The term 'industrialising town' by 1840 might be applied to a place which did rather more than make products for distant markets, to one which, whatever its current specialism, provided opportunities for vertical and horizontal integration, and for the growth of an expanding range of manufactures.

[111] A. Marshall, *Industry and Trade* (London, 1920), pp. 284–7.

· 25 ·

Conclusion

PETER CLARK

WALKING THE streets of Birmingham for the first time in 1803, John Francis, a Nottinghamshire lad, 'gazed and stared at everything that he saw that his eyes were bloodshot . . . and his mouth being open . . . he was almost choked with dust'. Such wonder at the sight of early nineteenth-century British towns was not confined to poor folk up from the country. The Franco-American businessman, Louis Simond, 'approached Leeds at night and from a height, north of the town, we saw a multitude of fires issuing, no doubt from furnaces, and constellations of illuminated windows (manufactories) spread over the dark plain'. Streets of good-looking shops, the vast, fire-proof clothiers' hall, the merchants' walk, the hospital with its good order and cleanliness, the library, and the many houses, a great part 'modern and comfortable, with gardens, planted squares, and flowers in every window', all impressed him.[1]

A bird's eye view of the island's cities and towns on the accession of Victoria would have seen them progressively bound together by the sinuous chains of navigable rivers, canals, improved roads and the new railways (see Plate 31), carrying unprecedented volumes of commercial and other traffic. Less visible but no less vital for integrating the urban system were the links forged by capital markets, by the growing postal system, by the London and provincial press, and by the imperative of cultural fashion. Certainly the British urban system had advanced dramatically over the period, particularly since the seventeenth century. This is in marked contrast to other parts of Europe, where early advanced urban networks (as in the southern Netherlands) had suffered major reverses and only started to revive towards the end of our period; or where (as in the case of the Dutch Randstad) highly integrated city systems actually de-urbanised in the late eighteenth and early nineteenth centuries; or where, as in

[1] Nottinghamshire RO, DD 311/2, p. 86; L. Simond, *An American in Regency England*, ed. C. Hibbert (London, 1968), pp. 112–13.

France, many cities were in decline after the French Revolution; or where, as in Scandinavia, towns were only slowly waking up from a bucolic past.[2] Admittedly, even in the Tudor era, England, and (to a lesser extent) Wales and Scotland, already had established and relatively developed networks of towns, but such networks were pervaded by a multitude of small towns, and headed by a bare handful of larger cities, of which London alone had a recognisable European status. As a result, urbanisation rates in Britain were lower than in most major European countries. In this post-Reformation urban world, agriculture preserved a powerful influence, heavily affecting flows of migrants, volumes of trade and levels of industrial output; urban elites (outside London) were small and had little of the wealth and power of continental patricians; trade and industries often lacked skilled labour and specialist roles; and the cultural voice and political autonomy of towns was generally circumscribed, operating under the wing of the crown and county magnates. Across the island, Scottish and Welsh towns were usually poor, paler cousins of English urban centres.

By the 1840s Britain not only had the highest level of urbanisation in the world, but also boasted a third of the biggest cities in Europe, helping to create an urban system with a recognisable rank order.[3] The Midlands, North of England, the central region of Scotland and South Wales were at the cutting edge of new forms of urban experience, creating shock cities. Striking, too, was the advent, alongside the older regional cities and country towns, of whole new classes of more specialist towns: industrial towns (with a variety of types according to product and manufacturing unit), seaside, spa and other leisure towns, military towns, canal and railway towns and the first satellite towns and conurbations. At the regional level, at least in the dynamic areas, specialist towns knitted together to form complementary, integrated networks of large and smaller centres, such networks buttressed by the advent of regional capital markets, and having in turn multiple financial, commercial and other connections to the metropolis and beyond. In this last respect the overseas hinterland of British towns, significant from the seventeenth century if not before, was increasingly global.

The ancient medieval ground plans which had corseted many British towns into the eighteenth century had been overlaid and overshadowed by greatly extended built-up areas, as suburbs began to appear on the outskirts of all but the smallest towns. The powerful influence of agriculture had been largely

[2] H. van der Wee, *The Low Countries in the Early Modern World* (Aldershot, 1993), esp. chs. 1–2; J. de Vries, *The Dutch Rural Economy in the Golden Age, 1500–1700* (London, 1974); B. Lepetit, *The Pre-Industrial Urban System: France, 1740–1840* (Cambridge, 1994); P. Clark, ed., *Small Towns in Early Modern Europe* (Cambridge, 1995), chs. 2–3.

[3] Nine British cities (plus two Irish ones) with over 100,000 inhabitants, against twenty-eight continental centres: cf. B. R. Mitchell, *European Historical Statistics*, 2nd edn (Basingstoke, 1981), pp. 86–8.

shaken off, except for the smaller towns in the agrarian regions. In addition to new manufacturing specialisms and staple industries geared to national or international markets, town economies boasted an army of specialist occupations, whether in the growing secondary profession, in retailing (with its profusion of food and drink traders) or in the transport sectors. Glass-fronted pastry shops, cloth shops, tea importers, jewellers, instrument makers, print shops, auctioneers, solicitors' offices, insurance agencies and banks, hotels, inns, gin-shops and beershops, coach and carrier offices, packed the main streets of towns. At the close of the period and following the earlier precedent of canal developments, the railway revolution carved its way through the townscape and shifted the centres of commercial gravity, towards new station areas with their goods yards, warehouses and hostelries, as well as redirecting (or consolidating) lines of communication and trade with the rest of the urban system.

By 1840 the old narrow town elites had changed out of recognition. Though the social composition varied greatly, in more traditional towns dominated by a miscellany of professional men, merchants, rentiers, manufacturers and even some old-style landowners, and in the larger industrialising centres by the largely commercial and manufacturing middle classes, these elite groups asserted and buttressed their power and authority through consumer expenditure, housing, education and participation in a mesh of social, religious and cultural organisations. Enjoying enlarged parliamentary representation after the 1832 Reform Act, and mobilising via extra-parliamentary associations, they exercised a growing voice in national politics, whilst at the community level their participation in municipal politics and in the voluntary sector buttressed urban pretensions to local autonomy. As the landed influence of the eighteenth century abated, the town wealthy likewise played the leading part in the growth of urban cultural activities, including music concerts and choral societies, learned and scientific societies and the new wave of provincial museums and art galleries, as cities competed with one another as centres of enlightenment and high seriousness. The same patronage cemented or at least articulated the powerful role of religion – with its many dissenting congregations, new-built churches, schools, missionary, visiting and other asssociated bodies – in the moral, political and cultural world of British cities, echoing the religious litany of town life after the Reformation.

Urban continuity is obvious in other respects. The transformation of British cities and towns, which has been such an important theme of this volume, was only part of the story. Towns in the early nineteenth century remained as much as they had ever been communities of immigrants, almost exclusively newcomers from the British Isles. For all the spectacular advance in manufacturing output since the eighteenth century, for all the advent of new extensive power-driven factories and mills, mainly in the textile sector, the organisation of production in many branches of industry remained biased towards traditional units of production. Up to 1840 the Industrial Revolution was strongly a workshop revolution: the factory and its distinctive ethos, infiltrating social and cultural as well as political relations in the city, was primarily a later Victorian creation (and even then had to contend with the continuing importance of the workshop tradition). No less important, skilled artisans with their networks of benefit, political, social and trade organisations conserved their position, acquired in the seventeenth and eighteenth centuries, as vital actors in the labour force and in the organisation of lower-class society.

Older features of the urban system also survived. A high proportion of those English, Welsh and Scottish towns functioning at the time of the Reformation remained important up to the accession of Victoria. True, from the Georgian era a clutch of high growth cities, particularly in the Midlands and the North, clambered fast up the urban league table, with exceptional surges of expansion in the 1820s and 1830s, and upended the top rankings, but only a small minority of the most successful towns before 1840 were actually new towns. No less striking, few ancient towns of importance had absolutely declined. Only towards the bottom of the urban hierarchy was there a loss of minor market towns.

This is not to argue for a seamless, painless, metamorphosis of British urban society. As we have seen, during the Tudor and Stuart period, many towns were buffeted by economic, social and political shocks – trade crises, the decay of old industries, influxes of pauper migrants, political faction-fighting, the disruption of the Reformation and the Civil War. Structurally, too many towns were competing for too little business at the local level. The late seventeenth century witnessed serious economic and demographic setbacks for Scottish towns. During the Georgian era, however, as the authors in this volume have explained, urban expansion was not only dynamic but wide-ranging, affecting most parts of the country. Indicative of the new urban buoyancy was the arrival of classical-style public buildings (theatres, assembly rooms, market houses and town halls) in even small market towns, the fashionability of notions of improvement, the increase of consumerism and material culture, improved private housing, the commercialisation of leisure (exemplified by the urbanisation of many sports) and the multiplication of those key vehicles for the fabrication of a sense of civil society – British clubs and societies. Parallel to the processes of urban integration occurred greater regional differentiation, but up to 1800 this was largely contained within the proscenium arch of urban and economic expansion. Or to put it another way, general urban growth and prosperity owed a good deal to increased specialisation. Specialisation between industrial and agricultural areas helped to provision urbanising centres. Urban specialisation within regional networks not only reduced competition between towns to a controllable level, but facilitated the division of manufacturing processes and the growth of component production and assembly towns. The coherence of urban Britain, though always fragile and repeatedly challenged, was sustained not only by a platform of more traditional structures and organisations, but also in the eighteenth century through a new complex array of commercial, voluntary and other structures and strategies, absorbing the pressures of urbanisation.

By the second quarter of the nineteenth century, if not before, the scenario is more problematic. The environmental consequences of urban and industrial growth, already visible earlier, appear to be taking an increasingly heavy toll, particularly in the bigger cities. In such places urban mortality rates are high and life expectancy is falling. The terrifying arrival of cholera from Asia in the 1830s underlined the demographic deterioration. Other evidence for the quality of life appears less clear-cut, as incomes and real wages improved but heights declined.[4] Certainly, the increase of pollution, smoke and dirt was commented on by almost all visitors to the bigger towns after 1800 and undoubtedly contributed to the accelerating exodus to the suburbs. As Louis Simond noted for London, the streets of the central districts are 'busy, smoky, dirty . . . a sort of uniform dinginess' affects everything, and its inhabitants are 'transferred from the centre to the extremities . . . [with their] better air, larger houses and at a smaller rent', though even here the risk of serious pollution from brick-works and other new industrial activity was never far away. Faced with these pressures, cities were increasingly unable to cope. Civic improvement, integral to the remodelling of Georgian towns as they faced the first wave of urban expansion, affected a diminishing proportion of the ever extending built-up area. Improvement was threatened with derailment by problems of funding, as rising expenditure and fiscal incapacity drove corporations into deficit during the 1820s, a financial situation which the Municipal Corporations Act of 1835 only partially resolved.[5]

Paradoxically, developments which had promoted the growth and coherence of urban communities during the earlier period now often proved divisive. Thus civic improvement increasingly demarcated and segregated urban quarters. In bigger centres the middle and respectable classes resided in orderly, regulated, improved streets and neighbourhoods; on the other side of town were poorer unimproved districts, with little sanitation, overcrowding, disorder and drunkenness, which were increasingly perceived as the terrain of the dangerous classes. In a similar fashion the urban system itself became more fragmented, as earlier

[4] S. Szreter and G. Mooney, 'Urbanization, mortality, and the standard of living debate . . .', *Ec.HR*, 2nd series, 51 (1998), 84–110; R. J. Morris, *Cholera 1832* (London, 1976), chs. 1, 3, 5; N. F. R. Crafts, 'Some dimensions of the "quality of life" during the British Industrial Revolution', *Ec.HR*, 2nd series, 50 (1997), 617–39.

[5] Simond, *An American*, pp. 5, 142–3; E. J. Dawson, 'Finance and the unreformed boroughs: a critical appraisal of corporate finance 1660 to 1835 with special reference to the boroughs of Nottingham, York and Boston' (PhD thesis, University of Hull, 1978), pp. 300–74; E. P. Hennock, 'Finance and politics in urban local government in England, 1835–1900', *HJ*, 6 (1963), 214–19. J. G. Williamson, *Coping with City Growth during the British Industrial Revolution* (Cambridge, 1990), ch. 10, stresses the underinvestment in urban infrastructure in the early nineteenth century, but fails to recognise the institutional, political and social reasons for this.

differentiation accelerated. This can be seen in two ways. First, there developed a growing preoccupation with the 'large towns', their problems and the issue of deficient public provision; in comparison country and smaller towns were marginalised in contemporary debates. With the exception of London, the big cities were increasingly identified with the dynamic industrialising regions. The mounting ferocity of industrial competition from the West Midlands, the North of England and the western Lowlands of Scotland, in conjunction with agricultural concentration, had a divisive effect on the older patterns of urban specialisation, undermining the relative stability of the Georgian urban system. Smaller towns in the more agrarian and traditional South-West and East Anglia witnessed the draining away of many of their older industrial specialities, and were forced into a greater dependence on the agrarian economy.[6] Divisions of this sort should not be exaggerated. Whether one uses historic or contemporary European criteria, most British county towns and quite a number of smaller towns enjoyed significant levels of growth during the Victorian era. But the broadly based coherence of the Georgian urban system had given way to a two-track system by the second quarter of the nineteenth century.

The early decades of the nineteenth century bequeathed a large legacy of problems for the Victorians. Parliamentary and municipal reform in the 1830s had only a limited effect in helping communities address these challenges, and many of the structures, organisations and attitudes which defined and conditioned the urban response after 1840 were the product of developments during the previous period: the ambition of improvement without the certainty of financial means; the reinforced and powerful identification of religion with moral reform and social control; the evolution of a mixed economy of welfare and of a devolved pluralistic system of government in which the state had a limited, ambiguous role, and in which municipal and voluntary organisations competed for power and status, more effective at asserting their own autonomy than in carrying out coordinated action in the social or other realms. For all its claims to modernity, the early Victorian city was, in part at least, a prisoner of its pre-modern past.

[6] *Liverpool Mercury*, 2 Dec. 1829, 25 June 1830, 25 Nov. 1831 (London School of Economics, Webb Collection, 148); J. P. Kay, *The Moral and Physical Condition of the Working Classes* (Manchester, 1832); R. Parkinson, *On the Present Condition of the Labouring Poor in Manchester* (Manchester, 1841), pp. 12–13. I am indebted to John Smith for information on the morphology of Wolverhampton. Joanna Innes, 'Big towns' (unpublished paper). I am grateful to Dr Innes for letting me see and refer to this. References to small or market towns in the titles of nineteenth-century publications were few and scattered.

Select bibliography

Abrams, P., and Wrigley, E. A., eds., *Towns in Societies* (Cambridge, 1978)

Adair, R., *Courtship, Illegitimacy and Marriage in Early Modern England* (Manchester, 1996)

Adams, I. H., *The Making of Urban Scotland* (London, 1978)

Adams, J., *Index Villaris* (London, 1690)

Adey, K. R., 'Seventeenth century Stafford: a county town in decline', *Midland History*, 2 (1974)

Aikin, J., *A Description of the Country from Thirty to Forty Miles around Manchester* (London, 1795; repr., Newton Abbot, 1968)

Alldridge, N., 'House and household in Restoration Chester', *UHY* (1983)

Alldridge, N., 'The mechanics of decline: migration and economy in early modern Chester', in M. Reed, ed., *English Towns in Decline 1350–1800* (Centre for Urban History Working Papers, 1, Leicester, 1986)

Anderson, M., *Family Structure in Nineteenth-Century Lancashire* (Cambridge, 1971)

Andrew, D. T., 'The aldermen and the big bourgeoisie of London reconsidered', *Soc. Hist.*, 6 (1981)

Andrew, D. T., *Philanthropy and Police: London Charity in the Eighteenth Century* (Princeton, N. J., 1989)

Archer, I. W., *The History of the Haberdashers' Company* (Chichester, 1991)

Archer, I. W., *The Pursuit of Stability: Social Relations in Elizabethan London* (Cambridge, 1991)

Armstrong, A., *Stability and Change in an English County Town: A Social Study of York 1801–51* (Cambridge, 1974)

Armstrong, W. A., 'The trend of mortality in Carlisle between the 1780s and 1840s: a demographic contribution to the standard of living debate', *Ec.HR*, 2nd series, 34 (1981)

Ashton, R., 'Popular entertainment and social control in later Elizabethan and early Stuart London', *LJ*, 9 (1983)

Aston, M., and Bond, J., *The Landscape of Towns* (Stroud, 1976)

Atherton, I., *et al.*, *Norwich Cathedral: Church, City and Diocese, 1096–1996* (London, 1996)

Bacon, N., *The Annalls of Ipswiche 1654*, ed. W. H. Richardson (Ipswich, 1884)

Baer, M., *Theatre and Disorder in Late Georgian London* (Oxford, 1992)
Bahlman, D. W. R., *The Moral Revolution of 1688* (New Haven, Conn., 1957)
Baigent, E., 'Economy and society in eighteenth-century English towns: Bristol in the 1770s', in D. D. Denecke and G. Shaw, eds., *Urban Historical Geography* (London, 1988)
Baines, E., *History, Directory and Gazetteer of the County Palatine of Lancaster* (Liverpool, 1825)
Barbeau, A., *Life and Letters at Bath in the Eighteenth Century* (London, 1904)
Barker, T. C., 'London: a unique megalopolis', in T. C. Barker and A. Sutcliffe, eds., *Megalopolis: The Giant City in History* (London, 1993)
Barker, T. C., and Harris, J. R., *A Merseyside Town in the Industrial Revolution: St Helens 1750–1900* (Liverpool, 1954)
Barrett, J., 'Spas and seaside resorts, 1660–1780', in *The Rise of the New Urban Society* (Open University, English Urban History course, Milton Keynes, 1977)
Barringer, C., ed., *Norwich in the Nineteenth Century* (Norwich, 1984)
Barron, C. M., 'The parish fraternities of medieval London', in C. M. Barron and C. Harper-Bill, eds., *The Church in Pre-Reformation Society* (Woodbridge, 1985)
Barry, J., 'Bourgeois collectivism? Urban association and the middling sort', in Barry and Brooks, eds., *Middling Sort*
Barry, J., 'The cultural life of Bristol 1640–1775' (DPhil thesis, University of Oxford, 1985)
Barry, J., 'The making of the middle class?', *P&P*, 145 (1994)
Barry, J., 'Popular culture in seventeenth-century Bristol', in B. Reay, ed., *Popular Culture in Seventeenth-Century England* (London, 1985)
Barry, J., 'Provincial town culture, 1640–1780: urbane or civic?', in J. H. Pittock and A. Wear, eds., *Interpretation and Cultural History* (London, 1991)
Barry, J., ed., *The Tudor and Stuart Town: A Reader in English Urban History, 1530–1688* (London, 1990)
Barry, J., and Brooks, C., eds., *The Middling Sort of People: Culture, Society and Politics in England 1550–1800* (London, 1994)
Beckett, J. V., *Coal and Tobacco: The Lowthers and the Economic Development of West Cumberland, 1660–1760* (Cambridge, 1981)
Beckett, J. V., ed., *A Centenary History of Nottingham* (Manchester, 1997)
Beier, A. L., 'The social problems of an Elizabethan country town: Warwick 1580–90', in Clark, ed., *Country Towns*
Beier, A. L., and Finlay, R., eds., *London 1500–1700: The Making of the Metropolis* (London, 1986)
Ben-Amos, I. K., *Adolescence and Youth in Early Modern England* (London, 1994)
Beresford, M., *East End, West End: The Face of Leeds during Urbanization 1684–1842* (Thoresby Society, 60–1, 1989)
Berg, M., *The Age of Manufactures: Industry, Innovation and Work in Britain 1700–1820* (Oxford, 1985; 2nd edn, London, 1994)
Berg, M., 'Women's work, mechanization and the early phases of industrialization in England', in R. E. Pahl, ed., *On Work: Historical, Comparative and Theoretical Approaches* (Oxford, 1988)

Berg, M., and Hudson, P., 'Rehabilitating the Industrial Revolution', *Ec.HR*, 2nd series, 45 (1992)

Berger, R. M., *The Most Necessary Luxuries: The Mercers' Company of Coventry 1550–1680* (Philadelphia, 1993)

Berlin, M., 'Civic ceremony in early modern London', *UHY* (1986)

Black, I. S., 'Money, information and space: banking in early nineteenth-century England and Wales', *Journal of Historical Geography*, 21 (1995)

Bond, S., ed., *The Chamber Order Book of Worcester 1602–50* (Worcestershire Historical Society, new series, 8, 1974)

Boorman, D., *The Brighton of Wales: Swansea as a Fashionable Resort, c. 1780–1830* (Swansea, 1986)

Borsay, P., '"All the town's a stage": urban ritual and ceremony 1660–1800', in Clark, ed., *Transformation of English Provincial Towns*

Borsay, P., *The English Urban Renaissance: Culture and Society in the Provincial Town, 1660–1770* (Oxford, 1989)

Borsay, P., 'The English urban renaissance: the development of provincial urban culture c. 1680–1760', in Borsay, ed., *Eighteenth Century Town*

Borsay, P., 'The London connection: cultural diffusion and the eighteenth century provincial town', *LJ* 19 (1994)

Borsay, P., ed., *The Eighteenth Century Town: A Reader in English Urban History 1688–1820* (London, 1990)

Borsay, P., and McInnes, A., 'Debate: the emergence of a leisure town: or an urban renaissance?', *P&P*, 126 (1990)

Boulton, J., *Neighbourhood and Society: A London Suburb in the Seventeenth Century* (Cambridge, 1987)

Braun, G., and Hohenberg, F., *Civitates Orbis Terrarum* (1572–1618; repr. with an introduction by R. A. Skelton, Cleveland, Ohio, 1966)

Brenner, R., *Merchants and Revolution: Commercial Change, Political Conflict and London Overseas Traders, 1550–1653* (Cambridge, 1993)

Brewer, J., *The Pleasures of the Imagination: English Culture in the Eighteenth Century* (London, 1997)

Brewer, J., and Porter, R., eds., *Consumption and the World of Goods* (London, 1993)

Brigden, S., *London and the Reformation* (Oxford, 1989)

Briggs, A., *Victorian Cities* (Harmondsworth, 1968)

Brodsky, V., 'Widows in late Elizabethan London: remarriage, economic opportunity and family orientations', in L. Bonfield, R. M. Smith and K. Wrightson, eds., *The World We Have Gained: Histories of Population and Social Structure* (Oxford, 1986)

Brown, A. F. J., 'Colchester in the eighteenth century', in L. M. Munby, ed., *East Anglian Studies* (London, 1968)

Brown, C. G., *The Social History of Religion in Scotland since 1730* (London, 1987)

Brown, F. E., 'Continuity and change in the urban house: developments in domestic space organisation in seventeenth-century London', *Comparative Studies in Society and History*, 28 (1986)

Burke, P., 'Popular culture in seventeenth-century London', *LJ*, 3 (1977)

Bush, G., *Bristol and its Municipal Government 1820–51* (Bristol Record Society, 29, 1976)

Byng, J., *The Torrington Diaries: Containing the Tours through England and Wales of the Hon. John Byng . . . between the Years 1781 and 1794*, ed. C. B. Andrews (London, 1934–8; repr., London, 1970)

Cadogan, P., *Early Radical Newcastle* (Durham, 1975)

Cannadine, D., 'The present and the past in the English Industrial Revolution, 1880–1980', *P&P*, 103 (1984)

Carter, H., *The Towns of Wales: A Study in Urban Geography* (Cardiff, 1965; 2nd edn, Cardiff, 1966)

Carter, M., 'Town or urban society? St Ives in Huntingdonshire, 1630–1740', in C. Phythian-Adams, ed., *Societies, Culture and Kinship, 1580–1850: Cultural Provinces and English Local History* (London, 1993)

Castle, T., *Masquerade and Civilization* (London, 1986)

Chalklin, C. W., *The Provincial Towns of Georgian England: A Study of the Building Process 1740–1820* (London, 1974)

Chalklin, C. W., *Seventeenth-Century Kent: A Social and Economic History* (London, 1965)

Chalklin, C. W., 'A seventeenth century market town: Tonbridge', *Archaeologia Cantiana*, 76 (1961)

Chalklin, C. W., 'The towns', in A. Armstrong, ed., *The Economy of Kent 1640–1914* (Woodbridge, 1995)

Chalklin, C. W., and Havinden, M. A., eds., *Rural Change and Urban Growth 1500–1800* (London, 1974)

Chamberlain, H., *A New and Compleat History and Survey of the Cities of London and Westminster* (London, 1770)

Chambers, J. D., 'Population change in a provincial town: Nottingham 1700–1800', in L. S. Pressnell, ed., *Studies in the Industrial Revolution* (London, 1960)

Champion, J. A. I., ed., *Epidemic Disease in London* (London, 1993)

Chaplin, R., 'The rise of Royal Leamington Spa', *Warwickshire History*, 2 (1972–3)

Chapman, S. D., 'Working-class housing in Nottingham during the Industrial Revolution', in S. D. Chapman, ed., *The History of Working Class Housing* (Newton Abbot, 1971)

Charles, L., and Duffin, L., eds., *Women and Work in Pre-Industrial England* (London, 1985)

Chartres, J. A., 'The capital's provincial eyes: London's inns in the early eighteenth century', *LJ*, 3 (1977)

Chartres, J. A., 'Market integration and agricultural output in seventeenth-, eighteenth- and early nineteenth-century England', *Agricultural History Review*, 43 (1995)

Chartres, J. A., 'The marketing of agricultural produce', in J. Thirsk, ed., *Ag.HEW*, vol. v (2) (Cambridge, 1985)

Church, R., *Social and Economic Change in a Midlands Town: Victorian Nottingham 1815–1900* (London, 1966)

Clark, A., *The Struggle for the Breeches: Gender and the Making of the British Working Class* (Berkeley, Calif., 1995)

Clark, P., *British Clubs and Societies 1580–1800: The Origins of an Associational World* (Oxford, 2000)

Clark, P., 'Changes in the pattern of English small towns in the early modern period', in A. Maczak and C. Smout, eds., *Gründung und Bedeutung kleinerer Städte im nördlichen Europa der frühen Neuzeit* (Weisbaden, 1991)

Clark, P., 'The civic leaders of Gloucester 1580–1800', in Clark, ed., *Transformation of English Provincial Towns*

Clark, P., *The English Alehouse: A Social History 1200–1830* (London, 1983)

Clark, P., 'Migrants in the city: the process of social adaptation in English towns 1500–1800', in Clark and Souden eds., *Migration and Society*

Clark, P., ' "The Ramoth-Gilead of the Good": urban change and political radicalism at Gloucester 1540–1640', in Barry, ed., *The Tudor and Stuart Town*

Clark, P., *Sociability and Urbanity: Clubs and Societies in the Eighteenth Century City* (Leicester, 1988)

Clark, P., 'Visions of the urban community: antiquarians and the English city before 1800', in D. Fraser and A. Sutcliffe, eds., *The Pursuit of Urban History* (London, 1983)

Clark, P., ed., *Country Towns in Pre-Industrial England* (Leicester, 1981)

Clark, P., ed., *The Early Modern Town: A Reader* (London, 1976)

Clark, P., ed., *Small Towns in Early Modern Europe* (Cambridge, 1995)

Clark, P., ed., *The Transformation of English Provincial Towns 1600–1800* (London, 1984)

Clark, P., and Corfield, P., eds., *Industry and Urbanisation in Eighteenth Century England* (Centre for Urban History Working Papers, 6, Leicester, 1994)

Clark, P., and Hosking, J., *Population Estimates of English Small Towns 1550–1851: Revised Edition* (Centre for Urban History Working Papers, 5, Leicester, 1993)

Clark, P., and Murfin, L., *The History of Maidstone: The Making of a Modern County Town* (Stroud, 1995)

Clark, P., and Slack, P., eds., *Crisis and Order in English Towns 1500–1700* (London, 1972)

Clark, P., and Slack, P., *English Towns in Transition 1500–1700* (London, 1976)

Clark, P., and Souden, D., eds., *Migration and Society in Early Modern England* (London, 1987)

Clarkson, L., 'The leather crafts in Tudor and Stuart England', *Agricultural History Review*, 14 (1960)

Clemens, P. G. E., 'The rise of Liverpool, 1665–1750', *Ec.HR*, 2nd series, 29 (1976)

Coad, J. G., *The Royal Dockyards 1690–1850* (Aldershot, 1989)

Coates, B., 'The impact of the English Civil War on the economy of London 1642–1650' (PhD thesis, University of Leicester, 1997)

Collier, S., *Whitehaven 1660–1800* (London, 1991)

Collinson, P., *The Birthpangs of Protestant England: Religious and Cultural Change in the Sixteenth and Seventeenth Centuries* (London, 1988)

Collinson, P., *The Religion of Protestants* (Oxford, 1982)

Colquhoun, P., *A Treatise on the Police of the Metropolis* (London, 1796)

Colvin, H. M., ed., *The History of the King's Works*, vol. IV: *1485–1660*, Part 2 (London, 1982)

Colvin, H. M., ed., *The History of the King's Works,* vol. VI: *1782–1851* (London, 1973)

Connolly, S. J., Houston, R. A., and Morris, R. J., eds., *Conflict, Identity and Economic Development: Ireland and Scotland 1600–1939* (Preston, 1995)

Corbin, A., *The Lure of the Sea: The Discovery of the Seaside in the Western World 1750–1840*, trans. J. Phelps (Cambridge, 1994)

Corfield, P. J., 'Class by name and number in eighteenth-century Britain', *History*, 72 (1987)

Corfield, P. J., ' " Giving directions to the town": the early town directories', *UHY* (1984)

Corfield, P. J., 'The identity of a regional capital: Norwich since the eighteenth century', in P. Kooij and P. Pellenbarg, eds., *Regional Capitals: Past, Present, Future* (Assen, Netherlands, 1994)

Corfield, P. J., *The Impact of English Towns* 1700–1800 (Oxford, 1982)

Corfield, P. J., *Power and the Professions in Britain 1700–1850* (London, 1995)

Corfield, P. J., 'A provincial capital in the late seventeenth century: the case of Norwich', in Clark and Slack eds., *Crisis and Order*; repr. in Clark, ed., *Early Modern Town*

Corfield, P. J., 'Small towns, large implications: social and cultural roles of small towns in eighteenth-century England and Wales', *British Journal for Eighteenth-Century Studies*, 10 (1987)

Corfield, P. J., 'Urban development in England and Wales in the sixteenth and seventeenth centuries', in D. C. Coleman and A. H. John, eds., *Trade, Government and Economy in Pre-Industrial England* (London, 1976); repr. in Barry, ed., *The Tudor and Stuart Town*

Corfield, P. J., 'Walking the city streets: the urban odyssey in eighteenth century England', *JUH*, 16 (1989–90)

Corfield, P. J., and Keene, D., eds., *Work in Towns 850–1850* (Leicester, 1990)

Corfield, P. J., and Priestley, U., 'Rooms and room use in Norwich housing, 1680–1730', *Post-Medieval Archaeology*, 16 (1982)

Cornwall, J., 'English country towns in the fifteen twenties', *Ec.HR*, 2nd series, 15 (1962)

Cowan, I., *The Scottish Reformation: Church and Society in Sixteenth Century Scotland* (London, 1982)

Creaton, H., *Bibliography of Printed Works on London History to 1939* (London, 1994)

Cross, C., 'The development of Protestantism in Leeds and Hull, 1520–1640', *NHist.*, 18 (1982)

Cross, C., *Urban Magistrates and Ministers: Religion in Hull and Leeds from the Reformation to the Civil War* (Borthwick Papers, 67, York, 1985)

Cruikshank, D., and Wyld, P., *London: The Art of Georgian Building* (London, 1975)

D'Cruze, S., ' "To acquaint the ladies": women traders in Colchester 1750–1800', *Local Historian*, 17 (1986)

D'Cruze, S., 'The middling sort in eighteenth-century Colchester: independence, social relations and the community broker', in Barry and Brooks, eds., *Middling Sort*

Dalgleish, A. J., 'Voluntary associations and the middle class in Edinburgh 1780–1820' (PhD thesis, University of Edinburgh, 1991)

Davidoff, L., 'The separation of home and work? Landladies and lodgers in nineteenth- and twentieth-century England' in L. Davidoff, ed., *Worlds Between: Historical Perspectives on Gender and Class* (Cambridge, 1995)

Davidoff, L., and Hall, C., *Family Fortunes: Men and Women of the English Middle Class, 1780–1850* (London, 1987)

Davies, M. G., 'Country gentry and payments to London, 1650–1714', *Ec.HR*, 2nd series, 24 (1971)

Dawson, E. J., 'Finance and the unreformed boroughs: a critical appraisal of corporate finance 1660 to 1835 with special reference to the boroughs of Nottingham, York and Boston' (PhD thesis, University of Hull, 1978) de Krey, G. S., *A Fractured Society: The Politics of London in the First Age of Party, 1688–1715* (Oxford, 1985)

de Vries, J., *European Urbanization 1500–1800* (London, 1984)

Deering, G. C., *Nottinghamia Vetus et Nova: Or an Historical Account of the Ancient and Present State of the Town of Nottingham* (Nottingham, 1751)

Defoe, D., *A Tour through the Whole Island of Great Britain*, ed. G. D. H. Cole and D. C. Browning (London, 1962)

Dennis, R., *English Industrial Cities of the Nineteenth Century: A Social Geography* (Cambridge, 1984)

Devine, T. M., 'The merchant class of the larger Scottish towns in the seventeenth and early eighteenth centuries', in Gordon and Dicks, eds., *Scottish Urban History*

Devine, T. M., 'The social composition of the business class in the larger Scottish towns 1680–1740', in T. M. Devine and D. Dickson, eds., *Ireland and Scotland 1600–1850* (Edinburgh, 1983)

Devine, T. M., *The Tobacco Lords* (Edinburgh, 1975; repr., 1990)

Devine, T. M., 'The Union of 1707 and Scottish development', *Scottish Economic and Social History*, 5 (1985)

Devine, T. M., 'Urbanisation', in Devine and Mitchison, eds., *People and Society in Scotland*

Devine, T. M., and Jackson, G., eds., *Glasgow*, vol. I: *Beginnings to 1830* (Manchester, 1995)

Devine, T. M., and Mitchison, R., eds., *People and Society in Scotland*, vol. I: *1760–1830* (Edinburgh, 1988)

Dickinson, R. E., *City and Region: A Geographical Interpretation* (London, 1964)

Dingwall, H. M., 'The importance of social factors in determining the composition of town councils: Edinburgh 1550–1650', *Scottish Historical Review*, 65 (1986)

Dingwall, H. M., *Late Seventeenth-Century Edinburgh: A Demographic History* (Aldershot, 1994)

Dingwall, H. M., *Physicians, Surgeons and Apothecaries: Medical Practice in Seventeenth-Century Edinburgh* (East Linton, 1996)

Dobson, C. R., *Masters and Journeymen* (London, 1980)

Docherty, J., 'Urbanisation, capital accumulation and class struggle in Scotland, 1750–1914', in G. Whittington and I. D. Whyte, eds., *A Historical Geography of Scotland* (London, 1983)

Dodd, A. H., *The Industrial Revolution in North Wales*, 3rd edn (Cardiff, 1971)

Dodd, A. H., ed., *A History of Wrexham Denbighshire* (Wrexham, 1957)

Donaldson, G., *The Scottish Reformation* (Cambridge, 1960)

Downes, K., *The Georgian Cities of Britain* (Oxford, 1979)

Dyer, A., *The City of Worcester in the Sixteenth Century* (Leicester, 1973)

Dyer, A., 'Crisis and resolution: government and society in Stratford, 1540–1640', in R. Bearman, ed., *The History of an English Borough: Stratford-upon-Avon 1196–1996* (Stroud, 1997)

Dyer, A., *Decline and Growth in English Towns 1400–1640* (London, 1991; 2nd edn, Cambridge, 1995)

Dyer, A., 'Market towns of southern England 1500–1700', *SHist.*, 1 (1979)

Dyer, A., 'Warwickshire towns under the Tudors and Stuarts', *Warwickshire History*, 3 (1976–7)

Dyer, C., 'Market towns and the countryside in late medieval England', *Canadian Journal of History*, 31 (1996)

Earle, P., *A City Full of People: Men and Women of London, 1650–1750* (London, 1994)

Earle, P., 'The female labour market in London in the late seventeenth and early eighteenth centuries', *Ec.HR*, 2nd series, 42 (1989)

Earle, P., *The Making of the English Middle Class: Business, Society and Family Life in London, 1660–1730* (London, 1989)

Elliott, V. B., 'Single women in the London marriage market: age, status and mobility, 1598–1619', in R. B. Outhwaite, ed., *Marriage and Society: Studies in the Social History of Marriage* (London, 1981)

Ellis, A., *The Penny Universities* (London, 1956)

Ellis, J., 'A dynamic society: social relations in Newcastle-upon-Tyne, 1660–1760', in Clark, ed., *Transformation of English Provincial Towns*

Estabrook, C., *Urbane and Rustic England: Cultural Ties and Social Spheres in the Provinces 1660–1780* (Manchester, 1998)

Evans, C., *'The Labyrinth of Flames': Work and Social Conflict in Early Industrial Merthyr Tydfil* (Cardiff, 1993)

Evans, J. T., *Seventeenth-Century Norwich: Politics, Religion and Government, 1620–1690* (Oxford, 1979)

Evans, N., ed., *Beccles Rediscovered* (Beccles, 1984)

Everitt, A. M., 'Country, county and town: patterns of regional evolution in England', *TRHS*, 5th series, 29 (1979); repr. in Borsay, ed., *Eighteenth Century Town*

Everitt, A. M., 'The market town' in J. Thirsk, ed., *Ag.HEW*, vol. IV (Cambridge, 1967)

Everitt, A. M., ed., *Perspectives in English Urban History* (London, 1973)

Falkus, M. E., 'The British gas industry before 1850', *Ec.HR*, 2nd series, 20 (1967)

Farr, M. W., *The Great Fire of Warwick, 1694* (Dugdale Society, 36, 1992)

Farrant, S., *Georgian Brighton 1740–1820* (Brighton, 1980)

Fawcett, T., *The Rise of English Provincial Art* (Oxford, 1974)

Ferdinand, C. Y., *Benjamin Collins and the Provincial Newspaper Trade in the Eighteenth Century* (Oxford, 1997)

Finlay, R., 'Natural decrease in early modern cities', *P&P*, 92 (1981)

Finlay, R., *Population and Metropolis: The Demography of London 1580–1650* (Cambridge, 1981)

Fisher, F. J., *London and the English Economy 1500–1700*, ed. P. J. Corfield and N. B. Harte (London, 1990)

Fissell, M. E., *Patients, Power and the Poor in Eighteenth-Century Bristol* (Cambridge, 1991)

Flinn, M., ed., *Scottish Population History from the Seventeenth Century to the 1930s* (Cambridge, 1977)

Floud, R., Wachter, K., and Gregory, A., *Height, Health and History: Nutritional Status in the United Kingdom 1750–1980* (Cambridge, 1990)

Foster, F. F., *The Politics of Stability: A Portrait of the Rulers in Elizabethan London* (London, 1977)

Foster, J., *Class Struggle and the Industrial Revolution: Early Industrial Capitalism in Three English Towns* (London, 1974)

Fox, C., ed., *London – World City, 1800–1840* (New Haven, Conn., 1992)

Friedrichs, C. R., *The Early Modern City 1450–1750* (London, 1995)
Galley, C., 'A model of early modern urban demography', *Ec.HR*, 2nd series, 48 (1995)
Galley, C., 'A never-ending succession of epidemics? Mortality in early-modern York', *Social History of Medicine*, 7 (1994)
Garrioch, D., *Neighbourhood and Community in Paris, 1740–1790* (Cambridge, 1986)
Gauci, P., *Politics and Society in Great Yarmouth 1660–1722* (Oxford, 1996)
George, M. D., *London Life in the Eighteenth Century* (London, 1925; 2nd edn, London, 1965)
Gerhold, G., 'The growth of the London carrying trade, 1681–1838', *Ec.HR*, 2nd series, 41 (1988)
Gibson, J., *The History of Glasgow from the Earliest Accounts to the Present Time* (Glasgow, 1777)
Girouard, M., *The English Town* (London, 1990)
Glass, D. V., 'Socio-economic status and occupations in the city of London at the end of the seventeenth century', in Clark, ed., *Early Modern Town*
Glen, R., *Urban Workers in the Early Industrial Revolution* (London, 1984)
Glennie, P., 'Consumption in historical studies', in D. Miller, ed., *Acknowledging Consumption: Interdisciplinary Studies* (London, 1995)
Goldberg, P. J. P., *Women, Work and Life Cycle in a Medieval Economy* (Oxford, 1992)
Goodacre, J., *The Transformation of a Peasant Economy: Townspeople and Villagers in the Lutterworth Area 1500–1700* (Aldershot, 1994)
Goose, N., 'Decay and regeneration in seventeenth-century Reading: a study in a changing economy', *SHist.*, 6 (1984)
Goose, N., 'Household size and structure in early Stuart Cambridge', *Soc.Hist.*, 5 (1980); repr. in Barry, ed., *The Tudor and Stuart Town*
Goose, N., 'In search of the urban variable: towns and the English economy, 1500–1650', *Ec.HR*, 2nd series, 39 (1986)
Goose, N., 'Urban demography in pre-industrial England: what is to be done?', *UH*, 21 (1994)
Gordon, G., and Dicks, B., eds., *Scottish Urban History* (Aberdeen, 1983)
Gowing, L., *Domestic Dangers: Women, Words and Sex in Early Modern London* (Oxford, 1996)
Gowing, L., 'Gender and the language of insult in early modern London', *History Workshop Journal*, 35 (1993)
Grady, K., *The Georgian Public Buildings of Leeds and the West Riding* (Thoresby Society, 62, 1989)
Gräf, H., 'Leicestershire small towns and pre-industrial urbanisation', *Transactions of the Leicestershire Archaeological and Historical Society*, 68 (1994)
Grassby, R., *The Business Community of Seventeenth-Century England* (Cambridge, 1995)
Green, D. R., *From Artisans to Paupers: Economic Change and Poverty in London, 1790–1870* (Aldershot, 1995)
Gregory, D., *Regional Transformation and Industrial Revolution: A Geography of the Yorkshire Woollen Industry* (London, 1982)
Griffiths, P., 'Masterless young people in Norwich, 1560–1645', in P. Griffiths *et al.*, eds., *The Experience of Authority in Early Modern England* (London, 1996)

Griffiths, P., *Youth and Authority: Formative Experiences in England 1560–1640* (Oxford, 1996)

Griffiths, R. A., ed., *Boroughs of Medieval Wales* (Cardiff, 1978)

Halliday, P., 'Partisan conflict and the law in the English borough corporations 1660–1727' (PhD thesis, University of Chicago, 1993)

Halliday, P., *Dismembering the Body Politic: Partisan Politics in England's Towns 1650–1730* (Cambridge, 1998)

Hancock, D., *Citizens of the World: London Merchants and the Integration of the British Atlantic Community 1735–1785* (Cambridge, 1995)

Harding, V., 'The population of London, 1550–1700: a review of the published evidence', *LJ*, 15 (1990)

Harris, T., *London Crowds in the Reign of Charles II: Propaganda and Politics from the Restoration to the Exclusion Crisis* (Cambridge, 1987)

Harris, T., ed., *Popular Culture in England, c. 1500–1850* (London, 1995)

Harrison, M., 'The ordering of the urban environment: time, work and the occurrence of crowds, 1790–1835', *P&P*, 110 (1986)

Hellmuth, E., ed., *The Transformation of Political Culture: England and Germany in the Late Eighteenth Century* (Oxford, 1990)

Hembry, P., *The English Spa 1560–1815: A Social History* (London, 1990)

Henderson, A. R., and Palmer, S. R., 'The early nineteenth century port of London: management and labour in three dock companies, 1800–1825', in S. P. Ville and D. M. Williams eds., *Management, Finance and Industrial Relations in Maritime Industries* (Research in Maritime History, 6, 1994)

Herbert, W., *The History of the Twelve Great Livery Companies of London* (London, 1834–7)

Hey, D., *The Fiery Blades of Hallamshire: Sheffield and its Neighbourhood 1660–1740* (Leicester, 1991)

Hill, B., *Servants: English Domestics in the Eighteenth Century* (Oxford, 1996)

Hill, J. W. F., *Georgian Lincoln* (Cambridge, 1996)

Hill, J. W. F., *Tudor and Stuart Lincoln* (Cambridge, 1956)

Hitchcock, T., 'Paupers and preachers: the SPCK and the parochial workhouse movement', in L. Davison *et al.*, eds., *Stilling the Grumbling Hive: The Response to Social and Economic Problems in England 1689–1750* (Stroud, 1992)

Hitchcock, T., King, P., and Sharpe, P., eds., *Chronicling Poverty: The Voices and Strategies of the English Poor 1640–1840* (London, 1997)

Holmes, G., *Augustan England: Professions, State and Society, 1680–1730* (London, 1982)

Hone, A., *For the Sake of Truth: Radicalism in London, 1796–1821* (Oxford, 1982)

Hopkins, E., *Birmingham: The First Manufacturing Town in the World 1760–1840* (London, 1989)

Horwitz, H., ' "The mess of the middle class" revisited: the case of the "big bourgeoisie" of Augustan London', *Continuity and Change*, 2 (1987)

Hoskins, W. G., 'The Elizabethan merchants of Exeter', in S. T. Bindoff, J. Hurstfield, and C. H. Williams, eds., *Elizabethan Government and Society: Essays Presented to Sir John Neale* (London, 1961)

Hoskins, W. G., *Industry, Trade and People in Exeter 1688–1800* (Manchester, 1935; 2nd edn, Exeter, 1968)

Hoskins, W. G., *Provincial England: Essays in Social and Economic History* (London, 1963)

Houston, R. A., 'Literacy, education, and the culture of print in Enlightenment Edinburgh', *History*, 78 (1993)

Houston, R. A., *Scottish Literacy and the Scottish Identity* (Cambridge, 1985)

Houston, R. A., *Social Change in the Age of Enlightenment: Edinburgh, 1660–1760* (Oxford, 1994)

Houston, R. A., and Whyte, I. D., eds., *Scottish Society 1500–1800* (Cambridge, 1989)

Howell, R., 'Neutralism, conservatism and political alignment in the English Revolution: the case of the towns 1642–9', in J. Morrill, ed., *Reactions to the English Civil War 1642–1649* (London, 1982)

Howell, R., *Newcastle-upon-Tyne and the Puritan Revolution: A Study of the Civil War in North England* (Oxford, 1967)

Hudson, P., ed., *Regions and Industries: A Perspective on the Industrial Revolution in Britain* (Cambridge, 1989)

Hughes, A., 'Coventry and the English Revolution', in Richardson, ed., *Town and Countryside*

Hunt, M. R., *The Middling Sort: Commerce, Gender and the Family in England, 1680–1780* (Berkeley, Calif, 1996)

Hutton, W., *A History of Birmingham to the End of the Year 1780* (Birmingham, 1781; 2nd edn, Birmingham, 1783)

Hyde, F. E., *Liverpool and the Mersey* (Newton Abbot, 1971)

Hyde, R., ed., *A Prospect of Britain: The Town Panoramas of Samuel and Nathaniel Buck* (London, 1994)

Innes, J., 'The local acts of national parliament: parliament's role in sanctioning local action in eighteenth-century Britain', in D. Dean and C. Jones, eds., *Parliament and Locality 1660–1939* (Edinburgh, 1998)

Ison, W., *Georgian Buildings of Bath, 1700–1830* (Bath, 1948; 2nd edn, 1980)

Jackson, G., *The British Whaling Trade* (London, 1978)

Jackson, G., *Hull in the Eighteenth Century: A Study in Economic and Social History* (Oxford, 1972)

Jackson, G., 'The ports', in M. Freeman and D. H. Aldcroft, eds., *Transport in Victorian Britain* (Manchester, 1988)

Jackson, G., *The Trade and Shipping of Dundee, 1780–1850* (Dundee, 1991)

Jackson, G., and Lythe, S. G. E., eds., *The Port of Montrose: A History of its Harbour, Trade and Shipping* (Tayport, 1993)

James, M., 'Ritual, drama, and the social body in the late medieval English town', *P&P*, 98 (1983)

Jenkins, P., 'Tory industrialism and town politics: Swansea in the 18th Century, *HJ*, 28 (1985)

Jenner, M., 'Early modern English conceptions of "cleanliness" and "dirt" as reflected in the environmental regulation of London c.1530–c.1700' (DPhil thesis, University of Oxford, 1991)

Johnson, D., *Music and Society in Lowland Scotland in the Eighteenth Century* (London, 1972)

Jones, E., *Towns and Cities* (Oxford, 1966)

Jones, E., 'The Welsh in London in the seventeenth and eighteenth centuries', *Welsh History Review*, 10 (1981)

Jones, E. L., 'The reduction of fire damage in southern England, 1650–1850', *Post-Medieval Archaeology*, 2 (1968)

Jones, E. L., and Falkus, M. E., 'Urban improvement and the English economy in the seventeenth and eighteenth centuries', in Borsay, ed., *Eighteenth Century Town*

Jones, E. L., Porter, S., and Turner, M., *A Gazetteer of English Urban Fire Disasters 1500–1900* (Historical Geography Research Series, 13, 1984)

Jones, P. E., and Judges, A. V., 'London population in the late seventeenth century', *Ec.HR*, 1st series, 6 (1935)

Jordan, W. K., *The Charities of London 1480–1660* (London, 1960)

Kellett, J. R., 'The breakdown of gild and corporation control over the handicraft and retail trade in London', *Ec.HR*, 2nd series, 10 (1957–8)

Kellett, J. R., 'Property speculation and the building of Glasgow, 1783–1830', *Scottish Journal of Political Economy*, 8 (1961)

Kitch, M., 'Capital and kingdom: migration to later Stuart London', in Beier and Finlay, eds., *London*

Koditschek, T., *Class Formation and Urban-Industrial Society: Bradford 1750–1850* (Cambridge, 1990)

Landers, J., *Death and the Metropolis: Studies in the Demographic History of London 1670–1830* (Cambridge, 1993)

Landers, J., and Mouzas, A., 'Burial seasonality and causes of death in London 1670–1819', *Population Studies*, 42 (1988)

Langford, P., *A Polite and Commercial People: England 1727–83* (Oxford, 1989)

Langford, P., *Public Life and the Propertied Englishman 1689–1798* (Oxford, 1991)

Langton, J., *Geographical Change and Industrial Revolution: Coalmining in South West Lancashire, 1590–1799* (Cambridge, 1979)

Langton, J., 'The Industrial Revolution and the regional geography of England', *Transactions of the Institute of British Geographers*, new series, 9 (1984)

Langton, J., 'Liverpool and its hinterland in the late eighteenth century', in B. L. Anderson and P. J. M. Stoney, eds., *Commerce, Industry and Transport: Studies in Economic Change on Merseyside* (Liverpool, 1983)

Langton, J., 'Residential patterns in pre-industrial cities: some case studies from seventeenth-century Britain', *Transactions of the Institute of British Geographers*, 65 (1975); repr. in Barry, ed., *The Tudor and Stuart Town*

Langton, J., and Laxton, P., 'Parish registers and urban structure: the example of late eighteenth-century Liverpool', *UHY* (1978)

Langton, J., and Morris, R. J., eds., *Atlas of Industrializing Britain 1780–1914* (London, 1986)

Large, P., 'Urban growth and agricultural change in the West Midlands during the seventeenth and eighteenth centuries', in Clark, ed., *Transformation of English Provincial Towns.*

Law, C. M., 'The growth of urban population in England and Wales, 1801–1911', *Transactions of the Institute of British Geographers*, 41 (1967)

Lees, L. H., *Exiles of Erin: Irish Migrants in Victorian London* (Manchester, 1979)

Life in the Georgian Town (Georgian Group Annual Symposium, London, 1986)

Lillywhite, B., *London Coffee Houses: A Reference Book of Coffee Houses of the Seventeenth, Eighteenth, and Nineteenth Centuries* (London, 1963)

Lindert, P. H., and Williamson, J. G., 'English workers' living standards during the Industrial Revolution: a new look', *Ec.HR*, 2nd series, 36 (1983)

Lindley, K., 'Riot prevention and control in early Stuart London', *TRHS*, 5th series, 33 (1983)

Lippincott, L., *Selling Art in Georgian London: The Rise of Arthur Pond* (London, 1983)

Lis, C., *Social Change and the Labouring Poor: Antwerp 1770–1860* (New Haven, Conn., 1986)

Lobel, M. D., ed., *British Atlas of Historic Towns*, vol. I: *Historic Towns: Maps and Plans of Towns and Cities in the British Isles* (London, 1969)

Lobel, M. D., ed., *British Atlas of Historic Towns*, vol. III: *The City of London from Pre-Historic Times to c. 1520* (Oxford, 1989)

Looney, J. F., 'Cultural life in the provinces: Leeds and York, 1720–1820', in A. L. Beier *et al.*, eds., *The First Modern Society* (Cambridge, 1989)

Lynch, M., 'Continuity and change in urban society, 1500–1700', in Houston and Whyte, eds., *Scottish Society*

Lynch, M., *Edinburgh and the Reformation* (Edinburgh, 1981)

Lynch, M., 'Preaching to the converted? Perspectives on the Scottish Reformation', in A. A. McDonald, M. Lynch, and I. B. Cowan, eds., *The Renaissance in Scotland: Studies in Literature, Religion, History and Culture Offered to John Durkan* (Leiden, 1994)

Lynch, M., 'The social and economic structure of the larger towns, 1450–1600', in Lynch, Spearman and Stell, eds., *Scottish Medieval Town*

Lynch, M., 'Urbanisation and urban networks in seventeenth century Scotland: some further thoughts', *Scottish Economic and Social History*, 12 (1992)

Lynch, M., ed., *The Early Modern Town in Scotland* (London, 1987)

Lynch, M., Spearman, M., and Stell, G., eds., *The Scottish Medieval Town* (Edinburgh, 1988)

Lythe, S. G. E., *The Economy of Scotland in its European Setting, 1550–1625* (Edinburgh, 1960)

MacCaffrey, W. T., *Exeter 1540–1640: The Growth of a County Town* (Cambridge, Mass., 1958; 2nd edn, 1975)

MacCulloch, D., and Blatchly, J., 'Pastoral provisions in the parishes of Tudor Ipswich', *Sixteenth-Century Journal*, 22 (1991)

McElroy, D. D., *Scotland's Age of Improvement* (Pullman, Washington State, 1969)

McInnes, A., 'The emergence of a leisure town: Shrewsbury 1660–1760', *P&P*, 120 (1988)

McIntyre, S., 'Bath: the rise of a resort town, 1660–1800', in Clark, ed., *Country Towns*

McKeown, T., *The Modern Rise of Population* (London, 1986)

Macky, J., *A Journey through England* (London, 1714, with further editions in 1722, 1724)

MacLean, S.-B., 'Drama and ceremony in early modern England', *UHY* (1989)

McNeill, P. G. B., and MacQueen, H. L., eds., *Atlas of Scottish History to 1707* (Edinburgh, 1997)

Macniven, D., 'Merchants and traders in early seventeenth century Aberdeen', in Stevenson, ed., *From Lairds to Louns*

McVeigh, S., *Concert Life in London from Mozart to Haydn* (Cambridge, 1993)

Malmgreen, G., *Silk Town: Industry and Culture in Macclesfield 1750–1835* (Hull, 1985)

Markus, T. A., ed., *Order in Space and Society: Architectural Form and its Content in the Scottish Enlightenment* (Edinburgh, 1982)

Marriner, S., *The Economic and Social Development of Merseyside* (London, 1982)

Marshall, J. D., 'Colonisation as a factor in the planting of towns in North-West England', in H. J. Dyos ed., *The Study of Urban History* (London, 1968)

Marshall, J. D., *Furness in the Industrial Revolution* (Barrow, 1958; repr., Whitehaven, 1981)

Marshall, J. D., 'The rise and transformation of the Cumbrian market town, 1660–1900', *NHist.*, 19 (1983)

Marshall, P., ed., *The Impact of the English Reformation, 1500–1640* (London, 1997)

Marwick, Sir J. D., ed., *Register Containing the State and Condition of Every Burgh within the Kingdome of Scotland in the Year 1692* (Miscellany of the Scottish Burgh Records Society, 13, 1881)

Mayhew, G., *Tudor Rye* (Falmer, 1987)

Mendenhall, T. C., *The Shrewsbury Drapers and the Welsh Wool Trade in the XVI and XVII Centuries* (Oxford, 1953)

Millward, R., 'The Cumbrian town between 1600 and 1800', in Chalklin and Havinden, eds., *Rural Change*

Minchinton, W. E., 'Bristol – metropolis of the west in the eighteenth century', *TRHS*, 5th series, 4 (1954)

Mitchell, C. J., 'Provincial printing in eighteenth-century Britain', *Publishing History*, 21 (1987)

Mitchell, D., ed., *Goldsmiths, Silversmiths and Bankers: Innovation and the Transfer of Skill, 1550 to 1750* (Stroud, 1995)

Mitchell, I., 'The development of urban retailing 1700–1815', in Clark, ed., *Transformation of English Provincial Towns*

Mokyr, J., 'Has the Industrial Revolution been crowded out? Some reflections on Crafts and Williamson', *Explorations in Economic History*, 24 (1987)

Money, J., *Experience and Identity: Birmingham and the West Midlands 1760–1800* (Manchester, 1977)

Morant, P., *The History and Antiquities of the Most Ancient Town and Borough of Colchester* (London, 1748)

Morgan, K., *Bristol and the Atlantic Trade in the Eighteenth Century* (Cambridge, 1993)

Morgan, N., *Vanished Dwellings: Early Industrial Housing in a Lancashire Cotton Town* (Preston, 1990)

Morris, C., ed., *The Journeys of Celia Fiennes* (London, 1947)

Morris, R. J., *Class and Class Consciousness in the Industrial Revolution 1780–1850* (London, 1979)

Morris, R. J., *Class, Sect and Party: The Making of the British Middle Class: Leeds, 1820–50* (Manchester, 1990)

Morris, R. J., 'Urbanisation in Scotland', in W. H. Fraser and R. J. Morris, eds., *People and Society in Scotland*, vol. II: *1830–1914* (Edinburgh, 1990)

Morris, R. J., 'Voluntary societies and British urban elites 1780–1850', *HJ*, 26 (1983)

Mowat, S., *The Port of Leith: Its History and People* (Edinburgh, 1995)

Muldrew, C., 'Credit and the courts: debt litigation in a seventeenth-century urban community', *Ec.HR*, 2nd series, 46 (1993)

Neale, R. S., *Bath 1680–1850: A Social History* (London, 1981)

Nenadic, S., 'Middle rank consumers and domestic culture in Edinburgh and Glasgow, 1720–1840', *P&P*, 145 (1994)

Nenadic, S., 'The rise of the urban middle class', in Devine and Mitchison, eds., *People and Society in Scotland*

Newton, R., *Eighteenth-Century Exeter* (Exeter, 1984)

Noble, M., 'Growth and development in a regional urban system: the country towns of eastern Yorkshire, 1700–1850', *UHY* (1987)

O'Gorman, F., *Voters, Patrons and Parties* (Oxford, 1989)

Oakes, J., *The Oakes Diaries: Business, Politics and the Family in Bury St Edmunds 1778–1827*, ed. J. Fiske (Suffolk Records Society, 32–3, 1990–1)

Owen, C. C., *The Development of Industry in Burton upon Trent* (Chichester, 1978)

Pagan, T., *The Convention of the Royal Burghs of Scotland* (Glasgow, 1926)

Paley, R., '"An imperfect, inadequate and wretched system": policing the metropolis before Peel', *Criminal Justice History*, 10 (1989)

Palliser, D. M., 'Popular reactions to the Reformation', in C. Haigh, ed., *The English Reformation Revised* (Cambridge, 1987)

Palliser, D. M., *The Reformation in York 1534–1553* (Borthwick Papers, 40, York, 1971)

Palliser, D. M., *Tudor York* (Oxford, 1979)

Patten, J., *English Towns 1500–1700* (Folkestone, 1978)

Patten, J., 'Population distribution in Norfolk and Suffolk during the sixteenth and seventeenth centuries', *Transactions of the Institute of British Geographers*, 65 (1975)

Patten, J., 'Urban occupations in pre-industrial England', *Transactions of the Institute of British Geographers*, new series, 2 (1977)

Patterson, A. T., *A History of Southampton 1700–1914*, vol. I: *An Oligarchy in Decline 1700–1835* (Southampton, 1966)

Pawson, E., *Transport and Economy: The Turnpike Roads of Eighteenth Century Britain* (London, 1977)

Pearl, V., 'Change and stability in seventeenth century London', *LJ*, 5 (1979); repr. in Barry, ed., *The Tudor and Stuart Town*

Pearl, V., *London and the Outbreak of the Puritan Revolution: City Government and National Politics, 1625–43* (Oxford, 1961)

Pelling, M., 'Appearance and reality: barber-surgeons, the body and disease', in Beier and Finlay, eds., *London*

Pelling, M., *Poverty, Health and Urban Society in England, 1500–1700* (Harlow, 1998)

Petchey, W. J., *A Prospect of Maldon 1500–1689* (Chelmsford, 1991)

Pevsner, N., *The Buildings of England: London*, vol. I: *The Cities of London and Westminster* (Harmondsworth, 1985)

Pevsner, N., *The Buildings of England: Northumberland* (Harmondsworth, 1957)

Pevsner, N., *A History of Building Types* (London, 1976)

Phillips, C. B., 'Town and country: economic change in Kendal c. 1550–1700', in Clark, ed., *Transformation of English Provincial Towns*

Phillips, J. A., *Electoral Behaviour in Unreformed England 1761–1802* (Princeton, N. J., 1982)

Phillips, J. A., *The Great Reform Bill in the Boroughs: English Electoral Behaviour 1818–41* (Oxford, 1992)

Phillipson, N., 'Culture and society in the eighteenth century province: the case of Edinburgh and the Scottish Enlightenment', in L. Stone, ed., *The University in Society* (Princeton, N.J., 1975), vol. II

Phillipson, N., 'Edinburgh', in *Cities and the Transmission of Cultural Values in the Late Middle Ages and Early Modern Period* (Brussels, 1996)

Phillipson, N., 'Towards a definition of the Scottish Enlightenment', in P. Fritz and D. Williams, eds., *City and Society in the Eighteenth Century* (Toronto, 1973)

Phythian-Adams, C., 'Ceremony and the citizen: the communal year at Coventry 1450–1550', in Clark and Slack, eds., *Crisis and Order*; repr. in R. Holt and G. Rosser, eds., *The Medieval Town: A Reader in English Urban History, 1200–1540* (London, 1990)

Phythian-Adams, C., *Desolation of a City: Coventry and the Urban Crisis of the Late Middle Ages* (Cambridge, 1979)

Phythian-Adams, C., 'The economic and social structure', in *The Fabric of the Traditional Community* (Open University, English Urban History course, Milton Keynes, 1977)

Phythian-Adams, C., 'Milk and soot: the changing vocabulary of a popular ritual in Stuart and Hanoverian London', in D. Fraser and A. Sutcliffe, eds., *The Pursuit of Urban History* (London, 1983)

Pooley, C. G., and D'Cruze, S., 'Migration and urbanization in North-West England circa 1760–1830', *Soc. Hist.*, 19 (1994)

Port, M., ed., *The Commissions for Building Fifty New Churches* (London Record Society, 23, 1986)

Porteous, J. D., *Canal Ports: The Urban Achievement of the Canal Age* (London, 1977)

Porter, R., *London: A Social History* (London, 1994)

Porter, S., *The Great Fire of London* (Stroud, 1996)

Pound, J. F., 'The social and trade structure of Norwich, 1525–75', in Clark ed., *Early Modern Town*

Pound, J. F., *Tudor and Stuart Norwich* (Chichester, 1988)

Pound, J. F., ed., *The Norwich Census of the Poor 1570* (Norfolk Record Society, 40, 1971)

Power, M. J., 'London and the control of the "crisis" of the 1590s', *History*, 70 (1985)

Power, M. J., 'Shadwell: the development of a London suburban community in the seventeenth century', *LJ*, 4 (1978)

Power, M. J., 'The east and west in early modern London', in E. W. Ives, R. J. Knecht, and J. J. Scarsbrick, eds., *Wealth and Power in Tudor England: Essays Presented to S. T. Bindoff* (London, 1978)

Priestley, U., *The Fabric of Stuffs: The Norwich Textile Industry from 1565* (Norwich, 1990)

Priestley, U., Corfield, P. J., and Sutermeister, H., 'Rooms and room use in Norwich housing, 1580–1730', *Post-Medieval Archaeology*, 16 (1982)

Prior, M., *Fisher Row: Fishermen, Bargemen and Canal Boatmen in Oxford 1500–1900* (Oxford, 1982)

Prior, M., *Women in English Society 1500–1800* (London, 1985)

Prothero, I., *Artisans and Politics in Early Nineteenth-Century London: John Gast and his Times* (Folkestone, 1979)

Pryde, G. S., *The Burghs of Scotland: A Critical List* (Glasgow, 1965)

Ramsay, G. D., *The City of London in International Politics at the Accession of Elizabeth Tudor* (Manchester, 1975)

Rappaport, S., *Worlds within Worlds: Structures of Life in Sixteenth-Century London* (Cambridge, 1989)

RCHM (England), *The City of Salisbury*, vol. 1 (London, 1980)

RCHM (England), *An Inventory of Nonconformist Chapels in Central England* (London, 1986)

RCHM (England), *The Town of Stamford* (London, 1977)

RCHM (England), *York*, vol. 1: *Historic Buildings of the Central Area* (London, 1981)

RCHM (Scotland), *The City of Edinburgh* (Edinburgh, 1951)

Records of Early English Drama (Toronto, 1979–)

Reddaway, T. F., *The Rebuilding of London* (London, 1940)

Reed, M., 'The cultural role of small towns in England 1600–1800', in Clark, ed., *Small Towns*

Reed, M., 'Decline and recovery in provincial urban network: Buckinghamshire towns 1350–1800', in M. Reed, ed., *English Towns in Decline 1350–1800* (Centre for Urban History Working Papers, 1, Leicester, 1986)

Reed, M., 'Economic structure and change in seventeenth-century Ipswich', in Clark, ed., *Country Towns*

Reed, M., 'London and its hinterland 1600–1800: the view from the provinces', in P. Clark and B. Lepetit, eds., *Capital Cities and their Hinterlands in Early Modern Europe* (Aldershot, 1996)

Reed, M., ed., *The Ipswich Probate Inventories, 1583–1631* (Suffolk Records Society, 22, 1981)

Rees, W., *Cardiff: A History of the City* (Cardiff, 1969)

Reid, D. A., 'Weddings, weekdays, work and leisure in urban England 1791–1911', *P&P*, 153 (1996)

Rennison, R. W., 'The supply of water to Newcastle on Tyne and Gateshead, 1680–1837', *Archaeologia Aeliana*, 5th series, 5 (1977)

Richards, P., 'R. A. Slaney, the industrial town, and early Victorian social policy', *Soc. Hist.*, 4 (1979)

Richardson, R. C., ed., *Town and Countryside in the English Revolution* (Manchester, 1992)

Ripley, P., 'The economy of the city of Gloucester 1660–1740', *Transactions of the Bristol and Gloucestershire Archaeological Society*, 98 (1980)

Risse, G. B., *Hospital Life in Enlightenment Scotland* (Cambridge, 1986)

Robson, B. T., *Urban Growth: An Approach* (London, 1973)

Rodger, R. C., 'The evolution of Scottish town planning', in Gordon and Dicks, ed., *Scottish Urban History*

Rogers, A., ed., *The Making of Stamford* (Leicester, 1965)

Rogers, N., 'Carnal knowledge: illegitimacy in eighteenth-century Westminster', *Journal of Social History*, 23 (1989)

Rogers, N., 'Money, land and lineage: the big bourgeoisie of Hanoverian London', *Soc. Hist.*, 4 (1979); repr. in Borsay, ed., *Eighteenth Century Town*

Rogers, N., *Whigs and Cities: Popular Politics in the Age of Walpole and Pitt* (Oxford, 1989)

Rosen, A., 'Winchester in transition, 1580–1700', in Clark, ed., *Country Towns*

Rowlands, M. B., *Masters and Men in the West Midlands Metalware Trades before the Industrial Revolution* (Manchester, 1975)

Rowlands, M. B., 'Government and governors in four manorial boroughs in the West Midlands', *Journal of Regional and Local History*, 13 (1993)

Roy, I., 'England turned Germany? The aftermath of the Civil War in its European context', *TRHS*, 5th series, 28 (1978)

Rubinstein, W. D., *Capitalism, Culture, and Decline in Britain 1750–1990* (London, 1993)

Ruddock, A. A., *Italian Merchants and Shipping in Southampton, 1270–1600* (Southampton Records Series, 1, 1951)

Rudé, G., *Hanoverian London 1714–1808* (London, 1971)

Sacks, D. H., 'Bristol's "wars of religion"', in Richardson, ed., *Town and Countryside*

Sacks, D. H., *Trade, Society, and Politics in Bristol, 1500–1640* (New York, 1985)

Sacks, D. H., *The Widening Gate: Bristol and the Atlantic Economy, 1450–1700* (Berkeley, Calif., 1991)

Sadie, S., 'Concert life in eighteenth century England', *Proceedings of the Royal Musical Association (1958–9)* (1959)

Sanderson, E. C., *Women and Work in Eighteenth-Century Edinburgh* (London, 1996)

Schofield, J., *The Building of London from the Conquest to the Great Fire* (London, 1984)

Schofield, J., ed., *The London Surveys of Ralph Treswell* (London, 1987)

Schwarz, L. D., *London in the Age of Industrialisation: Entrepreneurs, Labour Force and Living Conditions, 1700–1850* (Cambridge, 1992)

Seaver, P. S., *Wallington's World: A Puritan Artisan in Seventeenth-Century London* (London, 1985)

Seed, J., 'From "middling sort" to middle class in late eighteenth-century and early nineteenth-century England', in Bush, M. L., ed., *Social Orders and Social Classes since 1500* (Harlow, 1992)

Seleski, P., 'Women, work and cultural change in eighteenth- and early nineteenth-century London', in Harris, ed., *Popular Culture in England*

Sharlin, A., 'Natural decrease in early modern cities: a reconsideration', *P&P*, 79 (1978)

Sharlin, A., 'Natural decrease in early modern cities: a rejoinder', *P&P*, 92 (1981)

Sharpe, P., 'De-industrialization and re-industrialization: women's employment and the changing character of Colchester 1700–1850', *UH*, 21 (1994)

Sharpe, P., 'Literally spinsters: a new interpretation of local economy and demography in Colyton in the seventeenth and eighteenth century', *Ec.HR*, 2nd series, 44 (1991)

Sheils, W. J., 'Religion in provincial towns: innovation and tradition', in F. Heal and R. O'Day, eds., *Church and Society in England, Henry VIII to James I* (London, 1977)

Sheppard, F. H. W., *London 1808–1870: The Infernal Wen* (London, 1971)

Shoemaker, R. B., *Prosecution and Punishment: Petty Crime and the Law in London and Rural Middlesex. c. 1660–1725* (Cambridge, 1991)

Shoemaker, R. B., 'Reforming the city: the reformation of manners campaign in London 1690–1738', in L. Davison *et al.*, eds., *Stilling the Grumbling Hive: The Response to Social and Economic Problems in England 1689–1750* (Stroud, 1992)

Simpson, E., 'Aberdour: the evolution of a seaside resort', in G. Cruickshank, ed., *A Sense of Place: Studies in Scottish Local History* (Edinburgh, 1988)

Skeeters, M.C., *Community and Clergy: Bristol and the Reformation c.1530 – c.1570* (Oxford, 1993)

Slack, P., 'Dearth and social policy in early policy in early modern England', *Social History of Medicine*, 5 (1992)

Slack, P., 'The disappearance of plague: an alternative view', *Ec.HR*, 2nd series, 34 (1981)

Slack, P., *The Impact of Plague in Tudor and Stuart England* (London, 1985)

Slack, P., *Poverty and Policy in Tudor and Stuart England* (London, 1988)

Slack, P., 'Poverty and politics in Salisbury 1597–1666', in Clark and Slack, eds., *Crisis and Order*

Smail, J., *The Origins of Middle-Class Culture: Halifax, Yorkshire, 1660–1780* (Ithaca, N.Y., 1994)

Smith, C., 'Image and reality: two Nottingham market towns in late Georgian England', *Midland History*, 17 (1992)

Smith, D. L., Strier, R., and Bevington, D., eds., *The Theatrical City* (Cambridge, 1995)

Smith, L. T., ed., *The Itinerary of John Leland* (London, 1908; repr. 1964)

Smith, M., *Religion in Industrial Society: Oldham and Saddleworth 1740–1865* (Oxford, 1994)

Smith, R., 'Multi-dwelling building in Scotland, 1750–1970: a study based on housing in the Clyde valley', in A. Sutcliffe, ed., *Multi-Storey Living: The British Working Class Experience* (London, 1974)

Smout, T. C., 'The development and enterprise of Glasgow, 1556–1707', *Scottish Journal of Political Economy*, 7 (1960)

Smout, T. C., *A History of the Scottish People 1560–1830* (London, 1969)

Souden, D., '"East, west – home's best"? regional patterns in migration in early modern England', in Clark and Souden, eds., *Migration and Society*

Souden, D., 'Migrants and the population structure of later seventeenth-century provincial cities and market towns', in Clark, ed., *Transformation of English Provincial Towns*

Spufford, M., *Small Books and Pleasant Histories: Popular Fiction and its Readership in Seventeenth-Century England* (Cambridge, 1981)

The Statistical Account of Scotland (Edinburgh, 1791–9)

Stephens, W. B., 'The cloth exports of the provincial towns, 1600–1640', *Ec.HR*, 2nd series, 22 (1969)

Stephens, W. B., The overseas trade of Chester in the early seventeenth century', *Transactions of the Historic Society of Lancashire and Cheshire*, 120 (1968)

Stephens, W. B., *Seventeenth-Century Exeter: A Study of Industrial and Commercial Development 1625–1688* (Exeter, 1958)

Stephens, W. B., 'Trade trends in Bristol, 1600–1700', *Transactions of the Bristol and Gloucestershire Archaeological Society*, 93 (1974)

Stevenson, D., 'The burghs and the Scottish Revolution', in Lynch, ed., *Early Modern Town*

Stevenson, D., ed., *From Lairds to Louns: Country and Burgh Life in Aberdeen 1600–1800* (Aberdeen, 1986)

Stevenson, J., *London in the Age of Reform* (Oxford, 1977)

Stobart, J., 'An eighteenth-century revolution? Investigating urban growth in North-West England 1664–1801', *UH*, 23 (1996)

Stobart, J., 'Regional structure and the urban system: North-West England 1700–1760', *Transactions of the Historic Society of Lancashire and Cheshire*, 145 (1996)

Stobart, J., 'The spatial organisation of a regional economy: central places in North-West England in the early eighteenth century', *Journal of Historical Geography*, 22 (1996)

Stone, L., 'The residential development of the West End of London in the seventeenth century', in B. C. Malament, ed., *After the Reformation* (Manchester, 1980)

Summerson, H., *Medieval Carlisle: The City and the Borders from the Late Eleventh to the Mid-Sixteenth Century* (Cumberland and Westmorland Antiquarian and Archaeological Society, extra series, 25, 1993)

Summerson, J., *Georgian London* (London, 1945)

Sweet, R., 'Freemen and independence in English borough politics, c. 1770–1830', *P&P*, 161 (1998)

Sweet, R., 'Stability and continuity: Swansea politics and reform 1780–1820', *Welsh History Review*, 18 (1996)

Sweet, R., *The Writing of Urban Histories in Eighteenth-Century England* (Oxford, 1997)

Thomas, W. S. K, 'Tudor and Jacobean Swansea', *Morgannwg*, 5 (1961)

Thompson, E. P., *The Making of the English Working Class* (London, 1963)

Thompson, F. M. L., 'The rise of suburbia', in R. J. Morris, and R. Rodger, eds., *The Victorian City: A Reader in British Urban History, 1820–1914* (London, 1993)

Thompson, F. M. L., ed., *The Cambridge Social History of Britain 1750–1950* (Cambridge, 1990)

Thwaites, W., 'Women in the market place: Oxfordshire c.1690–1800', *Midland History*, 9 (1984)

Tilly, C., and Blockmans, W. P., eds., *Cities and the Rise of States in Europe A.D. 1000–1800* (Oxford, 1994)

Tittler, R., *Architecture and Power: The Town Hall and the English Urban Community c.1500–1640* (Oxford, 1991)

Tittler, R., *The Reformation and the Towns in England: Politics and Political Culture, c.1500–1640* (Oxford, 1998)

Tolmie, M., *The Triumph of the Saints: The Separate Churches of London 1616–1649* (Cambridge, 1977)

Torrie, E. P. D., *Medieval Dundee: A Town and its People* (Dundee, 1900)

Triffitt, J. M., 'Politics and the urban community: parliamentary boroughs in the South-West of England 1710–30' (DPhil thesis, University of Oxford, 1985)

Trinder, B., 'The textile industry in Shrewsbury in the late eighteenth century: the traditional town', in Clark and Corfield, eds., *Industry and Urbanisation*

Trinder, B., *Victorian Banbury* (Chichester, 1982)

Turnbull, G., 'Canals and economic growth in the Industrial Revolution', *Ec.HR*, 2nd series, 40 (1987)

Turner, H. L., *Town Defences in England and Wales* (London, 1971)

Tyson, R. E., 'Contrasting regimes: population growth in Ireland and Scotland during the eighteenth century', in Connolly, Houston and Morris, eds., *Conflict, Identity and Economic Development*

Underdown, D., *Fire from Heaven: Life in an English Town in the Seventeenth Century* (London, 1992)

Unwin, G., *The gilds and companies of London* (London, 1908; 4th edn, 1963)

Unwin, R. A., 'Tradition and transformation: market towns of the Vale of York 1660–1830', *NHist.*, 17 (1981)

Vaisey, D. G., ed., *Probate Inventories for Lichfield and District, 1568–1680* (Staffordshire Record Society, 4th series, 5, 1969)

Vanes, J., *The Port of Bristol in the Sixteenth Century* (Bristol Historical Association, 39, 1977)

Vickery, A. J., 'Town histories and Victorian plaudits: some examples from Preston', *UHY* (1988)

Vickery, A. J., 'Golden age to separate spheres: a review of the categories and chronology of English women's history', *HJ*, 36 (1993)

Wahrman, D., *Imagining the Middle Class: The Political Representation of Class in Britain c.1780–1840* (Cambridge, 1995)

Walker, M., 'The extent of guild control in England c.1660–1820: a study based on a sample of provincial towns and London companies' (PhD thesis, University of Cambridge, 1986)

Walsh, J., *et al.*, eds., *The Church of England c.1689–c.1833* (Cambridge, 1993)

Walton, J. K., *The English Seaside Resort: A Social History 1750–1914* (Leicester, 1983)

Walton, J. K., *Lancashire: A Social History 1558–1939* (Manchester, 1987)

Walton, J. K., 'The North-West', in Thompson, ed., *Cambridge Social History of Britain*, vol. I

Wanklyn, M., 'The impact of water transport on English river ports, c.1660–1760', *Ec.HR*, 2nd series, 49 (1996)

Wanklyn, M., 'Urban revival in early modern England: Bridgnorth and the river trade 1660–1800', *Midland History*, 18 (1993)

Wareing, J., 'Migration to London and transatlantic emigration of indentured servants 1683–1775', *Journal of Historical Geography*, 7 (1981)

Watson, M., *Jute and Flax Mills in Dundee* (Tayport, 1990)

Watt, T., *Cheap Print and Popular Piety, 1550–1640* (Cambridge, 1991)

Weatherill, L., *Consumer Behaviour and Material Culture in Britain 1660–1760* (London, 1998)

Webb, J., ed., *Poor Relief in Elizabethan Ipswich* (Suffolk Records Society, 9, 1996)

Webb, S., and Webb, B., *The Manor and the Borough* (London, 1908)

Webb, S., and Webb, B., *The Parish and the County* (London, 1906)

Webb, S., and Webb, B., *Statutory Authorities for Special Purposes* (London, 1922)

Weber, A. F., *The Growth of Cities in the Nineteenth Century: A Study in Statistics* (Ithaca, N.Y., 1899)

Weber, W., *Music and the Middle-Class: The Social Structure of Concert Life in London, Paris and Vienna* (London, 1975)

Weitzman, A. J., 'Eighteenth-century London: urban paradise or fallen city?', *Journal of the History of Ideas*, 36 (1975)

The Welsh Port Books (1550–1603), ed. E. A. Lewis (Cymmrodorion Record Series, 12, 1927)

White, A., 'The impact of the Reformation on a burgh community; the case of Aberdeen', in Lynch, ed., *Early Modern Town*

Whitehead, D., *Urban Renewal and Suburban Growth: The Shaping of Georgian Worcester* (Worcestershire Historical Society, Occasional Publications, 5, 1989)

Whiteman, A., *The Compton Census of 1676: A Critical Edition* (British Academy, Records of Social and Economic History, new series, 10, 1986)

Whiting, R., *The Blind Devotion of the People: Popular Religion and the English Reformation* (Cambridge, 1989)

Whyman, J., 'A Hanoverian watering place: Margate before the railway', in Everitt, ed., *Perspectives*

Whyman, J., ed., *Kentish Sources*, vol. VIII: *The Early Kentish Seaside (1763–1840)* (Gloucester, 1985)

Whyte, I. D., *Agriculture and Society in Seventeenth Century Scotland* (Edinburgh, 1979)

Whyte, I. D., 'The function and social structure of Scottish burghs of barony in the seventeenth and eighteenth centuries', in A. Maczak and C. Smout, eds., *Gründung und Bedeutung kleinerer Städte im nördlichen Europa der frühen Neuzeit* (Wiesbaden, 1991)

Whyte, I. D., 'The growth of periodic market centres in Scotland 1600–1707', *Scottish Geographical Magazine*, 95 (1979)

Whyte, I. D., 'The occupational structure of Scottish burghs in the late seventeenth century', in Lynch, ed., *Early Modern Town*

Whyte, I. D., *Scotland before the Industrial Revolution: An Economic and Social History c. 1050–c. 1750* (London, 1995)

Whyte, I. D., 'Urbanization in early modern Scotland: a preliminary analysis', *Scottish Economic and Social History*, 9 (1989)

Wiles, R. M., *Freshest Advices: Early Provincial Newspapers in England* (Columbus, Ohio, 1965)

Willan, T. S., *Early History of the Don Navigation* (Manchester, 1965)

Willan, T. S., *An Eighteenth-Century Shopkeeper: Abraham Dent of Kirkby Stephen* (Manchester, 1970)

Willan, T. S., *The English Coasting Trade, 1600–1750* (Manchester, 1938)

Willan, T. S., *River Navigation in England, 1600–1750* (Oxford, 1936; repr., London, 1964)

Williams, G. A., *The Merthyr Rising* (London, 1978; 2nd edn, Cardiff, 1988)

Williams, N. J., *The Maritime Trade of the East Anglian Ports, 1550–1590* (Oxford, 1988)

Williamson, J. G., *Coping with City Growth during the British Industrial Revolution* (Cambridge, 1990)

Wilson, K., *The Sense of the People: Politics, Culture and Imperialism in England 1715–85* (Cambridge, 1995)

Wilson, R. G., *Gentlemen Merchants: The Merchant Community in Leeds 1700–1830* (Manchester, 1971)

Wilson, T., 'The state of England anno dom. 1600', ed. F. J. Fisher, *Camden Miscellany*, vol. XVI (Camden Society, 3rd series, 52, 1936)

Wise, M. J., 'Birmingham and its trade relations in the early eighteenth century', *University of Birmingham Historical Journal*, 2 (1949–50)

Withers, C. W. J., 'Kirk, club and culture change: Gaelic chapels, Highland societies and the urban Gaelic subculture in eighteenth century Scotland', *Soc. Hist.*, 10 (1985)

Woodward, D. M., *Men at work: Labourers and Building Craftsmen in the Towns of Northern England 1450–1750* (Cambridge, 1995)

Woodward, D. M., *The Trade of Elizabethan Chester* (Hull, 1970)

Wright, N. R., *Lincolnshire Towns and Industry 1700–1914* (Lincoln, 1982)

Wright, S. J., 'Sojourners and lodgers in a provincial town: the evidence from eighteenth-century Ludlow', *UHJ*, 17 (1990)

Wrigley, E. A., 'City and country in the past: a sharp divide or a continuum?', *HR*, 64 (1991)

Wrigley, E. A., *People, Cities and Wealth: The Transformation of a Traditional Society* (Oxford, 1987)

Wrigley, E. A., 'A simple model of London's importance in changing English society and economy, 1650–1750', *P&P*, 37 (1967)

Wrigley, E. A., 'Urban growth and agricultural change: England and the continent in the early modern period', *Journal of Interdisciplinary History*, 15 (1985); repr. in R. I. Rotberg and T. K. Rabb, eds., *Population and Economy* (Cambridge, 1986); Wrigley, *People, Cities and Wealth*; and Borsay, ed., *Eighteenth Century Town*

Wrigley, E. A., and Schofield, R. S., *The Population History of England 1541–1871: A reconstruction* (London, 1981)

Wrigley, E. A., *et al.*, *English Population History from Family Reconstitution 1580–1837* (Cambridge, 1997)

Youings, J., *Tuckers Hall, Exeter* (Exeter, 1968)

Youngson, A. J., *The Making of Classical Edinburgh 1750–1840* (Edinburgh, 1966)

Zahedieh, N., 'London and the colonial consumer in the late seventeenth century', *Ec.HR*, 2nd series, 47 (1994)

Index

Note: page numbers in italic refer to Tables and Figures